LONG HOUSE

Upper west section of Long House.

Publications in Archeology 7H
Wetherill Mesa Studies

LONG HOUSE

Mesa Verde National Park, Colorado

George S. Cattanach Jr.

With contributions by
Richard P. Wheeler
Carolyn M. Osborne
Charmion R. McKusick
and Paul S. Martin

National Park Service
U.S. Department of the Interior
Washington, D.C.
1980

As the Nation's principal conservation agency, the Department of the Interior has responsibility for most of our nationally owned public lands and natural resources. This includes fostering the wisest use of our land and water resources, protecting our fish and wildlife, preserving the environmental and cultural values of our national parks and historical places, and providing for the enjoyment of life through outdoor recreation. The Department assesses our mineral resources and works to assure that their development is in the best interests of all our people. The Department also has a major responsibility for American Indian reservation communities and for people who live in Island Territories under United States administration.

Library of Congress Cataloging in Publication Data
Cattanach, George S
Long House, Mesa Verde National Park, Colorado.

(Publications in archeology; 7H)
At head of title: Wetherill Mesa studies.
Bibliography: P.
Includes index.
1. Long House site, Colo. 2. Mesa Verde National Park. I. Wheeler, Richard P., joint author. II. Title. III. Title: Wetherill Mesa studies. IV. Series.
E51.U75 no. 7H [E99.P9] 978.8'27 79-9990

For sale by the Superintendent of Documents,
U.S. Government Printing Office
Washington, D.C. 20402

Stock No. 024-005-00652-4

Foreword

The National Park Service, since 1916, has been charged with preserving and interpreting many of our nation's notable works of nature and significant works of man. Few archeological areas in the world exceed, in intrinsic interest for the visitor and in importance to scholars everywhere, that of Mesa Verde National Park.

This major archeological report of Long House concerns one of the largest cliff dwellings in the park—one in a virtually unspoiled natural setting, and containing much new evidence of the Indian farmers who lived there hundreds of years ago. In addition, the report interprets the artifacts and physical remains of three adjacent mesa-top sites occupied from roughly the mid-7th through the mid-13th centuries A.D.

We take pride in publishing this important book for several reasons. We have always been aware of our obligations to make known and readily available the researches the Service makes on the lands and sites it holds in public trust. This is particularly true of those of such extraordinary importance as Mesa Verde. It is appropriate that this publication follows so closely upon the action taken recently by an international committee of UNESCO in naming the park to the World Heritage List of "properties deemed of unusual significance for all mankind." Along with Yellowstone National Park and 10 properties in other countries, it becomes part of the first group to be placed on this international register.

Also, we are especially pleased to issue this report because of the long and fruitful relationship we have had with the National Geographic Society. Without the Society's financial assistance during the years 1959 through 1963, much of the research, and a significant part of this report as an end-product, would not have been possible.

RUSSELL E. DICKENSON
Director
National Park Service

Acknowledgments

During the active work period in Long House, from 1958 to 1962, a great number of Wetherill Mesa Project staff members and specialists from many institutions brought their talents and experience to bear on the problem of excavating and interpreting the cliff dwelling. I appreciate greatly all the assistance provided, and I want to acknowledge here the contributions of all those who were intimately involved in the Long House work or made significant contributions to it. In most cases, institutional affiliations given are those of 1958 to 1964.

James A. ("Al") Lancaster served throughout the project as excavations supervisor, and shared in all decisions made about the work in Long House. Without his experience in Southwestern archeology, and his enthusiastic and dedicated support and guidance in all of the fieldwork, the excavation and stabilization would have been far less effective. Al and I were partners—in the fullest sense of the word—in our work in Long House, and to him goes a large share of the credit for recognizing and interpreting the often poorly defined archeological traces of the Puebloan inhabitants.

Arthur H. Rohn was the assistant archeologist in Long House during the first summer season, and Robert F. Nichols during the 1961 season. Nichols was affiliated with the Laboratory of Tree-Ring Research at the University of Arizona in 1962, when he rejoined the project as dendrochronologist. From this time forward, he not only collected and recorded wood specimens from Long House, but also performed all the tree-ring dating under the general supervision of Bryant Bannister of the Laboratory of Tree-Ring Research.

Only during the first full season in 1959, and again during the final stages of the stabilization, was a professional photographer available to record the work in the ruin: Oswald Werner in 1959, and Fred E. Mang, Jr., in 1962. Fred Mang also photographed all artifacts and other specimens from the ruin, and made all of the final prints for publication. Working with him was a pleasure, particularly since Fred made what could have been a difficult chore into a pleasant and creative experience for me through his willingness to improvise and contribute freely his own artistic and photographic expertise to the project. Bob Nichols, Gerald F. Wood, David A. Hannah, and the author performed routine excavation and stabilization photography at all other times.

William Belknap, photographer from Boulder City, Nevada, spent many weeks on Wetherill Mesa to provide photographic coverage of the project for the *National Geographic Magazine.* While there, he devoted many hours to helping all of us solve our photographic problems.

The mapping of Long House was undertaken at different times by James E. Pond, Raymond Adkins, and Daniel Wolfman. Assistance was provided by James Sciscenti and Richard Williams. Lewis D. Anderson, Park Engineer, ran five of the six major sections of Long House. Architect George A. King, Durango, Colo., completed the final drawing of the Long House plan and began making drawings of the rooms and kivas. Edna Passaglia completed this large and difficult task, and made all final plan and section drawings of Long House and the various features illustrated.

It is not possible to give proper credit to each crew member who worked on the excavation and stabilization of the pueblo. Particularly devoted to the task were the members of the stabilization crew who worked each season throughout the project. These men, all trained in stabilization techniques by Al Lancaster, were under the immediate supervision of David A. Decker from the 1960 season on. Without their skillful efforts there would not be nearly so much of the ruin standing today. The members of the crew were Raymond Begay, Jim Bitsilly Begay, Lewis Joe, and Jim Frank.

The Long House crew included, on occasion and for widely varying periods of time, those who were working on the archeological survey team, at other sites, or in constructing and maintaining the base camp. All those known to have worked in Long House (except the permanent Project staff), and the seasons of their work, are listed below.

Richard P. Wheeler directed the Wetherill Mesa Project laboratory. Those most concerned with assisting in the artifact studies and collation of data were Ruth Chappell, Pauline Goff, and Jean Lee. Tillie Ellis labored mightily to straighten out mapping problems, and Marilyn Colyer made the line illustrations of specimens.

Since the Long House Camp was administered from Park headquarters, many members of former Superintendent Chester A. Thomas' staff—especially those in the Maintenance Division—found their workload considerably increased because of the field operation.

Analysis of material from the site was undertaken wherever possible by members of the Wetherill Mesa Project staff or other Park Service specialists. Through the generosity of the National Geographic Society, this work was greatly broadened by ancillary studies made by specialists in a number of academic institutions and other agencies of the Federal Government.

Major contributions to the Long House report were made by several fellow members of the Project staff. Although Richard Wheeler and I analyzed the stone and bone tools together, the classifications used are his, as well as the entire sections on these artifacts. He also described the detrital stone material previously analyzed by Douglas Osborne. Carolyn M. Osborne performed the same task for all of the perishable materials.

Thomas W. Mathews and Lyndon L. Hargrave, Southwest Archeological Center, Globe, Arizona, identified the mammal and avian remains, respectively. Hargrave was assisted in feather identifications by Norman Messinger. The data from the latter study is presented and discussed by Charmion R. McKusick, Southwest Archeological Center, in ch. 8 of this report. Mathews' tables of data and comments about the faunal stratigraphy are included in this chapter.

James A. Erdman, botanist, and Charles L. Douglas, zoologist, were stimulating office mates and readily available sources of information on plant and animal resources, respectively, of Mesa Verde. They not only identified a variety of material from the site but also contributed many thoughts on its paleo-ecology.

Frederick S. Hulse of the University of Arizona, assisted by Charles F. Merbs and Kenneth A. Bennett, identified the human skeletal material. James S. Miles, M.D., University of Colorado Medical Center, Denver, examined the "patients" (as he often put it) for evidences of osteopathology. Ellis R. Kerley, Orthopedic Pathology Branch, Armed Forces Institute of Pathology, Washington, D.C., also studied one specimen at Dr. Miles' suggestion. E. H. Hixon, D.D.S., Department of Orthodontics, Univesrity of Oregon Dental School, Portland, and Kemp Martin, D.D.S., oral surgeon in Durango, Colo., studied the dentition.

Stanley L. Walsh, Brigham Young University, identified the wild plant remains; Hugh C. Cutler and Winton Meyer, Missouri Botanical Garden, St. Louis, studied the corn and cucurbits, and Lawrence Kaplan, University of Massachusetts, Boston, the beans.

J. Alan Holman, Illinois State University, Normal, examined the reptiles and amphibians; Samuel A. Graham, University of Michigan, the insects and evidence of insect activity within the pueblo; and Robert J. Drake, University of British Columbia,

	1958	1959	1960	1961	1962
Raymond Adkins			x		
Douglas Anderson					x
Shelly Allen			x		
Jim Bitsilly Begay	x	x	x	x	
Raymond Begay	x	x	x	x	
Alan Brew			x		
William Burnett			x	x	
Richard Ellis			x		
George Fairer			x		
Jack Fitzgerald			x		
Jim Frank		x	x	x	
Al Gilliland		x			
William Gilmore				x	
J. Lester Goff					x
Gary Grove		x			
Harold Guide		x			
James Hammond		x			
David Hannah				x	
Loren Haury		x			
Marc Hayes		x			
Christopher Hulse		x			
Lewis Joe	x	x	x	x	
Carl Hugh Jones		x			
Gordon Lalander		x			
Richard Lee					x
Robert Lee			x	x	
George Lewis		x	x		
Arthur Loy			x		
Gerald McCaw		x			
F. Jerome Melbye, Jr.		x	x	x	
Kee Nez			x		
Willie Claw Nez	x				
Richard Parsons					x
Horace A. Ruckel			x	x	
Salvador Sanchez			x		
Curtis Schaafsma		x			
Fred Schack		x			
James V. Sciscenti		x			
Walter Stein		x			
Eugene Tapahonso			x		
John W. Wade		x	x		
Ansel Walters		x			
Oswald Werner		x			
Richard Williams			x		
Paul Willie				x	x
Daniel Wolfman				x	
Gerald Wood			x		
Ernest Yellowhorse		x			

Vancouver, and Halsey W. Miller, Jr., University of Arizona, the mollusks. The late Olas J. Murie, Moose, Wyo., identified mammalian and avian scats. The Federal Bureau of Investigation laboratory in Washington, D.C., studied specimens of human and animal hair and animal hide.

Paul S. Martin, Geochronology Laboratories, University of Arizona, assisted by William Byers and James Schoenwetter, identified the pollen from various soil profiles in Long House. Martin's discussion and interpretation are included in ch. 9.

Charles B. Hunt and Theodore Botinelly, U.S. Geological Survey, identified representative mineral and rock specimens as a guide for our classification of the rocks from which tools were made. Felix Mutschler, geologist, Shell Oil Company, Durango, Colo., identified several specimens. Orville A. Parsons, U.S. Soil Conservation Service, Fort Collins, Colo., studied the soils at Long House and in the possible agricultural areas on the mesa top nearby. Richard H. Brooks, University of Colorado, sampled the Long House trash for a mechanical and chemical analysis. The results were ambiguous, probably because the trash material was culturally mixed.

Robert Samuels, Mehary Medical College, Nashville, Tenn., studied human fecal samples for possible endoparasites. The results were negative. Bruno E. Sabels, University of California at Los Angeles, made a study of the trace elements in human feces from Long House to determine whether variations in the amounts present could be correlated with climatic changes. His findings were inconclusive, possibly because of the rather short occupation periods of the site.

Although typing of the mansucript was done by a number of typists, some unknown to me, major sections of the first draft were done by four Bureau of Indian Affairs secretaries in the former Gallup Area Office, Gallup, N. Mex.: Beth Higginbotham, Niki Gallegos, Lorraine Marsh, and Patsy Ramirez. All volunteered to assist when not otherwise occupied, and I am deeply grateful to them and to John Dibbern, Assistant Area Director (Economic Development), and Edward Kerley, Area Industrial Development Officer, who made this possible.

Bernard S. Katz began the chore of editing the Long House report, and Richard Wheeler completed the task of trying to make a reasonably concise book of a rather strung out manuscript.

Douglas Osborne provided professional guidance for the entire project, including the work in Long House. The Advisory Group appointed by the Director of the National Park Service—the late Frank H. H. Roberts, Jr., Emil W. Haury, J. O. Brew, and Robert H. Lister—also reviewed intermittently the work being done in Long House and offered many practical and useful suggestions in regard to the excavation and the site report then just begun.

Most of the data presented herein, and the conclusions reached, were discussed, before the manuscript was prepared, with fellow staff members of the Wetherill Mesa Project: Al Lancaster, Richard Wheeler, Robert Nichols, Arthur Rohn, Alden Hayes, and Jervis Swannack. These discussions were helpful in formulating ideas, and I value very much the opportunity presented during the course of the Project for this kind of give and take.

References are made in this report to materials from two sites on Wetherill Mesa which were excavated by the Project and will be reported upon in due course. These sites are the cliff dwelling Step House (Robert F. Nichols) and the mesa-top pueblo Two Raven House (Jervis D. Swannack).

G.S.C., JR.

Contents

Illustrations

Tables

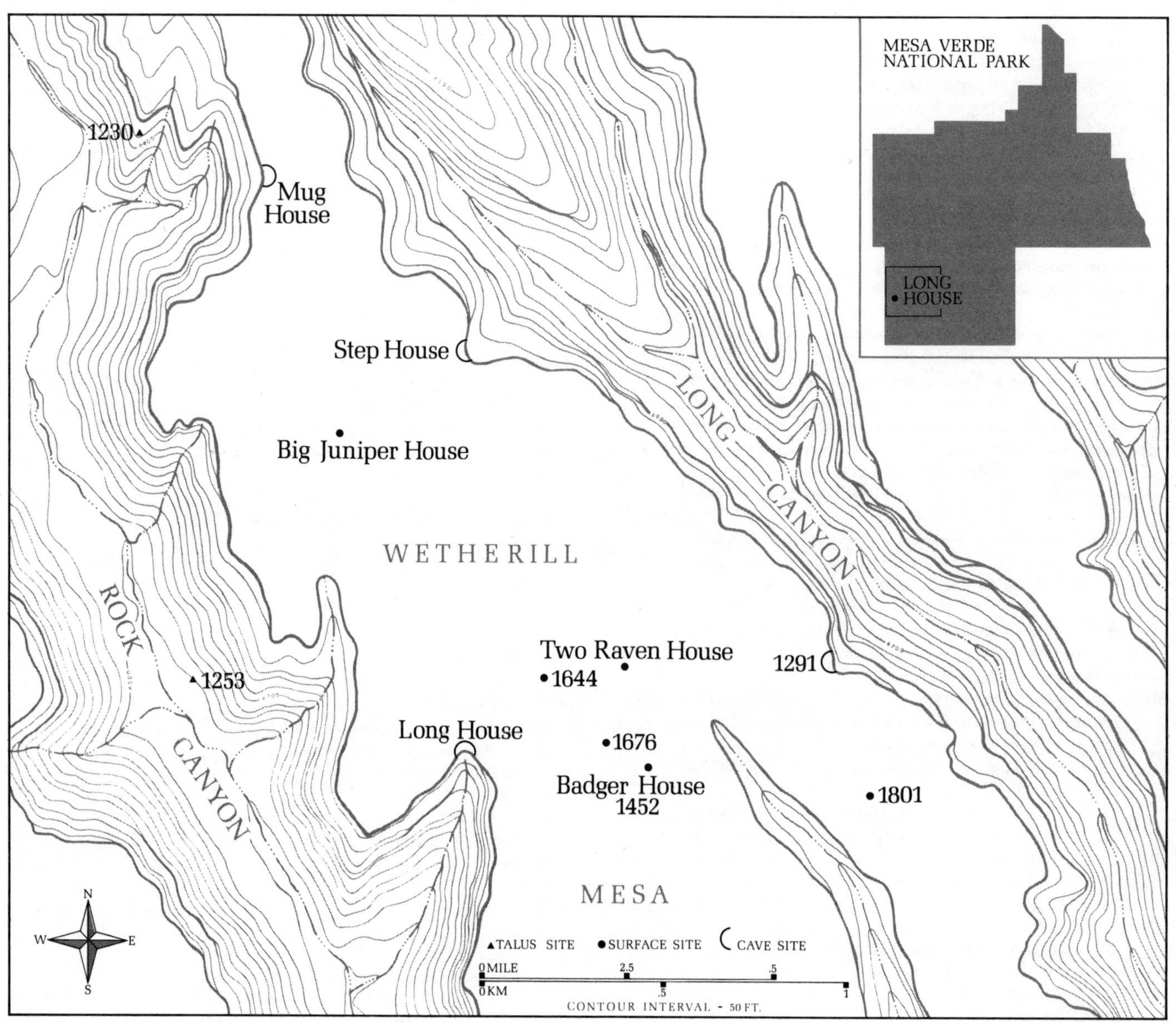

Figure 1. *Map of the west side of Mesa Verde National Park, showing the locations of Long House and 11 other excavated sites on Wetherill Mesa.*

Chapter One

Introduction

Hardly unique among Southwestern sites in its location and general construction, Long House nevertheless provides us with a rare insight into prehistoric Pueblo life because of the wealth of artifacts and information derived from its excavation.

Long House is a late Pueblo III structure built around A.D. 1200 and abandoned shortly before 1300. The pueblo had about 150 rooms, 21 kivas, and a plaza area which probably functioned as a great kiva. Underlying a portion of the east end of the cliff dwelling is a Basketmaker III pithouse, dated at A.D.648, and certain features which may have been associated with it. There were also suggestions of Pueblo I and Pueblo II occupations (A.D. 750 to 1100).

LOCATION

The ruin is situated in a shallow cave or rock shelter in the uppermost vertical scarp (Cliff House sandstone, of Late Cretaceous age), on the west side of Wetherill Mesa, about 100 feet below the rim rock. It faces almost due south down Long House Draw, a 600-foot-deep tributary of Rock Canyon. The elevation at Bench Mark "A", at the west end of the pueblo, is 6,983 feet above mean sea level. The site is located approximately at longitude 108°30′9″ W., and latitude 37°11′13″ N.

Wetherill Mesa forms part of the western boundary of Mesa Verde National Park (fig. 1), which embraces part of a high plateau or cuesta, as it is more accurately termed, called Mesa Verde. At its north rim, the mesa rises to an elevation of about 8,575 feet, or almost 2,000 feet above the Dolores Plateau to the north, and then slopes gently southward. It is drained by the Mancos River and its tributaries, two of which bound Wetherill Mesa: Rock Canyon on the west and Long Canyon on the east. The geological and physiographic character of the Mesa Verde area have been discussed in considerable detail by Douglas Osborne in his prologue to the Wetherill Mesa Project (in Hayes, 1964, pp. 14–17).

VEGETATION AND WATER SUPPLY

The mesa-top vegetation presents an appearance that is probably very similar to what it was before the Basketmaker-Pueblo occupation began some 14 centuries ago. But during the 700-year occupation the forest cover of large portions of the mesa must have been drastically reduced by clearing the land for farming plots and settlement areas, and also by the cutting of timber and brush for building purposes and fuel. It is impossible now to determine to what extent these activities affected the plant community as a whole.

In the vicinity of Long House, the mesa is covered by a mantle of rather dense pinyon-juniper forest (*Pinus edulis* and *Juniperus osteosperma*). The understory, generally devoid of shrubs where wind-deposited soils are deep, is dominated by mutton grass (*Poa fendleriana*). Big sagebrush (*Artemisia tridentata*) is found in areas that have suffered disturbances such as fire, cultivation, and building construction. The only climax or stable sagebrush communities are on the sandy terraces in the canyon bottoms.

James A. Erdman, plant ecologist for the Project, provided most of the above information in a letter of July 1, 1965. He gives more specific data about the Wetherill Mesa vegetation in his unpublished ecological study of the pinyon-juniper woodland (Erdman, MS.). In his letter, Erdman goes on to make the following noteworthy statement about the effect of the forest cover on ground water: "Although things like willow (*Salix exigua*) and reed (*Phragmites communis*) are a rarity in the immediate Long House area today, it is probable that they were not as scare then. From studies of the pinyon-juniper type today it is evident that these trees are intercepting precipitation to an amazing degree, and that in areas where the juniper is eradicated, springs and seeps are producing in much greater quantities."

It is likely that changes in ground water and plant cover were only local in nature, and that cessation of human occupation about A.D. 1300 saw a return to conditions very similar to those existing today. Plant remains and fossil pollen from Long House and other excavated sites reflect such a similarity in the flora. Moreover, changes in the pollen record following abandonment of the mesa do *not* demonstrate that a postulated change in climate occurred during the final stages of the occupation and contributed to the exodus from Mesa Verde (Martin and Byers, 1965, pp. 133–135).

The Mancos River, about 8 miles south of Long House at its nearest point, rises in the La Plata Mountains to the northeast of Mesa Verde and bisects the uplift in its southwesterly flow to the San Juan River. Although the river would have provided water for those living nearby, seeps and springs were the prime sources of water for most of the inhabitants. Ground water was supplemented by rainwater trapped in natural depressions in bedrock and by such a man-made reservoir (Site 1586) as the one near Mug House.

The Long House people developed a seep at the back of the cave by pecking small pits or catch basins into the bedrock floor. Here, as in other springs and seeps in the area, the water percolates down through the porous sandstone to an impervious shaly member, whence it moves horizontally. The cave itself undoubtedly owes its origin to differential weathering of moist and dry sandstone at their contact with shaly deposits.

Considering that today the flow from the Long House seep would not in itself provide sufficient water for the former inhabitants of Long House, Erdman's remark about the interception of precipitation by pinyon and juniper are most pertinent. The Mesa Verde people probably learned after years of observation that the clearing of trees from the mesa top, either accidentally through lightning-caused fires or deliberately, increased the flow of water to springs in the drainage area. In a prolonged dry season, even a slight increase might determine whether the people stayed or left an area. Such possible concern with small increases is reflected, perhaps, in the pecking of several long lead-in grooves and connecting channels for the catch basins.

The people of Long House probably augmented their water supply by using springs in Rock Canyon. The nearest of those now present, however, is about 3 miles down a rugged canyon from Long House and several hundred feet below the pueblo. Carrying water in pottery jars over this terrain for such a distance would have been no easy task.

CLIMATE AND GROWING SEASON

In their discussion of the environment of Mesa Verde, Erdman, Douglas, and Marr (1969, p. 18) make the following statement:

> According to Köppen's classification of world climates based on annual and monthly means of temperature and precipitation, Mesa Verde has a cold, middle latitude, semiarid climate. . . Though it lies in an area of dry climate, Mesa Verde is closer to a humid than to a desert climate because of the proximity of the San Juan Mountain massif to the northeast and of the rest of the southern Rocky Mountains farther east.

The term *dry climate* is defined in a quote from Trewartha (1954, p. 267), who says, in part: "The essential feature of a dry climate is that potential evaporation from the soil surface and from vegetation shall exceed the average annual precipitation. . . .In such a climate there is a prevailing water deficiency and a constant ground-water supply is not maintained, so that permanent streams cannot originate within such areas. It may be possible, however, for permanent streams to cross areas with dry climates. . . .provided they have their sources in more humid regions."

The U. S. Weather Bureau station near the park headquarters on Chapin Mesa (elevation 7,070 feet) undoubtedly reflects the general mesa-top climate which prevails near Long House, on Wetherill Mesa, about 2$^1/_2$ miles due west of the station. Its records go back to 1923, and are now augmented by data from three canyon-bottom and three mesa-top stations installed by the Wetherill Mesa Project and operated for almost 3 years.

From 1923 to 1964, the average annual precipitation at the Weather Bureau station has been 18 inches but has varied from about 9 to 33 inches. Snowfall, which has ranged from 22 to 151 inches, has averaged 19 inches in January, and rainfall has amounted to 2 inches in the peak month of August. The temperature has varied from −20° F. (in January 1963) to 102° F. (July). As Erdman et al. (1969, p. 19) point out:

> Winter moisture is a critical factor as it determines the vegetational aspect of the landscape in late spring and early summer, typically the driest period of the growing season. . . .During the late summer months the days begin with cloudless skies, but by noon, because of intense air turbulence, cumulus clouds develop and thunderstorms are common. Precipitation is usually localized and intense for a short period of time. Consequently, runoff is high and the precipitation is not nearly so effective as winter and spring precipitation in controlling the growth of indigenous plants.

With such fluctuations in local climate, it is not surprising that the growing season is rather variable. The average is 158 days, but this may differ by as much as 31 days from one year to another. Killing frosts have been recorded as late as May 29 and as early as September 14.

The growing season of varieties of corn and beans adapted to the climatic conditions of Mesa Verde is sufficiently shorter than the frost-free period to allow such crops generally to mature. But any one of several climatic factors—unseasonal frost, cool temperature, scanty precipitation—may cause crop failure if it occurs during germination, development, or ripening of these domesticated plants.

Because of the cold air drainage along the canyon bottoms at night, the frost-free period within the canyons is shortened considerably. It was only 102 days in 1962 at C–2, a weather station in the bottom of Navajo Canyon (Erdman et al., 1969, table 11, p. 40). The actual growing season for plants cultivated in the canyon below Long House would have varied not only with the height above the canyon bottom but also with the amount of solar radiation reaching the site. The latter is determined largely by the direction of the slope. "Slope direction, which affects the duration of snow cover and its relationship to soil moisture during the growing season, is probably the most important factor controlling the stand vegetation" (op. cit., p. 45). Conditions favorable to the growth of native vegetation would, presumably, be favorable to the growth of domestic plants also.

SUBSISTENCE

There are large areas of deep loess on the mesa above Long House that would have been suitable for raising the three staple crops—corn, beans, and squash. In addition, an effort was probably made by the Long House people to supplement the mesa-top fields with smaller plots formed by check dams built across gullies of intermittent streams and by terraces on the canyon slopes. The canyon bottom may also have been used.

Although soil moisture would depend to a large extent upon local precipitation and surface runoff, Parsons (MS.) notes that the "moisture relationships of soils developed from the loess [on Wetherill Mesa] are very good and fertility average to high." He adds that all the alluvial and colluvial soils tested, including those from behind check dams, in terraces, and in the canyon bottom, showed reasonably good fertility levels, and that the soil depth and moisture-holding capacity of these plots would have been adequate to permit farming.

Despite the presence of a number of check dams near Long House, both on the mesa top (Sites 1574, 1575, 1576, 1602, and 1683) and in Long House Draw (Sites 1252 and 1312), we can say only that they could have been made or used by the occupants of Long House. (For location of the check dams, see Hayes, 1964, p. 162). None of the sites, which had from 2 to 11 check dams, could be ascribed to a specific occupational phase or be attributed to a specific pueblo (ibid., pp. 140–151).

On the basis of several individuals' work, Parsons (MS.) estimates that the annual corn production of prehistoric Pueblo farmers ranged from 4 to 19 bushels, and averaged 11 to 12 bushels, per acre. This approximates the minimum nutritional needs of a people largely dependent upon corn for their food. At Mesa Verde, corn was supplemented by other foods and in seasons of plenty could easily be stored for future use.

Although it was not possible to determine accurately the total acreage of land cultivated on the mesa top and in the canyons, let alone delimit the fields worked by the inhabitants of Long House, Parsons estimated that about 2,200 acres on Wetherill Mesa were arable and thus would provide food for approximately the same number of people. Parsons is assuming, on the estimate of other researchers, that one acre is all an individual could take care of with his rather rudimentary tools and limited knowledge of agricultural techniques. Not all of this land was necessarily cultivated at any one time, so Parsons' figure of 2,200 people is not intended to indicate a peak population figure.

The hunter could readily find mule deer, rabbit, and other game in the immediate vicinity, as reflected in the refuse bones found in the ruin and dating to the period of occupation. During the time we were excavating Long House, bighorn sheep occasionally entered the ruin, evidently attracted by the spring, and bones of these animals were also found in ancient trash. Although not native to the Mesa Verde, elk may have been added to the larder now and then by hunters venturing onto the Dolores Plateau.

The Indians' diet was probably not restricted to the cultivated plants and game. Available seasonally were juniper berries, chokecherries, serviceberries, pinyon nuts, acorns, and the fruits and seeds of numerous other wild plants. It is possible that beeplant (*Cleome serrulata)* served as a source of food during years of poor crops (see p. 371).

SOURCES OF MATERIALS

The mineral and vegetal resources of mesa top and canyon were fully utilized in building and maintaining the pueblo, manufacturing tools and pottery, weaving, preparing food, and conducting all the other utilitarian and ceremonial activities.

The mere existence of the natural cave or rock shelter indicates that a mass of fragmented rock exfoliated from its roof and walls. Much of this sandstone, or at least that of workable size, was converted into building stone and spalls. A considerable amount of debris, large and small, was used to level building and work areas and to provide a rubble core for some of the walls.

The harder stone for tools and weapons probably came from several sources. Remnants of unconsolidated pediment gravels of late Tertiary or Quaternary age, on Chapin Mesa only a few miles southeast of Long House, contain polished pebbles and cobbles of jasper and quartzite, and also igneous material possibly derived from intrusive bodies in the La Plata Mountains (Wanek, 1959, p. 698). The Mancos River carries many kinds of igneous rock.

The small igneous plugs which intruded into the sedimentary strata of Mesa Verde in several places consist mainly of basaltic rocks and tuff breccias (op. cit., pp. 701–702). Without doubt, the tool maker made use of both the igneous material and the metamorphosed or altered country rock surrounding the intrusive bodies.

The trees and shrubs used most commonly in the construction of Long House and in wooden artifacts were all readily obtainable nearby. These include Utah juniper, pinyon pine, serviceberry, bitterbrush, mountain mahogany: rabbitbrush, and big sagebrush.

Perhaps more difficult to obtain was the reddish brown soil used extensively for wall plaster, floors, and even mortar. It undoubtedly made better adobe than the cave soil, much of which has a rather high sand content. But the nearest source that we could find for soil of this color was in the northern part of Wetherill Mesa, a considerable distance to haul construction material. It is conceivable, because of the small amount of water available in the pueblo, that soil was mined and dampened near Rock Springs, and then carried into the cave from there in the form of readymade adobe.

PHASE SEQUENCE

Table 1 (taken from Hayes, 1964, table 6, p. 88) gives the various classifications established over a period of many years for the purpose of correlating stages of cultural development in the Mesa Verde area with calendrical dates.

Only two periods of occupation have been established in Long House: the Basketmaker III period, dated at A.D. 648 by timbers from Pithouse 1; and the late Pueblo III period, during which the major occupation occurred, dated at A.D. 1200 to 1280 by roof timbers from various rooms and kivas. The former can be assigned to Hayes' La Plata Phase, the latter to his Mesa Verde Phase.

Table 1. Sequences of periods, foci, and phases suggested for the Mesa Verde area.

Date A.D.	Pecos Classification (Watson)	(Morris)	Gila Pueblo (O'Bryan)	Gladwin (Modified by Reed)	Roberts	Alkali Ridge (Brew)	Wetherill Survey
400	Basketmaker II				Basketmaker Period		
500					-----------		
600	Basketmaker III	Basketmaker III	Four Corners Phase	La Plata Focus	Modified Basketmaker Period	------?------	La Plata Phase
700		------?------			-----------	Abajo Focus	
800	Pueblo I	Pueblo I	Chapin Mesa Phase	Piedra Focus	Developmental Pueblo Period	Ackmen Focus	Piedra Phase
900		------?------					
		Pueblo II	Mancos Mesa Phase				Ackmen Phase
1000	Pueblo II	Early Pueblo III		Mancos Focus		Mancos Focus	Mancos Phase
1100			McElmo Phase		-----------	------?------	McElmo Phase
1200	Pueblo III	Late Pueblo III (Mesa Verde Phase)	Montezuma Phase	------?------ McElmo ------?------	Great Pueblo Period	McElmo Focus ------?------ Montezuma (Mesa Verde)	Mesa Verde Phase
1300				Mesa Verde Focus			

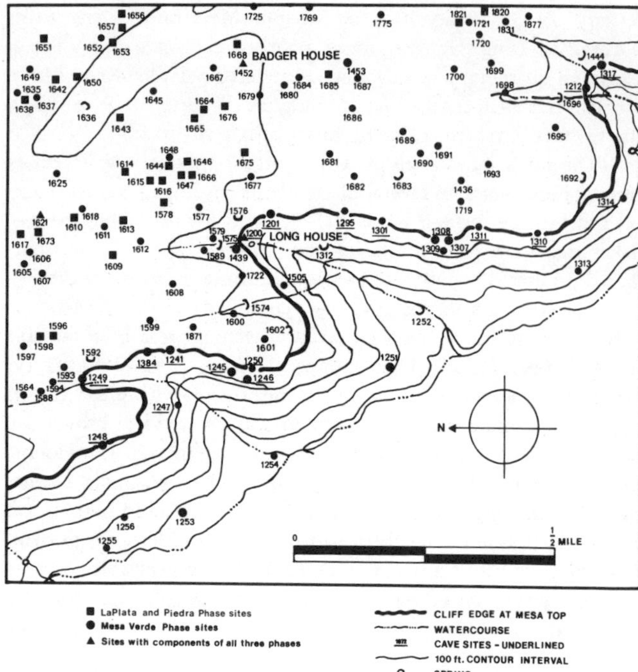

Figure 2. *Map of part of Wetherill Mesa, (above, left), showing the locations of La Plata and Piedra Phase sites, Mesa Verde Phase sites, and sites having components of all three phases.*

Figure 3. *Charcoal inscription (above, right), "John & Clate Wetherill 3 rd 9 1891," on Long House cave wall at east end of West Ledge Ruin.*

The distribution of all sites recorded by the Wetherill Mesa archeological survey crew in the general vicinity of Long House is shown in figure 2 (adapted from Hayes, 1964, p. 161, with additional data from pp. 173 and 197). With the exception of Long House, all sites in this area (which excludes Step House) known to have a Basketmaker III or Pueblo I component are on the mesa top. Also, with few exceptions (such as Badger House, Site 1452), all of the sites in the vicinity with a Pueblo III component are located in the canyons.

The lack of Basketmaker III-Pueblo I material in most of the cliff dwellings may signify only that not enough architecture and trash remain to make the presence of such components known without excavation. It is also likely that earlier structures were leveled by the Pueblo builders after they had salvaged reusable building materials from them. Only rarely, as in Step House (Nichols, MS.), do we find Basketmaker pithouses adjacent to a pueblo.

Although potsherds and other items of Pueblo I (Piedra Phase), Pueblo II (Ackmen and Mancos Phases), and early Pueblo III (McElmo Phase) were found in Long House and on the slopes below it, the bulk of this material was apparently washed into the ruin from sites on the mesa top above the cliff dwelling. Long House may have been inhabited from Basketmaker III through Pueblo III times, but the evidence for Pueblo I, Pueblo II, and early Pueblo III occupancy does not seem sufficient to demonstrate such a cultural continuum.

The concentration of Mesa Verde Phase sites in caves or rock shelters immediately below the canyon rim can be seen in figure 2. The reason for this is still not clear. Occupation of the canyon sites may reflect one or more broad factors which may ultimately have led to the abandonment of the Mesa Verde area: climatic and environmental change; social and political unrest or disturbance; or religious and ceremonial beliefs and practices.

Figure 4. *Panoramas of Long House; (above, center), before excavation; and (below), after excavation and stabilization.*

Figure 5. *East section of Long House before excavation (above, left), and after excavation and stabilization (above, right).*

DISCOVERY AND EARLY INVESTIGATIONS

In his discussion of previous archeological work on Wetherill Mesa, Hayes (1964, pp. 30–35) summarized the activities that led to the discovery of the Mesa Verde cliff dwellings in 1888 and succeeding years.

Long House was discovered and named during the winter of 1889–90, probably early in 1890, by the Wetherill brothers and Charlie Mason of Mancos, Colo. (Mason, MS.). Inscribed in charcoal on the cave wall at the east end of the West Ledge Ruin (east of Room 45) in Long House is "John & Clate Wetherill 3rd 9 1891" (fig. 3), evidence of further exploration of the site during the winter following its discovery.

Less clear, and dated in only one case, are five inscriptions at the east end of the East Ledge Ruin (Area VIII): "J. Wetherill" and "1891," and "A. Wetherill" (presumably for John and Alfred Wetherill), all in charcoal and located, respectively, 8 feet and 4 feet east of the east wall of the structure; the barely discernable "Nordenskiöld" scratched with a stone on the cliff face beneath "A. Wetherill;" the even more unreadable "A. W. . . . ." just below "Nordenskiöld;" and the initials "JW" and date "1891" scratched on the cave roof above loop hole number 11.

During the summer of 1891, Gustaf Nordenskiöld of Sweden learned of the discoveries at Mesa Verde while traveling in the west. After a preliminary trip to Chapin Mesa, he engaged Richard and Al Wetherill in helping him to investigate the ruins. Later, with John Wetherill as his foreman, he spent a month (July 14 to August 14) excavating in Long House. "No. 15," Nordenskiöld's site number for Long House, was carved in an ax-sharpening groove, in bedrock, at the back of the cave. In 1893, Nordenskiöld published the results of his observations and excavations in Long House and other cliff dwellings, thus giving us a reasonably clear picture of the ruins as they appeared at the end of the 19th century. Not until 1958, with the start of the Wetherill Mesa Project, was any additional excavation undertaken in Long House.

Evidence of early exploration of Long House was found near the top of unconsolidated fill in Room 71. A sheet from an undated film pack identifies it as Kodak S3S, Panchromatic. A fragment of newspaper gives a list of state officials, and another mentions William McKinley's bill. The only date given is July 1, in an advertisement. Although McKinley served as President from March 4, 1897, to September 14, 1901, he was also a member of the House of Representatives from 1876 to 1890, excepting 1882. The bill referred to is perhaps the McKinley tariff bill, which was enacted October 1, 1890.

EXCAVATION AND FIELD METHODS

Our objective, as was the case with most of the other sites excavated during the course of the Wetherill Mesa Project, was twofold: to prepare an in-place exhibit for the public through complete excavation and optimum stabilization of the cliff dwelling, and to derive as much information as possible by using the latest scientific techniques.

Although it was the largest of the three major cliff dwellings excavated by the Wetherill Mesa Project, Long House presented no great problems of access, supply, excavation, and stabilization, with several noteworthy exceptions which will be discussed later. The site can be entered by a moderately steep trail down the cliff several hundred feet southwest of the site. Steps cut in the bedrock at this point show that we were not the first to use this approach. The Pueblo Indians who lived in Long House, as well as in the other sites in Long House Draw, undoubtedly found this to be one of the easiest approaches to their homes.

During October 1958, Al Lancaster and I started work in Long House with a four-man crew. The bulk of the fallen building stone was cleared from the surface of the site, and the reusable blocks were stockpiled for stabilization. Living trees and brush were also removed where necessary to clear the work area. The extent of the problem can be seen readily in figures 4 through 6.

Twelve test trenches were dug through the trash fill in the lower, central part of the ruin and on the Upper East Trash Slope. Before bad weather forced us to stop work, we had located the outer pueblo walls in several places, and we knew fairly well the depth of trash fill and other occupational and natural debris that we would have to remove. The deepest fill overlaid the eastern end of the site and covered several rooms and kivas so completely that there was no evidence of their presence. We made our initial plans, accordingly, for the excavation sequence of the major portions of the pueblo. Work began in earnest in 1959, with a full crew to perform the excavation and concurrent stabilization, and extended on a seasonal basis through the summer of 1961. The final fieldwork was completed in an additional month during the summer of 1962.

A spur road from the main Wetherill Mesa dirt road into Long House Camp, the field headquarters for the Project, enabled us to take vehicles to the edge of the cliff just southwest of Long House. Here we built a platform that jutted out over the cliff edge and erected a commercial wooden derrick (fig. 7). By means of a winch, which could be operated electrically or manually, and with the aid of an old mine bucket, we lowered equipment and supplies of all kinds to the ruins trail about 70 feet below. We brought out all material excavated from the dwelling by the same mechanism.

Our water supply for the cliff dwelling consisted of a 200-gallon tank near the winch, several hundred feet of heavy duty garden hose secured to a nylon rope for the 100-foot drop to the pueblo from the cliff directly above, a hose nozzle, and several 50-gallon drums in the ruin.

Preliminary tests showed that the East Trash Slope was a prime burial area. So in order to salvage the burials before covering the slope with backdirt from the ruin above, we started our excavations here. A trench was cut parallel to the contour at the base of the trash deposits, and then extended uphill in a broadside to the pueblo walls. For convenience in recording and analysis, the slope was divided arbitrarily along a rough alinement of boulders. The lower section, which contained most of the burials, is southwest of the row of boulders; the upper section, northeast of it. A similar procedure was followed in excavating the West Trash Slope, but no subdivision of the area was made. Visible rooms, kivas, areas, and general features were numbered or lettered before excavation. The balance of the architectural features and the burials were designated consecutively as they were uncovered or demarcated. Only Rooms 2, 3, and 4 carry the same numbers assigned to them by Nordenskiöld in 1891.

With the trash slopes clear, excavation was started in the rather exposed rooms and kivas on the west end, and in the more sheltered central and eastern portions of the cave. Galvanized iron chutes were used in moving the dirt from Kivas A to F and associated rooms across unexcavated structures to the West Trash Slope (fig. 7). Backdirt from much of the central and eastern sections also had to be removed before the outer tier of kivas, rooms, and areas could be cleared. A long ramp of Douglas-fir planks was built from Area IV, across Kivas K and Q and several rooms, to a platform jutting out over the East Trash Slope (fig. 8). Secondary ramps led to the main ramp from various parts of the east end of the ruin. Debris was then simply carted out in wheelbarrows and dumped.

Although no attempt was made to sift all the fill from the site, we did use screens whenever we came upon concentrations of artifacts and refuse materials.

A difficult part of the site to reach was the East Ledge Ruin (Area VIII). Four sections of metal scaffolding, each consisting of two 5-foot-high end frames and four side braces, were stacked vertically on adjustable bases on top of deep, unexcavated fill in the Great Kiva (fig. 8). Outriggers of tubular pipe scaffolding erected on the south and west sides provided additional bracing. A wooden platform at the top of the tower supported a 20-foot ladder, which spanned the gap between tower and ledge. A similar construction, without the ladder, served as a photographic tower in various parts of the ruin.

Stabilization was carried on as an integral part of the archeological work. Often it was necessary to stabilize poorly preserved or leaning walls, made more precarious by uncovering their bases, before excavation could be completed. Only in Pithouse 1, however, was it necessary to clear fill from a large area beneath room walls. Here several walls of Rooms 54, 55, 56, and Kiva J were supported on wooden planks and masonry columns so the pithouse floor could be cleared in its entirety and left exposed as an exhibit.

In stabilizing Long House, we generally repaired or replaced sections of prehistoric masonry only where it was absolutely necessary. Occasionally we rebuilt walls, in part or entirely, because they served as fill-retaining structures. They often supported other structures in turn, and thus were subject to considerable lateral thrust. In addition, the top few courses of walls likely to be subject to heavy visitor traffic were reset in concrete.

We reshaped original building blocks to fit where needed, as long as the supply lasted, and then we turned to unshaped stone. In all cases, we tried to match the replaced masonry with the original. The joints in the new construction were packed with red adobe (derived from red, mesa-top soil), and finally a thin coating of red adobe was painted on all new exposed surfaces. When this washed or

Figure 6. *Long House from west overlook at start of excavation (left), and after excavation and stabilization (right).*

Figure 7. *Platform with wooden derrick at cliff edge southwest of Long House cave.*

Figure 8. *Ramp and platform jutting out over the East Trash Slope.*

flaked off shortly afterwards, depending upon whether it was exposed to rain or windblown dirt, these new surfaces looked much like those of the adjoining prehistoric walls.

A topographic survey was run and several semipermanent bench marks were established by transit. A brass marker was installed at bench mark "A," the only permanent reference point. Features in the ruin were mapped by telescopic or leaf alidade and plane table. Cameras used for the major coverage of activities were 4-by-5 press and view types, loaded with medium speed (ASA 200–400) black-and-white cut film. The 4-by-5 photographs were supplemented by 35 mm. color transparencies taken with a variety of rangefinder and single-lens reflex cameras and lenses. Heavy duty electronic flash and slave units were used extensively in photographing individual features.

All artifacts, unworked cultural material, soil samples, and other specimens of any type which we wished to preserve or record were first assigned field catalog numbers. They were then sent to the Wetherill Mesa Project laboratory on Chapin Mesa for cleaning, sorting, cataloging, and analysis or forwarding to specialists for study. Charcoal and wood specimens collected for dating, and occasionally other very fragile items, were treated at the site with appropriate preservatives.

Field notes were made on blank triplicate "forms," 8 inches by 10 $^1/_2$ inches, following a general outline agreed upon by all Project archeologists. Two copies of the notes were sent to the Wetherill laboratory once or twice a week for safekeeping, as were copies of other specialized triplicate forms which were used for the field catalog, burials, photographs, and the like.

Chapter Two

Architecture

By conservative estimate, Long House had approximately 150 rooms; 21 kivas, a large ceremonial plaza or great kiva, and various work areas. Beneath the Pueblo III structure we found evidences of earlier occupations of the cave: a Basketmaker III pithouse, a possible Pueblo I pithouse remodeled into a Pueblo III kiva, and hearths and walking surfaces probably associated with the early periods of occupation. As might be expected, the architecture is exceedingly varied, not only from one time period to another but within periods. The range of variation is due to the needs and desires of the builders, and also to the topography of the site (figs. 9 and 10).

The rock shelter served to protect the inhabitants from rain and snow, and a seep at the back of the shelter provided small amounts of water. In other respects, the cave presented problems in building rooms, storage areas, and the like. The floor of the shelter sloped downward sharply from the deepest recess of the cave to meet the head of Long House Wash, making construction of level walking surfaces difficult in places. Portions of the natural cave floor fill were unstable because of the steep angle. Although the seep provided water, it also created a drainage problem for the rooms built near it and no doubt made sections of the pueblo unpleasantly damp.

In parts of the rock shelter there is a fairly level floor, either of bedrock or sandy fill. It was in these areas that the first rooms were built, with construction continuing out to the edge of the wash in later times. Complexity of the structure—if we can consider anything this rambling a unit—also increased with the passing years. Rooms and kivas were abandoned, reoccupied, or perhaps remodeled from one type of unit to another. They were forced to conform not only to the cave topography but also to previously built features. The expansion was by no means limited to the floor of the cave: it was carried upward with equal zest though not always with sound engineering techniques.

The end results could hardly be unexpected, either by the original inhabitants or those of us who studied the ruin. The miscellaneous components were built in most cases without planning, were inadequately tied together, and were certainly poorly designed to support the upper stories that were added. The collapse of portions of the pueblo during occupation was not uncommon, as can be readily seen in at least four segments of the ruin. Prayer sticks found in several wall abutments, and in blocks of multistoried rooms, may have been placed there to ward off the possibility of wall collapse.

Perhaps this is too dismal a picture of Long House. Parts of it show excellent workmanship. Much of the trouble can be traced to the building stone itself. The Cliff House sandstone— the formation in which the shelter was formed and the source of the building stone—generally requires extensive working to obtain fairly rectangular blocks. Poorly shaped stones require more mortar, resulting in weaker walls. These factors, rather than a lack of interest or forsight on the part of the builders, contributed to the general instability.

ROOMS

Because of poor preservation or lack of significant features, few of the rooms merit individual description. A table giving the salient features of each numbered room is on file and available for study at Mesa Verde National Park. In most cases, upper-story rooms are not given separate numbers unless their walls do not lie directly above the walls of the rooms below. Upper-story rooms bear the same number as the ground floor rooms concerned, suffixed with a slash and a number indicating the story. For example, 4/3 indicates the third floor of Room 4.

Roofs

Unfortunately, in only two rooms—4/2, vent recess for Kiva A; and 4/3—was the roof either intact or partially intact (these are described in the discussion of Room 4). A small portion of what may have been the roof of Room 82 was present at the southwest corner of the structure. It consisted of three parallel sticks laid across the corner formed by the masonry wall on the south and the bedrock wall on the west. Adobe and rock were placed above the sticks, forming a small (1.4 feet across each end) section of roof, 5.9 feet above floor level.

Primary roof beams, door lintels and jambs, wall pegs, and other miscellaneous bits of prehistoric wood construction still remain in places, but in those rooms where there should have been roofs (because of almost perfect preservation of the rest of the room) the timbers apparently had been torn out deliberately after the pueblo was abandoned.

The extant timbers and beam seats do provide some information about roof construction in the larger rooms, however. Several major roof supports or *vigas*, about 6 inches in diameter, supported secondary roof poles or *latias*, approximately 3 inches in diameter (omitted in the Room 4 roofs), running at right angles to the *vigas*. For instance, in Room 17 there were three primary timbers and nine secondary, five once embedded in the north wall and interfingering with four embedded in the south (because of the length of the room). The closing material consisted of a mass of brush, split juniper poles, and bark or other available materials. Above this was usually up to half a foot of adobe.

Hatchways must have connected several superimposed rooms, but there was no clearcut evidence of such features. Some of the many slabs and the several fragments of rounded adobe "molding" found in the ruin may have come from hatchways.

Figure 9. *Map of Long House ruin and East Trash Slope, showing locations of human burials.*

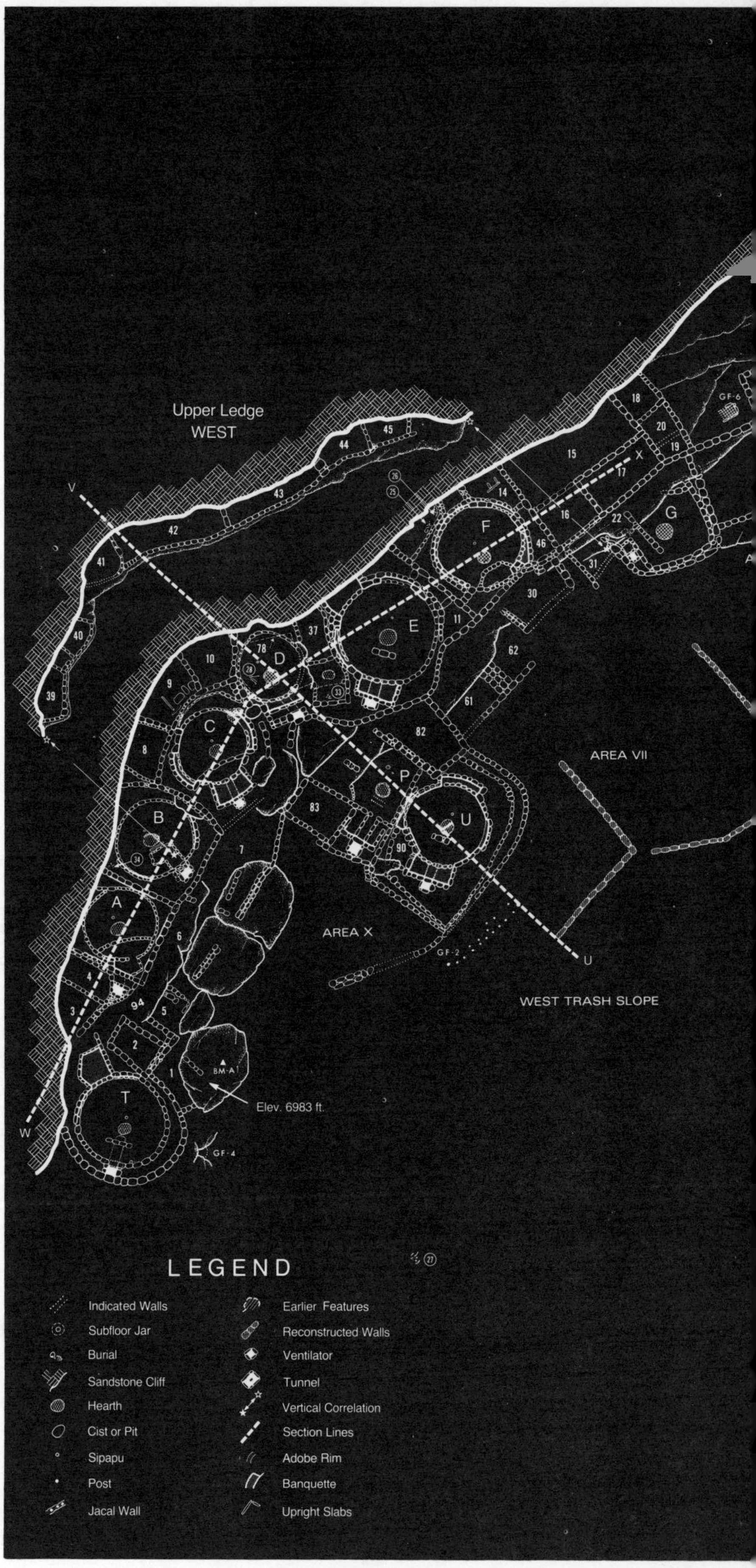

LONG HOUSE

SITE 1200

Showing Trash & Burial Areas

Wetherill Mesa

AREA VIII
Upper Ledge
EAST
AREA II
AREA III
AREA IV
GREAT KIVA
AREA VI
AREA IX
AREA XIII
AREA XI
AREA XII
PITHOUSE
UPPER EAST TRASH SLOPE
LOWER EAST TRASH SLOPE
Limit of Excavation
Limit of Excavation
FEET
METERS

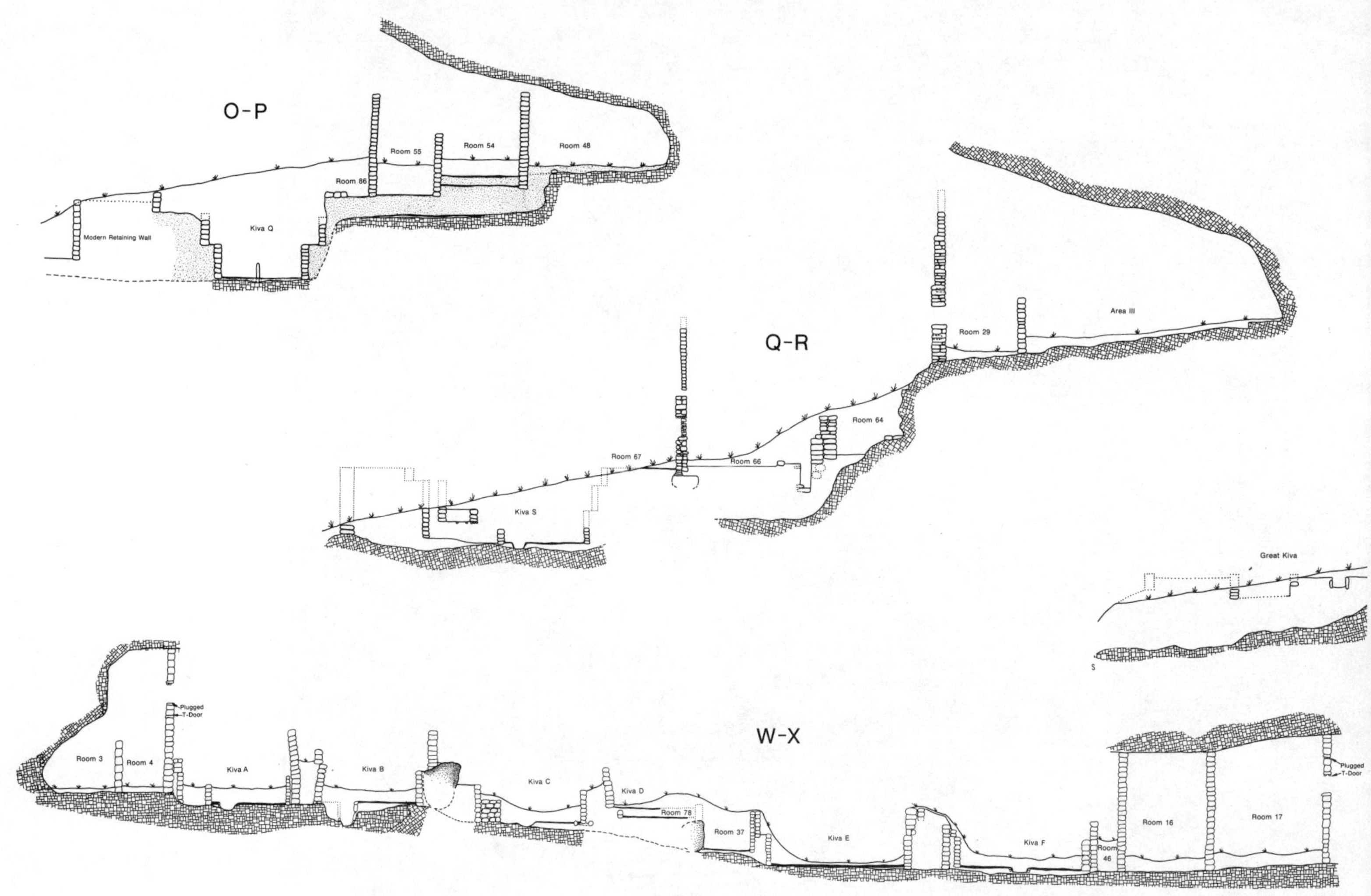

Figure 10. *Section of Long House ruin; a, Line O-P; b, Line Q-R; c, Line S-T; d, Line U-V; e, Line W-X; and f, Line Y-Z.*

Walls and wall features

Wall preservation of ground-floor rooms was generally good, except in those rooms built on sharply sloping surfaces or on unstable fill. In the case of the former, the downslope wall was often missing in its entirety. Mud lines (traces of adobe mortar) on a cave wall, as well as pecked beam seats in cave or man-made walls, helped us determine the extent of upper-story rooms. The amount of wall and floor debris in the fill—including timbers, shakes, brush, adobe, building stones, spalls, and artifacts—was also helpful in estimating the extent of collapsed architecture.

Except for two rooms, the walls of every structure were masonry. Room 41, West Ledge Ruin, is triangular in shape, with the cave wall forming the back wall of the room. The other two walls—one with a doorway—were *jacal* (wattle and daub). And in the case of Room 74, the south wall was built of wood and adobe; the other three were masonry. This room may not have been roofed, whereas Room 41 was roofed by the cave wall, which curved out over the ledge on which it was built. The jacal walls are described later, in the discussion of these two rooms.

Although the terms "single-coursed" and "double-coursed" have often been used to describe masonry walls, I believe that such use of the term "course" introduces a certain ambiguity. I prefer to restrict the use of the word to horizontal tiers of rocks, built one above another, rather than to both vertically and horizontally laid components of a wall. For the most part, the walls in Long House were laid up in courses but do not show banding or horizontal patterning. Practically all were superior to the so-called "rubble" wall, which consists of unshaped stones built up without regard to horizontal courses.

The three major types of masonry found in Long House are:

(1) Simple (formerly called "single-coursed"), consisting of a single thickness of masonry, coursed or uncoursed, and thus only as thick as the stones used in it. All the building stones are laid—usually horizontally—with the long axis in the same plane.

(2) Compound (formerly called "double-coursed," along with part of 3 below), with the stones usually laid horizontally and with their axes in two planes: parallel to the wall and perpendicular to it. The wall will usually be thicker than a simple wall because some stones are laid crosswise.

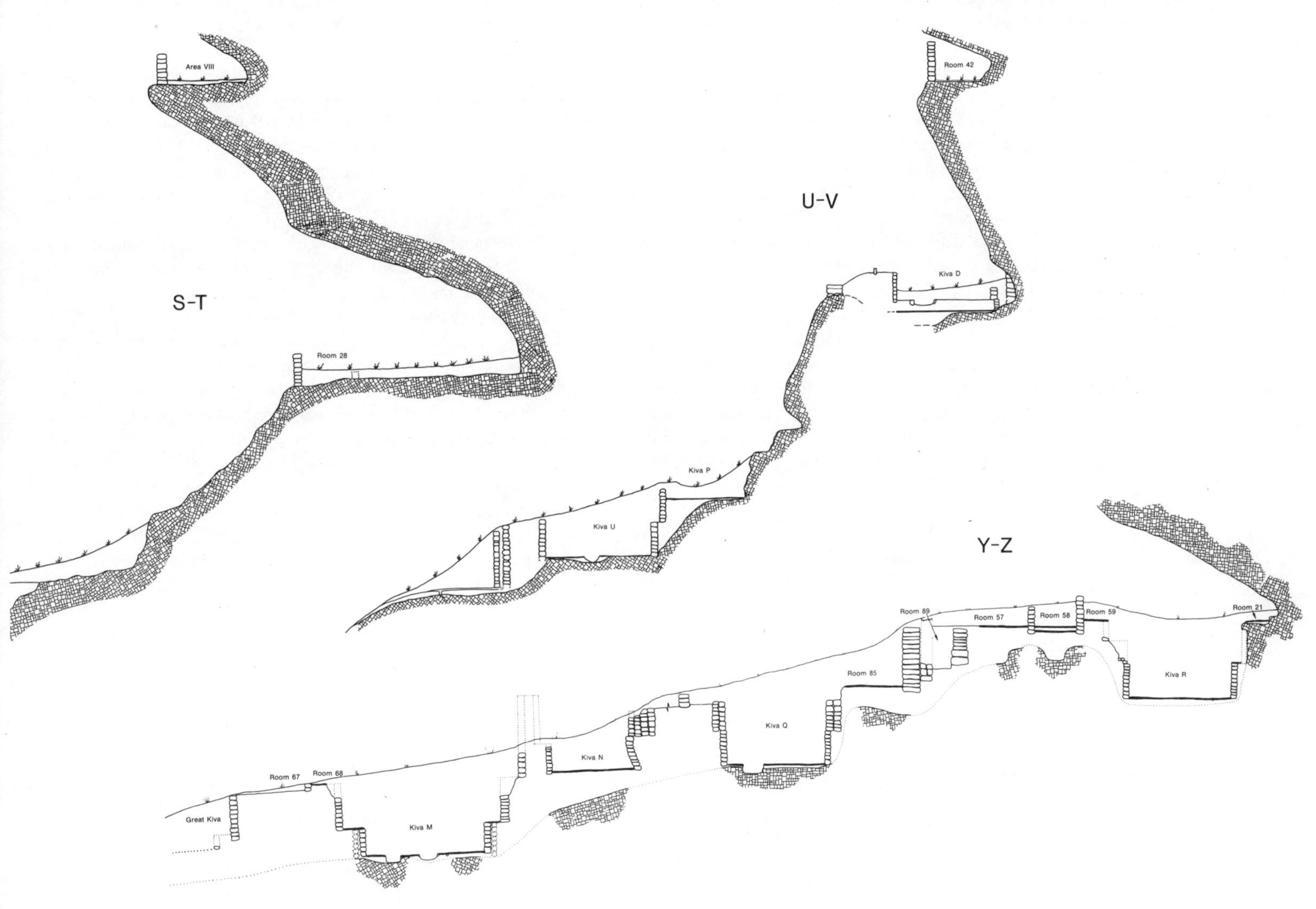

(3) Composite (some types were formerly called "double-coursed," with 2, above), which is rather rare in Mesa Verde and consists of all the other methods of construction not already discussed. Examples are the true double wall (built as two separate walls, side-by-side and one against the other), the rubble-cored wall faced on each side with a veneer of rock, and the rubble-cored wall that consists of two simple walls laid parallel to one another, with the space between filled with rubble.

The majority of the walls in Long House are simple, with compound the next most common. Composite walls are found in only a few places in Long House. Often a wall will start as one type at the base and, as the height is increased, change to a different type part way up. Others will vary in a similar manner, but longitudinally instead of vertically. No doubt there would have been many more compound and composite walls had the builders planned at first as many upper story rooms as were ultimately built. Perhaps the protection from wind, rain, and snow offered by the rock shelter was responsible in part for the large amount of simple wall construction.

In Long House, there was a lack of consistency not only in masonry types but in the finishing or dressing of wall faces. Any of the three types may be dressed on one or both faces, or may be entirely unfinished. The location of the wall and its function were apparently the prime factors considered during both the construction of the wall and the finishing of its faces. For example, exterior room wall faces were generally better finished than less visible interior faces which could be smoothed with thick plaster. In the tower, Room 60, the faces of the outer wall stones were also curved lengthwise to match the curve of the wall. Some fill-retaining walls showed no finishing whatever on the exposed face. The building stones were usually shaped by rough flaking and chipping, and were finished in some cases by pecking and grinding.

The inconsistencies found in room architecture were by no means limited to those common in one room as opposed to those in another. One room wall might be compound, the other three simple. One of the walls might show some dressing on one or both faces, the others being unfinished on both faces.

The average simple wall thickness was about 0.8 foot, with the range extending from 0.4 foot to 1.7 feet. That of the double walls was about 1.2 feet, and ranged from 0.8 foot to 2.2 feet. The composite wall forming the south wall of Rooms 57, 58, and 59 ranges in thickness from 1.7 feet south of Room 59 to 3.5 feet south of Room 57. This composite wall consisted, at its thickest, of the original compound wall on the north and a simple wall—possibly a brace—on the south, with rubble fill between. The composite north and east walls of Room 87 are true double walls, each part being a simple wall. The total wall thickness of each composite wall is about 1.5 feet. The other two room walls are compound.

Building stones varied widely in size, ranging from about 0.3 foot to 2.3 feet in length and 0.05 to 1.0 foot in height or thickness of the exposed face. The average size was far more uniform, being 0.8 to 1.0 foot long and 0.3 to 0.4 foot high. These figures do not include the large vertical slabs and small boulders which were used occasionally and were generally interspersed among the horizontally laid blocks.

Considerable mortar was used between the blocks to level them, and beneath the lowest course when it was placed on bedrock. Both the local yellow-brown soil and gray shaly clay, which outcrop in the back of the cave, were used for mortar along with red soil from the mesa top. We used the term "adobe" for the mud made from the red and yellow-brown soils to indicate that the mortar, plaster, and floor material was specially prepared and was thus distinguished from naturally deposited sediments which served a similar purpose in places. No sun-dried or sod bricks were used here, and vegetal material was not commonly mixed with the soil in preparing adobe.

Generally, unshaped chinking spalls, up to about 0.3 foot long and averaging about 0.2 to 0.3 foot wide, were pushed into the mortar in both horizontal and vertical mortar joints and in large gaps between building stones. They were often used on both sides of a wall, perhaps in the belief that they strengthened it as well as providing decoration.

Some walls were "plastered" in places by smearing surplus mortar extruded between blocks across the face of the surrounding wall. In most cases, however, the overall plaster was prepared and applied independently of the wall construction. The material was usually derived from the red or brown soils, and was probably tinted more often than we realized with pigments made from hematite, kaolin, and the like.

The general method of wall construction, the size and shaping of the stones used, and the chinking and plastering of the masonry were sufficiently uniform throughout the site to encourage the use of the term "conventional" for much of the masonry.

It was rather difficult to determine wall abutments in many parts of Long House because of both poor preservation, due to wall collapse and disintegration of damp sandstone, and inconsistencies in the method of bonding. Often walls were bonded—perhaps "tied" is a better term—only at several points rather than throughout the full height of the contact area. In some cases, one wall will abut another up to several feet above floor, and then the latter will abut the former for the rest of the junction.

There was considerable variation in doorways built into room walls. In general, most were rectangular in shape, often slightly narrower at the top, and at least six were T-shaped. Three of the

Table 2. Definite and probable room hearths.

	Lining		Shape			Location				
Room	Stone	Adobe	Circular	Rectangular	Quadrant of circle	Corner	Center	Other	Dimensions (in feet)	Evidence
*4/3						NW				Fire-reddened walls
*8								West side	Fire-reddened bedrock floor and cliff wall	
23		x			x	SW		Radius of arc: 1.4 Collar height: 0.15 Collar width: 0.6		
*26						SE				Smoke-blackened south wall
36	x		x					Southwest quadrant	Diameter: 2.0 Depth: 0.9	
37	x	x	x					Diameter: 2.0 Depth: 0.4		
*42								Against east wall in south half		Fire-reddened floor
*48								Centered along east against cave wall		Ash and fire-reddened wall
49		x	x				x		Diameter: 2.6 Depth: 0.8 (estimate)	
51	x				x	SW			Radius of arc: 2.5 (est.) Depth: 0.6 (estimate)	
*52				(irregular)				Possibly centered in south half (west wall of room gone)	Length/width: 4.5/3.0 (estimate)	Ash and fire-reddened floor
59	x		x		SW				Length/width: 2.1/1.8 Depth: 0.8	Ash and fire-reddened
60		x	x					Near east wall	Diameter: 1.4 Depth: 0.4	

latter were either partly or entirely filled in with masonry by the time the pueblo was abandoned. In some doorways, the wall masonry formed all four sides, with wooden lintels supporting the stones across the top of the opening. More commonly, a long slab, its edges flush with the wall faces, formed the lintel. Another slab usually formed the sill but projected out from the wall face a short distance. Vertical slabs were used in several doorways to form the jambs.

A molding, recessed from the face of the doorway and angled back toward its top, was often built to support a closing slab. Vertical poles, mudded into place at either side of the opening, and horizontal wooden poles running parallel to the wall just below the stone lintel supported the slab and provided a fairly snug fit.

Other openings in the walls, too small to be doors, were made only rarely. Examples include the square "windows" in Room 17/2, the possible draft openings in the east wall of Room 4 adjacent to the Kiva A ventilator shaft, and the loopholes in the East and West Ledge Ruins.

Wall pegs abounded in some of the rooms, generally at about the 5–to–6–foot level. They are generally on the inside of a room and imbedded in one or more walls. Where there are many in a room, as in Room 17, they are often alined roughly in rows and are sometimes fairly evenly spaced along the wall. They usually project about 0.5 foot from the wall face and angle up slightly, and average about 0.1 foot or slightly less in diameter.

Other wall features which occur irregularly include pole and rockledge "shelves;" niches, with some possibly remodeled from loopholes or beam seats; and loops outside and on either side of a doorway, possibly for a pole used to hold a door slab in place.

Floors and floor features

The fate of the floors in Long House rooms was generally determined by that of the walls: when at least a vestige of all walls remained, there was usually a portion of the floor remaining also. Despite a subfloor of bedrock in many rooms, a thin layer of adobe (at the very least) was usually laid down to provide a smooth surface. Often it was up to 0.1 foot thick and curved up onto the base of the room walls. More than one floor was placed in many rooms, especially those toward the front of the cave where they were more exposed to weathering.

Evidence of 28 hearths was found in 23 rooms, four of which had more than one hearth. Eight of the harths were rather nebulous because no part of the feature remained in place. As indicated in table 2, burned and smoke–blackened walls and floor, coupled with ash deposits in some cases, indicate the probable locations of six of the eight dubious features. The 20 clearly defined hearths—true fire-pits—were delimited by slab or adobe construction, or even by a raised clay collar in one case (fig. 29).

Seven of the definite hearths were circular, seven rectangular, and six quadrant-shaped. The quadrant-shaped features are corner fireplaces, defined by two room walls and a connecting arc of adobe. Two of these are hypothetical, being represented by large chunks of

Table 2. Definite and probable room hearths. (Continued)

	Lining		Shape			Location				
	Stone	Adobe	Circular	Rectangular	Quadrant of circle	Corner	Center	Other	Dimensions (in feet)	Evidence
60		x(?)		(semicircular)				Against wall in northeast quadrant	Diameter: 1.7 (estimate-poorly defined) Depth: ?	Smoke-blackened wall, in addition to unlined pit
67		x		x	NW				Radius of arc: 1.1 to 1.3 Depth: 0.7	
69	x	x	x					Centered along and near north wall	Diameter: 1.7 Depth: 1.0	
69	x	x	x					Centered along and near north wall	Diameter: 1.5 Depth: 1.0	
75	x			x				Against west wall near southwest corner	Length/width: 1.8/1.2 Depth: 0.8	
76	x			x				Centered along and against west wall	Length/width: 2.0/1.6 to 2.0 Depth: 0.6 (est.)	
79	x			x (roughly)				Centered along and against north wall	Length/width: 4.7/1.5 Depth: 1.5	
79	x			x (roughly)				South of and adjacent to pit no. 21	Length/width: 2.3 to 2.7(?)/ 2.3 Depth: 1.5	
80	x			x				Northeast quadrant	Length/width: 2.5/1.3 Depth: 0.7	
84	x				x	NW			Radius of arc: 1.8 to 3.0 Depth: 0.9	
87	x			x		NW			Length/width: 3.0/2.1 Depth: 1.2	
**87		x			x(?)				Radius of arc: 1.8 (est.)	
91	x		x					Southwest quadrant	Diameter: 2.0 (est.) Depth: 1.0	

*No part of structure remains.
**Fragments of adobe collars not in place.

an adobe collar found in the fill of Room 87. Had all the pieces fitted together, the hearths would have been semicircular. The evidence more strongly supports the possibility that the remains are from two corner hearths in the upper stories of the room.

Eleven hearths were lined with vertical slabs set in adobe, six with adobe alone, three with both stone and adobe, and one was possibly unlined. Eight hearths were in room corners, and several were aginst the wall near a corner. The northwest and southwest corners were preferred. One firepit was, centered in a room, another centered in the south half of a room. The remainder were built against or near the midpoint of one of the room walls, with the north and east sides being preferred.

The firepit in Room 36 was unique in being the only sealed one in any of the rooms. The firepit beneath the floor of Room 69, and probably a feature of Room 91, was filled and covered over but not deliberately sealed while the room was still in use. The Room 36 firepit was filled with soil to within 0.15 foot of the top, and then a hard-packed layer of red adobe placed over the fill to form a plug that was flush at its top with the room floor. Figure 11a shows the firepit with the plug in position and figure 11b shows the firepit after excavation.

The circular firepits ranged in diameter from 1.4 to 2.6 feet and in depth from 0.4 to 1.0 foot. The radius of the arc forming the quadrant hearths ranged from 1.1 to 2.5 feet, or to 3.0 feet with the elongated pit in Room 84 included. Depth varied from 0.15 foot, the height of the adobe collar laid on bedrock in Room 23, to 0.9 foot. The rectangular firepits ranged in width from 1.2 to 2.3 feet, in length from 1.8 to 4.7 feet, and in depth from 0.6 to 1.5 feet.

Corn and possibly other foodstuffs were ground on metates, some of which were built into mealing bins such as those in Rooms 9, 14, 21, 52, 56, and possibly 3. Some of these were removed during excavation to reach underlying features, others were stabilized in place. Four bins were found in each of four of these rooms, three in the fifth, and one to three in Room 3. They were arranged in all cases so that as many people as there were bins could use them simultaneously. It is quite possible, but could not be proved, that metates of different surface texture were arranged side-by-side so that one operator could produce meal of various degrees of fineness. Metates were found in kivas and rooms other than these six, occassionally embedded in the floor, but no other bins were located.

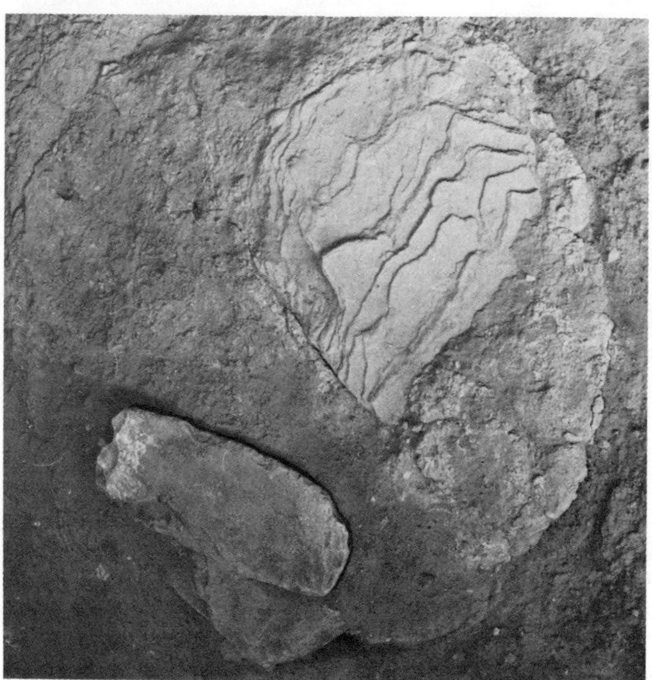

Figure 11. *Firepit in floor of Room 36, with plug in place (below) and after excavation (above).*

Upright slabs formed the four sides of the bins, small horizontal slabs and adobe the floor. The metate was embedded in adobe with its grinding surface just above floor, and sloped down and away from the front of the bin where the operator would have kneeled. In some bins a large potsherd was embedded in the adobe to the left of the metate at the foot of the sloping floor, but in others there was just an area of curved-up adobe or even a flat slab at either side of the metate and below it. These features provided a smooth backstop for the hand when scooping out meal. Few of the bins were sufficiently preserved to provide meaningful measurements. Those discussed in the section on Room 56 are probably fairly typical, however, except that they lack the well-defined scoops of those in Room 9. The grinding implements themselves, the metates and manos, are described in ch. 5 of this report.

In-place Wood

All in-place wooden items in the rooms, identified by Stanley Welsh of Brigham Young University, are listed by provenience in table 3. The specimens marked with an asterisk (*) are worked and possibly parts of digging sticks. The genus and probable species of the wooden items is given below rather than in the table.

Douglas-fir	*Pseudotsuga menziesii*
fourwing saltbush	*Atriplex canescens*
juniper	*Juniperus osteosperma*
mock orange	*Philadelphus microphyllus*
mountain mahogany	*Cercocarpus montanus*
oak	*Quercus gambelii*
pinyon pine	*Pinus edulis*
serviceberry	*Amelanchier utahensis*
willow	*Salix exigua*
yucca	*Yucca* sp.

Rooms 3 and 4, 5–7, and 94

The Room 4 "tower," rising four stories and almost perfectly preserved, is the focal point of interest in Long House (fig. 12a and b). Not only is it impressive, but it is useful in providing a key to a knotty archeological problem: How were the many three, four, and even five-story portions of the pueblo held together? The Room 4 block is the only such construction still standing in its entirety.

The first floor, formed by Room 3 on the south and Room 4 on the north, was built against the southern wall of Kiva A, or, at least, against the room in which Kiva A was built (fig. 13). The construction was then carried upward to the sharply sloping cave ceiling, which forms the roof of the top story. The north wall of the upper stories is supported by the south wall of Kiva A, and all but one of the room doors would have opened on the courtyard formed by the kiva roof.

Perhaps the prime reason for the presence of Room 4 today is that it was built on a flat, bedrock platform. The same may be said for the three-story section of wall still standing on the north side of Room 64. A sloping bedrock footing, or earth fill subject to some slight settling, had been the downfall of many of the higher buildings of Long House.

Part of the east wall of Room 3 had collapsed, but this is the only major break in the masonry of the tower-like room block. The two or three mealing bins that may once have existed in the room are poorly preserved, with only one upright slab and a few traces on the floor to mark their approximate positions.

An adobe lip projected from the north wall of the room, 2 feet above floor. Only the west end still remains, but its original extent is clearly shown by the scare in the plaster. The lip was about 2 feet long, and protruded from the wall about 0.1 foot. Because of its shallowness and rather fragile nature, the lip, made of adobe identical to that used as plaster in the supporting wall, seemed unsuited to support anything. There are no holes in the remaining section to provide an anchor for another object, nor is there any sign of physical use. There are no structures similar to this in other rooms or kivas of Long House.

Table 3. Identification of wood items in-place in rooms.

Room	Item / Location	Kind
2	lintels, south door, 1st & 2nd from N	
	3rd from N	juniper
	4th from N	oak
	5th from N	Douglas-fir
3	peg, north wall	serviceberry
4/1	peg, east wall*	serviceberry
4/2	jambs, T-door, east side, 1st from E	mock orange
	2nd & 3rd from E	serviceberry
	west side (2) from E	serviceberry
	lintels, T-door (3)	juniper
	east wall niche (1)	serviceberry
	east exterior wall, above two openings (1)	juniper
4/2	roof (numerous), room; north pole	pinyon
	other poles	juniper
	brushy material	willow
	ties	oak
4/3	lintel, north door	serviceberry
	peg, north exterior wall	serviceberry
	roof (numerous), E-W members	serviceberry
	N-S poles (3)	juniper
	loop on 1 N-S pole	yucca
13/1	roof, room	Douglas-fir
13/2	lintels, east door	serviceberry
14	pegs, north wall, 1st from E	serviceberry
	2nd & 3rd from E	mountain mahogany

(See Table 4, page 53)

*Worked, possibly part of a digging stick.

The floors of Rooms 3 and 4/1 were bedrock, leveled with adobe where necessary. There is no visible evidence that the floors were actually one or that these rooms were ever used as one. It is likely that some leveling of major depressions was done before the wall dividing the rooms was built. Although modified since construction, the east wall of the two rooms was probably built as a unit (fig. 13).

Unfortunately, neither floors nor walls provide a clue to an entranceway. Entry could have been by a hatchway from Room 4/2 or, more likely, through a door in the east wall of Room 3. The closeness of Kiva T, with its peculiar recess on the northwest side, would seem to support the door theory.

I won't argue here the function of the tunnels from kiva to kiva, or kiva to room, but in several cases in Long House the location of tunnels and the kivas in which they occur suggests possible use as an emergency exit. Anyone caught in an exposed kiva during an attack on the pueblo could move back into more protected rooms, thus possibly contributing to the pueblo's defense, without emerging through the commonly used roof hatchway. Kiva R, on the east end of the ruin, is in a location equivalent to that of kiva T on the west end. Kiva R has a passageway leading into Room 50; Kiva T may have had a similar exit into a room adjacent to Room 3 on the east. Or, possibly, there was a crawlway from the recess of Kiva T into Room 3 directly. There is no evidence for either of these suppositions.

Entry to Room 4/1 is through a very crude door in the east wall. *If* Room 4/1 was built against a room in which Kiva A was later constructed, then the inner east wall of the room was placed after the installation of the vent shaft for the kiva (see fig. 13). The inner wall feathers into the outer east wall at a fairly sharp angle. The point of intersection, and the doorway which cuts through it, are immediately north of the crosswall common to Rooms 3 and 4. The south side of the door is against the crosswall, thus placing it as far south as it could go and still open into Room 3.

The door itself gives the appearance, especially on the room side, of having been made in an already finished wall. The east (exterior) face of the door was fairly well finished, but the remainder presents quite a contrast. No lintel slab and no wooden lintel poles are present; the wall masonry merely continues across the top of the door.

A wall peg, 6.5 feet above the floor, is the only other east wall feature. The peg is probably part of a digging stick. There is a hole for another peg in the north wall, 6.4 feet above the floor. The former angles slightly up into the room, the latter probably inclined slightly downward.

Despite the fact that it extends over a part of Room 3 as well as over Room 4/1, the second story of the structure has been designated as Room 4/2. (The remaining two stories are more directly above Room 4/1.) No floor was found in place, but debris resulting from its collapse made up the bulk of the Rooms 3 and 4/1 fill (fig. 13).

At one time, a large T-shaped door in the north wall of Room 4/2 opened out onto the roof of Kiva A (fig. 14c and d). The lower half was filled, forming a smaller, rectangular door that could be easily closed with a slab. The wood and adobe inner jambs or supports, against which the slab could have rested, were also added after filling the base of the doorway. These consist of vertical brush stems, two on one side, three on the other, embedded in adobe at the top and bottom, and also adobe packed in and around the wood. The jambs lean slightly inward at the top to support the closing slab (fig. 15).

Figure 12. *Room 4 "tower" at west end of Long House, looking southwest (left), and south (right).*

Figure 13. *(Opposite page) Plan of Rooms 3 and 4, and of adjacent Rooms 1, 2, 5, and 6; Section A-A', Rooms 3, 4/1, and 4/2; and Section B-B', Rooms 4/1, 4/2, 4/3, and 4/4.*

The north wall of the room tapers sharply towards the top (fig. 16a). The east wall abuts the north up to about 2 feet above the room floor; above this point it is bonded to the north wall. The bonding of walls was apparently only done when absolutely necessary, and a lack of such bonding may have contributed to the collapse of various parts of the pueblo.

The two large niches in the east wall can be seen in figure 16a. One is especially interesting because of the wooden "lintel" across the front portion of it. The niche was roofed with a large slab whose support is not dependent upon the "lintel."

The west (cave) wall of the room is of interest because of a charcoal pictograph about 2.5 feet above the floor. The poorly preserved geometric drawing, which is inclined sharply to the south, is 0.59 foot long and 0.23 foot wide (fig. 17).

The top of the east wall marks the location of the roof of Room 4/2. The roof is entirely gone except for a portion of it over the Kiva A vent shaft recess, which opens into the north room wall from the roof of Kiva A. The primary timbers of the roof are pinyon and juniper; the closing material is willow brush. The ties used to secure the willow to the main supports are oak. Several of these can be seen in figure 16b. The maximum diameter of the primary beams ranges from 0.4 foot (north beam, directly under the north room wall) to 0.15 foot (southernmost beam). That of the willow ranged from 0.007 to 0.02 foot.

The adobe forming the rest of the roof is mixed in between layers of brush, and is also forced down between many of the layers. The total thickness of this portion of the roof of Room 4/2 ranges in thickness from 0.4 to 0.65 foot, with the brush and adobe occupying about 0.25 foot of this.

As is the case in the room below, Room 4/3 has only one doorway leading into it. Again, the door is in the north wall (fig. 14b). However, there is no convenient roof providing easy access to the room; a ladder from Kiva A's roof would have been the only method of reaching the door. The door is almost rectangular, being slightly narrower at top than bottom, and has a pecked channel in the sill for the door slab and one wooden lintel. The latter no doubt served as a support for the top of the slab. There is a wall peg on the outside of the north wall, slightly below the top and to the west of the door.

The north wall, and the northern half of the east wall, are continued upward from Room 4/2, and are still bonded in the

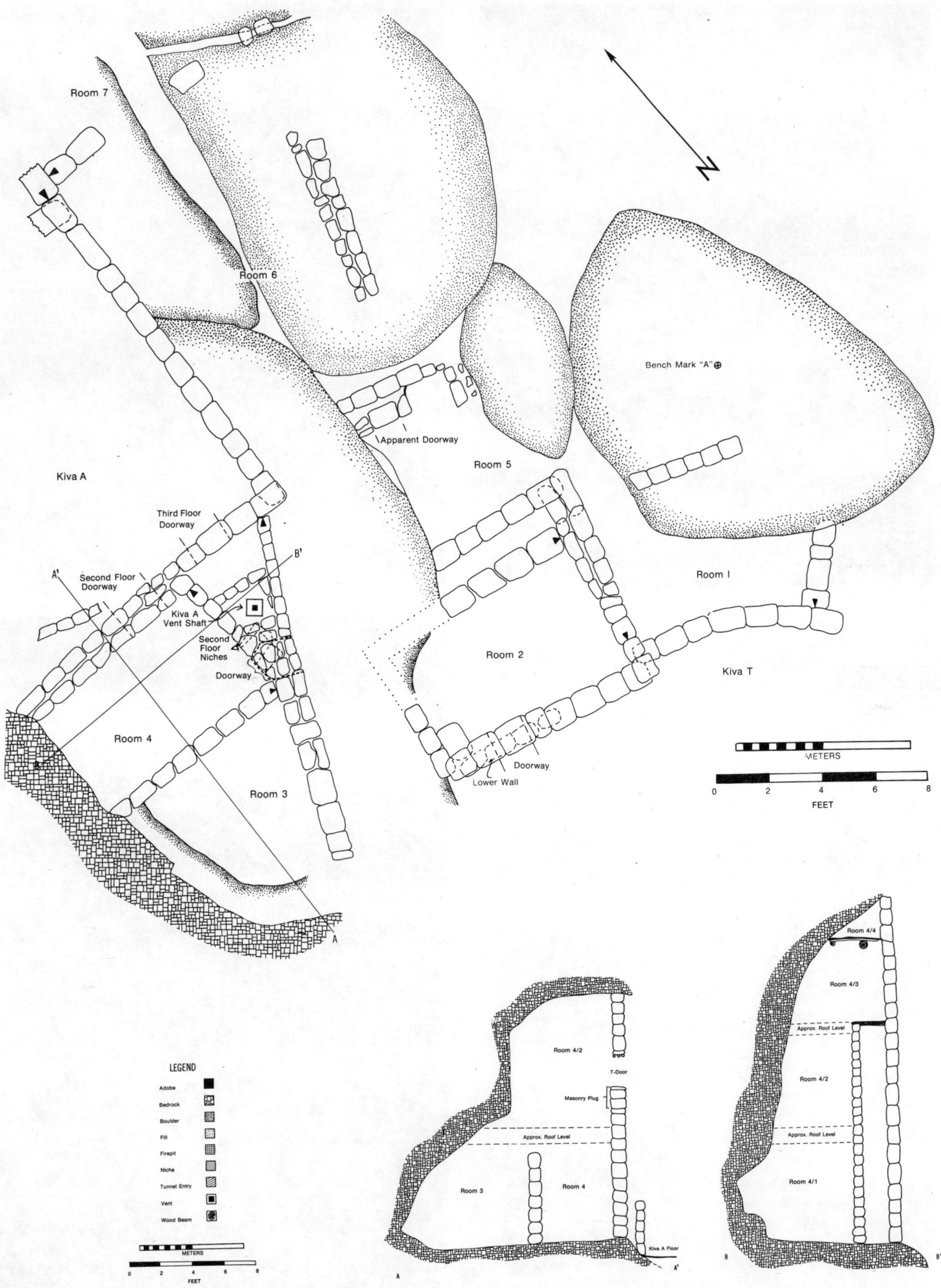

N
Room 7
Room 6
Bench Mark "A"
Apparent Doorway
Room 5
Kiva A
Third Floor Doorway
Second Floor Doorway
A'
B'
Kiva A Vent Shaft
Second Floor Niches
Doorway
Room I
Room 2
Kiva T
Room 4
Room 3
Doorway
Lower Wall
A
METERS
0
2
4
6
8
FEET
LEGEND
Adobe
Bedrock
Boulder
Fill
Firepit
Niche
Tunnel Entry
Vent
Wood Beam
METERS
0
2
4
6
8
FEET
Room 4/2
T-Door
Masonry Plug
Approx. Roof Level
Room 3
Room 4
Kiva A Floor
A
A'
Room 4/4
Room 4/3
Approx. Roof Level
Room 4/2
Approx. Roof Level
Room 4/1
B
B'

Figure 14. *Doors in Room 4 "tower:" subrectangular (a and b); and T-shaped door with lower part closed, exterior (c) and interior (d), in the north wall of Room 4/2.*

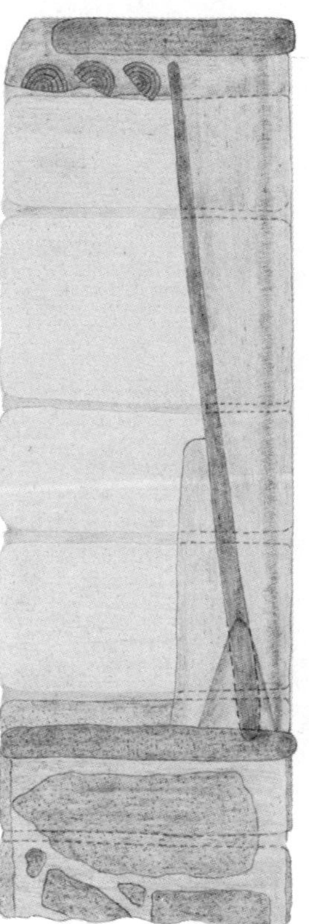

Figure 15. *Section of upper part of T-shaped door illustrated in figure 22c and d, showing provision for holding a closing slab in an inwardly oblique position.*

Figure 16. *North and east walls (a) and roof (b) of Room 4/2; and roof (c) of Room 4/3.*

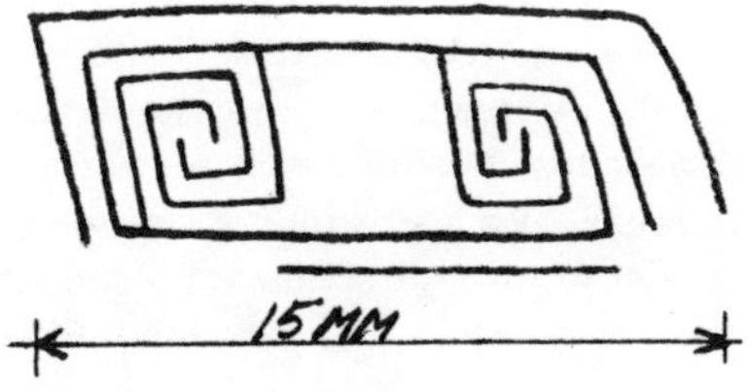

Figure 17. *Rendering of charcoal pictograph on west (cave) wall of Room 4/2.*

Figure 18. *End view of east wall of Room 6 (a), and split boulder with underlying bed on which east wall was built (b).*

northeast corner. The walls of Room 4/3 are of simple masonry, and the disparity in thickness between the compound masonry walls of Rooms 4/2 and those of 4/3 is shown by the presence of a ledge, where one is superimposed directly over the other. A thoroughly burned section of cave wall and plastered masonry in the northwest corner suggests the former presence of a hearth.

The sharply sloping cave wall left little of Room 4/3 to be roofed (fig. 16c), and the triangular shape of the upper portion of the room made roof construction a simple matter. Four primary timbers of juniper support the roof, although the easternmost member is embedded in, and is essentially a part of, the east wall. The overlying brush stems are serviceberry. The maximum diameter of the main supports ranges from 0.1 to 0.35 foot, that of the brush from 0.03 to 0.1 foot. Overlying the brush is 0.005 to 0.1 foot of hard-packed brown dirt (not the more common red adobe), which forms the floor of Room 4/4. The northeast corner of the floor is formed by a slab which was used to close the irregularly shaped opening not covered by brush. Possibly this was originally intended to be a hatchway opening into the storage room above (Room 4/4), but the slab had been mudded into place.

Room 4/4 is a very small, triangular room at the top of the tower. Entry must have also been gained by ladder from the roof of Kiva A. The rectangular doorway is as cramped as the room and is very rough in outline (fig. 14a). There is no evidence of wooden lintels or jambs. The north and east walls of simple masonry are a continuation of the walls of Room 4/3 and are bonded at the northeast corner. The cave wall forms not only the south and west sides of the room but also about half of the roof. The room walls curve in slightly at the top, and a large slab (2 feet by 0.9 foot by 0.13 foot) was mudded into position with red adobe over the portion of the room not roofed by the cliff.

One or possibly two structures were built up against the east wall of the Room 4 complex (Rooms 3 and 4, Kiva A ventilator recess). The room, or rooms if more than one story, designated as Room 94, must have extended out over a part of Rooms 2 and 5. With the exception of three sets of beam seats, two roughly at the first floor roof level of Room 4 and one at the second, there is no evidence of such a structure or structures.

The top row of beam seats at the lower level consists of three in place wood stubs and one empty socket. There may have been more at one time, possibly one against the southeast exterior corner of Kiva A. The lower set, less than a foot below the upper, consists of four or possibly five empty sockets, with a possible sixth seat in the southeast exterior corner of Kiva A. The upper set is probably the earlier, since the building stones appear to have been placed around the beams. Some of the stones of the lower set appear to have been chipped out to make room for the timbers.

At the level of the roof of Room 4/2, or about 5.5 feet above the uppermost of the two rows of beam seats, is a third row of at least three, more probably four, seats, with no wood present.

It is possible to make a reasonable guess as to what happened in this area, and my conclusions are based on two sets of data: (1) the remodeling of the upper walls of Room 2, and the location of the lower walls, which do not coincide precisely with the present upper walls; and (2) the possible orientation of the beams of Room 94, by projecting hypothetical beams from the remaining sockets in the east wall of Room 4.

Room 94 was undoubtedly built against the Room 4 complex using the middle of three sets of beam seats and over part of the roof of Room 2/2 and possibly all or almost all of the roof of Room 5/2. If Room 5 was constructed with only one high story, this would have been the roof of 5/1. The shifting of the large boulder on which Rooms 6 and 7 were built, and against which Room 5 was constructed, may have caused the collapse of Rooms 6, 7, and 94, and the partial collapse and extensive damage to the remaining portions of Rooms 2 and 5. The lower part of Room 5 was then filled, the upper part (story?) rebuilt, Room 2 reinforced and rebuilt where necessary, and Room 94 rebuilt and carried up to two stories. The lowest set of beam seats in the east wall of Room 4 would have been for the new roof of Room 94/1, the highest set for the roof of Room 94/2.

The north wall of Room 94 was probably slightly north of the southeast corner of Kiva A's exterior walls, and the northwest corner of Room 94/2 may have rested on this same corner. The south wall of Room 94 was probably located slightly south of the north wall of Room 2. The doorway through the east wall of Room 4/1 would have opened into Room 94/1. There is no evidence for a third floor to Room 94, and the wall peg on the east exterior of Room 4/3 could have been reached easily from the roof of Room 94/2.

I referred to the shifting of the boulder on which Rooms 6 and

Figure 19. *Beer Cellar Complex, Rooms 15–20.*

7 were built. Figure 18a shows the extent of the tilt (above 20°) of the east wall of Room 6. Underlying the boulder is fairly smooth bedrock (fig. 18b), and burrowing activity west of the boulder, or removal of fill from the downslope side, or both, might have caused the slide. (The position of the boulder has now been stabilized to prevent further movement).

Room 5 was built against the near end of the boulder, as shown in figure 18a. An apparent doorway led into a narrow room between the boulder and a bedrock ledge immediately west of it. The narrow crevice at the bottom of the photograph marks the location of problematical Room 6/1. A similar but wider crevice, also narrowed by movement of the boulder, exists between the north end of the boulder and the bedrock ledge, and may have formed Room 7/1. A considerable amount of trash, but no definite evidence of wall construction, was found in these "rooms."

It is equally difficult to determine the full extent of Rooms 6 and 7 at the upper level, immediately east of Kivas A and B, and on the same level. As figure 13 shows, an outer retaining wall for both rooms was built on the boulder. In the case of Room 7, an inner wall, also on the boulder, was built. Possibly the inner east wall of Room 7, along with a similar but hypothetical wall for Room 6, formed the true east walls of the rooms, with the outer east wall on the boulder serving only as a retaining wall for a walkway.

Rooms 14–20, and 46

One of the best preserved sections of the ruin is the room block consisting of Rooms 15–20. Room 15 is against the cave wall, and is entered only through a doorway in the south wall or a break in the north wall. It is a large room, very cool and dark, and is especially pleasant on a hot summer day. Through a bit of wishful thinking, it was dubbed the "Beer Cellar," and by extension the room block as a whole became known as the "Beer Cellar Complex." Although hardly scientific, the name has been carried onto room sheets and catalog cards as a useful replacement for a rather unwieldy official designation for these rooms. I will refer to the Beer Cellar (Room 15) and the Beer Cellar Complex (Rooms 15–20) where such designations are useful.

The Beer Cellar Complex occupies the full depth of the ledge on which it is built (fig. 19). The cave wall curves out over the top of

Figure 20. *Rooms 15 (a), 16 (b), and 17 (c).*

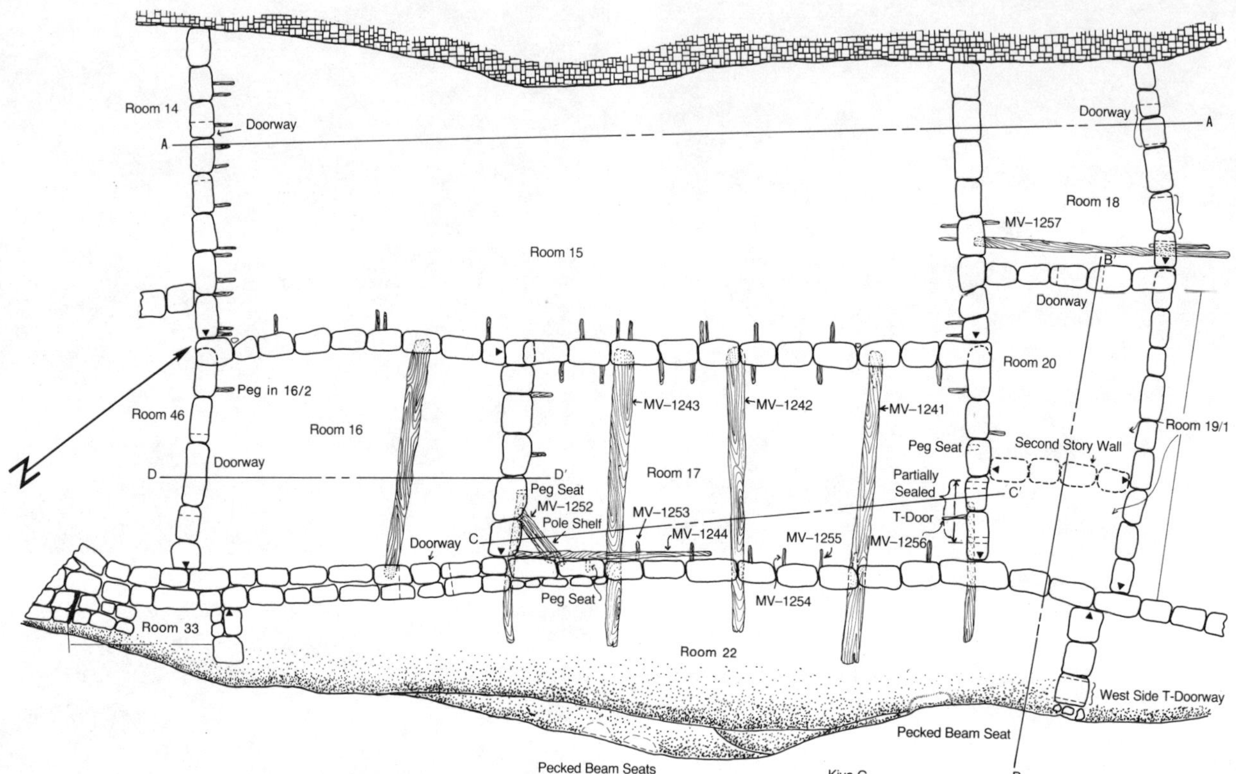

Figure 21. *Plan of Rooms 15–20.*

the room block to form the roof of four of the rooms, as well as the backwall of two of them. Area I—an open, work area—adjoins the complex on its north end; the west row of kivas and miscellaneous related rooms adjoin it on the south.

Both the room arrangement and the state of preservation can readily be seen in figures 21 and 22. With the minor exception of the southeast corner of Room 16, all room walls still extend upward to their original height. Room 15 is only one story high, but its east wall is shared with Rooms 16 and 17, which have two stories (fig. 20a–c). Room 18 also has two stories, although 18/1 has a very low ceiling. Room 19 occupies the first-floor level immediately east of Room 18, and Room 20 is superimposed over a part of Room 19 (figs. 21 and 22).

The room complex was not built as a unit, but rather shows several additions to the original construction as the need for more rooms arose. Apparently a retaining wall was built first along the ledge, and the base of this later incorporated into the east walls of Rooms 16, 17, and possibly a part or all of the east walls of Rooms 19 and 46. Room 17/1 was then built against the retaining wall or at least against part of its base. The rest of the retaining wall, and possibly related structures, may have been torn out to provide space for the new construction.

Room 16/1 was then added, leaving an open area between Rooms 16 and 17 and the back of the cave. Next, Rooms 15 and 17/2 must have been added at one time since Room 15 was built as a one-story room. Logically, 16/2 would have been added after this, thus completing the southern portion of the block. However, the construction sequence may not have followed our logic. In any case, Rooms 16/2, 18, 19 and 20 postdate Rooms 15 and 17. Rooms 19 and 20 may have been built as a unit (or Room 19 first), and then 18/1 and 18/2 may have been constructed as a unit.

Very little space was wasted south of the Beer Cellar Complex, as can be seen in figure 9. Room 14 occupies part of the space between Kiva F and Room 15. Room 46, adjacent to Room 14 on the east, takes up the remainder of the space.

Room 14 was probably never roofed, and most likely was entered from the roof of Kiva F or Room 46. The remains of three mealing bins were found on the lower floor level (fig. 23). They had been partially removed and covered with the later floor. Room 46 would have been served as a convenient storage room for foodstuffs prepared in this area, but its use may have been entirely different. Its function is even more dubious when the possible ceremonial function of Room 13, which is discussed in detail with Kiva F, is considered.

There are two sets of wall pegs on the north wall of Room 14, with the west pair 6.3 feet above floor 2, the east pair 6.0 feet above the same floor. Two possible beam seats on the southeast wall (Kiva F outer wall) suggest there may have been a second story to the room at one time. However, there are no seats in other walls which would have served to support the other end of beams placed in the two seats. Although conceivably such presumed timbers might have been supported by a structure that has been torn out, it seems unlikely considering the probably late construction dates of both the Kiva F and Beer Cellar complexes.

During its last years of use, Room 14 may have served only as a sort of hallway or general work area. (There was a surprisingly large number of sherds from this room, both between floors and on or immediately above the upper floor.)

One of the three rooms opening off Room 14 is Room 15 (fig. 20a), which could have been entered originally only through this one rectangular door. Other than its large size, the only distinctive trait of the room is its large number of wall pegs. There are 27 altogether: 4 on the north wall, 11 on the east, and 12 on the south (the west wall is bedrock). The height of pegs ranges from 5.1 to 7.7 feet, with most of those on the long east wall fairly well aligned in a horizontal row.

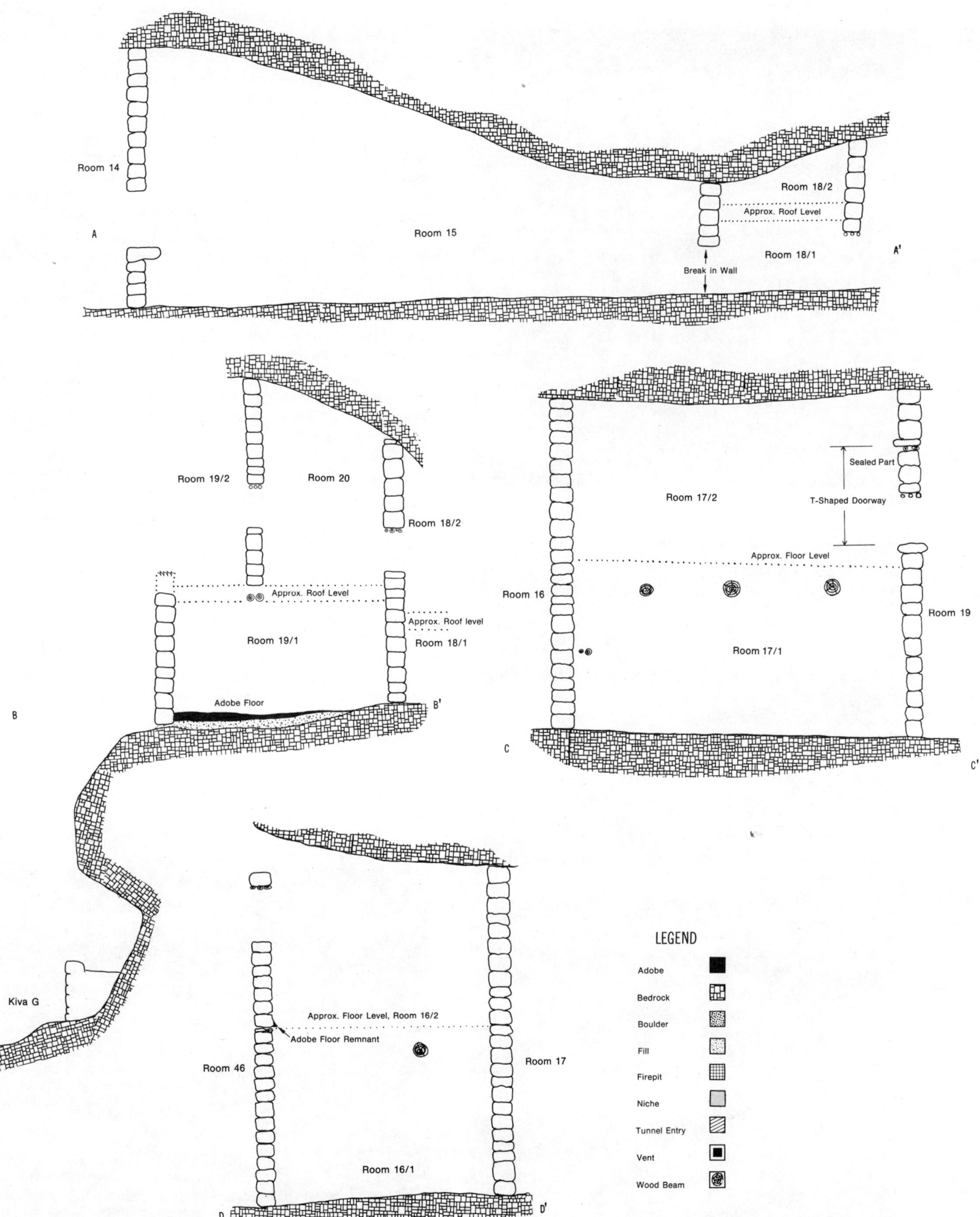

Figure 22. *Section A-A′, Rooms 15, 18/1, and 18/2; section B-B′, Rooms 19/1, 19/2, and 20; section C-C′, Rooms 17/1 and 17/2; and section D-D′, Rooms 16/1 and 16/2.*

Figure 23. *Room 14.*

Figure 24. *North wall (a) and south wall (b) of Room 17/1.*

Rooms 16 and 17, immediately east of Room 15, were well preserved but their first-story roofs were lacking except for the primary beams (fig. 20b and c). Most of the adobe portions of roof and floor were still in the rooms but nearly all of the wood was gone. Undoubtedly, some roofs were torn out deliberately. The same observation was made by several of the earliest explorers of other ruins in Mesa Verde. Although several recovered amd preserved many objects from the dwellings, others may have removed the wood for fuel. It is also possible that Puebloan or non-Puebloan (Ute or Navajo?) people might have removed the wood for new construction or fuel. Suffice it to say that the roofs were removed deliberately from many rooms, and that this could have occurred either before or after complete abandonment.

Room 16 could have been entered through either of two rectangular doors, one in the east wall of 16/1, the other in the south wall of 16/2. It is impossible to tell whether a hatchway connected the two floors. Each room had a niche in the east wall, that in 16/1 being 2.9 feet above floor, and the one in 16/2 about 2 feet above floor. The former may be a sealed hole which once extended entirely through the wall. There was one peg in the south wall of Room 16/2, 5.0 feet above floor.

The original room in the Beer Cellar Complex, Room 17/1, is reminiscent of Room 15 in that it is unusually long and has a great many wall pegs (figs. 24a and b). There was once a total of 22 pegs, three each in the north and south walls, eight each in the east and west walls. There are five niches in the room, one in the north wall and four in the east wall. They range from 2 to 3.4 feet above floor. The four in the east wall may have been niches in the end, but originally they probably were designed either as beam seats for the roof timbers of Room 22 or were deliberately placed holes which once extended through the wall before construction of Room 22.

An interesting feature of the room is the pole shelf in the southeast corner (fig. 25). Actually, there were three shelves at one time, the other two being in the same relative position, but one above and one below the existing shelf. Shelf heights are 1.7, 3.0, and 4.3 feet above floor, and each consisted of only two poles. There is one additional shelf in the room, but it is formed by a stone slab projecting from the wall. The shelf, 2.6 feet above floor, can be seen at the extreme left edge of figure 24a and at the extreme right edge of figure 24b.

There must have been a hatchway leading from Room 17/2 to

Figure 25. *Corner shelf in Room 17/1.*

17/1 as there would be no other way of entering the lower story. Room 17/2 shares several traits with the lower story—abundant wall pegs, niches, and holes—but is far more finished in that all of the walls are heavily plastered (fig. 26a–d). The room was entered from the outside through a rectangular door in the north wall. Like the door in the north wall of Room 4/2, this was once a large, T-shaped door. However, in this case the top of the doorway was filled in, leaving the bottom half open for use (fig. 26a). There is faint evidence of a rectangular sealed door in the south wall (fig. 26b).

Seven wall pegs were found in Room 17/2, one in the north wall, four in the east, and two in the south. There are also three niches, one in the north wall and two in the east wall. They are "shell-shaped," the greatest depth being at the base with the back sloping upward and outward (figs. 26a and d).

A very narrow "shelf" or ledge, 1.8 feet above floor, extends for 1.7 feet along the south wall from the southwest corner of the room (fig. 26b, right center). It may have been placed deliberately or may be an accident of construction.

Even more unusual are the large, nearly square openings through the east wall. The one to the left of the mug board in figure 26c is unique because the slab forming the sill juts out into the room slightly (a feature more common in doors). The opening had been closed by inserting—but not mudding—a shaped slab into the aperture. All three holes are about 1 foot square, or slightly less, and certainly do not resemble the smaller, common holes often called "loopholes," "ventilator," or "smoke" holes.

Just south of the niches in the east wall of Room 17/2 is a possible beam seat, 5.4 feet above floor. A break in the masonry of the west wall, directly opposite the beam seat, may mark the other seat for a horizontal beam. Such a timber could have been used to support a loom—or serve a variety of other purposes. Since the floor is gone, it is impossible to tell if there were anchors of any kind in or on the floor. The large openings in the east wall would have provided ample light for weaving.

If we postulate looms, we must then wonder who did the weaving, and where. There are definite loom anchors in the bedrock floor of Kiva E. Unless we accept this as a women's kiva, the implication is that men did the weaving. Into the early 1930's, Zuni weaving was done in rooms by women, but it is highly speculative to draw parallels between Zuni Pueblo and Long House.

There are two oak loops on the north exterior wall of Room 17/

Figure 26. *North wall (a), south wall (b), and east wall (c and d) of Room 17/2.*

2, one on either side of the door. One loop is now enclosed by Room 20, but I feel quite sure that it predates the room. Door slabs are often held in place by running a pole through loops on either side of the door, and I believe these loops had that purpose. Access to Room 17/2 was probably by ladder from the floor of Area I, or possibly from the roof of Room 19 if it was built at a different time than Room 20.

The two stories of Room 18—built against the cave wall—were probably the last additions to the Beer Cellar Complex (fig. 27a). The first floor had a very low ceiling, perhaps 3 feet on the average, as shown by the large beam seats in the photograph. It was probably entered only through a rather crude doorway in the north wall. There is no evidence of a hatchway leading from Room 18/1 to 18/2 and, considering the room size, I doubt that one existed.

Room 18/2 could be entered either from Room 20 on the east or from Area I (by ladder) on the north. The north door is unique because of the method used to support a door slab. Rather than resting against side supports or inner "jambs," the slab was supported by a horizontal structure across the top of the door, a short distance below the lintels. (The north face of the door is shown in fig. 27b). Also, the door slab could be somewhat shorter than the doorway to provide space for grasping the top of the slab when removing it, and yet it would still fit snugly against this upper support.

Above this adobe and wooden slab support are both wooden and slab lintels, a combination often repeated in Long House. Why both types of lintels were used in Room 18 we can only guess, especially since in several other rooms the building stones of the wall above the door rested directly on the wooden lintels alone. In some cases, the reason for the use of a double lintel is more obvious, as in Room 4/3, where the lower lintel served the same purpose as the slab support in Room 18/2.

Several features distinguish Room 18/2. One is the rather strange arrangement of lintels over the rectangular door connecting Rooms 18 and 20 (fig. 28a). Despite a massive slab serving as the main lintel for the door, four small sticks also span the opening, one pair near one face and the other close to the other face. A short stick was then jammed between the stone lintel and the two wooden "lintels" near the west face of the door.

A large timber running the length of the room can also be seen in fig. 28a, above the door and at the apex of the room. It may have served the same function as the wall pegs similarly positioned in the opposite side of the wall (fig. 28b). It is very unlikely that it could have served as a loom support, considering the door locations and the natural darkness of the room.

Also of unknown use is what appears to be a beam seat in the north wall. It is to the west of the door and about 0.5 foot above the floor of Room 18/2. There is a possible seat in the south wall, roughly opposite that in the north. If these actually had been beam seats, then the timber placed in them could have been used to support the lower end of a loom. However, as already mentioned, it seems impractical to set up a loom in such a cramped and ill-lighted room.

Rooms 19 (first floor level) and 20 were built before Room 18,

Figure 27. *Two stories of Room 18 (a); and door in north wall of second story of Room 18, showing north face (b).*

Figure 28. *Wooden lintels in door connecting Rooms 18 and 20 (a), and wall pegs at top of west wall of Room 20 (b).*

and this is reflected in the similarity in plastering of the lower half of all the walls in Room 20. There is no plaster in Room 18. The west wall of Room 20 (fig. 28b) has a niche about 1.5 feet above floor, and the plaster to the left (south) of the door bears several petroglyphs. A bird and several poorly defined designs have been scratched in the plaster.

Since Room 20 covers only a portion of the room over which it was built, the lower story (Room 19) was given a separate number. The west walls of the two rooms coincide, one above the other. The east wall of Room 20 was supported by one of the roofing timbers of Room 19, and the wall probably rested directly on the roof of the lower room. The part of the east wall resting on the roof or roofing timber had collapsed, so it was impossible to be sure.

Room 22

There is no known case in Mesa Verde of a room being built directly above the major portion of a kiva, but there are numerous instances of rooms extending part way out onto a kiva roof. Room 22 is a good example of this.

Because it was rather precariously perched on the bedrock ledge immediately east of the Beer Cellar Complex and on the roof of Kiva G, the collapse of the kiva roof destroyed almost all evidence of the room. The north wall, with half of a T-shaped-door, is partly preserved. Two possible sets of beam seats in the west wall (shared with Room 17) indicate that the room may actually have been two smaller rooms. The seats are at two levels. There is no trace of an intermediate wall between the two rooms, if such ever existed, or of the south wall. The east wall would have been footed on the kiva roof, and is now gone entirely.

Although the southward extent of the room cannot be determined precisely, I doubt that it reached as far as the doorway into Room 16. There is no evidence of beam seats in the wall near the door.

Spanning most of the distance across the central part of the cave is a well-preserved block of rooms. It extends from Room 23 on the west to Kiva I on the east. The rooms east of Kiva I, and on the same bedrock ledge (Rooms 36, 79, 76, and 80), are poorly preserved.

Figure 29. *Hearth with adobe collar in Room 23.*

Figure 30. *Parapet above roof level of Room 24.*

Figure 31. *Wooden lintels in door of Room 29.*

Rooms 23 and 24 were probably the first to be constructed, with Room 71 sandwiched between the two simultaneously or at some later date. From Room 24 east, the remaining rooms were added on, one after another. The area now occupied by Kivas H and I and Room 29 was probably taken up with other rooms at one time. Remnants of corners—and other irregularities in the present south wall of these three structures—indicate extensive rebuilding.

The wall abutments shown on the ground plan of Long House (fig. 9) for Rooms 71 to 28, inclusive, is accurate only for the lower portion of the walls—to a height of 4.6 to 7.0 feet, depending upon the room being considered. Above this, the abutment of walls is quite different, showing a two-stage but possibly almost simultaneous, construction of the rooms. In some cases, the break is above where the top of the roof would have been; in others, below the main roofing timbers. A more detailed account of the construction sequence of these rooms is given under Kiva H, below.

Room 23

Of all the hearths in Long House rooms, only one had an adobe collar (fig. 29). This hearth is in the southwest corner of Room 23, and because it was built on bedrock the collar was a necessity if the hearth were to be bordered on all sides. There were eight wall pegs in the room, another feature which sets it off from the other rooms in this row. Rooms 25 and 71 have three pegs each; the others have none. The pegs in Room 23 range from 5.5 to 5.9 feet above the floor, with two in the north wall, three in the east wall, and three in the south wall.

No roofing timbers remain in place in Room 23, but there is a remnant of an adobe beam seat on the top of its south wall.

Room 24

In at least two places in the pueblo, a parapet was erected in lieu of a second story. One of these is Room 24. where a low masonry wall, 3.4 feet in maximum height, was erected above the roof level and in line with the south wall of the room (fig. 30). The wall is fairly flat on top, and probably was never higher than it is now. The wall turns to the south at the east end of Room 24 and undoubtedly continued along the south side of Room 25. The other parapet is discussed in the section dealing with Kiva H.

Room 71

A unique feature of this room is the large rectangular cist in the southwest corner. The bedrock floor of the room breaks off sharply here, making the construction of a cist possible. The edge is built up with a thin masonry "wall." It is impossible to tell whether the cist was covered with a slab or other construction. The fill in the lower part of the cist was almost completely lacking in cultural material.

The only other remaining room features were three wall pegs in the south wall, about 5 feet above floor. The north and east walls, and a portion of the west wall, of Room 71 had been torn out deliberately while the pueblo was occupied. The north wall of Room 24 is gone, as is the west wall which it shares with Room 71. Three of Room 70's walls had also been removed, and the topmost walking surface in Area I extended over the wall footings into these three rooms.

Rooms 29 and 64

One of the most interesting rooms in the ruin is Room 29, whose south wall formed a part of the five-story structure which once stood just northeast of the Great Kiva (fig. 9). There is evidence of two roofs in this one-story room, probably as a result of partial collapse of the initial tower (Room 64) structure. In the southwest corner, a wall footing partly incorporated in the south wall shows the presence of earlier construction, probably a room. Later, with the construction of Kiva H and then Kiva I, the early room was removed and Room 29 was built. The lower roof of Room 29 was probably built first.

The tree-ring dates from the southwest corner of Kiva I, the second and higher roof over Room 29, and other irregularities in wall construction suggest partial collapse of the tower, as mentioned

Figure 32. *East wall of Room 64/1 before stabilization (a); beam seats for floor of Room 64/2 (b); and wall stubs of Room 64/3.*

above. When it was rebuilt, the south wall of Room 29 was greatly reinforced. Room 64 was carried up to five stories, using part of Room 29 and Kiva I for support on the north side and reaching a possible height of only 15 feet below the East Ledge Ruin. Access to the ledge was undoubtedly by ladder from the top of the tower.

A rectangular doorway in the south wall of Room 29 opened into the third story of Room 64. Because of the thickness of the wall, the top of the door is spanned by 10 wooden lintels, an unusually large number (fig. 31). Masonry typical of the wall extends across the top of the door and rests directly upon the wooden lintels. No stone lintel was used here, which is rather surprising considering the tremendous weight of the wall above the doorway. Such construction as this suggests that the use of stone and wooden lintels in one door was not for strength alone.

There is no evidence remaining that a roof hatchway may also have provided access to Room 29. Such an opening would certainly have been useful and in keeping with the pattern found in other rooms in this row. Although Room 29 is flanked by Kivas H and I, nothing was found that would suggest the room was part of a ceremonial complex.

Two niches were made in the exterior face of the north wall, facing into an alcove formed by the walls of Kivas H and I and of Room 29 (fig. 9). One is 5.4 feet above the base of the wall, the other is 4.0 feet. Another room could have been formed here, but nothing remains to indicate this.

It is unfortunate that more does not remain of the upper stories of Room 64, for this structure must have been an impressive sight. It is footed on bedrock on the north side and on fill on the south side. A portion of the thick east wall of Room 64/1 can be seen in figure 32a. Surprisingly, the east wall curves to the west to form the south wall of the room, rather than being built as a separate unit and bonded to the south wall. Such construction would have contributed to its strength.

In this remnant of the east wall, there is a rectangular doorway leading into Room 65. The lintels are split poles, and, as in the doorway connecting Rooms 29 and 64/3, the masonry above the door rests directly on the wooden lintels. The door slab would have been supported by two wood and adobe inner jambs, only one of which remains. It angles up to the west and consists of two split poles with adobe packed around them.

Room 64/2 would have occupied the existing space between the upper and lower sections of masonry shown in figure 32b. The timbers supporting the floor of the room were probably supported by the east and west walls, since no definite beam seats can be found in the face of the bedrock ledge. The roof of 64/2 can be definitely located by a series of beam seats, two of which were plugged with adobe and possibly belong to the first structure built in the place later occupied by Room 64. These may be seen below the door in figure 32b.

That the compound masonry of Room 64/1 continued up through 64/2 to 64/3 is shown by the east and west wall stubs of the third floor room (fig. 32c). The north wall, of similar masonry, was built above and behind the earlier "retaining wall" which forms its lower part. A ledge about 2 feet above the top of the doorway of Room 64/3 marks the level of the rooftop of the room (fig. 9, Sec. Q-R). A row of small beam seats above the door may indicate where the secondary roofing poles were placed. These are barely discernible in figure 32c. The only other feature of the room is a niche in the north wall, east of the door.

A second ledge in the north wall, about 5 feet above the first, undoubtedly marks the roof of Room 64/4 (fig. 9, Sec. Q-R). The masonry of the north wall is still compound to this point. Above the ledge, the masonry is simple and continues upward another 5 feet. The top of Room 64/5 was probably not much above the standing masonry.

Rooms 30, 31, and 33

A long row of rooms and kivas was built against the bedrock ledge immediately east of Kiva C–F and the Beer Cellar Complex. Several of these—Rooms 30, 31, and 62—are shown in figure 33a. Room 31 is unusual because of the construction of the east wall. Beam seats in the north and south walls of the room show that a large timber was incorporated in the wall in the manner shown in figure 33b, taken after stabilization.

A narrow corridor separates Room 30 from Room 31 to the south. Both the corridor and the remnants of a rectangular door into Room 30 can be seen in figure 33b. Just to the west of the door in Room 30, and 4.6 feet above floor, is a niche.

At the north end of this row of structures, Room 22 was built above, and partially supported by, Kiva G. Similarly, Room 33 was possibly built above Room 30. A stub projecting eastward from the east wall of Room 16 may be the north wall of the Room 33; conversely, it may be the south wall of a room extending north to Room 22. The latter theory gains some support by the superposition of the wall stub directly above the south wall of Room 31. The former theory seems plausible because of the fragment of a possible floor south of the stub.

A second stub of wall south of the first can be seen in figure 33a. If this is a remnant of an outer east wall for Kiva F, the wall may have formed part of the ventilator shaft of the kiva. There remains now only a portion of the opening in the wall through which the ventilator tunnel passed.

Rooms 39 and 40

The West Ledge Ruin consists of seven rooms, separated into two units of two and five rooms. The southernmost unit is comprised of Rooms 39 and 40 (figs. 34a and 35). It would have been easily accessible by ladder from the roof of Kiva C. In both rooms, the floor slopes down sharply to the east, and construction must have been both difficult and dangerous.

In entering the rooms, one had first to pass through a small antechamber which served as a landing. There may have been a doorway opening into the antechamber, as indicated primarily by the dressed masonry face at the north side and a possible seat for a stone lintel on the south. Getting into the rooms is difficult enough without a doorway to further restrict movement. With a door, entry would have been that much more difficult.

Two loops were fixed in the masonry about one-half foot below the top of the sill across the entrance to the antechamber. The southern one is located below the north end of Room 39, and the northern below the right side of the opening into the antechamber. The two loops may have been used to secure the upper end of the ladder, which provided access to the ledge ruin. A notch for one of the ladder poles was cut into the bedrock ledge just below the north loop.

The rectangular doorway into Room 39 has both stone and wooden lintels, as well as the supporting "molding" of wood and adobe across the top and down both sides. The west ends of the five pole lintels are tied with an oak strip, which in turn is tied between

Figure 33. *Rooms 30, 31, (a); beam seats in Room 31 after stabilization (b).*

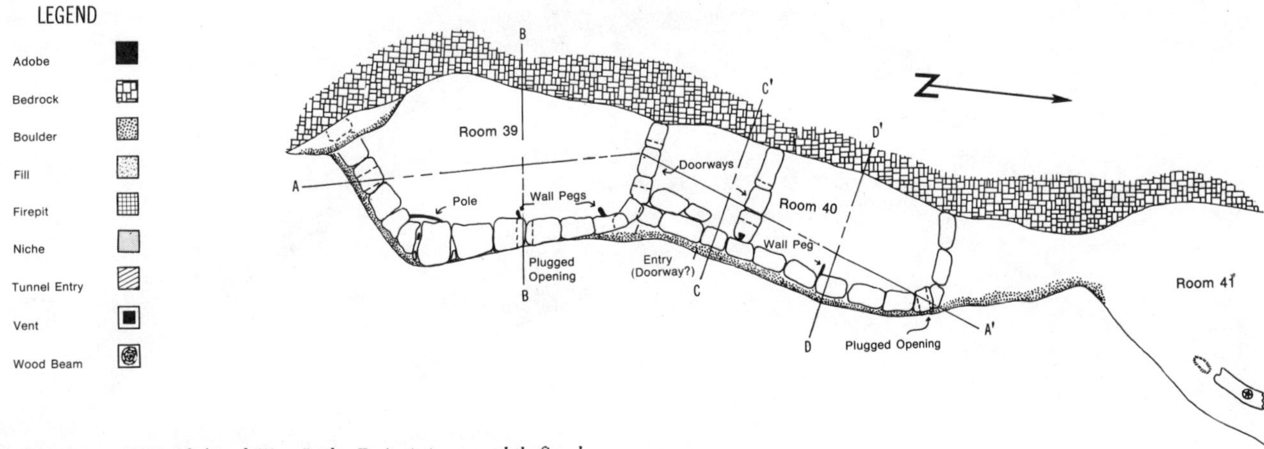

Figure 34. *Rooms 39 and 40 of West Ledge Ruin (a); stone slab fitted into rectangular door into Room 39 (b).*

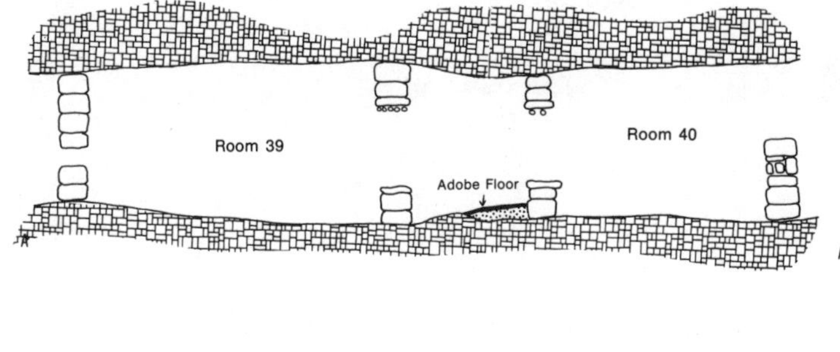

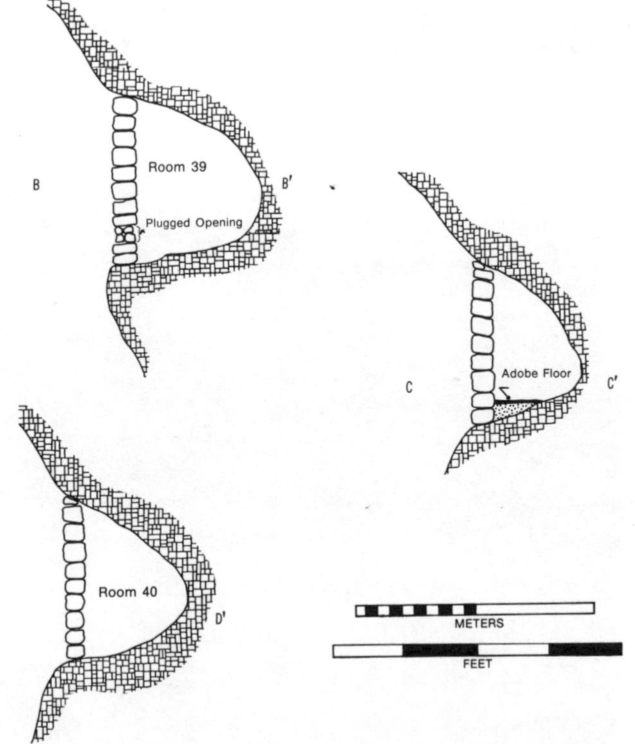

Figure 35. *Rooms 39 and 40, plan and sections A-A', B-B', C-C' and D-D'.*

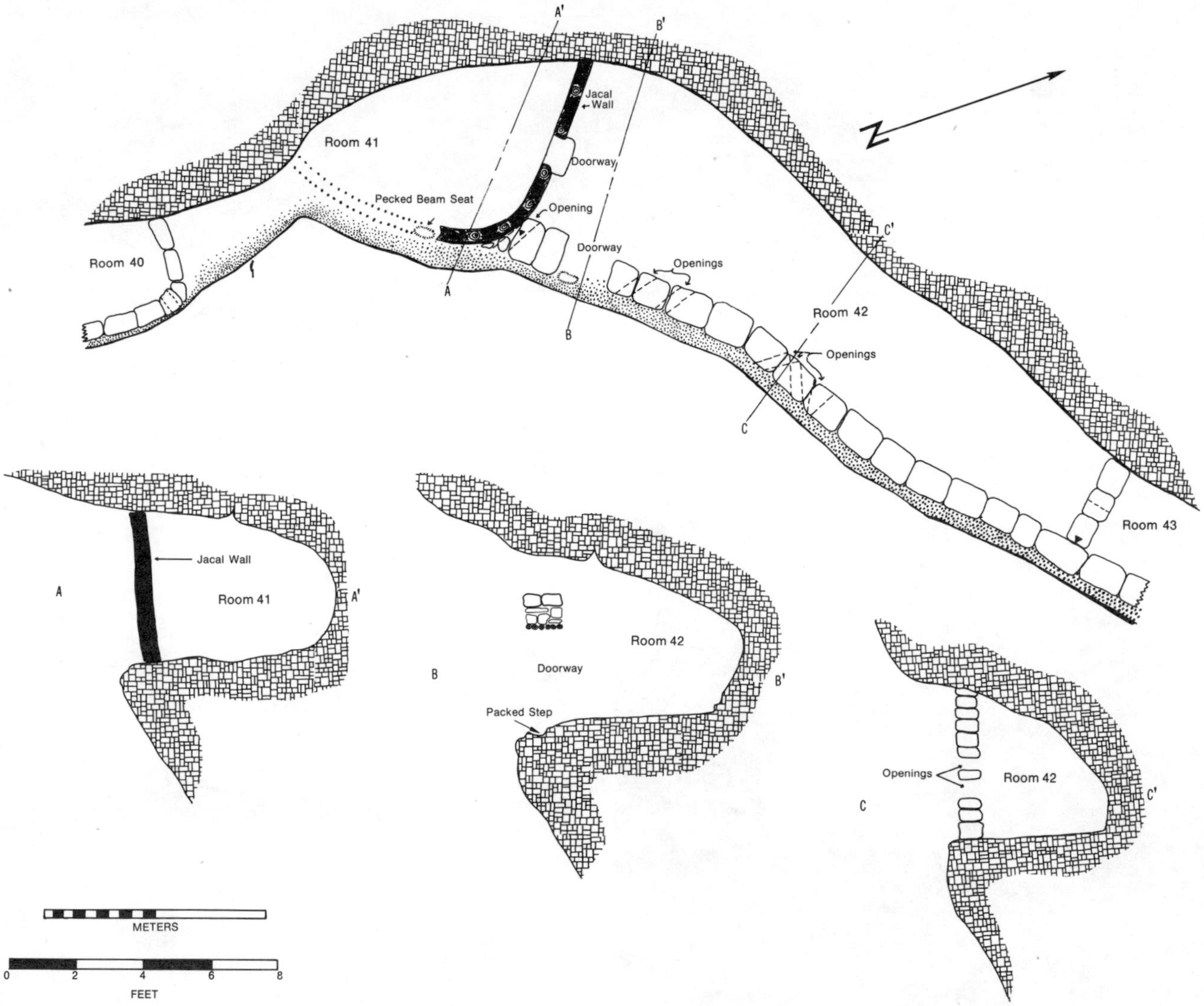

Figure 37. *Rooms 41 and 42, plan and sections A-A′, B-B′, and C-C′.*

the poles with yucca instead of being twisted. A slab found on the ledge was undoubtedly used to close the opening (fig. 34b).

The doorway into Room 40 is also rectangular, and has both stone and wooden lintels. However, it lacks the molding found on the doorway into Room 39.

No trace of adobe floor was found in either room. Along the walls, the adobe mortar was lipped out onto the floor, thus sealing the contact between walls and the bedrock floor.

The rooms share two other traits: the presence of wall pegs and small apertures in the walls. Room 39 has two pegs, one in the north wall, 3.3 feet above floor, the other in the east wall, 3.9 feet above floor. A horizontally placed pole in the southeast corner of the room, 3.9 feet above floor, could also have been used for hanging various materials. Room 40 has only one peg, in the east wall, 3.6 feet above floor.

Room 39 also has two openings, one through the east wall and the other in the south wall. The former has been closed with a plug of red adobe. Visible on the exterior face of the east wall of Room 40 is an opening that was blocked when the south wall of the room was built.

The blocked hole in Room 40 indicates that both the antechamber between the two rooms and Room 40 itself were part of a single larger room at one time. The sloping floor would preclude use of this room as a working or sleeping area, however. The function of these holes is unknown. As is the case with almost all of the openings of this nature found in the ruin, these would have commanded a view of large portions of the pueblo.

Rooms 41–45

Separated from Room 40 by a pinching out of the ledge on which they were built are Room 41 and the four rooms immediately north of it (fig. 36a). The room block was entered through a doorway in the east wall of Room 42 (fig. 37) and was probably reached by ladder from the roof of Kiva C. There is evidence of only two rooms with jacal walls in Long House. The better preserved of the two is Room 41 (fig. 36b and c). The walls consist of a series of vertical poles—one pinyon and five juniper—extending from the cave floor to ceiling. A great number of brush stems, placed vertically, were packed between the main uprights and secured with horizontal oak members and yucca ties. The whole structure was then packed with adobe. Two shallow, pecked seats in the bedrock floor and a mud line on the ceiling show that the wall continued to the south and thus included the remainder of the ledge within the room.

The only room features, other than the rectangular door, are the two pegs projecting from the wall above the highest horizontal member. The rather uneven bedrock floor was not leveled with adobe.

The construction of the north wall and most of the east wall of Room 42 is conventional in that the masonry was laid up with adobe. At the top of the east wall, however, is a section of dry masonry; that is, the rocks were placed without benefit of mortar. The rectangular door in this wall was the means of entry into the room block, as already mentioned. Two ladder grooves, each 0.3 foot wide and 0.1 foot deep, and spaced 1.2 feet apart, were worn into the cliff just below the door.

The east door differs from most of the others in Long House in that the lintels are split shakes (fig. 38). It was built directly on bedrock without a sill, as was the case with the doorway in Room 18/1.

The six openings in the wall command a view both to the east across Long House and to the south. The height of the holes above floor ranges from less than 1 foot to about 2.5 feet.

The floor of the room consists almost entirely of bedrock, but there is some adobe on the floor along the east and south walls. This may be the result of carrying the wall mortar out onto the floor. Against the east wall a section of this adobe, 1.2 by 2.6 feet, has been burned. There is no indication that this area was used continually as a hearth.

Rooms 42 and 43 are unusually long. The door connecting these two rooms is rectangular and has both slab and stick lintels. The door connecting Rooms 43 and 44 has wooden (split shakes) and stone lintels, and also a molding or slab support across the top. The molding consists of three sticks and adobe.

Figure 36. *Rooms 41–45 of West Ledge Ruin (a); exterior (b); and interior (c) of jacal wall of Room 41.*

Figure 38. *Room 42, split-shake lintels of east door.*

Figure 39. *Plan of Rooms 43, 44, and 45; and sections D-D′, Room 43, and E-E′, Room 44.*

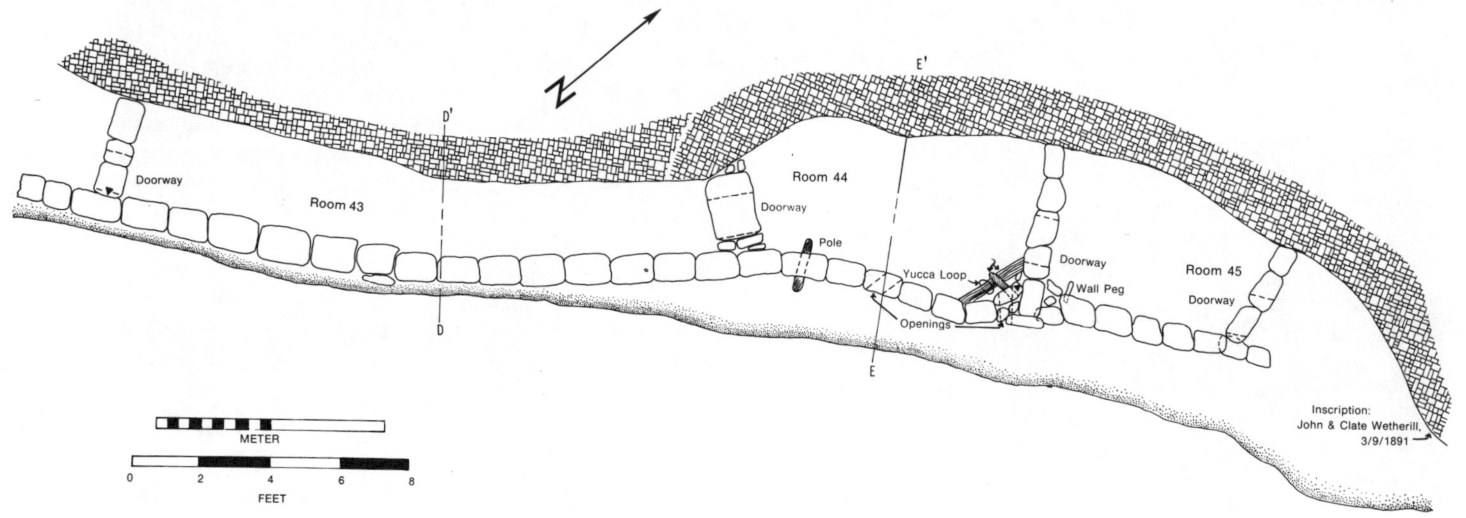

The extreme narrowness of Room 43, the absence of openings in the walls, and the relatively small amount of fill suggest that the room might have been used more for a passageway than for storage (fig. 39).

The ledge widens in Room 44, which in turn possesses several interesting features. The door common to Rooms 44 and 45 is generally rectangular in shape and has both slab and pole lintels. The length of the north wall made possible a more conventional construction of the doorway: wall masonry, rather than vertical slabs, forms its sides.

To the right of the door and near the base of the wall, is the east-facing wall opening. A second aperture, which opens to the south, is about the same height above floor. Above the wall opening in the northeast corner of the room are two split poles and a yucca loop. There is also a large wall peg near the top of the east wall, at its south end.

The large break in the east wall superficially resembles a door but, if so, construction was never finished. Because of the height of the room above the kiva block below, the possibility of a door in this wall might be considered absurd. However, an apparent beam seat in the cliff, about 15.5 feet above the floor of Kiva E, indicates that there may have been some structure above the walls shared by Kivas E and F. In this case, an attempt might easily have been made to enter Room 44 from immediately below.

Room 45 is the fifth and last room in this section of the ledge ruin. Beyond Room 45 the ledge pinches out, and it is not possible to continue eastward to the East Ledge Ruin (Area VIII).

Room 45 had at one time a doorway in the north wall, but the door is now gone except for the sill. A beam in the south wall, above the doorway into Room 44, indicates that a large wall peg or a pole extending the length of the room was seated here. If the latter, we have a situation analogous to that in Room 18.

Rooms 47–52, 54–56, and 21

An outward bulge of the cave wall separates the major portion of the pueblo from a very interesting complex of rooms and kivas at the east end. Rooms 47–52, together with Kivas J and R and other rooms south and west of this complex, appear to form one of the early parts of the pueblo. There are other sections whose architecture suggests that they were also among those first built, but evidence that would prove this is often less than satisfying.

One of the traits limited for the most part to this portion of the ruin is the use of vertical slabs in masonry walls. The builders of the wall common to Rooms 47 and 48 (fig. 40a and b) apparently used whatever rock was at hand, including massive blocks of sandstone, thin slabs, and a few rocks that are more typical of most of the masonry in Long House.

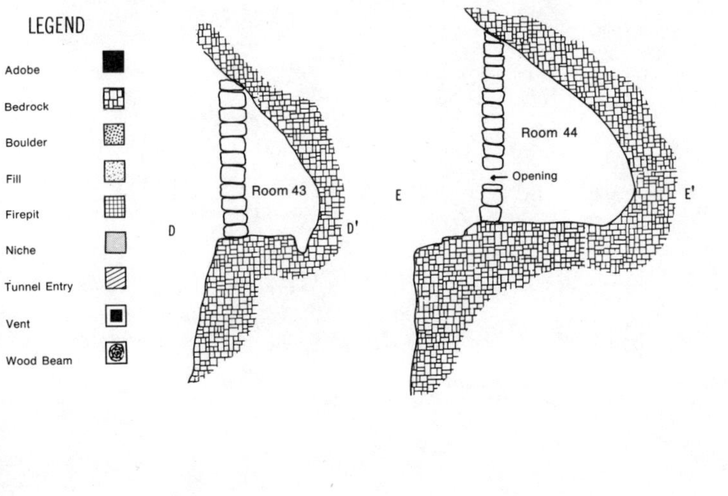

Slabs were also used in the west wall of Room 49 (fig. 41a and b). The stabilized wall in the lower photograph shows, fairly accurately, I believe, how the base of the wall originally looked. There was nothing to indicate how the rest of this wall was constructed.

A cist in Room 48 (fig. 40b and c) is also unique in Long House, being reminiscent of the Basketmaker II structures found by Morris and Burgh (1954) near Durango, Colo. The lower walls of the cist are composed of vertical slabs, one of which was probably a Pueblo III metate. Above the slabs horizontal coursed masonry was placed to raise the height of the rim. The floor of the cist was of hard-packed clay, and the fill above contained late Pueblo III pottery.

A more typical feature of the late occupation of the ruin is the Mesa Verde Corrugated jar buried to its rim in the floor of the same room (fig. 40d). The mouth of the jar was covered with an unworked stone slab. The base of another corrugated jar was found in the remains of a nearby pit, suggesting that a second storage vessel may have been placed in the same corner of the room.

The portion of a troughed metate found on the floor of Room 49 (fig. 41a, center foreground) suggests that the room was constructed during the earlier part of the Pueblo III occupation of Long House. In the same photograph the remnants of a possible bench along the back, or cave, wall of the room can be seen. The probable reconstruction of this bench, as well as that of a similar one in Room 50, is shown in figure 41b. A third bench, identical to the other two, was found in Room 51. A bench, if such it was, would also cover the irregular bedrock floor in the back of each of the rooms.

There is a significant amount of Chapin Gray pottery (Basketmaker III-Pueblo I, primarily), but very little of the more diagnostic Pueblo I types represented, in this section of the ruin. Most, if not all, of this pottery is undoubtedly from Pithouse I. More significant is the concentration here, as well as in a few other places in the ruin, of late Pueblo II-early Pueblo III pottery. The highest concentration of early Pueblo II pottery in the ruin is also from this area. (Identification here of the pottery from the rooms in this vicinity may make more meaningful what appear to be rather aberrant architectural features, at least from the point of view of the rest of Long House.)

The remaining room in this row along the cave wall is distinguished by two features: a small storage room, Room 21, at the south end, and the remains of four mealing bins at the north. The storage room was triangular in plan and probably had jacal walls. Only mud lines on the cave roof and adobe stubs on the floor mark the walls of this small, low-ceiling room.

Room 52 is one of only five rooms that appear to have contained mealing bins. They were positioned so that the operators of these would have faced each other while working. No metates were found in position in the bins; in fact, there were no metates in the room. Several of the more or less vertical slabs outlining the bins, the impression of the bottom of a metate in two bins, and several well-defined catch basins of adobe and flat slabs are all that remain.

Far better preserved are the four mealing bins in Room 56 (fig. 42). An extremely hard-packed, rough-surfaced layer of adobe is shown packed around the bins. Later, this material was removed and a smooth floor was found below. The upper layer of adobe may have been placed deliberately around the bins to provide greater support for the slabs.

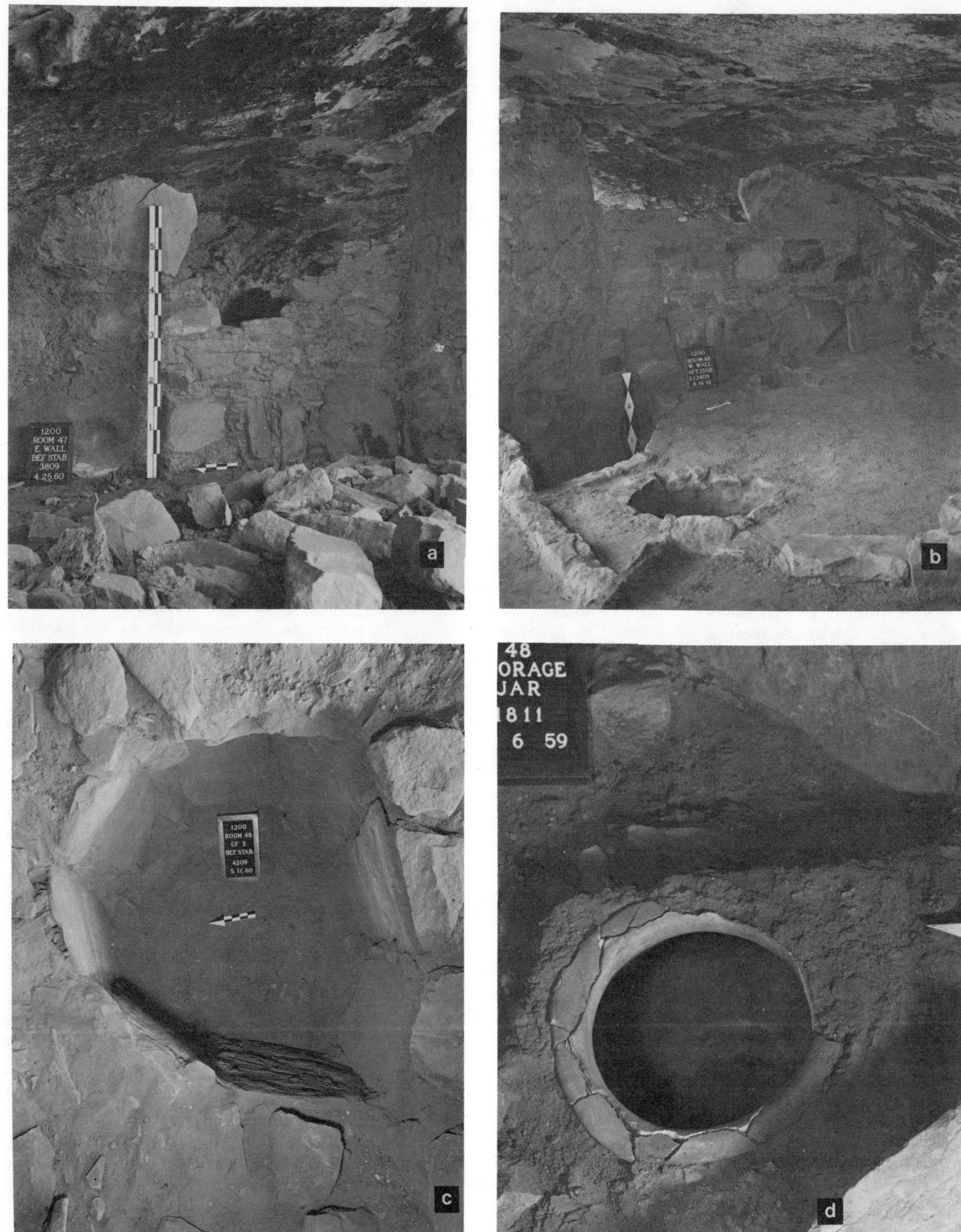

Figure 40. *Wall common to Rooms 47 and 48 (a and b); cist (c) and sunken Mesa Verde Corrugated jar (d) in the floor of Room 48.*

Figure 41. *West wall of Room 49, in foreground, before stabilization (a) and after stabilization (b).*

The northwest quadrant of the room, into which the doorway from Room 85 opens, and the southeast quadrant were clear of bins. The operators of the bins in the northeast quadrant would have faced the door, those in the southwest quadrant would have faced north.

The length (direction of mano movement) of the bins ranges from 1.7 to 2.1 feet, the width from 1.5 to 1.7 feet (inside dimensions). Depth from top of side slabs to slab-floored basin varies from 0.65 to 1.0 foot. Two metates were in place, and the supporting surface of a third was well preserved. These surfaces sloped down toward the far end of the bin (from the operator) at an angle of 18° to 35°. In all four bins the slab at the far end of the bin sloped inward; the other slabs delimiting the bins were roughly vertical.

The tops of the side slabs of two bins also sloped downward at angles of 15° to 17° toward the far end of the bins. The slabs in the third bin, and probably in the fourth also, were set level. The slabs were only roughly shaped, and one was a well–worn metate.

Seven manos were found in or near the bins. Two of these were stacked, one above the other, outside but against the wall of a bin nearest the operator.

The floor and bins of Room 56 were removed when Pithouse 1 was excavated. The same is true of the floors of Rooms 55 and 54, with two floors being removed from the latter. These last two rooms—and possibly Room 56—were either built before Rooms 47 and 48, judging by wall abutments, or else there has been extensive remodeling in the area (see fig. 9). Such remodeling would not preclude the use of what is now Rooms 47 and 48 as working areas. In fact, the extremely rough "floor" of Room 48 suggests this.

Two features encountered when excavating Room 54 to the pithouse floor strongly indicate some previous, but still Pueblo III, construction in this area. Immediately behind the south wall of Room 54 is a thin wall of small rock laid up with a lot of adobe

Figure 42. *Mealing bins in Room 56.*

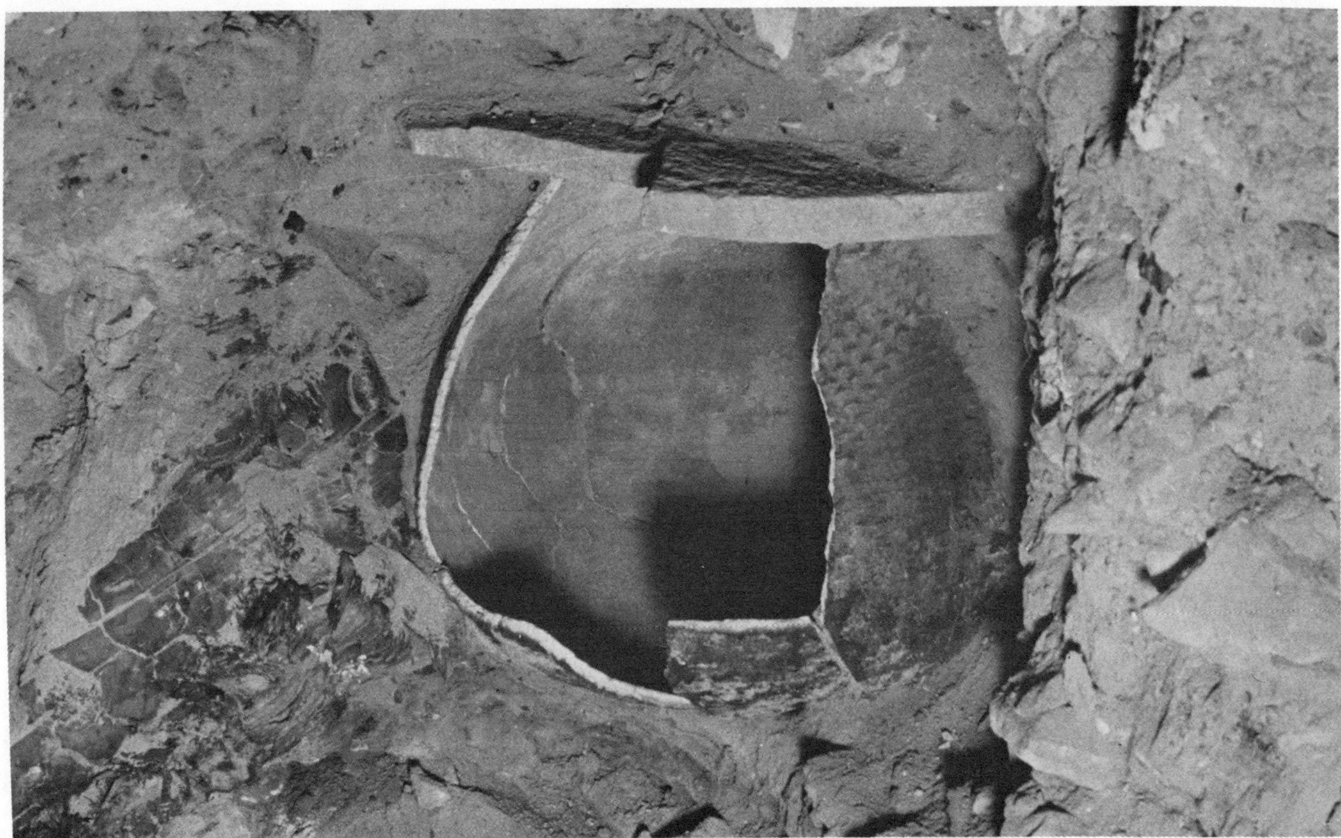

Figure 43. *Corrugated storage jar with slab cover at pithouse level in Room 54.*

mortar. It was probably seated at about the same level as the walls of Room 54, although not enough remains to be sure. It may have served as a fill-retaining wall for the upper portion of Kiva J. It is also possible, but less likely, that it is a part of a room built prior to the construction of Kiva J and Room 54.

The surface on which Room 54 was built was formed by leveling the burned debris of the pithouse, using fill as necessary. A corrugated storage jar with a slab cover (fig. 43) was apparently placed at this level, with the slab on what was either a walking surface or floor. The jar is below the thin wall discussed above and thus predates it. There is no other evidence of rooms or work areas in the section now occupied by Room 54, Kiva J, and adjacent rooms.

Upper Stories Rooms 55–59

I have already discussed two sections of the ruin where there is conclusive evidence that there were four and five story structures (Rooms 4 and 64). The collapse of several multistoried rooms blocks has made it difficult to estimate the original number of rooms in the pueblo.

Despite the absence of actual rooms, there is tangible evidence of numerous rooms on the cave wall above several ground floor rooms. Excellent examples of this are shown in figure 44a and b. The white lines show where there are traces of adobe left by the construction of walls and floors against the cliff; the black circles locate beam seats.

Between the two vertical white lines shown in figure 44a was a small third-story room built above a portion of Room 55/2. Conceivably, this room could be a fourth-story structure, but Rooms 55/2 and 55/3 would then have had very low ceilings to make this possible. The floor of this room is marked by the horizontal line between the uprights.

Immediately south (to the right) of the room overlying Room 55 is Room 56/3. The second vertical white line from the left marks the north wall of Room 56/3, the third (bent) line marks the east wall of the room. Once again, the floor level is shown by the horizontal white line. The upper portion of the line, above the five beam seats for the roof of 56/3, marks the fourth story.

The ground floor and subfloor levels of Room 57 present a confusing picture. Possibly there was a multistoried structure here, with possible collapse and rebuilding. In any case, there is no evidence on the cliff of any upper stories. The white square dot in figure 44a and b marks the location of the roof of Room 57/1.

Room 58 also shows no evidence of an upper story, with the possible exception of the circled beam seat to the left of the vertical white line marking the west wall of Room 59/2 (fig. 44b). The beam seat is angled toward Room 59. This, plus the patch of adobe on the cliff just to the right and below the seat, suggest that an angled brace of Room 59/2 was seated here.

To the right of the white line in the center of figure 44b can be seen traces of smoke-blackened plaster on the north or cave wall of Room 59. How far east the room reached cannot be determined, but it probably extended a few feet over the roof of Kiva R.

Rooms 60 and 88

There is only one circular tower, Room 60, in Long House. The total number of building stones, as well as the number of "tower stones"—building stones with slightly curved outer faces—in the fill, indicate a one-story structure. Entry was through a T–shaped door in the north side (fig. 45a). There were two hearths in the room: one with smoke-blackened wall behind it is shown in fig. 45b. The floor was hard–packed red adobe, but only traces of it remained.

The few fragments of wood in the fill undoubtedly came from

Figure 44. *Traces of adobe (white lines) and beam seats (black circles) marking locations of the upper stories of Rooms 55 and 56 (a) and Room 59 (b).*

the roof. They range in diameter from 0.15 to 0.30 foot and are up to 3.7 feet long. Nothing remains to tell us how the roof was constructed, but it probably resembled roofs placed on square or rectangular rooms.

Because the tower extended slightly over the southern recess of Kiva Q, the subfloor fill was probed carefully to see whether there might have been a connecting passageway. A large boulder underlies the north side of the tower, however, making such a connection an impossibility. See Kiva Q for further discussion of this tower-kiva complex.

Room 88 was rendered rather useless with the construction of the tower, since most of the room was torn out during the process. It now exists as a small, triangular-shaped structure, to the left of the tower in figure 45a. The reconstruction of the small "window" in it is problematical.

Rooms 63–69

The room block immediately east of the Great Kiva represents a tremendous amount of work on the part of the inhabitants of Long House. A retaining wall was built as the west wall of Rooms 66 and 67, and Kivas M and S served the same function on the south. At the north end are Rooms 63–65, built mostly on bedrock which slopes down to the south. There is about 6 feet of fill—all deliberately placed—between bedrock and the floor of Room 66, and a similar situation prevails in Rooms 67–69. Room 66 will be discussed in greater detail with the Great Kiva.

Room 67 is a prominent feature of Long House, with massive walls rising two stories (fig. 46a). A sealed T-shaped doorway once connected Rooms 66 and 67. Wooden lintels alone support the tremendous weight of the masonry above, as was the case in the doorway opening into Room 64 from Room 29. In both cases, it would have seemed logical for the builders to have used a thick stone lintel alone or in conjunction with the wood. The lintels were secured in a manner similar to that used in Room 39 (West Ledge Ruin). Oak strips encircled both ends of the lintels, and these in turn were tied between the lintels with yucca strips.

The room was floored with red adobe, which still bears the impressions of ears of corn (fig. 46b). One of the few quadrant-shaped corner firepits in the ruin was in the northwest corner of Room 67. It was entirely of adobe, excepting the sections of the north and west walls against which it was built.

Extensive room remodeling is shown not only by the masonry above but also by subfloor features. At about 0.6 to 0.8 foot below the adobe floor is the remainder of a walking surface or floor. Cut into this surface in the northeast corner of the room is an oval basin about 1.7 feet long and about 0.2 foot deep. Just south of this is a double basin—a small circular basin within a larger one—with a diameter of about 1.0 foot and a depth of 0.6 foot. A shallow, circular pit about 0.25 foot in diameter south of the double basin is the only other subfloor feature. I have no idea of the purpose of any of these features.

The subfloor level was apparently continuous into Room 68 before the high, north-south dividing wall was built. Here it was possible to discern traces of six floors or walking surfaces, with one of the upper ones being the continuation of that in Room 67. The fifth level passes directly under the north wall, which is built on it, into Room 69. The west wall of Room 68 is footed on this level, and the east wall of this room is footed on the second level.

Undoubtedly, after construction of the west retaining wall and Kivas M and S, the deep fill was leveled and it provided a large work-area on which Rooms 66–69 were built. Actually, the lowest level in Room 69 is the floor of Room 91. The construction of Kiva L split Room 91, the south half becoming Room 69 and the north half a part of the Kiva.

Figure 45. *T-shaped door (a) and hearths (b) in Room 60, the circular tower.*

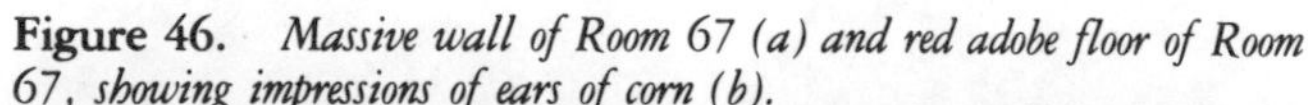

Figure 46. *Massive wall of Room 67 (a) and red adobe floor of Room 67, showing impressions of ears of corn (b).*

There are three circular firepits in Room 69, with the lowest belonging to Room 91. It was dug into a gray, ashy level which passes beneath the south wall into Room 68. The hearth was lined with upright sandstone slabs and has a flat, slab-lined bottom. The remaining two firepits belong to Room 69. The sides and bootom of these are also slab-lined.

With the obvious exception of Room 67, which has second-story masonry, there is no definite evidence that any of the rooms in the block, Rooms 66 to 69, had a second story.

In the southwest corner of Room 69 is an angled timber (fig. 47a) which would have helped tie together the west and south walls and would have provided additional support for the two-story construction in Room 67 and also in Room 68, if the latter had been carried up to two stories.

The north wall of Room 69 is directly beneath a wall stub jutting eastward from the west wall at the second-story level. The stub may be a remnant of the south wall of a room built above either the north half of Room 91 or the south half of Kiva L. The latter was formed by remodeling Rooms 91 and 92. The stub can be seen in figure 47b, above and slightly to the right of the doorway to Room 69.

It is also possible that the wall remnant is part of a parapet around the roof of Kiva L. This seems less likely, because all surrounding rooms probably extended either higher than the roof of Kiva L (Room 65 was probably two stories, and Room 66 may have been also), or else they were roofed at the same level (Rooms 69 and 73 and Kiva O). If the stairway area of Room 66 was not roofed, the parapet would then have served a useful purpose.

It seems unlikely that Room 68 ever had a second story. Much of its floor area would have extended out over the roof of Kiva M. Even its north wall, which it shares with Room 69, was originally supported by the kiva roof at its east end (fig. 47b). We know that there was considerable danger of collapse of the whole superstructure into Kiva M, and that this possibility (if such did not actually happen) was probably the reason for the construction of interpilaster wall supports in the kiva (fig. 47b).

Rooms 73–75

Like the room block just discussed, these rooms rested in part upon fill held in place by Kiva M. Rooms 74 and 75 had corrugated storage jars buried in the deep fill along their south walls, with the mouths of the jars flush with the room floors. Those in the southeast corner of Room 75 are shown in figure 48, after removal of the red adobe floor and subfloor fills. The same photograph shows the remains of a rectangular, slab-lined firepit in the southwest corner of the room.

Underlying all three rooms was a walking surface. In some places, bedrock was leveled with sterile fill or trash; in smoother places, the rock was leveled with red adobe. The gray, ashy trash beneath Rooms 74 and 75, as well as other rooms and kivas in the immediate vicinity, produced some Basketmaker III–Pueblo I pottery. Most of this is undoubtedly sheet trash from the pithouse and related areas to the east.

Room 74 is conspicuous because of other features, however. The north end of the room was remodeled to form the ventilator for Kiva O, and the south wall is of jacal construction. Although the wall was not as well preserved as that in Room 41, enough remained to show its construction clearly.

The wall is 8.5 feet long and averages 0.3 to 0.4 foot thick. It was built before the floor, which lips up against the wall, was completed. Six main vertical posts had furnished the primary support; the only two present are juniper. Numerous vertical members of serviceberry provided the framework for the bulk of the wall. The uprights were lashed together with strips of oak, and then the framework was packed with adobe. There was a doorway at the east end, between two upright posts.

South of the wall, a single course of masonry was laid up, undoubtedly to stabilize the jacal construction. This masonry, except for that portion forming the door sill, may have been covered by the courtyard fill of Kiva M. The east end of the jacal wall, which abuts the east room wall, was further stabilized by running a short wall against and parallel to the east room wall and letting it abut the end of the jacal wall.

Why a jacal wall in this room? Possibly this was an unroofed work area, and the wall was built as a windbreak. The large timber lying east-west across the room in the fill, along with juniper shakes and chunks of adobe that may have come from a roof, would indicate a roof, however. It could have been supported entirely by the east and west masonry wall, making it possible to have a jacal wall on the south. There is one other possibility. A jacal wall would greatly reduce the weight on this part of the courtyard, and thus reduce the pressure against the backwall of the northeast inter-pilaster space of Kiva M.

Figure 47. *Angled timber (a), and wall stub (b) in Room 69.*

Room 76

Excepting Kiva Q, only Room 76 had an extensive amount of fallen roofing in place. Two levels of roofing material (wood and adobe), possibly from the first and second floor roofs, were found on the floor of Room 76. There would have been very little space between a second–floor roof and the cave ceiling, however, as can be seen by the mud lines on the cave ceiling above Rooms 76, left, and 80, right, in figure 49.)

Two and a half feet below the floor of Room 76 is the top of a masonry wall. It is 1.4 feet high (two courses) at the north end, where it abuts the bedrock cave floor. Both the bedrock ledge on which the wall rests, and the next "step" or ledge south of and below the footing, are smoke-blackened. Subfloor tests in Room 79 and 36 also show extensive use of the bedrock area or lower fill (primarily for fires) prior to construction of the present rooms.

The orientation of the wall stub is north-south, and another short section of wall, similarly oriented, found behind the east pilaster of Kiva O may once have been part of the same wall. If extended farther south, this hypothetical wall would be, essentially, a part of the present east wall of Room 75. If this reconstruction is accurate, the wall would have been part of a room or rooms long since torn out and replaced by the present complex of rooms and kivas. Even some of these have been extensively remodeled, as shown by the conversion of rooms to kivas. Kivas O and L are examples of such remodeling.

Figure 48. *Corrugated storage jars buried in southeast corner of Room 75.*

Figure 49. *Mud lines on the cave ceiling between Rooms 76 and 80.*

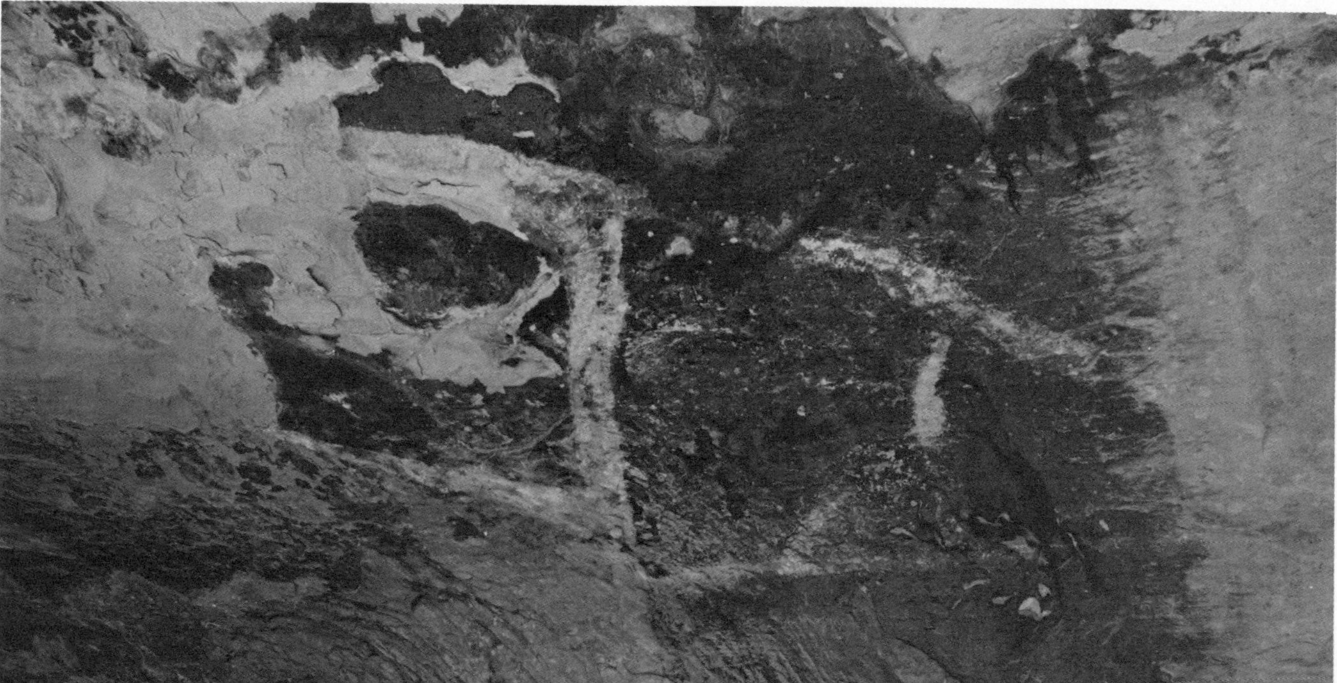

Figure 50. *Two "wall" stubs (a) and slabs lining deep firepits (b) in Room 79.*

Room 79

An even more confusing picture is presented by Room 79, adjacent to Room 76 on the west. About 1 foot below the room floor is an ash and charcoal level, which also extends east beneath the room wall into Room 76 and is probably related to the burned areas found below the floor of this room. Although the possible burning of earlier structures cannot be discounted as a source of the ash and charcoal, and the cause of the smoke-blackening of the bedrock ledges, it seems more likely, as Al Lancaster suggested, that this was an outdoor cooking area.

Slightly higher in the subfloor fill of Room 79 than the ash and charcoal deposit is a walking surface extending beneath the west room wall into Room 36. A circular, slab-lined firepit built on this surface was found beneath the wall common to the two rooms.

Room 79, a large rectangular structure, produced two very odd features. Two masonry "wall" stubs extend south over the room floor from the north wall (fig. 50a). They were built on a thin lens of ash-flecked brown soil about 0.2 foot thick. This suggests that the room floor was deliberately covered with fill before the features were constructed. It might have been necessary to place such a deposit to cover the top of slabs lining the deep firepits beneath the west wall stub (fig. 50b).

The two firepits were, originally, at least 1 foot deep. The stones of the north wall, which had collapsed into the room, were heavily smoke blackened. The south pit was probably the first constructed and was considerably larger at one time. Later, the north wall of the pit was torn out and the north firepit was built. (The stones which probably formed the north wall of the south pit were found in the fill of the north pit.) The south pit was entirely filled with ash and the north one was partly so.

Figure 51. *Painted hand and mud line on the cave wall indicating upper stories of Room 84.*

Rooms 84 and 87

An awareness of the problems of multistory construction on the part of the builders of the pueblo is certainly obvious in these two rooms. That Room 84 was at least two stories high (possibly three, if the rooms had very low ceilings) is shown by the mud line on the cave wall just north (left) of the painted hand (fig. 51). The hand is slightly above the floor levels marked in figure 44a. Room 87 was at least as high as shown by the reinforcing of all four walls, and could have been higher. The cliff breaks sharply upward at the south end of the room, so it is physically possible to add additional stories; such is not the case above Room 84. However, there is no evidence on the cliff that Room 84 was more than two stories high.

Five prayer sticks were found in this vicinity, three in the fill of Room 84, and two in a wall abutment of this room. The original room wall is common to Rooms 84 and 87. The inner east wall was then built against the original wall, the two touching throughout their length. Two other prayer sticks were placed vertically behind this reinforcing wall, in the northeast corner of the room. The inner wall certainly indicated construction of more than one story; the prayer sticks probably reflect fear of collapse.

The north wall of Room 87 was strengthened in a similar manner, but here the additional wall was placed outside the room. Both west and south walls were of compound masonry but may have been reconstructed (possibly replacing simple walls). The problem of the construction sequence in this area, along with the passageway leading from Kiva N to Room 87, is discussed in the description of Kiva N.

Room 87/1 was entered by a rectangular door in the south wall from the roof of Kiva Q. The tunnel or passageway, just mentioned, opens into the room floor, but crawling in was probably not the conventional manner of entering the room. With the collapse of the Kiva Q's roof, the doorway also collapsed, making it impossible to determine its precise size.

In the northwest corner of the room was a roughly rectangular, slab-lined firepit. The pit was lined all the way around, with no use being made of the nearby room walls. Six large fragments—about 5 linear feet—of a clay collar were found in the room fill. They could have come from one semicircular hearth, but more likely they were from two quadrant-shaped corner hearths. Two fragments were flattened on one end, as if they had abutted a wall, but the piece did not seem sufficiently uniform to have come from one collar. In either case, the radius of the arc formed by the inside of the collar would have been about 1.8 feet.

The hearth in Room 84/1 is also worth noting, since it is one of only two in the ruin—the other is in Kiva U—with a slab mudded into position in the middle of the pit. The hearth is lined with both slabs and adobe.

Rooms 85 and 86

These two rooms, just west of the pithouse, are somewhat questionable. The absence of the west walls does not prove that they are not rooms, because they could have rested on, or very near, the now collapsed roof of Kiva Q. All other walls, with the exception of the wall common to the two rooms, still exist, or did exist, as part of adjacent rooms.

The wall dividing the rooms is the enigma. There were only three courses of rock, laid up in brown adobe to form a simple wall about 4.6 feet long. The wall abuts the exterior of the west wall of Rooms 55 and 56. One of the long, east-west logs forming a part of Kiva Q's roof was embedded in the fill below the west end of the wall, suggesting that the wall had been built after the construction of the Kiva.

Lancaster recalls seeing in other ruins wall stubs of this type serving, apparently, as no more than a low divider in the plaza area formed by the kiva roof. Such may be the case here. There are three wall pegs in the east wall of Room 85, as well as at least three coats of plaster.

PITHOUSE 1

Underlying Rooms 54–56, and also parts of Rooms 47, 48, and Kiva J, is a Basketmaker III pithouse, bearing a construction date of A.D. 648, designated Pithouse 1 (fig. 9). The room block above the structure is shown in figure 52a; Kiva J is in the right foreground. First evidence of the pithouse was revealed by the excavation of Rooms 47 and 48. Two cistlike structures—one against the south wall of Room 47 (fig. 52b), the other against the west wall of Room 48 (fig. 52c)—are merely part of the dropoff from the lip of a rock ledge at room floor level to the bedrock floor on which the pithouse was built. To judge by the masonry collar or retaining wall on the north and east sides, respectively, these structures might have been used by the Pueblo III inhabitants. If so, they were probably not carried down to the full depth possible because of the danger of undermining the walls of rooms built above the pithouse.

The subfloor excavation of Rooms 54–56 and Kiva J revealed almost the full extent of the pithouse. Excavation was not completed beneath the northeast side of Kiva J because of the danger that the masonry above might collapse.

Unfortunately, the outline of the pithouse is poorly defined or entirely lost in several places. The section under Room 54 is the best preserved (fig. 53), with pole seats pecked into the bedrock floor visible at the right, and the remains of a storage bin built against the north wall at left. The globular object to the left of the bin is a Chapin Gray jar.

The walls of the superimposed Pueblo III rooms follow the outline of the pithouse fairly closely in Rooms 54 and 55. It then curves away from the west wall of Room 56, cutting across the south end of the room into Kiva J. The greatest difficulty in tracing the pithouse walls came in the kiva, as might be expected. The kiva floor is only slightly above that of the pithouse, and the latter was thoroughly disturbed or torn out in many places when the kiva was built.

The only floor features reasonably well defined are the hearth, a storage bin, and pecked seats. Even the floor itself was well preserved only in that section under Room 54. Portions of the floor under Room 55 were still intact, but most of the floor under Room 56 was torn out in subfloor testing of the room before the presence of the pithouse was recognized.

The pithouse floor was bedrock over three-fourths of the section below Room 54. The southwest corner of this section consisted of about 0.05 foot of heavily burned brown soil overlying the sterile yellow soil and rock. The soil floor under Room 55 was a continuation of that under Room 54, with the addition of numerous rocks protruding slightly through the floor and showing a very heavy burn where exposed. The floor under Room 56 was also soil and apparently identical to that in Room 55.

Possibly eight circular seats were pecked into the bedrock around the periphery of the northeast quadrant of the floor section under Room 54. These probably served to hold poles supporting the sloping wall of the pithouse. The diameter of the seats ranged from about 0.2 to 0.35 foot (unknown in two cases), and the depth from

Figure 52. *Room block above Pithouse 1 (a), cistlike structure against south wall of Room 47 (b), and cistlike structure against west wall of Room 48 (c).*

Figure 53. *Section of Pithouse 1 under Room 54.*

0.1 to 0.3 foot. A possible sipapu in the northeast quadrant of Kiva J would make better sense as a posthole for the pithouse. Although the alinement of pecked seats could not be traced under the north kiva wall without endangering the walls above, this "sipapu" appears to be in or very close to the alinement if it were extended. There is another posthole near the north wall of the kiva. This could belong to either the pithouse or kiva, but is too near the center of the pithouse to be part of the wall construction.

In order to support the masonry wall of Rooms 54–56 and Kiva J at their common corner, a rock support was extended down to bedrock from the base of the walls. Unfortunately, as we learned after excavation of the pithouse, the pillar was in the middle of the firepit. Lancaster had suggested that this might be the case after discovering the outline of the pithouse.

The firepit was probably formed by making a depression in rocky, sterile fill, using bedrock for the base. Large unshaped blocks of rock, from about 0.6 foot to 2 feet in length, were then laid up in hard-packed brownish soil (containing some shale and bits of charcoal) along the south and west sides. The firepit was probably subrectangular in shape, about 2.8 feet wide and 3.3 feet long.

A vertical slab, below and parallel to the east wall of Room 56, was positioned with one end against the south wall of the pithouse. This may be part of a wingwall or partition, but no other material was found to substantiate this bit of evidence.

Bin 1, the largest and most elaborate of three, is the only one to occupy part of the floor area. It was built against the north wall of the pithouse, and this common (pithouse-bin) wall extended upward, unbroken, for about 2 feet before it began to curve inward. Major irregularities in the wall had been filled with rock and brown adobe to form a somewhat smooth but very uneven surface.

All that remained of the other two walls of this somewhat triangular structure were vertical slabs, and the charcoal remains of a small vertical pole against the exterior face of the southernmost slab in the east wall. The remaining slabs, averaging about 0.1 foot thick, were still standing to a height of about 1.3 feet at the time of excavation. Slab length ranged from about 0.8 foot to 1.2 feet. The interior floor of the bin was probably about 3 feet northeast to southwest, and about 4.5 feet northwest to southeast.

It was not possible to determine whether the walls of the bin were constructed entirely of rock slabs and adobe. The fragment of vertical pole could have been part of a roof support, which in turn might have helped support one side of the bin. It was also not possible to tell if the roof of the pithouse formed the roof of the bin, or if the latter had a lower roof of its own.

Storage Bins 2 and 3 were cavities in the west wall of the pithouse, in the southwest quadrant of the dwelling. Both were excavated into the mixed sterile dirt and rock fill forming—with the addition of a facing of large vertical slabs—the wall of the pithouse at this point. As a result, both were somewhat nebulous in shape, especially Bin 2.

Bin 2 was about 2 feet deep and 1.25 feet across, with an opening 1 foot wide and 0.6 foot high. The height of the bin was at least 1 foot. The opening into the bin was covered with a small slab. It is entirely possible that this was intended to seal off this structure, a partial cavity before excavation, in which case the "bin" was the result of improper excavation.

More definite, but equally vague in shape, was Bin 3, which may have been two bins. The small section of the masonry which formed both the front wall of the bin and a part of the wall of the pithouse curved back into the bin and away from the pithouse wall.

Thus there seems to be no question as to the validity of this bin. There was no evidence of an opening into the bin, or of a roof for the structure. The bin could have been roofed with a large slab which, in turn, could have formed a crude bench unless the members of the pithouse wall were seated on this natural, benchlike mixture of rock and sterile soil.

Unlike the somewhat dubious Bin 2, Bin 3 was a fairly large structure. It was about 2.5 feet wide, and 2 feet deep. Unlike the other bins, it extended down below the room floor. The depth of the structure was about 1.3 feet and the height above room floor about 1.5 feet. The bench, if such ever existed in the pithouse, would have been about 2.25 feet above floor.

Beneath the west wall of Room 56 was a remnant of what was probably the base of the pithouse wall. At this point, the wall of the pithouse must have rested on a large boulder. At least the lower portion of this irregularly surfaced boulder was packed with adobe, applied in several applications, so as to form a smooth, curving surface from an apparent Basketmaker III walking surface, west of the pithouse, up onto the pithouse wall. The walking surface is certainly of Basketmaker III age, to judge by the associated pottery, and in all probability is contemporaneous with the Basketmaker III pithouse.

The surface slopes down slightly to the west from the pithouse. It is terminated abruptly at the roof of Kiva Q, which was cut through it. To the south, it extends under the north walls of Rooms 60 and 88, but it could not be followed to its limits because of the danger of undermining the room walls. Tests within these rooms showed no evidence of such a surface, but this was before it was discovered. The excavators could very easily have gone through the walking surface without being aware of it. The northern extent could not be determined because of the soil cement slab placed over the floor of Room 86 before discovery of the walking surface. The west walls of Rooms 55 and 56, built above the pithouse perimeter, would also collapse if undermined to any extent. Thus it was impossible to check thoroughly the contact of the pithouse walls with the walking surface along its east edge. A probable continuation of this surface was found beneath the west wall of Room 84, which is located immediately north of Room 86.

A series of possible pole seats was found in the walking surface below the south end of Room 85. Although several of these seem to be circular, well-defined "seats," there is no apparent pattern in their arrangement. Some others look to be the work of burrowing animals.

A far more definite feature is a round cist, cut through the walking surface but associated with it. A portion of the southern side of the cist was not excavated, to prevent collapse of the north wall of Room 60 immediately above. The cist is about 2 feet in diameter and about 1.2 feet deep in the center. The sides slope in gently, and the bottom is slightly basin shaped. The structure is slab lined up to within a few tenths of a foot of the rim. The balance of the lining is a mixture of gray shale, red adobe, and brown soil. It is at least 0.25 foot thick at the rim and feathers out onto the rock sides, sometimes covering them and sometimes leaving the rock exposed. The rim was about 0.5 foot wide and raised at least 0.1 foot above the walking surface, upon which it also feathered out smoothly.

The upper half of the south side of the pit shows evidence of heavy burning. The north side was also burned but to a lesser degree. Portions of the bottom and north and south sides show little or no evidence of fire. There was no ash or other evidence in the fill of use as a firepit, and the burning on the cist walls does not seem uniform enough for such use. It is more likely that the burning of a nearby structure—pithouse or ramada—caused the smoke blackening or partial burning of the rim and sides of the cist.

KIVAS

Although the architecture of the kivas is more specialized than that of the rooms, there is, perhaps, a greater standardization of features. The most commonly used terms, and the numbering sequence of pilasters and interpilaster spaces, are shown in figure 54.

The inner walls of the small kivas below the banquette are circular in outline, with three exceptions; those of Kivas G and P are roughly rectangular and those of Kiva J a modified D. The upper walls of many of the circular kivas are formed partly by discontinuous sections of a circular masonry wall concentric to the lower walls but larger in diameter, and partly by the back wall of the recess. The recess walls form, in a few cases, part of the arc of a still larger concentric circle. More commonly, the back wall is straight and runs at right angles to the kiva axis. Quite frequently the outer walls of a kiva—especially those built within a square room—also form part of the upper inner walls of circular kivas, as in Kivas A and I, as well as those of the rectangular kivas. The upper walls of Kiva J are unique in Long House.

The outer walls of the kivas conform to no particular pattern, but rather their presence and outline are dictated by location, need, and previous construction in the area. Some of the kivas, surrounded on all sides by natural artificial fill, needed no outer walls to be self-supporting.

The kiva axis is usually the center line of the kiva, and in a stylized structure would pass through the ventilator shaft and tunnel, deflector, firepit, sipapu, and (sometimes) a niche in the lower wall. In several of the Long House kivas, rearrangement of some features moved them off the axis or caused the axis to be skewed.

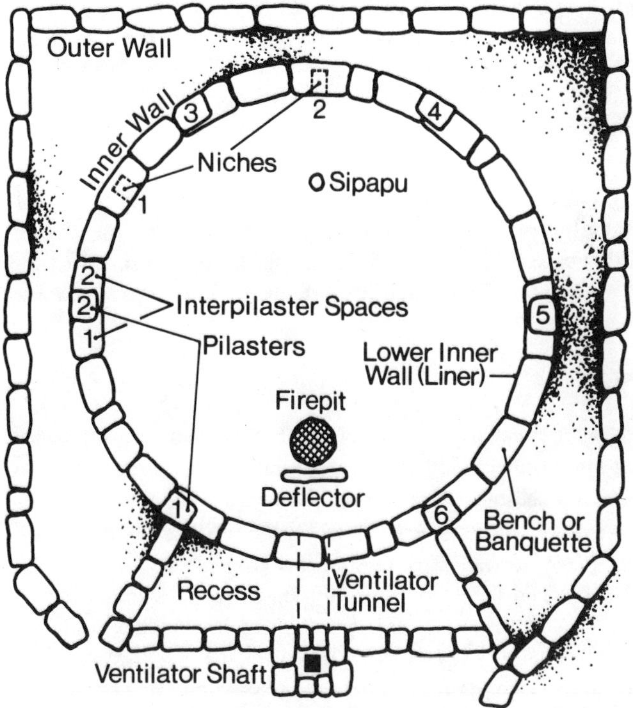

Figure 54. *Schematic drawing of a kiva, showing the numbering sequence of pilasters, interpilaster spaces, and niches, and terms for various other features.*

Walls

The description, under "Rooms," of the types of masonry and mortar used, dressing of individual stones, chinking, and plastering also applies to the kivas. The stones used in the lower kiva walls are probably slightly smaller on the average than those in the conventional room masonry. Those used in the pilasters and outer kiva walls, and in some of the upper inner walls, tend to be slightly larger than in conventional room masonry. The finest masonry in the kiva was often found in the pilasters, whose stones were usually larger in size than those in the lower walls. The core of these features was usually rubble, however. Also of higher quality workmanship were the stones forming the mouth of the ventilator tunnel. In both cases, the faces were usually rectangular and flat, the corners straight and alined with those of the stones above and below.

In many kivas, all of the inner walls, especially the lower walls and the face of the pilasters, show extensive replastering to a much greater extent than do the room walls. Major paintings were uncovered on the lower walls in Kivas E and Q, and the more limited art work found in Kivas J and R suggests that painted walls may have been quite common in the kivas. The walls were probably replastered and repainted frequently as they became smoke blackened.

Pilasters

At least ten of the circular kivas (A, E, F, H, K, M, O, Q, R, and S) had six pilasters; three (C, N, and U) probably had only four; and three others (B, I, and T) apparently had none. The two rectangular kivas (G and P) probably lacked pilasters also, and Kiva J (like Kiva I) does not have what can be called true pilasters. The remaining two (D and L) were too poorly preserved to determine whether they had pilasters. (There is one pilaster-like structure on the north side of Kiva L.)

Some of the pilasters in 12 kivas (A, C, E, F, H, K, M, N, O, R, S, and U) tapered radially from back to front. With the exception of Kiva U, the pilasters of all kivas possessing these features were set back from the edge of the banquette an average of 0.1 foot. The entire upper wall was probably set back in Kivas B and T.

In all kivas, the pilasters may have averaged about 3.0 to 3.5 feet high above the banquette. In six-pilasters kivas, the average width was probably 2.0 to 2.5 feet; in four-pilaster kivas, 3.0 to 4.5 feet (discounting Kiva I). Their depth, except in recesses, was about 1.0 foot to 1.5 feet.

Niches

All but four kivas (D, G, N, and P) have from one to 10 niches built into the inner walls. They are generally rectangular to square in shape, and slab-lined in many cases. Kivas C and M, which had been relined, have six niches each. However, counting each of the relined kivas as two separate structures for this purpose, we find that four niches— found in seven kivas— is the most popular number.

Most of the niches are in the lower kiva wall opposite the ventilator, but they can be found in all quadrants of a structure. They range in position from floor level to just below the banquette. In 11 kivas (B, H, J, K, L, M, O, Q, R, T, and U) there is at least one niche on the kiva axis. (Kivas H and M have two so positioned.) There are four kivas (C, E, J, and M) with a niche in a recess wall, two kivas (E and J) with a niche in the front of the deflector, and two kivas (E and U) with niches in the pilaster faces. More unusual is the niche in the north wall of the ventilator tunnel of Kiva C.

Wall Loops and Pegs

Oak wall loops, possible belt loom anchors, were found in Kivas I and L. Six loops were embedded in the lower walls of the former, and two in the lower walls of the latter. Wall pegs were found only in these two kivas. There were four in Kiva I—one in the face of the upper wall (but not centered) near the roof on all four sides—and two in the lower east wall of Kiva L.

Banquette

One of the more consistent features of the kivas was height of the banquette or bench. It averaged about 3.0 to 3.5 feet above the kiva floor, except in Kiva R; and in the kivas without pilasters, it was about 4.0 feet. The depth was more variable, but the intent of the builders in most cases was apparently to provide a bench 1.0 foot to 1.5 feet deep. The top of the lower kiva wall or liner formed the edge of the banquette. The banquette floor was usually plastered with adobe up to 0.1 foot thick, which in some kivas was brought forward over the top of the masonry liner to form a rounded corner at its junction with the wall face.

Recess

The recess—actually an expanded portion of the banquette in the circular kivas—is on the south side of 16 kivas. One of these, Kiva E, had a northwest recess also. In Kivas F and T, there was probably a northwest recess only because of inadequate room on the south side. The southwest corner recess of Kivas G and I was undoubtedly a substitute for the larger conventional recess. We were unable to determine the location of the recess, if any, in Kivas B and L. In addition to the conventional southern recess, Kiva J also has what can best be called a northern recess. Although it could be considered merely part of the banquette, its depth and features suggest a more specialized function.

The sides of several of the recesses in circular kivas (C, K, M, N, R, S, and U) converge radially, thus forming an area wider at the back (6.5 to 8 feet) that it is in front (4.2 to 5.8 feet). In some other kivas (D, probably E-southern recess, G, J, and P), the sides are parallel. As already mentioned, the back wall of the recess may be curved (as in Kivas C, K, and M) or straight. The side walls are generally straight except where deflected by large boulders or outcropping bedrock (Kivas Q and T), or forced to conform to the contour of an existing structure (Kivas H, I, and O).

The recess floor was probably hard-packed red adobe in most kivas and averaged about 0.1 foot thick. Up to at least three layers of adobe had been placed in some kivas. In Kiva U, there was once a corrugated jar embedded in the fill below each side of the recess, mouth flush with the floor, and in Kiva P there was a similarly positioned jar in the southwest corner of the recess. A third example occurs in Kiva J, where a corrugated jar was embedded in the fill below the east side of the north "recess," its mouth also flush with the bench floor.

Ventilator

Without exception, the kivas were equipped with a horizontal tunnel (reduced to only a horizontal entrance to the shaft in Kivas B, probably F, G, the remodeled ventilator of R, and T) and a vertical shaft (missing in F). The tunnel extended straight back from a floor-level rectangular opening in the lower kiva wall to the shaft, except in Kivas H and I. Here, it went to the south outer kiva wall, made a right-angle bend to the east, and followed the outer wall to a shaft inside the corner formed by the east and south outer walls. The tunnels averaged about 2.0 feet high by 1.3 feet wide; the shaft was about 1.0 foot square in 15 kivas and roughly 1.0 foot by 1.5 feet in four others.

Although masonry similar to that in the lower kiva walls forms most of the tunnel and shaft walls, vertical slabs were used alone in places or combined with block masonry. Most tunnels appear to have been roofed with whole or split tree or shrub stems and branches up to about 0.1 foot in diameter, or split juniper shakes up to perhaps 0.3 foot in width, which rested directly on the side walls and were covered with a layer of adobe. In Kiva A, slabs appear to have formed part of the tunnel roof; and in Kiva I, small poles resting on the tunnel walls supported juniper shakes running parallel to the tunnel walls.

Hard-packed red adobe or bedrock formed the floor of some tunnels, but compacted fill was commonly used. In several tunnels, the first foot or two were better finished on the sides and floor than farther back.

Kivas B and T had a subfloor ventilator which ran from the ventilator shaft to an opening in the kiva floor. When the tunnel was later filled and replaced by an above-floor tunnel, the shaft was retained and incorporated in the new construction. Subfloor ventilators are one of the most characteristic features of Chaco-type kivas (Judd, 1964, p. 183), but apparently this idea did not find favor with the Mesa Verde people.

Two crossed sticks, one immediately above the other, were found in the ventilator shaft of two kivas. In Kiva A, they were 2.15 feet below the top of the shaft and connected the mid-points of opposing sides. In Kiva H, they were about 1.0 foot below the top and connected diagonally opposed corners.

Deflector

A deflector was interposed between the firepit and the tunnel opening of all above-floor ventilators. It consisted of a low masonry wall in 15 kivas and a sandstone slab in three (or four) others (Kivas B, I, Q, and possibly P). No hint of its construction remained in Kivas D and L. As a rule, deflectors were better dressed on the side toward the firepit. Several were plastered, and at least one (in Kiva E) was painted.

Kivas A, C, and F (and possibly G) had a wall-to-wall masonry deflector. A central wall was built first in Kivas A and F, and then a wing was added to either side to form an arc which enclosed the area between the deflector and the ventilator. The wall was apparently built as a unit in Kiva C. There are two large rectangular notches in the top of the wing walls of Kivas A and F and in the equivalent location in the Kiva C deflector, as well as two small square-to-rectangular holes penetrating the same part of the feature, either near the base or at floor level.

There was definite evidence in seven kivas of low adobe or adobe-and-slab ridges—deflector "laterals"—running from the ends of the deflector to the kiva walls. Although there may once have been two laterals in each kiva, four kivas (N, Q, S, and T) had this number and the other three (K, M, and O) had only one. These features, only 0.2 foot high at most, may have served the same function as the wing walls mentioned above in delimiting the main, adobe-floored part of the kiva from the usually unfloored area behind the deflector.

Floor

The versatilitity of the kiva in its function as a multipurpose room is revealed clearly in the floor features. Layers of adobe, with a total thickness of up to 0.4 foot, and, occasionally bedrock form the various kiva floors. Evidence of considerable remodeling and reflooring was found in many kivas, and the work reached major proportions in Kivas C, D, and M.

About half the kivas had one floor, whereas the rest had two, three, or, in at least one case, four floors. These are full floors, not mere patches such as those in Kiva Q. Bedrock was used as a floor, or as part of a floor, in several kivas. Although difficult to determine in many cases because of erosion, there appear to be few kivas with a hard-packed floor between the deflector and the ventilator. Underlying a part of the floor in five kivas (E, I, K, M, and O) was a layer of coal against the north wall or in the northern or northeastern part of the kiva. A similar deposit was found behind part of the west wall of Kiva A and Room 78. Since coal was not found in any secular room, its presence in the latter structure suggests that Room 78, which underlies Kiva D, may also have been a kiva.

A circular firepit was centrally located in each kiva. It averaged about 2.0 feet in diameter and 0.8 foot deep, but several varied considerably in size and shape because of extensive relining. It was dug into fill, sterile soil and rubble, or even bedrock. The side walls and bottom were formed by adobe, vertical slabs, small rock, bedrock, or various mixtures of these. Many were basin shaped in cross-section, quite a few were flat bottomed. An adobe collar raised slightly above floor level was found in several kivas.

One other floor feature is usually found in kivas: the sipapu or symbolic "spirit hole," representing in some historic kivas the mythical opening through which the ancestors passed from the underworld to the earth's surface. But two kivas, G and H, lacked a sipapu. Kiva G's was probably destroyed along with other parts of the structure. Kiva H has a bedrock floor so the sipapu— if it ever existed—was most likely a shallow hole in a mound of adobe placed on bedrock. The sipapu is usually a cylindrical hole dug into cultural or sterile fill and, occasionally, bedrock at the bottom. Several kivas had two sipapus as a result of replastering the floor or, more rarely, changing the bearing of the kiva axis so that it passed through a new sipapu and a new wall niche.

Like the firepit, the sipapu sometimes had a raised adobe collar. More frequently, sherds or a jar neck were used at its mouth. In Kiva J, a large corrugated jar formed a sipapu. The remainder of the hole below the sherds or neck, in those so lined, was usually plastered with adobe, but vertical slabs were sometimes used. Excepting the jar in Kiva J, whose mouth was about 0.7 foot across, the openings ranged from 0.2 to 0.5 foot in diameter and averaged about 0.3 foot. Depth varied from 0.2 to 1.0 foot, and averaged about 0.7 foot.

Other features were found in the kivas, but not so frequently as to be considered customary: footdrum (M and Q), shrine (Q), metates or anvils (M, possibly Q, and S), tunnels (M, N, R, and possibly K and Q), masonry "flange" in front of the ventilator tunnel mouth to support (possibly) a cover slab (O), ashpit (C and M), loom loops in the bedrock floor (E), possible ladder sockets (H), stone-lined cist (K), small circular pits (C, N, and possibly O), and pot support (R). The area between the deflector and the ventilator tunnel perhaps served as an ashpit in some kivas. Subfloor "vaults" (foot drums), located west of the firepit, occur in a majority of Pueblo Bonito kivas in Chaco Canyon (Judd, 1964, p. 177) and thus provide—along with the subfloor ventilator—a second typical Chaco feature that was not so fully exploited at Mesa Verde.

Roof

Since only six kivas lack pilasters (B, G, I, J, P, and T, with the situation in D and L indeterminate), a cribbed roof would seem to have been the preferred construction for a kiva. Parts of both pilaster-supported (cribbed) and wall-supported roofs were preserved in several of the kivas, and are described fully under the appropriate heading. In Kiva E, there were three cribbed logs nearly in place on the pilasters; and in Kiva I, about half of the roof was still intact and in place. Kiva J had one main timber in place, spanning the center of the kiva, and two short sections of other primary timbers embedded in the walls. In Kiva M, the charred remains of two cribbed logs still rested on the pilasters. In Kiva Q, about half of the roof was found partly on the pilasters and partly in the upper fill.

The primary timbers used in the cribbing, and the secondary beams which closed the roof, ranged in diameter from 0.2 to 0.8 foot. (In some cases, of course, the primary timbers closed the roof and there were no secondary poles used.) Above the primary, or secondary, beams came split poles and shakes, juniper bark, brush stems or sometimes just masses of brush (Kivas E and M), and a thick layer of adobe. The entire roof was probably 2 to 2.5 feet thick, at least, in the cribbed structures, and about half this in roofs like that of Kiva I. Ceiling height (or the base of the cribbing) varied from a low 5.2 or 5.3 feet in Kiva M to perhaps 6.5 feet, and probably averaged about 6.0 feet. The height of the top of the roof above the kiva floor was probably 7.8 to 8.7 feet.

In-Place Wood

As in the rooms, all in-place wood was identified by Stanley Welsh. It is listed by provenience in table 4. The genus and species of the specimens are included in those given in the list on page .

Kiva A

Six of the 10 kivas in the west half of the pueblo were built in a row along the cave wall. Kiva A, the westernmost of the six, was built in a square room predating both Room 4 and Kiva B (fig. 55). Much of the inner wall construction of the kiva proper is gone, leaving only patches of smoke-blackened plaster on room and cave walls to indicate the location of pilasters and recess (fig. 56). Although this kiva is generally "conventional" in its shape and features, the need to conform to the shape of a pre-existing room resulted in modifications of pilasters, recess, and ventilator shaft. The kiva is oriented with the axis roughly northwest-southeast, with a small recess in the southeast corner of the original room.

Walls

Excepting the west exterior wall, which is formed by the cave, all walls are simple masonry. The exterior walls are made of large, roughly shaped stones, with only the east exterior being fairly well finished on the surface.

In several places, the inner wall or liner is no more than a thin veneer placed against fill or a portion of the outer walls. It is composed of stones of various shapes and sizes, some rectangular with pecked faces, and others irregular in shape and finish. Four coats of smoke-blackened plaster covered most of the remaining sections of the inner wall.

On the west side of the kiva, between the cave wall and the kiva liner, a shaly coal was packed between and at the base of the walls for a distance of several feet. Similar deposits of coal were found behind the west walls of Room 78 and Kiva E, and beneath the floors of Kivas E, I, K, M, O, and Q.

Pilasters

Although only one pilaster remained at the time of excavation, there were probably six originally. Judging by remnants of wall plaster, pilasters were located in the northwest and southwest corners of the room. The one remaining pilaster, roughly in the middle of the south wall, was probably matched by one in the middle of the north wall. A fifth appears to have been present near the southern end of the east wall, where it would have formed the north side of the recess. There was, almost surely, a sixth pilaster in the northeast corner of the room, but no evidence of it now exists.

The sides of the existing pilaster taper radially toward the center of the kiva. The face of the pilaster is covered with four or possibly five layers of smoke-blackened plaster. Each layer is less than 0.01 foot thick.

Niches

There are two niches in the north wall, Niche 1 near the base of the inner wall and Niche 2 at the base of an interpilaster space. The former is made entirely of slabs, the latter by a gap in the building stones. Neither is in line with the kiva axis.

Banquette

The fragment of the banquette remaining is joined to the surviving pilaster. The face of the pilaster is set back 0.1 foot from the face of the masonry liner at this point. Other evidence for a banquette is found in the lower limit of smoke blackening on the wall in presumed interpilaster spaces. The distance above floor is quite consistent in all cases, ranging from 3.4 to 3.8 feet.

Recess

Nothing remains of the recess floor, which was undoubtedly based on fill packed behind the walls of the ventilator tunnel and on top of the slab or wooden roof of the tunnel. The height of this floor was 3.7 to 3.8 feet, judging by the smoke-blackened walls of the recess.

At the back of the recess a triangular masonry structure was built into the room corner above the recess floor. This would have served as an extra roof support but would not have been a true pilaster. It would also have formed a straight or possibly curved backwall for the recess, thus bringing the recess shape more into conformity with that found in other Long House kivas.

Ventilator

The unique feature of Kiva A is the ventilator. The inner or horizontal portion can be seen in figure 56. The opening made in the original room wall is visible just to the right of the vertical scale. There is one serviceberry stick lintel across the opening, immediately below the rock lintel, but it serves no obvious useful purpose. The vent opening is reminiscent of niches, in both rooms and kivas, which also have wood lintels. It is quite possible, of course, that a niche in the room wall was converted to the kiva ventilator opening by removing the back slab.

Beyond the opening, the tunnel extends straight back 3.2 feet before turning upward. The sides of the tunnel are of masonry similar to that in the rest of the kiva, and the top is probably composed of horizontal slabs. The floors of the tunnel and of the vertical shaft are bedrock.

The masonry ventilator shaft extends up 8.6 feet, at which point it opens into the triangular-shaped vent shaft recess which I mentioned in discussing Room 4 (figs. 12b and 13). Near the top of the shaft is a pair of crossed sticks (fig. 57), a feature also found in

Table 4. Identification of wood in-place in kivas.

Kivas	Item / Location	Kind
A	crossed sticks (2), vent shaft, N-S	serviceberry
	E-W*	serviceberry
	lintel (1), vent shaft	serviceberry
E	lintels (2), northeast lower wall niche (Rohn niche #2)	serviceberry
	roof (numerous), vent shaft	mixed serviceberry, oak and juniper
H	crossed sticks (1), south end, NE-SW stick*	serviceberry
	roof (numerous split shakes), vent shaft	juniper
I	loops (6), north (4) and east (2) walls	oak
	pegs (4), north and south walls	serviceberry
	east and west walls	juniper
	roof (3 poles, lintel & numerous split shakes), vent shaft	juniper
L	lintel (1), north niche	juniper
	loops (2), east wall	oak
	peg (1), east wall	serviceberry
15	lintels, south door, 2nd & 3rd from N (north lintel missing, but probably serviceberry and a digging stick, to judge by impressions in the adobe)	serviceberry
	pegs, north wall, east (stub in wall)	(not checked)
	west	serviceberry
	east wall, 1st from N	oak
	2nd from N	serviceberry
	3rd from N	oak
	4th from N	willow
	5th, 6th, 7th, & 8th	serviceberry
	south wall, 1st from E	serviceberry
	2nd from E	mountain mahogany
	3rd from E	serviceberry
	4th from E	mountain mahogany
	5th from E	serviceberry
	6th from E	fourwing saltbush
16/1	lintels, east door, east	juniper
	west	serviceberry
16/2	lintels, south door	juniper
17/1	pegs, north wall, east (MV 1256)	serviceberry
	west	serviceberry
	east wall, 1st from N	oak
	2nd from N	serviceberry
	3rd from N (MV 1255)	serviceberry
	4th from N (MV 1254)	serviceberry
	5th from N	serviceberry
	6th from N (MV 1253)	serviceberry
17/1	pegs, south wall (2)	oak
	west wall,	
	1st, 2nd, 3rd & 4th from N	serviceberry
	5th from N	juniper
	6th from N	serviceberry
	7th from N	juniper
	8th from N	serviceberry
17/2	Lintel, T-door (1)	
	rectangular door (remodeled from	
	lintel, t-Door), north	serviceberry
	south	juniper
	loop, north exterior wall	oak
	pegs, east wall (2)	serviceberry
	north wall, east	juniper
	west	serviceberry
	east exterior (2)	(not checked)
18/1	lintels, north door	juniper
18/2	lintels, north door, 1st & 3rd from N	juniper
	east door (4)	willow
	E-W stick (1)	oak
	peg, south wall	serviceberry
	east door	
	E-W stick	
	pole, oriented N-S, MV 1257 (not roofing, which is bedrock)	juniper
	wedge, north exterior wall (1 stick used to wedge N-S pole above)	juniper

(continued)

Table 4. Indentification of wood in-place in kivas. (Continued)

Kivas	Item / Location	Kind
20	floor, room floor, and constituting a portion of the roof of Room 19; 1st & 2nd from E. replaced during stabilization (but may be Pueblo III logs); 3rd, 4th & 5th from E	juniper
	loops, east wall, forked stick	willow
	south wall	oak
	pegs, east exterior wall (1)	juniper
	west wall, 1st from N	willow
	2nd & 3rd from N	juniper
22	peg, south wall, identification probable (not sampled)	serviceberry
23	lintel, west door	serviceberry
	pegs, north wall (1)	serviceberry
	east wall, 1st & 3rd from N	serviceberry
	2nd from N*	oak
	south wall (2)	serviceberry
25	pegs, west & south walls, 1 each	serviceberry
29	lintels, south door	serviceberry
	roof, west wall, lower roof, pole stubs	juniper
39	jambs, north door, west side	juniper
	lintels, north door,	
	1st, 2nd, 3rd & 5th from N	serviceberry
	4th from N	juniper
	lintel retaining loop; west end of lintels	oak
	lintel retaining loop tie, west end of lintels	yucca
	pegs, north wall (1)	willow
	east wall (2)	serviceberry
	pole, extends from east to south wall	mountain mahogany
40	lintels, south door	serviceberry
	peg, east well	serviceberry
41	pegs, east wall	serviceberry
	jacal wall (numerous)	
	all horizontal members exposed inside Room 41 proper	oak
	vertical poles, 2nd east of door	pinyon
	all others	juniper
	small uprights	serviceberry
42	lintels, north door (2), north	juniper
	south*	oak
	east door (6)	juniper
44	lintels, north door (2)	serviceberry
	south door (5), 2nd from S	serviceberry
	all others	juniper
	pegs, east wall	juniper
	pole, east to north walls	juniper
	loop on pole	yucca
45	peg, east wall	serviceberry
46	peg, north wall	oak
47	peg, south wall	serviceberry
60	wall support, horizontal, in east wall	juniper
64/1	lintels, east door	juniper
	door-slab support (1), vertical stick, south side, east door	juniper
66	lintel, T-door (sealed—opened into Room 67), lintel on Room 66 side	juniper
67	lintels, T-door (sealed—open into Room 66),	
	lintel retaining loops, both ends of lintels, and in both rooms	oak
	lintel retaining loop ties rooms	yucca
68	peg, west wall	serviceberry
71	pegs, south wall	serviceberry
74	jacal wall (numerous):	
	vertical poles	juniper
	vertical brushy material, 1 member	oak
	all others	serviceberry
	horizontal ties binding vertical members together	oak
85	loop, east wall	oak
	pegs, east wall	serviceberry
86	peg, east wall	juniper

*Worked, possibly part of a digging stick.

Kiva H. The upper stick is 2.15 feet below the recess floor. Both the ventilator and the recess are an integral part of the Room 3 and 4 complex, and demonstrate an unusual way of incorporating a vertical vent shaft in other construction.

The recess is 3.5 feet long, north to south, 1.5 feet wide at the south end, and 3.8 feet wide at the north end. The vent opening occupies almost the entire south end of the recess. The height of the roof, already described with Room 4/2, averages 4.1 feet above the recess floor. The alcove opened onto the roof of Kiva A on the north, where the top of the south exterior wall of the Kiva A was probably flush with the recess floor and the kiva roof. The recess floor is composed of hard-packed red adobe, with some small rock mixed in, and is at least 0.5 foot thick.

The three remaining room walls, of compound masonry, are fairly well finished on the recess side. The two openings in the east wall of the room may have been intended to make the kiva ventilator draw in fresh air from east of the room block rather than more smoky air from the kiva roof. It certainly has no obvious use if it is not part of the ventilating system. The recess walls are not smoke blackened.

The lintel for the openings consisted of two poles extending across the top of both openings. One of these, a pole 5.1 feet long and 0.2 foot in diameter, is still in place. Beam impressions in adobe on the masonry dividing the openings and a beam seat in the south wall mark the location of the other. The north aperture is 1.05 feet long and 0.67 foot high, the south 1.2 feet long and 0.8± foot high. Both openings apparently had a sill, one of rock and the other of rock and adobe, about 0.3 to 0.4 foot above the recess floor.

Deflector

The deflector, built in two stages, consists of a short central segment and two wings which connect it to the kiva liner on either side. The central section is seated on bedrock, the wings on the uppermost adobe floor. All three parts are of simple masonry, with the stones of varying size, shape, and surface finish. There are two sets of openings in the wingwalls. The smaller set (0.45 by 0.5 foot and 0.4 by 0.6 foot) is at floor level and centrally located in each wing. The larger (1.7 feet by 0.9 foot) is either at, or near, the top of

Figure 56. *Location of pilasters and recess in Kiva A, indicated by patches of smoke-blackened plaster on room and cave walls.*

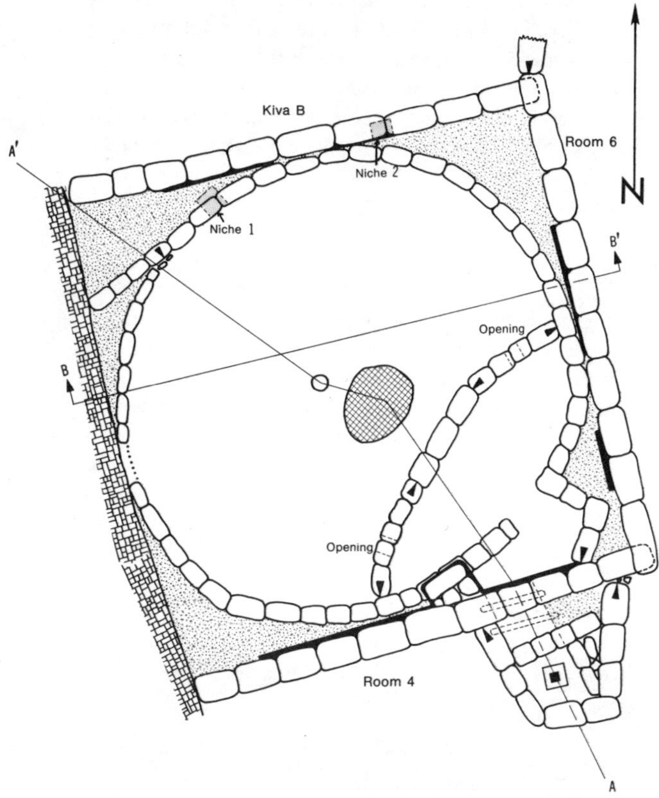

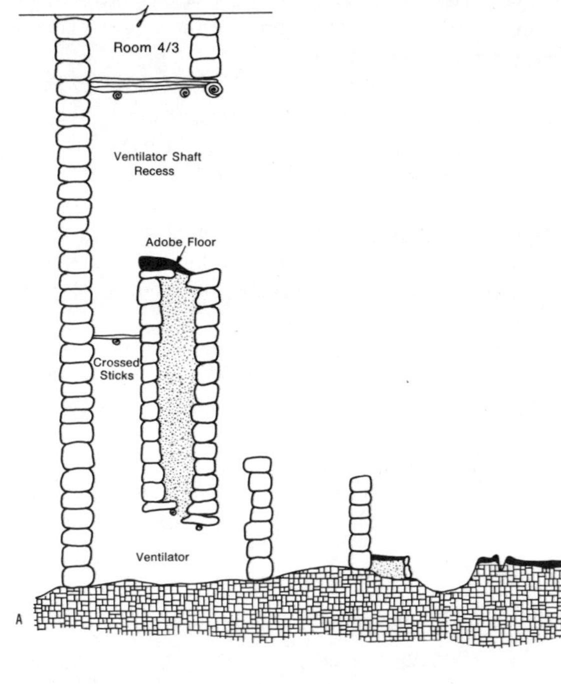

the wing, and adjacent to the central segment of the deflector. Although one of the small openings and a part of one of the larger ones are visible in figure 56, a better idea of the arrangement can be seen in Kiva C (fig. 62). All openings extend through the entire thickness of the wall.

There is no evidence that the deflector was ever higher than it is now. Thus the larger openings would merely be notches.

Floor

Over most of the kiva, the floor consisted of two to four layers of brown adobe, each up to 0.1 foot thick, overlying the bedrock. No adobe covered the bedrock floor behind, or south of, the deflector.

The only floor features are a firepit and a sipapu. The former was cut into the bedrock on the west side, and built up with stone slabs and adobe on the east side. The pit is roughly circular in outline and basin shaped in cross section. The sipapu is shallow, with a bedrock floor roughly circular in outline, and has an adobe collar raised about 0.1 foot above the kiva floor. The sipapu is slightly to the west of the axis through the firepit and ventilator opening.

Roof

A sharp break in the dressed masonry of the north wall of Room 4, a short distance below the doorway into Room 4/2, indicates that the top of the kiva roof was about 8.2 feet above the kiva floor. Smoke blackening of the cave wall bears this out and shows, further, that the kiva ceiling was probably between 5.8 and 6.1 feet above the floor.

To judge by the debris in the kiva fill, the roof was formed by layers of split juniper shakes, sagebrush stems, and juniper bark placed over large logs or poles which were probably supported by a cribbed-log base.

Figure 57. *Crossed sticks near top of ventilator shaft of Kiva A.*

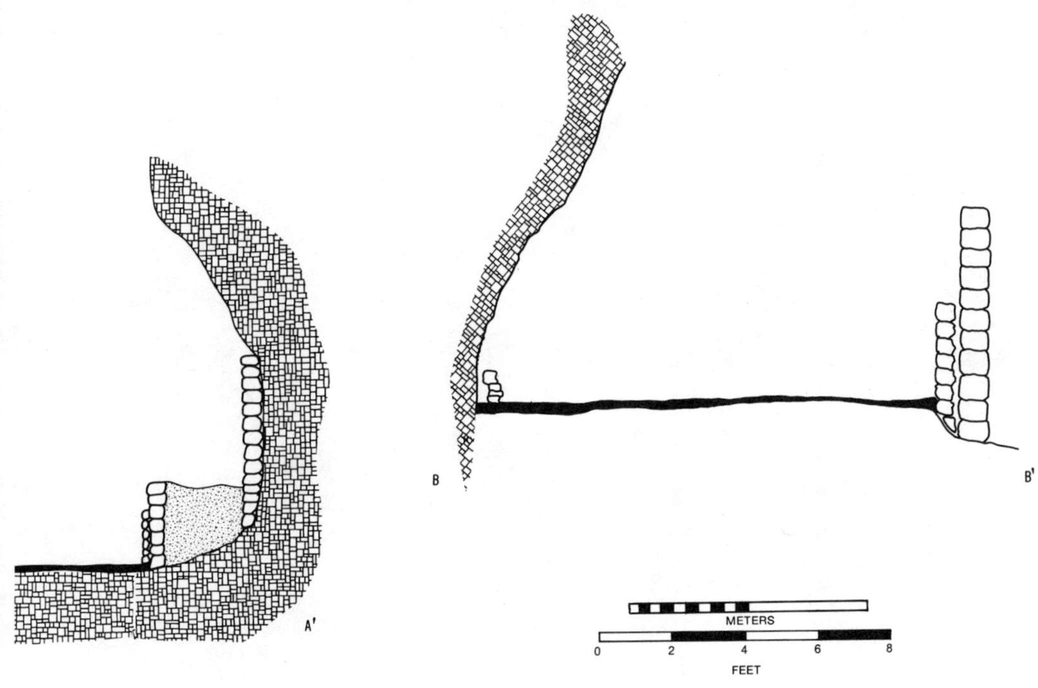

Figure 55. *Kiva A, plan and sections A-A′ and B-B′.*

Kiva B

The state of preservation of Kiva B, and especially of its walls, was very poor. This may account, in part, for the apparent simplicity of the structure. Although Kiva B is enclosed by other retaining walls, much like Kiva A, the structure they form was not built as a room originally and does not have the square shape of the room enclosing Kiva A (fig. 58). The kiva axis is roughly northwest-southeast, but it approaches the west-east line more closely than does the axis of Kiva A.

Walls

As in Kiva A, all walls are of simple masonry, with the exception of the west, or cave, wall. Both the north and east exterior walls are made of large rectangular to irregularly shaped stones. The north and east faces of the walls, exposed to view at the time of construction, are the better finished ones. The south exterior wall is formed by the north exterior of Kiva A.

The only remaining portion of the upper, inner wall (above banquette level) is along the south side of the kiva. It is concentric with the lower wall, and is built of large irregularly shaped blocks with fairly flat faces. The wall was covered with four coats of smoke-blackened plaster.

The lower, inner wall, preserved in part around the entire periphery of the kiva, was built of stones that were generally smaller but of irregular shape and size. Surface finish was inconsistent, with some of the building stones showing pecked faces and others not. Parts of the liner were covered with up to five layers of brown adobe plaster, most of which were smoked blackened. Part of one layer, at least, was painted white.

Pilasters, Banquette, and Recess

Where preserved on the south side of the kiva, the upper, inner wall is set back from the lower about 0.3 foot, thus forming a narrow ledge or banquette. There is no evidence of pilasters, or interpilaster spaces, either here or elsewhere in the kiva. With the ventilator shaft located almost immediately east of the kiva liner, it would not have been possible to build a recess above the ventilator tunnel. Only in the northwest corner, between inner and outer walls, would there appear to have been room for a recess, but there is no evidence that one was ever placed here.

Niches

Three of the four niches are in the northwest quadrant of the kiva, the fourth in the southwest quadrant. The sides, top, and bottom of Niche 1 are formed by building stones, the back by an upright slab. Niche 2, similar in construction, is on the kiva axis.

Niche 3 is oval, with sides and back rounded with adobe, and is much smaller than Niches 1 and 2. In recording this feature, Robert Nichols suggested that it might have been used to store a polished stone object.

Niche 4, in the north wall, is a possible double niche. The lower part, composed entirely of sandstone slabs, cannot be questioned. A small, partially collapsed section of masonry above the niche suggested to Lancaster that the niche was a double one. If so, the two sections were probably of equal size.

Ventilator

A subfloor ventilator tunnel, a feature shared only with Kiva T in Long House, was discovered in Kiva B (fig. 59). This structure is

Figure 58. *Kiva B, plan and section A-A'.*

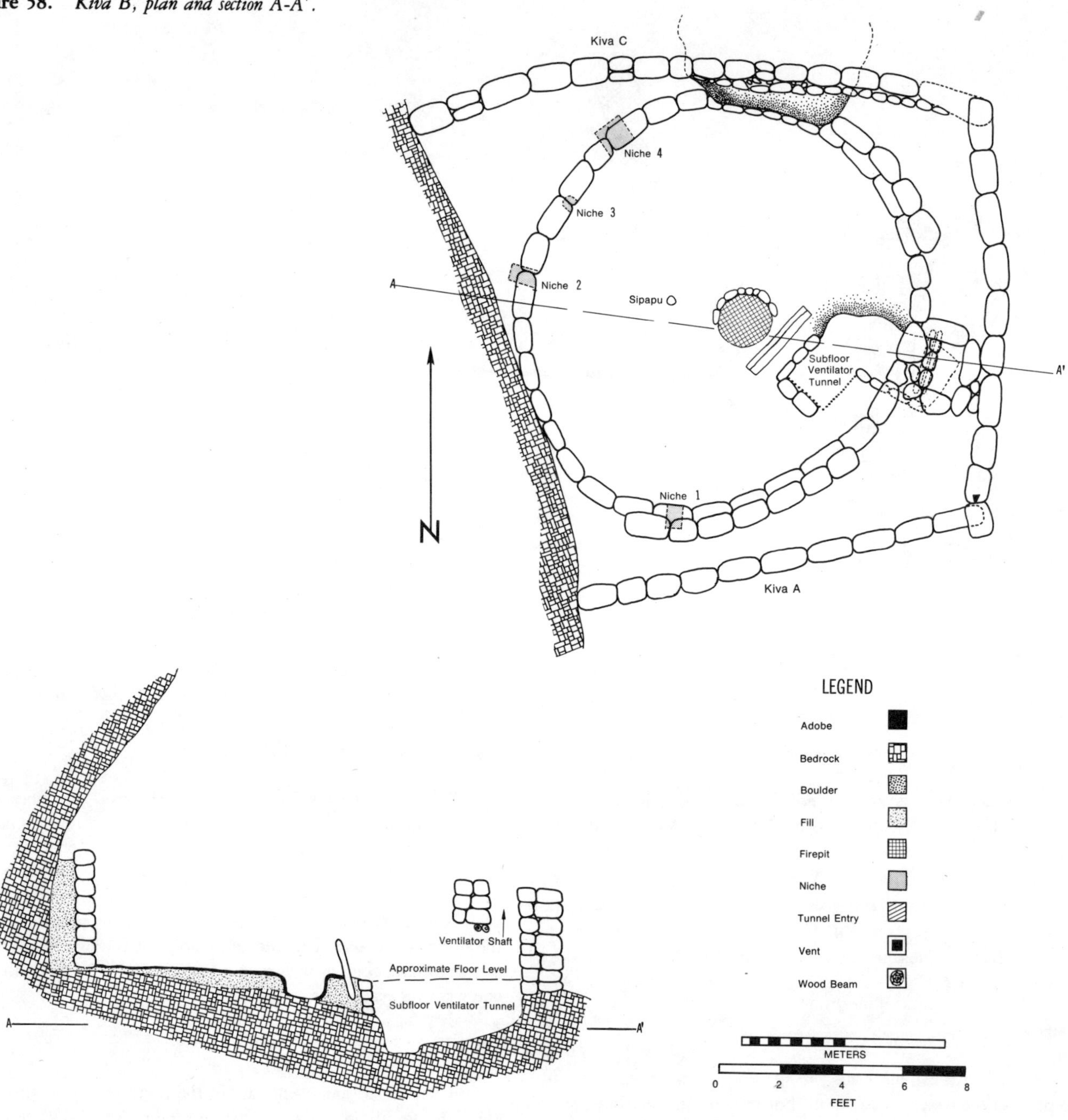

rather strange in that it is L-shaped. The shape was probably dictated by the location of bedrock beneath the kiva floor. It would not have been possible to extend the tunnel straight in from the wall without cutting it into bedrock at its western end.

For the sake of clarity, the ventilator is shown after stabilization. There is no question that the masonry in the jog came up to floor level, where it formed a collar for the ventilator opening in the kiva floor. Masonry present on the south side of the tunnel, as well as above the bedrock on the north side, would probably have been kept about 0.1 to 0.2 foot below floor level to allow room for roofing. The length of the main shaft is 4.6 feet, and that of the wing 1.8 feet. The tunnel is 1.3 to 1.5 feet wide, and 2.0± feet deep.

One artifact , a grooved stone ax, was found in the tunnel. It was on the ventilator floor, against the sidewall (to the left of the north arrow in fig. 59).

While the kiva was still in use, the subfloor ventilator was filled. An above-floor ventilator, found in all Long House kivas, was then built. The slab dividing the two ventilators (fig. 59) is a product of stabilization, and will hopefully make it easier for the visitor to visualize the relative location of the two ventilators. There is no evidence of such a slab in the original construction.

Deflector

A single, vertical slab forms the deflector, a feature definitely associated with the above-floor ventilator. The rather odd location of the deflector, which is placed in such a way as to block off the firepit from both ventilator openings, suggests that it may have been installed during the time the subfloor ventilator was open.

Floor

A single layer of hard-packed adobe, not over 0.05 foot thick, was laid over bedrock and rubble fill to form the floor. The floor adobe probably did not extend behind (southeast of) the deflector. There was no evidence of the low ridges I have called deflector "laterals," structures which occupied the same location on the floor in several kivas as did the wingwalls in Kiva A.

The firepit and sipapu were the only other floor features. The firepit is roughly circular and basin shaped, with a bottom partly formed by bedrock. The sides were built of small stones laid up in a large amount of red adobe. The sipapu is formed on two opposing sides by vertical slabs of rock; the floor adobe lips down into the opening to form the other two sides. The sipapu is on the kiva axis along with the ventilator opening, the firepit, and Niche 2.

Roof

Smoke blackening of the cave wall, where it formed part of the upper kiva wall, indicates that the roof top was at least 7.8 feet above the floor. Roof debris in the fill suggests that the roof consisted of large beams running across the kiva from wall to wall (since there were no pilasters), topped by a layer of split juniper shakes. These, in turn, were covered by juniper bark and adobe.

Figure 59. *Subfloor and above-floor ventilators of Kiva B.*

Kiva C

Unlike Kivas A and B, Kiva C is part of a room-kiva complex (fig. 60). Against the cave wall, and immediately west of the kiva, are Rooms 8, 9 (a mealing room), and 10. Both rooms and kiva show extensive remodeling. Beneath the east wall of Room 10 were parts of the walls of an earlier structure, but the number of rooms that were here at one time cannot be determined. The lower part of the south wall of Room 9 may be part of the structure. Kiva C was relined, as can be seen in figure 61, taken after stabilization. This revamping of the kiva may have been necessary because of changes made in Kiva D, which was converted from either a rectangular room or kiva (probably the former) to a circular kiva. It would have been very difficult to modify the underlying structure, designated Room 78, without doing considerable damage to the north wall and roof of the Kiva C. Decreasing the size of the kiva by a southward shift of the north wall would have made it quite easy to remodel and reroof Room 78 as a kiva.

A feature less easily explained, but which is also a result of remodeling, is the ashpit under the later north wall of Kiva C. This could have belonged to the original kiva but, if so, it is in a rather strange position on the kiva floor. The few possible ashpits in Long House are either close to the firepit or between the deflector and ventilator opening. A more logical explanation is that this ashpit was in a courtyard predating the original kiva and possibly associated with the earliest structures west of the kiva. The supposition would be stronger were the structure definitely a firepit, which does not seem to be the case.

Although the kiva was enclosed on all sides by either masonry walls or large boulders, it was not built within a room in the same manner as Kiva A or even Kiva B. It is possibly a more highly evolved, and certainly a better planned, feature than either of the other two kivas. It possesses formal pilasters, banquette, and recess, and shows no evidence of ever having had a subfloor ventilator. The kiva axis is northwest-southeast and closely parallels that of Kiva A.

Walls

All the remaining kiva walls, including the section of the outer wall formed by the east walls of Rooms 8, 9, and 10, are of simple masonry. Nothing remained of the short, east outer wall. Masonry of the remaining walls was of rectangular to irregular stones of varying surface finish.

In only two areas, the south interpilaster space and the recess, was there any portion of the upper, inner walls remaining. But a single course of large irregularly shaped rocks was in place in the south interpilaster space. The masonry in the recess was apparently similar in size but better shaped and finished. At least two coats of smoke-blackened plaster covered the recess walls.

Only the northwest quadrant of the original lower, inner wall of the kiva was intact at the time of excavation. It feathered out on the east wall of Room 9, and no continuation of the wall could be found elsewhere in the kiva. Had the present inner walls been torn out, it might have been possible to determine how much of the original kiva wall follows the later alinement. In other words, there may have been little change made in the kiva, especially in the recess area, except for tightening the arc of the west wall.

The masonry of the original liner consisted of small, generally rectangular rocks, with fairly well finished faces. That of the newer liner is more variable in size and often of more irregularly shaped blocks. The lowest two courses of rock are small and about the same size as that in the outer liner. The rest of the inner wall is of larger rock. Two layers of plaster still exist on the inner wall; traces of green and white paint can be detected on at least one layer.

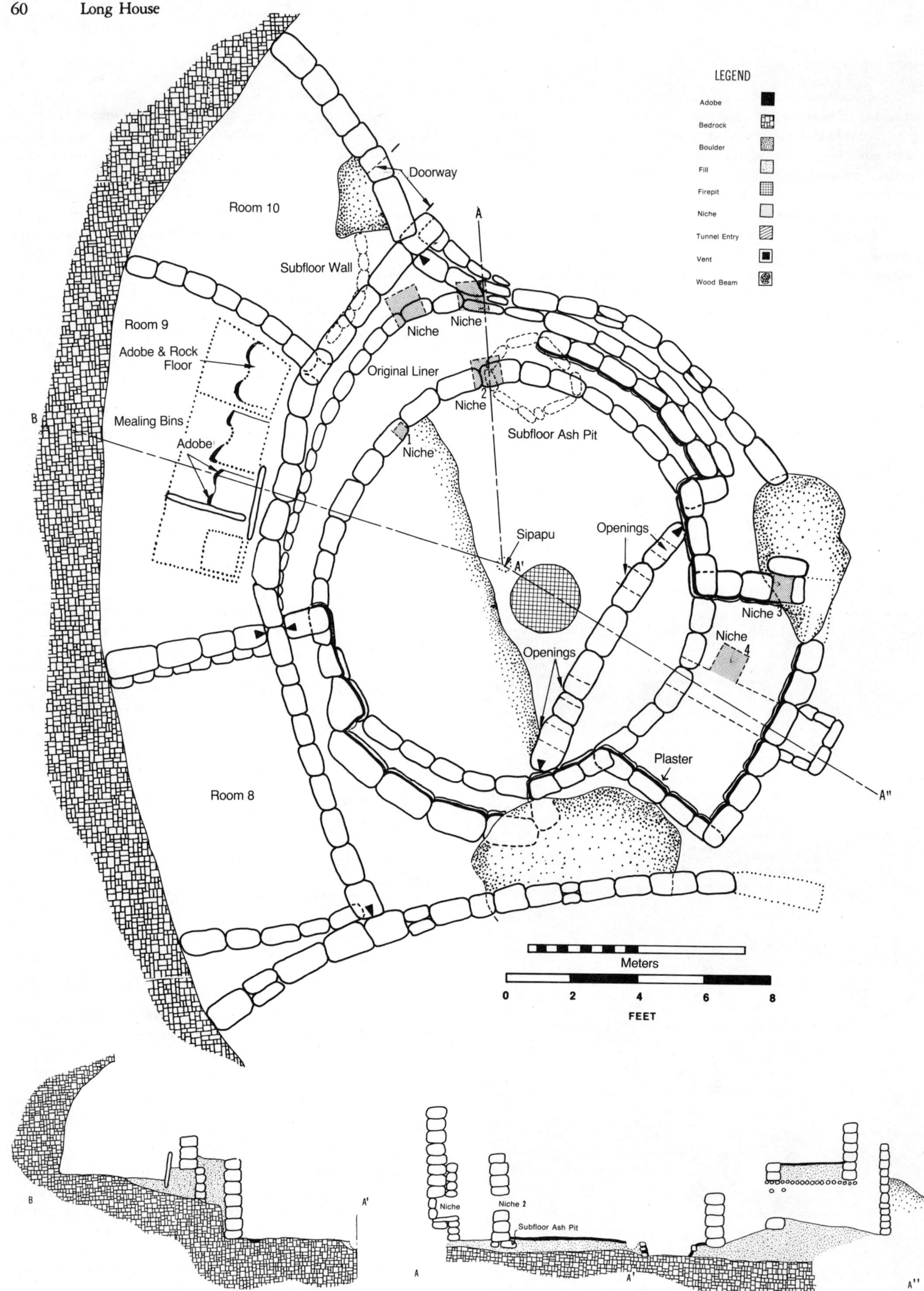

Figure 60. *Kiva C, plan and sections B-A′ and A-A′-A″.*

Figure 61. *Kiva C relined, showing two niches in the original liner and one niche in the later liner.*

Pilasters

There were undoubtedly four pilasters spaced evenly around the perimeter of the kiva, but only three were still standing at the time of excavation. These three all show a definite radial taper of the sides, and are set back 0.05 to 0.15 foot from the face of the kiva wall. Only Pilaster 4, immediately north of the recess, was fairly well preserved; the masonry consisted of rectangular blocks well dressed on the face. A single layer of smoke-blackened plaster covered the face of the pilaster.

Niches

Two niches, on the north side of the kiva, are the only features remaining in the original liner. Utilizing both slabs and the surrounding masonry to form the openings, the builders constructed the niches side by side, separated by only one building stone. This singular arrangement can be seen in figure 61.

Four niches are formed by the masonry of the inner liner, but none is on the kiva axis. Niches 1 and 2 are in the northwest quadrant of the kiva. Niche 1 is the size of a small building stone, but Niche 2 (visible in fig. 61) is of more conventional size. It is interesting to note that Niche 2 is in approximately the same relative position as the niches in the outer liner.

Niche 3, in the north wall of the recess, is a very unusual feature in Long House. Similar niches are found only in Kivas E and J, where they are on the opposite side of the recess, and in Kiva M on the side corresponding to the one in which Niche 3 is located. Even more unusual is Niche 4, which opens off the north side of the ventilator tunnel, 1.0 foot east of the ventilator opening into the kiva. Neither Niche 3 nor Niche 4 was plastered and, logically enough, only the recess niche was smoke blackened.

Banquette

Little is left of the banquette except in the recess and south interpilaster space. Its height can be determined at these sections, as well as at the pilasters, where a narrow strip is preserved between the pilasters and the lower kiva wall. The height varies from 2.9 to 3.6 feet and averages about 3.1 to 3.2 feet. The depth of 1.13 to 1.15 feet in the south interpilaster space can probably be considered typical of the remainder of the banquette.

Recess

The shape of the recess is typical of that found in several kivas on the east side of the pueblo: sides converging toward the center of the room, and the backwall curved so as to be roughly concentric with the inner kiva wall.

The recess floor is at the same level as the rest of the banquette. A small section of hard-packed adobe is all that remained of the floor, which was probably level across the full extent of the feature.

Ventilator

The above-floor ventilator is quite conventional in most respects. The tunnel roof, consisting of split juniper shakes covered with adobe, was very well preserved. Two additional shakes extended across the top of the shaft at 0.2 and 0.35 foot below the shake roof. One of these is 0.8 foot east of the vent opening in the kiva wall, the other 0.3 foot. The isolated shakes *could* have provided support for a sloping slab used to regulate air flow into the kiva. A flat rectangular stone in the floor at the mouth of the vent might have provided a seat or support for the hypothetical angled slab.

The horizontal shaft is 5.5 feet long and slopes downward almost a foot from ventilator mouth to the base of the vertical shaft. The tunnel floor is dirt, with the exception of the slab mentioned above. Both the vertical and horizontal portions of the ventilator were masonry lined.

Deflector

The slightly curved simple masonry wall, of moderately well-shaped rectangular stones, is almost identical to that found in Kiva A. Although this deflector appears to have been built in one piece, unlike that of Kiva A, it does have the two sets of openings found in the other structure (fig. 62). One of the smaller openings is 0.5 foot square, the other 0.45 foot square. The one large opening still intact is 0.8 foot wide and 0.9 foot high. There is no evidence here, as in the Kiva A structure, that the deflector was ever higher. Once again, the large openings were probably notches.

There are only three wall-to-wall deflectors in Long House. The third one, in Kiva F, is practically identical to those in Kivas A and C. All closely resemble a deflector in Kiva E, Cannonball Ruins, in southwestern Colorado, illustrated by Morley (1908, Plate XXXVIb). This deflector has the large notches at the top, and what appear to be the smaller, lower openings, situated as they are in the Long House deflectors.

Floor

The west half of the kiva floor is bedrock; the east half consists of two layers of adobe with a total thickness of about 0.1 foot. There is no adobe over the bedrock floor in the small area between the deflector and the kiva wall.

The sipapu shown in figure 60 is questionable. A jagged hole in the floor just west of the firepit may mark the location of a sipapu, but, if so, the feature was too badly damaged (by earlier digging?) to allow definite identification of the feature.

A circular, flat-bottomed firepit, about 2 feet in diameter and 0.5 foot deep, is one of three definite floor features. Bedrock forms the bottom and part of the south side of the feature, and irregularly shaped rocks set in a large amount of adobe form the other sides.

A circular pit, 0.4 foot in diameter and 0.05 foot deep, was pecked into the bedrock floor in the southwest quadrant of the kiva. Although many guesses can be made as to the use of such a depression, there is no archeological evidence to support any of them. Perhaps an analogous structure is present in Kiva N, but there the pit was deeper, clay lined, and contained sterile sand.

The only other floor feature is the shallow, roughly circular ashpit beneath the more recent kiva liner, on the north side of the room (fig. 61). The pit was built of vertical slabs, with the resulting shape closer, perhaps, to hexagonal than circular. It was filled with ash and had no clearly defined bottom other than the top of the underlying fill. It was almost entirely covered with the adobe of the kiva floor, leaving just the tips of a few of the slabs protruding through the floor. As mentioned above, the pit may belong to an occupation of this area pre-dating Kiva C. It could have been a feature of the kiva before it was remodeled but is certainly not situated in a location typical of either firepits or ashpits in other kivas.

Roof

Other than the smoke blackening of a large boulder forming part of an interpilaster space, there is nothing to indicate the height of the roof. The extent of the smoke marks suggests that the kiva ceiling was at least 6.1 feet above floor. All remains of the roof itself had evidently been removed during earlier excavations. The roof could have been supported by beams extending across the kiva from wall to wall, as is the case in Kiva I, or by a limited amount of cribbing seated on the four pilasters.

Figure 62. *Curved masonry deflector in Kiva C, with two sets of openings.*

Kiva D and Room 78

Kiva D was literally jammed between Room 10 and Kiva C on the southwest and Room 37 on the northeast (fig. 63). The cave wall to the northwest and an abrupt dropoff to the southeast further restricted the area occupied by the kiva. As a result, Kiva D is smaller than most kivas in Long House and possesses several odd features.

Although built in the same area as Room 78, no attempt was made to confine the kiva to the area occupied by the room, as was the case in Kiva A. Rather, the upper part of the room walls was removed, the floor was covered with almost a foot of fill, and the kiva was built on this level.

To judge from the relationship of the recess to the circular part of the kiva, the orientation of the kiva axis (northwest-southeast) should be practically identical to that of Kiva C. As defined by the ventilator, firepit, and sipapu, the axis is actually skewed, however. There is no apparent reason for this unless large rocks in the vicinity of the ventilator tunnel made such a shift desirable.

Walls

With the exception of the southeast exterior wall and the southwest recess wall, which are of compound masonry, all of the kiva walls were constructed of simple masonry. There was very little exterior wall construction. With other rooms and the cave wall forming the exterior walls on three sides, only the southeast wall, which incorporates the ventilator shaft, is actually part of the kiva. The masonry of the small portion of this wall still remaining is of irregular shape, size, and surface finish, and the same is true of the walls shared with Kiva C and Room 10. The wall common to the kiva and Room 37 was entirely gone.

Figure 63. *Kiva D and Room 78, plan and sections A-A' and B-B'.*

Only in the recess is any portion of the upper inner wall intact. The back (southeast) wall of the recess consisted of thick vertical slabs, the southwest wall of compound masonry. In both of these walls, and in the remaining segments of the lower inner wall, masonry was also irregular in shape, size, and finish.

Pilasters

No true pilasters were found, and the very limited space for such structures is a supporting argument for their absence in this kiva. The masonry structure on the south side of the recess was called a pilaster by Robert Nichols, who recorded Kiva D, and I agree that it served to support the roof. I would prefer to class this as part of the upper kiva wall, however, and not a pilaster as exemplified in most of the other Long House kivas. Perhaps a parallel for this sort of "right-angle pilaster" can be found in Kiva J (fig. 80). The similarity would probably end with four such features, at most, in the corners. Quite obviously, there is not room in Kiva D for the upper wall construction found in Kiva J.

Niches

No niches were found. Some of the remaining sections of the inner wall were so reduced in height as to make useless any speculation about the presence or absence of niches.

Banquette

Only in the recess, and immediately west of it, has the banquette been preserved. Its height above the kiva floor is about 3.3 feet. Originally, it was probably present only in the corners of the kiva and was thus of triangular shape in each case.

Recesses

Perhaps the strangest feature of Kiva D is the aborted recess. Apparently it was originally intended to be conventional in size and shape. Then, for some unknown reason, its depth was reduced by half with construction of a straight crosswall. Unlike the recess proper, the sealed off back portion was neither well finished on the wall surfaces nor smoke blackened. Thus the implication is that the back section was not just remodeled during use but was never used. Kiva J had at least two shallow recesses or interpilaster spaces resembling those in Kiva D, but it also had a full-sized southern recess.

The floor of the recess consisted of hard-packed, red-brown adobe. The sides were probably parallel, but this cannot be proved because the northeast wall had collapsed.

Ventilator

Much of the vertical shaft had collapsed, leaving only part of the horizontal tunnel intact. Both coursed masonry and vertical slabs were used for the sides of the tunnel, and probably masonry alone for the shaft. Most of the roof and floor of the tunnel were gone.

Deflector

The floor between the firepit and ventilator had collapsed, destroying all evidence of the deflector.

Floor

Only in the west half of the kiva is the floor preserved. It consists of a layer of red-brown adobe, 0.01 to 0.05 foot thick.

The firepit and sipapu are the only floor features remaining. The former is circular in outline, basin shaped in cross section. The sides of the pit were formed by small horizontal and vertical slabs laid up with a large amount of adobe. It was then remodeled by lining the west and south sides with vertical slabs set in adobe.

The sipapu is simply a circular hole dug into the subfloor fill, with the sides plastered with adobe. Apparently the inner lining did not extend over the bottom of the feature.

Roof

There was no definite evidence of roof material in the kiva fill. The logs found on the surface of the fill could have come from the roof, but this seems rather unlikely because of the extensive disturbance of this row of kivas. It is impossible to determine ceiling or rooftop height for this kiva on the basis of adobe remnants or smoke blackening on the associated cave and room walls.

It is possible that Room 78 was actually a kiva instead of a secular room. The door in the north wall of Room 10 could have opened into a clear area or court, but it probably led into Room 78. This would be an argument against the presence of a kiva. Since the

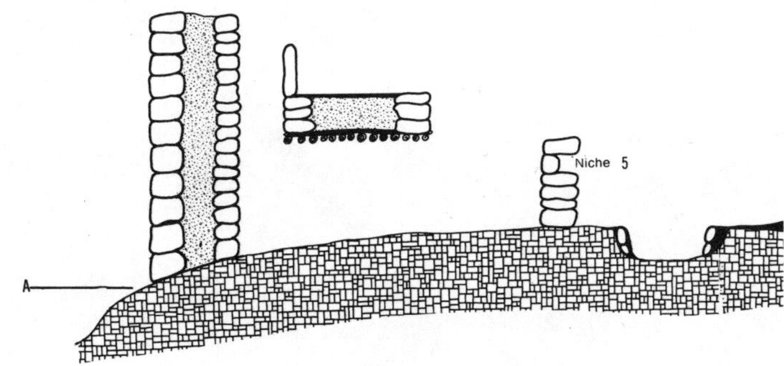

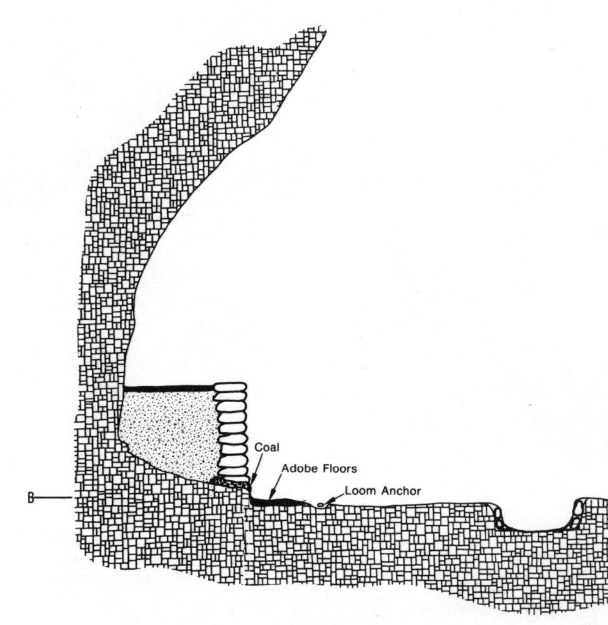

firepit and sipapu of Kiva D were not removed, it is impossible to be sure that equivalent structures did not exist on the floor immediately below. No features were found on that part of the room floor which was exposed by excavation. The floor itself is formed by a layer of adobe about 0.1 foot thick.

At first glance it might seem possible that the closed-off part of the recess for Kiva D could have been constructed for the hypothetical Room 78 kiva. However, the walls of this construction do not extend down to the Room 78 floor level. The roughly rectangular shape of Room 78 would certainly not rule out the possibility of ceremonial use. Kiva P and, to a lesser extent, Kiva G, are also somewhat rectangular in shape.

Only two architectural features of possible significance were found in Room 78 (fig. 63, plan & section B-B′). One is a large niche in the west wall, at the northwest corner. The niche is 0.9 foot wide, 0.8 foot deep, and at least 0.75 foot high (the top was gone). The sides and back of the opening are formed by vertical slabs, the bottom by the wall masonry.

A bit more significant, perhaps, is the coal packing behind the west wall of Room 78 and below the niche. In Long House, coal was found behind a wall, or under the floor, only in kivas.

Kiva E

Of the six tightly grouped kivas along the cave wall, only Kiva E was built in a location that allowed adequate room for full and unrestricted development (fig. 64). Possibly as a result of this, the kiva is larger and has features not found elsewhere in Long House.

Unlike the other five kivas in this group, Kiva E is oriented so that its axis runs almost due north-south. This was probably due less to an attempt to be different than to the restrictions in space imposed by the dropoff a few feet east of the kiva.

Unlike Kiva D, Kiva E apparently predates the rooms built around it. Rooms 11, 37, and 38 were built in open spaces between Kivas D, E, and F, and thus conform to the shape of Kiva E on one side (fig. 65).

Room 38 was floored at banquette level with thin sandstone slabs. It was probably roofed with Kiva E, and may have been accessible from within the kiva. It is also possible that this small storage (?) room may have been reached through a separate roof hatchway.

Figure 64. *Kiva E, plan and sections A-A′ and B-B′.*

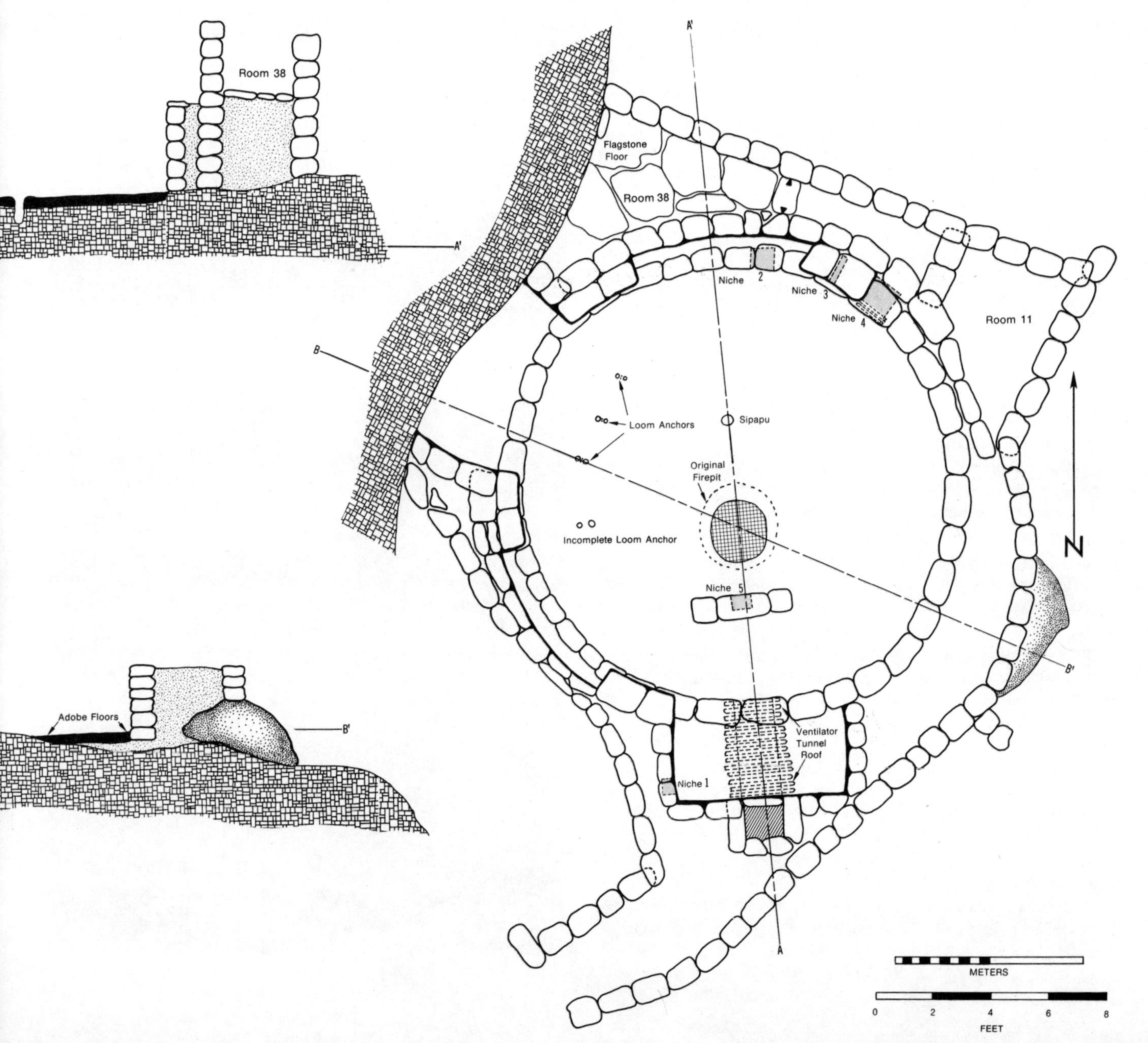

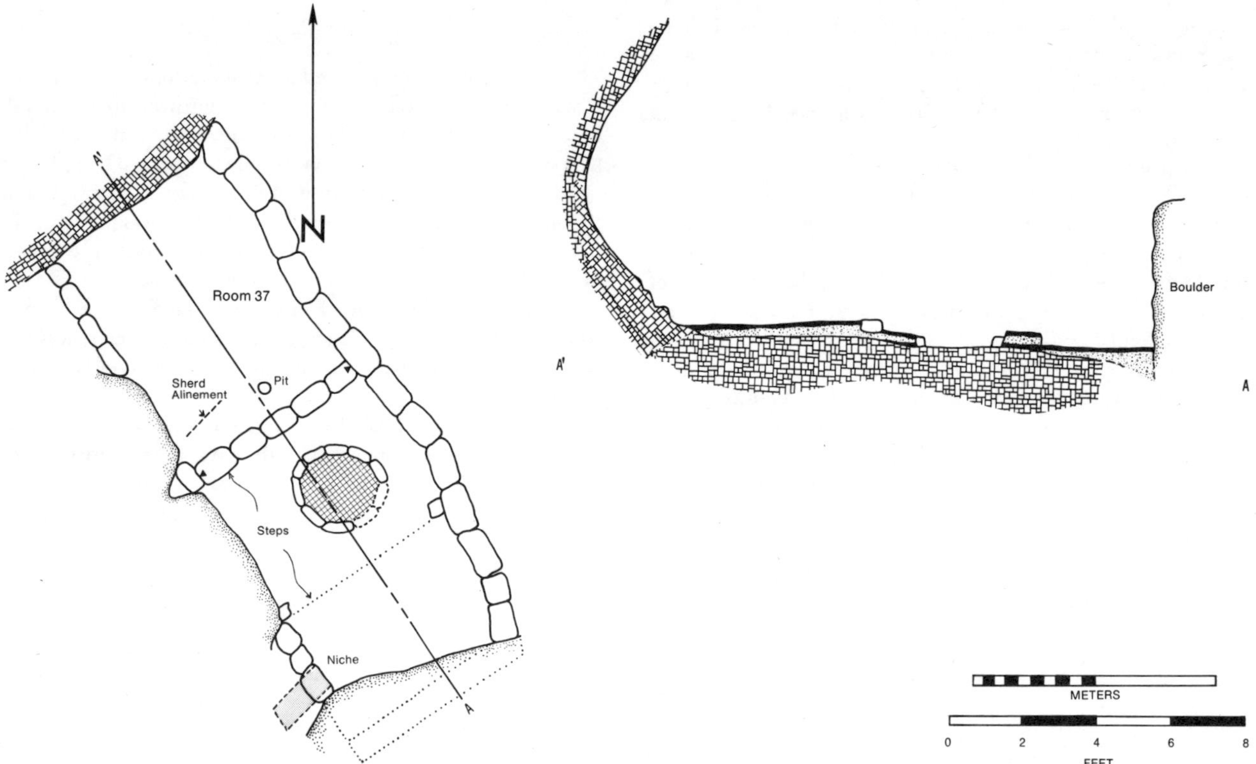

Figure 65. *Room 37, plan and section A-A'.*

Room 11 was floored with 0.1 foot of adobe at kiva floor level. Like Room 38, it was probably part of the kiva complex. Once again, there is nothing to indicate how this room was entered, or what function it served. Access might have been gained through a doorway in the east wall, but this wall had entirely collapsed.

Walls

Except where the cave wall forms a small part of the west kiva wall, all of the structure's walls are of simple masonry.

The wall shared by Kiva E and Room 37 is extremely crude, with great variety in the size and shape of the rocks. Along the north side of the kiva, the outer wall is essentially the inner wall finished on the north face with a small masonry veneer in Room 11 and with adobe and chinking spalls in Room 38.

The masonry of the upper, inner wall consists of fairly large blocks of very irregular shape, size, and surface finish. That of the lower wall consists of smaller blocks which show much better shaping and surface finishing. Along the west side of the kiva, the lower floor had been pecked into the bedrock outcropping at that point. The base of the inner wall here is also bedrock. From one to at least five coats of smoke-blackened tan plaster still cover parts of the upper and lower walls.

Immediately below and to the east of Pilaster 4, a well-preserved section of wall plaster gave us our only clue to the elaborateness of designs that may once have been placed on the walls of Long House kivas. Robert Nichols performed the delicate task of removing the outermost layer of plaster to reveal geometric designs and life forms (fig. 66).

The band design, consisting of two rows of opposed triangles separated by three parallel lines, can be seen above and to the right of the niche in figure 60a. There is a single framing line at the top and

Figure 66. *Fragmentary painting (band design) on wall plaster below and east of Pilaster 4 in Kiva E.*

bottom of the band, which is 14.0 cm. wide. The length of this fragment of the band is 57.0 cm. The design is common on pottery vessels.

A white plaster forms the background for this geometric design, which was executed in a red hematite pigment. A greenish-blue or greenish-gray pigment was applied to the space separating, longitudinally, each row of triangles in each half of the band. Thus, in shape, the greenish design approaches a sine curve.

To the right of the niche, and 20.5 cm. below the top of the band design, is a straight orange or yellowish line 2.0 to 2.8 cm. wide. A short distance below this is a broad red band on which were painted, with the same greenish pigment mentioned above, what appear to be two figures, a human and an animal. The top of the figures is 37.8 cm. below the top of the band design. The figure at the left could be a Kokopelli, or hunchbacked flute player, and the other appears to be an animal with forward jutting antlers. The length of the animal, less the antlers, is 8.8 cm.

Above the geometric band, with a background of white plaster, are two bighorn sheep. The antlers of one are above the center of the niche and at the top of the black blotch which obscures most of the animal. The second sheep is above the left or west edge of the niche. The length of the sheep, less the antlers, is 10.0 cm., the height (feet to back) is 6.5 cm.

The colors of the pigments used were checked against the Munsell Soil Color charts and can be designated as follows:

Red	10R 4/6 (closest to original color) to 10R 4/2 or 4/3. Original color was probably 10R 4/8.
Green-blue	5GY 7/1. Original color was probably 5G 6/2.
Orange	10YR 5/8. Original color was probably 10YR 6/8.

Behind the lower wall, in an area below the west recess, soft coal has been packed into the space between the wall and the bedrock ledge several tenths of a foot behind it. A similar concentration of coal was found between the two kiva floors, along at least a portion of the north wall.

In Kiva E, we have the second instance in Long House of coal being found behind a kiva wall. Kiva A is the other example. Coal found in other kivas was beneath the floor, but it is quite possible that many behind-the-wall pockets were never discovered. Lancaster recalled that coal was used as a subfloor packing in a room in Spring House in Mesa Verde, as well as below both kiva and some room floors at Awatovi in northeastern Arizona, but was never found behind walls in these cases.

Pilasters

Six pilasters were undoubtedly built in Kiva E, but only Pilasters 1 and 4 were intact at the time of excavation. Pilasters 2 and 3 were located by masonry remnants, but 5 and 6 were gone entirely. The extant pilasters were constructed of fairly large stones, similar in size to those of the upper, inner wall. The faces of the stones were well dressed, and the sides and faces of the pilasters were plastered.

The sides of Pilaster 4 are still covered with one to two layers of smoke-blackened plaster. From inside to outside, the front of the pilaster is covered with two layers of smoke-blackened plaster, two layers showing traces of red, white, and possibly black paint, and finally a layer of brown adobe.

Figure 67. *Niche 5 in the masonry deflector of Kiva E.*

The face and recess sides of Pilaster 1 still retain traces of about four layers of smoke-blackened plaster and possibly two layers of the red-white-black (?)-painted plaster.

Pilaster 1 is set back from the edge of the banquette about 0.07 foot, and has radially tapering sides. Pilaster 4 is set back about 0.05 foot, and its sides are roughly parallel.

Niches

There are five niches in the kiva, three in the north walls, one in the recess, and one in the deflector. Niche 2, which is close to, but not on, the kiva axis, is located at the base of the inner wall. Its floor is the bedrock floor of the kiva. When the kiva was refloored with adobe, the floor was apparently carried up to the niche but did not extend into it. The niche was built of thick slabs on sides and back.

Niche 4, in the lower wall just east of Niche 2, has a slab top, bottom, and back, but the wall masonry forms the sides. The niche is rather large and is distinguished by two "lintel" sticks across the top and near the front of the opening (fig. 66).

Only one other niche, in Kiva U, is located in a position similar to that of Niche 3. Both are built into the face of a pilaster. That in Kiva E is centered in the pilaster, with the banquette forming the base. Unlike the niche in Kiva U, and most other niches for that matter, this one is high and narrow, 0.5 by 0.2 foot. It is plastered with adobe carried into the opening from the face of the pilaster, and the top, back, and sides are smoke blackened.

Like the recess niche in Kiva J, Niche 1 in Kiva E is in the west wall of the recess, above the top of the banquette. The feature is formed by the wall masonry, and the interior is unplastered but heavily smoke blackened.

Niche 5 is centered in the north face, and near the top of the deflector (fig. 67). It, too, is merely an opening in the masonry deflector with the back formed by a vertical slab, and it was plastered throughout.

Banquette

Only in the southern recess, and around the two remaining pilasters, was the banquette preserved. The banquette probably averaged about 3 feet in height and 1 foot to 1.1 feet in depth. It was covered with a single layer of brown adobe, slightly under 0.1 foot thick. Like the surface of the pilasters, the top of the banquette was smoke blackened.

Figure 68. *Four sets of loom-retaining loops or anchors—three complete sets and one incomplete set— in the bedrock floor near the west side of Kiva E.*

Recesses

Kiva E possesses two recesses, a unique feature in six-pilaster kivas at Long House. One is located conventionally, above the ventilator tunnel, and is fairly well preserved except for the east side. The other, on the west side of the kiva, is actually an enlargement of an interpilaster space. An analagous structure may exist in Kiva F, although the western recess here is the second floor of Room 13.

Although the smoke-blackened cliff forming the backwall of the western recess shows the approximate size of the feature, little else could be determined because of poor preservation. The sides of the recess probably converged slightly toward the center of the kiva. The sides of the southern recess are parallel and the backwall is straight. Patches of red-brown adobe floor were found in both recesses.

Ventilator

Both the tunnel and the vertical shaft of the ventilator were built of a combination of vertical slabs and coursed masonry similar to that found within the kiva. The ventilator floor is bedrock, and its unusually well preserved roof is made of a large number of closely set branches of serviceberry, oak, and juniper covered with a layer of red-brown adobe. The location of both portions of the ventilator is conventional.

Deflector

The deflector is a simple masonry wall made of well-shaped and well-dressed rectangular blocks. Its present height of about 2 feet is probably its original height. A niche, mentioned above, is centrally located, east-west, in the north face. The deflector appears to have been covered with three or four coats of plaster. The next-to-last layer shows traces of white paint.

The ventilator, deflector, deflector niche, firepit, and sipapu are almost perfectly centered on the kiva axis. Such careful placement of features, coupled with the symmetrical shape of the kiva on either side of the axis, make Kiva E one of the best executed kivas in Long House.

Floor

Two floors were present in the kiva: a lower one of bedrock, leveled with adobe over fill or bedrock along the east side of the kiva, and an upper one of red-brown adobe, 0.15 to 0.25 foot thick. A coal packing was found between the floors along at least a portion of the north wall.

As can be seen in figure 68, three sets of loom retaining loops or anchors were pecked into the bedrock floor near the west side of the kiva. The distance between the sets is about 1.5 feet. Each set consists of two circular depressions, about 0.2 foot in diameter and about 0.12 foot deep, spaced 0.1 foot apart. Each pair of depressions has a small connecting hole formed by drilling opposing holes, at a slight downward angle, until they joined. A fourth, incomplete set of loops can be seen in the photograph, 2.15 feet south of the completed sets of loops.

Guernsey (1931, p. 64) found similar loom attachments cut into the bedrock floor of a kiva in Keet Seel Canyon, northeastern Arizona. There are examples of loom anchors, of varying construction, reported from other sites in the Southwest. Kidder (1958, p. 253) lists a number of these sites, and discusses the loops found at Pecos and in sites of the upper Rio Grande Valley. Of less certain function are the holes in the floor of a square kiva at Hawikuh. Hodge (1939, p. 205) reports that his Zuni workmen suggested that the holes could have been used for altar or loom uprights.

Victor Mindeleff (1891, p. 132) described in detail how looms were secured to planks, which in turn were fixed in the floor, in Hopi kivas of that time. No doubt a similar method was followed in Kiva E, with bedrock substituted for the plank.

Other than the loom loops, no floor features belonging solely to the lower floor were found. The other two floor features, the firepit and sipapu, extend down into bedrock, and the lower part of each structure was probably used with the bedrock floor.

The original circular firepit was cut into bedrock and used without further modification. Subsequent remodeling took the firepit through two additional stages. First, a lining of small stones set in red adobe was carried up to the edge of the bedrock floor. This was undoubtedly done while the lower floor was still in use. After this, following construction of the upper floor, the floor adobe was lipped down onto the top of the firepit liner but not into the pit proper.

The sipapu, somewhat oval in cross section, was unusually deep (0.9 foot) for its small diameter. Its mouth was formed partly by a broken jar neck, partly by the floor adobe. Although it is not possible to say definitely that the sipapu served both floor levels, its depth would seem to suggest this.

Roof

Three logs, which formed part of the lowest layer of the cribbed roof, were found almost in place. One end of each was still resting on Pilaster 1, the other end on the collapsed wall rubble where Pilaster 2 once stood and about 2 feet below their original position. Large piles of brush were found on top of these logs and in the area between the deflector and ventilator opening. The brush was identified by James Erdman as follows (with approximate percentage):

	Percentage
Amelanchier utahensis (serviceberry)	30
Artemisia tridentata (big sagebrush)	30
Cercocarpus montanus (mountain mahogany)	20
Chrysothamnus nauseosus (rabbitbrush)	10
Juniperus sp. (juniper)	10
Quercus gambelii (Gambel oak)	Trace
Purshia tridentata (bitterbush)	Trace

The brush was probably placed over the roof timbers, with adobe undoubtedly forming the top of the closing material. No further details can be suggested because the bulk of the roofing material was removed during the previous excavation of the kiva, presumably by Nordenskiöld.

Kiva F

Another kiva-room complex, very similar to that of Kiva C, is that of Kiva F and Rooms 12–14 and 46 (fig. 69). It is worth noting that Room 14 is a mealing room. Parallels to this situation can be found in three other definite combinations of kivas and mealing rooms: Kiva C and Room 9, Kiva Q and Room 56, and Kiva R and Room 52. Depending upon the access to Room 3, the Kiva T and Room 3 association may be another such combination.

These associations could be fortuitous, but they do suggest a pattern of related ceremonial and domestic functions. Such a pattern could be useful in interpreting the social organization from the archeological remains. Yet many sections of Long House do not manifest logical planning. The picture seems a little clearer on the east end than on the west, however.

The orientation of the kiva axis is northwest-southeast, so it closely approximates that of Kivas A to D. The reason for this orientation could be twofold: the limited space between the Beer Cellar Complex to the north and Kiva E and its related rooms to the south; and the desire to have a recess (remodeled to Room 13/2) on the west side of the kiva. I am assuming that Kiva F postdates Kiva E and Rooms 11 and 38, and predates Rooms 12–14 and 46, as the wall abutments suggest. The Beer Cellar Complex definitely predates Kiva F, and all or part of the east outer kiva probably does also. Were the kiva rotated clockwise to bring the next interpilaster space to the south into the line with the proposed location for the recess (Room 13, ultimately), there would not be room for the ventilator between the inner and outer kiva walls on the south side. The location of the recess could be shifted, but then construction of a rectangular structure would be more difficult. Also, the ventilator could open directly to the outside on the east without aid of a vertical shaft. This may not be the case, however, since a ventilator shaft may have been constructed outside the east exterior wall.

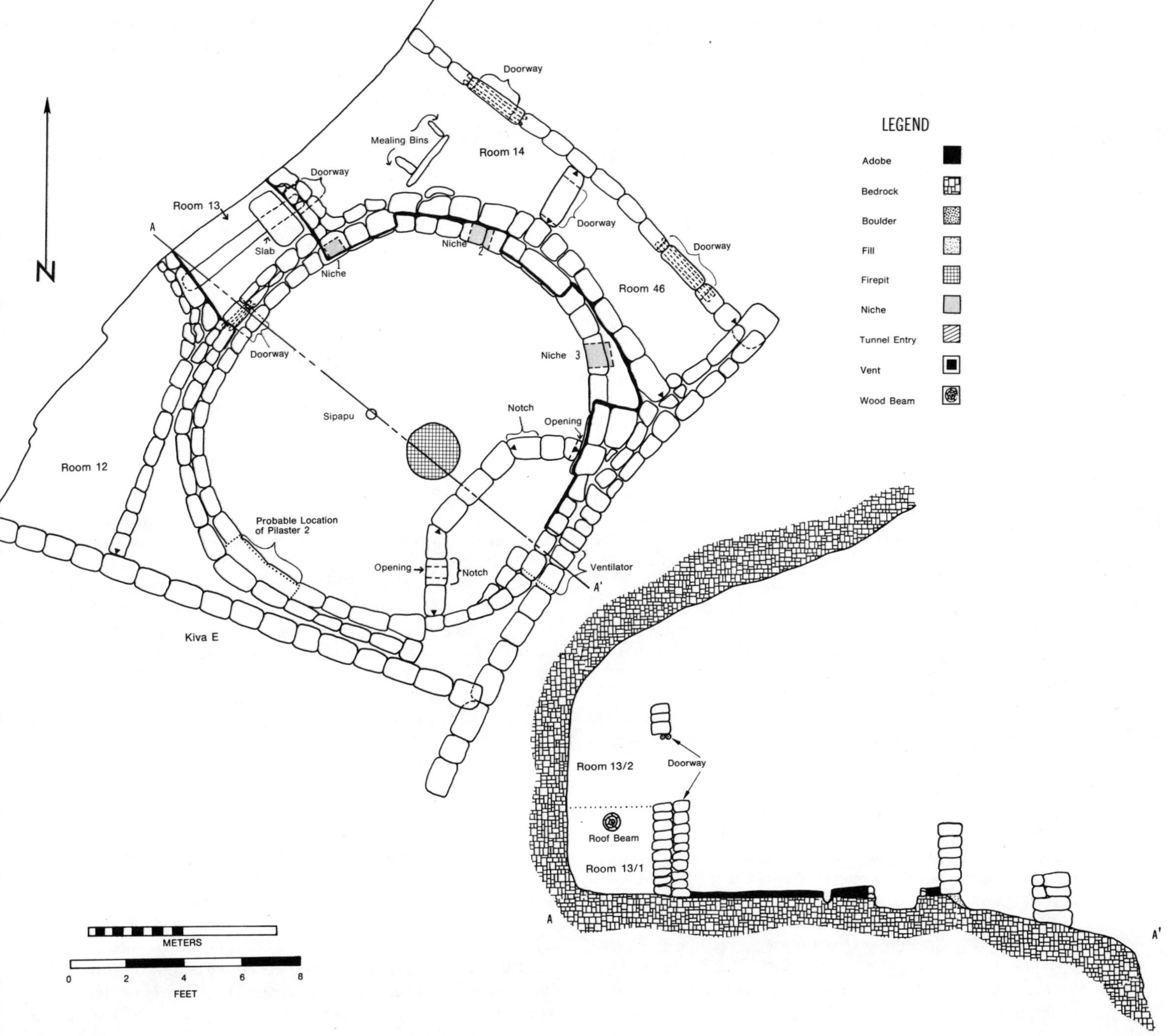

Figure 69. *Kiva F, plan and section A-A'.*

Walls

Along the north and west sides of the kiva, the outer walls are, in part, compound and composite masonry. Rooms 13 and 14 share an east and southeast wall, respectively, with Kiva F. In the case of Rooms 12 and 46, only part of the wall on the kiva side of the room is actually shared with the kiva. The lower portion of these shared walls is composite masonry, consisting of the lower kiva liner (simple masonry) back-to-back with the room or outer kiva wall (simple or compound masonry). Where a wall is shared above banquette level, the masonry varies, being either simple or compound.

Immediately north of the ventilator, and behind or east of Pilaster 6, the outside wall is compound masonry. The walls forming the north and south sides of the west recess are built of compound masonry but, once again, these are shared walls (Rooms 12 and 14 with Room 13/2). The back of the cave forms the west wall of the west recess. All other kiva walls, inner or outer, are built of simple masonry.

The masonry of the walls varies in shape, size, and surface finish. The dressed face of the north and east outer walls is to the outside of the kiva, that of the south wall to the north or inside of Kiva F. In other words, the north face of the north exterior wall of Kiva E was once an outside wall, and this is further evidence that Kiva E predates Kiva F.

The upper, inner walls were preserved only in the three extant pilasters (numbers 4, 5, and 6) and in the two interpilaster spaces they formed, as well as in the west recess and the wall added to close it off. At least two, and possibly three, layers of plaster still remain on parts of these walls. The lower layers of the red-brown and buff plaster were smoke blackened. Excepting the east face of the east wall of Room 13/2 (west recess), which was coated with a buff plaster, the upper and lower inner walls were covered with a very thin red "wash." This outermost coat was not smoke blackened, and so was probably applied shortly before the kiva was abandoned.

Pilasters

To judge by the location of the three extant pilasters, Kiva F undoubtedly had six such features at the time of abandonment. An attempt at radial convergence was made in the case of Pilasters 5 and 6, but the sides of Pilaster 4 are roughly parallel.

The masonry of the pilasters is considerably better than that in the kiva walls. The blocks are generally rectangular and many of the faces have been dressed by pecking. Several layers of plaster cover the faces of the pilasters, with the outermost being the thin red coat already mentioned. On the southern portion of the face of Pilaster 6 there was the fragment of a stepped design, with associated dots, executed in a black pigment. Once again we have a tantalizing hint of the extent and elaborateness of the decoration that was placed on the walls of the Long House kivas.

All three pilasters were set back from the edge of the banquette in the conventional manner. At Pilaster 6 the depth of the offset is less than 0.05 foot, but at Pilasters 4 and 5 it is the more common 0.01 foot.

Niches

Because of the collapse of much of the south half of the lower wall, it is impossible to determine the original number of niches. Two were preserved in the northeast quadrant of the kiva. A third niche, in the northwest quadrant, was located by one remaining side and the bottom. None of the three is on the kiva axis, which passes through the south side of the west recess. All are located within a foot of the kiva floor.

Single slabs formed the remaining side and bottom of Niche 1, and all parts of Niche 2. Slabs also form the top, bottom, and back of Niche 3. The sides were probably formed by slabs also, but the wall adobe extends into the niche here, thus concealing the sidewalls. In Niche 2, the adobe merely feathered out on the ends of the slabs forming the opening and did not extend into the niche itself.

Banquette

Except in the area east of the deflector, the banquette probably extended around the periphery of the room. It is somewhat irregular in shape in the northeast interpilaster space (between Pilasters 5 and 6) because of the location of the south wall of Room 46. In the northwest interpilaster space (between Pilasters 4 and 5), it is more uniform in depth, following the curve of the concentrically placed upper and lower kiva walls. The top of the banquette was formed by the top course of masonry of the lower kiva wall and a leveling layer of red adobe that may have covered most of the stones at one time. The height of the banquette above the kiva floor ranged between 3.0 and 3.5 feet.

Recess

During the final stages of the occupation of Long House, Kiva F apparently had no recess. Earlier, the area above Room 13/1 opened into the kiva and thus formed a western recess. Ultimately, this was converted to Room 13/2 by the addition of the east wall. The wall was set back from the edge of the banquette, and roughly in line with the backwall of the northwest interpilaster space. Access to the room from the kiva was provided by a door in the south end of the wall.

Once again, collapse of a large amount of upper and lower wall masonry in this area makes it impossible to determine the precise location of several kiva features. Possibly the south side of the recess could also be the north side of Pilaster 3, as suggested by the spacing of the three remaining pilasters. It is also possible that the recess did not occupy the whole interpilaster space, and that the north side of Pilaster 3 was perhaps 1.5 feet south of the recess wall. This last theory, which Lancaster favors, makes better sense when considering the distance at which the pilaster would have been set back from the edge of the banquette if it had been adjacent to the recess. During the stabilization of the kiva, one block was placed on the reconstructed banquette to mark the approximate location of the pilaster, but whether it represents the south or north end of the pilaster would depend upon which theory is favored.

The room formed by closing off the recess immediately brings to mind the small rooms opening off the recess of Kivas Q and U. Although the rooms may have served as storage chambers in all three cases, the fact that Room 13/1 can be entered from Room 14 offers the possibility of a ceremonial use in the case of Kiva F. Any sounds made in Room 13/1 would carry quite clearly into the kiva and would appear to come from the closed-off recess. In Room 90 (Kiva U), the evidence definitely indicates use of the structure for storage—three manos and 11 worked slabs were found in the room. Several of the slabs had been used as grinding tools.

The floor of Room 13/2 had collapsed into the room below, but there was nothing in the 3 feet of undisturbed fill of the lower room to suggest what use had been made of either room.

Originally, there were three wooden lintels over the small doorway into Room 13/2; two are still in place. The north and south walls of the recess were covered with three layers of plaster. The kiva face of the crosswall built when Room 13/2 was created was also plastered, having two and possibly three coats.

Ventilator

With the exception of the north side of the horizontal tunnel, all of the ventilator had collapsed. It might be inferred from this that the tunnel opened directly to the outside through the outer kiva wall, with no vertival shaft. I would not question this explanation were it not for a peculiar bit of masonry perched on the bedrock ledge against the east exterior of Room 46. It can be seen in figure 35a. The relationship of this structure to the kiva can be seen more clearly in figure 19. This masonry remnant appears to be the north end of a wall running against and parallel to the east wall of Room 46 and Kiva F. Although it could be part of some internal construction in Room 33, if such a room existed, this seems very doubtful. It seems more likely that it is the only remaining part of a wall built merely to house the vertical ventilator shaft for Kiva F. If so, it would have reached maximum thickness of a simple masonry wall at either end. Similar but more massive construction can be seen in Kiva N, so this hypothetical bit of building would not be unusual in the pueblo.

Floor

Three floors were apparently constructed in the kiva. Each was composed of red-brown or gray adobe and ranged in thickness from a thin veneer up to 0.05 foot. A gray, shaly clay was placed beneath portions of the top two floors, probably to level the earlier floor that was being covered.

The circular sipapu is slightly south of the kiva axis that passes through the center of the firepit, deflector, and ventilator (approximated). The opening extends slightly into the underlying bedrock. The floor adobe was carried down into the sipapu, completely concealing the sidewall construction (if any).

The firepit is circular, with a flat bedrock bottom that slopes down slightly from west to east. When first constructed, the firepit was probably lined with upright slabs. Successive floor levels changed the character of the feature, since each layer of adobe was carried over the rim and down the sides of the firepit. However, no attempt was made to create a raised collar or lip.

Deflector

The simple masonry deflector, like those in Kivas A and C, extends across the southeastern part of the kiva from wall to wall. Although built in three segments like the deflector in Kiva A, the curve of the deflector is not a smooth arc as it is in the other two cases. Moreover, the area enclosed is smaller than in Kivas A and C, and in shape is similar to the area delimited by the deflector and deflector "laterals" in Kivas M and Q.

The central segment of the deflector is 3.9 feet long and is seated at about the same level as the lower, inner kiva walls. The two wingwalls are footed at a higher level and were added later. There are two large notches, one in each wingwall, which open to the top. Each opening is about 0.8 foot wide and 1 foot deep. Two small openings were also present, each about 0.3 foot above the kiva floor. One is in the north wingwall and against the kiva wall, the other in the south wing and about 1.5 feet from the kiva wall. The width and height of the north and south openings are, respectively, 0.25 by 0.5 foot and 0.4 by 0.55 foot.

The masonry of the three deflector segments consists of fairly rectangular blocks. Most of the stones have fairly flat faces, with some showing evidence of pecking.

Roof

The base of the roof, or kiva ceiling, probably averaged between 6 and 6.5 feet above the floor, to judge by the height of Pilaster 4 and the extent of the wall plaster in the interpilaster space immediately to the north. A mud line on the extremely rough masonry wall directly above this same interpilaster space shows that the top of the roof was about 8.7 feet above the kiva floor. The presence of pilasters, coupled with a presumed roof thickness of over 2 feet, would seem to leave little doubt that a cribbed log construction was used.

Kiva G

Preservation of Kiva G was the poorest for this kind of structure at Long House. This is especially unfortunate because the kiva contains several rather unusual features.

Although the east wall had collapsed, allowing a large part of the subfloor fill and floor proper to bleed out, remains of the wall footing indicate that the kiva probably had a trapezoidal shape (fig. 70). In other words, the shape shown by reconstruction of this wall is probably quite close to the original. Only Kiva P, which is somewhat more rectangular, approaches Kiva G in shape. This statement should be modified, since Room 35—probably part of the Great Kiva complex—closely resembles Kiva G in shape. Not only that, but the masonry enclosing the ventilator shaft at the south end of Kiva G is conceivably analogous to the massive, pillar-like structure at the north end of Room 35. The latter construction does not now contain a ventilator, nor is there anything to suggest that it ever did. The floor area immediately east of the pillar in the room contains a shallow, circular basin. The corresponding area in the kiva appears to have been a recess.

I can draw no conclusions from any similarities in the two rooms; perhaps other researches will find additional structures of this nature which may shed some light on the problem.

The orientation of the kiva axis apparently has little significance in Kiva G. Although it is unusual, being northeast-southwest, the builders did not have much choice because of the location. Bedrock not only forms the sharply sloping footing for the kiva but also the entire west outer wall.

Kiva G was built as an isolated structure, predating both Room 31 to the south and the fill-retaining wall to the north. The latter could be the east wall of a hypothetical Room 32, but there is very little evidence for such a room.

Walls

The inner and outer kiva walls can, from the practical standpoint, be considered as one composite wall. The inner and outer components are simple masonry walls, each finished on the exposed side only. Little, if any, fill was placed between the members except in the vicinity of the ventilator shaft, where the components diverge to become, essentially, an inner wall of simple masonry and an outer wall of mixed simple and compound masonry. Bedrock forms both inner and outer walls on the west except in the northwest corner, where a short section of simple masonry forms the inner wall.

The outer part of the composite wall and the south exterior wall consist of blocks ranging in shape from very irregular to rectangular. The blocks are generally large, but there is considerable variation in their size. An attempt was made to expose naturally flat sides of the blocks, and a few faces had been pecked.

Better workmanship is evident in the north inner wall. The blocks are more uniform in size, rectangular in shape, and better dressed. The masonry of the south inner wall is of a similar size, but the quality of the shaping and dressing of the stones is inferior to that of the north wall.

A radical departure from most of the masonry in the kiva is found in the short west wall. The rectangular blocks are much thinner and, as Robert Nichols said, "very Chaco looking."

No plaster remained on the kiva walls except at the back or south side of the recess, where it completely concealed the masonry.

Pilasters—none.

Niches—none.

Banquette

At the time of excavation there was no encircling banquette, this feature being present in the recess and possibly in the northwest corner. The height of the short, west masonry wall and the inner north wall suggests that the builders may have created a banquette by maintaining the present height of the inner wall around the east side of the kiva.

Recess

The roughly rectangular area in the southwest corner of the kiva undoubtedly served as the recess. Whereas the floor of the recess is only about 2.3 feet above the upper kiva floor—unusually low for a recess floor or banquette—the height may have been influenced by the partial overhang of the cave wall at this point. The size of the recess, rather small to begin with, was increased 1.4 feet in north-south length by extending the supporting masonry out into the room. The addition was added after construction of the upper floor of the kiva.

The recess floor consisted of two layers of adobe, each about 0.05 foot thick. The center of the floor was broken away in a circular area, due possibly to settling of underlying fill and pressure from above. It is also possible that a jar may have been buried here (see Kivas J and U for examples of this) and then removed during previous excavations in the ruin.

Ventilator

Although located centrally in the masonry to the east of the

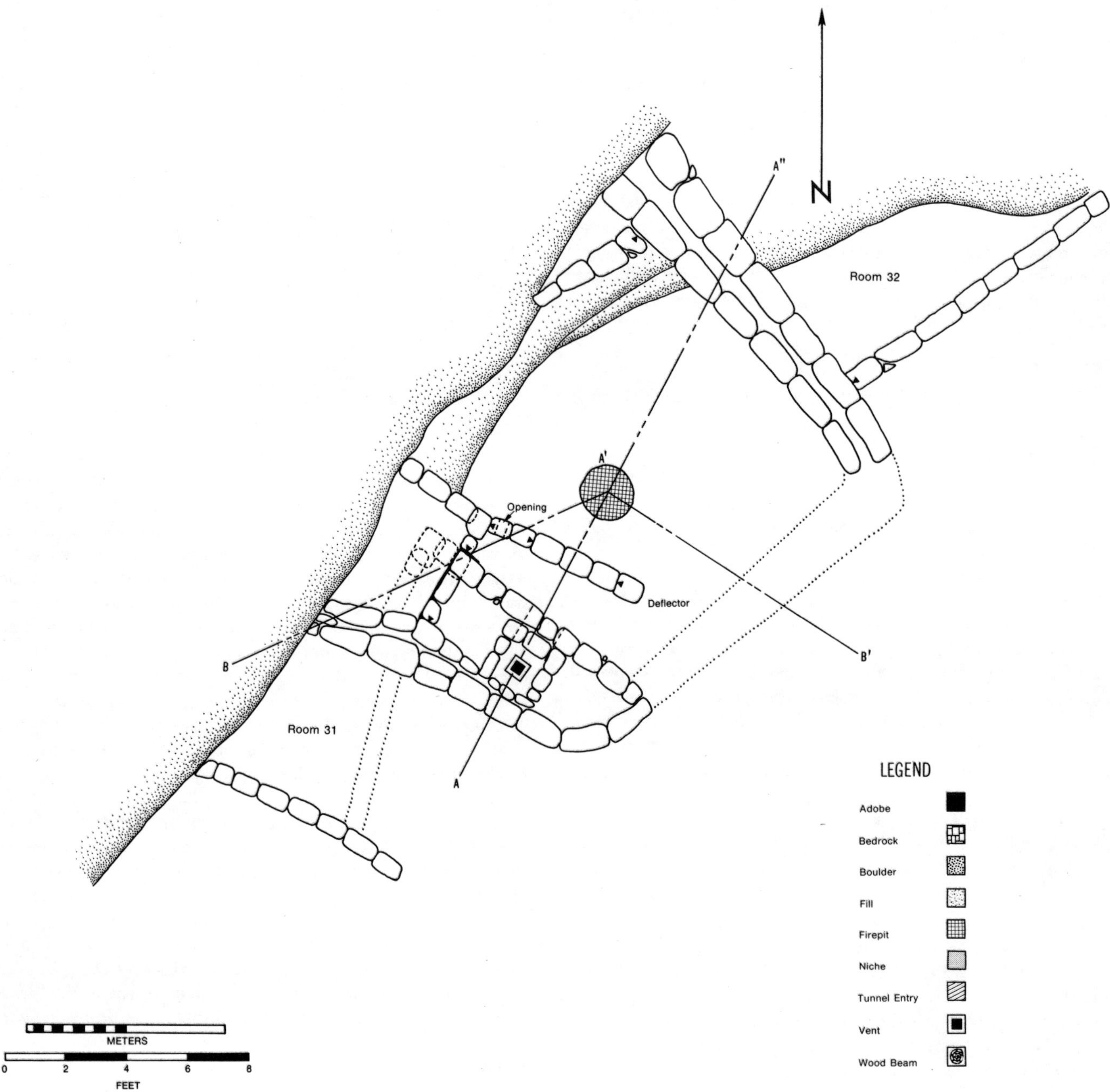

Figure 70. *Kiva G, plan and sections A-A′ and B-A′-B′.*

recess, the ventilator is offcenter in the south wall as a whole. In construction, it is similar to the ventilators in Kivas B and T, except that the horizontal tunnel passes beneath a straight, rather than a curved, kiva wall. In these three cases, the ventilator does not pass beneath the recess as was the case in most of the Long House kivas. The recess is in the northwest quadrant in Kiva T, but there is no recess in Kiva B.

The length of the ventilator tunnel is merely the thickness of the inner kiva wall. The floor of the tunnel is fill, the sides are masonry similar to that in the south inner wall. The roof of the tunnel consists of closely spaced wood members. The south side of the vertical shaft is formed by a veneer placed over the rough inner side of the south outer wall. The other three sides were built of rather rough masonry.

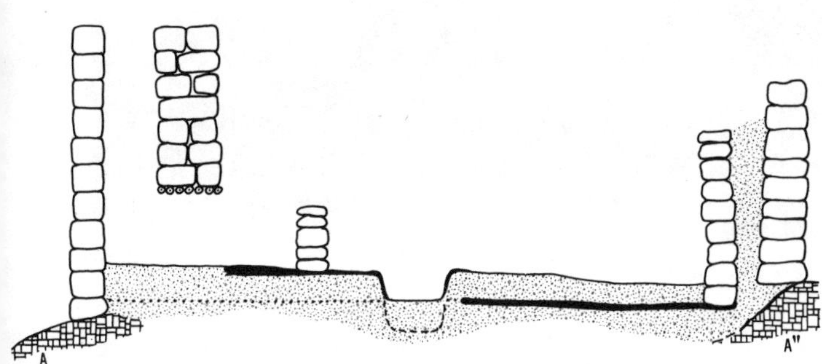

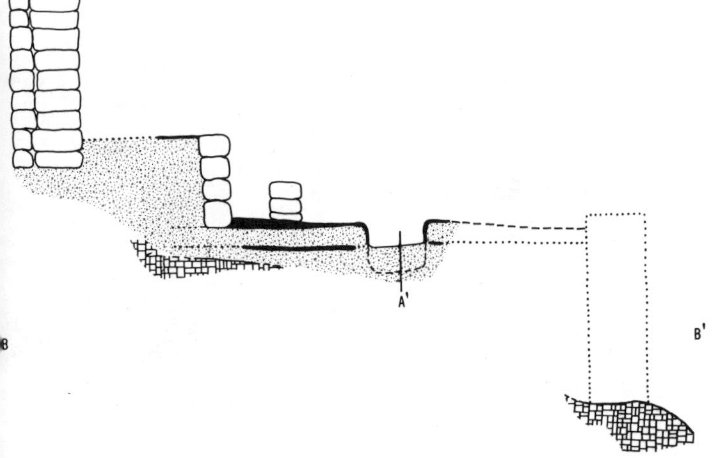

Deflector

It is likely that the deflector originally extended from the northeast corner of the recess to the east room wall. If so, it would have been similar to the deflectors in Kivas A, C, and F. Like those in Kivas A and F, this deflector was of simple masonry and built in three segments: center, or original segment, and two wingwalls, one on either side.

The eastern wing was destroyed when the kiva floor slumped from beneath it. The entire deflector appears to have been footed on the topmost floor. In the west wingwall, at floor level, and slightly to the west of the center of the wing, is an opening 0.3 foot wide and 0.4 foot high, which extends entirely through the wall.

Floor

Fortunately, the west half of the floor and the firepit were preserved, so it was possible to learn a little of the history of the kiva.

Three floors were present, with the lower two consisting of gray adobe, 0.1 to 0.2 foot thick in each case. Overlying the higher of these two was 0.4 to 0.6 foot of fill containing burned rock, ash, large chunks of roof adobe, and large slabs of sandstone which probably fell from the cave walls or roof. The roof adobe suggests that this rain of cave spall badly damaged or destroyed at least part of the kiva roof.

There is a greater percentage of McElmo Black-on-white or McElmo-Mesa Verde Black-on-white (indeterminate) in the fill overlying the second floor than in the fill above the third and uppermost floor, which was placed on top of the fallen rock and adobe. This may mean nothing, because of the very small number of sherds involved, or it could indicate a fairly long use of the kiva or a break between two periods of use. There is no evidence that the kiva was repaired immediately, and very little to suggest that there was a lapse in its occupation.

The uppermost floor was composed of one to three layers of red or gray adobe, depending on the location in the kiva. The average thickness of the floor was about 0.3 foot.

There is no sign of a sipapu, but if this feature had been located very far east of the kiva axis, it would have been destroyed by the collapse of the east wall.

The only other floor feature is the firepit. Although this circular feature was but 0.6 foot deep at the time of its last use, the accumulation of ash indicates an original depth of 1.2 feet and association of a lower floor level. The inside was lined with red adobe, which projected about 0.1 foot above floor level at the rim and formed a collar about 0.2 wide. The adobe of the collar lipped out onto the kiva floor, forming a smooth curve from the rim of the firepit to the floor.

Roof

Nothing remained of the roof, either on the surface or in the fill above the floor. Although lacking a series of good-sized beam seats in the cave wall for primary, east-west oriented timbers, we can still postulate longitudinally placed timbers as the prime roof supports. The possible beam seats in the cave wall are not of uniform height, and one, in fact, is about 8 feet above the kiva floor. This seems high for the base of the roof, but it is quite possible that upper structural members could have been seated this high. At least one room probably extended a short distance out onto the kiva roof, providing another reason for a strong tie of kiva roof to cliff. The smoke-blackened overhang of the cliff above the kiva indicates that the base of the roof was at least 6.5 feet above floor and possibly a little higher.

Kiva H

It is surprising that only two kivas, H and I, were built on the bedrock floor of the main cave. The presence of seeps along the back of the cave was probably one of the reasons greater use was not made of this area. Another factor might have been paucity of light: no sunlight, and little daylight, would have been available to brighten the interior of a kiva in such a location. There is little doubt that the kivas were used for a variety of purposes, and, as I can attest from notetaking in these rooms (and especially in re-roofed Kiva Q) under widely varying conditions of light and weather, a little sunlight or even a bright sky contributes far more illumination than does a fire.

Impossible as it is to determine the full sequence of events in the Kiva H area, some information can be gained from studying the wall abutments of the rooms located here. Of the rooms immediately west of Kiva H, Rooms 23 and 24 were built first. Then Rooms 25, 26, 27, and 28 were added, in this order, with all of these sharing a common south wall constructed prior to completion of any of the four rooms. The lower part of this wall abuts Room 24.

Actually, all the rooms in this group were probably built at the same time. Above a level ranging from 4.6 to 5.7 feet, the wall abutments on the south side of the rooms differ sharply from those below this level. Such a break in construction shows the building techniques used when more than one room was to be built at one time. The change in masonry (and masons, perhaps) comes below roof level in some cases, and so is not merely the result of room modification after construction. There is no evidence that more than one roof was built above these rooms, although this did happen in Room 29.

Figure 71. *Apparent room corners incorporated in the south wall of Kiva H and Room 29.*

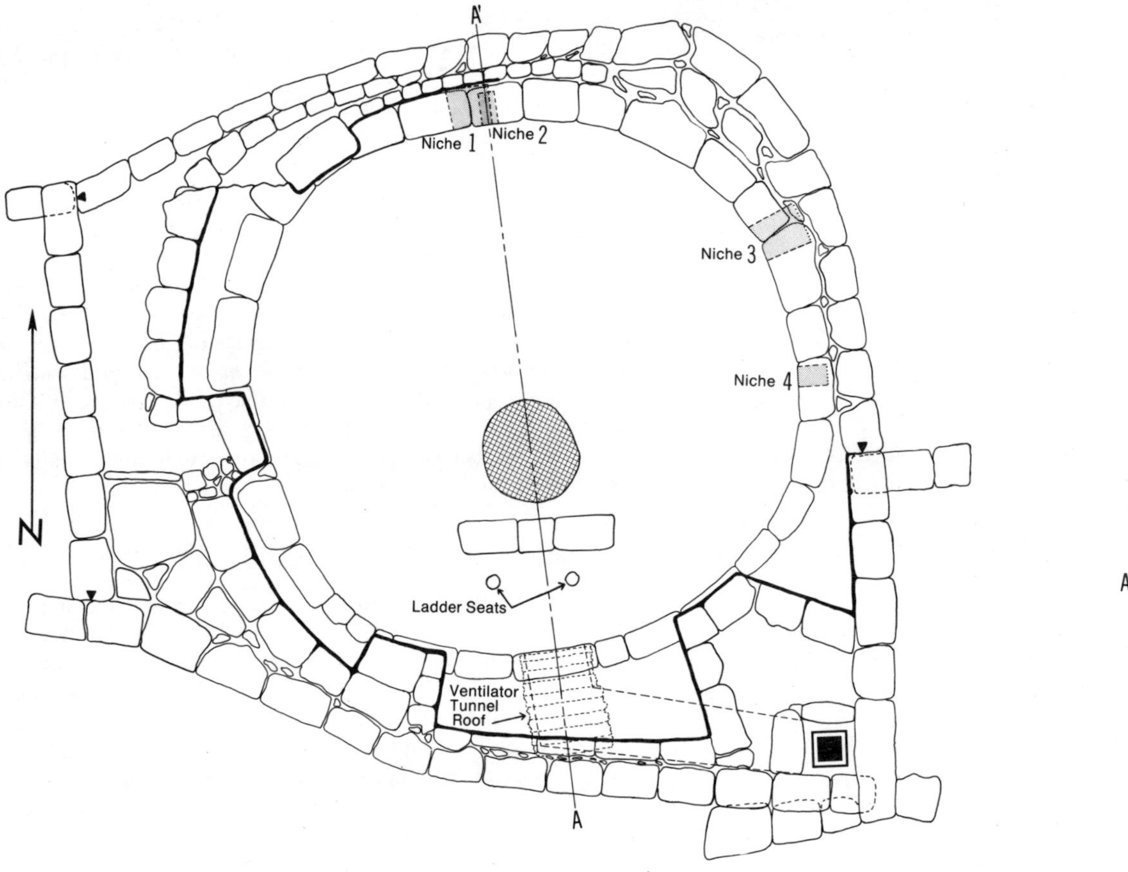

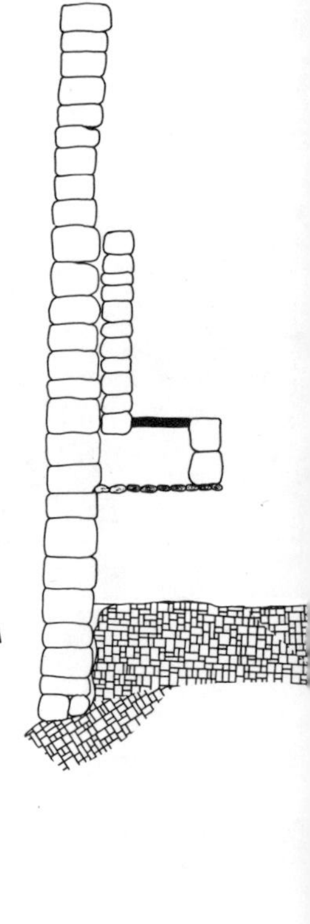

Two apparent room corners incorporated in the south wall of Kiva H and Room 29 suggest that a block of rooms existed in this area prior to construction of the present Room 29 and Kiva H. These corners can be seen in figure 71, one above and a few feet to the left of the wall stub perched on the ledge (Kiva H), the other almost on a level with and to the right of the stub (Room 29). The existing Room 29 was built above the early corner but was not perfectly alined with it. Both Kivas H and I postdate Room 29.

After construction of Kiva H, a parapet was built above the south wall. The change in masonry is readily visible in figure 71, and the location of the parapet on the roof can be seen in figure 72. A similar structure was placed on Room 24 (fig. 30) and may have continued along the entire row of rooms. Even a low wall such as this would have been a definite factor in preventing accidents in this very dangerous area, especially with small children undoubtedly running over the rooftops at full speed. A fall to the Great Kiva or other structures below could easily cause serious injury or death.

A very small interwall compartment was constructed in the southwest corner of the kiva. It is similar to Room 38 but was not assigned a room number because of its small size.

The floor of the compartment, like that of Room 38, is composed of horizontally placed slabs and is about 0.5 foot higher than the banquette. There is no evidence of an opening into the feature from the kiva bench, but then little remains of the backwall of the interpilaster space through which such an opening would have been made.

The unfinished faces of the inner and outer kiva walls form two of the three compartment walls. Only on the north side was a wall constructed for the chamber itself. All that is left of this is a large vertical slab roughly in line with the south side of Pilaster 2.

Kiva H is rather conventional in plan and construction, with two exceptions: the parapet, and the location of the vertical ventilator shaft in a corner of the outer kiva walls and off the kiva axis (fig. 73). The axis, presumably unaffected to any significant degree by topography or neighboring structures, is oriented north-south.

Walls

Along the south, north, and northeast sides of the kiva, the outer walls are merely retaining walls for the inner masonry and fill. On the west and southeast, the outer walls are actually part of Rooms 28 and 29, respectively, and are built of simple masonry. The outer walls become composite walls, in effect, where they run against or close to the inner walls, as is the case along part of the north side and in the northeast quadrant (fig. 72). The walls are composite both below and above banquette level. In the recess and the north interpilaster space, the inner wall is merely a veneer built against the outer wall and thus forms a composite rather than a compound wall.

As can be seen in figure 71, the masonry in parts of the outer walls varies from well-shaped rectangular blocks with pecked faces to irregularly shaped stones with unfinished faces. In the other outer walls, the masonry falls within the range exhibited in the south wall but is more uniform in any one wall. The better dressed faces of the north and south walls face away from the kiva, and those of the east and west walls face into the kiva. An exception to this is the upper part of the Room 29–Kiva H wall, which was built as a retaining wall for the roof of Kiva H and was finished only on the room side.

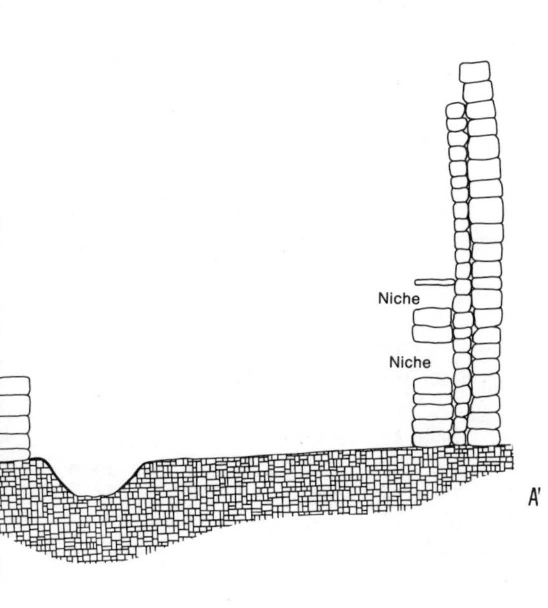

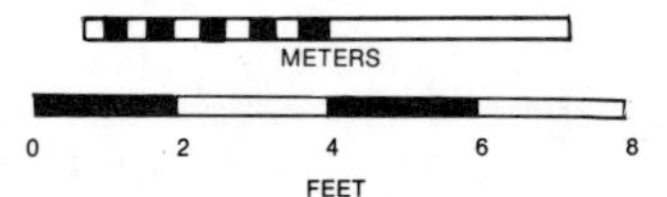

Figure 72. *Parapet (upper left) in south wall and above roof of Kiva H.*

Figure 73. *Kiva H, plan and section A-A′.*

The inner walls were built as simple masonry structures, becoming composite masonry only where they form a veneer against the outer wall, as already mentioned. The upper, inner wall was entirely missing in the northeast and southeast interpilaster spaces. The average-size block used in the remainder of the upper wall—as well as in the lower, inner wall—was generally smaller than that used in the outer walls. Once again, the shape and surface finish of the blocks vary widely except in the lower wall, where rectangular shape and pecked faces prevail. Plaster covered much of the masonry, with a single layer in the recess, at least two layers over the upper walls, and two to three layers over the lower walls. Most of the plaster was thoroughly blackened by smoke.

Pilasters

Kiva H had six pilasters, but only four remain today. Pilasters 4 and 5 collapsed along with much of the east wall. The four pilasters all show radial taper, with that of Pilaster 6 being extreme. All are set back from the edge of the banquette 0.05 to 0.1 foot.

The workmanship in the pilasters, excepting the angled sides of Pilaster 6, is far better than in the kiva walls. The stones are rectangular, with pecked faces, in Pilasters 1, 2, 3, and in the face of 6. The sides of the last are made of irregular stones with fairly flat faces. Two layers of plaster cover the faces and sides of the pilasters, and small patches of white "paint" are visible on the upper part of the face of Pilaster 2.

Niches

Two of the four niches are in the north wall and in line with the kiva axis. The third is in the northeast quadrant, the fourth in the southeast quadrant. Three of these are located vertically near or just below the center of the lower wall. The upper of the two north niches, Niche 2, is immediately below banquette level and slightly to the east of the center of the lower one.

A thin flat slab forms the top of Niche 1, and wall masonry forms its sides and bottom. Only the top is smoke blackened. Slabs form both top and back of Niche 2, and masonry forms the remainder (with the possible exception of the back, which has disintegrated). But here all surfaces, except the bottom and back, are smoke blackened. Masonry probably formed the sides and bottom of Niches 3 and 4, but poor preservation made it impossible to determine the construction of the back.

Banquette

Encircling the kiva at 3.2 to 3.7 feet above floor was a banquette of varying depth. The upper and lower kiva walls are roughly concentric except at the south end of the southeast interpilaster space, where the backwall is formed by the outer wall of the kiva (west wall of Room 29). The rest of the banquette proper in this space, as well as the northeast interpilaster space, was gone at the time of excavation. Flat stones or thin slabs at the top of the lower wall formed the front of the banquette, and a layer of adobe, up to 0.1 foot thick, was at the back of it.

Recess

Although it is located at the south end of the kiva and is centered on the kiva axis, and although it has radially converging sides and a straight backwall, the recess of Kiva H falls short of the "ideal" (as best exemplified in Kivas M and S, perhaps) because of its asymmetrical shape. Its floor is slightly lower than the rest of the banquette.

Two layers of smoke-blackened adobe form the floor of the recess. Smoke-blackened slabs underlying the adobe suggest the possibility of an earlier recess floor of stone rather than adobe.

Ventilator

Though conventional in construction, the ventilator is unusual because the vertical shaft is not in line with the kiva axis. Instead, the tunnel makes a right-angle turn just back of the lower kiva wall and runs about 4 feet to the east. From this point, the vertical shaft extends upward through Pilaster 6, finally emerging in the extreme southeast corner of the kiva block. Only Kiva I has a ventilator of this sort. Kiva A makes slightly different use of the same concept, since the ventilator shaft is outside of the outer kiva wall.

Masonry, of variously shaped small stones, lines the sides of the ventilator tunnel, and bedrock forms the floor. The well-preserved roof consists of a large number of closely spaced juniper shakes laid across the sidewalls. The sides of the ventilator shaft are also masonry but the rocks vary greatly in size and shape.

Crossed sticks were located in the shaft slightly more than a foot below the top of the kiva roof. The end of one stick, and an impression in the adobe mortar of the other, are all that mark the location. Unlike the sticks in the ventilator of Kiva A, these crossed the opening diagonally, northeast-southwest and northwest-southeast.

In his description of the features of Kiva H, Robert Nichols suggested that the sticks might have been used to prevent small children or small animals from falling into the shaft. But most ventilator openings are small and neither children nor little animals are in much danger of falling through them. Commenting on Eagle Nest House at Mesa Verde, Morris (1919; p. 170) noted, "Two sticks crossed at right angles are set into the masonry just below the top of the air shaft. Resting upon these was a block of stone which closed the opening and came almost flush with the level of the plaza." The position and orientation of the sticks in the Kiva H ventilator suggest, to me, that they may have had a ceremonial rather than a utilitarian purpose.

Deflector

A simple masonry wall forms the deflector. Its stones are rectangular, with flat faces, and were covered with a coat of plaster up to 0.05 foot thick. The present height of the deflector at its east end, 2.5 feet, is probably its original height overall.

Floor

Throughout Kiva H, the floor is bedrock, with only small patches of adobe to even out the larger irregularities.

There was no sipapu in Kiva H, at least at the time of excavation. One could have been constructed of adobe, but no attempt had been made to peck a hole in the bedrock floor. In only one other case, Kiva G, was there no sipapu, but collapse of the east half of the floor might have destroyed the feature there.

A circular, basin-shaped firepit was cut into the rock floor to a depth of about 0.7 foot. The sides of the pit were built up with a thick layer of adobe, which also formed its rim. No attempt had been made to create a raised collar.

About 0.55 foot south of the deflector is a pair of depressions which may have served as seats for the uprights of a ladder. The holes are about 0.25 foot in diameter and 0.07 foot deep. The centers of the two depressions are 1.7 feet apart.

A hammerstone and a stone ax were found on the floor just south of the deflector. This may reflect a practice similar to that observed by Hurst and Lotrich (1932, p. 196) in a pueblo in Yellow

Jacket Canyon: "In every case a stone axe was found about two feet in from the inside end of the horizontal tunnel of the ventilator shaft. This last is a most curious circumstance. The axe may have been kept in readiness to meet a possible invader, and, if viewed in this light, may be a possible clue to the reason for the abandonment of the dwelling." Were the ax in Kiva H the only one in Long House so located, I would think little about it. However, an ax was also found on the bottom of the subfloor ventilator, immediately behind or southeast of the deflector in Kiva B, and another was in the fill of the above-floor ventilator of Kiva E. Still another ax was found on the floor behind the deflector and against the lower wall in Kiva J.

A lone ax, even if found in every kiva, would seem to be a poor arsenal with which to repel an invader, especially if more than one person were in the kiva. Also, we do not know whether any of the axes, in Long House or Yellow Jacket Canyon, were hafted. If not, their use as a weapon is even more unlikely. The tools may coneivably have had a functional or ceremonial use in the kiva, but there is nothing in Long House to suggest what this use might have been.

Roof

Although a large amount of roof material was found in the kiva fill, no part of the roof was preserved in place. Much of this material—logs, brush, and adobe—was burned, as was the plaster and masonry in parts of the north lower wall of the kiva. This indicated that at least part of the roof burned and collapsed.

The pilasters, and the obviously large distance between the top of the upper kiva wall and the top of the roof (fig. 72), show that a cribbed roof was used. The cribbed logs, as well as the major cross logs immediately above, were large timbers (probably 0.5+ foot in diameter). The closing material consisted, in part at least, of brush stems and adobe. No additional information regarding roof components or their arrangement could be gained from the roof debris.

Judging by the height of the south recess wall, the base of the roof was about 6± feet above the kiva floor. The location of the top of the roof, clearly shown by the radical change in masonry of the south outer wall (fig. 72), is about 2 feet higher than the base.

Figure 74. *Kiva I, after excavation, viewed from above.*

Kiva I

Because of the excellent preservation of almost half of its roof, as well as of the kiva as a whole, Kiva I is one of the outstanding exhibits in Long House (fig. 74). Just one room separates Kiva I from Kiva H, the only other structure of this type built in the main part of the cave. Both kivas were built after, and against, Room 29, the room between them. Room 36 may also predate Kiva I, but the damp, rotted masonry of the walls east of the kiva provided very little information regarding wall abutments.

It is possible that a room between Rooms 29 and 36 was remodeled to form the square structure containing Kiva I, but subfloor tests provided no answer to this possibility.

Tighter construction is seen in Kiva I than in Kiva H, with little available space between inner and outer walls for storage rooms, or whatever these features may have been (fig. 75). The hard-packed dirt "floor" above the ventilator tunnel and between the south walls of the kiva is probably not a floor at all. A compacted surface here would protect the roof of the ventilator tunnel, and could also have served as a walking surface for the men constructing the vertical shaft, kiva walls, etc. No other surfaces of this type were found in the other, more cramped corners of the outer walls.

Although Kivas H and I are positioned alike, the axis of Kiva I is oriented slightly more northwest–southeast than that of Kiva H.

Walls

Basically, both inner and outer walls are made of simple masonry. In several places, the two run parallel to and against one another, thus becoming essentially the parts of a composite wall. The outer walls serve also as the inner walls in only one place, the southwest recess.

The masonry of the west exterior wall and of the upper third of the south exterior wall was quite good: squared blocks, most of which have pecked faces. The side facing into Kiva I is the better dressed of the two, and also bears remnants of reddish plaster. The masonry in the lower two-thirds of the south wall, and also in the east and west walls to judge by what little remained, is less uniform in shape and size, and shows rather poor surface finish.

The sections of inner walls not covered by plaster reveal good masonry. The stones of the upper wall are about the same size as those in the outer walls, and are slightly larger than the ones in the lower wall. Faces of most of the stones in both parts of the wall have been evened by pecking.

Several layers of plaster covered all of the interior walls, with at least five layers still remaining on the lower west wall. On the outermost layer, below the southwest recess and about 2.5 feet above floor, is a white handprint. Four fingers and the heel of the hand can still be seen. The fingers extend to the north, with the fifth or little finger angling down, the position that a right hand would normally assume if placed against the wall. On the east wall there are patches of a thin white plaster underlying the outermost layer, but no pattern could be discerned.

Pilasters

There are no true pilasters in Kiva I. The sections of the upper wall between the recesses vary widely in length, and thus differ considerably from pilasters in conventional four-pilaster kivas such as C and N. The four pilasters in Kiva U are larger than those in C and N, but are fairly uniform in width and much smaller than two of the "pilasters" in Kiva I. The primary roof timbers in Kiva I are embedded in the upper walls rather than being supported by masonry columns. The term "pilaster" is better restricted to weight-bearing pillars.

Niche

The only niche in the kiva is near the base of the inner wall, on the east side. The wall masonry forms all sides of the opening except the back, which was missing. The inside of the niche was plastered with adobe.

Two breaks in the masonry on the north side of the kiva might have contained niches, but nothing remains to suggest that this is the case. The larger gap is in line with the kiva axis.

Wall Loops

Six oak loops were built into the lower kiva walls, four in the north wall and two in the east. The latter are directly below the east wall peg, and each is 2.55 feet above the kiva floor and 1.0 foot below the banquette. The outside diameters are 0.19 and 0.23 foot, and the north loop protruded 0.06 foot from the kiva wall. Both loops were broken and partly gone. The distance between the loops is about 1.2 feet.

Figure 76 shows the location of the loops in the north wall. The loops are centered below the north wall peg, and a point midway between the loops is about 2 feet east of the kiva axis. The lower pair is 2.5 feet above floor; the upper pair is 0.8 foot above the lower and 0.35 foot below the banquette. The lower, unbroken loops have outside diameters of 0.12 and 0.14 foot and extend out from the wall 0.04 and 0.05 foot, respectively. The upper loops—broken but not

Figure 76. *Four oak loops in north wall of Kiva I (a).*

Figure 75. *Kiva I, plan and sections A-A" and B-A'.*

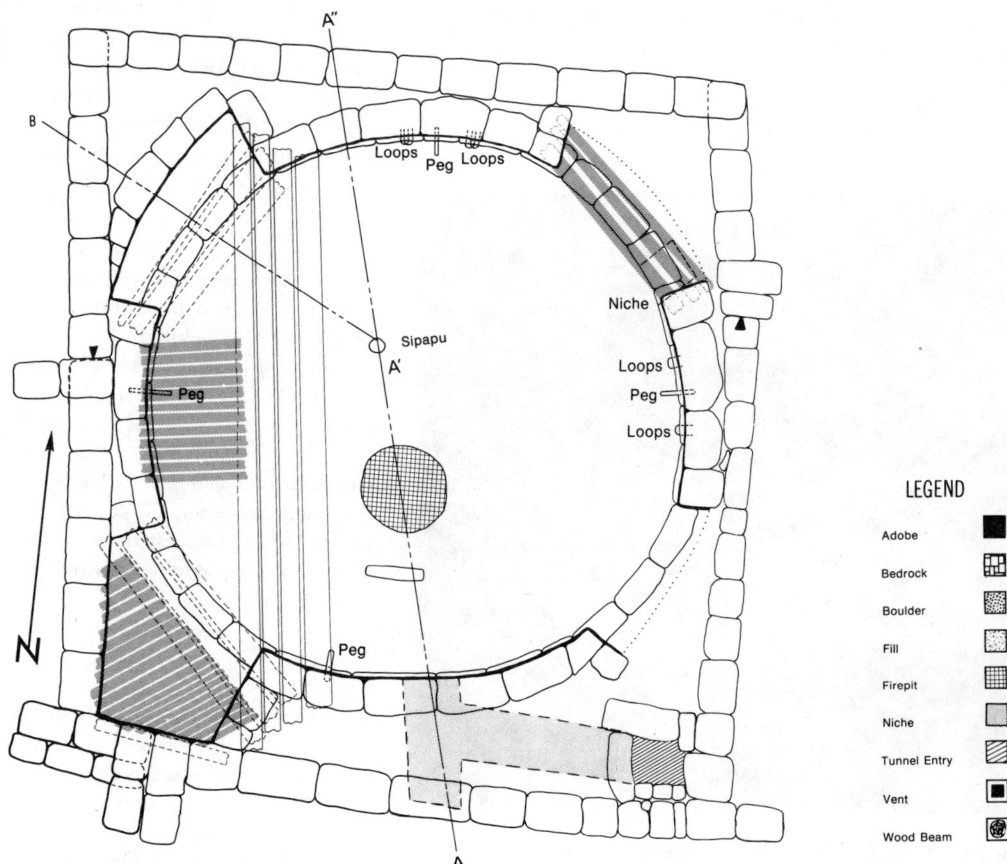

Figure 77. *Original roof and one of the wall pegs, just left of the bottom of the mugboard, in Kiva I.*

warped out of shape—have outside diameters of 0.17 and 0.19 foot, and each extends 0.07 foot from the wall. The distance between the members of each pair is 1.2 feet. The diameter of the wood in each loop is 0.025 foot.

I am inclined to call these "loom loops," although Carolyn Osborne, who studied the textiles for the Project, does not believe this is so. Admittedly, the orientation of the loops in each pair makes it impossible to slide the end rod of a belt loom into the loops (except vertically in the north loops, a theory which would not help explain the position of the east loops). In Kiva L, however, each loop of a similar pair is oriented vertically. It is impossible to say how a Long House weaver would have used these "loom anchors."

The loops could have served some function entirely unrelated to weaving. The perfect centering of the Kiva I loops below the wall pegs is intriguing. These pegs, and two more on the south and west sides of kiva, are all near the roof. Two of them could be used to suspend the unattached end of a loom when not in use, but this is probably stretching the imagination more than the evidence warrants and does not explain why four pegs were situated as they were.

Wall Pegs

The four pegs just mentioned are 2.2 to 3.0 feet above the banquette. One of these can been seen in figure 77, just to the left of the bottom of the mugboard. The pegs project 0.3 to 0.4 foot from the wall, and range in diameter from 0.06 to 0.1 foot.

Banquette

The banquette, composed of the floors of the four recesses, averages almost 4 feet above the kiva floor, except in the northeast

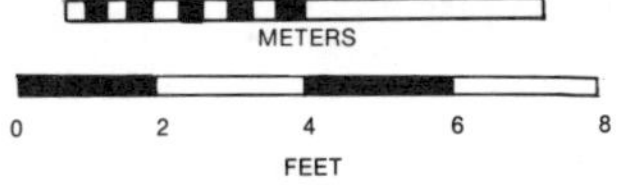

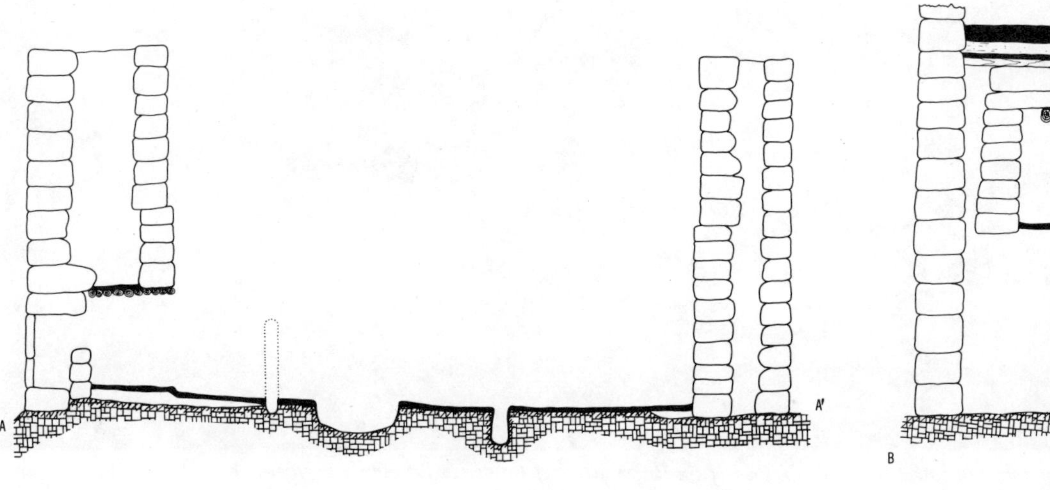

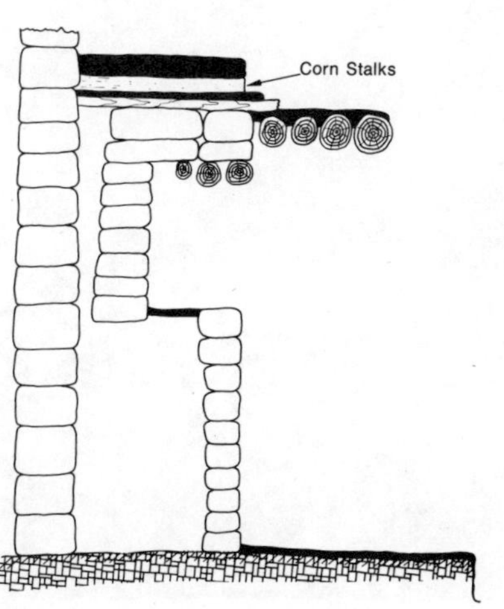

recess, where it is 3.3 feet above floor. Around the rest of the kiva's perimeter is a ledge, about 4 feet above the kiva floor, which was formed by setting the upper walls 0.1 foot back of the lower walls. Other details of the banquette are discussed below.

Recesses

At least two, and probably three, of the recesses are merely shallow spaces. The backwall of the southeast recess had collapsed, but the depth of the opening was probably similar to that of the northwest and northeast recesses. The southwest recess is much larger, occupying the entire corner formed by the outer walls, and probably served the function of the so-called southern recess.

The original roof was preserved intact over the southwest and northwest recesses. In the southwest recess, three parallel logs span the front of the opening, and a fourth lies across the south side of the recess, against the south wall. The logs, two juniper and two pinyon, average about 0.4 foot in diameter. The closing material consists of juniper shakes in the north half and whole pine poles, about 0.13 foot in diameter, in the south half. A layer of adobe, spread across the top of the poles and shakes, completed the roof. The main timbers are about 2.3 feet above the recess floor.

Tests in all the recesses revealed evidence of possible changes in the floor levels of the recesses during use of the kiva. In the southwest recess, the north wall extends down 1.1 feet and then an adobe lip at the base of the wall curves out to the south (but not onto a floor). The smoke blackening ends at the present floor level on both the north and west walls of the recess. The floor itself was missing entirely. Against the south wall the situation is even more confusing since the banquette masonry extends about 0.4 foot north of the wall before dropping off. It was not possible to determine what the construction is beneath the south wall of this recess.

The northwest recess has a fairly uniform depth of 1.5 feet. As in the southwest recess, three timbers span the recess, 2.1 feet above the recess floor. Two are juniper and one is pinyon, and they range in diameter from about 0.2 to 0.35 foot. Slightly more than half the space between the logs and the backwall of the recess is closed with three sandstone slabs, the remainder with juniper shakes. A layer of adobe forms the top of the recess roof.

The floor of the northwest recess, behind the topmost stones of the lower wall, consists of about 0.11 foot of adobe. There is evidence, once again, that an earlier recess floor may have existed about 1 foot below the present floor. The south wall of the recess probably extends at least 0.7 foot below floor. The north wall may have extended down about 0.35 foot below floor, jogged to the south 0.6 foot, and then dropped off.

In the northeast recess about half of the backwall had collapsed, as had the floor and all of the roof except the three main supporting timbers. These average about 0.27 foot in diameter and are about 2.3 feet above the recess floor.

The floor of the northeast recess, consisting of 0.1 foot of adobe, is about 0.35 foot below banquette level, in contrast to the other recesses, where the two are at the same level. On the north wall of the recess the smoked surface extends down below the present floor at least 0.3 foot. This suggests that either the outer kiva walls served as a room prior to construction of the kiva proper, or that the recess has been remodeled during use. The subfloor situation, which is similar to that in the southwest recess discussed above, suggests that the latter is more likely. An argument against it is that the south wall ends a very short distance below the recess floor, as is also the case with the north wall in the northwest recess.

The southeast recess was in the poorest condition of any, since the entire backwall and roof had collapsed. As in the southwest recess, there is a curved lip of adobe at the base of the north wall. It curves to the south at a point 0.65 foot below the banquette, but there is no floor here now. The south wall takes a jog of one-half foot to the north at floor level before it continues downward.

All of these lower recess "floors" may indicate only the construction sequence or foggy ideas on the part of the builders as to what they were trying to create.

Figure 79. *Kiva jar nested within two baskets found on the floor of the longer section of the horizontal ventilator tunnel, Kiva I.*

Figure 78. *Roof of the longer section of the horizontal ventilator tunnel, Kiva I.*

Ventilator

In layout and construction, the ventilator in Kiva I is almost identical to that in Kiva H. After passing through the lower wall, the tunnel takes a sharp bend to the east and runs horizontally about 5 feet before turning upwards. The vertical shaft opens in the extreme southeast corner formed by the outer walls.

The floor of the ventilator is hard-packed adobe, which lips up onto the sides of the passageway. The masonry walls of the tunnel and shaft, composed of stones showing widely varying workmanship, possess one interesting feature: a "niche" at the south end of the north–south segment of the tunnel, on the kiva axis. It was formed by closing off the lower part of a shallow recess in the wall, leaving an opening 1.1 feet wide by 0.7 foot high by 1.0 foot deep. The base of this aperture is 0.8 foot above the ventilator tunnel floor. The chamber thus formed is considerably larger than the opening, since it extends down behind the low masonry crosswall which separates it from the tunnel.

What appears to be a masonry patch on the south face of the south exterior wall marks the location of the niche. It seems quite likely that the tunnel extended through the outer wall at this point during some stage of the occupation. Whether or not it led into a vertical shaft to the south of the exterior kiva wall cannot be determined.

The roof of the longer section of the horizontal tunnel can be seen in figure 78. The main roof supports are three juniper poles, 0.13 to 0.20 foot in diameter, running north–south across the tunnel. A similar pole, also juniper, was positioned east–west across the top of the tunnel opening in the kiva wall, thus serving as a lintel. Overlying the poles are closely spaced split juniper poles and adobe.

Excavation of the ventilator of Kiva I produced a perfect kiva jar nested within two baskets, one of the more impressive discoveries made in Long House (fig. 79). The trio had been placed, as shown, on the floor of the longer section of the tunnel. The kiva jar is shown in its entirety in figure 190a. The two baskets, also in very good condition, are described by Carolyn Osborne in ch. 7.

Deflector

A large sandstone slab, 2.01 feet high, 1.15 to 1.38 feet wide, and 0.25 foot thick, found on the kiva floor to the west of the firepit, probably served as a deflector. To judge by the soil line across its narrower end, the slab was buried to a depth of 0.37 foot in a groove in the kiva floor a short distance south of the firepit. The top of the slab was carefully pecked to a convex shape.

Floor

A bedrock ledge forms the base of the floor across the western third of the kiva. This was leveled by pecking away the rock to a maximum depth of 0.38 foot. Rubble was used to level the remainder of the base, and then a 0.05-foot-thick layer of adobe was laid down to make the floor.

Bedrock forms the bottom of the circular, basin-shaped firepit. The sides were plastered with adobe, which contained a few small pieces of sandstone around the lip. The sipapu, too, is circular, and probably extends down into a depression in the rock ledge—or was pecked into the bedrock. The floor adobe was carried over a rounded lip into the sipapu, where it forms the sides and the rounded bottom. The sides taper slightly inward, so that the diameter of the shaft is greater at the base than at the top.

Against the north wall of the kiva, and beneath the adobe floor, is a layer of low–grade coal. It is packed in a shallow trench pecked into bedrock and extends slightly under the kiva wall. The deposit is 2.3 feet long by 0.5 foot wide, by 0.1 to 0.27 foot thick.

Roof

Four large, closely spaced timbers spanning the kiva from north to south provide support for the remaining section of original roof. The four beams, two juniper and two pinyon, range in diameter from 0.35 to 0.5 foot. A similar group of poles undoubtedly supported the eastern half of the roof, leaving a long, rectangular opening between the two main roof sections. Apparently, the 3±–foot gap was closed, except at the southern or hatchway end, by a series of east–west poles; impressions of several of these can still be seen in adobe just above the easternmost of the remaining beams.

A tightly packed layer of split juniper poles closes the space between the primary timbers and the west upper wall of the kiva. Unlike the main beams, which are seated in and near the top of the upper walls, the smaller poles rest on the topmost course of masonry in the upper west wall.

A section of the roof is shown in figure 75, section B–B′. In ascending order there are, first, the main timbers with the cracks between chinked with split juniper poles and adobe. Then come the east-west oriented split poles extending to the west wall of the kiva and no doubt to the east section of the roof (collapsed). Above these are three more layers of roof material. The first is adobe; the next is a mixture of cornstalks, leaves, husks, and cobs, with the material oriented north-south; and finally there is another layer of adobe. The overall thickness of the roof, from the bottom of the main beams to the top of the uppermost level of adobe, is about 1.05 feet. It is about 0.6 foot from the bottom of the shakes to the top of the adobe. The base of the roof is 6.5± feet above the kiva floor.

The rock and adobe forming the collar on the west side of the hatchway still remain. The size of the hatchway is not known precisely, but it must have been very close to 3 feet square. The opening is directly above the area between the ventilator tunnel mouth and the firepit.

Kiva J and Pithouse1

Despite variations, a clear pattern of architectural features seems to have been followed by the builders of kivas in Long House. Whereas Kiva J adheres to this pattern in some features, it departs from it radically in others. Most unusual is its shape, a modified D in its lower half (fig. 80). Apparently superimposed on this are masonry walls which do not conform to the shape of the lower inner walls. Rather, they jog in and out around the perimeter of the kiva to provide three recesses and an aborted fourth (at least at the time of abandonment).

In at least the northeast corner, the upper walls extend down to the floor behind the inner walls. In the remainder of the kiva, the walls seem to go only slightly below banquette level. Construction of a square kiva, like the original Kiva F in Mug House, may have been started and then modified during construction. If so, the lower walls were constructed after some of the "upper" walls. Whatever the sequence, the lower walls may have followed the alinement of earlier walls.

In outline, the lower portion of Kiva J closely approaches Kiva 3 in the Village of the Great Kivas near Zuni (Roberts, 1932, p. 81). Although Kiva 3 apparently dates to the A.D. 1000's, it resembles in shape earlier pithouses on the Long H Ranch, southwest of Zuni (op. cit., p. 77). The "notched" corners near the south end of Kiva J are very similar to those found in House 6, White Mound Village (Gladwin, 1945, p. 18). This is a Basketmaker III structure, and lacks the southern recess of both Kivas 3 and J. Similarities can be found in many other pithouses in the Anasazi area.

In the Mesa Verde region, Pueblo I pithouses tend to be deeper than Basketmaker III structures. The depth of Kiva J below banquette level would thus be more typical of pithouses or early kivas from Pueblo I on.

The foregoing is merely a way of saying that Kiva J gives the impression of being a remodeled pithouse, possibly of the Pueblo I stage. This cannot be proved, because in no part of Long House is Pueblo I pottery definitely associated with architecture. The black-on-white and red wares of this period are scattered across the ruin, but with a possibly significant concentration on the East Trash Slope, downslope from Kiva J. It is possible that there was a limited occupation of the cave during both Pueblo I and Pueblo II times, and, if so, the Kiva J area may or may not have been a part of it.

One quadrant of the pithouse floor was torn out almost entirely when construction was started on what is now Kiva J. Debris from the burned pithouse was probably used to level some of the surrounding area, as seems to have been the case beneath Rooms 54–56. These three rooms probably postdate the lower part of the kiva. The east wall of Room 56 overlies a part of the west wall of Kiva J but does not conform to the curve of the lower kiva wall. In the northwest quadrant of the kiva, the upper wall abuts the east wall of Room 56. It is quite likely that the three rooms and the upper kiva walls were built at one time. On the east side of the kiva, the upper walls also serve as fill–retaining walls for Rooms 49 and 50, which postdate the kiva and may have been part of a kiva–room complex. Room 48 can be included here also, but it may have seen considerable use prior to construction of the kiva.

The stabilized doorway in the south wall of Room 54 is, if valid, a very puzzling feature. Lancaster reconstructed it on the basis of a sill and one slab jamb. Only later did we think about the doorway in relation to the kiva roof, which would have covered the lower half of the door. If the door had ever been used, it must have been before the upper kiva walls were built. This is quite possible, of course, if we postulate either no structure or some other structure in the space now occupied by Kiva J.

Room 55 predates both Rooms 54 and 56, and so could have stood alone or with Room 54 before construction of the kiva and Room 56, with their problem of meshed walls. Although this is probably not the case, I can present no cogent arguments for alternate theories. There is one fact that should be mentioned again, since it bears on this situation. The thin masonry wall behind or south of the south wall of Room 54 was most likely a retaining wall or veneer for the upper kiva walls or some other construction. This implies that Room 54 came after, rather than before, the kiva.

The axis of the kiva is rotated slightly counterclockwise from a north–south orientation.

Walls

With the possible exception of the thin masonry wall mentioned above, there are no true outer kiva walls. The upper kiva walls serve as fill–retaining walls around the perimeter of the room except

Figure 80. *Kiva J and Pithouse 1, plan with overlay, and sections A-A′ and B-B′.*

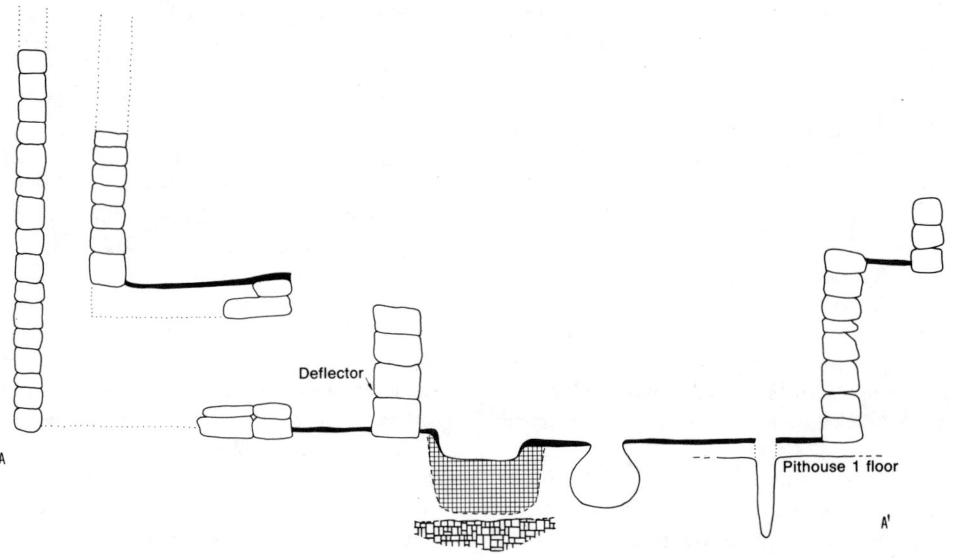

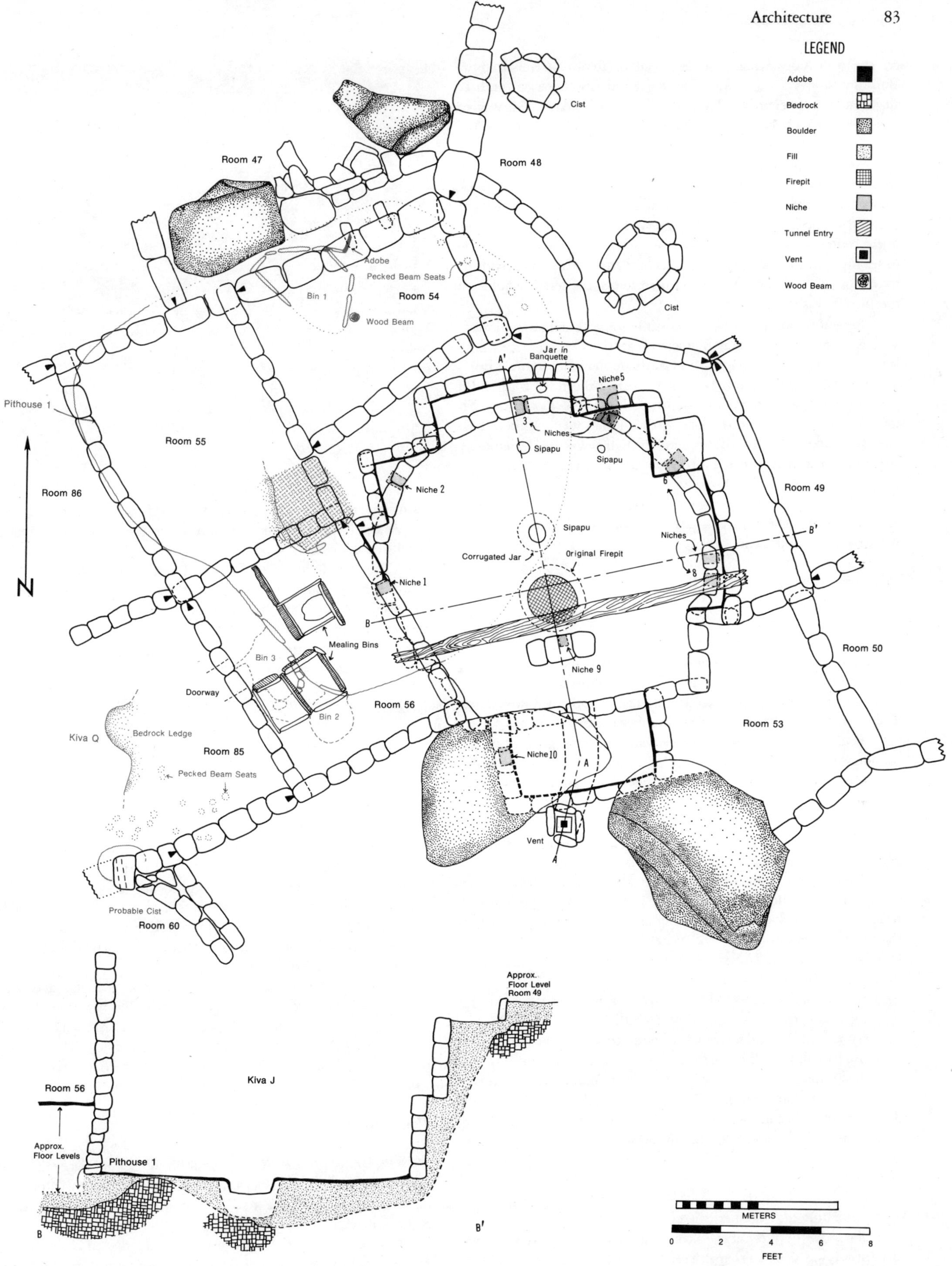
LEGEND
Adobe
Bedrock
Boulder
Fill
Firepit
Niche
Tunnel Entry
Vent
Wood Beam
Room 47
Room 48
Cist
Adobe
Pecked Beam Seats
Bin 1
Room 54
Wood Beam
Cist
Jar in Banquette
Niche 5
Pithouse 1
Niches
Sipapu
Sipapu
Room 55
Niche 2
Room 49
Room 86
Sipapu
Niches
Corrugated Jar
Original Firepit
Niche 1
Mealing Bins
Room 50
Bin 3
Niche 9
Doorway
Room 56
Bin 2
Room 53
Kiva Q
Bedrock Ledge
Room 85
Niche 10
Pecked Beam Seats
Vent
Probable Cist
Room 60
Approx. Floor Level Room 49
Kiva J
Room 56
Approx. Floor Levels
Pithouse 1
METERS
0 2 4 6 8
FEET

on the west side, where the east wall of Room 56 replaced it. Building stones in the upper walls are extremely varied in size, shape, and surface finish. The horizontally laid stones give way to vertically placed slabs in several places. Larger rocks were used in the pilaster-like structures in the northeast and northwest corners.

Most of the masonry of the lower walls consists of blocks that are smaller than those used in the upper walls. However, large, thick stones were used, probably on end, at either side of the ventilator opening in the lower wall. Well-preserved plaster, at least six layers in the southern recess and three to five elsewhere, made it impossible to see much of the masonry. All layers of plaster consisted of reddish, smoke-blackened adobe. In the southern recess, the total thickness of the plaster was 0.02 foot.

Several figures of birds, and possibly some of animals and men, were executed in a blue-gray pigment on at least the three outermost layers of plaster. The best-preserved birds are shown in figure 81a–c. The first two birds are on the west wall, and the third bird and a partial image (not shown) are on the east wall, 0.6 foot apart. All four are 1.4 to 2.2 feet above floor. Arthur Rohn, who recorded these wall paintings, thought the incomplete figure was ". . . remotely suggestive of a man pointing a bow and arrow at the bird. . . ."

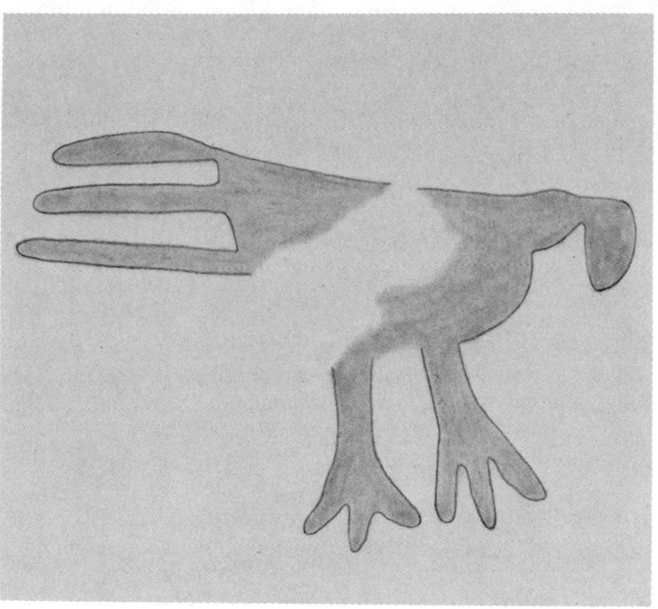

There are many other fragmentary depictions on the north, east, and west walls, but they are too poorly preserved to indicate what they may represent.

Pilasters—none.

Niches

Another striking characteristic of Kiva J is its unusually large number of niches: 10 altogether, of which eight are in the lower walls, one is in the southern recess, and one is in the deflector (Kiva R has six niches, the next highest number at Long House).

Five of the eight in the lower walls are rectangular, two are rounded at the top, and one is irregular in shape. With the exception of the last one mentioned, Niche 5, at floor level, all are located part way between the banquette and floor. One is 0.35 foot above floor, two are 0.7 to 0.9 foot, and four are from 1.75 to 2.5 feet above floor. All are in the northern two-thirds of the kiva, with only one, Niche 3, on the kiva axis.

Niche 5 incorporates an earlier niche built directly behind it in an earlier wall. This is a continuation of one of the straight upper walls discussed above. One stone chip and a potsherd were found in the fill of the newer part of the niche, but their presence may well have been accidental. Two stone chips were found in the fill of Niche 2, also probably accidental.

In all eight niches, the wall plaster was carried into the opening, thus rounding the corners and obscuring most of the masonry detail. To judge by what could be seen, sandstone slabs were used in almost all cases to form the sides of the niches.

The remaining two niches differ only in location from most of the niches in the lower wall. One is centered in the north face of the deflector, the other in the west wall of the southern recess. Both are roughly rectangular and plastered inside with adobe.

Banquette

Although the banquette is of fairly uniform height, ranging from about 3.7 to 4 feet above floor, what remains is broken up into areas of varying size and shape. There are small triangular sections in the northwest and northeast corners of the kiva, and two shallow recesses along the north and east sides. The eastern one is typical of an interpilaster space in its lack of features, but the northern one is deeper and has features more typical of a recess, under which heading it will be discussed.

The banquette level is carried over approximately into the southern recess, but there are no triangular areas in the southwest and southeast corners similar to those mentioned above. The configurea-tion of the lower kiva walls makes their presence impossible.

Where it remained, the top of the banquette consisted of hard-packed red adobe and the top of the inner kiva wall masonry.

Recesses

The northern recess is about twice the depth of the eastern "recess," and more symmetrical in shape. The sides are parallel and the backwall is slightly curved. Embedded in the floor in the northeast corner was a small corrugated jar containing a long, notched, double-bitted ax head. The mouth of the jar was slightly below the recess floor, with a lip of adobe spanning the gap.

Storage jars were found in the southern recess of two other kivas. In Kiva P, a corrugated jar was set in the southwest corner of the recess floor. In Kiva U, a corrugated jar was centrally located in each half of the recess (fig. 110). Preservation was poor in two cases, but it is probably safe to assume that the mouth of each jar was probably near the floor level of the recess.

The southern recess is fairly conventional in size and shape, although all walls are slightly curved (concave from within the kiva). The niche, already mentioned, is centered in the west wall. The floor shows extensive remodeling, with five levels defined. The top layers of adobe total only 0.05 foot in thickness. There is a possible mat impression in the east half of the top floor level.

Ventilator

Probably because of the position of several large boulders, which overhang the recess area, the alinement of the ventilator tunnel deviates slightly from the kiva axis. In other respects, the location of the ventilator is conventional.

In constructing the ventilator, the builders used both horizontal coursed masonry and vertical slabs for the side walls. The roof of the tunnel consisted of wooden members, probably split shakes, as evidenced by several remaining sockets and the wood "stain" on the

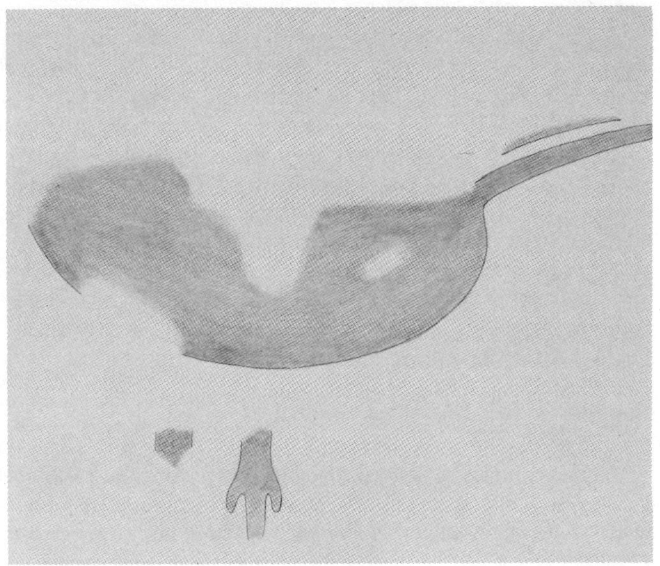

Figure 81. *Examples of wall paintings in Kiva J: a (left), b (center), and c (right), best-preserved birds.*

water–laid tunnel fill. The socket for the outermost lintel suggests that a complete digging stick was used. The tool was about 2.9 feet long and 0.08 foot in diameter, with a blade about 0.6 foot long by 0.2 foot wide by 0.1 foot thick.

The only unique feature of the ventilator is the sill, which is raised about 0.5 foot above the kiva floor. Part of the sill masonry extends under one of the sidewalls of the ventilator tunnel, indicating that the sill is not merely a short section of masonry inserted during some remodeling of the ventilator.

Deflector

The deflector is a simple masonry wall. The north face, with a niche positioned in the center, is well finished and still bears traces of plaster. The south face is uneven and lacks even the few pecked faces and plaster found on the opposing face. The stones forming the wall are somewhat irregular in size, shape, and surface finish. Except for the west end of the top course of stones, the deflector is intact.

Floor

Although at least three layers of red-brown adobe can be seen in the vicinity of the firepit, they cannot be followed across the remainder of the floor. There is a single layer of adobe between the opening of the ventilator shaft and the deflector. Most likely there was only one layer forming the kiva floor, which is 0.07 to 0.08 foot thick, except where remodeling of the firepit or patching of the floor resulted in additional coats of adobe.

There are two possible mat impressions in the adobe of the kiva floor. One is about 1 foot east of the firepit, the other immediately north of the jar sipapu. The latter covers an area about 1.2 feet east–west and about 0.8 foot north–south. The mat may have been 1.4 feet wide originally, and, although its length is unknown, quite likely covered the mouth of the sipapu. The main components of the mat, probably reeds, averaged about 0.02 foot in diameter and were spaced less than 0.01 foot apart. At least 39 shallow troughs could still be seen.

The circular, basin–shaped firepit shows four construction stages. The original pit was about 2.6 feet in diameter, and the floor adobe was carried down into the pit as a lining. A second layer of adobe was also carried over the rim, which was raised slightly by so doing. The firepit was then lined with rocks, reducing its diameter to about 2 feet, and finally another layer of adobe was carried over the rim from the kiva floor to cover the rocks.

A sipapu was formed by a large corrugated jar buried in the subfloor fill so that its mouth, about 0.7 foot in diameter, was flush with the kiva floor.

There are two other possible sipapus. One of these, on the kiva axis like the jar sipapu, is 0.5 foot in diameter and about 2 feet deep. A small stone slab was in place in the side of the shaft and three others were found in the fill, which consisted of sand and charcoal ranging from small flecks to large chunks. All identifiable pieces of charcoal were juniper. Robert Nichols recorded the feature as a posthole. If such was the case, it may have been associated with Pithouse 1 rather than Kiva J.

The other possible sipapu is in the northeast quandrant of the kiva, near the superimposed niches. It has a circular opening, 0.27 foot in diameter, and a shaft about 1 foot deep, lined with adobe and slabs and filled with clean yellow sand. The mouth was sealed with adobe.

A large slab metate was embedded in the kiva floor about 1.19 feet west of the jar sipapu. Its long axis was oriented roughly north-northeast by south-southwest.

Roof

One large Douglas-fir beam, spanning the kiva from east to west, was found in place. Two short sections of primary roof timbers were still embedded in the west wall, parallel to and against the complete beam. A number of fragments of charcoal and several additional wood specimens were found in the fill. Juniper was the predominant wood represented, with pinyon, Douglas-fir, and serviceberry also present. The upper 5 feet of fill consisted of water-laid sediments which probably washed into the east end of the cave from the mesa top. Many other structures in this part of the ruin were also partially filled or covered with this deposit. No doubt repeated flooding of the kiva contributed to poor preservation of the roof material.

Roof construction may have been similar to that of Kiva I. The primary roof timbers probably had a maximum diameter of about 0.6 foot, and were possibly placed about 7 feet above the kiva floor.

Kiva K

Directly below the floor of the main part of the Long House cave at its east end are Kivas L, O, and K, from west to east. The three kivas were built at about the same level, along with Kivas N and Q and several rooms nearby. The courtyard formed by the roofs of these structures must have been almost level and extensive enough to be a major work area. Unlike Kivas L and O, which appear to have been built within earlier rooms, Kiva K was probably intended as a kiva from the start. The kiva axis is oriented roughly north–northeast by south–southwest (fig. 82).

The walls of Rooms 76 and 80, which are immediately north of the kiva, extended out onto the kiva roof a short distance. The original south walls of these rooms are gone, but their location was easily determined by the wall outlines on the cave roof. The construction sequence of other rooms adjacent to Kiva K is less sure because of extensive remodeling of the area.

Walls

Sterile and occupational fill almost entirely surround the kiva. Only in the southwest corner is there an outside wall. The east wall of Room 75 may once have extended from the Kiva N area to a point under the present Room 76. If such was the case, the wall probably served as the west exterior wall of the kiva. The only remaining part of this hypothetical wall serves as the fill-retaining wall for the recess-ventilator area of Kiva K and as the east wall of Room 75. This is the same wall previously discussed under Room 76.

The west exterior wall, of which only a stub remained, is of simple masonry. The building stones are irregular in size, shape, and surface finish, with none of them well dressed.

The upper and lower inner walls are also constructed of simple masonry. Where preserved, the masonry of the upper walls is identical to that of the lower walls with one exception: there is a large, vertically placed slab in the north interpilaster space. Although the building stones are roughly rectangular, there is considerable variation in size, shape, and surface finish. A few of the stones have been pecked on the exposed face, but most have not. At least two layers of brown adobe plaster, each up to 0.05 foot thick, covered the upper walls. A large portion of the lower walls was still covered with up to six coats of plaster. All layers were smoke blackened and were applied over already smoke-blackened masonry. There was no evidence of decoration on any of the surfaces.

Pilasters

Kiva K undoubtedly had six pilasters, but the exact location of Pilasters 1 and 2 is uncertain. Pilasters 3–6 are fairly uniform in width and spacing, although Pilaster 3 has been pushed forward by pressure from behind. Pilaster 1 was completely missing, but it was probably located at about the same distance from the ventilator tunnel as Pilaster 6.

The location of Pilaster 2 near a possible opening into Kiva O (or merely a storage area or recess open only from the Kiva O side?) confuses the situation considerably. Lancaster believes that the pilaster was only 1.2 feet wide, and that an in-place stone against the south side of the pilaster was part of a wall built up between Pilasters 1 and 2. Such a wall would have eliminated the banquette in this area. An alternative theory would include the stone in question in the pilaster, thus increasing its width to 2.4 feet. This would make

Figure 82. *Kiva K, plan and sections A-A′ and B-B′.*

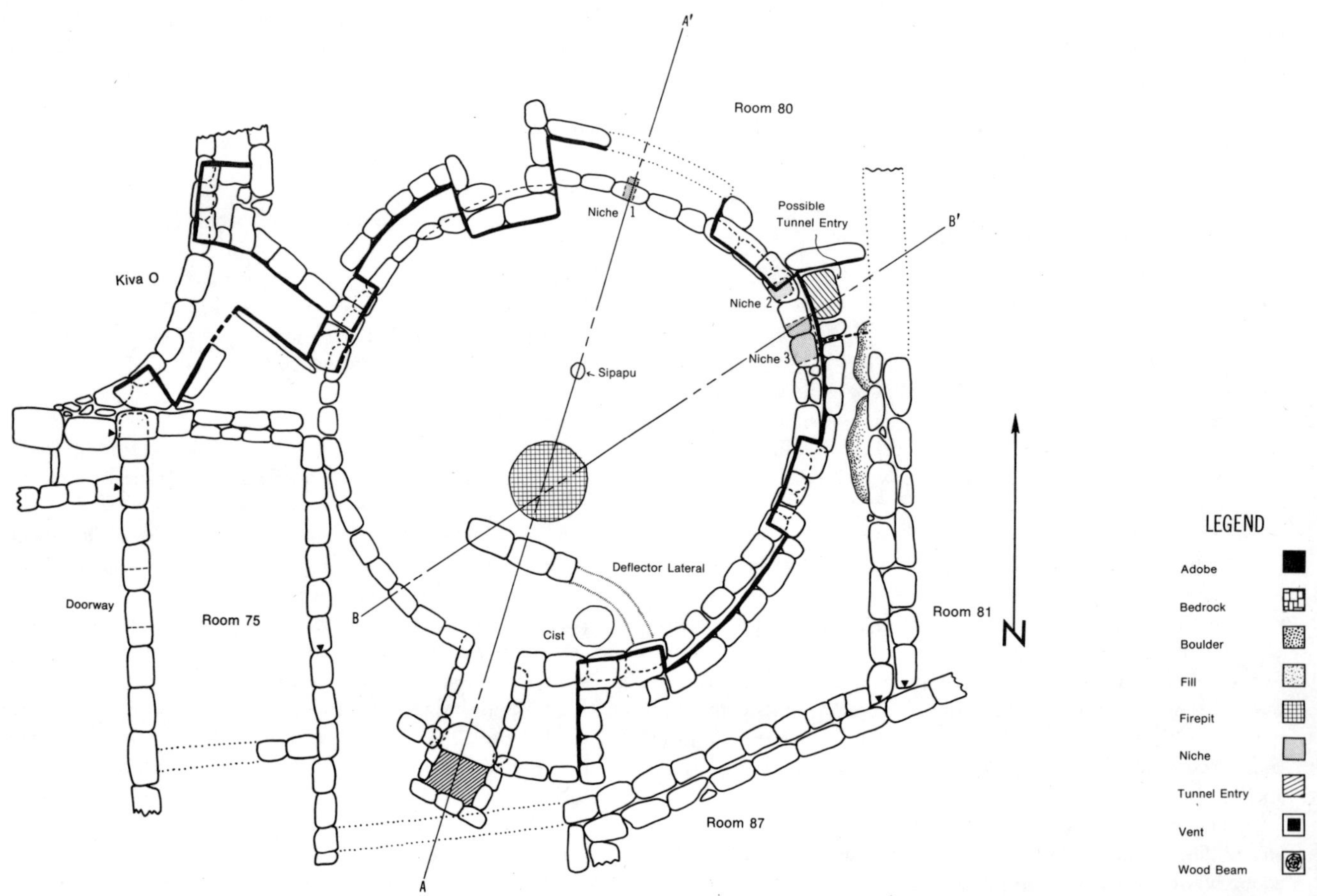

access to Kiva O an impossibility, apparently, since only the section north of the vertical slab in the "recess" between Kivas O and K is smoke blackened. Thus it would appear that the section south of the recess was filled, or at least closed off from both kivas. Lancaster's theory is probably the more logical. The wall between Pilasters 1 and 2 may have been the result of remodeling the recess area, which might have been open to Kiva K previously.

The majority of the remaining pilaster stones are large, rectangular, and pecked on the faces. From two to six layers of plaster cover the face and sides of the pilasters to a total thickness of about 0.1 foot.

All of the pilasters are set back from the edge of the banquette about 0.1 foot or slightly more. There is slight radial convergence of the sides of Pilaster 3, and an attempt at this was apparently made in Pilaster 4. The rest of the pilasters have parallel sides.

Niches

The three niches are roughly rectangular, and each is radically different from the others in size. Niche 1, on the kiva axis, is well up on the kiva wall, as is Niche 2. Niche 3, in the northeast quadrant of the kiva as is Niche 2, is only a short distance above the floor.

The coursed masonry of the lower walls forms the top, bottom, sides, and back of the niches, with the exception of a thin slab over the top of Niche 1 and similar slabs on the top, bottom, and north side of Niche 3. All the niches are lined with an adobe plaster.

On the north and south walls of Niche 3, about 0.1 foot back from the face of the inner kiva wall, are impressions in the adobe plaster of small sticks. The use of such sticks is problematical, but they could have served as supports for a slab cover.

Banquette

The concentric upper and lower walls form a banquette of fairly uniform depth and height around the perimeter of the kiva. The only exception to this is found in the northeast interpilaster space between Pilasters 4 and 5. The space extends back an additional 2.2 feet at its north end to form a small recess. The floor of the recess, raised 0.9 foot above banquette level, is formed by flat slabs near the front and red adobe at the back. The width of the recess can be argued, depending upon interpretation of remnants of adobe floor and footings of its south wall, but it has been reconstructed as Lancaster and I felt it should logically be.

Despite the mass of large rock, adobe, and rubble forming the base of the west wall of Room 81—a rather rough bit of construction now forming the east side of the small recess—I feel that the "recess" may actually be the west end of a tunnel which once extended from Kiva K into what is now Room 81. The construction of the interpilaster space is almost identical to that found in the north interpilaster space of Kiva R, from which a tunnel leads into Room 50. If a tunnel ever existed from Kiva K to Room 81, it was blocked by extensive remodeling.

Except in the "tunnel" area of the northeast interpilaster space, the banquette floor consists only of hard–packed adobe or clay, and the masonry forming the uppermost course of the lower kiva wall. In the northwest interpilaster space the floor consists of a thin layer of red adobe over a layer of brown adobe and gray shaly clay. The maximum thickness of the adobe portion of the floor is about 0.1 foot.

Recess

The walls of the recess were preserved only in the southeast

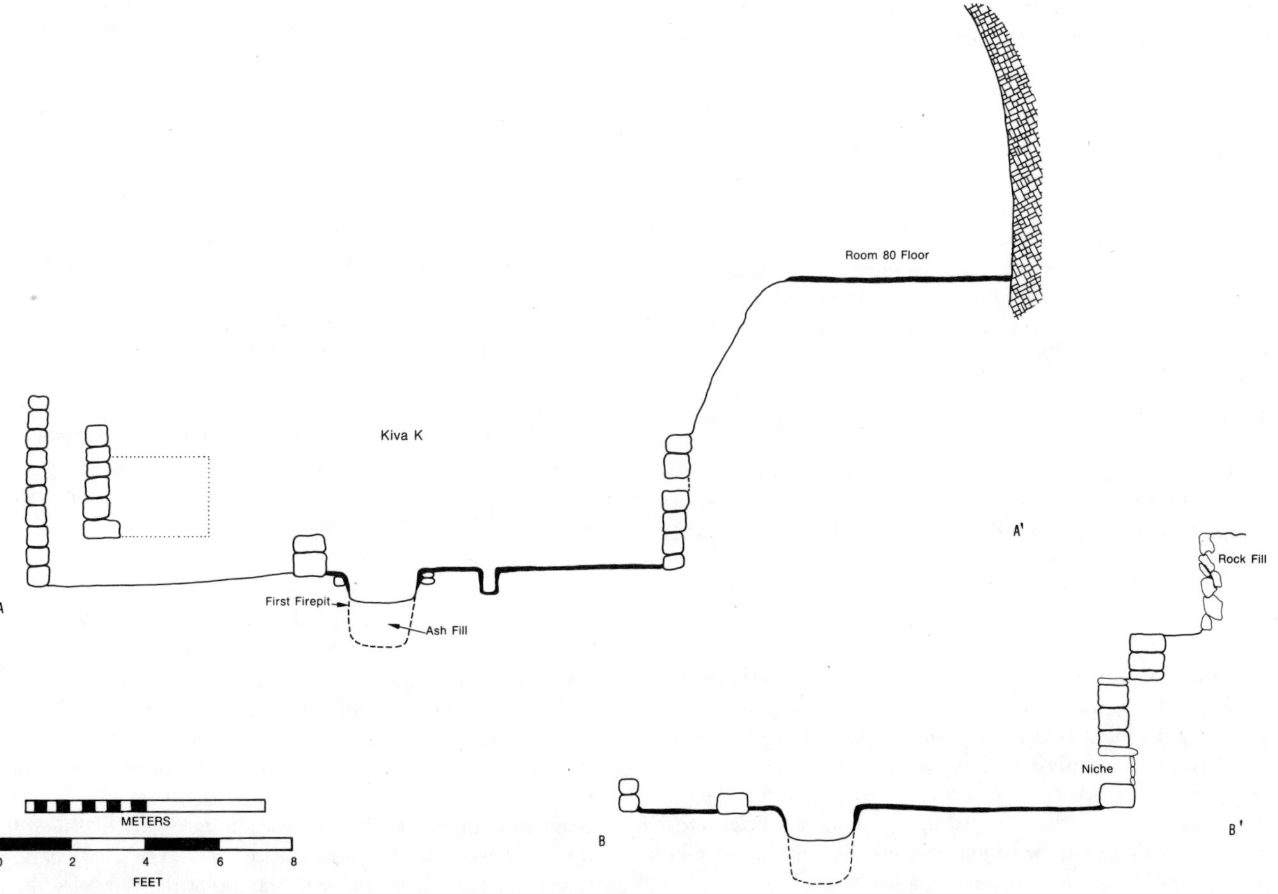

corner. The backwall of the recess probably curved slightly, thus conforming to the curve of the lower kiva wall. The sides of the recess probably converged radially, judging by the one remaining side. A narrow strip of adobe clinging to the east wall is all that remains of the floor, which consisted of at least three smoke-blackened layers of adobe.

Ventilator

With the collapse of the recess walls and floor, most of the vertical shaft and the roof of the horizontal tunnel of the ventilator were also destroyed. Horizontally laid masonry probably formed all of the ventilator walls, and at least some wood members formed the roof of the tunnel. At its south end, the soft dirt floor of the tunnel is 0.15 foot lower than the kiva floor. The tunnel floor slopes up to the north to meet the level of the kiva floor at the mouth of the ventilator. The location of the ventilator in the kiva is conventional.

Deflector

Except at the east end, where several isolated building stones still remained in place, the deflector now consists of a single course of rock. The construction is simple masonry, with at least some of the stones dressed on exposed (opposing) faces. The remaining blocks are rectangular and well shaped. The original height of the deflector cannot be determined.

Floor

A single layer of red adobe, averaging about 0.05 foot thick, forms the kiva floor. Underlying the adobe is a layer of gray shaly clay about 0.1 foot thick, and underlying part of this in turn is a layer of coal. The coal extends over at least the northeast third of the kiva. It is not possible to determine whether or not the adobe floor extended across the entire area behind or south of the deflector. Where it is present against the south kiva wall there are up to three layers of adobe overlying a layer of mixed gray clay and charcoal.

A deflector lateral or low adobe ridge, about 0.2 foot high and 0.5 foot wide, extends in a gentle curve from the east end of the deflector to the kiva wall, with which it forms a right angle.

The circular firepit shows two stages of construction. The pit was dug into sterile yellow soil, and then lined with stone and adobe. Later, after the lower 1.2 feet of the pit was filled with ash, the upper 0.8 foot of the firepit walls was again plastered with adobe. This last coat was carried over the rim and feathered out on the kiva floor.

The sipapu is simply a circular, adobe–lined hole. It is centered almost perfectly on the kiva axis, which extends through the midline of the ventilator, deflector, firepit, and Niche 1.

Immediately south of the deflector lateral is a circular, stone–lined pit. Like the firepit, it was dug into native soil and probably served as a storage cist. With the exception of the jar sipapu in Kiva J, there are no other large floor cists in Long House kivas.

Roof

Despite the amount of wood and charcoal found in the kiva fill, very little can be said about the roof construction. It probably consisted, as usual, of poles, brush, and adobe. Judging by the floor level of Room 80, immediately north of the kiva, the base of the presumed cribbing was probably between 6 and 6.5 feet above floor. None of the pilasters still extended up to its original height at the time of excavation, but the height to which the pilasters have been restored probably approximates the original height.

Kiva L

The shallow fill in Kiva L was clearly wind deposited and of quite recent origin. The kiva had been dug into prior to the work of the Wetherill Mesa Project.

The area now occupied by Kiva L and Room 69 was originally taken up by Rooms 91 and 92 (fig. 83). In order to create Kiva L, the wall dividing the original rooms was shifted to the south. Room 92 and the north half of Room 91 were converted to Kiva L; the south half of Room 91 is now Room 69. Figure 84 shows the kiva prior to excavation and stabilization. The sharp break in the floor marks the location of the wall common to Rooms 91 and 92.

The construction sequence of rooms and kivas in this part of the pueblo is rather confusing because of remodeling and poor preservation of the corners. Since much of the Kiva L subfloor fill, as well as that of Room 91, owes its ultimate support to Kivas M and S, these last structures probably predate all the adjacent rooms (67–69, 73, 74 and 91) and Kiva N. They may also predate other rooms and kivas farther north, but the underlying bedrock or sterile fill would make independent construction of some of these possible.

Because of the complete loss of the ventilator, the orientation of the axis of Kiva L cannot be determined accurately. Judging by the firepit and sipapu (and possibly by one of the wall niches, which may have been on the axis), it was oriented roughly north-south.

Walls

Since Kiva L was built within a room block, there are no true outside kiva walls. With the exception of a short section of compound masonry in the southwest corner and the bedrock which forms part of the north wall, the room walls enclosing the kiva are of simple masonry. The inner kiva walls are also constructed of simple masonry. Workmanship in all these walls varies greatly. Some are dressed on both sides, some on one side only. The shape, size, and extent of surface finish of the individual building stones also varies widely.

The lower, inner wall was present only in the northwest corner, where it rounded out one of the former room corners, and along the east side. The upper, inner wall was still present on the west, north, and east sides, but in parts of the first two is merely a continuation of the lower wall.

At least three coats of plaster cover portions of the east upper wall in the shallow recess or interpilaster space. The two inner layers are smoke blackened, and one of these may have been applied to the east wall of Room 92 prior to construction of the kiva. The north wall is not plastered, but the parts of it shared with Room 92 are smoked. It is interesting to note that other walls which may have served as both room and kiva walls lack the smoke-blackened plaster. No true plaster was found on the lower walls, but in some places in the east wall the mortar used in laying up the masonry was spread over the face of some of the stones.

Pilasters

There are only two possible pilasters in Kiva L. Any others that may have been built collapsed along with the south end of the kiva. The north pilaster was built in a break in the bedrock, as can be seen in figure 85. The northeast pilaster feathers out on the north wall on one end and forms the north side of the recess on the other. It would be more logical to consider this merely an extension of the upper wall used to round out the old room corner, rather than a pilaster. Several beam seats in the north wall probably belonged to Room 92, but they may also have supported the kiva roof. The seats can be seen in figure 85, roughly in line with the top of the vertical scale.

Niches

Three of the four niches are in the north wall, and can be seen in figure 85. Niche 1, above and to the left of the mugboard, may have been on the kiva axis. The feature was built in a crevice in the bedrock, which forms the top, east side, and back. Sandstone slabs form the other sides of the niche and create an opening that is roughly square.

The second niche is located just east of Niche 1, at about the same level. It is merely an oval depression pecked into bedrock. Both the niche and the bedrock wall are plastered with a single layer of reddish adobe.

Niche 3, which can be seen to the right of the vertical scale in figure 85, is now much larger than either Niches 1 or 2. Like Niche 1, it was built in a crack in the bedrock which forms the sides and back of the niche. Two parallel grooves, 0.05 to 0.07 foot deep, were cut into bedrock on each side of the niche. Both grooves are about 0.5 foot above the floor of the niche. Shakes or small sticks extended across the opening from groove to groove to form the top of the niche, but only one of the wooden members was found in place. There is no evidence that the cross members formed a double niche. The rough, irregularly shaped upper portion was probably filled with masonry. The bottom of the niche is bedrock covered with adobe.

Niche 4, in the east wall, can be seen in figure 84. It is trapezoidal in shape, with the bottom wider than the top. The wall masonry forms the sides of the niche, and the east exterior kiva wall forms the back. Although both the bottom and the top of the niche are formed by slabs, five shakes span the top of the feature. One of these runs across the front of the niche, the others across the back.

Wall loops and peg

Two oak "loom loops" were installed in the east inner wall, one above Niche 4 and the other 2.25 feet farther south. The north loop is 2.7 feet above floor, and the south one is 2.65 feet above floor. Each loop has an outside diameter of about 0.1 foot and protrudes about 0.05 foot out from the wall. The south loop is intact, and the north loop is broken in the center.

Unlike the loops in Kiva I, those in Kiva L are positioned vertically. Rather than being located below a pilaster (or a section of pilaster-like upper wall, as in Kiva I), the loops are below the east recess or interpilaster space. Whether they are loom anchors is open to question.

A possible wall peg is located in the back wall of the east interpilaster space, 2.0 feet above the banquette. The peg was broken off flush with the face of the wall and then plastered over. It may belong to Room 92 rather than to Kiva L.

Figure 83. *Kiva L, plan and section A-A′.*

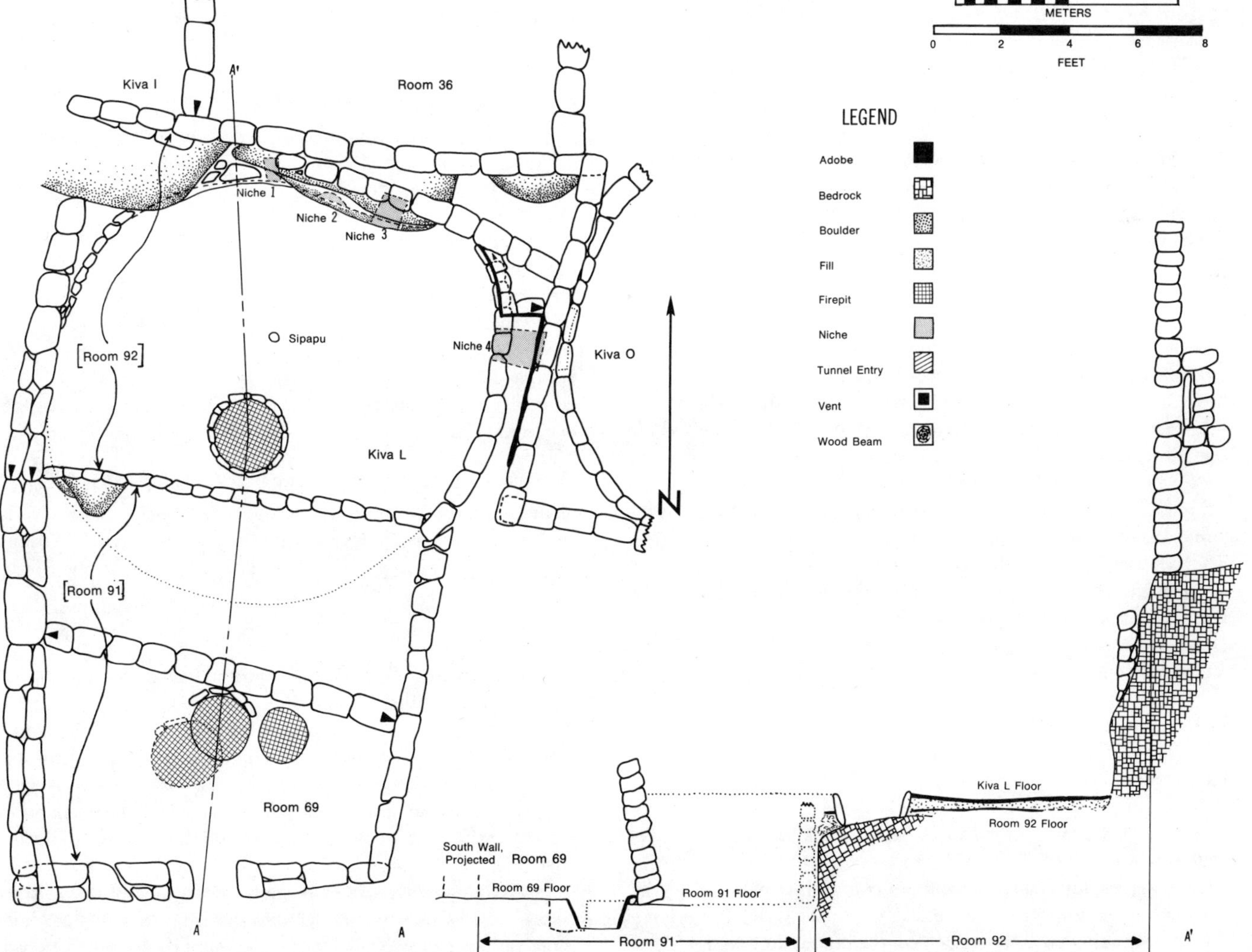

Figure 84. *Kiva L, before excavation and stabilization.*

Figure 85. *North pilaster built in a break in the bedrock, Kiva L.*

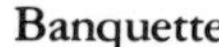

Banquette

The banquette was preserved only in the east interpilaster space. Even so, slumping of the fill at the south end of the space because of wall collapse had destroyed the top of the banquette. The height of the banquette above kiva floor is about 3.5 feet.

Recess

Any attempts the builders might have made to create a southern recess were completely obliterated when the southern end of the kiva collapsed. However, a glance at figure 83 will show that there is very little room for such a feature. If the vertical portion of the ventilator was on the kiva axis, there would probably not be room for a recess on the south side of the kiva. But if the ventilator shaft was in a corner, as in Kivas H and I, there would be room for a recess. In the former case, the east "interpilaster space" may have been the recess. The backwall is the straight exterior wall of Room 92. As a result, its depth is greater at either end than in the middle, and, judging by the north side, the sides coverged radially.

Ventilator—no evidence.

Deflector—no evidence.

Floor

One to two layers of red adobe formed the kiva floor. The upper floor was about 0.05 foot thick, the lower floor 0.01 foot thick. Underlying the kiva floors is about 0.3 foot of fill containing a large amount of unburned roof adobe and sandstone slabs. Underlying this, in turn, are two more adobe floors belonging to Room 92.

A feature of the upper kiva floor, a circular firepit, originally belonged to the lower floor. Vertical slabs lined the sides of the firepit, and small horizontal slabs lined the rim and adjacent floor. There was a thin layer of brown adobe covering the slab walls on the north and east sides of the pit. The upper adobe floor extended up to, but not over, the rim of the firepit.

A roughly circular, adobe–lined sipapu is a feature of the lower kiva floor. The hole was filled with clean sand and mudded over at the time the upper floor was put in.

One feature was uncovered below the upper kiva floor. Adjacent to the sipapu on the north is a shallow, rectangular, flat–bottomed basin about 2 feet long by 0.95 foot wide by 0.15 foot deep. Because of poor preservation in this area, it was not possible to determine whether this feature was related to the lower or the upper kiva floor.

There are several other subfloor features, but all appear to be related to one of the floors of Room 92. The presence of manos, slabs, and a possible supporting groove for the base of a vertical slab suggest that mealing bins might have existed in the room at one time.

Roof

The construction of the roof and the method used to support it are unknown. Pilasters could have been used to support a partially cribbed roof, but the conventional cribbing used in Kiva Q, for example, would present rather difficult construction problems if used in an irregular structure such as Kiva L. It is quite likely that pilasters and beam seats (pecked or constructed in or on the kiva walls) were used in conjunction with one another, especially in an obviously unstable area such as this.

To judge by the extent of smoke–blackened plaster in the east "recess" and by architectural features in the north half of the kiva, it is probably safe to estimate that the height of the lowest roof supports was at least 5.5 to 6 feet above the kiva floor.

Kiva M

No other kiva in Long House offers the variety of architectural features to be found in Kiva M. It is also one of the largest kivas in the ruin. A number of other kivas and rooms are dependent for support wholly or in part upon its walls, which serve as fill-retaining walls on three sides of the kiva. A corner of Room 69 and of former Room 91, and considerably more of Room 68, extended out onto the roof of the kiva, adding further to the pressure on the walls.

Kivas M and S were roofed at about the same level, and the courtyard thus formed would have provided a large work area, presumably for people living in nearby rooms. A doorway to Room 74 opened onto the roof of Kiva M, and a similar situation may have prevailed with Rooms 68 and 73. Collapse of several walls in these rooms makes it. impossible to tell whether there were doorways leading out onto the kiva roofs. The area occupied by Kivas M and S and Rooms 67 and 68 was designated Area IX before excavation revealed these units.

The axis of the kiva is rotated slightly counterclockwise from a north–south orientation.

Walls

Because it is one of the lowest structures in the pueblo, Kiva M has no true outer walls (fig. 86). There is deep fill on all sides except the west, where the lower inner wall of Kiva S serves as an "outer wall" for the lower liner of Kiva M. The two kivas share the upper, inner wall in this area.

As a whole, the masonry from the banquette upward is very rough, especially above the level of the top of the pilasters. The rock work consists of vertical slabs, large boulders (in place and incorporated in the wall), and more conventional horizontal masonry with both crudely shaped and unshaped blocks. Large sections of wall in the northeast and southeast interpilaster spaces had collapsed, as had the upper part of the wall shared with Kiva S in the southwest interpilaster space.

Surface finish of the building stones was generally poor, and few pecked faces were observed. Only in the recess and on the pilasters was there any evidence of plaster. The mortar used in laying up the south recess wall had been spread out over the face of the wall in many places to form a partial plaster. Over this was a layer of smoke-blackened adobe plaster less than 0.05 foot thick. The west and east sides of the recess (the east and west sides of Pilasters 1 and 6, respectively) possess 9 to 10 coats of plaster, with a total thickness of 0.025 foot. All layers are composed of a sandy, red-brown adobe, and are smoke blackened.

Because the kiva had been relined around its entire perimeter, the story presented by the lower wall masonry is far more complex than that revealed by the upper walls. Both lower walls were built of simple masonry, and each is about 0.5 foot thick. Both contain stones of about the same size, displaying about the same quality of surface finish .

Most of the rocks in the original wall are moderately well shaped, and those around the ventilator shaft are very well shaped. They are generally rectangular, with fairly flat faces. Many of the exposed faces show some evidence of pecking. Fragments of smoke-blackened red adobe plaster still cling to parts of the wall. On the north side there are up to five layers, two of which seem to be consistent along the wall. The remainder may be remnants of full coats but could well be parts of small patches applied to the underlying coats. There is no evidence of painted designs on any of the layers of plaster.

About one-third of the stones in the outer or second liner show pecked faces, and the remainder have flat faces. The shaping is somewhat crude, but about one-third of the stones are fairly rectangular in outline. No true plaster was found, but in a few spots the mortar was extruded between the building stones and was spread over the face of the wall.

Where a space exists between the two walls, as it does on the north side of the kiva, it is filled with rubble. In other places, about one vertical foot, more or less, of the upper part of the inner wall (including the banquette lip) has fallen or been removed before construction of the outer wall. As a result, the upper part of the later wall in some places overlaps the corresponding section of the original wall. This sort of construction suggests possible damage to the upper part of the inner liner and overlapping reconstruction only where wall strength was not the prime consideration.

It is interesting to note that the second liner does not extend across the ventilator area between Pilasters 1 and 6. Only in this one place was the original liner left exposed. The difficulties of extending a ventilator tunnel are obvious, and no doubt the original wall in this area had been damaged very slightly if at all.

Pilasters

As can be seen in figure 87, the six pilasters were extended toward the center of the kiva when the new lining was built. This could be done quite easily, since the later banquette was only slightly higher than the original one in places where both levels could be found. Also visible in the photographs are the northwest and north wall supports, which will be discussed later. These are located on the banquette between Pilasters 2 and 3, and 3 and 4, respectively.

The masonry of the original pilasters is considerably better than that of the upper kiva walls. The blocks are large and roughly squared at the edges, and they have pecked faces. The masonry in the front part of the original pilasters is more massive and generally a little better dressed than either the masonry in the original pilasters behind the front section or that found in the additions to the pilasters. The sides of each pilaster are almost parallel, but there is a slight radial taper in several of them. Pilasters 1 and 6 were set back from the edge of the original banquette a distance of 0.1 to 0.2 foot. All the pilasters may have been similarly positioned.

The masonry veneer used to extend the length of the pilasters was present except in Pilasters 1 and 6 (fig. 87). It was as wide, or almost as wide, as the original pilaster. The depth of the additional masonry construction ranged from 0.4 foot to 1.1 feet and averaged about 0.8 foot. All the remaining veneer structures were set back from the edge of the more recent banquette a distance of 0.05 to 0.2 foot.

From two to five coats of plaster were found on the face or sides of the pilasters. There were at least seven layers on the adobe lip curving up onto pilaster from the edge of the original banquette. The plaster layers range from 0.1 to 0.3 foot in thickness. There was no evidence of decoration on any of the pilasters.

Niches

Five of the six niches found in the kiva are in the lower walls, with two in the original liner. Niche 1 is almost obscured by the inner wall while Niche 2 is near the floor. More niches might have been found in this wall had more of the later wall been torn out.

Niche 1 is square and was formed by two thin slabs, top and bottom, and by building stones on the sides. It is roughly in line with the ventilator shaft, firepit, and south sipapu. Niche 2 was probably rectangular originally. It is formed by a thick slab at the top and by thinner slabs on the other three sides. Three of the joints between slabs in both niches were plastered with adobe to form a smooth curve, but no attempt was made to plaster the entire interior of the niches. No doubt all four joints in each niche were plastered at one time.

Niches 3 and 4, in the inner liner, are almost identical to Niche 1 in construction. Niche 4 is in line with the ventilator, firepit, and north sipapu. Niche 3, in the northwest quadrant of the kiva, is a bit more distinctive because it is lined up almost perfectly with the slightly larger Niche 5 behind it in the original liner. The depth of this expanded niche is 1.4 feet. All the niches except number 1 are in the upper middle part of the lower walls.

Niche 6, in the east wall of the recess, provides only the fourth example of a recess niche in Long House. The top and bottom are formed by the ends of large blocks, the sides by small stones and adobe. Plaster on the north side is 0.02 foot thick and is not smoked.

Interpilaster wall supports

There are two other pilaster-like structures on the banquette which I have designated "wall supports." Actually, they may have served both to support the roof and to shore up a buckling upper kiva wall, such as that behind the north wall support. The north support was definitely built on the original banquette before the kiva was remodeled, and the same is probably true of the northwest support. The height of the supports was apparently the same as that of the pilasters. The masonry of both supports resembles that placed behind the better–dressed facing of the original pilasters. The stones are crudely shaped and finished. No plaster was found on either support.

Lancaster and I argued considerably over the sequence of events which led to construction of the interpilaster supports and relining of the kiva. We both agreed to most of the following stages in the history of Kiva M: it was in use a considerable length of time before any modifications were made, and its walls became thoroughly smoke blackened. Kiva S was then built, and the backwall of the southwest interpilaster space in Kiva M was shifted closer to the edge of the banquette, to allow room for a similar feature in Kiva S. Then, present structures, or possibly others in a slightly different location, were built immediately north of Kiva M. The weight of the additional masonry exerted excessive pressure on the walls of the kiva, causing buckling of the upper walls in the northwest quadrant. The north and northwest supports were built, both to stabilize the walls and to help support the roof which, in turn, was bearing much of the weight of Room 68. Additional buckling, and possibly minor collapse of a part of the kiva masonry, may then have resulted in removal of a portion of the banquette and lower walls and complete relining of the kiva. A masonry buttress was also built against the north lower wall of Kiva S to help support the tremendous weight of the rooms and fill to the north.

The use of Kivas M and S was probably terminated abruptly by fire. I believe the position of the burned masonry on the pilasters and veneer extensions of Kiva M can be explained as follows: after the roof started burning and collapsing, it pulled portions of the pilaster facings down, allowing the fire to burn part of the face of the original pilasters. The heavy burn on both sides of the wall shared by Kivas M and S suggests simultaneous destruction of the two, since the burn on one side is not merely the result of "baking" by a fire on the other side. The mass of charcoal in the fill of both kivas suggests that they were permanently abandoned after the fire.

If Rooms 67 and 68 were still in place at the time of the fire, as suggested by the amount of building stone in the fill of the two kivas, they would have been damaged beyond repair. Perhaps this explains the sealed T-shaped door between Rooms 66 and 67.

Banquettes

The concentric construction of the upper and lower kiva walls created two banquettes of fairly uniform depth in each of the interpilaster spaces, both before and after the kiva was relined. The only exception is the northwest space, in which the east end is 0.9 foot deeper than the west end. The depth is less consistent from space to space. The height of the banquettes above the kiva floor ranged from about 3.0 to 3.5 feet. Where present, the floor consisted of red adobe, varying in thickness from 0.05 to 0.1 foot, and of masonry forming the edge of each of the two banquettes.

Recess

Other than the niche already mentioned, there is little to distinguish the recess. The sidewalls are straight and converge sharply toward the center of the kiva, and the backwall is curved. The recess is not symmetrical from side to side, being slightly deeper at the east end than at the west.

There are two floors in part of the recess, a lower one of brown adobe and associated with the original level, and an upper one of red adobe associated with the remodeled recess. Apparently the top course of rock had been removed from the lower kiva wall, and the reconstructed edge of the banquette was slightly higher than the original one. As a result, the red adobe floor slopes up and over the rock, feathering out on the new banquette edge and on the brown adobe floor. Maximum thickness of the brown adobe is 0.1 foot, that of the red adobe 0.15 foot.

Figure 86. *Kiva M, plan and sections A-A', B-B', and C-C' (through tunnel between Kivas M and N).*

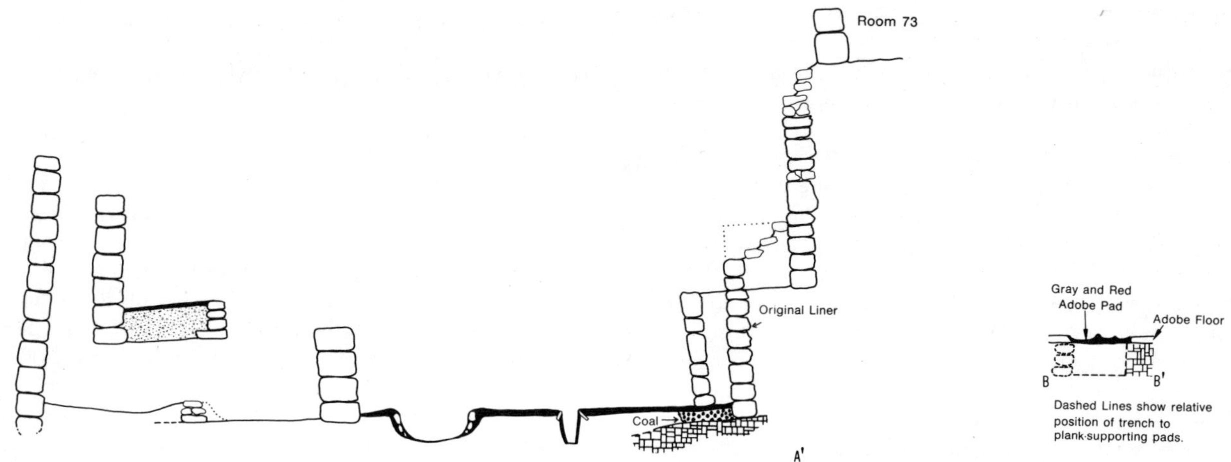

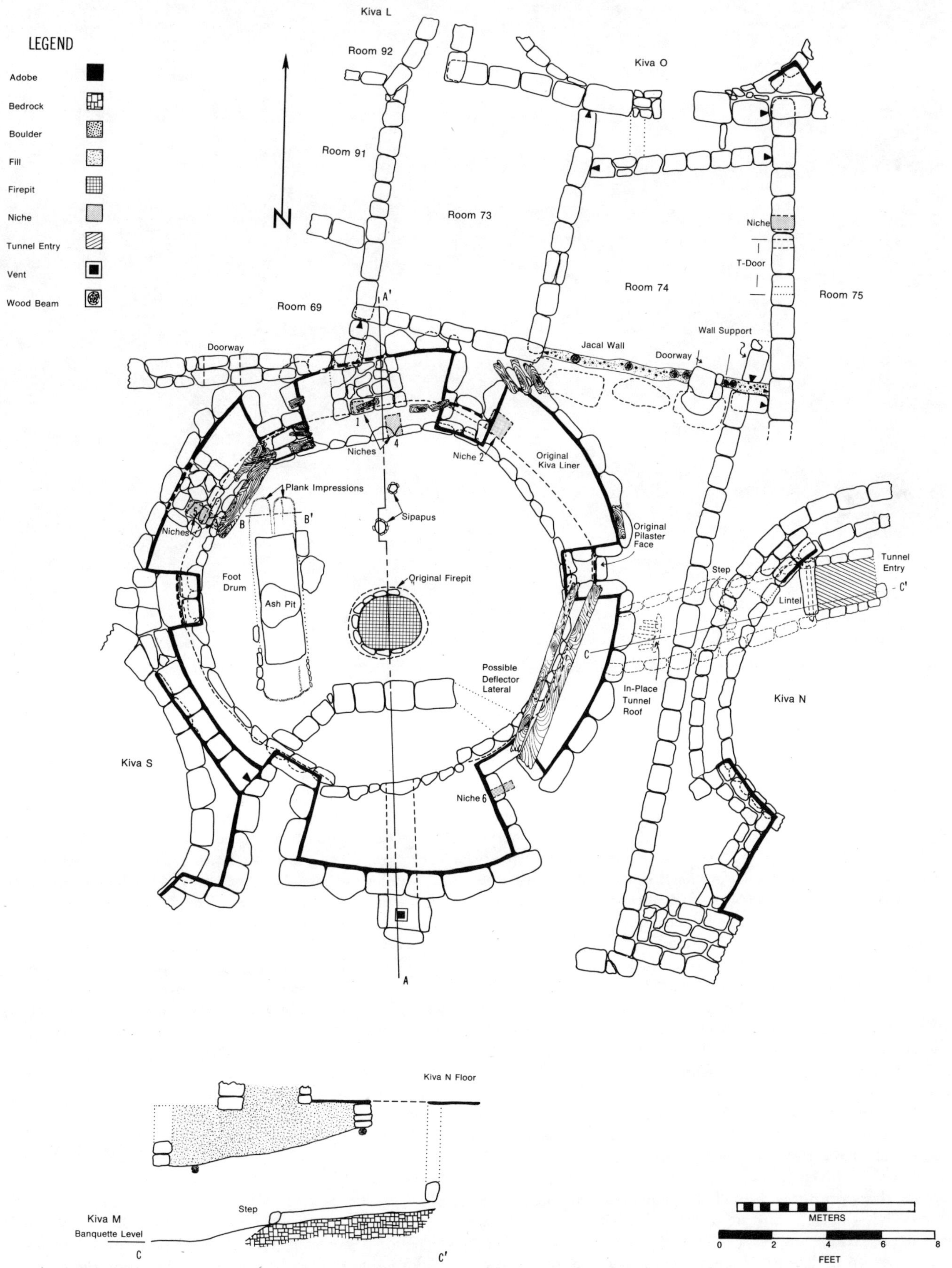
LEGEND
Adobe
Bedrock
Boulder
Fill
Firepit
Niche
Tunnel Entry
Vent
Wood Beam
N
Kiva L
Room 92
Kiva O
Room 91
Room 73
Niche
T-Door
Room 74
Room 75
Room 69
A'
Wall Support
Jacal Wall
Doorway
Doorway
Niches
4
Niche 2
Original Kiva Liner
Plank Impressions
Sipapus
Niches
B
B'
Original Pilaster Face
Tunnel Entry
Step
C'
Lintel
Original Firepit
Foot Drum
Ash Pit
C
Possible Deflector Lateral
In-Place Tunnel Roof
Kiva N
Kiva S
Niche 6
A
Kiva N Floor
Step
Kiva M Banquette Level
C
C'
METERS
0 2 4 6 8
FEET

Figure 87. *Pilasters extended inwardly when second liner built, Kiva M.*

Tunnel

Opening off the north end of the southeast interpilaster space is a tunnel or crawlway leading to a hatch–like opening in the floor of Kiva N. The base of the opening into Kiva M was either at banquette level or, more likely, about 0.2 foot above the top of the banquette because of the possible presence of a low rock sill. The 10-foot-long tunnel was sealed at the Kiva N end, but collapse of the back wall in the southeast interpilaster space made it impossible to tell whether the Kiva M end was also blocked, as would seem logical. The fill in the tunnel was sterile except for a considerable amount of charcoal, and it appears to have been placed there deliberately. If true, this provides additional evidence that the tunnel entrance to Kiva M was sealed. Possibly the tunnel was closed at the time the kiva was relined.

There was no evidence to indicate the type of masonry construction that formed the tunnel entrance to Kiva M, but quite likely it resembled the reconstruction. A combination of simple horizontal masonry and vertical slabs formed the tunnel walls. The base of the north wall of the passageway was constructed almost entirely of vertical slabs, with horizontal masonry of smaller-than-average stones forming the upper part of the wall. The individual stones are crudely shaped and, although there are quite a few flat faces, none shows evidence of pecking. In the Kiva N hatchway, the tunnel masonry was carried up to floor level, apparently without a masonry collar. Two lintels, one of stone and one of wood, span the mouth of the horizontal tunnel.

The roof of the tunnel consisted of a layer of red adobe about 0.2 foot thick overlying a series of closely spaced, wooden members oriented east–west. These were supported in turn by north–south wooden members. Because of very poor preservation, the length of the sticks could not be measured. The diameters ranged from 0.1 to 0.15 foot. All of the wood which could be checked was juniper. Although there is no direct evidence of a wood lintel across the Kiva M entrance, as there is at the Kiva N opening, I would be very surprised if there had not been one originally.

The floor consists only of bedrock and sterile fill. About 4.5 feet east of the Kiva M entrance is a "step:" three crudely shaped or unshaped rocks cemented in place with red adobe on the bedrock floor. This feature, which averages 0.3 foot high, may actually be a fill-retaining wall. As such, it would have made possible a fairly level floor area below the Kiva N hatchway.

The width of the tunnel ranges from 1.5 to 2.0 feet. The height, from floor to immediately below the location (or probable location, in most instances) of in-place wood, ranges from 2.2 feet at the "step" to 2.7 feet.

Ventilator

The masonry in both the horizontal and vertical parts of the ventilator is similar to that of the original lower kiva walls. The workmanship displayed in shaping and dressing the stones used in the first 1.5 feet of the tunnel is far superior to that found in the rest of the ventilator. The roof is formed by closely spaced poles averaging about 0.1 foot in diameter, some of which are possibly split, and an overlying layer of adobe. The stubs of many of the poles were in place at the sides of the tunnel when the kiva was excavated.

The ventilator floor slopes up about 10° from north to south and has a dip 0.2 foot deep near the center of the tunnel. The floor terminates at the north end in a crude rock wall, but at one time may have extended over the wall to lip out on the ashy brown fill forming the kiva "floor" south of the deflector. The wall is 0.6 foot high and is located in the tunnel about 0.5 foot from its mouth. It is possible that this apparent retaining wall was built on an earrlier tunnel floor. The present floor is a hard–packed, reddish–brown sandy fill containing flecks of charcoal.

Figure 88. *Two sipapus, oval firepit, foot drum, and superimposed ashpit, Kiva M.*

Deflector

This simple masonry feature, which was heated on sterile fill, is composed of roughly shaped blocks, some of which are rectangular. The faces had been dressed, with the north face smoother than the south. The exposed faces of the individual stones are roughly flat, but very few of them had been pecked. There was no true plaster, yet in a few places excess red adobe mortar had been spread over the face of the structure.

Floor

The red adobe floor appeared to be constructed as a unit, 0.01 to 0.2 foot thick, and was consistent over the entire kiva north of the deflector and laterals. There was no adobe south of these features. The floor breaks off sharply at the north side of the west deflector lateral or wingwall, which consisted of two flat slabs set in adobe, and at the south edge of a possible east lateral. No adobe ridge or masonry marked the location of the latter, which is merely suggested by the abrupt termination of the floor adobe. There was no evidence of a sipapu in this floor.

Subfloor excavation revealed a complex of features that had been smoothly and completely covered over by the floor laid during the final stages of remodeling. Sandwiched between bedrock and the floor adobe in the northeast quadrant of the kiva is an irregularly shaped deposit of coal, 0.25 to 0.4 foot thick. Both the coal, which was introduced by man, and the adobe floor above extend back under the inner kiva liner, presumably to the outer liner.

There is a sharp break between the coal and the subfloor deposit south and west of it, which consists of sterile fill. The red adobe floor extends across the top of the fill, and lips up onto the deflector. Complete removal of the upper part of the adobe floor revealed the two sipapus (fig. 88), but the original floor level could not be followed precisely through the overlying mass of extremely hard-packed, flaky adobe.

The southern sipapu, probably the earlier, is lined with red adobe and has the shape of an inverted, truncated cone. Seven black-on-white (probably Mesa Verde) jar sherds were embedded in the adobe to form a slightly incurving rim. All the sherds may be from the same jar, but one was placed with the painted side in rather than out, as was the case with the rest. The northern sipapu is square in horizontal cross section throughout most of its length, and the vertical slab walls slope in slightly toward the bottom. The elliptical top is formed by six sherds of a Mesa Verde Black-on-white jar corrugated rim, embedded in adobe. Both sipapus were filled with a sterile, yellow–brown soil and were covered with adobe, which undoubtedly feathered out on the original floor or floors.

The somewhat oval firepit had been remodeled once (fig. 88). The original basin-shaped, adobe-lined pit was relined with stone and adobe. The rock extended around three sides of the firepit and consisted of small stones and thin slabs laid up in red adobe. The newer lining was arched up about floor level to form a slightly raised collar, which feathered out on the original floor near the firepit. The slightly concave bottom existed during both stages of construction.

A large rectangular feature, which I have called a foot drum, and a later superimposed ashpit were found at the west side of the kiva (fig. 88). The resonating chamber for the foot drum was dug into the mixed sterile soil and bedrock forming the subfloor fill. The sides of the drum were formed by crude masonry on the west and south, by bedrock on the north, and by fill on the east side.

Pads, consisting of red adobe on the bottom and gray clay on top, were prepared adjacent to and immediately north and south of the rectangular pit. While the gray clay was still wet, planks were placed over the opening, with their ends resting on the clay. Both small and large rocks were placed alongside the planks, no doubt to hold them in position and to stabilize the edge of the red adobe floor, which was brought up to the edge of the foot drum. The large stone at the left of the ashpit in figure 88 has a concave depression in the upper face. Both this stone and the one adjacent to it are worn, possibly by feet. There is no evidence of grinding on either stone.

Wood impressions in the clay suggest that two, or perhaps four, planks were used. They were apparently placed rounded side down, producing troughs 0.1 to 0.2 foot deep. The small ridges formed by the planks suggest the irregularities common to juniper, but no wood remained to support this supposition.

A subrectangular vault or cist identical to the foot drums in Kivas M and Q was excavated in Kiva A at Badger House (Hayes and Lancaster 1975). Unlike the Long House foot drums, it was probably still in use at the time the site was abandoned. At one end and in the bottom of the pit were the charred remains of a large plank of ponderosa pine which, judging by wood impressions in the soil, measured 2.3 feet wide by about 8 feet long and 0.3 foot thick.

Less well–defined subfloor "cists," some of which may have been foot drums, have been seen by Lancaster in three ruins on Chapin Mesa, Mesa Verde—Square Tower House, west roofed giva; Site 16, kiva east of the tower; and Far View House, large kiva; and also in a deep, Chaco–type kiva excavated east of Lowry Ruin, near Pleasant View, Colo. At Square Towar House, Lancaster removed a log which was embedded in the floor along one side of the cist. At the Site 16 kiva there was a large cist on the west side and a small one on the east. In the Far View House kiva, a vertical pole just north of center of the slab–lined cist may indicate that this structure had some use other than as a foot drum.

A heart–shaped ashpit had been made in the foot drum in Kiva M after the planks had been removed (fig. 88). After construction of the ashpit walls, which are formed by the rubble fill in the resonating chamber of the foot drum, the remainder of the drum was plastered over with adobe. The ashpit was then plastered with adobe, which was carried over the rim (where it is about 0.1 foot thick) to lip out on the Kiva floor about 0.5 foot from the edge of the ashpit. All sides of the pit except the west one slope in slightly toward the bottom of the pit. The west side bows out about halfway down before curving inward to meet the floor. The adobe walls of the ashpit were not burned. The bottom 0.5 foot of fill in the pit was hard–packed ash and unburned rock. The upper 0.3 foot of fill, apparently placed at the time the pit was abandoned, consisted of yellow–brown soil containing bits of charcoal, rock, and a few potsherds. After the ashpit was filled, the entire west side of the kiva floor was covered with a thin layer of adobe.

South of the deflector and the southern edge of the adobe floor is an undeveloped area of the kiva that shows no definable floor levels. Above the native soil and rock base are several tenths of a foot of charcoal–flecked, gray–brown fill containing lenses of adobe which record the modifications made in the kiva. There may have been a very shallow, semicircular or elliptical depression adjacent to deflector, but the feature was poorly defined at the time of excavation.

Judging by the floor features, the sequence of events in the kiva was probably as follows:

(1) Construction of the outer liner, deflector, foot drum, adobe floor, firepit, and the south sipapu, which is on an axis extending through the ventilator, deflector, firepit, and Niche 1 (outer liner).

(2) Partial collapse of the kiva, with damage to the original floor.

(3) Relining of the kiva, placement of the new adobe floor over a portion of the kiva, with the foot drum left open (the new floor brought up to the east side of the drum), remodeling of the firepit, closing of the south sipapu, and construction of the north sipapu on the axis extending through Niche 4 in the inner liner. Construction of the masonry deflector lateral may have taken place at this time.

(4) Construction of the ashpit, and the filling and covering of the foot drum with adobe.

(5) Filling of the ashpit, and reflooring of the west portion of the kiva. Floor adobe carried onto the rim of firepit collar and probably over the north sipapu.

Roof

Although the roof had burned and collapsed, a few small sections were still in place. Charred timbers still spanned the interpilaster spaces between Pilasters 5 and 6, and Pilasters 2 and 3. In the latter case, the wood rested on the northwest wall support, and slightly above it but still in place was a mass of brush and juniper bark. The bark had been torn into strips which averaged 0.15 foot wide.

Besides the in-place wood, there was a great mass of burned wood and charcoal in the kiva fill. As shown by both preserved wood specimens and wood impressions in chunks of roof adobe, the poles ranged in diameter from 0.2 to 0.5 foot. Impressions in the adobe also showed that shakes, 0.1 to 0.2 foot wide, were used in building the roof. The thickness of the adobe above the impressions was 0.05 to 0.2 foot, and the upper surface of some of the chunks was obviously part of a fairly smooth but slightly undulating plaza floor. The wood used in the roof was almost entirely juniper, with only one specimen of ponderosa pine found. Two specimens were identified as *Populus* sp.; and the identifiable brush was *Artemisia* sp.

The six pilasters provided the main support for the roof, with probably an assist from the north and west interpilaster wall supports. As shown by the height of the pilasters, the base of the cribbed roof would have been 5.2 to 5.3 feet above floor. The southeast corner of Room 69 was apparently built on the kiva roof, which indicates that the top of the roof was about 8 feet above the kiva floor. The roof height was probably the same for both Kivas M and S. If the original Kiva M roof collapsed, or was badly damaged, the two kivas may have been roofed simultaneously. I believe there is very little doubt that the two roofs burned at the same time.

Kiva N

Few kivas in Long House were built in an area which saw such extensive remodeling as that carried on in the location now occupied by Kiva N. Although the kiva appears to be essential to the support of the west side of Kiva Q, I believe it actually postdates the latter structure. Remnants of three walls not part of the kiva were found in the interwall spaces behind Pilaster 4 and west of the west interpilaster space, and behind the upper wall in the north interpilaster space (fig. 89). We can only guess at the number and kinds of structures that existed here before Kiva N was built.

The wall stub behind Pilaster 4 is seated on bedrock, and is a continuation of the fill–retaining wall which superficially appears to abut the south exterior wall of Kiva N. At one time it continued north, probably toward the southwest exterior corner of Kiva K. It could also have curved to the east toward Kiva Q or Room 87. Whether or not it served only to support the fill west of Kiva Q, or also supported more directly a series of rooms on the same level as Room 87, could not be determined. The top of the retaining wall was at least as high as the top of the pilasters in Kiva N, so either situation is possible. It is worth noting that the subfloor wall in Room 76, the west exterior wall of Kiva K, and the retaining wall extending into Kiva N are lined up with one another fairly well.

The wall stub behind the north wall was found only at the 4–to–6–foot level above floor, but no attempt was made to excavate this area because of the danger of undermining other walls. It would seem logical for this wall to have extended down to the same level as the floor of Room 75 (and Kiva N), and to have formed the east wall of a room immediately south of Room 75. The west wall of Room 75 also continues south into this interwall space and could easily have formed the west wall of this hypothetical room. The wall remnant immediately east of and paralleling the west exterior wall of Kiva N may be a continuation of the west wall of Room 75. It is about 6 feet long, footed at the same level as the west outer kiva wall, and extended up to about banquette level at the time it was excavated. This could easily be the west wall of a second, hypothetical room south of Room 75. At one time there may have been a J-shaped block of rooms extending around part of three sides of Kiva M, with doorways opening onto the courtyard formed by the kiva roof.

Kiva N is connected with Room 87 by a passageway, and both kiva and passageway may have been built when the room was remodeled and extended upward to at least two stories, possibly more. It is quite likely that Rooms 87 and 84 are part of the Kiva Q complex and were built at about the same time. The walls of Room 87 were originally of simple masonry, and the fill on which the room was built was supported either by a retaining wall or a block of rooms in the location now occupied by Kiva N. Later, probably when Kiva

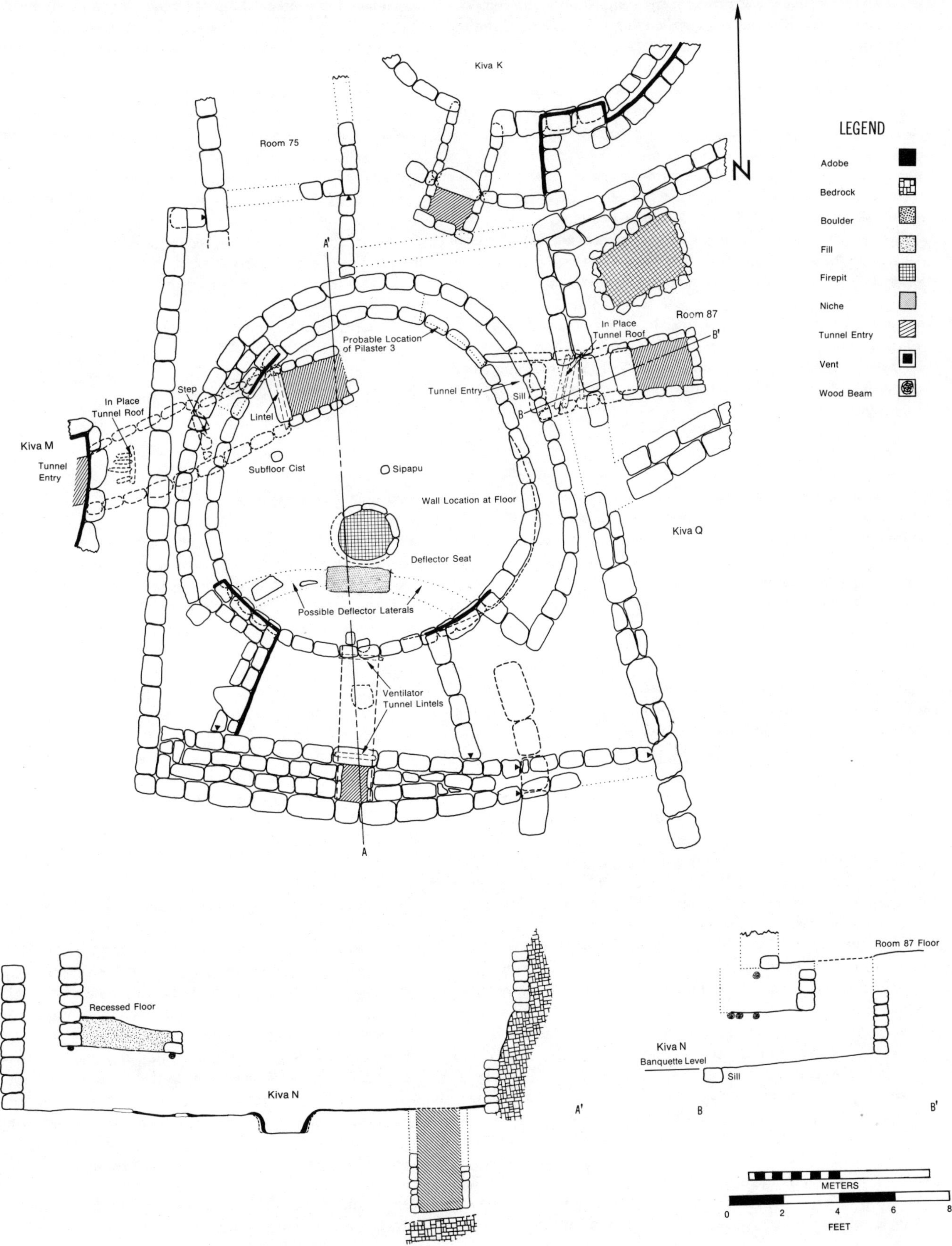

Figure 89. *Kiva N, plan and sections A-A′ and B-B′ (through tunnel between Kiva N and Room 87).*

N was built, a tunnel was run from the banquette to a hatchway in the floor of Room 87. The walls of the room were reinforced and the height of the dwelling was increased.

What function Room 87 served at the end is impossible to say. The floor was rather chopped up by the hatchway in the southwest corner and by a large firepit in the northwest corner. Both the south room wall, of compound masonry, and the doorway opening onto the roof of Kiva Q are probably features of the remodeled room. If so, they probably replaced similar features of simple masonry. Thus there may always have been a doorway from the Kiva Q area into the room. Whether or not it remained open after the tunnel was constructed into Kiva N cannot be determined because of partial collapse of the south room wall into Kiva Q. It is equally hard to know if inhabitants of the several stories of Room 87 used Kiva N.

The orientation of the kiva axis is very close to north–south, being rotated only slightly clockwise. In comparison with neighboring kivas, the orientation is closer to that of Kiva K than it is to the others. The orientation of Kivas M and S, and the intended orientation of Kiva Q, is considerably more to the northwest than in Kivas K and N.

Walls

Kiva N was one of the more poorly preserved kivas in Long House. Almost all of the west outer wall and possibly half of the south outer wall had collapsed. Also destroyed were the upper inner wall along the west side and a large portion of both upper and lower inner walls along the north and east sides.

Only along the west side of the kiva and along the western three–fourths of the south side are there true outer walls. The south wall of Room 75 and the inner walls of Kivas K and Q serve this purpose on the north side and on part of the east, but they are separated from Kiva N by a considerable amount of fill. All these walls except the south are built of simple masonry. The south wall is of composite masonry and consists of two simple, single–faced walls with a core of varying width (greatest at the ventilator shaft) composed of crude masonry and rubble. A major portion of the inner, simple wall forms the south wall of the recess.

The masonry in the west and south walls is composed of large, roughly dressed blocks. They are generally rectangular in the west wall but are rectangular and irregular in the south wall. There are few flat, pecked faces in either wall. The remnant of an earlier wall found just inside the west outer wall is practically identical to the latter in type of masonry used. It is not actually a part of the kiva, of course.

In the west interpilaster space, the upper, inner wall is missing except for one or two stones of the lowest course. It is partly preserved in the north and east interpilaster spaces and in the recess. What remains is single–faced, simple masonry, with smaller blocks than those in the outer walls. The stones are rather variable in size, shape, and surface finish. Most of them are roughly shaped but approach a rectangular outline on the exposed face. The faces are moderately flat but not pecked. There are remnants of a single, smoke–blackened, red adobe layer of plaster in the recess.

The masonry in the lower walls is also simple and single faced. The building stones are slightly smaller than those in the upper walls. Irregular to rectangular in shape, they are poorly to moderately well shaped. The faces are generally flat, with almost half showing evidence of having been pecked. No plaster remained on the lower walls.

Pilasters

There were only four pilasters. Pilaster 3 was entirely gone, but portions of the other three remained. The face of Pilaster 1 had collapsed except for the three rocks forming the lowest corner. Pilaster 4 was in place, but many of the building stones were somewhat eroded.

Judging by what little remains, the building stones used in the sides of the pilasters are about the same size as those in the upper walls but are better shaped and more uniform in size. The stones used in the pilaster faces were generally better dressed than those in the sides. The faces of the stones are fairly flat and rectangular in outline, and quite a few of them have been pecked. One of the stones in the northwest pilaster had been pecked and ground. There was no evidence of plaster except on the recess side of Pilaster 4, which still retained one to two layers of smoke–blackened red adobe.

The remaining pilasters were set back from the edge of the banquette between 0.1 to 0.2 foot. Pilasters 1 and 4 show a definite radial taper, and the part of Pilaster 2 still intact suggests a similar configuration.

Niches—None remaining.

Banquette

The banquette was entirely gone except for a narrow strip in front of the three remaining pilasters and in the recess. The height above floor probably averaged about 3 feet. The depth of the banquette was fairly uniform throughout, averaging just over 1 foot except in the southeast interpilaster space. Here the southern end was about 2 feet deep. The top of the banquette, present over much of the southern half of the recess, consisted of about 0.05 foot of hard–packed red adobe.

Recess

The recess has a straight back or south wall and straight, sharply converging sides. Like the recess in Kiva M, it is not symmetrical from side to side. It is about half a foot deeper on the east end than on the west. Only in the recess was any of the top of the banquette and wall plaster preserved, as mentioned above.

Tunnel to Room 87

A 5 1/2–foot–long tunnel leads from the north end of the east interpilaster space, at slightly above banquette level, to a hatchway in the southwest corner of the room floor. For the most part, the walls of the passageway consist of large vertical slabs. Small patches of crude masonry can be seen in several places, used apparently to fill in gaps around the slabs. The slabs are only roughly shaped, and the masonry is equally crude, composed of stones of varying size.

Except for three pole lintels, 0.07 to 0.08 foot in diameter, across the passageway near the west end, and a slab "lintel" across the east end and below the west side of the hatchway in Room 87, the tunnel roof had collapsed. About 1.3 to 1.4 feet above the pole lintels was at least one more pole, 0.1 foot in diameter, which served as a support for the west wall of Room 87. The upper wooden member, and one of the lower ones, can be seen in figure 90.

Hard–packed fill seems to have formed the poorly preserved floor of the tunnel. Two rocks were mudded in place at the kiva entrance to the tunnel and probably served as a low sill.

Ventilator

Both the construction and location of the ventilator are conventional. The well–shaped, pecked rocks which comprise the ventilator

Figure 90. *Upper and lower lintels above entrance to tunnel, Kiva N.*

Figure 91. *Hatchway, in floor of Kiva N, leading into tunnel to Kiva M.*

tunnel masonry at its mouth give way to more poorly worked stone about 1 foot in from the opening. The walls were constructed of both small rock masonry and large vertical slabs. In the vertical shaft, the walls consist of very crudely shaped stones, irregular in outline and with faces only roughly flat.

The roof was formed by closely spaced wood members set crosswise over the tunnel and resting on the walls. Only two were still in place, a split pole, 0.1 foot in diameter, and a juniper shake, 0.3 foot in diameter. Impressions in the dirt fill above the masonry walls marked the location of many other poles and shakes. Overlying the wood was a layer of adobe, 0.15 foot thick.

For the most part, the floor was merely packed, charcoal–flecked brown fill. In the first 2 feet of the tunnel, the floor consists of a layer of mixed red adobe and gray clay, which was used to cement three small slabs in place. Two extend part way out of the tunnel onto the kiva floor, and the third is centered in the tunnel about 2 feet from the mouth. Two of the stones have been worked, and one was probably part of a mano. About 3 ½ feet into the tunnel were two more stones, both manos, mudded in place on the floor with red adobe. These stones may have been used to raise the floor of the tunnel to the level of the upper kiva floor.

Deflector

No rock remained in place, but there were still impressions of a compound wall in the floor. The deflector was seated on, and embedded in, the lower kiva floor.

Floor

To the west of the deflector, the two levels of red adobe floor end at the possible location of a deflector lateral. On the west side of the deflector, at the edge of the upper floor (slightly farther north than the edge of the lower), are two rocks which were probably part of a west lateral.

The lower kiva floor directly overlies the subfloor fill (discussed later). It is hard–packed red adobe about 0.1 foot thick, and extends nearly across the kiva, covering the hatchway into the passageway leading to Kiva M. The location of the hatchway is shown in figure 91, taken during the stabilization of the kiva. The adobe also lips over into the firepit, thus forming the edges of the original pit.

The south end of this floor is roughly in line with the southern margin of the deflector and a southward curving arc extending from the deflector to the kiva liner. Apparently the area south of the deflector and probable laterals was used as an ashpit until the ashes reached the level of the top of the adobe floor, 0.15 foot above the floor of the ash area. The floor of the ventilator seems originally to have sloped down to the surface of the ash area.

The upper floor is also hard–packed red adobe, up to 0.1 foot thick, but covers only a portion of the original kiva floor. The area south of the deflector was filled in with flat slabs, small rock, and up to 0.2 foot of brown soil, so that its surface was level with the new floor. This second layer of adobe was placed over most of the southeast quadrant, part of the southwest quadrant, and possibly south of the firepit. It may have lipped over into the firepit, which was probably remodeled at this time.

The original firepit was a circular basin–shaped pit with adobe walls about 0.1 foot thick. When it was remodeled, vertical rock slabs were mudded into at least the north and east sides (none visible in the remainder of the pit) with a gray–brown, shaly clay. The firepit was then plastered inside with about 0.1 foot of red adobe. This construction rested on the compacted white ash of the partially filled original pit.

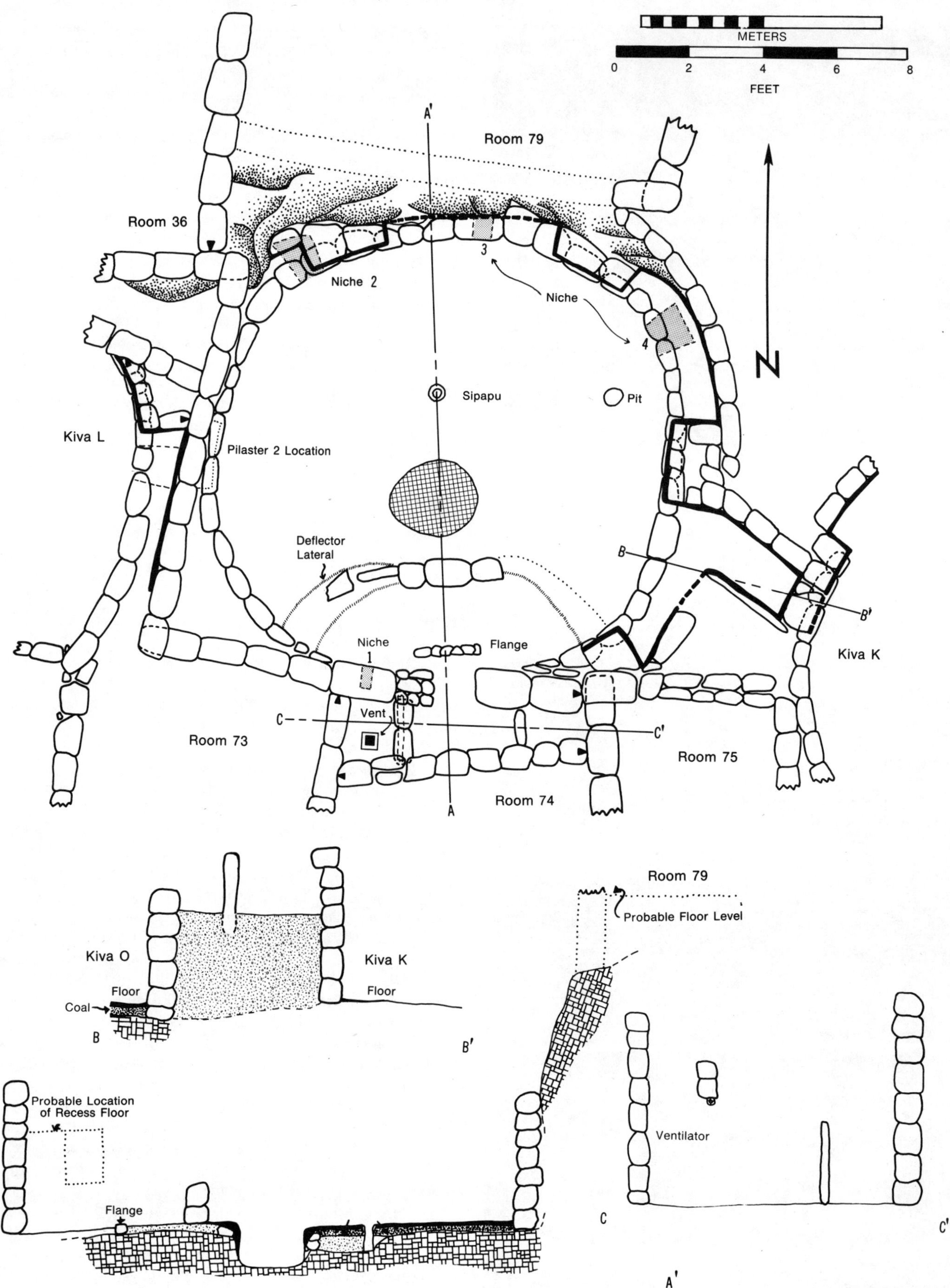

Figure 92. *Kiva O, plan and sections A-A', B-B' (through tunnel between Kivas O and K), and C-C'.*

The cylindrical sipapu appears to have been associated with both floor levels. The adobe lining extends upwards to form a collar, which is flush with the kiva floor. A small circular pit in the northwest quadrant was possibly a subfloor storage cist for small items. Being less than 0.2 foot deep, and far removed from the kiva axis, it did not appear to be a sipapu. It was filled with sterile yellow sand that was completely free of rock, adobe, or charcoal and was then covered with a patch of adobe 0.05 foot thick.

The only other floor feature was the tunnel hatchway, which has already been described with Kiva M. One additional feature must be noted: the liner of Kiva N extends over a portion of the masonry forming the tunnel hatchway. Although the entry *could* have been built under the liner after its construction, the superposition of walls suggests that the tunnel may have opened into a room that has been torn out and replaced with Kiva N.

Beneath the kiva floor is a deposit of trash at least 3 feet deep. It consists of building stone and unshaped stone, much of it burned, charcoal, small deposits of pure ash, and lenses of sterile yellow soil. Judging by the associated pottery, the lower part of the deposit is trash and debris from Pithouse 1, or from some Basketmaker III - Pueblo I occupation nearby. The rock and other debris in the upper part of the deposit are probably from the Pueblo III occupation and were used to level the fill below Kiva N and any structures which may have preceded the kiva.

Roof

With the exception of badly eroded beam fragments in the top part of the kiva fill, there was no direct evidence of the kiva roof. These fragments were too small to be of use in determining timber size and roof construction. To judge by the height of the footing, on fill, of a portion of the south retaining wall, and the back part of Pilaster 4, the base of what was probably a cribbed roof was most likely between 6 and 6.5 feet above the kiva floor. The section of the south retaining wall referred to seems to be nothing more than a roof–retaining wall. The top of the roof was probably 8 to 8.5 feet above the kiva floor, which would put it on about the same level as the rooftops of Kiva Q and Rooms 73–75.

Kiva O

Adjacent to Kiva K on the west, and possibly connected to it by a passageway at one time, is another kiva formed by extensive remodeling (fig. 92). Kiva O, like Kiva L, replaced several other structures and used existing masonry for parts of the kiva walls. It obviously postdates Rooms 73–75 and probably predates Kiva K. It may have been built before Rooms 36, 79, and 76, which were at least partly dependent for support either upon Kiva O or the rooms once present in the area now occupied by the kiva.

At first glance, the kiva axis appears to be alined with that of Kivas K and N. Actually it is skewed, as defined by the firepit and sipapu, and intersects the south outer kiva wall at an angle. The south wall of the recess–ventilator area is also skewed in relation to the wall immediately north of it (south outer kiva wall), possibly as a result of the orientation of the axis.

Walls

With the exception of the south recess wall, which was built across the north end of Room 74 and south of the original room wall, there are no true outside kiva walls. The north walls of Rooms 73–75 serve this function on the south side of the kiva, and the east wall of Room 92 acts both as an outer or dividing wall for Kivas O and L and as a backwall in at least two interpilaster spaces in the kivas. The upper and lower walls of Kiva K support the deep fill east of Kiva O, and the upper wall also forms the back of the L-shaped recess on the east side of Kiva O.

The south and west "outer" walls are generally composed of simple masonry, but they show a mixture of simple and compound masonry in a few places. They are faced on both sides. The building stones vary widely in size, shape, and surface finish. Most of the blocks tend to be rectangular, but there are very few pecked faces.

Although badly eroded in several places, at least part of the lower, inner wall is present around the entire perimeter of the kiva. The upper, inner wall is present in only about half of the kiva. On the north side, a large part of the upper wall is merely bedrock.

Masonry in the lower walls is simple and single faced. The building stones are smaller than those in the outer walls. They are roughly rectangular but vary considerably in size and shape. They are apparently better fitted than those in the upper wall. However, so little remains of the upper section that it is impossible to determine much about it. A large number of the exposed faces of stones in the lower liner have been pecked.

The base of the lower liner was plastered around most of the circumference of the kiva, and at least eight layers could be seen on the west wall. The three outermost layers were smoke–blackened red adobe, and the fourth layer can be described only as a coat of paper-thin whitewash. The four innermost layers were also smoked red adobe. Average thickness of the coats was 0.03 foot, and they ranged in thickness from that of the whitewash to 0.06 foot.

Pilasters

Although Kiva O can be considered a six-pilaster kiva, one pilaster is hardly conventional. Assuming that there *was* a Pilaster 1, it must have consisted of the existing section of the north wall of Room 74 just west of the ventilator. The remainder are free–standing structures of varying size. Pilasters 3–5 and part of Pilaster 6 are preserved well enough to show their construction. The position and size of Pilaster 2 are shown by traces of adobe and an unsmoked section of the kiva wall.

The pilaster masonry is similar to that in the lower, inner walls. The only traces of plaster found were remnants of two coats on Pilaster 3, each 0.01 foot thick or less. Pilasters 3–5 are set back from the edge of the banquette about 0.1 foot, and their sides show a slight radial convergence.

Niches

Only four niches were found in the remaining kiva walls. Well–preserved wall plaster around three of these made it very difficult to determine their construction. Niches 2–4 are rectangular, but Niche 1 (a questionable niche) is only approximately rectangular. Niche 1 is located just west of the ventilator, and is formed by horizontal and vertical building stones. Niches 2 and 3, in the northwest quadrant and on the kiva axis, respectively, are probably formed by horizontal blocks. Bedrock forms the backwall of Niche 2, and rocks of unknown size and adobe form the backwall of Niche 3. The inside corners of both are rounded with adobe.

Slightly more elaborate construction is seen in Niche 4, the largest of the group. Thin slabs comprise all four sides and the back, and, once again, the inside corners are rounded with adobe. Niches 1 and 4 are within 1 foot of the floor, and Niches 2 and 3 are close to the vertical center of the lower liner.

Banquette

The banquette is fairly well preserved in about half of the circumference of the kiva. Its height above floor is quite uniform, averaging about 3.2 feet, but its width varies considerably. This is especially true on the west side, where there was barely space enough to construct a very thin pilaster (front to back) and a shallow banquette.

An adobe lip extending from the lower wall onto the top of the banquette was present in a few places. In a few other places there were traces of an adobe floor remaining on the top course of the lower liner.

The L-shaped, southeast interpilaster space may be akin to similar features in Kivas K and R. There is a passageway from Kiva R to an adjoining room, and there may have been similar passageways leading out of Kivas K and O. The possibility of a Kiva K to Kiva O passageway has already been mentioned. A wooden shake protruding from the south side of Pilaster 5 could have been part of a lintel over the entrance to a tunnel, or part of the roof of the interpilaster space. It might even have been a portion of a shelf spanning the interpilaster space. The shake is 1.3 feet east of the pilaster face and 1.9 feet above the banquette.

Recess

A probable recess, as well as a ventilator, was created by modifying the north end of Room 74 (fig. 92). The east wall of Room 74 appears to have formed the west side of Pilaster 6. It is quite likely that all of the horizontal portion of the ventilator and the dead space immediately east of it were covered with poles or shakes and adobe to form the floor of a recess. Two building stones—resting on a single pole (but over the impression of a second)—marked the location of the west side of the recess and the east side of the ventilator shaft. None of the recess floor was in place, but it would have been at least 2.5 feet above the kiva floor.

Ventilator

Construction of the ventilator is similar to that in Kivas H and I, with the ventilator shaft to one side of the kiva axis. Since the feature was installed in the end of a room, there was a large but unnecessary open area incorporated in the ventilator tunnel. This was walled off, presumably to make the ventilator draw better. The masonry of the ventilator is merely that of the room walls forming it, and these have already been discussed. The exception to this is the east side of the vertical shaft, which is represented by only two building stones, with one pole and the impression of another immediately below the rocks.

Deflector

Only the lower courses of the simple masonry deflector were still in place. Its original height is unknown. The building stones are large and somewhat roughly shaped to provide a rectangular face. Surface finish varies considerably from stone to stone. The deflector is seated on bedrock.

Floor

Three layers of red adobe, each ranging in thickness from a thin plaster up to 0.1 foot, overlie a layer of coal throughout the entire kiva floor north of the deflector and laterals. Only the west lateral was actually constructed. Several flat slabs were placed on the floor in a curving line between the west end of the deflector and the kiva wall. Probably resting on the second adobe floor, they were plastered over by extending the adobe of the uppermost floor level over the top of the lateral. The abrupt termination of the adobe floors, on a curving line from the southeast corner of the deflector to the kiva wall, marks the possible location of the east lateral.

The coal layer, which consists of small chunks of coal and gray shale and of a few small rocks, is 0.05 to 0.1 foot thick. It was placed directly upon the bedrock floor of the rooms replaced by Kiva O. Two corrugated sherd disks, each 0.3 foot in diameter, were embedded in the surface of the coal layer near the east and west kiva walls. All four layers, three adobe and one coal, end at the inner edge of the lower kiva walls. They overlie the original bedrock floor, which extends back under the kiva walls.

The sipapu is subcircular in cross section and tapers inward slightly toward the bottom. The neck of a pottery jar (not identified as to type) forms the upper part of the sipapu. The feature was associated with the last adobe floor and may have been used—prior to the placing of the jar neck—with the other floors. The bottom of the sipapu was cut into the bedrock floor.

A circular hole, 0.5 foot in diameter and 0.15 feet deep, was cut into the second or middle adobe floor and extended down into the coal layer. It is in the northeast quadrant of the kiva, in the center of a possible mat impression, and is possibly analogous to a similar pit in the northwest quadrant of Kiva N. Owing to its location and shallowness, there is little likelihood that it is a sipapu.

The original firepit, roughly circular and basin shaped, had been remodeled at least three times. The pit was cut into bedrock and then rimmed with an adobe collar about 0.4 foot wide and 0.1 foot high. The lowest adobe floor was then carried over the collar into the firepit. When the other two adobe floors were laid down, they were also carried over the collar into the firepit. Finally, the north and east sides of pit were lined with masonry and another coat of adobe.

A masonry "flange" was set in trash fill, 0.3 foot in front of the ventilator opening and parallel to the kiva wall. It is 1.9 feet long and 0.3 foot wide, and it protruded about 0.1 foot from the fill. It may have supported a closing slab for the ventilator mouth.

Roof

Traces of adobe which outline Pilaster 2 indicate that the roof of Kiva O was probably at the same level as that of Kiva K. Thus the base of the cribbing would have been 6 to 6.5 feet above the kiva floor. Wood impressions in fragments of heavily burned roof adobe showed that the secondary roof timbers were at least 0.25 foot in diameter. The closing material consisted of shrub stems or branches about 0.05 foot in diameter and of shakes 0.08 to 0.2 foot wide. The thickness of the adobe above the wood impressions ranged from 0.05 to 0.35 foot.

Kiva P

Kiva P is one of two kivas in Long House that approach a rectangular shape (fig. 93). Unlike Kiva G, the other rectangular kiva, it has a conventional recess and ventilator.

Although the kiva is generally rectangular in shape, the north and south walls are not parallel. The west wall, consisting of a bedrock ledge and a short section of masonry, is irregular. Plainly, the kiva shows the results of being squeezed between Kiva U on the east and a rock ledge on the west.

Kiva P appears to postdate Room 82 and predate Room 83, but this cannot be proved because of extensive wall collapse on the east

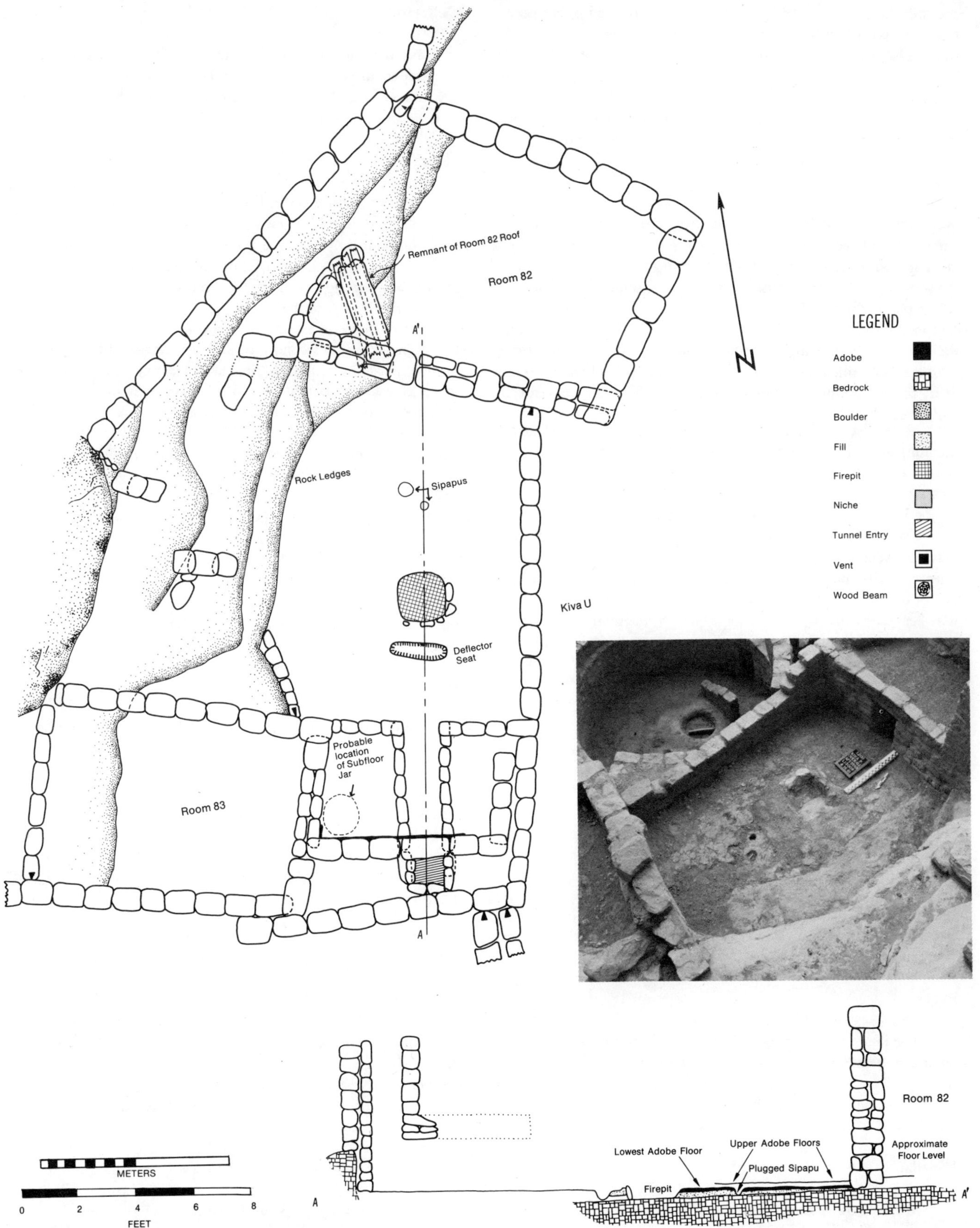

Figure 93. *(Inset) Kiva P, after stabilization.*

Figure 94. *Kiva P, plan and section A-A'.*

and west sides. It is quite possible that the kiva had either been a room or replaced one or two rooms that were associated with Kiva U. In any case, there is no question that Kiva U predates Kiva P, or was built at the same time, since the west walls of Kiva U support the fill and walls on the east side of Kiva P.

The orientation of the kiva axis is close to north northeast–south southwest, whereas that of Kiva U is closer to due north–south.

Walls

Only on the south side of the kiva were there true inner and outer walls. On each of the other three sides, one wall served as both inner and outer wall, with bedrock forming all but a small portion of the west wall. The west, east, and lower inner south walls were built of simple masonry. The east and west walls of the recess are compound masonry. Although the south outer and upper, inner walls are actually of simple masonry, above the banquette level they form a rubble–filled, composite wall on either side of the ventilator shaft. Several building stones in the south inner wall are vertically positioned slabs.

Generally, the blocks are fairly rectangular in shape and of medium size. The exposed faces are reasonably flat and quite a few of them were dressed by pecking. There are traces of smoke–blackened adobe plaster on the north wall, where there is at least one layer, and on the south recess wall, which is covered by at least two coats.

On the rock ledge just west of Kiva P are portions of three masonry walls (fig. 94). Two are apparently remnants of east–west oriented walls, but the third runs north–south and abuts the west end of the south wall of Room 82. It was not possible to determine whether these stubs are part of a structure or structures which postdated the kiva. The lowest wall is just barely high enough above the kiva floor to allow space beneath or even slightly above its footing for a low–roofed room. However, if the walls are part of structures that predate the kiva, why were just a few stones left in place? The bedrock ledge was undoubtedly leveled with fill after the kiva was roofed in order to provide a useable plaza.

Pilasters—none.

Niches—none.

Banquette

Other than the recess floor, which was probably between 2.5 and 3 feet above the kiva floor, there is no evidence for the existence of a banquette.

Recess

The floor of the rectangular recess was probably adobe, to judge by a few remaining traces. The concentration of sherds from a corrugated jar in the southwest corner of the recess suggests that there was a subfloor storage jar here. Similar features were found in Kivas J and U.

Ventilator

Much of the masonry in the side walls of the ventilator tunnel had collapsed. That which remained was similar in size, shape, and surface finish to the masonry of the lower, inner south wall of the kiva. With the exception of pole lintels still in place beneath the south wall of the recess, the roof of the tunnel was entirely gone. Loosely packed brown sandy fill formed the tunnel floor.

Deflector

No deflector remains, but there is a 2–foot–long depression in the floor about where the deflector should have been. The removal or destruction of a slab deflector, probably after abandonment of the kiva, would have left such a trough.

Floor

Directly above bedrock or sterile fill are four layers of adobe, two red overlying two gray. The total thickness of the four floor levels is about 0.4 foot. The floor apparently extended to the south wall in a strip immediately west of the firepit. Whether or not it was continuous directly south of the firepit could not be determined because the floor had been destroyed in this area. There was no evidence of deflector laterals or wing walls.

One sipapu, a second probable one, and the firepit are the only remaining floor features. A circular hole, only 0.3 foot deep in the lower gray adobe floor, and on the kiva axis, is undoubtedly a sipapu. A second circular hole, slightly larger in diameter, is probably associated with the upper gray adobe floor. Only 0.2 foot deep, and slightly west of the kiva axis, it is probably a second sipapu. Both sipapus were plugged with a gray shaly clay and were covered by the red adobe floors.

Bedrock formed the west side and about two–thirds of the floor of the circular firepit, with adobe forming the remainder of the floor. Both small rock masonry and small vertical slabs were used to form the other walls of the firepit. The upper red adobe floor may have extended over the lip and down into the firepit. The structure was not sufficiently well preserved to determine what modifications might have been made during the laying of the various floors.

Roof

Other than a few chunks of adobe, there is no clue to the construction of the roof. Nor is there any direct evidence of its height above floor. A probable remnant of the roof of Room 82, still in place in the southwest corner of the room, may match the kiva roof in height. The remnant if 5.9 feet above the room floor, and thus less than 1 foot above the base of the lowest wall remnant on the rock ledge west of Kiva P. The floors of the kiva and room are at about the same level, and the roofs were quite likely at the same height, to provide an uninterrupted plaza area.

Kiva Q and Room 93

It is safe to say that Kiva Q was more thoroughly dissected and studied than any other structure in Long House (fig 95). Its position is unique, both because of its propinquity to Pithouse 1 and its relationship to Room 60, the only circular tower in Long House. Other than Kiva I, it is the only kiva to have a part of the roof preserved (fig 96). Finally, it has been re-roofed to preserve several unusual floor features and the remaining section of wall decoration, while also serving as an in-place exhibit to show the original appearance of a courtyard formed by a kiva roof.

Kiva Q was cut through a work area or walking surface adjacent to, and obviously associated with, Pithouse 1. Although the evidence is not conclusive, the kiva appears to predate Kiva N. It definitely was built in conjunction with or before Room 60, whose north wall rests on part of the kiva recess and associated Room 93. There is little doubt in my mind that the kiva also predates Rooms 84–87, all of which rest on fill supported by the kiva walls. It is possible, though highly unlikely, that the somewhat dubious Rooms 85 and 86 could have been built before Kiva Q, with their west walls being removed at the time the kiva was constructed. If they were rooms, and were built after Kiva Q, a part of their walls must have rested on the kiva roof.

The doorways of Rooms 55, 56, 60, and 87, and possibly Room 84, opened onto the plaza restored through our reconstruction of the kiva roof. If Rooms 85 and 86 actually existed, we would then have had access to these two as well as to Rooms 60 and 87 from the plaza. Also adjacent to Kiva Q, and roofed at about the same level, is Kiva N.

Although the apparent axis of the kiva through the top of the ventilator shaft, firepit, and two sipapus is oriented roughly north–south, its actual orientation through the base of the angled shaft and the other features is rotated a few degrees counterclockwise from a north–south axis. The location of Room 60, the circular tower, forced the builders to shift the ventilator shaft opening to the west in order to clear the tower walls.

The location of the tower strongly suggests that it was built to form part of a kiva-tower complex, with a connecting tunnel. Unfortunately, as the inhabitants may have learned after erecting the one story tower, a large boulder underlies the tower floor on its north side. It seems likely that Room 93, perhaps intended only as a tunnel entrance, was retained as a small ceremonial or store room (fig. 97).

Walls

Before we knew what features, if any, occupied the area now known to be Kiva Q and Rooms 85 and 86, we designated it Area XIII. The wall forming the western limits of Area XIII funtioned primarily as a retainer for the roof of Kiva Q and would have been no more than about 3 feet high. It was seated on fill and built of large unshaped and crudely shaped stones.

With the exception of the pilasters, the upper walls were in very poor condition and many sections had fallen out. Only in the southwest and northwest interpilaster spaces was there any significant amount of masonry preserved. Generally the simple, single–faced masonry is crudely dressed, with no evidence of pecking. Large vertical slabs were intermixed with more conventional masonry in the recess and the southwest interpilaster space. Considerable mortar was used in laying up the rock, and in many places it was spread across the face of the walls to serve as plaster. All of the kiva and room walls were smoke blackened, including exposed sections of bedrock and the boulder underlying part of Room 60.

The manner in which the doorway in the south wall of Room 87 collapsed, coupled with the number of large building stones in the fill immediately below, strongly suggested that a tunnel may once have extended from the north interpilaster space—between Pilasters 3 and 4—of the kiva, under the doorway, and to the floor of Room 87. It was not possible to define such a feature during excavation, but collapsed walls would have obliterated much of the evidence of tunnel construction.

In the lower kiva walls, and where not covered by thick plaster, the masonry is also simple, single–faced and averages a little smaller in size. It varies from well shaped and rectangular to poorly shaped and irregular in outline. The faces are generally flat, and many show evidence of pecking.

Extensive sections of plaster are still intact, especially in the southern half, where there are remnants of a broad, red, horizontal band which once encircled the kiva immediately above the floor. Below Pilaster 6 there are at least 20 layers of plaster. On the upper part of the wall, above 1.6 feet, the tenth layer from the rock wall and the outermost four layers are white. The others are reddish or brownish adobe, and all except the outermost layer have been smoke blackened.

On the lower part of the wall, below the visible paint line, the situation is more complex. At 1.3 feet above floor, the colors of the plaster layers, starting from the outside, are red, yellow, white, red, white, and brown from then on. At 1.2 feet, the sequence omits the outer white layer. Below 1.2 feet, the inner white layer disappears. The red plaster is brightly colored, not the usual dull adobe red. There was no indication in the large sections of plaster removed that designs had been painted on the kiva walls.

Pilasters

The six pilasters are conventional in all respects. Although Pilasters 3 and 4, and the bench adjacent to them on either side, had slumped about 0.8 foot from their original position, the pilasters themselves were well preserved throughout their full 3–foot height. Pilaster 5 had also settled, but only about 0.1 foot.

Slumping may reflect construction of a second or third story for Room 87, with tremendous thrust being transmitted to the roof and Pilasters 3 and 4 of Kiva Q. The wall supporting the two pilasters obviously failed to hold up under the pressure against them, but the collapse was not total and the top of the banquette had been repaired. Masonry roof or wall supports such as we found in Kivas M, R, and S were apparently not deemed necessary. The settling of Pilaster 5 could indicate that hypothetical Rooms 86 and 85 were actually built, probably to only one story, and the additional pressure contributed to the thrust against Pilasters 4 and 5.

All the pilasters are similar in their masonry, which consists of building stones that are larger on the average than those used in the lower walls, as well as having the exposed faces more rectangular and better finished. Unlike the pilasters in many other kivas, these showed little if any radial taper. The sides of each pilaster, including Pilasters 3 and 4 before slumping, were roughly parallel. All the pilasters except number 5 were set back from the edge of the banquette about 0.1 foot. Pilaster 5 was recessed 0.15 foot on the north side and 0.25 foot on the south.

The number of layers of plaster found on the face and sides varied greatly from one pilaster to another. The faces were most frequently replastered, with the number of layers ranging from three to 13. On the sides, the range is from one to four. The layers average less than 0.01 foot thick, and the total thickness varies from this figure to about 0.03 foot. All layers are smoke–blackened, reddish–brown adobe, and none shows evidence of designs.

Niches

The four niches are in the lower walls, with three on the north side. The joints between components of the niches were plastered with adobe to make a smooth, curved surface, but there was no overall plastering of the niche interiors.

In cross section, Niche 1 is square at the base but domed on top. A slab forms the base of the niche, and building stones or slabs the remaining sides, the top, and the back wall. The niche is located in the north wall about halfway between floor and bench, and is lined up along the kiva axis with the two sipapus, firepit, and horizontal ventilator tunnel.

Niche 2, in the north wall below Pilaster 4, is an integral part of the shrine and is discussed more fully under this heading. The niche is rectangular and extends about 0.15 foot below the floor of the shrine. Slabs form the top, bottom, and right side of the niche, and probably the left as well. The back is formed by a rock and red

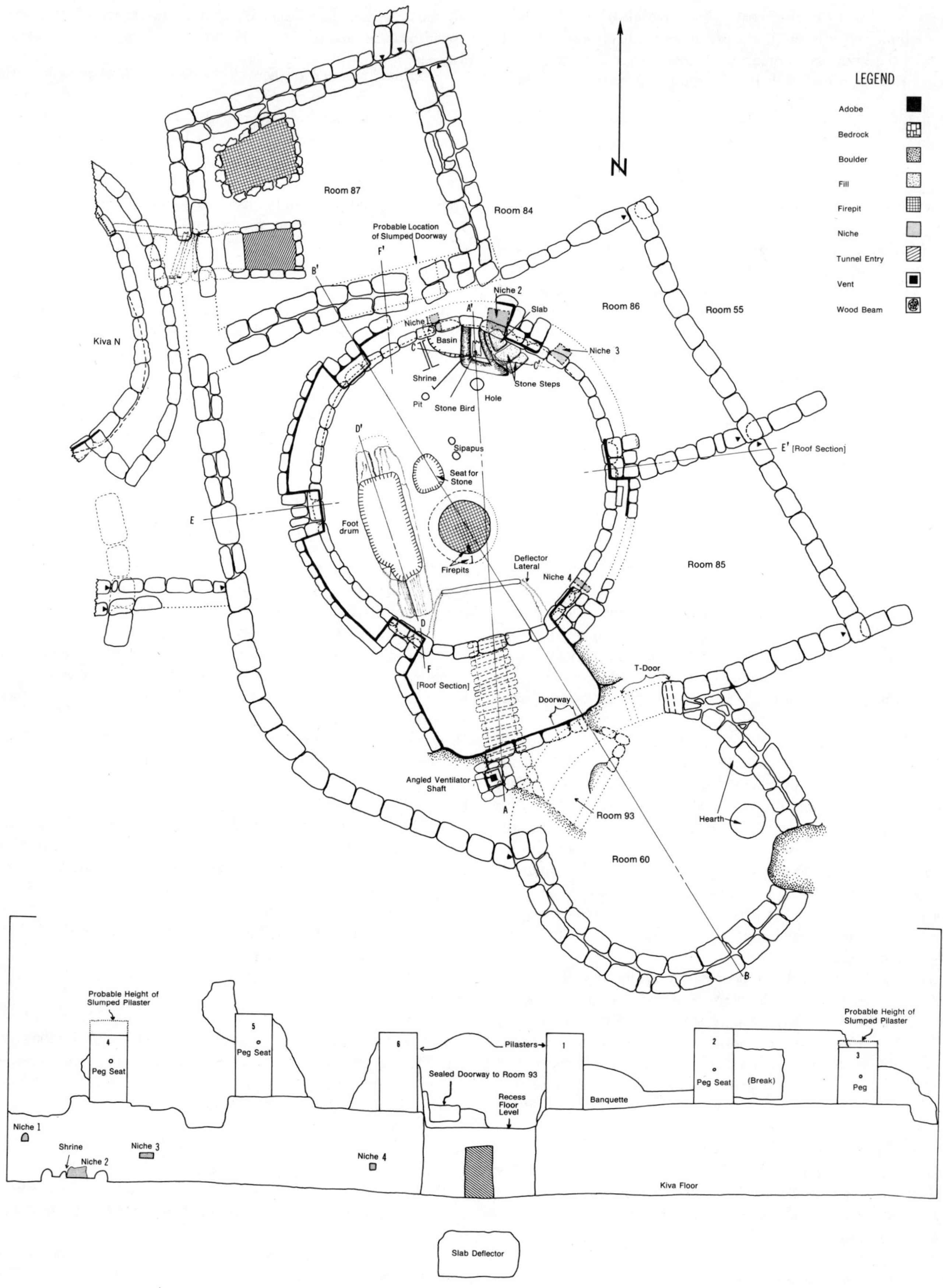

Figure 95. *Kiva Q, plan, roll-out elevation, and sections A-A', B-B', C-C', D-D', E-E', and F-F'.*

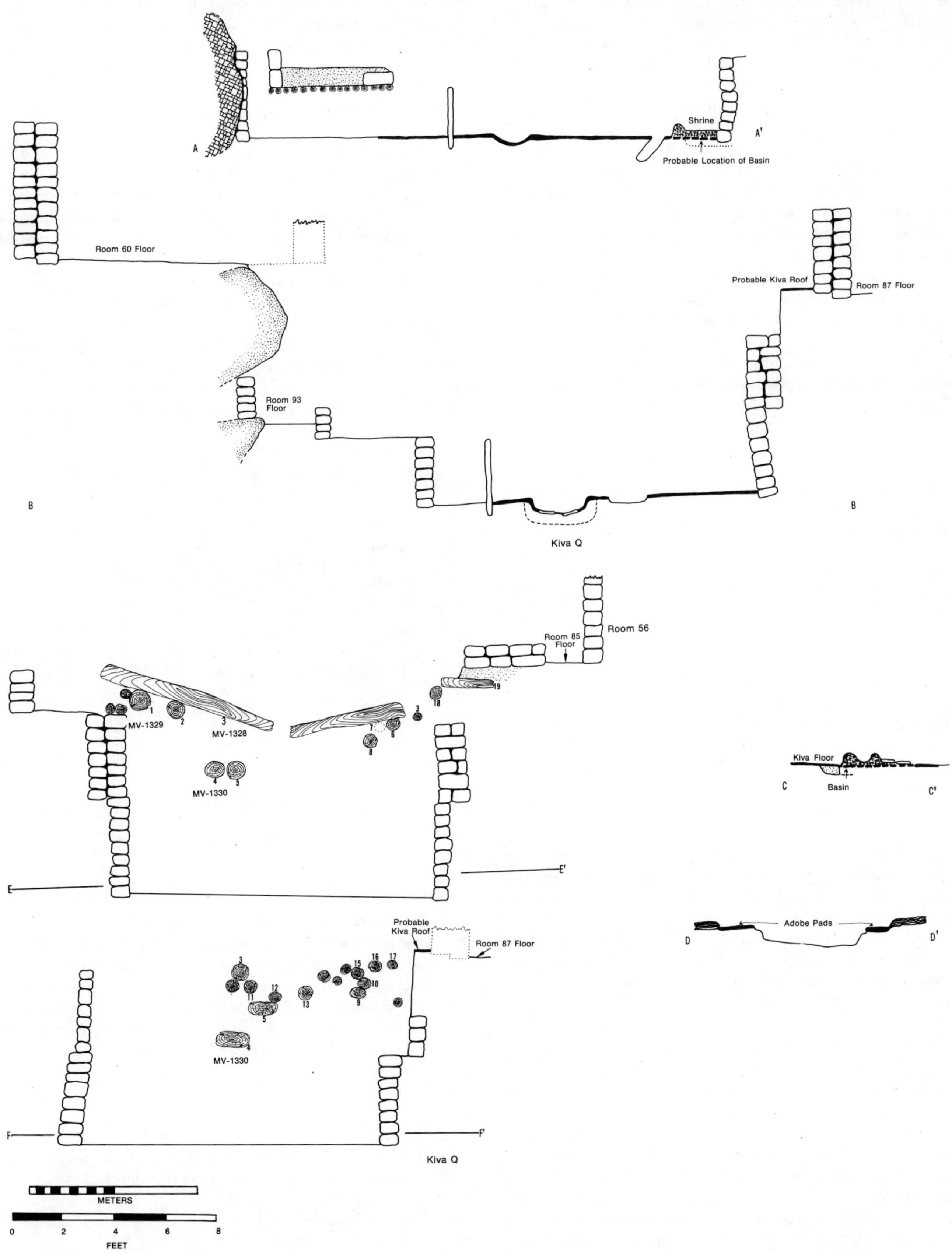

Shrine
A
A'
Probable Location of Basin
Room 60 Floor
Probable Kiva Roof
Room 87 Floor
Room 93 Floor
B
B
Kiva Q
Room 56
Room 85 Floor
MV-1329
MV-1328
MV-1330
Kiva Floor
Basin
C
C'
E
E'
Probable Kiva Roof
Room 87 Floor
Adobe Pads
D
D'
MV-1330
F
F'
Kiva Q
METERS
0
2
4
6
8
FEET

adobe which, along with the side slabs, apparently rest on the bottom slab. This, in turn, forms the roof of the cist below.

Niche 3, located about 1 foot above the floor in the northeast quadrant, may once have been several times its present size. Now 0.55 foot wide and 0.23 foot high, the niche may have been about 0.8 foot wide and 0.7 foot high. The niche is rectangular and is formed by slabs on the sides and back. A vertical slab to the left of the niche and the apparent extension of the slabs forming the top and right side suggest a larger original niche. Possibly pressure from the construction above caused the buckling and settling of Pilaster 4. This, in turn, may have caused the niche roof to buckle, making it necessary to repair and possibly remodel it to withstand the additional pressure.

Niche 4 is only roughly square in cross section, mainly because of thick adobe mortar across the top and on the east side. A slab forms the west side and a building stone the base. The niche ends in small-rock rubble about 0.8 foot from the face of the kiva wall, suggesting that originally it may not have been as deep as it is now. The niche is located in the southeast quadrant, less than a foot above the floor.

Wall Pegs

There were once pegs in the face of Pilasters 2 to 5, but only the antler peg in Pilaster 3 remains. In Pilaster 2, the peg seat is 1.65 feet from the top of the pilaster masonry, 0.77 foot from the south side, 0.04 foot in diameter, and angles back about 10° to the south to a depth of 0.12 foot. The antler peg in Pilaster 3 is broken off flush with the pilaster face. It is 1.05 feet from the pilaster top, 0.75 foot from the west side, 0.06 foot in diameter, and angles about 25° to the east. The peg seat in Pilaster 4 is 1.04 feet below the pilaster top and 0.65 foot from the east side. The size of the opening is about 0.03 by 0.08 foot, and the hole angles back about 25° to the west to a depth of 0.2 foot. The fourth peg was in Pilaster 5, 1.23 feet from the top and 0.65 foot from the south side. The size of the oval opening is about 0.03 by 0.05 foot, and it extends straight in 0.1 foot.

Shelf

On the north side of Pilaster 2 are two possible pole seats, one 0.11 foot in diameter and the other 0.25 foot. They are 0.35 and 0.2 foot deep, respectively, and angled out toward the west side of Pilaster 3. Possibly they supported one end of a pole shelf, which could then have been covered with brush and adobe. Although there was no evidence of similar seats in Pilaster 3, we can theorize that after the pilaster slumped the shelf was removed and the seats plastered over.

Banquette

Prior to the slumping of several pilasters, the banquette encircled the kiva at an average height of 3.5 feet. Except in the northeast interpilaster space, where it was entirely gone, the top of the banquette was composed of the top of the building stones that form the uppermost course of the inner kiva wall, and of hard-packed red adobe, ranging from 0.02 to 0.05 foot thick. The width of the banquette was fairly uniform within three of the interpilaster spaces and reached a maximum of 1.5 feet. In two other interpilaster spaces, it varied from 1.0 to about 1.5 feet wide.

In the northwest and north interpilaster spaces there was some remodeling after the pilasters slumped. In the former, a 0.6–foot depression against Pilaster 3 was packed with small unshaped rock and red adobe to restore the banquette top. In the latter case, similar depressions against Pilasters 3 and 4 were filled with thin-slab masonry and a rock-and-adobe packing, respectively, to level the top of the banquette.

Recess and Room 93

Because of the exposed rock faces which form part of its walls, the recess is rather ill shaped for a late Pueblo III kiva. The side walls not only curve in to the back wall of the recess, but they also parallel one another at an angle to the kiva axis. The recess is also deeper on the west side by about 0.5 foot. The uppermost courses of masonry above the ventilator tunnel were missing, as was the floor of the recess. The kiva wall forming the face of the recess below the original level of its floor was offset to the south about 0.2 to 0.3 foot.

The unique feature of the recess was a small room which once opened off the south recess wall. The small 1–foot wide doorway between the two had been deliberately sealed. The slab forming the east door jamb is 1.2 feet high, thus providing the information needed for its reconstruction. This was undertaken primarily to

Figure 96. *Part of roof of Kiva O* uncovered, in situ.

stabilize Room 60, whose north wall overlies Room 93.

The masonry of the short south wall of Room 93 is the same as that in the north wall it shares with the recess and in the other upper kiva walls: simple, single-faced, and crudely dressed without pecking. A veneer of small, crudely shaped masonry was placed against part of the exposed bedrock or boulder on the east side of Room 93. There was no evidence of plaster in the room, but all walls and exposed rock were smoke blackened.

Ventilator

Although the masonry is the same as that in the lower kiva walls for the first 2.5 feet of the horizontal tunnel, the average block length is about 1.0 foot on the east side of the tunnel and 0.6 foot on the west. South of this point, the masonry is more irregular in construction and shaping, and a large vertical slab was used on the east side for part of the wall.

The shaping of the building stones is good in the first 1.5 feet (west side) and 2.5 feet (east side) of the tunnel, with the blocks forming the sides of the tunnel mouth being the best shaped. The stones are rectangular, with faces either pecked or naturally flat. The

Figure 97. *Kiva Q, below, and adjacent Room 60 (circular tower), above, looking south-southeast.*

northeast corner stone of the tunnel, at the tunnel-kiva wall junction, is rounded on the corner; the northwest stone is grooved, possibly to accommodate an irregularly shaped ventilator cover–slab.

The tunnel roof consisted of poles laid east–west across the tunnel. The poles are 0.15 foot in diameter and are spaced about 0.3 foot apart, center to center. The northernmost pole is practically flush with the inner kiva wall and is one of four running beneath the lintel slab over the tunnel entrance. The roof extended to the vertical shaft, with two poles placed directly under the north shaft wall.

A mat of gray shaly clay, 0.1 foot thick, mixed with adobe, sterile yellow soil, and charcoal, formed the level floor of the tunnel for its first 0.5 foot. It also extends slightly under, as well as lipping up onto, the lower corner stones of the opening. The rest of the ventilator floor was apparently compacted (not hard–packed) brown fill, containing bits of charcoal and small rock.

The masonry of the vertical shaft was rather rough, judging by a few remnants of the west and south walls. The building stones vary greatly in size, and there is no indication that the surface was smoothed by pecking. The east and west walls, which the ventilator shares with Room 93 and the kiva recess, respectively, display the same kind of masonry as these features.

Deflector

A single, large vertical slab, set on edge in the kiva floor to a depth of about half a foot, constituted the deflector. The slab had been roughly shaped by chipping on the west end, by rather limited chipping and pecking on top, and by grinding of a north face that was already quite smooth.

Floor

At the time the kiva was abandoned, the floor consisted of hard–packed red adobe, 0.01 to 0.1 foot thick, which lipped up onto the kiva walls. The adobe also humped up slightly at either end of the deflector to form two ridges or deflector laterals, 0.05 foot thick. The structures are curved slightly, and extend from the ends of the deflector toward the opposing offsets in the kiva wall below each side of the recess. The adobe forming the laterals appeared to end abruptly at the side nearest the ventilator. It curved down onto another layer of adobe which terminated at the line of contact with a gray clay floor. This latter floor occupies the central part of the area between

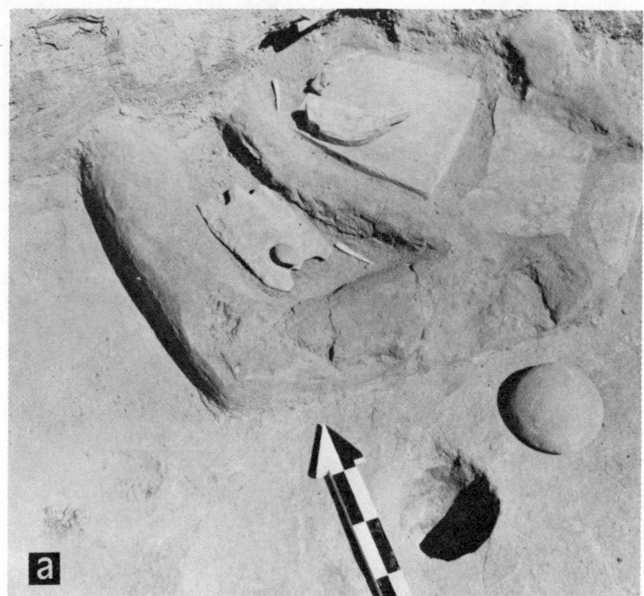

Figure 98. *Floor shrine, Kiva Q: a, artifacts and slab in place on top; b, after excavation of Niche 2 and subfloor cist; and c, artifact assemblage*

the deflector and the kiva wall, as well as forming the ventilator tunnel floor for about half a foot.

Subfloor testing showed not only that there was but one floor level around the periphery, but that there were several levels elsewhere. Full excavation of the entire floor to sterile soil and rock revealed an extremely complex maze of floor levels, floor patches, and plastered-over features. The three primary stages in the construction of the floor are described briefly below. Each "floor" has been given a numerical designation as well, to simplify its identification in the discussion of exposed and concealed floor features.

Floor I: This is the original kiva floor, of red adobe, with no evidence of patching.

Floor II: Above Floor I are a series of partial floors too scrambled to delimit clearly. They consist mainly of patches and small sections of adobe laid down during successive remodelings of the firepit, sipapu, and footdrum. Red adobe was the main material used, with gray clay being reserved for small patches.

Floor III: The topmost layer of red adobe, which was mentioned above as forming the final kiva floor, was placed to cover the footdrum and other features, and to provide a new firepit facing. It, too, is no more than a series of patches.

In addition to the deflector laterals, only three floor features were exposed when the kiva floor was cleared of fill: shrine, firepit, and sipapu. Once Floor III was removed, we found a footdrum, a second sipapu, a shallow basin beneath part of the shrine, a small pit of unknown use, and a possible rock seat. The various features will be described and then the probable construction sequence will be discussed.

The most prominent (and unique) floor feature was an adobe and rock "shrine," roughly 3 feet wide by 1.5 feet deep, front to back (fig. 98a and b). The structure was built against the north wall, just east of the kiva axis and partly below Pilaster 4. Ridges of red adobe, which abut the north kiva wall, form most of the shrine. They rise a maximum of 0.3 to 0.35 foot from the kiva floor, and range in width from 0.35 to 0.55 foot. Whether they were built on the adobe floor (Floor I), or form an integral part of it, was not determined. Depth of the shrine floor below the top of the dividing ridges is 0.25 to 0.28 foot in the west section, and 0.1 foot (at the step) to 0.2 foot in the east section. The height of the lower stone slab step is 0.1 foot, and its depth is 0.32 foot; the height of the upper step is 0.13 foot. With the exception of the upper step, the floor of the shrine consists of brown fill.

Further probing opened up Niche 2 behind the shrine and a subfloor cist which extended back under the thin slab forming the niche floor (fig. 98b). A slab formed the north part of the cist floor, and brown fill the rest. The sides are red adobe. It is very likely that Niche 2 is part of the original kiva construction, and was later incorporated in the shrine complex. The well-shaped slab covering the cist was ground on all edges and the exposed face. It was not fitted to any specific place but was merely on the cist opening.

The artifact assemblage from the shrine is shown in figure 98c. The artifacts are described, under the categories to which they belong, in chs. 5 and 6 of this report. The bird-like sandstone concretion (lower left), the large piece of petrified wood (upper left), the two bone awls, and the hematite concretion near the upper awl were all on the shrine floor. The beautifully smoothed chert nodule, which could be a crude bird effigy, was in the cist below the slab, accompanied only by a small stone flake. The chert nodule is naturally shaped but could have been smoothed by continual handling or hand rubbing. The balance of the items—two hematite concretions, three waterworn cobbles, a chipped stone artifact, and a small flake which may be intrusive—were in Niche 2 proper. The chert nodule may have been a prized possession of the Puebloans using the kiva, but we have no way of knowing what, if any, religious or ceremonial significance it possessed. This is also true of the shrine itself.

Immediately west of the shrine, and extending under the western half, was an oval basin, 0.25 foot deep and possibly 3 feet long, which had been cut into sterile yellow soil. It extends out 1.2 feet from the kiva wall, which was built on native soil in the basin, and 1.6 feet west of the shrine. Perhaps as much as a third of the depression is under the kiva wall, to judge by the curve of its sides, and a similar portion is under the shrine. The basin was filled with a brown trashy soil and was completely covered by the red adobe floor (Floor I). It was not determined whether the basin reflects an aborted attempt to build a shrine or some other feature, or belongs to an occupation level predating the kiva.

from all parts of shrine.

The firepit had been remodeled at least five times, the first two rather insignificant in that the overall shape was changed very little. The construction of the south side of the firepit, with series of six "firepits" indicated, is shown in figure 99. The 1–foot–long scale lies on Floor I, between the firepit and the deflector.

Firepit 1 was approximately 2.8 feet in diameter and 0.9 foot deep. Its red adobe lining (burned orange, as were Firepits 2, 3, and 4) is a continuation of Floor I. A new rim was added in Firepit 2, and this covers a layer of ash extending north from the deflector to feather out on the firepit rim. A third rim was added to Firepit 3, also over a layer of ash. The thick adobe wedge not only forms the rim of the firepit but also serves as a retainer for the ash lens. Firepit 3 corresponds to IIa, the lower part of the second floor.

Firepit 4 was remodeled more extensively. The pit was relined to a depth of 0.5 to 0.6 foot, with a thin layer of adobe overlying a hard–packed layer of ash. The new lining was carried over the wedge forming Firepit 3's rim to feather out on the floor.

Firepit 5 produced a major change which resulted in a smaller and much shallower pit, 1.8 to 2.0 feet in diameter and 0.5 foot deep. The floor of the pit is formed by at least six stone slabs set in red adobe and angled down slightly toward the center. The adobe is also carried upward to the rim, where it thickens out into a collar.

Figure 99. *South side of the firepit in Kiva Q, with succession of six firepits indicated.*

Figure 100. *Rectangular foot drum, Kiva Q.*

Firepit 5 corresponds to Floor IIb, the upper part of the second floor. Firepit 6, the final form, added a new rim which dropped off abruptly into the pit. This made its sides steeper and reduced its diameter slightly. Firepit 6 is merely a continuation of the adobe of Floor III, the topmost level.

Sipapu 1, the northern of the two and concealed during remodeling, was a feature of Floor I and extended into the sterile yellow soil below. It is slightly oval in cross section, unlined, and has a concave bottom. One side of the shaft is vertical, and the other curves in slightly at the bottom. Adobe was built up around the mouth of the opening to form a collar. A plain white sherd, probably from a black–on–white jar, is embedded flush with the floor in the collar and forms part of the rim. The sipapu was filled with a mixture of adobe, sterile soil, and cultural fill, and then covered with a thin veneer of red adobe.

Sipapu 2, located 0.5 foot southeast of Sipapu 1, center to center, extends from Floor IIb (?) into sterile soil. It is roughly cylindrical in shape, is lined in places with a thin veneer of red adobe, and has a concave bottom. A white rim sherd, probably from a black–on–white jar, was embedded flush in the slightly raised adobe collar. The collar extended to the north to form the adobe layer covering Sipapu 1.

Like the two sipapus, the small floor pit in the northwest quadrant of the kiva was cut through an adobe floor (Floor I, in this case) into sterile soil. Although 0.3 foot in diameter, both its depth of 0.25 foot and its location make it unlikely that the pit ever served as a sipapu. It was filled with material identical to that found in Sipapu 1, and then covered with adobe (probably Floor IIb).

The rectangular foot drum (fig. 100) is similar to the one found in Kiva M. The resonating chamber was cut into the sterile soil and rock deposits underlying the kiva. No masonry was used in its construction. The two red adobe pads, one at each end, rest on native soil. While the adobe was still plastic, planks (probably two, as was most likely the case in Kiva M) were placed across the pit, with their ends on the pads. Although none of the wood was preserved, the resulting wood impressions in the adobe still could be seen very clearly. The adobe of Floor IIa was then brought up to the edge of the wood. The seating was apparently quite shallow, perhaps only 0.1 foot below floor level, so the top of the planks may have extended above floor. When use of the foot drum was discontinued, the trench was first filled with hard–packed chunks of adobe (roofing material), small rock, and cultural trash. The adobe pads were covered with a mixture of yellow soil and trash, and the entire drum was covered with the 0.15–foot–thick red adobe of Floor III.

Adjacent to both the firepit and the foot drum was a roughly oval pit that was probably associated with Floor IIa. The floor of the pit is native soil covered with a thin veneer of red adobe. Its depth was 0.15 foot below the rim of Firepit 3 and the top of the intentional fill in the pit, and was even less below the level of Floor IIa. Although it may have been an ashpit, its shallowness and lack of ash deposits make this unlikely. The depression may have been the seat for a large stone (anvil), such as was found in essentially the same position in Kiva M. The pit was filled with hard–packed adobe and was covered with the 0.1–foot–thick Floor IIb.

The probable construction sequence and interrelationship of features is described below

(1) Floor I, 0.05 to 0.2 foot thick, was laid over the entire kiva floor. It was associated with four floor features: Firepit 1, Sipapu 1, the small floor pit, and probably the shrine.

(2) The firepit was remodeled, with Firepit 2's collar feathering out on Floor I over the site of the foot drum and the shallow pit or rock seat.

(3) The foot drum was cut through Floor I and the collar of Firepit 2. Firepit 3 was constructed, with the adobe collar extending to the east edge of the foot drum and down over the broken edges of the collars of Firepits 1 and 2. The adobe pads, which appear to have been placed at the same time, curve up smoothly to the edge of the depression. This level, designated Floor IIa, extended out over Floor I to form a low, incipient lateral at the east end of the deflector. There may have been a similar ridge at the west end, but it was not detected.

(4) Firepit 4 was created, with its adobe collar feathering out on the rim of both the foot drum and the possible rock seat. There was no construction west or south of the foot drum at this time.

(5) Several major changes accompanied the building of Firepit 5. The possible rock seat was filled and covered with Floor IIb, which also extended around the foot drum and thus raised the height of its collar. The new floor was present only in large patches west of the foot drum. Floor IIb was carried over the incipient lateral or laterals and south of the deflector, where it consisted of both gray clay in front of the ventilator opening and red adobe at either side. Also, at this time, Sipapu 1 was probably sealed by extending Floor IIb to within about 2 feet of the north kiva wall.

(6) With the construction of Firepit 6, the foot drum—and probably the small pit in the northwest quadrant—were covered by Floor III. The final deflector laterals were formed as part of this floor, and the preceding level (Floor IIb) was patched where necessary. The work was done so smoothly that there was no trace of subfloor features or obvious patches in the floor.

Roof

The large section of kiva roof preserved in the upper 4 feet of fill was an entirely unexpected bonus. Although it was not preserved nearly as well as that in Kiva I, it gave us our second chance to study original kiva roofing.

As figure 96 shows, the roof was still more or less in place, having slumped only slightly onto the supporting fill. The nature of the fill indicates that there were at least two kinds of material included: building materials from neighboring rooms which collapsed into the south side of the kiva; and water–deposited sediments washed in from the mesa top. There were no building stones or waterlaid sands on the kiva floor, which suggests that the collapse came from abandonment. On the other hand, several of the items left in the shrine suggest an abrupt departure from the kiva and perhaps from the pueblo.

The construction of the roof obviously started with cribbing of logs, as can be seen in the plan drawing (fig. 101). There may have been only two levels, however: one from pilaster to pilaster, the next from mid–point to mid–point of first–tier logs on either side of a pilaster. (Note this arrangement at Pilaster 2.)

Long beams were then laid roughly east–west across the kiva on top of the second tier of cribbed logs. The two timbers angling southeast from Pilaster 3 in figure 101 may have served as braces for the roof. They appear to have been seated at the level of the upper cribbed logs and in the wrong position to have only fallen out of a position parallel to the other cross–timbers. It is interesting that practically all of the wood used in the kiva roof was juniper, which quite likely was chosen because it could withstand weathering better than pinyon pine.

Removal of the roof and upper fill revealed wood impressions—and, of course, the angle at which the logs were placed—in red adobe pads on top of each pilaster (fig. 101). The impressions also suggest that smaller diameter poles were used as wedges to level the timbers or help hold them in place. Several objects which appeared to have been placed between the cribbed roof beams were recovered during roof removal. A tchamahia was found on top of the 0.05 foot–thick plaster covering the lower timber across the north interpilaster space, about halfway between Pilasters 4 and 5. A second tchamahia, a worked stone, and four bone awls with points to the north were found in the debris slightly to the east and above the first tchamahia.

Chunks of adobe bearing well–preserved wood impressions were found in the fill about 1.5 feet above floor. They provide a little more information about closing material in the roof, assuming they are from Kiva Q. The impressions are of brush stems, 0.08 to 0.09 foot in diameter. The thickness of the adobe above the impressions is about 0.2 foot, and the top surface was too rough ever to have been a well–smoothed or worn walking surface.

Although this report is concerned with the excavation rather than the stabilization of Long House, I believe a description of the new roof installed by Al Lancaster and Al Decker would be pertinent to the discussion.

No attempt was made to restore the roof as it was originally. We lacked the information for that, especially for the hatchway. Instead, a stylized kiva roof was built, with a square hatch above the firepit. Peeled juniper poles were used, and all saw–cut ends were concealed by adobe or closing material.

The first layer of the cribbed roof, three logs wide, was placed on the six pilasters (fig. 102a). The original builders probably used only two large or three small logs here. Two more layers of cribbed logs, rather than the total of two apparently used originally, were built on the lowest tier before the long cross–members were put in place (fig. 102b). Logs of varying lengths were then used to close the roof above the room itself, the recess, and the interpilaster spaces (fig. 102c). The main cross–members run north–south in our reconstruction, rather than east–west as in the prehistoric roof.

Once all major openings were covered with logs, a thick layer of juniper bark and hard–packed dirt sealed the roof against wind and rain (fig. 102d). A slab collar was placed around the hatchway above the wooden frame, and the roof was brought to the proper level by repeated filling with dirt, wetting, and packing (fig. 102e). Finally, on the inside, all the cracks between the logs were plastered with red adobe, and the logs were stained with roofing tar dissolved in gasoline to remove the shiny new look (fig. 102f).

Eighty timbers, 8 feet long, and 20 timbers, 10 feet long, were used in re roofing Kiva Q. Although fewer logs were used originally, the basic techniques used by the Puebloan builders were similar to ours. Without our modern tools—power saw, steel ax, and shovel—it was no easy task for the prehistoric Indians.

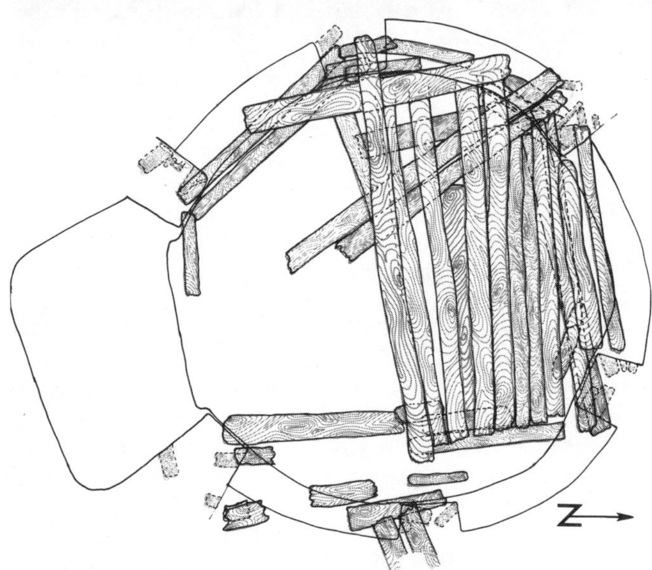

Figure 101. *Plan of original roof showing cribbing and beam impressions on top of pilasters, Kiva Q.*

Figure 102. *Restoration of the roof of Kiva Q: a, first layer of cribbed logs on the six pilasters; b, two additional layers of cribbed logs; c, logs of varying lengths used to close the roof; d, layer of juniper bark and packed earth; e, slab collar placed around hatchway; and f, interior cracks plastered with adobe and logs stained with roofing tar.*

b

c

e

5
4
3
2
1
1200
KIVA Q
S. WALL
AFT. STAB
L11601
7.25.61
f

Kiva R

Long House is "anchored" at the east end by Kiva R, the first structure encountered by one entering the site from that direction. The area occupied by the kiva was first designated "Area X, north half." The kiva is barely under the low cave roof, and is thus exposed to some weathering and water runoff from the mesa top. The 3.5 feet of waterlaid sediments in the upper kiva fill attest to the possible seriousness of the latter problem. These are cross–bedded, laminated sands, generally yellowish–brown in color but with several grayish laminae.

Kiva R apparently predates Rooms 52 and 59, whose west and east walls, respectively, would have been partly supported by the kiva roof. It may also predate Room 51, but here all the room walls could have been built on the rock ledge which adjoins the kiva on the east and north. Other nearby rooms, such as Rooms 50, 53, and 58, which are less directly dependent upon Kiva R for support, were probably also built after Kiva R.

The kiva axis is rotated slightly clockwise from a north–south orientation, and is practically the same as that of Kiva N (fig. 103).

Walls

Fill, boulders, and bedrock surround Kiva R on all sides, so there were no outer walls. Because of extensive collapse of masonry, as the result of moisture, root action, and pressure from adjoining rooms, little remained of the inner walls above bench level. All the masonry remaining was simple, single–faced, and built against rubble for the most part. The building stones in general were of average size, crudely shaped, with only a few showing evidence of pecking. Bedrock formed the wall in most of the northeast interpilaster space and at the extreme east end of the north interpilaster space, where the masonry feathers out on the rock face. There was at least one layer of red adobe plaster, less than 0.01 foot thick, on the walls. Both the plaster and the exposed bedrock were smoke–blackened.

In the lower walls, the masonry, where not covered by plaster, was about the same as in the upper walls. The building stones varied from irregular to rectangular in outline, and the faces were generally flat but showed little evidence of pecking.

Figure 103. *Kiva R, plans and sections A-A′ and B-B′.*

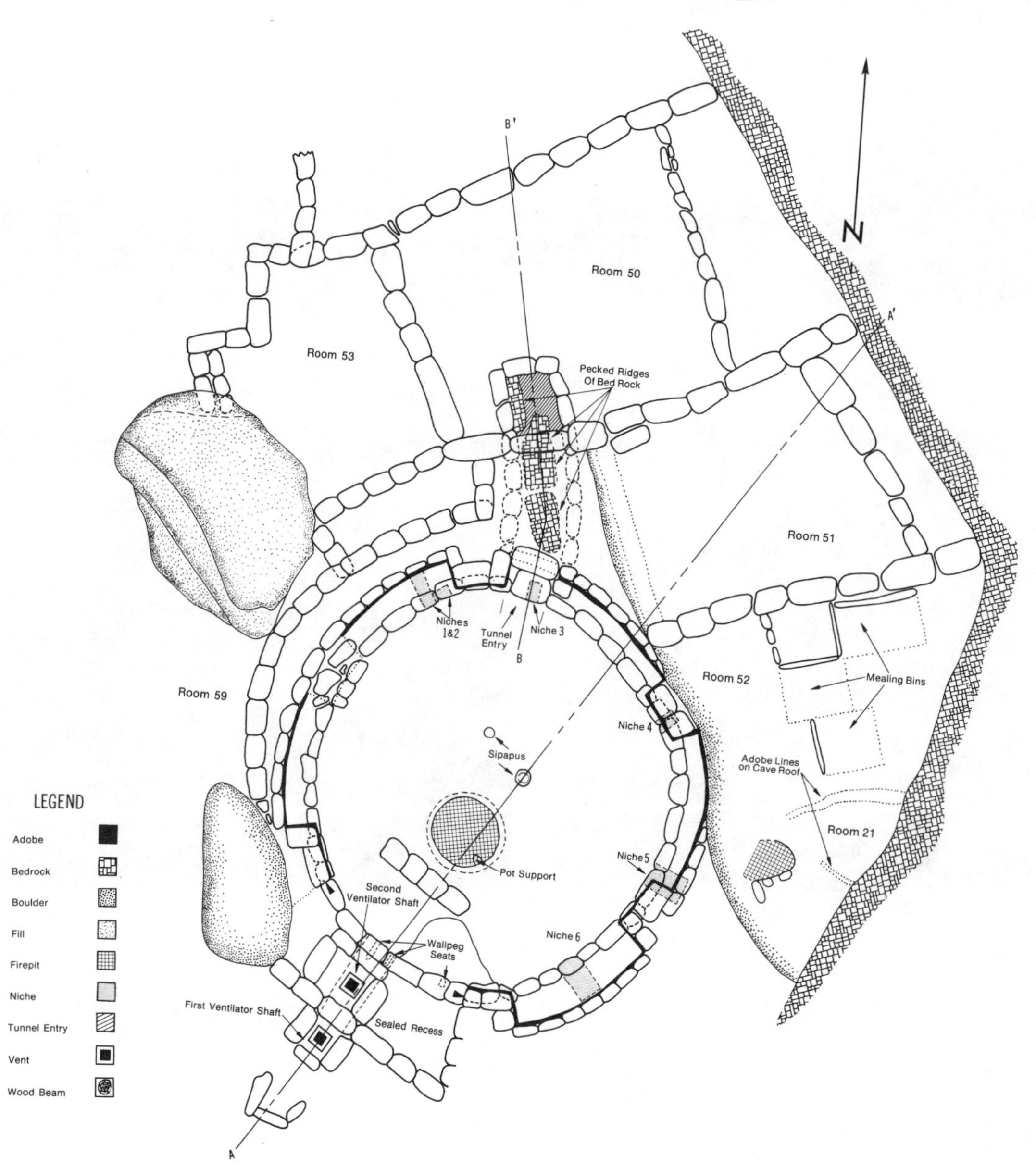

The lower walls were covered by at least eight layers of plaster. The lower 1.1 feet of the outermost layer was painted red, the upper part white. Faintly visible along the lower edge of the white band were a series of red triangles, extending from the red band up into the white, and a row of red dots, but not enough remained to determine the pattern.

Because of pressure against the west wall from fill behind and above the structure, it was apparently necessary to reinforce the section below Pilaster 2 (now gone) in an attempt to prevent it from collapsing. A masonry support, 1.3 feet wide and 0.4 foot deep at the base, was built below the pilaster (fig. 104). The support sloped back toward its top and probably supported a bulge in the wall about halfway to the bench and below the slumping pilaster. It is not possible to determine whether the support finally gave way during the period the kiva was in use, but it lasted long enough to acquire at least six coats of plaster.

Figure 104. *Masonry support built below Pilaster 2 (now missing), Kiva R.*

Another major change was made in the kiva, perhaps about the same time the wall support was built. Rain beating in on Kiva R and Room 59 may have resulted in considerable moisture in the fill behind the west wall and thus may have been the main cause of the collapse. Rain certainly penetrated to the kiva floor through the south ventilator shaft and must also have weakened the walls forming Pilasters 1 and 6. Pilaster 1 was subject to the same thrust from Room 59 above as was Pilaster 2. Perhaps it was to strengthen the entire south end that the ventilator shaft was moved north to just within the recess, a wall placed between Pilasters 1 and 6 to seal off the entire recess, and the space filled with rubble and cultural fill.

The masonry in the new wall was considerably more massive than that in the kiva walls, with the building stones being closer in size to those of the pilasters but not as well finished on the surface. The entire wall received at least two coats of plaster, one of which was white.

Three holes in this wall may have contained wall pegs. They range in diameter from 0.1 to 0.15 foot and are about 4.9 feet above the floor. They are spaced 0.45 foot, and 2.35 and 2.85 feet from Pilaster 6.

Pilasters

Six pilasters were present originally, but number 6 had been damaged when the wall below slumped and number 2 had collapsed entirely. The east side of Pilaster 1 and the west side of Pilaster 6 were completely concealed during remodeling of the ventilator and recess.

The masonry in the four fairly well–preserved pilasters (nos. 1 and 3–5) was much finer than in the kiva walls. The building stones were larger, with many showing a fairly rectangular outline. The faces were generally flat and most had been smoothed by pecking. Some of the stones in Pilaster 5 had been pecked and ground. The four pilasters which could be checked were set back from the edge of the banquette from 0.1 to 0.2 foot and showed a slight radial taper.

Two pilasters still showed traces of plaster. There were two layers of smoke–blackened plaster on the face and north side of Pilaster 1, and five coats, including several smoke–blackened, on all sides of Pilaster 3.

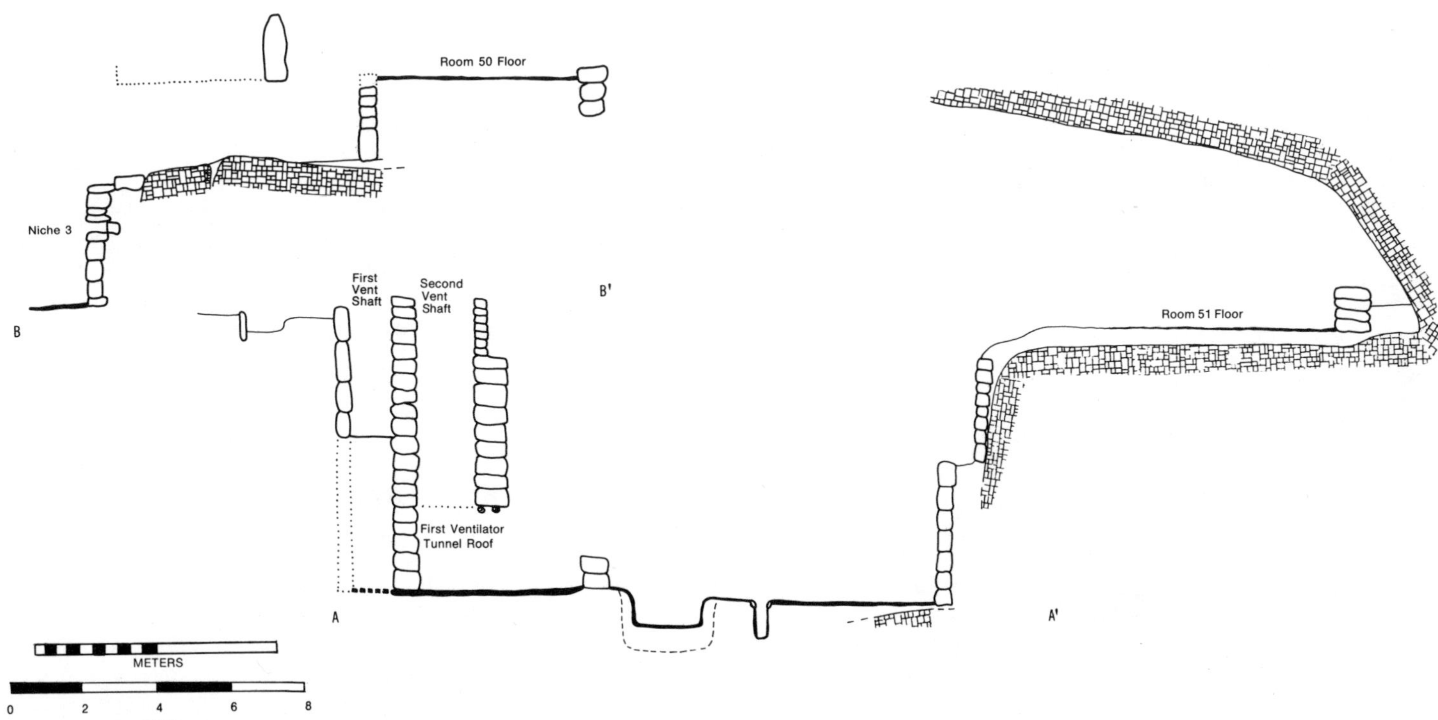

Niches

The six niches are ranged around the lower kiva wall in all quadrants except the southwest. They are near the midline of the wall except for Niche 6, which is at floor level.

Niches 1 and 2, located below the northwest interpilaster space, are adjacent to one another, with the bottom of Niche 2 level with the top of Niche 1 (fig. 104). The bottom and north side of Niche 1 are formed by slabs, the domed top and south side by a large boulder and adobe, and the back entirely by adobe. Adobe plaster lines the more arch–shaped Niche 2, concealing other construction details.

Niche 3 is directly below the entrance to the tunnel into Room 50 and on a possible kiva axis through the tunnel, west sipapu, and firepit, but not the ventilator. (The other possible axis is through the east sipapu, firepit, and ventilator.) It is very small and roughly square, with adobe lined sides which curve out to give it a slightly rounded shape.

Niche 4, a larger, square opening is below Pilaster 4. The top, bottom, and sides are formed by slabs.

Niche 5, partly below Pilaster 5, is a double niche as stabilized, but I do not believe that this is what the builders intended originally. The large, rectangular, northern section is lined on top, bottom, and back by thin slabs, and on the sides by thicker slabs smoothed with adobe plaster. The smaller and more irregular part may have been a building stone seat. It could, conceivably, reflect a late attempt to balance the combination of Niches 1 and 2 in the northwest quadrant with something similar in the southeast quadrant.

Niche 6, also large, is located at floor level below the southeast interpilaster space. Rocks in the fill behind the wall form part of the back, top, and north side, and masonry forms the other sides.

Banquette

The average height of the banquette was about 3.85 feet above the kiva floor, and its depth varied between 0.95 foot and 1.45 feet. The top course of rock in the lower inner kiva wall formed the base of the front half of the bench. Red adobe covered the back and probably extended forward over the top of the masonry originally.

Recess

Very little could be learned about the recess because of the remodeling. Although rather shallow, it had originally been quite conventional in shape: a straight south wall, except where a large boulder cut into the recess at its southwest corner; and the north side shorter across than the south because of the angled side walls formed by Pilasters 1 and 6.

Tunnel

Opening off the west end of the north interpilaster space was a tunnel leading under the south wall of Room 50 to an opening in the floor just inside the wall. The passageway is about 7 feet long and varies from 1.1 to 1.9 feet wide. The maximum height when in use was probably about 3 feet or slightly less. The west wall of the tunnel is a continuation of the east side of Pilaster 3. Unplastered masonry walls, 0.4 to 0.6 foot thick and now up to 2.3 feet high, form the sides of the tunnel except where bedrock juts out to form a part of the wall. The floor is bedrock, leveled with hard–packed yellow–brown soil averaging 0.1 foot thick. Projecting rock ridges were leveled and smoothed by pecking. A shallow step, 0.16 foot high by 0.64 foot deep, was probably placed, deliberately, in front of the tunnel by replacing a building stone at the edge of the banquette with a much thinner slab.

Ventilator

When the kiva was built, the vertical ventilator shaft was located outside but adjacent to the south recess wall. Its back or south wall was about 4 feet from the mouth of the horizontal tunnel, its opening perhaps 0.9 by 1.0 foot, and its height probably 8 feet. The three slabs about 2 feet south of the shaft, and probably 0.5 foot below the level of the top of the ventilator shaft when it was in use, formed a U open to the north. Coupled with the slabs, the depression within the U suggests that a rain trap may have been built, or at least started, before the ventilator and recess were remodeled. The trap would have consisted only of a right–angle jog in the ventilator shaft, and then a horizontal air tunnel leading to an opening not directly above the rest of the shaft.

After being used for some time, presumably, the vertical shaft was moved inside the recess, which was then sealed off by a wall along the north side. The ventilator tunnel was blocked off about 1.5 feet from its mouth, and an opening was cut through its top and the floor of the recess for the new shaft. The south recess wall, which had formed the north wall of the first shaft, now formed the south wall of the new shaft. The east and west walls were built, and then both the ventilator and the entire recess were closed by construction of the wall between Pilasters 1 and 6.

Much of the ventilator tunnel had collapsed, and little could be learned about the walls and roof. Wooden cross members, such as those preserved under the stone lintel of the tunnel entrance, undoubtedly formed the entire roof of the original tunnel. There were at least three layers of adobe on the tunnel floor, which extended back horizontally from the kiva floor.

Deflector

A simple masonry wall consisting of fairly rectangular stones formed the deflector. Some of the faces were quite flat, especially on the north side, and were covered with red adobe plaster.

Floor

A single layer of hard–packed red adobe, 0.05 foot thick, covered the entire floor, including the area between the deflector and the ventilator tunnel. It overlies sterile yellow soil. A firepit and two sipapus were the only floor features.

The circular firepit was originally about 2.6 feet in diameter and had been dug about 1.5 feet into sterile soil. It was reduced about half a foot in diameter and depth through remodeling. The fairly straight sides and flat bottom of the second pit are lined with adobe carried down over the rim from the floor. A sandstone pot support, projecting 0.15 foot above floor level, is embedded in the rim on the southeast edge, and similar stones may have been placed on the south and east sides where there were grooves in the adobe rim.

The west, or earlier, sipapu is on the axis through the tunnel, Niche 3, and the firepit. It is roughly cylindrical in shape and lined with adobe to a depth of 1.0 foot. The mouth of the sipapu is lined with a jar neck, only part of which remains. When abandoned, it was filled with clean sand and sealed with adobe.

The east, or later, sipapu is on the axis through the firepit and ventilator. It is slightly larger in diameter than the west sipapu but similar in shape and depth. A jar neck, 0.2 foot high, lines the mouth of the opening, and adobe lines the balance of the pit. It was not possible to determine whether the shift in the kiva axis indicated that the tunnel into Room 50 was no longer in use when the kiva was abandoned.

Roof

Little evidence of the roof proper, other than some adobe with shake impressions, was found in the fill. This may have been due to the exceedingly damp conditions in the kiva, unless the roof was removed deliberately before abandonment. The pilasters show that the base of the roof was 6 to 6.5 feet above floor. The surrounding rooms indicate that the top of the roof was about 7.5 to 8 feet above floor.

Kiva S

Squeezed in between Kiva M on one side and the Great Kiva and Long House Draw on the other, Kiva S also had to share with Kiva M the stress of supporting rooms above and to the north. Both Rooms 67 and 68 may have extended out a short distance over the roof of Kiva S. One or both of these may have had doors opening onto the kiva roof, but any evidence of this disappeared with the south room walls.

Kiva S was built after M, which was remodeled in the southwest interpilaster space to provide a narrow banquette in each kiva. Kiva S probably predates Rooms 66, 91, 92, and 73, in addition to the two mentioned above, since all of these rest on fill which must have been supported either by Kivas S and M or by a retaining wall no longer present.

Its axis, like that of Kiva M, is rotated slightly counterclockwise from a north–south orientation (fig. 105).

Walls

Neither Kiva S nor Kiva M was visible prior to excavation because of the low level at which they were built within the pueblo, and thus the great depth of debris and trash that accumulated above them. The area occupied by these structures, as well as by Rooms 67 and 68, was therefore designated Area IX during the initial part of the excavations. There were no outer walls of Kiva S standing, although originally there must have been a fill–retaining wall, at least along the west side of the area.

An upper inner wall was present only in the recess (south wall and four stones in the east wall), northwest interpilaster space (two stones), and along the east side of the kiva. The simple, single–faced masonry in the recess was apparently similar to that in the lower walls, but with stones slightly larger and much more crudely shaped. They vary from fairly rectangular to very irregular in outline and are not pecked.

The simple, double–faced wall dividing Kivas S and M was still standing to a height of about 1.3 feet above the banquette. It forms the back of a portion of the northeast and southeast interpilaster spaces in Kiva S but is farther east than the original Kiva M wall would have been. Its masonry is about the same as that in the lower walls and is better faced on the Kiva S side, where it shows some pecking. The Kiva M side was roughly shaped, with more adobe used to cover the joints. Both sides of the wall were burned, the Kiva S more heavily than the Kiva M side.

The lower inner walls were standing to bench height only across the south and east sides, and in a small section immediately west of Pilaster 3. Along the north side it was only one to two courses high. The masonry was simple, single–faced, and rather crude, of block size throughout the kiva except in the southwest quadrant. Here the stones were slightly smaller, generally rectangular in outline, and rather uniform, whereas elsewhere they were more poorly shaped. No true plaster remained, but both the gray shaly clay and red adobe mortars used in construction had been spread out over portions of the wall face to create a more even surface. The rock in the northeast and southeast quadrants, was heavily burned as high as 2 feet above floor.

In order to help support the weight of Room 67 and the fill behind the north wall, a masonry support, 3.2 feet wide, was built beneath Pilaster 3. The east end of the buttress is 0.8 foot thick, but the west end feathers out on the inner wall. Although it reached to within 0.3 foot of banquette height, it was not burned. The masonry is about the same as that in the northwest quadrant of the kiva. There is no evidence that Room 67 collapsed into Kiva S until after abandonment.

Pilasters

Judging by the size and location of the two extant pilasters, there must have been six pilasters originally. There is no trace of the remaining four, however, except for a break in the banquette and wall where Pilaster I had been.

Pilasters 3 and 6 stand about 1 foot high. The masonry is similar to that of most of the kiva, except in the southwest quadrant, but the blocks are thicker. The building stones are badly rotted but appear to have been only roughly dressed. None of the well–preserved faces are pecked, but the edges are either naturally straight or had been fairly well finished. Both pilasters are set back from the edge of the banquette about 0.1 foot, and they taper radially. Pilaster 6 shows no evidence of plaster; Pilaster 3 shown only smoke–blackened splotches of extruded and spread out mortar. The faces of both pilasters are burned.

Niche

The square niche in the wall brace, with its base 1.3 feet above the kiva floor, was the only one remaining. All four sides were formed by masonry, the back by the kiva wall behind. Three of the joints between blocks were plastered with adobe. Any niches in the north wall had been destroyed when this wall collapsed.

Banquette

There is a 1–foot–long and 1–foot–deep section of the banquette west of Pilaster 3. Its top is formed by a large rock slab at the top of the lower, inner wall. The banquette also extends about 8 feet along the east side of the kiva from Pilaster 6. Its depth ranges from 1.8 feet against the east side of Pilaster 6 to about 0.8 foot where Pilaster 5 once was. Another remnant of the banquette was found against Pilaster 6, where a layer of red adobe, 0.04 foot thick, overlies a practically sterile yellow soil and rock fill.

Recess

The 3.9–foot–deep east side of the recess indicates that in size and shape this poorly preserved feature was probably conventional. Only along the north side is preserved any of the hard–packed fill which served as a floor. A large, roughly shaped rock was mudded into position against the east recess wall and flush with the inner kiva wall. Whether this was part of a wall across the recess, as in Kiva R, could not be determined. The rock and the walls adjacent to it were burned.

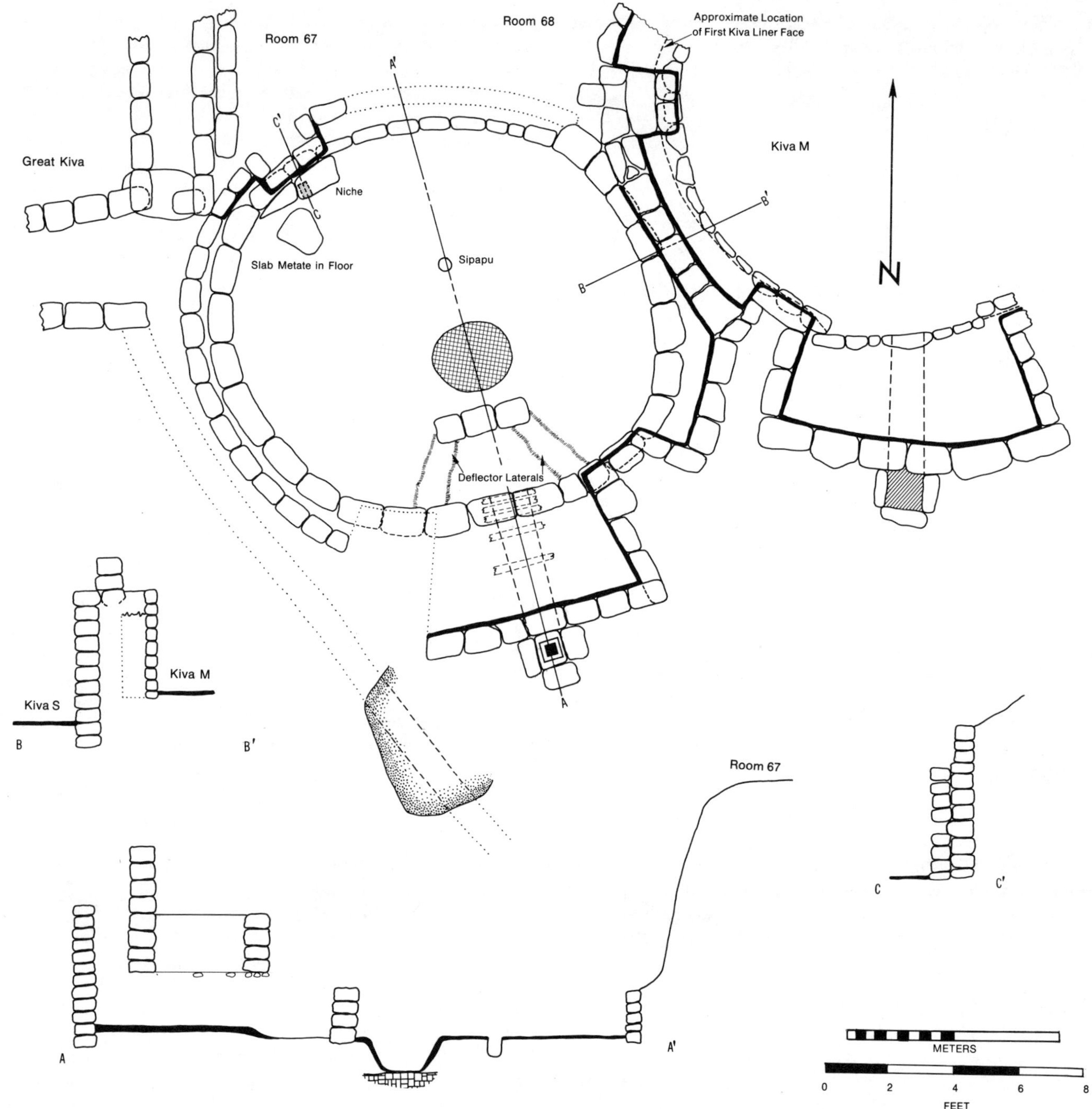

Figure 105. *Kiva S, plan and sections A-A′, B-B′, and C-C′.*

Ventilator

The tunnel mouth is slightly wider at the bottom than at the top. The masonry is similar to that of the adjoining walls but better dressed at the corners. To judge by the rotted remnants still in place, split shakes placed east–west across the tunnel formed the roof. A portion of the shaft may have been roofed by north–south shakes, since a large rock slab on the west side provided no seats (pecked or natural) over a portion of its surface.

For about half a foot south of the kiva wall the tunnel floor slopes up 0.3 foot and then extends back horizontally to the ventilator shaft. The floor consists of hard–packed, reddish–brown adobe up to 0.04 foot thick.

The ventilator shaft, 1–foot square, was formed by masonry similar to that in the south recess wall. The main blocks were fairly uniform in length, and most of the individual blocks extended across the full width of the shaft. The blocks sometimes touch at the corners, at other times abut one another.

Deflector

The unplastered wall forming the deflector is simple, single–faced masonry. The stones were roughly shaped and show no sign of pecking but have fairly rectangular outlines and flat faces on the north side. The major irregularities on the south side were filled with small rocks and additional mortar. For the most part, the mortar used in the wall and on the south face is red adobe, but at the base of the south face a large amount of gray shaly clay was used. The lowest visible course of rocks projects slightly south of the deflector, particularly near each end, but was covered by the deflector laterals and the up–curving fill between.

Floor

The one hard–packed adobe floor, generally red but brown in places, ranges in thickness from 0.03 foot on the south side to 0.13 foot on the north and averages about 0.08 foot over most of the room. The adobe curves up onto the kiva walls and the deflector, but ends at the inner (ventilator) edge of the two deflector laterals.

A slab metate, irregular in shape and slightly concave, is buried flush with the floor in the northwest quadrant of the kiva, immediately south of the wall brace. The floor adobe also extends up onto the edges of the metate. Perhaps its purpose was the same as that of the large stone seated in the floor in Kiva M and, possibly, a similar stone that may have been seated in the oval depression in Kiva Q.

The deflector laterals were fragmentary, with the east being the better preserved. It is 1 foot to 1.1 feet across and 0.1 foot high (0.2 foot at the end of the deflector). The west lateral was probably about the same width and height but is partially eroded away.

The southern edges of the laterals curve down onto the sterile yellow subfloor material, where they and the adobe floor end abruptly. The area between the laterals and in front of the ventilator tunnel was filled to a depth of 0.1 foot with brown soil containing quite a bit of charcoal and ash. The thin layer of adobe overlying part of this deposit was probably washed in by rain from the down–sloping ventilator tunnel floor.

The firepit, circular at the top but somewhat oval at the bottom, was dug into sterile yellow soil. The adobe sides, which were angled in slightly toward the bottom of the firepit, are a continuation of the floor adobe. This curves up slightly, then turns downward over a curved lip into the depression. Although part of the rim may have been repaired, there is nothing to suggest that the firepit was ever relined completely. Sterile soil and bedrock form the reasonably flat bottom.

The cylindrical sipapu was dug into sterile soil on the axis through the ventilator and firepit. Its mouth was formed by a corrugated (?) jar rim, and its straight sides were composed of rock and sterile soil.

Roof

Evidence of the roof found in the fill included burned timbers, 0.2 to 0.7 foot in diameter, overlaid by a mixture of roof adobe and brush up to 0.05 foot in diameter.

It is likely that six pilasters, their tops perhaps 6.2 to 6.5 feet above floor, supported one or possibly two levels of cribbed logs and a topmost level of parallel poles, brush, and adobe. The top of the roof would have been about 8.5 feet above the kiva floor, assuming it was no higher than the floor of Room 67, and probably on a level with Kiva M's roof, despite the lower pilasters in that structure.

As already mentioned under Kiva M, the two kivas could have been roofed simultaneously if the original Kiva M roof had collapsed or been badly damaged before Kiva S was built. In any case, the fire which destroyed the roofs of Kivas S and M probably ended the use of both kivas.

Kiva T

Anchoring the west end of the ruin, in a position equivalent to that of Kiva R, is Kiva T, the first structure encountered on entering the pueblo from the west (fig. 106). Unlike Kiva R, it is not sheltered from rain and snow by the protective overhang of the cave roof.

Although Kiva T predates Room 1, of which it forms the west wall, and Room 2, which it helps support, its relationship to Room 3 is not clear. I strongly suspect that the unusual recess in the northwest quadrant may have provided an undercover passageway into Room 3. However, Room 3 is not dependent upon the kiva for structural support.

The Kiva T axis through the ventilator, firepit, and sipapu—but not the recess—is oriented north–south.

Walls

Encircling the lower, inner kiva wall except in the northwest quadrant is a simple, single-faced outer wall built of rather large blocks. The wall is 1.0 foot to 1.3 feet thick, with blocks ranging from 0.4 foot to 2.3 feet and averaging about 1.2 feet long. The two similar walls, together with a rubble core, form a massive composite wall ranging in thickness from 2.2 feet on the north side to 3.6 feet at the ventilator.

In the outer wall, the exposed faces are generally rectangular in outline, but the stones are only moderately well shaped at the corners and edges. However, more than half of them have pecked faces, with many made slightly convex longitudinally to conform to the curve of the wall. The rock was laid up in red adobe mortar and, like most of the simple and compound walls in the ruin, had chinking spalls in both vertical and horizontal joints. Although the west wall of Room 1 abuts the outer kiva wall, the joints of both were probably mudded and chinked at the same time.

The south wall of Room 2 forms the outer kiva wall on the north. Here the masonry varies considerably, consisting primarily of small, unshaped or very crudely shaped stones in the lower section up to 2.3 feet above the banquette—a section normally concealed by the kiva roof. This grades irregularly into more conventional masonry, which would have been visible above the kiva roof line (fig. 107, at upper right).

The upper, inner wall was almost entirely gone. In the northwest quadrant, two courses remained to the south, and one course to the east, of the recess. Masonry in both is about the same as that in the lower, inner wall, and both sections were set back from the edge of the lower wall 0.15 to 0.2 foot.

Both the northwest and southwest corners of the recess were formed in part by bedrock, with simple, single–faced masonry between and across the top of the outcrops. The building stones here were larger than in the lower, inner wall but workmanship was about the same: moderately well–shaped, with many of the rectangular faces dressed by pecking. Several blocks were so rounded by erosion that the extent of their shaping could not be determined. Weathering may also have destroyed any plaster that might have been present.

Although the lower, inner wall was at least partially intact around the circumference of the kiva, it was reduced to only three courses on the east side. The wall is single-faced, simple masonry, with fairly well–shaped blocks. The exposed faces are generally rectangular, with more than half showing evidence of pecking, but few stones are well shaped at the ends and corners. Many of the blocks, especially on the north and west sides, are badly rotted.

Up to three layers of plaster still remained in patches on the north, west, and south sides of the kiva. The outer two layers are brown, the innermost cream colored, and all three are smoke–blackened. Except where heavily smoked, the cream–colored layer shows traces of a thin red wash, but no designs could be discerned.

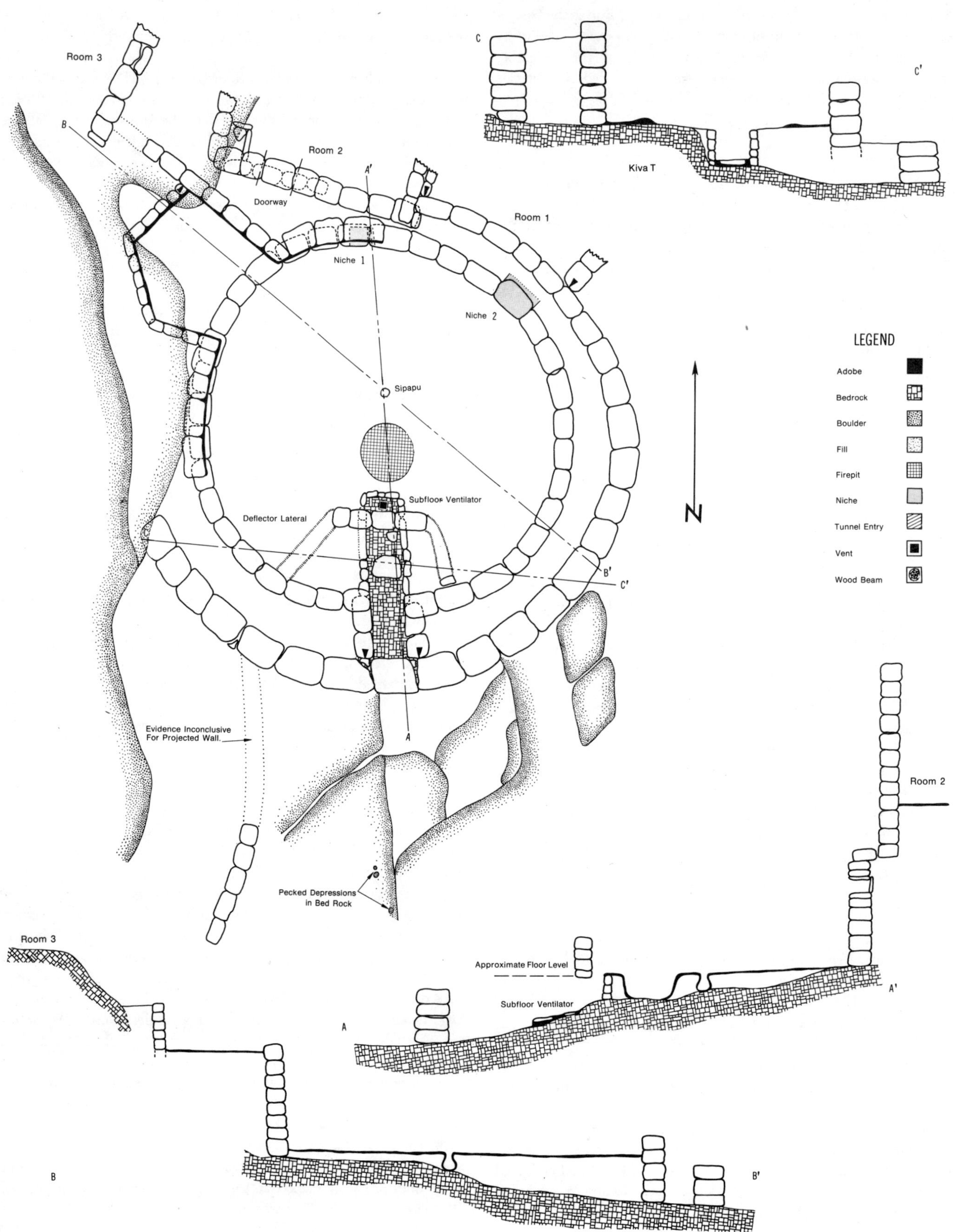

Figure 106. *Kiva T, plan and sections A-A', B-B', and C-C'.*

Figure 107. *Kiva T, after excavation, showing section of south wall of Room 2 above the roof line at upper right.*

Figure 108. *(Below) Subfloor and above-floor ventilators after stabilization, Kiva T.*

Pilasters

Probably none originally.

Niches

The two niches are in the lower, inner wall on the north side of the kiva. Niche I is in the upper part of the wall and on the axis through the ventilator, firepit, and sipapu. Thick slabs form the top and bottom of the niche, and thin slabs form the sides. A single slab or rock face is at the back.

Niche 2 is in the middle or lower part of the wall, depending upon its original size, in the northeast quadrant. Most of the east side, a portion of the west side, and all of the top were gone. The opening in the wall masonry is 1.4 feet wide and 1.7 feet high, but if the niche were slab lined, as seems likely, it may have been as small as 1 foot to 1.1 feet wide by 0.8 foot high. Presumably there was a back slab but, if not, the depth of the niche would be about 1.2 feet.

Banquette

A narrow ledge, 4 to 4.3 feet above floor, was formed by setting the upper wall back 0.15 to 0.2 foot from the face of the lower wall. It apparently continued around the circumference of the kiva and probably corresponded to the conventional banquette in location if not in function.

Recess

The location and shape of the recess are unusual, but there was nothing to indicate that the feature had ever been placed at the south side of the kiva and then shifted to the northwest quadrant because of exposure to rain and snow. The inward bend of the south wall of the recess is due primarily to the proximity of the cave wall at this point.

The north recess wall extends west to the east wall of Room 3, thus forming the north wall of a probable small chamber adjacent to the recess. This may have served as an entryway to Room 3 from the kiva or could even have been a small storage or ceremonial room such as Rooms 90 and 93, which open off the recesses of Kivas U and Q, respectively. The east "entry" wall, shared with the recess, supports fill which would have leveled part of the floor. The north wall of the recess–entry complex is continuous and smoke blackened on the south face.

There are several difficulties in arguing for a passageway here. That part of Room 3's east wall which might have contained either a doorway or an opening into a passageway had collapsed. Moreover, the kiva roof may not have been high enough to permit a person to crawl from one structure to the other over the bedrock ledge on which Room 3 stands. The problem could have been solved by angling or building up the roof over the entryway, or even by building an additional room above the entry chamber and adjacent to Room 3. There is no evidence that either of these steps was taken.

Ventilator

The ventilator in Kiva T has two parts, an earlier one below floor level and a later one above. Only in Kiva B is there a similar arrangement.

The subfloor ventilator tunnel presumably extended from the present vertical shaft, passing beneath the inner kiva wall to an opening in the kiva floor now partially covered by the deflector associated with the later above–floor ventilator. Because of a bedrock outcrop on the west side of the tunnel, it would not have been possible to make an L–shaped tunnel, as in Kiva B. The length of the ventilator is about 6 feet, its depth 0.8 foot (at the north end) to 1.2 feet below floor. Figure 108 shows both ventilators after stablization, with a slab divider in place between the two tunnels for interpretive purposes.

Most of the east tunnel wall consists of vertical slabs 1 foot to 1.2 feet long, 0.8 foot high, and perhaps 0.3 foot thick. There are also two sections of small–rock masonry. The stones are unshaped or

only roughly shaped and have fairly flat faces, which are pecked in a few instances. The stones average only 0.5 foot long and 0.2 to 0.3 foot high. The north end is similar, and so is the west side, except for a break of about 1.5 feet near the north end, where bedrock forms the tunnel wall. The masonry was laid up primarily in red adobe, but some gray clay was used at the north end of the tunnel.

The ventilator floor is bedrock from the vertical shaft to within 1.8 feet of where the south face of the deflector would later be. A 0.2–foot–thick layer of adobe, placed to level the floor at the north end, abruptly raised the floor level at this point. Two rocks were set in the adobe, their flat faces flush with the top of the floor. The upsloping bedrock again replaces the adobe floor at the north end of the tunnel. There is no evidence of the ventilator roof, which appears to have been torn out during the conversion from subfloor to above–floor ventilator. The subfloor ventilator was then filled with sterile and cultural fill and plastered over, apparently during the time of the third replastering of the firepit rim and kiva floor.

The roof and all of the west side of the above–floor ventilator tunnel, except one rock, had collapsed. So, too, had the north and south sides of the vertical shaft. The remaining masonry in both the horizontal and vertical portions of the ventilator is similar in size and extent of rock-shaping to that of the lower inner kiva wall. Most of the building stones still standing in the vertical shaft have pecked faces. The floor, which was probably hard–packed fill, was also entirely missing.

Deflector

The simple, single–faced masonry wall forming the deflector is associated with the later, or above–floor, ventilator. The masonry is similar to that in the lower kiva wall, with the faces on the north side being moderately even. Extruded mortar was spread over the face of some of the stones to further smooth the north face. No effort at all was made to aline and dress the much cruder south face.

Floor

The hard–packed red adobe, varying in thickness from a thin veneer over bedrock in the north and west portions of the room to at least 0.05 foot, covered the kiva floor north of the deflector and terminal edges of the laterals. A brown soil formed the floor between the laterals.

Both the east and west laterals are formed by slight upward swells of the adobe floor, which ends sharply at the edge of a shallow depression south of the deflector. The laterals are 0.8 foot wide and 0.15 foot high, and extend from the ends of the deflector to the kiva wall. The adobe forming these two features curves up onto both kiva wall and deflector.

Bedrock forms the floor and part of the west side of the circular firepit. The remainder of the vertical–sided pit is formed by fill lined with red adobe, a continuation of the original room floor which curves down in the firepit. Three additional layers of plaster, 0.01 to 0.05 foot thick, feather out on the firepit rim from the surrounding floor. They apparently were laid down to smooth irregularities in a well–worn floor, which was also charred and burned in places.

The circular sipapu is also lined with red adobe carried down from the top floor. It is 0.25 foot in diameter and 0.75 foot deep, and in vertical cross section it has the shape of a globular, straight–necked jar. It is located on the kiva axis through the ventilators, firepit, and niche.

Roof

We found no identifiable roofing material, beam impressions in adobe, or the like, in the kiva fill. There are no pilasters, or beam seats in the cave wall or the masonry walls of Rooms 2 and 3, to give us a clue to the method of roofing. We can only assume that timbers were supported by an upper wall broken only by the recess. Judging by irregularities in the masonry on the south exterior of Room 2, and by the floor level of Room 3, I believe that the probable height of the roof top above the kiva floor was 8.5 feet.

Kiva U

Because of its exposed position on the slope between the upper tier of rooms and kivas and the West Trash Slope, Kiva U was supported by massive fill–retaining walls on three sides. The area enclosed by the walls, as well as that immediately west of it but below the upper tier, was designated Area X, North Half, during the early part of the excavations. We learned, shortly, that Kivas U and P and Rooms 82, 83, and 90 comprised this part of Area X. Kiva U was built before and directly supports Kiva P and Room 82. Room 90, a feature of Kiva U, was presumably built at the same time as the kiva.

The orientation of the kiva axis through the ventilator, firepit, and sipapu is north–south, but slightly skewed through the structure because the kiva is not symmetrical (fig. 109).

Walls

The two simple masonry walls around the north, east, and west sides of Kiva U are separated by up to 2 feet of loose fill. They were not built as components of a composite wall but serve essentially the same purpose by providing greater support for the kiva than would a single wall. The outer wall may, in fact, have been necessary to support a rain–weakened inner wall.

The inner and earlier wall is apparently footed on sterile fill except at the southeast corner, where it overlies a short wall of unknown function and stands about 6 feet high in most places. It is extremely crude and is built of mostly unshaped blocks varying in size from cobbles 0.2 foot square to boulders 3.0 feet square.

The outer wall roughly parallels the inner, and the north and south walls and the northern half of the east wall are also footed on sterile soil. The southern half of the east wall rests on ash, which reaches a depth of 1.1 feet at the southeast corner. The east and south walls were probably bonded at their junction, which had collapsed. The masonry of the outer wall is considerably more regular in construction and shows greater uniformity in block size than that of the inner wall. The building stones are only roughly shaped and resemble those in the masonry of the upper kiva walls.

Remnants of the upper (inner) kiva walls remain standing to a height of 2.7 to 3.6 feet in the recess and the west and north interpilaster spaces (fig. 110). Along the east side they were gone entirely. The walls are generally simple masonry, and the building stones are large and irregular except in the recess, where they are roughly shaped. The faces are smooth but not pecked or ground, and rectangular in outline. In several places, especially the recess, gray clay mortar was used as plaster. It is heavily smoke blackened.

The masonry in the lower walls is considerably more even, and the building stones are smaller and much better shaped. The faces are fairly flat and frequently pecked, and rectangular in outline. As in the upper walls, the mortar used in laying up the building stones was gray shaly clay. It was spread out in a thin layer over the face of some of the stones to serve as plaster. It is also heavily smoke blackened.

Pilasters

There are remnants of four pilasters, each about 4.5 feet wide. Pilaster 2 was in poor condition, and Pilasters 3 and 4 had almost entirelly collapsed. Only Pilaster 1 was in good condition. The masonry is about the same as that in the lower walls, but slightly larger stones were used. Several of the stones in Pilasters 1 and 3 have pecked faces, and the corner stones were especially well shaped. Vertical slabs were used, also, on the recess side of Pilaster 4. Gray shaly clay was used as mortar. All four were set essentially flush with the face of the inner kiva wall, although Pilasters 2 and 3 show the faintest suggestion of a set-back. All tapered radially.

Niches

Three of the four niches are in the lower wall, two near the midline and one at banquette level, in or just below Pilaster 4. The fourth niche is in the face of Pilaster 2, near its base.

Niche 1 was a very small rectangular opening formed by building stones. It is located just north of center in Pilaster 2 and about 4 feet above the kiva floor.

Niche 2 is on the kiva axis and below the north recess and slightly west of its center. It is small and roughly square, being formed by building blocks above and below, and by two upright rectangular blocks on the sides. A flat slab forms the back of the niche.

Niche 3, beneath the west end of Pilaster 3, is the largest of the four. Flat building stones form the top, bottom, and east side of the rectangular niche; vertical slabs form most of its west side and back.

Niche 4 is at banquette level, just to the south of center of Pilaster 4 and thus squarely on a hypothetical line dividing the pilaster from the lower wall. It is a small rectangular opening formed by horizontal building stones. The back is apparently a rounded stone.

Banquette

Only the west and north interpilaster spaces had a true banquette, which ranged in depth from 1.3 to 1.9 feet. The east interpilaster space, now mostly gone, was merely a narrow ledge about 0.3 foot deep. The west interpilaster space was apparently topped with gray clay, and the north one with red adobe, 0.1 foot thick. The material in each apparently extended to the face of the lower kiva wall over the top course of rocks. In the east interpilaster space the rock formed the ledge, which may or may not have been plastered over.

Recess and Room 90

The straight back and radially angled sides of the recess made it quite conventional in appearance. However, its 0.1– to 0.2–foot–thick red adobe floor was apparently pierced at either side by the opening into a corrugated jar buried in the bench, with its rim flush with the floor. Figure 110 shows the mouth of a jar on the east side of the recess, and the base of a jar that was once on the west side. (Kiva J had only one jar in the northeast corner of the recess, and Kiva P one in the southwest corner.) The adobe floor probably did not cover the top course of lower–wall building stones which formed its inner edge.

A doorway in the west wall of the recess opened into Room 90, possibly a small storage area (fig. 111), which probably saw a use similar to that of Room 93 in Kiva Q. The room is entirely inside Pilaster 1. The rough inner (Room 90) face of the wall forming the front of the pilaster was plastered in places with gray clay and chinking spalls to smooth the surface. Parallel to this wall, and built against its base, was a bench–like wall, 0.6 to 0.7 foot high, with its building stones fairly smooth on the room side.

The north wall of Pilaster 1 was probably compound, with an inner face composed of flat, thick slabs. The west wall of the room is a continuation of the upper kiva wall in the west interpilaster space, and the south wall is formed partly by a boulder and partly by large, irregularly shaped building stones. The doorway occupied most of the short east wall. A vertical slab formed the north jamb, and a break in the adobe mortar at the door edge and lack of smoke blackening on the south side indicate that a slab may also have formed the south jamb.

Three manos, two rectangular worked slabs, and eight other slabs of various shapes, sizes, and degree of workmanship were found on the room floor or leaning against the walls. Removal of the loose slabs revealed a slab–lined floor over almost all of the room. Crevices between the slabs were filled with gray clay. The floor stones rested on practically sterile yellow fill consisting mostly of sand and rock.

Ventilator

The building stones forming the mouth of the horizontal tunnel have well–shaped, rectangular faces, some of which have been pecked. With the exception of the lower part of the east tunnel wall and the south wall of the vertical shaft, where vertical slabs were used, the masonry is similar to that in the lower kiva wall. The dirt floor sloped up very slightly to the south. The tunnel roof was evidently composed of small brush stems placed east–west across the ventilator, but all had rotted out.

Deflector

Remains of this feature consist of only a 1.5–foot–high remnant of a single–faced, simple masonry wall. The faces of the stones are generally rectangular on the north side, and several have been pecked.

Floor

Bedrock forms the western third of the kiva floor; red adobe, up to 0.1 foot thick, covers the rest of the floor, including the area south of the deflector. If there were ever deflector laterals, no evidence of them now exists.

A circular, round–bottomed firepit was dug into sterile soil, and the floor adobe was then carried just over the rim onto the sides of the pit. A vertical stone slab, 1.5 feet long, rests on ash fill 0.1 foot above the bottom of the pit. Although the slab may have been placed there as a support, it was not burned and may have fallen into the pit when the roof collapsed.

A roughly cylindrical, oval–mouthed sipapu was also dug into sterile soil, and the floor adobe was carried slightly over the rim onto its sides.

Roof

The exposed location of Kiva U resulted in almost no evidence of the roof in the fill. Some burned adobe, apparently from the roof, and small brush were all that was found. The standing masonry suggests the base of the roof was at least 6 feet above floor, and thus the top of the roof was probably 7.5 feet to 8 feet above the kiva floor.

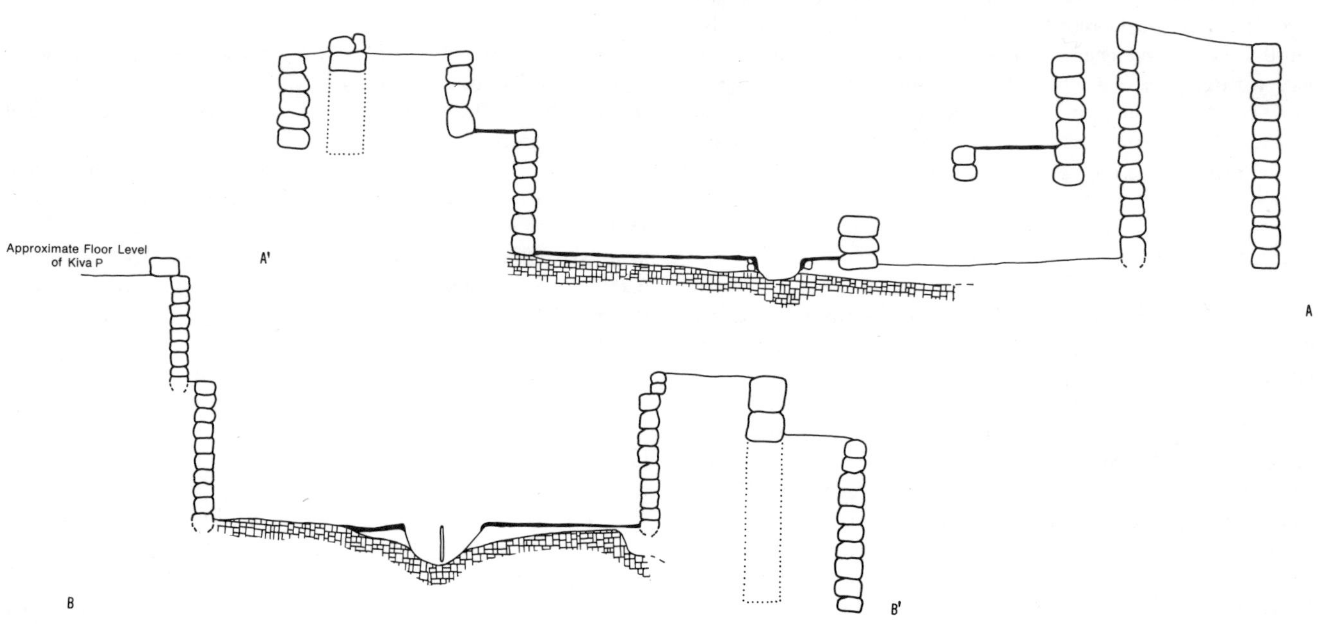
Approximate Floor Level
of Kiva P
A'
A
B
B'

Figure 109. *Kiva U, plan and sections A-A', B-B', C-C', and D-D'.*

Figure 110. *(Left) Kiva U, after excavation, viewed from above.*

Figure 111. *(Right) Room 90, a small storage area (?) for Kiva U, within Pilaster 1. Door at top, in west wall of Kiva U recess.*

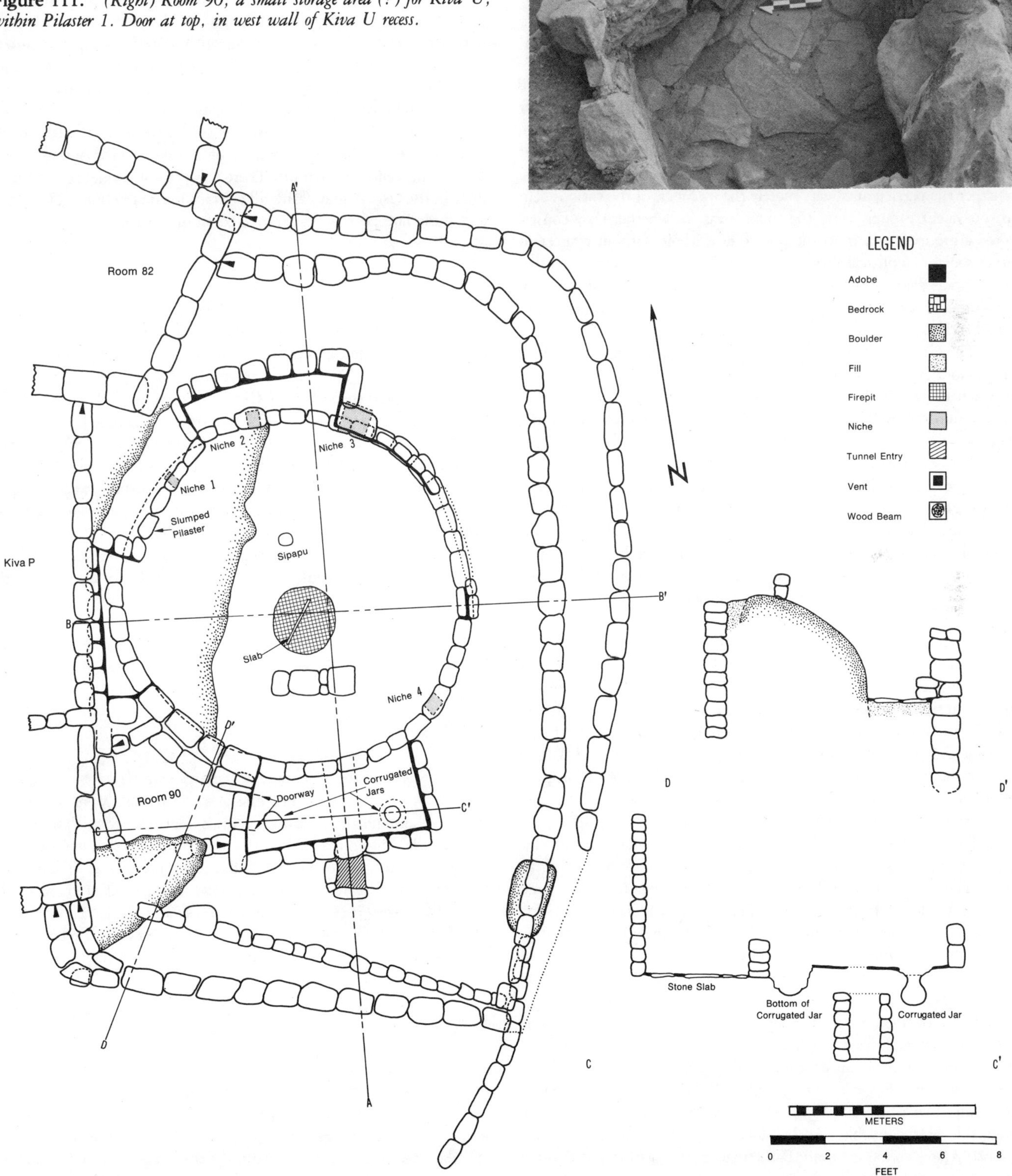

Great Kiva

No greater controversy has arisen from the excavation of Long House than that over the proper term for the central plaza or court which Lancaster and I prefer to call a great kiva (fig. 112). There is no point in reviewing here all the comparative data on great kivas and related structures that can be found in the archeological literature, or in trying to make any hard–and–fast rules about which attributes a feature must possess before it *is* a great kiva. Vivian and Reiter (1960) have already summarized much of the pertinent data about great kivas. Moreover, such a discussion would not answer the questions we have about the Long House structure, and would only lead us to a taxonomic impasse.

The Long House great kiva appears to be a large, specialized courtyard, roughly rectangular in shape, which was probably used for both ceremonies and secular activities. Events held here may have been significant to all the people in Long House and even to other Puebloan people living in the vicinity. It is not possible to determine whether the participants were merely the members of the various clan or equivalent groups using the small kivas, or whether they constituted a group drawn from the pueblo as a whole without respect to other social or political groups. No paintings, artifacts, or architectural details were unearthed that would establish a relationship to any structures in the ruin except Room 66 (and 67?) on the east and possibly Room 35 on the west.

The Great Kiva or Area VI, the designation applied to the kiva area before excavation, lies directly below that point on the canyon rim where the drainage above forms a 100–foot–high waterfall during rainstorms. The splash point depends upon the velocity of the water as it pours over the edge of the cliff. During heavy runoff, the impact is south of the kiva in the draw. As the flow is reduced, or during periods of light runoff, the water formerly flowed over and then slightly back under the rim, to fall on the south edge of the kiva. Heavy spray from the waterfall also splatters the kiva and structures on either side of it. The copper lip installed at the pouroff during the course of the Wetherill Mesa Project now deflects the water outward, so it tends to miss the structures below.

As a result of years of erosion, only the subfloor material, the base of architectural features, and remnants of the east and west benches have persisted. The wall stub at the southeast corner could have been part of a south bench or wall. Complete excavation, except along a test trench where we also burned trees and brush in 1958, revealed no early features or structures predating the kiva, with the possible exception of a shallow, oval–shaped hearth (fig. 113a). The floor of the stabilized kiva is at approximately the level of the original floor, and the stabilized features have been brought up to or just above this level (fig. 113b).

Floor level was probably at the base of the benches on either side of the kiva, and on a level with the exposed bedrock on the north side. The undisturbed fill remaining in the kiva (beneath huge mounds of debris from collapsed rooms) was primarily the sandy, yellow–brown soil which formed the base of the kiva floor. The deposit became gray–brown in places where there was considerable charcoal, ash, and other refuse mixed in, and gave way to red adobe part way beneath and south of the "firebox."

Some of the sterile material in the subfloor fill probably came from the bedrock faces immediately north of the Great Kiva. Perhaps debris cleaned out of this area was used to roughly level the bedrock and native soil below the southern side of the kiva. The trash deposits above and toward the north side of the kiva may have come from the west side of the pueblo. As Lancaster suggested, the trash would probably have contained more Basketmaker III–Pueblo I pottery had it come from the East Trash Slope.

Eight floor features were excavated in the kiva: a "firebox," a firepit, a shallow hearth, and five cists. Other construction may have disappeared along with the floor itself.

Cist 1

This feature is a rectangular box, 1.5 by 3.5 feet, which lies south of and possibly predates Cist 2. Both Cist 1 and Cist 2 are on the eastern side of the kiva. The long axis of Cist 1 parallels the east kiva wall. The north and east walls, and part of the west wall, were still standing to a maximum height of 1.6 feet. All are simple masonry, faced only on the inside, with stones laid up in a mixed gray clay and sandy red adobe mortar. There was no trace of the south wall. The building stones were of average size, roughly shaped, with faces generally rectangular and flat. Only a few showed any evidence of pecking. The floor of the cist was 0.05 foot above the base of the east and west walls and consisted of the compacted surface of the underlying yellow-brown fill. There was possible evidence of a higher floor in the cist. A gray, ashy fill containing small chunks of charcoal and some late pottery was recovered from the cist.

Cist 2

Although adjacent to Cist 1, Cist 2 angles more to the northwest, with its long axis parallel to the west kiva wall. It is also roughly rectangular, except for the skewed south wall, and measures 1.7 by 4.3 feet. The walls were built of masonry similar to but slightly smaller than that in Cist 1, and were still standing to a maximum height of 1.1 feet. The mortar used differed from that in Cist 1 only in not being sandy. The 1–foot–high slab, mudded into place against the northwest corner of the cist with a smooth curve of adobe, indicates that there may have been another feature here. It would probably have been south of the slab to incorporate the better finished face of that construction. No evidence of the floor was detected–it may have been merely the compacted surface of the subfloor fill. If so, it would have been almost 0.8 foot higher than the floor in Cist 1. The fill was identical to that in Cist 1.

Taken together, Cists 1 and 2 form a unit which seems to reflect doubt in the minds of the builders as to which side of the kiva the sides of the cists should parallel. Only the small firepit has the same orientation as Cist 1; all other features parallel the west wall.

"Firebox"

Centered in the south side of the kiva is the base of a rectangular firebox, 5.7 by 6.7 feet. The east and south walls were intact, but the west and north walls were almost entirely gone. The simple masonry, laid up in red adobe mortar, is similar to that in Cists 1 and 2, although the stones averaged slightly larger in size. The outside faces are generally rectangular and flat, and several of those in the south wall were pecked. There was no evidence of the floor or its location, or of fire ever having been built in the "firebox." The yellow–brown base material of the kiva constituted the fill above and around the feature.

Firepit

Three vertical slabs, with a maximum height of 0.9 foot above the base, form the west, north, and east sides of a small firepit several feet north of the "firebox". It measures 1 foot across on the inside and was probably square. A saucer–shaped depression forms the bottom, and the sides are seated on the edges of the depression, 0.1 foot above the deepest part of the pit. All slabs were fire-reddened, as were the small rocks exposed in the mixed, subfloor fill forming the bottom. The firepit contained a damp, 0.3–foot–deep deposit of whole pieces of charcoal in a compressed mat of pulverized charcoal, and small pieces of burned rock which probably came from the walls of the firepit. The maximum size of the charcoal fragments, which were not datable, was 0.1 foot. Above this deposit was the mixed subfloor fill found throughout most of the kiva.

Cist 3

Although in the same relative position on the west side of the kiva as Cists 1 and 2 on the east, Cist 3 is a single pit, measuring 1.3 by 4.8 feet on the inside. Its overall dimensions, including an exterior east wall; are 3.3 by 8.3 feet, thus making it almost as large as Cists 1 and 2 together.

The cist walls proper are simple masonry faced only on the inside, except where an inner masonry liner built on the cist floor converts the southern half of the east wall and the south wall to composite, single–faced walls. About three–fourths of the cist walls are upright slabs as much as 1.1 feet high; the balance is conventional masonry of average size. The shaping of both is very irregular, although the blocks tends to have flat, but not pecked, rectangular faces.

The outer wall is also simple masonry faced on the outside, and similar in extent of dressing to the inner wall. It may have been built to support the cist walls, or possibly to form a large structure incorporating the cist, but there is no evidence now that it ever extended entirely around the perimeter of Cist 3. It may also have been the west wall of another structure lying east of Cist 3, with the dressed face inside the feature. All stone in the complex inner and outer walls was laid up in red adobe and gray clay mortar. The floor consisted of the compacted surface of the yellow–brown fill, which also filled the cist, small rock and, in places, red adobe, up to 0.1 foot thick, used to fill holes and level the floor.

Cist 4

This possible double cist lies between Cist 3 and the west bench. The four simple masonry walls of the northern half, which measure 1.35 by 2.9 feet, were dressed on the inside only. They consist of vertical slabs in the south wall and at the base of the other three. Block masonry forms the construction above the slabs, resulting in a maximum standing wall height of 1.6 feet. The building stones are slightly smaller than those in the other floor features, excluding the large rock incorporated in the east wall of this cist. Natural cleavage, not pecking, formed the flat faces of the stones, which were roughly shaped to rectangular–faced blocks and square slabs. The mortar is primarily gray clay, but red adobe appears in few patches.

The hard–packed surface of the sandy, yellow–brown fill forms the floor of the cist. Centered in the cist floor is a circular pit, measuring 0.75 foot north–south by 0.65 foot east–west and 0.7 foot deep. The concave bottom curves gently down 0.1 foot below the base of the vertical side walls. It was completely filled with a black, ashy deposit containing carbonized remains of tiny plant stems, pine needles, small pebbles, and some chunks of gray clay, up to 0.2 foot in diameter, which were coated with black ash on the outside but "clean" on the inside. The surface of the cist floor, especially around the pit, was black from having ash packed down on it and from fire. Portions of wall masonry showed limited burning, as if fires had been restricted to the central pit.

In construction below the masonry walls, Cist 4 closely resembles a subfloor vault or possible foot drum reported by Roberts (1932, pp. 58–60) in Kiva A, House A at Village of the Great Kivas, New Mexico. Both features consist of a rectangular cist or vault, with a roughly circular pit dug into the bottom of the structure. (The pit described by Roberts is "jug-shaped," rather than straight-sided, as in Cist 4). The Kiva A structure has shelf–like features resembling the clay pads at either end of the foot drums in Kivas M and Q in Long House. As Roberts suggested, planks covering the vault could have rested on these features, to provide a drum surface flush with the kiva floor.

One simple masonry wall, faced on the north side, was standing 2.4 feet south of Cist 4 and may have been the south wall of another cist. If so, it probably shared with Cist 4 the south wall of that feature. A band of hard–packed soil extending north from the east end of the wall may show the location of the east wall of this possible cist. Vertical slab and block masonry similar to that in Cist 4 comprised the 1.3–foot–high wall stub. Its mortar was predominantly sandy red adobe, as in Cist 1, with a few patches of gray clay. Had there been a floor, and assuming that it was laid at the base of the masonry, it would have been 0.5 foot lighter than that of Cist 4. The usual yellow–brown subfloor fill covered both Cist 4 and the possible cist.

Hearth

Directly under the southwest corner of Cist 4, and lying mostly between that structure and the isolated wall stub, is an oval hearth, measuring 1.8 feet by 2.2 feet. It is 0.3 foot deep, saucer-shaped in cross section, and delimited by a burned rim of the yellow–brown fill into which it was dug. The floor consists of the same material and was covered with an ash deposit, 0.2 foot deep. A burned stone, 0.15 foot by 0.35 foot by 0.4 foot, was seated on 0.05 foot of ash and apparently packed down into the now–burned west rim. Possibly it served as a pot support. Unconsolidated fill in the pit consisted of ash and chunks of charcoal up to walnut size.

The hearth may be associated with an occupational level of Area VI, preceding construction of the kiva. However, it may be an early feature of the kiva, before the overall structure became formalized.

Cist 5

Corresponding to Cist 4 in relative position, but on the east side of the Great Kiva, was a poorly preserved structure which may have been a cist. (Neither this nor the possible south part of Cist 4 were restored during stabilization of the kiva.) Two vertical slabs, laid up one above the other in gray clay, mark the 1.1–foot–high south wall. Patches of red adobe and small rocks resting on fill may have formed part of a slightly curved west wall. A depression probably marked the location of the east wall, but there was no evidence of the north wall. The cist is 1.1 feet across, east–to–west, and the west wall is 0.8 foot long. The slabs are 0.8 foot wide and 0.2 foot thick, and the bottom slab is buried 0.2 foot below one of two possible levels of the floor. The other is about 0.1 foot below the base of the slabs, which would have rested on a gray clay pad.

A possible pit, 0.5 foot deep, poorly defined but apparently irregular in shape, curved west and north 2.3 feet from just under the west "wall." If this constituted part of the cist, and the west wall mentioned above is a spurious one, then the floor was saucer-shaped in cross section. The addition of this pit to the cist would still not give us its northern limits, however. The top 0.2 foot of fill into which the pit was dug contains chunks of red and brown adobe (one with a beam impression of a log at least 0.5 foot in diameter), burned rock, and gray clay. This material, identical to the fill under the east wall of the Great Kiva, overlies the ubiquitous yellow–brown fill.

Figure 113. *Excavated features (a) and stabilized features (b) in the floor of the Great Kiva.*

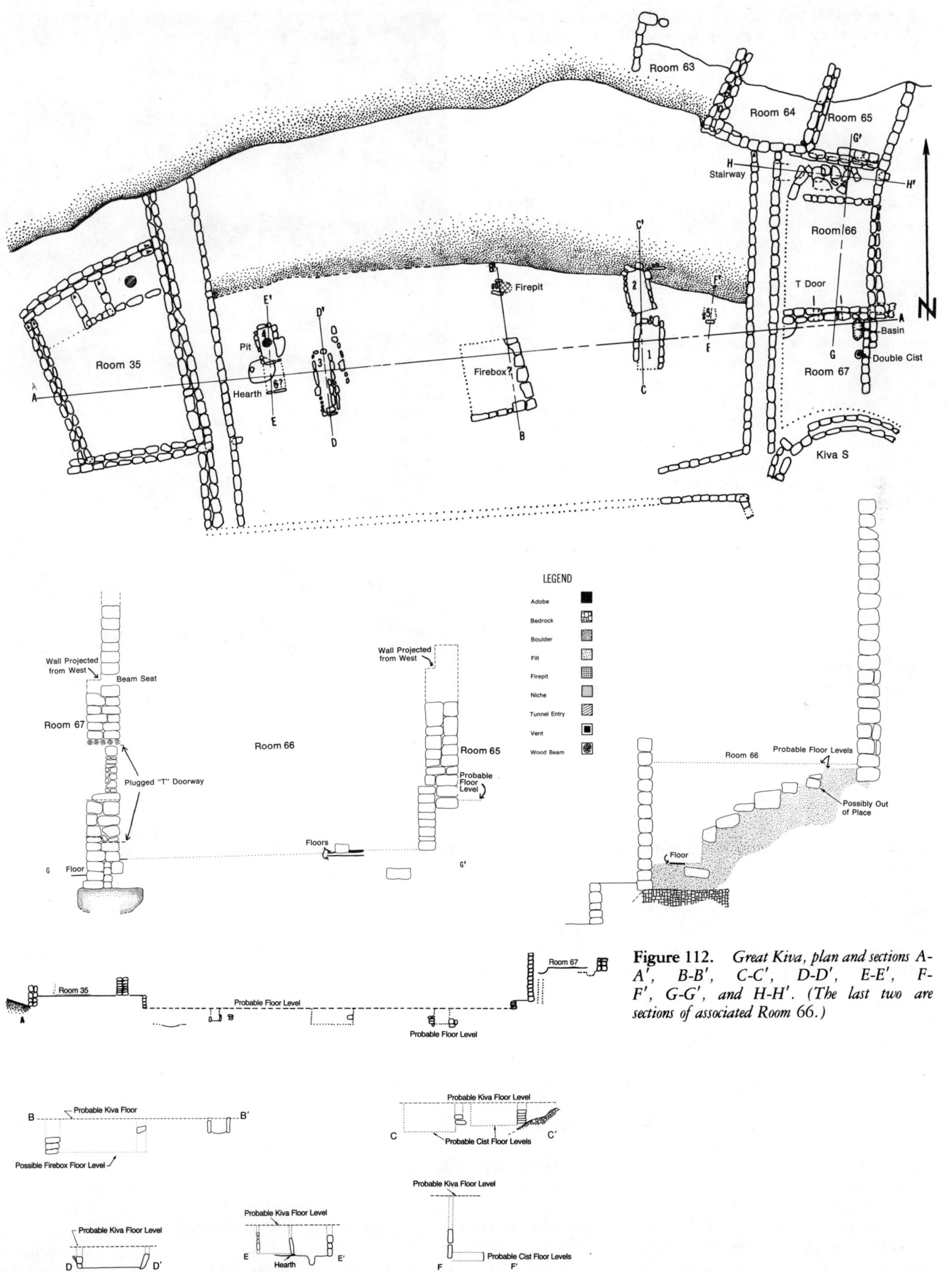

Figure 112. *Great Kiva, plan and sections A-A′, B-B′, C-C′, D-D′, E-E′, F-F′, G-G′, and H-H′. (The last two are sections of associated Room 66.)*

Cist 5 could have been built earlier than Cists 1 and 2, with its slabs removed for use in later structures. The pit adjacent to the supposed west cist wall might also have been only a borrow pit for salvaging old clay or red adobe from the trash.

Benches

The east bench was almost entirely gone except for a section of the base of the front (west) wall at the north end and part of the corner formed by this wall and a possible south bench or wall. The low front wall served as a retaining wall for the trash fill partly supporting the west wall of Room 66. A bench, 1.7 feet high and 2 feet deep, formed by these two walls, extended south from Room 64 along the entire eastern side of the Great Kiva.

Although both walls were simple, single–faced masonry laid up in red adobe mortar, the Room 66 wall was stabilized as a compound wall for greater strength. The lower part, below floor, is merely a retaining wall for the subfloor fill of Room 66; it had collapsed to a level about 2.5 feet below the room floor.

The better–preserved west bench shows the same construction as the east, except at the south end, where a low, compound masonry wall rather than a room wall forms its west side. A low simple, single–faced masonry wall forms the front (east side) of the bench, actually a trash–filled platform on which Room 35 was built. The east wall of the room was built of double–faced compound masonry, unlike the west wall of Room 66. The bench ranged from about 2 feet to 3.5 feet deep, and, like the east bench, was 1.7 feet high. The stones in both walls were fairly well shaped to provide flat, rectangular faces, many of which were pecked.

The short stub of wall extending west from the southeast corner of the kiva may have been part of a simple wall which extended entirely across the south side of the plaza, to form a retaining wall for the subfloor fill. It is more likely that the kiva wall was composite with the wall stub belonging to the north part of such a wall. The south part, for which there was only vague evidence, would probably have been an extension of the outer wall of Kiva S. It would presumably have formed the south wall of the wide part of the west bench, extending towards the draw from the south wall of Room 35. We built the short north–south wall connecting the components of the south kiva wall to retain wall fill. There was no wall there originally.

Construction of a composite wall across the kiva would have provided a third bench, probably not backed by any other structure. It seems very unlikely, therefore, that the kiva was fully enclosed. Even if there had been walls behind the possible south bench and the southern end of the west bench, there would also have had to be a wall from Room 63 to Room 35 to enclose the kiva. By the same token, we do not know by what approach the kiva was entered. Perhaps the low walls were simply stepped over.

Stairway

Leading from the level of the east bench, possibly before it was built, to the lower floor of Room 66 is a short stairway. The risers for the six steps are formed by stone slabs or blocks with flat tops and fairly straight front edges. Each step is 0.3 to 0.4 foot high, except the lowest, which is 1.7 feet. All but one of the stones ranged in width from 1.1 to 1.6 feet (the angled one was 2.2 feet), and in depth from 0.6 foot to 1.1 feet. Figure 114a shows the stairway before stabilization; figure 114b shows it from the doorway in the west room wall, after stabilization.

The upper part of the stair well was lined with large stones whose flattish faces formed the sides of the passageway. Those on the south side curved to the south, to form a wall inside or east of the west wall of Room 66. Other traces of the base of this wall were found near the south end of Room 66. The presence of an inner retaining wall makes more understandable the later construction of only a simple masonry outer reinforcing wall. There was probably no doorway in the outer wall at that time—the stair would have risen between the south walls of Rooms 64 and 65 and the curving west retaining wall of Room 66. There would then have been another step down to the level of the underlying bedrock from the base of the steps.

Figure 114. *Stairway from the level of the east bench of the Great Kiva to the lower floor of adjoining Room 66, before stabilization (left) and after stabilization (right).*

When the bench and the outer retaining wall were erected, the stairway was either blocked off or a doorway was left in the new wall. We created a doorway to show the stairway without weakening the buttressing action of the west wall of Room 66 against the south side of Room 64 (fig. 9). There was no archeological evidence, however, for its presence or absence.

Roof

There is no evidence that the Great Kiva had been roofed, or that any attempt was ever made to roof it.

Associated Rooms

Room 66 obviously played some part in the Great Kiva activities because of the stairway leading up to it. Possibly it equates with the antechamber of circular great kivas such as Casa Rinconada in Chaco Canyon, New Mexico. Although Room 66 may have had a

second story, we could not prove this. Room 67 was connected to Room 66 at one time by a large T-shaped door. The approach to the Great Kiva from Room 67 was blocked off when the doorway was sealed. Possibly this was done to restrict use of Room 66 to ceremonial activities, but it may have coincided with a reflooring of part of the room to cover the stair well.

The lower floor level, which was probably associated with the stairway, extended over the entire room. It consisted of a thin layer of red adobe overlying gray shale, twigs, and juniper bark. Later a wall, perhaps only one course high, was built just south of the stairs on top of the floor and parallel to the north room wall. The new wall, of simple masonry with the south face dressed, may have served only as a retainer for the second floor. The floor was red adobe, 0.2 foot thick, and extended from the low wall across the top of the filled–in stair well to the north room wall. It is possible that the floor level north of the new wall was raised still further with fill to form a low platform. If so, there was apparently no additional adobe floor placed flush with the top of the building stones.

With the possible exception of Room 66, none of the five rooms clustering around the east end of the kiva—Rooms 63-67—appears on the basis of architectural detail to have been built with any ceremonial purpose in mind. However, rooms other than Room 66 may have been used in conjunction with Great Kiva activities.

Room 35 presents quite a different picture, for its features are anything but conventional. It is a trapezium in shape, with no two sides parallel. Figure 115 shows the room from above, before the Great Kiva was discovered and the complex was stabilized. The north wall follows the angle of the bedrock ledge against which it was built, the south wall parallels the probable location of the south kiva wall, and the east wall roughly parallels the east wall of the west bench. It also forms the back of the bench. The south wall does not end at its junction with the west wall, but continues on as if it formed the south wall of another structure adjacent to Room 35.

All four walls were built of compound masonry. Although all had probably been faced on both sides, the remaining blocks in only the north and south walls show evidence of this. The outer part of the south wall extends down as a simple wall, 2.5 feet beyond the depth of the compound portion of the wall, and apparently it served as a prime fill–retaining wall for the platform on which the room was built. It rests on 0.8 foot of trash which, in turn, overlies the bedrock.

Built against and centered midway along the north wall is a square, pilaster–like block of masonry whose original height is unknown. Three simple masonry walls of mostly unshaped stones are bonded at the southeast and southwest corners, but abut the north room wall. The interior of the pilaster was filled with trash.

The floor in the west alcove between the pilaster and west room wall is hard–packed gray fill. It is probably at the level of the main room floor, which had been destroyed. The east alcove is floored with gray clay about one–half–foot higher than the floor in the west alcove. Three stones are all that remain of a rough retaining wall along the south side of the alcove and in line with the south face of the pilaster. Centered in the alcove floor is a subcircular, basin–shaped pit with a maximum diameter of 1.8 feet and a depth of 0.6 foot. (See Kiva G for a discussion of the similarities between the two features).

The disturbed fill in Room 35, up to 2 feet deep on the north side, contained a concentration of turkey droppings just above the probable floor level near the southwest corner. A small hematite effigy (chipmunk, squirrel, or gopher?) was found in the fill in the center of the room. This small object, only 2.0 cm. long, was carefully ground and polished all over.

Discussion

The Great Kiva in Long House closely resembles Fire Temple in Fewkes Canyon, Chapin Mesa (Vivian and Reiter, 1960, pp. 73–81). Both share the following features: large size (42 by 23 feet for Fire Temple, and approximately 56 by 34 feet for the Great Kiva in Long House); rectangular shape; benches (Fire Temple had north and south benches for a total of four); vaults (the west one in Fire Temple had one compartment, the east one two, thus resembling the single and double cists of Long House); raised firebox (circular in Fire Temple, rectangular in Long House); room blocks at either side, with the east ones entered through a doorway from the kiva; and no evidence of a roof. The sipapu in Fire Temple coincides in location but not shape (circular) with the small firepit in Long House. There was no evidence in Long House of a floor, subfloor pits, subfloor trough, or painted plaster.

No circular great kivas had definitely been found on Mesa Verde at the time of our excavations, despite their presence in nearby sites such as Lowry Ruin and Aztec Ruins, as well as in the Chaco Canyon sites such as Casa Rinconada and Chettro Kettle. Al Lancaster had long suspected, however, that a large depression in Morfield Canyon was a circular great kiva, and Lister (1968 pp. 494–495) proved this to be correct. It was roofed, and apparently possessed the formal arrangement of features typical of the sites mentioned above.

The interior features leave us with several unanswered questions. There was no evidence of fire in the "firebox," but this is not surprising since so much of the box and its original fill had been washed away. A lack of evidence of wood planks or wood impressions

in adobe in the fill of the cists makes it equally impossible to say that these structures, which correspond to those normally called "vaults" in other great kivas, were used for foot drums.

Although the small firepit might have belonged to an early level in the Great Kiva and later used as a sipapu, the ash fill would seem to rule this out. Furthermore, what was the function of the small pits in Cist 4 and the east alcove in Room 35? It is tempting to correlate the masonry pilaster of Room 35 with the "altar blocks" commonly found in the antechamber of many great kivas. We can say, at least, that the people in Long House were probably innovators, but we cannot tell what prompted this. The layout of the Great Kiva may reflect a need to adapt the features of the circular great kivas to physical limitations of the site, or perhaps just a desire to try something different. It is possible, also, that the Long House great kiva is merely a poor attempt to copy the layout of Fire Temple.

Figure 115. *(Left) Room 35, viewed from above, before the Great Kiva was discovered and the complex was stabilized.*

Figure 116. *Areas I through IV, a continuous stretch of floor in the deepest part of Long House cave.*

AREAS

Areas I–IV

The deepest part of the cave was divided arbitrarily into Areas I through IV, which form a continuous stretch of cave floor behind Kivas H and I and rooms on either side (fig. 116). Apparently no structures were built here except those shown in figure 9. Depth of fill ranged up to about 3 feet but generally averaged 1 foot or less. Bedrock ledges were exposed in places, especially in Area I. The fill from bottom to top included material of all kinds: sterile soil and rock, gradually deposited cultural trash, zones of turkey droppings mixed with plant debris and other trash (in Areas I–III), and fallen wall and roof material.

Several walls in Rooms 70, 71, and 24 were torn out following abandonment of these features, and the various walking surfaces (four were well defined) carried across the top of the wall footings. Part of the north wall of Room 28 was also missing, and the room was used as a trash dump and burial area (Burial 30).

A shallow, rectangular hearth (General Feature 6), 1.5 feet by 2.5 feet, was found in Area I, just west of Room 23. It was lined with vertical slabs on two sides and part of a third, and undoubtedly

had been completely encircled by rock originally. This was the only architectural feature found in Areas I–IV, and was probably used by the people living in the Beer Cellar Complex or Room 23 and adjacent structures.

Numerous ax–sharpening grooves, such as those in Area I, were ground into conveniently located bedrock ledges. Some of these were later filled in to level the surface, or were entirely covered by fill and the subsequently formed walking surfaces. Nordenskiöld carved his "No. 15" (for Long House) into one of these depressions, in the slanting face of a ledge in Area I.

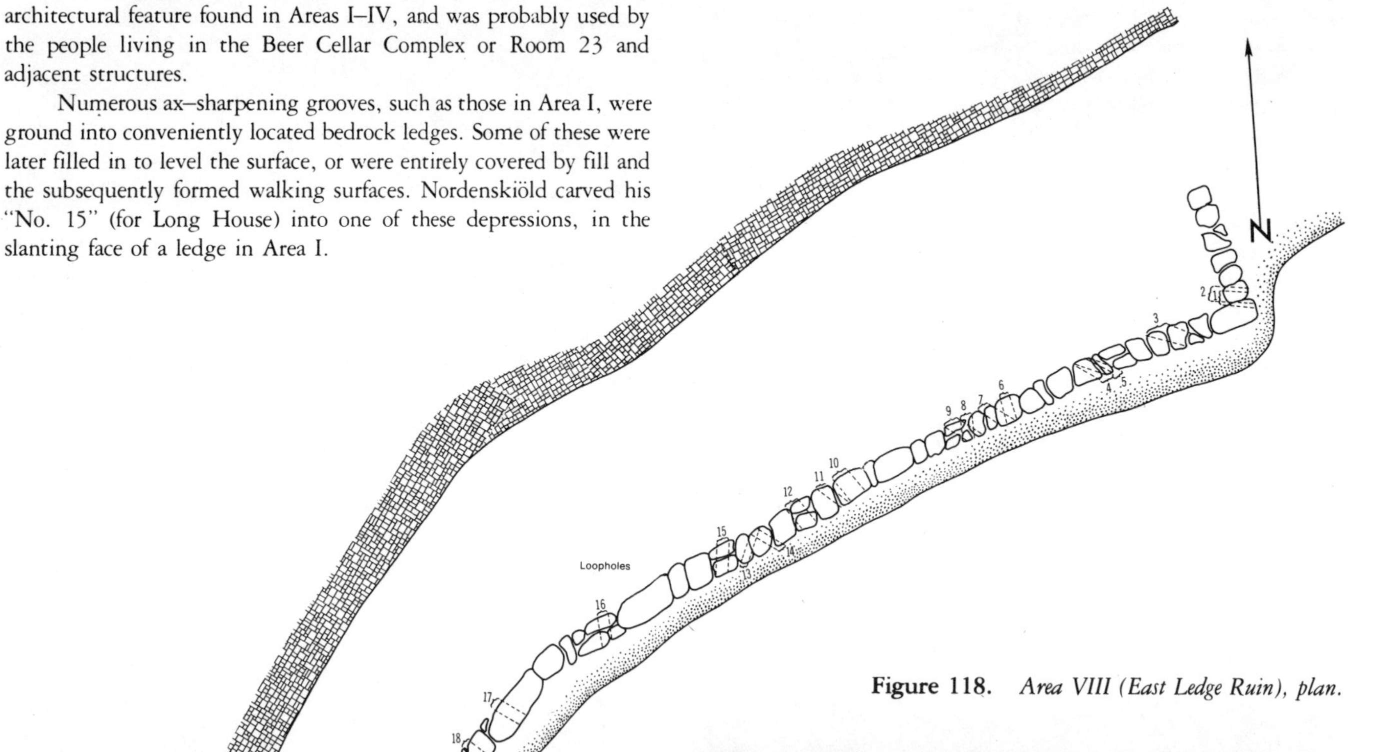

Figure 118. *Area VIII (East Ledge Ruin), plan.*

Figure 117. *Four water-collecting pits beyond the arrow in Area II.*

A series of water–collecting pits or catch basins was pecked and ground into the bedrock cave floor along a seep. A gray shale stratum, which outcrops where the cave roof and floor meet, serves as a aquifer by carrying to its exposed edge water percolating down through the sandstone above. The pits are located at the east side of Area II, at the east and west sides of Area III, and along almost the entire length of Area IV. They vary considerably in size, with the 20 or so major ones ranging from 0.3 foot to 0.7 foot in maximum diameter, and from shallow depressions to holes over 1 foot deep. Several had feeder grooves, both natural and manmade, which channeled water into the pits.

Figure 117 shows five pits directly north of Room 72 and a feeder groove leading to the one nearest the room wall. The four pits on the west are in Area II, the one on the east is in Area III. Unlike the other depressions, which are along the cave wall, these are below a slight slope in the cave floor to catch water seeping out in the damp (dark) area in the upper right corner of the photograph. The water level in Area IV remained about the same throughout the summers we worked in the cave. This is probably the same pool reported by Nordenskiöld (1893, p. 26). We could, undoubtedly, have secured considerably more water all along the seep by removing all vegetation and decomposed rock, thus leaving a freshly cut seep face, and perhaps by lining the pits with clay.

Area VIII: East Ledge Ruin

The East Ledge Ruin was designated Area VIII before we knew how many, if any, rooms or other features were concealed by the front wall (fig 118). It is perched on a shallow ledge about 53 feet above the floor of the Great Kiva (fig. 119) and was reached by

Figure 119. *Area VIII, perched on a shallow ledge above the floor of the Great Kiva.*

scaffolding and ladder, as mentioned briefly in the first chapter of this report. Access to the ledge during occupation was probably by ladder from the roof of Room 64/5 (see discussion of Rooms 29 and 64). Nordenskiöld and the Wetherills, who had preceded us by many years, devised an ingenious method of reaching the ledge (Nordenskiöld, 1893, p. 28). On the walls of Kiva I, they built a log platform, counterbalanced with rock, which supported a log tripod that supported, in turn, an upright log. The inscription they left in Area VIII were also discussed in ch. 1.

When we finally followed the early explorers up to the East Ledge Ruin, we found only two walls, bonded at their junction and pierced by 21 loopholes, most of which can be seen in figure 120. The short wall and Loopholes 1 and 2 are shown in figure 121a, taken from the ledge outside the walls. The same section of wall and the east end of the long wall, taken from within the enclosure with Loopholes 1 through 5 visible, is shown in figure 121b. The view of the ledge behind the long wall, from east to west, can be seen in figure 121c.

The short wall is 3.4 to 3.6 feet high above the bedrock floor, 0.8 foot thick, and 3.5 feet long. The simple, double-faced masonry is rather crude, with blocks only roughly shaped except at the north end. Here the stones forming the end of the wall are fairly well shaped and pecked on the north face. They are roughly dressed on the east and west faces but show some pecked faces.

The long wall, slightly under 50 feet long and about the same height as the short wall, is of the same construction except that it was very crudely dressed on the inner face and incorporated several massive slabs, up to about 5.8 feet long, which were undoubtedly on the ledge when the original inhabitants first climbed up to it. Quite a few thin slabs, 0.03+ foot thick, also probably on the ledge, were used in building both walls. Large amounts of adobe mortar were used in laying up the walls, and chinking spalls were jammed into crevices in the masonry in a very irregular manner.

Fill, up to a maximum of 0.5 foot, covered the unplastered bedrock floor. The fill was removed by bucket and rope, but contained nothing of cultural significance, unfortunately. Nordenskiöld (1893, p. 28) also reported that "no object of any great interest was discovered."

That the walls were intended for defense cannot be proved, but the loopholes—their only features—certainly suggest this. Each loophole is so angled as to command a view of a part of the ruin, its approaches, or the cliffs above. The closer one's eye is to the opening, the wider the field of view, of course. The loopholes are numbered in figure 18, and the height of the bottom of each above the ledge, its height and width, the approximate direction of view and dip below horizontal, and the point up which it centers are given in table 5.

Other Areas

Areas V, VII, XIV, and the south half of Area X are the highest section of the West Trash Slope, and Area XI and the south half of Area XII are the highest part of the East Trash Slope. The following areas, as mentioned in the discussion of the features involved, overlay the rooms and kivas shown parenthetically, with the original desig-

Table 5. Loopholes in walls of East Ledge Ruin.

No.	Height in feet above floor	Size in feet (Height/ width)	Bearing	Dip	Center of view
1	0.3	0.50/0.45	S 65° E	−30°	Room 75
2	2.0	0.50/0.50	S 55° E	−15°	Room 60
3	1.0	0.50/0.45	S 45° E	−8°	*Site 1201
4	1.65	0.40/0.45	S 45° E	−10°	*Site 1201
5	3.15	0.35/0.25	S 50° E	−10°	East approach (Trail between Sites 1201 and 1200)
6	0.25	0.30/0.25	S 20° W	−15°	West approach
7	2.5	0.30/0.30	S 45° E	0	*Site 1201 & east approach
8	0.65	0.40/0.30	S 35° W	−5°	*West approach
9	1.35	0.30/0.30	S 45° E	−6°	East approach
10	0.1	0.50/0.50	S 10° E	−10°	*East Trash Slope & east cliff, Long House Draw
11	1.1	0.25/0.30	S 45° E	−5°	*East approach
12	0.15	0.50/0.45	S 25° E	−25°	West side of East Trash Slope
13	1.8	0.35/0.20	S 50° W	−5°	*Kivas A and B
14	0.85	0.40/0.25	S 45° E	−10°	*Head of East Trash Slope
15	0.6	0.48/0.25	S 25° W	0	*Rock Canyon & Wild Horse Mesa
16	0.75	0.45/0.30	S 25° W	−10°	West Trash Slope and Wild Horse Mesa
17	0.3	0.35/0.40	S 55° E	−37°	Kiva M
18	1.0	0.42/0.40	S 50° E	−15°	*East side of East Trash Slope
19	1.5	0.35/0.30	S 65° E	−3°	*East entry to ruin
20	1.5	0.30/0.25	S 60° E	−10°	*Room 60
21	1.0	0.30/0.30	S 67° E	−28	*Kiva N

*Also commands top of either east or west cliff of Long House Draw.

nation remaining significant only for the fill above the features: Area IX Kivas M and S); the north half of Areas X (Kivas P and U. Rooms 82, 83, and 90) and XII (Kiva R); and Area XIII(Kiva Q). With the exception of three features in Areas X and XIV, no architecture was present in the various areas.

A triangular hearth (General Feature 4), measuring 3.9 feet by 5.2 feet, was built in the angle formed by two large boulders in the south half of Area X. The north and west sides (against the boulders), as well as part of the east side, were built up with small rocks and vertical slabs. A heavy red burn on the boulders showed that the top of the structure tapered sharply inward and upward, thus forming a triangular superstructure. The pit, which had a baked adobe floor, was filled with 0.9 foot of charcoal, ashes, and burned rock. Its construction is rather unusual for a conventional cooking or heating hearth, leading us to speculate that it might have been a pottery-firing oven.

A small cist (General Feature 9) was also found south of Room 83 in Area X. It was built on sterile soil beneath rock that had fallen from the cave roof, and measured 2.5 feet long by 2 feet wide by 1.7 feet high. Very crude masonry walls formed the slightly curved sides and back. It was filled with occupational trash and was not burned.

In Area XIV, immediately east of Kiva U and the Area X retaining wall, is a series of 17 postholes (figs. 122 and 9). They were dug into a surface extending west an unknown distance beneath the retaining wall. If the surface extended to the east beyond the holes, it was lost through erosion and trail construction before discovery of the feature. The surface slopes down to the north, losing about 1.3 feet in elevation along the 18-foot length of the posthole area. The holes ranged in diameter from 0.3 to 0.5 foot, and in depth from 0.25 foot to 1.2 feet. They are arranged, very roughly, in two parallel rows, and were dug into yellow fill containing charcoal and burned rock. Some extended down into the underlying native soil. The Area X retaining wall was built on trash fill overlying the postholes.

Most of the postholes are vertical, but a few angle slightly towards the east. Although we can probably assume fairly safely that the holes were pole seats, nothing that we found sheds any light on their function. Possibly they were part of a heavy-duty fence built to support fill to the west before construction of the retaining walls. Their size and spacing make it unlikely that a room wall was erected here, and the lack of turkey droppings would seem to rule out a turkey pen. They may have supported a brush shelter or ramada, but there is no direct evidence of such construction.

Figure 122. *Two rows of postholes in Area XIV (West Trash Slope).*

Figure 120. *(Above, left) Long and short walls of Area VIII, pierced by loopholes.*

Figure 121. *Views of Area VIII: a, exterior of the short wall with Loopholes 1 and 2; b, interior of short wall and east end of long wall with Loopholes 1-5; and c, ledge behind the long wall, from east to west.*

Chapter Three

Human Burials and Offerings

Forty occurrences of human remains were designated as "burials," but I do not know precisely how many individuals these bones represent. For example, Burial 36 consisted of bones from three individuals, and Burial 38 of bones from four individuals. It was not possible during the analyses made by the physical anthropologists for all of the bones to be laid out at one time and separated as to individuals.

Professor Frederick S. Hulse, University of Arizona, analyzed Burials 1 to 25 and 31 to 35, and, under his direction, two graduate students completed the task: Professor Charles F. Merbs, now of the University of Chicago, analyzed Burials 36 to 40; and Professor Kenneth A. Bennett, now of the University of Wisconsin, Burial 30. Bennett also examined a number of the burials previously studied by Hulse and Merbs. Dr. James S. Miles, Chairman of the Department of Orthopedics in the University of Colorado Medical School, Denver, made a pathologic study of the bones. Significant archeological and pathological traits of the burials are presented in table 6.

Twelve of the burials were found in rooms or kivas; the remainder were recovered from the trash slopes below and south of the ruin. Quite obviously, burials were placed where a minimum of digging was necessary, i.e., in soft, trashy fill within the pueblo, or in pockets of dirt or fill caught between or behind boulders or irregularities in the bedrock on the slopes below.

The problem of finding burials at Long House was no different than that at many other sites in the Southwest. There is no known burial area or cemetery, and the few burials recovered hardly correspond to the number of people that must have died during almost 100 years of occupancy in the 13th century, A.D. No burials can be assigned to the Basketmaker occupation during the 7th century, A.D.

The trash slopes below Long House at the head of the draw were excavated prior to dumping dirt here from the excavation of the pueblo proper. Trenches were cut on the contour at the base of the upper or main slope, on both east and west sides of the draw. These trenches were then extended broadside uphill. In this manner, most of the slopes were excavated, resulting in the discovery of three burials on the West Trash Slope and 23 burials on the East Trash Slope.

Two other burials were found on the slopes at about the same elevation but several hundred yards south of the ruin. One of these, Burial 11, was found by the survey crew while making an archeological survey of Wetherill Mesa. It is located near Site 1505, and may belong to this small pueblo rather than to Long House.

Graves

It was impossible to define clearly the size and shape of the graves. To judge by what little evidence there was, shallow, roughly rectangular hollows were scooped out of the fill, and were no larger than absolutely necessary to contain tightly flexed bodies.

The depths below surface at which the burials were found varied considerably, especially on the trash slopes. Here the depths on the downhill side were often considerably less than on the uphill. Also, the depths at the time of excavation may have coincided closely with the original depths of the burials, but in many cases they probably did not.

Thirteen of the burials were found from just below the surface to a depth of 1 foot. Six were located at the 1-foot level, four between 1 and 2 feet, and three at 2 feet. Only two were placed deeper than this, one at 3 feet and the other at $3^1/_2$ feet. The depths of the remaining burials lacked significance because of obvious disturbance, or great depth of room fill from collapsing walls and roof overlying an ill–defined level from which the burial was made.

Over the top of five graves (Burials 4, 5, 8, 9, and 12) were fragments or traces of wood. Apparently only two sticks were placed above the body in line with the long axis of the burial. Four burials had two sticks, and a fifth showed evidence of at least one and possibly two sticks. In Burial 4, the diameter of the pinyon stick was 3.0 cm., and it was dated A.D. 1236. Dimensions and dates were not obtained from the other burials.

In only three cases did there seem to be remains of a lining around at least part of the grave. Burial 6 may have been outlined with pieces of sandstone, but the evidence is very sketchy. On the

Figure 123. *Burial 12, East Trash Slope.*

Table 6. Significant archeological and medical traits of burials.

Bur. No.	Provenience	Cat. No.	Age (Years)	Sex	Stature	Position	Deformation
1	Test C: East Trash Slope	13636	Late teenage	F	5′1″ or 2″	Tightly flexed; on back	
2	East Trash Slope	13637	3 or 4	U		Flexed; on back and left side	
3	East Trash Slope	13638	20 to 25	F	ca. 5′	Flexed, knees drawn halfway to chin; on left side and partially face down	Lambdoid flattening: asymmetrical; right pterion, pronounced
4	East Trash Slope	13639	At least 30	M	5′5″	Flexed, knees drawn halfway to chin; on left side	Lambdoid flattening on left, moderate
5	East Trash Slope	13640	At least 40	M	at least 5′7″	Flexed, knees drawn halfway to chin; on left side	
6	East Trash Slope	13641	Not over 15	U		Flexed; on right side, face down	
7	East Trash Slope	13642	At least 40	F	ca. 5′	Flexed, knees drawn halfway to chin; on right side and face	
8	East Trash Slope	13643	45±	M	5′4″	Flexed, knees drawn toward chin; on left side	
9	East Trash Slope	13644	8 to 10	U		Flexed, knees drawn halfway to chin; on left side and back	
10	East Trash Slope	13645	Young adult	U	5′4″	Flexed, knees at right angle to torso; on left side and back	
11	Southwest of Long House	13646	30-35	M	5′5″	Semiflexed (Probably flexed originally); largely on face	Lambdoid flattening, slight
12	East Trash Slope	13647	Adult	M?	5′5″	Tightly flexed; on left side	
13	East Trash Slope	13648	1 or 2	U		Head on left side	
14	East Trash Slope	13649	Adult	U	Over 4′11″	Flexed?	
15	Upper East Trash Slope	13650	Adult	F?	5′2″±(?)	Tightly flexed; on left side	High lambdoid flattening, moderate
16	Upper East Trash Slope	13651	Adult	M	ca. 5′6″	Flexed, knees drawn halfway to chin; on left side	Lambdoid flattening, slight
17	Upper East Trash Slope	13652	Young child	U		On right side and face	Lambdoid flattening, pronounced
18	Upper East Trash Slope	13653	ca. 30	F?	5′4″	Tightly flexed, knees drawn halfway to chin; on left side and face	Lamboid flattening, slight
19	Upper East Trash Slope	13654	Less than 1 yr.	U			
20	Upper East Trash Slope	13655	Late teenage	U		On back	

Orientation: Head to (Burial Axis)	Orientation: Facing	Depth below surface	Grave: Stratification	Grave: Lining	Wood above burial	Artifacts	Other
North (N 30° W)	Up	1.5′±	In trash on sterile subsoil			B/W bowl B/W bowl	
West (N 80° W)	North and up	1.0′	In trash creeping down slope			Stone chip Corrugated potsherd	
Southeast (S 33° E)	South and down	Just under surface	Without top layer of trash			Stone chip Clay ball	
West (N 64° W)	East	4.3′	In trash and deeply intruded into sterile subsoil		2 sticks longitudinally over body	B/W mug, B/W bowl, Bone awl, Lignite hair ornament, several stone chips and sherds	
Northwest (N 58° W)	East	3.5′	In trash and intruded into sterile subsoil		Faint traces of 2 sticks longitudinally over body	Lap stone	
West (N 75° W)	South and down	1.0′-1.5′	In trash	Stones may have lined pit and extended over top of burial			
West (N 65° W)	South and down	0.2′	In trash			B/W mug B/W bowl	
Southwest (S 35° W)	Northwest	3.0′	In trash and intruded into sterile subsoil		Fragments of 2 sticks longitudinally over body	B/W mug, Corrugated jar, B/W bowl, Sherds covering bowl	
Northwest (N 42° W)	East (?)	2.0′	In trash		Faint trace of at least 1 stick longitudinally over body	Blue jar, B/W bowl	
Southeast (S 45° E)	Up (?)	2.0′±	In trash			With burial: 2 stone pendants, 3 cylindrical paintstones, Stone cone, Pair of eagle talons, Side-notched axe Back dirt: Bone pendant, Perforated eagle talon, 2 crystals All artifacts probably in container beside body	
West (N 75° W)	Down		In trash			Projectile point, Central portion of projectile point (intrusive?)	
Northwest (N 56° W)	Northeast	2.0′±	In trash	Large sherds of B/W bowls, olla, and seed jar (13767, 13773, 13778-9/700) used to line downslope side of grave	Faint trace of at least 1 stick longitudinally over body	B/W bowl, miniature plaindipper, B/W mug	
North (N 5° E)	East?		In trash	2 sandstone blocks along west side			
		0.5′	Disturbed—probably in trash originally				
North (N 29° W)	Northeast	0.2′ to 2.0′	In trash			B/W dipper, large bowl sherd	
North (N 4° E)	East	1.0′±	In trash and intruded into sterile subsoil				Pelvis directly above that of Burial 17
Due West	Down	1.0′±				B/W dipper bowl	
East (S 66° E)	South and down	0.3′ to 1.0′	In trash and intruded into sterile subsoil			B/W bowl	
Southeast (S 60° E)	Down	1.0′±	In trash and intruded into sterile subsoil				
North (N 20° W)	Up	0.1′ to 0.4′	In trash			Stone chip	

(Continued)

Table 6. Significant archeological and medical traits of burials.

Bur. No.	Provenience	Cat. No.	Age (Years)	Sex	Stature	Position	Deformation
21	Upper East Trash Slope	13656	Infant	U		Flexed? Head on back	
22	Upper East Trash Slope	13657	Infant	U		Flexed?	
23	Upper East Trash Slope	13658	7 to 8	U		Flexed, knees drawn halfway to chin; on right side and face	Lambdoid flattening, extreme
24	Upper East Trash Slope	13659	Mature (senile?)	M	5′5″	Flexed, knees drawn halfway to chin; on left side	Lambdoid flattening, slight
25	Room 12, against west wall in undisturbed fill (Level B)	13660	1 or 1+	U		Legs detached from body; on left side	
26	Room 12, N. end next to wall in undisturbed fill (Level B)						
27	West Trash Slope	13662		U			
28	Kiva D, Southwest quadrant in disturbed fill	13664	Adult	F		Leg semiflexed	
29	Room 48, Southwest corner below "floor" or walking surface	13665	10±	U		Head on left side	Lambdoid flattening, extreme
30	Room 28, Southeast corner	13666	3 to 4	F		Tightly flexed; on back	
31	West Trash Slope	13667	Infant (a few months)	U		Flexed? On left side	
32	West Trash Slope	13668	1±	U		Semi-flexed: On back	Lambdoid flattening, moderate
33	Room 37, from rodent burrow through sealed niche at floor level, east end	13669	Infant	U			
34	Kiva B, fill between walls in southwest corner	13670	Adult	U			
35	About 400 yards south of Long House	13671	Adult	M?		On back	
36	Room 81	23676	11±1	M?			
37	Room 8, against west wall	23678	Infant	U		On back	
38	Kiva O	23679	31±4	M			
39	Kiva K, Level III	23683	$1^1/_2$ to 2	U			
40	Kiva M, Levels VII (fill) and IX (floor)	23685	29±1	M		On back	

west side of the hollow in which Burial 13 was placed were rough sandstone blocks, which may have been laid up in a crude retaining wall or grave lining. Once again, it is impossible to be sure that the rocks did not fall accidentally into this position. Burial 12 presented more definite evidence of grave lining (fig. 123). Several large sherds of two black-on-white bowls, a black-on-white water jar, and a black-on-white seed jar were used to line the south or downslope side of the grave.

Position

Despite the fact that few of the burials were still in a tightly flexed position, there is very little doubt that most of them were so positioned originally. Figures 124a and b show the fully flexed position: legs folded, with knees under the chin, and arms either folded across the chest or extended along the trunk.

The arms were definitely flexed in nine burials. They were placed across the chest in seven or eight of these, and across the abdomen in one. In another case, the right arm was flexed across the abdomen, the left across the chest. In three other burials, the arms may have been flexed. If so, two probably had the arms folded across the chest and one across the abdomen. In one of the burials in which the arms were folded across the chest, the hands were directly in front of the face.

In two burials, the right arm was flexed and the left arm was extended along the trunk. Only five or six burials had both arms

Orientation			Grave				
Head to (Burial Axis)	Facing	Depth below surface	Stratification	Lining	Wood above burial	Artifacts	Other
North (N 28° E)	Up	0.5′	Disturbed—moved down slope				
West?		0.5′	In trash—probably on sterile subsoil				
Northwest (N 60° W)	West and down	Surface to 0.3′	In trash on sterile subsoil				
Northwest (N 60° W)	West	1.0′	In trash				
South (S 18° W)	West		In room fill			Stone chip, 2 potsherds	
East (S 65° E)	South?	0.9′	In room fill			Stone chip, 5 potsherds, charred stick	
		0.7′	In trash on sterile subsoil				
		0.4′	Disturbed				
North (N 5° E)	Northeast	1.0′ (in Level C)	Subfloor fill			B/W mug, Corrugated jar—intrusive into burial for subfloor storage	
South	North and up	1.0′ above bedrock floor	In trash fill of abandoned room			Feather robe wrapped around body; Turkey—mummified	Body mummified
Southeast (S 45° E)	Southwest		In trash on sterile subsoil				Directly above skull of burial 32
South (S 15° W)	Up	0.5′-1.0′	In trash on sterile subsoil			Numerous eggshell fragments	
			Disturbed				
			Disturbed				
Southwest (S 45° W)	Up	0.1′ to 0.2′	In trash			Piece of feather wrapped cordage—probably intrusive	
			Disturbed				
South (S 5° W)		Intrusive into Level II from surface above	In trash				
			Disturbed; probably fell from burial site in Room 79. In fallen wall debris				
			In trash fill				
Northwest (N 45° W)			In fill, mixed with fallen wall and roof material; torso only on floor			Portion of B/W bowl—associated or intrusive?	Head appeared to have been twisted off while some skin or ligaments remained

extended along the trunk. It was impossible to determine the position of arms in 19 burials.

Orientation

Most of the burials were placed with the head to the north. Seventeen ranged from N 20° W to N 80° W, with eight at N 56° W to N 75° W. Four others ranged from N 4° E to N 28° E, with three at N 4° E or N 5° E. Two burials were positioned with the head due west.

Of the 12 burials with the head to the south, four ranged from S 15° W to S 45° W. Two were oriented with the head due south, and the other six ranged from S 33° E to S 66° E. (All bearings are true.)

It was impossible to determine the orientation in nine burials because of extensive disturbance. Some of this was due to shifting of material on the trash slopes, some to collapse into another structure of the room in which the burial was originally placed. It is possible that disturbance in some cases can be traced to both animal and human activity, especially since quite a bit of human bone was found scattered across the surface of the ruin prior to excavation.

An interesting example of disturbance is seen in Burial 40 (fig. 125). Very little can be determined regarding its original orientation. At the time of excavation the head, if present, would have been pointed southwest. It also would have extended out over the rim of the firepit of Kiva M. The body appears to have been placed, or thrown, onto its back in the middle of the kiva floor. At some time

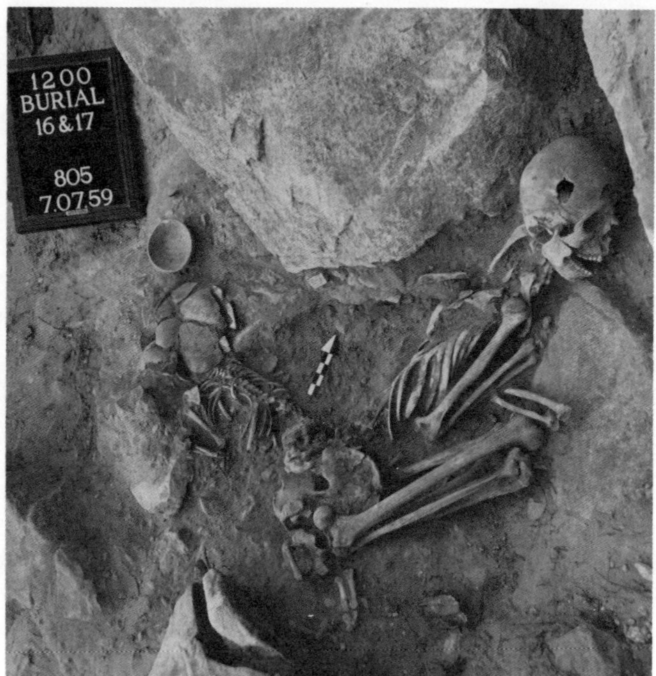

Figure 124. *Adult Burials 17 (above) and 8 (below) in East Trash Slope, showing fully flexed position.*

thereafter, apparently while some tissue was still holding the bones in an articulated position, the head, sternum, and ribs were twisted sharply down and to the left, and the head was removed. The legs and arms were also torn off. Several isolated human bones, probably from this burial, were found in the kiva fill nearby.

It would be interesting to know whether the body of Burial 40 was deliberately placed on the kiva floor, or at least in the fill in an abandoned kiva, or if it was thrown through the hatch of a kiva still in use. Kiva M burned, but the time of this event cannot be determined precisely. The extensive remodeling of the structure would suggest that it was in use during most of the final occupation of the cave. If so, the body was probably disturbed by animals after partial collapse of the roof made the floor accessible. The scattered bones in the kiva fill suggest that this alternative is the most likely.

Figure 125. *Remnants of Burial 40 found on the floor of Kiva M.*

It is also very difficult, if not impossible, to determine whether or not the direction in which the head faced had any significance. Head position depended, in many cases, upon shifting of the entire body or head alone after burial. Also, the skull was missing in some burials, or, in two cases (Burials 38 and 39), the skull *was* the "burial." Two additional crania were found in Kiva O with Burial 38 but were not assigned burial numbers. These loose skulls or parts probably came from fragmentary burials, such as 36 and 37, found in nearby rooms.

The most practical position in which a burial could be placed was generally parallel to the contour line of the slope at the burial location. Even when so placed, the steepness of the slope often resulted in a considerable variation in fill depth over the body. Thus very little natural erosion of the slope was necessary to uncover a portion of the burial. Erosion then became the prime factor in causing the shifting of the remains and, in some cases, entirely removed some or all of the bones from the original grave.

Nine of the trash slope burials were facing upslope, in most cases between north and east. At the time of excavation, seven of these were on the individual's left side, one on the back, and one on the left side and back (probably on the back, originally). Of the seven burials facing downslope, two were on the left side and face, one on the left side and back, and four on the right side and face. (Two had probably rolled from the back).

Two burials were perpendicular to the contour, one facing west with the head pointing downslope, the other facing east with the head pointing upslope. Four burials, placed on the back, were facing up. Two of these were on the East Trash Slope, one on the West Trash Slope, and one in Room 28. The burial in Room 48 faced the northeast and had been placed on the left side. In 17 cases, it was not possible to determine which way the head faced.

The significance of all this is debatable. There is an apparent trend toward burial on the left side or back, with the head to the north or west and facing east or north. Inclusion of burials which may have rolled from the left side or back to the right side would make the trend more significant.

In the case of the trash slope burials, more were facing upslope than downslope or straight up. This may be a function of preferred head direction and the side on which the burial was placed, rather than being meaningful in itself. The small size of the sample makes further attempts to determine patterns or trends rather futile.

Sex

In only 18 burials could sex be determined, or at least an opinion given, by the physical anthropologists. Eleven may have been males, but only seven are fairly definite. Seven may have been females, but, once again, only five appear to be definite.

If the remains of the five additional individuals found with Burials 36 and 38 are considered, the number of burials for which sex could be determined is increased by one, an adult female. Only the right innominate bone of this individual is present, and this may have come from another burial already tabulated. Therefore, this individual is not included in the above count.

Age

The range in age of the skeletal material covers the whole spectrum, from a few months to 45+ years, as shown in table 7. There are no sharply defined groups within the range, which forms, essentially, a continuum. However, there are several apparent categories, with the 3-years and under group being the most obvious. The large numbers of burials in the group probably reflects a high infant mortality. The few individuals above age 40 would indicate a relatively short average life span, if this sample is at all typical of the population as a whole.

A group of the 13 youngest ranges from a few months to 3 or 4 years in age. There are, at most, 6 in the next group, which includes the 7 to 10-year olds, 11± 1 year, and "young child." One other—"not over 15"—may belong to the group. Only two form the third, or "late teenage," group. These may actually fit in closely with another group of 14, which includes the "young adult" and those in the 20-to 35-year range. A possible break is found between the last group and individuals of 40 years of age and older. Two were considered to be "at least 40," one "mature (senile?)," and one 45+ years.

Table 7. Age distribution of Long House burials. All ages given in years

5–infant	2–late teenage
1–less than 1	—
1–1±	2
1–1+	
1–1 to 2	1 young adult
1–1 1/2	1–20 to 25
1–1 1/2 to 2	7–adult
2–3 to 4	1–29 ± 1
—	1–about 30
13	1–31± 4
	1–at least 30
1–7 to 8	1–30 to 35
1–9 ± 1	—
1–10±	14
1–11± 1	
1–young child	2–at least 40
1–not over 15	1–mature (senile?)
—	1–45±
6	—
	4

Total determinations: 39

Once again, if we also consider the 5 additional individuals represented in Burials 36 and 38, we could add to the above list three adults, a child or young adolescent, and an adolescent of 15± 1 year. Few bones of these five are present, and all could have come from burials already included in the above figures. Therefore, the five are not included in the counts above.

Stature

Stature could be estimated for only 14 individuals: six male, five female, and three indeterminate. The males ranged from a possible 5 feet 3 inches to 5 feet 7 inches, with one at 5 feet 4 inches and three at about 5 feet 5 inches to 5 feet 6 inches. One individual was placed at 5 feet 3 inches to 5 feet 6 inches. The females ranged from about 5 feet (two burials) to a possible 5 feet 4 inches, with two at about 5 feet 1 inch to 5 feet 2 inches. The most dubious is one placed at 5 feet 1 inch to 5 feet 4 inches. Heights of the three individuals for which sex could not be determined were 4 feet 11 inches + (two burials) and 5 feet 4 inches. All of the individuals for which measurements are available were late teenage or older, and thus of full stature.

The femur, tibia, and fibula were used in estimating stature in one burial, and the fibula alone in another. The femur and tibia were used in five burials, and the femur alone in another five burials.

Hair

The Federal Bureau of Investigation Laboratory, Washington, D. C., made a microscopic examination of eight hair specimens screened from human feces. The report, dated February 17, 1964, stated that "All of the hairs are human head hairs of Mongoloid origin. Most of them are dark reddish-brown and a few are black."

Burial Offerings

Although a large number of artifacts was associated with 18 burials, there was considerable variation from burial to burial in the objects placed with the body. There was much less variation in the location of the objects, since in 11 burials all or most of the artifacts were placed near or against the head.

A black-on-white bowl was found with nine burials. With four of these (Burials 4, 7, 8, and 12), there was also a black-on-white mug, with another (Burial 9) a black-on-white jar, and with yet another (Burial 15) a black-on-white dipper. One of these nine burials (Burial 1) was accompanied by two black-on-white bowls, as still another variation. Several large shreds served as a bowl cover in Burial 8 (fig. 124b).

In some graves containing pottery there was only one vessel. Burial 17 had a black-on-white dipper, and Burial 29 (fig. 126) had a black-on-white mug. The corrugated jar shown with the latter is a subfloor storage vessel; part of the burial was removed when the jar was put in place. Burials 18 and 40 had only one black-on-white bowl, each. In the case of Burial 12, a plain miniature dipper was added to the bowl and mug. Except for the corrugated jar with Burial 8, all of the whole or restorable vessels recovered from the burials were Mesa Verde Black-on-white or McElmo Black-on-white.

Several of the burials, including some already mentioned, contained artifacts other than pottery. Burial 4 had a bone awl and a lignite hair ornament, to judge by its position at the back of the head, besides the bowl and mug. The only artifact with Burials 6 and 11 was a projectile point, and the only item with Burial 21 a bone awl. To provide variety, a lapstone accompanied Burial 5, and a clay

Figure 126. *Black-on-White mug accompanying Burial 29 in Room 48.*

ball was with Burial 3. Also with Burial 3 was a stone chip, and small chips or cores may have been associated with Burials 3, 20, and 25. It was impossible to determine whether these were placed deliberately or merely happened to be in the fill near the burials. Numerous egg shell fragments were found near the skull of Burial 32.

Two burials departed radically from the general trend of placing one or two items of stone or pottery with the body. Burial 30 was wrapped in a feather and fur blanket (fig. 127a and b), as possibly less well preserved burials may have been, and was accompanied only by a turkey (fig. 127c). The bird (*Meleagris gallopavo*) and portions of the human burial were "mummified," or dessicated, to be more accurate. Details of the feather robe are discussed by Carolyn Osborne in ch. 7. A length of 2-ply, S-twist feather cordage with Burial 35 may have been from a similar robe.

An array of interesting objects accompanied Burial 10 (fig. 128). A side-notched ax, a large pendant, and a cone of green hornfels, a small pendant of turquoise, three cylindrical hematite paint stones, and a pair of eagle talons were found with the burial. When the backdirt from near the burial was screened, four other items were found: a bone pendant, a perforated eagle talon, and two crystals of quartz and fluorite. There is no question in my mind that all the objects were placed—probably in a container—beside the body at the time of burial. The container might have been a leather or cloth bag, or, less likely, a small basket. This individual may have been a "medicine man," but, if so, he was a young one, for the skeletal remains indicate a young adult. Sex could not be determined, but objects that might best be classed as ceremonial suggest that this was a man.

Artificial Skull Deformation

Lambdoid flattening was the only type of artificial deformation observed. Burials 11, 16, 18, and 24 showed a very limited amount of deformation, and Burials 4, 8, 15, and 32 showed a moderate

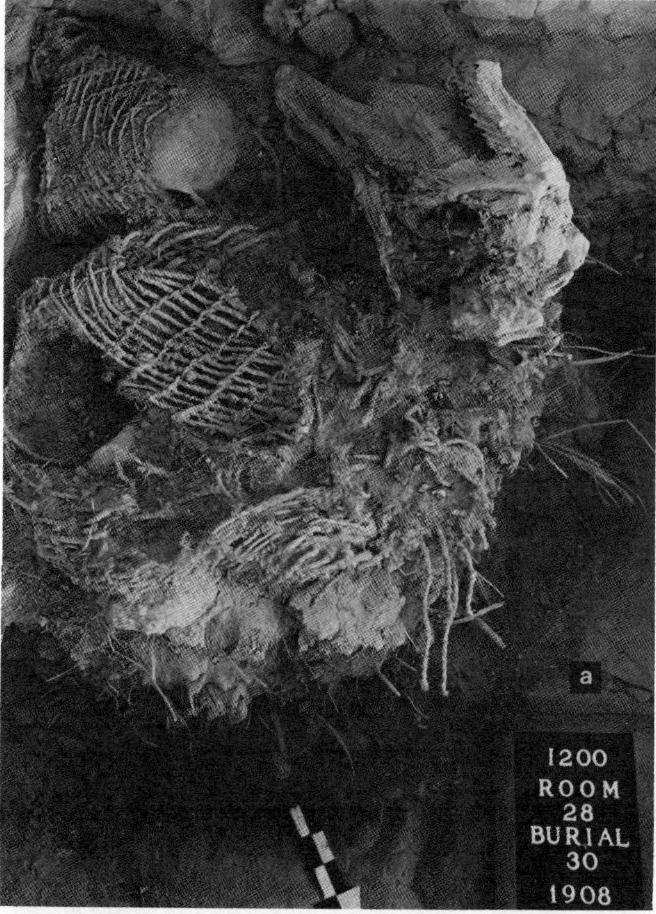

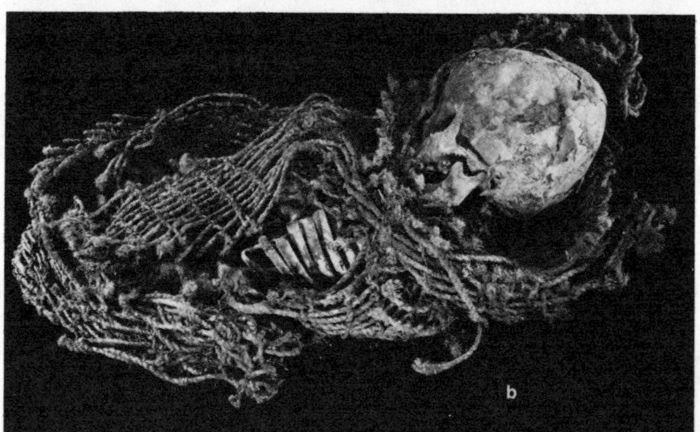

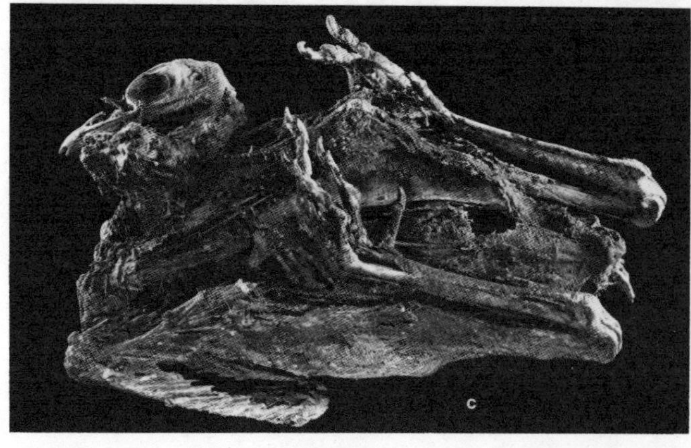

Figure 127. *Burial 30, in Room 28, wrapped in feather and fur blanket (a and b); and desiccated turkey accompanying Burial 30 (c).*

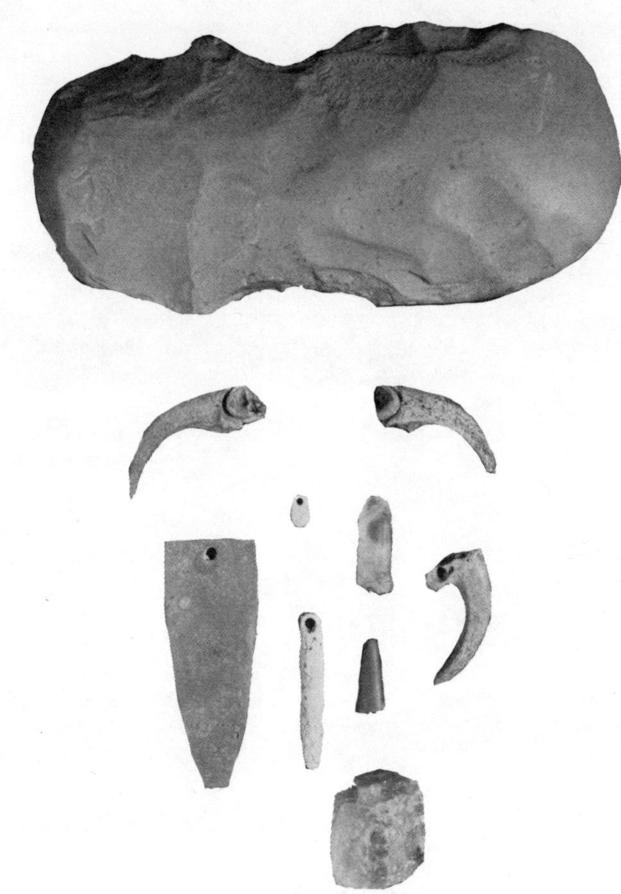

Figure 128. *Selected objects found with Burial 10: side-notched ax, large pendant, and cone of green hornfels; eagle talons; small pendant of turquoise; pendant of bone; and crystals of quartz and fluorite.*

amount. In Burial 4 the flattening was off center to the left; and in Burials 8 and 15 the flattening was located higher than usual. Considerable to extreme flattening was noted in Burials 17, 23, and 29. Burial 3 was very unusual in that it showed a pronounced asymmetrical right pterion form of lambdoid flattening.

Pathology

Dr. James Miles has discussed, in detail, bone pathologies of Wetherill Mesa burials in a report which has recently been published (Miles, 1976). A few of Dr. Miles' general observations regarding Long House burials may be mentioned briefly here.

Disturbances of prenatal origin are reflected in the fusion of vertebrae and of ribs 1 and 2 in Burial 24, and by the presence of an omohyoid bone in Burial 29. Osteoporosis, or a diminished density of the bone, is a metabolic disturbance observed in a vertebra of Burial 24.

The most frequent growth abnormalities are rotational deformities about the long axis of the lower extremity. Anteversion of the femoral neck, ranging from 27° to 35°, was noted in Burials 4, 7, 16, and 18, and in two bones not assigned to a specific burial. Regarding femoral anteversion, Dr. Miles has said, "I don't know whether this is a genetic deformity or not. I do know that it is developmental and that in most individuals the anteversion begins fairly high in children and that with subsequent development decreases. In other words, normal children may have an anteversion of 30 to 35 degrees whereas adults have an anteversion of only 18 to 20 degrees."

The commonest problem among the people of Long House was degenerative arthritis, which is evident in Burials 5, 7, 8, 11, 12, 15, and 24, and in two miscellaneous human bones (cat. nos. 14248/700 and 19489/700). Dr. Miles expressed the belief that the process began in the joints before age 35 and affected, in varying degree, almost all of the individuals who reached that age. He feels the process is the result of physical activity rather than living in a cave which can be rather damp and cold at times of the year.

As shown in Burial 12, there is indirect evidence for degenerative changes in the intervertebral disks. The subluxation of the facet joints and approximation of the spinous processes ("kissing spines") indicates a loss of vertical height of the disks.

Another degenerative change, a bunion, was observed in one of the miscellaneous human bones (cat. no. 27478/700). The bone is from an adult and shows mild osteophytosis of the medial aspect of the metatarsal head.

The only example of bone infection was in one of the miscellaneous bones (cat. no. 20069/700). Here we have pyogenic osteomyelitis in the femur of a child. At Dr. Miles's suggestion, further study was made of this bone on the chance that the lesion might be the result of syphilis. The bone was sent to Dr. Ellis R. Kerley, formerly Orthopedic Pathology Branch, Armed Forces Institute of Pathology, Washington, D.C., now University of Maryland. Dr. Kerley offered the following comments: "This specimen consists of an isolated femur of early adolescent age (about 12 years old). There is an eroding lesion of the medial aspect of the distal third of the femur. It is composed of a destructive focus surrounded by an expanding shell of reactive new bone. The marrow cavity appears to be normal, and the entire lesion seems to be the result of an inflammatory process eroding into the bone from overlying soft tissue. This active, chronic osteitis of the distal portion of the femur probably followed a local injury to the overlying soft tissue."

Burial 16 shows a giant cell turmor or "cyst" of the calcaneus. Dr. Miles considers this to be an example of benign neoplasia. He stated, further, that the precise nature of the lesion could not be determined but that it was unique for the calcaneus.

Surprisingly, considering the active life that these people must have led, there was evidence of only one fracture. This was a compression fracture of a vertebra in Burial 24, a mature (possibly senile) man.

Time period assigned to the burials

Tree-ring dates place the occupation of Long House at two time periods: the middle A. D. 600's (to?), Basketmaker III Stage; and from the late 1100's to perhaps A. D. 1280, late Pueblo III Stage. All of the burials are probably associated with the Pueblo III occupation; none can be assigned to the Basketmaker stage, nor is there any suggestion by provenience or associated material that any should be so assigned.

The burials that can be dated with most certainty to the late Pueblo III Stage, through architectural or ceramic associations, are as follows: Burials 1, 4, 7–10, 12, 15, 17, 18, 25, 26, 28–30, 33, 34, 37, and 40. The burial whose association with this stage is most dubious is Burial 11. It was in the trash slope about 70 feet below Site 1505. On the basis of pottery found on the talus below the cave, Alden Hayes believes that Site 1505 shows evidence of brief occupations in Pueblo II and Pueblo III times.

Chapter Four

Ceramics

Although the ceramics of Long House form only one facet of the Mesa Verde ceramic complex, they do bridge one of the most important stages in the occupation of the mesa: the movement of much of the population from mesa-top to cave sites during the early Pueblo III period.

The painted and utility potteries must go hand-in-hand culturally, although they have often been treated in analysis as two entirely separate aspects of the local ceramics. That is to say, the emphasis is placed on the classification of painted types, or of utility types, but only the gross associations of the two at specific time levels are noted.

The reasons for not attempting a closer association in analysis are obvious. The utility types often have a longer time span than the associated painted types, even extending through the life of two or more painted types of different chronological position. The changes made in utility pottery over a long period of time may be quite subtle, and they may be hard to recognize unless large sherds or whole vessels are present. Difficult though it may be to separate, in the analysis, certain local and intrusive painted wares of the same cultural stage, it is even more difficult to separate the utility wares. To further complicate the issue, the paste may be quite different in contemporaneous painted and utility types from one area.

The analysis of the Long House pottery produced no new methods for solving these and many of the other problems inherent in ceramic classification. However, most of the pottery is associated with the final stage of the prehistoric occupation of Mesa Verde. In relating the ceramic assemblage to the well–dated architecture of Long House, it is possible to suggest associations of painted and utility types with greater accuracy than has been done previously at Mesa Verde for this time period.

The locally made painted and utility wares of Mesa Verde appear to form a continuum from the earliest to the latest periods of occupation; that is, from Basketmaker III to Pueblo III times. All of the pottery has been influenced by that of other culture areas and has, in turn, influenced the pottery indigenous to these same areas. Certain techniques of construction, surface treatment, painted design, and the like, can be traced back through time and space to possible parent types, some far removed from Mesa Verde. Such relationships are rather vague, however, and are useful only when dealing with the broader aspects of Southwestern pottery evolution.

The Long House pottery not only reflects accurately the known periods of occupation of the pueblo, established by architecture and tree–ring dating, but it goes one step further. It permits a secondary division of the major periods, and thus makes possible a more subtle interpretation than could be gained by dated architecture alone. Pithouse I in Long House dates to the Basketmaker III period, but was it occupied into Pueblo I times? The major portion of the masonry pueblo dates to the late Pueblo III period, but were any parts of it possibly built during late Pueblo II or early Pueblo III times? Pottery is one of the major tools that can be used in an attempt to answer such questions.

In classifying the pottery, I have used existing type names so that comparisons can easily be made with other sites in the Southwest. I have also indicated throughout this section of the paper my suggested changes in the classification.

McElmo-Mesa Verde Black-on-white

The most significant pottery found at Long House is the painted type commonly known as Mesa Verde Black-on-white. It is the culmination, in design and technique, of all that had gone before. Nevertheless, it is not superior in all respects to the various pottery types which contributed to its development.

The prime reasons for the emphasis on Mesa Verde Black-on-white are twofold: it is distinctive in design, shape, and other physical attributes, and thus the better–made vessels (at least) can be recognized readily; and it had a short life span. The latter reason may not be plausible in light of dates that several archeologists working in the Mesa Verde area have assigned to the pottery, A.D. 1050 or 1100 to 1300. If this 200– to 250–year range is valid, Mesa Verde Black-on-white would then include the so-called McElmo Black-on-white and some material that might better be called Mancos Black-on-white: carbon paint variation. It would then also lose the first of the prime reasons for its significance—distinctiveness. Abel (1955: Ware 10B—Types 2 and 3) dates Mesa Verde Black-on-white at A.D. 1200 to 1300, or late Pueblo III stage, and McElmo (1955:Ware 10B—Type 1) at A.D. 1130 to 1200, or early Pueblo III stage.

Over a period of many years, archeologists have tried to define the cultural associations of Mesa Verde and Mancos Black-on-white, and to determine what occurred in the transitional period linking these types. The problem obviously involves more than just an exercise in pottery classification (Reed, 1958, pp. 102–109). It is also apparent that the transitional pottery, if it is to be named as a type or variety (and there may be more than one), must be sufficiently distinctive and culturally significant to warrant such classification.

McElmo Black-on-white is the name often given to the pottery transitional between Mancos and Mesa Verde Black-on-white. So far, it has been impossible to provide a clear-cut definition of the type, and the name has fallen into disrepute among many workers. McElmo Black-on-white has been treated as a catchall category by some archeologists, who throw into it vessels with design and shape identical to that of Mancos Blackon-white, execpt for having organic instead of mineral paint. They may include vessels with design and shape identical to that of Mesa Verde Black-on-white, differing only in having a more open design or possibly sloppier brushwork. Were it not for the preference for organic paint for Mesa Verde Black-on-white, rather than the mineral paint usually used on early Mancos and preceding black-on-white types, there probably would have been far less confusion over a transitional type.

It is particularly interesting to note that Joe Ben Wheat, in a discussion at one of the sites he was excavating in the Yellow Jacket area in 1963, expressed the opinion that McElmo is a valid type there. Possibly organic paint makes a later appearance on McElmo-Mesa Verda pottery at Yellow Jacket than it does on this pottery at Mesa Verde, since mineral paint may be predominant on McElmo at Wheat's sites. The sequences of pottery types for the two areas at this time period seem to be identical, and the appearance of organic paint—though it occurs at slightly different times—may be significant.

The extensive use of organic paint may have been one of several ceramic traits introduced into the Mesa Verde area from the Kayenta area. There are also similarities in design, rim, shape, and so forth in the two areas. But with some traits it is impossible to determine the direction of flow: did they go from the Kayenta area to the Mesa Verde, or the other way around? Or were both areas influenced by a third? In any case, what is the cultural significance of the extensive use of organic paint? I stress "extensive use" because organic paint also appears to a very limited extent on early black-on-white pottery at Mesa Verde (Hayes, 1964, table 4, p. 70). Brew (1946, p. 285) emphasizes the fact that mineral paint is basic in the Pueblo II and early Pueblo III stages of this general area, and that it probably continues throughout Pueblo III.

Rohn (1959), believing that Mesa Verde and McElmo Black-on-white were more closely related to one another than either was to Mancos Black-on-white, expanded the definition of Mesa Verde Black-on-white to include both "classic" Mesa Verde and McElmo. Following the type-variety concept of Wheat, Gifford, and Wasley (1958) and of Phillips (1958), he proposed two varieties, thus: Mesa Verde Black-on-white: Mesa Verde Variety (formerly Mesa Verde Black-on-white type); and Mesa Verde Black-on-white: McElmo Variety (formerly McElmo Black-on-white type). He also recognized a carbon paint variation of Mancos, and a mineral paint variation of McElmo Variety, to encompass vessels obviously transitional between Mancos and McElmo but with mixed diagnostic traits of the two. Abel's (1955) "Mesa Verde Polychrome" was reduced to "variation" status under the Mesa Verde Variety.

Although such a broad definition of Mesa Verde Black-on-white shows the close relationship between Mesa Verde and McElmo, there are several reasons why I believe it is not the best solution to the problem. First is the suggestion that McElmo Variety—although beginning earlier—coexists with Mesa Verde Variety throughout the life of the latter. Presumably, in the period of overlap of the two varieties, there would be many vessels with shape and finish typical of the Mesa Verde Variety but with designs typical or at least reminiscent of the McElmo Variety before creation of the Mesa Verde Variety. We would also expect to find vessels with the highly evolved designs of classic Mesa Verde but having the thinner walls and more rounded or tapered rims of the earlier McElmo. The evidence from Long House does not demonstrate— except to a very minor degree—the existence of either situation. It is hardly conceivable that the two varieties could exist side by side without extensive borrowing of traits, one from the other. If McElmo were in the process of being absorbed by the Mesa Verde Variety, it would be logical to expect the former of the above situations—at least to a greater degree than the latter. The thick, square-rim pottery seems more like the "style-of-the-moment" than does the McElmo style design, much of which is typical of Mancos Black-on-white. It is even more difficult to visualize the coexistence of Mesa Verde and McElmo without modification of shape and finish in the latter, especially when the two were being made in the same locality and probably in the same pueblo, as in Long House.

Jars and dippers present a problem in classification, mainly because the size of the field of decoration determines to a greater extent than on the large bowls the designs used by the potter. The majority of the dippers from Long House bear McElmo designs, but most were undoubtedly made at the same time as the larger bowls with Mesa Verde designs. Thus it is impossible to say whether the dipper is McElmo Variety or a "McElmo Style" within the Mesa Verde Variety. The usefulness of the McElmo Variety is therefore limited unless the time range can be shortened so as to restrict it primarily to the pre-Mesa Verde Variety period (with, necessarily, a certain temporal overlap). The tree–ring dates from Long House suggest that this can be done. The McElmo Variety would thus be a temporal, rather than a technological or areal, variant (Wheat, Gifford, and Wasley, 1958, pp. 36–37).

The recent excavations on Wetherill Mesa tend to substantiate the validity of a "transitional" pottery *type* between Mancos and Mesa Verde Black-on-white. We need to go a step beyond recognizing a transitional type, however, because I believe the transitional form is really the primary type, McElmo Black-on-white. Based mainly on the work in Long House, the "classic" Mesa Verde pottery would then become a late variety of McElmo Black-on-white. Wheat, Gifford, and Wasley (1958, p. 37–38) visualized the possibility of a situation in which it would be desirable to change an established type to a variety, or elevate a variety to a type.

Briefly, my reasons for suggesting this change in status of Mesa Verde Black-on-white are as follows. O'Bryan (1950, p. 109) discussed the possibility of a McElmo Phase, and cultural material from several of the sites excavated on Wetherill Mesa seems to support this classification. The transition from Mancos to McElmo Phase is coupled, roughly, with the beginning of McElmo Black-on-white pottery. The estimated date of transition is A.D. 1075. The introduction (or development) of practically all Pueblo III traits seems to occur at this time (Hayes, 1964, table 6, p. 88). The further development of early Pueblo III into Late Pueblo III culture, ca. A.D. 1225, brings refinements in at least two primary traits, architecture and pottery, with the latter reaching a peak of development in McElmo Black-on-white: Mesa Verde Variety. The last phase—the Mesa Verde— was a time not only for refinements in the material culture but also of social upheaval. A large percentage of the population, which had been living on the mesa top, now either moved into cave sites or left Mesa Verde entirely (Hayes, ibid., p. 109). Quite possibly both situations existed simultaneously, but the reasons for the disruption of an old living pattern are not yet known.

If the foregoing sequence proves to be true, then McElmo Phase and McElmo Black-on-white pottery are intimately related. Mesa Verde Phase and McElmo Black-on-white: Mesa Verde Variety stand in a similar relationship, but are specialized offshoots of the McElmo Phase and pottery.

I believe it is more logical to have the longer–lived and earlier (ancestral) aspect of the Mesa Verde–McElmo pottery carry the type name than to have the later, more temporally limited aspect carry it. If the type is named "Mesa Verde Black-on-white", some confusion is introduced because most archeologists associate the name with the "classic" pottery only, which has a limited number of design styles. McElmo, on the other hand, grows directly out of Mancos and has many design styles (only a few of which were adopted, along with styles more typical of Cortez Black-on-white, in a rather formalized manner for the classic pottery). If clearly defined as a type, McElmo becomes more than just an indeterminate, catchall category.

The Long House pottery is primarily "classic," with very little McElmo except in the earlier horizon. I believe that McElmo Black-on-white: McElmo Variety faded out between A.D. 1225 and 1250. If so, it is much more valuable as a taxonomic tool because of its primary association with the McElmo Phase. Certain McElmo design styles are carried over, essentially unmodified, into the classic pottery, but the limited amount seems to suggest that it is a design style, not a concurrent variety.

There is no intent here to change the name of pottery types purely for the sake of change. One of the problems that will arise, if such a change is made, is the question of name priority. Colton and Hargrave (1937, pp. 21–22) suggested seven "rules of priority" which have been followed (as far as I know) by most archeologists working in the Southwest. Such rules are needed, but since they cannot possibly cover all situations which may develop after their adoption, they should be interpreted and applied logically rather than blindly.

In the case of "McElmo" and "Mesa Verde," the type named earlier (Mesa Verde Black-on-white: Kidder, 1924, pp. 63–66) would be retained essentially as defined and understood by most archeologists concerned; only its status would be changed, from type to variety. Similarly, if we adopt Rohn's preliminary classification, the type would be expanded beyond what is generally accepted as "Mesa Verde Black-on-white," resulting in its redefinition. His "Mesa Verde Variety" would be the same as mine, the conventionally accepted "Mesa Verde Black-on-white."

A third alternative should be mentioned: retention of both Mesa Verde and McElmo as types. This classification, which is being used by Wheat at Yellow Jacket and has been adopted by Robert Nichols (MS.) and Jervis Swannack (1969) at Mesa Verde, certainly has merit and could—depending on the interpretation given the material by the three archeologists just mentioned—provide the best answer to the classification problem. For one thing, it would facilitate setting up temporal varieties within McElmo pottery, as Nichols and Swannack feel may be necessary. The separate-type classification fails only in not showing the intimate relationship between the two (intensified at Mesa Verde, at least, by having organic paint common to both). According to the two classifications suggested by Rohn and me, indeterminate sherds that cannot be classified as either McElmo or Mesa Verde Variety can be called "McElmo Black-on-white" or "Mesa Verde Black-on-white."

As implied in the foregoing discussion, the primary classificatory feature for this pottery is design style. All of us recognize the significance of temper, polish, slip, etc., as useful tools in pottery classification. Some writers consider them to be far more significant than design style for taxonomic purposes, and possibly their argument is valid for certain pottery types or even certain geographical areas. At Mesa Verde, at least when working with the Pueblo III black-on-white pottery, we find the range in variation of physical traits such that these traits become useful only when considering relative frequencies for the pottery as a whole. For example, how do Mesa Verde and Chaco Canyon types of the Pueblo III stage compare in regard to percentage of sand and sherd temper, or in regard to vessel–wall thickness? Can the traits be used to pinpoint the area in which a vessel was manufactured?

Shepard (in Vivian, 1959, pp. 26 and 28) has pointed out the great variation of temper found in Chaco hachured iron paint pottery and Chaco McElmo, and the difficulty of trying to determine intrusive temper and thus, possibly, intrusive pottery. Shepard found seven types of temper in the small batch of sherds sent her by Vivian, and she observed:

> I know of no practicable means of identifying intrusive, sherd-tempered pottery in Chaco. Although there may be other intrusives in Vivian's sample, I don't mean to imply that any considerable portion of the carbon paint pottery is intrusive, and I think the sanidine-basalt tempered sherd temper is a good indication of a Chaco product. Carbon paint and McElmo–like design suggest a foreign element moving into Chaco. They would have used local clays and potsherds, and they may well have been following their original technique of tempering.

I may seem to be going far afield to prove a point by using Chaco pottery as an example. The ceramics of the two areas are closely related, however, and any McElmo-Mesa Verde type classification should be flexible enough to allow inclusion of both Mesa Verde and Chaco "varieties," if such they prove to be. Needless to say, the variation in tempering material in this pottery is not limited to Chaco and Mesa Verde. Similar problems have been encountered at Aztec (Vivian, 1959, pp. 26, 28 and 31), and in that portion of the San Juan drainage covered by the Glen Canyon Project (Ambler and Lister, 1960, p. 219).

Other physical traits must also be considered, of course, and many times it is a cluster of such traits that will prove to be important, rather than any one alone. Mancos Black-on-white, for example, has a higher percentage of rock temper, mineral paint, and thinner walls on the average than does the McElmo-Mesa Verde pottery. These traits, coupled with differences in shape and design, make it possible to differentiate the two in the bulk of the specimens. Nevertheless, there are many McElmo or even Mesa Verde vessels with mineral paint, thin walls, rock temper, etc., or with a combination of several of these traits. The most consistently distinctive trait is the design. Similar design elements, units or even motifs are found on these pottery types, but the way in which they are arranged, or the combination of design components, is generally distinctive.

At only three Mesa Verde sites is McElmo Black-on-white known to be dominant (Swannack, 1969, p. 91). It is interesting to note that Vivian (1959, p.26) found McElmo to be the dominant type at Kin Kletso (Chaco Canyon), where it comprised 80 percent of the decorated wares in some refuse–filled rooms. Bannister (in Vivian, ibid., p. 69) has reported tree–ring dates as late as A.D. 1178 from Kin Kletso, but they are from charcoal specimens found in the fill rather than from in–place structural members. Roberts (MS., pp. 96–102) has very aptly termed this pottery "Chaco/San Juan." As Vivian (ibid., p. 28) points out, "substantially, the Chaco phase of McElmo is classic Chaco hachured paste bearing wide–line McElmo designs in carbon paint."

McElmo pottery does occur in limited quantities in several classic Chaco ruins, such as Pueblo Bonito, Chettro Kettle, and Pueblo del Arroyo. It occurs to a greater extent in ruins whose plan and architecture are not typically Chaco, such as the tri-wall structure at Pueblo del Arroyo, Bc–50, Bc–51, Bc–59, and, of course, Kin Kletso. A similar situation would be expected at Casa Chiquita and New Alto, which are contemporaneous with Kin Kletso, to judge from surface indications. In all the excavated ruins, McElmo pottery does not seem to lead into Mesa Verde, which is either entirely absent or represented by only a few sherds (Vivian, ibid., p. 69).

Vivian goes on to say that five or six rooms which he investigated near the Gallo Canyon "showed a total of Mesa Verde Black-on-white sherds of a rather decadent character, and no McElmo." He suggests a break between the late, indigenous Chaco occupation and "a reoccupation in quite small groups by carriers of well–developed or even decadent Mesa Verde Black-on-white (Montezuma Phase)."

Table 8. Provenience of sherds recovered in 1958-63.

Pottery Type	Rooms					Kivas					Areas					West Trash				
	Bowls	Jars	Mugs	Dippers	Total	Bowls	Jars	Mugs	Dippers	Total	Bowls	Jars	Mugs	Dippers	Total	Bowls	Jars	Mugs	Dippers	Total
Mesa Verde Black-on-white	784	71	22	7	884	780	104	24	9	917	1716	187	51	9	1963	611	62	30	2	705
Unslipped	13				13	9	4	1		14	26	5			31	7	7	1		15
Mineral Paint																				
Corrugated neck																				
McElmo Black-on-white	172	15	1	4	192	116	13	1	7	137	207	24	4	9	244	38	7	1	5	51
Unslipped	4	5			9	11	4			15	24	29	3		56	6	3			9
Exterior rimfillet																				
Indeterminate (M.V./McE.)	710	328	12	23	1073	645	192	13	21	871	1116	353	24	48	1541	274	85	6	5	370
Plain sherds from B/W vessels	15			1	16	11			1	12	25			1	26	2				2
Mancos Black-on-white	24	25			49	11	26	1		38	12	25			37	8	1		1	10
Unslipped																				
Corrugated exterior	1				1	4				4	3				3					
Carbon paint						1				1										
Ticked rim																				
Cortez Black-on-white	4	9			13	3	6			9	4	1			5	1				1
Corrugated exterior																				
Piedra Black-on-white	1				1	6				6						1				1
Carbon paint																				
Chapin Black-on-white	6				6	11				11	1				1					
Carbon paint						1				1										
Fugitive red						1				1										
Abajo Red-on-orange	1				1	1	1			2	1				1					
Bluff Black-on-red	1				1	3				3	2	1			3	2				2
Querino Polychrome																				
Gallup Black-on-white																				
Red Mesa Black-on-white																				
Wingate Black-on-red						1				1										
Unclassified or dubious	615	1007	4	46	1672	577	885	4	32	1478	978	1073	2	62	2116	241	324		10	575
Red ware	2	1			3	6	1			7		1			1	3				3
Mesa Verde Corrugated		1087			1087		534			534		581			581		139			139
Patterned		41			41		59			59		27			27					
Corrugated rim		93			93		138			138		89			89		8			8
Hovenweep Corrugated		68			68		55			55		25			25					
Mancos Corrugated		28			28		23			23		14			14		9			9
Diagonal ridged		8			8		4			4		11			11		8			8
Patterned		6			6															
Incised and punctuate		2			2															
Indeterminate corrugated		7823			7823		4500			4500		5039			5039		1522			1522
Patterned		8			8		12			12		30			30		15			15
Flattened coil		1			1		9			9		32			32					
Incised												1			1					
Hovenweep Gray												3			3		2			2
Mancos Gray		4			4		8			8		6			6		9			9
Moccasin Gray		5			5		4			4		3			3		6			6
Chapin Gray	6	26			32	6	33		1	40		17			17		6			6
Indeterminate plain gray	9	283		1	293	10	216			226	6	83			89		70			70

Table 8. Provenience of sherds recovered in 1958-63. (Continued)

Pottery Type	Upper East Trash Slope					Lower East Trash Slope						General						Tests					
	Bowls	Jars	Mugs	Dippers	Total	Bowls	Jars	Mugs	Dippers	Indeter.	Total	Bowls	Jars	Mugs	Dippers	Indeter.	Total	Bowls	Jars	Mugs	Dippers	Indeter.	Total
Mesa Verde Black-on-white	255	53	10	5	323	1988	333	75	30		2426	386	33	11	4		431	131	18	4			153
Unslipped	3				3	79	3	3	1		86	10	1				11		1				1
Mineral Paint							1				1												
Corrugated neck													1				1						
McElmo Black-on-white	104	8	3	3	118	441	26	11	28		506	31	3		7		41	17	4	1	2		24
Unslipped	2	3	1		6	56	10	4	2		72	8					8						
Exterior rimfillet						1					1												
Indeterminate (M.V./McE.)	223	88	7	7	325	1484	524	47	133		2188	134	55		15		204	62	29		3		94
Plain sherds from B/W vessels						7					7	6					6						
Mancos Black-on-white	10	18			28	54	116		8		178	6	11		1		18	1	12				13
Unslipped						2	5				7								1				1
Corrugated exterior						5					5												
Carbon paint									2		2								1				1
Ticked rim						3					3												
Cortez Black-on-white	2	2			4	18	18		1		37		2				2		1				1
Corrugated exterior						1					1												
Piedra Black-on-white	2				2	38	17				55							3					3
Carbon paint						2					2												
Chapin Black-on-white	4				4	38					38	10					10	4	1				5
Carbon paint																							
Fugitive red																							
Abajo Red-on-orange						24	1				25							1					1
Bluff Black-on-red	7				7	20	4				24							1					1
Querino Polychrome						1					1												
Gallup Black-on-white		1			1																		
Red Mesa Black-on-white	1				1																		
Wingate Black-on-red																							
Unclassified or dubious	219	297	3	17	536	2054	1418		91	278	3841	151	177		12		340	70	86		1	27	184
Red ware	7	3			10								1					1	1	1			2
Mesa Verde Corrugated		119			119		661				661		53				53		43				43
Patterned		8			8		2				2		4				4						
Corrugated rim		13			13		17				17		4				4		3				3
Hovenweep Corrugated		26			26								14				14						
Mancos Corrugated		8			8		23				23		1				1		4				4
Diagonal ridged		5			5		19				19		3				3		1				1
Patterned		1			1								2				2						
Incised and punctate																							
Indeterminate corrugated		1083			1083		6603				6603		693				693		235				235
Patterned		46			46		180				180												
Flattened coil							109				109												
Incised																							
Hovenweep Gray																							
Mancos Gray		3			3		11				11		1				1		2				2
Moccasin Gray		5			5		28				28		1				1		3				3
Chapin Gray	4	41			45	25	156			1986	2167	1	6				7		17			57	74
Indeterminate plain gray		303			303		25				25	14	31			20	65		3			48	51

Table 8. Provenience of sherds recovered in 1958-63. (Continued)

Pottery Type	General Features Bowls	Jars	Mugs	Dippers	Totals Total	Bowls	Jars	Mugs	Dippers	Indeter.				
Mesa Verde Black-on-white	23	2			25	6674	863	227	63		7827			
Unslipped											174	8003		
Mineral Paint							1				1			
Corrugated neck							1				1			
McElmo Black-on-white						1126	100	22	65		1313			
Unslipped						111	54	8	2		175	1489		
Exterior rimfillet						1					1			
Indeterminate (M.V./McE.)	8	3			11	4656	1657	109	255		6677			
Plain sherds from B/W vessels						66			3		69	6746		
Mancos Black-on-white	1				1	127	234	1	10		372			
Unslipped						2	6				8			
Corrugated exterior						13					13	400		
Carbon paint						1	1		2		4			
Ticked rim						3					3		27,728	
Cortez Black-on-white						32	29		1		72			
Corrugated exterior						1					1	73		
Piedra Black-on-white						51	17				68			
Carbon paint						2					2	70		
Chapin Black-on-white						74	1				75			
Carbon paint						1					1	77		
Fugitive red						1					1			
Abajo Red-on-orange						28	2					30		
Bluff Black-on-red						36	5					41		
Querino Polychrome						1						1		
Gallup Black-on-white							1					1		63,461
Red Mesa Black-on-white						1						1		
Wingate Black-on-red						1						1		
Unclassified or dubious	8	15		3	26	4914	5262	13	274	305	10,768	10,795		
Red ware						20	7				27			
Mesa Verde Corrugated		10			10		3227				3227			
Patterned								141			141	3733		
Corrugated rim							365				365			
Hovenweep Corrugated							188					188		
Mancos Corrugated							110				110			
Diagonal ridged							59				59	180		
Patterned							9				9			
Incised and punctate							2				2			
Indeterminate corrugated		67			67		27565				27,565		35,733	
Patterned							291				291	28,008		
Patterned coil							151				151			
Incised							1				1			
Hovenweep Gray							5					5		
Mancos Gray							44					44		
Moccasin Gray		1			1		56					56		
Chapin Gray	1	2			3	43	304		1	2043		2391		
Indeterminate plain gray		6			6	39	1020		1	68		1128		

Approximately 63,000 sherds were recovered from the surface and fill during the excavation of Long House (table 8). Twenty-five percent were McElmo-Mesa Verde Black-on-white. No attempt has been made to classify all pottery of this type by design style. Design analysis has been based on whole or restorable vessels (table 9), on approximately 5,200 sherds from the Lower East Trash Slope (thoroughly mixed and unstratified), and on selected sherds from other parts of the ruin. The measurements and provenience of illustrated whole or restorable vessels are given in table 14 at the end of this report.

McElmo-Mesa Verde Black-on-white pottery designs have been described in great detail by a number of students, especially Morris (1939), Shepard (1957), and Leavitt (1962). I will not attempt to duplicate the comprehensive work that has been done previously on Mesa Verde pottery as a whole. Rather, I am borrowing ideas in an attempt to set up a concise and simple framework into which I can fit, hopefully with a minimum of jamming, the designs most typical of this pottery as represented by the Long House collection. It should be flexible enough to encompass ramifications of the designs with which I am familiar. The pottery was undoubtedly bound by certain traditions which changed rather slowly, but there was also considerable latitude for individual expression within these traditions.

No one will ever know what observations or ideas led to the creation of the various elements of geometric design, especially since many of them can be created in various ways. This is of academic interest to the archeologist, whereas the student of art or psychology might find it a point of departure for a more esoteric discussion. Thus the few design classes which I am suggesting for the analysis of design do not imply any evolutionary step in the development of the designs. Nor do they imply that the potter laid out her design according to the symbols used to designate design class. I cannot stress too strongly that many components of design can be created in many different ways, and the difficulty in analyzing a design increases in direct proportion to its complexity. The problem is further confounded by not knowing with what components of design the potter worked. Shepard (1957, p. 267) stated the problem aptly:

> In the analysis of prehistoric pottery it is not always possible to recognize the potter's motifs, but the repetition of arrangements of elements on the same vessel and their appearance on other vessels will at least be significant. Because of the greater complexity, the motif is necessarily more varied and distinctive than the element. The same simple geometric figures appear again and again in various styles. Their usefulness in analysis depends on the complexity of the style. The simpler the style, the greater the probability that the element is the basic decorative unit, and the more significant it will be. The more complex the design, the greater the probability that the units of composition are combinations of elements. The concept of the element has been especially helpful in the study of sherds because a small part of design shows in the fragment when motifs and structures do not. The sherd at best, however, gives a sketchy and incomplete record of design and it would be unfortunate if dependence on sherds should dictate methods of analysis.

Rather than attempt to break down the various designs into elements, motifs, and the like, I am using for the most part the term "design component." The reader is referred to Leavitt (1962) for a thorough discussion of elements and their combinations. Note especially his definition of three terms: *element, unit,* and *motif* (Leavitt, ibid., pp. 189–192).

Such classification is important in detailed studies of design; it is less important for a discussion of the present material. I have used the term *element* in setting up classes of design, and the reader will recognize *units* and *motifs* in the combinations of elements illustrated herein.

The field of design on a vessel is another factor severely limiting the composition and thus its constituent parts. In the case of bowl interiors, for example, the limits of a band design are two parallel lines; those of an all-over design a circle. As these primary areas are further subdivided, the limits will again change. Only certain components of design can be used in these variously shaped sections. The complexity of the motif that the potter plans to use and its size relative to that of the section in which it will be used are two primary factors in fitting design to a field of predetermined shape. A third factor, which must have created trouble for many a beginning painter, is the vessel contour. It is very difficult to draw certain designs (such as life forms) on an area with a sharp break in curvature, such as a jar shoulder or the junction of a vertical jar neck with the sloping side wall of the vessel. Perspective is an ever–present problem in such cases, and can be just as difficult with simple, straight–line designs.

Field of Design (fig. 129). On McElmo-Mesa Verde pottery the field of design is generally sharply defined. The primary exceptions are the interior bottoms and, to a lesser extent, the entire exterior of bowls and dippers, and jar necks, interior and exterior. The field of design for the most conventional shapes (bowl, dipper, mug, and jar) will practically always fall into one of three categories: overall (fig. 130a-j) banded (fig. 130k-m), and isolated (fig. 130n and o). The first two of these—and occasionally the third—may in turn be subdivided, thus creating secondary and tertiary fields of design. Theoretically, the overall design would seem limited to bowl and dipper interiors. In actual practice, jar designs were apparently meant to be viewed from the top of the vessel, and thus were constructed in the same manner as an overall design in a bowl or dipper. Allowance had to be made for the mouth of the jar, but apparently this was not difficult.

The banded design is found on bowl and dipper interiors, and on bowl, jar, and mug exteriors. Mugs are generally too straight

Table 9. Whole or restorable vessels.

	Bowls	Large Worked Bowl Sherds	Jars	Canteens	Effigy Vessels	Mugs	Dippers	Totals
Black-on-white								
Mesa Verde	107	8	26	—	—	21	7	169
McElmo	19	1	3	1	—	1	12	37
Indeterminate **(Mesa Verde-McElmo)**	6	—	1	1	1	1	—	10
								216
Corrugated								
Mesa Verde	—	—	46	—	—	—	—	46
Hovenweep	—	—	13	—	—	—	—	13
Indeterminate **(Mesa Verde-Mancos)**	—	—	1	—	—	—	—	1
								60
Plainware								
Mesa Verde White Ware	2	—	1	—	—	1	3	7
Late Pueblo II III	—	—	—	—	—	—	4	4
Chapin Gray	2	—	3	—	—	—	—	5
Unclassified	—	—	2	—	—	1	—	3
								19
							Total	295

sided to make top viewing of the design possible. In the Long House material, isolated designs are generally confined to bowl exteriors and bottom interiors, and in one case to the bottom exterior of a small jar. I have omitted from the discussion so far the decoration of mug, dipper, and jar handles, and the rims of all vessel forms. Rim decoration will be treated in another section, as will the less formalized decorations found on handles; they do not conform to the pattern of design found on other parts of the vessels.

Division of the Field of Design (fig. 130). Rarely is the field of design covered by one design unit or motif (a). More commonly it is divided into bands, panels, or sectors (b-m). With a band design, only a portion of one surface of a vessel available for use (for example, a bowl interior) is covered with the design. With a sector or panel design, all or practically all of the surface is used, and thus these two are treated here as divisions of the overall field category. A band is an equally valid division of the overall design, but since it is usually analyzed as extended rather than in its circular context, it will be considered here as the second field category. The overall design and the divisions just mentioned, band included, comprise the primary layout.

A further sectioning of the band, panel, or sector—or, in some cases, a subdivision or elaboration of a main design unit—forms the secondary layout. Additional subdivision within the secondary layout would create the tertiary layout which, as Leavitt (1962, p. 191) points out, is rare.

The terms used to describe the primary layout leave much to be desired. They will serve, however, to describe the division of the design field without resorting to a more definitive, but far lengthier, verbal description each time a reference is made.

The primary layout of a circular field (bowl, dipper, and jar viewed from the top) usually will be banded (fig. 130k), bisected(b), paneled(c), trisected(g), or quartered(d). Although there were several examples of the offset trisected design, there were none of the true trisected from Long House. The sectoring lines in an overall design may meet at the center of the design (radii of a circle,d), or may be slightly offset so as to create a square or triangle at the center (partial chords of a circle,f and h). Panels are formed by full chords, with length of the panel determined by its distance from the center(c). If two central panels cross at right angles to one another, a variant of the quartered design is created(e). Unequal division of a bisected field will also result in a variant of the quartered design. If the "arms" of an offset-quartered design are removed, an overall design with a square section at the center remains(i). Similar treatment of an offset trisected field results in a triangular center.

Subdivision in a sector, panel, or band results in a secondary layout. The panel and band are both long areas bounded by parallel lines, and when divided are termed sectioned. The sections are usually square or rhombic but may be of other shapes. The most common secondary division of a sector is paneling. Additional sectioning of a panel in a sector would be an example of tertiary layout.

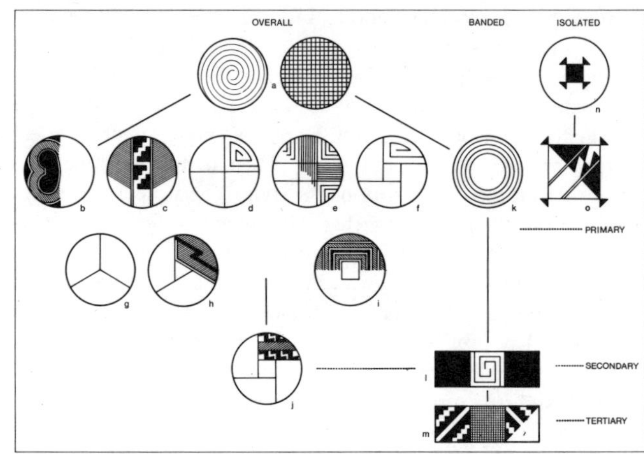

Design Classes. Five major design classes, with a sixth catchall category for miscellaneous designs, encompass all of the variations found on McElmo-Mesa Verde pottery from Long House (fig. 131). Several typical arrangements are given for each class and its subdivisions, and sherds and vessels illustrating several variations are also shown. Assignment to a class is based on the major design class present, with other classes being represented in the secondary and tertiary layout. Classes I and II (figs. 132 and 133) are examples of line structure. Shepard (1957, p. 297) used the term for what I have designated as design class IIA. She used the terms "net structure" for class IB and "striping" for Class IA. In all cases the principal element is the straight line, and I have taken the liberty of using her term "line structure" to cover all three categories. I have also added to the category, in class IA, right-angle or diagonal hatching between parallel lines. Shepard (1957, p. 299) would call this "filler."

Class III (figs. 134–136) is based on the zigzag line, with the oblique and right triangles and the stepped figure (variation of the right triangle) as the principal elements. Classes IIIB and IIIC display two methods of doubling the basic design, while still using the same elements. Doubling coupled with reversal in parts of the design, created a wide variety of patterns.

Class IV (figs. 137–140) consists of the fret and its variations. The principal elements are the rectangular and triangular fret and the spiral. Doubling, as seen in classes IVB and IVC, results in the S-

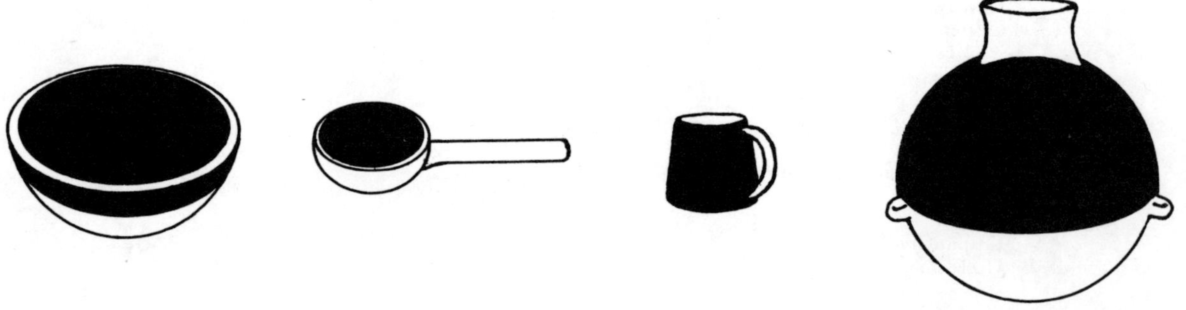

Figure 129. *Conventional vessel shapes: bowl, dipper, mug, and jar.*

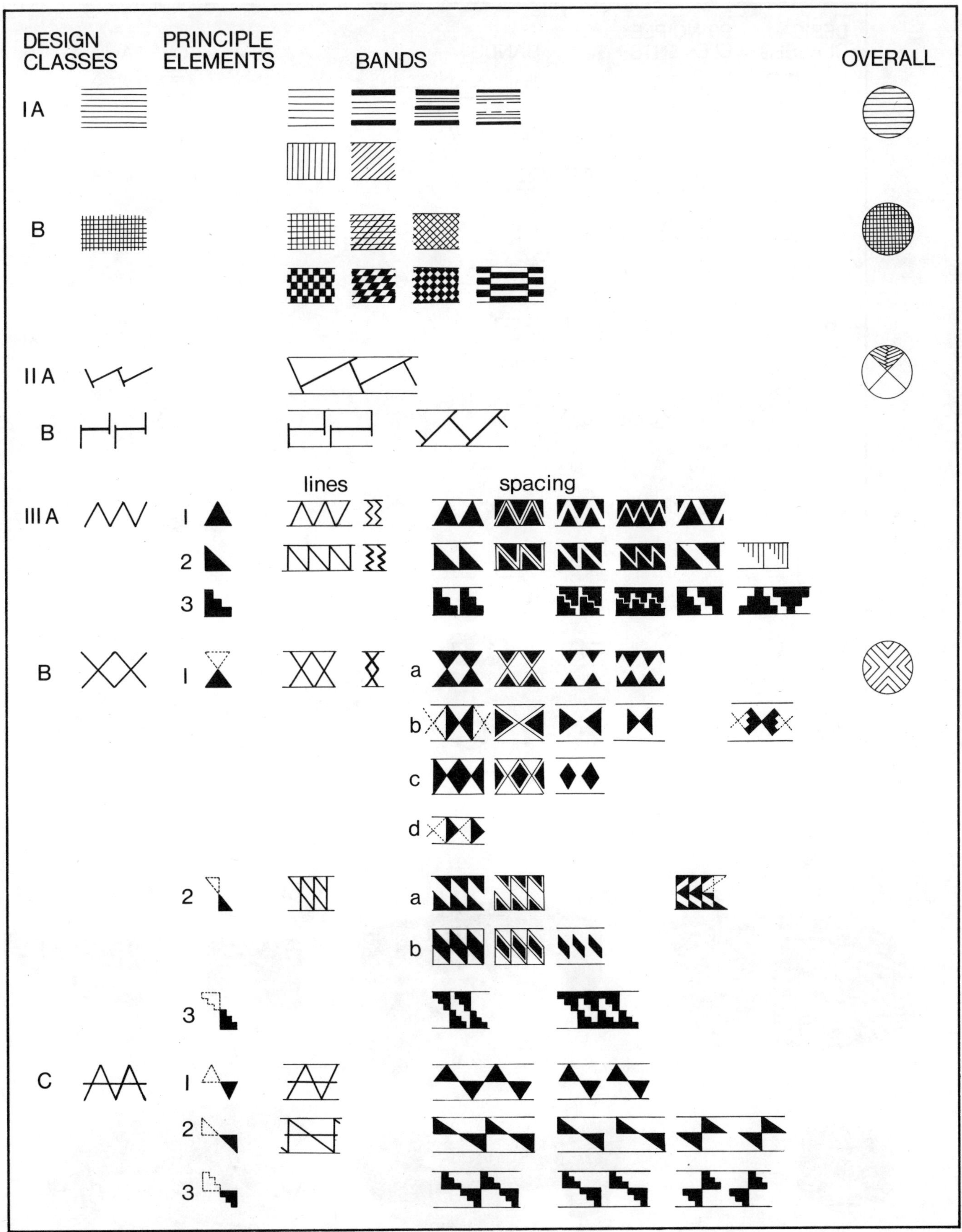

Figure 130. *(Above left) Field of design: overall (a-j), banded (k-m), and isolated (n and o).*

Figure 131. *(Above) Five major design classes, and a category of miscellaneous designs, found on McElmo-Mesa Verde Black-on-white pottery in Long House. (Continued on next page)*

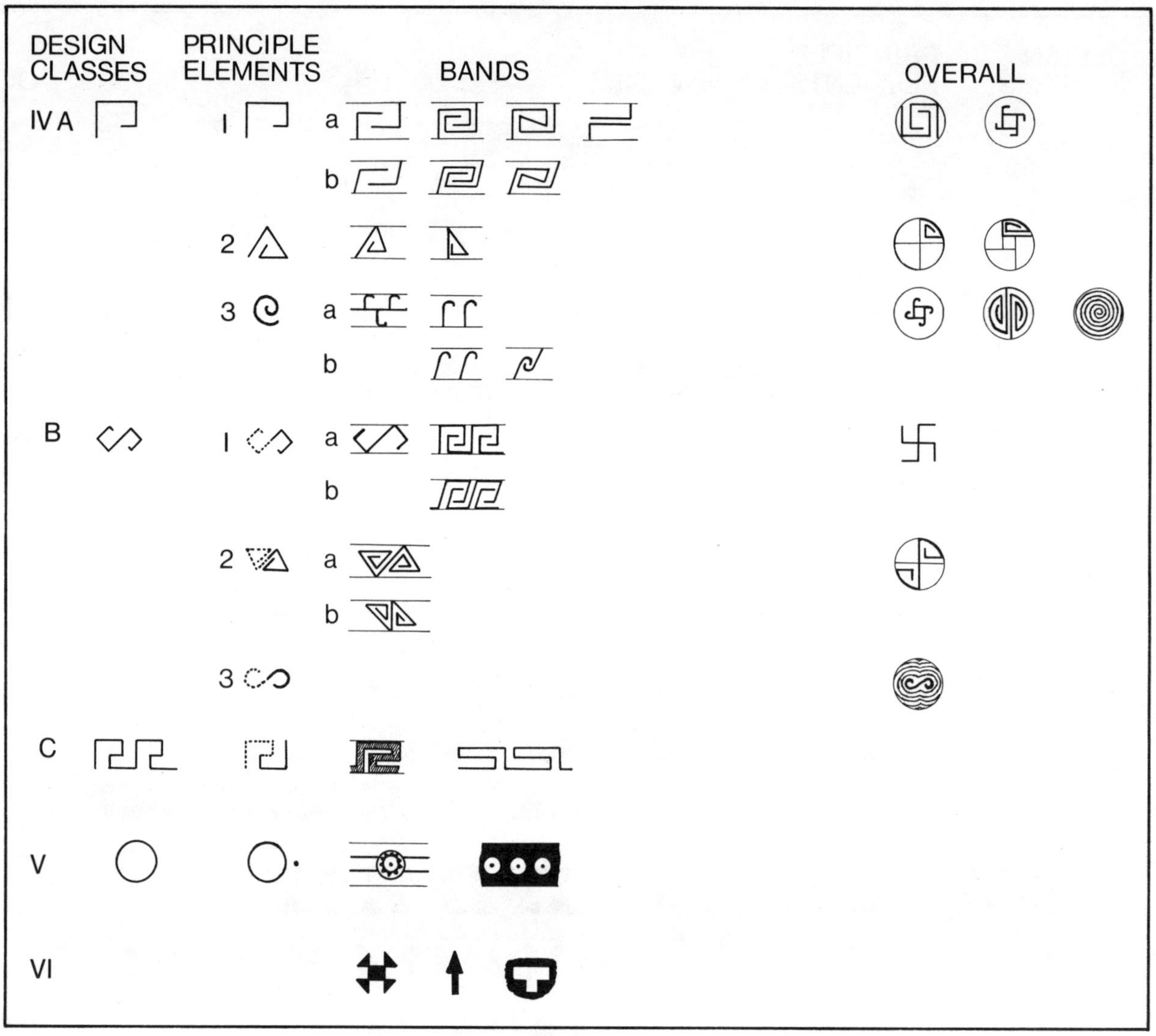

DESIGN CLASSES
PRINCIPLE ELEMENTS
BANDS
OVERALL
IV A
1
a
b
2
3
a
b
B
1
a
b
2
a
b
3
C
V
VI

Figure 131. *(Continuation)*

a
b
c
d
e
f

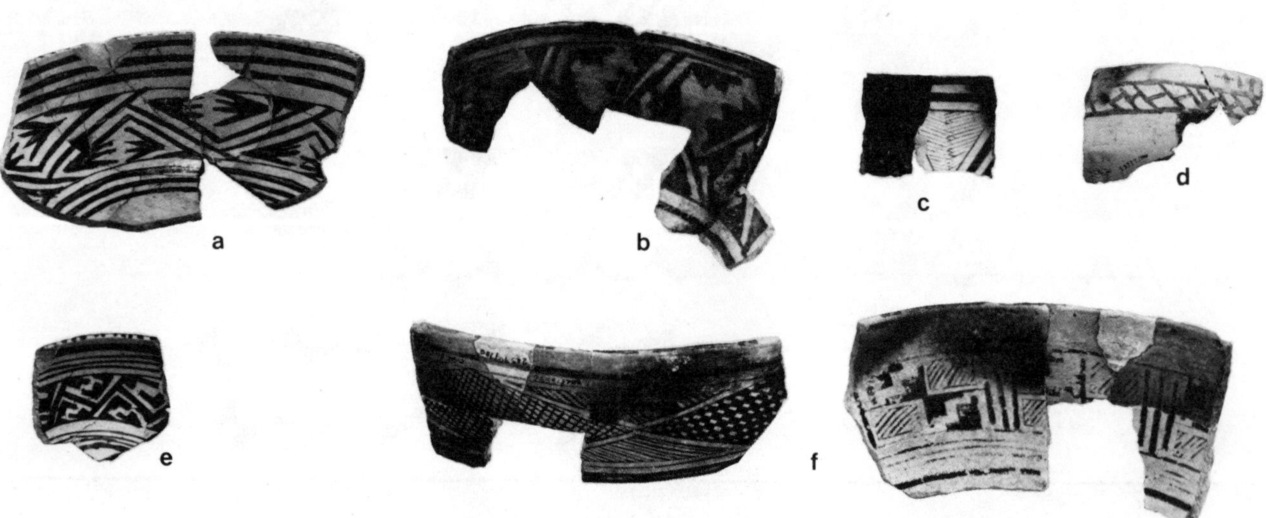

Figure 133. *Mesa Verde Black-on-white, design class II. Maximum estimated diameter of f, 28 cm.*

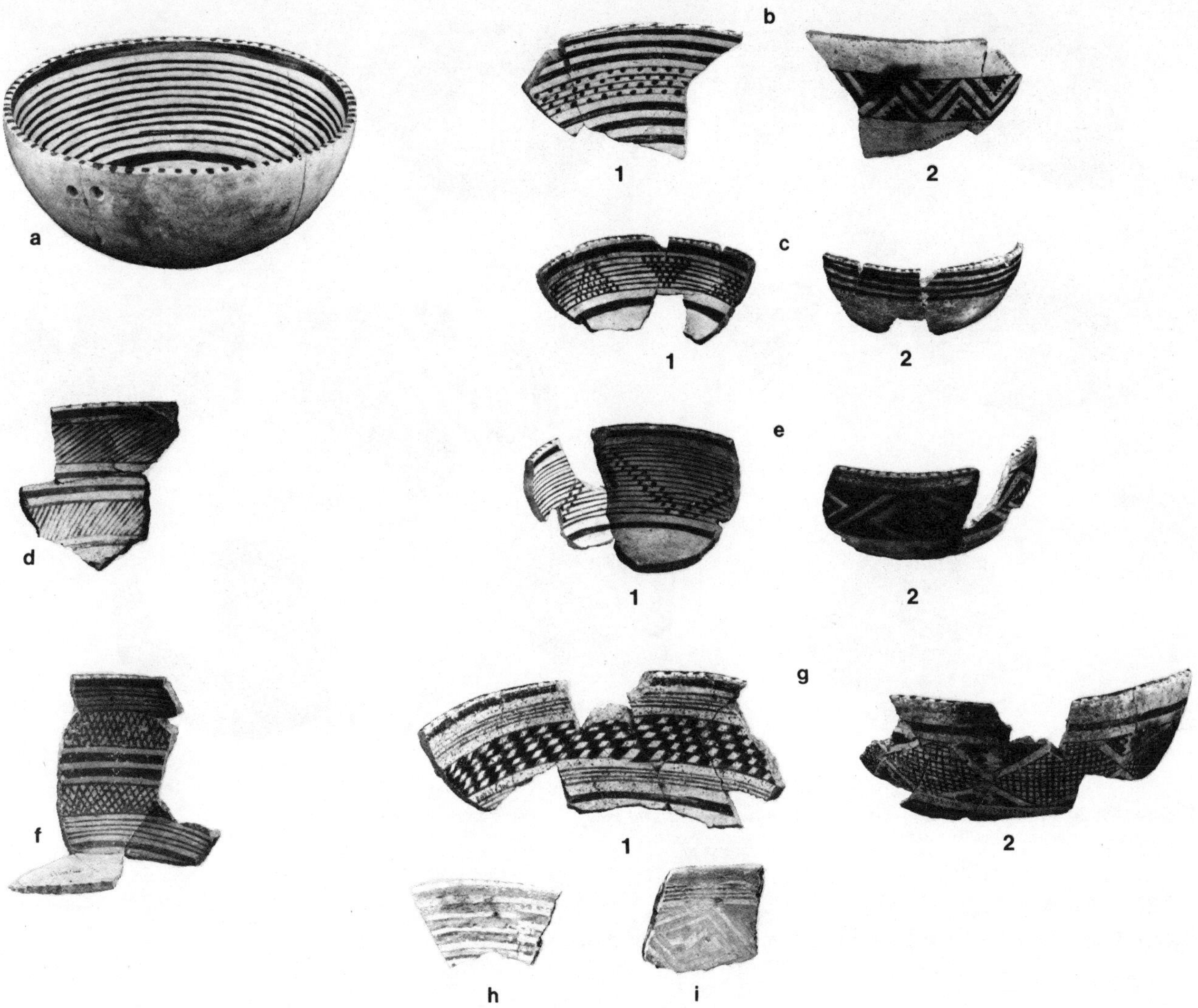

Figure 132. *Mesa Verde Black-on-white, design class I. Maximum diameter of a, 18.7 cm.*

Figure 134. *Mesa Verde Black-on-white, design class IIIA1. Maximum estimated diameter of i, 30 cm.*

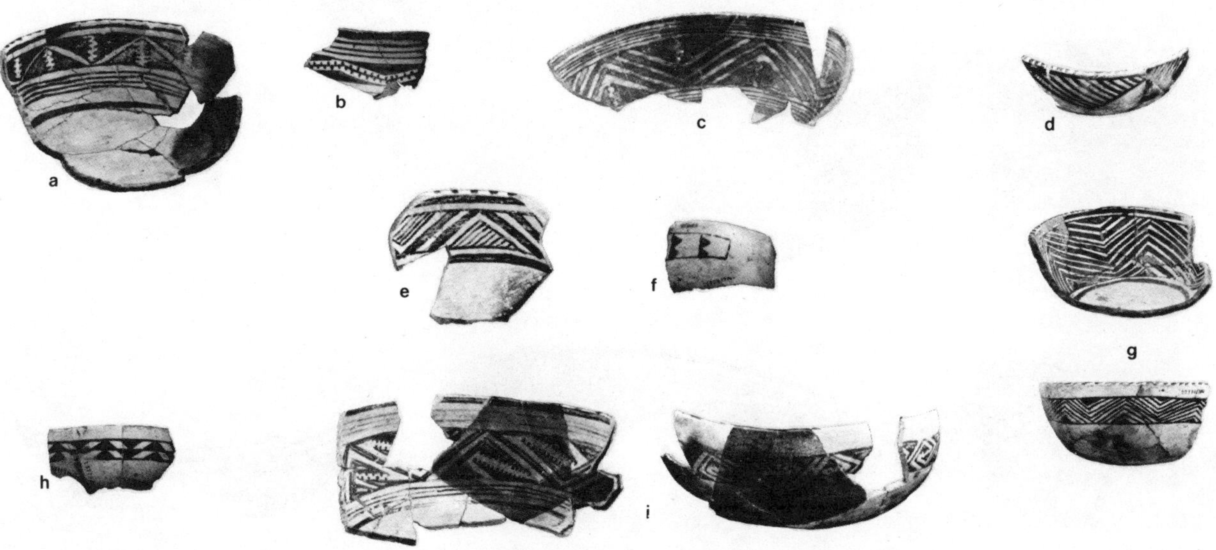

Figure 135. *Mesa Verde Black-on-white, design class IIIA2 and A3. Maximum diameter of c, 18.6 cm.*

Figure 136. *Mesa Verde Black-on-white, design class IIIB. Maximum estimated diameter of h, 27.8 cm.*

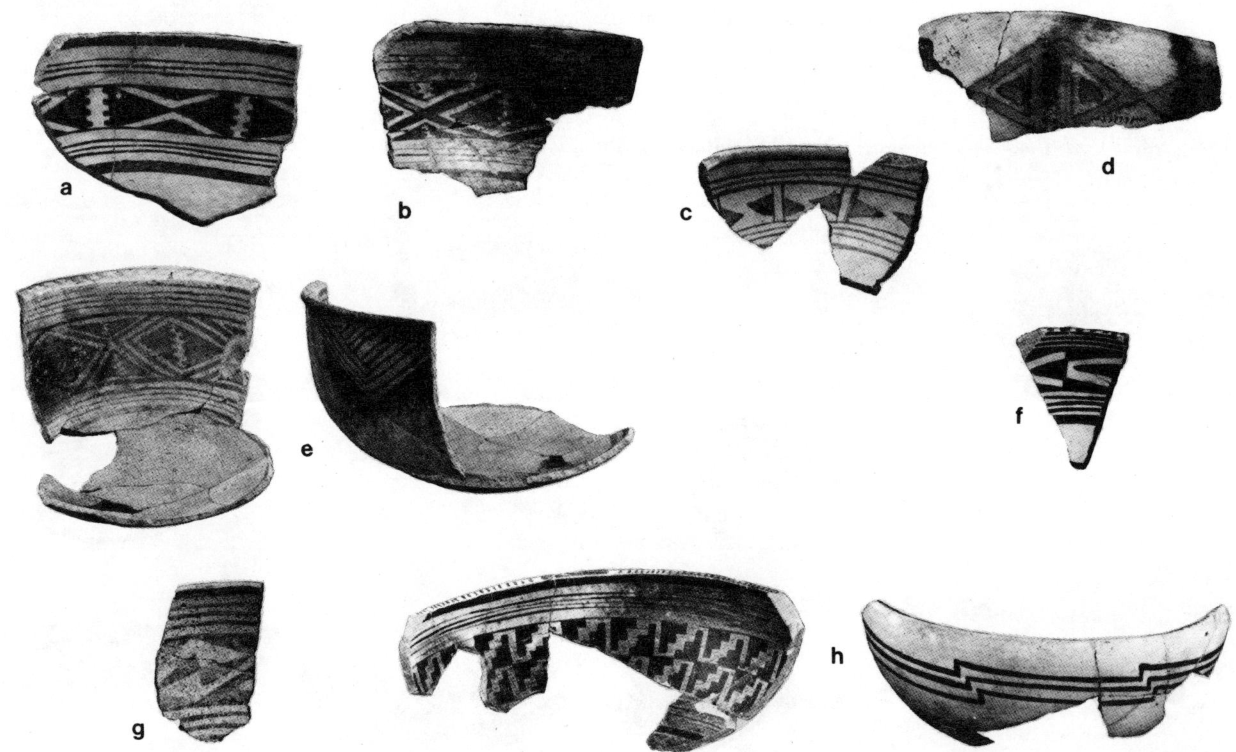

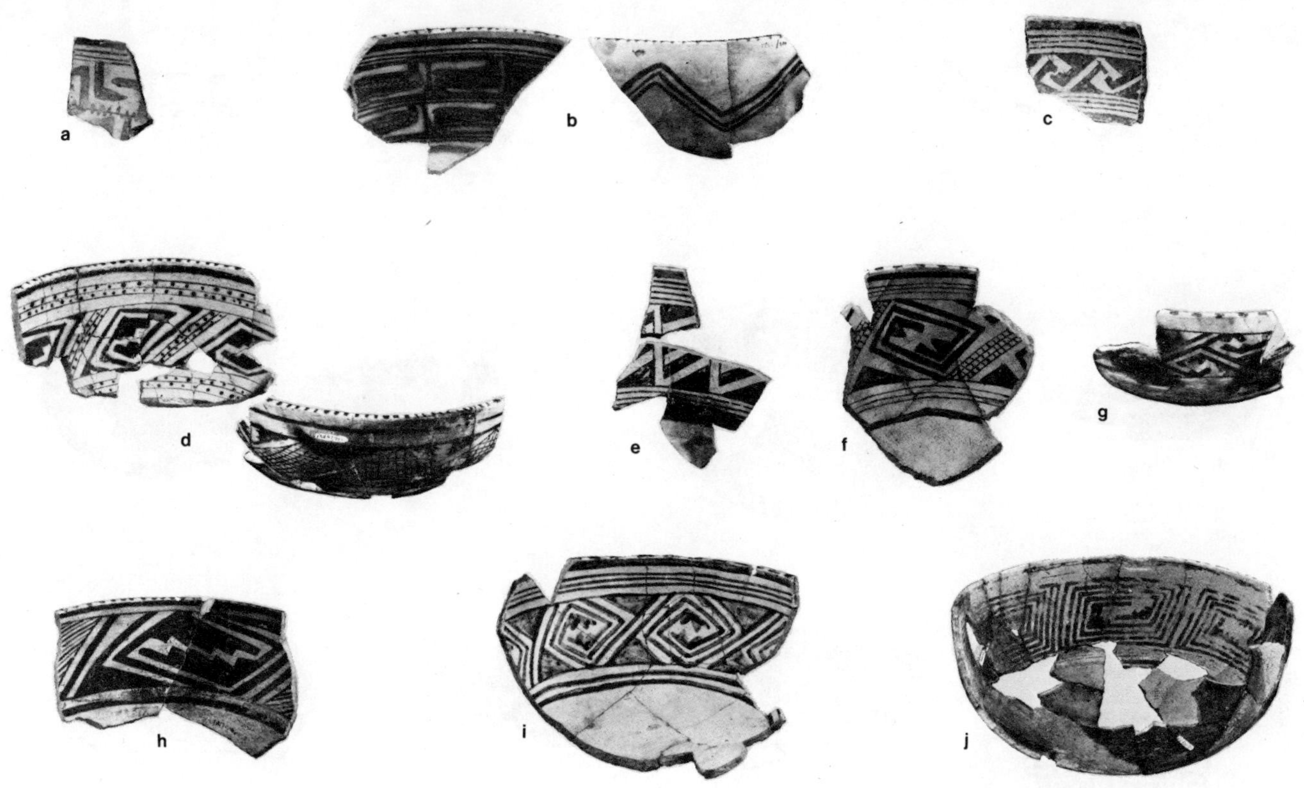

Figure 137. *Mesa Verde Black-on-white, design class IVA1. Maximum diameter of i, 28.9 cm.*

Figure 138. *Mesa Verde Black-on-white, design class IVA2.*

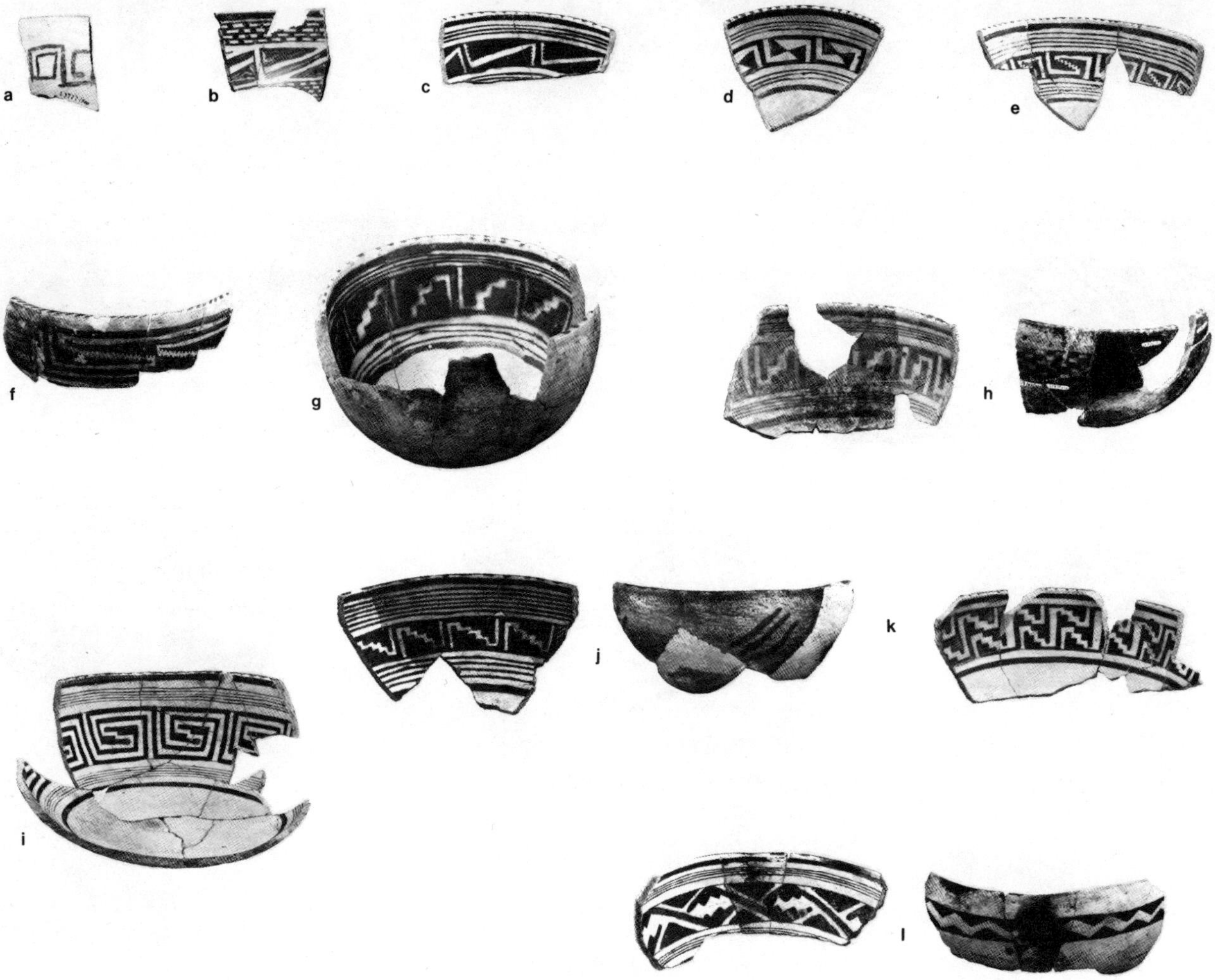

Figure 139. *Mesa Verde Black-on-white, design class IVB1. Maximum diameter of g, 17.8 cm.*

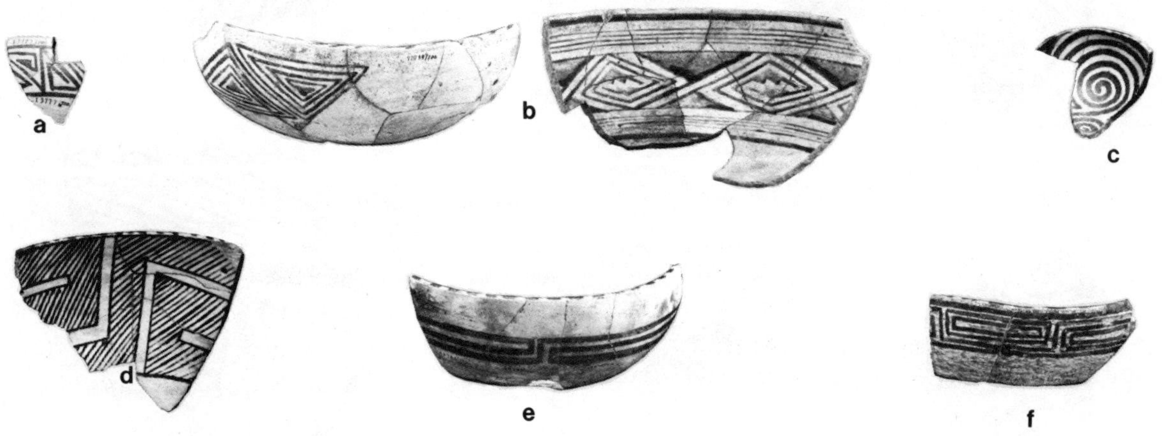

Figure 140. *Mesa Verde Black-on-white, design class IVB2, B3, and C. Maximum diameter of e, 29 cm.*

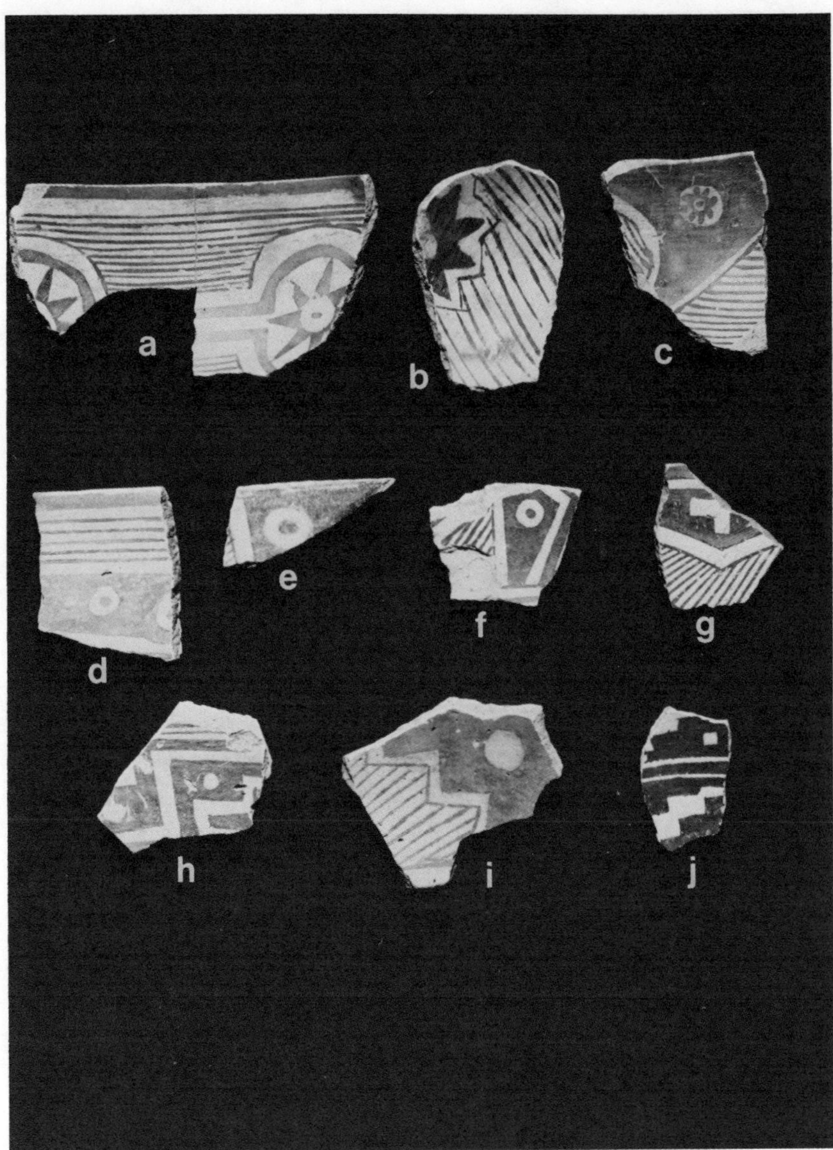

Figure 141. *Mesa Verde Black-on-white, design class V.*

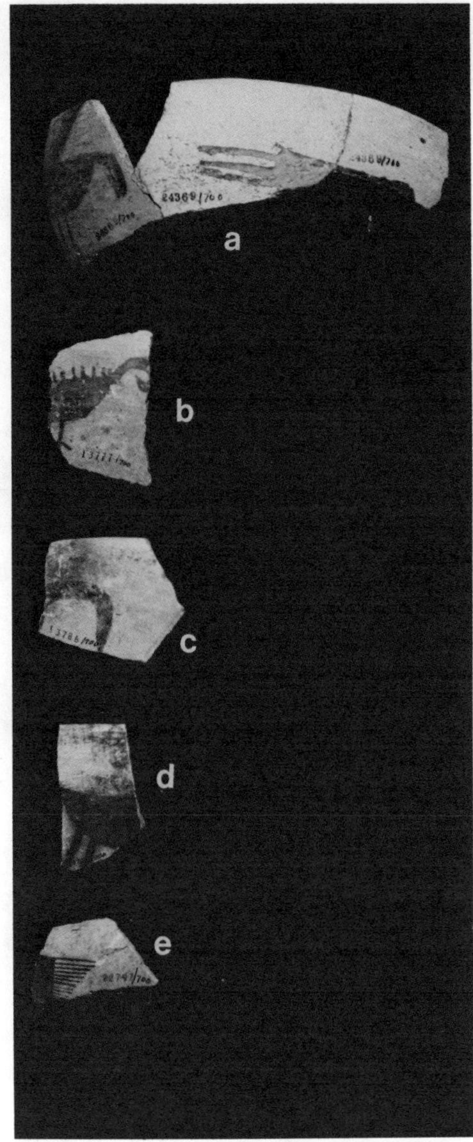

Figure 142. *Mesa Verde Black-on-white, design class VI, bird designs.*

scroll and its rectilinear counterparts, as well as in the classic meander. Designs in this class lend themselves especially well to a combination with the primary layout of overall design. Doubling and other more complex design ramifications have been described by Shepard (1957, pp. 267–293) as classes of symmetry (bilateral, rotational, radial) and motion (translation, rotation, reflection, etc.) or as spatial relations and value. These terms carry us into a subtlety of design classification beyond the scope of this report. The reader is referred to Shepard (1948 and 1957) for detailed discussions of the matter.

Class V is characterized by the circle, with the circle and circular dot being the principal elements. As primary design elements, they had very limited use with the Mesa Verde potters (fig. 141a, possibly d and e). Figure 141a is elaborated to form a rosette, a Class VI design. The dot, however, was used extensively for elaboration of triangles and lines (figs. 153 and 154). Here I would follow Shepard's terminology, with this example—"elaborations of lines and borders"—being one of three classes of her "elaborations of design" (Shepard, 1957, pp. 298–299).

Class VI consists of miscellaneous designs, primarily isolated, with the most important or at least most interesting one being the lifeforms. These, like the other isolated designs, are found primarily on the large bowl. Rarely are they seen on small bowls or dippers and on jars. On bowls, they are usually arranged in a band (unframed) around the exterior just below the rim. Less frequently, the interior bottom of a bowl, left undecorated by a band design, will show a centrally located figure or, occasionally, more than one figure.

The bird design—usually called a turkey, which may or may not be correct—is the most common life form. Figures 142 and 143 show varied portions of birds which differ slightly in certain features but are, in general, rather stylized. Figure 142b is unique in that the bird has sharp projections along its back. Figure 143a is also unique, because of its feet. Only one "toe" is shown, and the location of the feet suggests that there might also be a front pair of legs. This would make a very odd bird indeed. Don Ripley, then Park Ranger at Hovenweep National Monument, reported finding such a "bird" (with four legs) on a sherd from Hovenweep. The design shown in figure 142d is probably a bird, a little off balance, but it could be some other life form.

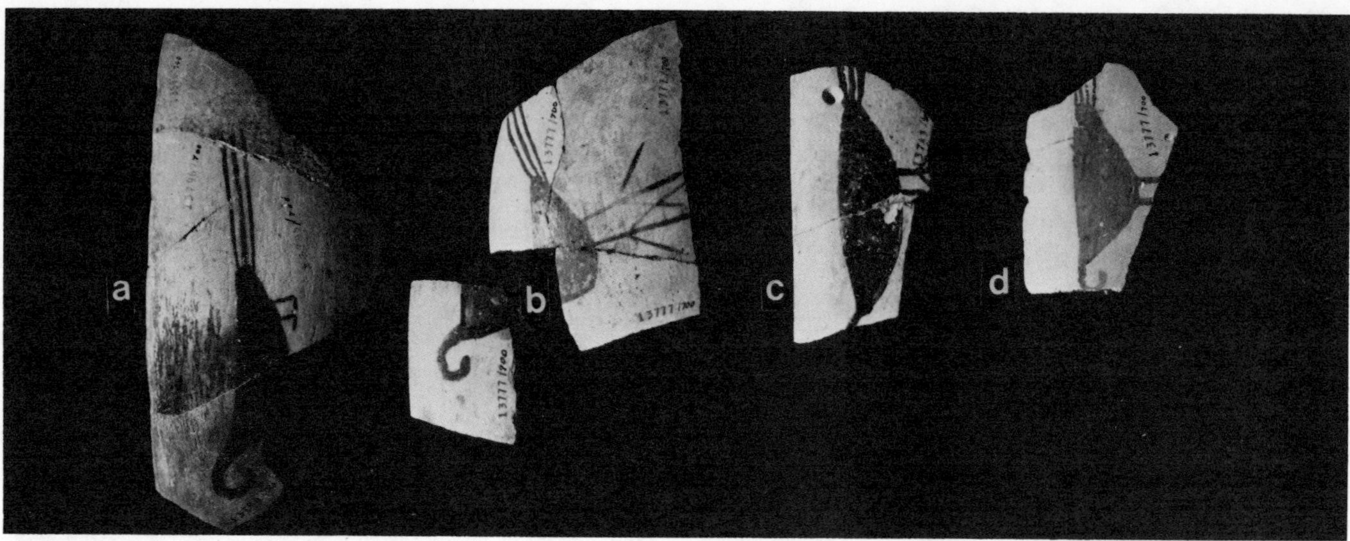

Figure 143. *Mesa Verde Black-on-white, design class VI, bird designs.*

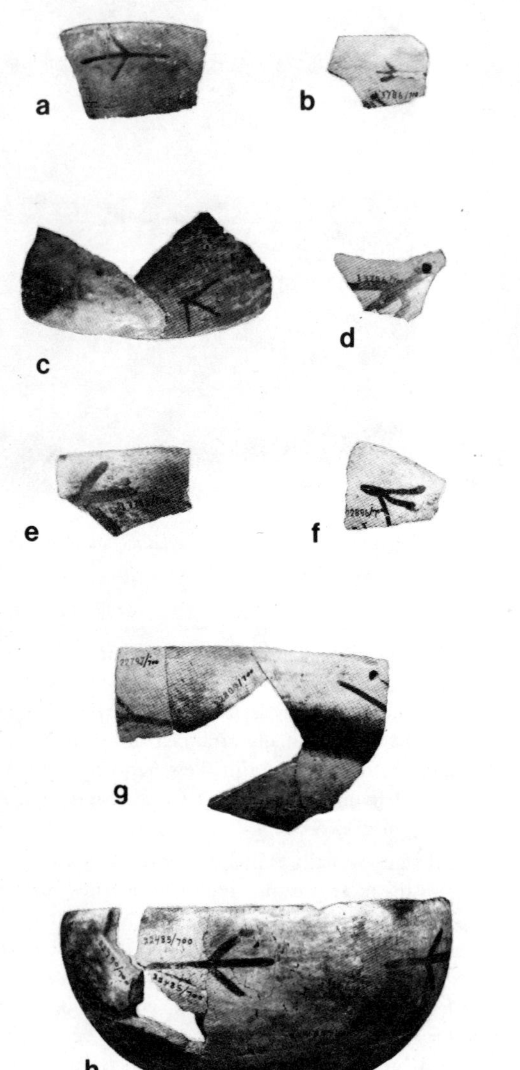

Figure 144. *Mesa Verde Black-on-white, design class VI, bird tracks; a-g, approximately to scale; maximum diameter of h, 17.4 cm.*

Closely related to the bird figures, but not associated with them, are bird tracks. They, too, are usually arranged in a band around the exterior of the bowl, the repeated track designs always pointing in the same direction in any one band. Figure 144 shows several good examples, some pointing to the left and some to the right.

I know of no definite examples in the Long House collection of birds or bird tracks appearing on any portion of a bowl other than the exterior. Only one dipper (fig. 144h) bears a bird design. There were no such designs on any mug, jar, or other vessel form recovered from the site.

Bird designs are found primarily on Mesa Verde Black-on-white, with the possible exception of the dipper just mentioned. Those in figure 144d, e, and f are probably Mesa Verde, with a McElmo style design. All others (figs. 142, 143, and 144) are definitely Mesa Verde.

Two definite horned lizards and three other figures that are probably lizards of one type or another are shown in figure 145. The complete horned lizard is centered in the interior bottom of a dipper (fig. 145a), the fragmentary one in the same location in a bowl (fig. 145b). Figure 145c, d, and f are sherds from a similar location; figure 145e is a jar sherd. There is no evidence of the lizard design on the exterior of a bowl, dipper, or mug.

A definite bighorn sheep appears on two sherds (fig. 146a–c). On one, it is an isolated element; on the other, part of a band design, wherein the sheep serves as a break in an otherwise geometric design. One other sherd possibly shows the hind feet of a bighorn sheep (fig. 146i), but too little of the design remains to be sure. Once again, the design seems to be restricted to the exterior of a bowl.

The human figure is equally rare. A sherd from the interior bottom of a large bowl (fig. 147) possibly depicts a dance scene, since one of four figures is shown holding an object which could be a rattle. The figure at the left seems to be sitting down, the next one standing up. The other two could be either lying down or sitting, depending upon the orientation of the design intended by the artist. Figure 146d and f could represent a human head and hand, respectively, but unfortunately there is not enough of the design left for a definite identification.

The remaining sherds illustrated in figure 146 seem to show various parts of animal anatomy and one possible human or bear footprint (fig. 146h). Despite the limits apparently imposed upon

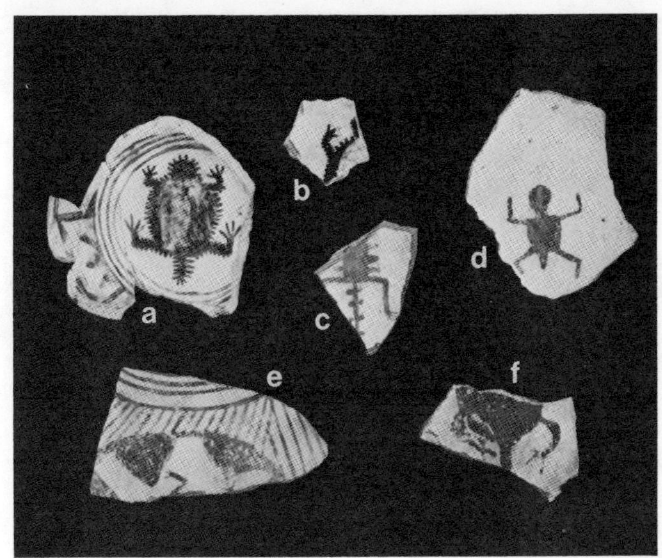

Figure 145. *(Left) Mesa Verde Black-on-white, design class VI, lizards.*

Figure 146. *(Left, below) Mesa Verde Black-on-white, design class VI, bighorn sheep and miscellaneous designs.*

Figure 147. *(Below) Mesa Verde Black-on-white, design class VI, human figures. Width 22.4 cm.*

the artist by the use of geometric designs on most of the vessels, artistic license certainly was indulged in to an extent.

One other possible life form is shown in figure 148a–f. This is an apparent claw design, but actually it may represent something entirely different. It is also shown, tentatively, in design class IVA3 as a modified spiral. The claw is usually suspended from a line encircling the exterior of a bowl just below the rim. The claw may be oriented with the hook up or down, or claws suspended from the same line may alternate position (fig. 148f). Figure 148d and e show two encircling lines, one with a series of claws turned up, the other with an identical set turned down.

Also seen in figure 148 are suspended elements of triangular shape (except fig. 148j, which probably is from an overall design). The orientation of figure 148i is definitive (a rim sherd), that of g and h open to argument. The triangular element is attached, symmetrically, to the end of a short straight line, forming a pattern reminiscent of the design a child of our times might draw to represent a tree.

The remainder of the designs found in Class VI are definitely not life forms, and most can be assigned to two major groups: the cross and its variations, and simple linear designs.

The cross is seen in its simplest form on the exterior bottom of a bowl (fig. 149d). The complexity is increased slightly in the swastika, in which the outer ends of the crossed lines are bent at right angles to the balance of the line. The swastika is actually an elaborated fret (Class IV), but is discussed here because it is used as an isolated figure rather than as an overall bowl design. Figure 149a and b show the swastika used as an isolated figure on the exterior of a bowl, perhaps one of several arranged in a band just below the rim. Figure 149c shows the inclusion of the figure in an interior band or overall design.

A more complex form of the cross is seen in figure 150. The design was limited to large bowls in the Long House material. It appears in both interior and exterior bands, and as an isolated element at the interior bottom and on the exterior just below the rim, possibly in a band arrangement with other identical figures. The design may have a solid or open center, and the outermost sides of the triangular elements may be ticked (fig. 150a).

The central portion of the figure may be expanded and contain an elaborate decoration (fig. 151a, b, and d). Locally this has been called a "blanket" design for obvious reasons, but there is nothing to indicate that it was ever derived from any such object. Figure 151c shows similar designs which lack the corner elaboration. These elaborate figures are always isolated, whatever their location. Although the design is usually limited to the exterior of a large bowl, figure 151e shows one in the interior bottom of a bowl. These are certainly among the more attractive designs used on Mesa Verde pottery.

The category of "simple linear designs" mentioned above consists primarily of what might be called exterior ticking. Often short lines are drawn straight down from the rim and may or may not be a continuation of the rim ticking. (Fig. 152a, b, and d are continuations of rim ticking, c is not). The lines may be drawn at an angle to, but not pendent from, the rim. In this case, the lines are usually found in groups of two or more (fig. 152e and f).

Finally, a design worthy of mention is the rosette. It could also be called a star-shaped or sunburst figure. Insofar as its context is concerned, in two examples (fig. 141a and c), it is merely an elaboration of the circle-and-dot design. A third example (fig. 141b) is not encircled, nor does it have a central dot. The rosette is very rare and apparently occurs only on Mesa Verde bowl interiors.

Other isolated designs which cannot be identified are found on bowls, both on the exterior and on the bottom interior. They may be portions of recognizable designs, or unique designs in themselves.

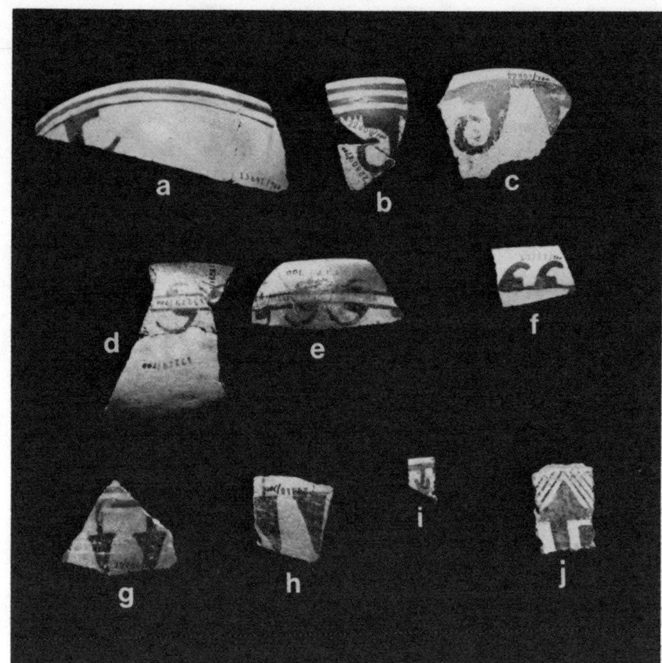

Figure 148. *Mesa Verde Black-on-white, design class VI, claws and triangles.*

Figure 149. *Mesa Verde Black-on-white, design class VI, crosses and swastikas.*

Space breakers, as montioned above, constitute one of the three classes of Shepard's (1957, p. 298) "elaboration of designs." As she states, they emphasize parallelism of line in an area and generally conform to its outline. They may also introduce a design class not used elsewhere in the design as a whole or repeat one already used in a different manner or place. Thus some space breakers may take the form of a secondary or tertiary layout in the design field. Others, as illustrated by Shepard, are merely eyelets placed more or less symmetrically in a solid element without conforming to its shape. Figure 141d–j illustrate several examples of this last type.

Figure 150. *Mesa Verde Black-on-white, design class VI, elaborated crosses.*

Figure 151. *Mesa Verde Black-on-white, design class VI, elaborated crosses.*

Hachure, cross hachure, and stippling are the fillers discussed by Shepard—with hachure being the only common filler—and these constitute the second class of design elaboration. The Long House material also demonstrates this. The filler may be placed between parallel lines or within an irregularly shaped area. Obviously, the filler will be essentially a space breaker in some cases. For ease of description, I have included hachure in Class I, but will still use Shephard's term "filler" where necessary in describing how the design is used.

Line elaboration, mentioned above, is the third class. Numerous minor designs fall in this class. Ticking on either or both sides of

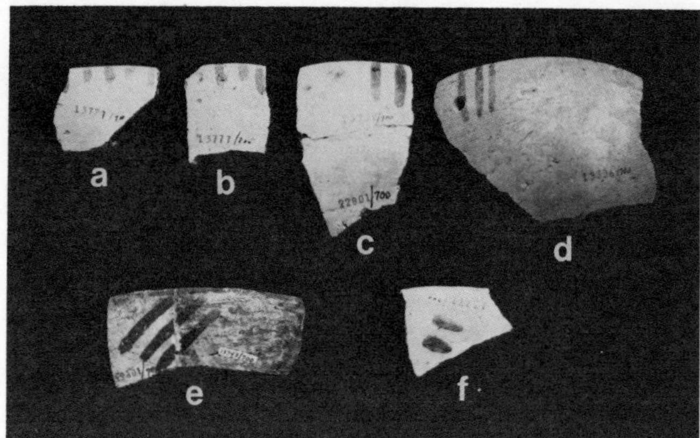

Figure 152. *Mesa Verde Black-on-white, design class VI, exterior ticking.*

a line, or on one or more edges of a solid, are two very common forms of elaboration found on Long House pottery. Ticking between (and connecting) parallel lines—Shepard's "brickwork"—is also quite common. The so-called "squiggle line" overlying a straight line would also be included in this class. With the possible exception of the circular dot, these designs defy inclusion in the main design classes without a considerable stretch of the imagination.

As seen in figures 153 and 154, the circular dot (discussed briefly under Class V) has been used in an almost unlimited number of ways. Most commonly, it is pendent from a line, especially the innermost framing line (fig. 153b), or it used to decorate the edge of a solid (fig. 153j). Perhaps the next most common use of dots is as a decorative filler between parallel lines (fig. 154). Triangles and diamond-shaped figures are often formed (fig. 154b and e-g) in interior bands consisting of horizontal, parallel lines (actually concentric circles). Rarely is a pattern of dots alone used (fig. 154c). The example illustrated is on the exterior of a bowl. The "brickwork" pattern (fig. 154m) is also very common, with the design used not only by itself but also as a framing unit (placed horizontally, vertically, or angled) for a more elaborate design.

Occasionally, dots will be used between (but not touching) lines or solid figures (fig. 154i-l), but this is one of the least common arrangements.

By no means are round dots always used for ticking and other decoration. Thin straight lines, triangular dots, and miscellaneous "blobs" are quite common (fig. 155).

I believe that it is apparent by now that the design on any one vessel is going to include several classes of design, with almost limitless combinations possible. Few designs will fall entirely into one design class. Vessels whose designs consist of a major class or combinations of major classes are illustrated (figs. 158 and 159), with arrangement based on the shape of the vessel profile rather than design class.

Mesa Verde Black-on-white design is typified by four primary aspects: (1) a preference for the band layout (found on about 75 percent of all vessels, with an interior band on about 80 percent of the bowls): (2) balanced sets of framing lines, one on either side of the band (on bowl interiors and, to a lesser extent, jar and mug exteriors), with the outermost lines generally wider than the others; (3) a tight but not negative pattern of rather stylized (usually geometric) designs, with very little open or white space between the various design components, and (4) a lesser preference for overall designs (except on dippers and very small bowls where overall designs predominate), again using tightly controlled but rather stylized designs.

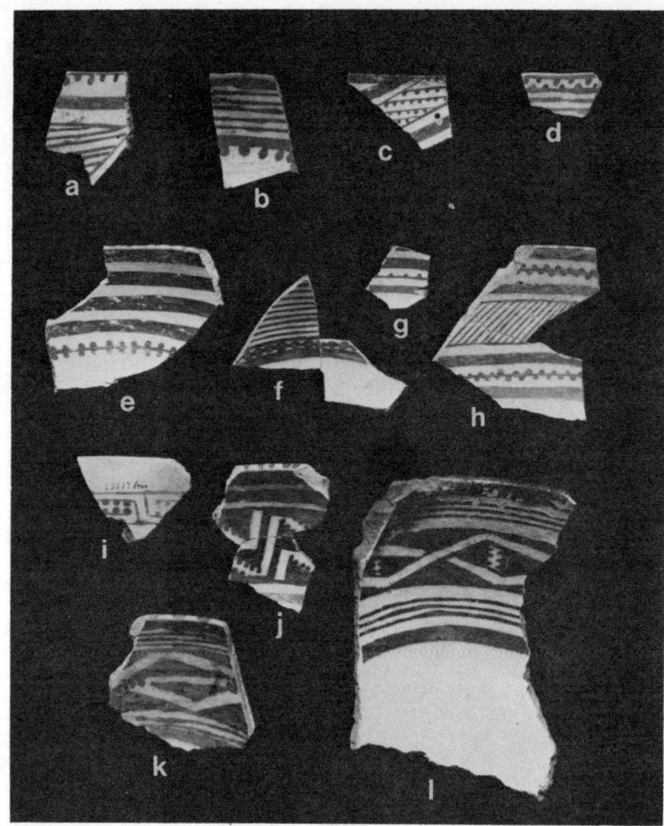

Figure 153. *Mesa Verde Black-on-white, circular dots used as decorative elements.*

These same aspects, but to a different degree, can also be used to describe McElmo Black-on-white. Band layout is again popular (found on about 65 percent of all vessel shapes, with an interior band on the same percentage of bowls). The exception to this is, once again, the dipper, on which the design is almost always overall. Often the band will extend all the way to the lip of a bowl. Framing lines may be absent, and when present usually all will be of the same size. The designs used are generally more open than those of Mesa Verde Black-on-white, and less stylized or formalized. McElmo pottery reflects a period of experimentation, with the earlier material firmly rooted in Mancos Black-on-white. There is a greater preference for overall designs, but simple paneled and sectored ones rather than the highly developed and elaborate ones found on Mesa Verde Black-on-white.

Classification of Vessels and Sherds

In classifying pottery as McElmo or Mesa Verde Black-on-white, specific design and technological aspects must be considered. To determine which aspects are most diagnostic, a twofold analysis was made of the sherds of these types from the Lower East Trash Slope. First, the sherds were separated according to vessel shape and by rim, body, and handle (where appropriate) within the vessel shapes. Then the sherds were classified as Mesa Verde, McElmo, or transitional McElmo-Mesa Verde. Sherd counts and percentages for the four major vessel shapes—bowls, jars, mugs, and dipper—are given in table 10. Frequencies of decoration and form in bowls, jars, and dippers of the three classes of black-on-white sherds are given in tables 11, 12, and 13.

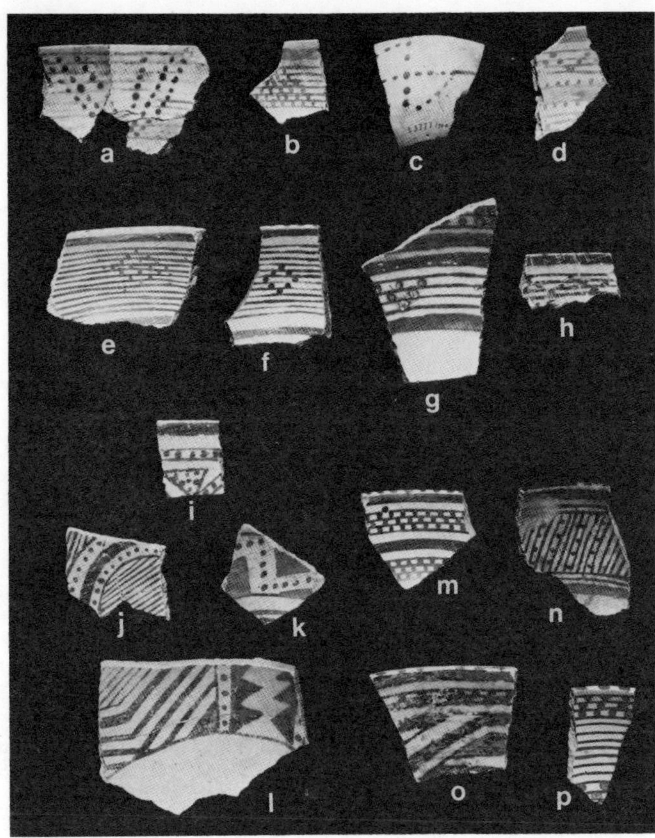

Figure 154. *Mesa Verde Black-on-white, circular dots used as decorative elements.*

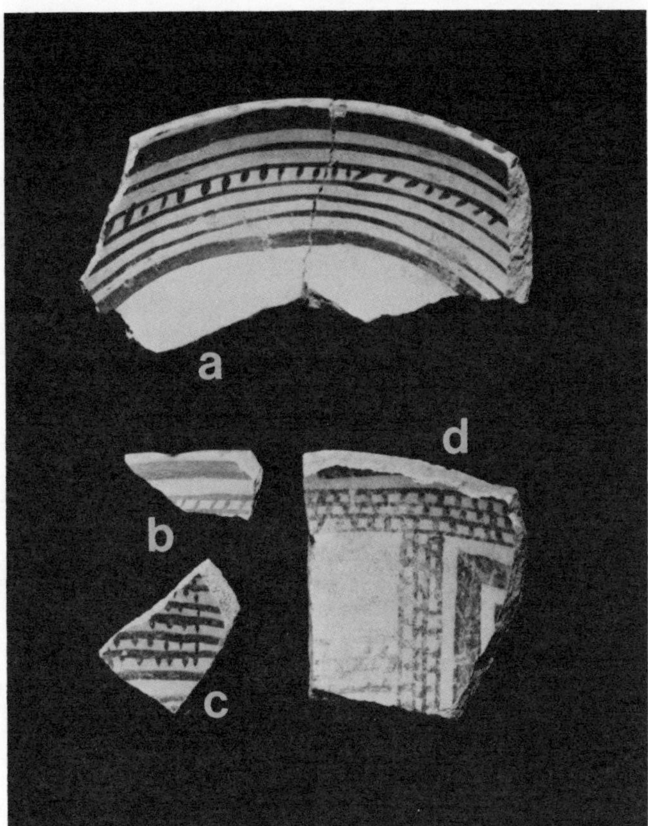

Figure 155. *Mesa Verde Black-on-white, straight lines, triangular dots, etc., used as decorative elements.*

The second step in the analysis concerned design, with emphasis on bowl sherds. Bowls constituted 76 percent of McElmo-Mesa Verde Black-on-white pottery from the Lower East Trash Slope and provided the largest sample for study. Also, the range of variation in layout, design components, paint, and the like found on bowls is unequaled by any other vessel form.

With few exceptions, the designs on bowl interiors can also be found on dipper interiors, bowl exteriors, and the exteriors of jars and mugs. Mesa Verde jars and mugs bearing interior decoration have been found, but there were none in the Long House collection. Thus a study of bowl designs covers almost the entire range found on the two pottery types. Restorable and whole vessels and sherds from other portions of the ruin were used to supplement the Lower East Trash Slope material in this discussion of design.

A third step in the study was not limited to the Lower East Trash Slope material. This was the physical analysis of such things as paste, temper, and slip, based primarily on restorable vessels and selected sherds from the ruin as a whole.

Bowls

Table 11 shows the difficulty encountered in separating Mesa Verde Black-on-white from McElmo Black-on-white. Of the bowl sherds studied, 52 percent were Mesa Verde, 13 percent McElmo, and 35 percent indeterminate Mesa Verde-McElmo. Following my proposed classification, the unclassified sherds would be merely McElmo Black-on-white. Some of these show too little design to be classified as to variety. Many others, however, show a less developed design than is commonly seen on Mesa Verde Variety pottery and certainly should not be included in this variety. Yet they obviously do not belong with the earlier McElmo pottery recovered from some of the surface sites excavated on Wetherill Mesa. A small percentage of sherds showed minor variations in construction which set them off slightly from the variety to which they would be normally assigned by design and physical characteristics.

All of these sherds form, essentially, one pottery type, and even though the variety is in doubt they should be assigned to this type. As will be discussed later, the stratigraphic evidence in Long House shows the fading out of the McElmo Phase and pottery, with a more developed form of McElmo Variety pottery than would be considered typical of the early Pueblo III stage being found in the lowest levels in Long House.

The same percentage of unslipped pottery is found in both the Mesa Verde and McElmo Varieties. It forms only 2 percent of these varieties, and 3 percent of the indeterminate group. Even less significant is the presence of an external rim fillet: two sherds, one McElmo (fig. 156a) and the other indeterminate. One sherd bearing a possible unindented corrugated exterior was found (fig. 156b), but it could not be assigned to a specific variety. Only one bowl handle was recovered from the ruin: a Mesa Verde sherd with a flared (Kayenta-type) rim (fig. 157).

A glance at table 11 shows a sharp difference between Mesa Verde and McElmo in the two categories of rim ticking and exterior decoration: 92 percent of Mesa Verde has some form of rim decoration, as compared to 71 percent of McElmo. It is interesting to note here that only 54 percent of unslipped McElmo had rim decoration, whereas 91 percent unslipped Mesa Verde had ticked rims. Practically all rim decoration was confined to the lip.

Table 10. Mesa Verde, McElmo, and Indeterminate (Mesa Verde-McElmo) Black-on-white sherds from the Lower East Trash Slope. NOTE: Percentages shown in parentheses.

Total count					5,166
Mesa Verde Variety				2,505(49)	
Slipped			2,419(47)		
Bowls		1,980(82)			
Rim	868(44)				
Body	1,112(56)				
Jars		334(14)			
Rim	6(2)				
Body	320(96)				
Handle	7(2)				
Mugs		75(3)			
Rim	25(33)				
Body	50(67)				
Dippers		30(1)			
Rim	4(13)				
Body	3(10)				
Handle	23(77)				
Unslipped			86(2)		
Bowls		79(91)			
Rim	43(54)				
Body	36(46)				
Jars		3(4)			
Body	3(100)				
Mugs		3(4)			
Rim	1(33)				
Body	2(67)				
Dippers		1(1)			
Rim	1(100)				
McElmo Variety				576(11)	
Slipped			504(10)		
Bowls		439(87)			
Rim	238(54)				
Body	201(46)				
Jars		26(5)			
Rim	8(31)				
Body	18(69)				
Mugs		11(2)			
Rim	6(55)				
Body	5(45)				
Dippers		28(6)			
Rim	22(79)				
Body	6(21)				
Unslipped			72(1)		
Bowls		56(78)			
Rim	26(46)				
Body	30(54)				
Jars		10(14)			
Rim	3(30)				
Body	7(70)				
Mugs		4(5)			
Rim	1(25)				
Body	3(75)				
Dippers		2(3)			
Rim	2(100)				
Indeterminate variety				2,085(40)	
Slipped			1,932(37)		
Bowls		1,275(66)			
Rim	325(25)				
Body	950(75)				
Jars		481(25)			
Rim	43(9)				
Body	362(75)				
Handle	76(16)				
Mugs		46(2)			
Rim	9(19)				
Body	32(70)				
Handle	5(11)				
Dippers		130(7)			
Rim	13(10)				
Body	20(15)				
Handle	97(75)				
Unslipped			140(3)		
Bowls		105(75)			
Rim	31(30)				
Body	74(70)				
Jars		31(22)			
Rim	1(3)				
Body	26(84)				
Handle	4(13)				
Mugs		1(1)			
Body	1(100)				
Corrugated exterior (unindented)			12(Trace)		
Jars		12(100)			
Rim	6(50)				
Body	6(50)				

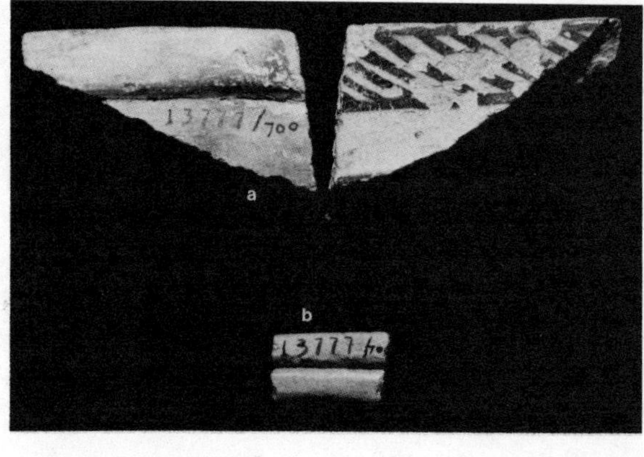

Figure 156. *External rim fillet on McElmo sherd (a) and indeterminate sherd (b).*

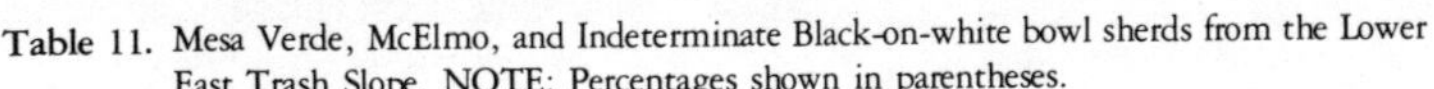
Table 11. Mesa Verde, McElmo, and Indeterminate Black-on-white bowl sherds from the Lower East Trash Slope. NOTE: Percentages shown in parentheses.

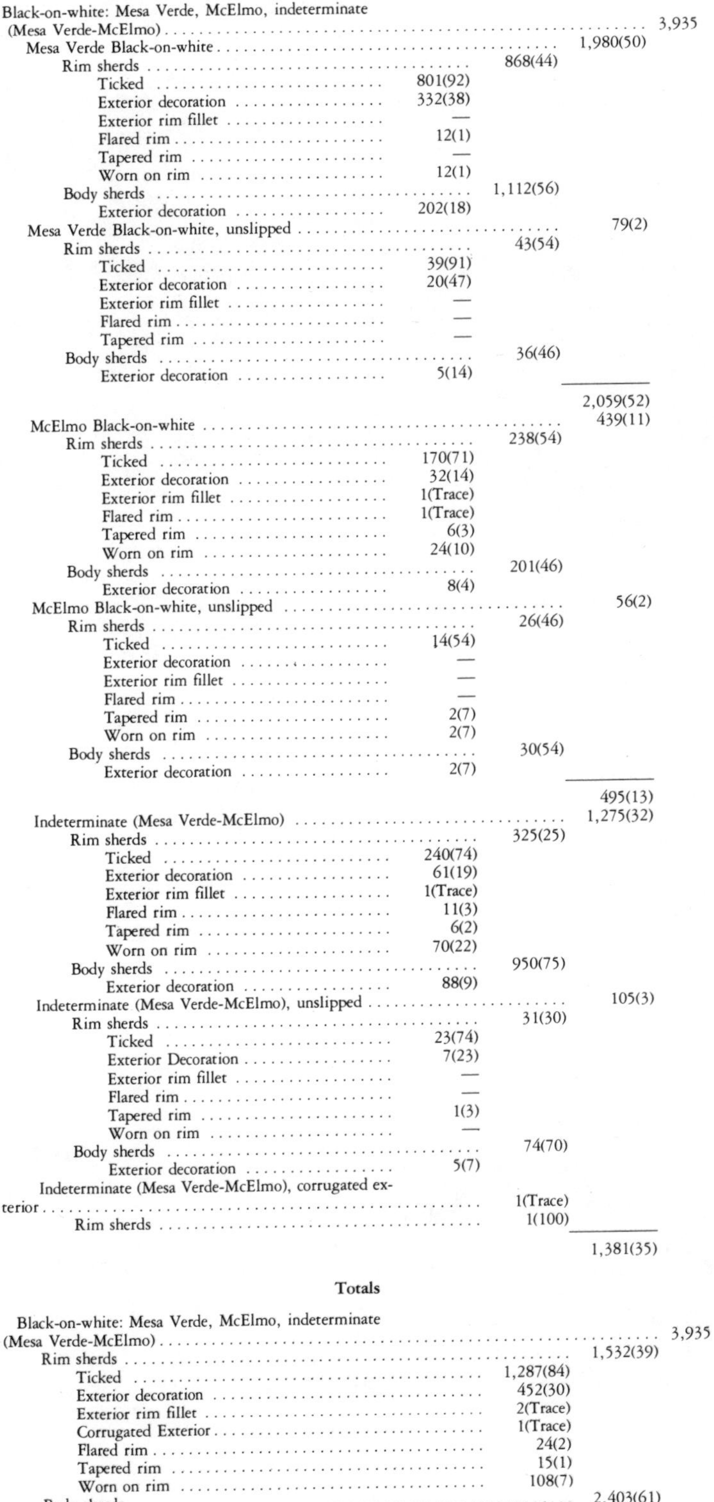

Black-on-white: Mesa Verde, McElmo, indeterminate (Mesa Verde-McElmo)				3,935
Mesa Verde Black-on-white			1,980(50)	
Rim sherds		868(44)		
Ticked	801(92)			
Exterior decoration	332(38)			
Exterior rim fillet	—			
Flared rim	12(1)			
Tapered rim	—			
Worn on rim	12(1)			
Body sherds		1,112(56)		
Exterior decoration	202(18)			
Mesa Verde Black-on-white, unslipped			79(2)	
Rim sherds		43(54)		
Ticked	39(91)			
Exterior decoration	20(47)			
Exterior rim fillet	—			
Flared rim	—			
Tapered rim	—			
Body sherds		36(46)		
Exterior decoration	5(14)			
			2,059(52)	
McElmo Black-on-white			439(11)	
Rim sherds		238(54)		
Ticked	170(71)			
Exterior decoration	32(14)			
Exterior rim fillet	1(Trace)			
Flared rim	1(Trace)			
Tapered rim	6(3)			
Worn on rim	24(10)			
Body sherds		201(46)		
Exterior decoration	8(4)			
McElmo Black-on-white, unslipped			56(2)	
Rim sherds		26(46)		
Ticked	14(54)			
Exterior decoration	—			
Exterior rim fillet	—			
Flared rim	—			
Tapered rim	2(7)			
Worn on rim	2(7)			
Body sherds		30(54)		
Exterior decoration	2(7)			
			495(13)	
Indeterminate (Mesa Verde-McElmo)			1,275(32)	
Rim sherds		325(25)		
Ticked	240(74)			
Exterior decoration	61(19)			
Exterior rim fillet	1(Trace)			
Flared rim	11(3)			
Tapered rim	6(2)			
Worn on rim	70(22)			
Body sherds		950(75)		
Exterior decoration	88(9)			
Indeterminate (Mesa Verde-McElmo), unslipped			105(3)	
Rim sherds		31(30)		
Ticked	23(74)			
Exterior Decoration	7(23)			
Exterior rim fillet	—			
Flared rim	—			
Tapered rim	1(3)			
Worn on rim	—			
Body sherds		74(70)		
Exterior decoration	5(7)			
Indeterminate (Mesa Verde-McElmo), corrugated exterior		1(Trace)		
Rim sherds		1(100)		
			1,381(35)	

Totals

Black-on-white: Mesa Verde, McElmo, indeterminate (Mesa Verde-McElmo)			3,935
Rim sherds		1,532(39)	
Ticked	1,287(84)		
Exterior decoration	452(30)		
Exterior rim fillet	2(Trace)		
Corrugated Exterior	1(Trace)		
Flared rim	24(2)		
Tapered rim	15(1)		
Worn on rim	108(7)		
Body sherds		2,403(61)	
Exterior decoration	310(13)		

Figure 157. *Bowl handle on Mesa Verde sherd with flared (Kayenta-type) rim; a, top view: and b, side view.*

Table 12. Mesa Verde, McElmo, and Indeterminate Black-on-white jar sherds from the Lower East Trash Slope. NOTE: Percentages shown in parentheses.

Black-on-white: Mesa Verde, McElmo, indeterminate (Mesa Verde-McElmo)				897
Mesa Verde Black-on-white			334(37)	
Rim sherds* (3 kiva jar)		6 (2)		
Ticked	6(100)			
Body sherds (3 kiva jar)		320(96)		
Mineral paint	1(Trace)			
Handle sherds		7 (2)		
Wide, flat strap	5(71)			
Narrow, flat-round strap	2(29)			
Mesa Verde Black-on-white, unslipped			3(Trace)	
Body sherds	3(100)			
			337(37)	
McElmo Black-on-white			26 (3)	
Rim sherds (4 seed jar)		8(31)		
Ticked (2 seed jar)	3(38)			
Body sherds		18(69)		
McElmo Black-on-white, unslipped			10 (1)	
Rim sherds (1 seed jar)		3(30)		
Ticked (1 seed jar)	1(33)			
Body sherds		7(70)		
			36 (4)	
Indeterminate (Mesa Verde-McElmo)			481(54)	
Rim sherds (7 kiva jar, 1 seed jar)		43 (9)		
Ticked (1 kiva jar)	24(56)			
Exterior decoration	10 (2)			
Body sherds		362(75)		
Handle sherds		76(16)		
Wide, flat strap**	53(70)			
Narrow, flat-round strap	15(20)			
Hollow	6 (8)			
Knob	2 (2)			
Indeterminate (Mesa Verde-McElmo), unslipped		31 (4)		
Rim sherds		1 (3)		
Ticked	1(100)			
Body sherds		26(84)		
Handle sherds		4(13)		
Wide, flat strap	4(100)			
Indeterminate (Mesa Verde-McElmo), corrugated neck			12 (1)	
Rim sherds		6(50)		
Ticked	4(67)			
Exterior Decoration				
Body sherds		6(50)		
			524(59)	

TOTALS

Black-on-white: Mesa Verde, McElmo, indeterminate (Mesa Verde-McElmo)			897
Rim sherds		67 (7)	
Ticked	39(58)		
Exterior Decoration	10(14)		
Corrugated neck	6 (9)		
Body sherds		743(83)	
Corrugated neck	6 (1)		
Mineral paint	1(Trace)		
Handle sherds		87(10)	
Wide, flat strap	62(71)		
Narrow, flat-round strap	17(20)		
Hollow	6 (7)		
Knob	2 (2)		

*All rim sherds from necked ("water") jar except where indicated otherwise.

**One side, flat-strap handle shows portion of perforation of either rectangular or "T" shape.

Table 13. Mesa Verde, McElmo, and Indeterminate Black-on-white dipper sherds from the Lower East Trash Slope. NOTE: Percentages shown in parentheses.

Black-on-white: Mesa Verde, McElmo, indeterminate (Mesa Verde-McElmo)				194
Mesa Verde Black-on-white			30(16)	
Rim sherds		4(13)		
Ticked	4(100)			
Exterior decoration	1(25)			
Body sherds		3(10)		
Handle sherds (separate)		23(77)		
Handle sherds (attached and separate)*	27(90)			
Decoration on handle	26(96)			
Flat	6(22)			
Oval-round	3(11)			
Compound	1 (4)			
Hollow	17(63)			
Mesa Verde Black-on-white, unslipped			1(Trace)	
Rim sherds		1(100)		
			31(16)	
McElmo Black-on-white			28(14)	
Rim sherds		22(79)		
Ticked	18(82)			
Exterior decoration	5(23)			
Body sherds		6(21)		
Handle sherds (separate)		—		
Handle sherds (attached and separate)*	9(32)			
Decoration on handle	7(78)			
Oval-round	5(56)			
Hollow	4(44)			
McElmo Black-on-white, unslipped			2 (1)	
Rim sherds		2(100)		
Ticked	2(100)			
Handle sherds (separate)		—		
Handle sherds (attached and separate)*	2(100)			
Decoration on handle	1(50)			
Oval-round	2(100)			
			30(15)	
Indeterminate (Mesa Verde-McElmo)			130(67)	
Rim sherds		13(10)		
Ticked	9(69)			
Exterior decoration	4(31)			
Body sherds		20(15)		
Handle sherds (separate)		97(75)		
Handle sherds (attached and separate)*	123(95)			
Decoration on handle	115(94)			
Flat	15(12)			
Oval-round	28(23)			
Compound	4 (3)			
Hollow	76(62)			
Indeterminate (Mesa Verde-McElmo), unslipped			3 (2)	
Body Sherds		2(67)		
Handle sherds (separate)		1(33)		
Handle sherds (attached and separate)*	3(100)			
Decoration on handle	1(33)			
Oval-round	3(100)			
			133(69)	
TOTALS				
Black-on-white: Mesa Verde, McElmo, indeterminate (Mesa Verde-McElmo)				194
Rim sherds			42(22)	
Ticked		33(79)		
Exterior decoration		10(24)		
Body sherds			31(16)	
Handle sherds (separate)			121(62)	
Handle sherds		164(85)		
Decoration on handle		150/91)		
Flat		21(13)		
Oval-round		41(25)		
Compound		5 (3)		
Hollow		97(59)		

* Handles attached to body and rim sherds are counted under these categories.

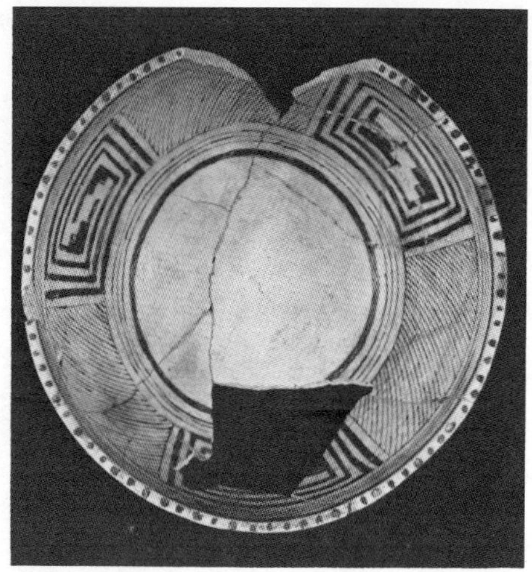

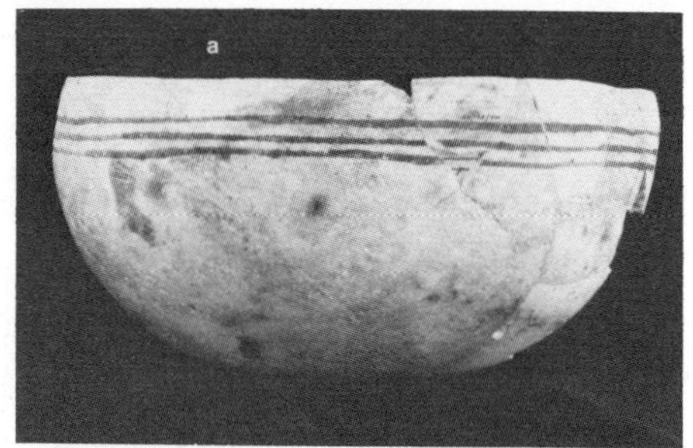

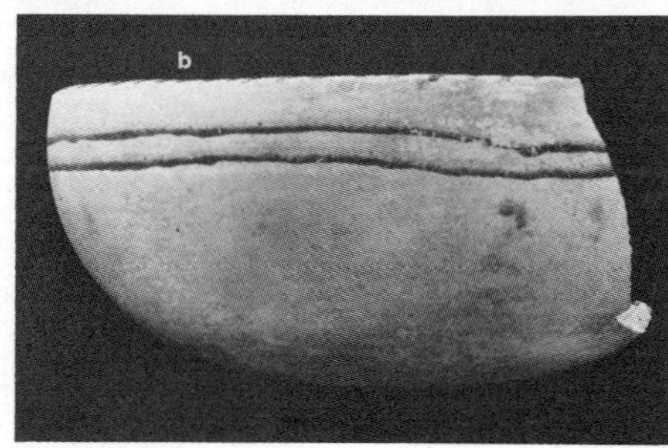

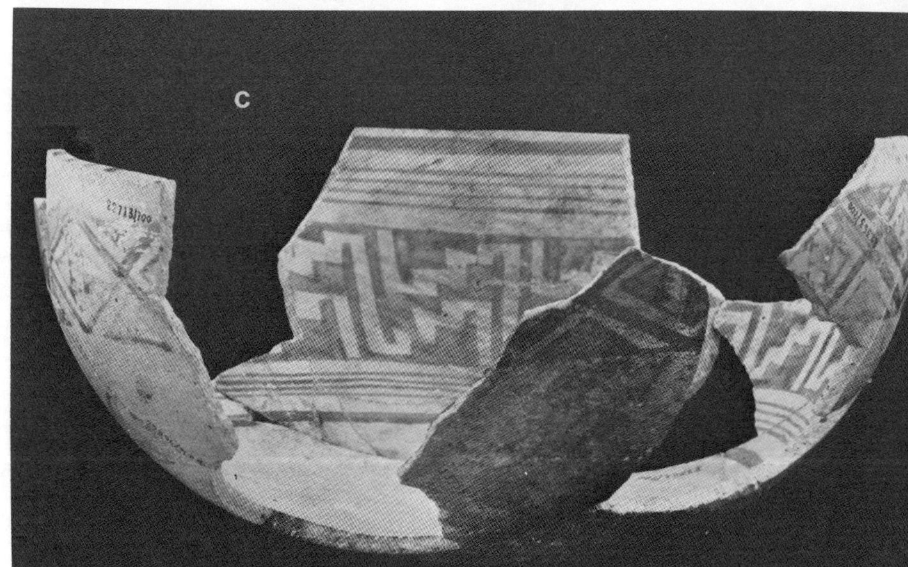

Figure 158. *Mesa Verde Black-on-white bowls, band designs. Maximum diameter of a, 28.1 cm.*

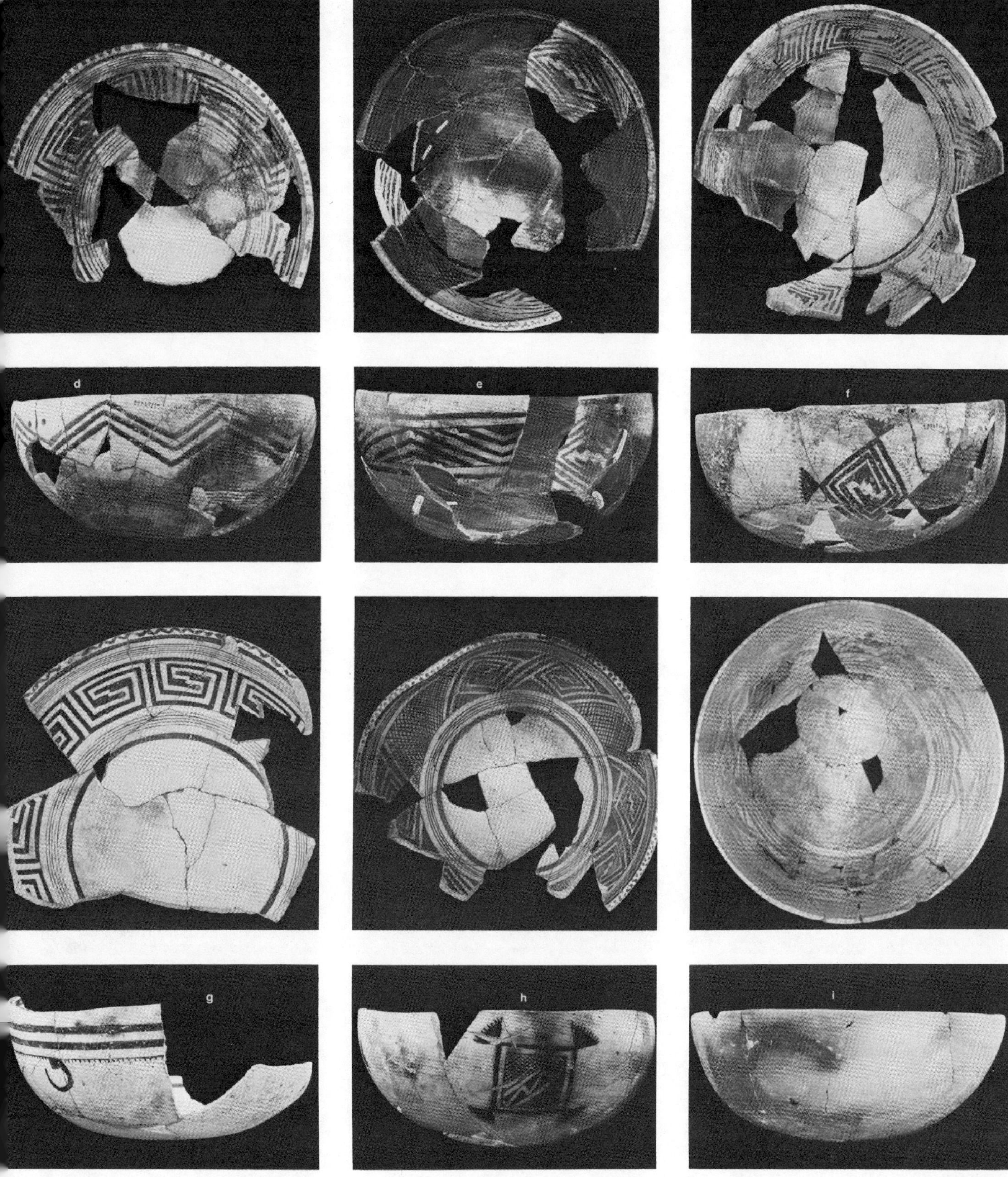
d
e
f
g
h
i

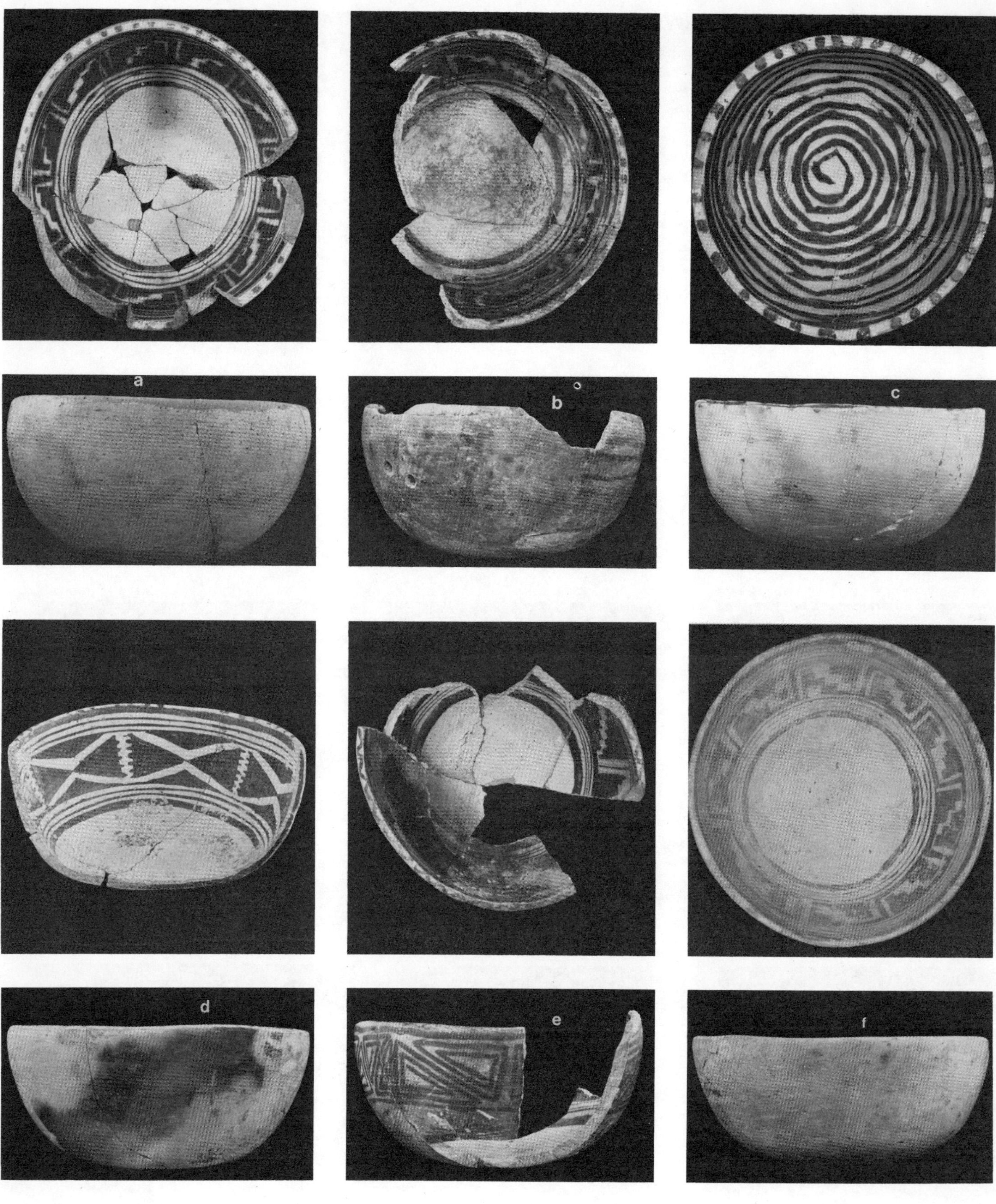
a
b
c
d
e
f

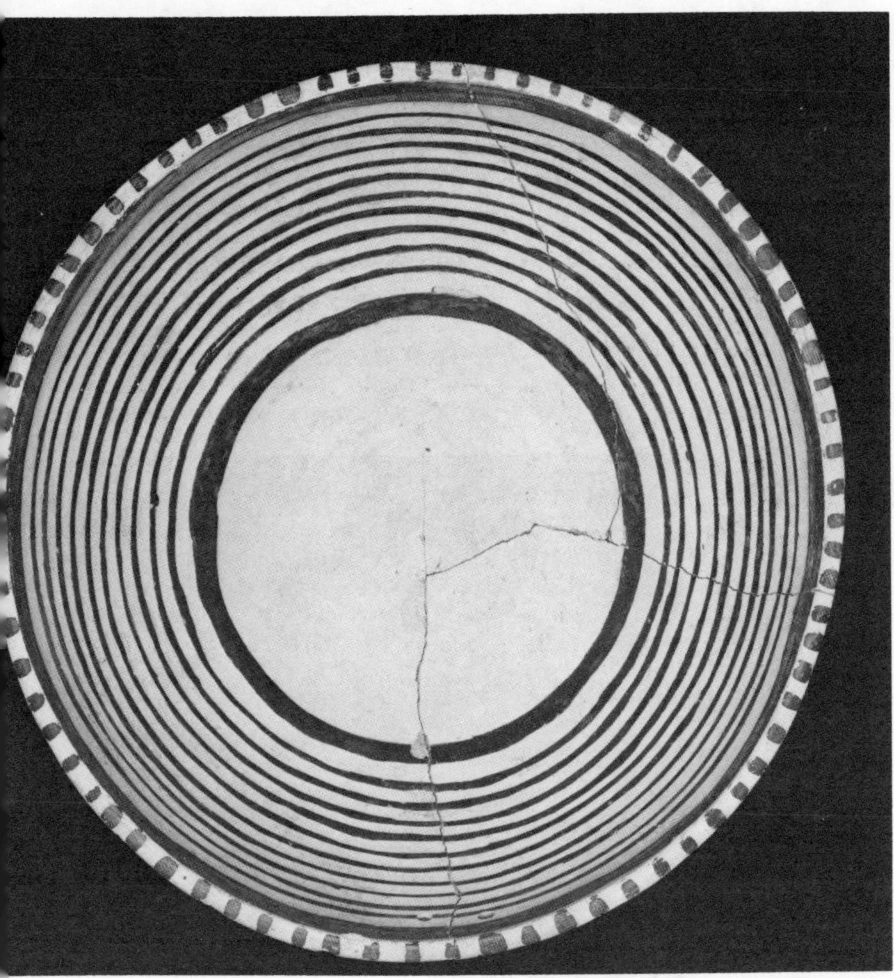

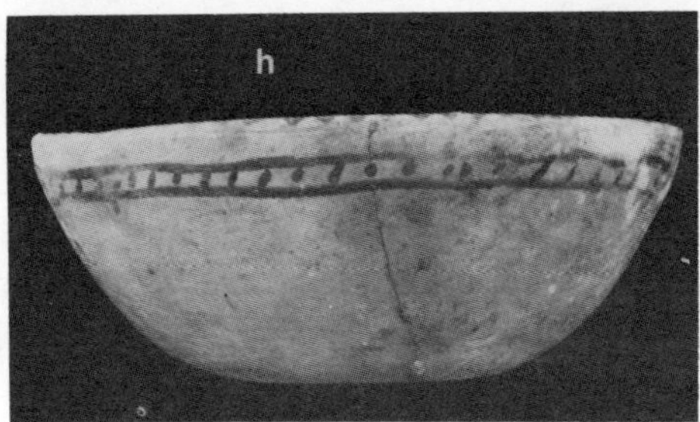

Figure 159. *Mesa Verde Black-on-white bowls, band designs except c (spiral, overall). Maximum diameter of g, 18.7 cm.*

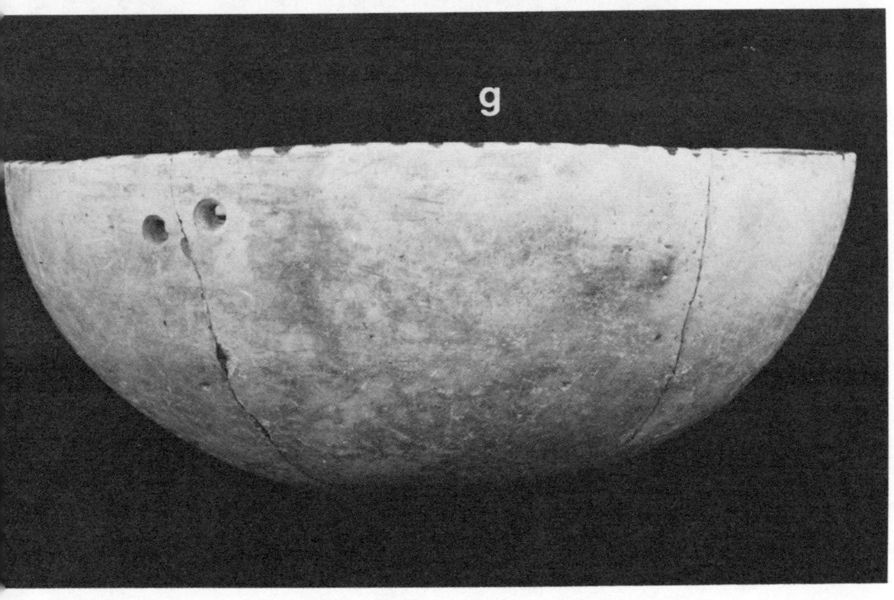

Exterior decoration was classified according to that found on rim and body sherds in order to get a general idea as to location of the bulk of this sort of decoration. On Mesa Verde, 39 percent of the rims and 18 percent of the body sherds were decorated on the exterior. McElmo had decoration on 12 percent of the rims and 4 percent of the body sherds.

Decoration on a greater percentage of body sherds of Mesa Verde Black-on-white than on McElmo Black-on-white suggests a wider design, or a design located lower on the vessel, or a combination of both. Inspection of the sherds and of whole vessels shows the first possibility to be the actual situation in most cases. Mesa Verde designs tend to be more elaborate, with band designs frequent, while McElmo often has only two or three parallel lines or some other simple and narrow design. However, some McElmo designs are closer to the rim, such as an extended diagonal ticking, running from or near the rim down and on to the side of the vessel.

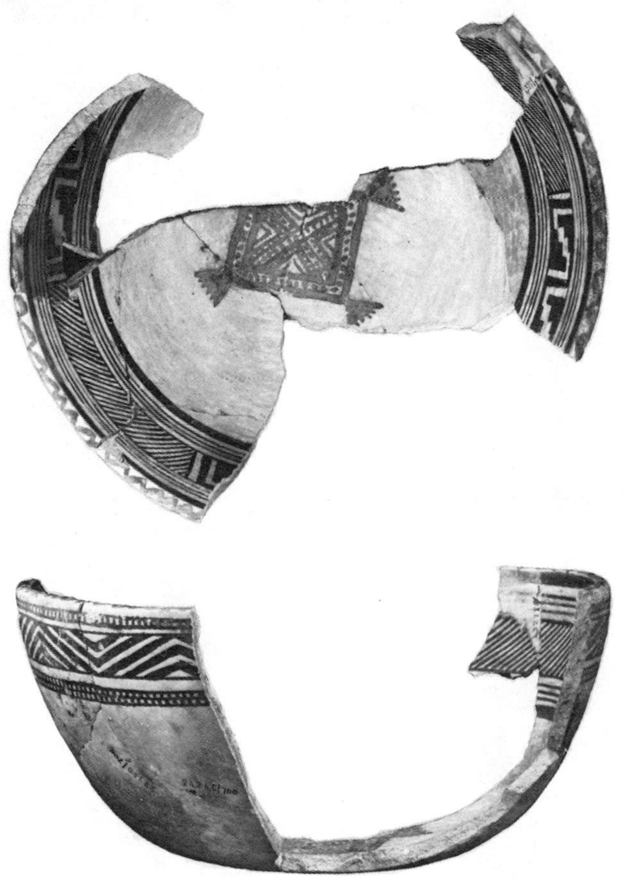

Figure 160. *Mesa Verde Black-on-white bowls, band and isolated designs. Maximum diameter, 25 cm.*

Figure 161. *Mesa Verde Black-on-white bowl, overall design. Maximum diameter, 28.8 cm.*

Rim shape is discussed in detail elsewhere, but two trends can be seen. Eight of the 264 McElmo sherds checked are sharply tapered or "pinched" but none of the Mesa Verde rim sherds have this shape. Twelve Mesa Verde rims were flared, a trait not found on any McElmo sherds in the sample. The flared rim is commoner in the Kayenta area than here, being found on such types as Flagstaff, Betatakin, and Polacca Black-on-white, Kayenta and Tusayan Polychrome, and so on.

A difference between Mesa Verde and McElmo Black-on-white in percentage of rim and body sherds recovered is noticeable in table 10. I believe that this is due to the comparative ease with which Mesa Verde body sherds can be recognized, primarily because of the elaborate band designs and framing lines found in this type. I am quite sure that a larger number of the indeterminate Mesa Verde-McElmo sherds were actually McElmo rather than Mesa Verde. Seventy-five percent of the indeterminates were body sherds, as compared to only 46 percent of the McElmo Black-on-white sherds. Considering the manner in which most vessels of these types broke, I would feel that both percentages distorted the actual proportions of rim to body sherds. The proportions of Mesa Verde Black-on-white rim and body sherds are probably closer to the true situation, though again the actual number of body sherds was probably slightly higher.

Of the 1,532 bowl rims included in the design analysis, 108 (7 percent) showed the rim edge (the original lip itself being gone in many cases) heavily worn by use-abrasion. Twelve of the sherds were Mesa Verde, 26 McElmo, and 70 indeterminate. I am sure that the larger percentage of the indeterminate sherds were McElmo, but once again the evidence was not strong enough to classify them as such. Most of these sherds were from small bowls. I think it safe to say that the majority of the "small bowls" were actually dippers, but handles or handle attachments were lacking so this cannot be proved.

The major designs of Mesa Verde Black-on-white have been illustrated in segments at least, in figures 132–152, showing design classes and elaboration of design. Vessels exemplifying designs consisting of a major class or combinations of major classes are illustrated in figures 158–167. The exterior of all the whole and many fragmentary vessels is also shown to indicate the great variety of designs found on Mesa Verde Black-on-white bowls.

Popularity of the band design is quite obvious in these illustrations, and even more so in the sherds from the Lower East Trash Slope. Equally obvious is a preference for the stepped or "keyed" figure, which appears on 10 of the 18 vessels illustrated in figures 158–160.

Although design classes are most useful in analyzing band designs, they are also applicable to the overall design. An example of this is the stepped figure (Class IIIA3), which is even more popular in the overall design than in bands. It appears on 10 of the 14 bowls in figures 161–163.

By no means is the highly elaborate, late Mesa Verde Black-on-white overall design incompatible with the band layout. The striking thing about this type of overall design is the balance of solid, stepped (or other) figures against hachure between parallel lines or within an irregularly shaped field bounded by a solid line. By means of paneling, a similar effect can be obtained in a band (fig. 164). The result is esthetically pleasing, and lends greater variety to the band without introducing new components of design. Within the panels of such designs there is still the traditional balancing of solid against solid, rather than solid against hatched figures. Exceptions to this are seen in figure 165a-c and possibly d, where a typical overall design is used within a band. Figure 165 a and b are probably from one bowl; d may be from an overall rather than a band design. Three additional sherds (fig. 166) show design somewhat similar, but closer in style to that of Tularosa Black-on-white. Figure 166a and b are probably from overall rather than band designs.

The vessels used to illustrate overall design also show clearly several types of primary layout: bisected (figs. 161 and 163f, offset

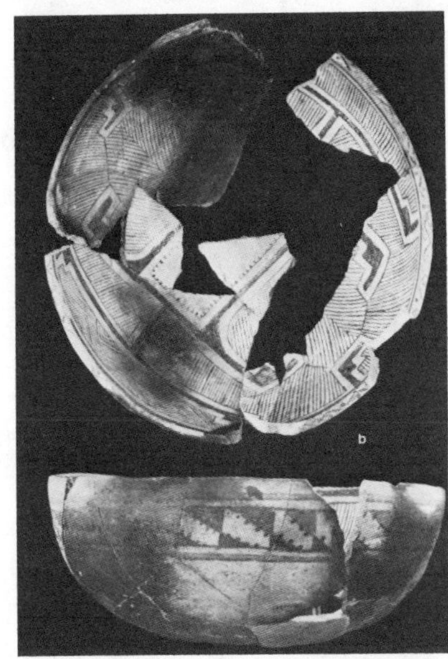

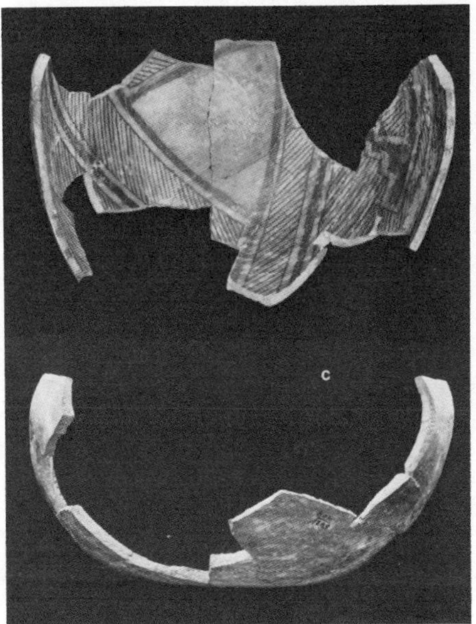

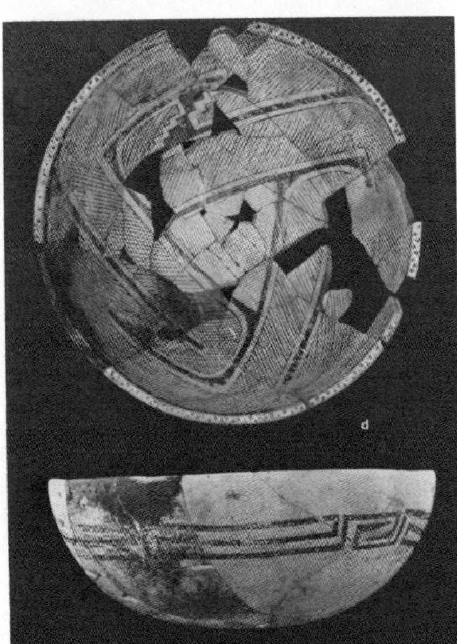

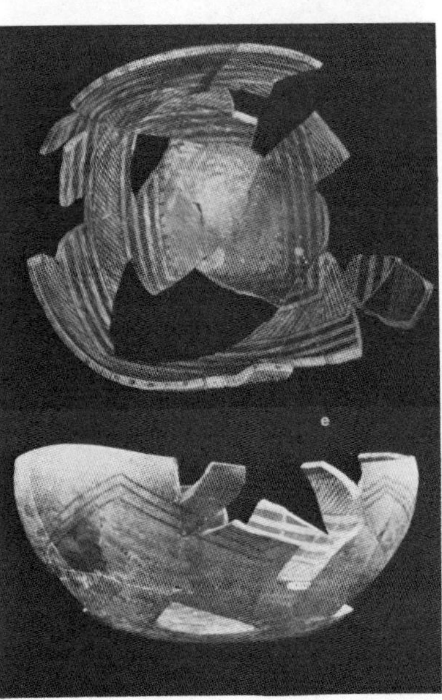

Figure 162. *Mesa Verde Black-on-white bowls, overall designs. Maximum diameter of d, 30.5 cm.*

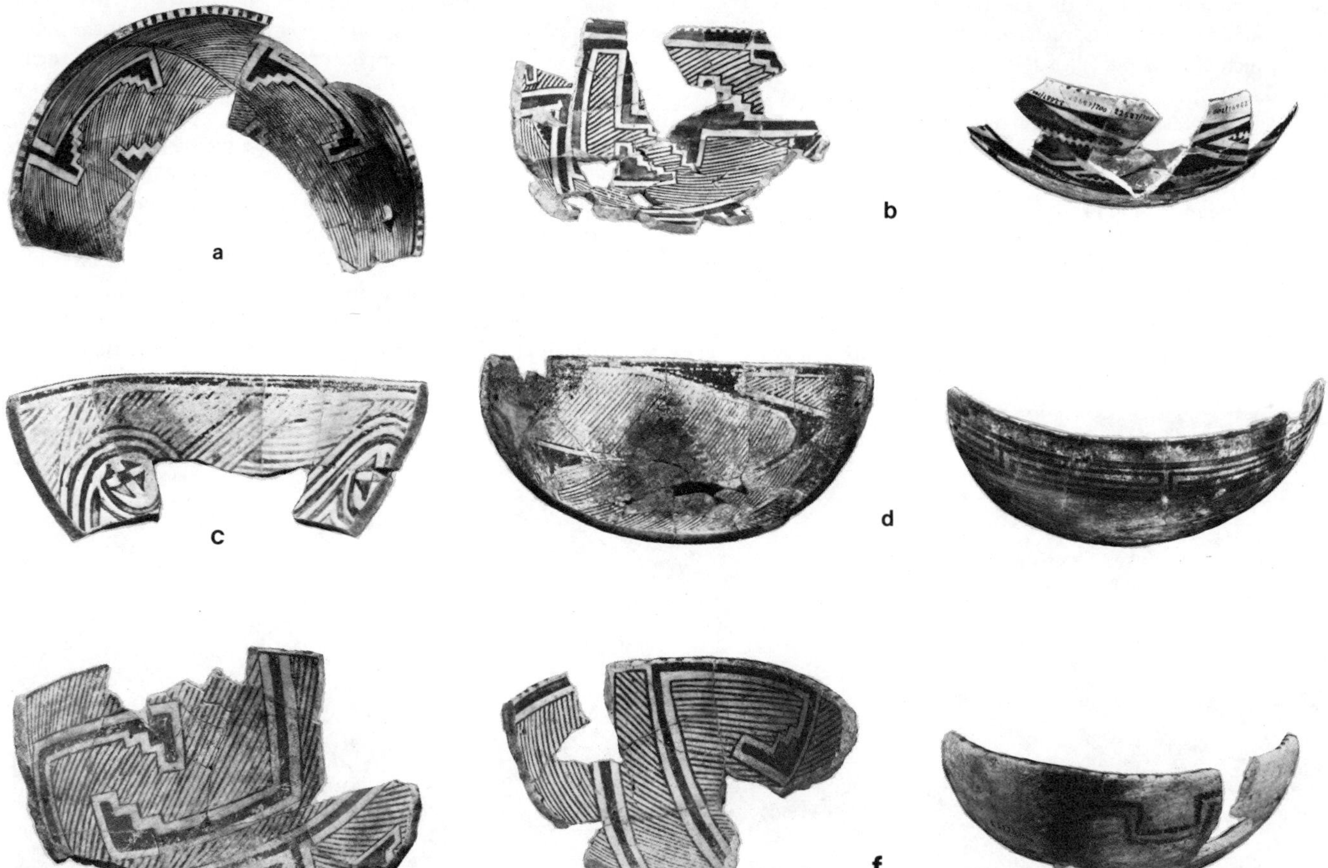

a

b

c

d

e

f

g

h

Figure 163. *Mesa Verde Black-on-white bowls, overall designs.*

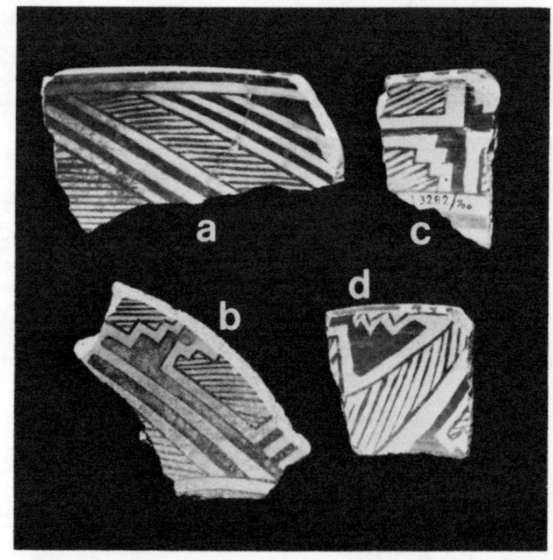

Figure 165. *Mesa Verde Black-on-white bowl sherds, overall designs used with a band.*

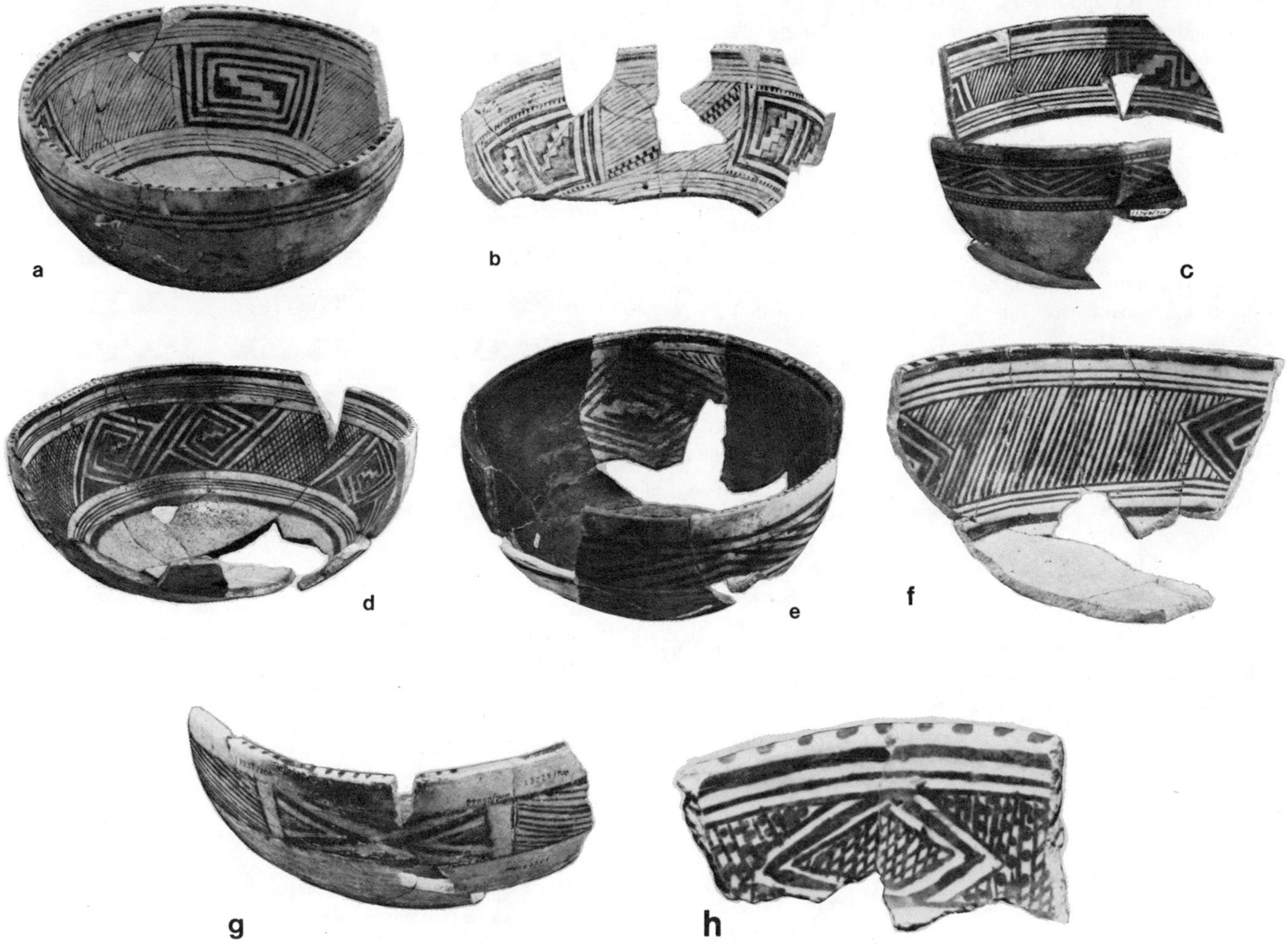

Figure 164. *Mesa Verde Black-on-white bowls, parallel band designs.*

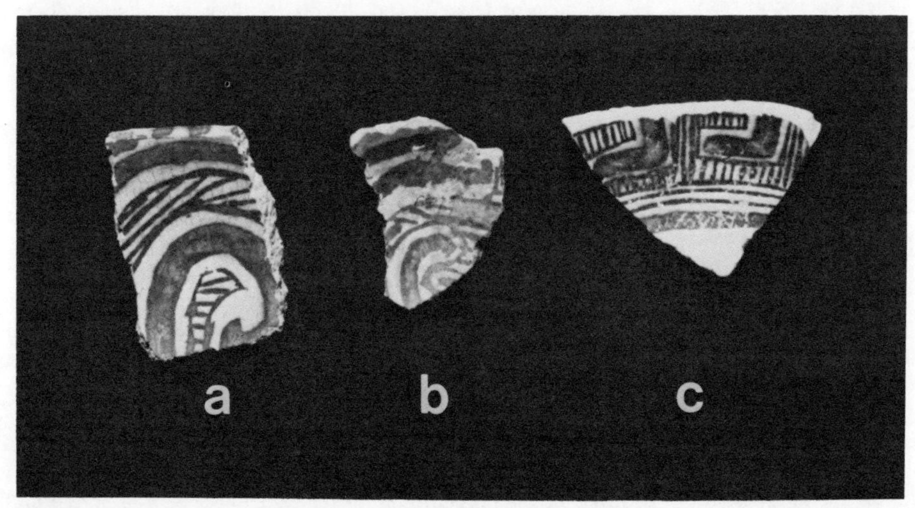

Figure 166. *Mesa Verde Black-on-white bowl sherds, overall designs (cf. Tularosa Black-on-white).*

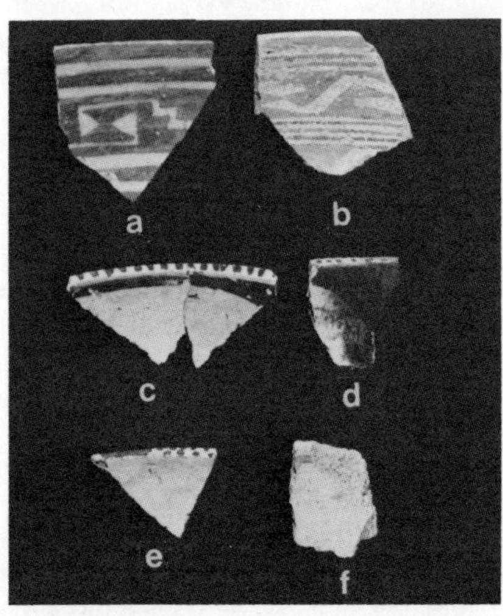

Figure 167. *Mesa Verde Black-on-white bowl sherds, triangles and frets in band pattern.*

trisected (fig. 162c and d), offset quartered (fig. 162b), paneled (fig. 163g), and a very unusual "square band" (fig. 162e). Bands are almost always based on the concentric circle, rather than the concentric square, layout.

Another significant characteristic of the overall layout, at least where more than one design is used, is the chevron-shaped sectoring device. It is most common in bisected or quartered designs, but may occur in overall designs that lack sectoring. At times, it is a secondary design between two crossed panels in a quartered design. In other cases, it may serve not only as a sectoring device (fig. 162a) but also to emphasize the composition (fig. 161). It may consist only of nested chevrons or may contain what can best be called a space elaboration.

I have already mentioned the popularity of the stepped figure. The relative frequency with which other components of design were used is also worth noting.

Bowls showing a predominance of white over black in the area of the interior band are extremely rare. Figure 167c-f shows examples of this, with the first three probably being sherds of one vessel. The rim ticking of the three varies in design from sherd to sherd, but this is not unusual from one portion of a bowl to another.

One of the most significant traits of Mesa Verde Black-on-white is certainly the elaboration of band framing lines, generally on the interior band only. The outermost lines are practically always heavier than the inner ones. Occasionally, the lines nearest the band design are of the same thickness as the outermost lines. The band border lines are usually thin. The framing lines may extend up to the lip or may start a short distance below it; they never extend to the center of the bowl. Rarely is there a difference between the sets of lines on either side of the band in number or thickness: one is the mirror image of the other. Sometimes more than one heavy line will be used, balanced above and below the band, and with or without the thinner lines. There may be considerable elaboration of the lines by dots or other figures, usually balanced above and below the band design except when dots are pendent to the innermost framing line. Figure 168 shows some of the variations found on sherds and whole vessels from Long House.

To judge from a sample of about 250 sherds, we can say that three or four thin framing lines, above and below the band design, were the most popular by a considerable margin. Three lines were found to be a little more common than four, but either will outnumber the next most common number, five, by a ratio of 4 to 1 or 3 to 1. The last number was followed, in descending order, by two, six, one, seven, eight, and nine lines.

Typical of Mesa Verde Black-on-white, but less significant than the framing lines, is lip decoration or "ticking." Figure 169 shows the commoner designs, and gives an idea of the variation that can be expected. The extent of patterning through spacing design elements (fig. 169j) or grouping of more than one element (figure 169w-z) can be suggested but not shown satisfactorily in sherds.

In the Lower East Trash Slope material, the most popular design was the repetition of closely spaced, rather circular dots. The ratio of this design to the next most common one (fig. 169e) was about 5 to 1. It is impossible to say more about design popularity, as the remainder illustrated were represented in different proportions in the different sherd lots checked, with none being particularly outstanding.

McElmo Black-on-white displays relatively little of the versatility of design seen in Mesa Verde Black-on-white. This is readily apparent in figures 170–176. The design classes are less numerous and the designs themselves are less stylized than they were later in time, but most of the components that make up the later, more elaborate designs are present.

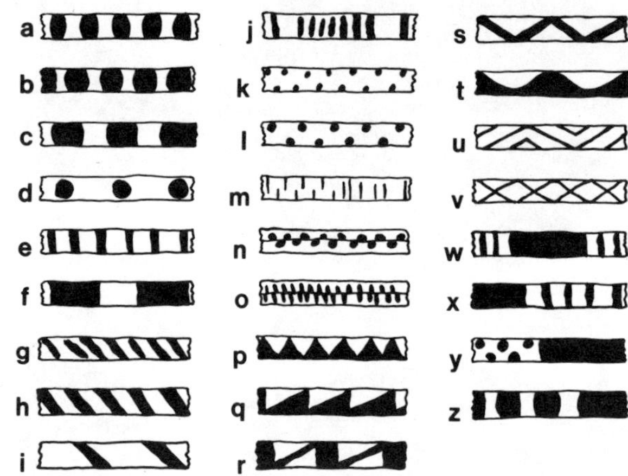

Figure 169. *Lip decoration or "ticking" on Mesa Verde Black-on-white bowls.*

The most striking difference in the two types is the absence of thin, sometimes elaborated framing lines, and the location of the band design at the lip rather than below it, on many of the bowls. The designs are more open than those of Mesa Verde Black-on-white, and the organization is not as good. As a whole, the linework is less carefully executed, but there are many examples that rival Mesa Verde in this respect.

Organic paint appears to a very limited extent on pottery types preceding McElmo, but it was not popular until the time of the transition from Mancos to McElmo Black-on-white. Perhaps a lack of familarity with such paint was partly responsible for the poor linework found on McElmo. If the paint lacked consistency, it would have been easier to apply in the broad-line designs so typical of Mancos Black-on-white. And it is in some of these designs, carried over from Mancos, that some of the better linework appears in McElmo (fig. 174a-c).

In the Lower East Trash Slope material, only design Classes I, III, and IV were represented in significant quantities. Of the Mesa Verde Black-on-white sherds, 60 percent were Class I, 18 percent Class III, and 22 percent Class IV. The triangle, in its various forms, was by far the commonest design. Although it outnumbered the stepped figure almost 4 to 1, it was combined with the stepped figure in many vessels in a Class IV design. In marked contrast with this, 67 percent of the vessels shown in figures 158–160 have Class IV, 13 percent Class I, and 20 percent Class III designs on the interior. The sample of whole vessels is too small to be useful in this case and probably presents a distorted picture.

Besides the more popular designs already discussed, there are, of course, many more that occur infrequently but are still typical of Mesa Verde Black-on-white pottery as seen in other collections. Good examples of this are shown in figure 167a and b, in which Class III and IV designs are combined in a band pattern. In a, neither design can be said to be secondary to the other. The more basic design in the other sherd is Class IVA.

It would be interesting to know what difference there may be in the slips of Mesa Verde and McElmo Black-on-white. Shepard (1957, p. 34) emphasizes the need for an absorptive clay to hold organic paint. Possibly slip clay was a factor in the paint behavior seen on McElmo. The Long House potters probably tried several slip clays before they found one that would hold the design during firing. But control of organic paint is difficult even with a proper slip, and this may be the prime reason for the poor linework seen in McElmo and, to a lesser extent, in Mesa Verde Black-on-white.

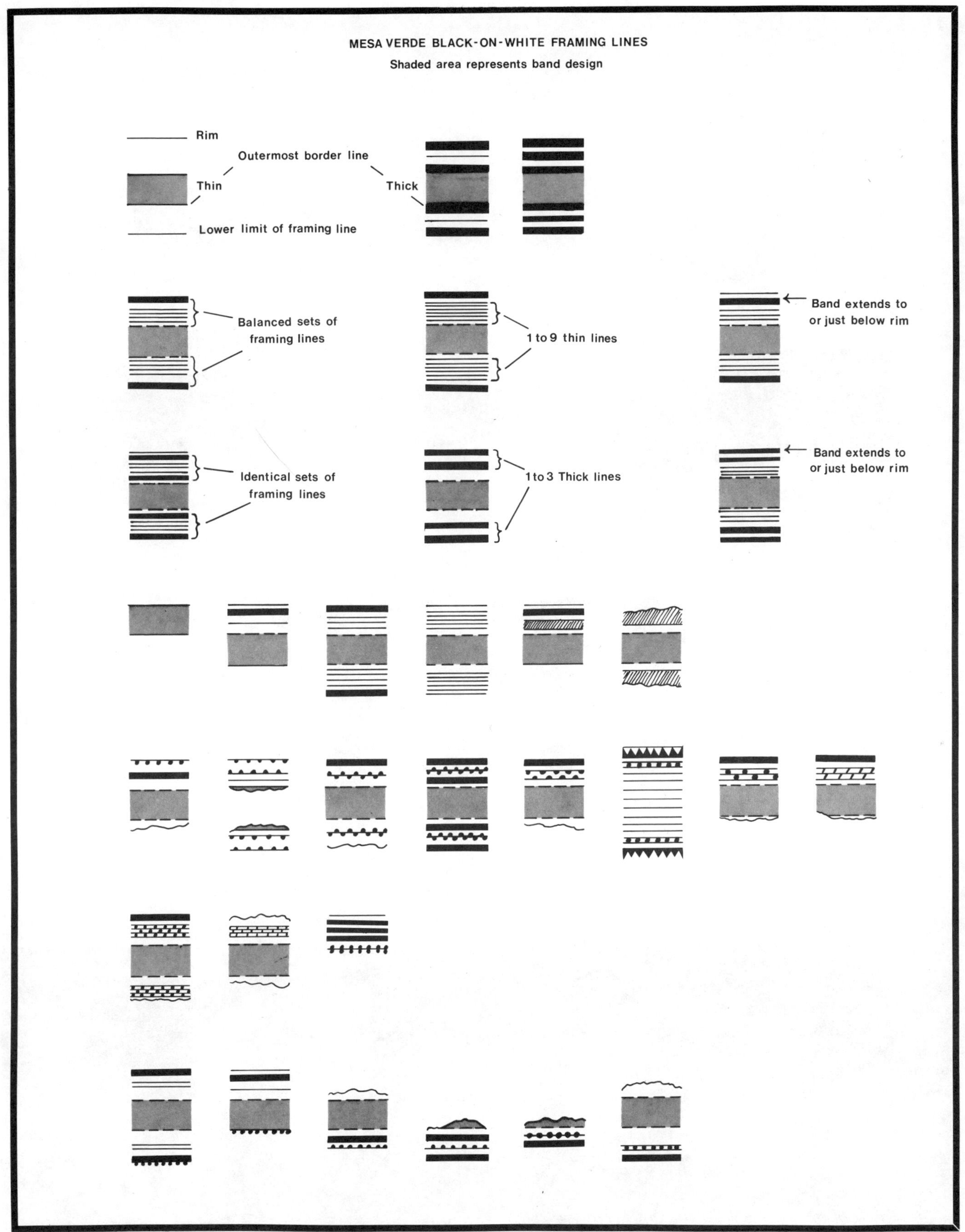

Figure 168. *Variations in framing lines on Mesa Verde Black-on-white sherds and whole vessels.*

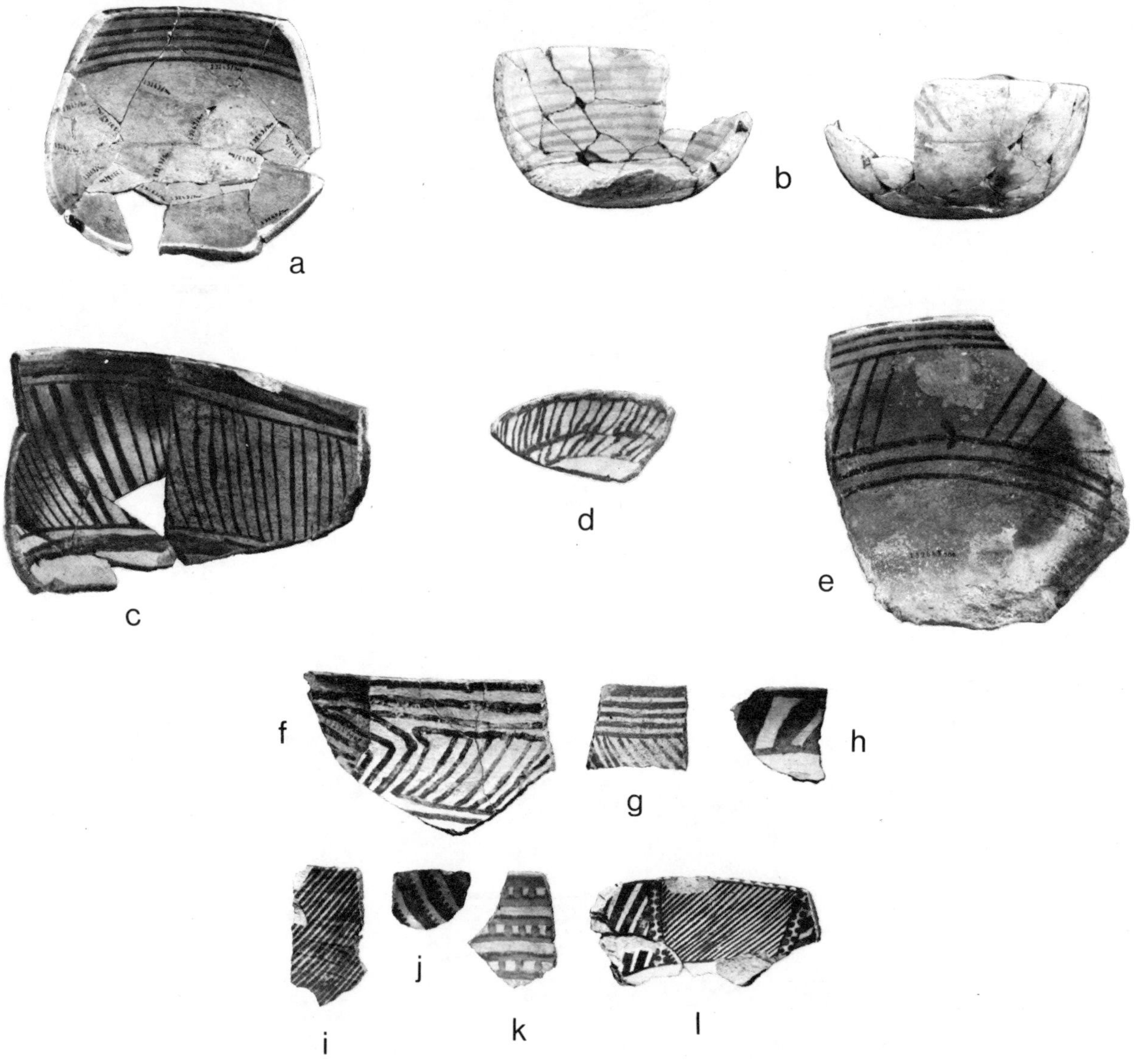

Figure 170. *McElmo Black-on-white, design class IA. Width of a, 20 cm.*

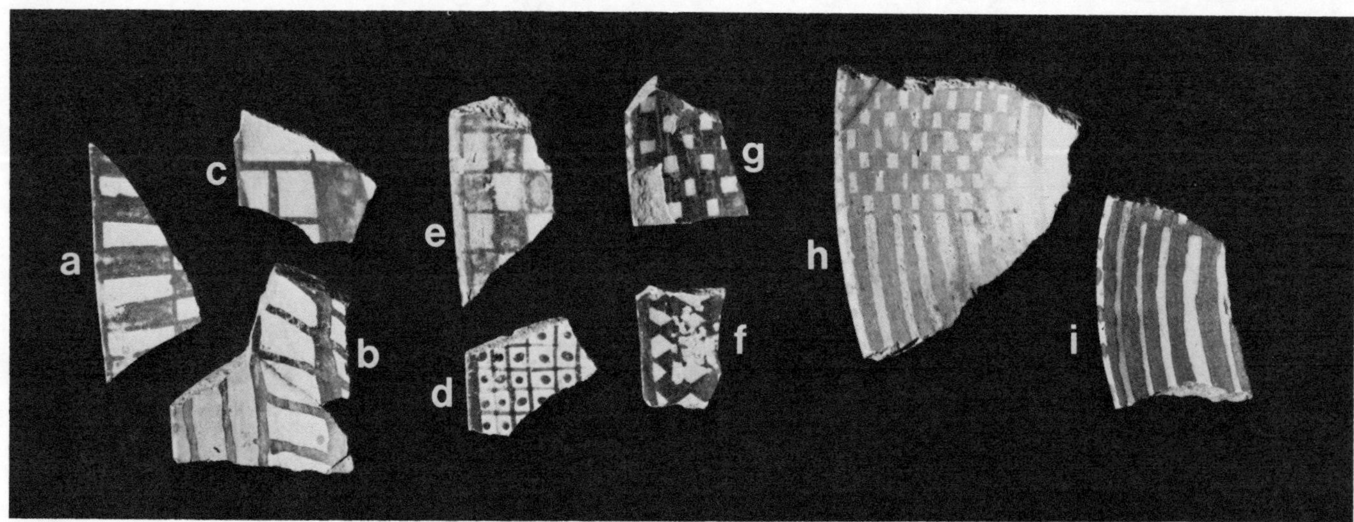

Figure 171. *McElmo Black-on-white, design class IB.*

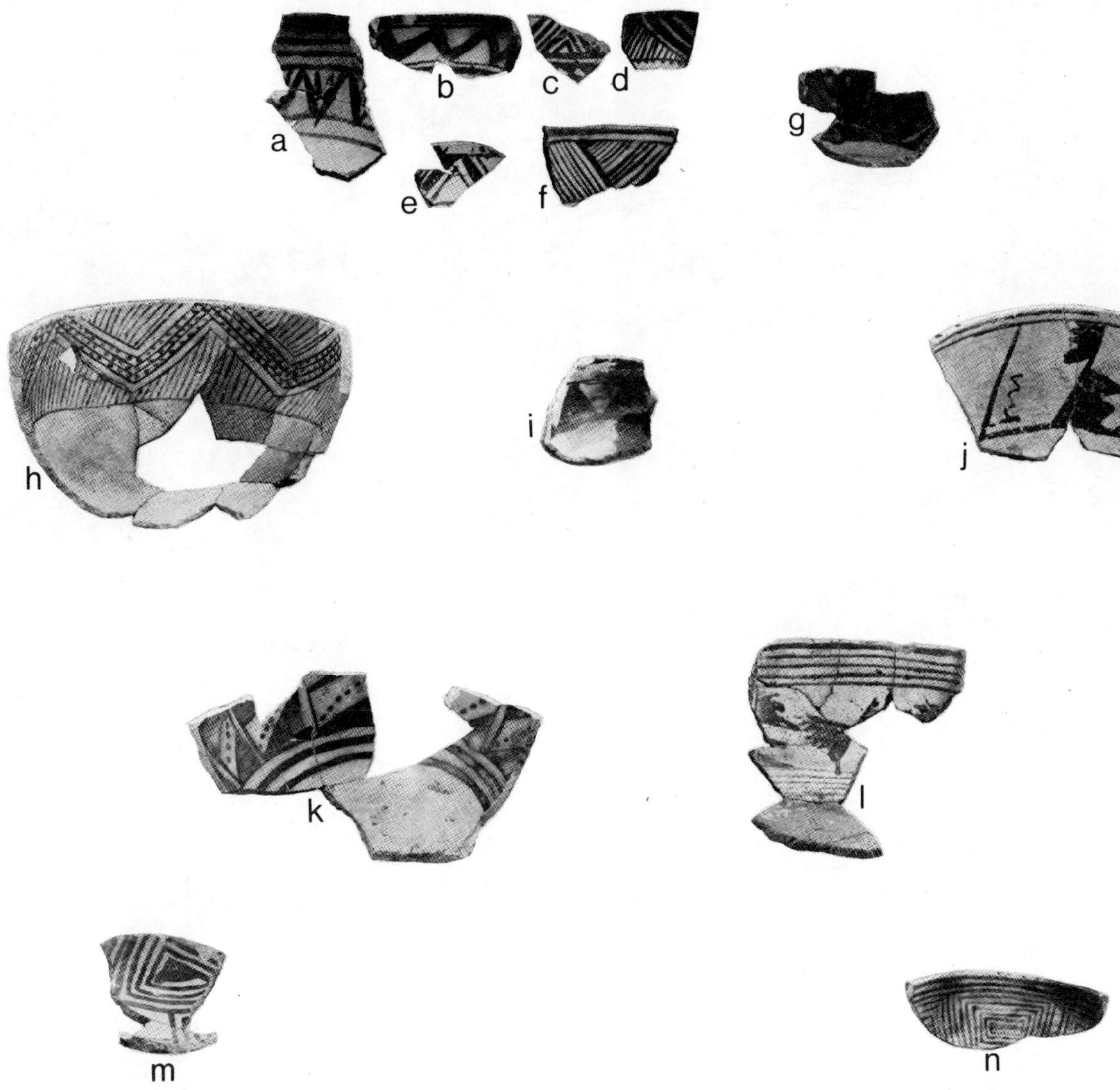

Figure 172. *McElmo Black-on-white, design classes IIIA and IVA. Maximum diameter of h, 24 cm.*

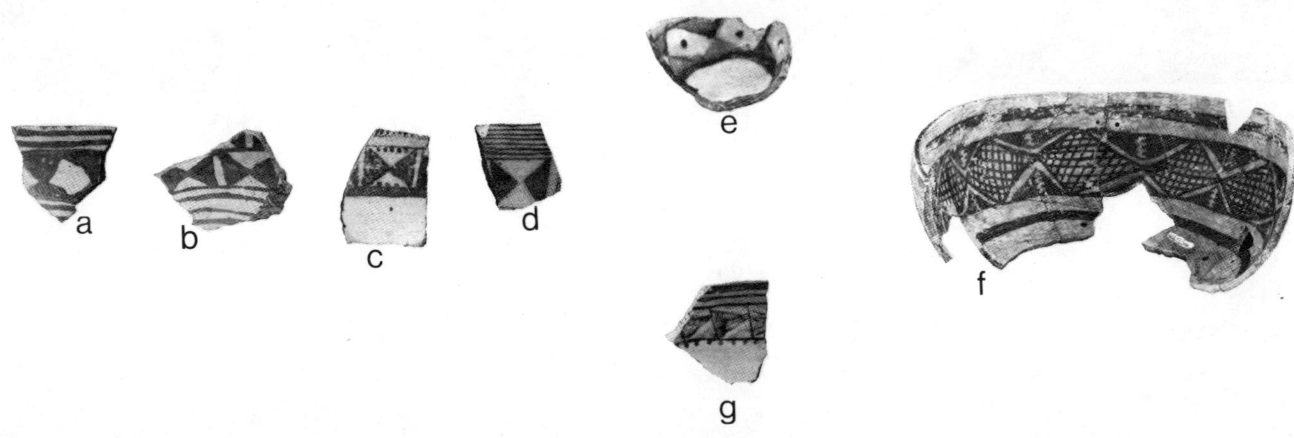

Figure 173. *McElmo Black-on-white, design class IIIB. Maximum diameter of f, 26 cm.*

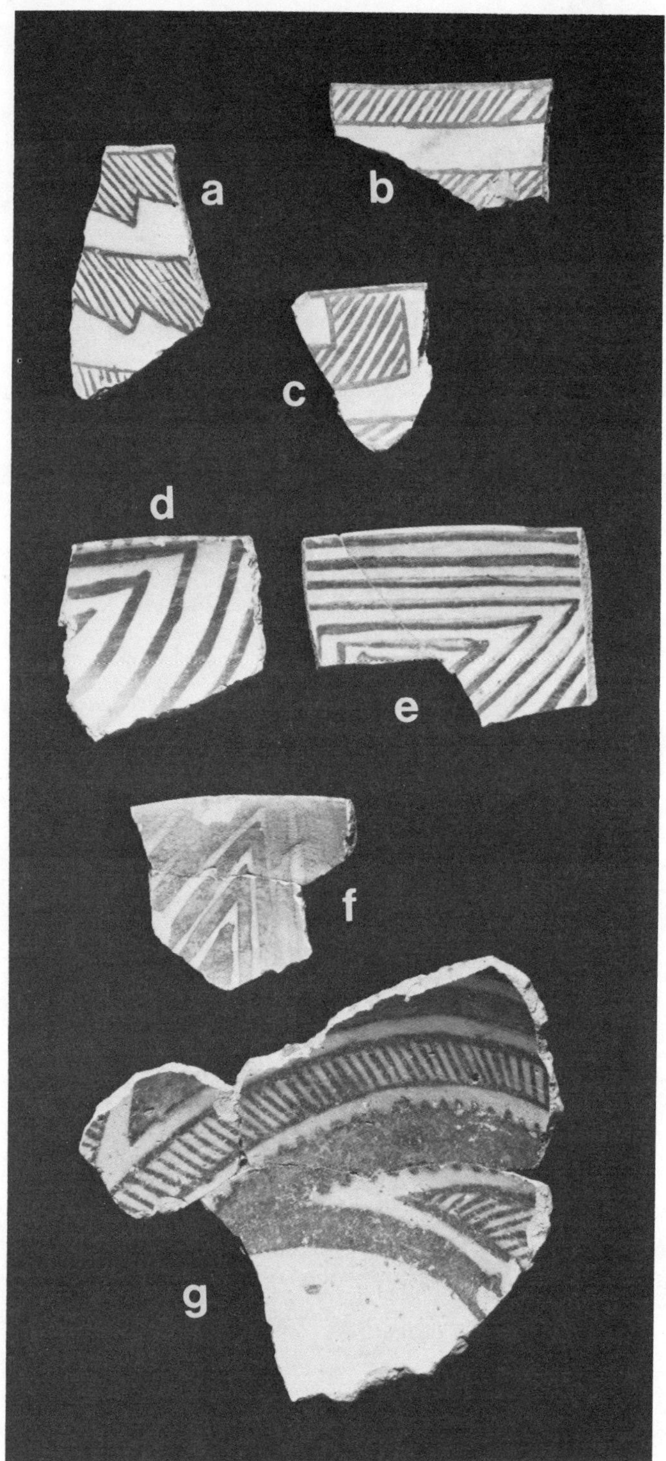

Figure 174. *McElmo Black-on-white bowl sherds.*

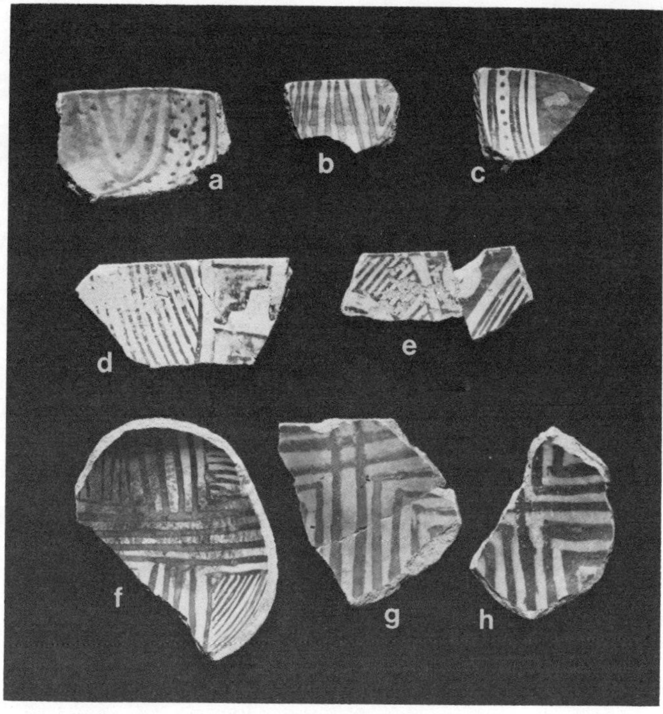

Figure 175. *McElmo Black-on-white bowl sherds.*

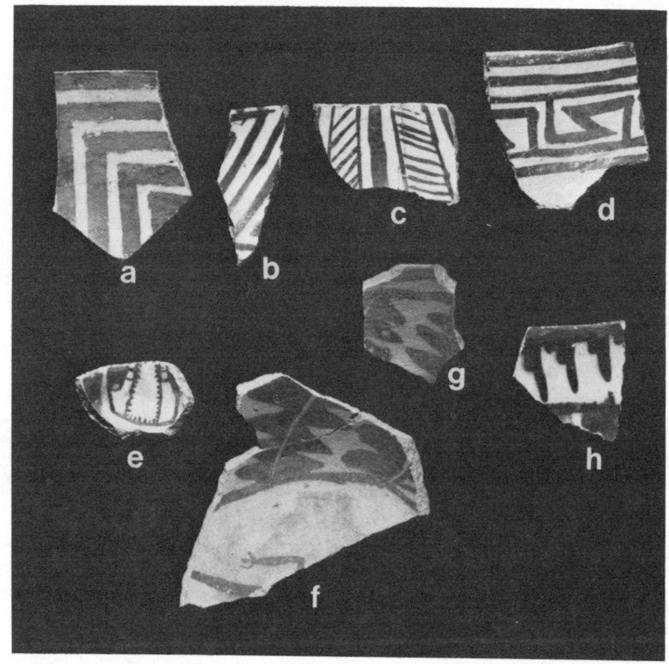

Figure 177. *Bowl sherds showing a combination of McElmo and Mesa Verde traits.*

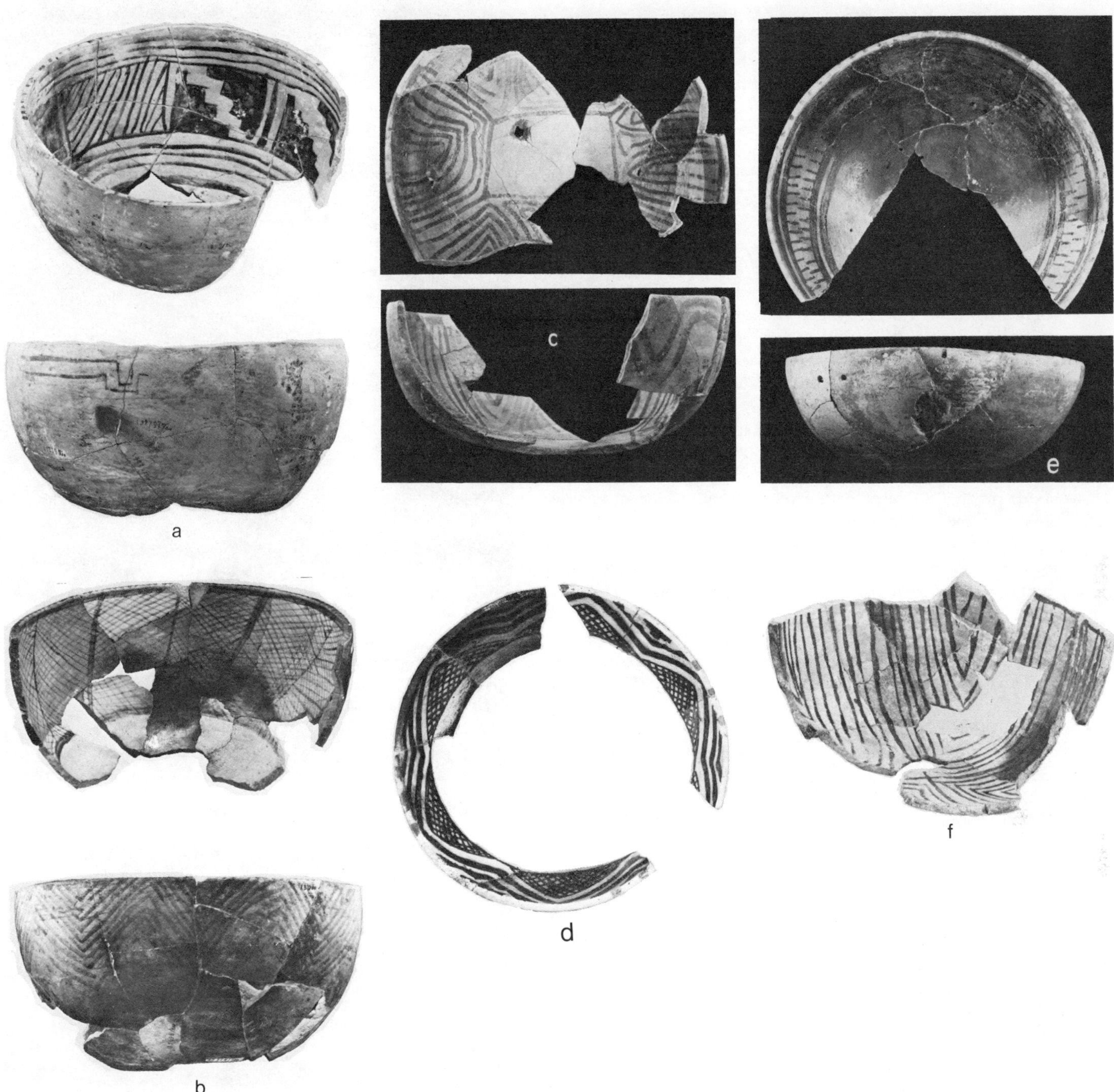

Figure 176. *McElmo Black-on-white bowls, band and overall designs. Maximum estimated diameter of c, 33 cm.*

So far, we have looked mainly at McElmo sherds because there are so few vessels that are definitely of this type. Figure 176 illustrates several of the best examples from Long House. Figure 176a, c, and f show a profile deeper and more straight-sided than is typical of Mesa Verde Black-on-white. In shape and design, figure 176c and f are close to Mancos Black-on-white. The others have "evolved" a step beyond this stage but not in all traits.

The identification of one vessel in this group (fig. 176b) will be open to argument, which is why I have chosen to illustrate it. In body and rim shape, finish, rim decoration (diagonal, closely spaced lines), and extent of exterior decoration, it is Mesa Verde. In placement and type of design, inside and out, it is closer to McElmo. It is the type of vessel that can be classified as one type one day, another the next. The design may be "aberrant" Mesa Verde, or it may be a step in the transition from McElmo to Mesa Verde. Another bowl (fig. 172k) shows the same problem. I hesitate to classify any of the sherds in figure 177. They all show a combination of McElmo and Mesa Verde traits.

Some McElmo designs may be very sloppy (fig. 172j and l), but sherds such as these are definitely McElmo in other respects. They are not merely sloppy Mesa Verde. I feel no hesitancy in calling all of the sherds in figure 178 Mesa Verde Black-on-white, taking into consideration all aspects of the pottery and its decoration. Two of the sherds (fig. 178a and b) show how radically different the workmanship on the exterior can be from that on the interior. Another example of how difficult the situation can get is shown in figure 179. Here two designs were painted on the bowl, one over the other. One consists of interlocking scrolls, the other of opposed triangles with a single line forming a running band spaced between the opposed sets. Possibly this is an example of the problem of paint consistency. The opposed triangles were applied first, and may have been so thin (or with so little coloring material) that the potter thought it would not stand out even after firing. Thus she painted a second design over the first and ended up with two designs, unintentionally.

The diameter of Mesa Verde Black-on-white bowls ranged from 14.0 to 33.0 cm. with a noticeable concentration in the 17.0 to 18.5 cm. range and another in the 22.0 to 30.0 cm. range. In the latter, the highest frequency occurred in the 26.0 to 28.0 cm. span. Vessel height varied from 6.3 to 14.7 cm. Again, two concentrations can be seen, one at 7.5 cm. and the other in the 11.5 to 13.0 cm. range (but with fairly even distribution). As expected, volume of the bowls can be split into two main groups. The smaller bowls range from 900 to 1,300 cc., with a peak at 1,000 to 1,200 cc. The larger ones extend from 3,800 to 7,500 cc., with a concentration at 5,000 to 5,500 cc.

McElmo bowls coincided in size with Mesa Verde bowls for the most part, differing primarily in extending farther down the small-size range. The diameter of the McElmo material varied from 10.1 cm. to 13.0 cm. Once again, there are two concentrations, with the smaller extending from 10.1 to 19.0 cm. and peaking at 13.8 to 16.0 cm. There is a considerable gap between this and the next concentration, which ranges from 24.0 to 33.0 cm., with the highest frequency occurring in the 25.7 to 27.0 cm. span. The bowls can also be placed in one of two groups by vessel height, which varies from 4.2 to 17.5 cm. The smaller group extends from 4.2 to 6.9 cm., with no peak, and the larger from 10.5 to 17.5 cm. There is no peak in this latter group either, but the maximum height, 17.5 cm., stands out as an isolated figure. The next largest bowl is 14.7 cm. high. With three exceptions, the McElmo bowls were too fragmentary to measure. These three had capacities of 200, 550 and 7,500 cc. The exterior bottom of both Mesa Verde and McElmo bowls was usually convex or slightly flattened. Only rarely was it slightly concave, as was common in jars.

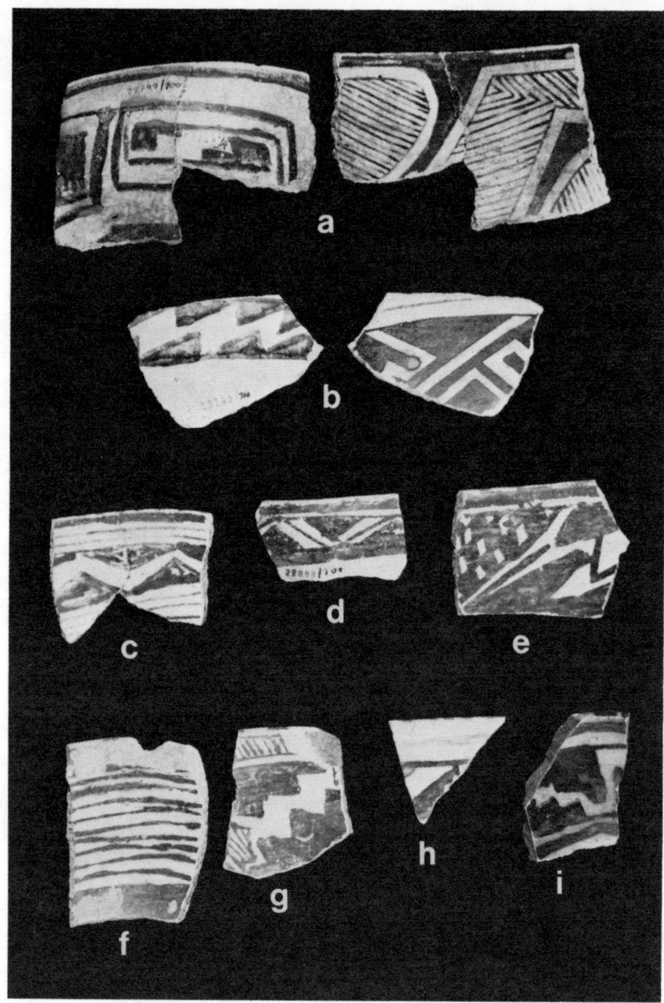

Figure 178. *Mesa Verde Black-on-white bowl sherds.*

Figure 179. *Black-on-white bowl sherd decorated with two designs: opposed triangles beneath interlocking scrolls.*

The range of primary rim shapes for Mesa Verde and McElmo Black-on-white bowls, mugs, dippers, and jars is shown in figures 180 and 181. The variety is overbalanced in favor of Mesa Verde Black-on-white, due in part to the much greater bulk of the later pottery. If comparative material from other sites were included, I believe that the number of rim shapes for McElmo would be increased substantially.

The typically squared and flattened Mesa Verde Black-on-white lip (fig. 180b, c, and g) is the commonest shape found on bowls, as well as on mugs and dippers, but the slightly rounded lip (a) is sometimes found. Also, the lip is occasionally slightly beveled,

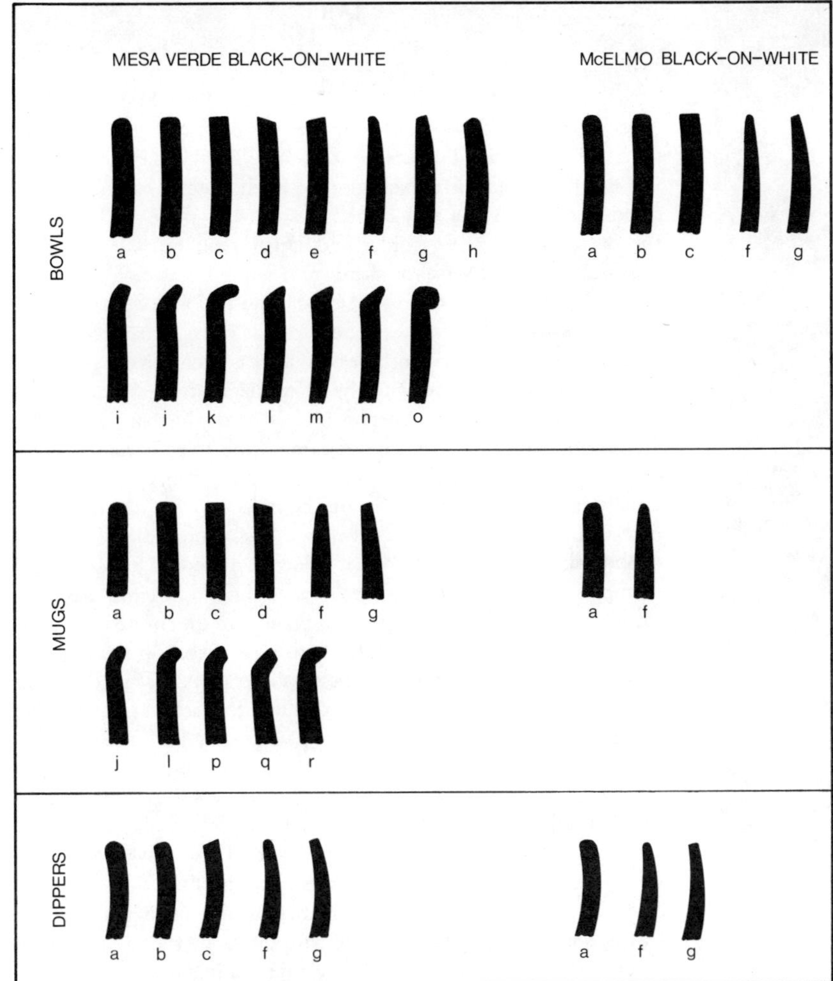

Figure 180. *Comparison of Mesa Verde and McElmo Black-on-white rim shapes of bowls, mugs, and dippers.*

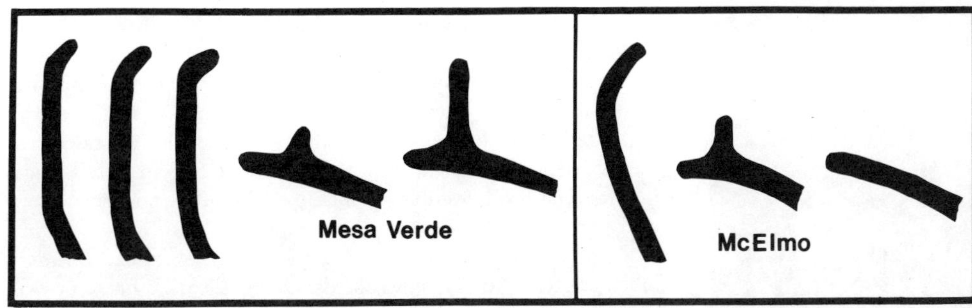

Figure 181. *Comparison of Mesa Verde and McElmo Black-on-white rim shapes of jars.*

sloping either in or out (d, e, and h). In cross section, the vessel walls may have parallel sides, thus forming a direct rim (Shepard 1957, p. 245), or taper slightly toward the lip (f-h) or toward the base (m). The tapered rim is more common in McElmo Black-on-white than in Mesa Verde, on all vessel shapes.

The term flared rim, which I have used several times, encompasses most of the remaining variations in rim form. The rim may be everted, while still holding its same thickness (fig. 180i, or it may taper slightly (j and k). More commonly, it will thicken slightly at the lip, thus creating a slight protuberance on the exterior vessel wall (l and m). This may be enlarged to produce a very rounded rim (o). When carried to the extreme, the flared rim will be sharply everted, with tapering of the rim starting at the point of eversion, and an insloping bevel (n). The everted rim is generally absent in McElmo pottery.

Wall thicknesses of Mesa Verde bowls have a wide range: 3 to 15 mm. The heaviest concentration is between 4 to 7 mm., with the average between 5 and 6 mm. Only a handful of sherds falls into the thick-walled category, 9 to 15 mm., where the average thickness is just under 11 mm. Within the total range given above, the rims fall between 3 to 7 mm., the average slightly higher than 5 mm.; the body sherds vary from 4 to 15 mm., and averages closer to 6 mm. The thickness of the base of the bowls is closer to the side thickness than in jars, ranging from 4 to 9 mm., and averaging just under 7 mm.

There is less variety in wall thickness in McElmo Black-on-white pottery. The range for all parts of the bowl is 3 to 11 mm., with the rim thickness apparently identical in the two types. Wall thickness varies only from 5 to 8 mm., whereas the bases range from 6 to 11 mm.

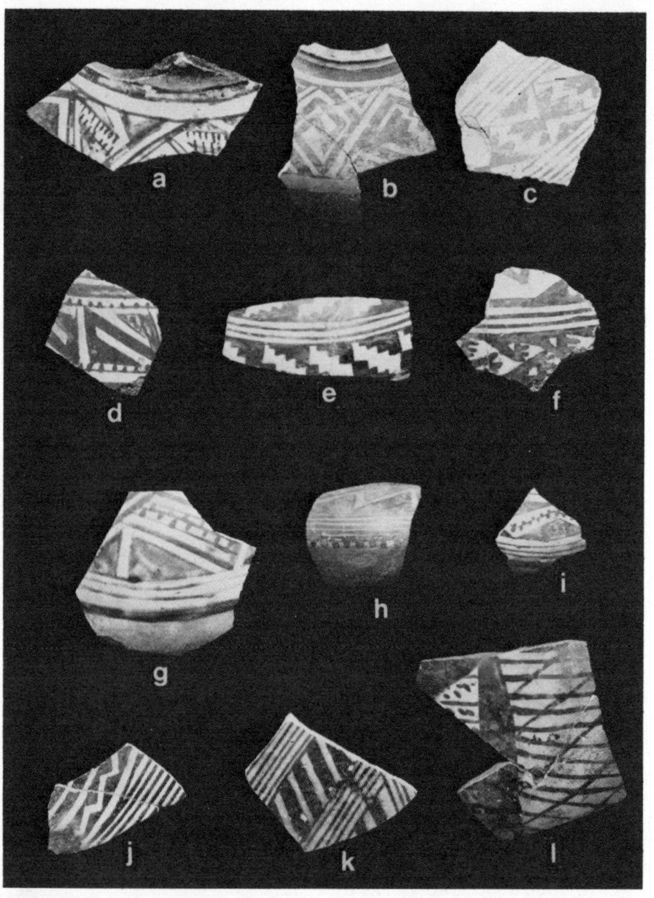

Figure 183. *Mesa Verde and McElmo (?) Black-on-white jar sherds.*

Figure 184. *McElmo Black-on-white jar sherds.*

JARS

Jar sherds (17 percent of the Lower East Trash Slope McElmo-Mesa Verde Black-on-white) form the second major group studied from the Lower East Trash Slope (table 12). Design alanysis of whole jars is difficult, and it is even more so in the case of jar sherds. The sherds into which a jar may break are small, like those of a bowl, but the design on a jar is bolder and larger than on a bowl. Thus classification of the vessel or sherd from rather insignificant portions of the design becomes at times a hopeless task. I also feel that many jar designs were less formal, or perhaps less classic, than those used on bowl interiors. Apparently less effort was spent on jar painting, with the result that several of the more diagnostic features of bowl design are often missing. There is usually no doubt that the vessel is McElmo-Mesa Verde, but it is often impossible to go beyond this.

Almost the entire range of bowl designs can appear on jars, usually in a band located in an area bounded by the junction of the neck and body and a point just below the maximum diameter of the jar but above the handles (when present). Figures 182–184 show examples of high-necked jar decoration, but no attempt has been made to group them by design class because of the limited material. A good example of a vessel difficult to type is seen in figure 182e. The design, rim decoration, and vessel shape are perfectly good Mesa Verde, but the execution of the design and the lack of framing lines make it appear more primitive. The painter may have been a child, an inexperienced adult, an elderly person with unsteady hand, or someone who didn't care what the end result looked like. I have classed the jar as Mesa Verde, but it is hardly a typical example.

A similar situation is seen in figure 182a, where again the workmanship is poor. I feel that the vessel is Mesa Verde, and its corrugated neck enhances this argument. Most, if not all, of the sherds shown in figure 183 are also Mesa Verde; the possible exceptions are j-l. Example k is closely related to a Mancos Black-on-white style of design, which is probably seen more commonly on McElmo than Mesa Verde pottery.

Design layout shown in figure 183j could be either McElmo or Mesa Verde, but not enough is present to make identification certain. The sherd is correctly oriented with respect to the horizontal in the illustration. Sherd 1 is obviously McElmo-Mesa Verde, but any attempt at further classification is futile. In all cases just mentioned, the paste, slip, and finish are of no help in the classification. Several good examples of McElmo Black-on-white can be seen in figure 184.

As table 12 shows, the proportion of indeterminate sherds is much greater in jar than bowl sherds. Of 897 sherds, 59 percent were classed as indeterminate. Only 37 percent were considered definitely to be Mesa Verde, and only 4 percent McElmo.

As with the bowls, the unslipped variation forms a very small percentage of the sample. The corrugated neck variation appears in the sample, but only in the indeterminate sherds, where it formed 1 percent of this class. It appears on three of the 28 restorable vessels. When it is possible to associate corrugation with a design that can be classified, as on whole or restorable vessels (fig. 182b and c) and on a few sherds from other parts of the ruin, the design is inevitably Mesa Verde Black-on-white.

Rim sherds form only 7 percent of the sherds of all varieties. The percentage of Mesa Verde rims is obviously too low, that of McElmo too high. Jar rims, except when attached to body sherds, are less diagnostic than those of bowls, and thus many Mesa Verde rims must have been placed in the indeterminate category.

All six Mesa Verde rims were ticked, but only three of the eight McElmo rims were so decorated. Twenty-four of the 43 indetermi-

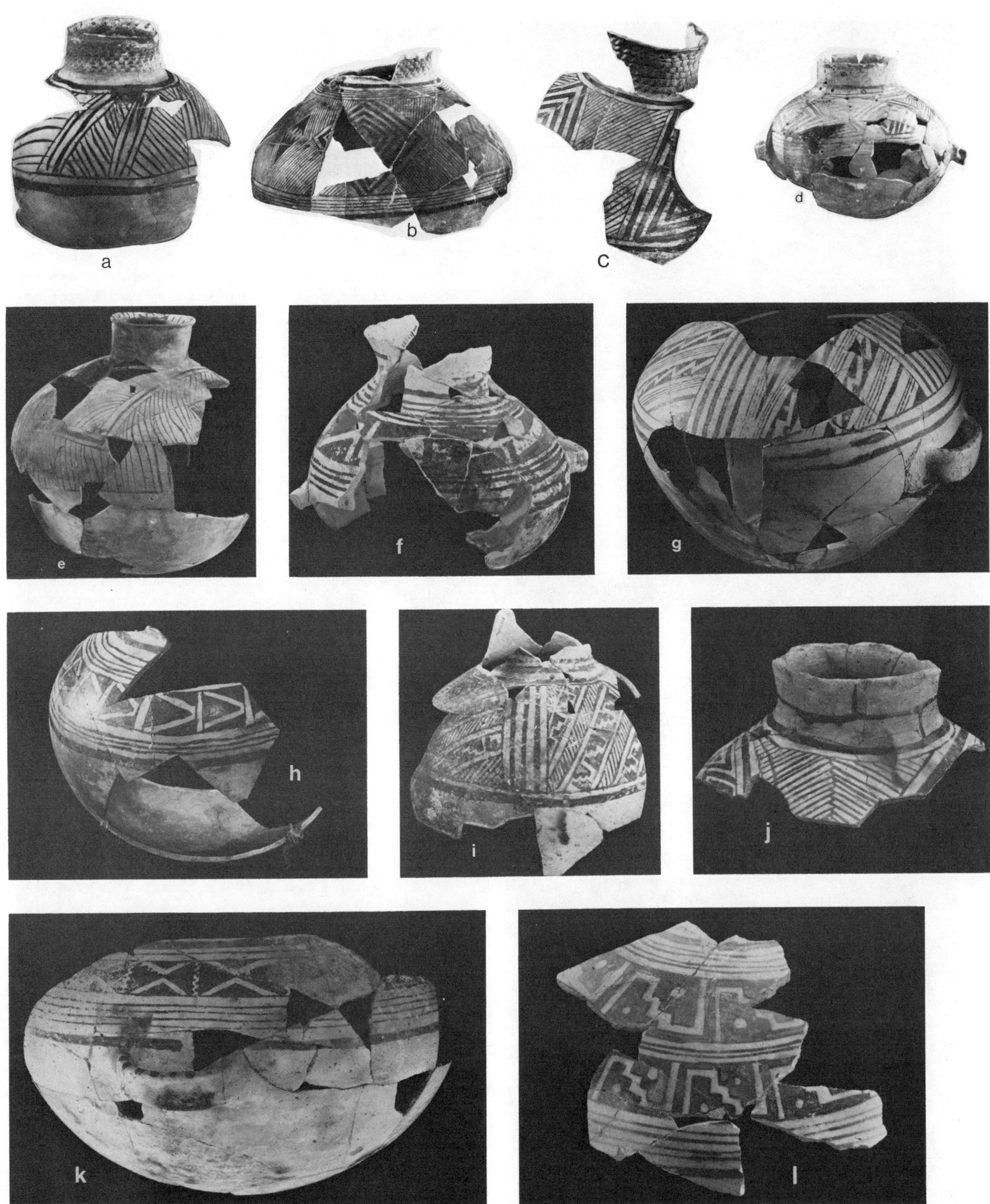

Figure 182. *Mesa Verde Black-on-white jars.*

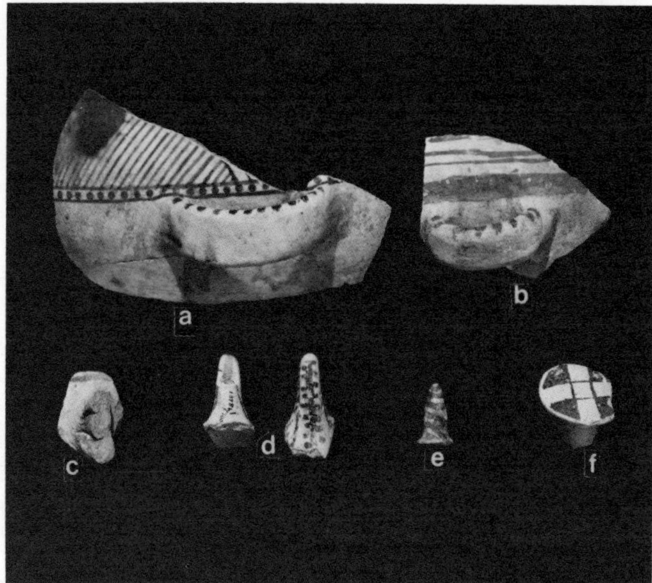

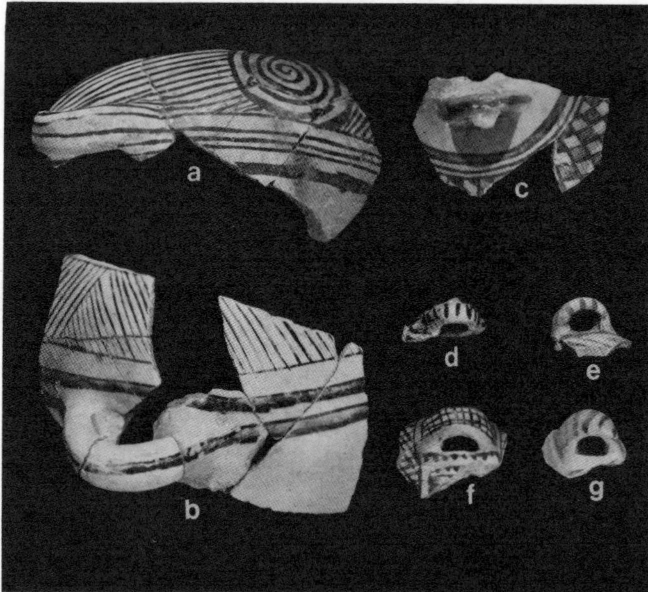

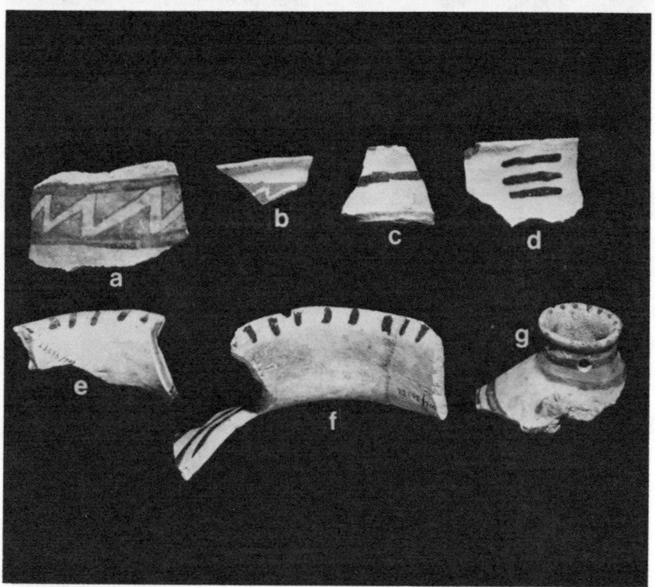

Figure 185. *(Above) McElmo Black-on-white jar handles.*

nate rim sherds were ticked. It is certainly safe to say—after studying whole vessels and sherds from other portions of the ruin—that ticking is far more common on Mesa Verde than on McElmo, but the proportion is still in doubt. The range in rim shape, for both whole vessels and sherds, is shown in figure 181.

Jar handles are even more difficult to contend with than the rest of the vessel, at least from the standpoint of classification. Four types were represented in the Lower East Trash Slope material, but only two of these were ascribable to Mesa Verde and none to McElmo.

The wide, flat strap handle (fig. 185a and b) was most common to the Mesa Verde type, with five specimens, and the narrow, flat-rounded least common, with two specimens (fig. 186a and b). With the 62 indeterminate handles, the proportion was almost identical. Two other handle types were represented in the indeterminate category only: hollow (fig. 185d) and knob (fig. 185f). There were seven examples of the former and two of the latter.

The knob handle was not found in place on any vessel in Long House, but Morris (1939, Pl. 297f) illustrates a good example. The hollow handle is merely a variant of the conical type (discussed below), and the one illustrated projected from the side of the jar. Its vertical position on the jar is unknown, however, A perforation about 0.4 cm. in diameter extends approximately 2.0 cm. into the handle through its tip. There are also two perforations symmetrically placed, one on either side of the handle, near the longest edge.

One of the two other types not found in the Lower East Trash Slope collection is a 3-rod, compound handle (fig. 185c), very similar to the compound dipper handle. Only one was recovered from Long House. The other type (fig. 185e), also represented by one specimen, is a long (3.0 cm.), conical handle. As can be seen in figures 185 and 186, handle decoration is rather varied in style. It is generally, and perhaps entirely, confined to the outer (convex) side and the top edge of strap handles but may be on any or all surfaces of the conical and hollow types. Decoration is usually restricted to the top of knob handles.

As a field for decoration, jar necks and rims present a problem similar to that of the handles. The designs are usually quite simple (figs. 187c and d) and thus very difficult to type unless more than just the neck of the vessel is present. Occasionally, the design is more elaborate and classification is possible (fig. 187a and b). Neck decoration seems to be extremely rare on McElmo jars, but when present, is invariably simple. Unfortunately, there are not many good specimens to document this observation.

Few high-necked (water) jars were sufficiently intact to allow measurement. The variation in size is apparently not great: height 20.0 to 26.5 cm.; maximum diameter 31.8 to 37.0 cm.; rim diameter 9.2 to 12.7 cm., with one specimen at 20.7 cm.; volume 11,000 to 11,650 cc. Neck height is difficult to measure on some specimens because of the transition from body to neck without a clear demarcation. Where such measurement could be made, it ranged from about 2.2 to 6.0 cm. Wall thickness varies from one part of the vessel to another: rim 3 to 4 mm., average 4 mm.; body 3 to 7 mm., average 5 to 6 mm.; neck 5 to 7 mm., average 6 mm.; base 6 to 7 mm., average 7 mm. The bottom of the highnecked jar is often slightly concave, as viewed from the outside.

A wide, flat strap handle was found on five vessels: length 8.8 to 10.0 cm., width 2.4 to 2.5 cm., and thickness 0.7 to 0.9 cm. Evidence of a narrow, flat-round handle was found on two jars. One was about 6.3 cm. long, but it was impossible to obtain other measurements.

Figure 186. *(Center) McElmo Black-on-white jar handles.*

Figure 187. *(Left) McElmo Black-on-white jar rim and neck decorations.*

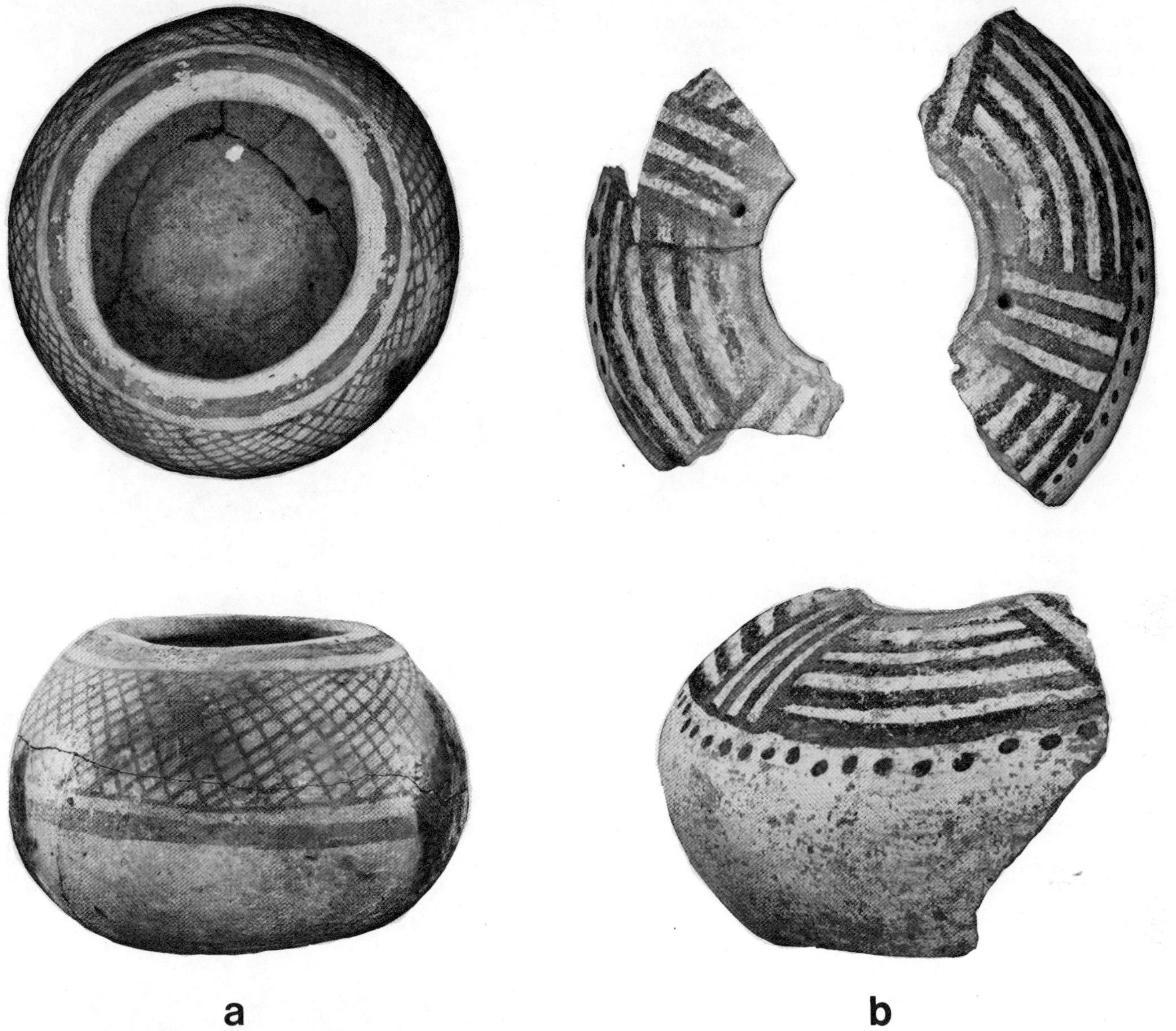

Figure 188. *McElmo Black-on-white seed jars.*

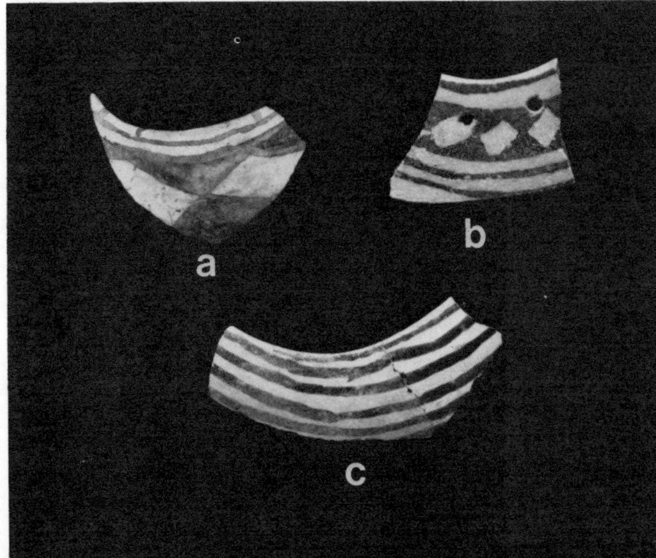

Figure 189. *McElmo Black-on-white seed jar sherds.*

The jar rim measuring 20.7 cm. in diameter, mentioned above, has a rim diameter almost twice that of the next largest, 12.7 cm. Rim shape and design would indicate Mesa Verde Black-on-white, despite sloppiness of design.

Included in the figures shown in table 12 are six sherds from seed jars and 13 from kiva jars. The balance are, for the most part, from high-necked jars. Both of the seed jars illustrated in figure 188, especially the fragmentary one, have McElmo designs. For what significance it may have, four of the five seed jar rim sherds were McElmo. Two of these five and one indeterminate sherd had ticked rims. Three rim sherds from elsewhere in the ruin (fig. 189) are also McElmo Black-on-white, with one having a ticked rim.

The one complete seed jar has a height of 8.4 cm., a diameter of 14.6 cm., and an orfice diameter of about 7.5 cm. Its volume is 950 cc. Wall thickness of the fragmentary jar is the same. The bottom of the complete jar is fairly flat except for a concave depression at the center.

As Morris (1939, p. 214) states: "Before the classic stage had been reached the squash pot (seed jar) as it had existed since the beginning of pottery making had, by an elaboration of its top, been transformed into the kiva jar." The Long House pottery seems to bear this out. Although both forms are very limited in number, kiva jars (sherds and whole or restorable vessels) do outnumber seed jars. Typical examples of kiva jars may be seen in figure 190.

Thirteen kiva jar sherds were recovered from the Lower East Trash Slope. Six of these were Mesa Verde Black-on-white, but, oddly, not one of the three rims was ticked. The remaining seven sherds were rims—one ticked—and were either Mesa Verde or McElmo Black-on-white. The lack of ticking on these sherds is interesting because on vessels with rims, from various parts of the ruin, ticking does appear (fig. 190).

The kiva jar is essentially the seed jar with the addition of a vertical rim fillet. This is shown clearly in figure 190d, where the vertical fillet has been broken off. The original seed jar rim has thus become merely a flange useful only to support a lid. Ticking may be found on both the flange and the vertical fillet, as seen in figs. 190c and 191. The diameter of the lid would be smaller than the inside diameter of the vertical rim, enabling the lid to fit within the circumference of the vertical rim and rest on the flange.

Although I have used the term "vertical rim," there is often a slight outward flare (fig. 191a). I have never seen a kiva jar with a sharply everted rim. The height of the vertical rim above the flange averages about 1.0 cm. An exception to this is shown in figure 190f, where the height is 2.4 cm. The jar is also unslipped, and has a design which defies classification. To judge by shape, and the elaborate rim ticking, it is probably Mesa Verde Black-on-white.

The other kiva jars illustrated are probably all Mesa Verde. Two of them (figs. 190a and e) bear what might be called a McElmo style design, although shape and surface finish would indicate Mesa Verde.

Figure 190b illustrates one of the finest examples of Mesa Verde pottery I have ever seen. The evolution of the shape of the kiva jar reaches its ultimate here. The vessel has very thin (3 to 4 mm.), strong walls, and is well slipped over the entire exterior. The layout of the design is quite uniform. It is also well balanced and esthetically pleasing. The linework is not precise, nor is the luster as high as that of many other vessels. However, this detracts not at all from the overall effect.

Lids were not in place on any of the kiva jars recovered from Long House. Two whole lids and 19 fragmentary specimens were found, and all but five of these (one whole and four sherds) were black-on-white.

The diameters of the lids range from 6 to an estimated 10 cm., thickness from 2 to 4 mm. at the edge to 4 to 7 mm. at the center. Five lids definitely had handles, and many of the others may have had. Figure 192a and g show the typical knob-type handle found on jar lids (and also, occasionally, on jars). The upper and lower faces of the lid are often parallel, especially where there is no handle. Handles, 2.0 to 2.4 cm. high, were seated, in some cases at least, on the upper surface of the lid and then anchored by building up clay smoothly from the lid face to the side of the handle. This resulted in a strongly convex upper surface on the lid. With or without a handle, lid profiles vary from slightly biconvex through planoconvex (most common) to concavo-convex.

Most of the specimens were slipped all over, but two were slipped on the upper face only, and two others apparently were not slipped at all. All surfaces may be painted but the design is commonly limited to the upper surface and handle top. Three lids, slipped on the upper side and on the edge, share one trait: extensive grinding on the nether surface. This is more than just wear—it is deliberate smoothing, and possibly shaping, of the lower surface, possibly to get a snugger fit of lid to jar. The original lower face of all of these may have been slipped. Several lids other than these show wear from repeated rubbing of the outer portion of the lower face on the flange of the kiva jar. The edges of one of the three also shows extensive grinding. This could result from original shaping or a reduction in size so that the lid would fit a jar with a smaller neck.

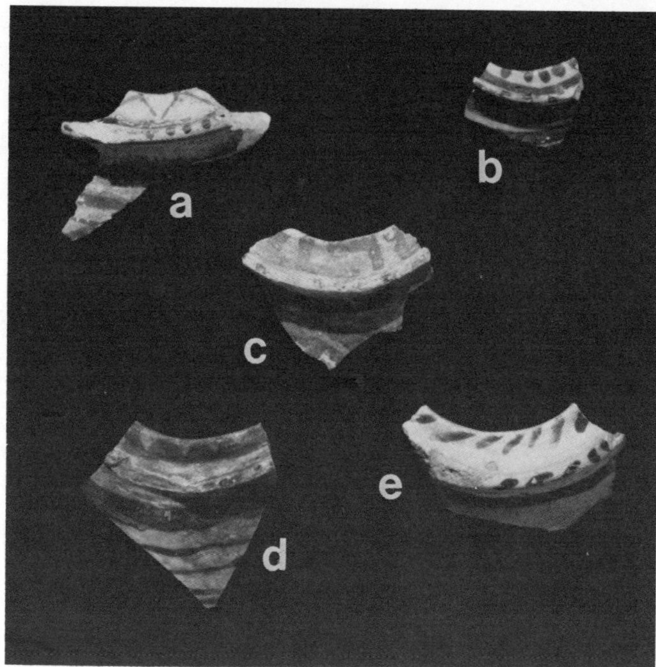

Figure 191. *Mesa Verde Black-on-white kiva jar rim sherds.*

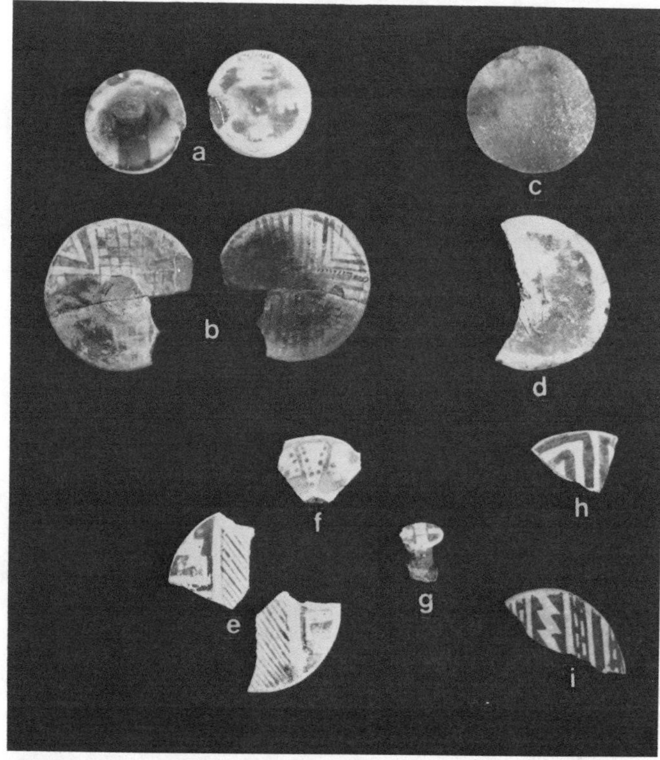

Figure 192. *Mesa Verde Black-on-white kiva jar lids.*

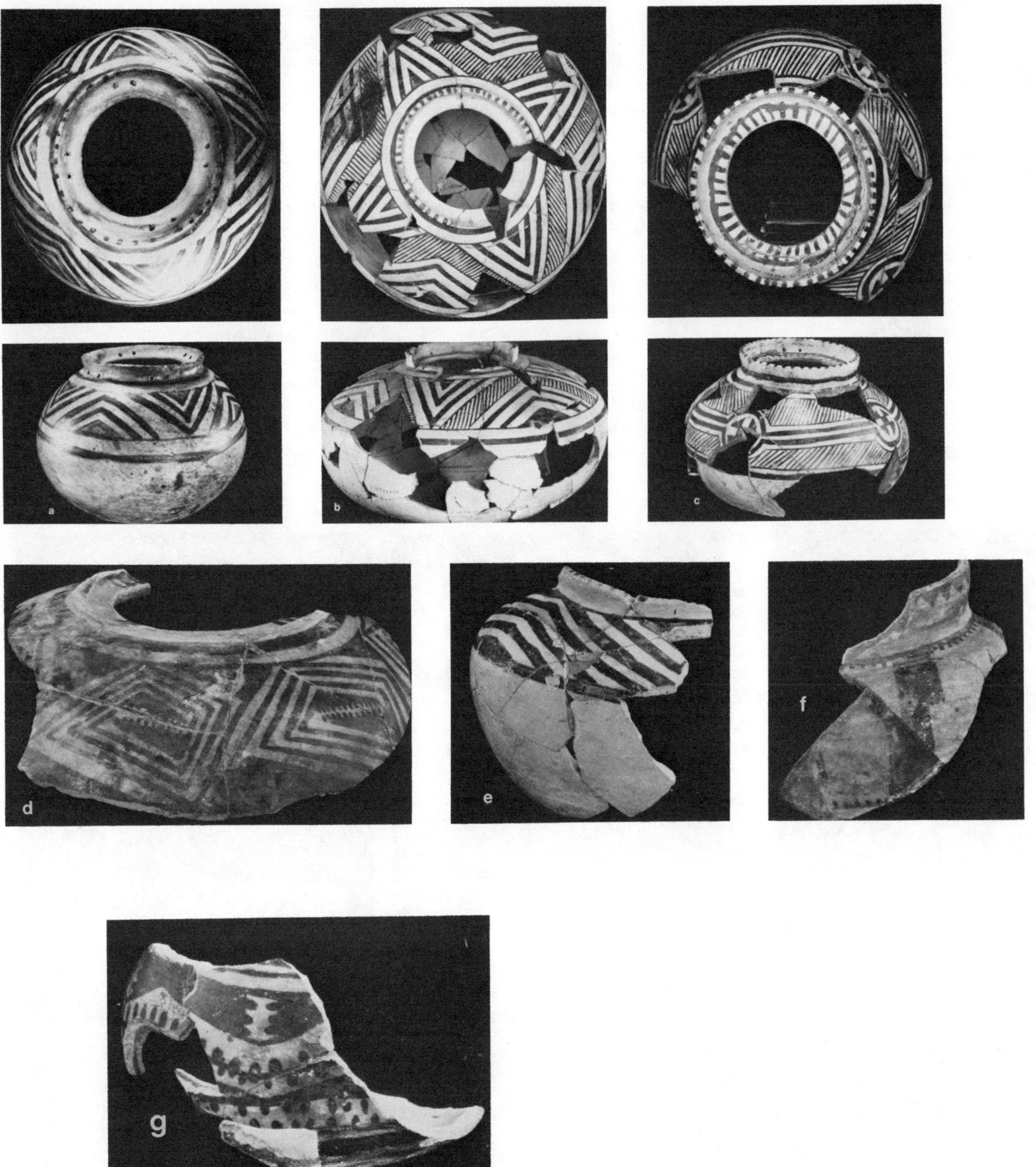

Figure 190. *Mesa Verde Black-on-white Kiva jars.*

The height of eight kiva jars (six Mesa Verde, one McElmo (?), and one Mesa Verde-McElmo) varies from 13.5 to 19.5 cm., with two at 15.0 cm. The maximum diameter ranges from 19.4 to 29.0 cm., the orifice diameter from 7.0 cm. (two jars) to 11.6 cm (with two jars at 11.5 cm.). The volume of two jars measured 2,150 and 4,450 cc. Thickness of the flange ranges from 4 to 6 mm., and averages 5 mm. The flange is generally 1 to 2 mm. thinner than the vertical rim. Walls are almost the same, ranging from 3 to 7 mm. and averaging 5mm. The base thickness of one specimen is 7 mm. The height of the rim ranges from 5 to 23 mm., and the width of the flange 8 to 11 mm. The bottom of the complete kiva jar shown in figure 190a is flat; that of the fragmentary jar, figure 190b, is slightly concave.

Dippers

Only 194 sherds (4 percent of the McElmo-Mesa Verde Black-on-white pottery from the Lower East Trash Slope) were classed as dippers (table 13). Unfortunately, most had to be considered indeterminate, primarily because of small size with very little design, the absence of diagnostic rim shapes (fig. 180) and decorations, and almost no knowledge of the evolution of handle design. Separate handles formed 62 percent of the group. Exterior decoration was far less common than with the larger bowls. Several examples of such decoration can be seen in figures 193b, c and f, and 194e. Table 13 summarizes what might be called expected trends, and requires no comment except for the handles.

Two handle counts were made, one of the separate handles mentioned above, and the other of separate handles and those attached to rim or body sherds. The counts for the latter are shown in table 13 under "rim" or "body" sherds. Thus we can say that there were actually 164 handles (85 percent of all dipper sherds).

Essentially, two aspects of the Pueblo III dipper handle must be considered: decoration and shape (figs. 195 and 196). Ninety-one percent of the handles were decorated with designs of varying complexity. Decoration was usually limited to the top of the handle, and may either extend from the bowl of the dipper to the end of the handle or be an isolated figure. Figure 194g shows a handle unique because of decoration on the underside. In only a few cases do I feel that a handle design—where the handle is not attached to the bowl—can safely be called Mesa Verde Black-on-white.

Simplicity of design in itself is no aid in classifying the handles because bowl exteriors, mugs, handles, and even jar necks may bear similar designs. Some handle designs are identical to bowl band designs except that they run the width of the handle (fig. 196m—handle with rattle). Others, running lengthwise on the handle, are identical to designs used on Mesa Verde and McElmo Black-on-white but lack both framing lines and the room to place them even if it were desired.

The cross section of dipper handles is probably a more useful trait. Five main shapes were recognized in the Long House material

Figure 193. *Mesa Verde (a-c) and McElmo (d-f) Black-on-white dippers. Maximum diameter of a (possibly a small bowl), 10 cm.*

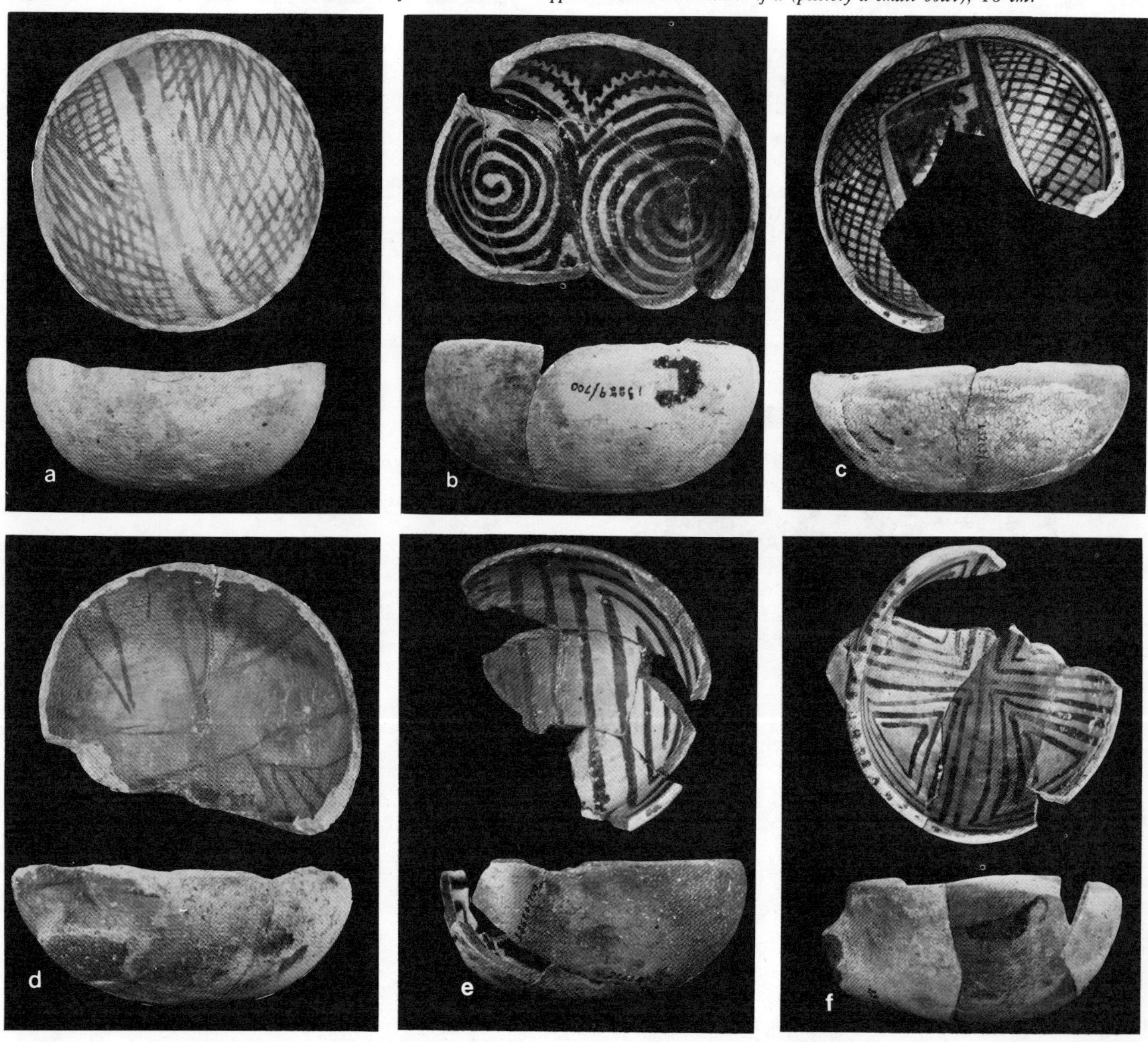

(fig. 195), with one troughed represented by only two sherds (fig. 195g and r). Four of the five classes of handles—flat, oval-round, compound, troughed—have solid cores. The fifth, actually a variant of the oval-round in shape, is hollow. The compound handles (fig. 195o and p) have only three components or rods, each circular in cross section. Morris (1939, p. 216) reported one dipper handle with eight rods clustered to form a cylindrical bundle, which was then twisted one-half turn to the right.

Handles may taper in thickness, width, or both, from the bowl toward the end. Although many handles are squared or slightly rounded at the end, further elaboration is quite common. Four handles without elaboration of the end are shown in figure 195c, d, g, and p. Figure 196 shows a series of more elaborate handles. Commonly, a fillet of clay is pulled out from the end of the handle and turned back over the top surface to form a slightly projecting "beak" (fig. 196a-c and m). In hollow handles, the tip of the fillet is pressed down into the handle to form a smooth junction (fig. 196a, b, and m) and an opening into the handle left beneath the fillet or at either side of it. This technique is also followed with some of the solid handles, but very often the tip of the fillet is only poorly smoothed down onto the top of the handle (fig. 196c) or left as a vertical projection (fig. 196g). One handle shows a similar treatment, but two fillets of clay were pulled out and turned back on the top surface (fig. 196f). Occasionally the projection, formed in the same manner, is carefully worked to form a smooth, symmetrical ridge (fig. 196i).

Other variations in handle construction are found, although they are not as common as those mentioned above. Figure 196h shows a handle with a horizontal loop at the end. The specimen in figure 196m is unique in that it is a rattle, the hollow handle containing several loose balls of clay or sand granules which roll freely throughout the length of the handle. Since there is more than one, it is probably safe to say they were placed there on purpose rather than being accidental inclusions.

Often there will be a series of small holes or perforations along the sides or the top of a handle. This is especially common with hollow handles (figs. 194e and 196b, j, and m) but also occurs with solid-core handles (figs. 194g, and 196d and n). When the holes are

Figure 194. *Mesa Verde (a and b) and McElmo (c-h) Black-on-white dippers.*

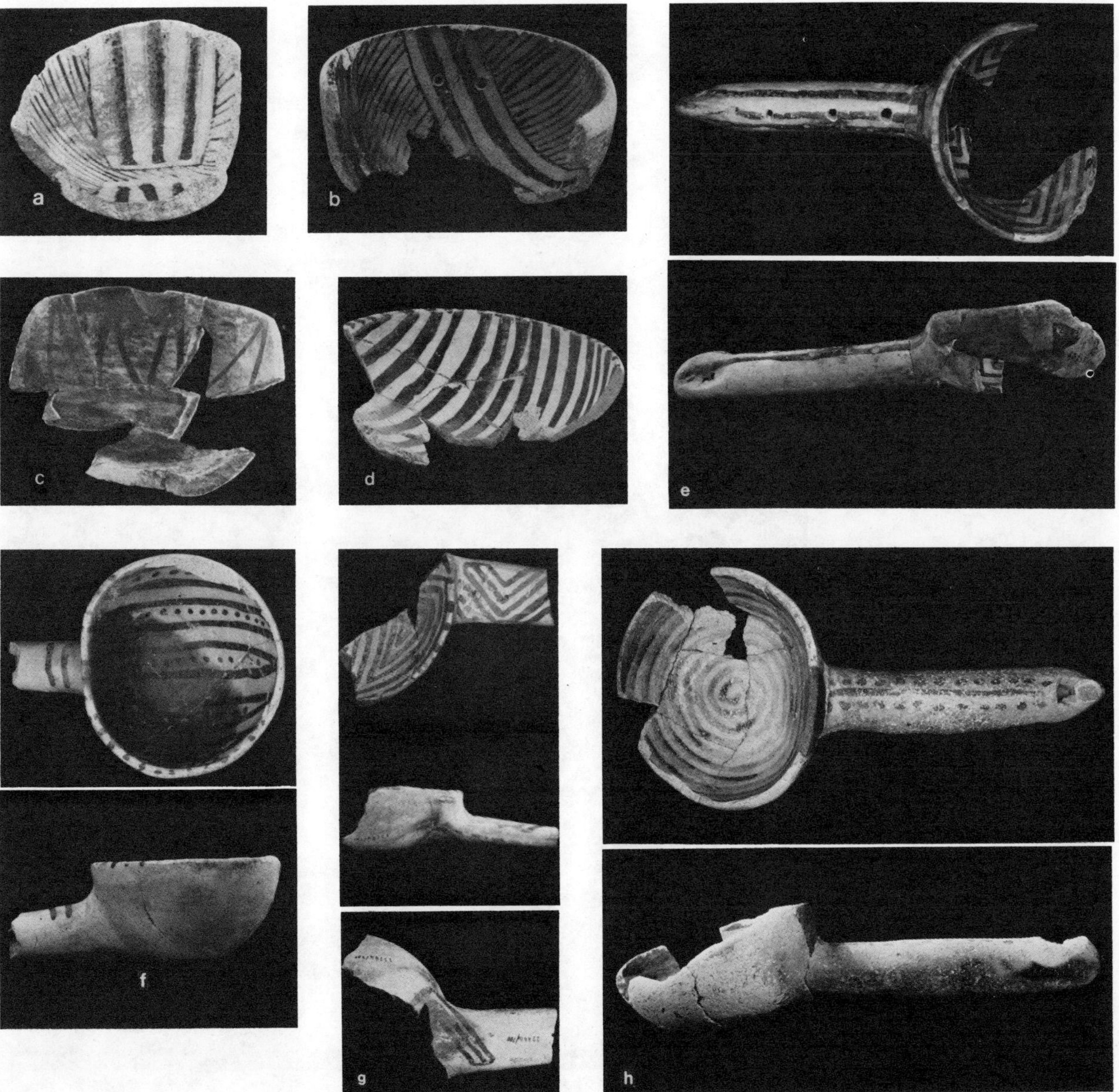

on the side of a hollow handle, they are usually symmetrically placed, one set on either side, or else there is only one set of holes on the top. As can be seen in figure 196j, they were punched into the core with a sharp-pointed instrument of circular cross section.

When the holes are in a solid handle, they may penetrate the entire handle (fig. 196n) or extend only into the core (fig. 196d). The former specimen, not painted, is included here because a portion of the quill of a feather is embedded in one of the perforations. This fragment was not embedded during the construction of the dipper since it would have burned out during firing.

A common method of attaching the handle to the bowl is seen in figure 196. A plug of clay is inserted into the handle during construction, leaving a thin neck projecting (fig. 196k). The handle is pressed down around the body of the plug to prevent it from pulling out. Then the neck is inserted into the side of the bowl, in these specimens going clear through the bowl side and forming part of the bowl interior. The junction is then built up with clay and smoothed.

Table 13 shows several interesting trends in the association of handle shape and pottery type. The hollow handle comprises 63 percent of the Mesa Verde specimens but only 44 percent of the McElmo. With the oval-round handle, the situation is reversed: 56 percent of the McElmo but only 11 percent of the Mesa Verde. The flat handle forms 22 percent of the Mesa Verde group but is nonexistent in the McElmo. The compound handle is rare in the Mesa Verde category, and not found at all in the McElmo.

Dipper handles were attached well below the bowl rim, thus forming an almost plane surface extending along the bottom of the handle and bowl. An occasional specimen will show attachment near the rim of the bowl, but this is rare.

As seen in figures 193 and 194, the overall design was found on almost all whole and large fragmentary dippers. Fig. 194c is an exception, having a simple band design. The designs are bisected, quartered (including offset), paneled, or asymmetrical (one example: the spiral). Although I have classified all of these vessels, I feel that many could be placed equally as well in one type as in the other. A few are definitely Mesa Verde (figs. 193c, and 194a and b). According to design alone, most of the others would be placed in the McElmo category. According to thickness, slip, rim shape, and ticking, quite a few could also be Mesa Verde. Two specimens (figs. 193d and 194c) show very simple designs. They are probably McElmo, but they may represent the doodling of a potter only

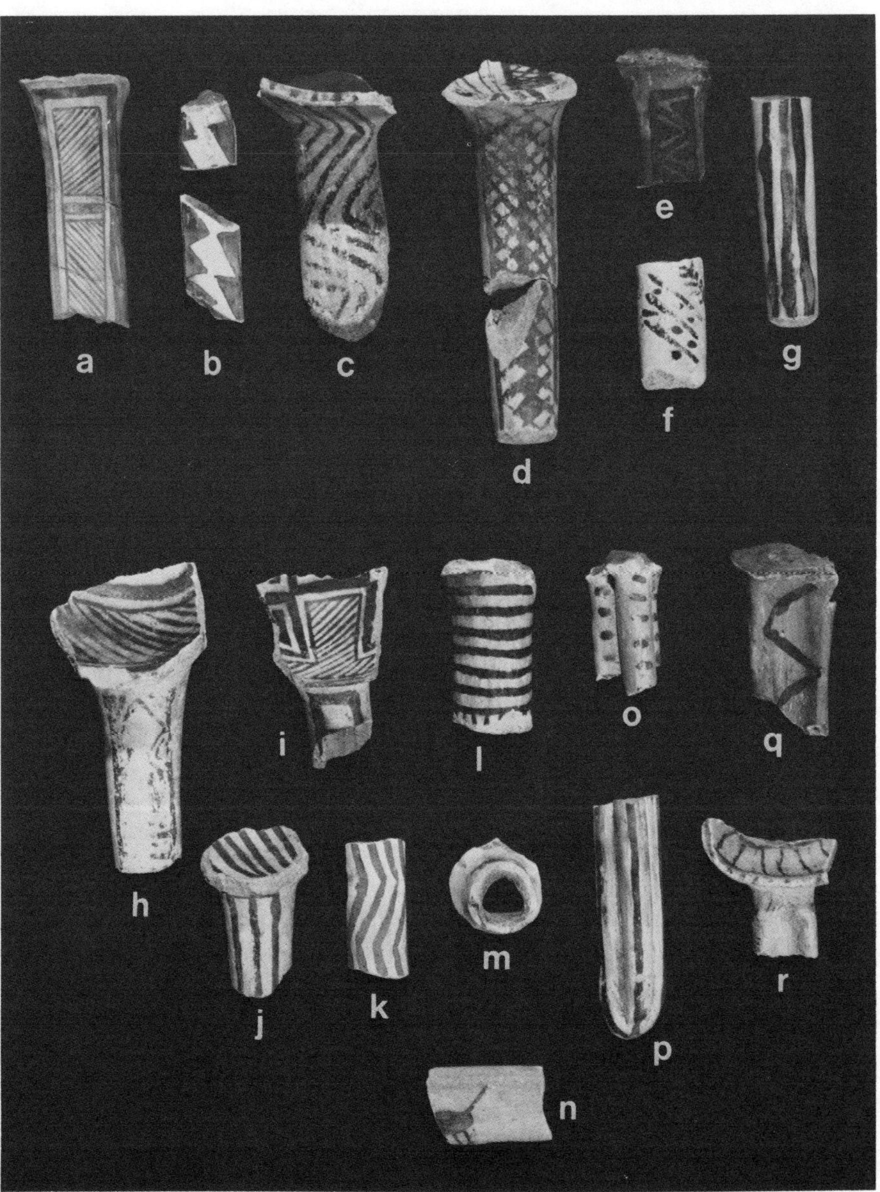

Figure 195. *Mesa Verde-McElmo Black-on-white dipper handles.*

slightly interested in what design went on the dipper or possibly what design her small daughter drew. For the most part, I believe we are dealing here with Mesa Verde Black-on-white, but with a McElmo style of design because it was easier to paint on a small area. I feel that dippers demonstrate a valid reason for combining McElmo and Mesa Verde into one pottery type.

The characteristic abrasion of the rim from use can readily be seen on several of the dippers illustrated (e.g., figs. 193c and 194h). With the exception of a short section near and on either side of the handle, such wear will extend entirely around the perimeter of the bowl. Often only the outside will be worn, creating a bevel, but in some cases the entire lip is worn away. Right- and left-handed use can sometimes be determined by the relative amount of wear on each side of the dipper bowl. Others, quite obviously, were held in such a manner as to wear only the portion of the rim farthest from the handle.

Few of the seven Mesa Verde dippers were complete enough to be measured fully. The depth of four dipper bowls ranged from 4.6 to 5.9 cm., with two at 4.9 cm. The diameter of these varied from 11.3 to 13.6 cm. The volume could be checked on only two: 250 and 400 cc. Vessel wall thickness extended from 3 to 11 mm., with rims restricted to the 3 to 5 mm. range and averaging 4 mm. Wall thickness varied from 4 to 7 mm., with no concentration at any one point. Thickness of the base extended from 7 to 11 mm., again with no concentration within the range. The exterior bottom was usually slightly convex or flattened; rarely was it slightly concave. Only one dipper had a complete handle attached; it was hollow and measured 19.8 cm. in length and 4.4 cm. in diameter.

I believe that 12 dippers can safely be considered as McElmo Black-on-white. The depth could be taken on the bowls of only five, and varied from 4.0 to 6.0 cm. The diameter of nine ranged from 10.3 to 14.0 cm., with a slight peak at 11.0 to 11.3 cm. As with the Mesa Verde dippers, volume could be measured on only two specimens: 150 and 300 cc. Wall thickness was practically identical to that of the Mesa Verde dippers. There was an observable concentration at 5 to 6 mm., and base thickness was 7 to 8 mm. Two dippers had complete hollow handles that measured 15.3 and 15.4 cm. in length and 3.3 and 3.4 cm., respectively, in diameter. A third, incomplete hollow handle had a diameter of 2.5 cm. An incomplete solid, flat strap handle was 4.5 cm. wide and 1.85 cm. thick.

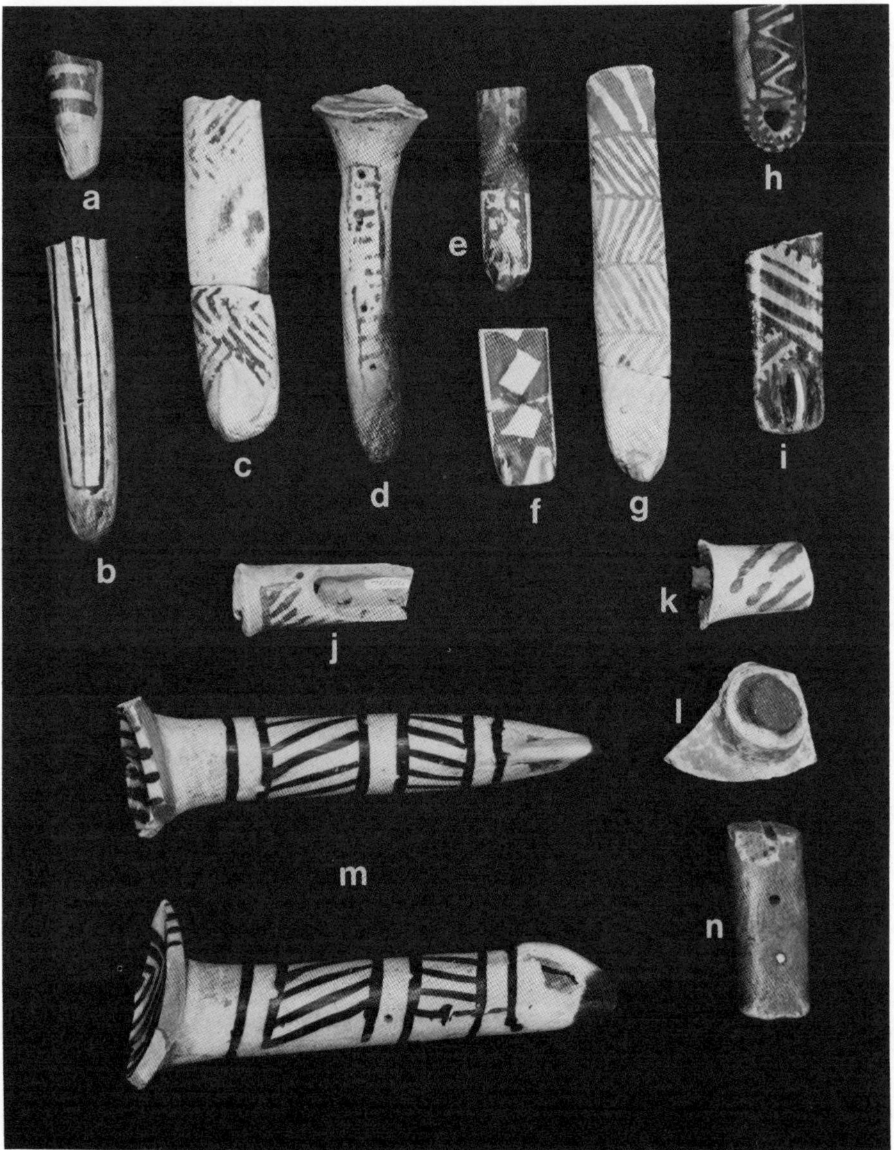

Figure 196. *Mesa Verde-McElmo Black-on-white dipper handles.*

MUGS

Perhaps the easiest pottery form to study is the mug. Unfortunately, mug sherds formed only 3 percent of the McElmo-Mesa Verde Black-on-white from the Lower East Trash Slope. The shape is more uniform than any other type of vessel, and the field of design is limited almost entirely to the full height of the side, the broad face of the handle, and the rim. With few exceptions, handles and rims are always decorated, but only one sherd (fig. 198c) shows an interior design. There are no mugs from Long House which show an exterior band of design narrower than the height of the mug.

The range of design on mugs certainly surpasses that on jars and dippers and rivals that of bowls (figs. 197–199). The mug seems to be a late development, derived from the earlier pitcher, so perhaps this diversity of design is understandable. The elaborateness of design is even more surprising when the space limitations are considered. Only in rim ticking does the mug show less diversity than the bowl. The circular and rectangular dot and the diagonal rectangular dot are most used. The bowl lip design shown in figure 169w also appears on the lip of a possible mug sherd. There is hardly room on the lip of a mug for the more elaborate bowl lip designs. Few sherds—11 percent of the Lower East Trash Slope mugs—could be classed as McElmo Black-on-white.

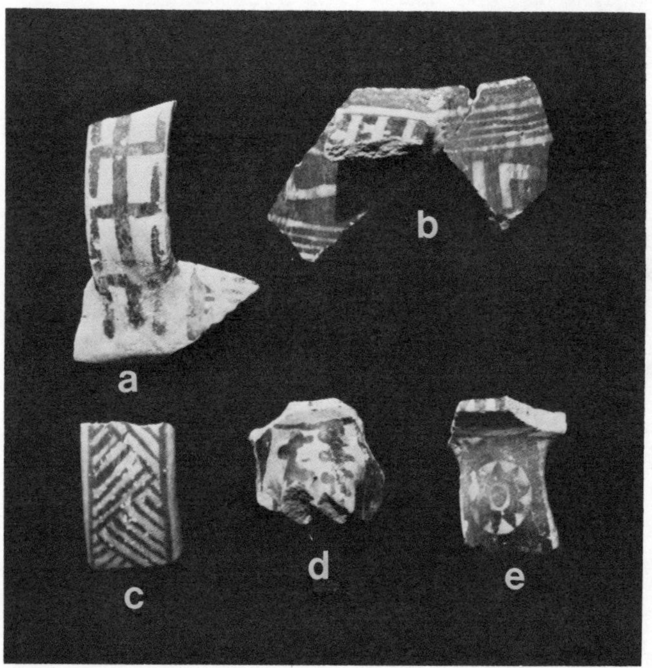

Figure 199. *Black-on-white mug sherds.*

As can be seen readily in figure 197, most of the mugs are larger at the base than at the mouth. The sides may slope down straight, and form a fairly sharp intersection with little rounding of the corner (fig. 197c and f); or more commonly, there is a slight convexity, with a pronounced incurve where side and base meet (figure 197a, b, d, e, g, and h). Occasionally, the shape is barrel-like, with end diameters approximately equal and the sides convex (fig. 197k). The exterior bottom is usually flat, occasionally slightly concave.

The range in rim shapes is shown in figure 180. Generally, the rim is direct and the lip is flat (b, c, and g), but somewhat rounded lips are not uncommon (a and f). Rarely is the rim flared (figs. 197o and p; and 180j-r), a style that might possibly be related to a similar treatment of bowls. Although this is probably a late development, there is little evidence to prove it. Figure 197o is from a burial on the Lower East Trash Slope which cannot be dated precisely. Figure 197p is from the fill of Kiva Q, about 1.5 feet above floor. Although the kiva may have an early construction date, it was extensively remodeled and was definitely used until the end of the occupation in Long House. Thus it is likely that the mug belongs to the late period.

Handles are usually attached just above the base and just below the lip. They bow out from the vessel wall in a smooth curve (fig. 197b), but occasionally will be slightly flattened (figure 197f), thus resembling some jar handles. In cross section, handles are usually flat, with squared edges, but some have rounded edges. A few are flat-oval in cross section. An unusual specimen (fig. 199d) has a compound handle composed of two fillets of clay with circular cross section.

Several of the sherds which I feel can be classified safely as McElmo Black-on-white are shown in figure 200. Designs are simpler, often consisting only of parallel lines placed horizontally or at an angle. The only other pattern clearly seen in these examples is the checkerboard. Four of the five rim sherds shown (a-c and e) are from vessels whose walls are tapered or "pinched," and the lips are rounded. Only one example, d, has a direct rim with a somewhat flattened lip.

Mesa Verde Black-on-white mugs varied in height from 8.7 to 11.2 cm., with equivalent concentrations at 8.8, 9.3, and 10.4 cm. The diameter of the 20 measurable mugs ranged from 6.9 to 12.9 cm. The two smallest were 6.9 and 7.1 cm. in diameter. The next size group extended fairly evenly from 8.5 to 11.9 cm., with slight peaks at 9.0 and 10.5 cm. The largest specimen, set off by itself, was 12.9 cm. in diameter. Orifice diameter ranged from 5.9 to 9.1 cm., with equivalent concentrations at 6.6 and 7.0 cm. The volume varied from 300 to 700 cc., with a concentration at 350 to 550 cc.

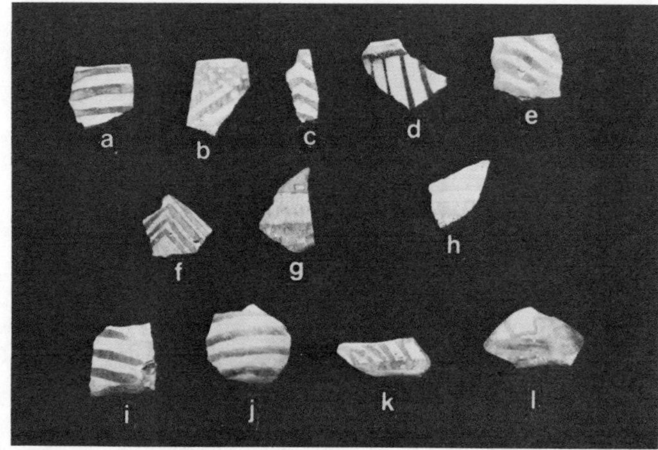

Figure 200. *McElmo Black-on-white mug sherds.*

Only one mug was classified, with reservations, as McElmo. Other than an orifice diameter of 9.0 cm., no measurements could be taken.

Vessel wall thickness for Mesa Verde mugs ranges from 3 to 7 mm. Rims vary from 3 to 6 mm. thick, with a concentration at 4 mm.; walls vary from 4 to 7 mm., with a concentration at 5 to 6 mm. The bases ranged from 5 to 9 mm., with no significant concentration. Handle width ranged from 2.5 to 2.9 cm., with the most common width being in the 2.5 to 2.7 cm. group. Thickness of the handles varied from 5 to 9 mm., and most commonly was 8 to 9 mm. All of these were flat strap handles. The small amount of McElmo material present falls within the range of the Mesa Verde mugs. The most common wall thickness is 5 mm., but there is not enough material to determine other average thicknesses.

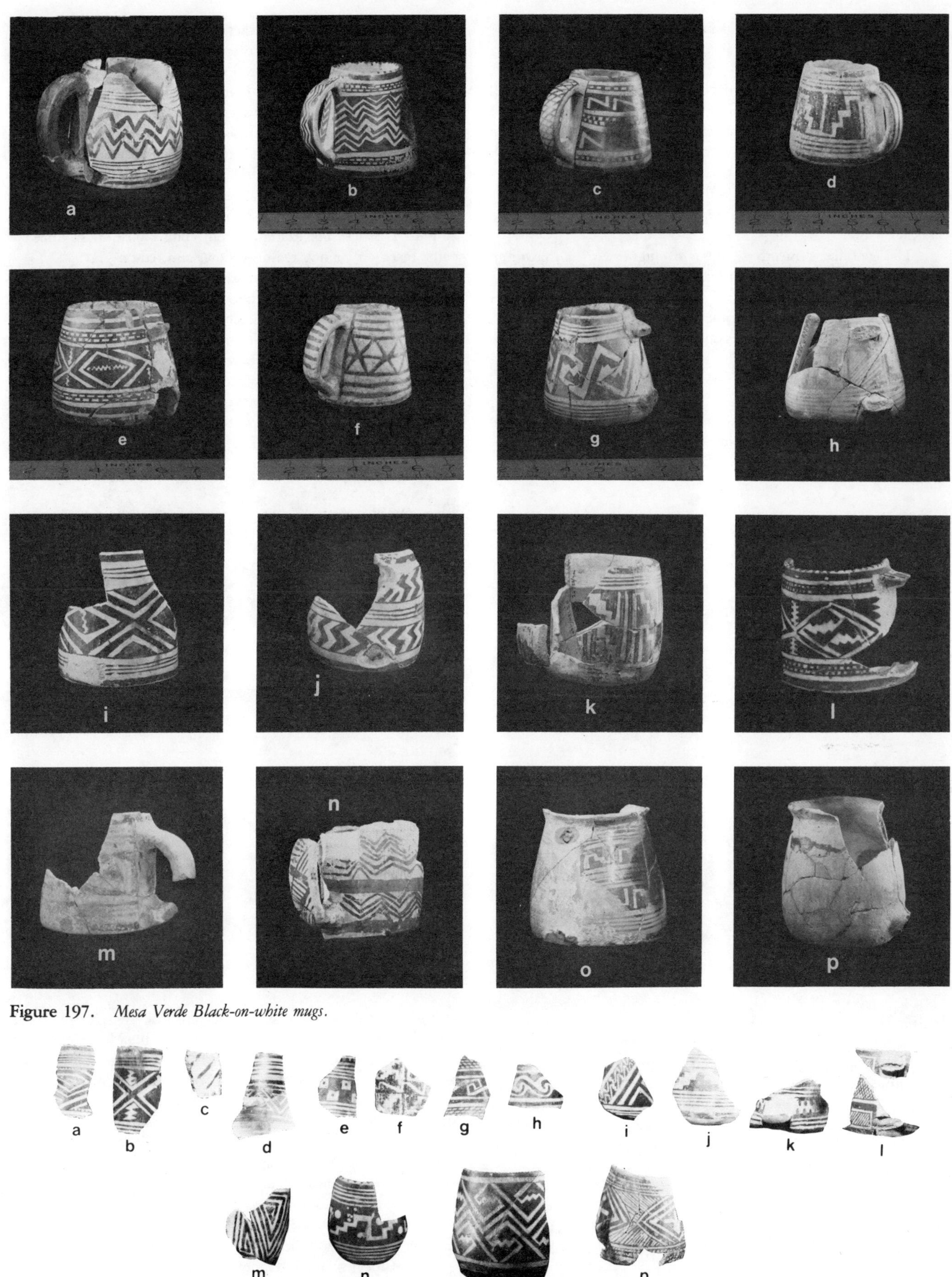

Figure 197. *Mesa Verde Black-on-white mugs.*

Figure 198. *Mesa Verde Black-on-white mug sherds.*

CANTEENS AND MISCELLANEOUS VESSELS

The two canteens in the collection share only one trait: small loop handles, with circular cross section, placed near the mouth of the vessel. One canteen is a globular, narrow-mouthed jar, with a slightly concave bottom when viewed from the exterior (fig. 201a); the other is what Morris (1939, p. 151) has called a submarine-shaped vessel (fig. 201b), which is flat on the bottom. The former is McElmo Black-on-white, the latter either McElmo or Mesa Verde Black-on-white.

The globular canteen is 12.0 cm. high, with a maximum diameter of 11.4 cm. and a rim diameter of 2.4 cm. Its volume is 400 cc. The submarine vessel is 16.5 cm. long, 5.8 cm. wide, and 8.2 cm. high, and has a rim diameter of 2.9 cm.

A possible effigy vessel (bird-shaped?) is represented only by the sherd shown in figure 201c. The left end has a rounded rim and undoubtedly formed part of an opening. The specimen is 9.8 cm. long.

Two sherds with sharp "tail-like" corners probably come from effigy vessels similar to the fragmentary one just described.

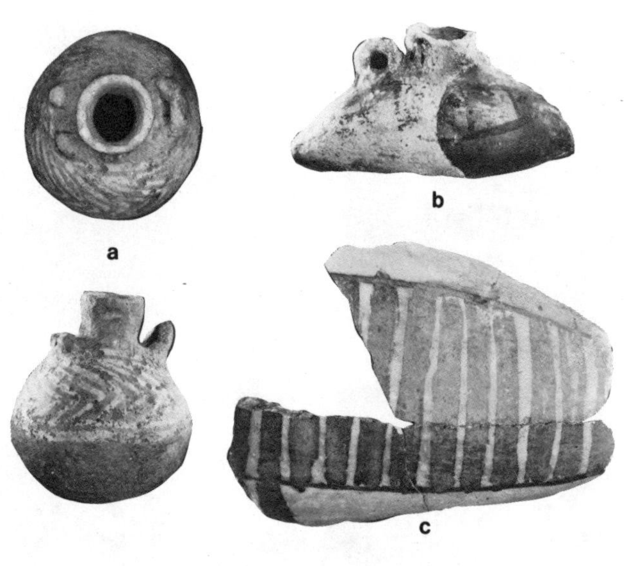

Figure 201. *Black-on-white canteens and miscellaneous vessels: a and c, McElmo; b, indeterminate.*

Technology

Occasionally, two tones of black paint are used on a vessel, with the outline of a figure darker than the filler. Figure 202a shows examples of this. Rarely are two kinds of pigment, organic and mineral, used to create what Abel (1955, Ware 10B—Type 3) has called "Mesa Verde Polychrome." No vessels from Long House show this treatment.

Not uncommonly, the potter will paint over her initial line work with a heavier coat of the same pigment or, in one case, of different pigment (mineral over organic). Erosion may also reveal a lighter-colored paint underlying the dark surface coat. These situations may indicate the use of an organic vehicle with mineral paint, possibly a technique followed much of the time but rarely seen clearly on the pottery.

I do not feel that any of these situations justify the naming of a separate pottery type. Rather, they can be described within the range of Mesa Verde Black-on-white. Probably such experiments in paint application occur on McElmo Black-on-white also, but all examples recognized in the Long House sherd collection were Mesa Verde.

As with any pottery, inconsistencies in the firing of Mesa Verde and McElmo Black-on-white produced some interesting results. Shepard (in Morris, 1939, p. 285) has pointed out the varieties of color that can be obtained by oxidizing the same clays and paints used in making the more conventional black-on-white pottery of the La Plata District. The examples from Long House are of three color pairs: black-on-yellow, red-on-yellow, and red-on-gray.

Possible partial oxidation has also resulted in a rather interesting effect (fig. 203). Here the black organic paint of the design appears to have been completely oxidized, but not the organic material in the slip and body of the vessel. The result is a complete reversal of design, with the painted design appearing light gray and the unpainted portions dark gray to black.

One hundred and two Mesa Verde Black-on-white bowls were checked under a binocular microscope at magnification up to 40x for tempering material. For a pottery described as having temper con-

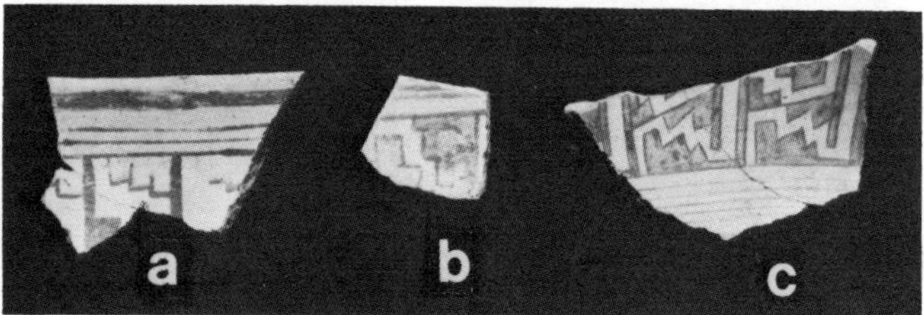

Figure 202. *Mesa Verde Black-on-white two-tone sherds.*

Figure 203. *Mesa Verde Black-on-white bowl, showing variations in paint due to firing.*

sisting of "crushed sherds; occasional pieces of crushed rock in some examples" (Abel 1955: Ware 10B—Type 2), the Mesa Verde Black-on-white that laboratory aids or I checked showed a phenomenal range in temper, or the proportions of tempering materials, used. The numbers of vessels with each type of temper are tabulated below. Mixed categories predominate in the materials listed first. All material is crushed except the sand, which was identified as such only when present in whole grains that were usually of large size when compared with uncrushed grains of what was obviously sandstone.

Sherd and igneous rock	52
Sherd, igneous rock, and sandstone	12
Igneous rock and sherd	11
Sandstone, sherd, and igneous rock	5
Sherd, igneous rock, and sand	4
Igneous rock, sand, and sherd	4

Sherd and sandstone	3
Sherd, sand, and sandstone	2
Sandstone and igneous rock	2
Mica, igneous rock, and sherd	2
Sandstone and sherd	1
Igneous rock, sandstone, sherd	1
Sherd, igneous rock, and mica	1
Sand and sherd	1
Igneous rock and sand	1
	102

Sherd tempering occurs impressively, but is not necessarily dominant, in 99 of the vessels. This is less impressive when one notes that igneous rock is present in 95 vessels. Sandstone is present in 26 vessels, sand in 12, and mica in three. Sherd temper is predominant in 74 vessels, igneous rock in 17, sandstone in eight, mica in two, and sand in one.

The detailed analysis shows that the temper of this pottery is certainly varied and that we should be cautious when making sweeping statements about it. I believe that care in identification of temper is especially important with sherd-tempered pottery, such as Mesa Verde Black-on-white, because with the naked eye or a 10-power lens sherd temper can often be very difficult to see or identify *as such.* Colton and Hargrave (1937, p. 12) use the phrase "light-colored angular fragments" because of this difficulty. When the core is black, sherd temper will often stand out clearly; when it is light-gray, as in most Mesa Verde vessels, it is often almost impossible to see without special equipment. Also, despite a possible dominance of sherd temper in many vessels, the temper that is readily apparent may be crushed rock and thus be misleading to the observer. Furthermore, it is difficult to separate tempering materials added directly from those included in or derived from crushed sherd temper. Thus there are undoubtedly cases where this distinction was not made successfully.

If identification cannot readily be made in the field or laboratory without recourse to the binocular microscope, temper is not a good criterion for the classification of great masses of pottery such as come from major excavations. Temper then becomes significant primarily in determining precisely the origin of sherds which appear—on the basis of other traits, such as design and layout—to be intrustive in an area.

The classification of grain size used in this report is based on the Wentworth scale (Krumbein and Pettijohn, 1938, p. 80, partially reproduced in Shepard, 1957, p. 118). Most of the inclusions in the Long House pottery can be described in terms of the size of sand grains, ranging from fine ($^1/_8$ to $^1/_4$ mm.) to very coarse (1 to 2 mm.). Occasionally granules occur (2 to 4 mm.), and without doubt there are large numbers of particles of the very fine ($^1/_8$ to $^1/_{16}$ mm.) or silt ($^1/_{16}$ to $^1/_{256}$ mm.) size. No attempt was made to record material of this size, nor were thin sections made of any of the pottery.

Where discussed, the roundness of particles is based on the description by Pettijohn (1949, pp. 51–53). In describing other physical aspects of the pottery, I have freely borrowed Shepard's (1957) terminology. Since she did not examine the Long House pottery, I am entirely responsible for any unintentional modification or misuse of her descriptive terms.

In more than four-fifths of the Mesa Verde Black-on-white bowls, tempering was moderate, with the remainder being either heavily or sparsely tempered. Grain size was predominantly coarse or medium, with the former being slightly more common. Quite a few vessels showed fine or fine to medium-size temper, but very few were in the very coarse category.

More than half of the vessels showed no carbon streak. Where present, it was often lenticular and occurred intermittently in the vessel wall. In some cases, it formed a band of fairly uniform width which might be located in the inner, outer, or central portion of the wall.

The paint was organic on all but one bowl, which showed mineral paint superimposed on organic paint in a series of dots along the edge of a solid figure.

All but one of the bowls was slipped, both inside and outside, and the slip was crazed slightly on 87 of the vessels. The exception was unslipped on both surfaces. The interior surface was only lightly polished in four vessels, producing a matte finish, and was polished to a medium to high luster on one bowl, to a medium luster on 15, and to a low luster on the remaining 82. Only a few sherds, and no whole vessels, were polished to a high, glassy luster. The figures are almost identical for the exterior, so apparently as much effort was expended on producing a good finish on the outside as on the inside.

Although generally smooth, the surface was bumpy or slightly undulating on 45 of the bowls and pitted on 25. Striations are visible in a large percentage of the bowls, especially where the slip is thin, and represent the initial scraping and smoothing which preceded the slipping and polishing. Spotty polishing on more than half of the bowls contributes to the visibility of the striations. Very shallow troughs left by the smoothing or polishing stone were visible on slightly more than half the bowls. In most cases, such marks are parallel to the coils, but occasionally they crisscross or are perpendicular to the coils. In some of the unslipped pottery (represented almost entirely by sherds), compaction and polishing of the surface produced a luster closely resembling that found on the best-finished slipped specimens. The surface is usually slightly grayer in such examples, but color alone is not a good criterion on which to base the presence or absence of a slip.

Analyses of the temper and surface finish of 19 whole or restorable McElmo Black-on-white bowls show a situation very similar to that of Mesa Verde. Despite the small sample, we found four of the temper "types" (proportions) that had been used in Mesa Verde Black-on-white. Practically all of the other types were found in checking McElmo jars and dippers. The four are among the most common with Mesa Verde pottery; sherd and igneous rock, nine; igneous rock and sherd, four; sherd, igneous rock, and sandstone, four; sherd and sandstone, one; sherd and soft, powdery particles (decomposed calcium carbonate?), one. Grain size and amount of temper were identical to that of Mesa Verde. Organic paint was used on all the McElmo vessels.

The only significant difference in vessel wall core between the two types was in the number of vessels showing a carbon streak. Nearly three-fourths of the McElmo bowls showed carbon streak, whereas less than one-half of the Mesa Verde bowls exhibited this trait. The location of the carbon streak in the wall was about the same in the two types.

There was very little difference in the interior and exterior of McElmo bowls with respect to slip, luster, and smoothness of the surface. However, there are differences in these traits between Mesa Verde and McElmo. Three of the 19 McElmo vessels were unslipped, a proportion that is greater than with Mesa Verde Black-on-white. The surface tends to be less lustrous than on Mesa Verde pottery, with only one vessel having a medium luster, five a matte finish, and the remaining 13 a low luster. Polishing—usually parallel to the coils—was spotty on 11 bowl interiors and 14 bowl exteriors, so finishing was not quite as thorough as on Mesa Verde. Also, the interior surface of six bowls was bumpy, while the exterior of nine showed a similar unevenness. About half of the bowls were pitted on both the interior and exterior surfaces. Striations were visible on all but two bowls.

Although this aspect of the study has been based on bowls because of the greater number of these vessels, the temper and surface finish of mugs, dippers, and jars within each type is practically identical to that found in bowls.

There are a few exceptions to this similarity, one being the extent of slipping on jars. Almost one-third of the jars were unslipped, a much higher percentage than found with any other vessel form. All but two of the jars are Mesa Verde Black-on-white; one of the two is a questionable McElmo, the other Mesa Verde-McElmo.

Another obvious difference is the surface finish of bowl interiors as compared to mug and jar interiors, neither of which were normally slipped or polished. Scraping marks were obvious on practically all of the jar interiors, which were finished by wiping the surface parallel to the coils. The interior of three jars had been roughly smoothed in places, but only one showed evidence of rubbing. In four jars the coils were not completely obliterated in places. The surface was predominantly grainy, although a few specimens had a fairly fine-textured surface.

With the exception of the neck, there was no slipping of an interior jar surface. Four of the jars were slipped inside the neck, and the slip was crazed in all cases. One was smoothed and compacted, and two were polished to a low luster. Both wiping (evident in places) and polishing were done parallel to the vessel coils.

Mug interiors present a similar picture: primarily scraped and wiped. More of the specimens showed further finishing, however, probably because mug interiors are both easier to work and more visible than jar interiors. The sides of about a fourth of the mugs were roughly smoothed, and those of another fourth smoothed and compacted. The remainder has a fine-textured surface. The interior bottom was also roughly smoothed in several cases. All rubbing marks were parallel to the vessel coils. As expected, the surface was bumpy in most of the mugs, and about a quarter of them showed pitting of the interior surface. Only one mug was slipped over the whole interior, but two others were slipped part way down the side of the vessel wall.

Certain physical aspects of the Mesa Verde-McElmo pottery have not been discussed. In the Long House material, some characteristics—firing atmosphere, friability of vessel walls—seemed of little signifcance except in a rather general way. Other traits, such as surface and core color, matched the earlier descriptions. The reader is referred to Abel (1955, Ware 10B—Types 1, 2, and 3) and the many other published references to the pottery for a description of these and other characteristics not discussed.

These same traits have been omitted from the discussion of other pottery types in this report, and once again the reader is referred to the type descriptions. The material discussed herein is not intended to serve as full type descriptions but to show, for comparative purposes, the range in traits of the Long House pottery.

MANCOS BLACK-ON-WHITE

So far, we have looked at the later end of the Mancos-McElmo-Mesa Verde Black-on-white continuum. The problem has been specifically one of taxonomy: are McElmo and Mesa Verde to be retained as separate pottery types, or would our objective be attained more readily by grouping them together? To understand the full extent of the problem we need to look at the earlier end of this continuum and thus see what distinguishes Mancos and McElmo. Also, if there is a sharp line of demarcation between the two, does it have any cultural significance? Although such questions may not be answered fully through an analysis of the material from one Pueblo III cliff dwelling, they should nevertheless be kept in mind.

As shown in table 8, of the 16,866 classified painted sherds (all types), only 400 or less than 2 percent were Mancos Black-on-white (Martin et al, 1936, pp. 80–94, revised by Abel, 1955, Ware 12A—Type 5. Abel dates Mancos Black-on-white at A.D. 950–1150. This situation accurately reflects the absence of any definite Pueblo II or early Pueblo III occupation in Long House. Some 16,170 sherds were classified as McElmo-Mesa Verde. I believe that this circumstance hints at a close relationship between McElmo and Mesa Verde Black-on-white—a relationship far closer than that between Mancos and McElmo Black-on-white.

Despite the limited number of sherds (and no whole vessels) from Long House, the range of design is fairly well covered by the examples shown in figures 204 and 205. Many of the design components used on Mancos Black-on-white can also be found on Mesa Verde and, especially, McElmo Black-on-white. If we ignore vessel shape and technological aspects of the pottery, can we still differentiate the types? I believe that we can in a fairly large percentage of the material, especially when separating the later McElmo from Mancos.

McElmo definitely shows greater development of the band design on bowls, a trait which leads directly into the highly developed Mesa Verde Black-on-white. McElmo also shares many designs or design components with Mancos, but the two types differ in the relative frequency of several of these designs. Checkboard designs (fig. 204a, b, e, f, j, and k) and straight-line hachure between parallel lines (fig. 205b-e) were popular with the potters who made both types. Broad-line designs (fig. 204v and w) are also quite common in both types. With some of the examples of these and other designs, it is difficult to classify the pottery as to type without making use of other criteria, such as vessel shape and type of paint.

The problem is further confounded by the presence of Mancos sherds with carbon paint (figs. 204c and f, and 205c) and of McElmo sherds with mineral paint. Four sherds with carbon paint were called Mancos; four of five sherds with mineral paint were classified as McElmo-Mesa Verde, the other as Mesa Verde Black-on-white. The fairly abrupt break at Mesa Verde, as contrasted with nearby areas such as Yellow Jacket, between Mancos and McElmo Black-on-white in regard to paint creates a division which may have little cultural significance. The two types are obviously part of a continuum, and the break in paint tradition is not reflected, as far as I know, by as radical a change in architecture, stone and bone artifacts, etc. Therefore, I feel that a breakdown by type on the basis of carbon or mineral paint is no more than a questionably useful field or laboratory tool. Also, its usefulness is apparently going to be limited to certain areas, such as Mesa Verde, which makes such a division even more arbitrary.

Returning again to designs, we find several which are not commonly shared to any great extent by McElmo and Mancos Black-on-white. Fine line work, seemingly more typical of Mesa Verde, is quite common on Mancos (fig. 204), but it appears on few sherds of McElmo Black-on-white, from Long House. Triangles are used on both types, but not in the same manner. Figure 204c and d show an arrangement not seen on McElmo sherds from Long House. Since there are no complete vessels of Mancos Black-on-white from Long House, and very little transitional material, Mancos to early McElmo, there is no point in discussing to any extent parallels or lack of parallels in design.

There are two other decorative techniques employed in Mancos pottery which help separate it from McElmo Black-on-white: corrugated exteriors on black-on-white bowls, and rim decoration. Corru-

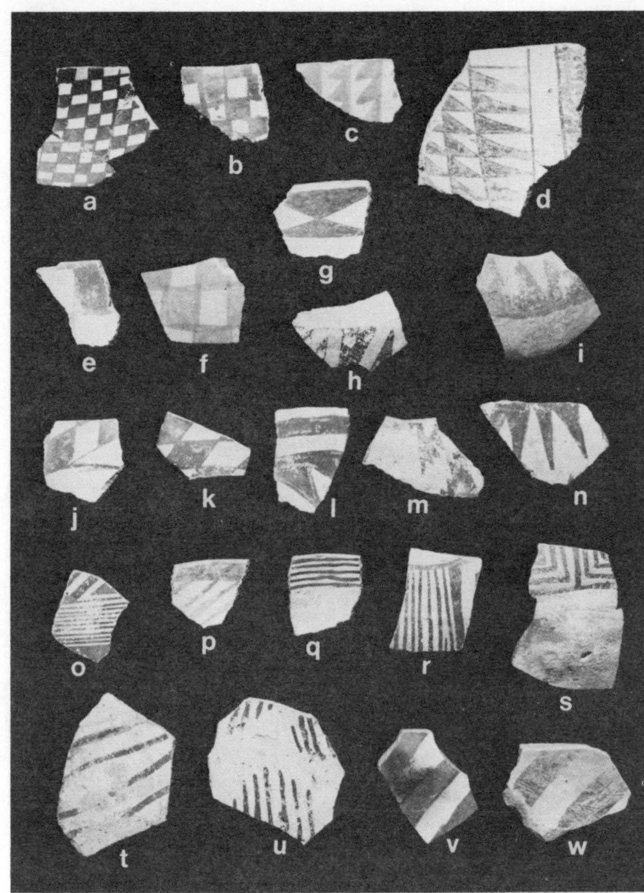

Figure 204. *Mancos Black-on-white sherds.*

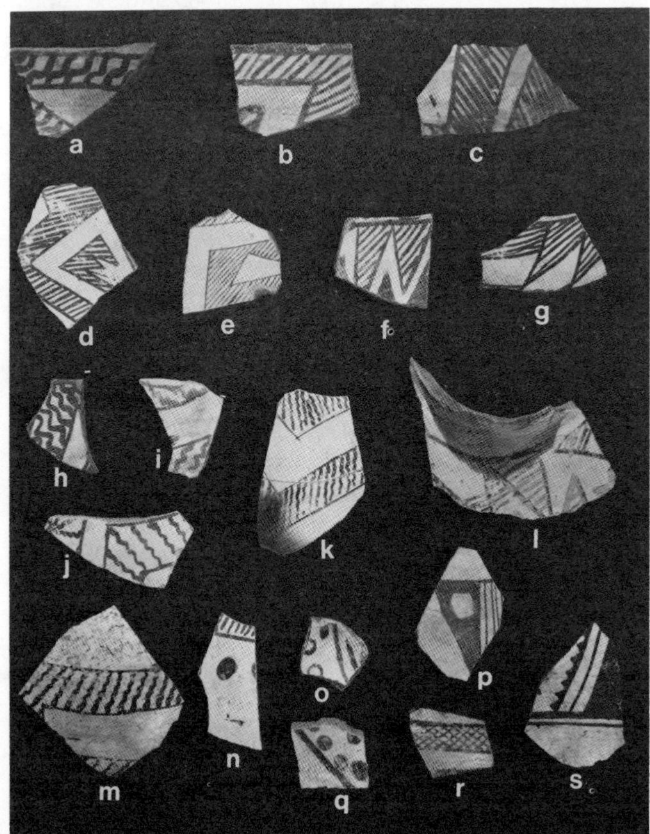

Figure 205. *Mancos Black-on-white sherds.*

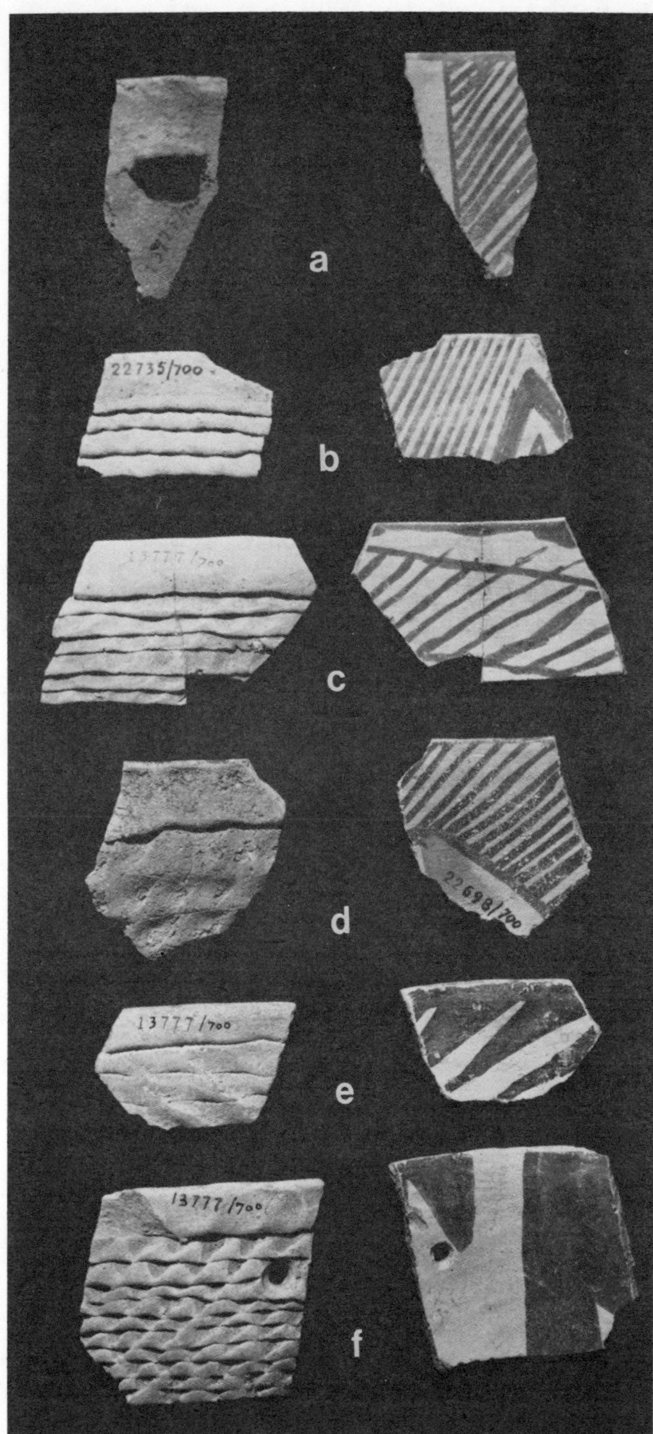

Figure 206. *Mancos Black-on-white sherds, corrugated on the exterior (left column) and painted on the interior (right column)*

gation produces an exceedingly attractive bowl (figs. 206b-f and 209f and g) and it is surprising that it was not carried over into the McElmo-Mesa Verde pottery other than in jar necks. There was only one bowl sherd classified as McElmo-Mesa Verde that had exterior corrugations; 17 jar neck sherds were corrugated. The Mancos Black-on-white bowl sherd with lug handle (figs. 206a and 209h) is unique in the Long House pottery, as is the handle on a Mesa Verde Black-on-white bowl (fig. 157).

Bowl rim decoration (fig. 207) was not as diversified as that on McElmo-Mesa Verde, but it does show what was to come. Of approximately 50 rim sherds checked for design, 28 were painted solid black (very uncommon on the later pottery) and 13 showed no decoration.

All of the Mancos Black-on-white sherds illustrated so far are from bowls or jars. There are no definite mug sherds from Long House, but the range in dippers can be seen in figure 208; three of the dipper handle shapes, found on McElmo-Mesa Verde Black-on-white, are present: flat (f), oval-round (e), and hollow (d). There are no examples of the compound handle. The dipper bowl was undoubtedly similar to that of McElmo and Mesa Verde. The majority of the dipper sherds (fig. 208g-l) are of a type not found in the later two types, the so-called scoop-handled dipper. Here the handle has a concave upper surface and slopes smoothly into the bowl proper. There is not the sharp break between bowl and handle that appears on McElmo-Mesa Verde pottery.

Little can be learned of bowl and jar shape from Mancos Black-on-white pottery from Long House. Figure 204d is a good example of the steep-sided vessels found at other sites. Figure 205l illustrates a high-necked jar, but the rim is broken off and could not be measured. The seed jar was present (figs. 204i and 205g) but there are no kiva jar sherds. The range of bowl and jar rim shapes (mostly the former) is shown in figure 209. Jar rim shape merely duplicates some of the bowl rim shapes. Most of the rims were tapered and rounded (d), but direct rims with flat lips (b) were becoming more popular. With previous pottery types even the flat lips were usually associated with more sharply converging sides.

Vessel wall thickness of 50 sherds ranges from 4 to 9 mm., and averages 5 mm. Crushed igneous rock temper is found in moderate amounts in about twice as many sherds (27) as crushed igneous rock and sherd, the next most common temper. Also present (all crushed) are the combinations of sherd and sandstone; igneous rock, sherd and sandstone; igneous rock and sandstone; and essentially pure sherd temper. The grain size is equally divided between medium and coarse, with a few fine or very coarse. Particle shape is primarily angular, but about one-fifth of the sherds had subangular particles.

About a third of the bowl and jar sherds were slipped on the interior, about a fifth of the bowl sherds on the exterior. Jar exteriors and both surfaces of the bowls were polished to a low luster in most cases. Bowl exteriors showed a slightly greater tendency to have a matte finish than the interiors. Polishing was spotty on about two-fifths of the bowl and jar sherds. About four-fifths of the bowl sherds showed crazing of the interior surface, about three-fifths crazing of the exterior.

Figure 207. *Mancos Black-on-white bowl rim decorations.*

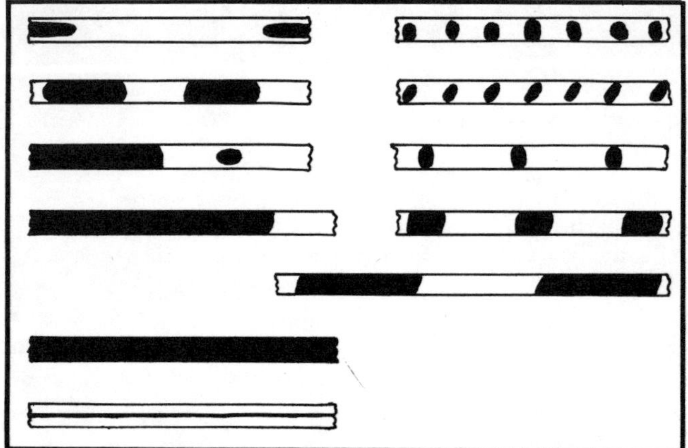

Slightly more than a third of the bowls and jars represented had a slightly bumpy or uneven exterior surface, but bowl interiors were more smoothly finished. Pitting was also common on the exterior of both vessel forms, and especially so on bowls. Surface texture was fine grained on the interior of all bowl sherds and the exterior of all but one of the jar sherds, but was slightly grainy on the exterior of about one-fifth of the bowl sherds.

The smooth contour of the vessel wall would imply scraping, but final finishing of the surface obliterated all marks of this process. Evidence of wiping of the surface is visible on the exterior of about four-fifths of the bowl sherds, but final rubbing or polishing obscured even this step on the majority of bowl interiors and jar exteriors. Jar interiors were scraped, wiped, rarely rubbed, and unslipped. The surface is bumpy or slightly uneven in most specimens. Surface texture is almost equally divided among fine grained, slightly grainy, and grainy.

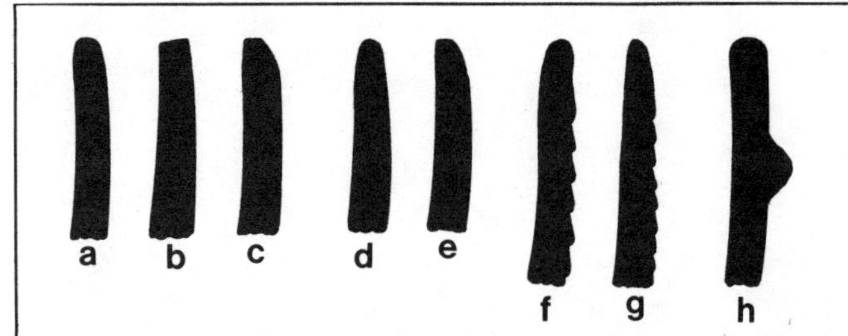

Figure 209. *Mancos Black-on-white bowl and jar rim shapes.*

CORTEZ BLACK–ON–WHITE

The 73 sherds of Cortez Black-on-white (Abel, 1955, Ware 12A—Type 3; early Pueblo II, A.D. 900 to 1000) have no obvious stratigraphic signifcance in Long House. The small amount reflects the apparent absence of an early Pueblo II occupation in Long House. Figure 217 presents representative samples of the designs and shapes present in Long House. Figure 210n shows a neck design which would allow classification as Mancos Black-on-white; the lines below are typical of Cortez. The squiggly lines, interlocking scrolls, and barbed triangles seem to imply a borrowing from Red Mesa and Kiatuthlanna Black-on-white from the area south of Mesa Verde and could be considered a variety of the former. Eight of the nine rims were painted black, the other was plain. One sherd had a corrugated exterior.

Many of the design components seen on Cortez Black-on-white from sites other than Long House make their appearance again on Mesa Verde Black-on-white. Although present on Mancos and McElmo, they are not as common. The interlocking scroll (fig. 210j-m and o) is an example of a design common in the highly developed bands of Mesa Verde Black-on-white. The small collection from Long House makes it impossible to show other similarities between Cortez and Mesa Verde. There were no examples of Cortez Black-on-white sherds with carbon paint from Long House.

The only vessel shapes indicated by the sherds in figure 210 are the bowl, jar (f, h, and m-o), and dipper (k, handle). As n and o show, the neck sloped gently into the body of the jar, in these specimens at least. The only definite dipper sherd is from an oval-round handle, with nothing whatsoever known about the bowl. To judge by these few sherds, the larger bowl seems to have less steep sides than the Mancos Black-on-white bowl. The bowl rim (fig. 211) shows very little variety in style. The tapered, rounded rim (c) was still the most common, but a flattened lip (b and d) appeared on

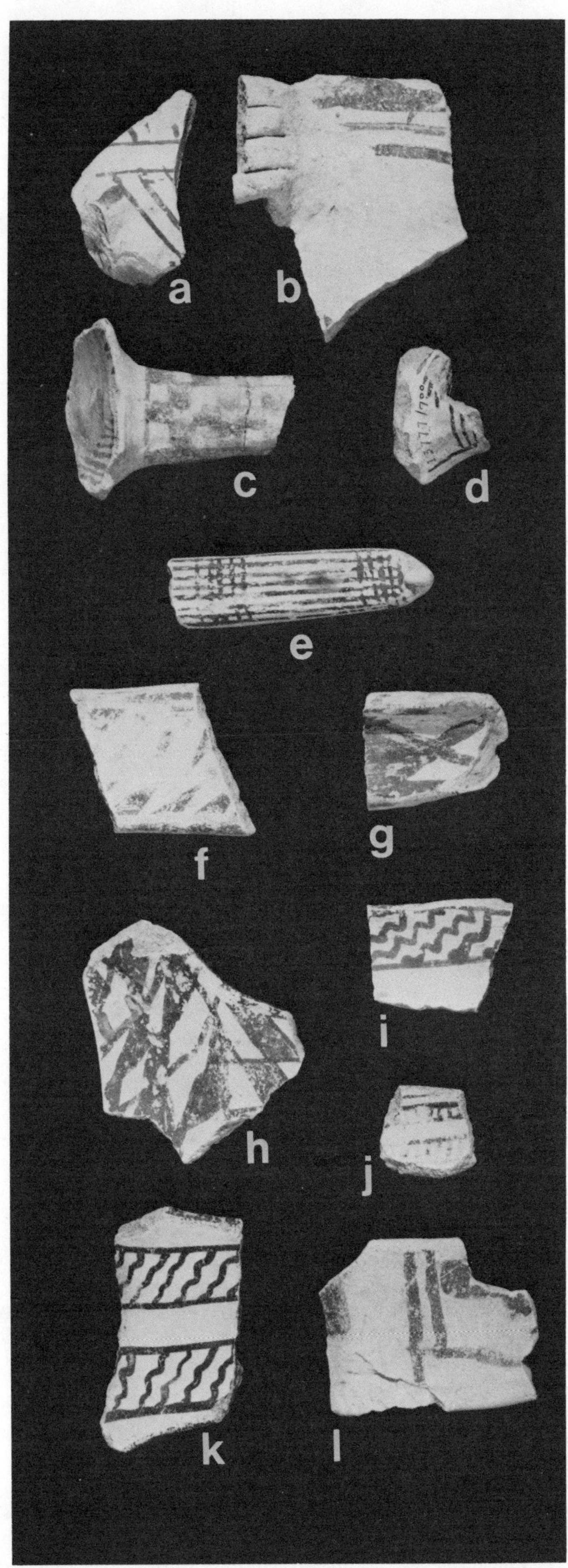

Figure 208. *Mancos Black-on-white dipper handle sherds.*

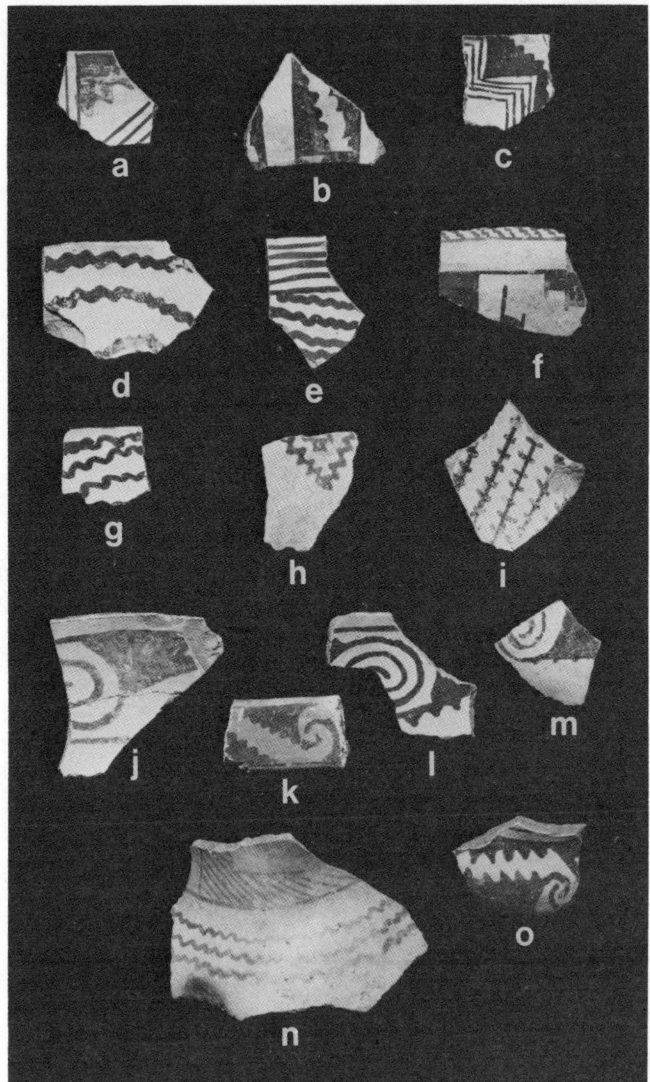

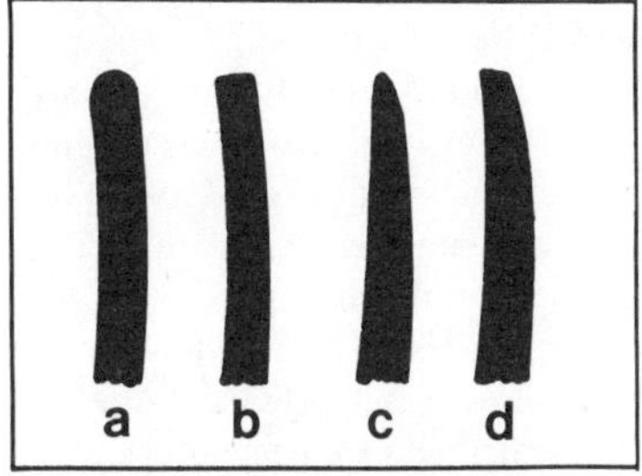

Figure 210. *(Above) Cortez Black-on-white sherds.*

Figure 211. *(Left) Cortez Black-on-white bowl rims.*

several sherds. No jar or dipper rims were recovered in the excavations.

The thickness of the vessel wall ranges from 4 to 6 mm., and averages just under 5 mm. Bowl and jar sherds were essentially identical with respect to temper. The pottery is moderately tempered with angular (rarely subangular) particles, which are crushed igneous rock in about half the sample. About a third of the sherds have a mixture of crushed rock and sherds. The remainder shows the same mixture but with sherd temper predominant. Unidentified, rounded gray inclusions were found in 10 of the sherds. In the bowls, grain size is medium in slightly more than half the specimens, with the remainder coarse; in the jars, coarse grains predominate, with medium and very coarse present to a slightly lesser extent.

Three-fourths of the bowl and jar sherds were slipped on the interior, but only one-fourth of the bowls were slipped on the exterior. All sherds were polished to a low luster, with the exception of one bowl exterior sherd, which was matte. The polished surface of a fourth of the bowl and jar sherds was crazed, and polishing was spotty on about half the sherds.

Jar exteriors and both bowl surfaces were somewhat bumpy or uneven on about half the specimens. Surface texture was fine grained on all sherds, excepting jar interiors.

As with all of the later black-on-white pottery, scraping was undoubtedly the method used in obtaining the smooth curves of the vessel walls. However, there is no definite evidence of this on any of the sherds. Wiping is visible on the jar interiors, and is less obvious on bowl interiors and jar and bowl exteriors. The final rubbing and polishing has obliterated evidence of most of the preliminary work. Jar interiors were unslipped and, for the most part, slightly grainy in texture.

PIEDRA BLACK–ON–WHITE

On the basis of design only, there is a sharper "break" between Piedra Black-on-white and Cortez Black-on-white than between any other two pottery types in the Mesa Verde White Ware continuum. Perhaps this is due only to the very limited material from Long House—70 sherds of Piedra, about the same number of Cortez and Chapin Black-on-white. Although the relationship between Piedra and Chapin is close, with many transitional sherds that defy classification, there seems to be little in the Piedra design to suggest what was to come in Pueblo II times with Cortez Black-on-white.

Piedra Black-on-white is a Pueblo I pottery dated by Reed (1958, p. 79) at about A.D. 750 to 900. Although not described for Mesa Verde, its appearance in the Mancos Canyon and the area around the Mesa Verde would suggest that it should be well represented on the mesa top. Most of the sherds illustrated in figure 212 show the relationship to Chapin Black-on-white, the Basketmaker III—early Pueblo I pottery from which it is derived. Several sherds (fig. 212c and k) show the trend toward Cortez Black-on-white design. Without evidence from other sites, such as the two Piedra vessels illustrated by Reed (ibid., p. 76), it would be very easy to separate the Piedra material from Long House into Chapin and Cortez Black-on-white and to place the "questionable" sherds in a transitional category. Rims were commonly painted solid black, but two showed possible ticking. Only one rim was undecorated. Two sherds bore carbon paint, the others mineral paint.

Bowl sherds were most common, although jar sherds were also present. For the most part, the bowl rims were tapered and rounded (fig. 213b) but several flat and almost flat rims were found (a and c).

Vessel wall thickness ranges from 3 to 7 mm., and averages just under 5 mm. All but two of the bowl sherds were tempered with crushed igneous rock. These two had a mixture of crushed rock and sherds. The jar sherds were tempered primarily with crushed igneous rock, but also represented were igneous rock and sherds, sandstone and igneous rock, and sherds and sand. Most of the sherds were moderately tempered, a few sparsely and a few heavily, with medium to coarse particles. The grains are primarily angular, with only a few sherds showing subangular particles.

All of the sherds were unslipped. As with other pottery types already discussed, the bowl interiors were better finished than the exteriors. Most of the interiors were polished to a low luster, the remainder being matte. About two-thirds of the bowl exteriors were matte, with the rest having a low luster. The surface finish on jar exteriors was almost equally divided between low luster and matte. Polishing was spotty on about a third of the sherds. Crazing of the surface was present in only four cases: the interior surface of three bowl sherds and the exterior of one jar sherd.

Few bowl sherds were uneven or bumpy on the interior surface, but about two-thirds of both bowl and jar sherds had a rather bumpy exterior. Pitting is found on all surfaces but is especially prominent on bowl exteriors, where it is present in slightly more than a fifth of the specimens. The surface texture of the interior of bowl sherds is overwhelmingly fine, with only a few slightly grainy. That of the exterior is slightly grainy for the most part.

Almost all of the sherds show both wiping and rubbing of the surface. This is in striking contrast to the later pottery, on which most evidence of wiping or scraping, or both, was usually obscured by final finishing. Jar interiors were unslipped, scraped, and wiped, with a slightly grainy to grainy surface. About half the specimens had a slightly uneven surface.

CHAPIN BLACK–ON–WHITE

La Plata Black-on-white, Lino Black-on-gray, and Chapin Black-on-white are essentially one pottery type, with Chapin being the local manifestation. Types of paint and temper definitely vary, at least in proportion, from one type to another, but all are Basketmaker III pottery types which undoubtedly extend into Pueblo I. There may be subtle temporal and spatial differences between the types, but these should not be allowed to obscure the broad relationship.

Abel (1955, Ware 12A—Type 1) has designated the earliest Mesa Verde black-on-white pottery as Chapin Black-on-white, dating it at A.D. 500–850 or 450–850 if the more polished Twin Trees Black-on-white is included. The material from Long House does not provide an adequate basis for arguing against the validity of this pottery type, so I am using the name he applies. I feel that adding another name to the literature confuses the picture and would much prefer to call this pottery La Plata or Lino (redefined). If it is necessary to separate the local development from that found elsewhere in the San Juan area, I would prefer to call it La Plata Black-on-white: Chapin Variety.

A similar situation exists with many other pottery types, both black-on-white and plain or corrugated, where the broad relationships are being buried under a mass of regional names. The local names are necessary for analysis, but surely there must be a better way of handling the taxonomy than by merely adding one name after another for every minor although perhaps significant variation of a "basic" type found. The type-variety concept offers a possible way out, but many archeologists have objected to tying up the word "variety" in this manner, and thus effectively deleting a rather useful word from the archeological vocabulary. It would seem to be a step in the right direction, however. It is certainly useful to be able to designate regional varieties, such as Mesa Verde and Chaco, but of course the designation does not have to be made part of the type name. In any case, the type descriptions need to be expanded to include these regional variants.

Despite the large amount of Chapin Gray, there were very few sherds (77) of the companion painted type, Chapin Black-on-white, from Long House. Figure 214 shows a rather limited number of designs which are, nevertheless, very typical of Chapin Black-on-white. There was one sherd each with carbon paint (fig. 214b) and fugitive red exterior.

Rim decoration was divided into three equal groups: painted

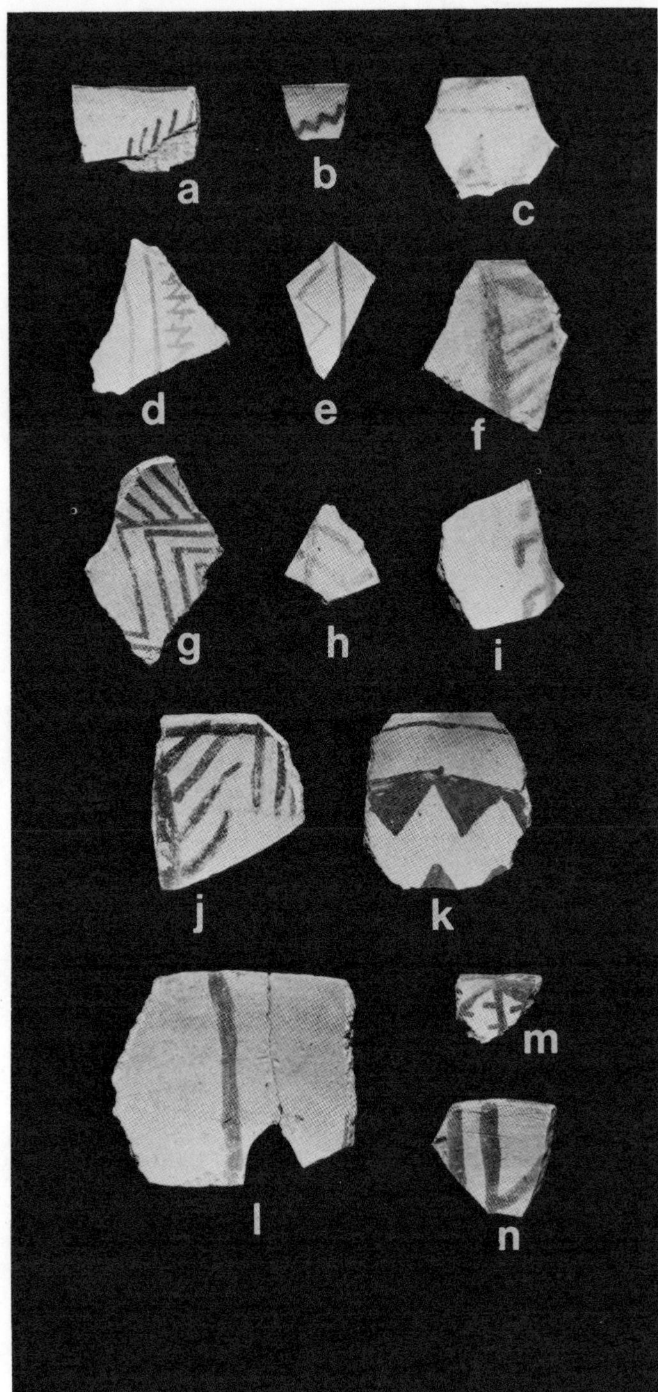

Figure 212. *Piedra Black-on-white sherds.*

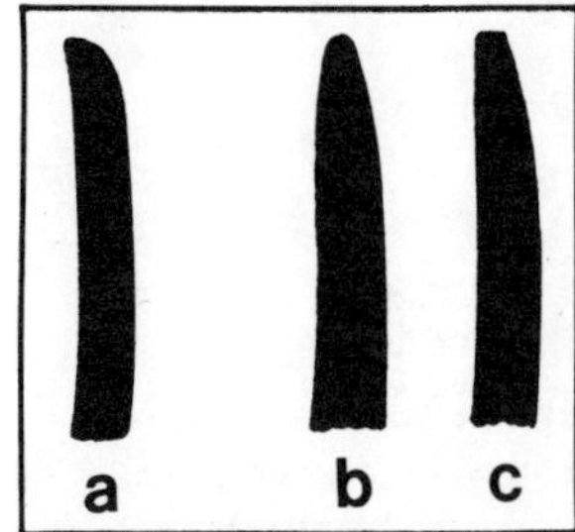

Figure 213. *Piedra Black-on-white bowl rims.*

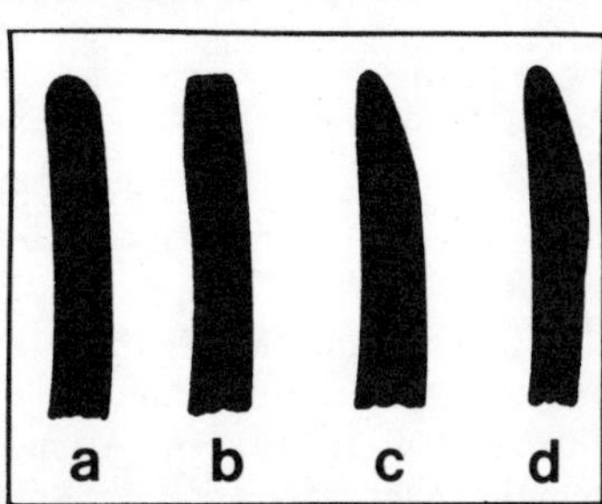

Figure 215. *Chapin Black-on-white bowl rims.*

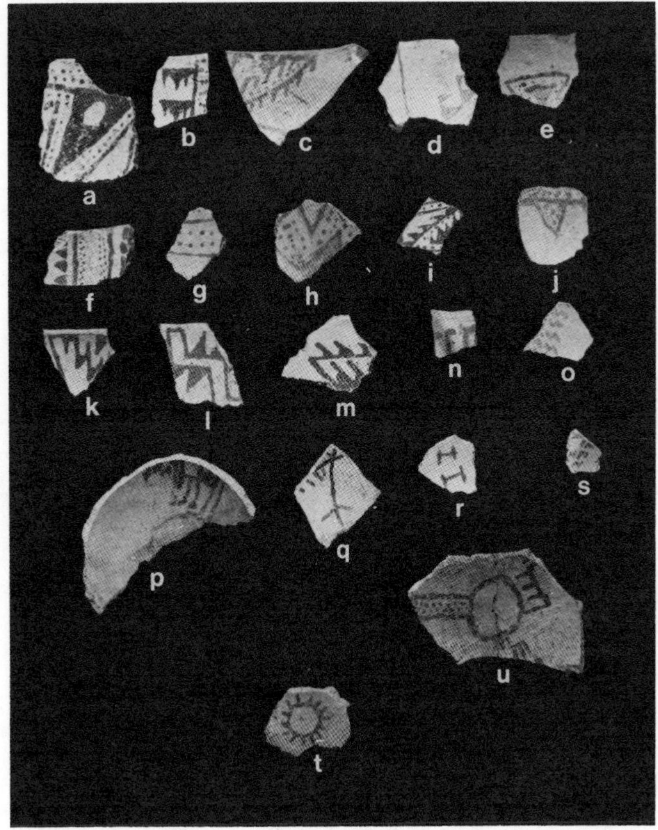

Figure 214. *Chapin Black-on-white sherds.*

solid black, plain, and possibly decorated (the weathered edges making it difficult to know for sure).

Once again little can be said about vessel form: all sherds but one are from bowls; the exception is a jar sherd. The bowl rim shape is usually tapered and rounded, (fig. 215c), with an occasional flat-lipped specimen (b). The outer vessel wall of one unusual sherd swelled outward slightly before tapering down to the lip (figs. 214k and 215d).

The thickness of the vessel wall ranges from 3 to 9 mm., and averages just under 5 mm. Temper is almost entirely crushed igneous rock and is moderate in most cases. Grain size is predominantly coarse, and becomes very coarse in about a third of the sherds. Almost all of the particles are angular, with the remaining few being subangular.

The interior and exterior surfaces of the bowl sherds were unslipped; both surfaces of most of the sherds show definite evidence of having been wiped and rubbed. All traces of wiping have been obliterated from the interior of about a fifth of the specimens, and to a slightly lesser extent, from the exterior. Rubbing of the interior surface has resulted in a spotty polish of low luster in about a third of the sherds, but similar results were obtained on the exterior in less than a fifth of the sherds. Except where a low luster was achieved, the surface was matte. None of the sherds showed the crazing of the surface so typical of the later pottery.

Strangely enough, few of the sherds were especially uneven or bumpy on either surface. As usual, the interior is somewhat better finished than the exterior. Only four sherds showed any significant amount of pitting. About two-thirds of the sherds showed an interior surface that was fine grained in texture, with the remainder slightly grainy. On the exterior the situation was reversed, with about two-thirds of the specimens being slightly grainy in texture and the rest roughly divided between grainy and fine.

SAN JUAN RED WARE

One of the anomalies of Mesa Verde ceramics is the red ware. There is no long sequence of red wares at Mesa Verde, and the center of manufacture of this pottery is not known. Red ware appears during a period extending, apparently, from late Basketmaker III to mid-Pueblo II, perhaps A.D. 700–1000.

One hundred sherds of black-on-red (including in this category the red-on-orange, black-on-orange, etc.) or plain red ware were recovered from Long House. Much of this material came from the East Trash Slope, and was also found scattered throughout the ruin. Examples are shown in figure 216. The sherds have been variously assigned: Abajo Red-on-orange (Colton, 1955, Ware 5A—Type 1), La Plata Black-on-orange (Martin and Rinaldo, 1939, p. 432) now dropped as a type, La Plata Black-on-red (Colton 1955, Ware 5A—Type 5), Bluff Black-on-red (Colton, 1955, Ware 5A—Type 4), and (possibly) Deadmans Black-on-red (Colton, 1955, Ware 5A—Type 6). This material may possibly be assigned to additional types other than synonyms for the above types). Reed (1958, pp. 122–133) presents an excellent discussion of San Juan Orange Ware, which includes pottery types formerly divided between San Juan Red Ware and Tsegi Orange Ware.

Sherds in figure 216a-1 and possibly r show more similarity in design (but not color) to sherds from southeastern Utah. The broad squiggle line is typical of Abajo Red-on-orange, but some of the other designs in this group also fall within the variations described for Deadmans, Bluff, and the like.

The so-called La Plata Black-on-red is represented by sherds such as those shown in figure 216m and n. As Reed (1958, p. 129) states, the slip is "not readily distinguishable in cross-section, but unmistakable on surfaces." The color is slightly more reddish than in the other sherds shown. Sherds in figure 216o-y fit in fairly well with the descriptions of La Plata Black-on-orange or Bluff Black-on-red, depending on how much emphasis one places on design, surface finish, paint color, or temper. The classification of the other sherds in this illustration may also vary with the emphasis placed on certain criteria. Whether or not slipping of the pottery is a later attribute with cultural significance (as suggested by Shepard *in* Morris 1939, p. 270) cannot be determined from the limited collection from Long House.

Three of the sherds in figure 216 are jar sherds (r, s, and w) with r being a rim sherd. Specimen h is from a scoop-handled dipper, and the rest are from bowls. Little more can be said about vessel shape. Most of the bowl rims have a flattened lip (fig. 217b-e,), unlike the majority of such early vessels definitely made in Mesa Verde, and the jar rim (fig. 216r) is rounded (fig. 217a). The walls taper slightly to the lip in most cases (c), but a few have walls essentially parallel (figs. 216e and 217a, b, and e). Several (figs. 216d and f and 217d) show a slight swell of the outer wall about 20 to 25 cm. below the lip.

Temper analysis was run on two types of pottery: one type was most likely Abajo Red-on-orange (22 bowl sherds), and the other Bluff Black-on-red or perhaps La Plata Black-on-orange (21 bowl and 4 jar sherds). Judging only from this small sample, the two types are practically identical with respect to temper. All of the Abajo and all but three of the Bluff sherds were tempered with crushed igneous rock. The exceptions were crushed igneous rock and sand (2) and crushed igneous rock and sherds (1). Generally, both types were moderately tempered with coarse particles of angular shape.

In other attributes, the two types varied slightly. Vessel wall thickness ranged from 3 to 6 mm. in both and averaged 4.2 mm. for Bluff and 4.4 mm. for Abajo. Both were unslipped, showed no crazing of the surface, and were polished to a low luster on both surfaces in about two-thirds to three-fourths of the specimens. The finish of the remainder was matte. The interior surface was slightly better than the exterior, with spotty polishing typical of both types in about a third of the sherds.

Figure 216. *San Juan Red Ware sherds.*

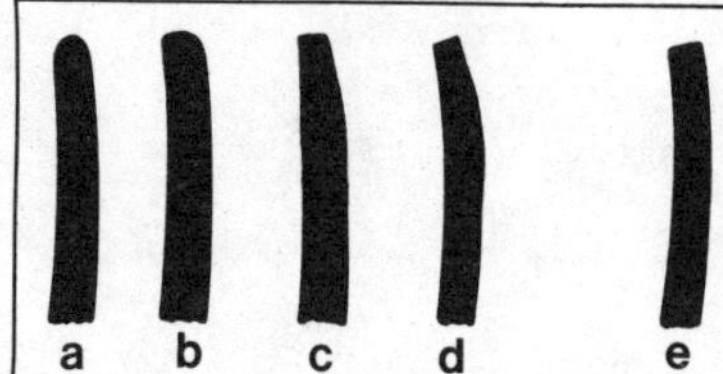

Figure 217. *San Juan Red Ware jar and bowl rims.*

The surface of Abajo and Bluff was slightly uneven on the exterior of about a third of the sherds. The interior surface of both was fairly even in all but a few cases. Indications of wiping and rubbing were visible on both surfaces of the two types, with wiping more visible on the exterior surface of the Abajo than on the Bluff. The surface texture on the interior of the two was fine in practically all of the sherds. Three Bluff sherds were grainy or slightly grainy. On the exterior, all but one Bluff sherd were fine grained, while the Abajo sherds were almost equally divided between fine grained and slightly grainy.

INTRUSIVES

One of the interesting things about the Long House ceramics is the almost complete lack of intrusive pottery. Possibly Pueblo II material from Hovenweep, Ackmen-Lowry, and nearby areas, or from the neighborhood of Aztec Ruins and farther south in the Chaco area might be overlooked in the Pueblo II pottery of Mesa Verde. Still, this does not account for sherds of other types and other time periods less likely to be confused with local products.

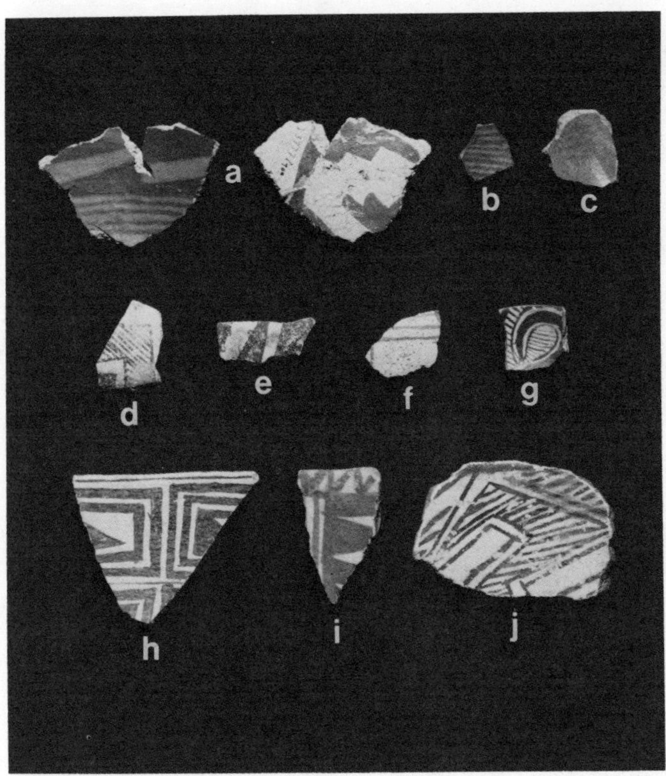

Figure 218. *Intrusive sherds.*

The few definite intrusives are shown in figure 218. Example a is Querino Polychrome (Colton and Hargrave, 1937, p. 122), black-on-red on the inside (left) and red-on-white on the outside (right), dated about A.D. 1250–1300. Wingate Black-on-red (Colton and Hargrave, 1937, p. 118) is also represented by one sherd (b). It is considered late Pueblo II, but is dated about A.D. 950 by Colton and Hargrave. Both of these types belong to White Mountain Red Ware, and as such were discussed at the Second Southwestern Ceramic Seminar, held September 19, 1959, at the Research Center of the Museum of Northern Arizona in Flagstaff. The "date of abundance" of Querino Polychrome was given as A.D. 1100 to 1200; the dates of Wingate Black-on-red were given as A.D. 975 to 1125. If the North Plains Variety were included, the terminal date would be almost as late as A.D. 1250 in the Acoma–Grants region.

Figure 218c can undoubtedly be assigned to the Tsegi Orange Ware, and is possibly Medicine Black-on-red (Colton, 1956; Ware 5B—Type 1). It is a Pueblo I–II trait, dating about A.D. 1050 to 1100.

Two sherds from the Chaco area are shown in figure 218d and e. Sherd d is Gallup Black-on-white, a Pueblo II–III ware, dating in the 11th century, according to Hawley (1936, p. 42). At the Cibola White Ware Conference in 1958, at the Museum of Northern Arizona, the type was given varietal status under Puerco Black-on-white, dating about A.D. 1050 to 1150. One other Chaco sherd (e), Red Mesa Black-on-white, was found. Red Mesa Black-on-white (Gladwin, 1945, p. 56) is a Pueblo II type dating around A.D. 870 to 930.

The remaining five sherds in figure 218f–j are probably northern Arizona types of the Tusayan White Ware. Sherd f appears to be Kana-a Black-on-white, a Pueblo I pottery dated by Colton (1955; Ware 8B—Type 1) about A.D. 700 to 900. Sherd j could possibly be Dogoszhi Black-on-white, a Pueblo II–III type dating about A.D. 1070 to 1150 (Colton, 1955: Ware 8B—Type 4). Sherds g–i are most likely Pueblo III black-on-white (type not identified) from northeastern Arizona.

About all that can be said of the intrusive pottery is that it covers the entire time range of the Long House occupation, but is present in such small quantities and from such poor proveniences as to be useless in dating portions of the ruin or in showing strong contacts with people peripheral to Mesa Verde.

MESA VERDE GRAY WARE

The companion utility pottery for Mesa Verde Black-on-white is Mesa Verde Corrugated (Abel, 1955; Ware 10A—Type 6). It is an outgrowth of Mancos Corrugated, yet with only sherds to deal with the transition between the two corrugated types is even more difficult to recognize than that between Mesa Verde and McElmo Black-on-white. Vessel shape is perhaps the prime diagnostic trait, and comparatively few whole or restorable vessels were recovered from Long House.

As shown in table 8, 51 percent of all sherds from Long House were corrugated. Of this group, 86 percent were either Mesa Verde or Mancos Corrugated, 11 percent were definitely Mesa Verde Corrugated, 0.5 percent were Mancos Corrugated, and 2.5 percent were Hovenweep Corrugated. The number of whole or restorable corrugated vessels of the various types is given in table 9.

There are several traits which help to distinguish Mancos Corrugated from Mesa Verde, and these will be discussed below. However, sherds which can be differentiated by these traits are few indeed. I believe that the two types (along with Hovenweep Corrugated, discussed below) should be lumped under Mancos Corrugated, with the Mesa Verde Variety covering the later material when it can be recognized. What is now called Mesa Verde Corrugated would then become Mancos Corrugated: Mesa Verde Variety. Mancos Corrugated would become Mancos Corrugated: Mancos Variety. Abel (1955; Ware 10A—Types 5 and 6) dates Mesa Verde Corrugated at A.D. 1200 to 1300, Mancos at A.D. 900 to 1200.

Comparison of corrugated wares from the nearby Kayenta and Chaco areas with that from Mesa Verde graphically points out the magnitude of the problem confronting the archeologist working with corrugated pottery. Before valid comparisons can be made from area to area, we need to classify better the pottery within a given area. I feel that lumping of these two types at Mesa Verde would be a step in the right direction.

Mesa Verde Corrugated

Vessel (jar) size varies widely for Mesa Verde Corrugated but can be broken down into four main groups. The smallest jars, Group I, represented by two examples—both fragmentary (fig. 219)—are so distinct from the larger jars as to be novelties. Figure 219a has a volume of about 300 cc., and a diameter of 11.3 cm.

Much larger, but still in the rather small category, are jars of Group II shown in figure 220. Figure 220a has a volume of 2,000 cc. and a diameter of 16.2 cm. Its height is 16.0 cm., but no comparison can be made here with the smaller jars because they are incomplete. The vessels shown are also more globular than those in the next group of larger jars. Maximum volume for this group—where it could be measured—is 6,200 cc.

Figures 221g and h and 222d and e are examples of Group III jars, which show a greater range in size than those previously described. At the smaller end of the scale is figure 221g, with a volume of 5,900 cc. Its diameter is 24.0 cm., and its height is 22.3

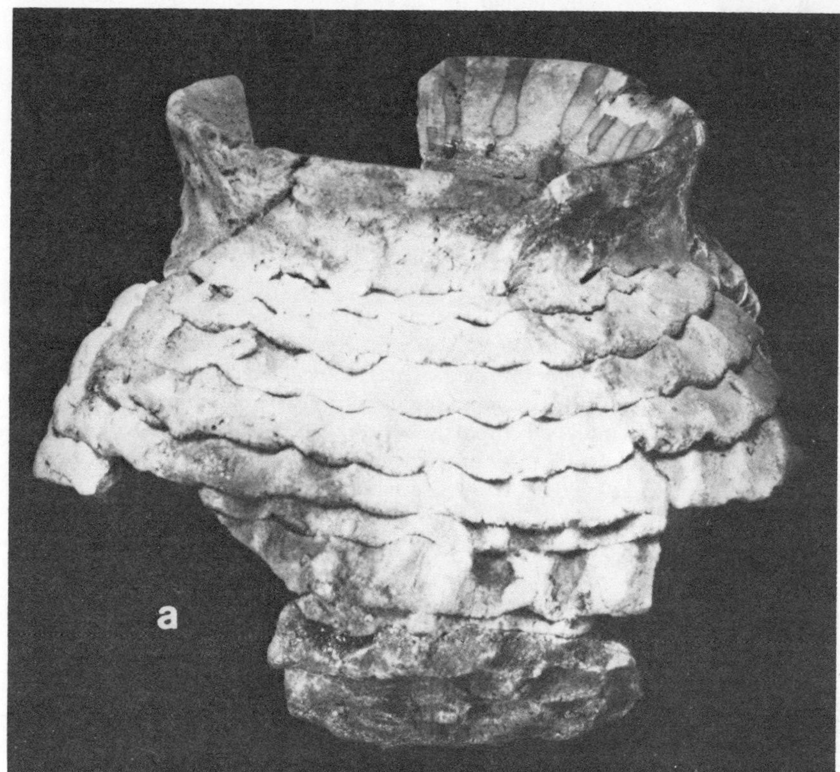

Figure 219. *Mesa Verde Corrugated, Group I jars.*

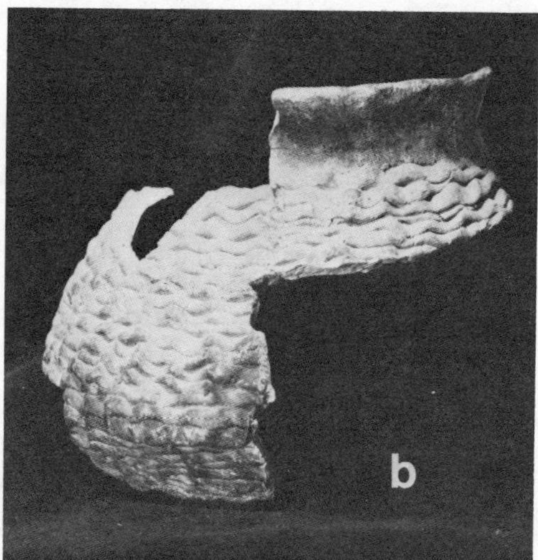

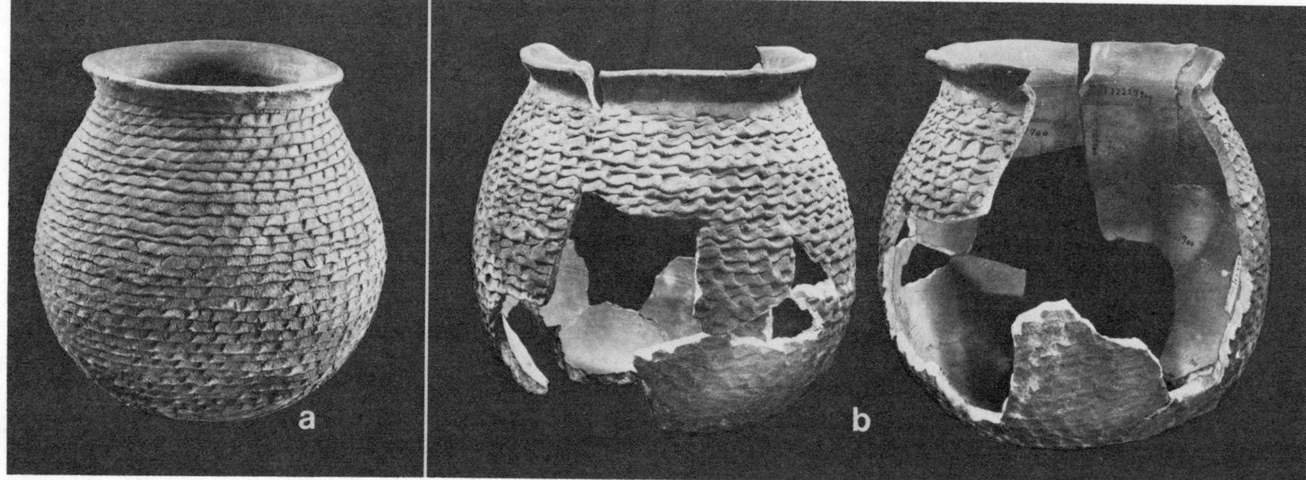

Figure 220. *Mesa Verde Corrugated, Group II jars; a, 16.2 cm. in maximum diameter; b, 17.9 cm. in maximum diameter.*

cm. One of the largest specimens is figure 222e, which has a volume of 9,200 cc., a diameter of 28.5 cm., and a height of 24.5 cm.

Group IV, the largest group in both size and number, also shows a wide range in size. The smallest measurable jar, figure 222b, with a volume of 13,500 cc., has a diameter of 30.5 cm. and an estimated height of 30.0 cm. The largest is about two and a half times the size of the smallest, with a volume of 31,000 cc. (fig. 221e). Its diameter is 40.5 cm. and its height is 38.8 cm. Despite size differences, the group is fairly homogeneous in regard to shape and general appearance, and I believe that the jars should be considered together. The average volume for the group is about 21,000 cc., the average diameter 35.0 cm., and the average height is 35.1 cm.

I have avoided mentioning rim diameter and the orifice or inside neck diameter because they can be measured on so few specimens except in the large-size group of jars. Expressed as a percentage of maximum diameter, the average diameters are (starting with the smallest jars):

	Rim	Neck
Group I	not measurable)	65%
II	do.	63%
III	do.	56
IV	66% (15 specimens)	55 (18 specimens)

In the last group, the range for rim diameter is from 56 to 76 percent; for jar opening, from 45 to 68 percent.

These figures mean little by themselves, but they would take on added significance if similar measurements could be made on Mancos Corrugated. (Mancos jars tend to be wider mouthed, with

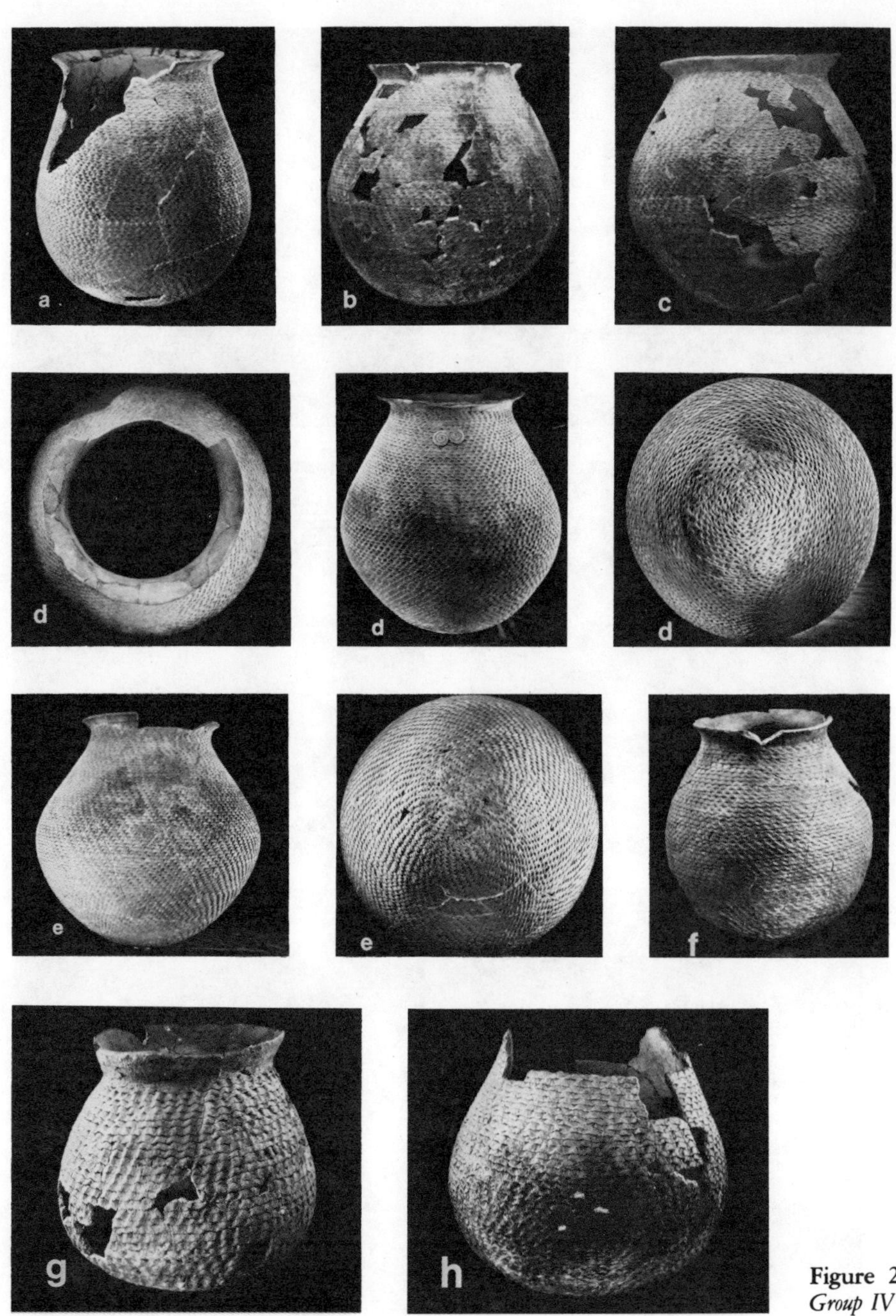

Figure 221. *Mesa Verde Corrugated, Group III and Group IV jars.*

less flared rims.) Unfortunately, there are only sherds of Mancos from Long House, so the data above are of no practical use in separating the Long House corrugated pottery into Mesa Verde and Mancos Corrugated.

As already suggested, the shape of the jar is one of the primary traits used for classification. Morris (1939, pp. 185–187 and 194–200) has described the Pueblo II and Pueblo III corrugated pottery in great detail. He refers to the earlier type as "bell-mouthed" and the later as "egg-shaped." Most of the Long House whole or restorable corrugated jars are of the latter form, especially the largest vessels. Shape of the smaller jars is more variable and certainly less distinctive. Variations in shape of the larger jars from Long House are shown in figure 221.

Only one specimen (fig. 221a) is suggestive of the earlier, bell-mouthed form. Figure 221b and e shows the varying degrees of convexity of the side of the jar, the trait which—when pronounced—produces the egg-shaped jar. The sequence in which these jars are pictured does not imply that the jar shape evolved in that order.

Rim shape is next to overall shape as an important criterion for determining jar type. Figure 223a–m shows the range in rim shape of Mesa Verde Corrugated from Long House. Sherds showing several of these shapes are illustrated in figure 224. The extent to which the rim is everted increases from sherd a to k. Generally, the point of eversion matches the termination of the corrugation. Sherd a is an exception to this, with no sharp eversion and the coiling extending up to the rim fillet. Sherd i is another unique example: there is a sharp point of eversion, but the coiling does not extend to it.

Because of pronounced rim eversion, many sherds could be classified fairly safely as Mesa Verde Corrugated. Care had to be taken here, however, because late Mancos Corrugated rims may show a

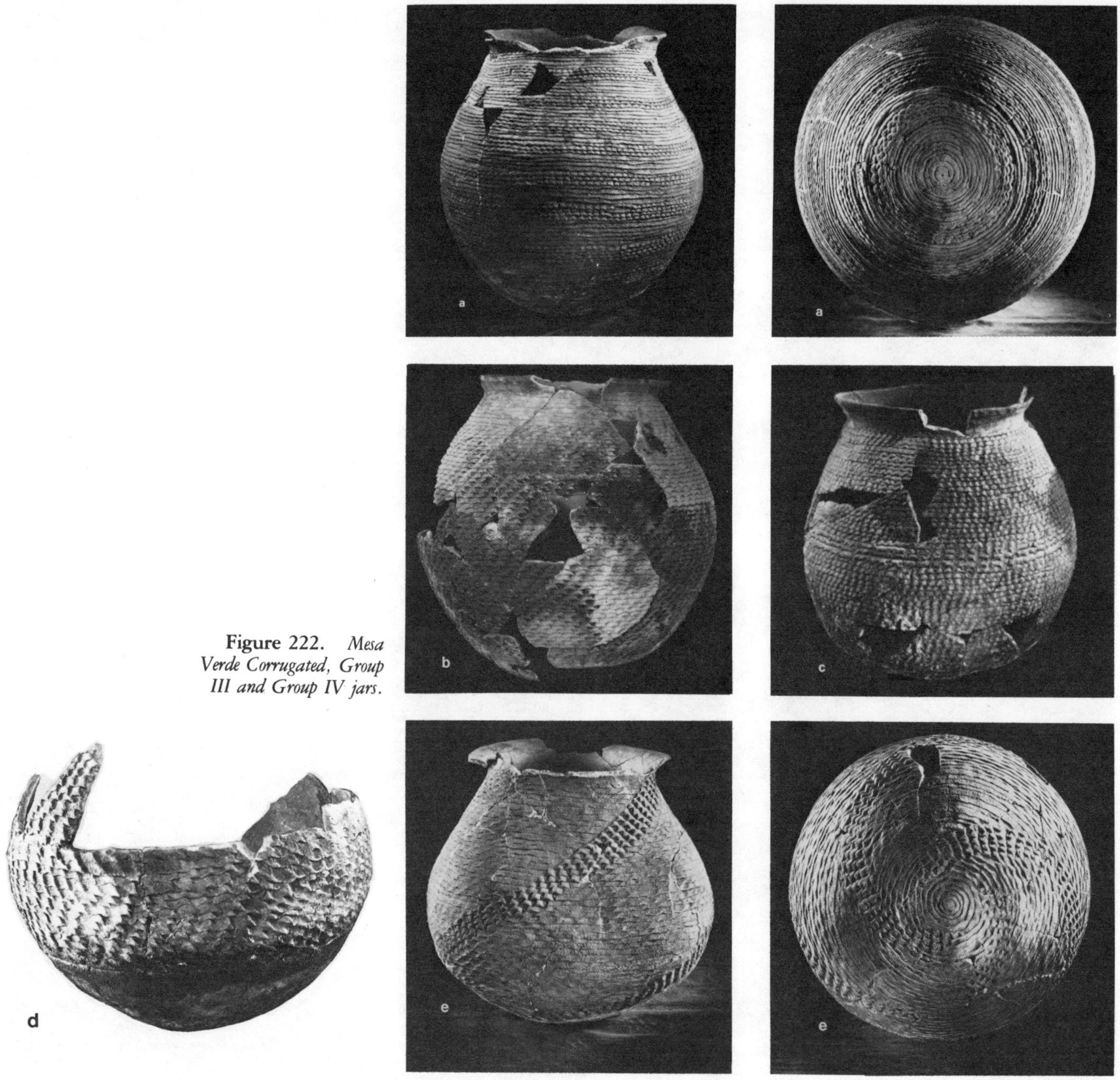

Figure 222. *Mesa Verde Corrugated, Group III and Group IV jars.*

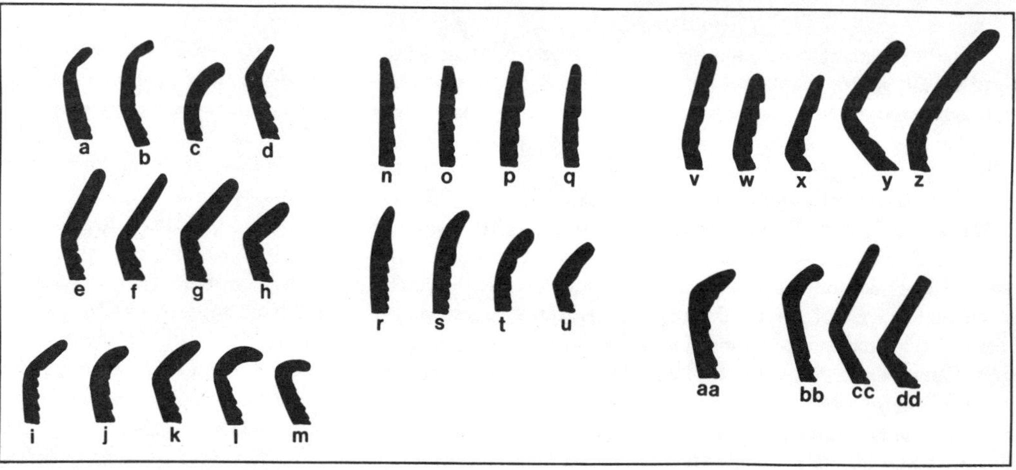

Figure 223. *Rim shapes of Mesa Verde Corrugated (a-m), Mancos Corrugated (n-u), and Hovenweep Corrugated (v-dd).*

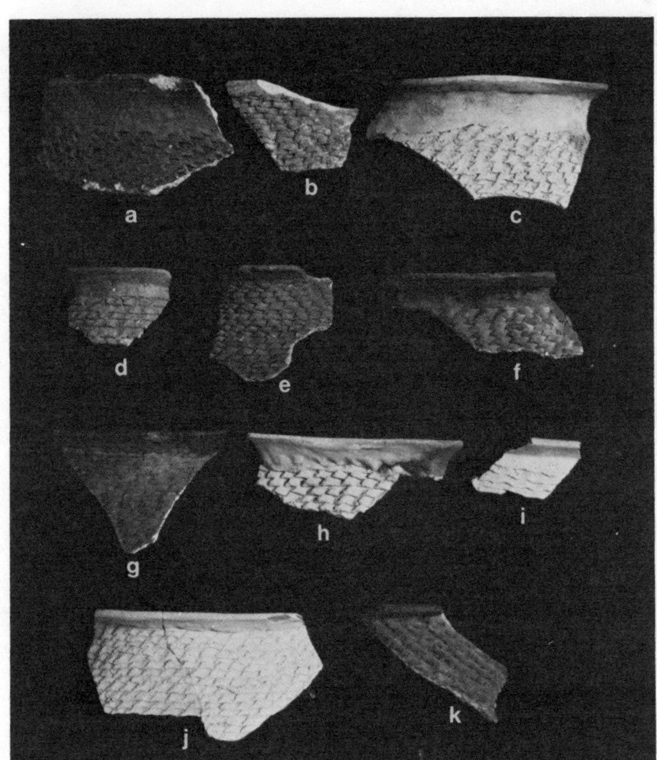

Figure 224. *Mesa Verde Corrugated rim sherds.*

similar eversion (fig. 223t and u). With the Mancos material, however, there is usually no sharply defined eversion point.

The classification of body sherds was impossible much of the time, other than to say that they are either Mancos or Mesa Verde Corrugated. Table 8 shows this quite clearly, since I have classified 86 percent of the corrugated pottery as "indeterminate" (Mesa Verde–Mancos). Coil width was of no help in separating the types since the range in one type is essentially identical to that in the other. With few exceptions, the pottery I am calling Mancos Corrugated: Hovenweep Variety can readily be distinguished from the more common Mesa Verde and Mancos.

The range in design as a result of variation in surface texture is very noticeable. Although not as marked as changes in design on black-on-white pottery, the variation in corrugated pottery from jar to jar is quite distinctive. Here the size, shape, depth, and alinement of indentations form the principal designs as the geometric elements form the designs on black-on-white pottery. Figures 225 and 226 show some of the more common variations found on the late Pueblo III corrugated pottery. No attempt at patterning has been made on the sherds illustrated in these two figures other than by the alinement of indentations.

Of the many methods of creating a pattern in corrugated pottery, the most common is intermixing indented and unindented coils (fig. 227). Usually at least three coils in a group will be unindented (fig. 227b), and the number may be much higher. Sherd c has 14 remaining, and the unindented portion is broken, with the probable loss of additional unindented coils. The bands may be located anywhere on the vessel but are often found one above and one below the widest portion. Occasionally, the band will be immediately below the rim (figs. 222b and 227a).

The unindented band may extend entirely around the vessel (fig. 222a and c), or only part way. In the latter case, the band may terminate in alinement with the diagonal "ridging" of the coils (fig. 227f), or be cut off more abruptly by rubbing out indentations so as to form a squared end (fig. 227d).

As mentioned above, the patterned band is usually formed by not indenting several coils. Occasionally the decorative coils (still unindented) are placed upon the thinned vessel wall as an applique (fig. 227d and g). As a result, they stand out in much greater relief than do unindented body coils.

A final touch—smoothing of the coils, or tooling between them—may be added to the band. Figures 228c and f, and 226h and i have been smoothed, but in the last mentioned example the whole vessel surface was also apparently smoothed. In figure 228k–m, sherds show scoring between the coils. A similar technique was employed with d, but a much larger tool was used to produce a broad groove. Tooling between coils was much more common on Mancos Gray and appears rarely on Mesa Verde or Mancos Corrugated.

Tooling or crude scoring occasionally appears on other parts of the jar but is usually poorly executed (fig. 228g–i). Deep fingernail impressions (fig. 228j, n, and o) were also used and resemble short, tooled strokes.

Various other ideas were used in decorating the corrugated pottery, and a few of these are illustrated in figures 228a, b and e, and 229. Figure 228a is either a mostly plain vessel with both indented and unindented corrugations, or else has a wide, smoothed band. Figure 222d is definitely a corrugated jar with plain bottom. In figure 228b and e, the unindented corrugated band is interrupted by indentations, and in the case of e the indentations are different than those in the indented portion of the decoration. A change in coil alinement (fig. 229a and b) and in coil width (fig. 229c and d) can produce a pattern. A more subtle way of introducing a pattern is seen

Figure 225. *Mesa Verde Corrugated jar sherds.*

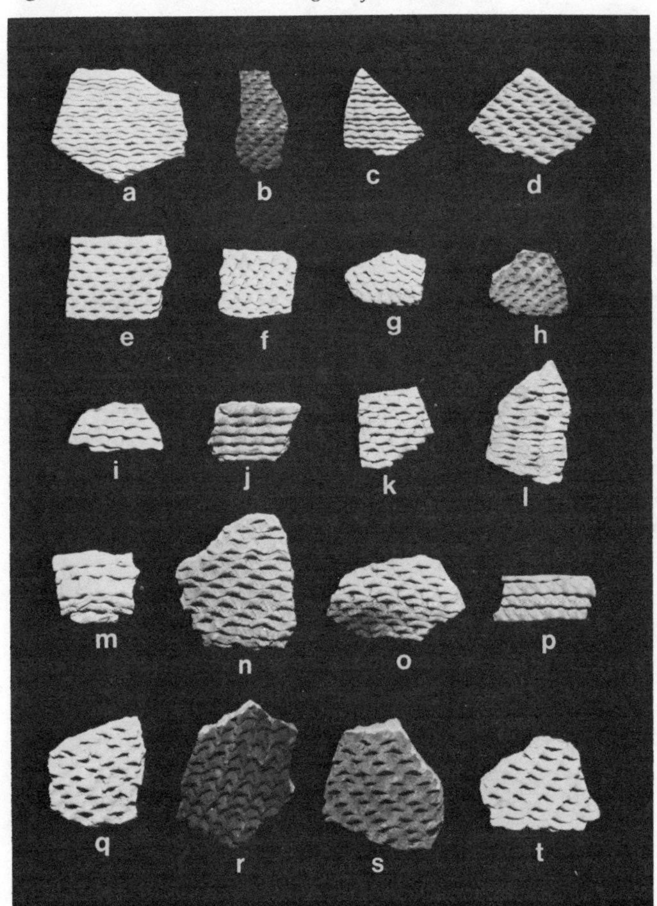

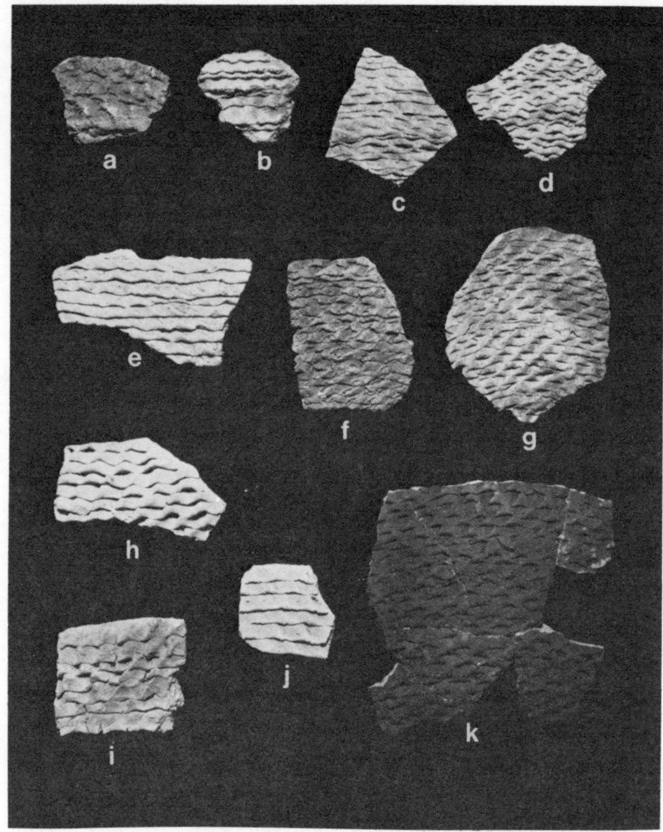

Figure 226. *Mesa Verde Corrugated jar sherds.*

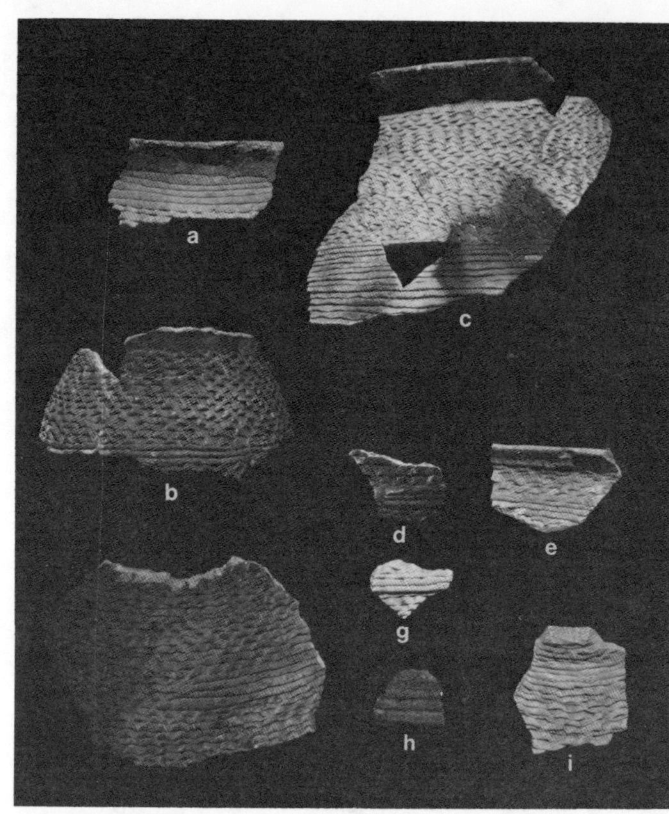

Figure 227. *Mesa Verde Corrugated, patterned jar sherds.*

Figure 228. *Mesa Verde Corrugated, patterned jar sherds.*

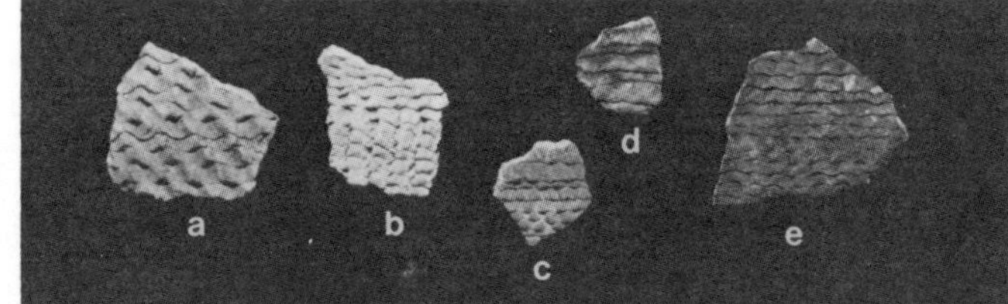

Figure 229. *Mesa Verde Corrugated, patterned jar sherds.*

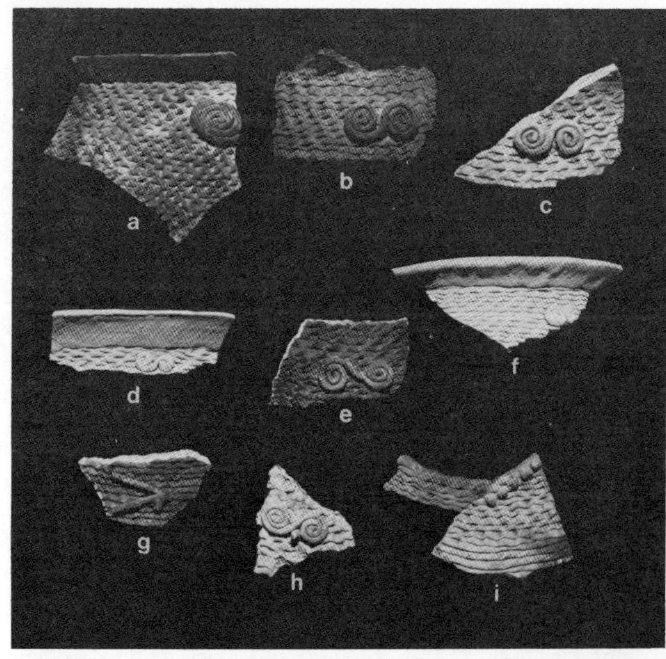

Figure 230. *Corrugated jar sherds showing different types of applique.*

in figure 229e. Here the potter apparently switched hands used to indent the coils, or in any case changed the angle from which the coils were indented. The four coils crossing the center of the sherd show this change in direction of indentation.

Perhaps the outstanding example of patterning from Long House is figure 222e. Three bands of deeply indented corrugations start almost at the center of the vessel base and spiral up to the rim, cross-cutting the more conventionally indented coils at an angle.

Apparently, a distinctive trait of the late Mesa Verde Corrugated is the addition of a more pronounced applique than that mentioned above. This usually takes the form of an S-scroll (figs. 221d and 230a–f, and h), but what seems to be a turgey track (fig. 230g), small flattened balls (fig. 230i), and a conical projection (fig. 230h) are also in evidence. One conical projection (not illustrated) was 7 mm. long. The appliques are almost always located a short distance below the rim of the jar.

No useful stratigraphic associations can be made for the patterned corrugated, nor can it be broken down into early or late styles. It is found in undisturbed levels of rooms which appear to belong to the early part of the occupation on the basis of architecture or tree-ring dating. It is also found in areas where the association appears to be with later material. It is from rooms or kivas in both main sections (east and west) of the ruin, as well as from miscellaneous areas and trash slopes. Possibly the only useful clue is negative: there are few sherds associated with structures producing the latest tree–ring dates (A.D. 1270 to 1280).

It is often difficult to differentiate light, deliberate smoothing of a jar surface from inadvertent smoothing due to handling or pressure, especially at the base of a large jar. Most of the smoothing appears to have resulted from rubbing the surface while damp with the hands, a cloth, or some other fairly soft or smooth article. There are few indications on the high spots, where most of the smoothing occurs, of striations or other marks resulting from scraping, polishing, and the like. Figure 231 illustrates sherds which show various degrees of smoothing of the corrugations. The evenness of surface on four sherds would suggest that some scraping was done (fig. 231c, f, h, and j), with possibly additional hand smoothing afterward. One sherd (fig. 231e) shows an entirely different treatment: grinding of the surface, and slight flattening, after the vessel was fired. It is quite possible, of course, that the ground surface resulted from use of a sherd broken from the vessel. The small size of the remaining sherd makes it impossible to determine the size of the ground area or to guess its purpose.

A certain amount of smoothing and flattening would be expected on the bottom of a jar because it is the primary weight-bearing surface. Wear on the bottom would also result from pivoting the vessel both during and after manufacture. Some vessel bases appear to have been deliberately smoothed by rubbing wile the clay was still plastic. Examples of the "smoothing process" due to the base being the weight-bearing surface are in figure 232a and c. That shown on b, d, e, and h may also be accidental, but could reflect a combination of deliberate and accidental smoothing. I believe that f and i show deliberate flattening and smoothing of the coils. The ground surface of j is probably the result of post-firing use. The sherds illustrated here also show clearly several slightly different ways of starting a vessel, but all are coiled spirally.

Of approximately 32,000 corrugated sherds, 162 show a marked flattening of the coils, but without any attempt to blur the line of demarcation between coils or to obliterate the indentations (fig. 233). In fact, quite a few of the specimens are patterned (fig. 233c and d). Coil width varies, as does the shape and alinement of the corrugations. A few sherds do show deliberate smoothing, with partial obliteration of the indentations (fig. 233g and i). These sherds

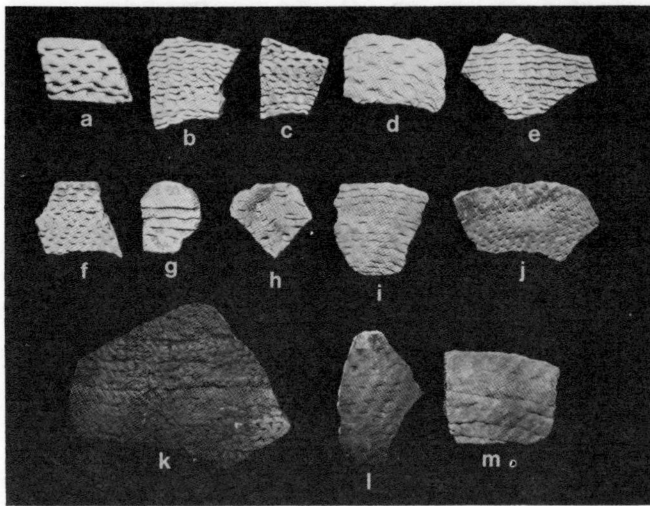

Figure 231. *Corrugated jar sherds showing various degrees of smoothing of the corrugations.*

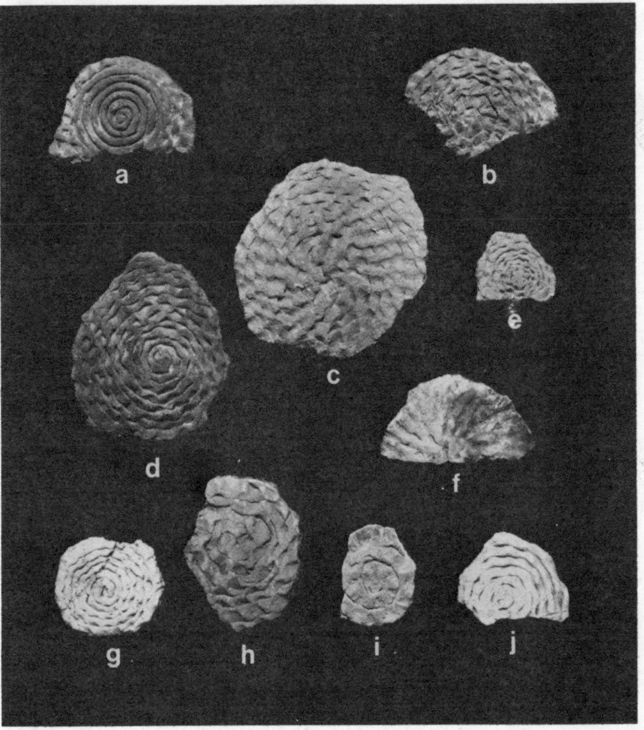

Figure 232. *Mesa Verde Corrugated, bottom sherds.*

resemble Moenkopi Corrugated (Colton and Hargrave, 1937, p. 197) and may be a Mesa Verde counterpart.

The date range ascribed to Moenkopi Corrugated is about A.D. 1075 to 1275. This style of surface treatment may have a similar range at Mesa Verde, since it is found not only in late cliff dwellings like Long House but also in earlier surface sites on Wetherill Mesa. Within Long House, the flattened coil pottery is found in both early and late proveniences but primarily the former. About two-thirds of the sherds come from the East Trash Slope and contribute nothing to the stratigraphic story. Only 11 sherds can be classified as Mesa Verde Corrugated by shape; the balance I would call indeterminate Mesa Verde-Mancos Corrugated.

Occasionally corrugated pottery will bear some painted design. On the Long House pottery it was always limited to the inside of the

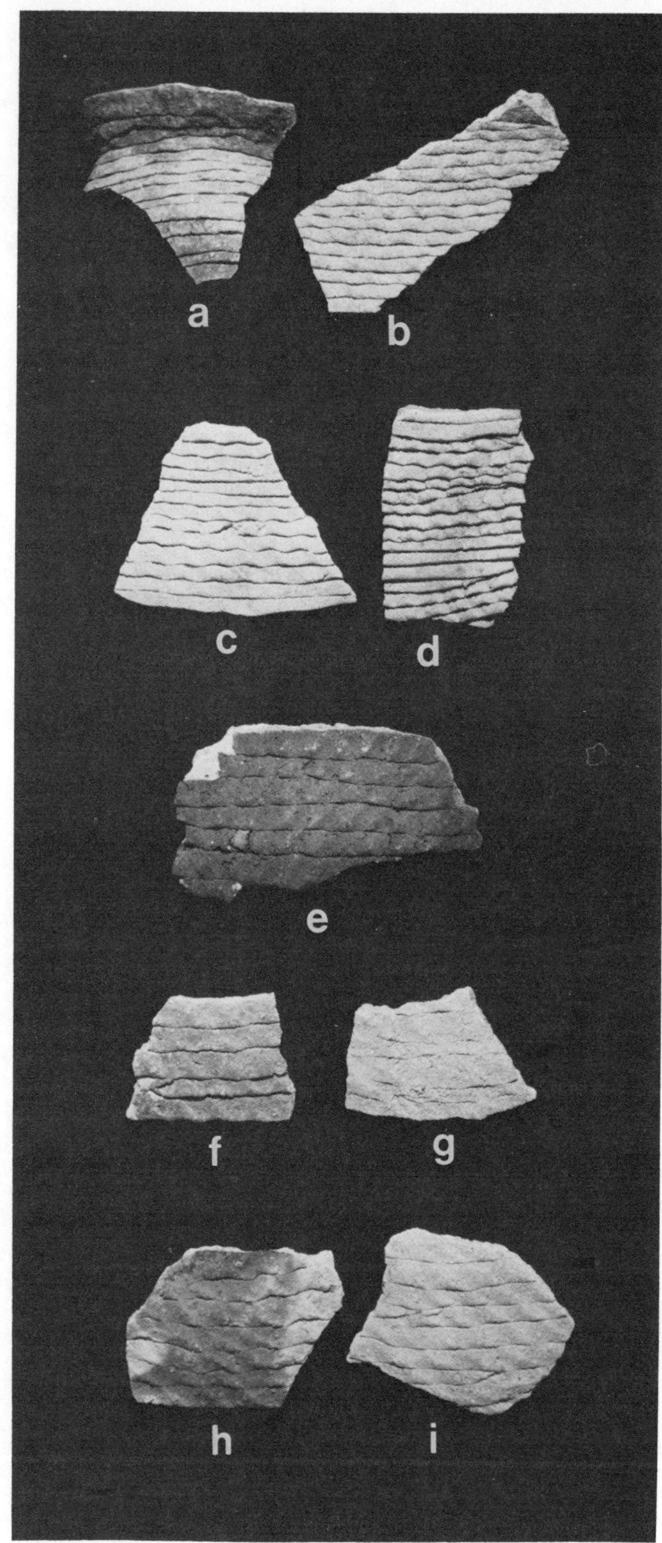

Figure 233. *(Left) Mesa Verde Corrugated, patterned coils.*

Figure 234. *(Above) Corrugated jar sherds with decorated interior rims.*

Figure 235. *(Right) Mancos Corrugated jar sherds.*

neck, the only accessible smooth surface. With one exception, a sort of rude cross (not illustrated), the decoration consisted of straight-line ticks in carbon paint (figs. 219a, 221a, and 234).

Mancos Corrugated

There are only 180 sherds (0.5 percent of the total corrugated sherds) which I feel can safely be called Mancos Corrugated. Such assignment is based primarily on two traits: rim shape (figs. 223n–u and 235) and pronounced diagonal "ridging" (fig. 236). Diagonal alinement is common in Mesa Verde Corrugated, but is not usually accentuated by running a finger between the ridges to partially obliterate the coils, or by the several other techniques used on Mancos Corrugated to achieve a similar effect.

All the rim sherds illustrated in figure 235 show the gently flaring rim so typical of the "bell-mouthed" jars of Pueblo II and early Pueblo III stages. Sherd e is a patterned and i is surely the unindented portion of a patterned vessel.

Abel (1955; Ware 10A—Type 5) feels that "Mancos Corrugated differs from Mesa Verde Corrugated in having heavier, rougher corrugations and in its diversity of treatment of the coils, such as alternating plain and pinched coils, diagonal lines incised through the coils, etc." Possibly this is true, but there is certainly a great variety of patterning in Mesa Verde Corrugated. Despite the disproportionately high number of indeterminate sherds, there are many obvious Mesa Verde Corrugated vessels—obvious because of form and rim shape—which show extensive patterning. I agree that certain types of surface manipulation are typical of Mancos Corrugated, but I am not sure the diversity of treatment is any greater in one type than in the other. Once again, shortage of whole vessels of Mancos Corrugated from Long House—and especially those from the Pueblo II stage—makes it impossible to compare Mancos and Mesa Verde Corrugated for their entire time span.

Several sherds in figure 236 are very similar to some already illustrated; a–d have strongly accentuated diagonal ridging without smoothing between the ridges; in e–g the emphasis is on vertical alinement, again without smoothing between the ridges. The remaining sherds, h–p, are quite different. Sherds h-l show a smoothing and consolidating of the ridge with a minimum disturbance of the troughs between; m–p show manipulation of the trough. In p, all traces of coils and indentations are removed to leave only the diagonal ridges. It is interesting to note that n also bears more conventional corrugations immediately above the diagonal-ridged portion.

Except for the trash slope material, many Mancos Corrugated sherds come from locations in the ruin that appear to be early in the

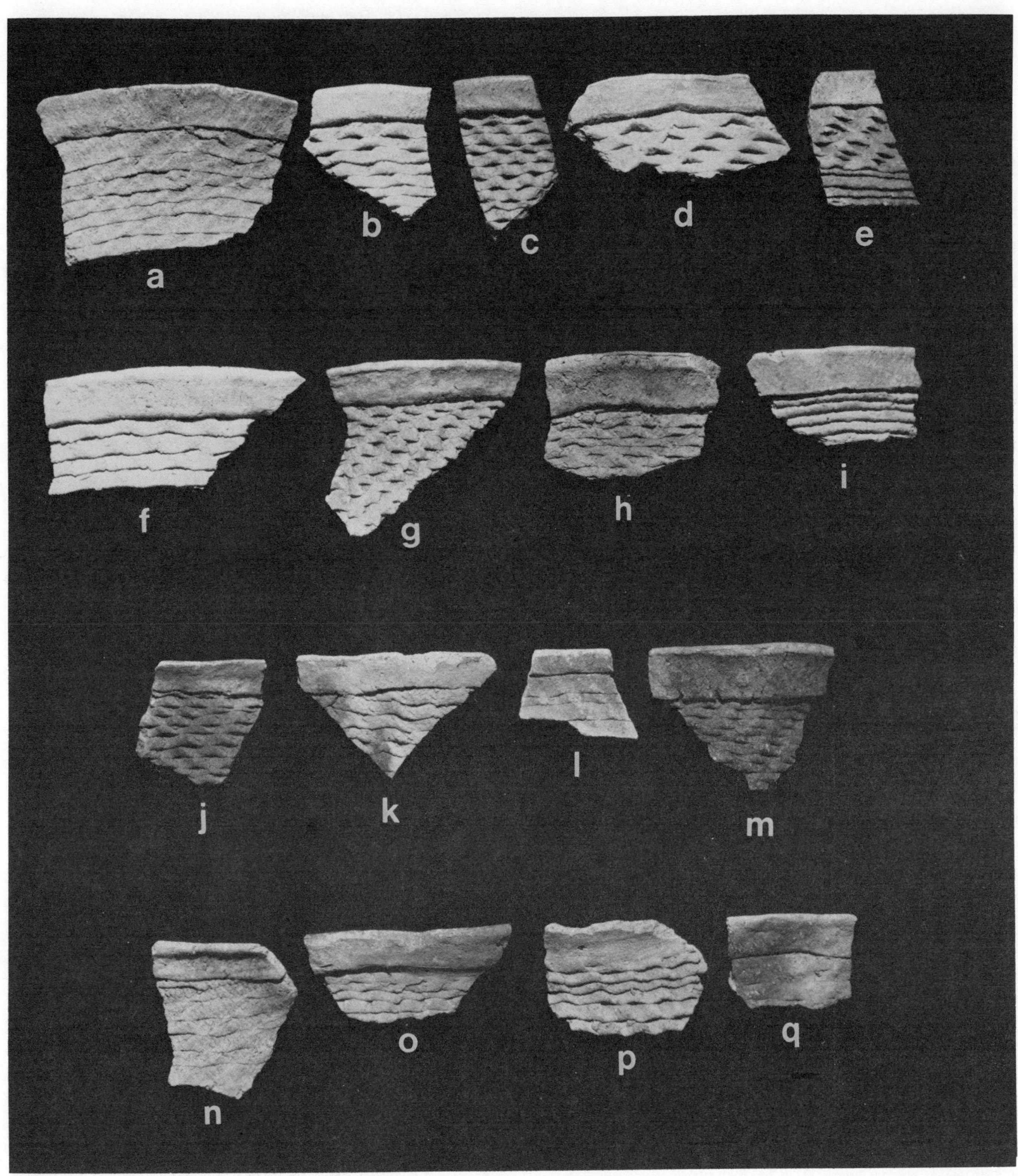

occupation. There is also a similarity in distribution with the flattened coil corrugated. This association may be further indication that the flattened coil pottery is found, generally, with the earlier part of the occupation. For once, the percentage of the type in question found on the East Trash Slope is no greater than that from the rooms. This is to be expected, since the lowest (and earliest) levels of trash would have been deposited nearer to the back of the cave than they would have been later on, when the pueblo was much more extensive.

Technology

Vessel wall thickness for Mesa Verde Corrugated ranges from 3 and 4 mm. (rim and body, respectively) to 8 mm., and averages 5 to 6 mm. Thickness of the bottom will often run 6 to 8 mm. A similar situation prevails with Mancos Corrugated, except that the average wall thickness is closer to 5 mm.

Practically all of the pottery of both types was moderately tempered, primarily with crushed igneous rock. A few specimens

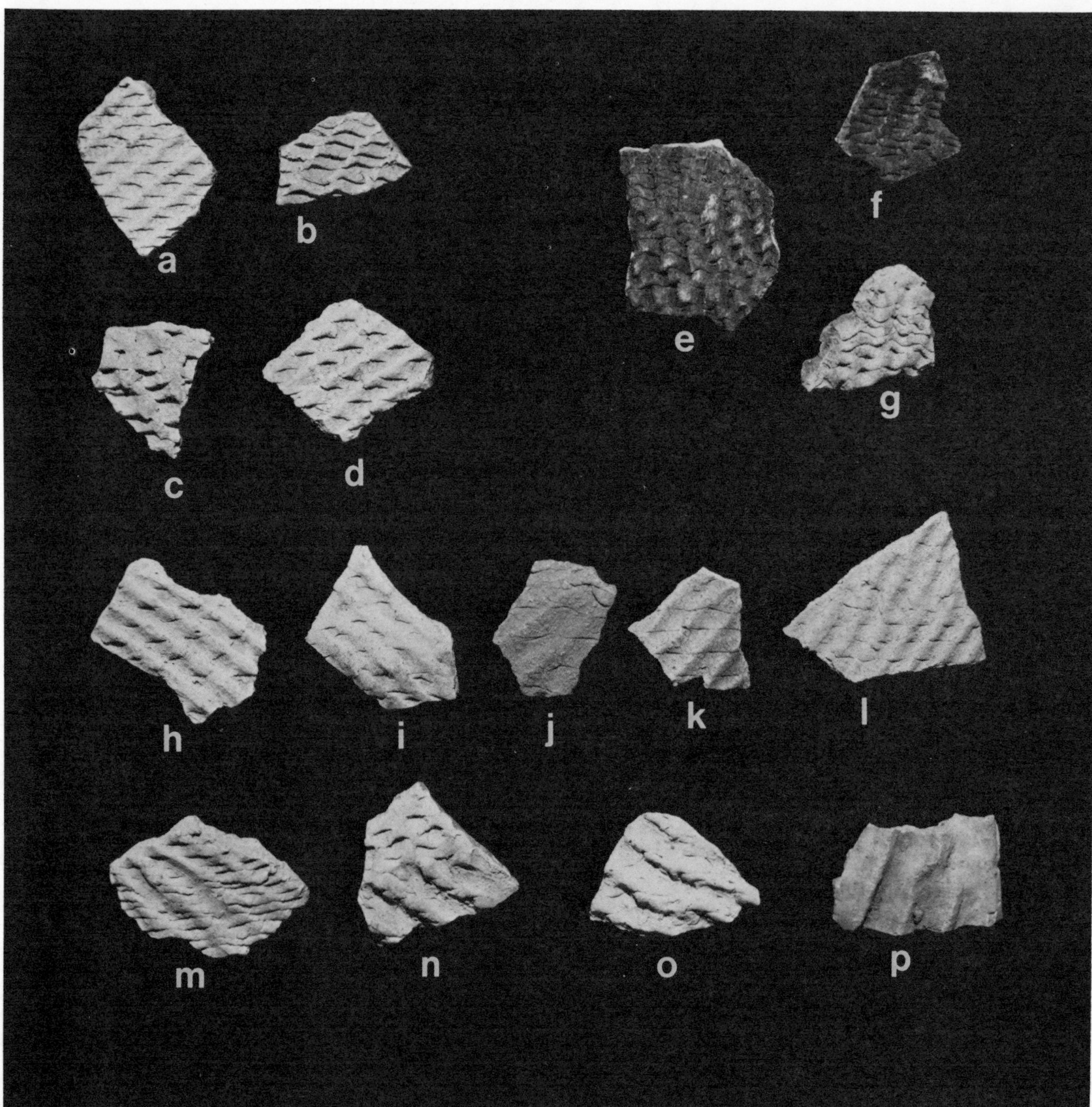

Figure 236. *Mancos Corrugated jar sherds.*

were tempered entirely with crushed sandstone, and several with a mixture of crushed igneous rock and sand, sandstone or unidentified gray tabular inclusions. Eight sherds of different vessels and numerous sherds of one patterned vessel, none of which was assignable to a specific type, were tempered with small specks of mica. The mica was primarily biotite, but muscovite appeared in several sherds. The mica temper is visible in the core and is especially prominent on both surfaces of the pottery. Particle size ranged from very fine to granular, but most vessels showed medium to coarse particles. The next most popular size was coarse to very coarse. Grains were generally angular, but about one-fifth of the vessels had particles tending toward subangular, and another one-fifth were definitely rounded.

About one-half of the material showed a carbon streak in the vessel walls, the result of incomplete oxidation of organic material in the paste. Where present, it generally forms lenses irregular in size and location rather than occupying a specific part of the wall. Occasionally it will form a strip of fairly uniform width through the center of the wall, occupying half to three-fourths of the wall's thickness. It may also be restricted to the inner one-fourth or one-third of the wall.

The interiors of most vessels are fine grained, the remaining few slightly grainy. Scraping marks are not visible on many specimens because of wiping over the scraping. Quite a few vessels show evidence of both scraping and wiping, or (rarely) scraping, wiping, and rubbing. The evenness of the surface of many vessels suggests initial scraping. The majority show wiping only, however.

Because of the corrugations, the exteriors are definitely grainier than the interiors but they are still only slightly grainy. Wiping is clearly evident on the high spots of most vessels, but only rarely can definite scraping marks be seen. Rubbing is even more rare on the exterior than on the interior.

Apparently all of the Mesa Verde and Mancos Corrugated pottery is spirally coiled. Careful observation of the exterior of corrugated jars will often reveal overlapping of the ends of coils (fig. 222a), but spiral coiling can be readily seen on the bottoms of jars (fig. 232). Fairly slender fillets of clay were pinched on from above as the vessel was built up by adding coils; the shingle effect is evident in figure 237, where the coils have separated because of poor attachment.

The flattening, indenting, or other manipulation of the coils was almost always restricted to the body of the vessel, except when the corrugations were carried onto the neck without interruption. A rare exception to this was a non-spiral fillet added at the top of the rim in a few specimens. The widths vary from 3 to 10 mm., and the fillet may be indented or unindented. In some cases, the fillet is irregular and partially obliterated, and may be merely a manipulation of the last coil placed on the vessel.

Many vessels and sherds, corrugated and black-on-white, have been mended by drilling conical holes from the exterior of the vessel on either side of a crack or break, and then binding them together with willow strips (fig. 238a) or yucca cordage (b and c). Rarely is the hole drilled from both sides. The shape of the holes in several typical cases can be seen better in figure 239, the general placement beside the crack in figure 221b and others. The size of the holes varies considerably; the largest shown (fig. 239c) is 13 mm. in diameter at the exterior end and 1.5 mm. at the inner end.

Undoubtedly many of the large, corrugated jars were used to store foodstuffs. Jars are often found buried in the subfloor fill of a room with the mouth flush with the floor. In many cases a slab cover will be found in place over the mouth of the jar. Some of the vessels, heavily coated with pinyon pitch on both sides, must have served as water containers. Water would quickly soak through the walls of a jar if it were not so coated. The total thickness of one pitch-coated sherd ranges from about 12 to 15 mm., and the thickness of the sherd itself is about 6 mm.

Figure 237. *Corrugated sherds showing shingle effect of superimposed spiral coils.*

Hovenweep Corrugated

One of the three or four main varieties of Mesa Verde Corrugated is the pottery called Hovenweep Corrugated by Abel (1955: Ware 10A—Type 8). I would call this pottery Mancos Corrugated: Hovenweep variety. It seems to appear late in the occupation of Mesa Verde (Abel suggests A.D. 1250 to 1300) and is probably a direct outgrowth of Mesa Verde Corrugated, into which it grades smoothly. On the basis of sherds only, Abel also named a plainware Hovenweep Gray, which is probably the counterpart of Keet Seel Gray, a northeastern Arizona type. Keet Seel Gray is dated about A.D. 1275 to 1300. Both of Abel's types were reported only from ruins in the Hovenweep National Monument area to the west of Mesa Verde. There were 792 sherds of Hovenweep Corrugated from Long House and five that might be Hovenweep Gray. They are probably Hovenweep Corrugated rim sherds on which the corrugations end slightly lower down on the vessel than usual.

In overall form, Hovenweep Corrugated is identical to Mesa Verde Corrugated (fig. 240). Most vessels from Long House would fall in the category of largest jars (Group IV) set up for Mesa Verde Corrugated. Unfortunately, complete sets of measurements can be taken on very few jars because of their fragmentary condition. The largest measurable vessel (fig. 240a) has a volume of 21,600 cc., is 40.5 cm. high, and has a maximum diameter of 36.1 cm. Its rim diameter is 22.4 to 23.0 cm., with an orifice diameter of 18.3 cm. The smallest specimens (fig. 240e and f) fall between Groups II and III in size. Jar e has a height of 17.4 cm.

The rim shape of Hovenweep Corrugated (fig. 223v–dd) is essentially the same as that of Mesa Verde Corrugated. There is less variety, but then there are far less sherds and vessels. The one noticeable difference is the height of the rim above its point of eversion: it is definitely higher on Hovenweep than on most Mesa Verde Corrugated vessels.

Hovenweep Corrugated differs from Mesa Verde Corrugated in several more significant aspects: surface treatment, temper, and rim

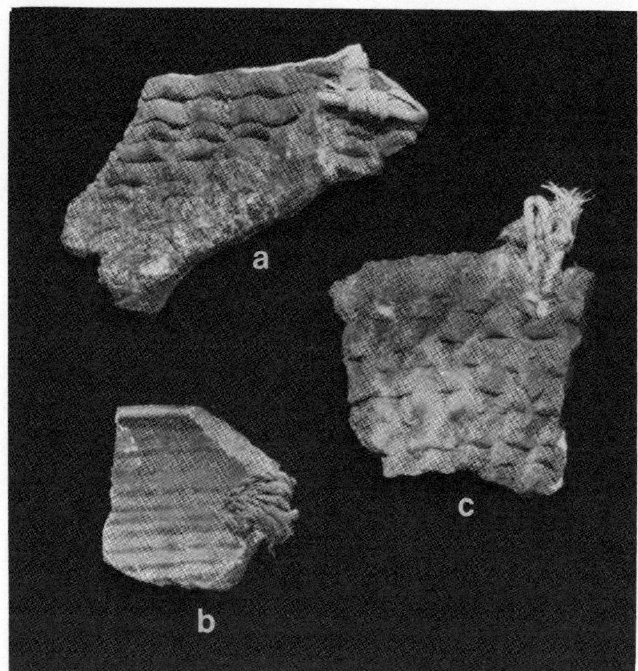

Figure 238. *Corrugated sherds mended by conical holes and willow strips (a) or yucca cordage (b and c).*

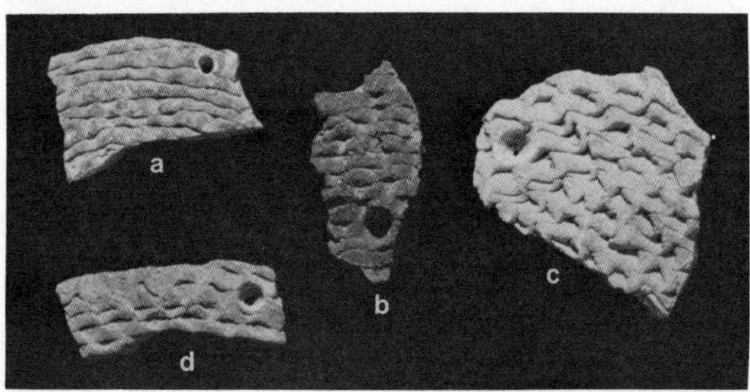

corrugation. The indentations are usually large and often squared. Occasionally they are smeared, a term that seems more accurate here than does smoothed or rubbed. The temper protrudes from inner and outer-wall faces, thus creating a pottery with a grainy surface more typical of Chapin Gray than Mesa Verde Corrugated.

The most distinctive and most common feature is the continuation of the corrugations to the rim on most of the vessels or rim sherds in the Long House collection. Figures 240 and 241 show several good examples of this. Note also the variation in surface finish and indentations in this and following figures.

With some vessels, the potter seems to have made some attempt to create a more pronounced rim fillet than was customary (fig. 242). On others, she produced an unindented corrugated rim (fig. 243a, b, and c). Occasionally the rim would be left plain (fig. 243h), with the corrugations extending to or almost to the eversion point.

Another interesting trait occurring on some vessels is diagonal ridging similar to that found on some Mancos Corrugated jars (fig. 244). On two sherds (fig. 244a and c) it is coupled with an indented corrugated rim.

Quite a few jars bear all the hallmarks of Hovenweep Corrugated except for coil and indentation size. Practically all of the obvious Hovenweep jars have wider coils and deeper indentations. Two sherds have the rough surface and squared indentations of some Hovenweep Corrugated, but the coil size is unusually small and the rim is not indented. Other sherds, apparently transitional between Mesa Verde and Hovenweep, are shown in figures 245 and 246.

The sherds in figure 245 lack the typical rough surface of Hovenweep Corrugated. However, they all have corrugated rims, some with a pronounced rim fillet, and are more typical of Hovenweep than Mesa Verde, but the body corrugation is typical of Mesa Verde Corrugated. A similar situation prevails with the sherds shown in figure 246. Here again, the surface finish is typical of Mesa Verde and, except for the size and depth, so is the indentation. Undoubtedly many sherds with equally large indentations have been called Mesa Verde Corrugated during analysis. The unique feature is the

Figure 239. *(Above) Corrugated sherds with conical mend holes.*

Figure 240. *Hovenweep Corrugated jar sherds.*

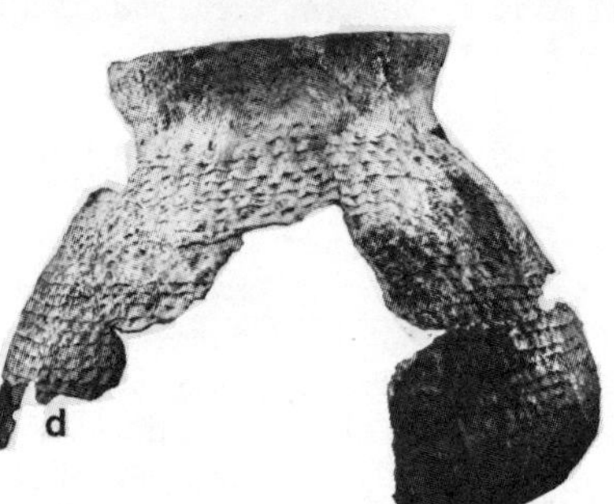

indented rim. Also, as seen in figure 246a–c, the rim is higher above the eversion point than is common with Mesa Verde Corrugated.

Additional examples of Hovenweep Corrugated, showing the tremendous range of surface manipulation, are illustrated in figures 247 to 251. Figure 248b displays an applique of unknown design; c, the beginning of the spiral coiling; d, a possible attempt at patterning by periodically alternating wide and narrow coils. Figures 249 and 250 show various degrees of smoothing. Figure 250a–d reveals a progression from barely smoothed to almost obliterated on sherds whose surfaces are more typical of Hovenweep Corrugated than those in figure 249.

Patterning is also common in Hovenweep Corrugated. Interspersing bands of unindented coils among indented ones can be seen in figure 251a–e; a–c are probably from one jar. Figure 251g has short, tooled marks running vertically across two or three coils, and h–k bear fingernail impressions. Only one sherd (f) bearing interior rim ricks in carbon paint, was found.

The provenience of a good part of the Hovenweep material would place it in the period A.D. 1250 to 1280. Quite a bit of it is either from rooms or kivas with tree–ring dates for the period mentioned or from structures which, by virtue of their physical position, were built later in time. In several rooms, it is stratigraphically above Mancos Corrugated and McElmo Black-on-white, which would tend to emphasize its position in the later part of the occupation. It is also associated with these types in some instances, primarily in upper levels of possibly earlier structures, but never below them or even associated with them in the lowest stratigraphic level.

Technologically, the definite Hovenweep Corrugated and the indeterminate material that might be Mesa Verde Corrugated are identical.

The thickness of the vessel wall varies from 4 to 11 mm. and, like that of Mesa Verde Corrugated, averages 5 to 6 mm. The bottom tends to be thicker, ranging from 8 to 11 mm., with the lower figures being more common.

The temper is predominantly crushed igneous rock, but there is

Figure 241. *Hovenweep Corrugated jar sherds.*

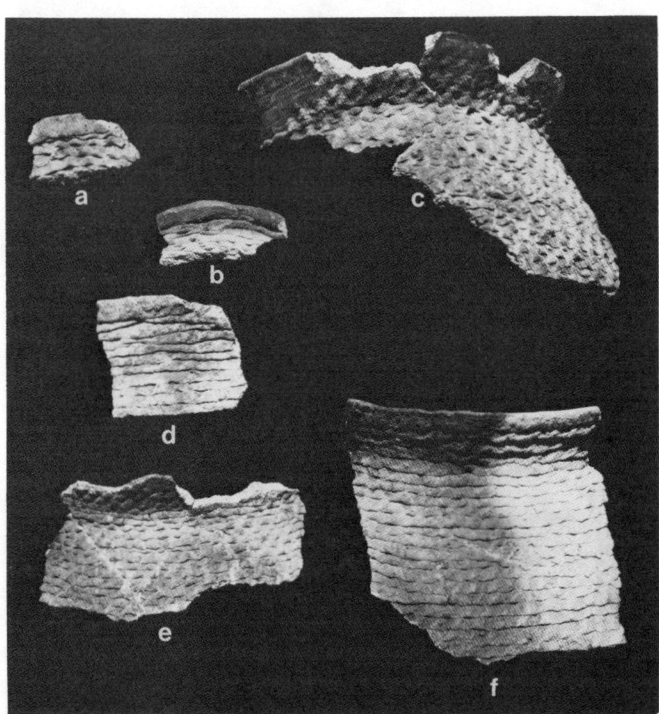

Figure 242. *Hovenweep Corrugated jar sherds.*

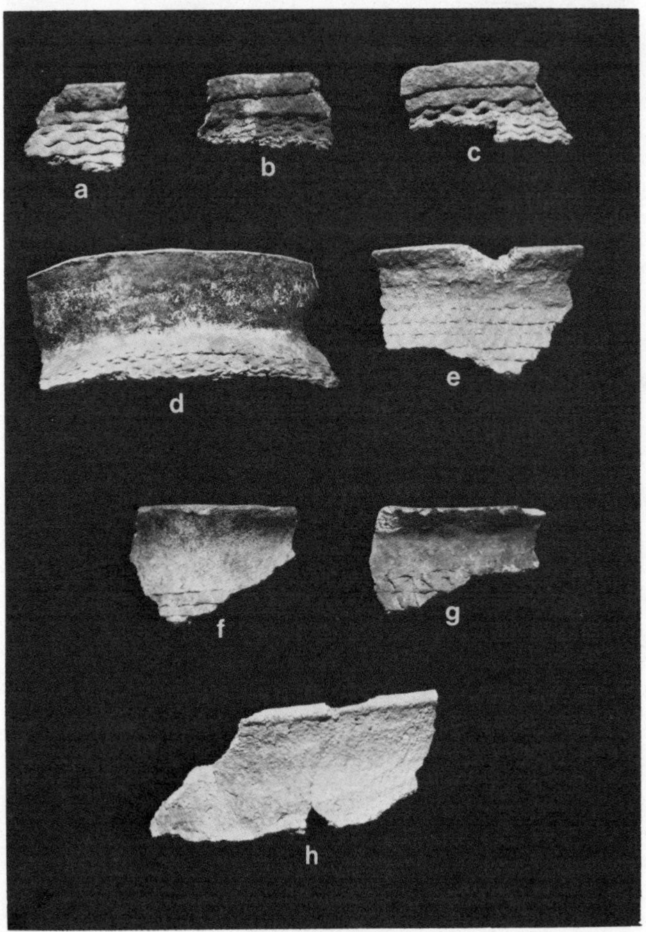

Figure 243. *Unindented corrugated jar sherds.*

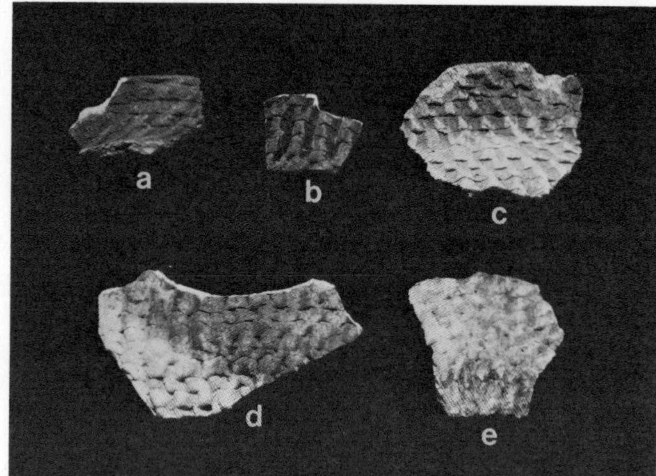

Figure 244. *Corrugated sherds with diagonal ridging.*

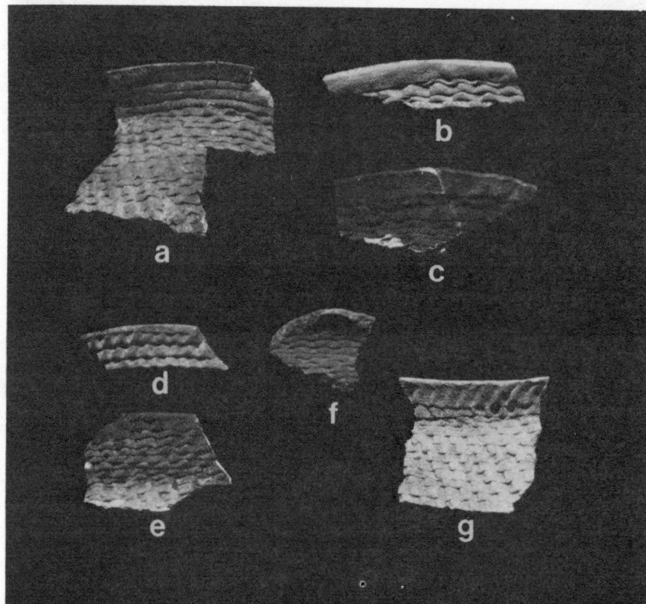

Figure 245. *Corrugated jar sherds apparently transitional between Mesa Verde and Hovenweep.*

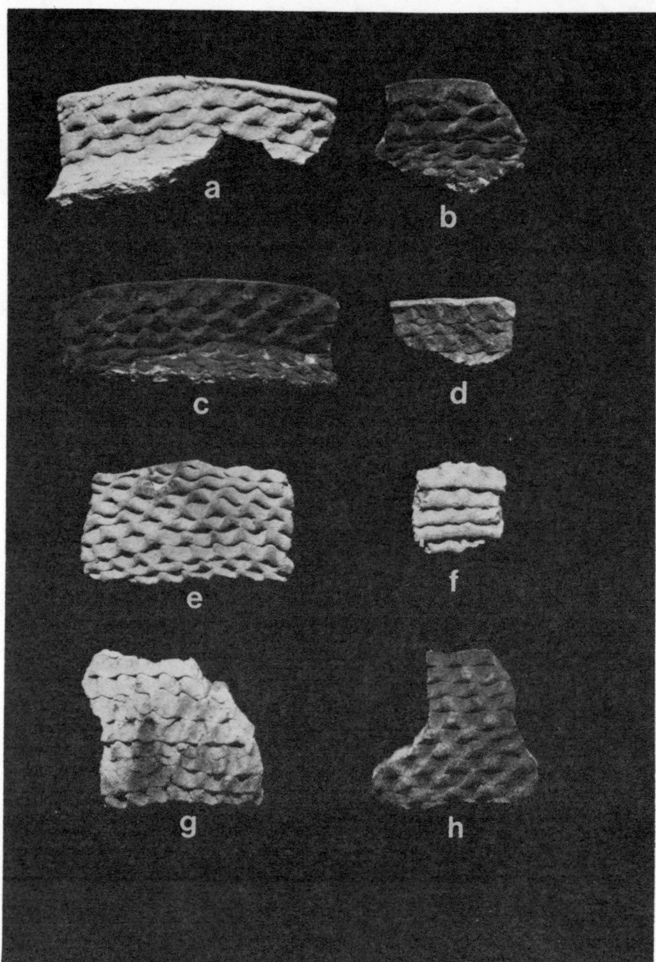

Figure 246. *Corrugated jar sherds apparently transitional between Mesa Verde and Hovenweep.*

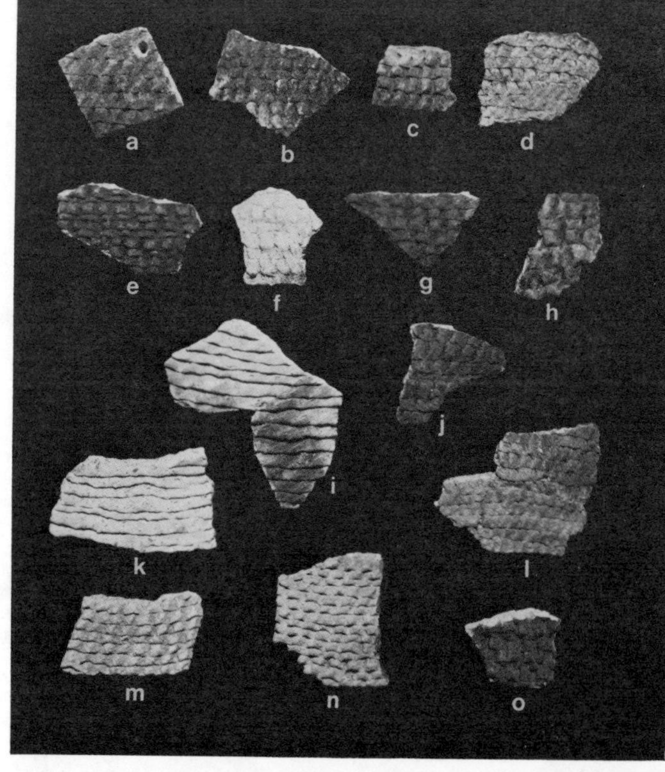

Figure 247. *(Right) Hovenweep Corrugated jar sherds.*

a small amount of crushed rock combined with sand, sherd, or crushed sandstone. Grain size is almost equally divided between coarse and very coarse, and sorting is about equally divided between poorly and fairly well sorted. With only one exception, the particles are angular in shape.

Unlike Mesa Verde Corrugated, Hovenweep Corrugated shows very little difference in surface finish from interior to exterior. With the exception of a few sherds and vessels that show evidence of scraping and rubbing on the inner and outer surface, the method of finishing was by wiping. As with the other varieties of corrugated pottery, the vessel may have been scraped first and then wiped, but all traces of the scraping have been obscured. On the interior, the resulting texture was slightly grainy in the largest number of specimens, but with almost an equal number being grainy; a smaller but still surprisingly large number show a fine texture. Since the wiping was limited to the high spots on the exterior, the finish was mainly grainy, with a few being slightly grainy and an occasional specimen showing a fine texture.

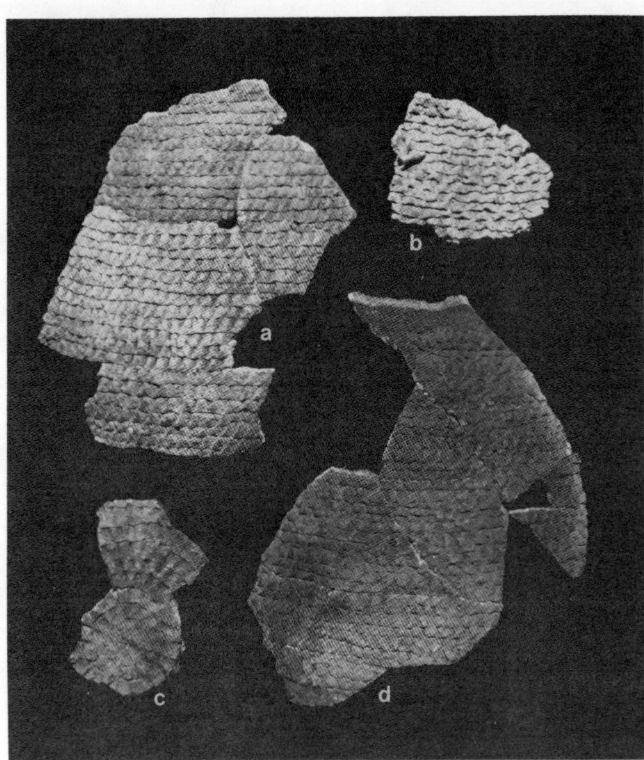

Figure 248. *Hovenweep Corrugated jar sherds.*

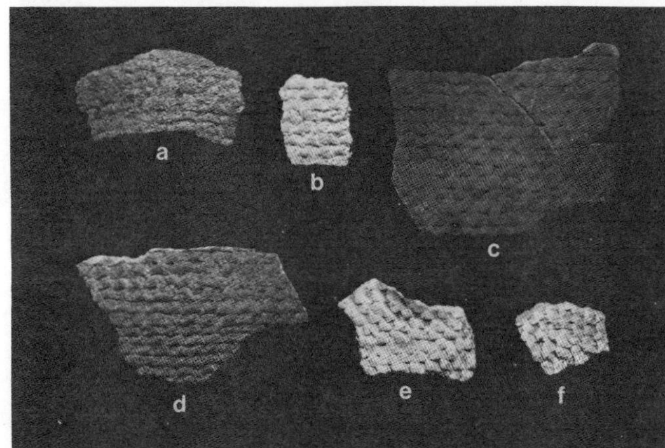

Figure 249. *Hovenweep Corrugated jar sherds.*

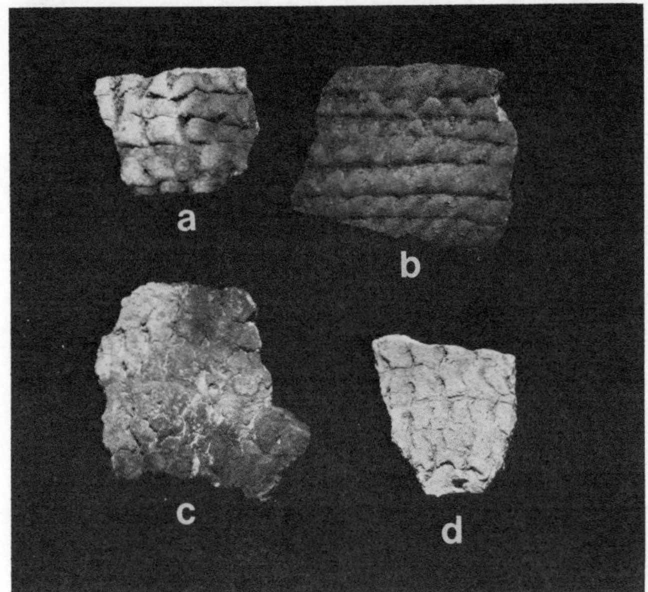

Figure 250. *Hovenweep Corrugated jar sherds.*

Figure 251. *Hovenweep Corrugated jar sherds, patterned.*

Few vessels showed evidence of a carbon streak. Where present, it formed lenses in the central one-third of the vessel wall.

Coil width ranges from 4 to 8 mm., and averages about 5 mm. The width of the rim fillet is spread evenly from 6 to 11 mm. The diagonal alinement of the indentations is almost equally proportioned among poor, fair, and good. The most common variation of those illustrated or discussed is the corrugated neck indented to the rim with no rim fillet.

The four pottery types of Mesa Verde Gray Ware which preceded Mancos Corrugated are Mancos Gray, Moccasin Gray, Chapin Gray, and Mummy Lake Gray. The first three are represented in the Long House pottery, although in relatively small quantities. There seems little point in discussing these in detail because of lack of architectural association—with the exception of Pithouse I (Basketmaker III stage)—and the limited number of sherds of each type. Instead, I have followed the published descriptions in classifying this pottery and have illustrated a few examples of each type. For comparative purposes, a brief description of each type, as represented in Long House, follows.

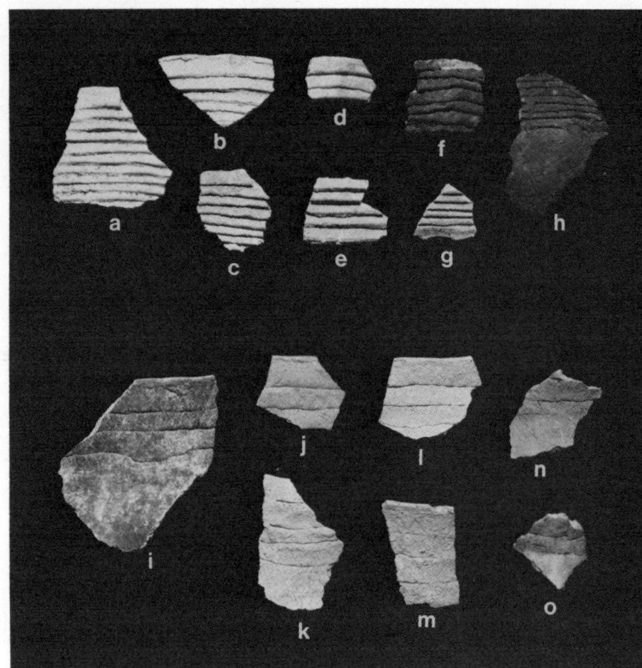

Figure 252. *Mancos Gray sherds (a-g), and Moccasin Gray sherds (i-o).*

Mancos Gray

Mancos Gray (Abel, 1955: Ware 10A—Type 4) is an obvious outgrowth of Moccasin Gray, and an equally obvious ancestor of Mancos Corrugated. Abel places it in the early Pueblo II stage, giving dates of A.D. 875 to 950. There are only 44 sherds in the Long House collection. They came from all parts of the ruin—rooms, kivas, trash slopes, and other designated areas. The distribution and stratigraphic position tells us nothing of their original association.

The sherds in figure 252a–g convey little of the vessel form, other than that they were apparently high-necked jars or pitchers. Only two rim shapes were present (fig. 253). To judge by figure 252, the unindented spiral coiling comes well down onto the shoulder of the jar. Rough scoring between the coils can be seen in a and b, and g shows the use of a sharper tool for the same purpose. This last sherd was also smoothed, thus flattening the coils slightly. Some indentation of the coils can be seen in sherd f but is probably inadvertent. Coil width on most specimens is apparently the same as that found on Mancos Corrugated and Mesa Verde Corrugated. Occasionally it approaches Moccasin Gray in width.

Wall thickness of the pottery varies from 4 to 7 mm., and averages 4 to 5 mm. The temper is either coarse or very coarse. It was poorly or fairly well sorted in all but two sherds, where temper was well sorted. All of the temper is crushed rock, and the particles are angular.

Both interior and exterior surfaces were wiped only, resulting in a slightly grainy texture in most cases. A few sherds were either quite fine or very grainy in texture.

Moccasin Gray

Moccasin Gray (Abel, 1955: Ware 10A—Type 3) is essentially the same pottery as Chapin Gray, from which it is derived, except that the concentric coils around the neck have not been obliterated (fig. 252i–o). It is a Pueblo I stage pottery, dated by Abel at about A.D. 800 to 900. As with Mancos Gray, the Moccasin sherds—56 in all—were scattered throughout the ruin. There was a heavier concentration of sherds on the East Trash Slope than was the case with Mancos Gray, perhaps lending slight support to a questionable Pueblo I occupation at the east end of the ruin.

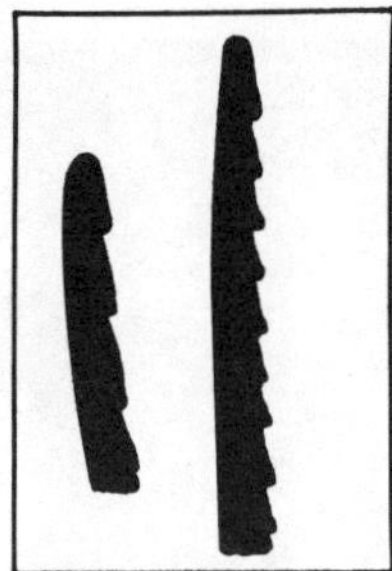

Figure 253. *Mancos Gray rim shapes.*

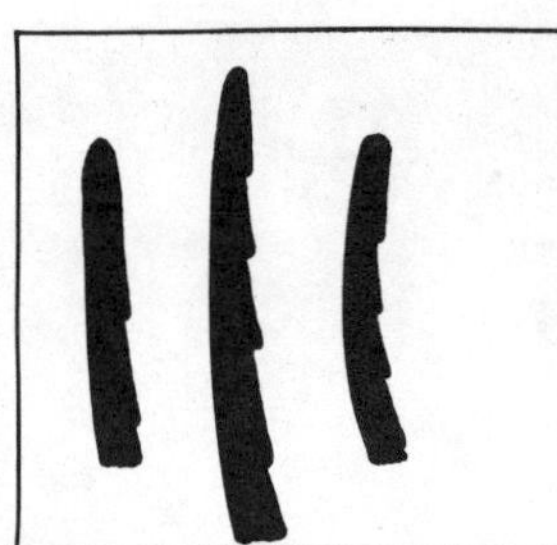

Figure 254. *Moccasin Gray rim shapes.*

Judging from the fragmentary remains of Moccasin Gray vessels, the general form was probably similar to that of Mancos Gray. Figure 252i shows a high neck, with just the beginning of the swell into the sidewall of the jar. As in Mancos Gray, rim forms were limited (fig. 254). There is no evidence of a sharp break in curvature between sidewall and neck on most sherds. Figure 252o is an exception, with a distinct break at the junction of body and neck. Coil widths range from 10 to 20 mm., generally, but occasionally approach the narrower width typical of Mancos Gray. Quite a few sherds are obviously transitional between the two types and cannot be classified as one or the other.

Wall thickness of the sherds varies from 4 to 6 mm., and averages 5 mm. The temper is predominantly crushed rock, but a few sherds show a mixture of crushed rock and sand, and crushed rock and sherds. The grain size varies from medium to granular, but is mostly coarse and very coarse. Sorting is divided between poorly and fairly well sorted, with a few sherds showing well-sorted temper. Both angular and subround particles are present in a few sherds, the remainder having angular particles only.

Evidence of scraping is visible on the exterior and interior of a few sherds, but the balance show that wiping was the common method of finishing. The exterior of the sherds tend to be largely grainy, but with quite a few sherds being only slightly grainy. This situation is reversed for the interior, and a few sherds have a fine texture.

Chapin Gray

Chapin Gray (Abel, 1955: Ware 10A–Type 4, AD 450–900), the base type of Mesa Verde Gray Ware, shows more variety in shape than those that follow it. Probably this is due to black-on-white pottery taking over functions first provided by the plain ware. There were five whole or restorable vessels (table 9), and 3,519 sherds of Chapin Gray—6 percent of the total recovered from Long House.

The form of Chapin Gray includes jars or pitchers with vertical necks up to 6.4 cm. high, some of which join the body in a smooth curve (figs. 255a and 256b), and jars with very short, vertical necks, about 0.7 cm. (fig. 255e). A variation of this form is figure 255b, which has a moderately short and recurved or everted neck. The "seed jar" was another very popular shape (fig. 256b and d, and 255f, possibly g). Bowls are also in evidence (figs. 255c and 256a), but because of the rough surface finish it is often difficult to determine whether a sherd is from a bowl or a jar. The full range of rim shapes for Chapin Gray from Long House is shown in figure 257.

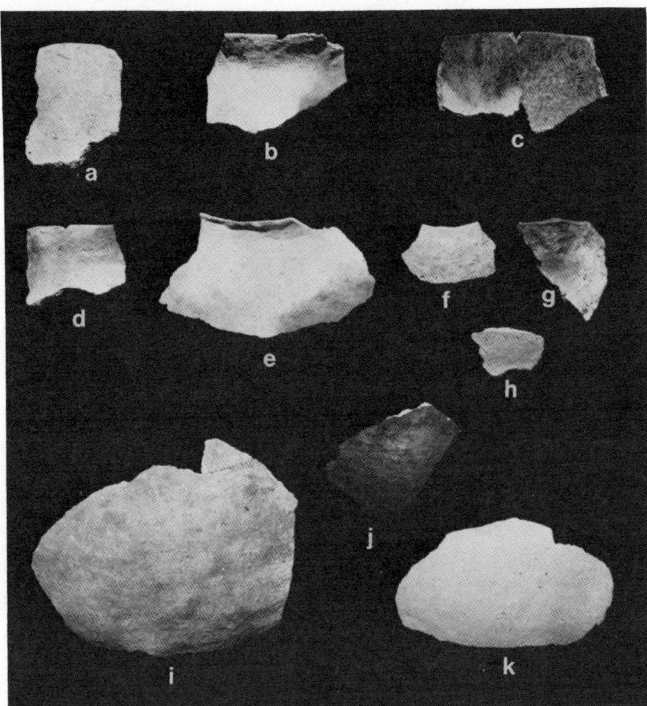

Figure 255. *Chapin Gray bowl and jar sherds.*

Figure 256a shows very well the similarity in finish on some bowl interiors and exteriors. Figure 255c has been well smoothed on the exterior (not shown) and polished to a low luster on the interior. This and jar sherds, figure 255j and k, would have been called Twin Trees Plain by Abel (1955: Ware 10A—Type 2). Twin Trees is merely a polished variety of Chapin Gray; as treated herein, the description of Chapin Gray is expanded to include the so-called Twin Trees material.

A few jar sherds of Chapin Gray bear an impermanent red (hematite?) paint on the exterior surface (fig. 255i). This is generally called "fugitive red." There is no obvious stratigraphic significance to either the fugitive red or polished variations of Chapin Gray.

I must admit that many of the sherds classified as Chapin Gray may be plain portions of Moccasin or Mancos Gray, or even Chapin Black-on-gray or Piedra Black-on-white. Hence, table 8 shows the breakdown by Chapin Variety sherds, as shown by rim shape or other obvious features, and indeterminate sherds, i.e., those that appeared to be Chapin on the basis of surface finish and temper.

Other than smoothing or polishing there is no working of the surface on the Chapin Gray pottery, with one possible exception. Figure 255h—probably Chapin Gray—bears part of a sharply incised design.

One characteristic of quite a few Chapin Gray sherds, not seen on sherds definitely identified as later types, is a smoky, greasy stain

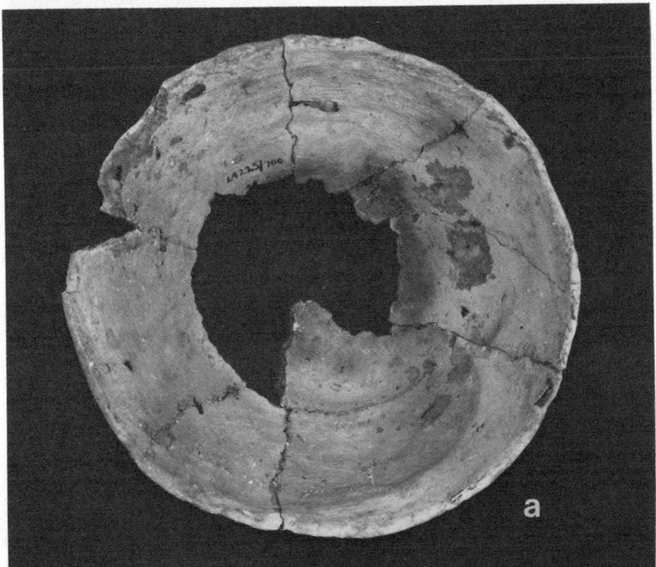

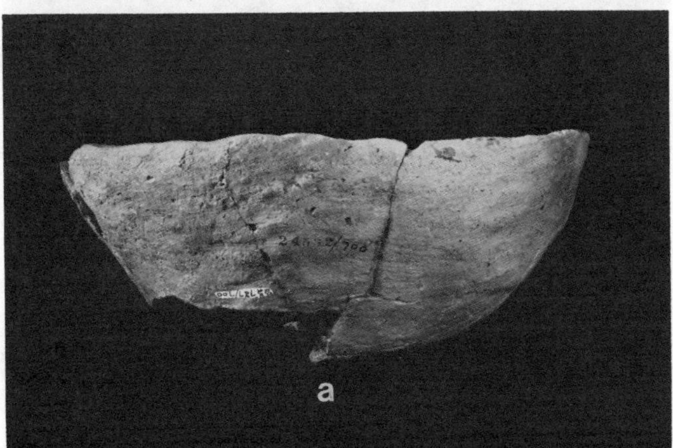

Figure 256. *Chapin Gray bowls and jars.*

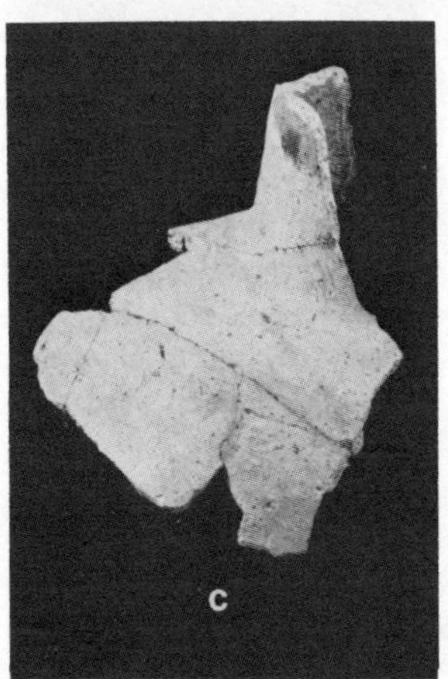

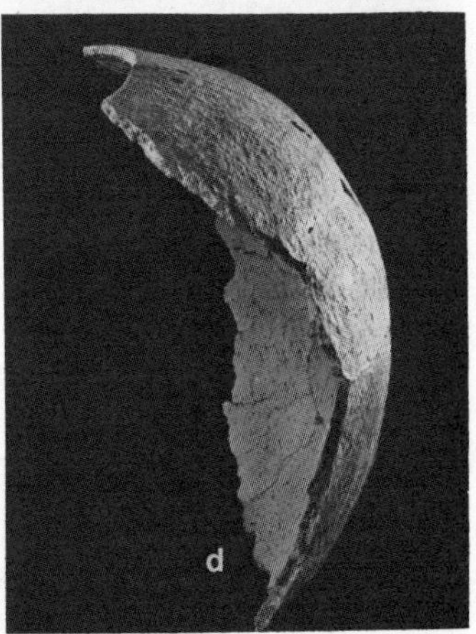

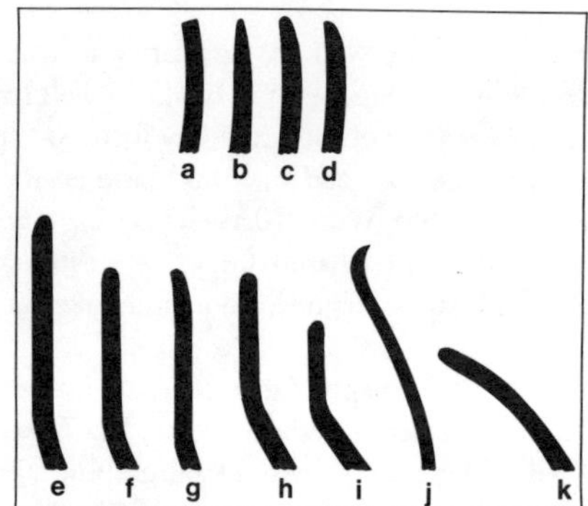

Figure 257. *Chapin Gray bowl rim shapes (a-d) and jar rim shapes (e-k).*

which may give the sherd a slightly lustrous appearance (fig. 255j). This is probably the result of using the vessel for cooking, but why it does not appear on other types I do not know. Some of the sherds are burned, both in use and as a result of firing.

The thickness of the vessel wall ranges from 3 to 7 mm., and averages 5 mm. for the 50 sherds of Chapin Gray analyzed in detail. Once again, the temper was almost entirely crushed rock, with only a few sherds showing crushed rock and sandstone or sand alone. There were also a few sherds with a tabular gray material that could not be identified. The temper was almost equally divided between coarse and very coarse particles, with only a few grains being of medium size. Sorting was poorer than in Mancos Gray or Moccasin Gray, with most of the sherds showing temper that was poorly sorted. In a few sherds, the temper was well sorted or fairly well sorted. As in Moccasin Gray, both angular and subround particles were present in a few sherds, and rounded particles only were found in two sherds. Most of the sherds were tempered with angular particles.

Wiping, or wiping and rubbing, were the common ways of finishing the vessel surface, both inside and out. Scraping marks were obvious on a few sherds. Undoubtedly, many of the vessels were first roughly scraped and then wiped or rubbed, with only the latter step being visible on the finished surface of some bowls and jars. The surface of the restorable vessels was bumpy and pitted, definitely more so than on Mancos or Moccasin Gray. The potter apparently expended little effort in producing an even surface. About a fifth of the sherds examined showed a low surface luster and would have been called Twin Trees Plain by Abel.

PLAIN WARE

As might be expected in any pottery collection, there are numerous sherds, and a few whole vessels, which are unpainted counterparts of Mesa Verde Black-on-white and the types which preceded it at Mesa Verde. With the exception of the McElmo-Mesa Verde material, most of these sherds cannot be assigned to a specific type. Needless to say, rim sherds form the basis of these categories, because plain body sherds—especially from low on the vessel—could as well have come from the undecorated portions of black-on-white vessels.

Figure 258 is a good example of a jar that can be assigned fairly safely to McElmo or Mesa Verde Black-on-white on the basis of such attributes as shape, surface finish, and wall thickness. The jar is slipped but bears no painted decoration. A similar situation prevails in the case of a slipped but unpainted dipper (fig. 259c), which is certainly either McElmo or Mesa Verde Black-on-white. There were 69 sherds, slipped and unslipped, from the ruin that can be placed in the McElmo-Mesa Verde category, and many more that were doubtful. Although the squared rim of bowls and dippers is a prime diagnostic trait of this pottery type, many rims show up that are slightly rounded and have vessel walls that are thinner and more tapered toward the lip. Thus many rim sherds could just as well be Mancos Black-on-white as Mesa Verde or McElmo. Temper is of no help here because all three types are rather similar in this trait, and all can show considerable variation from the expected "norm."

More difficult to classify are miniature vessels, such as the dippers shown in figure 258a and b. Both are probably unslipped and unpainted Mesa Verde or McElmo Black-on-white, however, judging by shape and archeological context. Smaller, subminiature vessels are discussed in the following section of this report.

Two more vessels difficult to classify are shown in figure 260. Jar a is probably Basketmaker III or Pueblo I plain ware, and thus probably Chapin Gray. Morris (1939 Pls. 188, f and l, and 227, x) illustrates miniature vessels from these stages that are similar to the one from Long House, both in rim shape and general appearance.

The other jar (fig. 260b), a miniature seed jar, defies classification. Its height is 4.5 cm., its diameter 6.5 cm.; the diameter of the opening is 1.8 cm. It is very crudely made and shaped but polished to a low luster. It was fired to a red-orange color over most of the vessel. The temper is crushed sandstone and ranges in size from fine to granule. It was probably a toy, accidentally overfired when included with other larger vessels for firing.

Several plain handles, not necessarily all from plain vessels, that cannot be assigned to specific pottery types are shown in figure 261. The large, down-curved lug handle (one specimen, top view, fig. 261a; another, bottom view, fig. 261c) is typical of some jar handles described for Pueblo I by Morris (1939, p. 172). The horizontal loop handle (fig. 261b) is well established in Pueblo I, also, according to Morris, but the flattened cross section and squared corners are certainly more typical of Pueblo II and III. The sherd shown is most likely from a Pueblo II–III black-on-white jar.

The two-strand handle (fig. 261e) can be found from Basketmaker III to Pueblo III times on pitchers and jars. The handle shown is different from most in that the break between the two fillets of clay forming the handle has been accentuated by drawing a twig or some such object between the strands.

The simple lug handle is prevalent in Basketmaker III jars and continues into Pueblo I (Morris, 1939, p. 172). The one shown (fig.

Figure 258. *Plain Ware jar.*

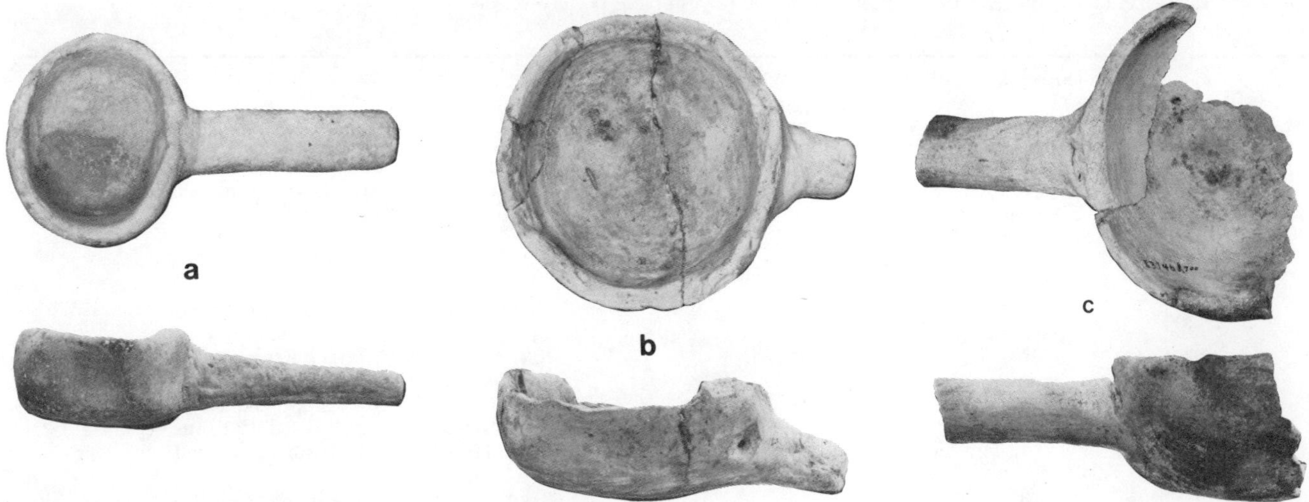

Figure 259. *Plain Ware dippers; bowl of b, 7.8 cm., and of c, 11.5 cm.*

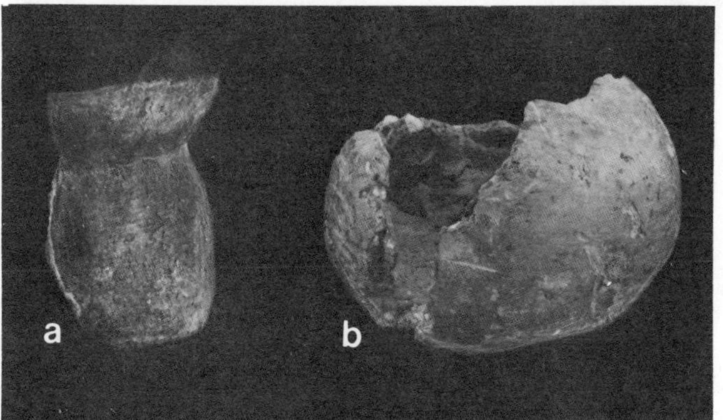

Figure 260. *Plain Ware miniature jars.*

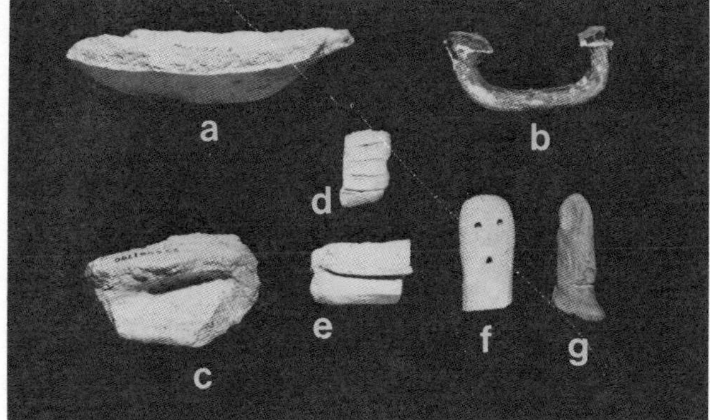

Figure 261. *Plain Ware handles.*

261d) is unusual only in having sharply incised lines on the upper surface. Morris (1939, Pl. 234, b) illustrates similar work on a lug handle.

Figure 261g is probably a jar handle from an unknown time period. Its prime decoration consists of a squeezed-up "beak" at its outer end. There is also a short groove running crossways near the attachment to the vessel. The groove may have been an additional attempt at decoration.

The handle shown in figure 261f has three small holes punched in it—giving it a face-like appearance—and possibly comes from a dipper.

UNFIRED POTTERY

It was extremely difficult to classify the 357 unfired sherds recovered from the fill, but most were probably on the way to becoming McElmo or Mesa Verde Black-on-white. Only eight were tentatively identified as Basketmaker III pottery. There were several others that definitely predate the Pueblo III stage, but they could fall anywhere between the Basketmaker III and late Pueblo II stages. Two sherds were either Mesa Verde or Mancos Corrugated. These were the only corrugated sherds in the group. In many cases it was impossible to differentiate bowl, dipper, jar, and mug sherds because of erosion, and the classification according to shape of quite a few is open to argument.

Of the 41 sherds which appeared to bear traces of paint, only three showed a fairly dark and clear design. In most cases, the paint was light in tone and difficult to see.

The rough classification of unfired sherds is given in table 15.

WORKED SHERDS

Few of the 341 worked sherds from Long House were well-shaped artifacts. Most showed little or no attempt at shaping, either by breaking or grinding of the edge. A sherd from a broken vessel was often used as found, regardless of vessel type or portion of the vessel from which it came.

The size of the worked sherds varied tremendously, with the largest—an obvious scoop—being roughly one-third of a large black-on-white bowl. This unusual specimen (fig. 163d) is 27.4 cm. long, and the bowl from which it came had an estimated diameter of 28 cm. The smallest specimen which appeared to be complete was 2.3 cm. long.

More as a matter of curiosity than in the hope of learning anything significant, the sherds were separated into three categories: worked on one edge, worked on two or more edges, and worked all around the perimeter. Because of the fact that many sherds were fragments of larger worked sherds, the first two categories are not clearly distinct. Table 16 shows the classification of these two categories by pottery type and vessel shape.

Table 14. Measurements and provenience of illustrated whole or restorable pottery vessels.

Figure	Size (cm) Height	Diameter	Thickness	Weight (gm. or lbs. oz.)	Miscellaneous	Provenience	M.V.N.P. Catalog No.
158a	12.8	28.1				Kiva Q, Level I; Area X, $5^{1}/_{2}$, Level II	12969
b	12.2	30 estimate				General Feature 9, Area X, $5^{1}/_{2}$, Surface, fill and Level III; West Trash Slope	25980
c	12.5	32.5 estimate				Kiva C, upper fill; Kiva D, dist. fill; Kiva P, Level I and II, Room 37, near floor; Room 6, Level I, backdirt	33809
d	10.8	26.5 estimate				Kiva Q, Level I; Kiva M, Level III and VI	22670
e	12.6	27 estimate				Kiva A, fill; Kiva H, Level I; Room 1, fill and inside basket; Room 5, surface and fill	33804
f	12.8	28.9				Kiva N, Level V; Kiva J, upper and lower levels; Room 56, Levels II and III; Room 48, Level II; Room 57, surface, fill and subfloor II	13747
g	12.6	28 estimate				Kiva Q, Levels I, III, V; Kiva R, Levels III, IV, Room 51, fill	22760/ 700
h	12.8	28 estimate				Kiva T, Levels II, IV, V; Room 3, 4, fill	22782
i	12.5	30.5				With Burial 12, lower East Trash Slope	13767
159a	8.5	17.8				Burial 18, upper East Trash Slope	13770
b	8.2	13.8				Room 75, fill; Kiva N, interplastic space	22486
c	6.7	13.8				With Burial 9, East Trash Slope	13761
d	8.5	18.5 estimate				With Burial 12, Lower East Trash Slope	13779
e	—	20 estimate				Kiva P, Level I; Room 6, Level I	22711
f	7.4	18.4				With Burial 12, Lower East Trash Slope	13766
g	7.4	18.7				Burial 8, East Trash Slope	13757
h	7.1	18.6				Burial 8, East Trash Slope	13757
		estimate				East Trash Slope, below Burial 4	13774
161	12.5	28.8				With Burial 1, Lower East Trash Slope	12112
162a	12	29.7				Kiva P, Levels I and IV; Kiva U, Level X, Area X, $5^{1}/_{2}$, Levels I and III	33810
b	11.6	29.2				Kiva K, Levels I and V; Kiva O, Level V; Room 35, fill (floor); Areas V and VII, fill	28401
c	119	254				Room 82, Level II; Rooms 37 and 61; Kiva E; Area VII; Area X; surface and fill E of Kiva C, $5^{1}/_{2}$, Levels I and III	33818/ 700
d	117	305				Kiva U, Levels II, III, IV; Area X, Surface and East of Kiva P; West Trash Slope	24339
e	124	246 and 293				Kiva A, fill; Kiva C, upper fill; Kiva D, West trench; Room 37; Area XII; Area X, surface and fill	33819
163a	—	29.2 estimate				Kiva T, Level IV and V (floor); Room 1, fill; West Trash Slope	22784
b	—	—				Room 73, surface and fill; Room 79, Level II; Kiva O, surface and fill	28306
c	—	26 estimate				Kiva Q, levels I, III and IV; Kiva N, Level I	29154
163d	17.2 length	12.1 width		worked sherd		Kiva E, against West wall, floor undisturbed	22727
e	—	28 estimate				Kiva U, Level V, floor	24250
f	7.5	16.5 estimate				Kiva J, Lower level, on floor	28678
g	—	28				Kiva Q, Level II	22731
h	—	25 estimate				Kiva P, Levels I, III, fill and vent shaft; Kiva A, fill; Kiva D, dist. fill; Room 37, upper fill, Room 30, fill, backdirt	22725
164a	12.8	28.1				Kiva Q, Level I; Area X, $5^{1}/_{2}$, Level II	12969
b	—	—				Room 26, undist. fill; Room 36, dist. fill, Areas II, III, and IV; backdirt	29426
c	11.5	25				Kiva B, fill-2" above floor; Kiva P, Levels I and III; Kiva V, Level II; Room 82, Level III, Room 15, dist. fill; Area V, fill; Area X, surface	33811
d	12.8	28				Kiva T, Levels II, IV, V; Rooms 3, 4, fill	22782
e	12.6	27				Kiva A, fill; Kiva H, Level I, Room 1 fill and inside basket; Room 5, surface and fill	33804/ 700
f	12	29 estimate				Kiva Q, Level II; upper East Trash Slope; Lower East Trash Slope	22732

Table 14. Measurements and provenience of illustrated whole or restorable pottery vessels. (Continued)

Figure	Size (cm) Height	Diameter	Thickness	Weight (gm. or lbs. oz.)	Miscellaneous	Provenience	M.V.N.P. Catalog No.
g	—	25				Room 12, Level II, undist. fill; Area VII, fill	30506
176a	12	24.7				Room 37, upper fill; on and near floor	13280
b	13.5 estimate	25.7				Room 7, Levels V, VI; Kiva E, fill; Kiva F, fill; Area X, surface E of Kiva P, $5^1/_2$, Levels I to III	33812
c	14.7 estimate	33 estimate				Kiva U, Level III; West Trash Slope above post hole section; Area X, $5^1/_2$, Levels I and II; Area VII	25966
d	—	21.6				Kiva R, Levels IV, V and VI	28589
e	·11.4	29.9				Room 81, Level II; West Trash Slope	22603
f	12.3	27 estimate				Area X, $5^1/_2$, Levels I to III; Area VII; West Trash Slope	13826
182a					124 mm orifice diameter	Room 4, floor fill; Kiva T, fill and Level IV; West Trash Slope	12169
b		33.7 estimate				Room 83, Level I; Kiva C, fill; Kiva P, Level I; Kiva N, Level II; Room 9, fill; Area X, surface and fill E of Kiva P; Trash Slopes; Room 8; Area IX	13224
c					127 orifice diameter	Room 5, surface and fill; Kiva A, fill; Kiva P; Level I; West Trash Slope	13589
d	26.5 estimate	31.8 estimate			12.7 orifice diameter	Room 81, Level II, on flat slab	22496
e	—	—			11.4 orifice diameter; 57 neck height	Room 47 and 56, Level II; Room 81, Levels I, II, IV; Room 84, Level I; Kiva K, Levels III, IV; Kiva N, Level III and subfloor fill; Kiva B, fill; Kiva L, surface	24591
f	20 estimate	23 estimate				Kiva R, Levels I, IV, V, VI and fill; Room 50 subfloor; Room 28, fill; Room 72, fill	22743
g		37 estimate				Kiva P, Level I; Kiva Q, Level I; Upper East Trash Slope	22721/ 700
h	—					Area VII, below Room 31	13750
i	—	—			11.1 orifice diameter	Room 12, Level II; Room 13, fill; Room 14, fill 2 on or near floor 2, Eastern half, Level II, top of floor	13249
j	—	—			11.5 orifice diameter	Room 14, Level II and top of floor 1; Room 37, against wall N of firepit	13248
k	—	—				With Burial 12, Lower East Trash Slope	13778
l	—	—				Room 2, fill between floors 3 and 5; Room 10, fill; Area X, fill E of Kiva P, West Trash Slope and Lower East Trash Slope	33821
188a	9.4	14.6			7.5 orifice diameter	With Burial 12, Lower East Trash Slope	13773
b	—	—			7 orifice diameter	With Burial 10, Lower East Trash Slope	13775
190a	13.55	19.4			11 exterior rim diameter	Kiva I, ventilator shaft	12158
b	14.7	25.6			7.5 orifice diameter 8.5 interior rim diameter	Room 35, Subfloor; Room 12, Level II; Kiva E, fill; Kiva F, fill	13244
c	15	19.8			7 orifice diameter	Room 47, Levels I and II; Room 54, Level II; Room 81, Level II	22382
d	—	—				Room 37, against wall, N of firepit, 0.1-0.2 above floor	13286
e	—	—			7 estimate orifice diameter	Kiva L, surface, fill, subfloor, NE interwall space; Kiva O, Level III, V, VI	28308
f	—	—			2.4 exterior rim height	Kiva K, Levels II and III	29107
g	—	—				Room 14, Levels I and II, top of floor 1; Room 15, disturbed fill	30509
193a	4.5	11				With Burial 1, Lower East Trash Slope	12111
b	5.4	12 estimate				Room 12, Level II	13235
c	4.9	13.6				Room 28, fill; Room 26, disturbed fill	13269
d	4	11.2				Kiva P, Level III	22715
e	5.3	12.6				Room 85, Level II	22624
f	6	11.8				Kiva O, Level VI; Kiva K, Level II; Room 80, Level II	22708
194a	4.2	11 estimate				Kiva H, floor	13704/ 700
b	—	12.2				Kiva U, Levels III and IV	24249
c	5.8	—				Room 16, fill	29628
d	4.2 estimate	12.5 estimate				Room 75, Level I	22472
e		11 estimate			153 handle length 33 handle diameter	Room 11 and between walls of Kiva E, loose fill; Kiva E, fill; Area VII, fill	33816

Table 14. Measurements and provenience of illustrated whole or restorable pottery vessels. (Continued)

	Size (cm)			Weight			
Figure	Height	Diameter	Thickness	(gm. or lbs. oz.)	Miscellaneous	Provenience	M.V.N.P. Catalog No.
f	5	10.3				With Burial 15, Upper East Trash Slope	13764
g	—	—			4.5 handle wide 1.85 handle thick	Room 60, Levels II, III, IV; Upper East Trash Slope	30786
h	4.8	11.7			154 handle long 34 handle diameter	Kiva U, Levels III and IV, and fill in and around Kiva walls	24338
197a	8.7	9.5			6.4 orifice (inside) diameter	Room 12, Level II	13233/700
b	10.3	10.6			6.5 orifice (inside) diameter	Burial 29, Room 48	13293
c	?	?				Burial 12, Lower East Trash Slope	13769
d	9.3	9.7			6.7 orifice (inside) diameter	Burial 4, surface Lower East Trash Slope	13772
e	10.3	13			8.2 orifice (inside) diameter	Kiva Q, Level II	22723
f	9	9.9			6.1 orifice (inside) diameter	Burial 8, East Trash Slope	13758
g	10.5	11.4			7.1 orifice (inside) diameter	Burial 7, East Trash Slope	13763
h	8.4	10.9			6.5 orifice (inside) diameter	Room 12, Level II	13250
i	9.4	8.8				Area VI, 1.5′ below E. wall of Great Kiva, in fill beneath E. wall of Great Kiva	24554
j	8.9	9				Kiva C, surface—fill	22642
k	9	9.2				Kiva Q, Levels III and IV	22734
l	9	10.4				Room 56, Level II; Room 74, Surface; Upper East Trash Slope	29091
m	8.9	9				Room 50, subfloor test and fill	22401
n	8.8	8.6				Kiva D, disturbed fill	13593
o	10	11.5			7.2 orifice (inside) diameter	Burial 9, East Trash Slope	13762
p	9.7	94.5			7.8 orifice (inside) diameter	Kiva Q, Level IV	22736
198n	—	—			6.0 orifice diameter estimate	Lower East Trash Slope	27489/700
o	8.8	9.1			9.1 orifice diameter—exterior	Room 7, Level VI	22377
p	8.7	10.2 estimate			7.0 orifice diameter estimate	Room 12, Level II	13245
201a	11.8	11.5				Room 60, Level III	22444
b	8.1	16.8			length, 5.7 width, 2.9 orifice diameter	Room 7, Level IV	22371
219a	—	11.3 estimate			7.3 orifice diameter exterior	Area IV, Level III	22830/700?
b	—	—			8.0 orifice diameter	Room 12, Level II, undisturbed fill	30508
220a	16	16.2	9.9			Burial 8, Lower East Trash Slope	13760
b	17.5	17.9	11.6			Room 9, fill	13226
221a	34.7	40.3	26.7			Room 74, subfloor	22468
b	34.7	34	22.6			Kiva T, Levels III and IV	30908
c	36.2	34.8	26			Kiva Q, Levels III and IV	29108
d						Burial 29, Room 48, Level III	13298
e	40.5	39.9	—			Room 75, subfloor	25490
f						Kiva J, banquette	13724
g						Kiva H, floor	13721
h						Kiva H, floor	13720
222a	36	34.5				Room 47, Level II and III	22383
b	—	30	20.5			Kiva O, Levels IV and V	28207
c	—	33.3				Kiva P, fill below recess, floor level SW corner of S. recess	24188
d	—	24.7				Room 48, Level III	27958/700
e	25.2	28.1				Room 54, general Feature 8	24203
240a	40.5	36.1		20		Kiva J, 6" above floor	13726
b	32.9	34.5		21.2		Room 60, Levels III and V floor	30513
c		28	20 exterior			Kiva Q, Levels I, II, III, IV	12187
d		31		15		Kiva P, fill below recess, floor level	24190
e		17.4				Kiva J, Lower level	28676
f			14			Kiva Q, Levels I, II, III, IV, VI	24225
256a	7.4 estimate	16.6				Room 55, Level IX floor; Kiva Q, Level I and NE interpilaster space	22425
c	9.8	12.2	8			Pithouse 1, floor	25576
d						Pithouse 1, floor	20587
259a		4.6			8.6 total length 4.9 handle length	Burial 12, Lower East Trash Slope	13768
b	2.7	6.45			1.6 handle length 1.6 handle diameter	Room 55, Level IV, floor	22419
c	5.4	11.4			3.4 handle diameter	Area V, fill	30907
260a					1.6 rim height	Room 66, subfloor fill	29094/700
b	4.5	6.4				Kiva Q, in fill behind NE pilaster	24223

Table 15. Unfired sherds.

Painted (all probably McElmo-Mesa Verde Black-on-white) . . .			41
Jar		26	
Bowl		13	
Dipper		2	
Unpainted	316		
Jar		221	
Mesa Verde-Mancos Corrugated . . .	2		
Probably P III	194		
Probably BM III	8		
Unclassified	17		
Bowl		43	
Probably P III	22		
Unclassified	21		
Dipper		7	
Shape unknown		45	
Total:			357

Bowl sherds were the commonest worked sherds. These figures probably reflect nothing more than breakage of a large number of bowls because they were used for so many tasks. Also, black-on-white jars were not as common as bowls, and mugs and dippers were even rarer. More surprising is the small number of corrugated sherds, considering the large number recovered from the excavations. Possibly there are three reasons: corrugated sherds are not as attractive to look at as black-on-white ones, they are more friable (as suggested by Kidder, 1932, p. 147), and they are not as smooth to the touch. The last reason might be important, from the standpoint of skin abrasion, if one were to use a sherd for any length of time.

A representative sample of worked sherds of the two categories can be seen in figure 262. Sherd a has been ground extensively on the right and bottom edges, and to a limited extent on the top edge. Example b has probably been chipped around the periphery and may have been a disk in the making. Both faces have been ground, leaving the concave inner surface of the bowl in the center of the side shown in the photograph and the convex outer surface around the outer margin of the reverse side.

Sherd c shows pronounced and beveled wear on opposite sides, and no work on the rim. Sherd f, a mug base, has been worn at the top of the broken side as well as on the point where the base meets the side. Sherds d (the corrugated neck of a black-on-white water jar) and e (the rim of a black-on-white kiva jar) have been ground at the point at attachment to the top of the jar.

Sherds g and h (dipper handles) and k (jar handle) have also been ground extensively at the end once attached to the rest of the vessel. Two other dipper handles, sherds i and j, have been shaped much more extensively, forming objects of unknown use.

The three corrugated sherds, m, n, and o, were formed in the same way that the black-on-white ones were. The first two have been ground on one edge, the third on two edges. This last is interesting because it is from a jar that had been covered with pinyon pitch inside and out. Smoothness of the sherd was certainly not considered here.

A special class of sherds worked only part way round the perimeter, and not covered by the two categories already mentioned, is illustrated by figure 262p, q, and r. The three sherds have been bifacially ground on one edge to form an apparent tool closely resembling the so-called stone saws which were ground in a similar manner. One of these, p, is a rim sherd, but the edge has been ground so thin that no rim features remain.

Table 16. Worked sherds.

	Bowls		Jars			Mugs		Dippers			Totals
	R*	B	R	B	H	R	B	R	B	H	
Worked on one edge											
Black-on-white:											
Mesa Verde	28	70	4	2	—	1	2	—	—	—	107
Indeter. (MV-McE)	5	31	1	6	—	—	—	1	—	3	47
McElmo	12	13	—	1	—	—	—	—	—	—	26
Mancos	1	—	—	2	—	—	—	—	—	—	3
Cortez	—	1	—	—	—	—	—	—	—	—	1
Corrugated:											
Indeter. (MV-Mancos)	—	2	—	13	—	—	—	—	—	—	15
Unclassified:											
Black-on-white	2	3	—	4	—	—	—	—	—	—	9
Plain	—	15	1	20	—	—	—	—	—	1	37
Worked on two or more edges											
Black-on-white:											
Mesa Verde	22	10	1	3	—	—	2	1	1	1	41
Indeter. (MV-McE)	2	6	—	1	1	—	—	—	—	4	14
McElmo	9	3	—	—	—	—	—	—	—	—	12
Mancos	1	—	—	1	—	—	—	—	—	—	2
Corrugated:											
Indeter. (MV-Mancos)	—	—	—	3	—	—	—	—	—	—	3
Unclassified:											
Plain	1	11	1	9	—	—	—	—	—	1	23
Black-on-red:											
Bluff	1	—	—	—	—	—	—	—	—	—	1
Total											341

*Key: R = rim
B = body
H = handle

The third category of worked sherds is composed of those which have been worked entirely around the perimeter. There are three main groups of artifacts in this category: large disks; small disks and similar—but oval—sherds; and pendant-shaped items. Also included in the category—but not typical of the three main groups—is a rhomboidal sherd, its shape being unique in the Long House collection (fig. 262l).

The top and bottom edges (as oriented in the illustration) have been slightly ground. The portion of these two edges—as well as that of the right edge—adjacent to the painted face has been ground to form a bevel. The left edge was not ground but was probably shaped by breaking so as to make a more or less square object.

The large disk class consists of five sherds: two black-on-white and three corrugated (figs. 263 and 264). The maximum diameter ranges from 7.5 to 15.0 cm. The edges of all five have been broken off to form a somewhat circular sherd. The breaking was probably deliberate around part of the edge, possibly accidental in places. The edges of the black-on-white disks have also been ground in several places.

The smaller of the two painted sherds (a bowl rim) is of interest because the concave side has been leveled with a hard-packed (but not burned), ashy material (fig. 264a and b). The claylike substance—containing small fragments of charcoal and tiny chunks of sandstone—closely resembles that found on the bottom of firepits which have been used over a long period of time. The deposit is slightly rounded at the edges of the sherd and in one place lips over onto the edge.

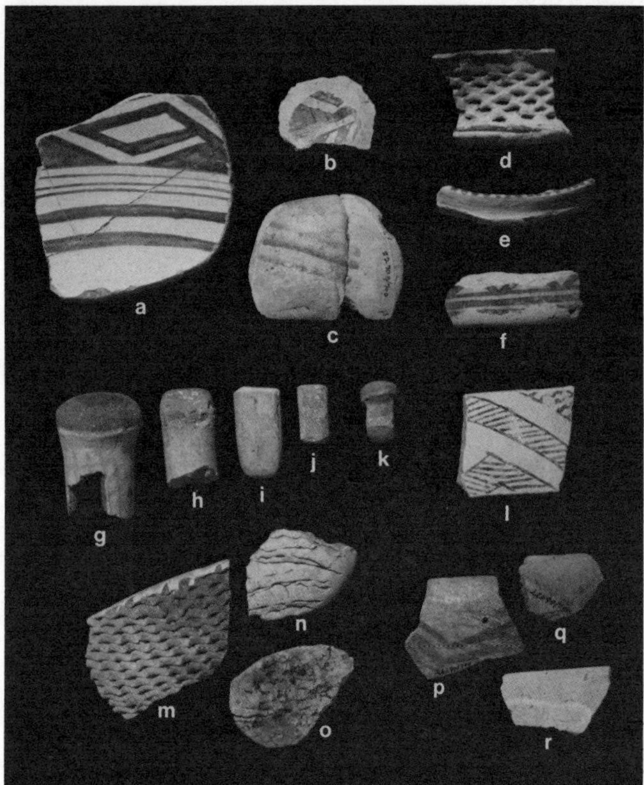

Figure 262. *Black-on-white and corrugated sherds worked on one edge and on two or more edges.*

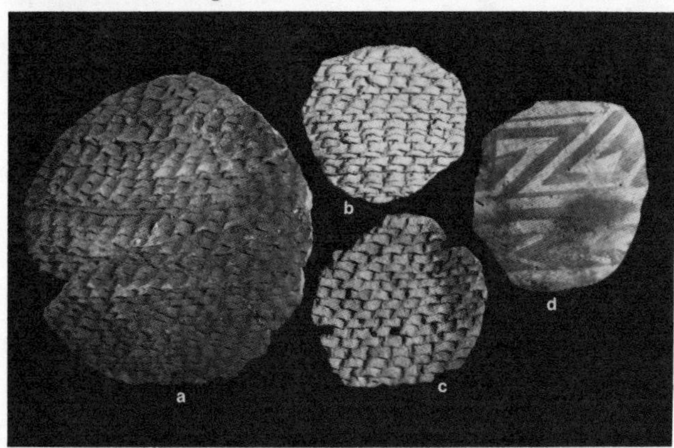

Figure 263. *(Left) Worked sherds: large corrugated and painted disks.*

Figure 264. *(Above) Worked sherds: large painted sherd (a. exterior; and b. interior).*

It is certainly worth noting that all but one of the large disks were found in kivas. Figure 263a is from the fill of Kiva A; b, from the fill of Kiva E; c, from the subfloor fill of Kiva O; and figure 264 from the fill of a wall niche in the northeast corner of Kiva J.

The large size of the sherds suggests their possible use as jar covers. There is no direct evidence for this, however. In fact, the only jar lid found in place was an unworked stone slab (General Feature 8, in ch. 2). The sherds, except for one shown in fig. 264, could also have been used as shallow containers for pigment, meal, pollen, or the like.

Of similar shape, but in a size class by itself, is a group of 26 small sherds. Actually, shape varies from circular to oval, and the workmanship is considerably better than that of the large disks. Seven of the sherds are from corrugated jars, nine from plain jars and bowls—or at least plain parts of probably decorated vessels, in the case of the bowl sherds—and 10 from black-on-white bowls. The maximum lengths range from 2.9 to 6.4 cm.

Kidder (1932, p. 147) has described in detail the probable method of manufacture. As can be seen in figure 265, which shows the better-made but still typical specimens, only two, c and g, are ground smoothly around the entire perimeter so as to form an almost circular object. (One of the corrugated sherds, i, is well shaped, but the edges are not ground.) There is some grinding on the edges of all the sherds shown except d and e (black-on-white) and i and j (corrugated).

I have also included in this third main category those sherds in which use was made of the bowl rim or what might be called a "pre-worked" edge. Sherds k–o are examples. All edges except the rims show some grinding. Sherds n (Bluff Black-on-red?) and o may actually belong to the previously discussed class of small circular and oval artifacts, since they approach these quite closely in shape. However, the unworked rim allies them more closely with the pendant-shaped specimens, k–m. These last may be pendant blanks, excepting m, a possible pendant with a slightly off-center (mend?) hole drilled at one end. They may also be merely rectangular worked sherds that were never intended to be pendants. If so, sherd pendants would be absent in the Long House material.

Only three of the circular sherds are from rooms (48, Level II—upper fill; 10 and 58, subfloor), and none are from kivas. The room proveniences suggest association with the earlier stage of the occupation (early A.D. 1200's), but the painted sherds are not limited to McElmo Black-on-white. Undoubtedly, the objects were made during the entire occupation. The remainder of the artifacts are from areas (IV, VII, VIII—East Ledge Ruin, X, XII) and from the East Trash Slope.

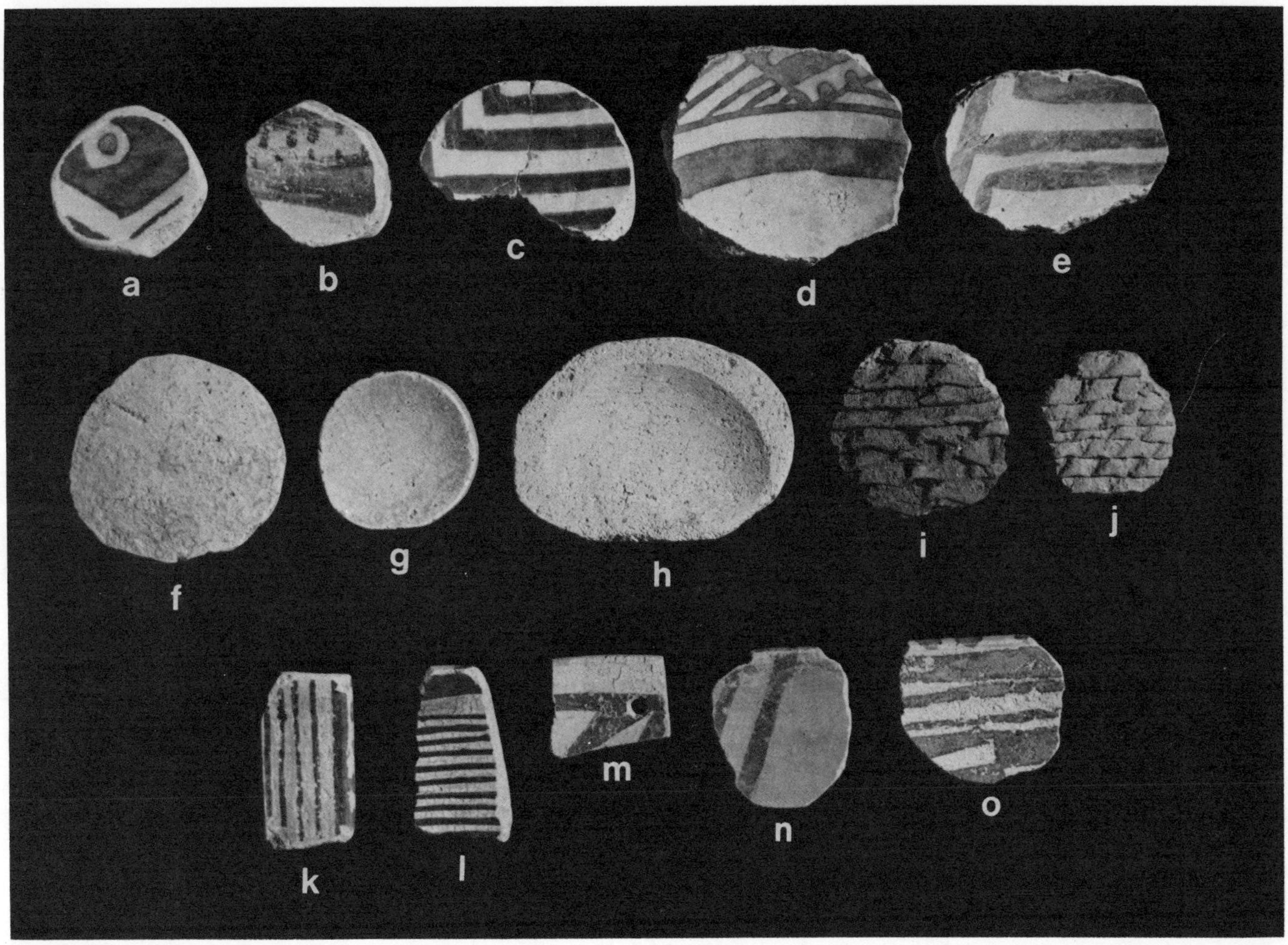

Figure 265. *Worked sherds.*

Of the possible pendants and blanks (including the two disk-like objects with intact rim), one is from Room 36 fill (fig. 265k), another from Kiva O, Level II—upper fill (l), and the third from Kiva Q, Level V—within a foot of the floor (n). The remaining two (m and o) are from the East Trash Slope.

Kidder (1932, pp. 154–155) suggested several uses for the well-shaped worked sherds he found at Pecos but considered none of the explanations very satisfactory. There is certainly nothing unusual about the Long House specimens—including provenience—that would suggest anything to add to Kidder's remarks.

PERFORATED DISK

Even more mystifying than the worked sherds discussed above is the large object from the subfloor fill of Room 58 (fig. 266). This large Mesa Verde Black-on-white rim sherd has been broken around the periphery to form a somewhat oval-shaped object. Six biconical holes were then drilled around the perimeter, all near the edge but spaced somewhat irregularly. At least some, if not all, of these holes can be ruled out as mend holes. I have no idea as to their use or function. One of the small black-on-white disks (not illustrated) comes from the same provenience.

Figure 266. *Perforated disk.*

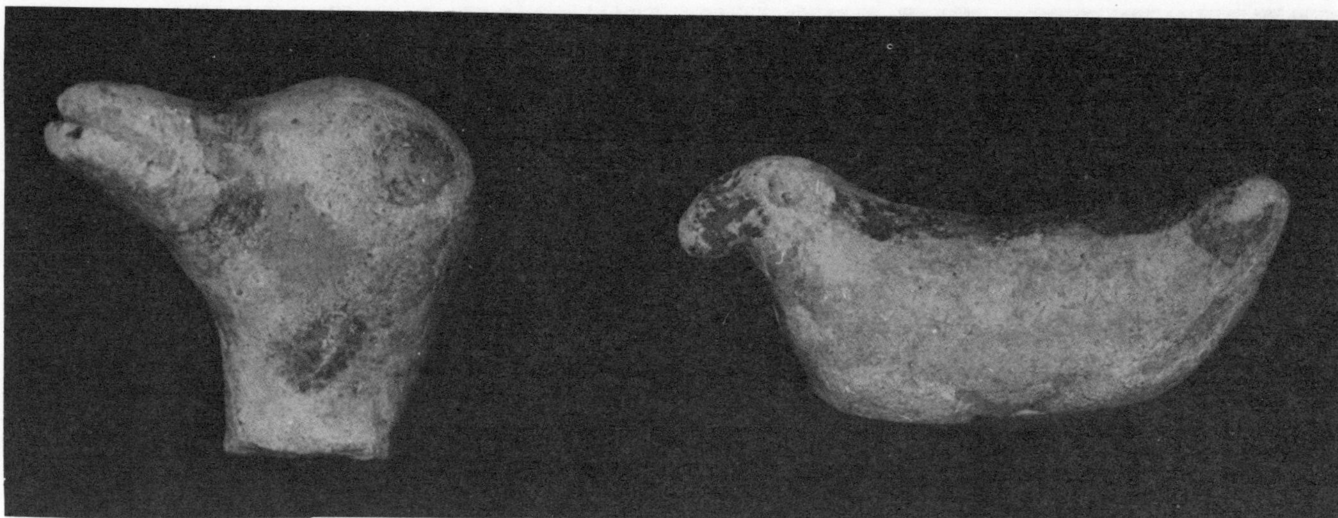

Figure 267. *Bird effigies.*

BIRD EFFIGIES

The bird head shown in figure 267a is probably a handle for either a small jar or a kiva jar lid and is 2.7 cm. from tip of bill to back of head. It is unslipped and decorated with carbon paint. The design consists of two eyes, a line encircling the beak, and a blotch on the left side of the neck. An incised line divides the upper and lower portions of the bill. The effigy was found on the East Trash Slope.

The other bird-shaped object (fig. 267b) gives the appearance of having been ground down on the base. Not completely removed are slight humps where the legs on a four-legged animal would have been. Thus the effigy may not have been a bird. The humps may be points of attachment used to connect the effigy to a jar or kiva jar lid as a handle. The object is 3.8 cm. long, apparently unslipped, and decorated with carbon paint. The design consists of a single stripe down the back, with a slight broadening of the stripe to cover at least part of the head and tail area. The effigy came from the subfloor fill of Kiva D.

Figure 268. *Clay pipe.*

PIPE

Only one definite pipe fragment (fig. 268) was found: a slightly globular bowl, with practically all of the stem gone. The exterior diameter of the bowl is about 3.5 cm., and the interior is fairly shallow, being only 1.6 cm. deep. The bore or smoke-passage is about 0.3 cm. in diameter, straight but slightly off-center in the bowl. The pipe is made of unfired clay, and there is no evidence of burning inside the bowl. If tempering material was added to the clay, it was, generally, very fine in size. There is no slip or painted decoration.

The method of making the bore was probably that described by Kidder (1932, p. 157): "The smoke-passage was made by moulding the moist clay around a small reed or grass stem. This is surely proved by well-defined imprints to be seen in many pipes." A few longitudinal striations in the bore would seem to bear this out. In the Long House specimen, these would have been due to pulling the stem out, not just to molding the clay around a stem. The bowl interior could have been shaped quite easily with the potter's finger.

Although the pipe was recovered from the fill of Pithouse 1, it is impossible to be sure of the validity of this association. In the process of leveling the burned and collapsed pithouse, to provide a base for the Pueblo III rooms overlying it, considerable material from the later period became mixed with the pithouse fill.

SUBMINIATURE VESSELS

Several small vessels, which were actually large enough to be used, were discussed under plain ware in a preceding section of this report. Besides these, four tiny vessels—obviously nonfunctional—were found.

Three are shallow "bowls," one being indented corrugated on the exterior (fig. 269b), the other two are plain (one is shown in figure 269c). The corrugated bowl has a diameter of 2.9 cm. and height of 1.1 cm.; the other two have dimensions of 3.1 cm. by 0.9 cm. (illustrated) and about 4.5 to 5.0 cm. by 1.2 cm. (fragmentary, not illustrated). The fourth specimen is a tray-like object, with upturned edges and a flat bottom (fig. 269a). It is 3.8 cm. long, 3.0 cm. wide, and 1.1 cm. high.

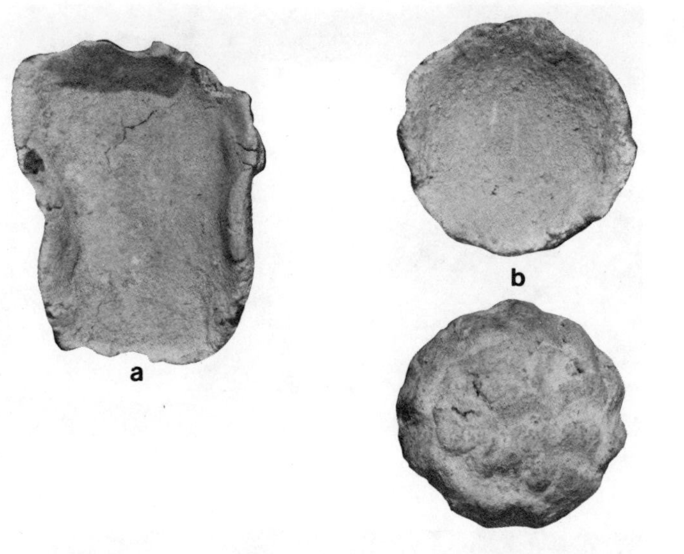

Figure 269. *Subminiature vessels: a, traylike object; and b and c, "bowls," obverse above and reverse below.*

The three smallest vessels appear to have been shaped and smoothed by fingers alone. Tempering material—if any was added deliberately—is very fine grained. The tray and the plain bowl have not been fired. The corrugated bowl was probably fired, but this conclusion was not tested thoroughly because of the perfect condition and small size of the object.

The largest bowl was scraped inside, leaving obvious striations; the outside was smoothed with the fingers. The bottom is slightly ground, probably from use. Either it was tempered with poorly sorted material, apparently shale for the most part, or else it was made from poorly ground or sorted potter's clay.

The provenience of the three bowls would suggest a late Pueblo III date of manufacture. The corrugated and large plain bowls are from the fill of Area X. The smaller plain vessel is from the firepit of Room 60 (but is not burned, so apparently arrived there after the hearth was no longer used). The tray-like object is from the surface of the ruin, no specific provenience assigned.

BALLS

Three clay "balls"—actually ellipsoidal in shape—were found in the ruin. Two are shown in figure 270; the third and largest of the three is fragmentary. The smaller of the two illustrated is 1.8 cm. long, the larger 3.3 cm. The fragmentary specimen probably had a maximum length of from 4 to 5 cm. All are solid clay, and only the middle-sized one has not been fired or only partially fired.

The largest ball was slipped but shows no evidence of paint; the other two are unslipped and unpainted. The temper in the largest ball is fairly fine grained. The other two were either not tempered or were tempered with very fine-grained material.

The ball in figure 270b is from Area III and can be ascribed to the Pueblo III occupation. The other two lack a definite provenience. The smallest ball is from the West Trash Slope, the other from the surface of the ruin, with no specific provenience assigned.

Figure 270. *Clay "balls."*

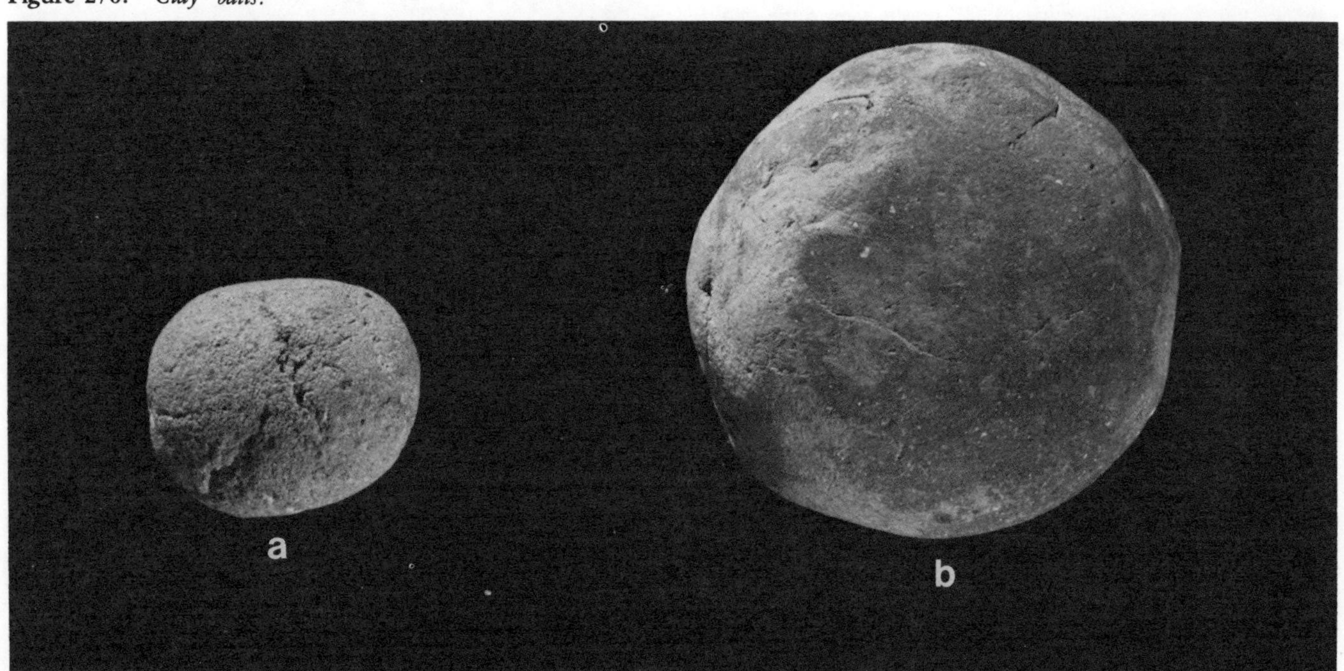

FIGURINES

Of the three items that may be human effigies, only one (fig. 271b) has recognizable features. The one shown in figure 271a, is of similar shape but lacks all other attributes. Figure 271c is probably the bottom portion of a third figurine but, if so, is unique because it has been painted, apparently with organic pigment. Both the figurine with the features and the fragment are of unfired gray clay. The third has been fired, either deliberately or accidentally. Once again, if temper had been added deliberately, it was very fine grained.

The facial features and possible breasts of figure 271b closely resemble those of several of the Basketmaker figurines shown by Morss (1954, fig. 19). The shape is closer to those of Pueblo II or III origin shown by Morss (ibid., fig. 29b) from Marsh Pass, Ariz., and by Judd (1959, fig. 37a) from Pueblo del Arroyo.

The provenience of the painted fragment (Room 82, Level II) would seemingly place it late in the occupation. However, the fill was disturbed by rodent activity, making the association uncertain. The figurine with the features was found in shallow fill on the West Trash Slope, not far from Room 82. Both figurines may have come from earlier structures higher up on the west end of the ruin.

The remaining figurine (the only one that may have been fired, a trait apparently more common in later times) is from Room 12, Level II. Here the fill is undisturbed, and wood specimens associated with the object have been dated in the A.D. 1270's.

Figure 271. *Figurines.*

JAR SUPPORT

Possibly akin to the stone items it resembles (see ch. 5) is a rectangular clay object (fig. 272) from the fill of Kiva R, within a foot of the floor. It is somewhat oval in cross section, and one end has a groove, possibly made by a stick, running across its longer dimension. The small portion still remaining of the other end is smooth and flat. The support measures 10.7 by 9.0 by 6.5 cm.; the groove is about 0.8 cm. wide and 0.4 cm. deep. The object was probably made of unfired clay, baked to a light brown. Except for the wide face (not shown in photograph), all surfaces show some smoke blackening.

It is difficult to say how the object was used, or which end or side was up if it was fixed in place in a hearth. It may have supported a stick, which in turn helped support a pottery vessel or other object. A similar item of stone was found embedded in the adobe liner of a firepit in Kiva R, and it may have been one of three originally in place around this hearth. It is interesting that the two stone objects illustrated (but not found *in situ*) are both from kivas (R and B). Fragments of two clay objects—probably similar in size and shape to the one from Kiva R—were found, but both lack a useful provenience. One is from Area III, the other from the Lower East Trash Slope.

Figure 272. *Jar support (?).*

PLUG

Only one clay plug (fig. 273) was found in Long House. Like the possible jar supports, this also came from a kiva: the fill of the subfloor ventilator shaft in Kiva B. It is only roughly modeled, being rounded at one end and flattened at the other. The flattened surface extends beyond the sides of the plug to form a flange. Its length is

5.6 cm., its maximum diameter is 8.0 cm. The plug is made of unfired, perhaps sun-dried, clay. Although it may have been used as a jar plug, its diameter suggests possible use as a sipapu plug.

Figure 273. *Plug.*

Chapter Five

Stone Artifacts and Minerals

Richard P. Wheeler

The 2,452 whole or broken artifacts of stone and 10 mineral specimens described in this chapter represent not all but the vast majority of the portable lithic items found in Long House in 1958–1963. A few stone artifacts were incorporated in the ruin, inadvertently, during the stabilization operations and were left undisturbed. Several scores of mainly slab-like pieces, too fragmentary to provide information other than mere presence, were discarded in the field and at the laboratory.

The analysis of most of the items and the selection of all the specimens illustrated were made jointly by George Cattanach and the writer. The numerous classes of stone objects are discussed under "functional" categories rather than by such unsatisfactory rubrics as Chipped Stone, Ground and Pecked Stone, and so on, in order to bring out their cultural connotations insofar as possible. Artifacts of multiple uses are assigned to one class, among the several possible classes, and re-used objects are assigned to the class indicated by the latest inferred use, although prior uses are noted.

Identification of lithic materials is often precarious for the archeologist who is not also a geologist possessing knowledge of the local lithology. The bulk of the non-sedimentary materials from Long House were identified by reference to examples of recurring rock-types in the Wetherill Mesa collections identified by Charles B. Hunt and Theodore Botinelly of the U.S. Geological Survey. Even so, conscientious checking is not proof against erroneous judgments. Several puzzling objects from Long House were graciously identified in the laboratory, in May 1964, by Felix Mutschler, a geologist with the Kennecott Corporation, Durango, Colo.

Modified and unmodified waterworn stones in this collection are characterized according to standard maximum-diameter classification: *pebbles*, 0.4 to 6.4 cm.; *cobbles*, 6.5 to 25.6 cm.; *boulders*, more than 25.6 cm. Linear measurements of the specimens are recorded in centimeters, and weights are given in grams and kilograms. It may be observed that if weights were regularly included in descriptions of lithic objects, these data could be found to have considerable value in comparative studies.

IMPLEMENTS FOR QUARRYING, SHAPING, AND FINISHING

The stone tools used for fashioning other tools and objects (of rock, mineral, vegetal, and faunal materials) displayed few formal attributes. The six classes recognized in the Long House collection comprise 989 items and account for 40 percent of the stone artifacts reported on from the site.

Hammerstones. These show varying amounts of battering and spalling as a result of quarrying and shaping rough stones and of maintaining the effectiveness of certain kinds of stone implements, e.g., the sharpening of grinding implements. Tools such as these, showing no evidence of having been hafted or mounted while in use, have often been designated as "hand hammers" and "pecking stones" without clear-out distinctions. The larger implements, held by the thumb and fingers against the palm of the hand (and perhaps frequently manipulated by both hands in this manner), may have served for the heavier work. The smaller implements, grasped by the thumb and finger tips, may have been employed for lighter and more precise tasks. The 829 hammerstones from Long House are described under six styles, according to their origins and particular characteristics.

Style 1: *Waterworn pebbles or cobbles and fragments, battered, sometimes spalled, on naturally rounded or on broken, angular edges.* 56 specimens—4 pebbles, 21 cobbles (fig. 274a)*, and 31 fragments.

Materials: quartzite (31), diorite (13), claystone (4), indurated sandstone (3), basalt (2), granite (1), gabbro (1), and syenite porphyry (1).

Shapes: pebbles—ovate, discoidal; cobbles—ovate, oval, subrectangular, oblong, subsquare, spheroidal, cylindrical, lozenge.

Measurements: pebbles—length 3.1 to 5.8 cm., width 2.5 to 4.7 cm., thickness 1.8 to 3.1 cm., and weight 19 to 102 gm.; cobbles—length 7.1 to 14.2 cm., width 4.5 to 10.6 cm., thickness 2.0 to 8.6 cm., and weight 72 to 1,692 gm.

Provenience: floor, Rooms 12 and 14, Kivas B and K (1 each); on banquette, Kiva R (1); fill, Rooms 1, 3, 7, 35, 48, 52, 57, 72, 74, 80, 84 (1 each), and 81 (2), Kivas D, E, H, I, M, N, O, Q, T, U (1 each), C, K, S (2 each), and R (4), Areas V (1), IV and VII (2 each), and X (4); surface and fill, Lower East Trash Slope (5) and Upper East Trash Slope (1), West Trash Slope (2), and backdirt (1).

*The measurements, materials, provenience, and catalog numbers of the illustrated stone artifacts are given in table 17 at the end of the report.

Style 2: *Cores and flakes, and fragments, derived from waterworn pebbles or cobbles (with varying amounts of smooth, rounded cortex present), battered, sometimes spalled, on edges; narrower edges and protuberances often blunted (by abrasion?), possibly for comfort in handling.* 340 specimens—317 cores (fig. 274b), 22 flakes, and 1 fragment.

Materials: claystone (186), quartzite (59), chert (24), diorite (21), indurated sandstone (15), basalt (13), syenite porphyry (13), granite (3), gabbro (2), schist (2), peridotite (1), and travertine (1).

Figure 274. *Hammerstones.*

Shapes: cores—ovate, spheroidal, subtriangular, subrectangular, discoidal, oval, lunate, wedge, trapeze, pentagonal, irregular; flakes—subtriangular, ovate, discoidal, subrectangular, oval, lunate, irregular.

Measurements: cores—length 3.7 to 10.9 cm., width 3.3 to 10.1 cm., thickness 2.0 to 9.2 cm., and weight 50 to 986 gm.; flakes—length 4.4 to 8.8 cm., width 3.6 to 6.3 cm., thickness 1.6 to 3.7 cm., and weight 28 to 166 gm.

Provenience: below floor, Rooms 57 and 91 (2 each), Rooms 58 and 76 and Great Kiva (1 each); floor, Pithouse I and Kiva Q (3 each), Room 76 (2), Rooms 14 and 49, Kivas J, O, and R (1 each); fill, Room 48 (31), Room 52 (20), Kiva J (11), Rooms 1, 2, 7, 9, 10, 11, 12, 13, 14, 15, 28, 30, 35, 37, 38, 47, 49, 50, 53, 54, 55, 56, 58, 60, 66, 69, 73, 76, 79, 81, 82, 88, 89 (1 to 7), Areas I, III, IV, V, VI, VII, IX, X, XII (1 to 6), Kivas A, B, C, E, F, G, H, I, K, L, O, P, Q, R, T (1 to 5); surface and fill, Lower East Trash Slope (68), Upper East Trash Slope (5), West Trash Slope (14), general (8), and backdirt (3).

Style 3: *Cores and flakes derived from outcrops or colluvium fragments (with varying amounts of angular cortex present), battered, sometimes spalled, on edges; narrower edges and protuberances often blunted (by abrasion?), possibly for comfort in handling.* 119 specimens—117 cores (fig. 274c), and 2 flakes.

Materials: chert (70), claystone (47), basalt (1), and quartzite (1).

Shapes: cores—ovate, oval, spheroidal, discoidal, conoidal, subrectangular, rectangular, cuboidal, square, subtriangular, wedge, lunate, lozenge, trapeze, pentagonal, irregular; flakes—ovate, subrectangular.

Measurements: cores—length 3.8 to 9.1 cm., width 2.6 to 8.2 cm., thickness 1.8 to 6.1 cm., and weight 29 to 491 gm.; flakes—5.0 by 4.3 by 2.3 cm. (length, width and thickness), and 59 gm., and 5.3 by 4.1 by 2.4 cm., and 61 gm.

Provenience: below floor, Rooms 49 and 69 (1 each); in Bin 3 in Room 14 (1); in ashy fill of firepit in Room 87 (1); in ventilator shaft of Kiva H (1); fill, Room 48 (25), Room 81 (14), Rooms 3, 9, 12, 14, 24, 28, 37, 47, 51, 52, 54, 56, 63, 87 (1 to 6), Areas III, V, VI, VII, IX, X (1 to 4), Kivas A, B, C, E, J, L, N, O, Q, R, S, U (1 to 2); surface and fill, Lower East Trash Slope (8), Upper East Trash Slope (2), West Trash Slope (7), general (4).

Style 4: *Cores and flakes, and fragments, with no cortex showing, battered, sometimes spalled, on edges; narrower edges and protuberances often blunted (by abrasion?), possibly for comfort in handling.* 260 specimens—249 cores (fig. 274d), 8 flakes, and 3 fragments.

Materials: claystone (143), chert (103), quartzite (7), indurated sandstone (5), basalt (1), and diorite (1).

Shapes: cores—ovate, oval, spheroidal, discoidal, conoidal, lunate, subtriangular, subrectangular, cuboid, subsquare, lozenge, pentagonal, irregular; flakes—ovate, discoidal, subtriangular, subrectangular.

Measurements: cores—length 3.2 to 9.3 cm., width 2.4 to 8.4 cm., thickness 1.8 to 7.5 cm., and weight 27 to 778 gm.; flakes—length 4.9 to 6.9 cm., width 4.2 to 5.3 cm., thickness 1.7 to 3.2 cm., and weight 67 to 107 gm.

Provenience: below floor, Room 81 (2), Room 85 (1), Area III (2), Kivas J and L and Great Kiva (1 each); on floor, Room 12 (1), Room 14 (2), and Kivas I and Q (1 each); in General Feature 3, Room 48 (2); in Pit 3, Room 48 (1); in ventilator shaft of Kiva H (2); on banquette of Kiva K (1); in fill of firepit in Kiva L (1); on floor of niche in Kiva O (1); fill, Room 48 (25), Room 81 (18), Room 52 (11), Room 47 (10), Rooms 3, 5, 7, 9, 12, 14, 18, 28, 37, 54, 55, 56, 58, 63, 66, 74 (1 to 5), Areas III, IV, V, VI, IX, X (1 to 6), Kivas A, B, C, D, E, F, H, I, J, K, L, M, N, O, P, Q, R, S, T, U (1 to 5); surface and fill, Lower East Trash Slope (49), Upper East Trash Slope (5), West Trash Slope (11), general (16), back dirt (3).

Style 5: *Dulled implements, or fragments of implements, of other classes, battered, sometimes spalled, on edges and protuberances.* 45 specimens, of eight classes of implements.

a. Fragments of Notched or Grooved Hammer Heads or Ax Blades (see fig. 294–297). 21 specimens—end-edge and median-edge fragments with one notch present (8); end fragments with one notch in each edge (5); longitudinal fragment, full-grooved (1); end-edge fragments, full-grooved (2, fig. 274e); end fragments, full-grooved (4); median fragment, full-grooved (1).

Materials: diorite (8), claystone (5), granite (3), syenite porphyry (2), basalt (1), quartzite (1), schist (1).

Shapes: ovate, oval, subrectangular, subtriangular, lunate.

Measurements: length 4.6 to 8.7 cm., width 3.1 to 8.1 cm., thickness 2.7 to 6.0 cm., and weight 63 to 570 gm.

Provenience: below floor, Room 81 (1); floor, Room 14 (1); on banquette, Kiva R (1); fill, Rooms 28, 48, 81, 87, Areas V, VI, VII, X, Kivas O, R, U (1 to 3); surface and fill, Lower East Trash Slope (2), West Trash Slope (1).

b. Bit fragments of Ax Blades. 5 specimens.

Materials: claystone (2), diorite (1), basalt (1), quartzite (1).

Shapes: subrectangular, subtriangular, ovate.

Measurements: length 5.4 to 6.7 cm., width 4.8 to 6.1 cm., thickness 2.1 to 3.4 cm., and weight 80 to 187 gm.
Provenience: in Bin 3, Room 14 (1); fill, Room 14 and 48 (1 each); surface and fill, Kiva G and Lower East Trash Slope (1 each).
c. Fragments of Rubbing Stones. 4 specimens.
Materials: quartzite (3), claystone (1).
Shapes: subtriangular, lunate.
Measurements: length 7.1 to 12.5 cm., width 4.3 to 6.6 cm., thickness 2.4 to 5.2 cm., and weight 96 to 616 gm.
Provenience: subfloor, Room 57 (1); fill, Room 37 and Area X (1 each); surface and fill, Upper East Trash Slope (1).

d. Dulled Choppers. 4 specimens.
Materials: claystone (4).
Shapes: oval, ovate, subtriangular, trapeze.
Measurements: length 5.6 to 6.3 cm., width 4.3 to 5.3 cm., thickness 2.1 to 2.8 cm., and weight 69 to 79 gm.
Provenience: fill, Room 81 (1); surface and fill, Lower East Trash Slope (2); general surface (1).
e. Dulled Planes. 6 specimens.
Materials: claystone (5), chert (1).
Shapes: suboval, ovate, conoidal, subrectangular, pentagonal.
Measurements: length 4.1 to 6.3 cm., width 3.2 to 4.5 cm., thickness 2.7 to 4.1 cm., and weight 53 to 196 gm.
Provenience: floor, Room 14 (2); fill, Room 48 (2); Area X and Kiva U (1 each).
f. Dulled Scrapers. 1 specimen.
Material: chert.
Shape: subrectangular.
Measurements: 5.5 by 3.7 by 2.1 cm., and 53 gm.
Provenience: fill, Kiva I.
g. Fragments of Handstones. 2 specimens.
Material: indurated sandstone.
Shapes: oval, irregular.
Measurements: 8.4 by 9.3 by 4.7 cm., and 401 gm., and 11.0 by 9.7 by 5.6 cm., and 717 gm.
Provenience: fill, Rooms 48 and 57 (1 each).
h. Fragments of Pitted Pounding and Rubbing Stones. 2 specimens.
Materials: indurated sandstone (1), quartzite (1).
Shapes: suboval, subtriangular.
Measurements: 8.4 by 6.2 by 5.3 cm., and 420 gm., and 7.5 by 7.0 by 6.1 cm., and 425 gm.
Provenience: fill, Room 35 and Kiva F (1 each).

Style 6: *Whole or broken pieces of hematite, battered, sometimes spalled, on edges and protuberances*. 9 specimens (fig. 275).
Materials: dark brown or dark red hematite.
Shapes: ovate, spheroidal, discoidal, subrectangular.
Measurements: length 4.6 to 8.3 cm., width 4.0 to 7.0 cm., thickness 2.8 to 6.2 cm., and weight 112 to 595 gm.
Provenience: floor, Kiva H (1); fill, Room 48 (2), Room 56 and Kiva A (1 each); surface and fill, Rooms 6–7, Area VI, West Trash Slope, backdirt (1 each).

Hammer Heads. Twenty-seven objects, showing varying amounts of spalling and battering on one or both blunted ends, possess notches (in one or more sides), and sometimes also grooves (in one or both faces) that provided "seats" for wooden handles, none of which were found attached. Designated as "hammer heads" rather than simply "hammers," in order to indicate their function as members of *hafted* quarrying and shaping implements, the specimens are described under four styles based on different provisions for hafting.

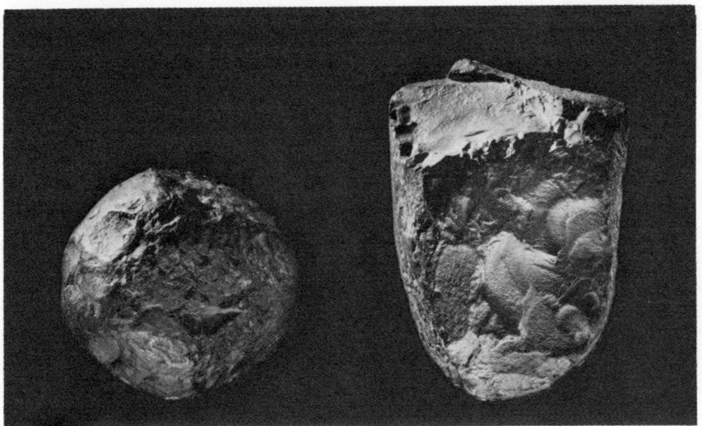

Figure 275. *Hammerstones.*

Style 1: *Notched.* 13 specimens. Commonly, a single transverse notch occurs in each side, about midway between the ends (8 specimens, fig. 276a). Variations include a single transverse notch near one end of each side (2 specimens, fig. 276b), a dual transverse notch in the middle of one side and a single transverse notch near the middle of the other side (1 specimen, fig. 276c), three oblique notches in one side and a single transverse notch near the middle of the other side (1 specimen, fig. 275d), and a single notch near the middle of each of three sides (1 specimen, fig. 276e). The notches are symmetrically concave. Single notches range in width from about 1.5 to 4.0 cm., and in depth from about 0.1 to 0.7 cm. The dual notch is 3.7 cm. in total width and 0.5 cm. in maximum depth. The three oblique notches mentioned above vary from about 1.4 to 1.8 cm. in width and are about 0.3 cm. in depth.

Ten of the implements are waterworn cobbles, shaped mainly around the perimeter, including the notches, and less commonly on the faces, by spalling, pecking, and grinding. One of these is a blunted single-bitted axe blade, with the foreshortened bit bifacially ground. Two hammer heads are notched handstones, and the remaining example of Style 1 is a revamped pitted pounding and rubbing stone (fig. 276d).

Figure 276. *Hammer heads.*

Materials: diorite (3), gabbro (3), claystone (2), indurated sandstone (2), syenite porphyry (1), schist (1), sandstone (1).
Shapes: oval (5), irregular (8).
Measurements: length 7.3 to 14.0 cm., width 5.6 to 9.7 cm., thickness 2.5 to 6.7 cm., and weight 188 to 1,339 gm.
Provenience: fill, Rooms 48, 75, 88 (1 each), Area X (2), and Kivas G, J, R (1 each); surface and fill, Kiva O and Lower East Trash Slope (2 each), and West Trash Slope (1).

Style 2: *Full-grooved*. 8 specimens. Usually, a single transverse groove completely encircles the specimen about midway between the ends (fig. 276f). In two cases, the encircling transverse groove is expanded to a dual groove in the middle of one side—one specimen (fig. 276g) is a blunted single-bitted ax head, with the foreshortened bit bifacially ground. All eight hammer heads in this group are waterworn cobbles, shaped mainly around the perimeter, including the groove, by spalling, pecking, and grinding. The grooves are symmetrically concave. Single encircling grooves range in width from about 1.4 to 4.0 cm., and in depth from about 0.1 to 0.5 cm. The dual groove in two specimens each measured 3.7 cm. in total width and 0.5 cm. in maximum depth.

Materials: claystone (4), granite porphyry (2), diorite (1), quartzite (1).
Shapes: oval (4), spherical (2), irregular (2).
Measurements: length 7.8 to 14.1 cm., width 5.4 to 9.2 cm., thickness 3.7 to 5.9 cm., and weight 280 to 1,195 gm.
Provenience: fill, Rooms 37, 80, Areas V, X, XII, and Kivas J, N (1 each); surface and fill, Lower East Trash Slope (1).

Style 3: *C-grooved*. 4 specimens. A single transverse groove in *one* face and in each side, like the letter C, commonly occurs nearer one end ("poll") than the other ("head"); 3 specimens (fig. 276h). Rarely, the C-shaped groove is present about midway between the ends; 1 specimen. The four implements in this group are waterworn cobbles, shaped principally around the perimeter, including the groove, by spalling, pecking, and grinding. The grooves are symmetrically concave, and range in width from about 1.3 to 3 cm., and in depth from about 0.1 to 0.5 cm.

The manner of hafting these hammer heads, and also certain ax heads in the Long House assemblage, here called "C-grooved," is to be distinguished from the U-shaped groove (in two faces and one side), known as "three-quarter-grooved," which occurs in aboriginal stone hammer heads and ax blades found in the central and southern sections of the Southwest. C-grooved, but not three-quarter-grooved, pounding and cutting tools have been recovered from several other sites on Wetherill Mesa. The contrivance may provisionally be regarded as an attribute developed independently in the Mesa Verde district, or, perhaps less restrictively, in the Four Corners region of the northern Southwest.

Materials: gabbro(2), granite porphyry (2).
Shapes: subtriangular (1), irregular (3).
Measurements: length 8.0 to 13.5 cm., width 7.2 to 8.2 cm., thickness 3.4 to 4.7 cm., and weight 433 to 679 gm.
Provenience: below floor, Room 84 (1); floor, Kiva I, (1); ventilator shaft, Kiva H (1); fill, Room 48 (1).

Style 4: *L-grooved*. 2 specimens. A single transverse groove in one face and one side, like the letter L, occurs nearer one end ("poll") than the other ("head"). The two specimens in this group are waterworn cobbles; one is shaped by spalling, pecking and grinding (fig. 276i), the other is shaped by spalling and pecking only. The grooves are symmetrically concave, and vary in width from about 1.7 to 2.8 cm. and in depth from about 0.2 to 0.35 cm.

The device for hafting these hammerstones, here labeled "L-grooved," appears to be an independently developed attribute, like the one discussed under the preceding style.

Materials: schist (1), claystone (1).
Shapes: ovate (1), irregular (1).
Measurements: 8.1 by 6.0 by 4.0 cm., and 266 gm.; and 9.2 by 6.7 by 3.5 cm., and 373 gm.
Provenience: fill, Room 7 and Area VI (1 each).

Maul Heads. Three objects comparable to hammer heads are identified as maul heads. Although similar in use and form, maul heads are more massive and appear to have been designed for quarrying and shaping large stones. The two styles below are based on different features for hafting.

Style 1: *Notched*. 2 specimens. In both cases, a single transverse notch is present in each side, nearer one end ("poll") than the other ("head"). One maul head is a tabular piece of sandstone, shaped on one face and around the perimeter, including the notches, by spalling and pecking (fig. 277, top). The other implement appears to be the revamped end section of a humpback mano of loaf-form with a single grinding surface (see section on Style 7), shaped by spalling (including the notches), pecking, grinding, and use-abrasion (fig. 277, center). The notches of the former are symmetrically concave and

Figure 277. *Maul heads.*

Figure 278. *Abrading stones: plain surface.*

measure about 2.8 and 3.5 cm. in maximum width and about 0.5 and 0.6 cm. in maximum depth, respectively. The notches of the second specimen are very irregular and measure, respectively, about 3.5 and 4.0 cm. in maximum width and about 1.0 and 1.1 cm. in maximum depth.

Materials: sandstone (1), breccia (1).

Shapes: subtriangular, subrectangular.

Measurements: 16.3 by 12.7 by 4.7 cm., and 1,528 gm.; and 17.9 by 13.0 by 5.0 cm., and 1,890 gm.

Provenience: fill, Kiva E (1); surface, Kiva A (1).

Style 2: *Partially grooved.* 1 specimen (fig. 277, bottom). Single transverse pecked grooves occur in the upper half of one face and in the upper third of the opposite face, both in the same plane and nearer one end ("poll") than the other ("head"). This implement is an ovate cobble or block of indurated sandstone, heavily spalled by use on faces and ends (and considerably dimished in size thereby?), and battered spottily on the ends. The one intact groove is about 2.5 cm. in maximum width and about 0.4 cm. in maximum depth. The specimen measures 14.5 by 8.9 by 9.1 cm., and weighs 848 gm. It was found below the floor in Room 32.

Abrading Stones. Sixty-seven objects of gritty stone, showing varying signs and degrees of use-abrasion, are here labeled "abrading stones." They are described under three styles.

Style 1: *Plain surface.* 45 specimens. Forty-four of the implements are either (a) unshaped or roughly shaped by spalling and possess one wear-facet (27 specimens, fig. 278, top) or two or three wear-facets (8 specimens); or they are (b) dressed by intentional grinding on parts or all of the perimeter and possess one wear-facet (3 specimens), two wear-facets (4 specimens, fig. 278, center and bottom), or five to six wear-facets (2 specimens). Two of the tools shaped by spalling, with two and three wear facets, are re-used medial fragments of manos of Style 4, wedgeshaped in cross section, and Style 5, triangular in cross section. In the case of the former, the thinner irregular side is bifacially beveled to a sharp edge, and the irregular ends are unifacially beveled on opposed faces by use-abrasion.

Figure 279. *Abrading stones: plain surface (whetstone?).*

The other implement in this group, of very fine-grained sandstone, ovate in outline, with sides and ends rounded by intentional abrasion, possesses two parallel wear-facets (fig 279). It might be characterized as a whetstone, analogous to abrading tools of similar appearance and quality in our culture.

Materials: sandstone (42), micaceous volcanic rock (2), breccia (1).

Shapes: irregular(25), subrectangular (15), pentagonal (2), ovate (2), lozenge (1).

Measurements: length 5.3 to 13.2 cm., width 3.0 to 12.5 cm., thickness 1.1 to 6.1 cm., and weight 51 to 681 gm.

Provenience: below floor, Kiva N (2) and Kiva M (1); fill, Rooms 2, 48, 58, Kiva R (3 each), Kiva F, J, K (2 each), Rooms 28, 35, 59, 79, 82, Areas IV, VI, X, Kivas A, D, F, G, N, Q, U, Pithouse 1 (1 each); surface and fill, Lower East Trash Slope (5), Upper East Trash Slope (1), West Trash Slope (1); and general (1).

Style 2: *Narrow-groove.* 18 specimens. Seventeen of these implements are (a) unshaped or roughly shaped by spalling and exhibit one to seven U-shaped grooves on one surface (9 specimens, fig. 280a), 12 U-shaped grooves on two surfaces and three edges (1 specimen, fig. 280b), seven U-shaped grooves on four surfaces (1 specimen, fig. 280c), or one to six U-shaped grooves on one surface (4 specimens, fig. 280d and e); or (b) are dressed all over by intentional grinding and exhibit one U-shaped or contracting U-shaped groove on one surface (2 specimens, fig. 280f).

The other implement in this group is a large, flat block, unshaped but nearly square in outline, with 17 U- or V-shaped grooves in one surface (fig. 281).

The size ranges of the grooves are: length 0.8 to 28.6 cm., width 0.2 to 1.9 cm., and depth 0.05 to 1.2 cm.

Materials: all sandstone (Mesaverde group).

Shapes: irregular (16), oval (1), subrectangular, multifaceted (1).

Measurements: length 2.8 to 21.0 cm., width 3.4 to 15.8 cm., thickness 1.7 to 12.2 cm., and weight 24 gm. to 2.4 kg. (17 specimens); and 31.2 by 27.0 by 13.9 cm., and 15.3 kg. (block).

Provenience: below floor, Rooms 42, 52, Areas III, VI, VII, X, Kivas A, F (1 each); surface and fill, Lower East Trash Slope (3), West Trash Slope (1).

Style 3: *Broad-groove.* 4 specimens. Two of these implements are small, irregular spalls of sandstone (Measverde group), with a relatively broad, smooth "groove" worn by use-abrasion in one

Figure 280. *Abrading stones: narrow-groove.*

Figure 281. *Abrading stones: narrow-groove.*

surface, in each case. They measure 4.6 by 4.0 by 2.7 cm., and weigh 51 gm., and 5.6 by 5.0 by 2.3 cm., and 51 gm. (fig. 282, center), and were found, respectively, in the trash fill of Area V and on the surface or in the fill of the Upper East Trash Slope.

The other two implements are large, irregular, roughly shaped flat blocks of sandstone (Mesaverde group), with a broad, straight, transverse groove worn by use-abrasion near the middle of one surface and enclosed by "borders" on the sides and at one end (fig. 282, left), and with two broad, straight grooves worn by use-abrasion at one corner of one surface and running parallel to each other and obliquely to the long axis of the block (fig. 282, right). The former measures, overall, 32.5 by 22.5 by 9.2 cm., and 7.8 kg., and the single groove is about 25.0 cm. in length, 11.5 cm in width, and 3.0 cm in maximum depth. The second implement measures, overall, 29.0 by 25.5 by 14.0 cm., and 12.6 kg., and the grooves are about 21.5 cm. in length, 7.0 to 9.0 cm. in width, and 1.6 cm. in maximum depth, and about 13.0 cm. in length, 5.1 cm. in width, and 0.3 cm. in maximum depth. Both implements were found on the surface at the east side of the site.

Figure 282. *Abrading stones: broad-groove.*

While the two small broad-groove abrading stones would have had varied uses in tool-making, the two large broad-groove implements appear to have had at least one clear purpose, namely, the production and maintenance of the smooth bit and thin, sharp cutting edge on many single- and double-bitted stone axes.

Rubbing Stones. The 22 complete and 2 broken implements assigned to this group are hard or dense stones of varying shape, showing one to three flat or convex wear-facets which are occasionally rough but are generally smooth and dull or glossy. Most of the specimens are unaltered whole or fragmentary waterworn cobbles (16 specimens; fig. 283, bottom). The illustrated example and two other whole cobbles show traces of battering on the faces and one end, in each instance. These batter-marks may be fortuitous, yet they suggest that the implements may have been used additionally and briefly

Figure 283. *Rubbing stones.*

as hammerstones. The other eight specimens include two cobbles trimmed on parts of the perimeter by spalling, one split cobble fragment (fig. 283, center), one split concretion (fig. 283, top), and four re-used mano fragments—an end section and a corner section of Style 9 manos, and end fragments of Style 15 manos.

Materials: indurated sandstone (6), quartzite (6), diorite (3), gabbro (3), syenite porphyry (2), conglomerate (2), granite (1), concretionary sandstone (1).

Shapes: irregular (9), ovate (6), discoidal (2), subrectangular (2), suboval (1), subtriangular (1), hemispherical (1).

Measurements: length 7.0 to 19.8 cm., width 5.8 to 12.7 cm., thickness 2.7 to 8.6 cm., and weight 230 gm. to 2.4 kg.

Provenience: floor, Kivas K, Q, U (1 each); niche, Kiva J (1); fill, Kivas A, F, K (2 each), Rooms 28, 37, 72, Areas VI, X, Kivas H, N (1 each); surface and fill, Rooms 6–7, Areas I, XII, Kiva N (1 each); and general (3).

Rubbing stones, like abrading stones, probably had many and varied uses in the production of other tools and objects. Whereas the invariable grittiness of the Long House abrading stones implies specialization in their use as shaping and sharpening tools, the hardness or denseness and relative heaviness of the rubbing stones in the collection suggest an emphasis on certain finishing operations, for example, in the smoothing or buffing of shaped objects of considerable size, including architectural elements such as door and niche covers and household objects such as cooking slabs.

Polishing Stones. The 36 complete and 3 broken implements termed "polishing stones" are small hard stones or rock fragments of variable shape, showing one to five flat or convex wear-facets which are sometimes striated but are commonly smooth and dull or glossy. Most of the specimens are unaltered or lightly spalled or battered, whole or broken waterworn pebbles (31 specimens, fig. 284a–d), or unaltered whole or fragmentary and occasionally lightly battered waterworn cobbles (5 specimens, fig. 284e). Three specimens are

Figure 284. *Polishing stones.*

tabular pieces of travertine. One of these is shaped around the perimeter by grinding and has one striated wear-facet. The other two are unshaped, with one and five striated wear-facets, respectively.

Materials: claystone (18), quartz (8), quartzite (5), travertine (3), diorite (2), granite (1), chert (1), carnelian (1).

Shapes: suboval (9), subtriangular (5), lozenge (5), ovate (4), subrectangular (4), discoidal (3), irregular (3), oval (2), trapeze (1).

Measurements: length 2.0 to 7.8 cm., width 1.4 to 6.2 cm., thickness 1.0 to 3.0 cm., and weight 4.6 gm to 166 gm.

Provenience: floor, Kiva O (1); fill, Room 3 and Kiva N (4 each), Room 37 (3), Room 48 and Area X (2 each), Rooms 2, 29, 35, 56, 81, Areas VII, IX; Kivas D, I, J, O, R, and Pithouse 1 (1 each); surface and fill, Lower East Trash Slope (4), Upper East Trash Slope (1), Areas VI, X, Kiva O (1 each); and general (2).

In contrast to the heavy finishing work performed by the more massive rubbing stones described previously, the small and lightweight polishing stones probably served in many delicate smoothing and buffing operations—particularly in producing the even surfaces on pottery at Long House.

IMPLEMENTS FOR PIERCING, CUTTING, SAWING, AND SCRAPING

A variety of implements with points or edges, prepared by several technics or simply modified by use, are present in the Long House assemblage. By analogy and inference, the tools were employed in hunting and butchering, in harvesting timber for building purposes and possibly fuel, or in the working of wood, hides, bone and antler, animal and vegetal fibers, and soft stone. The nine classes of (mainly) intentionally fashioned implements and the three classes of use-modified implements described below embrace 434 items and amount to 18 percent of the stone objects dealt with herein.

Projectile Points: Sixteen whole or broken objects and seven blade sections of similar objects are considered, by virtue of their form, size, and condition, to be the hard, piercing tips of arrow or dart shafts used in hunting and possibly also in warfare. All the specimens are flakes or spalls that have been shaped, or at least finished, by pressure-retouch flaking. Five styles of "small points" and two styles of "large points" (Fenenga, 1953, pp. 317–319) are represented in the collection.

Style 1: *Small, with notched straight or convex sides and straight or concave base.* 8 complete or nearly complete specimens (fig. 285a–d). Six specimens are fully retouched on both faces, one is fully retouched on one face and marginally retouched on the reverse face, and one specimen is marginally retouched only on both faces. Lateral and basal edges are straight, even or slightly wavy, and sharp.

Materials: chert (4), quartzite (3), chalcedony (1).

Measurements: length 1.5 to 3.6+cm., width 1.1 to 1.7 cm., thickness 0.2 to 0.4 cm., and weight 0.5 to 1.4+gm.

Provenience: floor, Room 36 (1); fill, Rooms 11, 57, Kiva Q (1 each); surface, Area VI and Lower East Trash Slope (1 each); with Burial 6, Lower East Trash Slope (1), with Burial 11, on slope southwest of site (1).

Style 2: *Small, with notched angled sides and concave or straight base.* 2 complete or nearly complete specimens (fig. 285e). The two examples are marginally retouched only on both faces. Lateral and basal edges are straight, even or faintly wavy, and sharp. The illustrated specimen is made of quartzite and measures 2.3 by 1.2 by 0.4 cm., and weighs 0.8 gm.; it came from the fill of Kiva U. The second specimen, of jasper measures 2.4 by 1.4 by 0.3 cm., and weighs 0.9 gm.; it was found in backdirt.

Style 3: *Small, with straight-sided blade, short barbed shoulders, and wide expanding stem with straight base.* 1 intact specimen (fig. 285f). Fully retouched on both faces, and also marginally retouched on one face, with blade and stem edges straight, slightly uneven, and sharp, this point is made of chert and measures 2.7 by 1.7 by 0.4 cm., and weighs 1.7 gm. It was found on the Lower East Trash Slope.

Style 4: *Small, with concave-sided blade, long barbed shoulders, and narrow expanding stem with convex base.* 1 nearly complete specimen (fig. 285g). This point is fully retouched and marginally retouched on both faces, and blade and stem edges are straight, even, and sharp. Made of chert, it measures 2.8+by 1.8+by 0.3 cm., and weighs 1.2+gm. It came from the fill of Room 82.

Style 5: *Small, with convex-sided blade, short barbed shoulders, and narrow expanding stem with convex base.* 1 intact specimen (fig. 285h). This point is fully flaked and marginally retouched on both faces, and blade and stem edges are straight, slightly uneven, and sharp. Made of chalcedony, it measures 3.4 by 2.0 by 0.4 cm., and weighs 2 gm. It was found on the surface of Area VI.

Style 6: *Large, with straight or convex-sided blade, straight or insloping shoulders, and narrow expanding stem with convex base.* 1 incomplete and 1 nearly complete specimen (fig. 285i). These points are fully flaked and marginally retouched on both faces, and blade and stem edges are straight, even or slightly uneven, and sharp. The illustrated specimen, made of chalcedony, measures 4.0+by 2.3 by 0.5 cm., and weighs 5.1+gm. It came from the fill of Kiva A. The other specimen, of quartzite, measures about 5 cm. in length, 2.5 cm. in width, and 0.6 cm. in thickness, and weighs 5.9 g,. It was found on the floor of Kiva U.

Style 7: *Large, with straight-sided blade, short barbed shoulders, and narrow straight-sided stem with slightly convex base.* 1 nearly complete, restored specimen (fig. 285j). This point is fully retouched and marginally retouched on both faces, and blade and stem edges are straight, slightly uneven, and sharp. Made of chert, it measures 4.4+by 2.1 by 0.5 cm. (disregarding the "peak" which may be seen in the illustration, near the base of the blade), and it weighs 4.6+gm. The point had been broken, at some time or other, into two pieces, near the middle of the blade; the proximal section of the point came from the fill of Area IV, and the distal portion was found in backdirt.

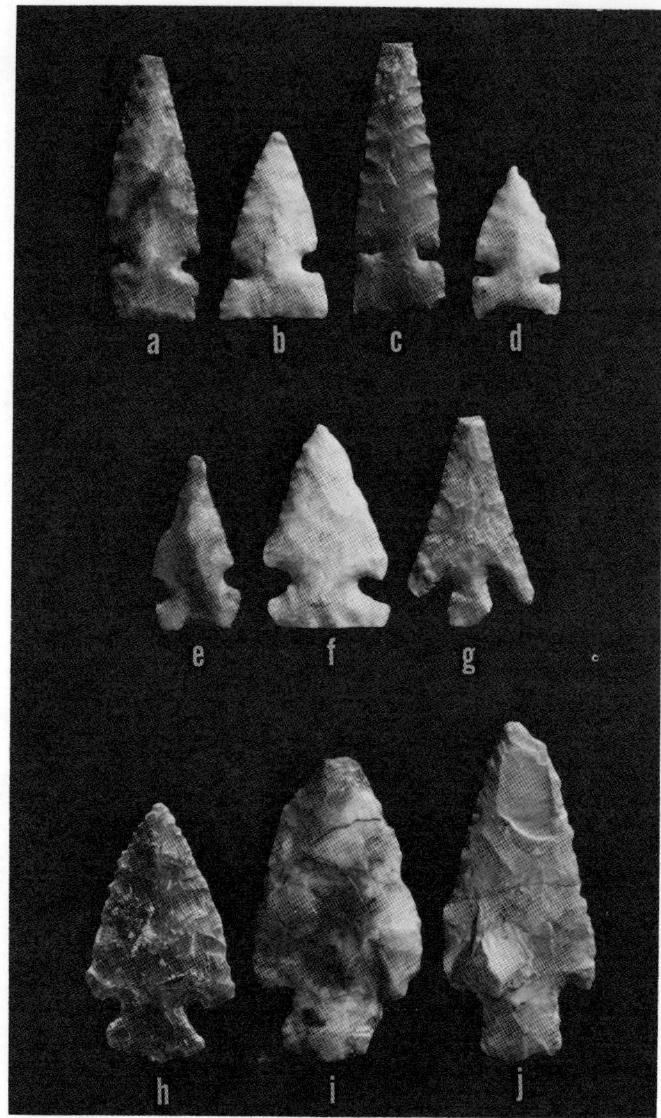

Figure 285. *Projectile points.*

The provisional styles, the characteristics, and the provenience of the seven blade sections of projectile points are presented in the following tabulation.

Style	Material	Blade Measurements (in cm.) Length	Width	Thickness	Provenience
1 or 2	chert	1.4+	1.1	0.3	West Trash Slope, surface
1 or 2	chert	2.2+	1.2	0.2	Burial 11, on slope southwest of site
1 or 2	quartzite	4.3+	1.1	0.35	Room 75, fill
1 or 2	chalcedony	2.6	1.0	0.3	Kiva N, fill
6 (?)	chert	—	2.5+	0.5	Kiva O, fill
6 (?)	chalcedony	3.2	2.1	0.6	Room 2, fill between floors 1 and 2
7 (?)	chalcedony	3.5+	1.9+	0.6	Kiva Q, fill

Figure 286. *Knives.*

Figure 287. *Knife fragment (Angostura point fragment?).*

Knives. Thirty-two complete or incomplete implements of varying size and shape are considered to be knives or portions of knives used in butchering and other cutting operations. One large stemmed specimen and many of the other thinner and more carefully flaked specimens were probably mounted in handles of wood or bone. The thicker and cruder implements may have been merely grasped in the hand. Six styles of knives are recognized.

Style 1: *Lanceolate, double-edged.* 8 complete or incomplete specimens. Most of these implements—two nearly complete specimens (fig. 286a and b), and two distal, one medial, and one proximal fragments—are fully retouched in a random fashion, and are also marginally retouched on both faces; the lateral edges are straight, even or uneven, and sharp or slightly dulled by use.

The remaining two are of unusual interest. One of them, which is complete (fig. 286c), bears on one face and the distal half of the reverse face oblique and transverse, narrow and shallow flake scars running from the lateral edges to or beyond the midline; the bifacially flaked portion is symmetrically lenticular, the rest is planoconvex, in transverse section. Edges are marginally retouched and slightly dulled by use. The other, an incomplete implement (fig. 287, left, obverse; right, reverse), has parallel oblique, narrow and shallow (ribbonlike) flake scars on most of both faces, which are oriented from upper left (tip) to lower right (base) and run, on both the obverse and the reverse face, from one lateral edge more than halfway, and from the other lateral edge less than halfway, across the face, resulting in an asymmetrically lenticular transverse section.

The lateral edges are unifacially edge-retouched on opposed faces, and they are slightly dulled with use. One lateral edge is also use-flaked and nicked near the tip end. Judging from the shape (asymmetrically lenticular transverse section and the probable outline form), the overall flaking pattern and the minor edge-retouching, and the dimensions, this specimen appears to be identifiable as the proximal section of an Angostura point (Wheeler, 1954, pp. 3–4).

The complete implement with ribbonlike flake scars may be a Paleo-Indian relic, like the Angostura point fragment. Despite their exotic appearance, these implements seem to have been put into ordinary service by the residents of Long House, together with cutting tools finished by far less specialized flaking technics.

Materials: chert (5), quartzite (3).

Measurements: length 6.1 to 8.0+cm. (3), width 1.9 to 3.4 cm. (6), thickness 0.6 to 1.0 cm., and weight 11.9 gm and 19.7 gm. (2).

Provenience: fill, Rooms 36 and 37, Area X, Kivas J, K, Q, U (1 each); surface, West Trash Slope (1).

Style 2: *Ovate, double-edged.* 9 complete or incomplete specimens. These implements range from spalls or flakes that are fully retouched in a random manner on both faces and are also marginally retouched on both faces (fig. 286g and k), or fully retouched on one face and marginally retouched on both faces, to planoconvex flakes that are bifacially retouched along the lateral edges only (fig. 286f). Bases are symmetrically or asymmetrically convex and tips are rounded or pointed. Lateral edges are straight or sinuous, even or slightly uneven, and sharp or, more commonly, slightly dulled and sometimes minutely flaked and nicked by use.

Materials: chert (5), chalcedony (3), quartzite (1).

Measurements: length 28+ to 11.0+ cm (5), width 1.3 to 5.4 cm., thickness 0.5 to 1.4 cm., and weight 3 to 5 gm. (4).

Provenience: floor, Kiva O (1); fill, Rooms 52 and 82, Area X, Kivas D and R (1 each); surface, Lower East Trash Slope (2); surface, east part of site (1).

Style 3: *Triangular, single-edged.* 6 whole specimens. Five of the implements are bifacially retouched along the margins of one side. They include two bladelike flakes (fig. 286d), a small concavo-convex flake, a tabular piece of travertine with alternate edge-flaking on opposed faces, and a small flat flake with finely serrated edge (fig. 286e). (Cutting tools with one or more serrated edges have often been identified, incorrectly, as saws.) Knives with toothed edges are not uncommon utensils in our own culture; for example, bread knives or frozen food knives. The other implement of Style 3 is fully flaked on both faces, and also bifacially retouched along the margins of one side. In all cases, the working edge shows evidences of dulling, flaking, and nicking as the result of use.

Materials: chert (3), chalcedony (1), quartzite (1), travertine (1).

Measurements: length 3.2 to 7.0 cm., width 2.1 to 5.1 cm., thickness 0.6 to 2.2 cm., and weight 4.2 to 58 gm.

Provenience: floor, Kiva T (1), Rooms 23 and 81, Kiva M (1 each); surface and fill, Lower East Trash Slope and West Trash Slope (1 each).

Style 4: *Irregular, double-edged.* 5 complete or incomplete specimens. The two complete implements are flat flakes, bifacially retouched only along the margins of opposite sides, which are uneven, straight or sinuous, and slightly flaked and nicked by use (fig. 286h and i). The fragmentary specimens include a distal section with rounding tip, fully retouched on one face and alternately retouched along the margins on both faces; a proximal section fully retouched and marginally retouched on both faces; and a proximal section only marginally retouched on both faces. The working edges of the first and third fragments are sinuous, uneven, and sharp; those of the second fragment are straight, slightly uneven, and dulled by use.

Materials: quartzite (3), chert (2).

Measurements: length 4.0 to 6.4 cm. (2), width 2.8 to 4.7 cm., thickness 0.7 to 1.7 cm., and weight 10 to 24 gm. (2).

Provenience: fill, Areas IV and X, Kivas H and P (1 each); and backdirt (1).

Style 5: *Irregular, single-edged.* 3 whole specimens. These implements are flat flakes, retouched by percussion flaking alternately along the margins of one side (fig. 286j) or along the margins of one side and one end. Edges are sinuous, uneven, and slightly dulled by use.

Materials: chert (2), claystone (1).

Measurements: length 4.6 to 5.2 cm., width 3.1 to 4.1 cm., thickness 1.2 to 1.4 cm., and weight 26 to 36 gm.

Provenience: fill, Area XI and Kiva R (1 each); surface and fill, West Trash Slope (1).

Style 6: *Large, with rounded tip, straight-sided blade, short barbed shoulders, and narrow expanding stem with straight base.* The single complete specimen, of chert (fig. 288), is fully retouched in a random fashion, and also marginally retouched, on both faces. Blade edges are straight, even, and slightly flaked by use; stem edges are straight, even, and sharp. The implement measures 9.8 by 3.9 by 1.0 cm., and weighs 38 gm. It was found in the fill of Kiva H.

Shaft Cutters. A subtriangular, planoconvex flake of chert and a roughly ovate, planoconvex flake of chert feature, in each case, an inset or notch near the middle of one side. The notch in the former, which is asymmetrical and measures 1.4 cm. across and 0.25 cm. deep, is finely retouched on the convex face (fig. 289, left). No other modification of this flake is evident. The notch in the second flake, which is symmetrical and measures 1.2 cm. across and 0.2 cm. deep, is delicately retouched on the concave face (fig. 289, right). This flake shows traces of use-flaking on the convex face—along the edges of the notch, the convex end, and the side opposite the notch. The flake with the asymmetrical notch measures 4.5 by 1.7 by 1.2 cm., and weighs 7.4 gm.; it came from the general surface of the site. The other flake measures 3.2 by 2.7 by 1.1 cm., and weighs 7.1 gm.; it was found in the fill of Kiva A.

The effectiveness of tools such as these in cutting reed cane for arrowshafts was discovered experimentally a decade or more ago by Aaron J. Cosner (1956).

Saws. Four implements, identified as saws, are thin, tabular pieces of fine-grained sandstone that have been beveled by intentional grinding along only one side, either unifacially (fig. 290, upper left) or, more commonly, bifacially (fig. 290, upper right and lower). The straight or slightly concave working edge is evened longitudinally, and is rounded or flattened transversely, by use-abrasion. The other edges and the faces show varying amounts of spalling, pecking, and grinding. Lunate, subrectangular, and irregular in outline form, these tools measure as follows: length 4.1 to 10.8 cm., width 3.2 to 5.7 cm., thickness 0.6 to 0.9 cm., and weight 13 to 47 gm. They were found in the fill of Test D, Area IV, and Kiva E (1 each), and on the surface of the Lower East Trash Slope (1).

Similar implements have been reported, in small numbers and under different designations, from several other archeological locations and sites in the Southwest. Two single-edged "rasping and scouring implements" of sandstone were found in the La Plata

Figure 288. *Knife.*

Figure 289. *Shaft cutters.*

Figure 291. *Drills.*

district in southwestern Colorado and northwestern New Mexico (Morris, 1939, p. 129, Pl. 135 *c, d*). Twelve single-edged or double-edged "sandstone saws" were recovered from Pueblo Bonito, in Chaco Canyon, northwestern New Mexico (Judd, 1954, pp. 124–125, Fig. 35). Five sandstone implements with one to three beveled edges, provisionally termed "stone files," were obtained at Pecos pueblo, in north-central New Mexico (Kidder, 1932, pp. 82–83, Fig. 58). Three single-edged implements of fine-grained sandstone, called "smooth-edged stone saws," were found at the Swarts ruin in southwestern New Mexico (Cosgrove, H. S. and C. B., 1932, p. 46, Fig. 4). Our experiments with the Long House saws indicate that these implements are useful for cutting wood and bone but *not* stone materials. The results accord with the findings of Kidder (wood) and of the Cosgroves (bone), but they do not substantiate Judd's assertion and Kidder's speculation that such tools were used, or might be useful, for working stone as well as various organic materials.

Figure 290. *Saws.*

Drills. The seven implements of this class are described under three styles as follows.

Style 1: *Triangular.* 5 complete or nearly complete specimens. Three of these implements are marginally retouched along the lateral and basal edges on both faces (fig. 291d); another is marginally retouched along the lateral edges on one face; and another implement—mounted at the end of a small barked and trimmed shaft of saltbush and secured by a narrow strip of yucca leaf—is marginally retouched along one lateral edge on both faces (fig. 291a, and inset enlargement). The tips on four specimens are blunted and smoothed by use. The other specimen, lacking the tip, is nicely rounded and polished all over. It seems not unlikely that this implement served ultimately as a turkey "gizzard stone."

Materials: chert (4), quartzite (1).

Measurements: length 2.5 to 3.2 cm. (4), width 0.9 to 1.3 cm.,
thickness 0.3 to 0.7 cm., and weight 1.3 to 2.4gm. (4)

Provenience: floor (floor3), Room 4 (1); fill,Room 2 (1); surface and fill, Lower East Trash Slope (3).

Style 2: *Irregular.* The single specimen is a bladelike flake of chert with a short triangular projection at the end opposite the bulb (fig. 291b). The projection is unifacially retouched on each side, and the tip is blunted and smoothed. The sides of the flake are bifacially flaked and dulled by use, suggesting that the implement was also used for cutting. The specimen measures 5.3 by 3.4 by 1.1 cm., and weighs 18 gm. It was found in the fill of Kiva N.

Style 3: *Bipointed.* The single specimen has a long, tapering pile at one end and a short, broad, triangular point at the other end (fig. 291c). Made of quartzite, it is fully flaked and marginally retouched on both faces. The lateral edges are straight, even, and sharp, but the tip at each end is blunted and dulled. The implement measures, overall, 6.1 by 2.1 by 1.0 cm., and weighs 8.4 gm. The pile portion measures 4.1 by 1.5 by 0.8 cm., and the triangular point portion measures 2.0 by 2.1 by 1.0 cm. This unusual specimen was found in the fill of Test L.

Choppers. Seventy-two complete implements of varying size and shape, which exhibit from one to three edges that are bifacially retouched by percussion flaking and are (usually) blunted or flaked and nicked by use, are considered to be choppers, or hand-held tools employed in severing meat, bone, wood, and other organic materials. Four styles are recognized.

Style 1: *Large core.* 15 specimens. The majority of these implements (8) have a single working edge on the long axis, or side, of the core (fig. 292a). Four specimens have two working edges each, on the long axis of the core (fig. 292b). Two implements have two working edges, each, on the long and short (end) axes, of the core. The prepared edges range from straight to sinuous, even to uneven, and sharp to dull (blunted by crumbling, or use-flaked and nicked).

Materials: claystone (9), chert (3), basalt (1), syenite porphyry (1), indurated sandstone (1).

Shapes: suboval (5), ovate (4), irregular (3), oval (1), discoidal (1), subrectangular (1).

Measurements: length 7.7 to 11.9 cm., width 5.1 to 9.8 cm., thickness 2.0 to 6.1 cm., and weight 170 to 702 gm.

Provenience: fill, Area VII and Kivas I and O (3 each), Rooms 15, 48, 55, Kivas D, E, F, (1 each).

Style 2: *Small core.* 28 specimens. Over half of these implements (16) have a single working edge on the long axis of the core (fig. 292c). The rest have two working edges, each, on the long axis (4 specimens; fig. 292d), or two working edges, each, on the long and short axes (4 specimens), or on the short axis (1 specimen); or a single working edge on the short axis (3 specimens). The prepared edges range from straight to sinuous, even to uneven, and sharp to dull.

Materials: chert (16), claystone (12).

Shapes: irregular (12), ovate (6), suboval (5), subrectangular (4), subsquare (1).

Measurements: length 3.7 to 7.0 cm., width 3.3 to 6.1 cm., thickness 1.7 to 3.5 cm., and weight 30 to 103 gm.

Provenience: subfloor fill, Great Kiva (1); floor, Room 14 (1); firepit, ash fill, Room 87 (2); fill, Room 48 (6), Area VII (3), Room 81 and Kiva R (2 each), Rooms 3, 52, 56, 57, 88, Kivas D, F (1 each); surface and fill, Area IV (1), Upper East Trash Slope (1), West Trash Slope (2).

Figure 292. *Choppers.*

Figure 293. *Chopper.*

Style 3: *Flake.* 28 specimens. The majority of these choppers (12) have a single working edge on the long axis of the random flake (fig. 292e). The other implements have two working edges, each, on the long axis (4 specimens) or on the long and short axes (7 specimens), or three working edges on the long and short axes of the random flake (5 specimens, fig. 292f). The prepared edges range from straight to sinuous, even to uneven, and sharp to dull.

Materials: claystone (17), chert (8), quartzite (2), basalt (1).

Shapes: irregular (12), suboval (5), ovate (5), subrectangular (5), subsquare (1).

Measurements: length 4.2 to 8.5 cm., width 3.4 to 7.0 cm., thickness 1.3 to 2.7 cm., and weight 29 to 126 gm.

Provenience: subfloor fill, Rooms 57 and 81 (1 each); floor, southern recess, Kiva U (1); fill, Room 48 (9), Room 81 (2), Rooms 36, 47, 52, 55, Areas III, VII, IX, Kivas D, J, M (1 each); surface and fill, Lower East Trash Slope (2) and Upper East Trash Slope (1); and general (1).

Style 4: *Slab.* The single specimen is a tabular piece of indurated sandstone, subrectangular in outline, which has been bifacially flaked along one side and part of one end (fig. 293). The prepared edges are straight and slightly uneven; they are flaked back and blunted as a result of use. The specimen measures 23.5 by 12.0 by 2.3 cm., and weighs 1,139 gm. It was found in the fill of Room 12.

This implement, unlike the other more generalized choppers from Long House, looks as though it may have been designed and used specifically as a cleaver.

Ax Heads. Thirty-three complete or nearly complete single-bitted and seven complete double-bitted implements and five bit sections of implements are present in the Long House assemblage. The complete or nearly complete specimens possess notches in the sides, and sometimes also grooves (in one or both faces), for "seating" wooden handles, none of which were found associated with the stone objects.

The group as a whole is here designated "ax heads" rather than simply "axes," in order to suggest their function as parts of *hafted* cutting or chopping implements. Robert F. Nichols, an archeologist on the staff of the Wetherill Mesa Project, suggested to us that wooden handles for ax heads and hammer or maul heads could have been fashioned easily at the work-site and may have lasted for only brief periods of time. Thus, stone heads are the durable, valuable, easily transported portions of these hafted implements, and the wooden handles are the frangible and readily replaceable accessories.

The complete or nearly complete specimens are described under five styles.

Style 1: *Notched, single-bitted.* 13 complete and 2 nearly complete specimens. Commonly, a single transverse notch occurs in each side, slightly nearer the poll than the bit (10 specimens, fig. 294 a and b, and fig. 295); and possibly two additional specimens whose bit, in each case, has presumably been greatly foreshortened by repeated sharpening, as in fig. 294e. Variations include (a) a deep transverse notch in each side, near the poll, plus three shallow transverse notches—two on the upper or outer side, and one on the lower or inner side, of the ax blade (one specimen, fig. 294c); (b) two sets of single transverse notches in each side, the deeper pair nearer the poll (one specimen, fig. 294d); and (c) a dual transverse notch in one side and a single transverse notch, not in alinement with the former, in the other side (one specimen, fig. 294f).

The variations are interpreted as follows: the supernumerary notches in (a) seem to indicate an unusually elaborate device for hafting; the two pairs of notches in (b) suggest an adjustment for proper balance, with the deeper poll-ward pair of notches made later than the shallower, forward pair of notches, as the bit became considerably foreshortened by repeated sharpening; and the differing, unalined notches in (c) are aspects of the re-fashioning of an ax head whose original bit was broken off. The remaining portion of the bit of this specimen was converted to a poll; the central part of the poll was bifacially ground to a cutting edge; and the single transverse groove in one side replaced the original (dual) groove, which was shattered along with the bit.

The notches are symmetrically concave in 29 cases, asymmetrically concave in five cases. Single notches range in width from 0.7 to 3.8 cm., and in depth from 0.1 to 0.9 cm. The one dual notch is 3.2 cm. in total width and 0.7 cm. in maximum depth.

Thirteen of the implements in this group are waterworn cobbles, shaped mainly around the perimeter, including the bifacially beveled bit and the notches, and less commonly on the faces, by spalling or flaking, pecking, and grinding. The other two specimens are a core of cream-colored chert roughly spalled all over, with the notches neatly pecked, and a core of lime-green hornfels spalled all over, with the bit and portions of the poll and faces ground and polished, and with the notches spalled and pecked (fig. 295).

Figure 295. *Ax head.*

Figure 294. *Ax heads.*

The cutting edge of the bits ranges in width from 2.9 to 6.9 cm. The cutting edge is intact in 13 cases (eight are sharp, two are dull, and three are minutely edge-flaked by use) and is unifacially flaked back in two cases (one is sharp, the other is dull). In seven specimens the poll is spalled or battered by use.

Materials: claystone (3), basalt (3), diorite (2), granite (1), porphyry (1), chert (1), hornfels (1), quartzite (1), schist (1), sandstone (1).

Shapes: subrectangular (12), irregular (3).

Measurements: length 7.0 to 14.9 cm., width 3.8 to 10.2 cm., thickness 2.4 to 4.6 cm., and weight 84 to 774 gm.

Provenience: floor, Room 49 and Kiva H (1 each); in niche, Kiva J (1); fill, Rooms 6, 28, 37, 47, 58, Kivas F, R (1 each); with Burial 10, Lower East Trash Slope (1); surface and fill, Lower East Trash Slope (3); surface, Kiva I (1).

Style 2: *Notched, double-bitted.* 5 complete specimens. In each instance, a single transverse notch occurs in each side, about midway between the ends. Generally, the notches are symmetrically concave, and they range in width from about 2.1 to 3.8 cm. and in depth from 0.4 to 0.9 cm.

Four of these ax heads are cores. One of these, including the notches, is spalled all over; another is spalled almost all over and has pecked notches; another is spalled all over except for parts of each face, is partly ground, and has pecked grooves (fig. 296, top); and the fourth is ground and polished all over except for the notches, one of which is pecked or spalled and the other is pecked (fig. 296, center). The remaining specimen in this group is a tabular piece of sandstone, bifacially spalled around the ends (bits) and along one side. The notches are pecked; one face is pecked and partly ground, and the obverse face is partly ground (fig. 296, bottom).

The "cutting" edge of the bits ranges in width from about 5.8 to 10.8 cm., and is intact in every case. In two specimens, one edge is sharp and the other is slightly dull; in two cases, both edges are slightly dull; and in one case, one edge is sharp and the other is flaked by use.

Materials: quartzite (1), hornfels (1), hematite rock (1), slaty shale (1), indurated sandstone (1).

Shapes: subrectangular (3), suboval (2)

Measurements: length 12.8 to 17.3 cm., width 7.0 to 11.0 cm., thickness 2.5 to 3.8 cm., and weight 337 to 551 gm.

Provenience: floor, Kiva J (1); on banquette, Kiva R (1); fill, Room 37 (2) and West Trash Slope (1).

Style 3: *Full-grooved, single bitted.* 13 complete specimens. All have a single transverse groove that completely encircles the ax head, nearer the poll than the bit. The grooves vary considerably in contour and dimensions. In seven specimens, the grooves are asymmetrically concave and range in width from 1.8 to 3.6 cm. and in depth from 0.05 to 0.7 cm. In two specimens, they are symmetrically concave and range in width from 1.3 to 2.6 cm. and in depth from 0.15 to 0.35 cm. The grooves in three specimens have insloping sides and a slightly convex bottom, and range in width from 2.6 to 3.9 cm. and in maximum depth from 0.3 to 0.6 cm. The groove in the remaining specimen is symmetrically concave in the sides and irregular in the faces, and measures from about 0.6 to 2.2 cm. in width and from about 0.15 to 0.5 cm. in depth.

Eight of these ax heads are cores shaped by spalling and pecking, with bifacially ground bit, ground groove, and ground or partially ground poll (fig. 297a and b). Four specimens are cobbles, with bifacially ground bit, pecked or pecked and ground groove, and ground or unground poll (fig. 297c). The remaining specimen, which has the symmetrical-irregular groove noted above, is a slab of hematitic sandstone roughly shaped around the perimeter, including the bit, by spalling. The groove is ground on one face is pecked on the reverse face and the sides.

Figure 296. *Ax heads.*

The cutting edges of the bits range in width from about 2.9 to 6.4 cm. The cutting edge is intact in 12 cases (six have a sharp edge throughout and two are sharp but nicked at one corner, three are dull, and one is dull and nicked in the middle of the edge). The cutting edge of one blade is flaked back, nicked, and dulled by light battering. The poll in five specimens is spalled by use.

Materials: claystone (4), basalt (2), diorite (2), syenite porphyry (2), schist (1), chert (1), hematitic sandstone (1).

Shapes: subrectangular (7), irregular (5), suboval (1).

Measurements: length 7.8 to 22.7 cm., width 4.8 to 8.5 cm., thickness 2.1 to 6.6 cm., and weight 151 to 1,378 gm.

Provenience: subfloor ventilator shaft, Kiva B (1); floor, Room 80 and Kiva T (1 each); fill, Room 12, Area VII, Kiva J (2 each), Room 88, Kiva O, R, Test K (1 each).

Style 4: *C-grooved, single-bitted.* 5 specimens. In each case, a single transverse groove in *one* face and in each side, like the letter C, occurs nearer the poll than the bit. The grooves are symmetrically concave and range in width from 2.0 to 3.3 cm. and in depth from 0.1 to 1.0 cm.

Four of the ax heads are cores shaped by spalling and pecking, with bifacially ground bit, pecked or pecked and ground groove, and ground or unground poll (fig. 297d). The fifth specimen is a cobble, with bifacially ground bit, pecked groove, and unground poll.

The cutting edge of the bits varies in width from 3.0 to 6.5 cm. The cutting edge is intact, but dull, in two cases, is partly intact and partly flaked back in two cases (one is sharp, the other dull), and is flaked back and sharpened by regrinding in one case. The poll may be spalled by use in one specimen but not in the other four.

Materials: claystone (2), basalt (2), quartzite (1).

Shapes: subrectangular (3), irregular (2)

Measurements: length 9.5 to 16.3 cm., width 5.4 to 10.1 cm., thickness 2.9 to 6.8 cm., and weight 264 to 1,581 gm.

Provenience: subfloor ventilator shaft, Kiva B (1); ventilator shaft, Kiva E (1); floor, Kiva T (1); fill, Kivas O and Q (1 each).

***Style 5:** C-grooved, double-bitted.* 2 specimens. In each case, the single transverse, C-shaped groove occurs about midway between the ends. One specimen, restored from two pieces fractured through the groove, is a core of slate, shaped by overall spalling and pecking (fig. 297e). It measures 12.5 by 6.9 by 3.3 cm., and weighs 431 gm. The spalled and pecked groove varies in width from 1.3 to 2.4 cm. and in depth 0.2 to 0.5 cm. The "working" edges of the bits, bifacially percussion-flaked and blunt, are 5.5 cm. and 5.9 cm. wide.

The other specimen is a core of indurated sandstone, shaped mainly around the perimeter by spalling. It measures 11.7 by 6.8 by 3.5 cm., and weighs 285 gm. The spalled and pecked groove varies in width from about 1.8 to 2.6 cm. and in depth from 0.3 to 1.0 cm. The working edges of the bits, bifacially spalled and very blunt, are 2.9 and 3.5 cm. wide.

The first specimen was found on the floor of Kiva O, the second in the fill of Room 81. Both appear to be unfinished.

The five bit fragments, which cannot be assigned to any of the styles recognized above, are portions of cobbles of syenite porphyry (two specimens) or parts of cores of claystone (two specimens) and granite (one specimen), with the cutting edge in each case bifacially spalled and ground. The cutting edge of the bit fragments varies in width from about 3.6 to 6.7 cm. (or within the range of widths of the cutting edges of the ax heads described previously), and is intact in every instance. In two fragments, the cutting edge is sharp; in three fragments, it is edge-flaked and dulled by use. One fragment was found in the fill of Room 37, one of the surface of Area I, and three were taken from the surface or fill of the Lower East Trash Slope.

Figure 297. *Ax heads.*

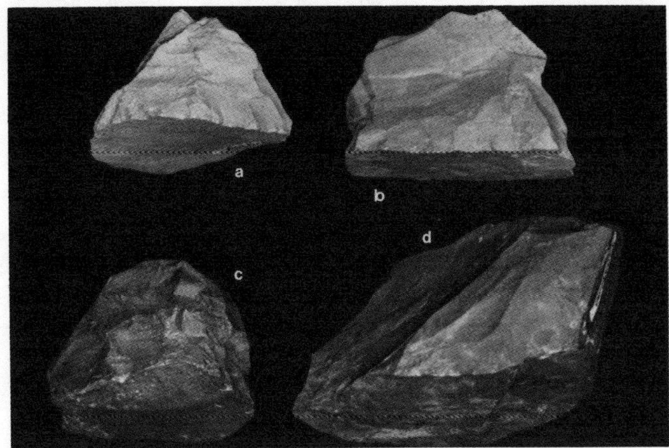

Figure 298. *Planes.*

Most of the ax heads in the Long House assemblage appear, in view of the materials (hard and resilient igneous or metamorphic rock) and of their condition, to have been used for heavy and light cutting or chopping tasks. But a few ax heads, excluding the two unfinished (?) specimens of Style 5, seem to be either too friable (two of sandstone and slaty shale, of Style 2; and one of hematitic sandstone, of Style 3) or too finely finished (one of hornfels, of Style 1; and one of "hematitic rock," of Style 2) to have served purely utilitarian purposes unless the objects of work were of exceptionally fragile consistency. The occurrence of the notched, single-bitted ax head of polished lime-green hornfels (Style 1) with a human burial (Burial 10), together with several other objects which will be described later, suggests that this artifact may not have been an implement in the usual sense but a status symbol or an object of personal veneration.

It is interesting to note that in 12 or 13 of the 33 single-bitted stone ax heads from Long House the poll has been spalled and/or battered by use. The dual chopping-and-hammering function of these implements is often seen in single-bitted steel ax heads in our culture.

Planes. The 33 implements assigned to this class are relatively small and relatively thick cores (19) and flakes (14) possessing a flat or slightly concave nether face and an upper face with steep facets, one or more of which are flaked by percussion to form a working (or cutting) edge or edges. Nine specimens are conoidal and retouched on all or most of the perimeter (fig. 298a). Seven specimens (three with keeled backs) have two working edges, each, on the long axis (fig. 298d); four specimens (two with keeled backs) have two working edges, each, on the long and short (end) axis; one specimen has three working edges—one on the long and two on the short axis (fig. 298b); and five specimens (one with a keeled back) have three working edges, each—two on the long axis and one on the short axis (fig. 298c). The angle of the working edges of the implements ranges from 50° to 80° and averages about 65°. The working edges are generally straight and uneven, and are dulled or flaked back and nicked by use.

Materials: chert (27), claystone (5), quartzite (1).

Shapes: subtriangular (11), conoidal (9), ovate (5), subrectangular (4), suboval (1), lunate (1), lozenge (1), irregular (1).

Measurements: length 3.2 to 8.6 cm., width 2.0 to 6.1 cm., thickness 1.7 to 4.3 cm., and weight 14.3 to 93 gm.

Provenience: subfloor fill, Great Kiva (1); on banquette, Kiva R (1); fill, Area X (4), Area IX and Kiva N (2 each), Rooms 3, 28, 48, 81, 84, Kivas Q, R (1 each); surface and fill, Areas IV, X (1 each), Lower East Trash Slope (6) and Upper East Trash Slope (3), West Trash Slope (3); general (1); backdirt (1).

The hand-held implements described above were probably employed mainly for barking and dressing wood and other moderately resistant vegetal materials used for many purposes.

Scrapers: The 85 complete or fragmentary implements of this class in the Long House assemblage include 67 random flakes, 4 end fragments of random flakes, 8 blades, 4 bulbar-end sections of blades, 1 piece of tabular stone, and 1 spall from a *tchamahia.* The working (or scraping) edges of three specimens, all of chalcedony, are retouched by pressure-flaking: a blade (fig. 299c) and the bulbar-end fragment of a blade, each with two working edges on the long axis, unifacially retouched on the upper or convex face; and a random flake with two working edges on the long axis, one unifacially retouched on the convex face and the other unifacially retouched on the bulbar face, and with an inset or notch for hafting on one side which may or may not have been fortuitous (fig. 299j). The working edge or edges of all the rest of the specimens are retouched by percussion-flaking in the following ways (on the long axis or side; on the short axis or end):

Unifacial, upper or convex face: one side only—23 random flakes (fig. 299a), 2 end fragments of random flakes, and 3 blades; one end only—4 random flakes (fig. 299e), and the end fragment of a random flake; one side and one end—16 random flakes (fig. 299d), and on spall from a *tchamahia* (fig. 299i); two sides—4 random flakes, 1 fragment of a random flake, 1 blade, and 1 bulbar-end section of a blade; two sides and one end—1 random flake; three sides—1 random flake; and four sides—1 random flake (fig. 299g).

Figure 299. *Scrapers.*

Unifacial, lower or bulbar face: one side only—9 random flakes and 1 bulbar-end section of a blade; one side and one end—1 random flake; two sides—4 random flakes, 1 blade, and 1 bulbar-end section of a blade.

Unifacial, opposite edges or opposite and adjacent edges, upper and lower facets: two sides—1 random flake and 2 blades (fig. 299b); two sides and one end—1 random flake (fig. 299f); two ends—1 tabular piece of stone (fig. 299h).

The angle of the working edges of these implements ranges from 10° to 80° and averages about 35°. The working edges are generally straight and uneven, and are minutely flaked and nicked by use.

Materials: chert (43), claystone (32), chalcedony (7), quartzite (1), obsidian (1), metamorphosed shale (1).

Shapes: irregular (37), subrectangular (20), ovate (9), subtriangular (6), pentagonal (4), lozenge (2), subsquare (1), suboval (1), lunate (1), trapeze (1) (82 specimens).

Measurements: length 2.2 to 11.3 cm. (81 specimens), width 1.7 to 5.3 cm., thickness 0.5 to 2.4 cm., and weight 3.3 to 72 gm. (81 specimens).

Provenience: subfloor fill, Great Kiva (2), Rooms 54, 65, 74, 76, 84, Kiva N (1 each); floor, Room 79, Kivas I, R (1 each); floor of niche, Kiva R (1); fill, Area X (10), Kiva Q (5), Room 12, Area VII, Kivas I, R (3 each), Room 81, Areas IV, XII, (2 each), Test F, Rooms 2, 6, 14, 25, 35, 64, 84, 87, Pithouse 1, Areas I, IX, Kivas B, C, E, N, T, U (1 each); surface and fill, Area X, Upper East Trash Slope, West Trash Slope (5 each), Lower East Trash Slope (2), Areas VI, XII (1 each); general (2); and backdirt (1).

The six implements retouched on the short axis only (fig. 299e and h) and the 20 specimens retouched on both the long and short axes (fig. 299d and f) might be dubbed, respectively, "end scrapers" and "side-and-end scrapers;" and the other 59 implements, retouched on the long axes, might be called "side scrapers." However, the forms of the implements seem so amorphous (except for those made on blades and blade fragments) and the attention given to their manufacture seems so perfunctory (with the exception of the three implements retouched by pressure-flaking) that we feel it is more appropriate simply to designate the entire group as "scrapers." With one possible exception (fig. 299j), these implements were seemingly hand-held. As a class, they were probably used in working a variety of organic materials.

Utilized Flakes. One hundred and three implements in the Long House assemblage are small random flakes whose edges and angles or projections are altered by use and not by secondary flaking. The various modifications are described, and the different uses that presumably produced these modifications are suggested, under the following eight styles.

Style 1: *Small random flakes with one or more edges showing irregular, shallow scars and nicks on one face, resulting from use as scraping (?) tools.* 60 specimens (fig. 300a). The 91 use-modified edges of these specimens are sharp in 88 cases and slightly rounded or dulled in only 3 cases.

Materials: chert (44), claystone (10), quartzite (3) basalt (2), chalcedony (1).

Shapes: irregular (35), subtriangular (11) suboval (5) subrectangular (3), discoidal (2), lozenge (2), lunate (1), trapeze (1).

Measurements: length 2.1 to 6.7 cm., width 1.6 to 5.9 cm., thickness 0.3 to 2.5 cm., and weight 1.3 to 50.7 gm.

Figure 300. *Utilized flakes.*

Provenience: subfloor ventilator shaft, fill, Kiva B (1); subfloor fill, Rooms 32 and 66 (1 each); floor fill, Room 30 (2), Kiva N (1); fill, Room 12 (4), Rooms 37, 48, Area IX, West Trash Slope (3 each), Rooms 28, 35, 46, 52, Areas VII, X, Kivas N, U (2 each), Rooms 2, 26, 47, 54, 76, 81, 88, Kivas I, M (1 each); surface and fill, Area X and Lower East Trash Slope (4 each), Upper East Trash Slope (3), Area VIII and general (1 each).

Style 2: *Small random flakes with one or more edges showing irregular, shallow scars and nicks on opposed faces, resulting from use as cutting (?) tools.* 9 specimens (fig. 300b). The 14 use-modified edges of these specimens are sharp in 12 instances and slightly rounded or dulled in 2 instances.

Materials: chert (4), claystone (3), basalt (1), chalcedony (1).

Shapes: irregular (5), suboval (2), ovate (1) subtriangular (1).

Measurements: length 2.8 to 6.1 cm., width 2.6 to 4.6 cm., thickness 0.4 to 1.9 cm., and weight 1.7 to 4.08 gm.

Provenience: fill, Room 14 (2), Rooms 12, 26, 48, 84, Area X, Kiva N (1 each); surface, Area X (1).

Style 3: *Small random flakes with two or more edges showing irregular, shallow flake scars and nicks on one face and on opposed faces, resulting from use as scraping (?) and cutting (?) tools.* 8 specimens (fig. 300c). The 18 use-modified edges of these specimens are sharp.

Materials: chert (4), claystone (1), basalt (1), chalcedony (1), metamorphosed shale (1).

Shapes: irregular (5), subrectangular (2), subtriangular (1).

Measurements: length 2.2 to 6.5 cm., width 2.2 to 4.5 cm., thickness 0.5 to 1.6 cm., and weight 4 to 36 gm.

Provenience: General Feature 3, Room 48 (1); fill, Rooms 12, 48, Area IX, Kivas M, U (1 each); surface and fill, Area IX and general (1 each).

Style 4: *Small random flakes with a notch or concavity and one or more edges showing irregular, shallow flake scars and nicks on one face, and sometimes one edge showing irregular shallow flake scars and nicks on opposed faces, resulting from use as shaft cutting (?) and scraping (?), and also cutting (?), tools.* 4 specimens (fig. 300d). The three notches range from 0.7 to 0.9 cm. in width and from 0.1 to 0.2 cm. in depth. The concavity measures 1.1 cm. in width and 0.1 cm. in depth. The use-modified edge of the notches and of the concavity and the nine additional use-modified edges in the four specimens are sharp.

Materials: chert (2), chalcedony (2).

Shapes: subtriangular (2), irregular (2).

Measurements: length 3.6 to 5.8 cm., width 3.2 to 4.1 cm., thickness 0.8 to 1.4 cm., and weight 12 to 17 gm.

Provenience: fill, Room 75 (1); surface and fill, Room 66, Upper East Trash Slope, and general (1 each).

Style 5: *Small random flakes with a triangular point or projection showing irregular, shallow flake scars and sometimes evidences of abrasion, and one or more edges showing irregular, shallow flake scars and nicks on one face, resulting from use as drilling (?) and scraping (?) tools.* 3 specimens. The tip of the point or projection is blunted in each case by flaking and/or abrasion (fig. 300e). Two of the use-modified edges (on two specimens) are sharp, and two of the use-modified edges (on one specimen) are rounded or dulled.

Materials: chalcedony (2), chert (1).

Shapes: irregular (2), subtriangular (1).

Measurements: length 2.9 to 4.3 cm., width 2.1 to 3.0 cm., thickness 0.7 to 1.2 cm., and weight 2.9 to 9.7 gm.

Provenience: fill, Room 35 and Area X (1 each); surface and fill, Area X (1).

Style 6: *Small random flakes with one "beaked" point or projection showing irregular, shallow flake scars and evidences of abrasion, and one edge showing irregular, shallow flake scars and nicks on one face or on opposed faces, resulting from use as engraving (?) and scraping (?) or cutting (?) tools* 2 specimens. Both implements are flakes of chert. One of them, lunate in outline, measuring 4.8 by 3.9 by 1.4 cm. and weighing 20.1 gm., has a flaked and abraded "beaked" projection and a unifacially flaked and nicked, and sharp, edge (fig. 300f). It was found in the fill of Room 28. The other, subtriangular in outline, measuring 4.0 by 3.0 by 0.9 cm. and weighing 7.6 gm., has a flaked and abraded "beaked" point and a bifacially flaked and nicked, and slightly dulled, edge. This implement came from the fill or Room 35.

Style 7: *Small random flakes with one or two edges which are wholly or partly abraded by use (round or flat, or partly round and partly flat in transverse section) and, often, with one or more edges which are nicked and/or flaked unifacially or bifacially by use.* 16 specimens (fig. 300g and h). On the basis of recent experimentation, I have observed that the edge-abrasion seen on these 16 random flakes from Long House—and the 6 utilized blades and 1 utilized core from this site, to be described below (as well as on numerous implements of these classes from other sites in the district)—resulted from their use in incising and cutting or sawing the local soft, fine-grained sandstone (Wheeler, 1965).

Materials: chert (13), basalt (2), claystone (1).

Shapes: irregular (7), subtriangular (4), trapeze (2), suboval (1), ovate (1), subrectangular (1).

Measurements: length 2.5 to 5.2 cm., width 1.8 to 5.0 cm., thickness 0.6 tog 2.0 cm., and weight 3.4 to 42.6 gm.

Provenience: subfloor, Room 32 (1); firepit, ash fill, Room 87

(1); fill, Rooms 2, 12, 28, 35, Kivas A, C, G, R, West Trash Slope (1 each); surface and fill, Area X, Lower East Trash Slope, West Trash Slope (1 each), and general (2).

Style 8: *Small random flakes with one sloping side grooved and horizontally striated.* The single specimen, of metamorphosed shale, irregular in outline, measures 3.5 by 3.8 by 1.1 cm., and weighs 11.1 gm. (fig. 300i). It was found in the fill of Kiva P.

The unusual modification of this specimen seems to have resulted from its use as a scraping (?) tool. But questions as to how it was used and on what material elude explanation at this time.

Utilized Blades. Twenty-two implements from Long House are complete blades or portions of blades; i.e., "long, parallel-sided, thin flakes" (Burkitt, 1963, p. 49), whose edges are modified by use. They are described under five styles, showing various modifications presumably produced by different uses.

Style 1: *Blades with one or more edges showing irregular, shallow flake scars and nicks on one face or alternately on opposed faces, resulting from use as scraping (?) tools.* 4 complete blades (fig. 301a), and the section of a blade below the bulbar end. The eight use-modified edges of these specimens are sharp in seven cases and rounded or dulled in one case.

Materials: chert (4), petrified wood (1)
Shapes: subrectangular (2), suboval (2), irregular (1).
Measurements: length 3.7 to 8.7 cm., width 1.5 to 4.4 cm., thickness 0.9 to 1.7 cm., and weight 5 to 70 gm.
Provenience: fill, Room 48 (3), Kiva B (1); surface, Area IV (1).

Style 2: *Blades with one or more edges showing irregular, shallow flake scars and nicks on opposed faces, resulting from use as cutting (?) tools.* 6 complete blades (fig. 301b), and the bulbar end-section of a blade. The 14 use-modified edges of these specimens are sharp in six cases, dulled in six cases, and partly sharp and partly dulled in two cases.

Figure 301. *Utilized blades.*

Materials: chert (5), chalcedony (1), basalt (1).
Shapes: subrectangular (5), irregular (2).
Measurements: length 3.6 to 7.9 cm., width 2.0 to 4.9 cm., thickness 0.4 to 1.5 cm., and weight 5.6 to 48.6 gm.
Provenience: fill, Room 12 (3); Rooms 2, 56, 84, Area VII (1 each).

Style 3: *Blades with two or more edges showing irregular, shallow flake scars and nicks on one face and on opposed faces, resulting from use as scraping (?) and cutting (?) tools.* 2 specimens. One of these implements, a subrectangular blade of claystone, measuring 8.8 by 6.3 by 2.1 cm. and weighing 99 gm., has two unifacially flaked and nicked edges, and one bifacially flaked and nicked edge; all are sharp. This specimen was found in the fill of Kiva I. The other implement, a suboval blade of chert, measuring 4.7 by 2.4 by 0.9 cm. and weighing 9.7 gm., has one bifacially flaked and nicked edge which is dulled and one unifacially flaked and nicked edge which is sharp (fig. 301c). This specimen came from backdirt.

Style 4: *Blades with one or two notches showing irregular, shallow flake scars and nicks on one face or opposed faces, and sometimes one or more edges showing irregular, shallow flake scars and nicks on opposed faces, resulting from use as shaft cutting (?) and cutting (?) tools.* 2 specimens. One of these implements, a subrectangular blade of chert, measuring 4.2 by 2.3 by 0.6 cm. and weighing 6.5 gm., has two unifacially flaked notches in one edge which are about 0.4 and 0.8 cm. in width and 0.1 cm. in depth, and are sharp. No other modifications are noted in this specimen, which was found in the fill of Area X. The other implement, a subrectangular blade of banded chert, measuring 5.1 by 2.7 by 0.8 cm. and weighing 9.9 gm., has one bifacially flaked notch in one sharp edge, which is bifacially flaked and nicked along much of its length, and two additional bifacially flaked and nicked and slightly dulled edges, one opposite the edge with the notch, the other at the bulbar end of the blade (fig. 301d). The sharp-edge notch measures 0.9 cm. in width and 0.2 cm. in maximum depth. This specimen was found in the fill of Room 9.

Style 5: *Blades with one to three edges which are wholly or partly abraded (flat or round in transverse section), and are sometimes also unifacially flaked, by use, and often with one or two edges which are nicked and/or flaked unifacially by use.* Four complete blades (fig. 301e and f), and two bulbar end-sections of blades. The suggested explanation of the edge-abrasion seen on these specimens, as well as other use-modified implements from Long House, was given above (see Style 7 of the utilized random flakes).

Materials: chert (5), claystone (1).
Shapes: subrectangular (6).
Measurements: length 3.2 to 6.8 cm., width 2.1 to 4.2 cm., thickness 0.9 to 1.8 cm., and weight 7 to 47.9 gm.
Provenience: fill, Kivas I and T (1 each); surface and fill, Areas VI and VII, and general (1 each); and backdirt (1).

Utilized Cores. Six implements in the Long House assemblage are cores whose edges or pointed end are modified by use. They are described under four styles, showing different modifications presumably resulting from different uses.

Style 1: *Cores with one or two flat or nearly flat faces and one or two steep ends or sides, the edges of which show irregular, shallow flake scars and nicks, resulting from use as planing (?) tools.* 3 specimens. One of these implements, a small subrectangular core of chert, measuring 4.6 by 3.4 by 3.5 cm. and weighing 84 gm., has one steep end which is unifacially flaked and nicked, and dulled by use. It was found in the fill of Room 74. Another specimen, an ovate core of chert, measuring 5.5 by 4.1 by 2.9 cm. and weighing 74 gm., has one side which is unifacially flaked and nicked by use. It was recovered from the fill of

Figure 302. *Utilized cores.*

Area X. The third implement, a large irregular core of chert, measuring 12.8 by 8.6 by 5.7 cm. and weighing 814 gm., has two sides which are unifacially flaked and nicked, and dulled, by use, on opposed faces (fig. 302d). It was found in the fill of Kiva O.

Style 2: *Core with one edge showing irregular, shallow flake scars and nicks on one face, resulting from use as a scraping (?) tool.* The single specimen, of chert, irregular in outline, measures 5.3 by 3.6 by 2.1 cm. and weighs 37.4 gm. (fig. 302a). The use-modified edge is sharp. This implement was found on the Lower East Trash Slope, accompanying Burial 3.

Style 3: *Core with a triangular point showing irregular, shallow flake scars and evidence of abrasion, resulting from use as a drilling (?) tool.* The single specimen, of chert, subtriangular in outline, measures 4.5 by 3.1 by 1.8 cm. and weighs 19.2 gm. (fig. 302b). It was found in the fill of Kiva C.

Style 4: *Core with one edge abraded (flat in transverse section).* The single specimen, of chert, subtriangular in outline, measures 5.9 by 4.2 by 3.2 cm. and weighs 96 gm. (fig. 302c). It was found in the fill of Room 37.

The suggested explanation of edge-abrasion manifested in this implement, and in other use-modified implements from the site, has been given previously (see Style 7 of the utilized random flakes).

IMPLEMENTS FOR GRINDING

The grinding of foodstuffs and pigments at Long House was done by means of pairs of simple stone or stone and wooden implements, one element representing a solid resisting force at rest and the other a solid opposing force put in motion and made to exert pressure by the hand(s) in either a reciprocating or a rotating direction. The six classes of grinding implements discussed below comprise 505 items and account for 21 percent of the stone artifacts reported on from the site.

Figure 303. *Metates, Style 1.*

Metates. Ninety-six complete or fragmentary implements are considered, in view of their form, size, proportions, and condition, to be metates or metate "blanks," used or intended to be used with manos for the principal if not the exclusive purpose of grinding shelled corn, and possibly also wild seeds, into coarse meal or fine flour by the reciprocating technic.

Metates uncovered *in situ* are, as a rule, either stationary—embedded in adobe mortar in slab-lined enclosures or "bins"—or are free-standing and supported by stones. In either case, the metate invariably slopes away from the operator, presumably so that the meal will fall easily from the working surface and concentrate in one place.

The complete and fragmentary metates from Long House are described under six styles.

Style 1: *Plain-faced, with one grinding surface.* 87 specimens, including 58 complete or nearly complete, whole or restored specimens, 20 end fragments, 4 corner fragments, and 5 complete "blanks".

The "used" complete or fragmentary metates in this group, numbering 82 specimens, are preponderantly of fine-grained sandstone (77 specimens, or 94 percent of the sample). Of the 53 complete or nearly complete specimens of tabular to blocky, soft to

Figure 304. *Metates, Style 1.*

Figure 305. *Metates, Style 1.*

Figure 306. *Metates, Style 1.*

indurated sandstone, 42 are subrectangular in outline (figs. 303b-d and 304, center), seven are suboval (fig. 305, upper right), two are ovate (fig. 305, lower right), and two are irregular. One of the last (fig. 306, left and right) is the re-used end fragment of a metate of Style 6 (see below), with the remnant of the scoop-shaped trough having widths of ca. 22.3 cm. (top) to about 19 cm. (bottom) and a maximum depth of slightly more than 4.9 cm. The length-width ratio of these specimens ranges from 1.25:1 to 5.5:2.

The edges of the 77 complete and fragmentary sandstone metates are rarely unmodified (in only 30 out of 278 cases). The modifications vary from unifacial spalling (25 cases), bifacial spalling (58 cases), pecking (18 cases), and grinding (one case), to pecking over unifacial spalling (22 cases), pecking over bifacial spalling (116 cases), overall spalling and pecking (five cases), and grinding over unifacial spalling (three cases).

The nether face of the metates, with one exception, ranges from uneven to flat to convex. It is unmodified in 61 cases (but somewhat "worn" in 12 cases, probably from being moved about). In 15 other cases, the nether face is spalled all over (one case), pecked all over or in part (four cases), ground in part (eight cases), and pecked and ground over much of the face (two cases). In the case of the reversed and re-used end fragment of what was once a scoop-shaped troughed metate, the border on each side and the platform or shelf at one end, on the "nether" face, are partly ground over spalling.

The upper face, or grinding surface, of the sandstone metates is, in transverse section, symmetrically concave in 35 cases (varying from 0.15 cm. to 1.2 cm. in maximum depth), flat in 25 cases, and slightly convex in 17 cases. In longitudinal section, it is asymmetrically concave in 70 cases (varying from 0.2 cm. to 2.7 cm. in maximum depth), flat in six cases, and slightly convex in only one instance. In 64 cases, the upper surface shows slight to extensive use-grinding over pecking, especially in the middle of the working surface. (Metates showing slight use-grinding over pecking are illustrated in figs. 303b and 306, left, and metates showing extensive use-grinding over pecking are illustrated in figs. 303c and d; 304, center; and 305, upper right and lower right. In five specimens, the upper surface is dimpled by pecking, with no subsequent grinding, and in eight specimens the upper surface is worn very smooth. These observations indicate that in the majority of cases the sandstone metates received maximum attrition in their center, and that, because of their fine abrasiveness, they all required repeated "sharpening" by pecking with hammerstones in order to maintain their cutting power.

The sandstone metates range in size and weight as follows: length 30.6 to 55.0 cm. (53 specimens), width 17.4 to 36.5 cm. (73 specimens), thickness 3.2 to 18.1 cm. (all specimens), and weight 6.0 to 27.9 kg. (53 specimens).

One of the remaining five metates of Style 1 is a broken but restored, blocky piece of micaceous basalt, subrectangular in outline. The edges are bifacially spalled and the nether face is irregular and unmodified. The upper face, or grinding surface, is symmetrically concave in transverse and longitudinal sections (the former is 0.4 cm. and the latter is 2.3 cm. in maximum depth); the surface shows slight use-grinding over pecking. The metate measures 44.0 by 29.5 by 11.3 cm., and weighs 23.8 kg. The length-width proportion of this specimen is 3:2.

The other four metates of Style 1 are complete tabular to blocky pieces of conglomerate (three specimens) and of fossiliferous shale (one specimen). Two of the conglomerate metates are oval in outline. The irregular edges are bifacially spalled and the convex nether face is spalled and pecked or unmodified (fig. 304, top). The third conglomerate metate is subrectangular in outline. Two edges are bifacially spalled and two edges are bifacially spalled and pecked. The nether face is uneven and unmodified (fig. 304, bottom).

The metate of fossiliferous shale is suboval in outline. The irregular edges are bifacially spalled and the nether face is uneven and unmodified (fig. 305, left).

The upper face, or grinding surface, of these four metates is flat or symmetrically convex in transverse section (two cases of each) and symmetrically concave in longitudinal section (all cases), with the maximum depth ranging from 0.2 to 1.6 cm. The grinding surface in each case is even, and it is smooth except where it is broken by small pits (figs. 304, top and bottom, and 305, left). The sharp-edged "pits" are the spaces left when, in the grinding process, particles became dislodged from the matrix. These four metates did not have to be "sharpened" repeatedly by pecking with hammerstones to keep them effective. They may be characterized as *self-sharpening* metates, and they range in size and weight as follows: length 29.5 to 45.0 cm., width 21.5 to 29.0 cm., thickness 7.5 to 13.4 cm., and weight 8.1 to 12.8 kg. The length-width ratio varies from 1.25:1 to 3:2.

The provenience of the 82 complete or fragmentary "used" metates of Style 1 is as follows: subfloor fill, Kiva N (1); in "mealing bins," Room 56 (4); embedded in floor, Rooms 49 and 79 (1 each); in sealed firepit, Room 36 (1); floor, Kiva H (2), Rooms 46, 49, 56, 76 (1 each); in ventilator shaft fill, Kiva P (1); fill, Area VII (6), Kiva R (5), Rooms 16, 52, 81, Area XII, Kivas F, O (2 each), Rooms 7, 14, 30, 37, 56, 82, Area V, Kivas A, B, D, K, U (1 each); surface and fill, Kiva L (2), Rooms 14, 57, 66, Area IV, Kivas C, G, N (1 each), West Trash Slope (4), Lower East Trash Slope (3), Upper East Trash Slope (1), general, east side of ruin (4), general, west side of ruin (2), and general (9).

The five complete metate-"blanks" assigned to Style 1 are tabular or blocky pieces of fine-grained sandstone (fig. 303a). The edges are modified in 14 cases—pecked in seven cases, and pecked over bifacial spalling in seven cases—and unmodified in six cases. The nether face of one specimen is partly evened by spalling, but in the other four it is uneven and unmodified. The upper face of two specimens, supposedly intended to become the grinding surface, is dressed by overall pecking (fig. 303a), with a little smoothing noted on one specimen. The "blanks" range in size and weight as follows: length 34.4 to 51.0 cm., width 24.8 to 33.8 cm., thickness 8.2 to 12.2 cm., and weight 9.3 to 25.3 kg. The length-width proportion is 3:2 in every instance. One of the "blanks" was found in the fill of Kiva O. The other four came from the general surface of the site.

Figure 307. *Metates, Style 2.*

Style 2: Plain-faced, with two grinding surfaces. 2 whole specimens and 1 end fragment, all of tabular, fine-grained sandstone. The two complete specimens are subrectangular in outline. One of these (fig. 307, top) has bifacially spalled edges and grinding surfaces that are symmetrically concave in transverse and longitudinal sections, and are 1.2 cm. and 0.5 cm. in maximum depth. The deeper grinding surface is use-ground over pecking, the shallower one is pecked or sharpened over grinding (fig. 307, center and bottom, respectively). The metate measures 42.4 by 29.0 by 5.1 cm. and weighs 8.2 kg. The length-width proportion is 3:2. The metate was found in the fill of Kiva M.

The other complete metate has one unmodified and three pecked edges. Both grinding surfaces are flat in transverse section and symmetrically concave in longitudinal section (0.3 cm. in maximum depth in each case), and they are ground over pecking. The specimen measures 60.5 by 36.8 by 9.4 cm., and weighs 27.2 kg. The length-width proportion is 3.25:2. The specimen was found in the fill of Kiva R.

The end fragment of Style 2 has three pecked edges. One grinding surface is symmetrically concave in transverse and longitudinal sections; the other grinding surface is flat in transverse section and symmetrically concave in longitudinal section. Both surfaces are pecked or sharpened over grinding. The fragment measures 26.5 cm.

Figure 308. *Metates, Styles 3, 5, and 6.*

in width and 7.3 cm. in thickness. It came from the general surface of the site.

Style 3: *Plain-faced, with one grinding surface, markedly concave from side to side and end to end, and showing traces of a spalled-off border on each side.* 1 complete specimen and 1 end fragment, both of fine-grained sandstone. The complete metate is blocky and subrectangular in outline (fig. 308b). The unmodified nether face slopes sharply toward one side; the ends are partly spalled unifacially and bifacially, and are slightly pecked; and the irregular sides are roughly spalled along the edges of the upper face, or grinding surface. One side is partly pecked over the spalling. The grinding surface is deeply concave in both transverse and longitudinal sections (1.7 cm. and 3.5 cm. in maximum depth, respectively) and is sharpened by pecking. The pronounced concavity of the grinding surface and roughly spalled sides of the upper face, which extend up to 2.3 cm. beyond the actual grinding surface on one side and up to 2.0 cm. beyond this surface on the other side, indicate that this specimen is a remodeled troughed metate with open ends and lateral borders. The specimen measures 39.5 by 27.4 by 11.0 cm., and weighs 6.8 kg. The length-width proportion is 2.75:2. The metate was found in the fill of Kiva R.

The end fragment is tabular and probably subrectangular in outine (fig. 308a). The nether face is fairly flat, worn but not modified; the intact rounded end and irregular sides are shaped by overall spalling, and the sides are additionally spalled along the edges of the upper face, or grinding surface. The grinding surface itself is markedly concave in transverse section (1.6 cm. in maximum depth), and also in longitudinal section (not measurable), and it is pecked over grinding. The unusually deep concavity of the grinding surface and the rough spalling along its sides suggest that this fragmentary metate, like the whole one described above, is remodeled troughed metate with open ends and lateral borders. This specimen measures 25.9 cm. in width and 6.8 cm. in thickness. It, also, was recovered from the fill of Kiva R.

Style 4: *Plain-faced, with one grinding surface, markedly concave from side to side and end to end, and showing traces of spalled-off borders on sides and one end.* The single specimen is the upper end fragment of a metate, based on a boulder of fine-grained, hard sandstone. The convex nether face, the rounded upper end, and the rounded sides are all unmodified. The edges of the upper surface, or grinding surface, are roughly spalled along the sides and along the upper end. The grinding surface, whose width is 6.5 cm. less than the width of the object, is deeply concave in transverse and longitudinal sections, and is ground over pecking. The pronounced concavity of the grinding surface and the rough spalling of its margins suggest that this fragment is from a remodeled troughed metate (scoop-shaped) with a border on each side and at the upper end (see Style 5, below). The specimen measures slightly more than 27 cm. in width and 11.0 cm. in thickness. It was obtained from the surface of Kiva G.

Style 5: *Troughed (scoop-shaped), with a border on each side and at the upper end.* The single specimen is the upper end fragment of a metate of thick, tabular, fine-grained sandstone (fig. 308 c). The uneven nether face is worn but not modified; the straight upper end is unmodified; one irregularly straight side is bifacially spalled and pecked along the edge of the upper face, the other irregularly straight side is pecked only along the edge of the upper face. The borders on the sides (12.0 cm. and 9.0 cm. wide) and at the upper end (11.0 cm. wide) of the upper face are generally uneven, with a little pecking and grinding here and there.

The scoop-shaped trough, which has insloping sides, measures 23.2 cm. wide at the top, 19.8 cm. wide at the bottom (at the edges of the grinding surface), and slightly more than 5.9cm. in maximum depth. The grinding surface is symmetrically concave in transverse section and supposedly concave in longitudinal section. The surface is roughened by pecking.

The fragmentary metate measures 44.8 cm. in width and 10.8 cm. in thickness. It was found on the surface of the West Trash Slope.

Style 6: *Troughed (scoop-shaped), with a border on each side and a platform or shelf at the upper end.* 1 specimen, lacking most of one side and most of the lower end; and 1 upper end fragment, with the edge of one side partly missing. Both specimens are of tabular, fine-grained sandstone, probably subrectangular in outline.

In the more complete metate (fig. 308 d, the nether face is uneven and unmodified; the intact upper end is unifacially spalled and partly pecked, and the partial lower end is bifacially spalled and pecked; the intact side is spalled along part of the upper edge, and the other partial side is bifacially spalled. The intact border on one side (ca. 6.8 cm. wide) and the intact platform or shelf at the upper end (ca. 15.0 cm. wide), of the upper face, are uneven and only lightly ground here and there. The scoop-shaped trough, which has insloping sides, measures about 30 cm. long, about 23 cm. wide at the top and about 20 cm. wide at the bottom (at the edges of the grinding surface), and 4.7 cm. in maximum depth. The grinding surface is symmetrically concave in transverse and longitudinal sections. The surface is ground fairly smooth over pecking. The metate measures, overall, 55.8 by 36 by 6.5 cm. It was found in the fill of Room 48.

In the upper end fragment, the nether face is uneven and unmodified; the straight upper end is unifacially spalled; the intact side is bifacially spalled, and the broken side is spalled along the edge of the upper face. The intact border on one side (7.3 cm. wide) and the intact platform or shelf at the upper end (15.2 cm. wide), of the upper face, are uneven, with light grinding on the high spots. The scoop-shaped trough, which has insloping sides, is about 23 cm. wide at the top, 20.0 cm. wide at the bottom (at the edges of the grinding surface), and 4.8 cm. in maximum depth. The grinding surface is symmetrically concave in transverse and longitudinal sections. The surface is ground smooth over pecking. The fragment measures, overall, about 38 cm. in width (estimated) and 6.5 cm. in thickness. It was recovered from the fill of Room 47.

Manos. Three hundred and thirty-eight complete or fragmentary implements from Long House are considered to be manos used, or intended to be used, in conjunction with metates for the main if not the sole purpose of grinding corn, and possibly also wild seeds, into meal or flour by the reciprocating technic. The specimens are described under 16 styles, according to the end-to-end contour of the grinding surface(s), the general form of the implement, and the location and number of the grinding surfaces. These criteria were worked out, and then were symbolized for convenient reference, by the writer and Arthur H. Rohn when they were members of the staff of the Wetherill Mesa Project, as follows: V=grinding surface concave from end to end; X=grinding surface convex end to end; S=slablike back; H=humped back; U=unifacial; B=bifacial; 1, 2, 3, 4 = number of grinding surfaces.

Style VSUI: 70 specimens, including 38 complete or nearly complete, whole or restored specimens, and 32 end fragments.

The manos in this group are spalls, mainly of fine-grained sandstone (66 specimens). Other materials sparsely represented are fine-grained basalt (two specimens) and "micaceous igneous rock" (one specimen), and coarse conglomerate (one specimen). Of the 38 complete or nearly complete specimens, 35 are subrectangular in outline (fig 309a–c), two are suboval, and one is oval. The length-width ratio of these specimens ranges from 1.75:1 to 2.75:1.

The sides of these complete or fragmentary manos are rarely unmodified (two cases). Modifications include unifacial spalling (15 cases), bifacial spalling (37 cases), pecking over unifacial spalling (26 cases), pecking over bifacial spalling (28 cases), grinding over unifacial spalling (two cases), grinding over bifacial spalling (12 cases), pecking and grinding over unifacial spalling (10 cases), and pecking and grinding over bifacial spalling (eight cases). Round or oval indentations or "finger-grips," produced by pecking and grinding, occur in seven manos as follows: one in one side (three cases), one in each side (three cases), and two in one side and one in the opposite side (one case). The sides of two specimens are medially constricted by intentional shaping (fig. 309 c). Finger-grips would provide firmer purchase on the mano by fingers and thumbs, and medial constrictions would aid in grasping a wide and heavy mano.

The ends of complete and fragmentary manos of Style VSU1, like the sides, are rarely unmodified (two cases). Modifications consist of unifacial spalling (10 cases), bifacial spalling (43 cases), pecking over unifacial spalling (14 cases), pecking over bifacial spalling (35 cases), pecking and grinding over unifacial spalling (two cases), and grinding over bifacial spalling (two cases).

The upper face or the "back" of these manos varies from uneven to flat or slightly convex. It shows no modification in seven cases. Modifications include grinding of the high spots (34 cases), grinding over pecking on the high spots (four cases), partial pecking (one case), partial grinding (six cases), grinding over pecking (four cases), and some pecking and grinding (14 cases).

The lower face or grinding surface of these manos is concave or very slightly concave from end to end, and is convex (62 cases), flat (seven cases), or slightly concave (one case), from side to side. The surface itself is moderately use-ground over pecking or "sharpening" (41 cases; fig. 309a), well ground over pecking (11 cases; fig 309b), or slightly ground over pecking (17 cases; fig 309c). The grinding surface of one other mano, of conglomerate, is smooth on the surface and slightly pitted below the surface, because of the coarse nature of the material. This is another example of a *self-sharpening* grinding implement (see metates of Style 1, described above).

Measurements: length 19.0 to 32.7 cm. (38 specimens), width 9.5 to 13.9 cm. (all specimens), thickness 1.2 to 5.4 cm. (all specimens), and weight 546 gm. to 2.9 kg. (38 specimens).

Provenience: subfloor fill, Rooms 50, 60, 65 (1 each); fill below cist, Room 48 (1); General Feature 3, Room 48 (1); firepit fill, Kiva L (1); in "mealing bin," Room 56 (1); floor, Room 60 (3), Rooms 49, 50, 90, Kivas H, J, K (1 each); fill, Room 48 (5), Room 54, Kivas F, R (3 each), Rooms 7, 52, 58, Area IV, Kivas K, U (2 each), Rooms 1, 6–7, 14, 37, 38, 56, 74, 79, 80, 83, Kivas B, L, O, T (1 each); surface and fill, Lower East Trash Slope(3), Kivas I, L (2 each), Rooms 48, 69, Area IX, West Trash Slope (1 each); backdirt (2); general (1).

Style VSU2: 123 specimens, including 47 complete or nearly complete, whole or restored specimens, 73 end fragments, and 3 medial fragments.

The specimens in this group, the largest group of manos identified in the Long House collection, are spalls of fine-grained sandstone (122 specimens) and coarse conglomerate (one specimen). Of the 47 complete or nearly complete manos, 42 are subrectangular in outline (fig. 309d), three are suboval (fig 309e), and two are oval. The length-width ratio of these specimens range from 1.75:1 to 2.5:1

The sides of the complete and fragmentary manos are unmodified in only six instances. Modifications consist of unifacial spalling (33 cases), bifacial spalling (95 cases), pecking over unifacial spalling (24 cases), pecking over bifacial spalling (39 cases), grinding over unifacial spalling (eight cases), grinding over bifacial spalling (21 cases), pecking and grinding over unifacial spalling (12 cases), and pecking and grinding over bifacial spalling (eight cases). Two manos have one finger-grip each, and two specimens have one finger-grip in each side. One mano has medially constricted sides.

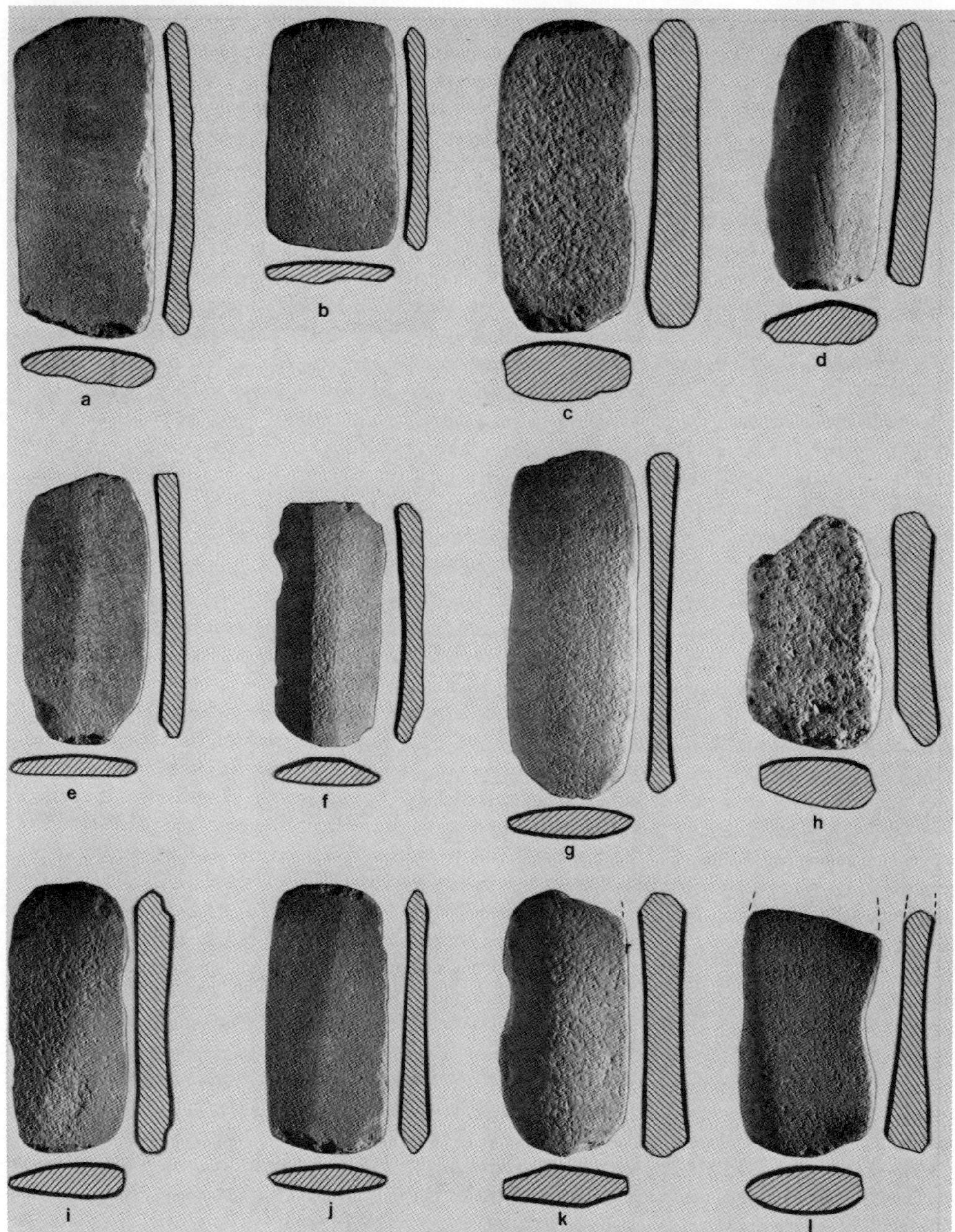

Figure 309. *Manos, Styles VSU1, VSU2, VSU3, VSB2, VSB3, and VSB4.*

The ends of the complete and fragmentary manos of Style VSU2 are unmodified in 12 specimens. Modifications include unifacial spalling (11 cases), bifacial spalling (70 cases), pecking over unifacial spalling (23 cases), pecking over bifacial spalling (39 cases), grinding over unifacial spalling (two cases), grinding over bifacial spalling (two cases), and pecking and grinding over bifacial spalling (two cases).

The upper face or "back" of these manos varies from uneven to flat or slightly convex. It is unmodified in 26 cases. Modifications include grinding on the high spots (60 cases), partial grinding (19 cases), grinding over pecking (three cases), and some pecking and grinding (15 cases).

The lower face of these manos possesses two adjacent grinding surfaces which are concave from end to end and are convex (242 cases) or flat (four cases) from side to side. The grinding surfaces are of unequal width in 102 manos and are of approximately equal width in only 21 manos. The grinding surfaces are moderately use-ground over pecking (130 cases; fig. 309e, left grinding surface), well ground over pecking (92 cases; fig. 309d and e, right grinding surface), or slightly ground over pecking (22 cases), or is "self-sharpened" (two cases).

Measurements: length 22.1 to 32.2 cm. (47 specimens), width 6.8 to 14.0 cm. (all specimens), thickness 1.3 to 4.1 cm. (all specimens), and weight 672 gm. to 2.2 kg. (45 specimens).

Provenience: subfloor fill, Room 49 (4), Rooms 57, 81 (1 each); on banquette, Kivas K, O (1 each); in firepit, Kiva R (1); on floor, Kiva J (5), Rooms 14, 51 (2 each), Rooms 12, 49, 50, Kivas B, E, H, I (1 each); fill, Room 48 (14), Kiva O (5), Room 37 (4), Room 9, Areas VII, X, Kivas B, K (3 each),

Rooms 53, 54, Area IV, Kivas E, F, J, N, Q, (2 each), Rooms 7, 29, 49, 50, 57–58, 75, 83, 88, Areas II, III, V, IX, Kivas D, H, I, P, R, U (1 each); surface and fill, Lower East Trash Slope (8), West Trash Slope (3), Room 48, Kiva L (2 each), Room 66, Areas IV, X, Kivas E, G, N, Upper East Trash Slope (1 each); and surface, on east side of site and on west side of site (1 each), and general (2).

Style VSU3: The single complete specimen is a spall of fine-grained sandstone, subrectangular in outline, with a length-width proportion of 2:1 (fig. 309f). One straight side is pecked over unifacial spalling, the other irregular side is bifacially spalled. One irregularly straight end is pecked over bifacial spalling, the opposite convex end is pecked over unifacial spalling. The upper face or "back" is slightly uneven and ground on the high spots. The three grinding surfaces on the lower face are all concave longitudinally and convex transversely. The outer grinding surfaces are well ground over pecking or sharpening, the interior grinding surface is only slightly ground over pecking.

The specimen measures 22.8 by 11.0 by 2.3 cm., and weighs 814 gm. It was found on the surface at the east side of Long House.

Style VSB2: 24 specimens, including 9 complete or nearly complete, whole or restored specimens, and 15 end fragments.

The specimens in this group are spalls of fine-grained sandstone (21 specimens), fine-grained basalt (1 specimen), coarse breccia (1 specimen), and coarse conglomerate (1 specimen). All nine complete or nearly complete manos are subrectangular in outline (fig. 309g, of fine-grained sandstone, and h, of coarse conglomerate). The length-width proportion of these specimens ranges from 1.75:1 to 2.75:1.

The sides of the complete and fragmentary manos are modified by unifacial spalling (one case), bifacial spalling (eight cases), grinding (one case), pecking over unifacial spalling (23 cases), pecking over bifacial spalling (five cases), grinding over bifacial spalling (five cases), pecking and grinding over unifacial spalling (three cases), and pecking and grinding over bifacial spalling (two cases). Two manos have one finger-grip each, and three manos have one finger-grip in each side.

The ends of the complete and fragmentary manos are rarely unmodified (two cases). Modifications include unifacial spalling (four cases), bifacial spalling (six cases), pecking over unifacial spalling (12 cases), pecking over bifacial spalling (five cases), grinding over bifacial spalling (one case), pecking and grinding over unifacial spalling (two cases), and pecking and grinding over bifacial spalling (one case).

The grinding surface on each face of the manos of Style VSB2 is concave longitudinally and convex transversely. The grinding surfaces show variations in the degree of use-grinding: both grinding surfaces are moderately ground over pecking or sharpening in eight specimens, both grinding surfaces are well ground over pecking in two specimens, both grinding surfaces are slightly ground over pecking in one specimen. In seven specimens, the grinding surface on one face is well ground over pecking and the one on the opposed face is moderately ground over pecking; in two specimens, the grinding surface on one face is moderately ground over pecking and the one on the opposed face is slightly ground over pecking. In the remaining two manos, made of coarse breccia and coarse conglomerate, both grinding faces on each specimen are self-sharpened.

Measurements: Length 21.5 to 32.3 cm. (nine specimens), width 10.1 to 13.5 cm. (all specimens), thickness 1.7 to 4.8 cm. (all specimens), and weight 1,071 gm. to 2.2 kg. (nine specimens).

Provenience: subfloor fill, Room 85 (1); floor, Room 56 and Kiva O (1 each); ventilator shaft fill, Kiva P (1); fill, Rooms 2, 60, 82, 90, Areas IV, IX, Kivas B, F, O, R (1 each); surface and fill, Lower East Trash Slope and West Trash Slope (2 each), Room 5, Kivas L, N, O, and west side of site (1 each); and surface, east side of site (1).

Style VSB3: 24 specimens, including 7 complete, whole or restored specimens, and 17 end fragments.

The manos in this group are spalls of fine-grained sandstone (23 specimens) and fine-grained "micaceous igneous rocks" (one specimen). All seven complete specimens are subrectangular in outline (fig. 309i). The length-width proportion of these manos ranges from 1.5:1 to 2.5:1.

The sides of the complete and fragmentary manos are modified by unifacial spalling (four cases), bifacial spalling (13 cases), pecking over unifacial spalling (five cases), pecking over bifacial spalling (nine cases), grinding over unifacial spalling (five cases), grinding over bifacial spalling (seven cases), pecking and grinding over bifacial spalling (four specimens). One mano only has finger-grips, one in each side near opposite ends (fig. 309i).

The ends of the complete and fragmentary manos are modified by unifacial spalling (one case), bifacial spalling (12 cases), pecking over unifacial spalling (five cases), pecking over bifacial spalling (10 cases), grinding over bifacial spalling (two cases), and pecking and grinding over bifacial spalling (one case).

The adjacent grinding surfaces of the manos of Style VSB3 are concave longitudinally and convex transversely. The paired grinding surfaces are of unequal width in 19 manos and are of approximately equal width in five manos. The grinding surfaces show considerable variation in the degree of use-grinding over pecking or sharpening. These observations are tabulated below (s=slight grinding; m=moderate grinding; w=well ground):

No. of specimens	Single grinding surface	Paired grinding surfaces (on reverse face)
3	1m	2m
4	1w	2w
2	1m	2s
2	1s	2m
3	1m	2w
2	1w	1s, 1m
1	1m	1s, 1m
2	1s	1s, 1w
2	1m	1m, 1w
3	1w	1m, 1w
—	—	—
24		

In the illustrated example (fig. 309i), the paired grinding surfaces are slightly ground over pecking and the grinding surface on the opposed face is moderately ground over pecking.

Measurements: length 18.6 to 31.0 cm. (seven specimens), width 8.1 to 13.5 cm. (all specimens), thickness 1.4 to 4.6 cm. (all specimens), and weight 954 gm. to 1,878 gm. (seven specimens).

Provenience: floor, Rooms 56, 79 (1 each); fill, Room 81 (3), Room 48 (2), Rooms 74, 76, 79, 86, 90, Area X, Kivas B, F, H, I (1 each); surface and fill, Rooms 6–7, Areas IV, VI, VII, IX, XII (1 each); backdirt (1).

Style VSB4: 15 specimens, including 8 complete or nearly complete specimens and 7 end fragments.

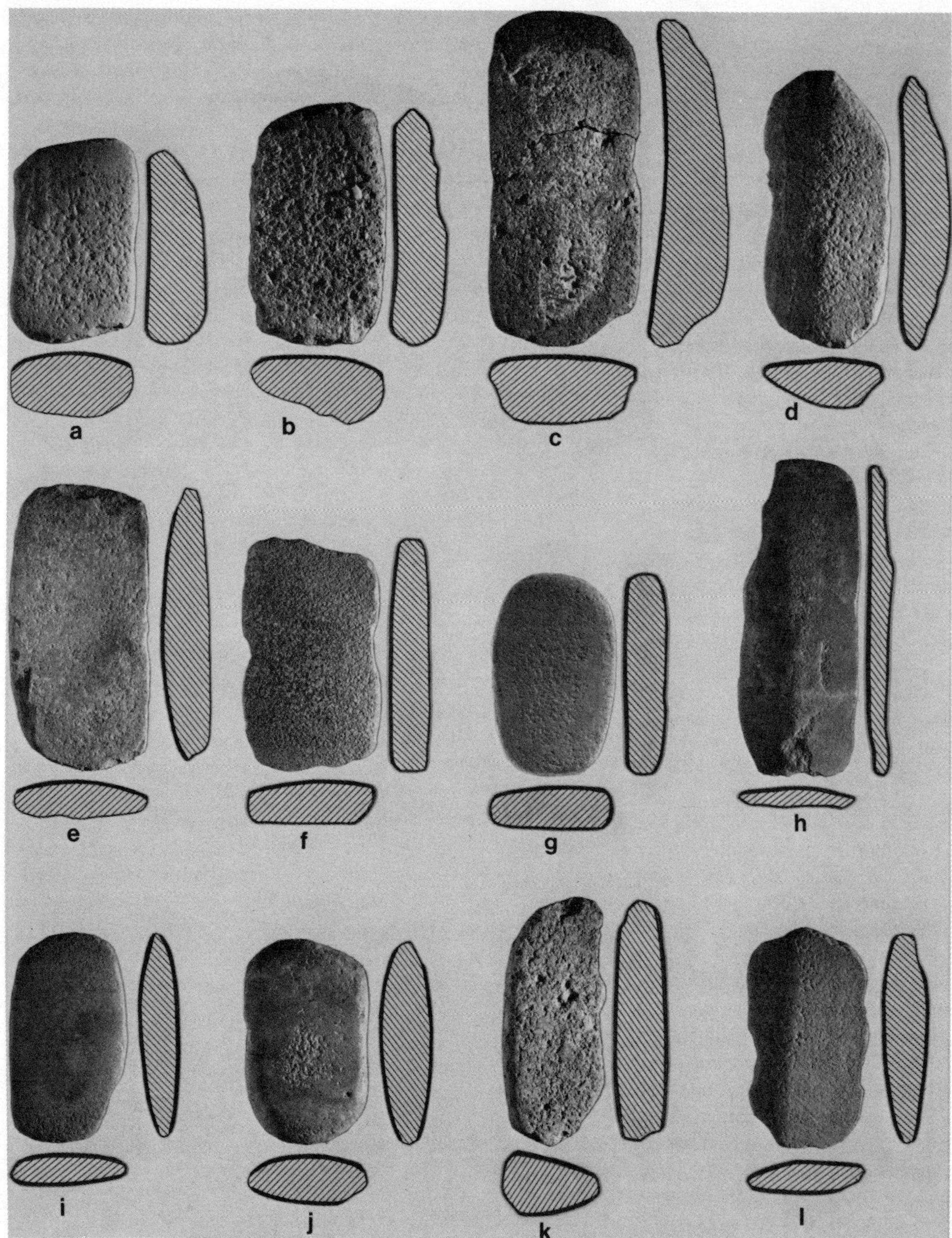

Figure 310. *Manos, Styles VHU1, VHU2, XSU1, XSU2, XSB2, and XSB3.*

The manos in this group are spalls of fine-grained sandstone (14 specimens) and fine-grained "micaceous igneous rock" (one specimen). All eight complete or nearly complete specimens are subrectangular in outline (fig. 309j and k). The length-width proportion of these manos ranges from 1.75:1 to 2.5:1.

The sides of the complete or nearly complete and fragmentary manos are modified by unifacial spalling (two cases), bifacial spalling (11 cases), pecking over unifacial spalling (15 cases), pecking over bifacial spalling (one case), and pecking and grinding over bifacial spalling (one case).

The ends of the complete or nearly complete and fragmentary manos are modified by unifacial spalling (three specimens), bifacial spalling (four specimens), pecking over unifacial spalling (12 specimens), and pecking over bifacial spalling (four specimens). One complete mano has a finger-grip near the middle of one side (fig. 309k), and one incomplete mano has a finger-grip near the middle of each side (fig. 309l).

The grinding surfaces of the manos of Style VSB4 are concave longitudinally and convex transversely. The paired grinding surfaces are of unequal width in 14 manos and are of approximately equal width in one specimen. The grinding surfaces show a good deal of variation in the degree of use-grinding over pecking or sharpening. The variations are tabulated below (s=slight grinding; m=moderate grinding; w=well ground):

No. of specimens	Paired grinding surfaces	Paired grinding surfaces
2	2m	2m
1	2w	2m
1	2m	1s, 1w
3	2w	1m, 1w
1	1s, 1m	2s
1	1s, 1m	1s, 1m
1	1s, 1m	2m
1	1s, 1m	1m, 1w
1	1m, 1w	1s, 1m
1	1m, 1w	2m
2	1m, 1w	1m, 1w
—		
15		

In the illustrated examples, the grinding surfaces shown are well ground over pecking (fig. 309j), slightly ground and moderately ground over pecking (fig. 309k), and moderately ground over pecking (fig. 309l).

Measurements: length 22.9 to 28.4 cm. (eight specimens), width 9.6 to 13.3 cm. (all specimens), thickness 1.7 to 4.5 cm. (all specimens), and weight 1,117 gm. to 1,598+ gm. (seven specimens).

Provenience: subfloor fill, Rooms 81 and 85 (1 each); floor, probably in "mealing bin", Room 9 (2); floor of ventilator shaft, Kiva N (1); fill, Rooms 7, 12, 52, 82, Area X, Kivas B, K (1 each); surface and fill, Area VII, Lower East Trash Slope, and West Trash Slope (1 each).

Style VHU1: 32 specimens, including 16 complete, whole or restored specimens, and 16 end fragments.

The manos in this group are spalls of fine-grained sandstone (24 specimens), coarse conglomerate (seven specimens), and coarse breccia (one specimen). The 16 complete manos are subrectangular in outline (14 specimens; fig. 310a-c; and fig. 311, which is a three-quarter veiw of the mano shown in fig. 310c), or oval in outline (two specimens). The length-width ratio of these specimens ranges from 1.5:1 to 2:1.

The sides of the complete and fragmentary manos are modified by unifacial spalling (five cases), bifacial spalling (four cases), pecking over unifacial spalling (34 cases), pecking over bifacial spalling (17 cases), grinding over bifacial spalling (one case), and pecking and grinding over bifacial spalling (three cases). Three complete manos and one end fragment have one finger-grip near the middle of one side, in each example, and one complete mano and one end fragment have a finger-grip near the middle of one side and a medial constriction on the opposite side, in each instance. Six complete manos and seven end fragments have one finger-grip near the middle of each side (figs. 310a and c, and 311).

The ends of the complete and fragmentary manos are unmodified in two cases. Modifications include unifacial spalling (five cases), bifacial spalling (eight cases), pecking over unifacial spalling (20 cases), pecking over bifacial spalling (12 cases), and grinding and pecking over unifacial spalling (one case).

The convex or irregular upper face or "back" of the manos of Style VHU1 is unmodified in two cases. Modifications include pecking, grinding, or pecking and grinding on the high spots (five cases), and small amounts of pecking or grinding, or both (24 cases), or of pecking over grinding (two cases).

The lower face or grinding surface of these manos is concave longitudinally and convex transversely. The surface itself is slightly use-ground over pecking or sharpening in 15 specimens (fig. 310a), moderately ground over pecking in 12 cases, and self-sharpened in five cases (fig. 310b, of coarse breccia, and c, of coarse conglomerate).

Measurements: length 17.9 to 28.9 cm. (16 specimens), width 11.0 to 14.2 cm. (all specimens), thickness 3.0 to 5.6 cm. (all specimens), and weight 1,197 gm. to 3.3 kg. (16 specimens).

Provenience: subfloor fill, Room 57 (1); floor, Room 56 (2) and Room 50 (1); on banquette, Kiva O (1); fill, Room 56 (2), Rooms 9, 47, 48, 57, 64, 80, 85, Area IV, Kivas A, N, P, Q, T (1 each); surface and fill, Area VII and Kiva G (2), Areas IX, X, Kiva L, Lower East Trash Slope, Upper East Trash Slope, West Trash Slope (1 each); and general (2).

Style VHU2: 2 complete specimens and 1 end fragment.

The manos in this group are spalls of fine-grained sandstone. The two complete specimens are subrectangular in outline, with a length-width proportion of 2:1.

The sides of the three manos are pecked over unifacial spalling. The two complete specimens have one finger-grip near the middle of one side in each instance. The ends of these manos are bifacially spalled; the intact end of the fragmentary specimen is pecked over unifacial spalling.

The convex upper face or "back" of the three specimens is dressed, in each case, by a small amount of pecking and grinding. The adjacent grinding surfaces in each specimen are concave longitudinally and convex transversely, and they are of unequal width. In

Figure 311. *Mano, Style VHU1.*

the illustrated example (fig. 310d), both grinding surfaces are slightly use-ground over pecking or sharpening. In the fragmentary specimen, both grinding surfaces are well ground over pecking, and in the other complete mano one grinding surface is moderately use-ground and the other is well ground over pecking.

Measurements: length 23.8 to 24.0 (two complete specimens), width 10.8 to 12.4 cm., thickness 3.2 to 4.2 cm., and weight 1,327 to 1,606 gm. (two complete specimens).

Provenience: fill, Room 88, Kivas O, Q (1 each).

Style XSU1: 17 specimens, including 14 complete manos and 3 end fragments.

All of the implements in this group are of fine-grained sandstone. Of the 14 complete specimens, 11 are subrectangular in

5.9 cm., and weighs 1,814 gm.; the conglomerate mano measures 24.2 by 11.3 by 4.3 cm., and weighs 1.573 gm.

Provenience: the sandstone mano was found in the fill of Kiva Q; the conglomerate mano came from the surface or fill of Area VII.

Mano "blanks": Two tabular, subrectangular objects of fine-grained sandstone, with edges pecked over bifacial spalling, and with one slightly uneven face lightly ground over pecking and the opposed uneven face ground on the high spots, in each specimen, are identified as mano "blanks."

Measurements: One of the "blanks" measures 29.6 by 12.5 by 2.7 cm., and weighs 1,715 gm. The other specimen measures 28.9 by 13.4 by 3.0 cm., and weighs 1,990 gm.

Provenience: The slightly smaller "blank" was found in the fill of Kiva B; the other one came from the surface or fill of Area VII.

Certain statistics pertaining to the 338 complete or fragmentary manos from Long House, which were incorporated in the detailed description of the 16 styles of manos recognized in the collection, are drawn together in accompanying table 18. These data are discussed under the following nine points:

(1) The vast majority of manos in the Long House sample have from one to four grinding surfaces that are *concave* from end to end (292 specimens, or 86.4 percent of the sample). Within this grouping, the manos with one grinding surface and with two adjacent grinding surfaces on one face, with slablike back and mainly subrectangular in outline, are enormously predominant (70 specimens, or 24 percent of the grouping, and 123 specimens, or 42 percent of the grouping, respectively).

(2) A small minority of manos in the sample have from one to four grinding surfaces that are convex from end to end (45 specimens, or 13.6 percent of the sample). Within this grouping, the manos with one grinding surface, with slablike or humped back and largely subrectangular in outline, considerably out-number the other styles of manos with convex grinding surfaces (17 specimens with slablike back, or 38 percent of the grouping, and 10 specimens with humped back, or 22 percent of the grouping).

(3) One mano fragment in the collection has two adjacent, longitudinally *concave* grinding surfaces on one face and one longitudinally *convex* grinding surface on the opposed face, with the intact end canted. This implement was undoubtedly used with a plain-faced metate, on which the two adjacent *concave* grinding faces were developed, and had previously been used with a troughed metate, on which the *convex* grinding surface and canted ends had been developed.

(4) The dominance of manos with longitudinally concave grinding surfaces over manos with longitudinally convex grinding surfaces in the Long House sample is even surpassed by the prevalence of plain-faced metates with transversely flat or convex grinding surfaces (excluding five metate "blanks") over plain-faced metates with transversely concave grinding surfaces (presumably re-shaped troughed metates) and troughed metates with concave grinding surfaces. In the sample of 91 used metates, there are 85 plain-faced metates with transversely flat or convex grinding surface, or 93 percent of the sample, as compared to three plain-faced metates with transversely concave grinding surface and three troughed metates with transversely concave grinding surface, representing 7 percent of the sample. Assuming, on logical grounds, that longitudinally concave grinding surfaces could only have been developed in manos used on plain-faced metates with flat or convex grinding surface, we find that the ratio of manos with longitudinally concave grinding surfaces (292 specimens) to plain-faced metates with transversely flat or convex grinding surfaces (85 specimens) in the Long House sample is approximately 3.5:1.

(5) The relationship between the manos with longitudinally convex grinding surfaces and the metates with which they were used is not, we believe, so clearly inferable as in the case of manos with longitudinally concave grinding surfaces. Of the 46 manos in the collection that have longitudinally convex grinding surfaces, only 19 specimens have canted ends, which presumably resulted from contact between the ends of the manos and the sloping sides of the troughed metates with which they were used. The ratio of these manos to the troughed and reshaped troughed metates (6 specimens) in Long House is approximately 3:1, and thus is quite comparable to the ratio of manos with longitudinally concave grinding surfaces and plain-faced metates with transversely flat or convex grinding surfaces, as noted above. It seems likely that the other 27 manos with longitudinally convex grinding surfaces but without canted ends were used not on troughed metates but on plain-faced metates in a manner that can be regarded as other than "habitual."

(6) Inspection of the ranges of measurements recorded in table 18 indicates that within the grouping of manos with longitudinally concave grinding surface, the manos with slablike backs tend to be longer, narrower, thinner, lighter in weight, and slightly more variable in length-width proportion than do the manos with humped backs, and that within the grouping of manos with longitudinally convex grinding surfaces, the manos with slablike backs tend to be slightly narrower, thinner, and more variable in length, width, weight, and length-width proportion than the latter.

(7) Finger-grips are present in only 46 of the 338 manos in the Long House collection (13.6 percent of the sample). In the 46 manos, two finger-grips, one in each side, occur in 26 manos, a single finger-grip occurs in 19 manos, and three finger-grips are present in 1 mano only. Proportionately, finger-grips are present much more commonly in manos with humped backs than in manos with slablike backs (in 21 of 35 manos with humped backs compared to 19 of 257 manos with slablike backs in the grouping of manos with longitudinally concave grinding surfaces; and in 4 of 12 manos with humped backs compared to 2 of 33 manos with slablike backs in the grouping of manos with longitudinally convex grinding surfaces). It is possible that finger-grips were originally present in numerous manos with slablike backs and were obliterated as these implements were worn down (cf. Woodbury, 1954, p. 68 ff.).

(8) The medial constriction of one or both sides of manos was noted in only six specimens in the Long House sample. Medial constriction occurs in both sides of three manos with slablike backs, and in one side of two manos with humped backs, in the grouping of manos with longitudinally concave grinding surfaces; and medial constriction occurs in one side of one mano with slablike back, in the grouping of manos with longitudinally convex grinding surface. The feature occurs in wider and heavier manos with one grinding surface or two adjacent grinding surfaces on one face; it would seem to have been provided as an aid in grasping such cumbrous implements.

(9) The 338 used manos in the Long House collection are made principally of fine-grained sedimentary and igneous rocks—sandstone (316 specimens, or 93.5 percent of the sample), basalt (3 specimens, or 0.9 percent of the sample). The other materials represented among the used manos are coarse sedimentary and volcanic rocks—conglomerate (14 specimens, or 4.1 percent of the sample) and breccia (two specimens, or 0.6 percent of the sample). The two mano "blanks" are of fine-grained sandstone.

The manos made of fine-grained rocks had two patent disadvantages in comparison with those made of coarse-grained rocks: (a) they required constant "sharpening" with hammerstones in order to

Table 18. Manos, totaling 338 specimens, from Long House. Note: Counts of specimens are indicated in parentheses.

End-to-end contour of grinding surfaces	Material					Outline form				Range in length (cm.)	Range in width (cm.)	Range in thickness (cm.)	Range of weight (gm. or kg.)	Range of length-width ratio	No. of finger-grips	No. of medially constricted sides	No. of specimens with canted ends
	sandstone	basalt	"mic. ig. rock"	conglom.	breccia	rectangular	suboval	oval	irreg.								
VSU1(70)	66	2	1	1	—	35	2	1	—	19.0–32.7 (38)	9.5–13.9 (70)	1.2–5.4 (70)	546 gm.–2.9 kg. (38)	1.75:1 to 2.75:1 (38)	1(3), 2(3), 3(1)	2(2)	—
VSU2(123)	122	—	—	1	—	42	3	2	—	22.1–32.2 (47)	6.8–14.0 (123)	1.3–4.1 (123)	672 gm.–2.2 kg. (45)	1.75:1 to 2.51:1 (47)	1(2) 2(2)	2(1)	—
VSU3(1)	1	—	—	—	—	1	—	—	—	22.8 (1)	11.0 (1)	2.3 (1)	814 gm. (1)	2:1 (1)	—	—	—
VSB2(24)	21	1	—	1	1	9	—	—	—	21.5–32.3 (9)	10.1–13.5 (24)	1.7–4.8 (24)	1,071 gm.–2.2 kg. (9)	1.75:1 to 2.75:1 (9)	1(2) 2(3)	—	—
VSB3(24)	23	—	1	—	—	7	—	—	—	18.6–31.0 (7)	8.1–13.5 (24)	1.4–4.6 (24)	954 gm.–1,878 gm. (7)	1.5:1 to 2.5:1 (7)	2(1)	—	—
VSB4(15)	14	—	1	—	—	8	—	—	—	22.9–28.4 (8)	9.6–13.3 (15)	1.7–4.5 (15)	1,117 gm.–1,598+ gm. (7)	1.75:1 to 2.5:1 (8)	1(1) 2(1)	—	—
VHU1(32)	24	—	—	7	1	14	—	2	—	17.9–28.9 (16)	11.0–14.2 (32)	3.0–5.6 (32)	1,197 gm.–3.3 kg. (16)	1.5:1 to 2:1 (16)	1(6) 2(13)	1(2)	—
VHU2(3)	3	—	—	—	—	2	—	—	—	23.8–24.0 (2)	10.8–12.4 (3)	3.2–4.2 (3)	1,327 gm.–1,608 gm. (2)	2:1 (2)	1(2)	—	—
XSU1(17)	17	—	—	—	—	11	2	—	1	18.2–29.5 (14)	8.9–13.3 (17)	1.4–4.3 (17)	1,028 gm.–2.5 kg. (14)	1.5:1 to 2.5:1 (14)	1(1) 2(1)	1(1)	11
XSU2(5)	5	—	—	—	—	3	1	—	—	20.0–29.2 (4)	10.3–13.4 (5)	2.0–4.3 (5)	875 gm.–1,555 gm. (4)	1.5:1 to 2.5:1 (4)	—	—	1
XSB2(6)	5	—	—	1	—	3	—	—	—	18.8–21.9 (3)	9.3–12.0 (6)	2.0–5.4 (6)	987 gm.–1,383 gm. (3)	1.5:1 to 2.25:1 (3)	—	—	3
XSB3(4)	4	—	—	—	—	3	—	1	—	20.3–25.3 (4)	11.0–13.2 (4)	2.3–4.9 (4)	746 gm.–1,732 gm. (4)	1.5:1 to 2.25:1 (4)	—	—	1
V/XSB3(1)	1	—	—	—	—	—	—	—	—	—	12.6 (1)	3.4 (1)	—	—	—	—	1
XSB4(1)	1	—	—	—	—	1	—	—	—	26.0 (1)	12.2 (1)	3.0 (1)	1,330 gm. (1)	2:1 (1)	—	—	—
XHU1(10)	8	—	—	2	—	4	—	—	—	19.4–26.1 (4)	9.1–13.4 (9)	3.3–6.3 (10)	1,532 gm.–2.3 kg. (4)	2:1 (4)	1(2) 2(2)	—	2
XHU2(2)	1	—	—	1	—	2	—	—	—	23.8–24.2 (2)	11.3–12.1 (2)	4.3–5.9 (2)	1,573 gm.–1,814 gm. (2)	2:1 (2)	—	—	—

outline (fig. 310e and f), two are suboval (fig. 310g), and one is irregular. The length-width ratio of these manos ranges from 1.5:1 to 2.5:1.

The sides of the complete and fragmentary manos are modified by unifacial spalling (three cases), bifacial spalling (five cases), pecking over unifacial spalling (13 cases), pecking over bifacial spalling (two cases), grinding over unifacial or bifacial spalling (one case of each), pecking and grinding over unifacial or bifacial spalling (six cases and one case, respectively), and pecking over grinding (two cases). One mano has a single finger-grip near the middle of one side, one mano has a finger-grip near the middle of each side (fig. 310f), and one mano has one side medially constricted.

The ends of the complete and fragmentary manos are modified in 30 out of the 31 cases. Modifications include unifacial or bifacial spalling (two and 14 cases, respectively), grinding (one case), pecking over unifacial or bifacial spalling (five cases of each), pecking and grinding over bifacial spalling (one case), and pecking over grinding (two cases).

The convex or irregular upper face or "back" of the manos of Style XSU1 is unmodified in two cases, or is modified by grinding on the high spots (six cases) or by small amounts of pecking, grinding, or grinding over pecking (nine cases).

The lower face or grinding surface of these manos is convex longitudinally and convex transversely. The surface itself is slightly use-ground over pecking or sharpening (three cases, fig. 310f and g), moderately ground over pecking (11 cases, fig. 310e), and well ground over pecking (three cases). The ends of eight complete manos and the intact end of the three fragments are canted or probably canted on the grinding surface. The term *canted* denotes the beveled or upward curving, smoothed or sometimes glossily polished surfaces observed at the very ends of the grinding face(s) of some but not all of the manos from Long House with longitudinally convex grinding surface(s). The feature is believed to have resulted from contact between the ends of such manos and the sloping sides of troughed metates with which the manos were used. The feature was previously observed and similarly accounted for by Woodbury (1954, p. 67). (Note: The three illustrated specimens of Style XSU1, like the three other manos of this style, do not have canted ends. A mano with canted ends, of Style XSB2, described below, is illustrated in fig. 310i).

Measurements: length 18.2 to 29.5 cm. (14 specimens), width 8.9 to 13.3 cm. (all specimens), thickness 1.4 to 4.3 cm. (all specimens), and weight 1,028 gm. to 2.5 kg. (14 specimens).
Provenience: floor, Rooms 76, 80 (1 each); in "mealing bins," Room 56 (1); fill, Kivas B, R (2 each), Rooms 36, 37, 38, 54, Kivas C, F (1 each); surface and fill, Room 48, Area IX, Kiva E, Lower East Trash Slope (1 each).

Style XSU2: 4 complete or nearly complete, whole or restored manos, and one end fragment, all of fine-grained sandstone. Three complete or nearly complete specimens are subrectangular in outline (fig 310h), the fourth is suboval. The length-width ratio of these manos ranges from 1.5:1 to 2.5:1.

The sides of the complete and fragmentary manos are modified by unifacial or bifacial spalling (two and three cases, respectively), grinding over unifacial spalling (two cases), pecking over bifacial spalling (one case), and pecking and grinding over unifacial spalling (two cases). The ends are modified by unifacial or bifacial spalling (one and five cases, respectively), pecking over unifacial spalling (one case), and grinding over bifacial spalling (two cases).

The uneven upper face or "back" of the manos is unmodified in one case, ground on the high spots in three cases, and slightly pecked and ground in one case. The paired grinding surfaces on the lower face are convex longitudinally and convex transversely. Both grinding surfaces are slightly use-ground over pecking or sharpening in two manos, both are moderately use-ground over pecking in one mano, and both are well ground over pecking in one mano (fig. 310h). The fifth specimen has one grinding surface moderately ground, and the other well ground, over pecking. The grinding surfaces are of unequal width in three specimens and are of approximately equal width in two specimens (as in the illustrated example). In one complete mano (not illustrated), the ends of the mano on the grinding surface are canted.

Measurements: length 20.0 to 29.2 cm. (four specimens), width 10.3 to 13.4 cm. (all apecimens), thickness 2.0 to 4.3 cm. (all specimens), and weight 875 to 1,555 gm. (four specimens).
Provenience: floor, Rooms 49, 81 (1 each); fill, Rooms 12, 37 (1 each); surface and fill, Area VII (1).

Style XSB2: 3 complete manos and 3 end fragments. The specimens are spalls of fine-grained sandstone (five specimens) and fine-coarse conglomerate (one specimen). The three complete manos are subrectangular in outline (fig. 310i-k). The length-width ratio of these specimens range from 1.5:1 to 2.25:1.

The sides of the complete and fragmentary manos are modified by unifacial or bifacial spalling (two cases and one case, respectively), pecking over unifacial spalling (eight cases), and pecking over bifacial spalling (one case). One mano has a finger-grip in the middle of one side (fig. 310j). The ends of the complete and fragmentary specimens are modified by unifacial or bifacial spalling (two cases and one case, respectively), and pecking over unifacial spalling (six cases).

The grinding surfaces, one on each face, are convex longitudinally and convex transversely. Both grinding surfaces of one fragmentary mano are moderately use-ground over pecking or sharpening, and the intact end is bifacially canted. Both grinding surfaces of one fragmentary and one complete mano are well ground over pecking, and the ends of the complete mano are bifacially canted (fig. 310i). One grinding surface of a fragmentary mano is slightly ground over pecking and the opposed grinding surface is moderately ground over pecking. One grinding face of a complete mano is slightly use-ground over pecking and the opposed grinding face of this mano is well ground and freshly pecked in the center; the ends of the latter grinding surface, but not of the former, are canted (fig 310j). Lastly, both grinding faces of one complete mano, of conglomerate, are self-sharpened (fig. 310k).

Measurements: length 18.8 to 21.9 cm. (3), width 9.3 to 12.0 cm. (all specimens), thickness 2.0 to 5.4 cm. (all specimens), and weight 987 to 1,383 gm. (3).
Provenience: fill, Kivas K, N (1 each); surface and fill, Area VI, Lower East Trash Slope, west end of site, and general (1 each).

Style XSB3: 4 complete specimens, all of which are spalls of fine-grained sandstone, subrectangular in outline (three specimens, fig. 310l), or oval in outline (one specimen). The length-width ratio varies from 1.5:1 to 2.25:1.

The sides of these manos are pecked over unifacial or bifacial spalling (four and two cases, respectively), or pecked and ground over bifacial spalling (two cases). The ends are pecked and ground over bifacial spalling (two cases).

The three grinding surfaces on each of these manos are convex longitudinally and convex transversely. The paired grinding faces are of unequal width in three manos and are of approximately equal width in one mano. Variations in the degree of use-grinding over pecking or sharpening and the presence or absence of canted ends are recorded in the following tabulation (s=slight grinding; m=moderate grinding; w=well ground):

No. of Specimens	Single Grinding Surface	Paired Grinding Surfaces	Canted Ends
1	1m	2s	Present, one face
1	1s	1s, 1m	Absent
1	1m	1s, 1m	Absent
1	1m	1m, 1w	Absent
—			
4			

In the illustrated example (fig. 310l), the paired grinding surfaces are slightly and moderately use-ground over pecking, and are of unequal width, and the grinding surface on the opposed face is slightly ground over pecking. The ends are not canted.

Measurements: length 20.3 to 25.3 cm., width 11.0 to 13.2 cm., thickness 2.3 to 4.9 cm., and weight 746 to 1,732 gm.

Provenience: fill, Room 58, Kivas J, R (1 each); general (1).

Style V/XSB3: The one example of this style in the Long House assemblage is the end fragment of a presumably subrectangular mano made from a spall of fine-grained sandstone (fig. 312a). The sides are pecked over unifacial or bifacial spalling, and the extant end is bifacially spalled. The single, longitudinally convex grinding surface on one face is convex in transverse section; it is moderately use-ground over pecking or sharpening, and the extant end is canted. The paired, longitudinally concave grinding surfaces on the opposed face are convex in transverse section and are of approximately equal width; one is slightly ground and the other is well ground over pecking.

The fragmentary mano measures 12.6 cm. in width and 3.4 cm. in thickness. It was found on the surface of Room 48.

Style XSB4: The single example of this style in the collection is a complete mano, subrectangular in outline, made from a spall of fine-grained sandstone (fig. 312b). The length-width ratio is a little over 2:1.

The sides of the mano are ground over bifacial spalling and the ends are pecked over bifacial spalling. The two pairs of grinding surfaces are convex longitudinally, and each grinding surface is convex transversely. The grinding surfaces are of unequal width on both faces, and the narrower and wider grinding surfaces on one face occur in reversed position on the opposed face. All four grinding surfaces are moderately ground over pecking or sharpening. The mano measures 26.0 by 12.2 by 3.0 cm., and weighs 1,330 gm. It was found in the fill of Room 14.

Style XHU1: 4 complete specimens, five end fragments, and 1 corner fragment. The manos are spalls of fine-grained sandstone (eight specimens, fig. 312e) and coarse conglomerate (two specimens). All of the complete manos are subrectangular in outline, with a length-width ratio of 2:1.

The sides of the complete and fragmentary manos are modified by unifacial spalling (two cases), pecking over unifacial or bifacial spalling (11 and four cases, respectively), and pecking (two cases). Two manos have one finger-grip each near the middle of one side, in one case, and near the end of one side, in the other case; and two manos have one finger-grip near the middle of each side, in each case.

The ends of the complete and fragmentary manos are modified by unifacial or bifacial spalling (three and four cases, respectively), pecking over unifacial spalling (six cases), and pecking and grinding over bifacial spalling (one case).

The convex or uneven upper face or "back" of the complete and fragmentary manos is ground on the high spots in three cases, and pecked, ground, or ground over pecking in seven cases. The lower or grinding face of each specimen is convex longitudinally and convex transversely. It is slightly use-ground over pecking or sharpening in three cases (fig. 312e), moderately use-ground over pecking in two cases, well ground over pecking in three cases (fig. 312c and d), and self-sharpened in two cases (end fragments made of coarse conglomerate). The intact end of two fragmentary manos—the single corner fragment and one of the five end fragments (fig. 312e)—are canted in each case. The ends of the other fragments and of the complete mano of Style XHU1 are not canted.

Measurements: length 19.4 to 26.1 cm. (four specimens), width 9.1 to 13.4 cm. (nine specimens), thickness 3.3 to 6.3 cm. (all specimens), and weight 1,532 gm. to 2.3 kg. (four specimens).

Provenience: subfloor, Room 49 (1); fill, Rooms 47, 54, 57, 81, 88, Kiva R (1 each); surface and fill, Kiva L, Lower East Trash Slope, West Trash Slope (1 each).

Style XHU2: 2 complete specimens made, respectively, from spalls of fine-grained sandstone and coarse conglomerate (fig. 312f). Both manos are subrectangular in outline, with a length-width ratio of 2:1.

The sides, ends, and upper face or "back" of the sandstone mano are all unmodified; the two grinding surfaces on the lower face, which are longitudinally and traversely convex and are of unequal width, are moderately use-ground over pecking or sharpening. The sides of the conglomerate mano are pecked over unifacial and over bifacial spalling, and the ends are pecked over unifacial spalling. The upper face or "back" of this mano is ground on high spots, and the two adjacent grinding surfaces on the lower face, which are longitudinally and transversely convex and are of unequal width, are self-sharpened (fig 312f). The ends of the grinding surfaces on the two manos are not canted.

Measurements: the sandstone mano measures 23.8 by 12.1 by

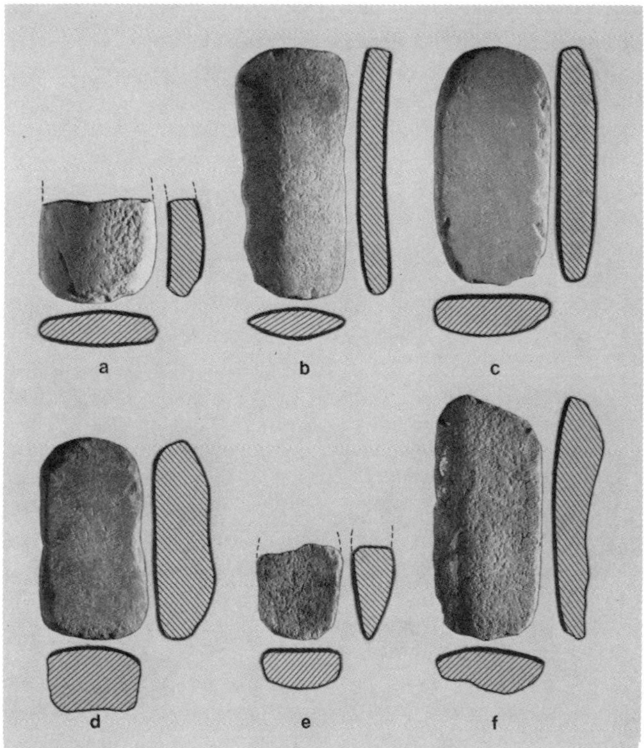

Figure 312. *Manos, Styles XSB4, XHU1, XHU2, and V/XSB3.*

maintain their cutting power, whereas those made of coarse-grained conglomerate and breccia were "self-sharpening;" and (b) they were subject to rapid exhaustion and fracture because of the softness and brittleness of the stone, whereas those made of conglomerates and breccia were resistant to abrasion and breakage because of their hardness and toughness. Nevertheless, the immediate availability of the fine-grained rocks, particularly the sandstones, clearly outweighed other considerations in the selection of materials suitable for manos. This factor also holds true for the metates in the Long House assemblage, where 86 of 91 used metates (or 94.5 percent) and all five metate "blanks" were made of local sandstones.

A comparison between the Mug House and Long House samples of manos is of some interest. The Mug House sample (Rohn, 1971, table 26, p. 206) is roughly half again greater, 492 classified specimens, than the Long House sample, 338 specimens, but comprises 13 styles as contrasted to the 16 styles of Long House manos. The proportion of manos with longitudinally concave grinding surface(s) to the total number of specimens is comparable in the two samples: Mug House, 451, and Long House, 293; yet when it comes to manos with longitudinally convex grinding surface(s), the Mug House series is slightly smaller than the Long House series, 41 to 45. In both samples, sandstones are about equally preponderant; Mug House, 424 or 86 percent of the total number of specimens; and Long House, 316, or 90 percent of the total.

Mortars. Four implements in the Long House assemblage with one hemispherical, angular, or oval depression each are designated as mortars, used in grinding of seeds and other materials by the rotating technic. Three styles are represented.

Style 1: *Discoidal.* 1 complete specimen, made from a spall of fine-grained sandstone (fig. 313, left). The uneven bottom and most of the perimeter are dressed by pecking. The flat upper face is pecked and partly ground. The shallow hemispherical depression near the center of the upper face is pecked and ground; it is 6.2 cm. in diameter and 2.0 cm. in maximum depth. The implement measures, overall, 17.0 by 14.6 by 7.3 cm., and weighs 2.8 kg. It was found in the subfloor fill of Room 31.

Style 2: *Irregular Block.* 2 complete specimens, of fine-grained sandstone. One of these (fig. 313, center) is unmodified except for the pecked and ground depression, near the center of the upper face, which has insloping sides and a flat bottom, and is 6.1 cm. in maximum diameter and 5.2 cm. in depth. This implement measures, overall, 18.9 by 16.5 by 14.6 cm., and weighs 4.5 kg. It came from the fill of Kiva R.

The other mortar of Style 2 is partly dressed by pecking (fig. 313, right). The hemispherical depression near the center of the upper face is pecked; it is 10.4 cm. in diameter and 5.7 cm. in maximum depth. The implement measures, overall, 19.4 by 18.8 by 12.9 cm., and weighs 5.5 kg. It was obtained from the southern recess of Kiva D.

Both of these implements may originally have been concretions with a natural bowl-shaped depression which was only slightly modified for and by use.

Style 3: *Slab.* 1 complete specimen, restored from three pieces, of tabular, fine-grained sandstone (fig. 314). One side only is modified, by bifacial spalling. The off-center, asymmetrically oval, shallow depression in the upper face, worn smooth by use, is 22.5 cm. long by 19.0 cm. wide by 3.3 cm. in maximum depth. This "mortar" measures, overall, 39.5 by 30.0 by 8.7 cm., and weighs 12.0 kg. It was found on the floor of Kiva R.

Figure 314. *Mortar, Style 3.*

Figure 313. *Mortars, Styles 1 and 2.*

Figure 315. *Unspecialized grinding (nether) stones, Styles 1 and 2.*

No stone implements recognizable as pestles turned up in the Long House collection. It is possible that wooden rather than stone pestles were used with the mortars described above.

Unspecialized Grinding (Nether) Stones. Some 35 complete or fragmentary tabular pieces of stone of varying forms and sizes, upon which seeds and other materials were presumably ground or pulverized with handstones (see below) by either the reciprocating or rotating technic, are identified as "unspecialized grinding (nether) stones." Two styles are represented.

Style 1: *Plain-faced, with one grinding surface.* 28 specimens, including 21 complete specimens, 5 end fragments, and 2 corner fragments.

All are of fine-grained sandstone except for one of coarse conglomerate. Of the 21 complete specimens, 13 are rectangular or subrectangular in outline (fig. 315, center), one is oval, three are suboval, one is ovate (fig. 315, right), one is trapezoidal, one is subtriangular, and one is irregular (figs. 316 and 317).

The edges of the complete and fragmentary grinding stones are unmodified in 27 cases. Modifications include unifacial or bifacial spalling (14 and 19 cases, respectively), pecking (eight cases), pecking and spalling (five cases), pecking over unifacial spalling (four cases), pecking or pecking and grinding over bifacial spalling (22 cases), and pecking or grinding with bifacial spalling (two cases). Two specimens are re-used fragments of metates of Style 1 (plain-faced, with one grinding surface): an end fragment, rotated 90°, and a corner fragment.

The lower face or "bottom" of these implements is unmodified in 19 specimens. In six specimens, it is ground or pecked and ground on the high spots. In three specimens, the bottom is partly pecked, partly ground, and partly pecked and ground, in each instance.

Figure 316. *Unspecialized grinding (nether) stones, Style 1.*

Figure 317. *Unspecialized grinding (nether) stones, Style 1.*

The upper face or grinding surface of these implements is concave both longitudinally and transversely in 15 specimens (fig. 315, right, and 316 and 317), flat both longitudinally and transversely in four specimens, convex both longitudinally and transversely in one specimen; and concave longitudinally and flat transversely (five specimens), concave longitudinally and convex transversely (two specimens), and convex longitudinally and flat transversely (one specimen). The grinding surface is slightly ground over pecking or sharpening in two cases (fig. 315, right), moderately ground over pecking in five cases (figs. 316 and 317), well ground over pecking in 10 cases (fig. 315, center), ground smooth or fairly smooth with no evidence of pecking or sharpening in 10 cases, and self-sharpened in the case of the grinding stone of coarse conglomerate.

Measurements: length 17.6 to 50.0 cm. (21 specimens), width 11.7 to 35.5 cm. (26 specimens), thickness 2.2 to 9.7 cm. (all specimens), and weight 1,241 gm. to 20.1 kg. (23 specimens).
Provenience: floor, Kiva Q (2), Kivas H, J, Pithouse 1 (1 each); fill, Kivas B, F, J, O (2 each), Rooms 3, 57, 80, 82, 85, Areas V, VI, Kiva K (1 each); surface and fill, Area VII, West Trash Slope (2 each), Kiva I, surface at east side of site (1 each); and general (1).

Style 2: *Plain-faced, with one grinding surface on one face and one grinding surface on the opposed face.* 7 complete specimens, all of fine-grained sandstone and subrectangular in outline (fig. 315, left).

The edges of these grinding stones are unmodified in four cases. Modifications include bifacial spalling (eight cases), pecking (two cases), pecking and grinding (three cases), pecking over bifacial spalling (two cases), and grinding over pecking or over pecking and spalling (five cases and four cases, respectively).

The two grinding surfaces, one on each face, are flat both longitudinally and transversely (two specimens), concave both longitudinally and transversely (one specimen), convex both longitudinally and transversely (one specimen), flat longitudinally and concave transversely (one specimen), convex longitudinally and flat transversely (one specimen), and flat and convex longitudinally and concave transversely (one specimen). Considerable variation obtains in the degree of use-grinding observed in these implements: in one specimen, one surface is slightly ground and the opposed surface is moderately ground over pecking or sharpening; in one specimen, one surface is slightly ground over pecking, the other is well ground; in two specimens, one surface is moderately ground, and the other is well ground, over pecking; in one specimen, both surfaces are well ground over pecking; in one specimen, both surfaces are pecked over grinding; and in one specimen, both surfaces are ground smooth, with no evidence of pecking or sharpening noted (fig. 315, left).

Measurements: length 15.5 to 32.2 cm., width 12.6 to 20.0 cm., thickness 2.5 to 6.9 cm., and weight 1,326 gm. to 5.3 kg.
Provenience: floor, Kiva R (1); floor, horizontal portion of ventilator shaft, Kiva N (1); fill, Kiva O (2), Kivas H, R (1 each); surface and fill, Area VII (1).

Handstones. Twenty-four complete or fragmentary implements, which are considered to have been used in conjunction with the unspecialized grinding (nether) stones for grinding or pulverizing seeds and other materials by the reciprocating or rotating technic, are designated as handstones. Tools such as these are often called "one-hand manos." We prefer the term handstones, in order to connote their diverse manipulation in contrast to the particular way in which manos were used. Five styles are represented in the Long House assemblage.

Style 1: *Cobbles with one grinding surface.* 3 complete or nearly complete, whole or restored specimens, all of fine-grained sandstone and oval in outline. One of these cobble implements, a nearly complete, restored specimen, is shown in figure 317 resting on an unspecialized grinding (nether) stone of Style 1 (described previously). The two implements are in approximately the same positions in which they were found on the floor of Pithouse 1.

In the three cobble implements, one or both ends are battered and the convex upper face or "back" is unmodified or slightly spalled or lightly battered. The single grinding surface on each specimen is longitudinally flat or convex and transversely convex; it is ground smooth in one specimen and pecked or sharpened over grinding in the other two.

Measurements: length 12.4 to 13.5 cm., width 7.2 to 9.4 cm., thickness 4.5 to 5.4 cm., and weight 659 to 1,094 gm.

Provenience: floor, Pithouse 1 and Room 49 (1 each); fill, Room 49 (1).

Style 2: *Cobble with one grinding surface on one face and one grinding surface on the opposed face.* 13 complete specimens and 3 end fragments.

These implements are cobbles of sandstone (10 specimens), quartzite (3 specimens), diorite (2 specimens), and granite (1 specimen). Of the 13 complete specimens, three are subrectangular in outline (fig. 318a) and nine range from oval to ovate (fig. 318b and c).

The edges of these handstones are unmodified in three specimens. Modifications of the edges of the other specimens include pecking or battering on one or both ends and sometimes on one or both sides also (10 specimens, one of which may have been used additionally as a hammerstone, so pronounced is the battering on the ends), pecking around the entire perimeter (two specimens), and grinding around the entire perimeter (1 specimen).

The grinding surfaces, one on each face, are longitudinally convex and transversely convex in 11 specimens. In three specimens, the grinding surfaces are longitudinally flat and transversely convex, in one specimen they are longitudinally convex and transversely flat, and in one specimen they are longitudinally flat and convex, and transversely convex. The degree of use-grinding and the amount of pecking or sharpening of the surfaces varies considerably. In four handstones, both surfaces are ground smooth (fig. 318a); in five specimens, one surface is ground smooth and the surface on the opposed face is pecked over moderate grinding (fig. 318b); in four specimens, both surfaces are smoothly ground and lightly pecked (fig. 318c); and in three specimens, both surfaces are smoothly ground over pecking.

Measurements: length 8.5 to 17.1 cm. (13 specimens), width 8.0 to 12.9 cm. (all specimens), thickness 3.5 to 6.4 cm. (all specimens), and weight 406 to 1,963 gm. (13 specimens).

Provenience: floor, Kivas H, U (1 each); fill, Kiva K (2), Rooms 38, 60, 64, 85, Kivas A, B, Q, R, T, (1 each); surface and fill, Kivas E, L. Lower East Trash Slope (1 each).

Style 3: *Cobble with five adjacent grinding surfaces.* The single specimen present is an end fragment (approximately one-half) of diorite. The extant end is slightly modified by pecking or battering. The three wider and two narrower grinding surfaces adjacent to one another (with an unmodified edge separating two of the wider grinding surfaces) are all longitudinally and transversely convex. All five surfaces are ground very smooth, and only one of them has been pecked or sharpened over the smooth surface.

Figure 318. *Handstones, Styles 2 and 5.*

The specimen measures 7.6 cm. in width and 6.1 cm. in thickness. It was found in the fill of Kiva M.

Style 4: *Re-used fragments of manos, with one grinding surface.* 2 complete specimens, of tabular, fine-grained sandstone.

One specimen is discoidal. Approximately three-quarters of the perimeter is pecked over bifacial spalling; the remaining portion (fracture surface) is pecked. The uneven upper face or "back" is ground on the high spots; the convex lower face or grinding surface is ground smooth over pecking or sharpening. The specimen measures 15.0 cm. in maximum diameter and 3.9 cm. in thickness, and weighs 998 gm. It was found on the floor of Room 50.

The other specimen is subrectangular. The sides and one end are pecked over bifacial spalling, and a shallow, circular finger-grip occurs near one end of one side; the other irregular end (fracture surface) is partly spalled bifacially and lightly pecked. The uneven upper face or "back" is ground on the high spots; the convex lower face or grinding surface is ground smooth over pecking or sharpening. The specimen measures 15.8 by 12.5 by 4.0 cm., and weighs 1,507 gm.

Both handstones of Style 4 are re-used and partially reshaped end fragments of manos of Style VSU1.

Style 5: *Re-used fragments of manos, with one grinding surface on one face and one grinding surface on the opposed face.* Two complete specimens, of tabular, fine-grained sandstone, suboval in outline.

The larger of the two specimens (fig. 318d) is neatly dressed by pecking on the sides and at one end (one corner of this end is spalled, probably accidentally). The other end (fracture surface) is partly spalled bifacially and partly pecked. The convex grinding surfaces are well ground over pecking or sharpening. The specimen measures 17.4 by 12.4 by 2.5 cm., and weighs 707 gm. Like the discoidal hammerstone of Style 4, it waş found on the floor of Room 50.

The smaller specimen of Style 5 is pecked over bifacial spalling on one side and one end. The other side and the other end (fracture surface) are bifacially spalled. The convex grinding surfaces are pecked or sharpened over grinding. The specimen measures 14.7 by 11.1 by 2.4 cm., and weighs 495 gm. It came from the fill of Kiva J.

Both handstones of Style 5 are re-used and partly re-shaped end fragments of manos of Style XSB2.

Paint-grinding (Nether) Stones: Six shaped or partially shaped pieces of tabular, fine-grained sandstone with one surface, each, lightly or heavily coated or stained with bright red or reddish brown pigment (hematite?) are designated as paint-grinding (nether) stones. Four of these implements are subrectangular, one is suboval, and one is irregular, in outline. The edges of these specimens are unmodified, or are bifacially spalled and pecked, or partly pecked or ground; the lower face or "bottom" is unmodified, or ground on the high spots, or partly pecked or ground. The upper face or grinding face of three specimens is longitudinally and transversely concave, and is moderately well ground over pecking in each case. The grinding face of two specimens is uneven, and is partly ground or partly pecked and ground. In the sixth specimen, the well-ground working face has a shallow oval depression (0.4 cm. in maximum depth) in the center, evidently the result of use-grinding.

Measurements: length 10.2 to 26.7 cm., width 9.5 to 17.4 cm., thickness 2.8 to 5.2 cm., and weight 666 gm. to 2.2 kg. *Provenience:* floor, Kiva J (2); fill, Rooms 9, 12, 83, Kiva F (1 each).

Presumably handstones, described previously, were used in conjunction with these implements for grinding the pigments.

OBJECTS OF PERSONAL ADORNMENT

Personal adornment is a universal human trait, and its character and amplitude vary widely from culture to culture and from individual to individual within cultures. The ornaments, paint stones, and lumps of colorful pigment present in the Long House collection add up to only 51 items and represent a mere 2 percent of the stone objects reported on from the site.

The ornaments in the collection include finished or unfinished pendants, each provided with, or presumably intended to have, a perforation near one end for suspension; beads, each having a central perforation or a perforation near one end for threading or suspension; and toggles, each with a double perforation on the obverse and reverse face, for securing the ornament to the clothing or the person.

The 25 objects identified as pendants are described under three categories.

Finished Pendants—11 specimens of two styles.

Style 1: *Geometric.* 10 specimens of five forms:

Lanceolate. The single whole pendant of this form, made of speckled green hornfels, is flat, with tapered ends, in longitudinal section and flat in transverse section (fig. 319a). The faces and edges are finely ground but not polished. The perforation near the wider end, drilled from each face at right angles to the long axis of the specimen, is 0.3 to 0.45 cm. in diameter. *Measurements:* 6.1 by 2.4 by 0.4 cm., and weight 7.8 gm. *Provenience:* found with Burial 10 in the Lower East Trash Slope.

Cylindrical, with one pointed end. The single complete specimen of this form, made of cream-colored mineralized bone (?), is planoconvex in longitudinal and transverse sections (fig. 319b). The faces and edges are slightly ground. The perforation, very near the rounded end, is drilled for each face at right angles to the long axis of the pendant; it is 0.2 to 0.35 cm. in diameter. *Measurements:* 3.8 by 0.6 by 0.5 cm., and weight 2.1 gm. *Provenience:* found with Burial 10 in the Lower East Trash Slope.

Trapezoidal. One whole pendant of this form, made of jet, is flat in longitudinal and transverse sections (fig. 319c). The faces and edges are ground. The slightly off-center perforation, very close to the narrower end and 0.2 to 0.5 cm. in diameter, is drilled at right angles from the obverse face and at an oblique angle from the edge of the narrower end.

One pendant of trapezoidal form, made of brown travertine, lacks one corner of the narrower end and all of the lower

Figure 319. *Finished pendants, Style 1, and unfinished pendants.*

end. The fragmentary specimen is convex in longitudinal and transverse sections. The faces and edges are ground. The slightly off-center perforation near the narrower end (only half of which is still extant) is 0.2 to 0.4 cm. in diameter; it was drilled from each face at right angles to the faces. *Measurements:* length 1.9 cm. and width 1.4 to 1.7 cm. (whole specimen), thickness 0.5 to 0.6 cm. (whole and fragmentary specimens); weight 1.6 gm. (whole specimen). *Provenience:* Area VI, below extended floor level of Room 66 (whole specimen); surface, Area X (fragmentary specimen).

Discoidal. Three whole pendants of this form, made of pink (burned) shale (2) and jet (1), are flat in longitudinal and transverse sections (fig. 319e). The faces and edges are ground and the perforation, drilled from each face at right angles to the faces, ranges from 0.1 and 0.3 cm. to 0.15 and 0.4 cm. in diameter.

Another whole specimen of discoidal form, made of jet asymmetrically convex on the obverse face and flat on the reverse face (fig. 319d). The faces and edges are ground and polished, and the perforation, 0.3 to 0.8 cm. in diameter, is drilled from each face at right angles to the faces.

One fragmentary pendant of discoidal form, made of pink shale, has smoothly ground edges, and one flat and smoothly ground face and one concave face ground only around part of the perimeter. A cluster of three shallow and two very shallow, parallel horizontal incisions occurs in the edge, near the perforation. The perforation, 0.3 to 0.4 cm. in diameter, is drilled from each face at right angles to the faces.

Measurements: maximum diameter 1.8 to 2.5 cm. (four specimens), maximum thickness 0.5 to 1.0 cm. (five specimens) and weight 1.8 to 2.0 gm. (four specimens). *Provenience:* fill, Test A (1); surface and fill, near Room 66, Area IV, Lower East Trash Slope (1 each); back dirt near back of cave (1). *Ovate.* The single whole specimen of this form, made of pink shale, is flat in longitudinal and transverse sections (fig. 319g). The faces and angular edges are lightly ground. The perforation near the wider end, 0.3 to 0.5 cm. in diameter, is drilled from each face at right angles to the faces. *Measurements:* 3.3 by 2.2 by 0.3 cm., and weight 2.7 gm. *Provenience:* surface or fill, Lower East Trash Slope.

Style 2: *Zoomorphic.* 1 specimen.

The single pendant of this style is an effigy of a small mammal (chipmunk, squirrel, or gopher?), with triangular muzzle, forward-pointing ears, and flat back. Made of dark brown hematite, it is ground and polished all over (fig. 320, upper, three-quarter view; lower left, frontal view; lower right, view of left side). The transverse perforation, 0.3 to 0.4 cm. in diameter, is drilled from each side at right angles to the sides. *Measurements:* 2.0 by 0.9 by 1.0 cm., and weight 3.4 gm. *Provenience:* fill, Room 35.

Unfinished Pendants—9 specimens of four geometric forms:

Trapezoidal. There are four complete specimens, two made of cream-colored and amber-colored travertine and two made of jet (fig. 319g, h, and j), and two fragmentary specimens (the narrower end of one specimen, and the corner of the wider end of another), made of pink shale. The faces of all these unfinished pendants are flat or nearly flat in longitudinal and transverse sections. Faces and edges are ground but not polished. The marks for a perforation—shallow, hemispherical depressions—occur near the upper edge of the corner fragment (fig. 319h). *Measurements:* length 2.0 to 2.7 cm. (4 specimens), maximum width 1.4 to 2.5 cm. (4 specimens), thickness 0.25 to 0.8 cm. (all specimens), and weight 0.8 to 5.7 gm. (4 specimens). *Provenience:* fill, Room 14, Area X (in crevice west of Room 83), Kiva A, Pithouse 1 (1 each); surface and fill, Lower East Trash Slope (2).

Figure 320. *Finished pendant Style 2.*

Pentagonal. The single complete specimen of this form, made of pink shale, is flat in longitudinal and transverse sections (fig. 319i). The faces and edges are ground. *Measurements:* 2.7 by 2.5 by 0.35 cm., and weight 3.2 gm. *Provenience:* fill, Area X.

Subsquare. The single complete specimen of this form, made of buff-colored travertine, is slightly convex in longitudinal and transverse sections (fig. 319k). The faces and edges are finely ground but not polished. The mark for a perforation occurs on one face, slightly off-center near one edge. *Measurements:* 3.5 by 3.3 by 0.6 cm., and weight 15.3 gm. *Provenience:* fill, Kiva U.

Ovate: The single complete specimen of this form, made of very fine-grained, dark gray sandstone, is flat in longitudinal and transverse sections (fig. 319l). The face and nearly all of the edges are ground. *Measurements:* 3.8 by 3.3 by 0.35 cm., and weight 6.5 gm. *Provenience:* fill, Kiva I.

Fragmentary Pendants of Indeterminate Form—5 specimens.

Four of the five objects in this category are made of pink shale; the fifth is brown travertine. All seem to be flat in longitudinal and transverse sections. The faces are slightly to well ground but not polished, and the striaght or curved edges present in four specimens are ground. The five objects vary from 0.4 to 0.5 cm. in thickness. *Provenience:* fill, Test A (levels I and II), Kivas R, U, Area IV (1 each); surface and fill, Lower East Trash Slope (1).

Four objects in the Long House collection are identified as beads. The three complete specimens are described according to form, as follows:

Annular. The two complete specimens of this form are made of pink shale (fig. 321, lower left) and of jet (fig. 321, lower right). The flat faces and vertical edges of both specimens are ground but not polished. The central perforation in the shale bead is 0.15 cm. in diameter; the central perforation in the jet bead is 0.3 cm. in diameter. In both cases, the perforation is

Figure 321. *Beads.*

drilled from each face at right angles to the faces. *Measurements:* maximum exterior diameter 0.45 and 0.8 cm., thickness 0.1 and 0.3 cm. (shale bead and jet bead, respectively). *Provenience:* fill, foot drum, Kiva Q (shale bead), and upper West Trash Slope (jet bead).

Ovate. The single complete specimen of this form is made of clear pale blue turquoise (fig. 321, upper center). The faces, flat in longitudinal and transverse sections, and the vertical edges are finely ground and polished. The slightly off-center perforation at the narrower end is 0.15 cm. in diameter; it is drilled from both faces at right angles to the faces. *Measurements:* 0.8 by 0.5 by 0.1 cm., and weight 0.1 cm. *Provenience:* found with Burial 10 in the Lower East Trash Slope.

The fourth bead is a corner (?) fragment of greenish blue turquoise obtained from the fill of Room 14.

Two ornaments in the collection are identified, provisionally, as toggles. One of these, made of jet, is discoidal in outline and planoconvex in longitudinal and transverse sections. The faces and edges are ground and highly polished. Two connecting, oblique, tapered perforations, each 0.4 to 0.8 cm. in diameter, are present in the center of the convex face.

Measurements: 5.8 cm. in maximum diameter, 1.8 cm. in maximum thickness; weight 18.2 gm. The ornament was found with Burial 4 in the Lower East Trash Slope. (The object is not illustrated because it has all but disintegrated.)

The other ornament, also of jet, is a bird effigy (raven?), planoconvex in longitudinal and transverse sections (fig. 322, top, upper convex face; center, lower flat face; bottom, view of left side). All surfaces are ground and highly polished. Two connecting, oblique, tapered perforations, each 0.2 to 0.3 cm. in diameter, are present in the center of the flat face, toward the "head." The bridge between the perforations has broken out, giving the perforations a groove-like appearance.

Measurements: 3.9 by 2.9 by 1.0 cm., and weight 6.3 gm. *Provenience:* fill of Room 48.

The 15 paint stones in the Long House collection are of two forms:

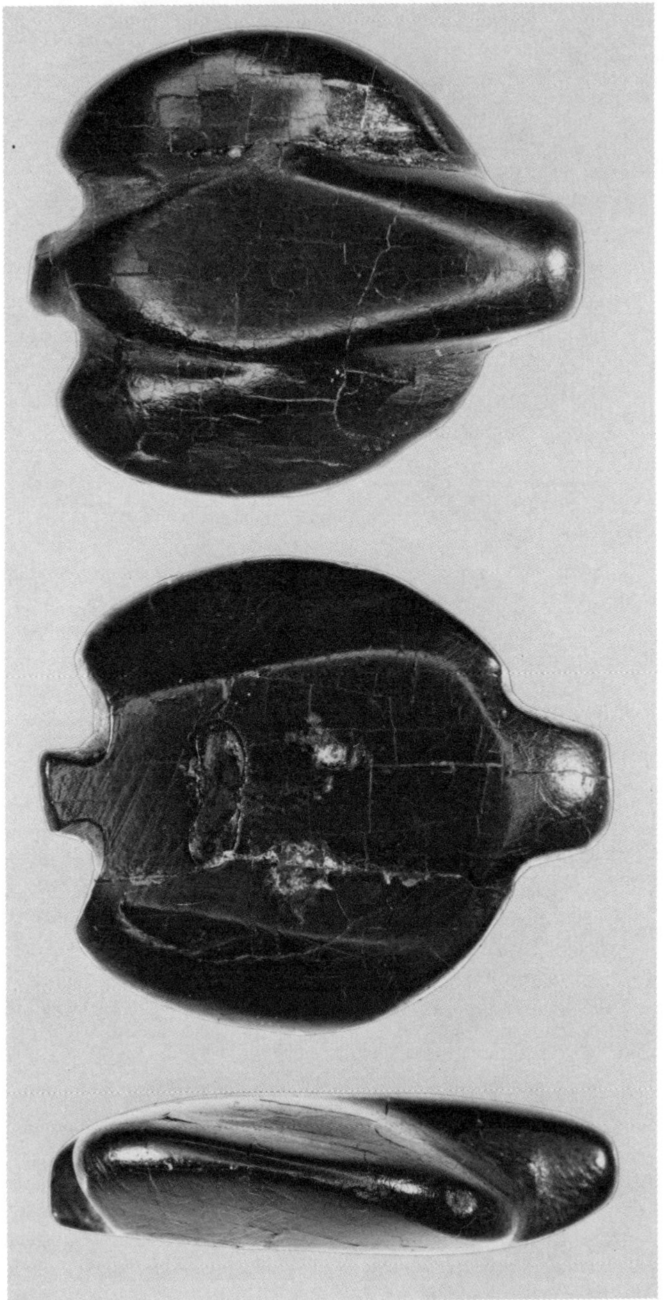

Figure 322. *Toggle (?).*

Cylindrical. 7 specimens, of reddish brown hematitie. Four of the paint stones of this form are nearly perfect cylinders of varying length, ground smooth on the perimeter and ends by use (fig. 323b, c, and f). Another faceted specimen tapers toward one end; it is also ground smooth on the perimeter and ends (fig. 323a). Another faceted specimen is longitudinally split; it is ground smooth on the faceted portion and on the ends, and is partially ground on the spalled portion (fig. 323e). The other paint stone of this group, which is somewhat oval in cross section, is broken transversely at one end and irregularly at the opposite end; it shows little or no grinding. The other cylindrical paint stones may have looked much like this specimen before they were put to extensive use.

One of the cylindrical paint stones has a shallow, horizontal groove incised about midway between the ends (fig. 323c). This groove possibly secured a tiny cord worn in a loop around the user's neck or wrist.

Measurments: length 1.5 to 3.4 cm., maximum diameter 1.0 to 2.2 cm., and weight 2.5 to 19.5 gm. *Provenience:* found with Burial 10, Lower East Trash Slope (3); fill, Rooms 16, 60, Area V, Kiva T (1 each).

Irregular. 8 specimens. Six of these paint stones are of bright red to dark reddish brown hematite (fig. 323d), one is of kaolinite, and one is of grayish black magnetite. Some specimens have a few facets, while other specimens have numerous facets, resulting from use-grinding.

Measurements: length 1.5 to 4.6 cm., width 1.0 to 4.1 cm., thickness 0.4 to 3.3 cm., and weight 0.6 to 84.5 gm. *Provenience:* subfloor fill, Kiva L (1); floor, Kiva O (1); fill, Rooms 37, 48, Areas II, V, VII, Kiva U (1 each).

Five irregular lumps of colorful stone material in the collection were presumably gathered and saved as pigments to be used in body painting or for the decoration of clothing and other personal items. Three of the specimens are of red to dark reddish brown hematite and two are of green clay.

Provenience: fill, Room 51, Area X (in crevice west of Room 83), Kiva R (1 each); surface and fill, Area X (2).

OBJECTS OF UNCERTAIN PURPOSE

There are 326 stone items in the Long House assemblage whose purpose, for various reasons, is not self-evident. They are described here under 16 named classes. The inferred uses of many of the objects may be valid in some cases but off the mark in others. The group as a whole comprises 13 percent of the stone objects reported on.

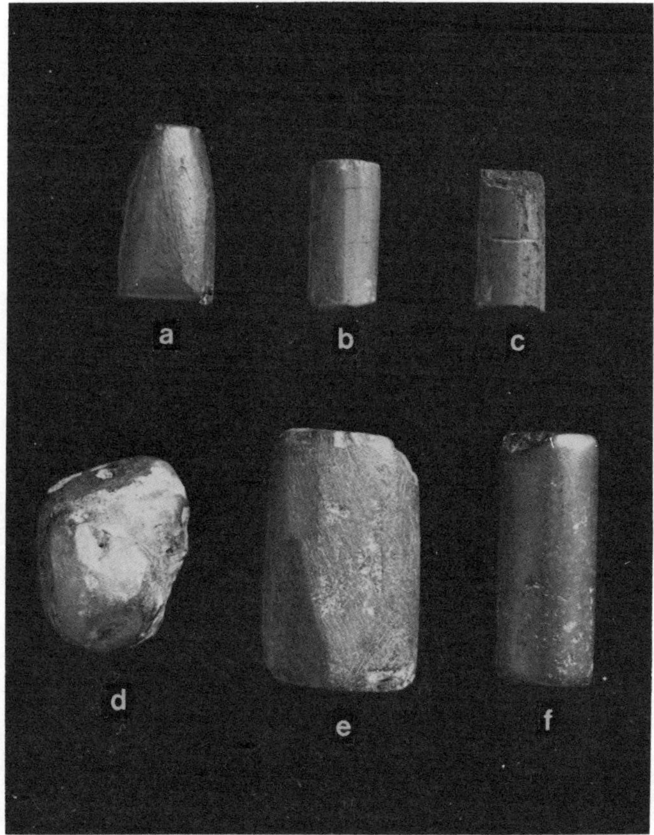

Figure 323. *Paint stones.*

Figure 324. *Pitted pounding and rubbing stones.*

Pitted Pounding and Rubbing Stones. Thirty-seven complete implements and the corner fragment of another implement exhibit from one to six pits and from one to four wear-facets each (fig. 324a–d). All are made of hard waterworn cobbles save for one made of a fine-grained sandstone spall. The pits are shallow to deep, oval or circular indentations, measuring about 1.5 to 4.5 cm. in diameter, produced by pecking in every case except one, which is pecked and ground (fig. 324b). The pits occur singly and are invariably located in or near the center of the face(s), side(s), and ends, as the case may be. Placement of the pits and wear-facets is indicated in the following tabulation:

Pits	Number of cases	Wear-facets	Number of cases
In opposed faces only	8	On opposed faces	25
In one face only	7	On one face only	9
In opposed faces and in opposite sides	5	On four faces	2
In one face and in opposite sides	5	On two faces & two sides	1
In one face and one side only	4	Two on one face	1
In opposed faces and one side	3		
In opposite sides only	2		
In opposed faces, opposite sides, and opposite ends	2		
In three faces	1		
In four faces	1		
	38		38

Of the 75 intact or partly intact ends (of the 38 specimens), 42 are spalled and pecked or battered, 32 are pecked or battered, and only one is unmodified. Of the 37 sides lacking pits, 20 are pecked or battered, seven are spalled and pecked or battered, and ten are unmodified. Of the 73 wear-facets (on the 38 specimens), 56 are slightly worn to well worn and 17 are partly pecked or battered.

Materials: cobbles—indurated sandstone (23), granite (5), diorite (3), quartzite (3), syenite porphyry (2), and "micaceous igneous rock" (1); spall-sandstone (1).

Shapes: subrectangular (14), suboval (10), oval (4), ovate (4), discoidal (4), spherical (1) (37 specimens).

Measurements: length 8.9 to 17.5 cm. (37 specimens), width 6.5 to 12.8 cm. (37 specimens), thickness 2.7 to 8.5 cm. (all specimens), and weight 324 to 1,966 gm. (37 specimens).

Provenience: floor, Kiva Q (2), Room 80 and Kiva B (1 each); fill, Room 88, Area VII, Kivas E, H, R (2 each), Rooms 9, 12, 17, 48, 54, 56, 58, 61, Area X, Kivas A, I, J, S, T, U (1 each); surface and fill, Kiva L (2), Rooms 6–7, 69, 74, Kiva G, Lower East Trash Slope, West Trash Slope, and general (1 each).

Several attributes of these implements—the preponderance of tough materials used, the shapes, size, and weight, evidences of spalling and/or pecking or battering on the ends and less commonly on the sides, and the presence of pits (providing a grip for the thumb and fingers)—suggest that they were employed primarily as pounding instruments. Additionally, all of the specimens have from one to four wear-facets each, suggesting that the implements had a secondary use as rubbing tools or, in the case of the sandstone slab, possibly as a grinding tool.

Similar, although somewhat smaller, implements, called "pitted rubbing and pounding stones," have been reported from the La Plata District of southwestern Colorado and northwestern New Mexico by Morris (1939, pp. 128–129, and Pl. 134); and similar tools, designated "elongated pitted hammerstones," have been described from Awatovi and nearby sites in Jeddito Wash, northeastern Arizona, by Woodbury (1954, p. 91 and Fig. 19, *h*). To Morris's statement, "the arts or industries for which this type was specifically intended are not evident," we can add nothing so far as the Long House specimens go. Implements of this class occurred with almost equal frequency in kivas and secular units of the site.

Club Heads. Four complete objects possessing single notches in the sides or a single encircling groove, probably for securing wooden handles, are present in the Long House assemblage. Two styles are recognized.

Style 1: *Notched.* 3 specimens. A single transverse notch occurs in each side, about midway between the ends (fig. 325, top and center). All three specimens are spalls of indurated sandstone, shaped around the perimeter, including the notches, and on the faces by spalling and pecking. The faces are partly ground. The convex ends are thick and blunt and evened by pecking. The single notches range in width from about 2.5 to 3.5 cm., and in depth from about 0.3 to 1.0 cm.

Measurements: length 11.7 to 13.1 cm., width 7.0 to 7.9 cm., thickness 3.1 to 4.0 cm., and weight 367 to 486 gm.

Provenience: fill, Rooms 14, 58, Kiva H (1 each).

Figure 325. *Club heads, Styles 1 and 2.*

Style 2: *Full-grooved.* 1 specimen, with a single transverse groove completely encircling the object midway between the ends (fig. 325, bottom). Made of indurated sandstone, the specimen is shaped around the perimeter, including the groove, and on the faces by spalling and pecking. The faces are partly ground. One convex end is thick and blunt, and evened by pecking; the other end, originally convex and evened by pecking, is irregularly spalled back (by use?) on both faces. The symmetrically concave groove ranges in width from 2.4 to 3.0 cm., and in depth from 0.3 to 0.5 cm. The specimen measures 15.2 by 5.9 by 4.7 cm., and weighs 499 gm. It was found in the fill of Kiva I.

The friable materials of the four double-headed, notched or full-grooved implements, plus the thickness of their nicely dressed ends (which show no signs of spalling or battering except in the case of one end of the full-grooved specimen), suggest the likelihood that they are "club heads," used or intended for use in hunting and possibly in warfare.

Lapstones. There are 12 complete or partially complete and broken waterworn cobbles and three complete waterworn boulders of hard rock that show evidences of use. Of the seven complete cobbles, five are unaltered (fig. 326, left and center), and two are partly spalled on the perimeter. Of the three partially complete cobbles, two are unaltered and one 5-sided specimen is bifacially spalled and pecked on four sides. Two broken cobbles have intact edges unmodified. Of the three boulders present, two are partly spalled (fig. 326, right), and one is unaltered around the perimeter.

The cobbles show the following signs of use: one wear-facet on one face (four specimens); one wear-facet on opposed faces (two specimens); one slightly dimpled or battered wear-facet on opposed faces (three specimens); one wear-facet on opposed faces, one of which is battered (one specimen); four wear-facets, each of which is battered (one specimen); and opposed faces battered only (one specimen).

Two boulders have one wear-facet on one face, and the third specimen has one wear-facet on opposed faces, with one of these showing some battering.

Materials: cobbles—diorite (5), quartzite (4), granite (1), indurated sandstone (1), iron concretion (1); boulders—quartzite (1), syenite porphyry (1), iron concretion (1).

Shapes: cobbles—subrectangular (3), discoidal (2), irregular (2), subtriangular (1), 5-sided (1), 6-sided (1); boulders—suboval (2), subtriangular (1).

Measurements: cobbles—length 13.1 to 22.1 cm. (10 specimens), width 10.2 to 19.7 cm. (11 specimens), thickness 3.4 to 8.0 cm. (12 specimens), and weight 1,085 gm. to 4.0 kg.; boulders—length 26.3 to 35.5 cm., width 15.4 to 24.3 cm., thickness 4.8 to 13.1 cm., and weight 3.8 kg. to 16.7 kg.

Provenience: cobbles—with Burial 5 in Lower East Trash Slope (1); floor, Pithouse 1 (2), Room 60, Kivas J, O (1 each); fill, Kivas A, B, D, Q, U (1 each); surface and fill, Room 57 (1); boulders—floor, Kiva O (1); fill, Kiva O (1); and surface, near Kiva N (1).

All but one of the 15 waterworn cobbles and boulders, or fragments thereof, described above have from one to four wear-facets, each; only seven of the specimens are dimpled or battered on one or more faces. Thus these implements appear to have served as portable, sturdy platforms on which various materials, e.g., vegetal substances, hides, were commonly scraped or rubbed or less commonly pounded or pulped. The term "lapstone" seems appropriate for these artifacts.

Anvil. A massive object of fine-grained sandstone, with a small hemispherical depression in one flat face, is provisionally identified as an anvil (fig. 327). It is the re-used corner fragment of a troughed (scoop-shaped) metate of Style 5. The fractured edges of the metate are trimmed by spalling. The depression, whose surface is pecked or battered by work (?), measures 5.7 cm. in diameter and 1.3 cm. in depth. It is located near the center of the former nether face of the metate. The surface of the face is pecked or battered all over. The specimen measures 28.8 by 22.7 by 10.7 cm., and weighs 11.6 kg. It was found on the surface of the Lower East Trash Slope.

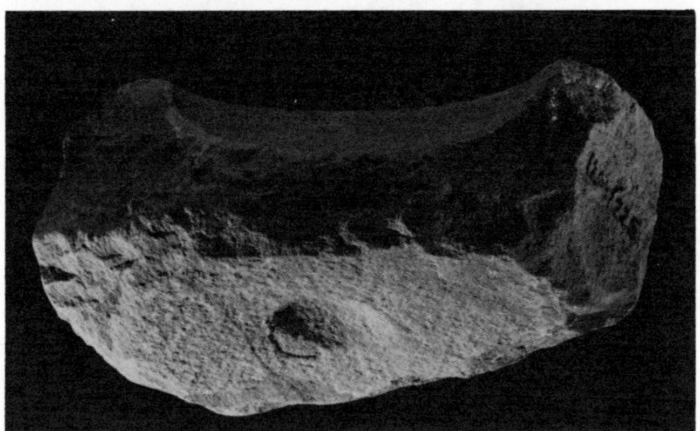

Figure 327. *Anvil.*

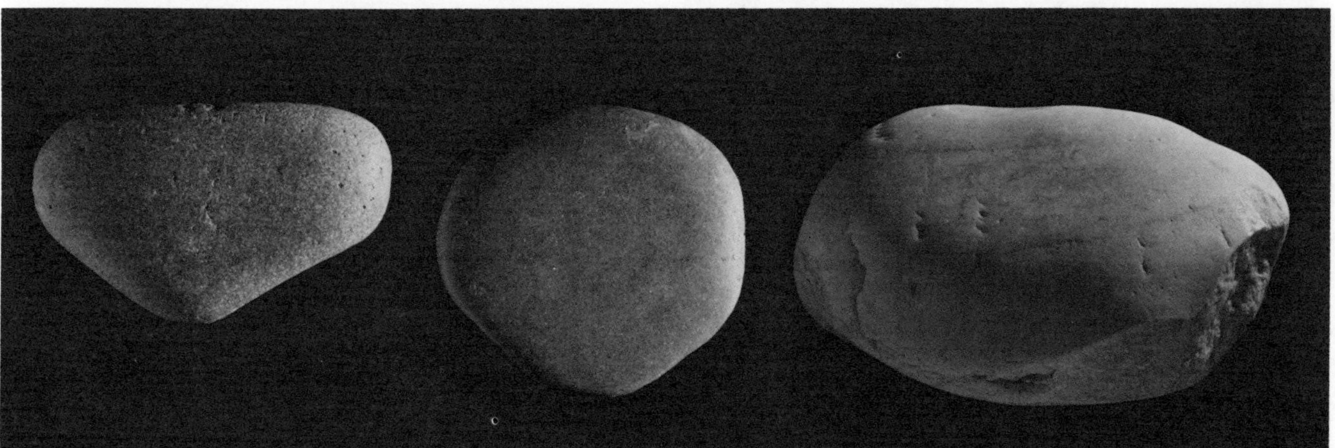

Figure 326. *Lapstones.*

Crushers. There are 20 complete and four fragmentary implements in the assemblage which are relatively large and blocky and possess from one to four "working surfaces," each. The complete specimens include one waterworn boulder, five waterworn cobbles (fig. 328b and c), and 14 spalls (fig. 328a and d). The four fragmentary specimens, all end fragments, are made of spalls.

The implements vary in the number of working surfaces as follows: single working surface, flat from end to end (nine specimens); single working surface, concave from end to end (eight specimens); single working surface, convex from end to end (three specimens); two working surfaces, flat and convex from end to end (two specimens); two working surfaces, both flat from end to end (one specimen); and four working surfaces, all convex from end to end (one specimen). The working surfaces are slightly ground to well ground over pecking in 20 cases, pecked or pecked and ground in 4 cases, pecked over spalling in 1 case, and self-sharpened in 5 cases. The upper face (when not used as a "working surface") is unmodified in 4 cases, and pecked or ground, or both, in 16 cases. The sides are unmodified in 4 cases, unifacially or bifacially spalled (4 and 4 cases, respectively), pecked over unifacial or bifacial spalling (15 and 8 cases, respectively), and pecked or pecked and ground in 12 cases. The ends are unmodified in 2 cases, unifacially or bifacially spalled (5 and 6 cases, respectively), pecked over unifacial and bifacial spalling (11 and 5 cases, respectively), and pecked or pecked and ground in 15 cases. A "finger-grip" is present in one side of one specimen and in each side of seven specimens. One implement has constricted sides.

Materials: boulder—"micaceous igneous rock"; cobbles—indurated sandstone (2), syenite porphyry (2), and "micaceous igneous rock" (1); spalls—sandstone (14), conglomerate (4).
Shapes: boulder—subrectangular; cobbles—subrectangular (4), elongated oval (1); spalls—subrectangular (9), oval (2), suboval (1), trapeze (1), irregular (1).
Measurements: boulder—28.0 by 12.6 by 8.0 cm., and 5.7 kg., cobbles—length 15.7 to 24.0 cm., width 8.0 to 12.9 cm., thickness 6.6 to 8.6 cm., and weight 981 gm. to 4.0 kg.; spalls—length 13.0 to 26.9 cm., width 8.8 to 15.8 cm., thickness 4.6 to 9.3 cm., and weight 1,284 gm. to 3.6 kg.
Provenience: subfloor fill, Room 49 and Great Kiva (1 each); floor, Room 60 and Kiva R (1 each); fill, Rooms 12, 15, 17, 56, 57–58, 76, 86, Area X, Kivas D, K, U (1 each); surface and fill, Area VI (2), Area VII and Kiva O (1 each), Lower East Trash Slope (3), and general, probably Area I and in vicinity of Room 81 (2).

These implements differ in form and relative massiveness from both manos and handstones, the two classes of hand-held grinding stones in the Long House assemblage described previously. The designation "crushers" is suggested for them, although it is not known just how they were used.

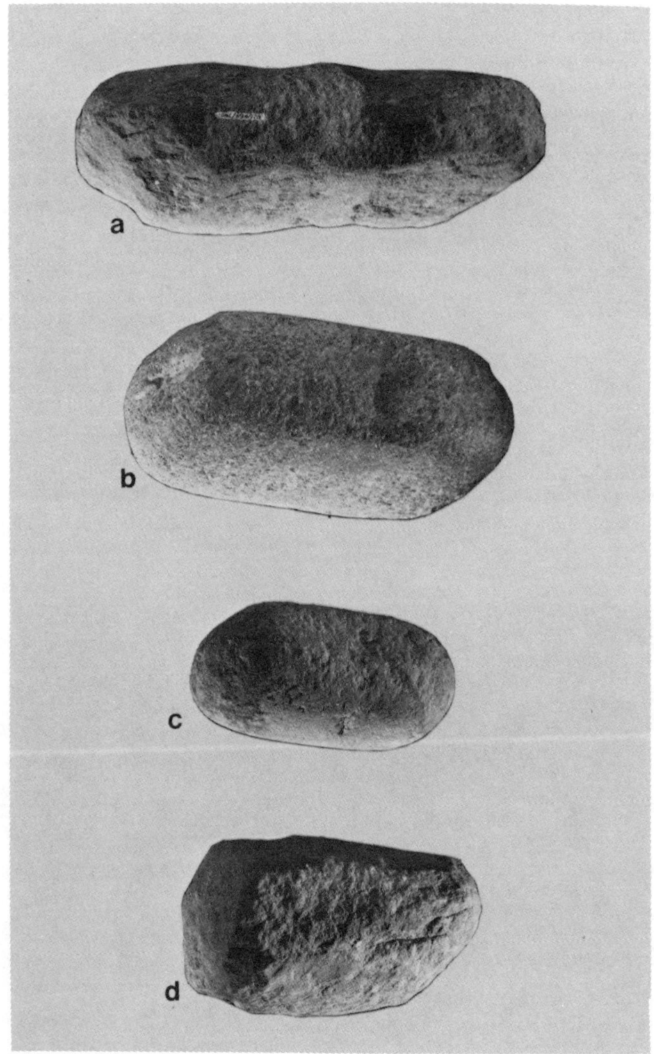

Figure 328. *Crushers.*

Tchamahias. In the Long House assemblage there are nine complete and eight fragmentary examples of a tool-type which occurs, archeologically, in greatest numbers in the San Juan area and is identified among the Hopi by the Keresan term, *tchamahia* or *tcamahia.* Five complete specimens, made of cream, tan, or reddish brown hornfels, often with dark gray laminae, are subtriangular in outline and lenticular in longitudinal and transverse sections. Four are relatively small (fig. 329), and one is relatively large (fig. 330, left). The sides diverge symmetrically from the narrow squared, rounded, or pointed end, or "butt," to the wide convex end or "cutting edge," which varies from thick and rounded (fig. 329a), to thin and blunted (fig. 329b and c), to thin and sharp (figs. 329d and 330, left). The faces, sides, and narrow end of each specimen are finely ground and polished except where the flaking scars are very deep.

One large, complete, reworked (?) specimen, of black metamorphosed shale or slate, is shouldered (fig. 330, right). One face,

Figure 329. *Tchamahias.*

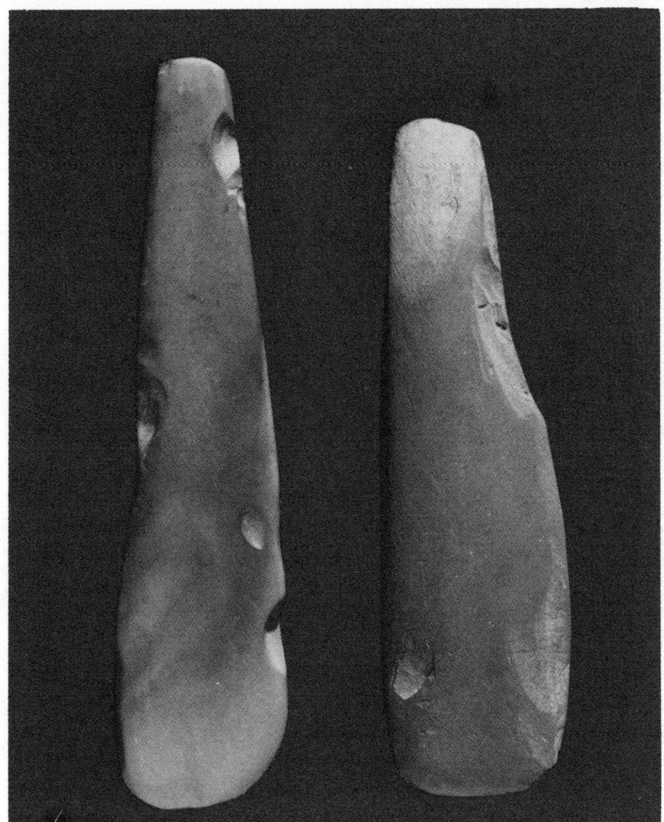

Figure 330. *Tchamahias.*

Figure 331. *Tchamahias.*

lenticular in longitudinal and transverse section, the convex ends, one side and half of the opposite side are ground and slightly polished. The uneven reverse face is flaked all over but not ground. Half on one side, forming the shoulder, is bifacially flaked and partly ground. The thin edge is minutely nicked.

The other three complete specimens are tanged. All are lenticular in longitudinal and transverse sections. One of them, of cream-brown hornfels, is ground and polished on the faces, sides, and wider, convex end, which is thin and sharp except for nicking and flaking at one corner; the short tang and butt-end are bifacially flaked and pecked (fig. 331, left). The other two specimens, of metamorphosed shale or slate, black with gray speckles and solid black, are ground on faces, sides and wider, convex or asymmetrically convex end, which is thin and sharp except for nicking and flaking. The long tang and butt-end, in each case, is bifacially spalled (fig. 331, center and right). The speckled object is moderately well polished, but the solid black specimen shows no polish.

The eight fragmentary *tchamahias* include: the distal end of a small subtriangular specimen of gray-brown hornfels, ground and highly polished, with wide, convex end thin and sharp except for nicking and flaking; the distal end and the longitudinally split distal corner fragment of two tanged specimens, of black shale or slate, ground and slightly polished, with nicked cutting edges; and the proximal end, two distal ends, and one small edge fragment, all of black shale or slate, ground and slightly polished, and the midsection, of tan-brown hornfels, ground and highly polished, of small or large subtriangular or tanged specimens. The "cutting edges" of the two distal end fragments of shale or slate are, respectively, thick and rounded, and deeply flaked back on each face.

Measurements: overall, length 14.2 to 25.0 cm. (9 specimens), width 5.3 to 8.7 cm. (13 specimens), thickness 1.2 to 2.2 cm. (16 specimens), and weight 194 to 408 gm. (9 specimens). The tangs of three complete specimens range in size as follows: length 4.4 to 8.8 cm., width 3.5 to 5.1 cm., and thickness 1.3 to 1.7 cm.

Provenience: subfloor fill, Great Kiva (1); floor, Room 49 (1); in southern recess, Kiva C (1); fill, Kiva O (3), Room 76, Kivas F, Q, U (2 each), Rooms 28, 56, Kiva H (1 each).

It is difficult to determine whether the *tchamahias* from Long House were actually used by the residents of the village as cultivating tools or were objects of symbolic and ritualistic significance, as they have come to be among two living Puebloan groups, the Hopi and the Keres (Woodbury, 1954, pp. 166–169). Almost half of the Long House specimens are fragmentary, and in 11 of the specimens, with all or part of the "cutting edge" remaining, this edge is nicked or flaked, or blunted by wear. Their condition suggest use or intended use. Still, the association of most of these implements with kivas implies that they may be tools inherited from the past, that had come to serve purposes no longer purely utilitarian.

Fragmentary Notched or Grooved Artifacts: Seven fragmentary objects with notches or parts of notches and four fragmentary objects with portions of grooves are present in the collection. The specimens are described and commented upon as follow:

The end (?) section of an object made of a spall of fine-grained sandstone, with a transverse spalled and pecked notch in each side (fig. 332d). The irregularly convex end (?) is unifacially spalled and pecked or battered. One face has three moderately well-ground facets; the reverse face is uneven, partly pecked but not ground. The object measures 8.7 cm. in width and 2.0 cm. in thickness. It came from the surface or fill of the Lower East Trash Slope. *Comment:* The notched object appears to be the remodelled section of a mano of slab-form, with three longitudinally concave grinding surfaces on one face (Style VSU3). The friable material is not suitable for an ax or hammer head. The function of the object is unknown.

The midsection of an object, made of a cobble of indurated sandstone, with one transverse spalled and pecked notch in each side (fig. 332b). The notches are ca. 2.4 cm. wide and 0.4 and 0.6 cm. deep. The convex faces and the intact portions of the rounded edges are naturally smoothed. The fragmentary object measures 6.1 cm. in width and 1.9 cm. in thickness. It came from the surface or fill of the Lower East Rash Slope. *Comment:* The friable material of this notched specimen is not suitable for an ax blade or hammer head. Its purpose is unknown.

Figure 332. *Fragmentary notched and grooved artifacts.*

An object, lacking one end, made of a cobble of quartzite, oval (?) in outline and subtriangular in transverse section, with a transverse pecked notch in each of its three edges (fig. 332c). The notches range from 1.0 to 1.7 cm. in width and are all ca. 0.25 cm. deep. The intact rounded end and the flat, smooth faces seem to be unmodified. The object measures 3.1 cm. in width and 2.5 cm. in thickness. It was found in the fill of Kiva F. *Comment:* The missing end of this notched object may have been broken in "use." Its small size suggests that it may have been a toy rather than a tool.

An object, lacking one end, made of a spall of fine-grained sandstone, with a transverse pecked notch in each side (fig. 332d). The notches are 1.2 and 1.8 cm. wide and 0.3 cm. deep. One longitudinally concave face is ground smooth; the reverse face is uneven and pecked. The edges are unifacially or bifacially spalled. The "poll" is lightly battered. The object measures 4.5 cm. in width and 1.5 cm. in thickness. Like the object described above, it came from the fill of Kiva F. *Comment:* This notched object appears to be the remodeled portion of a mano of slab-form. The friable material is not suitable for an ax blade or hammer head. It may have been a toy.

The midsection of a longitudinally split object, made of a cobble of diorite, with a transverse pecked groove in the intact face (fig. 332e); and the end section of a longitudinally split object, made of a cobble of claystone, with a transverse pecked and ground groove in the intact face and portions of the intact sides. The groove in the first is 3.8 cm. wide and 0.6 cm. deep; the groove in the second is not complete enough to permit measurements. The faces of the two specimens are naturally smoothed. The partially intact end of the second specimen is spalled and battered by use. The first object was found in the fill of Kiva E; the second object came from backdirt, probably from Area IX. *Comment:* These grooved objects are too incomplete to tell if they are fragments of full-grooved or partially grooved ax blades or hammer heads.

One edge fragment, made of a cobble of gabbro, has a complete, transverse, pecked and ground notch, ca. 2.7 cm. wide and 0.6 cm. deep, with a rounded ridge on each side of the notch (fig. 332f); and one edge fragment, made of a cobble of basalt, with a partially complete, transverse, pecked and ground notch, and a rounded ridge on the intact side of the notch. The edges of both specimens are spalled and pecked. The intact face of the first object and both faces of the second object are naturally smoothed and polished; they measure, respectively, slightly more than 4 and 3 cm. in thickness. The first object came from the surface or fill of the Lower East Trash Slope; the second was found in the fill of Area VII. *Comment:* These notched objects may be fragments of hammer heads or, possibly, of ax blades.

The corner fragment of an object, made of a cobble of claystone, with a transverse, pecked and ground notch in the intact portion of one side (fig. 332g). The notch measures 3.5 cm. wide and 0.5 cm. deep. The convex end ("poll") is spalled and battered by use. The

Figure 333. *Tether stones.*

faces and the part of the side adjacent to the notch are naturally polished. The object measures 2.5 cm. in thickness. It was found in the fill of Kiva Q. *Comment:* This object could be the poll-section of a notched, single-bitted ax blade (Style 1).

The corner fragment of an object, made of a cobble of gabbro, with a transverse, pecked and ground groove in one intact side and in one face, measuring from 1.0 to 1.2 cm. in width and 0.1 to 0.15 cm. in depth (fig. 332h); and the corner fragment of an object, made of a cobble (?) of hematite, with a transverse pecked groove in one intact side and in one face, measuring about 1.5 cm. in width and from 0.1 to 0.4 cm. in depth. The convex or irregular end (poll?) of each specimen is spalled and battered by use. The faces are naturally (?) smoothed. The object of gabbro measures 3.4 cm. in thickness; it came from the surface of the Lower East Trash Slope. The object of hematite measures 3.1 cm. in thickness; it was found in the fill of Area VII. *Comment:* These grooved objects may be fragments of C-grooved hammer heads (Style 3) or, in the case of the corner fragment of gabbro, possibly of a C-grooved, single-bitted ax blade (Style 4).

Tether Stones. There are five large, spheroidal, grooved stones in the assemblage. Four are sandstone concretions and one is a blocky piece of fine-grained sandstone (Mesaverde group). They are shaped to some extent by spalling and pecking, with a little grinding here and there. Each specimen has a single encircling V-shaped or U-shaped groove, made by pecking or pecking and grinding, situated about midway between the rounded or irregular ends (fig. 333). The grooves range in width from 0.7 to 2.7 cm. and in depth from 0.1 to 0.8 cm.

Measurements: length 16.4 to 19.2 cm., width 12.8 to 16.7 cm., thickness 12.9 to 13.6 cm., and weight 3.4 to 4.7 kg.

Provenience: fill, Room 50, Kivas B, E (1 each); surface or fill, Area IV and Upper East Trash Slope (1 each).

These heavy, friable objects are ostensibly weights or anchors of some sort. Fewkes (1898, p. 731) suggested that large, unworked stones with "equatorial grooves" which he found archeologically in Arizona may have been used in tethering eagles or domesticated turkeys. We are inclined to accept this suggested purpose for the similarly grooved, albeit rather well shaped, objects from Long House.

Slabs. Seventy-one complete or nearly complete, whole or restored slabs and 27 fragmentary slabs are present in the collection. The specimens vary greatly in shape, size, and degree of finish. Three styles are recognized.

Style 1: *Subrectangular to subsquare, with angular to rounded corners.* 8 complete or nearly complete, whole or restored specimens, and 9 fragmentary specimens.

All are made of fine-grained sandstone. The faces range from uneven and roughly spalled (fig. 334) or uneven but ground on the high spots, through flat and well ground on one face and uneven and

Figure 334. *Slab, Style 1.*

Figure 335. *Slab, Style 1.*

roughly spalled on the reverse face (fig. 335), to flat and well ground (fig. 336). Edges are unmodified in 11 cases, unifacially spalled in 1 case, ground in 4 cases, ground over unifacial spalling in 2 cases, pecked or ground, or both, over bifacial spalling in 13 cases (fig. 337).

Measurements: length 14.2 to 45.3 cm. (8 specimens), width 9.1 to 33.2 cm. (13 specimens), thickness 0.8 to 4.6 cm. (all specimens), and weight 192 gm. to 9.8 kg. (8 specimens).

Provenience: subfloor fill, Kiva L (1); on floor or footed on floor, Rooms 60, 76 (1 each); fill, Room 37 (2), Kivas F, U (1 each); fill, Room 37 (2), Kivas F, U (1 each); surface and fill, Areas III, VI, IX, Kivas I, L, Lower East Trash Slope, Upper East Trash Slope (1 each), and general (3).

One large, not quite complete slab, seemingly impregnated with grease and coated on one side with charred material, may have been a griddle stone (fig. 335). The larger slabs (figs. 334, 336, and 337) probably served as door covers, and many of the small ones may have been used as covers for niches and for small openings (windows ?) in walls.

Style 2. *Long rectangular, with one or two ground faces, parallel or tapered sides, straight to convex ends, and squared to slightly rounded corners.* 61 complete or nearly complete, whole or restored specimens, and 16 fragmentary specimens.

All of these specimens are made of fine-grained sandstone. In 42 of the 76 specimens, one flat face is dressed by pecking (1 case), grinding (8 cases), slight to extensive grinding over pecking (7 cases; fig. 338a, a thin slab with parallel sides), pecking and grinding (26 cases; fig. 338b, a thin slab with tapered sides; fig. 338c, a medium-thick slab with parallel sides; and fig. 338d, a thick slab with parallel sides). In the other 34 specimens, both flat faces are dressed by

Figure 336. *Slab, Style 1.*

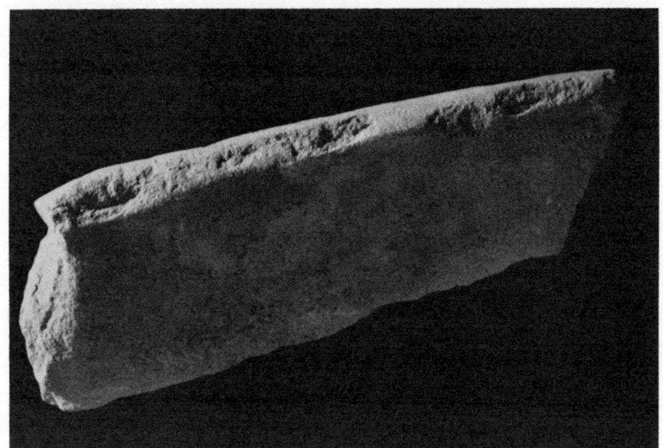

Figure 337. *Slab, Style 1.*

pecking (2 cases), slight to extensive grinding (8 cases), slight to extensive grinding over pecking (19 cases), and pecking and grinding (5 cases). Edges are unmodified (13 cases), unifacially or bifacially spalled (27 and 81 cases, respectively), pecked over unifacial or bifacial spalling (54 and 65 cases, respectively), ground over unifacial or bifacial spalling (1 case and 9 cases, respectively), pecked only (5 cases), and pecked and ground (13 cases).

> *Measurements:* length 14.8 to 40.6 cm. (61 specimens), width 10.7 to 16.9 cm. (76 specimens), thickness 0.8 to 6.3 cm. (all specimens), and weight 464 gm. to 4.6 kg. (61 specimens).
>
> *Provenience:* subfloor fill, Room 50 (1); floor, Room 49 (4), Kiva O (2), Rooms 12, 76, 80, 90, Kivas B, D, I, J, K, S, U (1 each); floor of ventilator shaft outside Kiva N (1); fill, Room 37 (7), Kiva F (3), Rooms 12, 14, 47, 75, 80, Kiva K (2 each), Rooms 9, 27, 38, 48–51, 56, 72, 76, 79, 83, 90, Area IX, Kivas B, O, P, Q, R (1 each); surface and fill, general (6), Kiva L (3), Kiva I and West Trash Slope (2 each), Room 5, Area VII, Kivas G, N, Lower East Trash Slope (1 each); and backdirt (1).

The slabs of Style 2 possess no distinctive features which would indicate their functions. The proveniences of two of the longer complete slabs—one, measuring 35.0 cm. in length, was footed in the floor and leaning against the wall of Kiva S, and the other, measuring 31.5 cm. in length, was standing on edge on the floor against the west wall of Room 90—suggest the possibility that, cushioned with hide or matting, they could have been used as backrests. Following this slender clue, we would suggest that perhaps 12 other complete specimens, measuring from 31.2 to 40.6 cm. in length, were similarly used. The remaining, shorter slabs may have had various uses as platters, trays, and shelves.

Style 3: *Sandal-form.* 1 complete and 1 nearly complete, restored specimens and 2 fragmentary specimens. The four items are described individually, as follows:

1. One complete, restored specimen, made of hard, fine-grained, yellowish brown sandstone, has nearly straight sides which taper from a wider, asymmetrically convex end with a short, rounded corner projection ("jog"), to a narrower, convex end (fig. 339, right). The flat faces and rounded edges are well ground over pecking. The specimen measures 29.0 cm. in length, 12.9 cm. in width at the "jog" and 10.8 cm. in width at the "heel," and 1.3 cm. in thickness, and weighs 914 gm. The wider end section ("toe" portion) was found in Area III directly behind Kiva H.

2. One nearly complete, restored specimen, made of black shale or slate, has one straight and one slightly convex side, both of which

Figure 338. *Slabs, Style 2.*

taper from a wider, asymmetrically convex end with a short, rounded lateral projection ("jog"), to a narrower, convex end (fig. 339, left). The flat faces and rounded edges, now pitted and flaked by weathering (?), were well ground over spalling. The object measures 31.0 cm. in length, 14.5 cm. in width just back of the "jog" and 12.1 cm. in width at the "heel," and 1.3 cm. in thickness, and weighs 971+ gm. It was recovered from the floor of Room 76.

Figure 339. *Slabs, Style 3.*

3. One end fragment ("toe" portion), made of black shale or slate, has straight sides that taper inward from the intact end, which is asymmetrically convex with a short, angular corner projection, like (1) described above. The faces, flat in longitudinal section and slightly convex in transverse section, and the rounded or vertical edges are well ground over spalling. The fragmentary specimen measures 12.8 cm. in maximum width at the "jog" and 1.4 cm. in thickness. It was found in the fill of Room 4.

4. One end fragment ("heel" portion ?), made of hard, fine-grained gray-tan sandstone, has slightly convex (?) sides that diverge outward from the intact end, which is irregularly straight. The flat faces are smoothly ground. The edges are trimmed bifacially by spalling and are slightly ground. The fragmentary specimen measures 7.6 cm. across the "heel" end and 0.9 cm. in thickness. It was found in the fill of Room 48.

Except that they are considerably larger, the first three sandal-form slabs bear a striking resemblance in outline to a nearly complete, right-foot, "jog-toed" fiber sandal from Long House found in the upper fill of Room 47. (Diagonally twilled of yucca-leaf strips, measuring about 27 cm. in length and about 10.5 cm. in maximum width at the "jog," this sandal and other twilled and twined sandals from Long House are described on pp.).

In their discussion of twilled and twined sandals, with a "little jog on the outer side," obtained from sites in the Kayenta District of northeastern Arizona in 1914 and 1915, Kidder and Guernsey (1919, p. 105) observe: "This sandal type suggests a possible use for certain flat stones, shaped like "jog-toed" sandals, that have been commonly found in the ruins of the San Juan drainage. These stones have always been called 'sandal lasts,' but their large size and the fact that none of them have any holes or grooves for the attachment of strings have made the method of their employment uncertain. Their form, however, is so exactly that of the 'jog-toed' sandals that it seems certain that they must have had some connection with the making of them."

In 1930, Morris excavated 12 complete or incomplete, finished or unfinished "sandal form" slabs at a large open site on the La Plata River in New Mexico, just south of the Colorado border (Morris, 1939, pp. 131–132, and Pl. 144). He quotes, *in extenso,* the comment of Kidder and Guernsey quoted briefly above, and he states: "While the exact manner of their use cannot positively be stated, there can be no doubt that the sandal forms were primarily utilitarian in function. I think it probable that when used in fashioning plaited sandals they served as lapboards. Thus they would have provided a smooth flat surface to work upon, and having the shape of the object that was being woven, would have served as a guide to regulate the contour of the sandal. . . . However, there would seem to be little doubt that sandal forms had their place in myth and resultant ceremonies."

Two points noted by Kidder and Guernsey concerning the sandal-form slabs—their large size and the lack of holes or grooves for the attachment of strings—seem to argue against the likelihood that the slabs had some connection with the making of fiber sandals. Figure 340 shows how large the larger of the two complete or nearly complete "jog-toed" specimens from Long House is. The left sock-foot measures 28.0 cm. in length and 9.8 cm. in width, whereas the "jog-toed" slab beneath the foot—described under (2) above—measures 31.0 cm. in length and 14.5 cm. in width just back of the

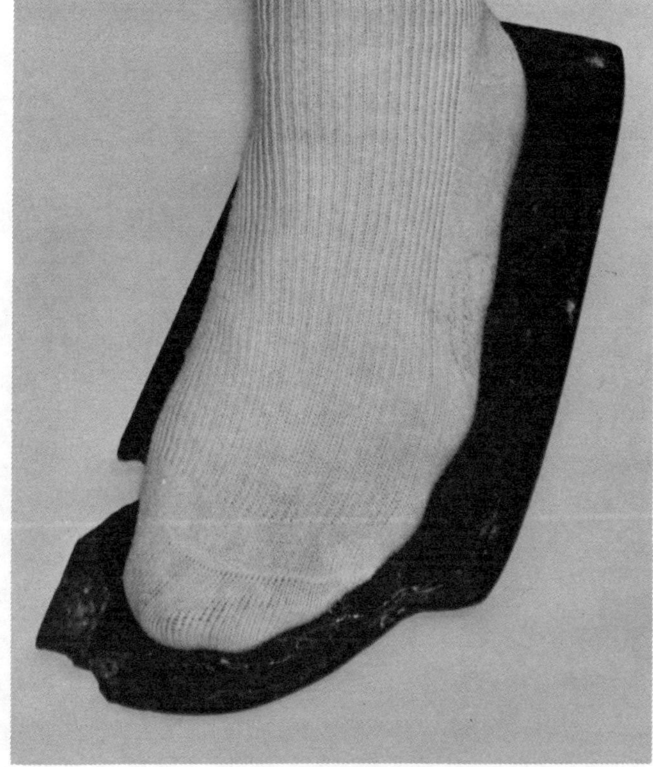

Figure 340. *Left-sock foot superimposed on sandal-form slab shown in figure 339, left.*

Figure 341. *Jar covers.*

"jog," or the considerable difference of 3.0 cm. in length and 4.7 cm. in width. (The left sock-foot is that of a White American who is 6 feet tall and wears 10B shoes; this is to say, an individual who is taller and who probably has a longer and narrower foot than all but the most exceptional prehistoric Puebloans.)

Two suggestions offered by Morris in support of this notion that the slabs were "primarily utilitarian in function"—that they served as lapboards "to work upon" and as "guides to regulate the contour of the sandal"—seem logically somewhat far-fetched. As to the first suggestion: fiber sandals, like baskets and other light woven objects, are supported by the free hands during manufacture, so that they can be worked on alternately from both faces; a stationary working surface would serve no useful purpose in such an operation. As to Morris's second suggestion: the great variability in even highly stylized objects made by hand indicates that such things are most often produced according a general preconceived idea but not by prefabricated patterns; in other words, it seems likely that "jog-toed" fiber sandals were made without reference to "guides" of stone (or wood ?). In the present context, moreover, oversize patterns would appear to have been more of a hindrance than a help.

Morris's additional suggestion that sandal-form slabs had "their place in myth and resultant ceremonies" seems to approach a far more acceptable interpretation of these objects than his arguments for their utilitarian function. We would suggest, tentatively, that "jog-toed" slabs from Long House and elsewhere in the San Juan drainage played no part in the manufacture of fiber sandals, but rather were symbols of such footwear, perhaps used in rites and ceremonies, and that their large size was an important aspect of the symbolization.

Jar Covers. There are 36 complete or fragmentary shaped pieces of sandstone, discoidal to subrectangular in outline, in the Long House assemblage. Three sizes are recognized:

Large. 2 complete or nearly complete, discoidal specimens; 1 complete subrectangular specimen; and 4 edge fragments of discoidal (?) specimens. Edges are bifacially spalled only (two specimens), bifacially spalled and partly pecked (two specimens), bifacially spalled and partly ground (two specimens), and well ground over spalling (one specimen).

Three of the specimens have one flat, moderately to well-ground face only (the opposed face in each specimen is uneven and roughly spalled). The other four specimens are pecked on both faces (fig. 341b, with bifacially spalled and partly pecked edge), pecked and partly ground on both faces (fig. 341a, subsquare in outline, with the corners bifacially spalled), and moderately to well ground on both faces (two fragmentary specimens).

Measurements: discoidal specimens—maximum diameter 23.2 to 27.0 cm. (three specimens), thickness 0.7 to 2.1 cm. (all six specimens), and weight 1,229 and 1,959+ gm. (two specimens); subrectangular—30.1 by 27.0 by 1.5 cm., and weight 1,920 gm.

Provenience: subfloor, Room 49 (1); fill, Room 37-Kiva E, Rooms 55, 56, Kivas O, R (1 each); surface and fill, Lower East Trash Slope (1).

Medium. 4 complete or nearly complete, discoidal specimens, and 11 edge fragments. Edges are unifacially or bifacially spalled only (four and five cases, respectively), or unifacially and bifacially spalled and partly ground (four cases), or well ground (two cases).

Two of the specimens have one flat, moderately or well-ground face only (the opposed face in each specimen being uneven and roughly spalled). The other specimens have both faces worked in varying degrees, from pecking only (two specimens), to pecking and some grinding (nine specimens; fig. 341c, with smoothly ground edge), to smooth grinding (two specimens; fig. 341d, with bifacially spalled edges).

Measurements: Maximum diameter 12.3 to 16.9 cm. (5 specimens), thickness 0.7 to 2.7 cm. (all specimens), and weight 17+ to 634 gm. (4 specimens).

Provenience: subfloor fill, Room 35 and Great Kiva (1 each); floor, Room 12 (1); fill, Area X (2), Rooms 12, 26, 58, Kivas I, J, R (1 each); and surface and fill, Area IV (1), Lower East Trash Slope (3).

Small. 4 complete or nearly complete, discoidal specimens, and 10 edge fragments. Edges are bifacially spalled only (three cases), bifacially spalled or pecked and partly ground (five cases), or smoothly ground (six cases). Two of the well-ground examples, both edge fragments, have a slight to pronounced unifacial bevel.

Two of the specimens have one flat or slightly concave, well-ground face only (the opposed face is uneven and roughly spalled, in each case). The other specimens have both flat or slightly convex faces either pecked and partly ground (four specimens) or smoothly ground (eight specimens; fig. 341e, with convex faces and smoothly ground edge; one short segment of the edge and about half of the surface of the reverse face are spalled off, the latter along a bedding plane, supposedly by accident).

Measurements: maximum diameter 8.5 to 10.0 cm. (4 specimens); thickness 0.6 to 1.9 cm. (all specimens), and weight 116 to 196 gm. (4 specimens).

Provenience: fill, Rooms 12, 48 (2 each), Rooms 28, 47, Areas IV, XIII, Kivas B, N, R (1 each); surface and fill, Upper East Trash Slope, West Trash Slope, and general (1 each).

The objects here labeled jar covers have been called "pot-covers," "pot lids," "jar lids," etc., by other writers. Woodbury (1954, pp. 179–180) notes: "Although jar lids have been found in place at several sites, thus justifying the use of the term, other purposes are known for such disks"—archeologically, as a sipapu cover; and ethnologically, in games. Many of the fragmentary specimens from Long House (25 specimens, or 70 percent of the sample) may have been broken as a result of use in games of various kinds. Since none of the so-called jar covers from Long House were found in or over the orifices of vessels, the designation given the specimens is clearly open to question.

Tablets. There are 19 complete or fragmentary objects of ground or polished stone, rectangular or presumably rectangular in outline, in the collection. They may be described conveniently under four headings:

End or corner fragments. 9 specimens. Six of these specimens are of soft to hard, fine-grained sandstone, gray and red in color; two are of black shale or slate; and one is of mottled buff-brown sandstone. Tabular in form, they range from partly ground to smoothly ground or faintly polished on faces and extant edges (fig. 342, left, of sandstone). They measure in width from 4.3 to 11.6 cm. (6 specimens) and in thickness from 0.4 to 0.9 cm. (all specimens).

Edge Fragments. 7 specimens. Four of these specimens are of black shale or slate, and three are of fine-grained, gray and brown sandstone. All are tabular in form. The faces are ground or slightly polished, and the extant edges are lightly ground over bifacial spalling, thoroughly ground, or faintly polished. They range in thickness from 0.4 to 1.2 cm.

Midsection. The single tabular fragment, of black shale or slate, is well ground on both faces. It is 1.0 cm. thick.

Subrectangular. One complete and one nearly complete specimen, of black shale or slate, lenticular in transverse section, well ground and slightly polished on faces and edges, except where the spalling scars are deep. The complete specimen (fig. 342, right) measures 7.3 by 4.3 by 1.5 cm., and weighs 89.2 gm. The nearly complete specimen measures 6.1+ by 4.4 by 0.7 cm., and weighs 36.4+ gm.

The provenience of the 19 specimens is: subfloor fill, Great Kiva (1); fill, Area IV, Kivas I, O (2 each), Room 2, Areas III, X, Kivas Q, R (1 each); surface and fill, Room 35 (1) Upper East Trash Slope (2), West Trash Slope (1), and general (3).

The purpose of these objects, provisionally designated as tablets, is not known.

Small Ground Objects. Nine small complete or fragmentary ground objects are present. They are described individually or in groups as follows:

Conoidal. Two complete specimens with flat, smoothly ground base. One, made of a pebble of diorite, measures 3.8 cm. in height and 3.7 cm. in maximum diameter, and weighs 79.5 gm. (fig. 343a). The other, made of a pebble of black claystone, measures 1.3 cm. in height and 1.9 cm. in maximum diameter, and weighs 4.2 gm. (fig. 343b). The former, which bears traces of red and green pigments on the perimeter, was found in the fill of Room 12; the latter came from the fill of Room 11. They are both tentatively identified as paint pestles.

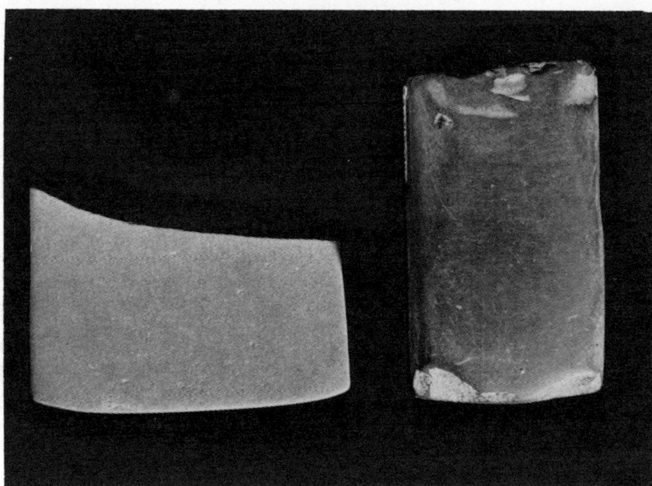

Figure 342. *Tablets.*

Cylindrical. The single complete specimen, of fine-grained, yellow sandstone, is ground on the ends and on the faceted perimeter (fig. 343c). It measures 3.1 cm. in length and 1.8 cm. in diameter, and weighs 11.7 gm. It was found on the Lower East Trash Slope. Its purpose is unknown.

Discoidal. The single complete specimen, of fine-grained, reddish (burned ?) sandstone, is partly ground on one face and pecked on the reverse, convex face (fig. 343d). It measures 4.5 cm. in maximum diameter and 1.5 cm. in thickness, and weighs 22.4 gm. It came from the general surface of the site. Its purpose is not known.

Rectangular. The two complete specimens are of fine-grained, yellow and reddish brown sandstone. The former, well ground all over, with short flanges at one end, measures 5.0 by 2.6 by 2.1 cm., and weighs 40.8 gm. (fig. 343e). It was found on the Lower East

Figure 343. *Small ground objects.*

Trash Slope. The second specimen, pecked and partly ground, measures 3.7 by 3.3 by 1.7 cm., and weighs 29.8 gm. (fig. 343f). It came from the subfloor fill of Room 85. The purpose of these objects is unknown.

Tabular. One complete and one fragmentary specimen, of fine-grained, yellow sandstone. The former, rectangular in outline and well ground on faces and edges, measures 3.8 by 1.4 by 0.6 cm., and weighs 5.4 gm. (fig. 343g). It was found in the fill of Kiva F. The fragmentary object, smoothly ground on faces and extant, thin edges, measures 3.0 cm. in width and 0.5 cm. in thickness (fig. 343h). It was found in the fill of Room 17. The purpose of these objects is unknown.

Tabular, incised. The single specimen, of red shale, is 4-sided, is smoothly ground on faces and edges, and has a deep, narrow, V-shaped groove in the longest side, near one face (fig. 343i). The object measures 4.5 by 2.1 by 0.7 cm., and weighs 7.6 gm. It came from the Lower East Trash Slope. Its purpose is not known.

Small Cones and Cylinders. There are six small, complete or nearly complete, finely ground or polished objects in the collection. They are described individually or in groups as follows:

Cones. 2 specimens. One elongated cone, of buff-colored travertine, is finely ground on the perimeter and at the rounded tip and slightly convex base (fig. 344a). It measures 3.8 cm. in length and 0.9 cm. in maximum diameter, and weighs 5.7 gm. It came from the subfloor fill of Kiva L. The second, short specimen, of green hornfels, is finely ground and polished around the perimeter and at the rounded tip and at the oblique, slightly convex base (fig. 344b). It measures 1.7 cm. in length and 0.8 cm. in maximum diameter, and weighs 1.0 gm. It was found with Burial 10 on the Lower East Trash Slope. The purpose of these objects is not known.

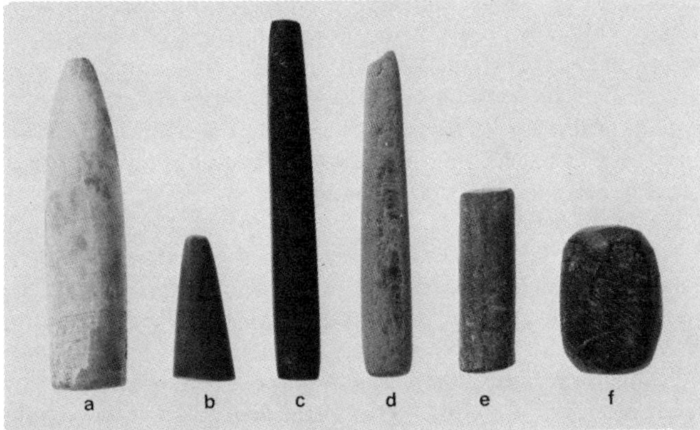

Figure 344. *Small cones and cylinders.*

Cylinders. Two of the three specimens are elongated and tapered at one end. One of these, made of black shale or slate, is finely ground and slightly polished around the perimeter and at the convex ends (fig. 344c). It measures 4.3 cm. in length and 0.6 cm. in maximum diameter, and weighs 2.5 gm. It was found in the fill of Area IV. The second tapered specimen, made of gray petrified wood, is complete except for a tiny nick at the smaller end. The object is finely ground around the perimeter and at the ends (fig. 344d). It measures 3.9+ cm. in length and 0.6 cm. in maximum diameter, and weighs 1.8+ gm. It came from the subfloor fill of Kiva M.

The third object, of buff-black shale, is finely ground and slightly polished around the perimeter and at the oblique and convex ends (fig. 344e). It measures 2.2 cm. in length and 0.7 cm. in diameter, and weighs 1.9 gm. It came from the fill of the West Trash Slope.

The purpose of the three objects is unknown. Woodbury's suggestion that similar objects from Awatovi, in northeastern Arizona, may be nose plugs has interesting possibilities (Woodbury, 1954, pp. 183–184, Fig. 28, *o–t*).

Keg-shaped. The single complete specimen, of black shale or slate, is finely ground and slightly polished around the perimeter and at the convex ends (fig. 344f). It measures 1.7 cm. in length and 1.2 cm. in maximum diameter, and weighs 1.9 gm. It came from the fill of the West Trash Slope. Its purpose is not known.

Objects of Petrified Wood. Eight complete or nearly complete and three fragmentary shaped slivers of opaque gray to reddish brown petrified wood are present in the collection from Long House. Three styles are recognized:

Style 1: *Long and narrow, with convex ends.* 1 specimen, complete except for a missing piece at one corner (fig. 345a). The nearly flat faces and all edges are finely ground. The object measures 11.9 by 1.7 by 0.4 cm., and weighs 12.9+ gm. It was found in the fill of Room 4.

Style 2: *Short and narrow, with convex or squared ends.* 5 complete and 1 fragmentary specimens (fig. 345b–e). The flat or slightly convex faces and all edges are finely ground. *Measurements:* length 2.9 to 6.9 cm. (5 specimens), width 1.0 to 1.6 cm. (all specimens), thickness 0.3 to 0.8 cm. (all specimens), and weight 1.7 to 14.6 gm. (5 specimens). *Provenience:* floor, Kiva P (1); fill, Areas V, X, Kiva P (1 each); surface and fill, Room 58 and Upper East Trash Slope (1 each).

Style 3: *Short to long and wide, with squared or rounded ends.* 1 complete, 1 nearly complete, and 2 fragmentary specimens (fig. 345f). The flat or uneven faces vary from partly ground to well ground, and the edges range from partly ground over spalling to smoothly ground. *Measurements:* length 5.1 to 7.6 cm. (2 specimens), width 2.6 to 2.8 cm. (3 specimens), and weight 8.1+ to 33.0 gm. (2 specimens). *Provenience:* floor, Kiva P (1 specimen); fill, Area V (2) and Area VII (1).

Figure 345. *Objects of petrified wood.*

The purpose of these objects of petrified wood is uncertain. The fact that six of the 11 specimens show a gloss presumably resulting from handling suggests the possibility that they were used or were intended to be used as talismans.

Carved Stones. In the Long House collection there are three blocks and three fragments of blocks, all of buff to brown, soft, fine-grained sandstone, which bear designs or parts of designs carved in one face. The specimens are described individually as follows:

1. An irregular block with one ground face bearing narrow, deeply incised horizontal, vertical, and oblique lines forming a frieze of squares, triangles, and other geometric patterns (fig. 346b). The specimen, which is slightly eroded by weathering on one side, measures 18.7 by 18.4 by 12.0 cm., and weighs 4.9 kg. It was found in the fill of Room 35.

2. A subsquare block with two adjacent pecked and partly ground faces, one of which bears two large and one small 3-element incised figures, all oriented in the same horizontal plane and placed near one edge of the block (fig. 346d). Figures of this kind are commonly identified as "turkey tracks." The specimen measures 23.0 by 21.7 by 15.1 cm., and weighs 12 kg. It came from the surface of Area III.

3. A triangular block with one partly ground face bearing one pecked and incised anthropomorphic figure with round head, upraised arms, and 3-digit hands, and bent-knee legs indicated in intaglio, and with the body indicated in cameo (fig. 347). The figure measures, overall, 11.0 cm. in height and 8.0 cm. in width. The block measures 18.9 by 11.0 by 18.9 cm., and weighs 3.8 kg. It was found on the Lower East Trash Slope.

4. The edge fragment of a flat block, obliquely fractured into two pieces that do not quite fit together. One smoothly ground convex face, lacking part of one end and one corner, bears a long narrow frieze which is bordered by single horizontal and vertical incised lines and contains parallel zigzag incised lines that suggest a large and a small serpentine figure, the latter below and parallel to the former (fig. 346a). The block fragment measures slightly more than 25 cm. across and 9.2 cm. in thickness. It was found on the surface of Area VI.

Figure 346. *Carved stones.*

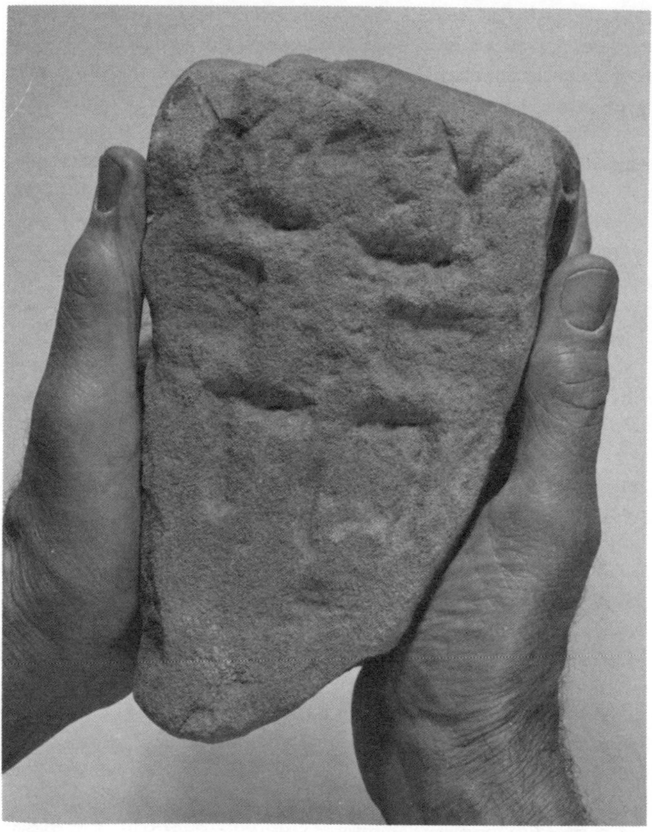

Figure 347. *Carved stone.*

5. The corner fragment of a flat block with one smoothly ground convex face bearing segments of two pairs of broadly incised, curvilinear lines which arc in opposed directions (fig. 346c). The fragment measures 11.7 cm. across and 7.6 cm. in thickness. It was found on the surface of the West Trash Slope.

6. The edge fragment of a block with one smoothly ground convex face bearing segments of eight parallel, curved, incised lines (fig. 346e). The fragment measures 12.3 cm. across and 6.8 cm. in thickness. It was found in the trash fill of Area V.

The six carved stones appear to be structural elements or fragments of such elements. Whether the designs have ritual significance or are manifestations of man's urge to embellish his surroundings cannot be determined from the evidence available.

Pot Supports. Nineteen sandstone concretions, and six end fragment and one longitudinally split end fragment of sandstone concretions, with one or both ends transversely or obliquely spalled and/or pecked, are present in the collection. All of them show signs of fire-reddening and, in many instances, of smoke-blackening as well. They are tentatively identified as "pot supports" on analogy with similar objects found *in situ* in other Puebloan sites, where they stand upright in firepits, usually in sets of three.

The intact concretions are of five forms: roughly cylindrical (eight specimens, fig. 348, lower), loaf-shaped (four specimens, fig. 348, upper), dumbbell-shaped (three specimens), irregular (three specimens), and ovate (one specimen). The end fragments were originally cylindrical in 3 cases, loaf-shaped in 2 cases, and irregular in 1 case. The longitudinally split end fragment was once cylindrical, with a naturally formed hollow, vertical shaft.

Measurements: length 6.1 to 20.8 cm. (19 specimens), width 6.6 to 12.4 cm. (all specimens), thickness 4.8 to 10.2 cm. (25 specimens), and weight 668 gm. to 2.1 kg. (19 specimens).

Provenience: in firepit, Kiva S (1); floor, Kivas R and U (2 each), Rooms 37, 80, Kiva K (1 each); fill just above floor, Room 37 (2); fill, Kiva R (4), Rooms 2, 54 (2 each), Rooms 52, 76, Area X, Kivas B, E (1 each); and general surface or fill (3).

The sandstone concretions are fine-textured and extremely dense, and thus more resistant than other rocks to fracturing and spalling when exposed to high temperature or sudden changes in temperature. Observation of this characteristic may have led to the regular employment of such stones to hold the cooking pot steady and the griddle stone firm above the level of glowing coals in firepits at Long House and many other Puebloan sites.

Figure 348. *Pot supports.*

POTPOURRI

At archeological sites occupied by people for any length of time, objects are usually found which cannot be fitted neatly into a category but nevertheless should be mentioned. This is the case with 147 items, designated as potpourri and representing 6 percent of the stone objects reported on from Long House. The miscellaneous items include concretions, waterworn cobbles and pebbles, pieces of petrified wood, and gizzard stones.

Concretions. The 74 whole or fragmentary concretions in the collection are of two kinds: sandstone concretions and iron-impregnated sandstone concretions, or simply iron concretions. The specimens are described under these headings, as follows:

Sandstone concretions—51 whole or fragmentary specimens of three styles:

Style 1: *Geometric*—47 specimens described according to form:

Spherical. The 16 specimens vary in color from gray through buff to yellowish brown and range from marble-size to cobble-size. Four of the concretions are spalled on one face or one end, by intention or accident (fig. 349a), and the largest one of this form appears to be slightly ground on one face by use. The other 11 specimens seem to be unmodified.

Measurements: maximum diameter 2.2 to 13.4 cm., and weight 11 to 1,743 gm.

Provenience: subfloor fill, Room 60 (1); fill, subfloor ventilator shaft, Kiva B (1); fill, Test Trench L, Rooms 37, 54, Area VI, Kivas I, Q, S (1 each); surface and fill, Lower East Trash Slope (5), and Areas IV, X (1 each).

Cylindrical. The 11 specimens of this form vary in color from gray through buff to yellowish brown. Only two specimens, each square or round at one end and pointed at

Figure 349. *Concretions.*

the opposite end, appear to be complete (fig. 349b). The other specimens include a pointed end fragment, an irregular cylinder lacking one end, four midsections, two bipointed specimens (?) lacking one end, and a squared end fragment. The last three specimens only seem to be modified, by grinding.

Measurements: maximum diameter 0.8 to 2.9 cm. (all specimens), length 5.5 to 8.7 cm. (2 specimens), and weight 23 to 49 gm. (2 specimens).

Provenience: fill, northeast firepit, Room 60 (1); fill, Room 12, Kiva F (1 each); surface and fill, Area XII (3), Lower East Trash Slope and West Trash Slope (2 each), Upper East Trash Slope (1).

Discoidal. The two examples of this form have biconvex faces. The smaller, buff-colored specimen, measuring 4.9 cm. in maximum diameter and 3.1 cm. in thickness, and weighing 89 gm., seems to be slightly ground on one face (fig. 349c). The larger specimen, brown in color, measuring 6.2 cm. in maximum diameter and 4.4 cm. in thickness, and weighing 147 gm., is unmodified. *Provenience:* fill, Room 48 (larger specimen; surface and fill, Lower East Trash Slope (smaller specimen).

Subrectangular. The single specimen, brown in color, has one end transversely spalled by intention or accident; otherwise, it seems to be unmodified (fig. 349d). *Measurements:* 6.7 by 4.9 by 2.9 cm., and weight 188 gm. *Provenience:* fill, Area X.

Ovate. The two small specimens of this form, reddish gray and buff in color (the latter with a nipple-like projection at the narrow end), appear to be unmodified (fig. 349e and f). *Measurements:* length 3.0 cm. (both specimens), width 2.2 to 2.4 cm., thickness 2.0 to 2.2 cm., and weight 13.1 and 23.3 gm. *Provenience:* surface and fill, Lower East Trash Slope (both specimens).

Dumbbell-shaped. The single buff-colored example of this form appears to be slightly spalled at one end, possibly by accident, and is otherwise unmodified (fig. 349g). *Measurements:* length 5.4 cm., maximum diameter 3.5 cm., and weight 77.1 gm. *Provenience:* surface and fill, Upper East Trash Slope.

Eccentric. Four complete concretions and one fragmentary concretion are joined, buff-colored spheres and cylinders of "eccentric" form (fig. 349h and i). All of these specimens are unmodified. *Measurements:* length 4.0 to 7.0 cm. (4 specimens), maximum diameter 1.4 to 3.0 cm. (all specimens), and weight 8.2 to 53.4 gm. (4 specimens). *Provenience:* fill, Rooms 36, 52 (1 each); surface and fill, Lower East Trash Slope (3).

Irregular, with hollow center. The three complete examples are sections of yellow or buff-colored concretions with hollow centers. The edges of each section may be intentionally spalled but the concave interior surfaces do not appear to be modified by intention or use (fig. 350a). *Measurements:* length 11.5 to 12.7 cm., width 6.9 to 9.3 cm., thickness 1.7 to 4.8 cm., and weight 158 to 445 gm. *Provenience:* subfloor fill, Kiva N (1); surface and fill, Area XII and West Trash Slope (1 each).

Irregular, with one or two hollow shafts. Three of the six complete examples, buff to reddish brown in color, have one hollow shaft each, and the other three have two hollow shafts apiece. Two of the former may be intentionally spalled on one end (fig. 350b) or on both ends (fig. 350c). Otherwise, these two concretions, the third one with one shaft, and the three specimens with two shafts each (fig. 350d) do not seem to have been modified by man. *Measurements:* length 8.0 to 21.0 cm., width 7.3 to 20.5 cm., thickness 5.5 to 14.2 cm., and weight 348 gm. to 5.2 kg. *Provenience:* fill, Kiva R (4), Kiva K (1); surface and fill, Lower East Trash Slope (1).

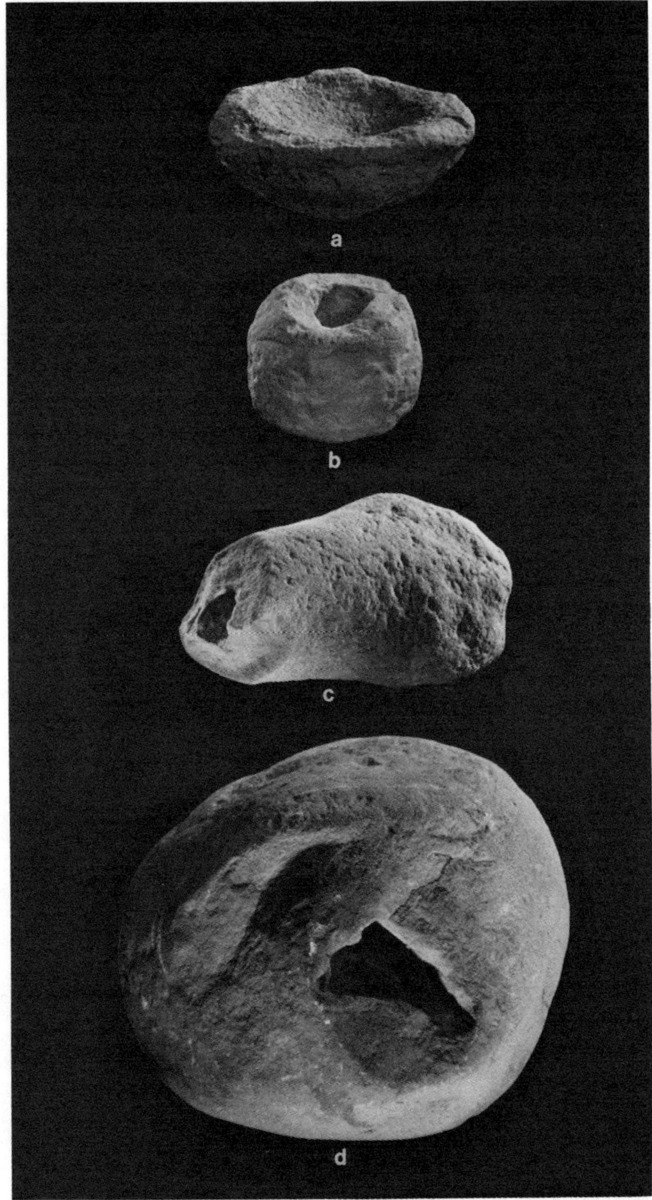

Figure 350. *Concretions.*

One of the three concretions of this style is cobble-like, gray-brown in color, with a flattish projection at one end. The "head" and upper surface or "back" are fairly smooth; the perimeter of the "body" is knobby. The lower surface or "belly" is roughly spalled, perhaps in order to make the object sit level. The concretion suggests a horned toad without a tail (fig. 351, upper). It measures, overall, 14.2 by 10.4 by 6.3 cm., and weighs 981 gm. It was found on the upper portion of the West Trash Slope.

Another concretion, of tabular form, brown in color, has three flat projections and a pedestalled ovate projec-

Figure 351. *Concretions.*

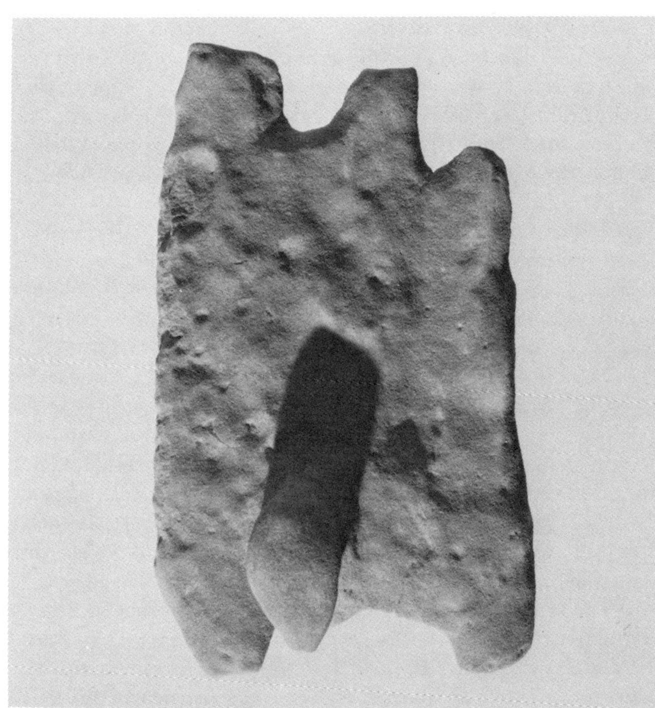

Figure 352. *Concretion.*

tion at one end and three flat projections (one of which is slightly spalled or broken) at the opposite end. The middle section of one side is bifacially spalled but no other modifications are evident. The concretion suggests a nesting bird (fig. 352). It measures 20.2 by 12.3 by 4.5 cm., and weighs 682 gm. It was found in the floor-level shrine in Kiva Q, at the base of the liner opposite the southern recess and firepit.

The third concretion of Style 2 is a large, pitted block of gray-brown sandstone. The top is concave, the bottom is flat. A natural groove, possibly deepened by intentional grinding, extends upward on both sides from the rounded end. The other, ungrooved end is very irregular and possibly spalled. The concretion suggests the head of a long-muzzled creature, more supernatural or fantastic than real (fig. 353, left, view of left side; right, frontal view). It measures 33.5 by 15.9 by 18.4 cm., and weighs 12.4 kg. It was found in the fill of Room 87, along the south wall.

Style 3: *Vegetable-like*—1 specimen.

The single example of this style is a nearly symmetrical, cone-shaped concretion with an extremely rough surface. Except for a little grinding or wear on the convex bottom, the specimen has apparently not been altered in

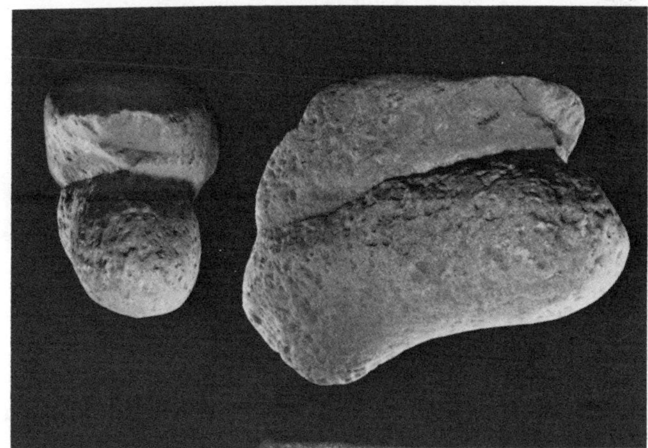

Figure 353. *Concretion.*

any way. It suggests a bottle gourd (fig. 351, lower). The concretion measures 15.5 cm. in length and 12.5 cm. in maximum diameter, and weighs 1,961 gm. It was found in the fill of Area IV.

Iron concretions—23 whole or fragmentary specimens, all but two of which, being dark reddish brown in color, are described according to form as follows:

Hemispherical, with hollow center. The single complete specimen may have been spalled around the "orifice," but otherwise the naturally even exterior and interior seem to be unmodified (fig. 354a). It measures 3.0 cm. in diameter and 1.8 cm. in height, and weighs 17.7 gm. It came from the fill of Kiva M.

Spherical. The three complete examples of this form include two small, naturally even-surfaced specimens, each measuring 2.5 cm. in maximum diameter and weighing 15 and 15.5 gm. (fig. 354b), and one large, uneven, apparently unmodified specimen measuring 7.0 cm. in maximum diameter and weighing 398 gm. The latter specimen was found in the fill of

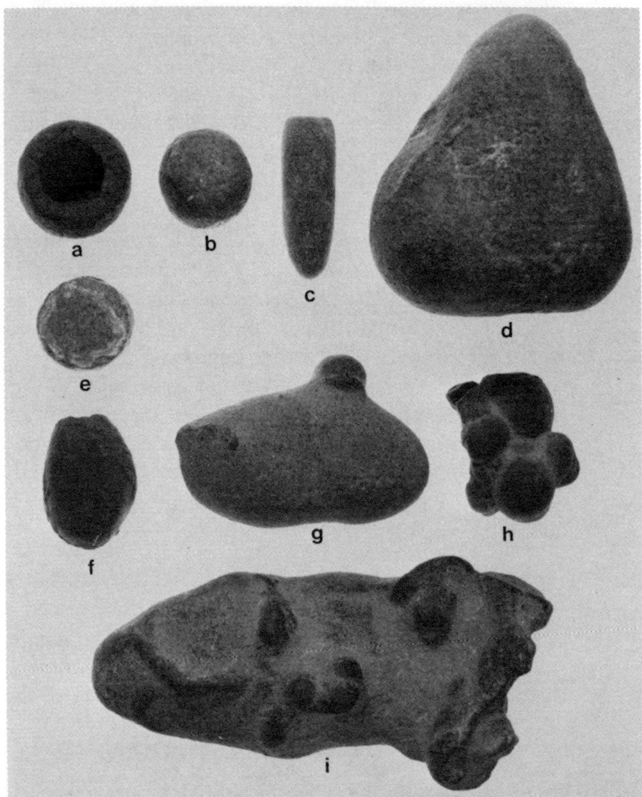

Figure 354. *Iron concretions.*

Room 54. The two small ones came from the general surface and fill of the site.

Cylindrical. The single complete specimen is pointed at one end and nearly square at the opposite end. An oval recess in the square end measures 0.6 cm. in maximum diameter and 1.3 cm. in depth. Both the recess and the smooth exterior seem to be wholly natural (fig. 354c). The specimen, which resembles a pipe, measures 4.2 cm. in length and 1.4 cm. in maximum diameter, and weighs 14 gm. Like the hemispherical concretion described above, it was found in the fill of Kiva M.

Subtriangular. The single complete specimen of this form is unevenly concave on one face and evenly convex on the reverse face. Except for a spall scar on the latter face, the object appears to be unmodified (fig. 354d). It measures 7.1 by 6.4 by 4.4 cm., and weighs 211 gm. It was found in the niche back of the shrine in Kiva Q.

Discoidal. The single example is naturally rough around the perimeter; its uneven faces may or may not be the result of intentional spalling (fig. 354e). The specimen measures 2.6 cm. in maximum diameter and 1.1 cm. thick, and weighs 10 gm. It was found in the fill of Room 12.

Suboval. One large specimen and two of the three small specimens of this form are spalled at one end (fig. 354f). The third small specimen, yellowish brown in color, is roughly spalled on one side. Otherwise, these concretions seem to be unmodified. *Measurements:* length 3.5 to 9.0 cm., width 1.9 to 4.5 cm., thickness 1.6 to 4.4 cm., and weight 9.6 to 225 cm. *Provenience:* fill, Area VII (2), Test B (1); surface and fill, Upper East Trash Slope (1).

Dumbbell-shaped. The two complete examples of this form have evened surfaces. They appear to be unmodified by intention or use. *Measurements:* 5.6 by 2.1 by 1.5 cm., and 25 gm., and 8.3 by 3.8 by 3.3 cm., and 127.5 gm. *Provenience:* surface and fill, West Trash Slope (smaller specimen) and general (larger specimen).

Eccentric. Five complete concretions are joined spheres and cylinders of "eccentric" form (fig. 354g–i). All are unmodified. *Measurements:* length 4.0 to 11.9 cm., width 2.1 to 5.7 cm., thickness 2.0 to 4.9 cm., and weight 13.9 to 270 gm. *Provenience:* in floor-level shrine, Kiva Q (1 specimen, fig. 354h); in niche back of shrine, Kiva Q (2 specimens, fig. 384g and i); fill, Room 83 and Area X (1 specimen each).

Irregular, with hollow center. The three complete examples (one of which is yellowish brown in color) and the single fragmentary example are sections of concretions with hollow centers. The edges of each section may be intentionally spalled but the uneven concave interior surfaces do not appear to be modified by intention or use. The bottoms of two specimens are smooth, possibly merely worn from being moved about. *Measurements:* length 7.3 to 9.9 cm. (3 specimens), width 4.2 to 9.2 cm. (all specimens), thickness 1.8 to 3.1 cm. (1 specimen), and weight 116 to 195.7 gm. (3 specimens). *Provenience:* subfloor fill, Kiva N (1); fill, Room 75 (1); surface and fill, Area IV and Lower East Slope (1 each).

Irregular (lump). The single complete specimen shows no definite evidence of having been modified. *Measurements:* 6.1 by 4.8 by 2.8 cm., and weight 105.2 gm. *Provenience:* surface, West Trash Slope.

Less than half of the sandstone and iron concretions in the collection (31 specimens, or 42 percent) seem to be modified in any way, and the modifications noted—spalling on 24 specimens and grinding on 7 specimens—may often be fortuitous rather than intentional. Of the 46 specimens having precise or reasonably certain provenience, 26 came from rooms and areas and 19 were found in kivas. The condition of most of the specimens and location of many of them suggest that concretions were collected and saved by the residents of Long House not for utilitarian purposes but in part as curiosities and in part as objects of veneration. The latter quality seems attributable particularly to the sandstone bird effigy and the iron "eccentric" found in the shrine, and to the three iron concretions found in the niche back of the shrine, in Kiva Q.

Waterworn Cobbles and Pebbles. Five cobbles and 16 pebbles, shaped and smoothed by stream action are present in the Long House assemblage. Except for two pebbles, spalled respectively on one end and one side, probably by accident, these specimens appear not to be modified by intention or use.

The five cobbles vary in form and material: oval (1 specimen of sandstone), ovate (1 specimen of quartzite), subrectangular (1 specimen of claystone), and irregular (1 specimen each of chert and travertine). *Measurements*: length 6.5 to 12.5 cm., width 4.1 to 8.5 cm., thickness 2.1 to 7.8 cm., and weight 126 to 1,048 gm. *Provenience*: in niche back of shrine, Kiva Q (1, of chert, irregular form); fill, Area V, Kivas Q, R (1 each); surface and fill, Lower East Trash Slope (1).

The 16 pebbles also vary in form and material: oval (1 specimen each of sandstone, chert, claystone, and quartzite), ovate (2 specimens each of claystone and quartzite), subtriangular (3 specimens of quartzite), and irregular (2 specimens each of claystone and quartzite, and 1 specimen of quartz). *Measurements*: length 1.7 to 5.7 cm., width 1.4 to 5.3 cm., thickness 1.0 to 4.5 cm., and weight 3.4 to

174.4 gm. *Provenience*: subfloor fill, Great Kiva (1); in niche back of shrine in Kiva Q (1 ovate pebble and 1 subtriangular pebble, both of quartzite); in fill of firepit, Kiva K (1); fill, Rooms 4, 37, 81, Area IV, Kiva T (1 each); surface and fill, Lower East Trash Slope (5), Areas VI, XII (1 each).

The presumably unmodified cobbles and pebbles in the assemblage seem to have been collected and saved either because of their arcane significance—which may be inferred, specifically, in the case of the two pebbles found in the niche back of the shrine in Kiva Q—or as "stock" to be worked into artifacts of various sorts.

Petrified Wood. Twenty-six unmodified pieces of petrified wood of varying sizes and shapes occur in the collection. A majority of the pieces (22 specimens or 80 percent of the lot) are dull gray to black and may have come from a single source. The other pieces are glossy brown or black and may derive from a different source. *Measurements*: length 2.3 to 16.8 cm., width 1.2 to 5.6 cm., thickness 0.7 to 4.0 cm., and weight 4.3 to 473.2 gm. *Provenience*: in shrine of Kiva Q (the largest specimen, of dull gray-black material); fill, Area X (3), Kiva F (2), Rooms 12, 17, 87, Kivas C, Q (1 each); surface and fill, Lower East Trash Slope (7), West Trash Slope (3), Upper East Trash Slope (2), Room 7 and Area VII (1 each).

The pieces of petrified wood, like the waterworn cobbles and pebbles, may have been collected and saved because of their ritual value (inferred from the presence of the largest piece in the shrine of Kiva Q), or as "stock" for fashioning objects similar to those described previously.

Gizzard Stones. Twenty-five small stones of gray, greenish gray, and brown chert and one small stone of gray-tan chalcedony exhibit rounded edges and polished surfaces in every case. They are probably identifiable as gizzard stones of the turkeys bred, raised, and slaughtered in Long House. The stones were originally minute flakes or spalls which the birds picked out of refuse deposits in and near the site.

Shapes: irregular (21), ovate (3), subtriangular (2). *Measurements*: length 1.0 to 2.8 cm., width 0.7 to 1.5 cm., thickness 0.2 to 0.8 cm., and weight 0.4 to 2.7 gm. *Provenience*: subfloor fill, Kiva N (1); fill, Room 81 (4), Rooms 44, 47, 76, Areas IV, VII, X, Kivas C, I, J, U (1 each); surface and fill, Lower East Trash Slope (7), Area VII and West Trash Slope (2 each).

MINERALS

Ten minerals were recovered from Long House. They are described individually, or in a group, as follows:

One flat, irregular lump of coal or lignite, measuring 4.2 by 3.3 by 1.6 cm., and weighing 15.3 gm. It was found in the fill of Room 64.

Six flat, irregular pieces of lignite. They give the following measurements: length 1.3 to 2.7 cm., width 1.0 to 1.6 cm., thickness 0.5 to 0.9 cm., and weight 1.1 to 4.1 gm. All these pieces were found in the fill of Room 4.

One lump of coal or lignite broken into 30 tiny fragments, which together weigh 3.6 gm. The specimen came from the surface or fill of the Lower East Trash Slope.

One subsquare lump of calcite, battered on edges and corners, possibly by handling. The specimen measures 2.3 by 2.2 by 2.0 cm., and weighs 30.2 gm. It came from the surface or fill of the Lower East Trash Slope.

One elongated quartz crystal, spalled at the ends and worn on the sides by handling (?). The specimen measures 2.4 by 0.9 by 0.8 cm., and weighs 2.7 gm. It was found with Burial 10 on the Lower East Trash Slope.

Table 17. Measurements, material and provenience of illustrated stone artifacts.

Figure	Length	Size (cm.) Width or Diameter	Thickness	Weight	Material	Provenience	M.V.N.P. Catalog No. /700*
274, a	13.4	9.8	7.4	1587gm.	Quartzite	Room 74, Level II (1.5′-2.1′)	17735
b	5.8	5.8	2.6	100gm.	Claystone	Room 47, Level II (0.6′-1.5′)	17465
c	5.7	4.7	3.8	198gm.	Chert	Kiva N, fill	20741
d	7.2	5.7	3.5	185gm.	Claystone	Room 48, Pit 3	15650
e	5.7	4.1	3.7	112gm.	Diorite	Kiva U, Level III (8.5′-9.5′)	24316
275, left	6.9	6.4	5.3	413gm.	Hematite	Kiva H, floor	16091
right	8.1	6.3	6.2	595gm.	Hematite	Rooms 6-7, surface area of two floors	13901
276, a	7.3	6.8	3.3	255gm.	Gabbro	Room 48, Level B	14311
b	13.6	7.7	6.7	885gm.	Claystone	Kiva O, surface	20763
c	11.4	8.5	5.4	364gm.	Syenite Porphyry	Area X, fill	22288
d	14.0	9.0	6.7	1339gm.	Indurated Sandstone	Kiva R, Level IV	20941
e	9.0	8.6	4.2	473gm.	Gabbro	Lower East Trash Slope	16614
f	9.2	7.6	5.9	602gm.	Quartzite	Kiva N, fill	20738
g	12.4	8.2	4.7	1195gm.	Granite Porphyry	Kiva J, Lower level	16232
h	11.4	8.2	3.4	506gm.	Granite Porphyry	Room 48, Level C	15638
i	9.2	6.7	3.5	373gm.	Schist	Area VI, fill	16349
277, top	16.3	12.7	4.7	1528gm.	Indurated Sandstone	Kiva E, surface	20640
center	17.9	13.0	5.0	1890gm.	Breccia	Kiva A, Level VI (7.8′-8.2′, floor)	20812
bottom	14.5	8.9	9.1	848gm.	Indurated Sandstone	Room 32, subfloor	14058

(continued)

Table 17. Measurements, material and provenience of illustrated stone artifacts. (Continued)

Figure	Length	Size (cm.) Width or Diameter	Thickness	Weight	Material	Provenience	M. V. N. P. Catalog No. /700*
278, top	8.3	7.8	2.9	930gm.	Sandstone	Kiva R, Level VI	20958
center	8.1	7.8	2.1	73gm.	Sandstone	Kiva R, Level VI	20959
bottom	7.7	5.6	2.4	163gm.	Sandstone	Room 58, fill	15828
279	16.4	6.2	3.0	569gm.	Sandstone	Kiva Q, Level I	20862
280, a	17.0	13.8	5.2	1148gm.	Sandstone	Kiva R, Level VIII	20982
b	9.6	6.4	4.5	261gm.	Sandstone	Kiva I, floor	16124
c	6.2	5.9	3.8	112gm.	Sandstone	Lower East Trash Slope	16687
d	11.3	8.5	2.9	279gm.	Sandstone	Area VII	16415
e	11.6	9.9	3.8	374gm.	Sandstone	Kiva R, fill	20985
f	6.9	4.4	1.7	56gm.	Sandstone	Room 60, subfloor fill	25915
281	31.2	27.0	13.9	16.3kg.	Sandstone	Area VI, fill	22174
282, left	32.5	22.5	9.2	7.8kg.	Sandstone	Surface at east side of site	22087
center	5.6	5.0	2.3	51gm.	Sandstone	Upper East Trash Slope	16781
right	29.0	25.5	14.0	12.6kg.	Sandstone	General surface, east side of site	22086
283, top	—	13.8	6.0	1429gm.	Concretionary Sandstone	Kiva Q, Level VII, floor	20907
center	16.3	8.5	5.8	1126gm.	Gabbro	Kiva K, Level III	20653
bottom	16.4	10.8	8.6	2.4kg.	Quartzite	Area I, surface	16263
284, a	3.5	2.3	1.5	19gm.	Chert	Area X, surface	22281
b	2.0	1.4	1.1	4.6gm.	Quartzite	Area X, Level II	22304
c	3.2	2.8	1.7	24gm.	Carnelian	Room 37, fill, northwest corner	14079
d	5.0	4.4	1.3	51gm.	Claystone	Lower East Trash Slope	16665
e	6.8	6.2	2.5	166gm.	Diorite	Kiva J, upper level	16194
285, a	3.4+	1.3	0.3	1.4+gm.	Quartzite	Area VI, surface	16130
b	2.5	1.5	0.3	1.0gm.	Chert	Lower East Trash Slope, Burial 6	16543
c	3.6+	1.3	0.3	1.2gm.	Chert	Room 11, fill	24380
d	2.0	1.2	0.3	0.5gm.	Quartzite	Lower East Trash Slope	17093
e	2.3+	1.2	0.4	0.8gm.	Quartzite	Kiva U, Level IV	24303
f	2.7	1.8	0.4	1.7gm.	Chert	Lower East Trash Slope	16519
g	2.8+	1.8	0.3	1.2+gm.	Chert	Room 82, Level II	20578
h	3.4	2.0	0.4	2gm.	Chalcedony	Area VI, surface	16185
i	4.0+	2.3	0.5	5.1+gm.	Chalcedony	Kiva A, fill	15863
j	4.5+	2.1	0.5	4.5+gm.	Chert	Area IV, Level A, 2nd backdirt	22134
286, a	8.0+	2.9	1.0	19.7	Quartzite	Area X, fill	22282
b	7.5+	2.5	0.6	11.9	Chert	Kiva K, Level II	20643
c	6.1	2.2	0.8	—	Chert	Room 36, Level C	17415
d	7.0	4.6	2.2	58	Chert	Room 23, fill	17100
e	3.2	2.3	0.6	4.2	Chalcedony	West Trash Slope	24265
f	3.6	2.0	0.6	4.6gm.	Quartzite	Lower East Trash Slope, surface	16712
g	3.2	1.3	0.6	3.1gm.	Chalcedony	Kiva R, fill	22030
h	6.4	4.7	0.7	24gm.	Quartzite	Kiva H, Level B	16068
i	4.0	2.8	0.7	10.0gm.	Quartzite	Backdirt	17063
j	4.7	3.1	1.4	25.6gm.	Chert	Kiva R, Level X	20997
k	—	5.3	1.4	—	Chert	Kiva O, Level VII (floor)	20813
287, left and right	—	1.9	0.9	—	Chert	West Trash Slope, surface	16952
288	9.6	3.8	1.0	38gm.	—	Kiva H, Level C	16081
289, left	4.5	1.9	1.2	7.4gm.	Chert	General surface and fill	22124
right	3.2	2.7	0.9	7.1gm.	Chert	Kiva A, fill	15864
290, upper left	4.1	3.2	0.6	12.9gm.	Sandstone	Test D, Level 1	12108
upper right	6.7	4.2	0.8	35.4gm.	Sandstone	Lower East Trash Slope	16707
lower	10.8	5.3	0.9	78.5gm.	Sandstone	Kiva E, fill	15970
291, a	—	0.9	0.3	—	Chert	Room 4, floor 3	24735
b	5.3	3.4	1.1	17.8	Chert	Kiva N, fill	26446
c	6.1	2.1	1.0	8.4	Quartzite	Test L, fill	12110
d	2.5	1.0	0.4	1.3gm.	Chert	Lower East Trash Slope	16526
292, a	10.9	7.7	5.2	495gm.	Syenite Porphyry	Kiva O, Level V	20794
b	9.2	8.8	2.7	324gm.	Chert	Kiva I, Level A	16148
c	6.7	4.9	2.4	90gm.	Chert	Room 48, Level B	14176
d	6.6	6.1	3.3	96gm.	Claystone	Kiva R, fill	22034
e	7.2	7.0	1.8	111gm.	Claystone	General surface and fill	23461
f	5.3	5.1	2.1	58gm.	Claystone	Room 57, subfloor fill	26370
293	23.5	12.0	2.3	1139gm.	Indurated Sandstone	Room 12, Level A	13928
294, a	9.5	5.8	2.4	225gm.	Basalt	Room 49, on floor	15665
b	14.8	7.2	3.8	590gm.	Claystone	Kiva F, fill	16013

Table 17. Measurements, material and provenience of illustrated stone artifacts. **(Continued)**

Figure	Length	Size (cm.) Width or Diameter	Thickness	Weight	Material	Provenience	M.V.N.P. Catalog No. /700*
c	9.6	5.5	3.4	294gm.	Claystone	Room 58, fill	15833
d	10.3	6.5	2.8	318gm.	Schist	Kiva H, floor	16090
e	9.3	6.8	3.0	291gm.	Basalt	Kiva J, northeast niche	16240
f	12.2	10.2	4.0	691gm.	Diorite	Lower East Trash Slope	16711
295	13.8	6.5	3.3	384gm.	Hornfels	Lower East Trash Slope, with Burial 10	16548
296, top	13.5	7.3	2.5	361gm.	Quartzite	Kiva J, floor	16244
center	12.8	7.0	3.8	551gm.	Hematite Rock	West Trash Slope, fill	17034
bottom	17.3	11.0	2.6	337gm.	Indurated Sandstone	Room 37, fill	14091
297, a	10.2	5.9	4.3	314gm.	Basalt	Kiva J, upper level	16195
b	15.6	8.1	6.6	1224gm.	Diorite	Area VII, fill	16412
c	22.7	8.5	5.0	1378gm.	Diorite	Kiva J, upper level	16241
d	14.0	8.8	6.2	1266	Basalt	Kiva B, subfloor ventilator shaft	24742
e	12.5	6.9	3.3	431	Slate	Kiva O, Level IV, floor	20797
298, a	4.9	4.2	3.0	55gm.	Chert	Lower East Trash Slope	16802
b	5.3	2.2	3.9	54gm.	Chert	Room 28, fill	15511
c	5.0	4.4	3.4	93gm.	Claystone	Lower East Trash Slope	16584
d	8.6	6.1	4.3	223gm.	Chert	Kiva R, Level IX	20993
299, a	6.0	4.4	1.6	41gm.	Chert	Lower East Trash Slope	16829
b	6.5	3.9	1.8	39gm.	Claystone	Kiva N, subfloor fill	25545
c	6.7	2.6	0.8	17gm.	Chalcedony	Room 12, Level B	13942
d	4.7	4.3	2.2	40gm.	Claystone	Kiva B, fill	12498
e	4.2	3.8	2.0	26gm.	Claystone	Room 12, Level B	17095
f	5.6	4.3	1.7	40gm.	Claystone	Room 35, undisturbed fill	17102
g	5.6	4.6	1.7	36gm.	Claystone	Kiva R, Level IX	20994
h	5.7	2.4	0.9	21gm.	Metamorphosed Shale	Area IV, Level B	23448
i	4.3	2.8	1.1	11gm.	Claystone	Area X, Level II	22316
j	4.5	3.2	0.7	9gm.	Chalcedony	Room 64, fill	13375
300, a	4.8	4.1	1.3	27.2gm.	Chert	Room 12, Level B	13947
b	3.7	4.3	0.8	11.5gm.	Chert	Room 84, Level II	23436
c	4.6	4.0	1.6	26.7gm.	Chert	Room 12, fill	13950
d	5.5	4.1	1.4	16.6gm.	Chert	Room 75, Level 1	20008
e	4.3	3.0	1.0	9.7gm.	Chert	Room 35, fill	14427
f	4.8	3.9	1.4	20.1gm.	Chert	Room 28, fill	14039
g	4.1	4.1	1.3	21.8gm.	Chert	Lower East Trash Slope	16685
h	4.7	4.4	1.3	25.8gm.	Chert	Kiva A, fill	14134
i	3.5	3.8	1.1	11.1gm.	Metamorphosed Shale	Kiva P, Level III	20832
301, a	5.7	2.9	0.8	11.0gm.	Chert	Room 48, Level B	14168
b	6.4	4.9	1.8	47.2gm.	Chert	Room 84, Level II	20598
c	4.7	2.4	0.9	9.7gm.	Chert	Backdirt	17077
d	5.1	2.7	0.8	9.9gm.	Chert	Room 9, fill	13907
e	4.4	2.4	1.1	12.5gm.	Claystone	Area VII	14125
f	6.8	4.2	1.8	46gm.	Chert	Kiva T, fill	22073
302, a	5.3	3.6	2.1	37.4gm.	Chert	Lower East Trash Slope, with Burial 3	16540
b	4.5	3.1	1.8	19.2gm.	Chert	Kiva C, fill	15910
c	5.9	4.2	3.2	96gm.	Chert	Room 37, fill	14106
d	12.8	8.6	5.7	814gm.	Chert	Kiva O, Level VI	20799
303, a	51.0	33.8	8.2	25.3kg.	Sandstone	Kiva O, fill	20776
b	49.0	33.3	8.5	27.9kg.	Sandstone	Kiva H, floor	16088
c	48.5	32.5	6.0	17.5kg.	Sandstone	Lower East Trash Slope	16620
d	48.0	26.8	5.8	11.1kg.	Sandstone	Area IV, surface	16300
304, top	35.6	23.0	12.6	11.8kg.	Conglomerate	General surface, east side of site	22088
center	46.0	26.2	9.2	21.8kg.	Sandstone	Kiva R, Level VII	20971
bottom	45.0	29.0	8.0	10.2kg.	Conglomerate	Kiva L, surface	20706
305, left	34.7	21.5	7.5	8.2kg.	Fossiliferous Shale	West Trash Slope	17008
upper right	39.2	25.9	7.8	12.6kg.	Sandstone	Room 56, Level III, floor	17618
lower	37.7	29.0	10.9	15kg.	Sandstone	West Trash Slope	17009
306, left & right	39.0	26.3	8.3	13.5kg.	Sandstone	Room 49, embedded in floor	15682
307, top, center, bottom	42.4	29.0	5.1	8.2kg.	Sandstone	Kiva M, Level III	20715
308, a	—	25.9	6.8	—	Sandstone	Kiva R, Level IV	20947

Table 17. Measurements, material and provenience of illustrated stone artifacts. (Continued)

Figure	Length	Size (cm.) Width or Diameter	Thickness	Weight	Material	Provenience	M.V.N.P. Catalog No. /700*
b	39.5	27.4	11.0	6.8kg.	Sandstone	Kiva R, Level V	20948
c	—	44.8	10.8	—	Sandstone	West Trash Slope, surface	16951
d	55.8	ca. 36.0	6.5	—	Sandstone	Room 48, Level C	15591
309, a	30.0	13.6	2.6	1764gm.	Sandstone	Room 49, on floor	15671
b	22.0	13.1	1.9	855gm.	Sandstone	Kiva L, fill	25529
c	28.0	13.0	4.8	2.9kg.	Sandstone	Room 69, surface	17708
d	24.8	11.2	3.8	1552gm.	Sandstone	West Trash Slope, surface	16991
e	25.5	12.6	1.7	1015gm.	Sandstone	Room 37, fill	14088
f	22.8	11.0	2.3	814gm.	Sandstone	General surface, east side of site	22081
g	32.3	12.5	2.4	1729gm.	Sandstone	Room 2, fill	26300
h	21.5	12.8	3.9	1669+gm.	Conglomerate	Kiva R, fill	22021
i	25.3	11.5	2.9	1228gm.	Sandstone	Room 56, Level III	17626
j	25.3	11.9	2.5	1309gm.	Sandstone	Kiva B, fill	15893
k	24.3	12.5	3.6	1485gm.	Sandstone	Room 82, Level IV	20583
l	—	13.3	4.0	—	"Micaceous Igneous Rock"	Kiva K, Level IV	20659
310, a	17.9	11.4	5.3	1511gm.	Sandstone	Upper East Trash Slope	16926
b	21.5	12.4	5.1	1872gm.	Breccia	Room 56, Level II	17614
c	28.3	13.6	5.6	3.3kg.	Conglomerate	Kiva L, surface	20686
d	24.0	11.5	4.2	1327gm.	Sandstone	Kiva O, Level VI	20809
e	26.1	13.3	2.9	1662gm.	Sandstone	Room 37, upper fill	14111
f	20.9	12.9	3.8	1706gm.	Sandstone	Kiva F, fill	16017
g	18.2	11.8	3.7	1259gm.	Sandstone	Kiva R, fill	22037
h	29.2	11.6	2.0	875gm.	Sandstone	Room 12, Level B	13965
i	19.5	11.2	2.8	987gm.	Sandstone	Kiva K, fill	20666
j	18.8	11.8	3.6	1321gm.	Sandstone	Area VI, surface	22181
k	21.9	9.3	5.4	1383gm.	Conglomerate	Kiva N, Level V	20745
l	20.3	11.5	3.0	882gm.	Sandstone	Kiva J, fill	25521
11	28.3	13.6	5.6	3.3kg.	Conglomerate	Kiva L, surface	20686
312, a	—	12.6	3.4	—	Sandstone	Room 48, surface	20686
b	26.0	12.2	3.0	1330gm.	Sandstone	Room 14, fill	13992
c	24.0	12.2	3.6	1850gm.	Sandstone	Kiva L, surface	20683
d	20.0	10.8	5.9	2.3kg.	Sandstone	West Trash Slope, surface	16960
e	—	9.1	4.0	—	Sandstone	Room 54, Level II	17540
f	24.2	11.3	4.3	1573gm.	Conglomerate	Area VII	16460
313, left	17.0	14.6	7.3	2.8kg.	Sandstone	Room 31, subfloor fill	14057
center	18.9	16.5	14.6	4.5kg.	Sandstone	Kiva R, Level II	20946
right	19.4	18.8	12.9	5.5kg.	Sandstone	Kiva D, southern recess	15952
314	39.5	30.0	8.7	12.0kg.	Sandstone	Kiva R, Level XI, floor	22011
315, left	32.2	17.9	2.9	3.3kg.	Sandstone	Kiva O, Level VI	20805
center	30.5	13.1	4.3	2.4kg.	Sandstone	Kiva B, fill	15888
right	27.5	18.1	5.1	3.3kg.	Sandstone	Surface, east side of site	22091
316	37.5	30.0	8.1	9.8kg.	Sandstone	Pithouse 1, floor	26525
317 (hand-stone)	13.5+	9.7	5.4	1094gm.	Sandstone	Pithouse 1, floor	26524
stone)	37.5	30.0	8.1	9.8kg.	Sandstone	Pithouse 1, floor	26525
318, a	11.8	9.3	3.5	782gm.	Sandstone	Room 85, Level II	20606
b	13.4	9.6	5.0	1090gm.	Quartzite	Kiva H, floor	16092
c	14.8	8.6	5.5	1202gm.	Diorite	Kiva Q, Level II	20857
d	17.4	12.4	2.5	707gm.	Sandstone	Room 50, floor	15704
319, a	6.1	2.4	0.4	7.8gm.	Hornfels	Lower East Trash Slope, Burial 10	16550
b	3.8	0.6	0.5	2.1gm.	Mineralized Bone (?)	Lower East Trash Slope, Burial 10	14532
c	1.9	1.7	0.5	1.6gm.	Jet	Area VI, below extended floor level of Room 66	22173
d	1.8	—	1.0	1.9gm.	Jet	Backdirt, near rear of cave	15580
e	2.5	—	0.3	2.0gm.	Shale	Area IV	16315
f	3.3	2.2	0.3	2.7gm.	Shale	Lower East Trash Slope	16628
g	2.0	1.4	0.3	0.8gm.	Jet	Pithouse 1, Level I	24767
h	—	—	0.25	—	Shale	Lower East Trash Slope	16629
i	2.7	2.5	0.35	3.2gm.	Shale	Area X, fill	22283
j	2.8	1.6	0.2	3.0gm.	Travertine	Room 14, fill	13815
k	3.5	3.3	0.6	15.3gm.	Travertine	Kiva U, fill	25554
l	3.8	3.3	0.35	6.5gm.	Sandstone	Kiva I, Level A	16167
320	2.0	0.9	1.0	3.4gm.	Hematite	Room 35, fill	15581
321, upper center	0.8	0.5	0.1	0.1gm.	Turquoise	Lower East Trash Slope, Burial 10	16555

Table 17. Measurements, material and provenience of illustrated stone artifacts. (Continued)

Figure	Length	Size (cm.) Width or Diameter	Thickness	Weight	Material	Provenience	M.V.N.P. Catalog No. /700*
lower left	0.45	—	0.1	—	Shale	Kiva Q, foot drum	33837
lower right	0.8	—	0.3	—	Jet	West Trash Slope	25988
322	3.9	2.9	1.0	6.3gm.	Jet	Room 48, Level C	15639
323, a	2.3	1.3	—	8.2gm.	Hematite	Lower East Trash Slope, Burial 10	16551
b	2.0	0.9	—	3.2gm.	Hematite	Lower East Trash Slope, Burial 10	16551
c	1.9	1.0	—	2.7gm.	Hematite	Lower East Trash Slope, Burial 10	16551
d	2.6	2.1	2.2	26.8gm.	Hematite	Kiva L, subfloor fill	25526
e	3.4	2.2	1.4	18.3gm.	Hematite	Room 16, fill	14014
f	3.4	1.3	—	19.5gm.	Hematite	Room 60, fill	17677
324, a	11.5	10.0	5.8	1171gm.	Diorite	Kiva H, Level B	16067
b	12.4	9.6	7.4	1203gm.	Sandstone	Kiva Q, Level VII, floor	20820
c	14.0	10.1	6.8	1617gm.	Granite	Area X, fill	22286
d	10.1	—	7.9	1245gm.	Sandstone	Lower East Trash Slope	16538
325, top	12.0	7.0	4.0	427gm.	Sandstone	Room 14, Level B, West end	13977
center	13.3	7.9	3.9	468gm.	Sandstone	Kiva H, Level B	16065
bottom	15.2	5.9	4.7	499gm.	Sandstone	Kiva I, Level A	16132
326, left	26.3	15.4	6.3	3.8kg.	Syenite Porphyry	Room 60, floor	17674
center	21.9	19.7	4.0	2.8kg.	Dyorite	Kiva D, fill	15953
right	35.5	24.3	13.1	16.7kg.	Quartzite	Surface near Kiva N	26302
327	28.8	22.7	10.7	11.6kg.	Sandstone	Lower East Trash Slope	16621
328, a	18.8	12.5	9.3	1771gm.	Sandstone	Kiva O, surface	20767
b	17.2	9.1	7.0	1767gm.	Sandstone	Area X, fill	22284
c	21.6	12.9	7.3	4.1kg.	"Micaceous Igneous Rock"	Room 49, subfloor	17522
d	26.0	13.0	7.3	3.3kg.	Sandstone	General, vicinity of Room 81	26464
329, a	16.9	5.3	1.6	210gm.	Hornfels	Kiva Q, fill	20851
b	16.0+	5.6	1.8	215+gm.	Hornfels	Room 56, fill	17610
c	15.6	5.6	1.9	206gm.	Hornfels	Kiva Q, fill	20852
d	14.2	6.2	1.6	194gm.	Hornfels	Room 76, fill	20022
330, left	25.0	6.0	2.2	408gm.	Hornfels	Kiva O, fill	20788
right	22.7	6.5	1.8	3.3kg.	Shale or Slate	Room 76, fill	20041
331, left	19.3	7.9	1.2	252gm.	Hornfels	Kiva U, fill	24301
center	17.1	8.7	1.3	274gm.	Hornfels	Kiva U, fill	24302
right	15.0	6.6	1.7	232gm.	Shale or Slate	Room 49, on floor	15666
332, a	—	8.7	2.0	—	Sandstone	Lower East Trash Slope	16809
b	—	3.1	2.5	—	Quartzite	Kiva F, fill	16011
c	—	—	—	—	Gabbro	Lower East Trash Slope	16572
d	—	4.5	1.5	—	Sandstone	Kiva F, fill	16037
e	—	—	2.5	—	Claystone	Kiva Q, Level II	20855
f	—	6.1	1.9	—	Sandstone	Lower East Trash Slope	16709
g	—	—	—	—	Diorite	Kiva E, fill	15986
h	—	—	3.4	—	Gabbro	Lower East Trash Slope, surface	16566
333	19.2	14.4	13.0	4.5kg.	Sandstone	Room 50, fill	15699
334	45.3	30.7	3.6	8.9kg.	Sandstone	Kiva F, fill	16021
335	—	24.2	4.6	—	Sandstone	Area III	16284
336	—	18.5	1.1	—	Sandstone	Kiva L, subfloor fill	25528
337	—	—	2.0	—	Sandstone	Room 60, floor	17675
338, a	29.0	13.1	1.9	1219gm.	Sandstone	Room 12, fill	13964
b	26.1	12.1	2.0	1090gm.	Sandstone	Room 37, fill	14086
c	33.0	12.8	3.4	2.6kg.	Sandstone	Room 38, fill	14143
d	31.5	14.6	6.3	4.6kg.	Sandstone	General surface and fill	22105
339, left	31.0	14.5	1.3	971+gm.	Shale or Slate	Room 76, floor	20038
right	29.0	12.9	1.3	914gm.	Sandstone	Kiva H and Area III	16087
340	31.0	14.5	1.3	971+gm.	Shale or Slate	Room 76, floor	20038
341, a	10.0	—		150+gm.	Sandstone	Area XIII, fill	22358
b	13.7	—	1.6	420gm.	Sandstone	Kiva R, fill	20923
c	12.3	—	0.7	173+gm.	Sandstone	Room 26, fill	14029
d	24.0	—	2.0	1229gm.	Sandstone	Kiva O, fill	20807
e	30.1	27.0	1.5	1920gm.	Sandstone	Room 55, fill	17581
342, left	—	6.9	0.4	—	Sandstone	Kiva Q, fill	20902
right	7.3	4.3	1.5	89gm.	Shale or Slate	Kiva R, fill	22023
343, a	3.8	3.7	—	79.5gm.	Diorite	Room 12, fill	13940
b	1.3	1.9	—	4.2gm.	Claystone	Room 11, fill	24531
c	3.1	1.8	—	11.7gm.	Sandstone	Lower East Trash Slope	16612

Table 17. Measurements, material and provenience of illustrated stone artifacts. (Continued)

Figure	Length	Size (cm.) Width or Diameter	Thickness	Weight	Material	Provenience	M.V.N.P. Catalog No. /700*
d	—	4.5	1.5	22.4gm.	Sandstone	General surface	26468
e	5.0	2.6	2.1	40.8gm.	Sandstone	Lower East Trash Slope	16501
f	3.7	3.3	1.7	29.8gm.	Sandstone	Room 85, subfloor fill	26405
g	3.8	1.4	0.6	5.4gm.	Sandstone	Room 17, fill	17334
h	—	3.0	0.5	—	Sandstone	Kiva F, fill	16003
i	4.5	2.1	0.7	7.6gm.	Shale	Lower East Trash Slope	16536
344, a	3.8	0.9	—	5.7gm.	Travertine	Kiva L, subfloor fill	25527
b	1.7	0.8	—	1.0gm.	Hornfels	Lower East Trash Slope, Burial 10	16552
c	4.3	0.6	—	2.5gm.	Shale or Slate	Area IV, fill	22154
d	3.9+	0.6	—	1.8+gm.	Petrified Wood	Kiva M, subfloor fill	25533
e	2.2	0.7	—	1.9gm.	Shale	West Trash Slope, fill	16537
f	1.7	1.2	—	1.9gm.	Shale or Slate	West Trash Slope, fill	17051
345, a	11.9	1.7	0.4	12.9+gm.	Petrified Wood	Room 4, fill	13893
b	6.9	1.6	0.8	14.6gm.	Petrified Wood	Kiva P, Level V	20835
c	5.0	1.2	0.4	4.6gm.	Petrified Wood	Upper East Trash Slope	14567
d	5.8	1.2	0.5	7.2gm.	Petrified Wood	Room 58, surface and fill	17656
e	—	1.0	0.4	—	Petrified Wood	Kiva P, Level V, floor	20834
f	7.6	2.8	0.8	33gm.	Petrified Wood	Kiva P, Level V, floor	20833
346, a	25.0+	—	9.2	—	Sandstone	Area VI, surface	16186
b	18.7	18.4	12.0	4.9kg.	Sandstone	Room 35, fill	14063
c	11.7	—	7.6	—	Sandstone	West Trash Slope, surface	16946
d	23.0	21.7	15.1	12kg.	Sandstone	Area III, surface	16274
e	12.3	—	6.8	—	Sandstone	Area V, trash fill	16389
347	18.9	11.0	18.9	3.8kg.	Sandstone	Lower East Trash Slope	16617
348, upper	12.9	8.2	8.3	1305gm.	Sandstone Concretion	Kiva E, fill	15981
lower	16.8	8.6	5.7	1013gm.	Sandstone Concretion	Kiva R, Level I	20927
349, a	—	5.9	—	170gm.	Sandstone Concretion	Lower East Trash Slope	16635
b	8.7	2.2	—	49gm.	Sandstone Concretion	Lower East Trash Slope	16766
c	—	4.9	3.1	89gm.	Sandstone Concretion	Lower East Trash Slope	16562
d	6.7	4.9	2.9	188gm.	Sandstone Concretion	Area X, Level III	24610
e	3.0	2.4	2.2	23.3gm.	Sandstone Concretion	Lower East Trash Slope	16746
f	3.0	2.2	2.0	13.1gm.	Sandstone Concretion	Lower East Trash Slope	16725
g	5.4	3.5	—	77.1gm.	Sandstone Concretion	Upper East Trash Slope	16915
h	6.2	2.8	—	28.1gm.	Sandstone Concretion	Lower East Trash Slope	16677
i	7.0	3.0	—	53.4gm.	Sandstone Concretion	Room 52, fill	15791
350, a	11.5	9.3	4.8	445gm.	Sandstone Concretion	Kiva N, subfloor fill	25543
b	8.0	7.3	5.5	348gm.	Sandstone Concretion	Lower East Trash Slope	16683
c	14.5	8.3	7.4	748gm.	Sandstone Concretion	Kiva K, Level I	20642
d	18.0	17.8	15.2	4.8kg.	Sandstone Concretion	Kiva R, fill	22025
351, upper	14.2	10.4	6.3	981gm.	Sandstone Concretion	West Trash Slope, upper portion	25990
lower	15.5	12.5	—	1961gm.	Sandstone Concretion	Area IV, fill	22163
352	20.2	12.3	4.5	682gm.	Sandstone Concretion	Kiva Q, in floor level shrine	20903
353	35.5	15.9	18.4	12.4kg.	Sandstone Concretion	Room 87, fill	26303

Table 17. Measurements, material and provenience of illustrated stone artifacts. (Continued)

Figure	Length	Size (cm.) Width or Diameter	Thickness	Weight	Material	Provenience	M.V.N.P. Catalog No. /700*
354, a	—	3.0	1.8	17.7gm.	Iron Concretion	Kiva M, fill	20722
b	—	2.5	—	15gm.	Iron Concretion	General surface and fill.	26507
c	4.2	1.4	—	14gm.	Iron Concretion	Kiva M, fill	25931
d	7.1	6.4	4.4	211gm.	Iron Concretion	Kiva Q, in niche back of shrine	20919
e	—	2.6	1.1	10gm.	Iron Concretion	Room 12, Level B	13961
f	3.5	2.5	1.8	16.7gm.	Iron Concretion	Test B	12100
g	6.5	4.3	3.3	94.5gm.	Iron Concretion	Kiva Q, in niche back of shrine	20920
h	4.0	3.2	2.3	34.4gm.	Iron Concretion	Kiva Q, in shrine	20904
i	11.9	5.7	4.9	270gm.	Iron Concretion	Kiva Q, in niche back of shrine	20921

*All catalog numbers have an accession number suffix of /700

Chapter Six

Bone and Antler Artifacts

Richard P. Wheeler

BONE ARTIFACTS

Four hundred and thirty-four complete or fragmentary bone artifacts were obtained from Long House during the course of the Wetherill Mesa Project's investigations. Of these, 301 or 70 percent are tools, 58 or 13 percent are ornaments, and 75 or 17 percent are "problematical objects."

Tools

The most numerous bone tools by far are awls, made from mammal or bird bones, or from elements so changed that they cannot be identified as either mammal or bird. Awls are considered to be generalized perforating implements, and as such they almost invariably show moderate to high degrees of use-polish which seemed to aid in their preservation. Some Long House specimens have constricted tips like certain awls from Hawikuh which Hodge (1920, pp. 102 and pls. XVI and XVII) suggested may have been used for sewing or weaving. A few mammal bone awls from Long House possess one or more shallow, tranverse, use-polished grooves in the sides near the tip. Morris (1920, p. 39) described three awls from Aztec Ruin to be "deeply notched as if by drawing a cord between the implement and the thumb and finger," and he inferred that "they may have been used in straightening cords or thongs."

Mammal bone awls. Ninety-three complete or fragmentary awls from Long House are made from mammal bones. Every one is single pointed. Six styles are recognized:

Style M1 (figs 355 a-d and 356)*: longitudinally split distal end of metapodial of *Artiodactyla* (mule deer, bighorn sheep, or undifferentiated deer). The shaft tapers symmetrically to a point, which is oval or round in cross section; the butt or grip is the unmodified or slightly modified segment of the distal joint. Nine complete and three fragmentary specimens.

Measurements: complete specimens range in lengths from 8.5 to 23.3 cm.

Provenience: Rooms 6, 54, 55, Pithouse 1, Kivas H, O, Q, Areas IX, X, Lower East Trash Slope (one each); Kiva B (two, shown in fig. 356).

Style M2 (fig. 357 a-g): longitudinally split distal or proximal end of long bone of *Artiodactyla* metapodial, radius, ulna, or tibia. The shaft tapers symmetrically, or constricts sharply, to a point; the articular joint (butt) has been removed or greatly modified by cutting and grinding, and the base is rounded or squarish. Some examples have polished grooves on one face and one edge near the tip. Twenty-one complete and three fragmentary specimens.

Measurements: complete specimens range in length from 6.8 to 19.4 cm.

Provenience: Test A, Rooms 2, 33, 55, 84, 86, Kivas L, M, R, U, Area V, Lower East trash Slope, Upper East Trash Slope (one each); Room 56, Kiva H, Area X (two each); Kiva Q (five).

Style M3 (fig. 358 a-m): distal or proximal end of whole long bone of species other than *Artiodactyla* (cottontail, bobcat, gray and

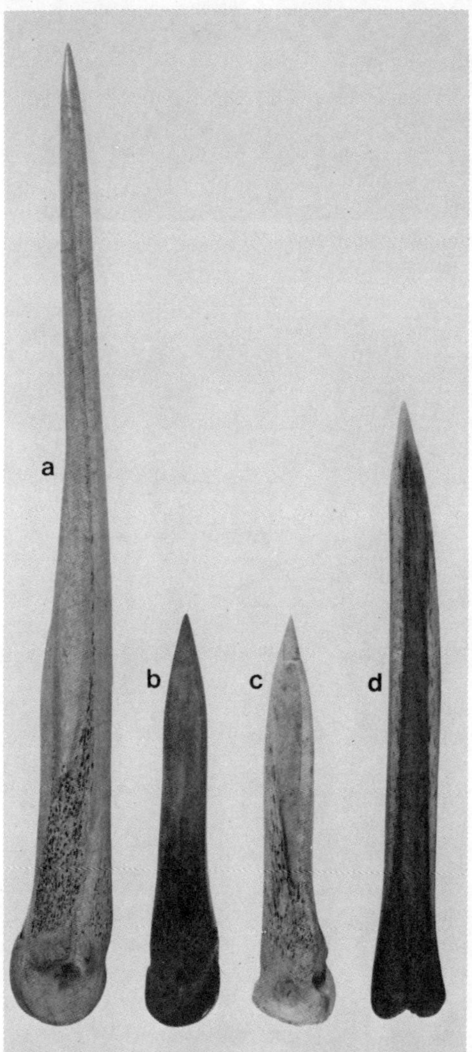

Figure 355. *Mammal bone awls, Style M1.*

---

*Measurements, species, element, and provenience of illustrated bone and antler artifacts are given in table 19 at the back of the report.

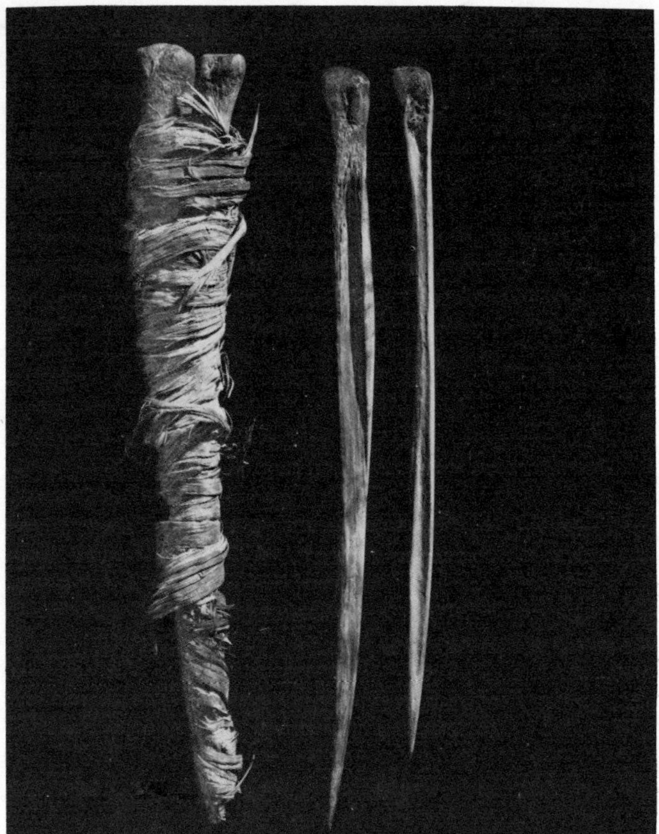

Figure 356. *Mammal bone awls, Style M1.*

Figure 357. *Mammal bone awls, Style M2.*

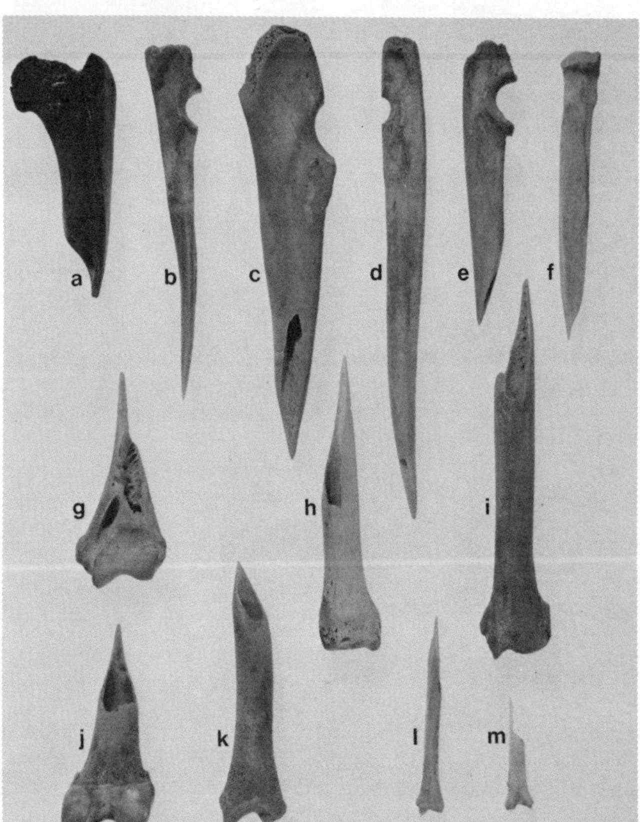

Figure 358. *Mammal bone awls, Style M3.*

red fox, badger, coyote, wolf). The shaft tapers symmetrically or asymmetrically, or constricts sharply, to a point; the articular joint (butt) is unmodified or slightly modified by cutting and grinding. Twenty-one complete and 13 fragmentary specimens.

Measurements: complete specimens range in length from 3.3 to 14 cm.

Provenience: Rooms 30, 56, 82, Kivas A, I, M, O, R, U, Areas IV, VII, X, XII, Upper East Trash Slope, backdirt (one each); Room 12, Kiva O Lower East Trash Slope (two each); Room 48 (three); Kiva J (four); Kiva Q (five).

Style M4(fig. 359a): distal or proximal end of whole long bone of species other than *Artiodactyla* (bobcat, wolf). The shaft tapers to a short, asymmetrical point; the articular joint (butt) is greatly modified by cutting and grinding. One complete and one fragmentary specimen.

Measurements: complete specimens range is 7.75 cm. long.

Provenience: Room 28 and Upper East Trash Slope (one each).

Style M5(fig. 359b): section of whole long bone of species other than *Artiodactyla* (cottontail, bobcat, coyote). The shaft tapers to a symmetrical point at one end and is roughly broken and unaltered at the other end. Two complete and one fragmentary specimens.
Measurements: Complete specimens 5.65 and 9 cm. in length.
Provenience: Room 14, Kiva T, and Upper East Trash Slope (one each).

Style M6(fig. 359c-f): splinters of long bone of *Artiodactyla* and other species. One end tapers to a symmetrical point; the other end is cut and ground to a rounded or squarish butt. Thirteen complete and five fragmentary specimens.

Measurements: Complete specimens range in length from 5.3 to 12.6 cm.

Provenience: Rooms 7, 12, 37, 54, Kivas B, G, H, J, T, Areas IV, V, West Trash Slope (one each); Kivas A, R, Lower East Trash Slope (two each).

Bird bone awls. There are 197 complete or fragmentary bird bone awls in the Long House assemblage. Like the mammal bone awls from Long House, every one is single pointed. Five styles are recognized:

Style B1(fig. 360 a, b, e, g, i, and j): proximal end of whole long bone of domestic turkey, *Meleagris Galloparo*—tibiotarsus, tarsometatarsus, carpometacarpus, humerus, radius. The shaft was cut obliquely and ground to a sharp point; the articular joint, used as a grip, is unmodified. Fifteen complete and four fragmentary specimens.

Measurements: complete specimens range in length from 5.3 to 12.5 cm.

Provenience: Room 87, Kivas I, K, M, O, Q, S, U, Areas III, X, XIII, Lower East Trash Slope (one each); Area IV, West Trash Slope (two each); and Upper East Trash Slope (three).

Style B2(figs. 360 c, d, f, and h, and 361 a and b): distal end of

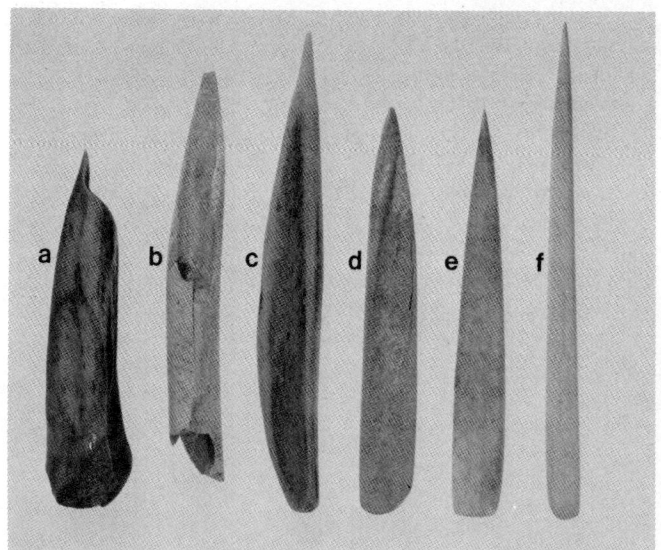

Figure 359. *Mammal bone awls, Styles M4 (a), M5 (b), and M6 (c-f).*

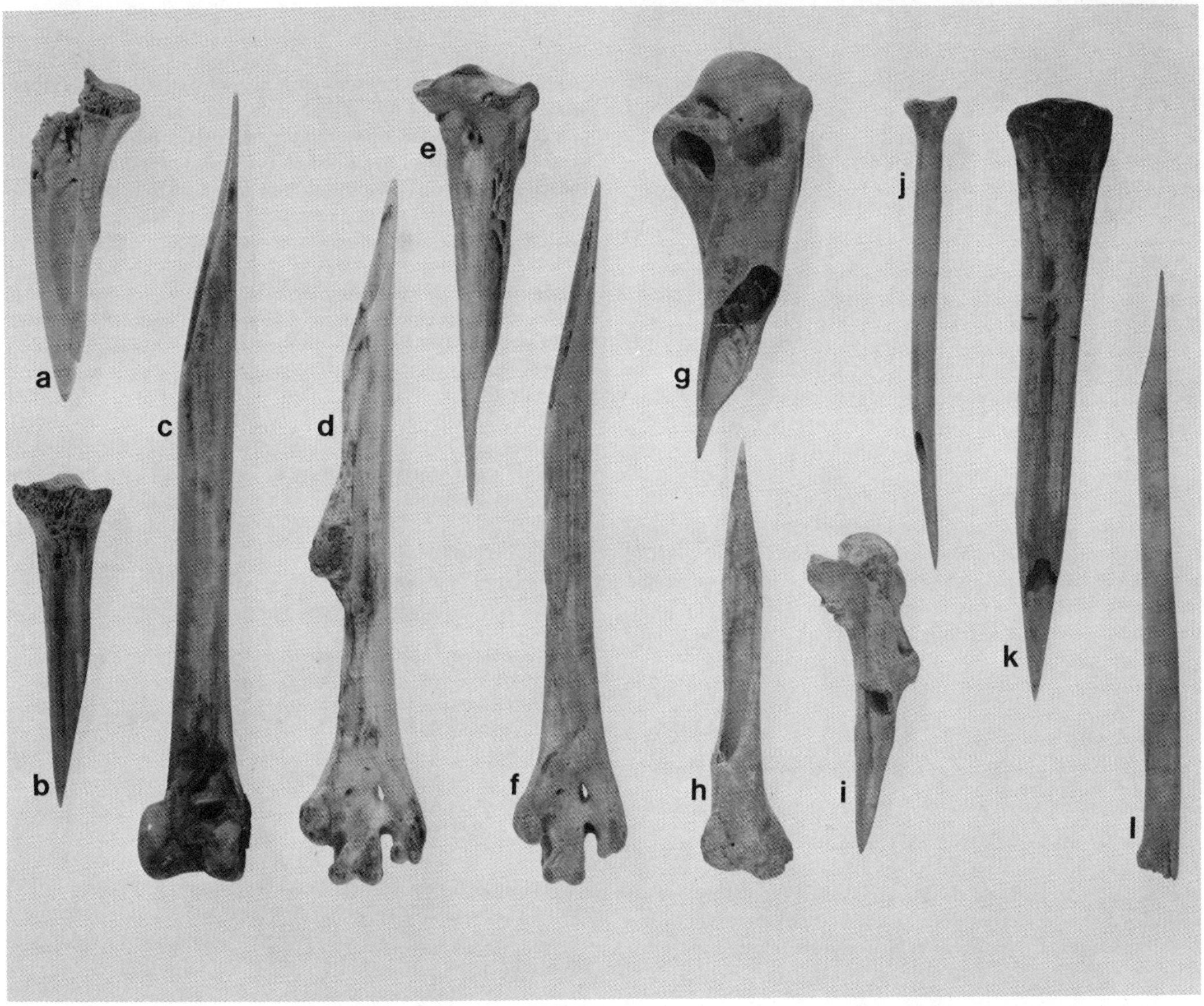

Figure 360. *Bird bone awls, Style B1 (a, b, e, g, i, and j), Style B2.*

whole long bone of domestic turkey-tibiotarsus, tarsometatarsus, ulna, radius. The shaft was cut obliquely and ground to a sharp point; the articular joint, used as a grip, is unmodified. Sixty-six complete and 26 fragmentary specimens.

Measurements: complete specimens range in length from 5.7 to 18.1 cm.

Provenience: Rooms 26, 28, 36, 43, 45, 46, 47, 48, 61, 64, 66, 75, 89, Kivas F, H, M, N, P, Q, Great Kiva, Areas III, XII, Test J, West Trash Slope (one each); Rooms 2, 54, Kivas A, J, K, S, backdirt (two each); Kivas B, U, Upper East Trash Slope, General (three each); Room 12, Kivas I, O, Area VII (four each); Area X (six); Kiva R (seven); Lower East Trash Slope (13 specimens).

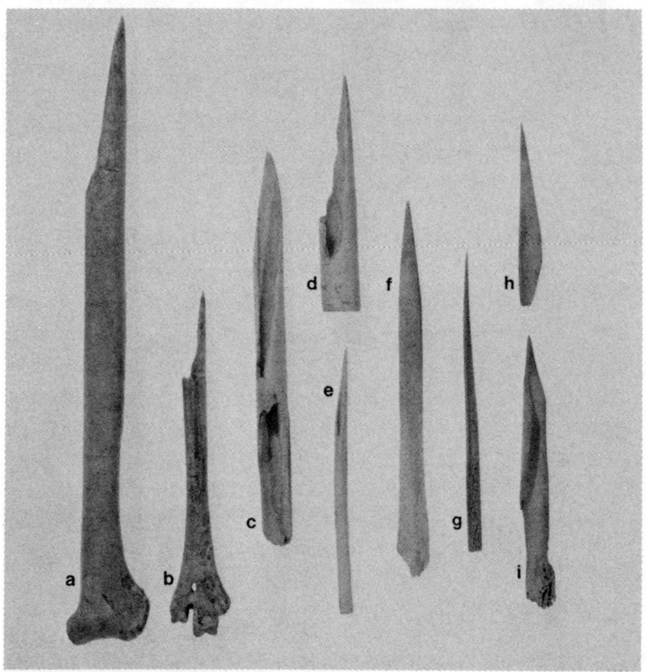

Figure 361. *Bird bone awls, Style B2 (a and b), Style B4 (c-3), and Style B5 (f-i).*

Style B3(fig. 360 k and l): distal or proximal end of whole long bone of domestic turkey-tibiotarsus, tarsometatarsus, radius. The shaft was cut and ground to form a short to long, symmetrical or asymmetrical point; the articular joint or butt was removed or nearly removed by cutting and grinding. Thirteen complete and three fragmentary specimens .

Measurements: Complete specimens range in length from 4.7 to 12 cm.

Provenience: Rooms 48, 74, Kivas H, S, T, Areas V, X (one each); Room 56, Kiva R, Upper East Trash Slope (two each); and Kiva K (three).

Style B4(fig 361c-e): proximal or distal end, or central section, of whole long bone of domestic turkey- tibiotarsus, tarsometatarsus, ulna, radius. The shaft was cut and ground to form a short to long symmetrical or asymmetrical point at one end; the other end (butt) is rounded or squared. Nineteen complete and six fragmentary specimens.

Measurements: complete specimens range in length from 6.3 to 11.8 cm.

Provenience: Rooms 2, 4, 37, 48, 66, Kivas A, J, O, T, U, Areas IV, V, Surface (one each); Area X and West Trash Slope (two each); Kiva R and Lower East Trash Slope (four each).

Style B5 (fig. 361 f-i): splinter of long bone of domestic turkey or, in one instance, of hawk (*Buteoninae*)-tibiotarsus, tarsometatarsus, ulna often identifiable. One end cut and ground to form a symmetrical or asymmetrical point; the other end usually irregular, unmodified. Forty complete and five fragmentary specimens.

Measurements: complete specimens range in length from 3.9 to 11.5 cm.

Provenience: Rooms 3, 8, 12, 29, 35, 48, 50, 58, Kivas C, F, J, R, T, U, Area VI, Trash Slope below Area II (one each); Rooms 52, 55, 84, Kivas D, H, I, Area VII (two each); Kiva O (three); Area X, Lower East Trash Slope, West Trash Slope (four each).

Mammal or bird (?) bone awls. The four complete single-pointed specimens from Long House (fig. 362 a-d), all splinters of mammal or bird long bone, are cut and ground to a short to long symmetrical point at one end and unmodified or cut and ground to a rounded or squarish base at the other end (butt). They range in length from 5.3 to 9.2 cm. One each was found in Kivas A, K, R, and on the Lower East Trash Slope.

Bodkins or Needles. Two complete and one incomplete artifact made of splinters of metapodial of *Artiodactyla* or other long bone were cut and ground to a symmetrical point at one end; near the other (butt) end is a central perforation, from about 2 to 6.5 cm. in diameter (fig. 363). The complete specimens are 9.3 and 8.5 cm. in length. The three artifacts, presumably used for sewing, were found in Room 89, Kiva J, and on the surface.

Fleshers. Four implements that have been cut and ground to a convex or subtriangular working edge are made from the left or right humerus of *Artiodactyla*. Two of these (fig. 364 a and c) retain the articular joint unmodified or only slightly modified as a grip or

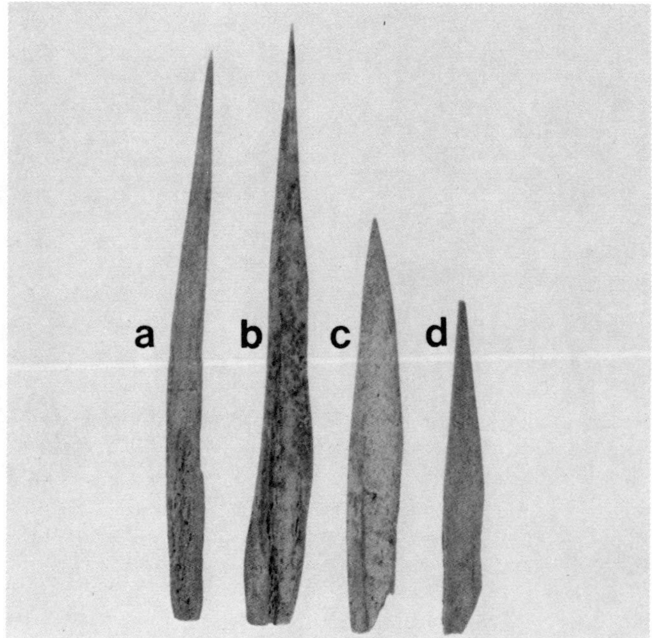

Figure 362. *Sliver awls of unknown mammals or birds.*

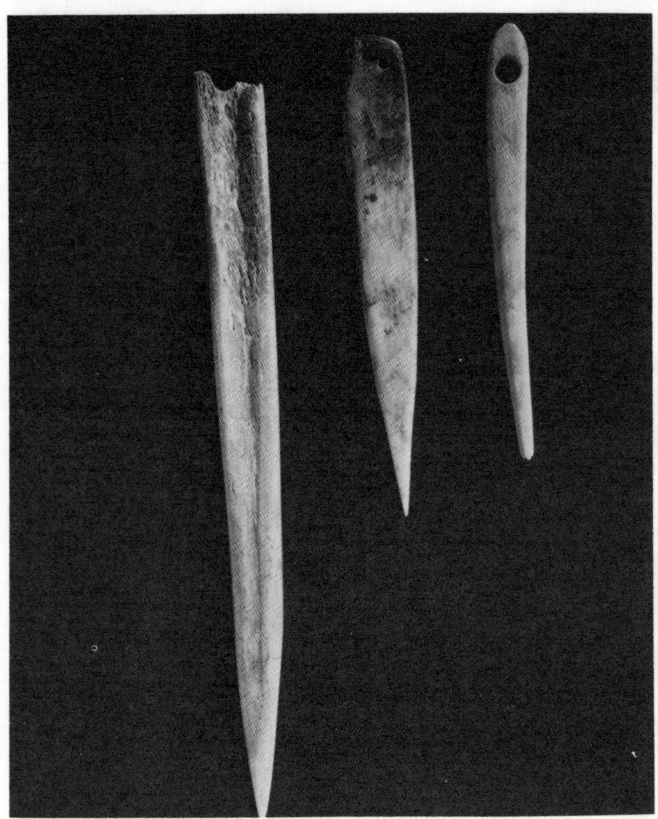

Figure 363. *Eyed needles or bodkins of mammal bone.*

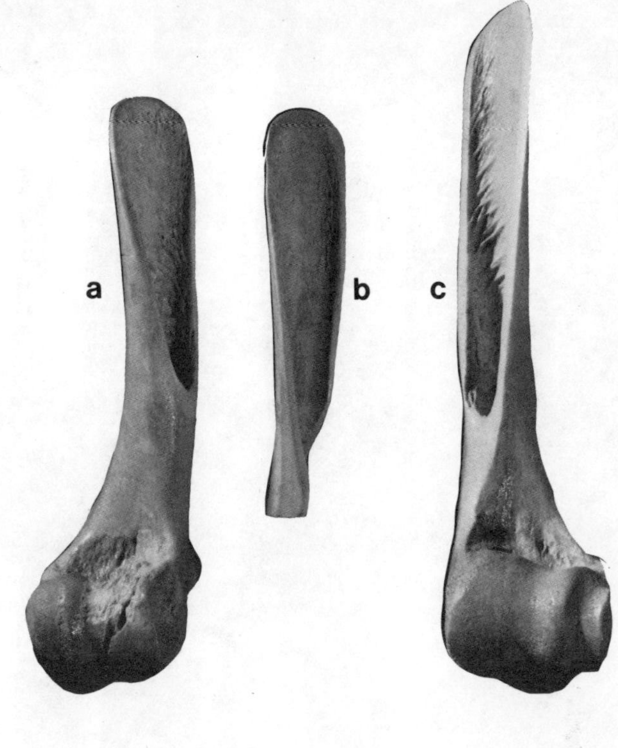

Figure 364. *Scraper of mammal bone.*

handle. Measuring 14 and 16.3 cm. in length, they were found in Kiva B. The articular joint of the third specimen, which is 7.8 cm. long and came from the surface, is considerably altered by grinding. The fourth specimen, lacking the articular joint entirely, may or may not be intact (fig. 364b). It was found in Area IV.

These implements show a high degree of use-polish around the beveled working edge. Their shape and condition suggest that they were used particularly for scraping hides.

Ornaments

There are 58 bone tubes in the Long House assemblage (figs. 366 and 367). The ends were cut more or less squarely and were frequently smoothed; the body is usually unmodified, but in rare instances it is smoothed and decorated by incising (fig. 367 a and b). The specimens range in length from 7 to 96 mm. They were all made from bird bones: 58 from domestic turkey, *Meleagris Gallopavo* (ulna, tibiotarsus, radius, humerus, and femur, in declining order of frequency); and one each from turkey vulture, *Cathartes aura* (radius), golden eagle, *Aquila chrysaetos* (ungual), red-tailed hawk, *Buto jamaicenses* (ulna), hawk, *Accipitrinae* or *Buteoninae* (femur), and goshawk, *Accipiter gentilis*.

The proveniences of the bone tubes were: Rooms 2, 6, 8, 12, 30, 32, 37, 54, 57, 66, 85, Kivas A, D, F, P, T, Great Kiva, Area IX, Trash Slope below Area V, Backdirt (one each); Kivas N, R, T, Area III, Upper East Trash Slope (two each); Area VIII (three); Area IV, West Trash Slope (four each); Area X (eight); and Lower East Trash Slope (nine).

It is possible that the bone tubes were "beads," strung on yucca cord or thongs and were worn as bracelets and necklaces.

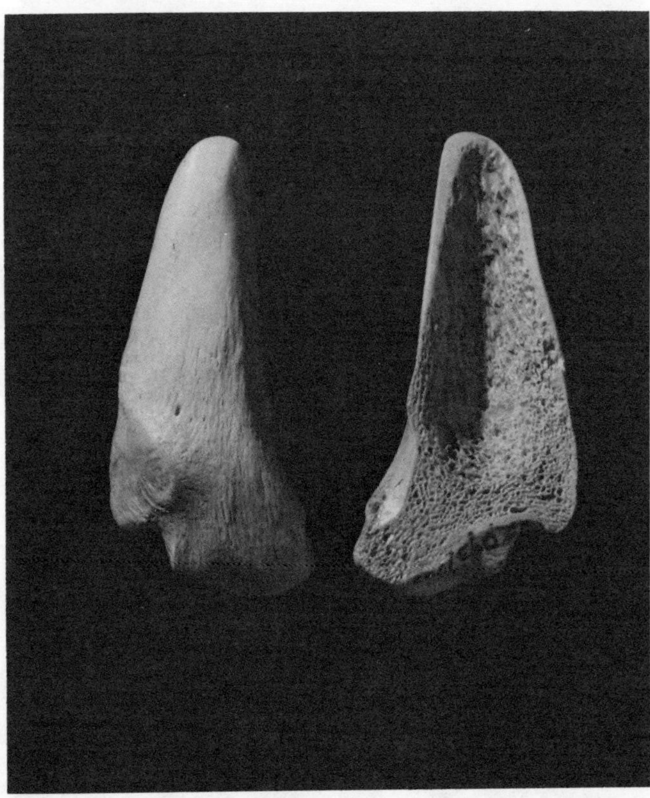

Figure 365. *Scraper of mammal bone—obverse left, reverse right.*

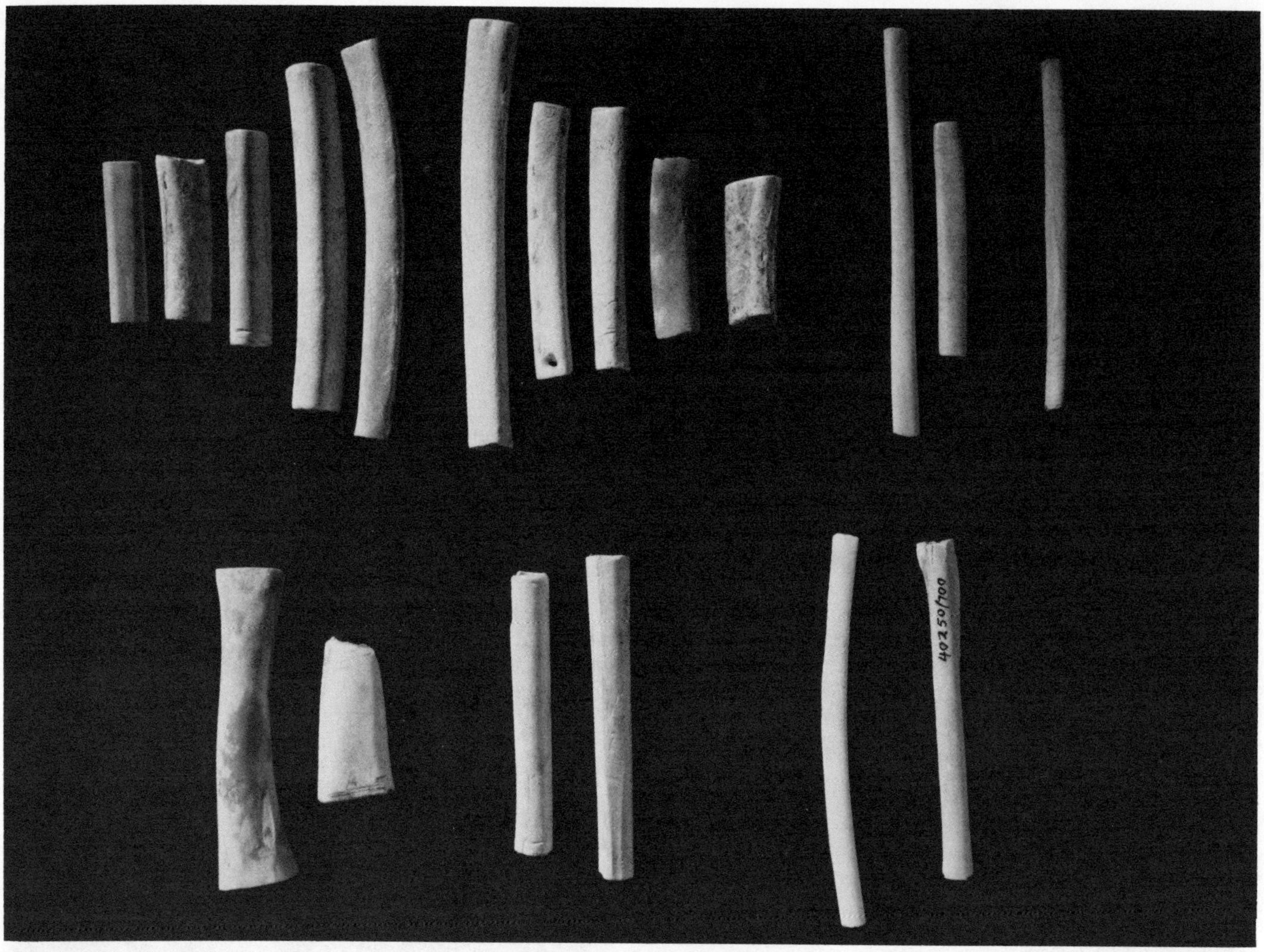

Figure 366. *Tubes of bird bone.*

Figure 367. *Tubes.*

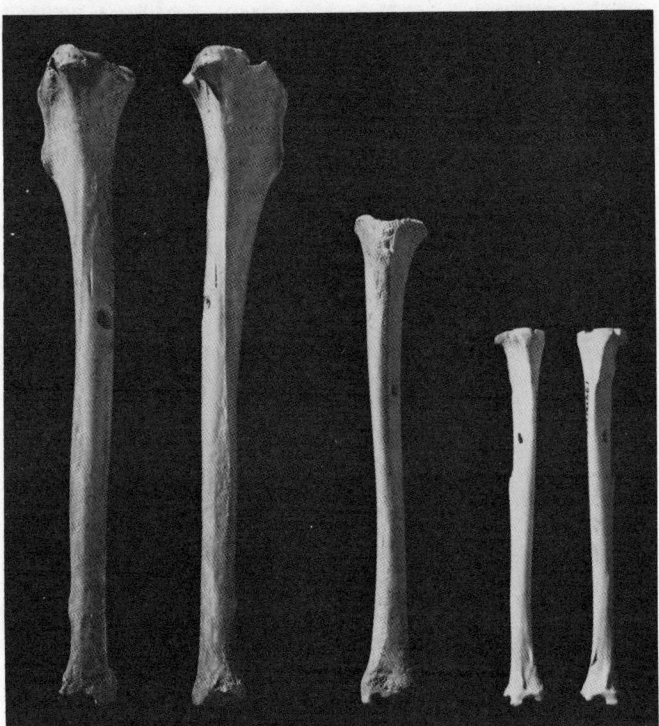

Figure 368. *Perforated mammal tibias.*

Figure 369. *Perforated mammal tibias.*

"Problematical Objects"

Seventy-five bone artifacts from Long House are "problematical." They have been sorted into four groups for purposes of convenient description.

Figure 370. *Flakers of mammal bone.*

Perforated Mammal Tibias. Nine complete and 11 incomplete mammal tibias–10 right and 10 left tibias-were cut off squarely and cored out at the proximal end but were unaltered at the distal end. Almost invariably a single round or oval perforation, 2 to 3.5 mm. in diameter, is present on the dorsal face of the shaft, one-quarter to one-third down from the proximal end (figs. 368 and 369). The specimens have been identified as rabbit, *Leporidae* (9), cottontail (7), fox (2), and coyote (2). Their proveniences were: Rooms 12, 76, Kiva D, Area V (one each); Kivas J, R, Area X, Lower East Trash Slope (two each); and Room 12 (eight).

Perforated mammal tibias have been recovered from other excavated sites on Wetherill Mesa, viz., Big Juniper House, Mug House, Badger House, Step House. Their purpose has not been established, but it has been suggested that they may have been strung together on yucca cords or thongs and used as tinklers in various ritual dances.

Flakers(?) Three splinters of mammal long bone, with one narrowed and nicked end, may have been used in flaking stone artifacts (fig. 370). They were found in Room 12, Kiva B, and on the Lower East Trash Slope, and range from 7 to 9.6 cm. in length.

Counters or dice(?) Three cut and ground splinters of mammal long bone or rib, subcylindrical or rectangular in shape and ranging in length from 2.4 to 7 cm., may have been gaming pieces (fig. 371). They were found in Room 13, Room 55, and Area V.

Stock(?) Twenty-three complete or fragmentary mammal bones show traces of work, such as the longitudinally sawed left metatarsal of bighorn sheep illustrated in figure 372, left, and are taken to be "stock" from which various artifacts were made or were intended to be made. The proveniences of 22 of these specimens were: Rooms 66, 85, Kivas N, R, S, T, Areas IV, IX, XI, Lower East Trash Slope, Upper East Trash Slope, backdirt (one each); Room 12, Kivas K, O, Q, V (two each).

Figure 371. *Gaming pieces (?) of mammal bone.*

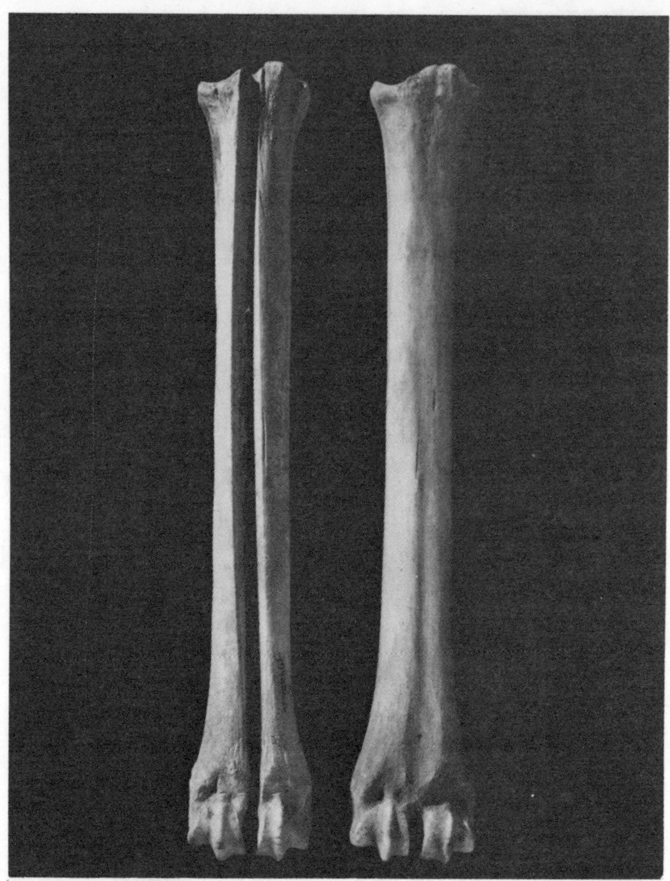

Figure 372. *Cut and uncut mammal metapodials.*

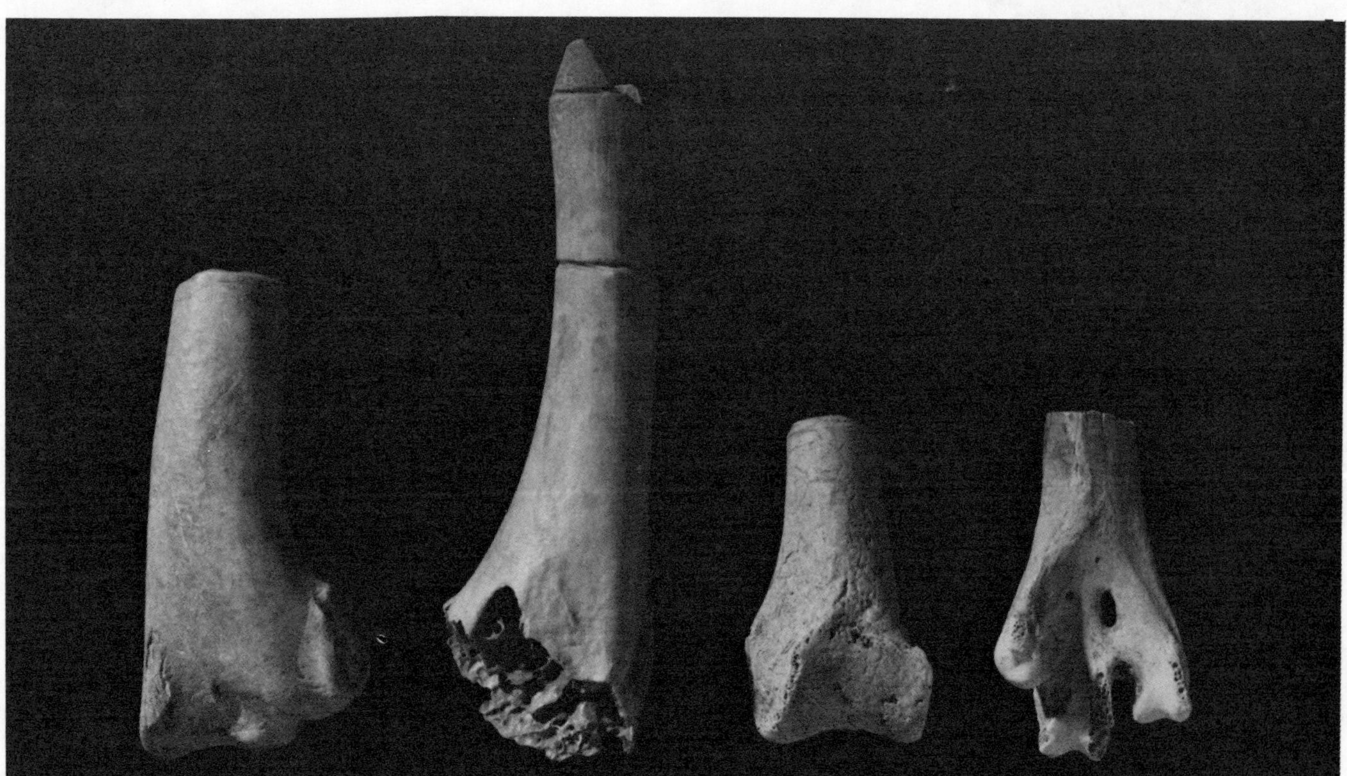

Figure 373. *Cut bird bones.*

Figure 374. *Antler handle.*

Nineteen complete and seven fragmentary bird bones show signs of work; as, for example, the cut end pieces illustrated in fig. 373 are considered to be stock from which awls, tubes, and other artifacts were manufactured. The proveniences of the 26 specimens were: Rooms 2, 11, 12, Kivas I, J, N, T, Areas IV, V, VII, XII, General Feature 9, Lower East Trash Slope, Upper East Trash Slope, Trash Slope below Area V, backdirt (one each); Kivas D, H, O (two each); and Area X (four).

ANTLER ARTIFACTS

Only two artifacts of antler—a handle and a wall peg—were found in Long House. The nearly complete absence of objects of this material must be ascribed to conditions unfavorable for the preservation of antler, or to the deliberate removal of antler artifacts such as antler-tip flakers, rather than to the non-availability of antler in prehistoric times.

The antler handle, recovered from Kiva R, has been identified as a section of the main trunk above the burr of an adult male deer, *Cervidae* sp. Cut at both ends, and slightly broken off on one side of one end, the specimen measures 4.7 cm. long and 2.7 cm. in diameter (fig. 374).

The antler wall peg, from the south face of the northwest pilaster in Kiva Q, is a section of the right antler beam of a young adult male mule deer, *Odocoileus hemionus*. Measuring 11 cm. in length and 2.3 cm. in diameter, it is in generally good condition albeit slightly cracked and chipped.

Chapter Seven

Objects of Perishable Materials

Carolyn M. Osborne

Life in ancient villages can be described more fully wherever circumstances of preservation permit the study of perishable remains. From the rooms, kivas, and working areas of Long House, various kinds of perishables were recovered, although not in sufficient abundance to give us the complete picture of the site that we would like to have. There are several possible explanations for this. First of all, it seems likely that clothing, as well as wooden and woven household items, never existed in surplus quantities—there is little to suggest stockpiling of any kind. Moreover, Long House was probably abandoned gradually, and the dwindling population may have appropriated many of the remaining serviceable items. Another possibility that might have diminished our finds is that the Project's excavation of Long House was not the first one. In his report of 1893, Nordenskiöld commented on the paucity of artifacts in Long House, and his list of perishable items found there is indeed short. Perishables recovered by him are now at the National Museum of Finland in Helsinki. His description of them was not complete. Additional notes on his collection and photographs of some of the items were made by Charlie R. Steen in 1960 and have been incorporated in this chapter.

Marilyn Colyer, a museum aid with the Project, produced the drawings of perishable objects illustrated herein. In many cases, close study of the intricacies of construction was required of the artist.

Professor Stanley L. Welsh of Brigham Young University identified all the wild plant materials, and Charles L. Douglas of the Wetherill Mesa Project identified the leather and fur by microscopic observations of epidermal patterns of hair. Gisele Eberling, another museum aid, prepared the hair impressions on slides. Lyndon L. Hargrave, a Park Service collaborator, made macroscopic identifications of whole feathers, and Norman Messinger, National Park Service, made microscopic identification of barbules of feathers when the quantity was considerably smaller.

It would be difficult to imagine prehistoric Pueblo culture without the yucca plant. The Mesa Verde Indians were fortunate in that the broadleafed *Yucca baccata* is ubiquitous in this area—on the forested and brushy mesa top, canyon slopes, and valley floors. Rarer, but also available, is *Yucca harrimaniae*, the narrow-leafed yucca. This species was preferred by the Indians for brushes and head rings. Its use, of course, made the extra task of splitting the wide *Yucca baccata* leaves unnecessary.

Strips of the wide-leaf yucca and leaves of the narrow-leaf yucca were woven into sandals and baskets. Strips were also used to make jar rests, to tie bundles of raw materials, for binding, sandal ties, and network around jars. Yucca fiber, when extracted, was the primary material for making twine; the fiber was also semifelted and sewed.

Prepared but unused yucca strips were found throughout Long House: 318 individual strips were more or less isolated occurrences, but 667 strips were found in four bundles or groups.

A bundle of 380 prepared strips, 3 to 4 mm. wide and from 12 to 60 cm. long, was found in Kiva A (fig. 375). There were none of the filiferous edge strips (i.e. strips with the coarse, thread-like growths) in this group. All had been removed. The second large accumulation was found untied in Room 46; this consisted of 180 filiferous edge strips (fig. 376), all discards from strip preparation. Ninety of these were greater than 30 cm. in length. One Long House jar rest makes use of these discard yucca edge strips as a core. The third group, also unsecured, in Room 28, consisted of 59 strips, 2 to 3 mm. wide. The fourth group was a well-tied bundle of strips, 3 to 6 mm. wide and 50 cm. long (fig. 377), found in Room 80/2. The width and length of this last group would conform to those used in both sandals and ring baskets.

Including these four large groups, yucca strips of varying widths and lengths were found almost equally in kivas (448) and rooms (511).

Nordenskiöld (1893, Pl. XLVIII, 3) illustrates a large bundle of yucca strips secured with a binding of yucca twine. The length of the strips is around 48 cm.; the diameter of the bundle, 14 cm.

Yucca strips, used and discarded, appear in archeological contexts as knots, loops, chains, and other forms. In considering these forms separately from yucca strips, we are simply making a distinction between used materials and stock. Of the 549 yucca strips with knots from Long House, 48 percent were found in rooms, 34 percent in kivas. Most of the total ranged in length from 1 to 2 cm. and were obviously broken fragments of jar harnesses, sandal ties, and many other objects. Square knots are so much the prevailing knot in this collection (96 percent) that the occasional use of a granny or other knot is hardly worth noting. The slip knot, called the "slippery reef" (fig. 378) (Graumont and Hensel, 1946, fig. 69 on pl. 26, and p. 64), which was occasionally used, is a variation of the square knot. Its counterpart, the "bundle knot" (ibid., fig. 343 on pl. 48, and p. 102), is a slip variation of a granny and does not appear. Two running eye knots and three clove hitches were undoubtedly used for special purposes.

We have observed no variation in knots, strip widths, numbers of knots, or total lengths of knotted strips between rooms and kivas, although these were tabulated and counted. The few specimens that still retained whole strips (i.e., with two or more knots joining strips end to end) indicate that the bulk of the broken fragments we now have were originally strips 25 cm. or more in length (76 percent). One rope of knotted yucca strips, 85 cm. long, consisted of four whole strips and sections of two others. Yucca had to be tied when green and supple; untying and retying is not evidenced in the material from the ruin.

Yucca strips with the sharp leaf tips retained as needles (fig. 379) were undoubtedly used for mending, as seen in the knotless netted fabric of human hair twine (20118/700), for stringing ears of

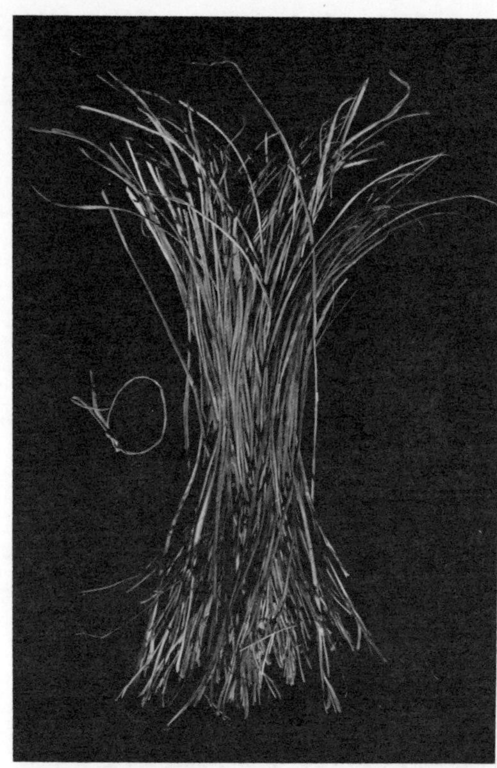

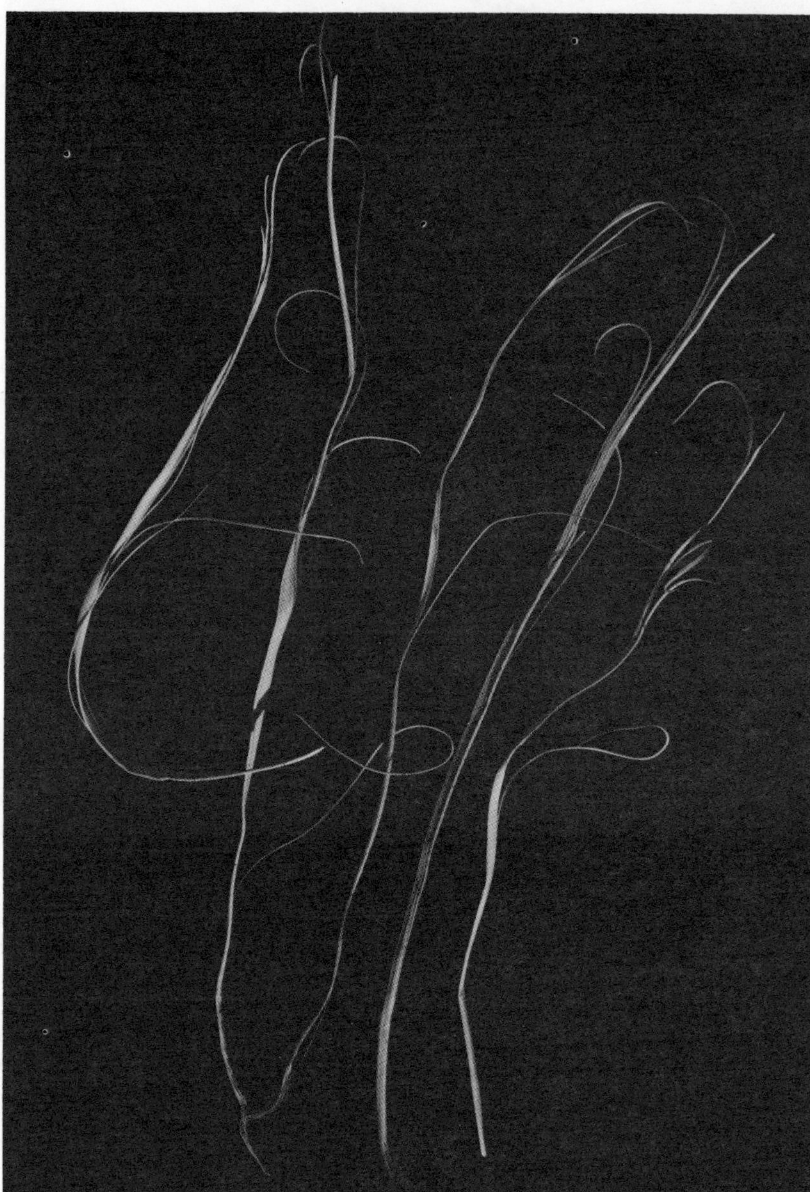

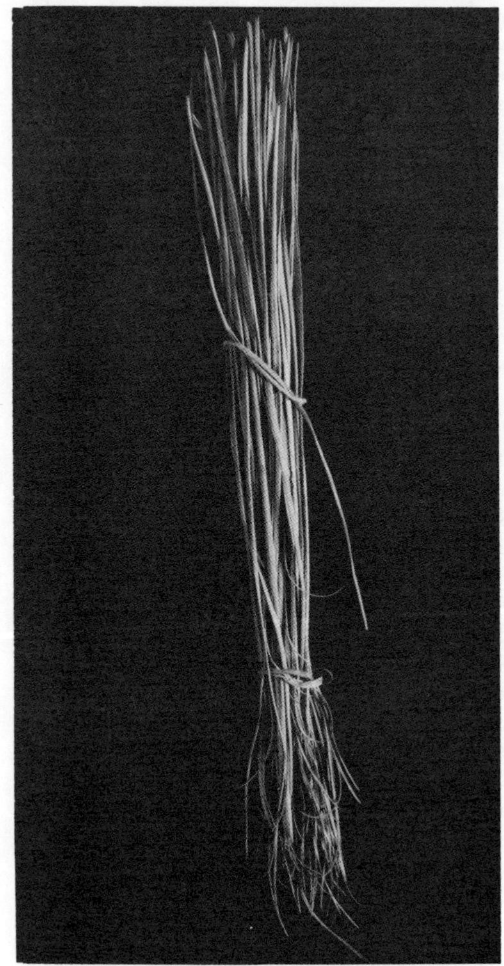

Figure 375. *(Above, left) Bundle of 380 prepared strips of* Yucca baccata, *with associated loop, from the fill of Kiva A.*

Figure 376. *(Above, right) sample of filiferous edge strips of* Yucca baccata *from the fill of Room 46.*

Figure 377. *(Left) Tied bundle of yucca strips from the floor of Room 80/2.*

Figure 378. *(Below) Drawing of a "slippery reef" knot, a variation of the square knot, used almost exclusively in Long House.*

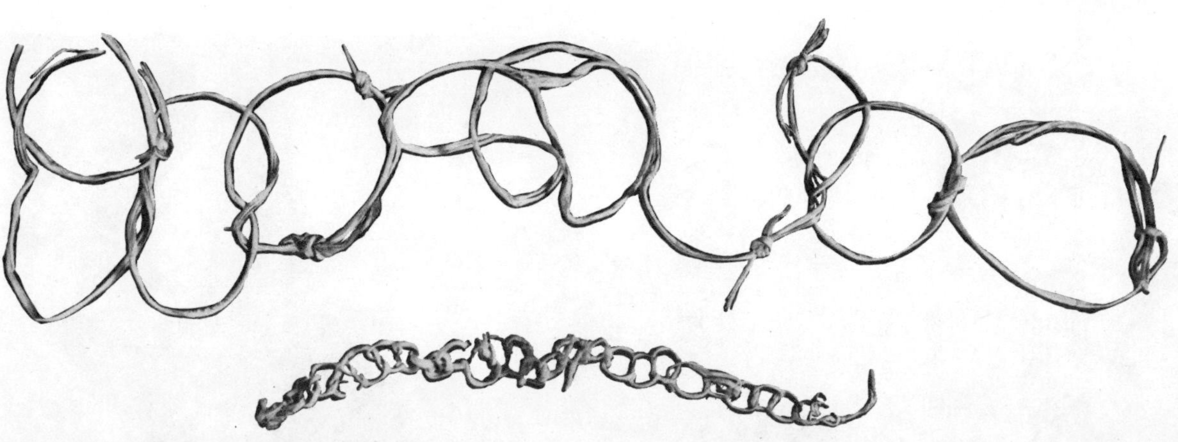

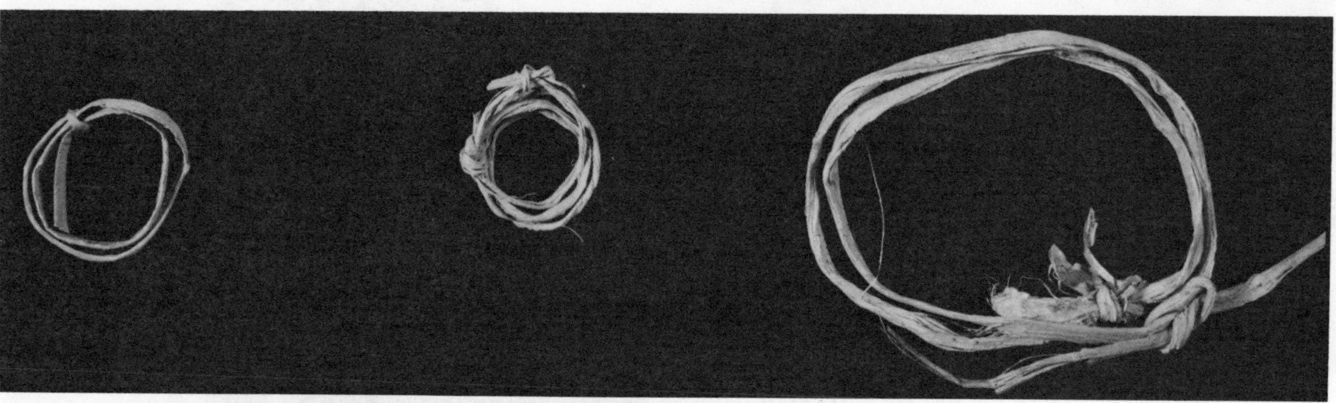

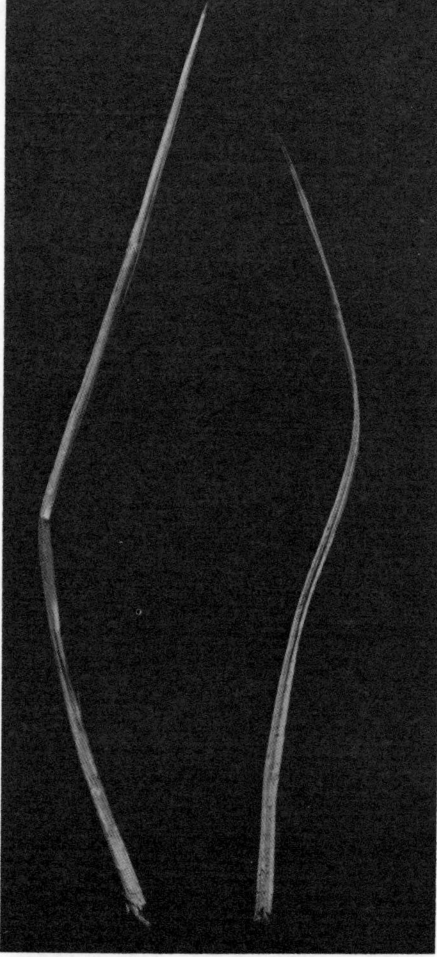

corn, and for repairing baskets. The point, even if not strong enough to penetrate a basket coil or a corn peduncle, made a natural threading device. Yucca strip perforators like these have been found in other Southwestern sites and are used in the pueblo of Santa Ana today for making coiled baskets (Ellis, 1959, p. 189). Their use in the past was probably more widespread than the literature indicates.

Loops which at one time held bundles of raw materials or various objects are numerous in Long House (fig. 380). Most consist of a single strip of yucca leaf which was once wrapped around some object as many times as length permi•ted and tied with a square knot. The majority of these probably secured objects for household use. This is indicated by their location; approximately 60 percent were found in rooms, 25 percent in kivas, with the remainder dispersed in various spots in the village.

Chains of yucca strips (and occasionally of twine) held objects in series (fig. 381). The loops vary from 6 cm. to 40.5 cm. in diameter, as the objects themselves varied. Nearly all have overhand knots between the loops; if these loops were pulled tight, granny knots would result. Figure 382 illustrates the overhand knots used by the Long House people and a series which, if pulled tight, would produce square knots. It can be seen that the former would tend to rotate the object enclosed to nearly right angles, wereas the latter would hold them in a straighter line. If the objects contained between the ties were to be dried, the rotating would be of value. The granny knot is so contrary to usually expressed motor habits of the Long House people that we must assume its use here was deliberate.

Figure 379. *(Left) Strips of yucca with sharp leaf tips retained as needles.*

Figure 380. *(Upper top) Yucca loops for securing bundles or various objects.*

Figure 381. *(Lower top) Chain of yucca strips.*

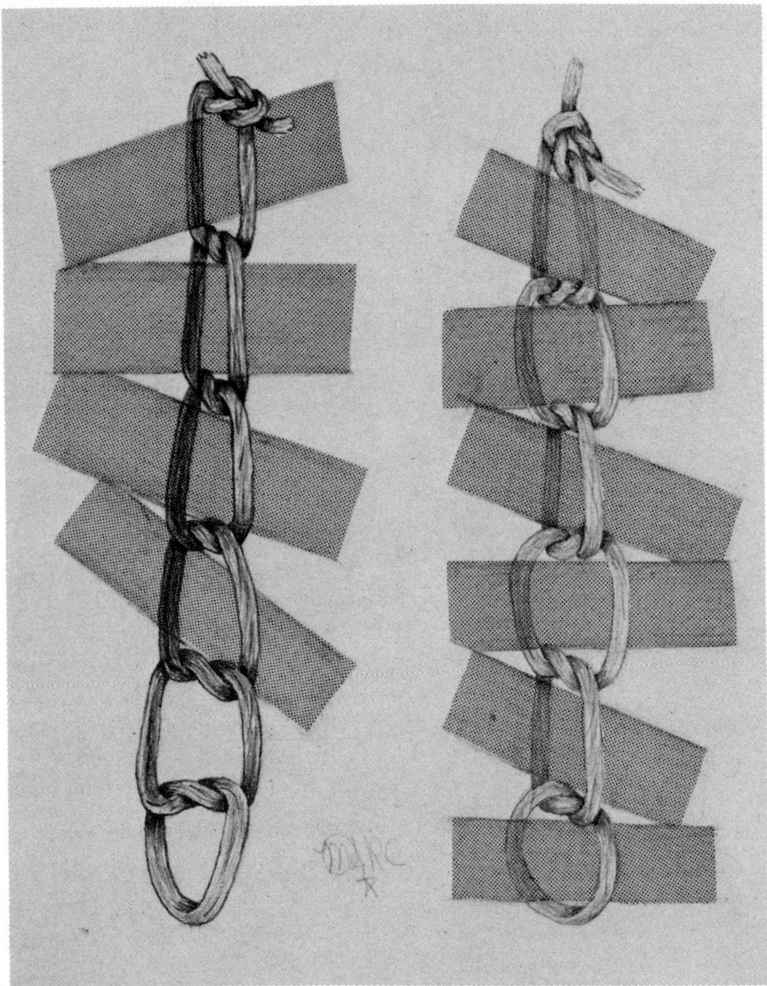

Figure 382. *Drawing showing comparison of two chains of yucca strips with overhand knots; left, if pulled tight, chain would form granny knots (used in Long House); right, if pulled tight, chain would form square knots (not used in Long House).*

Figure 383. *A binding with yucca strips from Kiva D.*

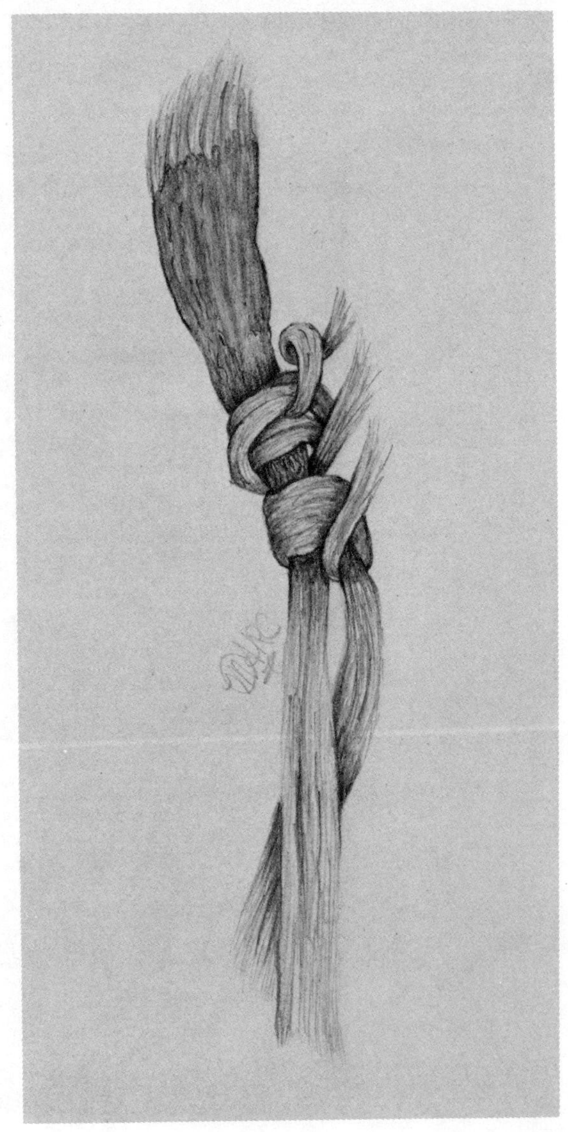

Figure 384. *Drawing of a wide strip of yucca, split and served above with yucca binding, from an unknown object.*

A binding with yucca strips is shown in figure 383. This specimen, found in Kiva D, probably held two slender rods apart. Bindings such as this one can be seen in prayer sticks. A wide strip of yucca, partially split and served above with yucca binding to prevent its extension (fig. 384), is the fragment of an object of unknown use.

The same is true of a Nelson sennit found in Kiva I, Level A. This item, which is complete, is 4.4 cm. long and averages 1 cm. in diameter; it narrows at the upper end as the yucca strips narrow (figs. 385 and 386). Begun on a fold of the strips, this is the sennit commonly produced by Boy Scouts as "busy work." Its utility for the ancient Indians, who did not posses the watches, keys, or whistles associated nowadays with the construction, is problematical.

A dumbbell-shaped bundle of compressed yucca flower stalk measures 10 cm. long by about 6 cm. at each end and 2.5 cm. through the center ; it is flat and only 12 mm. thick (fig. 387). The compressed fibers are wound concentrically; at each end, they pass around a core of twisted stalk, about 5 mm. in diameter, which regulated to some extent the width of the flare at the ends; the entire straight center section was once wrapped, but only the grooves caused by the wrapping are now present. Similar objects, of unknown use, occurred in several sites at Mesa Verde.

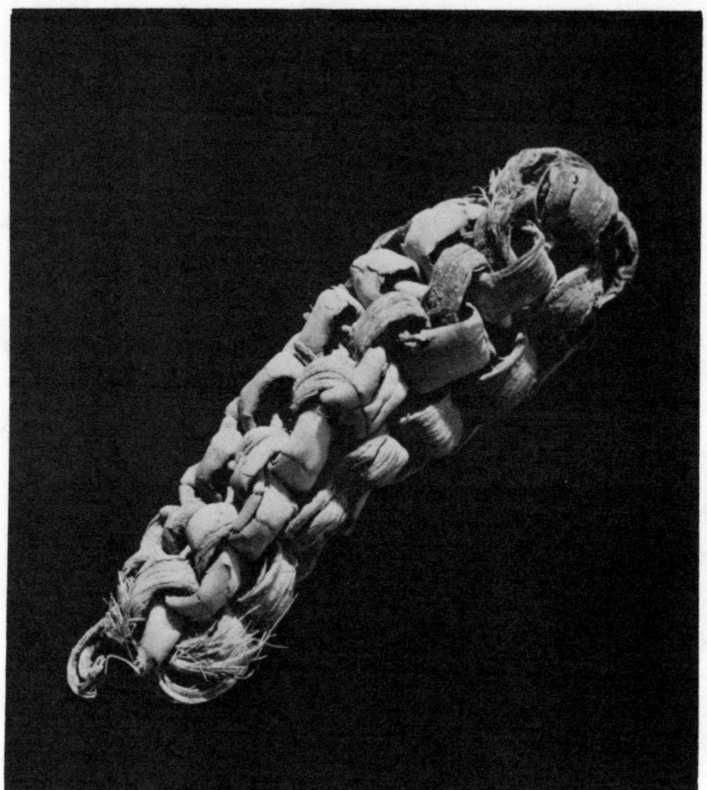

Figure 385. *A Nelson sennit of two yucca strips folded in midsection to provide four ends (12796/700), found in Level A, Kiva I.*

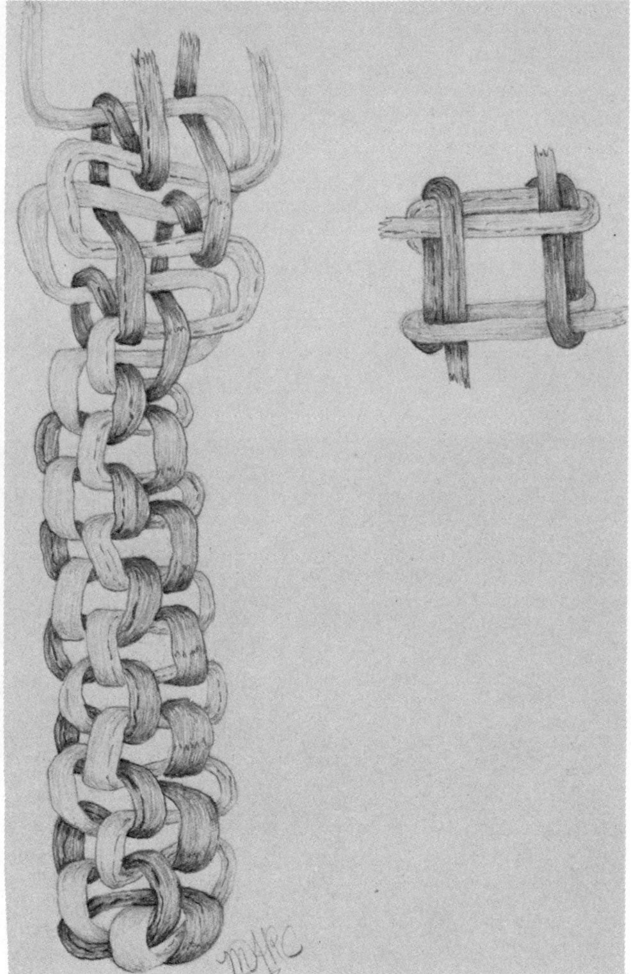

Figure 386. *Drawings of the Nelson sennit shown in figure 385.*

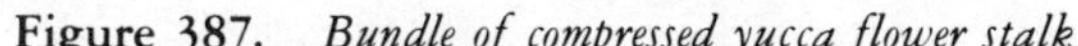

Figure 387. *Bundle of compressed yucca flower stalk.*

Although brushes of *Yucca harrimaniae* occur in other Mesa Verde sites, the lone specimen from Long House (fig. 388) is probably too supple to be a hairbrush but could have been useful for sweeping ground meal from a metate into a container. The leaves are split, with the edge strips forming the brush and held in midsection with seven wraps and a square knot tie of the common 2–ply Z-twist yucca twine. The present length is about 30 cm. The ends are worn and straggly.

Two unfinished objects of plaited yucca strips were found. It is evident that more work was intended on one of them, a band 2.5 cm. wide, with about 6 cm. of completed plaiting, using eight elements (fig. 389). The long ends of the elements were divided in half and loosely tied to hold them in position. No complete object in Mesa Verde collections is constructed in this way. The yucca strip plaiting on the outside of the ring baskets, although similar, is attached to the basket by the individual elements before plaiting itself begins. I have never seen a strip woven separately and then appliqued on Mesa Verde baskets.

The other unfinished plaited object resembles the corner section of a sandal beginning (fig. 389b). It is a 2/2 twill, as are sandals, but unlike the twilled sandals the bases of the leaves are not present to be tied off shortly on the under surface. Rather, the plaiting was started in the midsection of the leaves. Both objects may be teaching or practice devices.

Associated with a corrugated jar was part of a net of yucca strips, 0.7 to 1.0 cm. wide and running the full length of the yucca leaves, including portions of their bases. Square knots join the strips into a frame of no regular mesh size. A jar with a net such as this was clearly used for storage and not (at least any longer) for cooking.

Nordenskiöld (1893, pl. XLVII, 11), illustrates a ball, between 3.5 and 4.0 cm. in diameter, from Long House. Steen described this as a tight ball of shredded yucca, tied and held together with split yucca leaves. The Wetherill collection in the Colorado State Museum includes two of these items. I would identify them as balls, probably used in games.

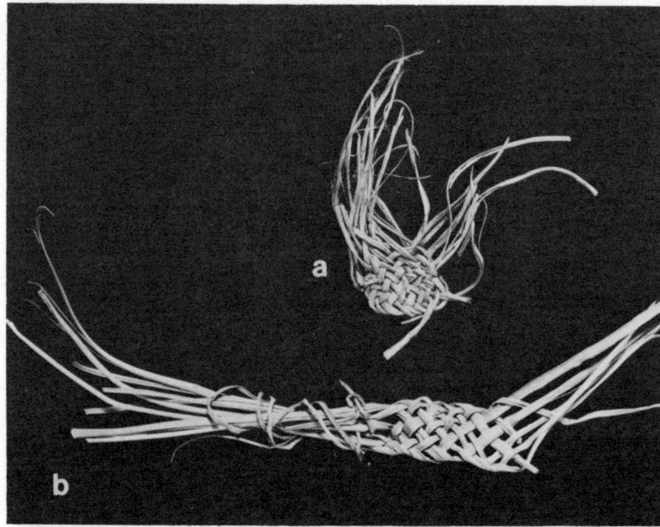

Figure 389. *Unfinished objects of plaited yucca strips; a, narrow band from fill behind northwest recess of Kiva H; and b, corner section from loose fill in Room 11.*

Figure 388. *Brush of edge strips of the narrow leaf* Yucca harrimaniae.

RESTS

The first item taken from Long House by the Wetherill Mesa Project in 1958 was a jar rest picked up on the surface (table 19). Although not a very attractive specimen (or perhaps because of this), it had "survived" many visitors. The core of this jar rest is juniper bast, and the wrapping, which must once have been complete, is of tough yucca strips (fig. 390a). It has a slightly oval shape and is decidedly thicker in one section than elsewhere. A disintegrating jar rest (fig. 390b) has a juniper bast core and a loose juniper bast wrapping which must originally have covered the foundation.

Far better made, and in better condition, is a juniper bast and yucca strip ring (fig. 390c). The bundle core was neatly coiled, and the yucca strip was knotted to give sufficient length to spiral around the bast. This jar rest shows considerable use. It differs from the others from Long House, and indeed from most of these items, in the large inner diameter and lack of height of the wall; it would support few round-bottomed bowls or cooking jars. Only a depression in the earth under it would make it useful, and with such a depression the jar rest would hardly be needed. It may have been made to support a specific jar; or we may be mistaking its function.

Only one other specimen from Long House is a properly constructed jar rest (fig. 390d). Its core is a compactly coiled bundle of the filiferous edge strips of yucca; the binding is of 2–ply Z-twist yucca twine which is feather quill wrapped in some sections, an obvious remnant from a feather blanket. The jar rest is flat on one surface, slightly concave on the other. Both surfaces are sooty—evidence that cooking pots had been set on it.

The remainder of the rests were probably not for jars. Present-day Pueblo Indians visiting the Project's laboratory commented on the use of small rings to support various objects on kiva floors. The loosely constructed rest of juniper bast (fig. 390b), one of the two specimens of cornhusk (fig. 391a, right), and the two rests of grass were found in kivas. The two of grass have a nest-like construction; they may have supported or protected some fragile object. The quickly constructed and not too sturdy cornhusk rings show no use. One has no binding; the other is loosely bound in one section only. They may possibly have been temporary head rings discarded after slight use. The same is true of a small yucca strip ring, which consists of six strips individually knotted with a square knot, the knots assembled at one section of the circumference, and the whole loosely tied together with a single yucca strip.

A tiny ring (fig. 391b) could possibly have served a child as a head ring. Its maximum diameter is only 5.7 cm. The core of juniper bast was once probably completely concealed by the wrapping which is also of juniper bast.

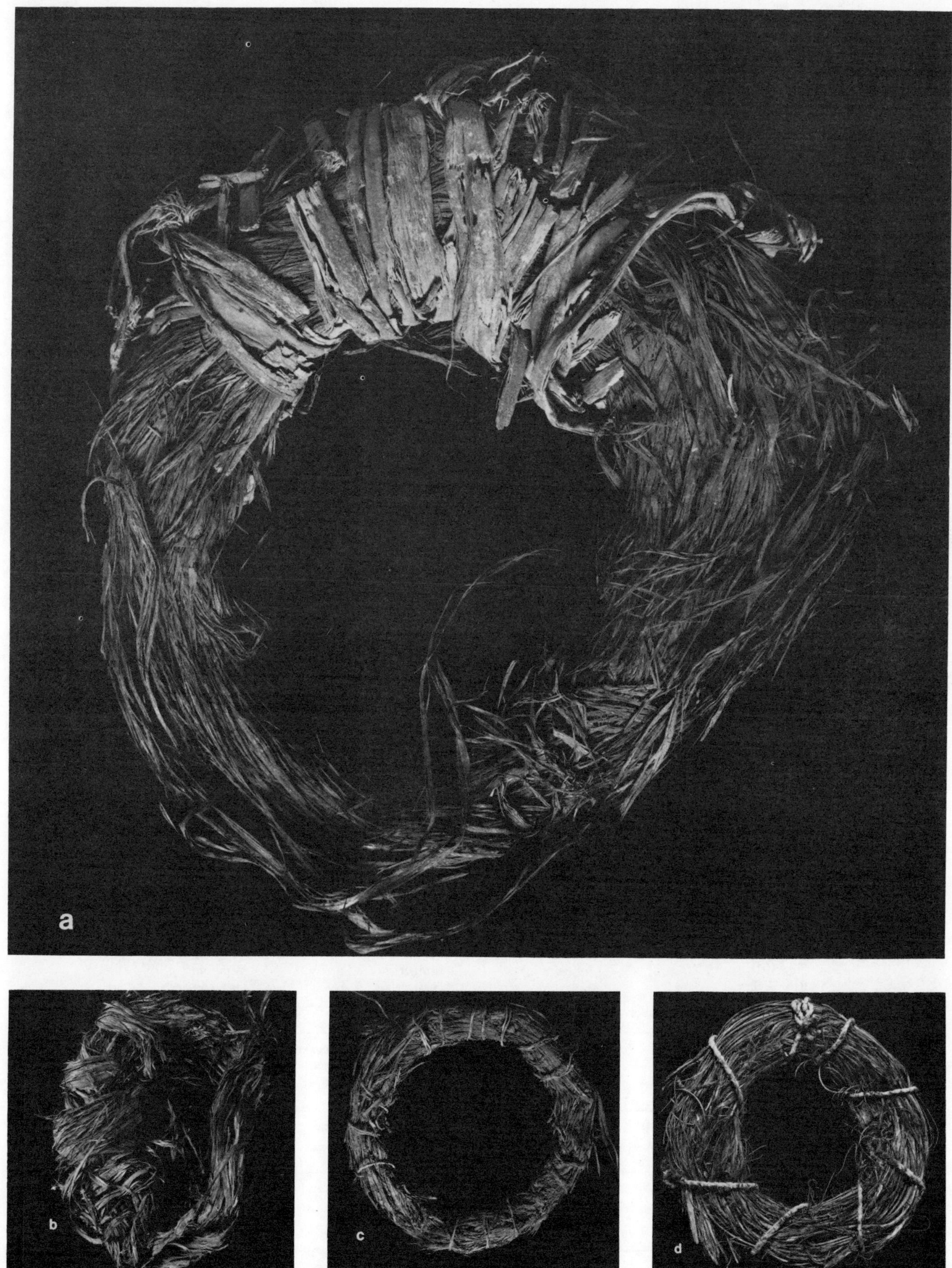

Figure 390. *Jar rests of juniper bast.*

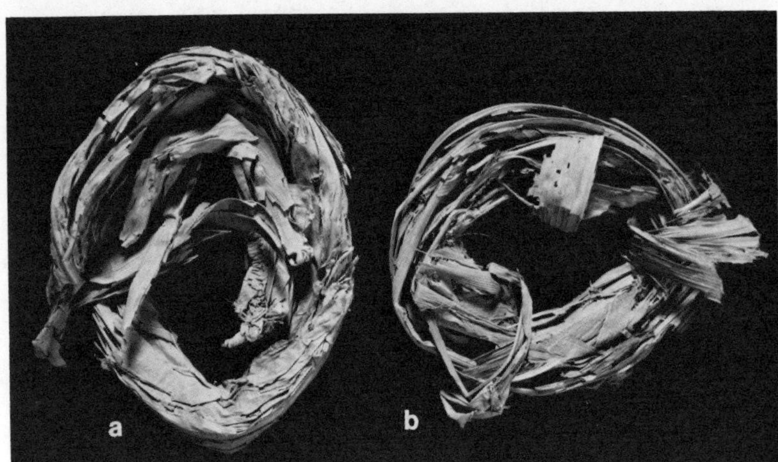

Figure 391. *Rings of cornhusk and juniper bast.*

Table 19. Rests.

Illus. Proven. Cat. No.	Diameters (cm.) Outer	Inner	Thickness (cm.)	Coil foundation	Binding	Remarks
Fig. 390a Surface 12000/700	20 by 10 (oval)	11 by 9.5 (oval)	2.6 at 1 edge, 1.1 at opposite	juniper bast, untwisted	yucca strip	See text.
Fig. 390b Kiva H, Lev. A 12733/700	21 (broken)	13	2	juniper bast	juniper bast	Loose coil of base.
Fig. 390c Rm. 47, Lev. I 17416/700	16	11.5	1.5	juniper bast	yucca strip	Spiral wrapping.
Fig. 390d Rm. 80, fl. Lev. II 20071/700	20.5	11	2.3	yucca strip	yucca twine	Twine in spiral binding.
Fig. 391a, left Surface, west end 12003/700	14 by 10.5 (oval)	8 by 4 (oval)	3.5	cornhusk	none	See text.
Fig. 391a, rt. Kiva D, disturbed fill 12667/700	13 by 11	7 by 5	2.5	cornhusk	cornhusk	Husks, untwisted.
Fig. 391b Rm. 7, Lev. VII 17387/700	5.7	2	1.5	juniper bast	juniper bast	Wrapping once concealed core.
Rm. 46, fill 16095/700	12	7	2	yucca strip	yucca strip	Six strips individually square knotted.
Kiva F, fill 12718/700	13.4 by 10 (oval)	solid	3.5	grass, sp.?	none	Two bundles loosely twisted.
Kiva H, inside northeast wall 12771/700	23 by 14.5	solid	3.7	grass, sp.?	none	Loosely twisted; nestlike.
Surface, west end 12008/700	fragment; 3.6 wide	bundle	ca. 4.5	yucca strip; many edge strips	yucca strip	

SANDALS

The excavation of Long House revealed two type of sandals worn by the occupants: twill-plaited, of yucca strips; and fine twined, of yucca twine. No other kind is represented, even by small fragments. Sandals were not abundant. Four reasonably complete twilled sandals[1] give shape, size, and an idea of ties; and 14 fragments add to the total count of twilled sandals and to details such as selvage construction. Only one twined sandal is present. These 19 specimens must represent only a small fraction of the number in use when Long House was at its prime. Table 20 gives details on all sandals and fragments from the site.

Yucca in two forms—strips and twine—is the only plant material used in sandal construction. Carefully prepared yucca strips, 3 to 5 mm. wide, eliminating the edge strips but often using a portion of the leaf base and maximum length, are used for twilled sandals. Two varieties of yucca twine are used for the twined "cloth" sandals.

The most complete twilled sandal, for the right foot, measures approximately 28 cm. long; it is 10.2 cm. wide through the ball of the foot and narrows slightly at the heel (fig. 392a and b). Plaiting of the 2/2 twill was probably begun at the heel, using a leaf strip folded or bent approximately 2.5 cm. from the base of the strip. The broad bases of the leaves were maintained on the lower surface of the sandal at the beginning of the weaving, and were later, during finishing, tied two together with an overhand knot and cut off just under the heel. The heel selvage is thus the simple turning of the other selvages. Because of the increase of tension and the curving of the heel where these knots are tied on the lower surface, the upper surface has a row of simple twilling which appears different from the rest of the sandal. The twill weave is continued at the side and toe selvages, with the yucca strip elements going under 2, turning, and over 2 at the left selvage (fig. 393) and over 2, turning, and under 2 at the right selvage. As can be seen along the bottom edge of figure 392b, new elements were added as needed along the left selvage and knotted off on the under surface about 1.3 cm. inside the edge.

Unfortunately, the toe end of the sandal is too worn and disintegrated to analyze the final stages of the weaving. It has, however, the slight jog formed by a minor displacement of the elements (fig. 394) characteristic of sandals of the period in this area. Extant ties consist of a series of loops, 5 to 6 cm. apart, of yucca strips reduced almost to fiber. The strips pass through the sandal in a backstitch, with about 1 cm. on the lower surface. In addition to this, there is a three-strand braid of untwisted yucca fiber, which tapers from 1 cm. in width at the left, where it is anchored through the sandal, to 0.4 cm., where it is terminated with a self knot. This braid probably formed a double toe loop, although the narrow end is now free. No heel ties are present.

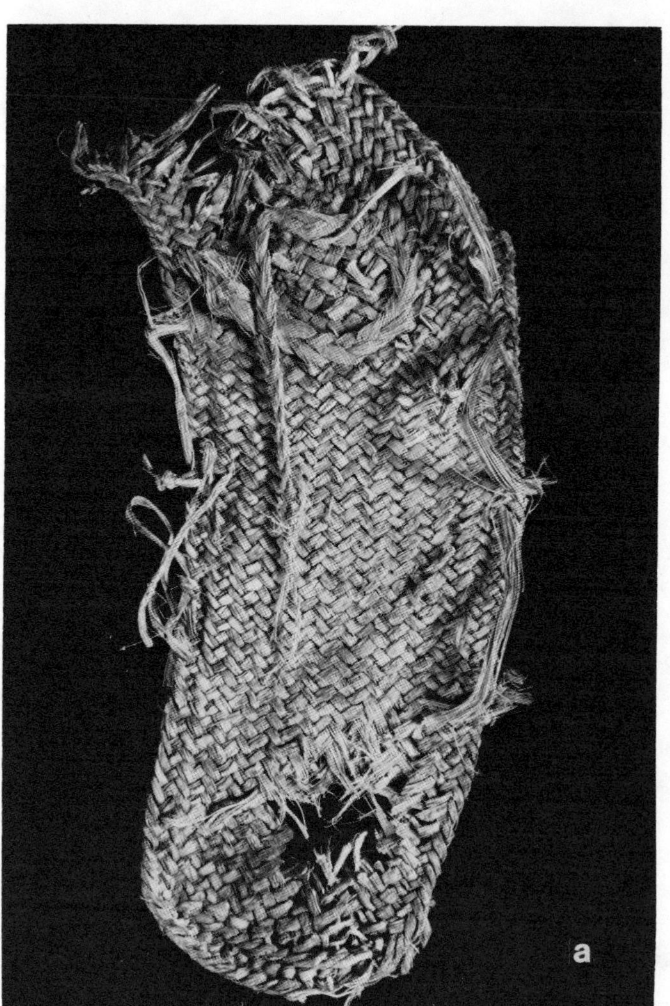

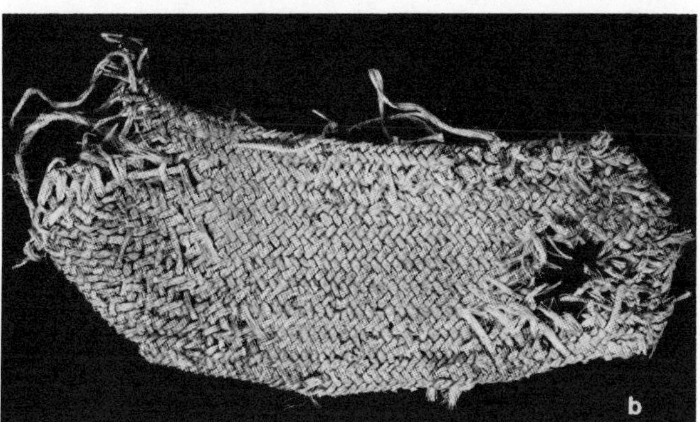

Figure 392. *Twilled sandal: a, upper surface; and b, under surface.*

Figure 393. *Drawing showing single turning of elements at left side of selvage of twilled sandal illustrated in figure 392. (Note: under 2, over 2 selvage spread out at top.)*

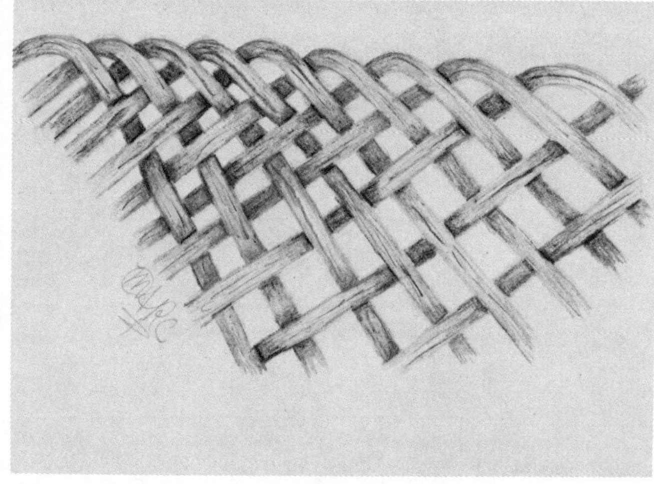

[1]For the sake of brevity, these sandals will be referred to as twilled sandals; they are, of course, twill-plaited, as the elements move from one selvage to the opposite and back again.

Table 20. Sandals.

Illus. Proven. Cat. No.	Size in cm.	Selvages present	Weave	Elements	Remarks
Fig. 392a,b, 393, 394 Rm. 47, Lev. I 17417/700	2.8 x 10.5 (across ball of foot)	nearly complete sandal	2/2 twill	yucca strip 3–5 mm. wide	Right foot; jog toe; simple selvage (see fig. 393). See text for construction details.
Fig. 395 Kiva K, Lev. I 20176/700	23.5 x 9.5 (across jog) 75 (nr. heel)	4 side	2/2 twill	yucca strip 3–5 mm.	Left foot, jog toe; turned up at heel with knotting of initial elements on under surface. See text for construction details.
Fig. 396 Rm. 46, 3.7–5 ft. below 2d flr. 12545/700	25.5 x 9	2 side, heel and toe broken	2/2 twill	split strips of *Y. baccata,* 4–5 mm.	Right foot; heel worn, toe section missing, no jog apparent, portions of heel and instep loop, toe loop. See text for construction details.
Fig. 397 Rm. 80, Lev. II 20070/700	17 x 12	2 side; toe	2/2 twill yucca strip 3–5 mm.	Right foot, jog toe; elements pass over three, under three at selvage, reinforced with running stitch of yucca strip. See text for construction details.	
Fig. 328, 329 Kiva B, fill 12619/700	5.5 x 2.7	fragment of one side	2/2 twill	yucca strip ca. 3mm.	Small fragment almost reduced to fiber. See text on elaborate selvage.
Fig. 400a,b, 401 Rm. 47, Lev. I 17422/700	20 x 10.5 (toe) x 8.2 (at midstep)	2 side; portion of toe	twined, pitch up to the right	warp: 2-ply S-twist yucca weft, 2-ply, S-twist yucca twine; dyed brown	Left foot; probably jog toe. See text for construction details.
Rm. 11 & between walls of Kiva E 15224/700	3 x 5.5	portion of heel	2/2 twill	yucca strip 3–4mm. wide	Heel turned up, highly disintegrated; no knotting of initial elements.
Same as above 15225/700	7.5 x 5	portion of one side	2/2 twill	yucca strip 4–5 mm. wide	Simple selvage (see fig. 393).
Rm. 37, upper fill 12503/700	3.5 x 4	none 2/2 twill	yucca strip ca. 3mm.	Fragment in poor condition; purple stain on one surface.	
Rm. 62, fill 12804/700	6 x 3.2	1 side, probably	2/2 twill	yucca strip 3–4 mm. wide	Simple selvage (see fig. 393); closely whipped over selvage with yucca strip for 3.5 cm. of edge present; almost reduced to fiber.
Rm. 81, Lev. II 20107/700	28 x 7.5	1 side, heel	2/2 twill	yucca strips 5–6 mm. wide	Yucca strips almost reduced to fiber; Simple selvage (see fig. 393). Series of 5 side loops of 2-ply Z-twist yucca twine, 4 mm. in diameter, backstitched through the sole; loops 5.5 cm. long x 4 cm. deep.

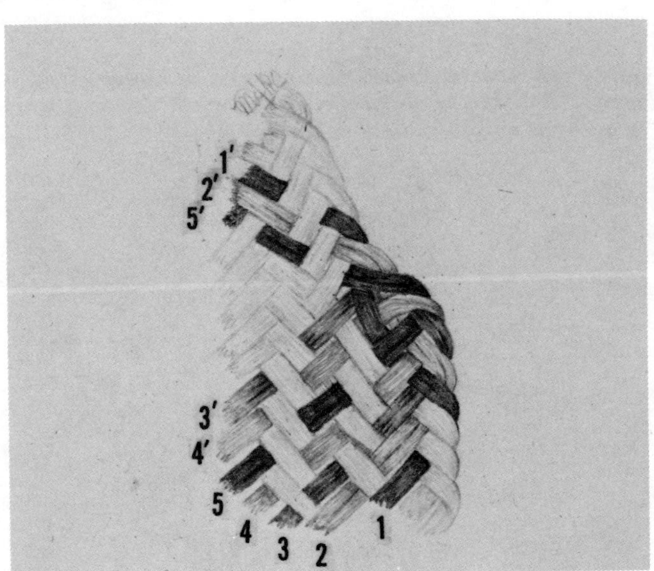

Figure 394. *Drawing showing detail of construction, proceeding from the heel, of jog in twilled sandal illustrated in figure 392.*

The second nearly complete sandal, for the left foot, has no ties and no indications of former ties (fig. 395). It measures 23.5 cm. long by 9.5 cm. wide across the jog. The selvage is a turning, maintaining the 2/2 twill of the weave. The heel is slightly turned up, with the row of knots of the initial elements just under the heel and with the irregularly pulled strips showing plainly on the upper surface. New elements were knotted to the old on the lower surface, primarily near the selvages. Regrettably, the strips just above the jog are broken and could not be followed through the rearrangement.

A heavily worn twilled sandal (12545/700) has an unusual selvage which may have been sturdier than the simple selvage turn. This sandal was made for the right foot; the heel and the ball of the foot are completely worn through, and the toe section is missing. The sandal is approximate 25.5 cm. long and 8.9 cm. wide. As with the others, weaving was begun at the heel; elements are tied off with a simple overhand knot just under the heel, which is slightly cupped. The right selvage (fig. 396) involves one of the two elements forming the edge (marked 1 in the illustration) passing over 2 (including its partner), turning over 1, under 2, etc.; its counterpart (marked 2 in the illustration) passes under 2 (one its partner), turn, under 1, over 1, etc. The element shown lightly hatched in the figure was an error on the part of the maker; she (or he?) compensated for this in the next

Table 20. Sandals.—(Continued)

Kiva A, fill 12609/700	22.5 x 9.8	Fragments of 2 side selvages; fragment of heel 2/2 twill	yucca strips 3–5 mm. wide	Probably right foot; toe jog not apparent; simple selvage maintaining twill (fig. 393). Heel turned up with elements knotted on under surface. New strips added along both edges; knotted to previous element with simple overhand on under surface. Portions of toe and heel ties.	
Kiva D, disturbed fill 12672/700	8 x 5.8	1 side, toe?	2/2 twill yucca strip 3–4 mm. wide	Simple selvage (see fig. 393), portion of tie.	
Kiva E and Rm. 11, loose fill & trash beyond edge of floor 12704/700	1 x 5	heel only	2/2 twill?	yucca strip 3–4 mm. wide	Heel turned up with overhand knots holding elements on under surface.
Kiva K, Lev. II 20184/700	11 x 11	1 side	2/2 twill	yucca strip 3–5 mm. wide	Simple selvage (see fig. 393), with reinforcement of running stitch of yucca strip near selvage. New elements added near edges, knotted on under surface to old strip.
Area V, 6 feet east of Rm. 32 & 8 feet north of Kiva G; loose in trash	2 frags., 5 x 5 and 6.5 x 5	fragment of one side	2/2 twill	yucca strip 3 mm. wide	Simple selvage (see fig. 393).
Area V, fill 12863/700	2 frags. totaling 3.5 x 3.5	fragment of one side	2/2 twill	yucca strip 3 mm. wide	Simple selvage (see fig. 393).
Area VII 15484/700	small	may be heel turning	2/2 twill?	yucca strip	Highly disintegrated fragment; has one knot like those seen on under surface of other sandals.
Upper West Trash Slope, between Kivas E & F 12942/700	14.5 x 8.5	fragments of 2 side selvages 2/2 twill	yucca strip 3–5 mm. wide	Simple selvage (see fig. 393); new elements added by knotting on under surface, running stitch reinforcement of yucca strip along one edge.	

turning. When tightly pulled, the latter lies nearly on top of the former, making a double strip along the edge. The edges of the sandal are in excellent condition, perhaps because of the doubling of the elements there. Yucca strips were used for the ties. The toe loop is broken, but the strip that went behind the heel and high over the instep is intact. Attached to the instep strap is a broken strip which probably connected with the toe loop.

The other 2/2 twilled yucca strip sandals have unusual selvages. A sandal half (20070/700) was woven for a right foot, with a slight toe jog on the right selvage. At the edge, elements break the normal 2/2 twilling by passing over 3 strips, turning, and then under 3 (fig. 397). The edge seems to be slightly irregular and the longer floats, although decorative, may have formed a weaker selvage. New elements were added in a cluster on the under surface around the arch of the foot, tied with overhand or square knots to the ends of the exhausted strips. There are remnants of an overlapping double toe loop.

The fragment of a twilled sandal, 12619/700, measuring a little over 5 cm. long by 2.5 cm. wide, has the most complex selvage of any found in Long House. The slight detour of each element before it reaches the edge produces the double row seen in the figure 398. In the drawing showing the selvage construction (fig 399), one strip has

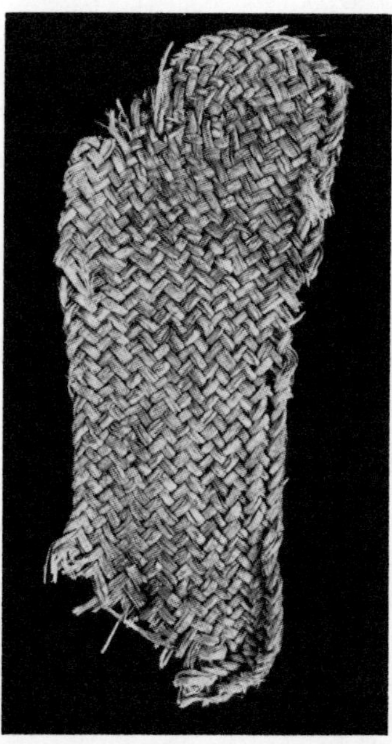

Figure 395. *Twilled sandal, upper surface.*

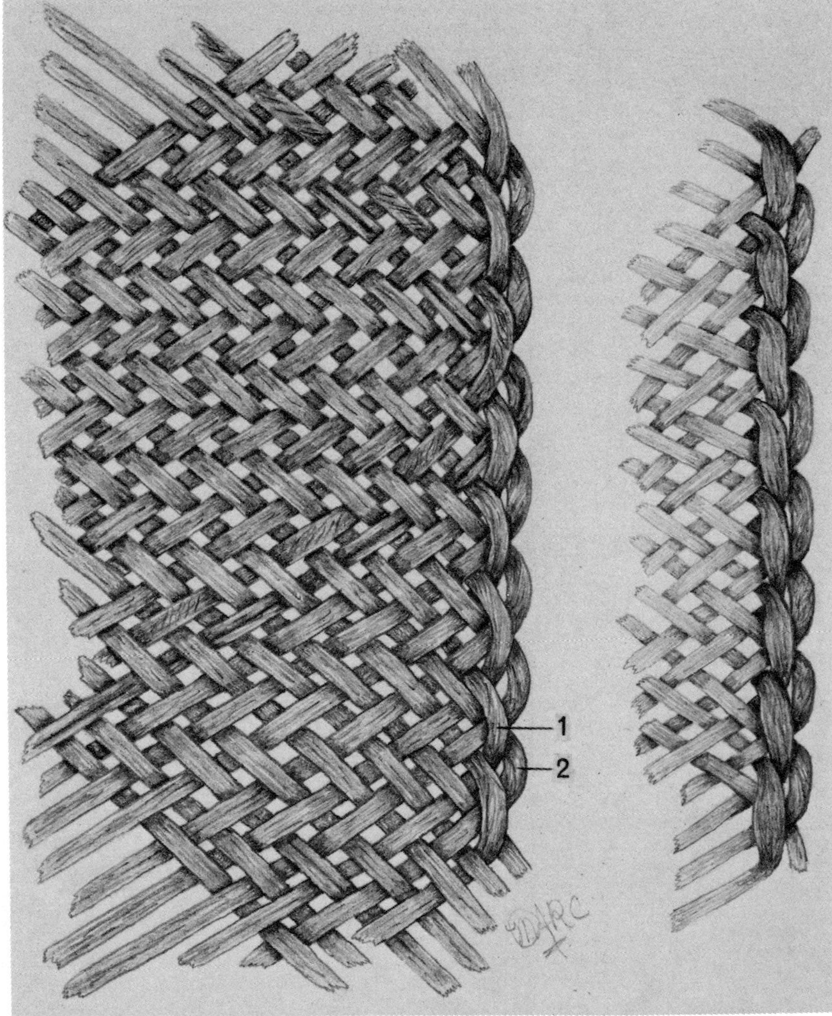

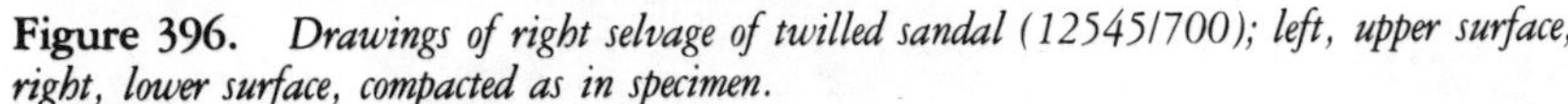

Figure 396. *Drawings of right selvage of twilled sandal (12545/700); left, upper surface; right, lower surface, compacted as in specimen.*

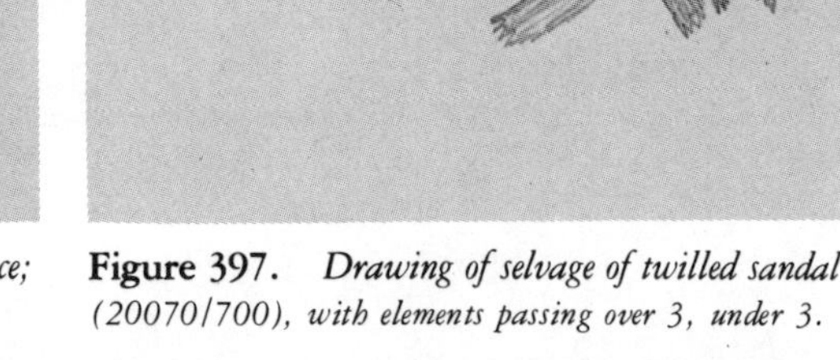

Figure 397. *Drawing of selvage of twilled sandal (20070/700), with elements passing over 3, under 3.*

been darkened to indicate the movement of each element as it approaches the edge and turns back into the plaiting order.

The single twined, or "cloth," sandal found in Long House was made for the left foot (fig. 400a and b). Lacking the heel section, it measures 20 cm. in length by 10.5 cm. across the toe section by 6.2 cm. at the instep. The jog is broken, probably from wear, and the entire toe section is worn around the edge.

The warp is 2–ply S-twist yucca twine, 2 mm. in diameter, loose to medium degree, of well-separated Class B fibers. This slick twine of a warm gold color facilitated the extremely tight packing of the weft yarns. The weft is also 2–ply S-twist of fine, well-processed Class C fibers, off-white in color and superficially resembling cotton. This yarn was dyed a soft brown for the narrow stripes, and there may have been a lighter shade of the same color used in the heel section. The warping was set up, insofar as we could follow it (fig. 401), with the maximum number of warps at the toe of the sandal and secured there with what was surely the initial twining, a wedge-shaped section (A), which can be seen also in figure 400a. This is the only section of the weaving which secures *all* of the initial warps. The left portion of the toe section (B, C, E) was woven, as was the first, with radiating wefts, using "fill-in"[2] wefts (D) when necessary. Warps begin to be eliminated in the curve (B) which moves around to the

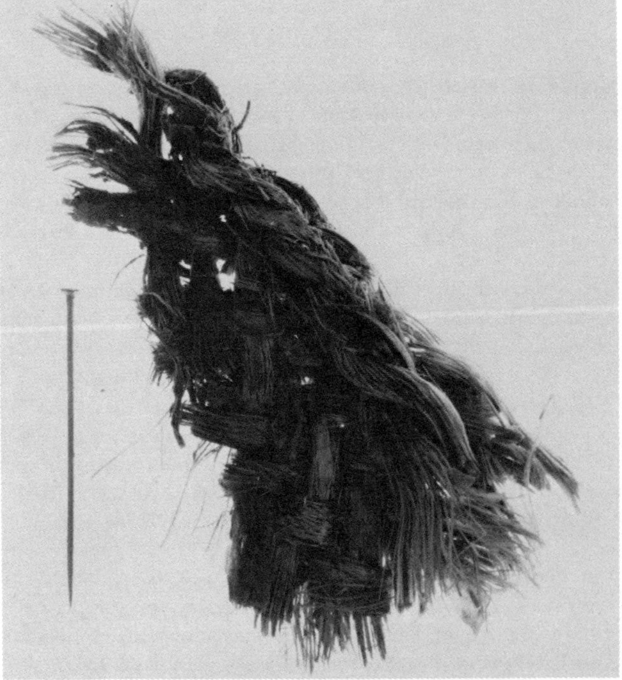

Figure 398. *Selvage fragment of twilled yucca sandal (12619/700).*

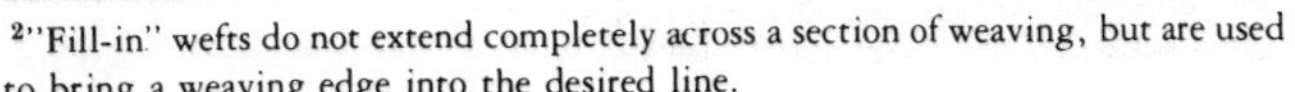

[2]"Fill-in" wefts do not extend completely across a section of weaving, but are used to bring a weaving edge into the desired line.

left; the maximum of 17 warps at the right toe section, which would equal 34 for the width of the sandal, is cut to 28 across the complete brown strip, and to 25 where the sandal is being narrowed for the heel at the broken end. The job added two warp elements along the left selvage at approximately the same height as the innermost loop of the warps. This elaborate warping is executed to produce the pointed right corner, the rounded left, and the toe jog which apparently were the height of fashion at this period at Mesa Verda.

Yucca strip sandals strive to produce the same shape, but the diagonal twilled plaiting, because of its bias nature, cannot produce the exact shape that this twined one exhibits. Wefts are tightly compacted with a count of 10 pairs to the centimeter; pitch is up to the right. Brown wefts were used for both elements of the twining pair in one band, which completely crosses the sandal, and for two short bands extending from the right selvage part way into the sandal, where they turn and move back to the selvage. The lower band of color uses a light and a dark yarn to make the pair, producing the "beaded" band. The lowest section, directly below this, is either stained or dyed a lighter shade of the brown.

The raised pattern of the sole is much worn. No yarns are used for this other than the weft pairs. When the tension on the weft on the upper surface is slightly released the wrapping is pulled to the lower surface.[3] In order to compensate for the thicknes of this wrapping and to keep the upper surface smooth, a row of plain twining is inserted between rows of the wrapped wefts. On the lower surface, these are concealed beneath the patterning, with is not elaborate (fig. 400b). It is obvious that these ridges took a great deal of the wear; indeed they must have offered an excellent "gripper" sole. Those parts of the pattern at the edge of the sandal are almost completely worn, exposing the warps in some sections. Still, the sandal is firm and tough; the wefts were so tightly compacted that the breaking of a number of them did not cause disintegration of the fabric.

[3] The handling of tension of one of the elements of a pair of turning wefts is shown clearly in Mason, 1904, figs. 23 and 24, p. 237, and figs. 25 and 26, p. 238. The two examples were designated "wrapped twining."

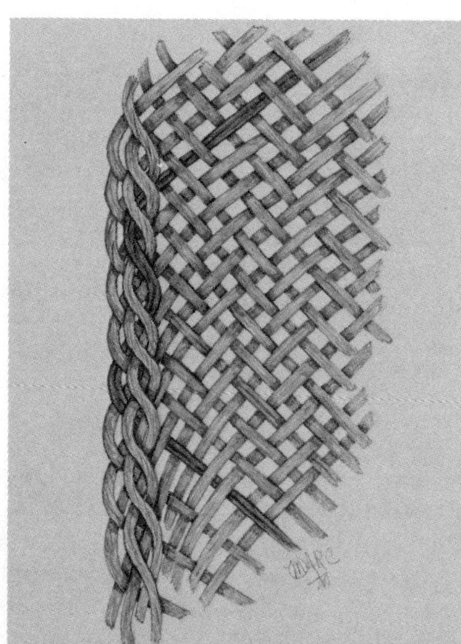

Figure 399. *Drawing showing construction of the selvage of sandal fragment illustrated in figure 398. One strip has been darkened to indicate the movement of each element as it approaches the edge and turns back into the plaiting order.*

Figure 400. *Twined, or "cloth," yucca twine sandal: a, upper surface with brown and natural wefts; and b, lower surface with wrapped pattern.*

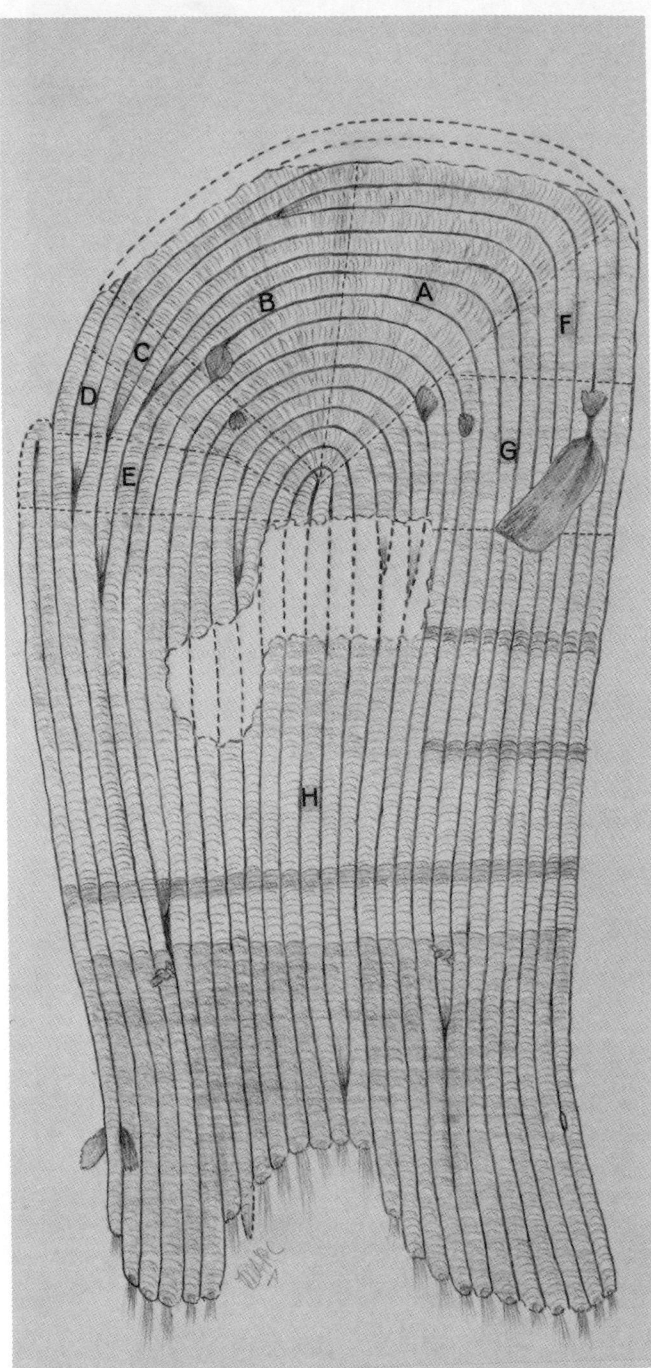

Figure 401. *Drawing of the upper surface of the sandal illustrated in figure 400.*

The sandal has basal segments of leather thong toe ties that appear to be overlapping double loops. A leather thong was inserted through the left side just above its break and a hole occurs on the opposite selvage. If these are remnants of ankle-instep loops, the length of the sandal is almost complete.

Much has been written by Southwestern archeologists about the use or non-use of "sandal lasts" for construction of jog-toed sandals. The construction of twill-plaited sandals at Mesa Verde began at the heel, and the formation of the jog was simply an alteration in the arrangement of elements; only nimble fingers were needed. The making of these sandals is simply an aspect of twilled basketry making, and no forms are ever used for such things.

Lacking the heel selvage of this twined sandal, it is impossible to see whether the warp was set up as illustrated in Kidder and Guernsey (1919, fig. 38, p. 104). However, unlike the coarser sandal illustrated from Ruin 7 in the Comb Ridge area, not all warps were continued to the heel in the Long House specimen. The warp, as I visualize it, consisted of 17 lengths of twine, secured by an initial row of twining and then by the outline wedge shaped section A (fig. 401), which set the curve of the toe end.

In making a trial reconstruction of the setup, I used a pair of wefts to secure the 17 warps with a row of twining. This was accomplished in the fingers simply by adding each warp as the wefts were twisted; the fold of the twining wefts was designated as the center of the sandal. This pair of wefts was then tied temporarily at the selvage. Three additional twining rows were set in beside the first, using it as a guide, each starting with a fold at the center and with the ends of the twining wefts temporarily tied at the selvage edge. These four were now spread apart into radiating lines, to be plainly seen in figure 400a, thus shaping the whole toe end of the sandal. The triangular wedges could now be filled, using the weft ends temporarily tied off at the selvage.

Immediately after section A was filled in with weft, the weaver began eliminating warps on the left to narrow the sandal. Weaving was flexible: warps were simply eliminated as the weaver desired a narrowing or shaping of the fabric. Yet at a point before which she had already eliminated several warps, she added the looped-end warp which forms the jog. No pattern or template would be needed for this; the two elements of the warp with the fold at the top could simply be added as the weft pair reached that selvage. The ends of all warps appear to have been loose and open throughout construction. This situation, also true of the Kidder and Guernsey sandal, was probably necessary because of the variation of takeup on the warps caused by the tight packing of the wefts and the wrapped pattern that falls only between some warps. When the weaver reached the desired length, the open warps were secured in some way (not known, in the case of the Long House sandal).

Weavers of fine twined bags, baskets, and blankets such as the Chilkat, using a non-rigid warp, generally work with the warp suspended, pushing the wefts upward for compaction (Mason, 1904, p. 516, fig. 147, and pls. 18 and 150). Fingers are used for this work. I would assume that the twined sandals with their non-rigid (yucca twine) warps were also woven suspended, the free ends of the warp dangling below the woven section. This makes it possible for the weaver's hands to operate on both surfaces, and it would have been almost a necessity in alining the wrapped weft elements.

To sum up, "sandal lasts" would not aid in shaping the warp and would be an actual hindrance in weaving insofar as they would limit finger manipulation of wefts to one surface. Indeed, technologically, there are no such things as sandal lasts.

YUCCA TWINE

Twine fragments were amazingly scarce in Long House. The excavations yielded only 553 lengths of yucca twine, totaling about 313 feet. The greatest single length of twine is a fur-strip wrapped piece from Area X, measuring 83.5 cm. Fourteen other lengths of fur-strip and/or feather wrapped twine were over 40 cm., the longest of these being slightly less than 68.5 cm. Nine additional pieces of twine measured over 40 cm., but these achieved their length by knots joining two or more fragments. There was no stockpile of unused twine.

Yucca fiber is easily obtained from the leaves of the plant. Dr. Welsh could make no distinction between fibers of the broad-leafed yucca (*baccata*) and the narrow-leafed yucca (*harrimaniae*) growing at Mesa Verde. We can probably assume that they were used as available without discrimination and that, therefore, the fiber for the bulk of our cordage was from *Yucca baccata.* For most of the twine, fiber was removed rather carelessly from the parenchymatous tissue: a twisting and untwisting of the twine will often discharge dried fleshy particles of the tissue.

Seven small bundles of prepared fibers were found. The three illustrated (fig. 402) show the poor separation of the fibers from tissue; but all of these were obviously prepared for twine making. Fibers for thigh twisting should be kept in parallel position and bundles of fibers were often tied in a loose overhand knot (fig. 402c) or were otherwise secured to maintain evenness.

Two specially prepared yucca fibers were used to make twine: well-separated fibers, warm gold in color, with all of the parenchymatous tissue removed, designated Class B fibers; and soft, white fibers which appear to have been pounded or rubbed and which superficially resemble cotton in its twine form, designated Class C fibers. Neither class of fibers is represented in the raw state at Long House, although there are fragments of twine and woven objects of both classes.

In this period of concern about standard terminologies, it is well to define the terms one has adopted. I have followed the terminology of the American Society for Testing Materials (1952): "Ply. The number of single yarns twisted together to form a plied yarn; also the number of plied yarns twisted together to form a cord." Herein, a 2-ply twine or cord is one in which the final twisting is of two plies even though each of these may already be plied yarns. *Twine* is used for simple 2-ply and 3-ply constructions. *Cord* is reserved for multitwists; the succession of twists is recorded in text and tables, beginning with the twist of the single and ending with the final twist.

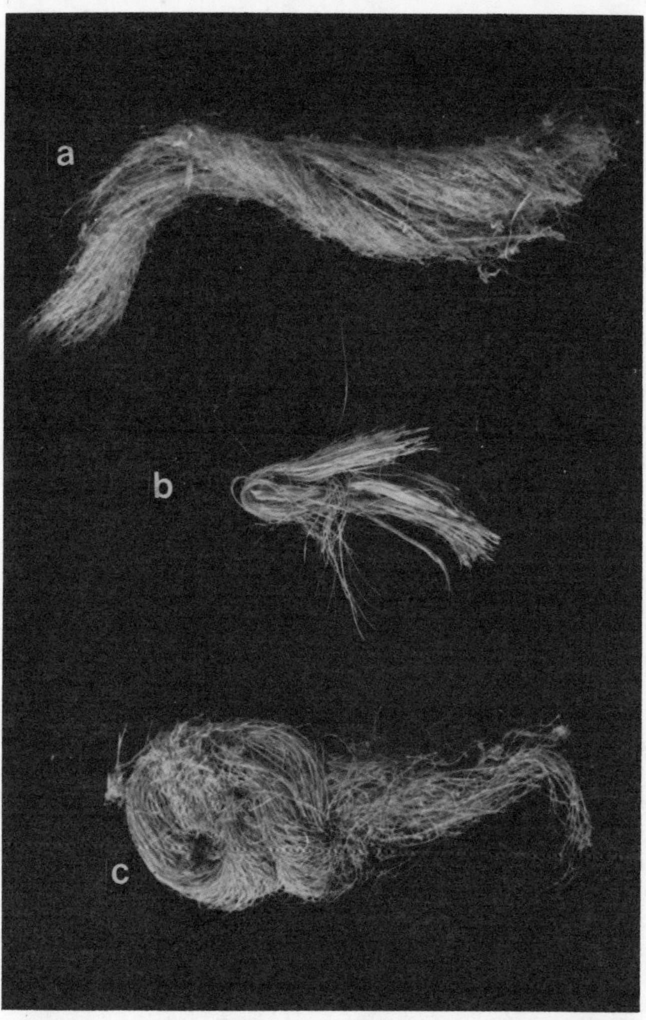

Figure 402. *Three bundles of prepared fibers; one of these (c) is tied in a loose overhand knot.*

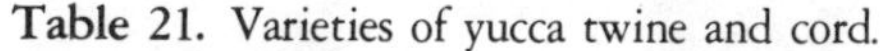

Table 21. Varieties of yucca twine and cord.

Total number of specimens: 553. Total length of twine: 9,540 cm. (312 feet, 10 inches). Twelve specimens unmeasurable. Average length: 17.6 cm. (7 inches).

Final Ply	Twist	No. of specimens	Percentage of total	Length of specimens (cm.)	Percentage of total
1-ply	S(1) Z(8)	9	1.4	130.5	1.4
2-ply	Z(singles S) (Fig. 403)	495	89.5	8,665.5	90.8
2-ply	S(singles Z) (Fig. 404)	22	4	282	3
3-ply	S(singles Z)	2	.4	18.5	.2
Multitwist cord final 2-ply					
4 singles	final Z (Fig. 406a)	13		187.5	
	final S	2		18	
8 singles	final Z (Fig. 406b and d)	2		49.5	
	final S (Fig. 405a)	1		20	
12 singles	final Z (Fig. 406c)	1		10	
final 3-ply					
6 singles	final Z	3		131	
	final S (Fig. 405b)	3		27.5	

Twist is expressed as S and Z. I do not use S-spun or Z-spun. The purpose of the American Society for Testing Materials standardization of spinning terminology is to remove any implication of motor activity from the finished product. Hence the recommendation to drop such terms as "clockwise," "anticlockwise," "left spun," and "right spun" in favor of S and Z hyphenated with the word "twist." It is intended to apply only to the angle of twist of the finished product as viewed by the analyst. By coupling the S- and Z- to the action verb "spin" or its past tense "spun," the motor activity is again being used and we are once more confronted with the complexity which prompted Amsden and others to call for clarification. Since there is no such action as S-spin and Z-spin, I reject S-spun and Z-spun as applied to yarn.

Spinning is used only when the dual processes of drawing out and twisting prevail; and *twisting* is used when drawing out is nonexistent or minimal.

The varieties of yucca twine found in Long House are summarized in table 21.

The yucca twine found in Long House was commonly 2-ply, with the singles given an S-twist and two singles plied to produce a Z-twist (89 percent), and was between 1 and 3 mm. in diameter (73 percent) and twisted to a hard degree (77 percent). The range of diameter, degree of twist, and types of yucca fiber are given in table 22. Figure 403d, f and h represent the more common varieties. The heavy emphasis on certain types of twine demonstrates both habit in motor action and, probably, limited uses of twine. The most prevalent type is that observed as twining wefts in the feather down blankets, certainly one of the primary uses of plain yucca twine.

The Class B and Class C fibers are represented sparingly in the twine series (figs. 403a-c and 404 a and c). The Class B fibers are observed as 2-ply twine three times as often with Z-twist as S-twist; the Class C fibers are almost equally seen with S-twist as Z-twists. This is interesting, because two woven objects we have from Long House—a twined sandal, 17422/700, and a twined tumpline fragment, 26512/700— make use of B fibers in 2-ply S-twist twine for warps, but the sandal has C fibers in 2-ply S-twist twine for wefts and the tumpline weft, though 2-ply S-twist, is not of the special fiber. The observation on the use of the special fibers in S-twist twine is not limited to Long House. Certainly the short lengths of these twines in Long House would hardly prompt a weaver to begin a sandal. Most of them are raveled from sandal destruction, but one twine length of Z-twist Class B fiber from Kiva H (12729/700), tapered to a few fibers at one end, represents either the beginning or the end of twine making. It appears to have been cut at the even end. Twines of Class B fibers also saw use as sewing twines; their slick surfaces and lack of fuzzy fibers not completely caught into the twist would facilitate pulling through.

Two-ply twines and S-twist (fig. 404) make up only 4 percent of the total by count. It should be noted that these twines are generally smaller in diameter (75 percent between 0.5 and 3 mm.) and of looser degree of twist (70 percent medium and loose) than 2-ply Z-twist twines. Furthermore, whereas the B fiber was used for

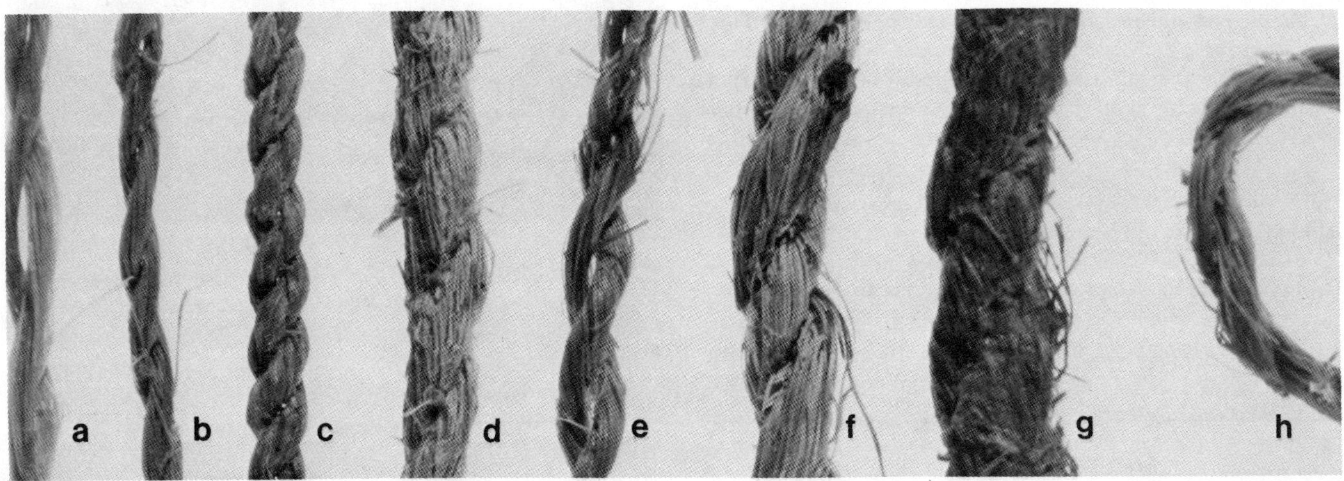

Figure 403. *Range of 2-ply Z-twist yucca twines; a-c use Class B fibers.*

Table 22. Range in diameter, degree of twist, and fibers of 2-ply yucca twine. Numbers reflect specimen counts and their respective percentages are in parentheses.

	Diameter					Degree			Total
	1 mm.	1–3 mm.	4–7 mm.	7+ mm.	crêpe	hard	medium	loose	
2-ply Z-twist									495(96)
Plain twine	3(.8)	263(73)	95(26.3)	1(.3)	5(1.4)	277(76.9)	72(20)	7(1.9)	
Feather wrapped		58(47)	65(53)	—	1(.8)	77(62.6)	45(36.6)	—	
Fur strip wrapped	—	3(60)	2(40)	—	—	3(60)	2(40)	—	
Fur-strip and feather wrapped	—	—	7	—	—	4(57.1)	3(42.6)	—	
2-ply S-twist									22(4)
Plain twine	4(20)	11(55)	3(15)	2(10)	—	6(30)	5(25)	9(45)	
Feather wrapped	—	—	—	—	—	—	—	—	
Fur-strip wrapped	—	—	2	—	—	1	1	—	
Fur-strip and feather wrapped	—	—	—	—	—	—	—	—	

only 4 percent of the 2-ply Z-twist twine, it was used for 25 percent of the S-twist twine; the C fiber, used for only 1 percent of the Z-twist twine, was used for 15 percent of the S-twist twine. We can do little more now than record this observation. The absence of these fibers in a raw state at Long House, their association primarily with the unusual (for Mesa Verde) direction of twist, and their use in the only two twined objects from Long House, pose problems of origin or selection which cannot be answered at present.

Of the 495 lengths of 2-ply Z-twist twine, 27.3 percent (135 lengths) were feather and/or fur strip wrapped. Neither of the special fibers was used for these constructions; they were not necessary. Nor was the 2-ply S-twist twine wrapped except for two lengths, both of which were fur-strip wrapped.

Fur strip wrapping in Long House was apparently a supplement to downquill wrapping, occasionally a mending, as it covers quills. Strips of fur, primarily from small animals, were cut to widths of 2 to 5 mm. and spirally wrapped on the twine. An unusual length is fur strip wrapped around 3-ply S-twist twine (12613/700). Although in the San Juan area fur strip wrapping generally appears in blankets of Basketmaker vintage, these fragments of twine can hardly be taken for remnants of that period. Nearly every feather blanket from Mesa Verde has a few strips of fur on some warp length.

Down-wrapped twine lengths are surely fragments from blankets and knotless netted socks. They often see secondary use such as jar rest wrappings and sandal ties. Most of the fragments have no down remaining, so an occasional bit of twine fully covered with bird down is the main evidence of the warmth and softness of these old constructions. Remaining quills are usually of the dull gray-brown color of the breast down of the turkey. A rare length of twine shows white quills from light colored down. Rarer still are the lengths of twine with light and dark quills in sections of the length. On one length of this twine (17433/700), it was noted that certain sections were stained with red color. No reason for this could be seen at the time the Long House twine analysis was made. Later I studied two blankets from Mesa Verde with patterns of light and dark down (one in the Colorado State Museum, one at the University Museum, University of Pennsylvania). Both had red ocher stains to mark the areas of wrapping with white down. Long House apparently at one time had such blankets.

A bundle of feather sections, split from the quills and retaining enough quill wall to hold the vanes, may have been prepared for twine making 12200/700). The downier feathers seem to have been preferred, but feathers from other sections of the turkey were used on twine. This bundle measures 9 cm., individual lengths are slightly shorter. As they now exist, they are too short to have been used for feathering arrows, and split feathers are not used on prayer sticks, apparently. A length of 2-ply Z-twist twine was mixed in with the bundle. The feathers were identified as *Meleagris gallopavo* by Lyndon Hargrave.

Multitwist cords (figs. 405 and 406) of both cable and hawser types made up 4.5 percent of all the twine (25 lengths). Their average length, in spite of their greatest strength, is no more than that of the 2-ply twines, that is about 17.5 cm. Cables, alternating direction at each twisting (i.e., S-Z-S, Z-S-Z, and S-Z-S-Z), make up half of the cords (13 lengths). The hawser twist, in which the first two twists are in the same direction and the final twist in the opposite direction (S-S-Z and Z-Z-S), is seen in only four specimens. The remainder of these multitwist cords use mixtures of twists such as S-Z-Z, and Z-S-S, and S-Z-Z-S. In many cultures, including our own, ropes and cords use the more even surface of the hawser (fig. 406a, although not a true hawser, shows this smoothness) for constructions in which easy slipping is desirable. Finding no objects made with these cords, we cannot know if the Long House people purposely made these twists or if the cords were constructed fortuitously. Two of the lengths were feather quill wrapped, one was fur strip wrapped. It is interesting, if not significant, that half of the multitwist ropes and cords were found in kivas.

Three other raw materials were used for yarn and twine construction: juniper bast, human hair, and cotton.

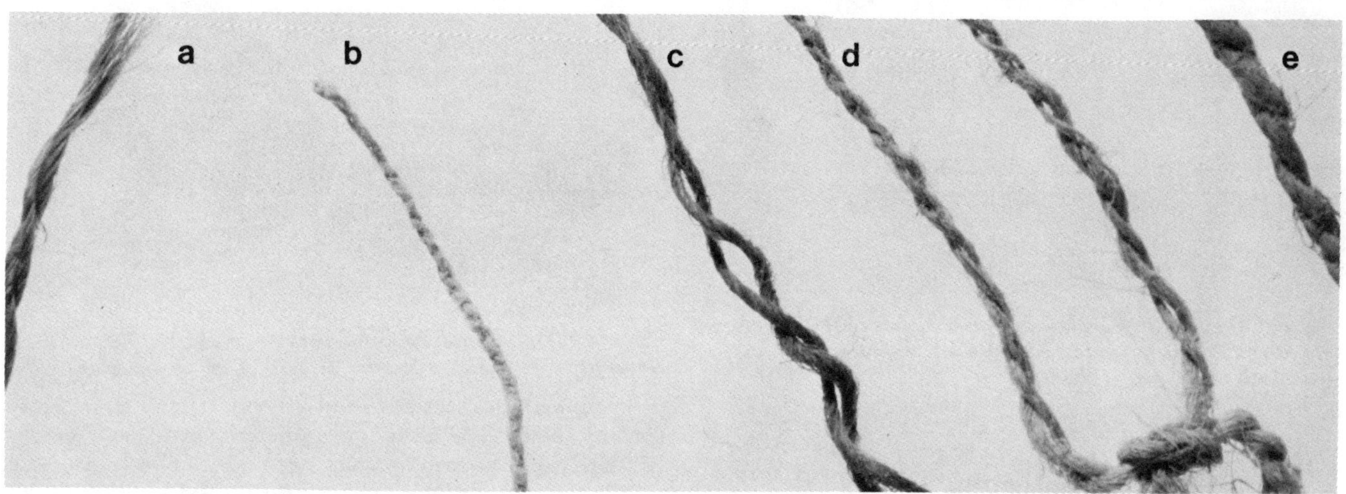

Figure 404. *Two-ply S-twist twines.*

Juniper bast was apparently twisted into twine occasionally for immediate use. The excavations turned up four lengths totaling 45 cm. There are no constructions making use of juniper bast twine. Two of the isolated lengths are 2-ply Z-twist; the other two are 1-ply extremely loose Z-twist. These bast twines have little strength.

Human hair twine, on the other hand, is seen primarily in finished form, as in a large fragment of knotless netting. The twine for this is 2-ply S-twist, about 1 mm. in diameter and twisted medium to hard in degree. One other length (fig. 407) had evidently been wrapped around some object: this is the only length of 2-ply human hair twine with Z-twist. It measures 54.6 cm. long, is a little greater than 1 mm. in diameter, and was twisted primarily to a hard degree. One untied bundle of human hair (fig. 408), from the surface at the west end of Long House, was probably saved for twine making. The maximum length of this hair is about 11.5 cm.

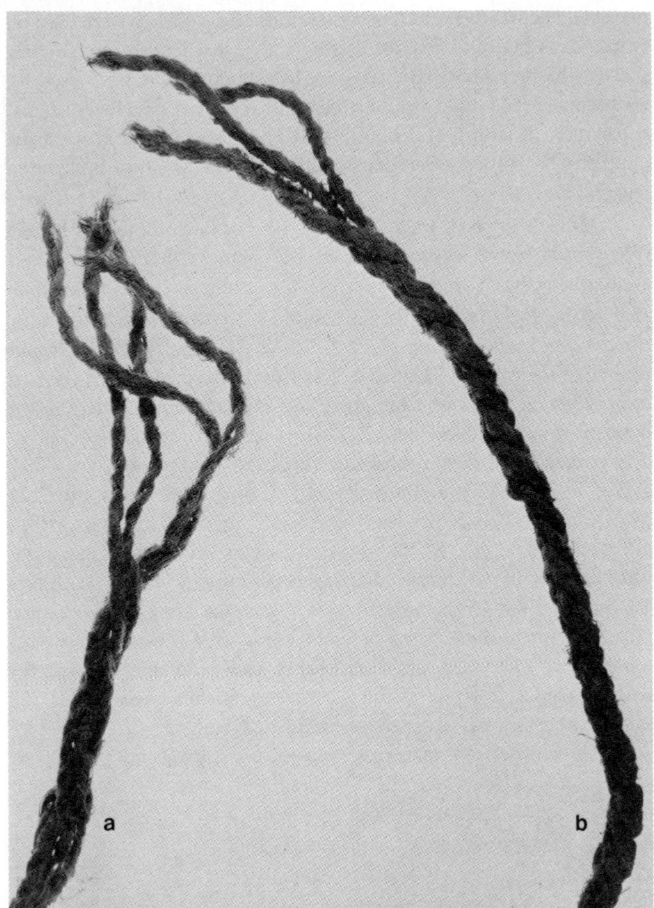

Figure 405. *Multitwist cords with final S-twist.*

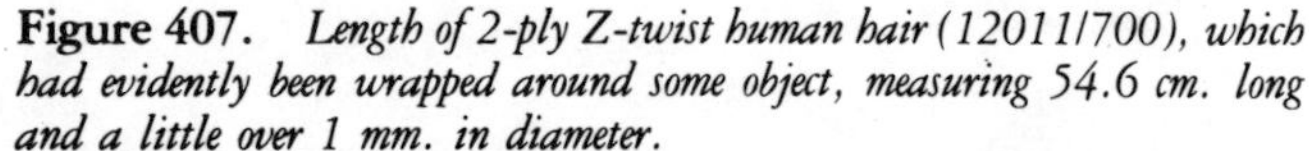

Figure 407. *Length of 2-ply Z-twist human hair (12011/700), which had evidently been wrapped around some object, measuring 54.6 cm. long and a little over 1 mm. in diameter.*

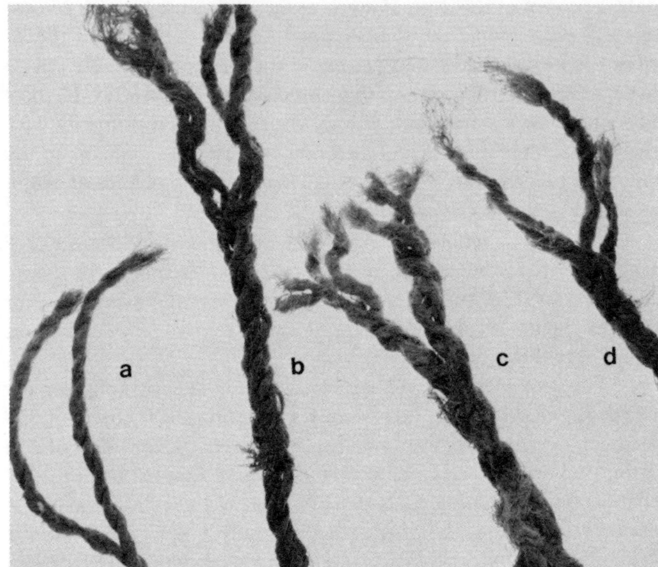

Figure 406. *Multitwist cords with final Z-twist.*

Figure 408. *Untied bundle of human hair (12091/700), probably saved for twine making, measuring about 11.5 cm. in maximum length.*

Cotton yarns are rare: there are only 10 lengths. None are unused yarns; all of them are apparently raveled from textiles. Examples are illustrated in figure 409: a, 2-ply S-twist (singles Z) (4); b, 6-ply S-twist (1); c, 3-ply S-twist (1); and 1-ply Z-twist (4), not shown. All are products of the same method of spinning, and all of them fall into the range of woven cotton yarns. One cotton yarn, 2-ply S-twist, was used to sew two lengths of leather together.

There was no raw cotton in Long House, nor even clumps of unspun staple. There are no hanks or bundles of yarn prepared for weaving. There are no complete spindles (probable whorls will be discussed later), much less any yarn on a spindle.

The presence of S-twist and Z-twist in the 2-ply yarns and twines may be summarized as follows: (1) yucca fibers of the common variety were generally plied in a Z-twist (96 percent); (2) yucca of B fiber was plied primarily in Z-twist (75 percent); (3) yucca of C fiber was plied about equally in Z-twist and S-twist; (4) juniper bast (if it is to be considered) was plied in Z-twist; (5) human hair was plied in both S- and Z-twist, but S-twist was the predominant form; and (6) cotton yarns were plied entirely in S-twist.

If the motor habit for thigh twisting at Long House produced 2-ply Z-twist twines, and if the ply known to have been produced by the spindle is S-twist (cotton), can we conclude that human hair and possible C yucca fiber were twisted and plied on a spindle? Or is it

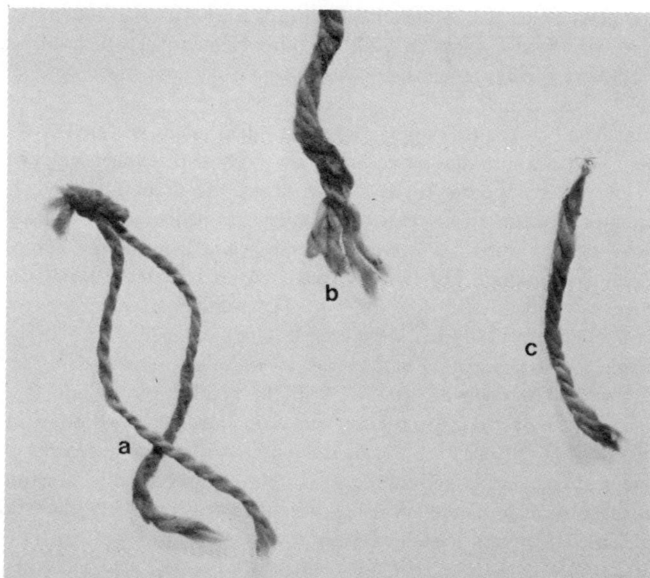

Figure 409. *Cotton yarn fragments; a, measuring 7.5 cm. in length, is the longest free cotton yarn found in Long House.*

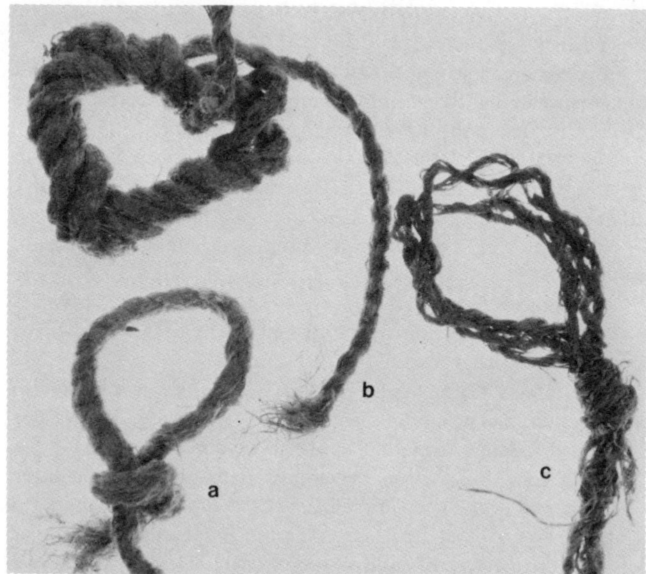

Figure 410. *Eye loops of yucca twine: a, openhand eye knot; b, running eye knot; and c, wrapped eye knot.*

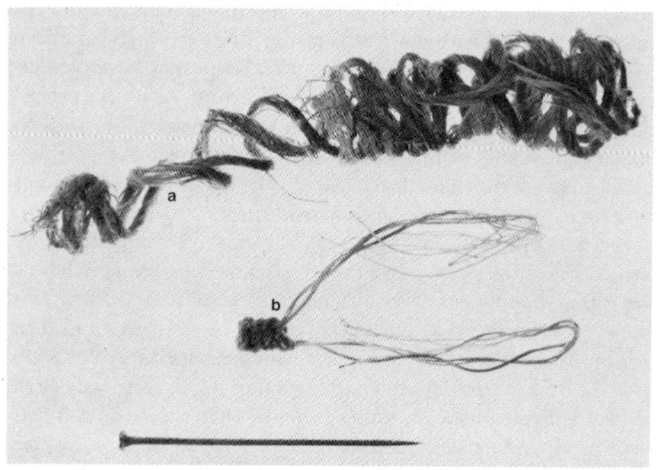

Figure 411. *(Left) Yucca twine objects: a, binding for a small object; and b, section of twine consisting of overhand knots. (Straight pin at right for scale.)*

Figure 412. *(Below) Three-strand flat braid of twisted yucca fiber.*

possible that the S-twist twines were not produced locally? Discussion of these questions is included in my study of larger collections of these materials from the Mesa Verde area.

Although it is probable that the bulk of yucca twine was used in the weaving of blankets, sandals, and tumplines, twine and cord served the ancient Indians for the myriad purposes they serve modern man. Sandal ties and loops along the sides of sandals, wrappings or bindings for wooden items, and mending of cracked pottery vessels are a few of the uses observed. Uncommon knots were featured in certain articles of which we have only fragments.

Three eye loops illustrated in figure 410 may be ends of nooses or snares, or simply slips for ties; a is an open hand eye knot (Graumont and Hensel, 1946, fig. 9, Pl. 1), formed by folding two lengths of twine and tying them at the base of the eye with a simple overhand knot; b, the simplest, is a running eye knot or bight (ibid., fig. 66, Pl. 26); and c was made by winding a length of twine into a circle and wrapping it completely with its own length.

The binding for some object, probably a small rod, is 6 mm. in inner diameter and 5 cm. long (fig. 411a). A section of fine 2-ply S-twist Class B yucca twine, consisting of a series of overhand knots, is 3 mm. in diameter and has no visible function (fig. 411b).

A 3-strand flat braid of untwisted yucca fiber is plaited from a fold at one end and knotted at the other (fig. 412). It shows no use.

BLANKETS

Excavations uncovered four blanket fragments and a small blanket enveloping the infant mummy placed in Room 28 (fig. 127b). All of these share the following characteristics:

(1) Warps of 2-ply Z-twist yucca twine, 4 to 5 mm. in diameter, set approximately two to the centimeter; for the most part, feather quill wrapped.

(2) Wefts of 2-ply Z-twist yucca twine, 3 to 4 mm. in diameter.

(3) Construction by twining; weft rows spaced irregularly, 1.5 to 4 cm. apart, with the pitch alternating from up to the left to up to the right, in adjacent rows.

The largest of the fragments (12613/700) is a much-mended corner section, measuring 41 cm. long by 21 cm. wide. The warp is primarily of the common twine, but there are variations up to a 3-ply multitwist cord (S-Z-S), and the edge warp is greater in diameter than the warps in the body of the blanket. The majority of the warp elements have no wrapping at present but indentations show that there was formerly tight quill wrapping, augmented by more fur strip wrapping than in any other blanket in the collection. In setting up the warp for this blanket (and the others which have an end selvage present), the warp loops were overlapped and were secured at the one selvage end remaining, with a twined row of four strands of 2-ply Z-twist twine. The pairs of twining wefts for the body of the blanket twist around each other between the second and third warps before beginning the return passage (fig. 413).

The second fragment (12009/700), found on the surface at the west end, is 20.3 cm. long by 6.4 cm. wide. No end selvages are present. The third fragment, found on the surface of Room 36, measures 15.2 cm. by 6.4 cm., and includes a section of corner construction. The warps have both down quill and fur strip wrapping with no apparent system of alternation. The end selvage section is, judging from the complete blankets studied, the opposite end from that of 12613/700. The warp loop ends are similarly overlapped but, instead of the twined row, a double weft beginning with a larkshead at the selvage weaves across the warps in plain weave. This probably represents the lower edge of weaving and may not have been inserted until weaving was finished. It presents a good argument for the twining of these blankets on loose hanging warps.

The fourth fragment (17324/700) is largely unwoven and tangled. There is a portion of end selvage with a heavy twined row; one element of the twining loomstring is a multitwist 2-ply yucca cord with final Z-twist (S-Z-Z); the other element, of which only a very short portion remains, appears to be a 6-ply cord made up of 2-ply-Z-twist twine.

The blanket enveloping the mummified infant was tied at the head area and near the lower end of the body with feather-wrapped twine. There appears to have been also a tie around the whole bundle. It seems to me that the blanket was deliberately cut away from the face: warps are severed in a straight line here and the selvage section is missing. The twined loomstring end is at the head, the plain-woven loop end is at the foot. The blanket measures 80 cm. long (warp) by 130 cm. wide (weft). There are 127 warps in the blanket, making a total of 333 feet of warp, fur strip and feather wrapped. There are 26 weft rows in the blanket proper and four lengths of weft twined at the top and plain woven at the bottom. A total of 273 feet of twine was used for weft. (All of the fragments of wrapped twine in Long House totaled 87 feet, and the total amount of twine suitable for weft was 138 feet. It can easily be seen that the ancient inhabitants wasted nothing.)

The bulk of the warps are wrapped with down; both the light down and the more common taupe were used, but no pattern could be seen except for an area of light down at the lower edge. There is no red ocher on these bare warps. However, of the 127 warps, the four nearly central ones (53–57) were wrapped with fur strips. This change must once have made a decorative stripe down the middle of the back of the wearer. Other isolated fur strips may have provided contrast, possibly of color and certainly of texture. As it once existed, the blanket had an area of light down at the lower edge, with the body of the textile of mottled taupe and light down and a stripe of about 5 cm. of fur through the center. The infant that wore it must have been warmly and elegantly provided for.

The upper selvage (fig. 413a) consists of overlapped warps secured below the loops with a row of heavy twining with pitch up to the right. The weaver used for this four lengths of 2-ply Z-twist twine, loosely twisted together (Z-twist) and begun with a fold at the corner. At the bottom of the blanket, four wefts used together weave in and out of the overlapped warp loops (fig. 413c). The body of the blanket is twined with rows alternating in pitch and with weft pairs twisting around each other between the first and second or the second and third warps in descending to the next row (fig. 413b). Wefts are spaced 4.5 to 5 cm. apart. The blanket is more closely woven than many such specimens.

Figure 413. *Selvages of remnants of feather quill-wrapped blanket: a, upper selvage with heavy twined row; b, side selvage showing twisting of weft pairs between second and third warps; and c, lower selvage with four wefts in plain weave.*

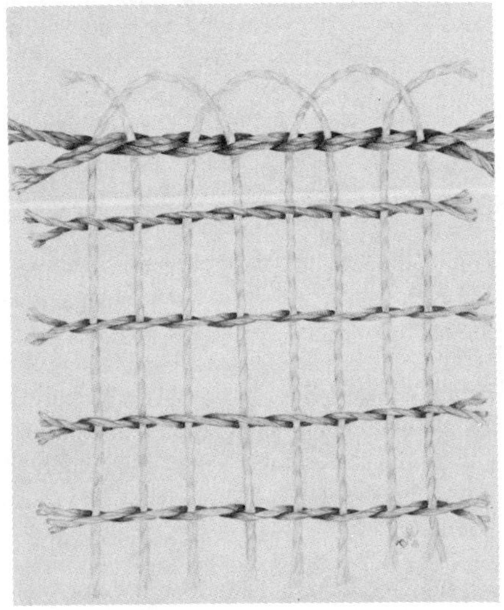

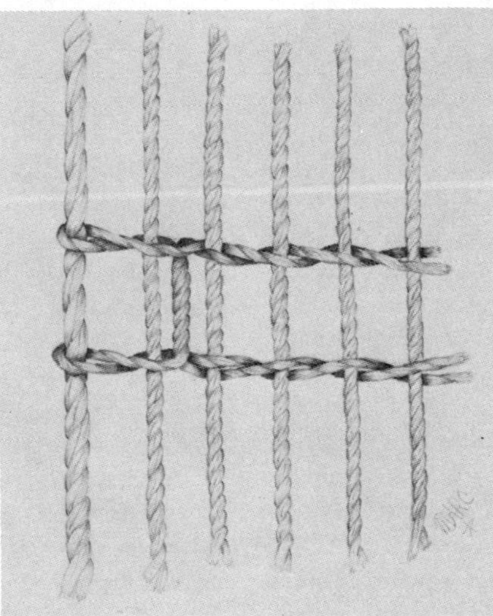

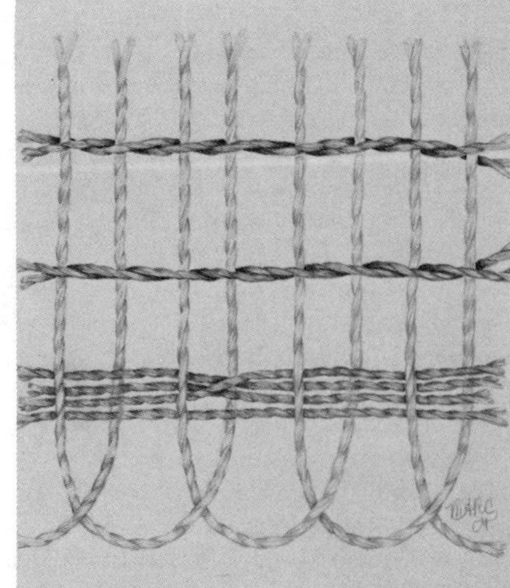

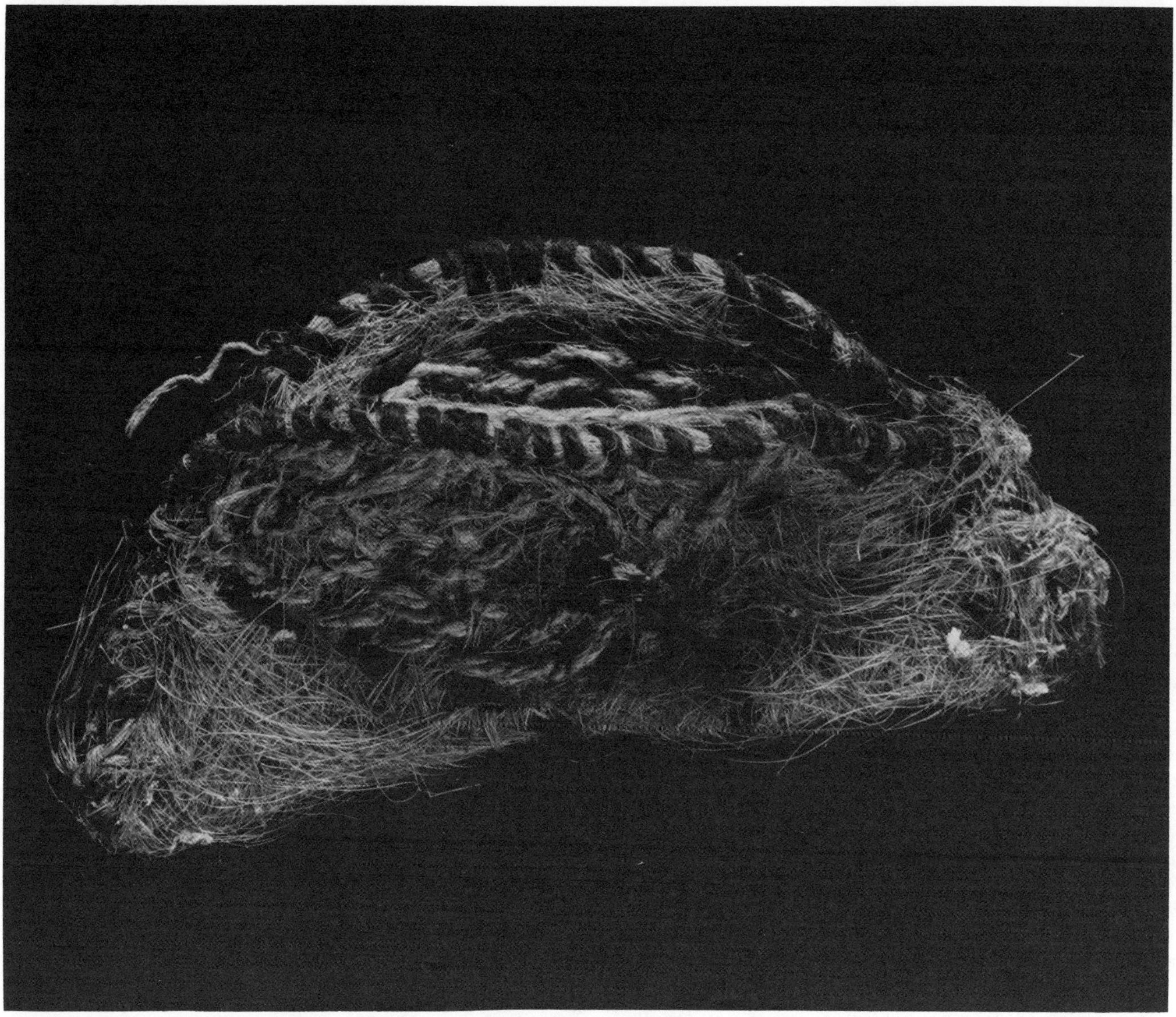

Figure 414. *A small pouch of semifelted or matted yucca fiber (12288/700) from fill in Room 3.*

Figure 415. *Schematic drawing of construction of pouch illustrated in figure 413.*

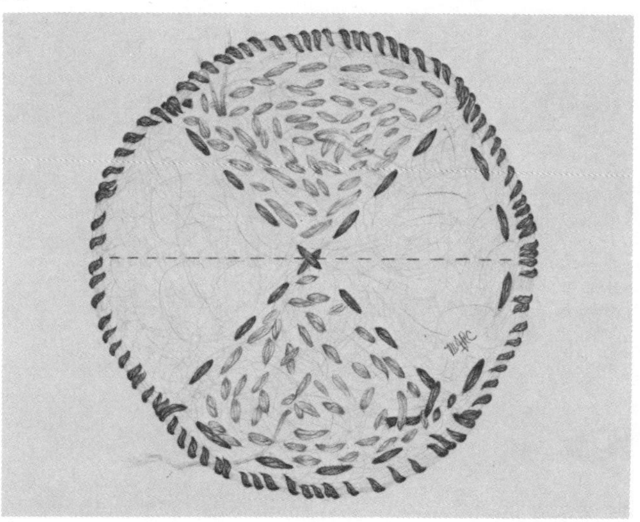

POUCH

A small pouch of semifelted or matted yucca fiber (fig. 414) was made in the following way: separated yucca fiber was laid out in a flat circle, 12.5 cm. in diameter, with fibers crossing in all directions to a thickness of about 4 mm. The two opposite quarter sections were then outlined with a running stitch of dark brown twine (2-ply S-twist) and randomly stitched in the segments with 2-ply S-twist yucca fiber C twine (fig. 415). The whole outer circumference was whipped over the edge with the dark brown twine, then folded in half, and the two edges were whipped up the sides from the fold for about 4 cm., forming a small, partially closed pouch. I have seen identical items from other Mesa Verde proveniences and from southeast Utah. One from Grand Gulch (Colorado State Museum, Mellinger Collection) was in a woman's work basket containing twines of various types and a sharp bone awl. Their most obvious function would be as awl cases, the openness of the yucca fiber mass permitting the threading of a sharp point many times into the wall. Several of the items seen are partially sewed up the sides, as is this one.

BASKETS

Twilled ring baskets are well known from Mesa Verde, but only a fragment of one was found during the Project's excavations of Long House (fig. 416). The estimated diameter of the basket is 38 cm. and the depth is approximately 5 cm. (the fragment had been considerably flattened). Yucca strips of natural color, 4 to 5 mm. wide, were woven into a 3/3 twill mat. There is evidence of a design pattern toward the center of the basket, where some elements pass over five of the strips moving in the opposite direction. After weaving, the elements around the edge of the mat were folded over a rod of willow (*Salix* sp.), 8 to 9 mm. in diameter, and were secured with a twisted row of split yucca strips.

The number of elements held in one twining stitch varies from three to seven. Figure 417 shows the plaited band of yucca strips as it now appears; no attempt has been made to reconstruct it according to any one of several methods of completing this type of plaiting. It is a loose 6-element band, begun by looping the strip at midsection through the basket above every other twined stitch. These elements, moving to the left, proceed in an over 1, under 1 plain weave; the darkened strip in the figure shows the movement of one of these strips.

Two hoops of oak (*Quercus gambelii* Nutt. and *Quercus* sp.) were found in Long House. Weavers of ring baskets in present-day pueblos (Williamson, 1937, p. 38) usually prepare such items in a variety of sizes when the wood is cut and easily bent, and tie them in rings as they are drying so that they will retain their shape. One of the hoops is complete (fig. 418, left). It was peeled, trimmed for an overlap of 13.5 cm., and bound in three places with yucca strips, each individually wrapped by starting at midsection and square knotting the ends together. There is some evidence that this hoop was once used in a ring basket and saved for re-use. A series of indentations on the inside of the hoop was, perhaps, left by the tight binding of basket elements. The diameter of the hoop is 15.5 cm; that of the withe is 6 mm.

The second hoop is incomplete (fig. 418), right). It was peeled and measures 14 cm. in maximum diameter. Unfortunately, no ties remain on this hoop.

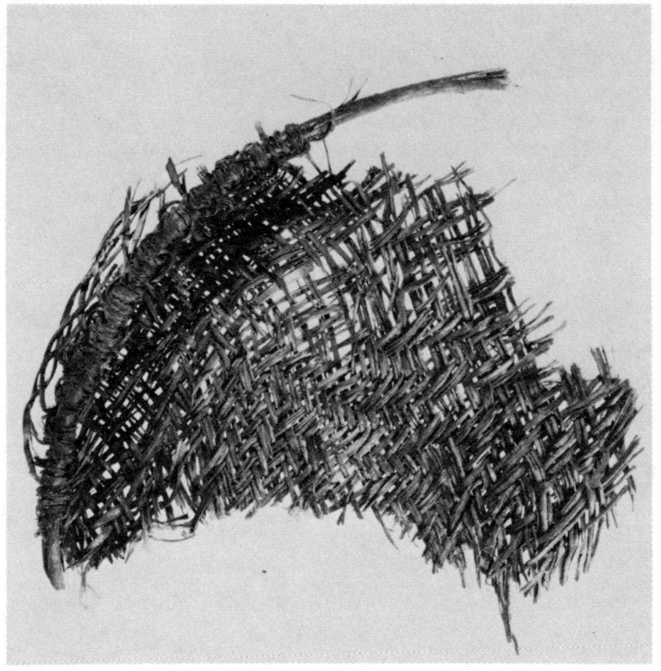

Figure 416. *Fragment of twilled yucca strip ring basket, with twined row of split yucca strips on the outside of the rim (17377/700), from Level VI, Room 7.*

Figure 417. *Drawing of exterior of fragmentary twilled yucca strip ring basket illustrated in figure 416, showing twined row of split yucca strip securing the elements over the rod and the plaited six-element band of yucca strips covering the cut-off ends of the elements.*

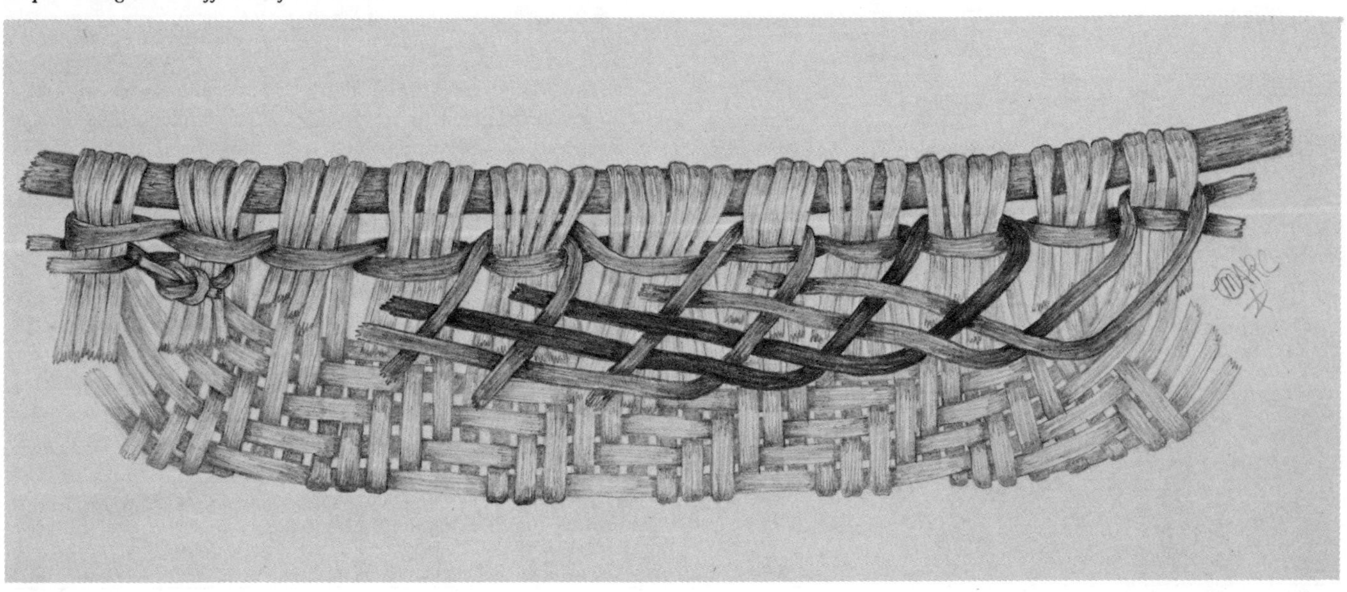

Figure 418. *Two rings of oak, presumably prepared hoops for ring baskets: left, complete peeled ring, 13.5 cm. in diameter, bound in three places with yucca strips (12164/700), from niche in ventilator shaft, Kiva I; and right, incomplete peeled ring, 14 cm. in maximum diameter (12417/700), from disturbed fill, Room 17.*

Table 23. Coiled basketry.

Illus. Proven. Cat. No.	Size (cm.)	Foundation	Sewing	Remarks
Fig. 419a and b, & 420a and b Kiva I, vent. shaft. 12156/700	complete, 40 in diam. at mouth, 12.5 deep	*Salix* sp.; 2-rod and bundle, 3-rod bunched; 2 coils to 15 mm.	*Salix* sp.; 5 stitches to 10 mm.	Simple stitch, non-interlocking (Morris & Burgh, 1941, figs. 3, *j*, and 4, *b*). See text for details.
Fig. 421a and b Kiva I, vent. shaft. 12157/700	complete, 22 in diam. at mouth, 6.5 deep	*Salix* sp.; 3-rod bunched, 2 coils to 12 mm.	*Salix* sp.; 4–5 stitches to 10 mm.	Simple stitch, non-interlocking (Morris & Burgh, 1941, fig. 4,*b*). See text for details.
Fig. 422 Room 3, fill 12286/700	bottom missing, 32 in diam. 9 deep	*Salix* sp. & *Yucca* sp.; 2-rod & bundle, bunched, 2-coils to 10 mm.	*Salix* sp.; 6 stitches to 10 mm.	Simple stitch non-interlocking (Morris & Burgh, 1941, fig. 3, *j*). See text for details.
Fig. 423 Kiva I, vent. shaft. 12222/700	fragment, 4.5 in diam.	1-rod & 2-ply Z-twist yucca twine, 2 coils to 13 mm.	*Salix* sp.	Beginning coils: simple stitch, non-interlocking. See text for details.
Fig. 424 Surface, west end. 12002/700	fragment, 13.5 wide x 2.5 deep	*Chrysothamnus*; 3-rod bunched, with 2-rod bundle at top coil; 2 coils to 10 mm.	*Salix* sp.; 7 stitches to 10 mm.	Simple stitch, non-interlocking (Morris & Burgh, 1941, figs. 3, *j*, and 4, *b*). See text for details.
Fig. 425 Room 44, fill 12533/700	fragment 3.5 wide x 1 high	*Salix* sp.; splint bundle	*Salix* sp. 3 stitches to cm.	Simple stitch, non-interlocking (Morris & Burgh, 1941, fig. 3, *e*). See text for details.
Room 10, fill 12369/700	fragments, largest is 10.5 wide x 4 deep	*Salix* sp.; 3-rod bunched, 2 coils to 10 mm.	*Salix* sp. 6 stitches to 10 mm.	Simple stitch, non-interlocking, splitting the top rod (Morris & Burgh, 1941, fig. 4, *b*).
Room 60, Lev. V. 17667/700	5 fragments, largest 3.5 wide x 5 deep	*Salix* sp.?; 3-rod bunched, 2 coils to 10 mm.	? 6 stitches to 10 mm.	Reduced to charcoal; simple stitch, non-interlocking (Morris & Burgh, 1941, fig. 4,*b*).
Kiva O, surface 20228/700	fragment, 4.2 wide x 2 deep	*Salix* sp.; 2-rod & bundle, bunched; 2 coils to 12 mm.	*Salix* sp.; 5 stitches to 10 mm.	Simple stitch, non-interlocking (Morris & Burgh, 1941, fig. 3,*j*).
Area X 20352/700	fragment, 4.5 wide x 2 deep	*Salix* sp.; 2-rod & bundle, bunched; 2 coils to 11 mm.	*Salix* sp.; 6 stitches to 10 mm.	Simple stitch, non-interlocking (Morris & Burgh, 1941, fig. 3, *j*).

Figure 419. *Coiled basket, 40 cm. in diameter and 12.5 cm. deep (12156/700), from tunnel, Kiva I: a, three-quarters view; and b, interior view.*

Coiled baskets are much better represented in the Project's collection from Long House than twilled baskets (table 23). Two very fine bowl-shaped baskets, with a kiva jar nested within them, had been thrust into the longer section of the ventilator tunnel in Kiva I (fig. 79). The larger basket (fig. 419) measures 40 cm. in diameter and 12.5 cm. deep. One section of the rim of the basket has disintegrated but the basket itself shows little wear, even on the base. No colored sewing elements and no design are visible.

The foundation of the coiling consists of two rods of willow (Salix sp.) and a third rod, also of willow, so split by the sewing element that it resembles a splint bundle, or was a splint bundle originally. These elements are bunched (Morris and Burgh, 1941, fig. 3, *j* and 4, *b*); two rows of coiling measure 15 mm. at the top of the basket and are slightly narrower toward the base.

Stitching is with willow splints, 2 to 3 mm. wide and spaced about five to the centimeter. The stitches are not interlocked; they penetrate the splints (?) at the top, and there are few split stitches. Coiling proceeded counterclockwise. Except for 1.5 cm., the rim of the basket was finished with false braiding (fig. 420). The lacing of this single element construction through the top coil to cover the final stitching served both as a reinforcement of the edge and an ornamentation. The drawing shows the progression of the elements (including the mistakes of the weaver) in one section of the rim. In most instances, the element passes straight through the coil but occasionally, in going through the basket between grouped stitches, it is on a diagonal line and emerges at the next group.

Nested in the large coiled basket was a slightly smaller one in almost perfect condition (fig. 421). It measures 22 cm. in diameter by 6.5 cm. in depth. Very similar to the former in construction, the foundation is three-rod bunched throughout, of willow, with each row about 6 mm. wide.

The sewing is of willow splint, 4 to 5 stitches to the centimeter and entirely of natural color. Each stitch penetrates the upper rod with few split stitches and with the stitches non-interlocking. Coiling proceeds counterclockwise. The rim is finished with only 3.5 cm. of false braiding where the foundation tapers and terminates.

Another coiled basket, much worn but beautifully constructed, lacks its base (fig. 422). The Long House people probably would have sewed in a replacement base had circumstances not intervened. Many such mendings have been observed in Mesa Verde specimens and the general condition of the basket warranted this repair. The coil foundation is of two rods of willow and a splint bundle (in some areas at least, this bundle is of yucca strip), bunched, with two coils to the centimeter. Stitching is of willow, non-interlocking, and it

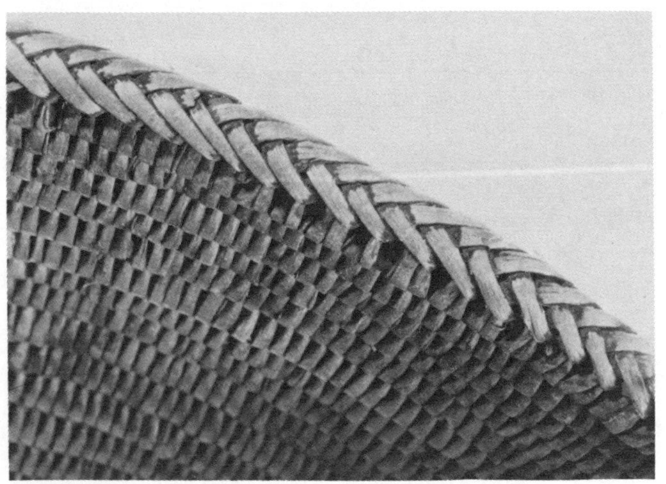

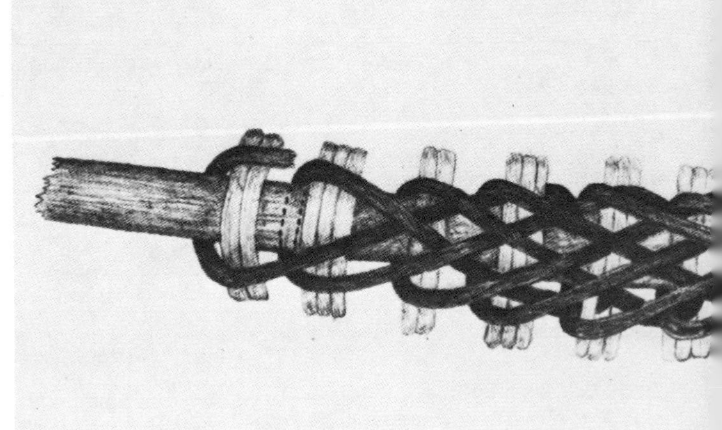

Figure 420. *False braid on rim of coiled basket illustrated in figure 419: a. three-quarters view of about 6 cm. of the rim; and b. drawing of false braid construction as viewed from the top.*

penetrates the bundle only. The rim is irregularly broken but there is no false braiding present in any intact section. There are four isolated dark figures about 2.5 cm. below the rim that vaguely resemble ducks. Because of wear on the interior of the basket, these are visible only on the exterior. The basket measures 32 cm. in diameter by 9 cm. in depth.

A coiled basket beginning, or possibly the broken out base of such a basket, 4.5 cm. in diameter, uses for foundation a single rod bent and pinched, and a length of 2-ply Z-twist yucca twine (fig. 423). Stitching is non-interlocking even here, with stitches penetrating or going under the yucca twine.

A small fragment, measuring only 13.5 cm. wide by 2.5 cm. deep, was cross sectioned to show use of three-rod foundation, with a two-rod and bundle foundation at the top coil. The foundation material is rabbitbrush (*Chrysothamnus* sp.), and the sewing material is willow splint. The shallow penetration of the non-interlocking stitching into the top rod or bundle of the foundation may be clearly seen (fig. 424.)

A tiny fragment is the lone representative of a coiled basket with a splint bundle foundation (fig. 425). Stitching is non-interlocking. Judging by the lack of curve, this fragment was not the coiling beginning. Morris and Burgh (1941, fig. 3, *e*) refer to this type as Basketmaker III and Pueblo IV-V (Hopi).

Profile drawings of the three whole baskets from Long House are shown in figure 426. The upper two baskets, from the tunnel in Kiva I, are essentially the same bowl shape; the straight-sided, finely woven basket at the bottom, from the fill of Room 3, is also a Pueblo III type, but this seems to be rarer at Mesa Verde than the bowl shape. All of the constructions, except for the tiny fragment (fig. 425), fall into the classic Pueblo period; we could dismiss this fragment, with a splint bundle foundation, as a freak of Pueblo III times if it were not for the known Basketmaker III horizon at Long House. The fragments present on the upper ledge may be due to the agility of our wild feathered friends.

Parts of a twig, a partially split twig, and a splint of willow (*Salix* sp.) are shown in figure 427. All parts of small willow stems were used: whole stems such as a, when peeled, made up the foundation of many baskets; twigs with two sections of outer bark and two of inner bark, such as b, made up the bundle of the foundation, while fine sections of these formed the sewing elements; and splints, such as c, were suitable for sewing. The last were found in various places, but no large coils of prepared basketry materials, either for foundation or sewing, were found in Long House.

Figure 421. *Coiled basket, 22 cm. in diameter and 6.5 cm. deep (12157/700), from tunnel, Kiva I: a, three-quarters view; and b, interior view.*

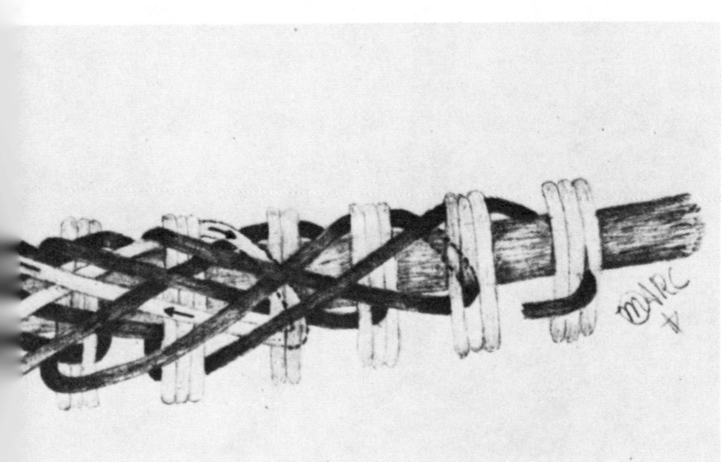

Figure 422. *Coiled basket, lacking the base, is decorated with small ducklike figures on the exterior (12286/700); from the fill of Room 3.*

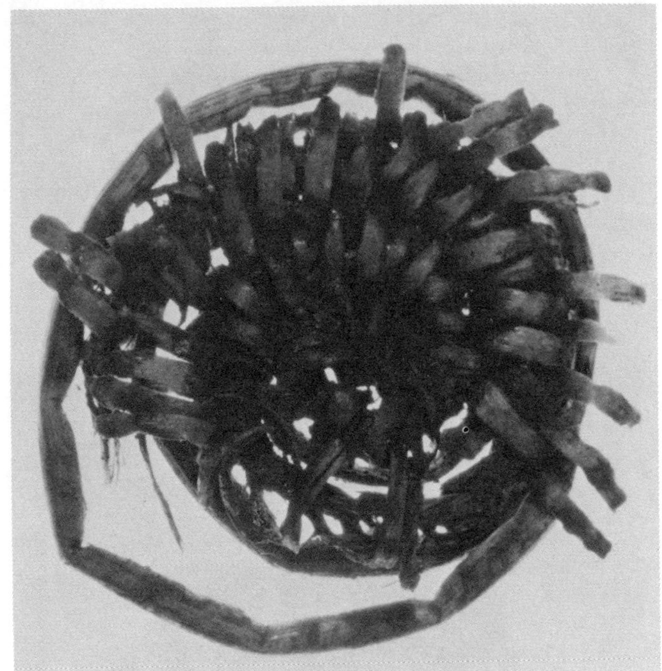

Figure 423. *Coiled basket beginning or broken-out base (12222/700) from tunnel, Kiva I.*

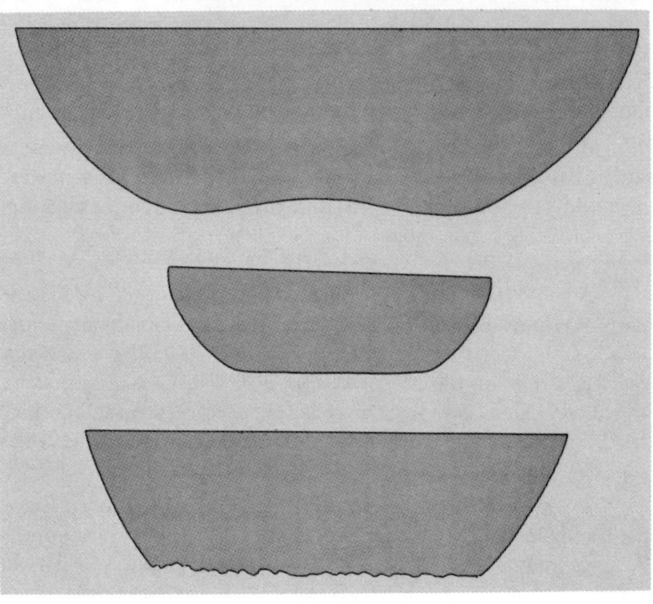

Figure 426. *Cross section drawing of the three baskets illustrated in figures 419, 421, and 422.*

Figure 424. *Cross section of a coiled basket fragment using three-rod bunched foundation, with a two-rod and bundle foundation at the top coil (12002/700), from the surface at west end of Long House.*

Figure 425. *Tiny fragment of a coiled basket with splint bundle foundation (12533/700) from fill of Room 44.*

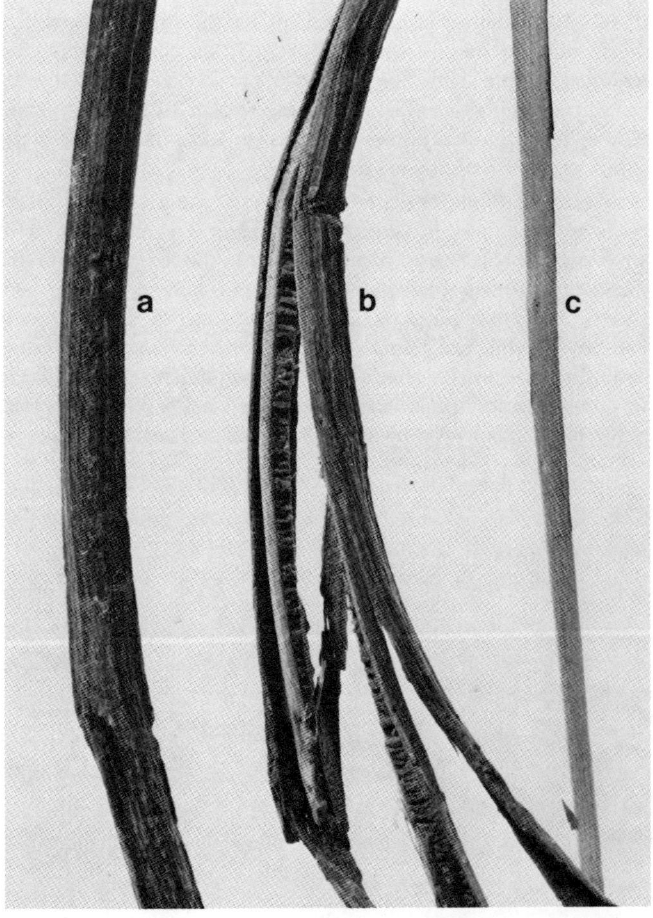

Figure 427. *Part of a twig (a), a partially split twig (b), and a splint (c) of willow used in coiled basketry at Long House.*

TUMPLINE

A small selvage fragment of a tumpline (26512/700), measuring 66 by 3.5 cm., was found at the head of the East Trash Slope. The warp of the fragment is 2-ply S-twist twine of Class B yucca fiber; the weft is 2-ply S-twist yucca, scratchy, perhaps partly because of its hard twist. Warp-weft count is three by seven (twined pairs) to the centimeter; construction is twined with pitch up to the right and a simple turn at the selvage.

KNOTLESS NETTING

A fragment of knotless netting of human hair twine measures 25 cm. long by 29 cm. wide (fig. 428). The fragment has no definable finished form, but the great majority of human hair network specimens from Mesa Verde are leggings. The netting element is 2-ply S-twist, diameter about 1 mm., and twisted to a hard degree. Kent (1957, fig. 98, G) calls this "closed loop netting." The mesh is very fine, between 3 and 4 mm.; meshes touch each other (fig. 429). In reconstructing the netting with this fine mesh, we found small sticks extremely useful: they served not only as gages to maintain evenness of mesh size but prevented the loops from turning or rotating and having to be straightened for each looping. O'Neale (1945, fig. 75, *d*) illustrates sticks being used in Guatemala for close knotless netting. Small peeled and smoothed wooden rods of the proper diameter for this network have been found in all sites at Mesa Verde. One of these from Long House (12287/700) is shown in figure 428.

Netting, in contrast to knitting, is a construction using a finite yarn; that is, an end is needed for its construction. The length of the element can be, and usually is, extended by the use of a bobbin, commonly called a netting shuttle, or needle, on which a quantity of yarn can be wrapped. In this case, the bobbin itself is an end. I have never seen a winding device from this area. We must assume, therefore, that the end of the human hair twine was itself used for passing through the loops; this would have been aided by the use of stick gages, and even more by slender eyed needles. Long House produced only two tools which might have been used as lacing or netting needles: a bone needle or bodkin (fig. 363c) and a wooden needle (fig. 441), although neither of these will pass through the mesh of this net. If an end of the twine itself was used, lengths would have had to be short. There is no visible knotting of these ends, and the maker apparently twisted the ends together carefully to give a knotless continuity. The finished piece was probably highly valued: it had been much mended with a fine yucca strip and fine 2-ply Z-twist yucca twine. Human hair lacks elasticity, and although looped networks by their open construction have some "give," the fine mesh of this example lessens the quantity so that undue strain would snap the twine.

Figure 428. *(Above, right) Fragment of knotless netting of human hair twine, measuring 25 cm. long and 29 cm. wide (20018/700), from the floor of Room 81. (Divider tips 1 inch apart.) A small peeled wooden rod of a diameter suitable for the network is shown at right.*

Figure 429. *(Right) Detail of knotless netting illustrated in figure 428, showing close mesh and yarn twist. (Divider tips 1 inch apart.)*

COTTON TEXTILES

Thirteen ragged fragments of cotton cloth were found. Their proveniences, dimensions, and descriptions of selvage, yarns, and construction are set forth in table 24. Two of the fragments have embroidery in natural white cotton yarn. All of the woven fragments are in plain weave, one-over-one. The small fragment of plaiting could not be analyzed because of the lack of both selvages and sufficient length.

Embroidery on a small fragment is limited to a rectangle, 2.5 by 1.2 cm., near the side selvage, with stitches of 2-ply S-twist cotton yarn parallel to the warp (fig. 430). The embroidery is in running and double running stitches (Pesel, n.d., pls. 36 and 37) and whipping stitches beginning or ending with a thumb knot. This rectangle appears to have been rubbed at one time with red ocher.

The medallion with tassels illustrated in figure 431, about 4 cm. in diameter, is not necessarily a fragment, although this object was made from a former textile and has no portions of selvage remaining. On a plain weave foundation, running and double running stitches were spirally applied to form a firm and considerably thicker circle. The raveled warps extend at both ends; at one end these warps are gathered, loosely twisted (S-twist) in a group. Throughout this tassel are fragments of wefts in place, showing that it was not left unwoven originally. The embroidery yarn is 2-ply S-twist cotton. One surface and parts of the raveled ends were heavily coated with red ocher.

The cotton textile fragments in the Project's collection from Long House may be briefly summarized: (1) all of them are small; (2) only two have portions of end selvages (loomstring), and two have portions of side selvages; (3) with one exception, all are plain weave, one-over-one; and (4) all are woven with 1-ply Z-twist warp and weft of natural white color. The two loomstring ends have an identical technique for securing the warp loop ends. Textiles were well woven, even, fine, showing excellent control of both spinning and weaving techniques but little variety. The lone attempt at decoration is a bit of crude embroidery with cotton yarns of natural fiber color.

MISCELLANEOUS VEGETAL OBJECTS

Twig bundles

Bundles of plant sections, probably gathered at specific times of the year and carefully preserved (and dried?) for future use, are of considerable interest. Two of these are bundles of stems and leaves loosely wrapped and tied with yucca strips. One, of rabbitbrush (*Chrysothamnus* sp.), is a slightly curved bundle of twigs including dried leaf remnants, 14 cm. long and 3 cm. in diameter. A tie of narrow yucca strips is now quite loose, because individual twigs have been removed or because of centuries of drying. One coiled basket from Long House uses rabbitbrush twigs for foundation material. Whiting (1950, p. 95) lists several uses of the plant by the Hopi—most of these are concerned with its excellent dyeing properties. A more unusual use, in view of the provenience of this bundle on the floor of a kiva, is that *Chrysothamnus* is one of the four fuels used in kivas, as reported by Hough (1897).

The other bundle, of sage (*Artemisia* sp.), is also a loosely wrapped and tied bundle of twigs and leaves, 15 by 5.5 by 1.5 cm. Narrow yucca strips wrap the bundle with a cross on one surface and are square knotted for length and for the ending. Since none of our manufactured items make use of the leafy twigs of sagebrush, it may perhaps be assumed that this is an herb bundle.

A tightly bound bundle of juniper sprigs, laid parallel, may possibly have been a brush, although it might have been a medicine bundle. The twig lengths, around 5.5 cm., are wrapped 20 times with yucca, split to around 1 mm. in width, and the ends are neatly pulled under the binding. The ends of the juniper appear to be broken or bruised. The many medicinal uses of juniper leaves and twigs are summed up by Whiting (1950, p. 62) for the Hopi, by Stevenson (1915, p. 55) for the Zuni, and by Robbins, Harrington, and Freire-Marreco (1916, pp. 39–40) for the Tewa. The uses are very similar among all three Pueblo groups.

Two other bundles may be very different objects, but still of

Figure 430. *Embroidery on a rectangle near the side selvage of a cotton textile fragment (12641/700) from the upper fill of Kiva C.*

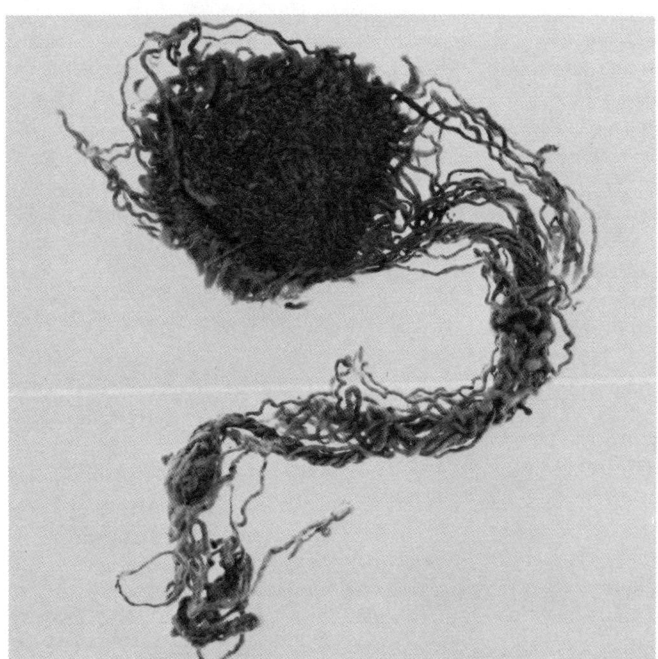

Figure 431. *Medallion of cotton cloth embroidered with cotton yarn, with tassel of raveled warps (15382/700), from subfloor of Room 32.*

Table 24. Cotton cloth.

Illus. Proven. Cat. No. 62	Dimensions Length (warp) cm. 62	Dimensions Width (weft) cm.	Selvages present	Warp Type	Warp Count to cm.	Weft Type (all are natural white)	Weft Count to cm.	Construction
Fig. 430 Kiva C, upper fill 12641/700	24	4.2	1 side and part of 1 breadth	1-ply Z-twist, hard, even, .5 mm. in diam.	11	1-Ply Z-twist, loose, fuzzy, 1 mm. in diam.	10	Fragments of two breadths with both side selvages rolled and whipped individually, then whipped together for the length illustrated. Plain weave, one-over-one; weft heavier than warp. Embroidered (and whipped) with 2-ply S-twist cotton yarn, showing remnants of red ocher rubbing. A fine 2-ply S-twist yucca sewing yarn may have been mending twine near the selvage. See text for details.
Fig. 431 Rm. 32, subfloor 15382/700	40, of which 4 are woven	3.5	none	1-ply Z-twist, 1 mm. in diam., hard	9	1-ply Z-twist, loose, 1 mm. in diam.	9	Plain weave, one-over-one; warps extend unwoven. Embroidered; topical application of red ocher. See text for details.
Rm. 27, undisturbed fill 12445/700	29.2	2.7	none	1-ply Z-twist, hard, 5 mm. in diam.	10	1-ply Z-twist, soft, fuzzy, >1 mm. in diam.		Plain weave, one-over-one; almost square count in spite of disparity of warp and weft sizes.
Rm. 28, fill 12448/700	13	15	none	1-ply Z-twist, hard, .5 mm. in diam.	9	1-ply Z-twist loose, fuzzy, >1 mm. in diam.	9	Plain weave, one-over-one; almost weft face.
Rm. 32, subfloor 12143/700	2	9	1 loomstring	1-ply Z-twist hard, fine	?	1-ply Z-twist, fuzzy	?	Loomstring end of plain weave one-over-one; rolled and whipped over end; 2 yarns of 2-ply S-twist cotton hold warp loops (Kent, 1957, fig. 93,b.), with pitch up to left.
Rm. 83, Lev. I 20137/700			almost completely raveled	1-ply Z-twist, hard, <1 mm. in diam.	11	1-ply Z-twist, loose, 1 mm. in diam.	8	Plain weave, one-over-one.
Kiva C, upper fill 15566/700	10	13	none	1-ply Z-twist, hard, <.5 mm. in diam.	10	1-ply Z-twist, loose, fuzzy, >1 mm. in diam.	8	Plain weave, one-over-one; weft predominant; firm even texture.
Kiva C, upper fill 15567/700	11.2	11.7	small portion of 1 loomstring	1-ply Z-twist, hard, .5 mm. in diam.	11	1-ply Z-twist, loose, fuzzy, >1 mm. in diam.	9	Plain weave, one-over-one cloth. Loomstring end has warp ends secured with twined row, as in 12143/700, using 2-ply S-twist cotton yarn.
Kiva C, fill 25975/700	11 6 of which is raveled warp	7.5	none	1-ply Z-twist, hard, .5 mm. in diam.	8	1-ply Z-twist, loose, 1 mm. in diam.	8	Plain weave, one-over-one; square count.
Kiva D, disturbed fill 12669/700	4	12	none: warp end rolled and whipped	1-ply Z-twist, hard, .5 mm. in diam.	9	1-ply Z-twist, fuzzy, loose, >1 mm. in diam.	9	Plain weave, one-over-one.
Area III, surface 15367/700	15.5	.7	none	1-ply Z-twist, hard, .5 mm. in diam.	9–10	1-ply Z-twist, loose, fuzzy, >1 mm. in diam.	8	Plain weave, one-over-one, sewed with 2-ply S-twist yucca twine, 1 mm. in diameter.
Area X, surface 20321/700	9	9.5	none	1-ply Z-twist, hard, .5 mm. in diam.	11	1-ply Z-twist, loose, fuzzy, 1 mm. in diam.	10	Plain weave, one-over-one; weft heavy but not predominant.

unknown function. A bundle of compressed twigs of rabbitbrush (?) from Kiva I (12197/700) appears to have been somewhat constricted in its center section. Another bundle, with an hourglass shape, suggests a bobbin, but I do not believe that anyone has ever reported finding yarn or twine wound on such a bundle. This bundle (12294/700, from the fill of Room 3) measures 8.6 by 2 by 1 cm.

Bark and bast items

The ready availability of juniper bark and bast at Mesa Verde is comparable to that of yucca: juniper is everywhere. But, unlike yucca, little bark and bast have been recovered from the ruin. Short lengths of bast twine are found, and loosely tied bundles of juniper bast were obtained from Kiva F (12714/700 and 12715/700), Kiva E and Room 11 (12705/700), Room 46 (15076/700), and Kiva B (12624/700). All of these appear to have been collected for tinder to start or speed fires. Each bundle has either a self overhand or square knot. A similar bundle of sage bark and bast, loosely self tied, was found in Room 44.

Two bundles of juniper bast were more carefully prepared. Tapering from a charred concave end to a narrow base, they were spirally bound with yucca strips, 2 to 3 mm. wide, and were tied with square knots when needed. The bindings hold the bundles rather tightly. Both have been burned almost to the yucca binding. One of them is 18 cm. long by 3.5 cm. in diameter at the charred end and 2.3 cm. in diameter at the base. The other is 20 cm. long by 4 cm. in diameter at the charred end and 2 cm. in diameter at the base. Whiting (1950, p. 62), Robbins, Harrington, and Freire-Marreco (1916, p. 39), and Stevenson (1915, p. 93) all mention the use of juniper bast for tinder and for carrying fire from house to house (i.e., slow matches). The Tewa, at least, bound juniper bast with yucca for the latter purpose.

An unusual use of strips of juniper bast is an awl sheath, which held two fine mammal bone awls (fig. 356). Perhaps because of its flimsiness, this should not properly be called a sheath or case since the bast strips simply wrap the tools spirally. They can be removed and replaced, but the bast would not survive this action many times. On the other hand, as a tip protector, the bast wrapping could be replaced quickly and may in fact have been constructed simply to protect two fairly new awls until they were needed.

Objects of cane

A fragment of matting of narrow cane *Phragmites* sp. was picked up on the surface of Long House. In the portion of upper selvage present, the warp elements are bent over a rod about 8 mm. in diameter (rod no longer present but interstice is well preserved), and both the ends and warps in groups of six or seven were caught in a row of tie-twining. Since the pitch of these overhand knots is invariably in one direction, the tying is the granny seen in yucca chains (fig. 382, left). Tie-twining was used for only the top binding row. The weft row, 8 cm. below this, is in simple twining, with pitch up to the left; it embraces fewer warps and splits the selvage bundles. The yucca twine weft is 2-ply Z-twist about 4 mm. in diameter. This item very likely served as a door closing mat; the elements maintain their round shape, which they would not have

Table 25. Cane "cigarettes."

Illus. Proven. Cat. No.	Length (mm.)	Diameter (mm.)	Mouth to node length (mm.)	Remarks
Fig. 432a Area V, fill 13891/700	121	6	13	Mouth end squarely cut, other end charred on interior; node perforated. No dottle remaining.
Fig. 432b Room 44, fill 31263/700	73	5	17	Mouth end cut; node perforated. Charred end contains dottle.
Fig. 432c Room 28, fill 30281/700	28	7	21	Charred to perforated node; mouth end smoothed from use (?). Some dottle remaining.
Fig. 432d Room 26, undist. fill 31255/700	43	8	24	Node reamed to great diameter; mouth end cut but not smoothed; smoking end charred almost to node. Almost no dottle remaining.
Room 12, Lev. B 31257/700	38	7	27	Mouth end cut but rough; node perforated; charred to node. No dottle remaining.
Room 12, disturbed fill 12960/700	33	8	20	Mouth end squarely cut, other end charred on interior; node perforated. No dottle remaining.
Room 46, fill 31264/700	30	7	14	Mouth end cut, partially smoothed; other end broken; node perforated.
Room 82, Lev. III, 20127/700	43	6	28	Charred almost to perforated node.
Kiva C 31256/700	28	8	15	Node perforated; end charred to node; mouth end cut and smoothed. Some material inside.
Kiva H, Lev. A 31262/700	35	7	28	Mouth end cut and partially smoothed; node perforated; charred to node. No dottle remaining.
Area III 33895/700	34	7	?	Mouth end cut; node perforated. Charred end contains dottle.
Area IV, undist. fill, probably same as Lev. A 15415/700	60	7	32	Node at approximate mid-length; perforated.

done if it had been used as a floor mat.

Twelve cane "cigarettes" (*Phragmites communis*) were found in Long House. The provenience and measurements of the specimens, and comments on them, are given in table 25. Perhaps they should be called tubular pipes, since they were only containers for the smoking material, which was probably inserted many times over (fig. 432a-d). With use, the cane became charred and decreased in length, and many of the "cigarettes" were no longer serviceable. The longest one is 121 mm., and the average mouth-to-node length is 21 mm. The diameter of the cane selected was around 7 mm. Mouth sections seem to have been cut to a length of from 15 mm. to a little over 25 mm. from the node. The perforated node is invariably at this end. None of the cigarettes have cotton in the mouth end. Samples of the dottles from three of the Long House specimens were examined for the presence of nicotine and related alkaloids by spectromorphic analysis with negative results."

Ten cut lengths of cane, lacking the perforation of the node characteristic of "cigarettes," were found (table 26). Two long sections, in which one end has been cut close to the node, may be partially prepared items. The first one, 21 cm. long, would make two excellent smoking pipes if a second cut were made close to the next node. Two cylinders of cane, with the ends cut and smoothed, are of unknown use. Both appear to have been much handled.

Seven other lengths of cane, with one end cut and ground or partially ground, may have been used as small rods. They average about 7 mm. in diameter and range from 5 to 19 cm. in length. Cane arrowshaft fragments will be discussed with wooden arrowpoints below.

Worked sections of cultivated plants

The Long House people used the rinds of pumpkin, *Cucurbita pepo L.*, and squash, *Cucurbita* sp., for tools, containers, and household utility items (the specimens were identified by Winton Meyer of the Missouri Botanical Garden, St. Louis). Four items of pumpkin rind, with one or more edges beveled by use, are easily recognizable as pottery scrapers (fig. 433). The curve and bevel of two of the specimens (fig. 433b and c) indicate their use on the interior of a jar or bowl. Another example (fig. 433d) leaves little doubt as its function; its excurvate edge is beveled on the exterior and its interior is packed with a mass of light gray clay. A fifth rind pottery scraper was identified as *Cucurbita mixta*. As with others, the interior is clay-packed, and the exterior edge is use-beveled.

A large object of pumpkin rind appears to have been a scoop. All the edges, except the (broken) upper end, are finished by grinding. The item is cracked from drying and is so warped that it cannot be restored. It is possible that the crack prevented it from being used extensively and thus showing much wear.

Figure 432. *"Cigarettes" of cane,* Phragmites communis; *a, 12.1 cm. long (13891/700), from the fill of Area V.*

Table 26. Cut lengths of cane.

Proven. Cat. No.	Length (mm.)	Diam. (mm.)	Remarks
Rm. 7, Lev. VI 17385/700	210	7	2 nodes unperforated; both ends cut and partially smoothed.
Kiva A, fill 15145/700	145	6	Two nodes present; one end cut and well smoothed.
Area X, surface and fill 20329/700	33	9	Both ends cut and ground smooth; surface appears to have been handled. This object and 25503/700 appear to be identical objects but no function can be assigned.
Kiva C, fill between inner liners 25503/700	34	7	Both ends cut, one end well smoothed. This object and 20329/700 appear to be identical, but no function can be assigned to them.
Rm. 12, disturbed fill above top of west wall 15517/700	40	6	End near node broken; opposite end cut and ground smooth.
Rm. 36, disturbed fill 15000/700	52	7	End near node cut and ground; opposite end broken.
Kiva E 15199/700	223	5	Both ends cut and partially smoothed.
Kiva H, fill of vent. shaft 14896/700	138	7	Both ends cut and ground; one node present.
Kiva I, Lev. A 15330/700	107	6	One end broken; opposite end, at a node, notched 3 mm. deep on opposing edges, with the notches cut to the node itself and ground. No evidence of wrapping. Notches apparently too shallow for hafting an object.
Kiva O, surface 20225/700	66	8	Both ends cut but unsmoothed.

Figure 433. *Scrapers of pumpkin rind,* Cucurbita pepo L.: *a, exterior, 6.2 cm. long (14391/700), from fill of Kiva A; b, exterior (21681/700), from undisturbed fill, northeast corner of Room 48; c, exterior, 10 cm. long (12602/700), from fill of Kiva A; and d, interior, with packed clay, 4.9 cm. long (27753/700), from Level A, Kiva I.*

Figure 434. *Two remnants of large vessel of the rind of pumpkin,* Cucurbita pepo L. *(20072/700), from Level II, Room 80. Maximum diameter of top fragment, which shows aboriginal mending with narrow yucca strips, is 24.5 cm.*

Remnants of an extraordinary large vessel of the rind of *Cucurbita pepo L.* were found. Three sections were reconstructed, but these could not be attached to each other even with the aid of the many small pieces. The rind is badly warped so that its shape and approximate size are not determinable. Aboriginal mending is shown in one of the two sections illustrated (fig. 434). As with cracked pottery, holes were drilled on each side of the crack and narrow yucca strips were threaded through and knotted.

A perforated disk of pumpkin rind (fig. 435) might be assumed to have been a spindle whorl were it not for its light weight (3 gm.) and the small diameter of the central perforation (2 mm.). It is circular and concavo-convex, and it has ground perpendicular edges. The hole is not circular; it appears to have been punched rather than drilled. As the flywheel of a spindle, it would not have been functional; moreover, no sticks were found in the site with such a small diameter. Fewkes (1892, pp. 72–73) describes a *baho* (currently spelled *paho* in the literature) used in the Nimankatcina dance at Hopi which has 16 little disks of "gourd" rind, perforated, each suspended from cotton yarn with a feather at the end, attached to twigs. These disks were about 2 inches in diameter. The Long House object corresponds closely to Fewkes's drawing.

Among the perishables at Mesa Verde sites are squash and corn peduncles tied or pierced and strung with yucca strips or twine for drying. Pierced peduncles, with the stringing material no longer present, are quite common.

Occasionally, cornhusks were knotted end-to-end to make strings or ropes for tying; when dried, these ropes are brittle. However, as any maker of tamales knows, they can be dampened and will regain strength and flexibility. An accurate measurement of the lengths could not be made because the specimens could not be straightened without wetting. Seven such ropes were found in Long House, ranging in overall length from 13.5 to 64 cm.

Two rings of slightly S-twist cornhusks may be bundle ties, although their smallness (both are under 2.5 cm in diameter) suggests "finger" rings. Another specimen, an eye loop of cornhusk, seems to have been extended into a rope of cornhusk. The diameter of the eye is 3.5 cm.

There are 11 small cornhusk items. Three tightly rolled cornhusks must have been wrapped around small twigs; there is no binding to preserve the tight coil. Two small bundles of cornhusks are folded at one end and bound at the other with narrow strips of cornhusks.

All of these are "made" items; they would have functioned as spills. The same use may suggested for a narrow leaf bundle which is wrapped near one end with split twisted (Z-twist) cornhusks.

These objects may have been connected with ceremonial life for two reasons. First, there would have been no need to make such items for purely utilitarian purposes. Any cornhusk rolled between the palms would serve as a spill (none of these are charred), but these husk were split, folded, and tied. Secondly, their very presence seems to testify to a desire for them as objects. On the other hand, many small objects regarded by some ancient housekeeper as very useful might seem totally unnecessary to her own contemporaries, and even more so to modern housewives.

Figure 435. *Perforated disk of pumpkin rind (20102/700), from Level I, Room 81. (Divider tips 1 inch apart.)*

Quids

Vegetal quids were found in rooms, kivas, and areas, and also in undesignated general areas, in Long House. The specimens were identified by Stanley L. Welsh and Glenn Moore as to material and were subsequently sorted by Jean Lee according to their appearance—"chewed," "crumpled," or "folded."

Of the 411 specimens in the collection (table 27), 362, or 88 percent, are corn leaves, husk, and stems. Other materials represented are yucca leaves and fruit (30 specimens, or 7 percent); a mixture of yucca and beans (4 specimens, or 1 percent); bean stems and mixed stems and pods (11 specimens, or 2.7 percent); Amaranth (3 specimens, or 0.7 percent); and dock (*Rumex*) (1 specimen, or 0.24 percent).

Most of the corn quids, 211, were found in rooms, and 156 of these were found in the fill of Room 28 (74) and of Room 46 (82). Some 118 corn quids came from kivas.

"Chewed" quids include 56 of corn (fig. 436a), 2 of yucca, 1 of bean, and 1 of Amaranth. These spicemens, and the more numerous "crumpled" and "folded" quids of corn (fig. 436b and c) and of the other vegetal species, may have had diverse uses. One possible use for all of them was as an actual or potential source of plant juices for paint applied to bodies and clothing (Roediger, 1961, pp. 99–102).

Table 27. Quids.

Type	Corn	Yucca	Yucca and Bean	Bean	Amaranth	Dock
Chewed	56	2	0	2	1	0
Crumpled	296	27	3	9	2	1
Folded	10	0	0	0	0	0
Prepared leaf	0	1	0	0	0	0
Prepared bundle	0	0	1	0	0	0
Totals	362	30	4	11	3	1

Figure 436. *a, "Chewed" corn leaves, or quid; b, crumpled wads; and c, folded wads of corn leaves.*

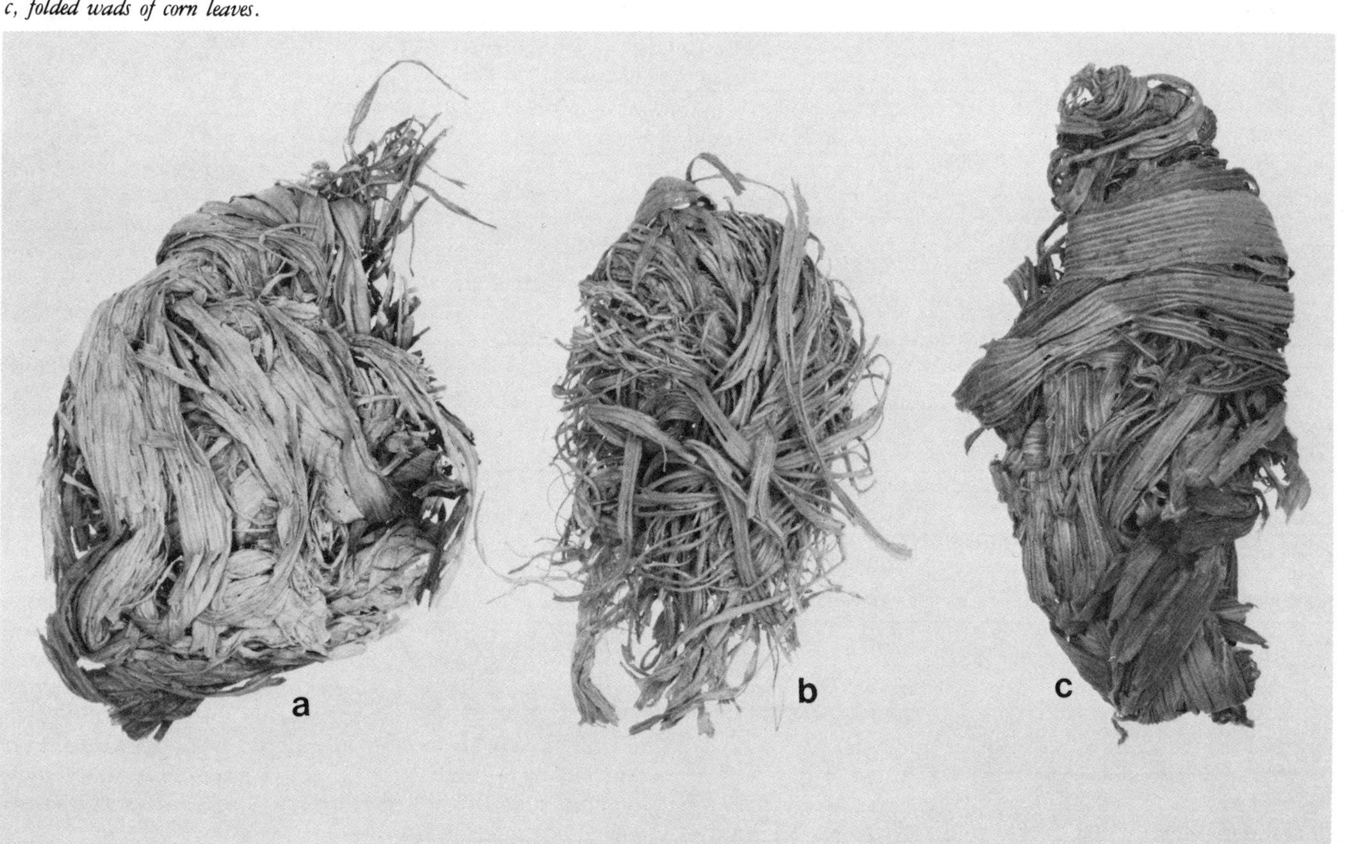

WOODEN OBJECTS

Wall pegs and construction rods

Wall pegs and construction rods are in place in 2 kivas and 23 rooms of Long House. Others became part of the rubble fill as walls of the pueblo collapsed. All are peeled sticks with crudely rounded ends, and some are smoothed. Hardwoods, notably serviceberry (*Amelanchier* sp.), were used primarily, although willow (*Salix* sp.) was used for the long peg. They are between 1.4 and 4 cm. in diameter and from 12.5 to 64.5 cm. in length (table 28). From one-third to one-half of each length had been imbedded in the masonry, and the previously exposed part of each is stained with soot.

Wall loops

Wooden loops of various sizes were found in place in the walls of two kivas and three rooms. Paired loops in suitable positions can possibly be designated as "loom loops." Displaced wall loops are described in table 29. The crossed ends of the complete wall loop had been imbedded in a wall and the loop itself is barked, perhaps through use. As in the case with wall pegs and construction rods, hardwoods such as serviceberry and oak were preferred for wall loops.

Agricultural tools

The three varieties of agricultural tools represented at Long House are a curved blade cultivator, broad blade cultivators or

Table 28. Wall pegs and construction rods.

Proven. Cat. No.	Plant ident.	Length (cm.)	Diam. (cm.)	Remarks
Area III 29099/700	Willow (*Salix* sp.)	32.4	1.4	Peeled and bluntly pointed at one end; smudged 14 cm. from tip. Wall peg.
Rm. 15, disturbed fill 12405/700	Oak (*Quercus* sp.)	26	1.9	Peeled; outer end is chopped, rounded. Stained by soot for 11 cm., remainder imbedded in wall. Wall peg.
Rm. 17, fill 17395b/700	Serviceberry (*Amelanchier* sp.)	29.5	2	Peeled and slightly smoothed, slightly curved, one end partially smoothed. Wall peg.
Rm. 49, undisturbed fill 12581/700	Serviceberry (*Amelanchier* sp.)	28.8	1.8	Unbarked; one end rounded, rough, smudged for 17 cm. from this end. Wall peg.
Rm. 61, fill 12801/700	Serviceberry (*Amelanchier* sp.) and yucca	22	3.2	Rod broken at both ends. Rod wound with wide yucca strips (7-10 mm. wide), square knotted for length, tied in larkshead. Probably roofing element, with yucca strip for suspending some object.
Rm. 3 or 4 12881/700	Serviceberry (*Amelanchier* sp.)	64.5	2.7	Peeled; one end rounded, other broken. Much weathered.
Rm. 13, fill 12970/700	Serviceberry (*Amelanchier* sp.)	45	1.7	Partially peeled; chopped and bluntly rounded at each end.
Rm. 13, fill 15521/700	Serviceberry (*Amelanchier* sp.)	45	2.1	Split lengthwise (post-occupation?).
Rm. 7, Lev. III 17345/700	Mt. Mahogany (*Cercocarpus* sp.)	12.5	1.7	Rounded and ground at one end, split and broken at the other. Wall peg.
Rm. 17, fill 17395a/700	Serviceberry (*Amelanchier* sp.)	29	2.5	Partially peeled, unsmoothed; both ends scored and broken.
Rm. 61 12802/700	Serviceberry (*Amelanchier* sp.)	52	2	Barked; one end rounded, other broken.
Kiva B, fill 12631/700	Juniper	33	2.4	Peeled; smudged on lower surface. Construction rod?
Kiva I, vent. shaft 14770/700	Serviceberry (*Amelanchier* sp.)	35	2	Peeled; blunt at one end, broken at other.
Area IV, undisturbed fill 15419/700	Serviceberry (*Amelanchier* sp.)	37.5	2.1	Peeled, slightly curved rod; chopped at one end and rounded; broken at other end after heavy scoring. Probably wall peg.
Area VII, fill 12922/700	Serviceberry (*Amelanchier* sp.)	35	2.2	Barked; end rounded.
Backdirt 12946/700	*Pinus* sp.	18.5	4	Peeled; chopped at one end. Construction rod.

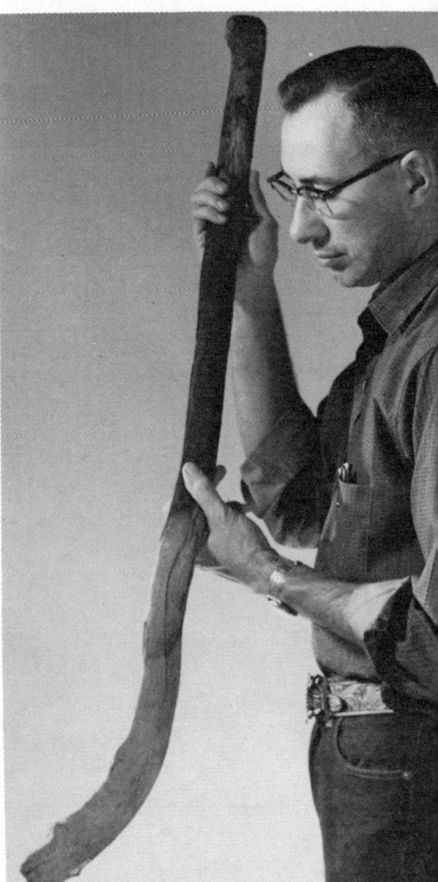

Figure 437. *Curved blade cultivator from Level III (upper roof fill), Room 76.*

Table 29. Wall loops.

Proven. Cat. No.	Plant ident.	Diam. of stick (mm.)	Loop Diam. (mm.)	Remarks
Rm. 44, fill 12532/700	Serviceberry (*Amelanchier* sp.)	5	45 Acrosss base.	U-shaped, unpeeled twig, split on the back from bending.
Rm. 11 and between walls of Kiva E, loose fill and trash beyond edge of broken floor. 15235/700	Oak (*Quercus* sp.)	6	57	Peeled twig, U-shaped with one long side.
Area X, surface and fill. 20330/700	Oak (*Quercus* sp.)	12	95 × 50 (inside)	Unpeeled except for loop proper; ends crossed for better stability.
Kiva G, loose fill. 12724/700	Serviceberry (*Amelanchier* sp.)	7	130 max.	Peeled twig; loop partially closed; both ends broken.
Rm. 29, fill. 12470/700	Skunkbush (*Rhus rilobata* Nutt.)	4	95 incomplete across base	Approx. one-half circle; unpeeled except for approx. mid-section, where a section was barked and scored.
Kiva C, upper fill 14835/700	Oak (*Quercus gambelii.*)	250	8 mm. diam. rod int. 39 mm.	Unpeeled except for loop proper; ends not crossed.
Kiva F, fill 14870/700	possibly Brickellbush (*Brichellia* sp.)	3	81 across base	Partially peeled in midsection.

Table 30. Agricultural tools and re-used fragments.

Illus. Proven. Cat. No.	Wood	Length (cm.)	Diameter (cm.)	Remarks
Fig. 437 Rm. 76, Lev. II, upper roof 20052/700	Serviceberry (*Amelanchier* sp.)	121	4.3 (handle) and 5.8×2.2 (blade)	Complete; unfinished or finished, unused. Curved flat blade with shaping beginning 48 cm. from tip; chopping marks plainly visible; no smoothing. Natural expansion for knob at top, trimmed. Shaft slightly charred. Inner and outer curves show no beveling.
Rm. 82, Lev. III 20128/700	Serviceberry (*Amelanchier* sp.)	21	4.2×1.1	Blade only, thickening near break for shaft. Tip thinned to tip, which has fine edge.
Rm. 83, Lev. I 20146/700	Serviceberry (*Amelanchier* sp.)	17	4.6×1.6	Blade fragment only: straight, sharply pointed to tip, symmetrical.
Area VII 12920/700	Serviceberry (*Amelanchier* sp.)	47.5	2.2 (shaft) and 2.4×.8 (blade)	Blade and portion of round shaft. Blade no wider than shaft, tapered to flat and bluntly pointed tip. Dibble or planting stick.
Surface, east end. 12285/700	Juniper	32.5 incomplete	5×3	Blade only: straight, broad, thick, flat; edges and tip blunt.
Area VI 14393/700	Serviceberry (*Amelanchier* sp.)	11.5	2.5×1.1	Blade section only: flat, narrow, much weathered. Apparently part of a dibble stick.
Rm. 84, Lev. I 20152/700	Indeterminate			Tip of blade only: thick, sharply pointed.
Area VI, surface and fill 20275/700	Oak (*Quercus* sp.)	34.2	3.9 (knot) and 2.8 (shaft)	Rounded, smoothed knob handle, and upper end of shaft.
Rm. 42 No Cat. no.	Serviceberry (*Amelanchier* sp.)	60.5	4×1	Blade straight,flat, 37.5 cm. long. Re-used as door jamb.
Rm. 4/3 No Cat. no.	Serviceberry (*Amelanchier* sp.)	ca. 40		Blade section straight, flat. Re-used as lintel.
Rm. 23 No Cat. no.	Oak (*Quercus* sp.)	ca. 18	2.5×2	Handle section. Re-used as wall peg.
Kiva H No Cat. no.	Serviceberry (*Amelanchier* sp.)	17	3×1	Upper portion of blade, straight, flat, thick. Re-used as one of crossed sticks over ventilator shaft.

thrusting hoes, and dibble or planting sticks. The first, the only complete specimen, shows no use and may not be a finished implement (fig. 437). It is a rather massive stick of serviceberry (*Amelanchier* sp.) measuring 121 cm. in length and 4.3 cm. in diameter at the handle. The curved, flat blade is 5.8 cm. wide and 2.2 cm. thick, and it projects at an angle of about 35° from the vertical. The implement resembles a hockey stick. Whereas used tools of this sort are tapered to an edge on the outside of the curve, this one is blunt and retains whittling marks. The knob at the top of the handle is a natural expansion that has been trimmed somewhat; the shaft is slightly charred. Tools with a broad, flat blade are used at present in most pueblos. Forde (1950, fig. 76 on p. 228) pictures a Hopi stick that was used as a weedcutter and soil loosener. Cushing (1920, Pl. III) illustrates the same type from Zuni, with a foot rest added.

The complete and fragmentary agricultural tools and re-used fragments from Long House are described in table 30.

ARROW PARTS

All of the arrow parts excavated in Long House indicate a two-part arrow: a cane shaft and a wooden arrow point or head (fig. 438). The presence of stone arrow points refutes the evidence of perishable parts; yet no foreshafts were found. Five whole or nearly complete wooden arrow points, one hafted into a section of cane shaft, are made of shrubby hardwoods, serviceberry, 4-wing saltbush, and fendlerbush.

Three of the points were shouldered (15198/700, 12943/700, and 12793/700). Two made use of natural branching or growth nodes as a shoulder to prevent the head from being rammed into the shaft and splitting it (12752/700 and 12700/700, in a shaft fragment). The tang of the point of one arrow rests on the node of the cane—a second precaution against splitting. All of the points are sharp except 12700/700, which is eroded along the entire shaft.

The shafts of the arrows are cane (*Phragmites communis Trin.*), approximately 6 mm. in diameter. The lone shaft specimen with fletching is notched at the butt. Three split feathers were symmetrically arranged and bound at both ends with sinew. The exposed feather sections were 8.5 cm. in length. Red ocher was applied to 2 cm. of the shaft under the feathers (fig. 438f).

The two fragmentary arrows and five arrow parts recovered by the Project from Long House, as well as the Long House arrow and arrow part illustrated by Nordenskiöld (1893, Pl. LXII, 16 and 23), are described in accompanying table 31. Information on the latter two items was supplied by Charlie Steen.

Table 31. Arrows and arrow parts.

Illus. Proven. Cat. No.	Plant ident.	Length (cm.)	Diameter (mm.)	Remarks
Fig. 438a Kiva E and Rm. 11, loose fill and trash beyond broken edge of floor. 12700/700	Four-wing saltbush (*Atriplex* sp.), *Phragmites*, *Yucca* sp. binding.	Point 20.5, of which 6 is in shaft.	3.5 7	Incomplete. Tip bluntly pointed; head warped and eroded. Not shouldered, inserted into cane to natural protuberance. Shaft is split at upper end, wrapped with narrow (1 mm.) strips of yucca for 15 mm. at area of insertion of point. Yucca strip pulled under 2 or 3 wraps at lower end for tie. Light arrow.
Fig. 438b Kiva E 15198/700	Serviceberry (*Amelanchier* sp.) head, Cane (*Phragmites*) shaft.	4.9	 9	Base of point or foreshaft inserted in reed shaft, of which only a collar below the shoulder remains. Tang tapers, is squarely cut at base and ground.
Fig. 438c Kiva I, Lev. A 12793/700	Serviceberry (*Amelanchier* sp.)?	18.5 tang, 3.3 long	6.8 at shoulder	Complete; sharply cut at shoulder to 6 mm. in diameter. Tang tapers to base, tip sharp and slightly flattened.
Fig. 438d Upper West Trash Slope 12943/700	Serviceberry (*Amelanchier* sp.)	20	9 at base	Broken at shoulder; this base was subsequently ground and the item probably used secondarily as an awl. Tapers smoothly to tip, which is bluntly pointed. Fire darkened at base.
Fig. 438e Kiva H, vent. shaft 12752/700	Fendlerbush (*Fendlera* sp.)	26	6 to 7	Complete, straight. Not shouldered but made use of natural protuberance, 4.8 cm. from base, as a stop. Tang is smooth, tapers evenly to tip, which is sharp. All nodes smoothed.
Fig. 438f Rm. 24, undisturbed fill 12430/700	Cane (*Phargmites communis Trin.*)	18.9	6	Shaft fragment, butt end. Notch broken, 3-4 mm. deep, U-shaped. Bound with sinew strip from base of notch for 30 mm. up shaft, securing feathers at upper end. Three split feathers (quills) exposed for 85 mm. and caught at nock end under 23 mm. of sinew wrapping. Red ocher 20 mm. under feathers at butt end.
Kiva D, disturbed fill 14841/700	possibly Serviceberry	5.9	8	Small fragment, which appears to be tang of a foreshaft or an arrow head. Tapers to base, which is blunt.
4834.130 (Nordenskiöld #213; Pl. XLII, 16)	Hardwood point in cane shaft	ca. 4 14.7	ca. 5 ca. 5	Slender reed with short blunt wooden point, lashed with sinew. Called a "child's arrow."
4834.146 (Nordenskiöld #232; Pl. XLII, 23)	Cane shaft	14.7	ca. 8	Sinew lashing at one end, nock at other.

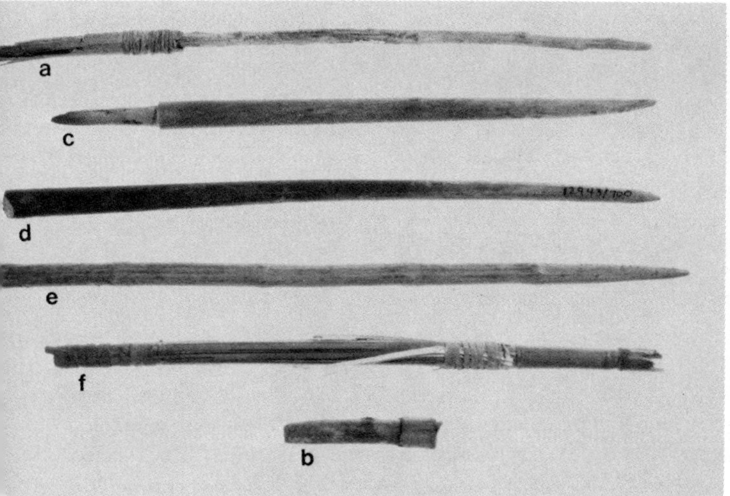

Figure 438. *Arrows of wood and cane (a and b); arrow points or heads of wood (c-e); and fletched arrow shaft of cane with notched butt (f).*

Hafted drill

One of the stone drills found at Long House, described and illustrated in ch. 5 (fig. 291), was mounted on a twig of fourwing saltbush (*Atriplex* sp.), 4 mm. in diameter and now 18.8 cm. long (broken at the proximal end). The twig was smoothed as much as the knobbiness of the wood permitted. No slit for the insertion of the point seems to have been made; instead, the stone flake was set on the end of the stick and was lashed with 2 mm.-wide yucca strips. The wrapping conceals the point of contact between the drill point and the wooden haft. A natural knob on the flake keeps the yucca strips from slipping down the shaft, but the drill point wobbles at the present time.

Knotted twigs, twig bundles, and bent sticks

Knotted twigs of willow, *Salix* sp., and of skunkbush, *Rhus trilobata,* may be raw materials or broken remnants of once usable items. Perhaps some of them secured bundles, as did yucca strips. The bundle of willow twigs could be considered material for use in basketry.

Two bent sticks appear to be broken hafts for hammers or axes. Both are oak *Quercus gambelii* Nutt.) with a trimmed section on the inside of the bend and with the outer section and the extensions unpeeled. They are 5 mm. in maximum diameter.

Data on these specimens are given in table 32.

Table 32. Knotted twigs and twig bundles.

Proven. Cat. No.	Plant ident.	Length (cm.)	Diameter (mm.)	Remarks
Kiva I, Lev. I 12788/700	Willow (*Salix* sp.)	14.5 27 21	6 6 3	Square knots of willow joining two lengths end to end. Three specimens.
Rm. 7, Lev. I 17301/700	Willow (*Salix* sp.)	13	4	Peeled curved rod of willow with split willow wrapped around it in loose knot.
Rm. 36, Lev. C 17407/700	Skunkbush (*Rhus trilobata* Nutt.)	11	2-3	Eye loop of slippery reef knot.
Area X, fill in crevice immediately west of Rm. 83 20378/700	Willow (*Salix* sp.)	7.5	ca. 5	Figure 8 weave of willow splint around forks of folded willow twig.
Kiva A, fill of southeast corner between walls 12196/700	Willow (*Salix* sp.)	21.3	4 max.	Stem with long shoots drawn together and tied with loose overhand knot. Raw material?
Rm. 6, Lev. I 17259/700	Willow (*Salix* sp.)	ca. 17	4	Overhand knot of willow around another length of willow.
Rm. 36, disturbed fill 14996/700	Willow (*Salix* sp.)	18.5 13.2	4 3	Disintegrated square knots.
Rm. 56, in wall of building 17640/700	Oak (*Quercus* sp.)	34	5 max.	Two small branches untrimmed, unpeeled, loosely wrapped at bases with split yucca strip. Not heavy enough for wall loops.
Kiva C, lower fill 15172/700	Willow (*Salix* sp.)	12	3	Distintegrated square knot.
Kiva I, surface 15315/700	Willow (*Salix* sp.)	5.5	6	Half a square knot.
Kiva I, Lev. A 15323/700	Serviceberry (*Amelanchier* sp.)	5.5	5	Disintegrated square knot.
Kiva I, NW corner 15301/700	Willow (*Salix* sp.)	7	5	Disintegrated square knot.

Willow splint matting

Sewed mats of willow splints barked and shaved to one flat surface are a prominent feature of the Mesa Verde artifact complex. They do not seem to appear in such large quantities elsewhere in the Southwest with the possible exception of Chaco Canyon. One fragment of sewed willow mat (fig. 439) and many scattered splints were found in Long House. Whatever their household use, willow mats were almost invariably the outer wrappings of burials. The splints are 6 to 12 mm. in width and 4 to 12 mm. in thickness. Their lengths are the lengths of the mats. No splicing has been observed. After preliminary splitting of the under surface, the splints were beveled at the ends from the upper surface and then pierced from one side. There is nearly always some splitting on both sides of the holes, which are 2 to 3 mm. in diameter. Yucca twine, 2-ply Z-twist and 3 mm. in diameter, was inserted and the splints were pulled together tightly. The single matting fragment has beveled ends but no sewing selvage. There appears to have been, on most specimens, additional abrading of the flat surfaces after the mat was made.

Table 33 describes the willow splints from Long House.

Rods and sticks of various possible uses

Table 34 provides data on a number of wooden rods and sticks, and fragments thereof, whose exact uses cannot be determined on the basis of association and wear characteristics. They are described under several groups. One complete peeled rod, rounded and flattened at each end and showing wear in the middle (Group A) is a possible ladder rung.

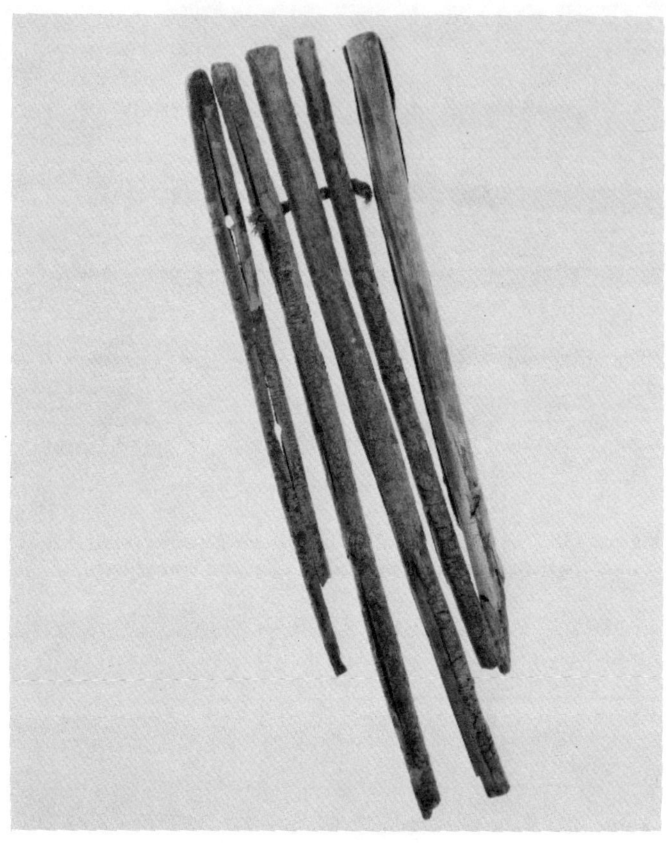

Figure 439. *End fragment of sewed willow mat (12676/700) from disturbed fill of Kiva D. Longest splint measures 26 cm.*

Table 33. Willow matting splints.

Illus. Proven. Cat. No.	Length (cm.)	Width (mm.)	Thickness (mm.)	Remarks
Fig. 439 Kiva D, disturbed fill 12676/700	21 22 25.4 26 21	12 8 11 9 10	12 9 10 9 10	Five splints: three, sewed with intact twine, are almost round, only slightly abraided on lower surface with some portions of bark remaining. End of mat beveled from upper surface. First sewing row 5 cm. from end, second at 13, third at 20.5 cm., equalling sewing intervals of 5, 8, and 7.5 cm.
Rm. 26, undisturbed fill 15278/700		small fragments		All have been split, probably at sewing holes.
Rm. 28, fill 12452/700	31.5 14.5 14 11.7 5	8 8 6 8 7	4 6 4 5 5	Five splints: mid-fragment split, probably from sewing hole; end fragment, top beveled at end, one sewing hole; mid-fragment, split; mid-fragment, split; and flat on lower surface, partially barked on upper, no sewing holes.
Rm. 32, subfloor 12142/700	17.5 7	8 10	6 7	Two splints. End fragment with bevel on upper surface to tip. One sewing hole 5 cm. from end.
Rm. 36, disturbed fill 12494/700	11.5	7	6	End fragment beveled from top, one sewing hole 5 cm. from end.
Rm. 46, fill 15083/700	33.5 5.5	6 6	5 5	Two splints: one partially flattened on 1 surface with four sewing holes spaced 10, 10.5, and 11 cm. apart; other, end fragment, beveled from upper surface, with one sewing hole 5 cm. from end.
Rm. 49, undisturbed fill 15115/700	51	11	11	Unbarked mid-fragment with four sewing holes at intervals of 11.5, 11, and 11 cm.
Kiva I, intentional fill 14688/700	9.5 9.5	7 6	4 4	Two splints: each a mid-fragment with one sewing hole.
Area X, crevice east of Kiva D 25592/700	11.2	8	8	Unbarked end fragment with bevel on one surface at end; two sewing holes at interval of 7 cm.

Table 34. Rods and sticks of various possible uses.

Illus. Proven. Cat. No.	Plant ident.	Length (cm.)	Diameter (mm.)	Remarks
		Group A: Possible Ladder Rung		
Rm. 14 12390/700	Serviceberry (*Amelanchier* sp.)	52.7	26	Complete; peeled, rounded at each end; the rod is slightly flattened at each end, shows wear in the center.
		Group B: Possible Fire Drills		
Rm. 3, fill 12297/700	Gooseberry (*Ribes* sp.)	14.3	7	Peeled and smoothed rod, rounded and charred at one end.
Rm. 47, Lev. I 17448/700	Four wing saltbush (*Atriplex* sp.)	13.4	10	Peeled rod, ground at one end, not charred at tip but shaft above is fire darkened.
Kiva C, lower fill 12647/700	Four-wing saltbush (*Atriplex* sp.)	10.8	8	Peeled rod, knobby but smooth. One end rounded, smoothed, uncharred.
		Group C: Possible Pokers		
Rm. 16, fill 15557/700	Greasewood (*Sarcobatus* sp.)	23.5	13	Charred at one end.
Kiva I, Lev. A 15322/700	Serviceberry (*Amelanchier* sp.)	18.5	14	Peeled rod; broken at one end, charred at the other.
Areas III & IV surface 12859/700	Skunkbush (*Rhus trilobata*)	29	12	Peeled rod, charred at both ends. Too massive to have been firedrill.
		Group D: Short Rods		
Rm. 64, fill 14390/700	Serviceberry (*Amelanchier* sp.)	16.1	7	Peeled, completely smoothed; both ends rounded, one is slightly charred.
Area IV, undisturbed fill 12857/700	Willow (*Salix* sp.)	13.9	12	Unpeeled rod, ground and finished at both ends. Resembles stick used at end of tumpline.
Backdirt 15502/700	*Populus* or Willow (*Salix* sp.)	16	10	Straight rod; peeled and smoothed the entire length; ends cut squarely, not smoothed.
		Group E: Blunt-ended Sticks		
Rm. 27, undisturbed fill 12982/700	Serviceberry (*Amelanchier* sp.)	9.5	12	Poor condition.
Rm. 28, fill 27975/700	Four-wing saltbush (*Atriplex* sp.)	17.1	6	Peeled stick, unilaterally beveled to blunt, flat tip.
Rm. 64, fill 12816/700	Serviceberry (*Amelanchier* sp.)	10.4	8	Peeled and smooth; fire darkened or hardened; tapered to slightly flat point.
Rm. 66, subfloor fill 26391/700	Serviceberry (*Amelanchier* sp.)	6.3	14	Split wood; distal end bluntly pointed; fire-darkened.
Rm. 84, Lev. IV 20155/700	Oak (*Quercus* sp.)	23	6	Peeled rod; bluntly pointed and smooth at distal end.
Kiva B, fill 12623/700	Gooseberry (*Ribes* sp.)	5	8	Split stick; tip beveled to blunt point.
Kiva E, fill 15205/700	Serviceberry (*Amelanchier* sp.)	18.5	8	Unpeeled stick, broken at proximal end; split at distal end with edge smoothed, slight fork peeled, notch worn.
Kiva H, beneath northeast recess, north of vent shaft	Indeterminate (possibly *Amelanchier* sp.)	25	10	Sliver with used tip.
Kiva I, Lev. A 15329/700	Indeterminate	4.3	11	Dull, charred tip; proximal end appears cut, smoothed.
Kiva I, southeast corner between walls 12194/700	Willow (*Salix* sp.)	3.8	6	Peeled rod.
Kiva I, southeast corner between walls 27970/700	Willow (*Salix* sp.)	5.3	10	Peeled, smooth.
Kiva I, southeast corner between walls, Lev. A, intentional fill 14745/700	Indeterminate (possibly *Amelanchier* sp.)	9.6	10	Split rod.

(continued)

Table 34. Rods and sticks of various possible uses. (Continued)

Kiva I, southeast corner between walls, Lev. B 12180/700	Greasewood (*Sarcobatus* sp.)	28.4	6	Slightly bowed, peeled but unsmoothed; broken at proximal end, unilaterally beveled at the end to a blunt tip.
Kiva I, northeast corner between walls 14728/700	Indeterminate, possibly *Amelanchier*	4.6	7	Unpeeled except near point, which is quite sharp.
Area V, fill 12865/700	Gooseberry (*Ribes* sp.)	14.2	6	Peeled and smoothed rod; broken at proximal end; distal end smooth with a wear-bevel on one surface.
Area VII, fill 20304/700	Willow (*Salix* sp.)	19.3	8	Peeled, partially smoothed; knob at distal end is partly natural, partly cut.
		Group F: Sharply Pointed Sticks		
Fig. 440a 12416b/700	Fendlerbush (*Fendlera* sp.)	29.4	4	Fire darkened; tip slightly flattened. A third stick was found with figure 440a and b but is no longer in the group.
Fig. 440b Rm. 46, fill 15085/700	Mockorange (*Philadelphus* sp.)	15.5	4	Tip end broken; proximal end squarely cut. Peeled stick, smooth, even.
Fig. 440c Kiva E, fill 12697/700	Four-wing saltbush (*Atriplex canescens* [Pursh] Nutt.)	11.2	5	Broken at proximal end; peeled, evenly tapered to point.
Fig. 440d Rm. 81, Lev. II 20115/700	Fendlerbush (*Fendlera* sp.)	16.5	3-4	Promixal end broken. Peeled stick with dull tip.
Fig. 440e Rm. 17, disturbed fill 12416a/700	Fendlerbush (*Fendlera* sp.)	28.8	4	Peeled stick, partially smoothed. Fire darkened near proximal end, tip slightly flattened.
Fig. 440f Rm. 3, fill 12287/700	Fendlerbush (*Fendlera* sp.)	30	3	Found inside the coiled basket, 12286/700. Smooth peeled stick, fire darkened at one end. (This was pointed at time of museum cataloging, but in course of transit to the botanist and back pointed end was broken.
Fig. 440g Rm. 17, disturbed fill 14108/700	Chokecherry (*Prunus* sp.)	29.5	4	Unpeeled except for last 4 cm. at distal end, which tapers to point; the bark is quite smooth. Proximal end is ground, rounded. A possible perforating tool.

Three rods (Group B) may be designated as possible fire drills although they are not precisely comparable to recognized fire drills found in association with hearths elsewhere; no hearths were encountered in Long House. Three rods (Group C) are possible pokers. In modern pueblos, pokers are also used to remove pottery from the firing "oven."

Short rods, both peeled and unpeeled, are to be seen in the ends of some of the twined tumplines of Mesa Verde. They formed the loom bars of the warp and remained as toggles. The three short rods (Group D) could have been intended for such use.

Sixteen blunt-ended sticks (Group E) are invariably peeled and are at least partially smoothed. Some of these appear to be tools, whereas other fragmentary specimens may be parts of cradle rods, wooden arrow points, or even *pahos*.

The seven sharply pointed sticks of Group F (fig. 440) may have served as perforators, pins, skewers, or mesh gages for knotless netting such as the legging of human hair (fig. 428). Cushing (1920, p. 266 and Pl. XI) pictures pointed sticks like these that were used by the Zuni in a bundle as stirring rods for parching corn. Each of these tools might have served all of these purposes in the household.

Perforator

The base of what was probably a wooden perforator (14396/700, from Area VII) is made of fendlerbush. Measuring 19 cm. in length by 7 mm. at the broken proximal end, it has a natural knob at the base with a crook providing a "pistol grip." The smooth shaft tapers toward the tip, which is missing. This well-made tool is similar to several complete ones present in early Wetherill collections from Mesa Verde.

Needle

A flat, double-ended needle has an eye in the midsection measuring 6 mm. long by 3 mm. wide. The tool itself, which is quite eroded and may not be complete, measures 8.2 cm. long by 7 mm. wide by 3 mm. thick. It would have been an excellent lacing needle for knotless netting. It is shown with a length of twine not found in association (fig. 441).

Spatulate Tools

Two split sections of juniper have ends which were ground to sharp edges. One tool, measuring 13.9 cm. long by 1.9 cm. wide by 5 mm. thick, has one end that is sharply beveled and slightly excurvate; the long edges are smoothed from handling. The second is broken and charred at one end; its present measurements are 11.9 cm. long by 2.9 cm. wide by 8 mm. thick. It is possible that this a fragment of a weaving batten, although one end is more beveled than necessary and the implement is smaller than a batten would ordinarily be. The long edges are smooth.

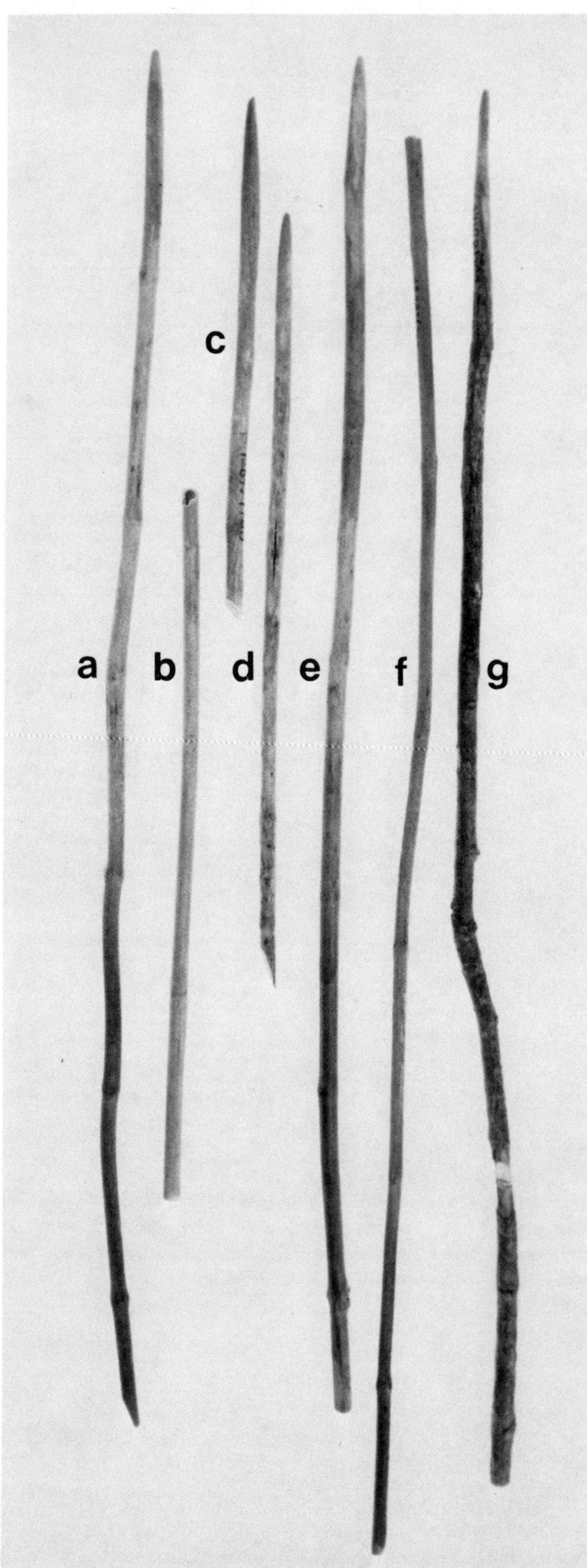

Figure 440. *Sharply pointed sticks, possibly used as perforators, pins, mesh gages, or stirring rods. Specimen at extreme right is 29.5 cm. long and 4 mm. in diameter.*

Figure 441. *Double-ended wooden needle (12483/700) from the fill of Room 30.*

Kidder and Guernsey (1919, Pl. 49 *k-m*) show three tools, one from Grand Gulch, that are comparable in size (11.5 cm. long) and general appearance. These were, however, stained red at the tips, and Kidder and Guernsey considered them delicate skinning knives (assuming the staining to have been blood). The Long House tools are not stained.

Possible loom parts

No rods from Long House could be positively identified as loom bars. The three specimens described here are so identified on the basis of surface finish and straightness of the wood, the latter being more of a requirement than the former. No two were found in association. None are from proveniences of rooms or kivas where wall or floor loops occurred, and none came from the same location as either of the two spindle whorls.

The best possibility is the well-finished rod found in Level I of Kiva O (fig. 442a). It is 61.6 cm. long and 4.3 cm. in diameter. It is a straight, peeled bar of poplar, rounded but rough at both ends, with a cut groove 2 cm. wide near one end which encircles less than half of the circumference. If the rod were used as an end bar, this partial groove would secure the suspending rope. The other end has no groove, but there is wear on the surface indicating some wrapping or tie. A textile using this rod for a loom bar would necessarily be narrow but probably adequate for the average width of the cotton textiles found at Mesa Verde. As a possible loom bar in twining feather robes, it would have been useful only for infant sizes.

The second bar is probably too well finished to have been a loom bar (fig. 442b). Only a reticence about calling many items "ceremonial" prevents me from referring to this as a baton, yet it may well have been one. The surface of this cottonwood or willow bar is smoothed, with longitudinal striations, and there is a brown stain or dye coating the surface. There are no grooves or protuberances for securing ropes, and there are no signs of its having been tied at the ends. The bar is 32.3 cm. long and 2.7 cm. in diameter. As a loom bar, this would have been serviceable only for quite narrow fabrics.

The third bar illustrated (fig. 442c), of juniper, is fragmentary; it measures 1.9 cm. in diameter and its present length is 32 cm. The rod is smoothed and straight, with a slight knob at the finished end. It is of too soft a wood and probably too small in diameter to have served as an end bar, but it would have made an excellent heddle bar. A similar fragmentary rod, of serviceberry, peeled and smoothed, might also have served as a heddle bar. Both of these rods resemble the wall pegs, but neither has the line of imbedding nor the smudged surface characteristic of such items.

Spindle whorls

Two wooden disks are probably spindle whorls. If rods had accompanied them, the identifications would have been decisive. No sticks or rods found in the excavation of Long House fit them, but both were tested on slightly tapered rods and are most satisfactory spindle whorls by my standards. The rectangular disk is of juniper and measures 8.1 cm. long by 6.9 cm. wide by 9 mm. thick (fig 443, upper). Both surfaces are smoothed and the edges are roughly smoothed. The central hole is conically drilled and easily wedged onto a tapered stick about 7 mm. in diameter. The object weighs 24.5 gm. and is light for its size. It has excellent balance for top twirling (which may never have been practiced) and produces a fine momentum. If the Long House people made a habit of spinning most of their yarns with the shaft rolled on the thigh, as the Hopi and Navajo do today, the light weight and good balance of this object would not be necessary. It serves its purpose as a fly-wheel so well that I cannot believe it was used in the thigh-rolling method exclusively.

The roughly circular disk is 6.6 cm. in diameter and 9 mm. thick, and it weighs only 6 gm. (fig. 443, lower). Dr. Welsh lists the deteriorated wood as indeterminate, possibly juniper. The surfaces are irregular but the edges are smooth. The perforation is 6 mm. in diameter, with straight sides. At present, this object is almost too light for good balance and, when mounted on a spindle of appropriate size, it tends to creep.

Daubing sticks

Four twigs or splinters found in Long House have pine pitch at one end or on one surface. Identified as daubing sticks, they are described in table 35.

One of several matchlike sticks heavily coated with white and coral-orange paint at one end was submitted to the Federal Bureau of Investigation for possible identification of the paint. The Bureau reported that the paint was composed of "calcium carbonate, zinc oxide and phosphorus." These sticks, which resemble block matches of the late 1800's, undoubtedly belonged to one of the early explorers. According to the Encyclopedia Britannica, phosphorus ceased to be used in matches in 1906 by international agreement. The presence of these items in "undisturbed fill" must be the result of rodent activity.

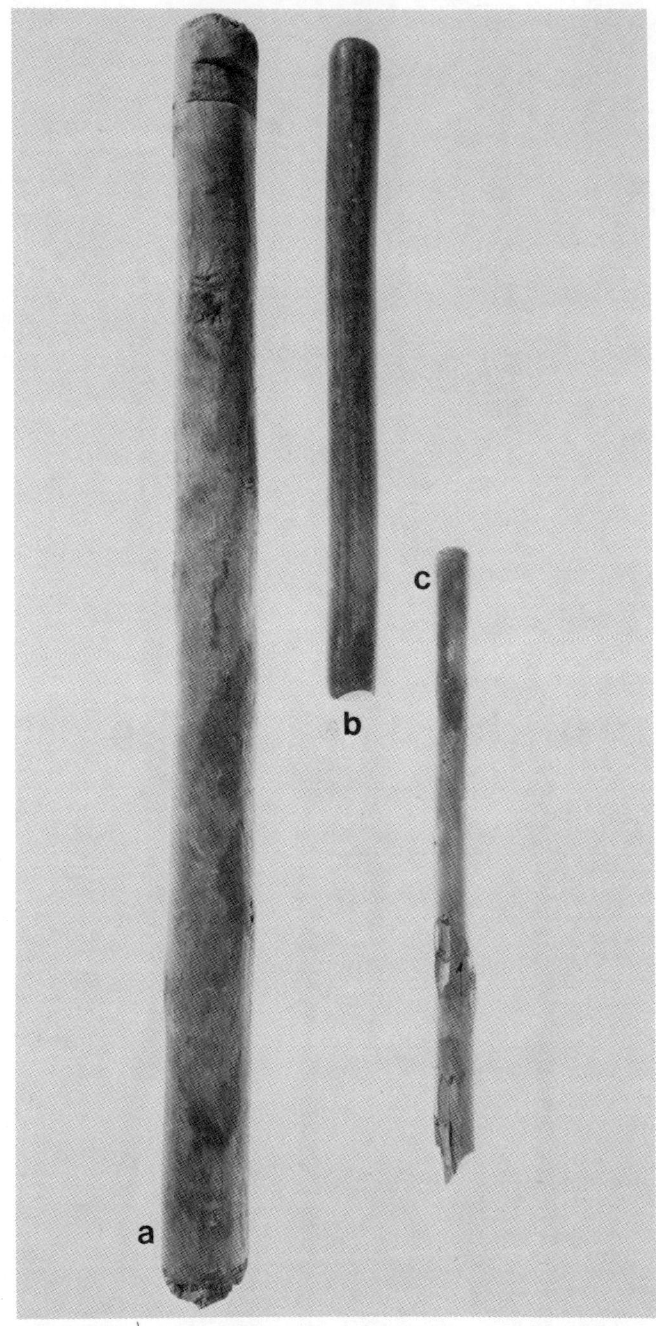

Figure 442. *Possible loom parts: a, loom bar of poplar (20230/700) from Level I, Kiva O; b, loom bar of cottonwood or willow (12546/700) from Room 46; and c, heddle bar fragment of juniper (17374/700) from Level V, Room 7.*

Pahos and other ceremonial items

More than any other site known at Mesa Verde, Long House abounded in ceremonial items of a perishable nature. Many of these are comparable to objects used at the present time.

Two feather aspergills were found in Kivas D and C. Hargrave identified the feathers as turkey (*Meleagris gallopavo*) flight feathers. The larger item (fig. 444a) consists of 19 feathers arranged in two rows, overlapping on the edge. The bases of the feathers have been rodent gnawed, and possibly one row of the sewing is lost. The intact sewing is about 10 cm. above the gnawed quill bases. The quills are threaded on one length of 2-ply S-twist yucca twine which is tied on

Figure 443. *Spindle whorls (?): right, rectangular (12560/700) from undisturbed fill, Room 48; left, roughly circular (12601/700) from fill of Kiva A.*

Table 35. Daubing sticks.

Proven. Cat. No.	Plant ident.	Length (cm.)	Diameter (mm.)	Remarks
Rm. 12, Lev. 8 15534/700	Four-wing saltbush (*Atriplex* sp.)	3.1	3	Twig with clear reddish pitch at one end.
Rm. 43, fill 12528/700	Serviceberry (*Amelanchier* sp.)	12.5	5	Dollop of charred pitch at one end.
Rm. 46, fill 27971/700	Serviceberry (*Amelanchier* sp.)	14	7	Unpeeled twig except for shaved end, which is covered with pitch.
Rm. 47, Lev. III 17502/700	(*Juniperus* sp.)	6.1	20×4	Flat splinter with one rounded and one square cut end. There is pitch on much of one surface.

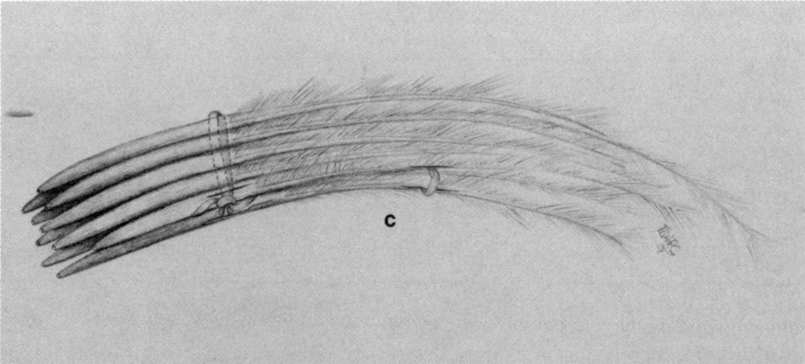

Figure 444. *Feather asperqills: a (14366/700), from the fill of Kiva D; b (14365/700) and d (14364/700), knotted split quill sections, probably part of b, from south recess of Kiva C; and c, schematic arrangements of feathers and sewing in b.*

the inside of the curve with a square knot. The length of the bundle is 21 cm., the width at the base is 4.2 cm., and the thickness is 1.8 cm. This must once have been a fine aspergill, but time has altered its appearance considerably.

The other aspergill (fig 444b) consists of 10 flight feathers arranged in two rows of five each so that the feather vanes overlap the rows. The sewing was accomplished with flat split feather quills. The first row is 8.5 cm. from the base of the feathers; the second, 18 cm. from the base, is broken and the knot and a part of the sewing quill is not present (fig. 444c). Two split quill sections tied end to end with a square knot, also found in Kiva C (fig. 444d), may be the missing sewing element. The length of this aspergill is 29.5 cm., the width at the lower tie is 3.4 cm., and the thickness is 1.8 cm.

A lone feather pierced with 2-ply Z-twist yucca twine, found in the lower fill of Kiva C, may be the remnant of a third aspergillum. It is also *Meleagris gallopavo*.

A corncob with the base of a broken feather quill inserted in its base is a possible ceremonial item (fig. 445). The entire cob is mudpacked. Whether or not this was deliberate, it is impossible to say, but a like specimen was found in Mug House. The cob and quill combination is 11.3 cm. long.

The Wetherill Mesa Project's excavation of Long House yielded two nearly complete and six fragmentary carved prayer sticks or *pahos* (fig. 446a and b). Seven fragmentary *pahos* of the same type were found in Long House by Nordenskiöld (1893, Pl XLII, 2–8) and approximately 100 similar *pahos* were found by the Wetherill brothers at a site that may have been on Wetherill Mesa. Table 36 gives data on all 15 specimens from Long House, including measurements and observations made by Charlie Steen in 1960 on the seven Nordenskiöld fragments housed in the National Museum of Finland.

The shapes and sizes of all of the Mesa Verde carved stick *pahos* are in close agreement. They are essentially the same as those from Pueblo Bonito illustrated by Pepper (1920, fig. 53, p. 142), and by Judd (1954, pl. 38, *a-f*). However, there are sufficient differences in the handling of the heads by these ancient peoples to indicate that the two groups are typologically distinct.

The grooved prayer stick lacking the head may not properly belong in this group (fig. 446a and b). The grooved lashing section has some sinew intact; no feathers appear to have been caught under the sinew as it now exists. Nor do any of the other Long House sticks have binding or feathers in the "lashing section." This section was so labeled from more complete specimens in the Colorado State Museum collections from Mesa Verde, which retain portions of feathers under binding, and from Pepper's illustration of a *paho* with the

Table 36. Carved prayer sticks or *pahos*.

Proven. Cat. No.	Plant ident.	Length (cm.)	Diam. (mm.)	Remarks
Room 15, N wall 26076/700	Serviceberry (*Amelanchier* sp.)	38.5	17	Nearly complete. Head missing; base double beveled. Peeled and smoothed shaft and base.
Room 84, surface 20147/700	Skunkbush (*Rhus trilobata*)	52.5	11	Nearly complete. shaft curved, possibly from warping. Completely peeled, partially smoothed. Flat head, double beveled, peaked top.
Room 84, surface 20148/700	Serviceberry (*Amelanchier* sp.)	28	10	Fragmentary. Flat head; double beveled; sharply pointed top. Completely barked; partially smoothed.
Kiva I, Lev. A 15328/700	Willow (*Salix* sp.)	15.3	10	Fragmentary. Main shaft peeled and partially smoothed. Beveled head with peaked top.
Area VI, fill 20284/700	Skunkbush (*Rhus trilobata*)	8.5	11	Fragmentary. Head missing; only ring intact, 6-7 mm. wide. Shaft barked and partially smoothed.
Room 84, 1.5′ above datum 20150/700	Serviceberry (*Amelanchier* sp.)?	32.4	11	Fragmentary. Flat head double beveled with peaked top. Completely barked, smoothed.
Room 84, 0.5′ above datum 20151/700	Serviceberry (*Amenlanchier* sp.)	38	11	Fragmentary. Flat head, double beveled with rounded peak at top. Unbarked section on main shaft.
Room 46, fill 15084/700	(*Juniperus* sp.)	5.3	12	Fragment, split lengthwise.
Nat. Mus. Finland/ 4834.120 (Nord. 202) Nord., 1893, Pl. XLII, 2		25		Fragmentary. Once painted red (?).
4834.121 (Nord. 203) Nord., 1893, Pl. XLII, 3		26		Fragmentary.
4834.122 (Nord. 204) Nord., 1893, Pl. XLII, 4		26		Fragmentary. Traces of red Paint (?).
4834.123 (Nord. 205) Nord., 1893, Pl. XLII, 5		21.2		Fragmentary.
4834.124 (Nord. 206) Nord., 1893, Pl. XLII, 6		12		Fragmentary. Head of *paho* once painted black.
4834.155 (Nord. 247) Nord., 1893, XLII, 7		22		Fragmentary.
4834.156 (Nord. 246) Nord., 1893, XLII, 8		19		Fragmentary.

Figure 445. *Mud-packed corncob with inserted feather quill (14789/700) from undisturbed fill, Room 24.*

Table 37. Wrapped twigs.

Proven. Cat. No.	Plant ident.	Length (cm.)	Diameter (mm.)	Remarks
Kiva E and Rm. 11 12708b/700	Boxelder (*Acer negundo* L.) with cornhusks	9	3	Twig with split cornhusks laid parallel and along it, wrapped with narrow split lengths of husk. Partially unwrapped.
Rm. 7, Lev. IV 17358/700	Four-wing saltbush (*Atriplex* sp.) and yucca	9.4	3	Twig with feather (quill) bound to stick with narrow yucca strip for length of 2.5 cm. Twig cut when leaf budded.
Kiva D, disturbed fill 12665/700	Four-wing saltbush (*Atriplex* sp.), yucca strip	9.4	4	Twig pointed at the base. At upper end a lashing of 2 mm. wide yucca strip secures the quill of a feather. Wrapping now loose.
Kiva B, fill 12622/700	Oak (*Quercus* sp.) and yucca twine	5.1	4	Twig (now splitting) tightly wrapped at one end with 2-ply Z-twist yucca twine 1 mm. in diameter. Wrapping started at top, with first end of twine covered; final end pulled under previous wrapping. Nothing visible under the twine.
Kiva D, disturbed fill 12677/700	Skunkbush (*Rhus trilobata*), yucca	9.8	2	Twig folded so that both ends are together and with the fold bent into the shape of a triangle with the base up. The apex of the triangle is the merging of the two sections that are wrapped below with a narrow yucca strip. The yucca strip makes three figure-8 wraps, then proceeds around both to the end of the sticks. Nothing is visible under the lashing. The twig was visibly budded when cut.
Kiva I, northeast corner between walls, intentional fill 12207/700	Fendlerbush (*Fendlera* sp.) with cornhusk and yucca strip	9.5	4	Unpeeled twig wrapped with cornhusks longitudinally and bound with sections of narrow yucca splints at top and bottom. Nothing is visible under the husks.
Kiva E and Rm. 11 12708b/700	Boxelder (*Acer negundo* L.) with cornhusks	9	6	Twig with split cornhusks folded over the top and extending down to the base of the stick. Narrow cornhusk strips spirally wrap the bundle from top to the lower end of the stick to form compact bundle.
Rm. 7, Lev. I 17301b/700	Rabbitbrush (*Chrysothamnus* sp.) and cornhusks	11.7	4	Twig wrapped in one section with narrow cornhusk strips.
Kiva P, Lev. I 20241/700	Serviceberry (*Amelanchier* sp.) and yucca	7.9	5	Twig broken and splitting at one end, wrapped with yucca strip at the other end, which is now too loose to secure anything.

lashing complete (op. cit., fig. 85, p. 193).

Two curved rods are identical to those pictured by Pepper (ibid.), attached to carved stick *pahos* (fig. 446c). The Long House specimens are isolated; in fact, none in the Mesa Verde collections are attached to the longer sticks although they exist as tied pairs in the early collections. The thicker of the Long House curved stick *pahos* is made of skunkbush, *Rhus trilobata*. It measures 16 cm. long and 6 mm. in diameter, and is completely peeled and smoothed. The interior of the curve has a series of parallel oblique lines, spaced irregularly from 9 to 15 mm. apart, lightly incised or indented into the wood. These lines do not extend around the stick and could have been caused by a binding or used for binding only if there were a heavy padding such as a group of feathers on the outside of the curve. The other curved stick, of fendlerbush, is 18.2 cm. long and 5 mm. in diameter. It has a similar incising or indenting on the inside of the curve only, with lines 5 to 8 mm. apart and as if spirally wrapped in a lower-left to an upper-right direction, but frequently crossed in the opposite direction to form light crosses (cf. Judd, 1954, fig. 77b, p. 277).

Three examples of crook *pahos* are carved of oak sticks (*Quercus* sp.) (fig. 446c). Known from many archeological sites in the San Juan drainage area and still produced in most pueblos, crooks seem to be sometimes associated with longevity and death (Judd, 1954, p. 269). The most complete of these prayer sticks measures 36.5 cm. in length and 7 mm. in diameter. It is completely peeled; at the upper end, the stick is cut away on one side and the trimmed portion is bent into the crook, 15 mm. in diameter. The end of the crook and the base of the stick are missing.

The delicate bend of the crook of one of the prayer sticks has survived remarkably well. The "eye," 15 mm. in diameter, is closed and the end of the trimmed wood extends for 2 cm. parallel to the main shaft. The broken staff is only partially peeled; it measures 9.2 cm. in length and 7 mm. in diameter.

The crook of the third prayer stick is also well preserved. The stick was trimmed, and the eye formed by the reduced section, 13 mm. in diameter, is not completely closed and the extension parallels the main shaft for a distance of 2.5 cm.

All three of the crook *pahos* had leaf bases or branchlets which had been removed; the wood was partially smoothed over these. Pepper (1920, fig. 55) illustrates a variety of crooks from Pueblo Bonito. In only one of these is the crook head closed to form an eye.

The crossed stick *paho* has a staff of cane (*Phragmites* sp.), and measures 25.5 cm. in length and 5 mm. in diameter (fig. 446c). At the top is bound a cribwork of four sticks, two parallel underneath with two in the opposite direction above. These are held with a firm but disorganized wrapping of fine split yucca strips. The crossed sticks could not be identified as to wood. Mug House produced the cap fragment of an identical object; and a yucca binding with the sticks removed, found in Kiva D in Long House, may have been part of another such object.

Wrapped twigs

Nine wrapped twigs (fig. 446d) are described in table 37. Two of these have feathers bound with yucca strips, and four have cornhusk covering and binding. One is a triangular hoop of a budding twig and one is a twig fragment with a tight binding of yucca twine. Nearly all of them were found in kivas or in rooms closely associated with kivas. They seem to have been ceremonial paraphernalia.

Figure 446. *Carved prayer sticks or* pahos *(a); sketch of carved prayer stick (b); curved stick, crook, and crossed stick* pahos *(c);*

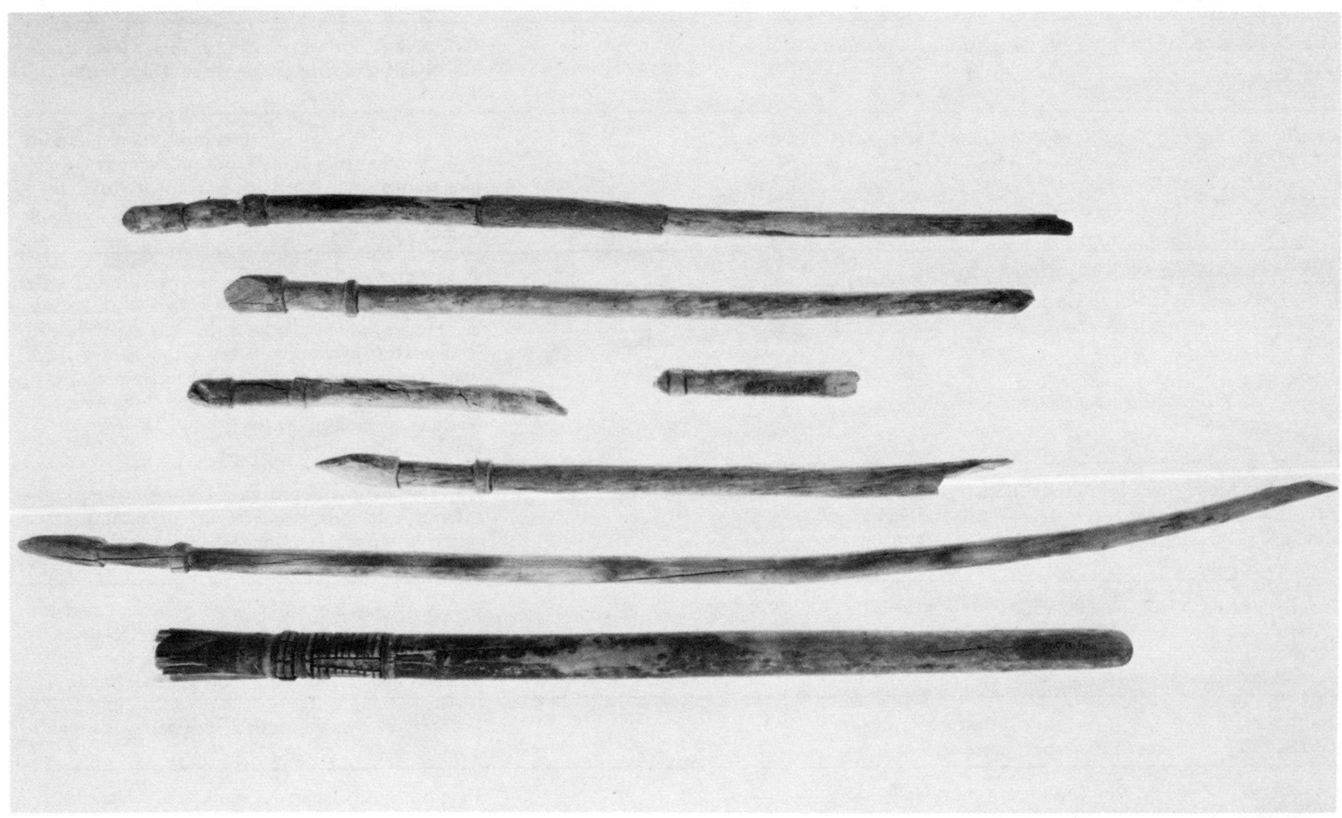

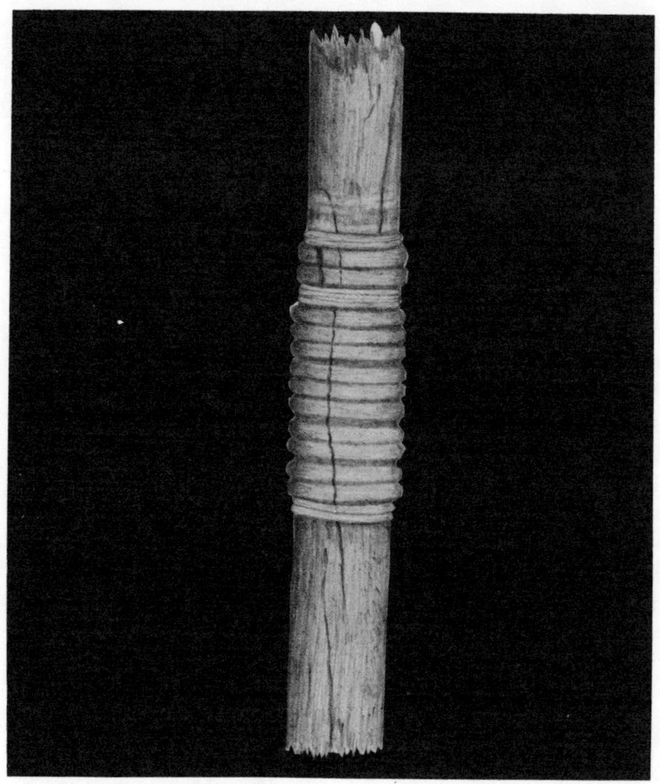

Figure 446. *(b)*

Shaved sticks

The final group of items of possible religious or ceremonial import is a series of shaved sticks (fig. 446e). Comparable objects have been reported from Tularosa Cave by Hough (1914, figs. 129 and 130, p. 60) and by Grange (in Martin et al, 1952, fig. 149, g and h, on p. 407). The specimens described by Grange had feathers caught in the shredded wood, and Grange considered that they might be some type of a feather carding device but did not press the point. The Long House items did not have feathers, but the cylinders themselves are identical in the two series. The specimens most closely resemble the shaved sticks of religious import among the Ainu (Hitchcock, 1891, fig. 86, p. 474), but I hasten to add that I draw no inferences from this.

Data on the Long House items are given in table 38. I do not feel that they could have served as brushes: the delicacy of the curled shavings precludes such practical use. There remains the possibility that they are discards from the manufacture of other objects, and that the shavings represent fine cuts of wood, with the breaking of the sticks the final goal. This was Hough's conclusion (op. cit., p. 60). His examples retained a fine spindle which was characteristic of one of his types of *pahos*. If this were the ultimate goal, the shavings were certainly carefully preserved.

Three of the Long House specimens, of serviceberry exhibit very delicate curled shavings that were pushed down around the stick. The fourth of the shaved sticks is oak. The shavings around the core of the wood are short at present but appear to have once been curled. This specimen retains a spindle-like core. The bases of two of the cylinders are finished; the shafts of two others are broken.

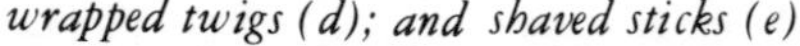

wrapped twigs (d); and shaved sticks (e).

Figure 446. *(c)*

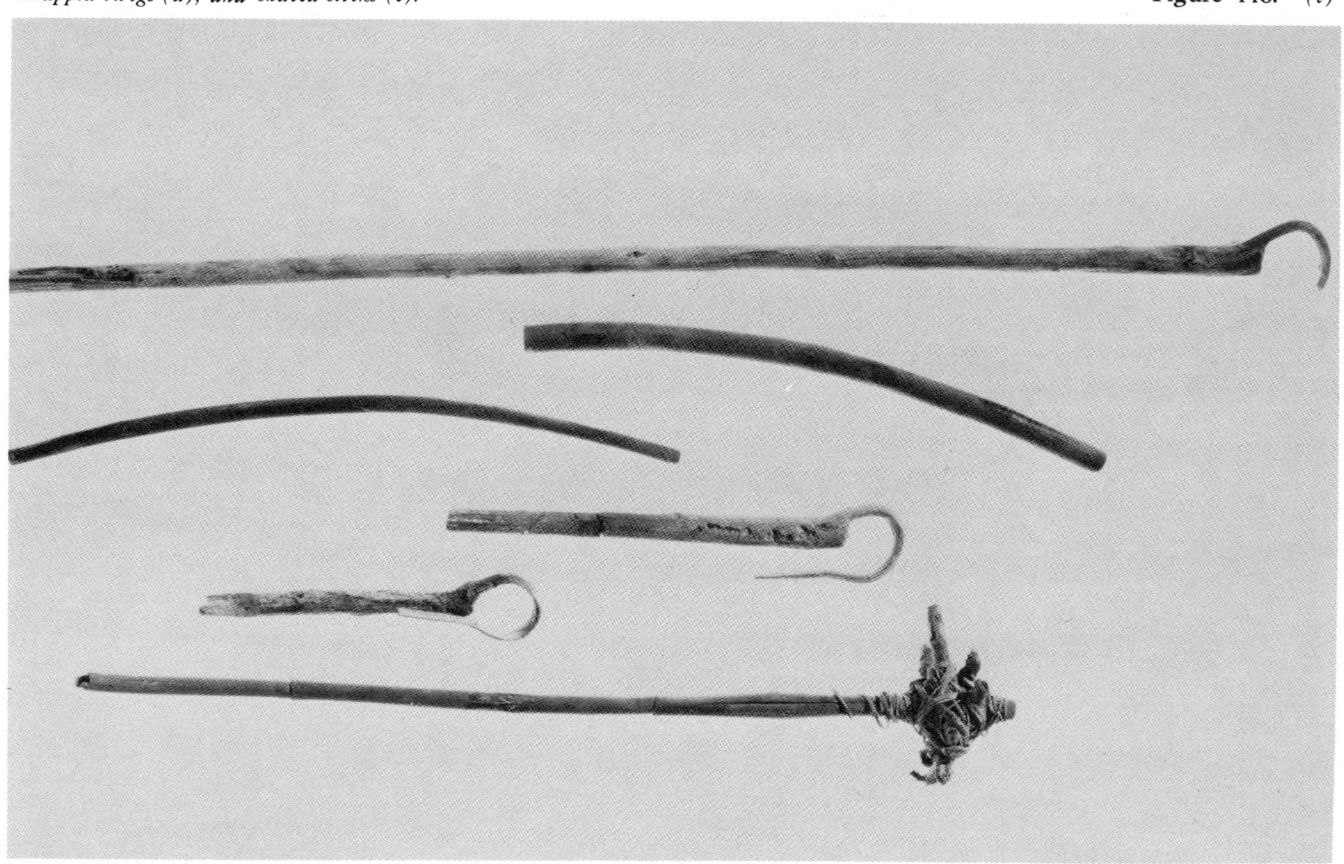

The remaining two items illustrated may not belong with the other four. The first is yucca, partially shredded at one end. It is too large to have been a brush for painting pottery and not sturdy enough to have been a hair brush or scrubbing brush. Grange (op. cit., p. 402 and fig. 146,j) describes a similar brush coated with glue. The Long House specimen may have been intended, but never used, for such purpose. The second item is a corn stalk frayed at one end, in the same manner as the wooden sticks. The outer fibers have been delicately separated from the stalk. This may have been the result of chewing or biting to extract the sweetness of the stalk. It resembles lengths of sugarcane with the fibers pulled by the teeth to get at the core of the stem.

Two possible antecedents of these in the Anasazi area should be noted. Kidder and Guernsey (1921, p. 102 and pl. 40, *b*) found, with a Basketmaker mummy in White Dog Cave, a stick with a brushlike arrangement of coarse fibers protruding from one end, which they assumed to be ceremonial. An identical item from a cave in one of the canyons of the Colorado River above the confluence with the San Juan is in the McLoyd and Graham collection in the University Museum, University of Pennsylvania.

The following are single objects which merit a few words of description:

A root of indeterminate species (12014/700) was folded and was wrapped twice with a yucca strip and tied off with a square knot. This may be simply an eye loop, but more likely it is a plant collected for medicinal or food use.

A slightly concave paddlelike split section of wood with a blunt end and smoothed edges may have been a scraper used in pottery construction (23410/700). At present, it is eroded and split, and it measures 4.2 cm. long by 2.1 to 3.8 cm. wide by 7.5 mm. thick.

In order to round out the use of varieties wood in Long House, mention should be made of worked fragments. There are six flat shakes of split juniper; several of these have one cut and finished end. A corner fragment of what may have been a small tablet was made of indeterminate wood, possibly *Populus*. An oak billet fragment may be a construction item. A split stick of willow or *Populus* is not a matting splint and its function is unknown. Two small sections of aspen bark, one with a finished edge, may be remnants of bent aspen bark objects (17365/700 and 14392/700).

Other items, listed as "barely worked," include splinters showing some use. They were identified as Prince's Plume (*Stanleya* sp.), 1; willow (*Salix* sp.), 7; fendlerbush (*Fendlera* sp.), 1; juniper, 5; mockorange (*Philadelphus* sp.), 1; serviceberry (*Amelanchier* sp.), 5; oak (*Quercus* sp.), 1; gooseberry (*Ribes* sp.), 2; pine (*Pinus* sp.), 2; rabbitbrush (*Chrysothamnus* sp.), 1. Six were indeterminate because of rotting, charring, or inadequate size.

Figure 446. *(d)*

Table 38. Shaved sticks.

Illus. Proven. Cat. No.	Wood ident.	Length (cm.)	Diameter (mm.)	Remarks
Fig. 446a Rm. 14, Lev. A 12399/700	Serviceberry (*Amelanchier* sp.)	10.4	9	Twig with secondary budded twig; shavings curled and peeled down around stick.
Fig. 446b Rm. 47, Levs. I and II 17444/700	yucca	13	9	Split yucca leaf with base shredde, left fuzzy at the end.
Fig. 446c Rm. 28, fill 12450/700	Serviceberry (*Amelanchier* sp.)	8.8	20	Rod with rounded base; shaved from below with tufts partially retained; center of stick is twisted and broken.
Fig. 446d Rm. 46, fill 27973/700	Oak (*Quercus* sp.)	6.4	14	Unpeeled rod; base rounded; shavings quite short at present; center twisted and broken.
Fig. 446e Rm. 37, fill 30291/700	corn	4.9	10	Length of corn stalk with one end frayed, which appears to have been deliberate; the center of the stalk is rounded on top.
Fig. 446f Rm. 14, Lev. A 12396/700	Serviceberry (*Amelanchier* sp.)	6.7	8	Incomplete. Stick shaved from above with curled shavings pushed down around this section, base broken.

Figure 446. *(e)*

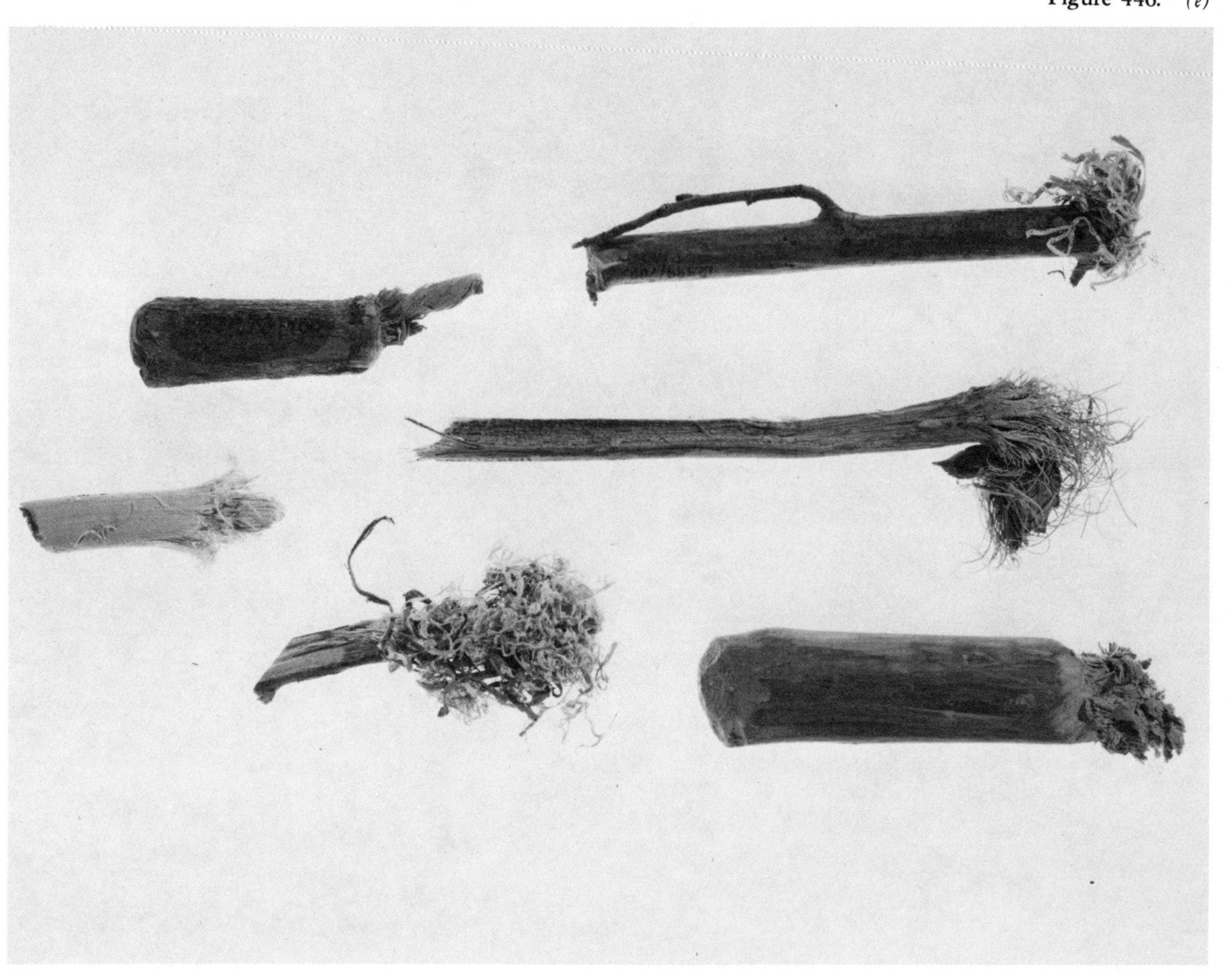

LEATHER

A moccasin illustrated by Nordenskiold (1893, Pl. XLVI, 4) came from Long House, but its exact provenience is not known. This is most unfortunate in view of Steen's description of this specimen as a possible Fremont-type moccasin and of the evidence of early occupation of Long House adduced by the Wetherill Mesa Project excavations. Figure 447 was made for Steen while he was restudying the Nordenskiöld collection in the National Museum of Finland in 1960.

The foot was small, with the sole length only 21 cm.; it is apparent that the moccasin had become molded to a foot. The buckskin (?) is quite thin; the hair side was on the inside. In this respect, it is unlike the Fremont moccasins illustrated by Morss (1931, pl. 38). The sole, heel, and uppers around the foot and over the toe are of a single piece of hide from near the hoof of the animal and the dew claw was attached at the flap of skin at the left, near the toe. The tube of shank hide was sewed around the toe before the fur side was turned to the inside. The hide is split at the heel and the ends are long, presumably for tying around the ankle. A triangular piece of leather is set in to form a section on the top of the foot. Sewing is with yucca twine. The moccasin is much worn. Steen thinks this may have been a winter foot covering to have been worn with a sandal, though it may have been simply a moccasin with fur interior. As far as I know, it has no exact counterpart at Mesa Verde, although a skinned, small mammal pouchlike object in the Colorado State Museum had been worn on a foot.

Mere fragments of leather were found in the Project's excavation of Long House; they are described in table 39. One specimen, having a whipped seam joining two lengths of hide with the fur remaining, is illustrated in figure 448. The sewing thread is 2-ply S-twist cotton yarn.

A bundle of six leather thongs, held together by a seventh thong (12360/700), measures 14 cm. in length. These are extraordinarily soft and pliable. One twisted fur strip (17325/700) was undoubtedly once part of twine. It maintains the S-twist of the fur-strip wrapping of blanket twines.

Two objects of unknown material—vegetal or animal— are small concentrically wound disks. One of these (17423/700) was started with an S-fold and then wound to a bundle 13 mm. in diameter and 3 mm. thick. A cactus spine was thrust through the flat material to hold the disk. The other specimen (12908/700) is essentially the same, although the disk has one concave surface and there is no securing pin.

Figure 447. *Buckskin (?) moccasin with the fur side turned inside; found in Long House by Nordenskiöld (1893, Pl. XLVI, 4).*

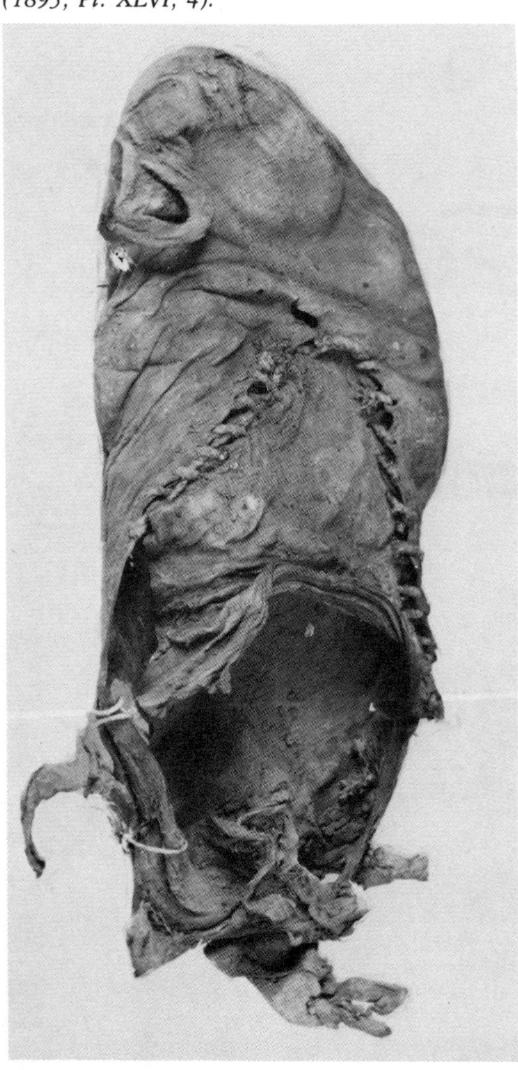

Figure 448. *Fragment of leather with whipped seam joining two lengths of hide, with the fur remaining (12749/700).*

Table 39. Leather and hide fragments.

Illus. Proven. Cat. No.	Ident.	Length (cm.)	Width (mm.)	Remarks
Fig. 448 Kiva H, vent. shaft 12749/700				Two pieces of leather, with fur remaining, sewed together along short edges with 2-ply S-twist cotton yarn; whipped seam with stitches touching. Along lower edge of the right piece there is a running stitch of 2-ply Z-twist yucca twine beginning with a self knot. Along the lower edge of the left piece is a running stitch of 2-ply S-twist cotton yarn. This is obviously a small fragment of a sewed leather item but it is impossible to guess what it had been.
Room 3, fill 12360/700		14	3 (each)	Bundle of six soft thongs wrapped and tied with another thong.
Room 7, Lev. II 17325/700		11.3	ca. 8	Twisted fur strip, probably a wrapping of twine.
Room 26, undisturbed fill 15275/700	rabbit sp.	(very small)		Unworked bits of hide with adherent long, grayish brown hairs.
Room 46, fill 15568/700		4	12	Fragment of soft leather; no sewing.
Room 45, fill 12540/700		8.3	70	Irregular fragment of hide with red ocher rubbed on both surfaces; no sewing.
Kiva C, fill between walls 15149/700	woodrat sp.	ca. 12.5	1-4	Strip of hide, twisted (S-twist) but unworked; white and grayish brown hairs are adherent throughout most of the length.
Kiva E and Rm. 11, loose trash beyond broken edge of floor. 12702/700		10.8	80	Rectangular fragment; whipping along one edge with 2-ply S-twist cotton yarn.
Kiva G, loose fill in south-west recess 12723/700		21.5	10	Thong.
Kiva I, vent. shaft fill 27981/700		4.5	30	Triangular fragment (red stained?) with running stitch along one edge and whipping stitch along another edge that joins it to another fragment. Sewing with 2-ply Z-twist yucca twine about 1 mm. in diameter.
Kiva I, vent. shaft fill 12223/700		9		Triangular fragment; sewing at one corner with 2-ply Z-twist yucca twine.
Kiva O, surface 20222/700		9	Narrow	Two lengths of thong of irregular widths joined end to end with square knot.
Area IV, Lev. A 20255/700		18	9	Two strips of hide joined end to end with square knot.
Burial 35 14402/700				Small irregular bits of raw hide which could be human.

Chapter Eight

Refuse

REFUSE

Great masses of refuse material were recovered during the excavation of Long House. They reflect a broad spectrum of available resources, including plant and animal foodstuffs (wild and domestic), unworked architectural and artifact materials, and debris resulting from the manufacture of building components and artifacts. Several types of material have been studied extensively and reported upon elsewhere by experts in the particular field of study concerned. No attempt will be made here to repeat this information in detail, but the basic data will be summarized.

PLANT MATERIAL

Domestic Plants

Corn and Cucurbits (2,964 specimens). Hugh Cutler and Winton Meyer analyzed both the corn and cucurbits from Long House and other Wetherill Mesa sites. In the abstract of their article, the authors describe concisely the major findings of their study of the Wetherill Mesa corn:

> Most corn from the Mesa Verde area belongs to a complex derived from hybridization of a small-cobbed flint-pop corn with an 8-rowed flour corn. This cross produced 12- to 14-rowed flint and flour corn (the typical Basketmaker corn) and the variable Pima-Papago corn. After Pueblo I, probably late Pueblo II, there was an increase in the number of 8-rowed cobs and a decrease in 12- to 14-rowed cobs. The corn is similar to collections from sites of comparable age excavated in northern Arizona near Navajo Mountain. The uniformity and the slow development of corn types probably reflect peripheral conditions, especially adaptation to short growing seasons and limited cultural interchange. (Cutler and Meyer, 1965, p. 136).

In Long House, the percentages of cobs of each row number (based on the median of collections from any room or area with 26 or more cobs) is as follows: 8 rows—42 percent; 10 rows—35 percent; 12 rows—21 percent; and 14 rows—1 percent (Cutler and Meyer, ibid., p. 149, table 5). As near as we could determine, all of the corn cobs came from Pueblo III deposits.

The 2,651 corncobs taken out of Long House came from the surface, fill, or below the floor of 50 rooms and 15 kivas. The distribution, which Cutler and Meyer (ibid., pp. 144–145, Table 2) give by room and kiva, shows several areas of concentration. These, in turn, probably reflect both storage of corn in rooms and the use of trash to level floors and fill interwall spaces.

The largest concentration of cobs (1,105) came from a portion of the central room block—Rooms 23–28, 36, 70, and 71, and Kiva I— and, by probable association through wall collapse, Room 64 and Kiva L immediately below Kiva I. A large number of these came from trash fill packed between Kiva I's walls and in rooms known to have been abandoned and partially torn out while the pueblo was still occupied (Rooms 70, 71, 24, and 28). The figures suggest, further, that Room 26 may also have been abandoned.

The next largest concentration of cobs (515) is from the west end of the ruin—Kivas A, B, and C, and Rooms 3, 4, 6, and 7. Many of these cobs were from the subfloor area of Rooms 6 and 7, which was filled with trash, and probably from trash placed between the walls of the three kivas. Other locations in the ruin which produced large numbers of corncobs are Rooms 14 and 46 (between Kiva F and the Beer Cellar Complex); Kivas D and E and adjacent Rooms 12, 37, and 61; Rooms 47 and 81 (northwest of Pithouse 1); and Rooms 40, 42, 44, and 45 (part of the West Ledge Ruin).

What the location of these concentrations signifies is uncertain, but we should note the presence of mealing bins in Rooms 9, 14, and possibly 3, as well as the correlation between the distribution of metates and features in which cobs were found. Perhaps two-thirds of the rooms and kivas in which metates were found are either in or closely peripheral to the areas of cob concentration. No cobs were found, however, in Room 56, which had four mealing bins, or in Rooms 49 and 79, where a metate was embedded in the floor. Another strange exception, due in part, perhaps, to ground moisture, is the area centered about Kiva R. Almost no cobs were found here, but mealing bins were located in Room 52 and a dozen metates were found in or near the kiva. (In most cases, metates in the kivas were probably on the roof or came from nearby rooms.)

In addition to the cobs, 34 corn tassels were found below the floor of Room 32 and 59 tassels were recovered from Room 44. There is little obvious significance in the presence of tassels in Room 32, adjacent to Kiva G on the north, which consisted of only one wall and a floor when excavated. However, Room 44, one of the rooms in the West Ledge Ruin, may well have been a storeroom.

All of the squash from Long House that could be identified specifically was—with one possible exception—*Cucurbita pepo* ". . . the species which spread over all agricultural areas of the United States" (Cutler and Meyer, 1965, p. 136). Included in the material studied by Cutler and Meyer (ibid., pp. 144–145, plus additions given in personal communications) were 101 rind fragments, 14 seeds, and 3 peduncles of unidentified *Cucurbita*. These were found primarily in four locations: Rooms 6 and 7 (42 specimens); Room 46 (20 specimens); Area I (8 specimens); and Rooms 47 and 48 (19 specimens).

Specimens of *Curcurbita pepo* were found in the following quantities: vine—1; rind fragments—12; seeds—48; and peduncles—29. The areas of concentration were Rooms 6 and 7 (34 specimens); Room 46 (14 specimens); Area I (6 specimens); Kiva I (17 specimens); and Rooms 47 and 48 (6 specimens).

One of the *Cucurbita* sp. rinds was probably *Cucurbita mixta*, the only other species of squash found at Mesa Verde. Cutler and Meyer (ibid., p. 151) state that "*C. mixta* is not as cold-tolerant as *C. pepo*, and conditions at Mesa Verde probably were marginal."

Only 12 fragments of the bottle gourd, *Lagenaria siceraria*, were found in Long House.

Beans (90 specimens). Kaplan (1965), who studied the Wetherill Mesa beans, reported that all bean pods, pod fragments, and seeds found in Long House are of one species, *Phaseolus vulgaris* (common bean). Of the 90 specimens found, eight are variety C1 (cylindrical, solid orange-red), 18 are variety C11 (semiround, violet, striped), and 64 are indeterminate (Kaplan, ibid., p. 155, Table 1, plus additions given in personal communications). Kaplan (ibid., p. 153) states, "The violet, striped bean (C11) with a non-curling, often purple-mottled pod predominates at Wetherill Mesa and was also the most abundant and widespread common-bean variety of the pre-Columbian Southwest."

The major concentrations of beans within Long House closely parallel those of other vegetal refuse: Rooms 6 and 7 (13 specimens); Rooms 14 and 46 (32 specimens); Kivas H and I, and Room 28 (11 specimens); Room 69 (5 specimens); Rooms 47 and 80 (9 specimens); and Room 44 (12 specimens). The remaining eight specimens came from Rooms 12, 24, 26, 30 and 40, and Area VIII.

Wild Plants

All of the unworked wild plant materials in Long House were identified by Dr. Stanley Welsh of Brigham Young University at various times during the course of the Project. Most of the specimens were in trash fill, including those placed between kiva walls and the like, from the drier portion of the ruin. (Few specimens came from Kiva R and associated rooms in the rather damp east end of the site.) With the exception of Jimson week (*Datura metaloides*) and miner's lettuce (*Montia* sp.), all plants represented by the archeological material are still present in the Mesa Verde flora (Welsh and Erdman, 1964). The materials will be discussed according to the nine generalized categories into which we sorted them.

Yucca (150 specimens). Leaves or leaf fragments and other parts of the yucca formed one of the groups of refuse material. Yucca fiber was also found in small lots or bundles, as wads, and in large masses. The fiber may have been derived from naturally dessicated leaves, but it could also have been obtained by deliberately removing the fleshy tissue from freshly cut leaves. It was not possible to distinguish specific differences in most of the yucca, but the bulk of the material was probably *Yucca baccata*, the broad-leafed yucca. Sixteen leaf bases were recognized as *Yucca harrimaniae*.

The yucca fibers came from three general locations: the west end (Kiva C, Room 83, and Area X); part of the central room block (Rooms 26, 28, and 36, and Kivas H, I, and nearby K, and Area I; and the Beer Cellar Complex (Room 19) and Room 32. The distribution of the greater part of the yucca remains was similar: the west side (Rooms 4, 6, 7, 12, and 37, Kivas A–E, and Areas V, VII, and X); the central room block (Rooms 27–29, 36, and Kiva I); and Areas VI (Great Kiva) and IX (above Kivas M and S). The specimens of *Yucca harrimaniae* came from the nested baskets in the ventilator shaft of Kiva I.

Grass (425 specimens). A considerable amount of grass, primarily crowns, was found in the trash fill. Most of it was of undetermined species, with only three identified: Indian ricegrass—*Oryzopsis hymenoides* (21 specimens definite, 7 tentative); needle-and-thread grass—*Stipa comata* (2 specimens); and bluegrass—*Poa* sp. (1 specimen definite, 16 tentative). The distribution covered a majority of the more sheltered rooms and kivas, generally those against or near the cave wall, including Rooms 43–45 of the West Ledge Ruin.

Bark and Bast (471 specimens). Juniper (*Juniperus* sp.) bark and bast, which was used in roof construction, as a source of fiber, and in many other ways, was the most common plant in this category. A few specimens of serviceberry (*Amelanchier* sp.), willow (*Salix* sp.), sagebrush (*Artemisia* sp.), skunkbush (*Rhus trilobata*), Douglas fir (*Pseudotsuga menziesii*)—possibly, pine (*Pinus ponderosa* and, probably, *Pinus erulis*), poplar (*Pipulus* sp.), and mountain mahogany (*Cercoccarpus* sp.) were also represented. This material was found, once again, in the more protected rooms and kivas, including both ledge ruins (Rooms 40 and 43–45 and Area VIII).

Wood (3,813 specimens). A large quantity of many plants, primarily woody, formed one of the largest categories of refuse material. The specimens ranged in size from slivers of wood and small pieces of charcoal to large stems and masses of brush. The plants identified are given below.

Mormon tea—*Ephedra viridis*
juniper—*Juniperus* sp.
pinyon pine—*Pinus edulis*
ponderosa pine—*Pinus ponderosa*
Douglas-fir—*Pseudotsuga menziesii*
amaranthus—*Amaranthus* sp.
skunkbush—*Rhus triblobata*
elderberry—*Sambucus* sp.
snowberry—*Symphoricarpos* sp.
fourwing saltbush—*Atriplex canescens*
greasewood—*Sarcobatus vermiculatus*
tarragon—*Artemisia dracunculus*
big sagebrush—*Artemisia tridentata*
brickellia—*Brickellia* sp.
rabbitbrush—*Chrysothamnus* sp.
snakeweed—*Gutierrezia sarothrae*
wirelettuce—*Stephanomeria* sp.
prince's plume—*Stanleya pinnata*
Gambel oak—*Quercus gambelii*
serviceberry—*Amelanchier* sp.
mountain mahogany—*Cercocarpus montanus*
chokecherry—*Prunus virginiana*
bitterbrush—*Purshia tridentata*
willow—*Salix* sp.
fendlerbush—*Fendlera rupicola*
mockorange—*Philadelphus* sp.
gooseberry—*Ribes leptanthum*
cattail—*Typha* sp.

The material was widely distributed across the site, for the most part in relatively dry areas, including all of the ledge ruins except Room 40.

Reed (219 specimens). All fragments were from the common reed, *Phragmites communis*. The distribution coincided roughly with that of other refuse, and included Rooms 44 and 45 and Area VIII.

Seeds, cones, pods, and other plant parts (1,042 specimens).

Included in this catchall category are parts of plants not included in the sections above. These items did not serve, generally, as raw material for tools, ornaments, and other artifacts, but a number were obviously foodstuffs. Others may have played a part in ceremonial activities, but there is no specific evidence to indicate such a use. The specimens forming this category are listed below by plant.

star puffball—*Geastrum* sp. (1 fungus)
juniper—*Juniperus* sp. (446 seeds & berries, 1 gall)
pinyon pine—*Pinus edulis* (393 seeds, 3 seed shells, 18 cones, 1 cone scale, 2 chunks of resin)
Douglas-fir—*Pseudotsuga menziesii* (2 cones)
amaranthus—*Amaranthus* sp. (1 seed)
fourwing saltbush—*Atriplex canescens* (8 seeds, 1 seed pod)
sagebrush—*Artemisia* sp. (10 stems with seed pod, 1 root)
rabbitbrush—*Chrysothamnus* sp. (1 flower, 3 involucres)
thistle—*Cirsium* sp. (2 seed pods)
sunflower—*Helianthus* sp. (2 composite heads)
Gambel oak—*Quercus gambelii* (30 acorns)
onion—*Allium* sp. (1 bulb scale)
yucca—*Yucca* sp. (76 seeds, 6 pods, 1 bud scale)
evening primrose—*Oenothera* sp. (1 seed pod)
mountain mahogany—*Cercocarpus montanus* (1 seed plume)
mockorange—*Philadelphus* sp. (2 galls)
gooseberry —*Ribes leptanthum* (1 seed)
Jimson weed—*Datura metaloides* (1 seed pod)

The distribution corresponded to the previously shown pattern, including Area VIII and Rooms 39 and 40 of the West Ledge Ruin.

Cactus (363 specimens). All but two identified specimens of cactus were *Opuntia* sp. These two, both stems, were probably *Echinocactus* sp. The material consisted of 357 seeds, 3 ponds, 5 ovaries, 4 vascular skeletons, 29 fruits, 5 stems, 7 cladophyll fragments, and 3 unidentified specimens. The cactus was found across the ruin from the west to the east end, but not in either ledge ruin.

Miscellaneous vegetal material from adobe (122 specimens). This category, and the following one, have a cultural basis for sorting. The vegetal materials in other categories was merely gathered en masse and sorted by the plant or part of the plant present. The techniques used in separating the materials from adobe and fecal samples are described in detail by Colyer and Osborne (1965). Most items recovered were probably included during the prehistoric occupation period, and thus we eliminated to a large extent the possibility of recent intrusives in this rare instance.

Several of the most common trees and plants, and others less common, were represented in the items recovered from adobe. The specimens are listed below by plant.

corn—*Zea* (leaf, kernel)
Mormon tea—*Ephedra viridis* (twigs)
juniper—*Juniperus* sp. (bark, bast, twigs, splinters, berries, seed, and charcoal)
pinyon pine—*Pinus edulis* (bark, splinters, needles, seeds)
sagebrush—*Artemisia* sp. (not indicated)
rabbitbrush—*Chrysothamnus* sp. (twigs and splinters)
oak—*Quercus* sp. (twigs)
reed—*Phragmites communis* (not indicated)
yucca—*Yucca* sp. (fiber)
serviceberry—*Amelanchier* sp. (twigs and bark)
willow—*Salix* sp. (not indicated)

Seeds only of the following were recovered:

squash—*Cucurbita* sp.
amaranthus—*Amaranthus* sp.
?(Borage Family—Boraginaceae (*Lappula* sp.?)
cactus—*Opuntia* sp.
beeplant—*Cleome* sp.
?(Pink Family)—Caryophyllaceae
lambsquarter—*Chenopodium* sp.
sunflower—*Helianthus* sp.
sedge—*Carex* sp.
wheatgrass—*Agropyron* sp.
needlegrass—*Stipa* sp.
lupine—*Lupinus* sp.
Jacob's ladder—*Polemonium* sp.
ground cherry—*Physalis* sp.
nightshade—*Solanum* sp.

The adobe, presumably all construction material, came from trash east of Kiva D, south of Kiva P in Area X, and just outside the Area XIV retaining wall on the Upper West Trash Slope.

Miscellaneous vegetal material from human feces (67 specimens). Seeds predominate in this category, which also includes such surprising items as juniper bast and an oak twig. These, and other items listed, probably became embedded in the specimens and were not deliberately ingested. The cactus spines may have been eaten accidentally with the fruit, or probably acquired in the same way the bast and twig were. The inclusions are listed below by plant.

corn—*Zea* (leaf fiber, kernel fragments)
beans—*Phaseolus vulgaris* (seed, seed fragments)
squash—*Cucurbita* sp. (seed, seed fragments, rind)
fungus—? (capillitia, peridia, spores)
juniper—*Juniperus* sp. (bast)
amaranthus—*Amaranthus* sp. (seed, immature seed)
skunkbush—*Rhus trilobata* (seed)
cactus—*Opuntia* sp. (spines, epidermis, vascular skeleton)
cactus—*Opuntia phaeacantha* (seed)
beeplant—*Cleome* sp. (seed, seed fragments)
chenopodium—*Chenopodium* sp. (seed)
oak—*Quercus* sp. (twig)
miner's lettuce—*Montia* sp. (seed)
ground cherry—*Physalis* sp. (seed)

The specimens were collected from fill in Rooms 44 and 47, and in the following locations along the central room block: Room 26, Kiva H, Areas I and III, and in corners formed by the walls of Room 29 with Kivas H and I.

FAUNAL MATERIAL—MAMMALIAN

Desiccated remains (3 specimens). Complete specimens of the bushy-tailed wood rat (*Neotoma cinerea*) and chipmunk (*Eutamias* sp.) were found in Rooms 17 (disturbed fill) and 19 (undisturbed fill), respectively. The skeleton of a deer mouse (*Peromyscus* sp.) came from the undisturbed fill of Room 26.

Hide, hair, and claws (29 specimens). Four human hairs from human feces, one lot of gray rabbit hair, and two lengths of twisted wood rat hair were identified by the Federal Bureau of Investigation in Washington, D. C.

Eighteen fragments of hide were found, but only the five sent to the FBI laboratory were identified:

mouse (possibly)—Room 36, disturbed fill
wood rat (with tawny pelage)—Room 42, fill
wood rat (twisted strip of hide)—Kiva C, fill between early and late lower inner walls
bighorn sheep—Room 46, fill
rabbit—Room 26, undisturbed fill

Four of the other 11 fragments were tentatively identified in the Wetherill Mesa Project laboratory as deer. Three fragments, two from the ventilator of Kiva I and one from Room 45, were stained or dyed red. The other identified fragments came from Rooms 7, 14, 46, Kiva 0, Area IV, and Burial 35.

Four claws, possibly dog, were found in Room 54, and one other unidentified claw came from Kiva U.

Feces (30 specimens). Only about 30 of the 170± fecal specimens identified by the late Olaus J. Murie were mammalian. The animals represented, excluding man, were bobcat, coyote, ringtail, bear, mule deer or bighorn sheep, wood rat, and unidentified small mammals. All of these are part of the modern Mesa Verde fauna (Anderson, 1961). Most of the specimens came from the west side (Kivas A, C, E, and F; Rooms 4 and 30; and Area X) and the central room block and vicinity (Kivas H and I; Rooms 24, 27, 64, and 73; and Area IV).

Unworked bone. All mammal bones were identified by Thomas W. Mathews of the National Park Service. In addition to preparing the tables used in this discussion, Mathews also outlined the faunal stratigraphy in personal correspondence with the author. His remarks form the basis for this discussion.

Table 40. Unworked bone.

		All Specimens				Mammals Only			
	Totals	%	%	%	%	%	%	%	%
Mammalia-Aves, Unknown	25	00.8							
Mammalia sp.	23	00.7				00.7			
Sorex sp.	1	00.0				00.0			
Lepus sp.	5	00.1	00.5			00.1	00.5		
Lepus californicus	13	00.4				00.4			
Sylvilagus sp.	1,353	44.1		44.8		44.5		45.2	
Sylvilagus nuttalli	1	00.0	44.2			00.0	44.6		
Sylvilagus auduboni	1	00.0				00.0			
Rodentia sp.	81	02.6				02.6			
Sciuridae sp.	11	00.3				00.3			
Marmota flaviventris	56	01.5				01.8			
Cynomys gunnisoni	4	00.1				00.1			
Citellus sp.	34	01.1	03.6	06.0		01.1	03.7	06.0	
Citellus variegatus cf. *grammurus*	79	02.5				02.6			
Eutamias sp.	2	00.0				00.0			
Geomyidae sp.	1	00.0				00.0			
Thomomys sp.	44	01.4	01.6			01.4	01.6		
Thomomys umbrinus	6	00.1				00.1			
Dipodomys sp.	5	00.1				00.1			
Cricetidae sp.	4	00.1				00.1			
Peromyscus sp.	39	01.2	01.3			01.2	01.3		
Peromyscus crinitus	2	00.0				00.0			
Neotoma sp.	824	26.9	31.0	33.7		27.1	31.2	34.0	
Neotoma cinerea	126	04.1				04.1			
Microtus sp.	29	00.9				00.9			
Microtus montanus cf. *fusus*	8	00.2	01.2			00.2	01.2		
Microtus mexicanus cf. *mogollonensis*	1	00.0				00.0			
Carnivora sp.	5	00.1				00.1			
Canidae sp.	11	00.3				00.3			
Canis sp.	17	00.5				00.5			
Canis lupus	2	00.0	01.5			00.0	01.5		
Canis familiaris	16	00.5				00.5			
Canis latrans	11	00.3			02.4	00.3			02.5
Vulpes sp.	2	00.0	00.1			00.0	00.1		
Vulpes fulva	2	00.0		00.6		00.0		00.6	
Urocyon cinereoargenteus cf. *scotti*	15	00.4				00.4			
Mustelidae sp.	1	00.0				00.0			
Mustela (Putorius) sp.	1	00.0				00.0			
Taxidea taxus cf. *berlandieri*	6	00.1	00.3			00.1	00.3		
Spilogale gracilis	2	00.0				00.0			
Felidae									
Lynx sp.	6	00.1	02.5			00.1	02.6		
Lynx rufus cf. *baileyi*	73	02.3				02.4			
Artiodactyla sp.	34	01.1				01.1			
Odocoileus sp.	10	00.3	01.2			00.3	01.2		
Odocoileus hemionus	29	00.9		03.6		00.9		03.6	
Ovis canadensis	38	01.2				01.2			
Perissodactyla									
Equus caballus	3	00.0				00.0			
Totals	3,062				3,037				

The Long House excavation produced 5,476 mammal bones, 418 worked and 5,058 unworked. All categories of unworked bone are listed by number of specimens and percentage of the total collection in table 40, which further breaks down the mammal totals by order. As indicated in table 41, 45 taxonomic identifications below the level of Class (Mammalia) were made. Several of these figures, which form the final totals, will differ slightly from those used elsewhere in this report because they include miscellaneous material examined after completion of various parts of the study.

Two additional tables list in detail the results of Mathews' study. Table 42 gives the total number and percentage of unworked bones each taxonomic unit represented, and table 43 the distribution of mammal bones by features within the pueblo.

Table 41. Resume of mammalian faunal list of unworked bones.

Mammals		
Insectivores	1	1 genus
Lagomorphs	5	2 genera, 3 species
Rodents	19	1 order, 3 families, 7 genera, 8 species (3 suggested sub-species)
Carnivores	15	1 order, 2 families, 4 genera, 8 species (1 suggested subgenus; 3 suggested sub-species)
Perissodactyls	1	1 species
Artiodactyls	4	1 order, 1 genus, 2 species
Total	45	

Forty-five identifications have been assigned to this collection below the level of Class (*Mammalia*).

Orders	–	3
Families	–	5
Genera	–	15
Species	–	22
Total		45
Suggested subgenus	–	1
Suggested subspecies	–	6
Total		7

Table 42. Total number and percentage of unworked bones in each taxonomic unit represented.

	No.	Percentage
Total Sample	5,058	100
*Bone, unknown	2	(T)
*Fish, Amphibians, and Reptiles	25	(T)
*Mammal or bird, unknown	25	(T)
Mammals	3,037	60.04
Birds	1,889	37.34
*Man	80	1.58
*(other = 2.6%)		
Mammals	3,037	100
Mammals, unknown	23	(T)
Insectivores	1	(T)
Lagomorphs	1,373	45.21
Rodents	1,356	44.64
Carnivores	170	5.59
Perissodactyls	3	(T)
Artiodactyls	11	3.65

As Mathews stated (personal communication, 1964), "The unworked bone collection from Long House is characterized by clearly stratified faunal assemblages. While dominated quantitatively by lagomorphs and rodents derived chiefly from post-occupational contexts, taxonomically there is great faunal diversity throughout the site." He further pointed out that the bird bones reflect considerable diversity among the wild species but felt that they are probably far less significant stratigraphically than the mammal material.

The first question raised by Mathews concerns the source of jackrabbits and marmots, both of which seem to appear during the earliest occupation of the cave. The former was found in the lower levels of Room 48, the subfloor level of Room 85, the fill of Kiva Q–Area IX, and the upper fill of Kiva J—all adjacent to the pithouse—as well as from fill immediately above the floor of the pithouse itself. Specimens also came from the fill of Room 9 and Kivas H and K. These last three may date to the early 1200's, but not to the Basketmaker occupation. The specimens in Kiva K could easily have drifted in there from the pithouse area, and the Room 9 and Kiva H specimens may also be floaters.

The marmot remains come entirely from the pithouse (fill directly above floor) or from rooms adjacent to or near it: the lower fill of Rooms 47, 48, and 81; the floor of Room 49; the subfloor (pithouse) levels of Rooms 54 and 55; the subfloor level of Room 85; the fill and subfloor levels of Room 87; the upper fill in Kivas N and Q; and the lower fill and floor of Kiva R.

Mathews suggests that pockets of early faunal material predate and were disturbed by the Basketmaker III occupation. This is based, in part, upon mineralization of the marmot bones, implying a different depositional history than that of the rest of the faunal assemblage from the earliest parts of the pueblo.

Whatever the origin of these particular marmot remains, that animal and the jackrabbit were probably found in limited numbers throughout the occupation, just as they are on the Mesa Verde today. It is probably more accurate to assume that the earliest inhabitants made greater use of the marmot than those who moved in later, rather than postulating any significant climatic variations between periods of occupation.

Also from the early (Basketmaker) horizon, apparently, are Gunnison's prairie dog (lower levels of Rooms 47, 48, and Kiva J), gray fox (subfloor levels of Rooms 54 and 55, and the fill directly above the pithouse floor), and ferret (middle level, Room 47). As Mathews observed, all of these animals with the exception of the marmot are referable to a dry, open country environment (Upper Sonoran).

Material which can be attributed to the Pueblo III occupation is, as Mathews termed it, ". . . almost a residual category, and is, in many respects, the most unsatisfactory of the series." I would certainly agree with this statement, since the time period represented is far shorter (perhaps 100 years or less) than either the long post-occupational period (A.D. 1300± to present) or the even longer pre-Pueblo period interrupted only briefly, perhaps, by the builders of the pithouse.

The late Pueblo III period is high in carnivores (wolf, dog, coyote, vulpid fox) and is distinguished by the absence of the animals characteristic of the lower horizon. Exceptions are the mule deer and bighorn sheep, which appear in both the Basketmaker III and Pueblo III horizons.

The post-occupational deposits are extensive, but in many areas very difficult to separate from those of the late occupation. This is especially true in fill disturbed by both burrowing animals and man. Mathews has described these post-occupational materials as a constant "fall-out" over the surface of the site, a process which is periodically interrupted by man. That this process continued at the

Table 43. Distribution of unworked mammal bones by feature.

	General Feature 9, fill	General vicinity of Room 80, surface	General surface & fill	Surface	1: Datum to 4.1 (bedrock)	2: Fill between floors 1, 2	2: Fill between floors 3, 5	3:	4: Fill	5: Surface & fill 0–4.0′	6: Level III	7: Level III	7: Level IV	7: Level VI	9: Fill	10: Fill
**Mammalia—Aves,* Unknown	1				1											
Mammalia sp.					1											
Sorex sp.																
Lepus sp.															1	
L. californicus																
Sylvilagus sp.	4		3			7	23	1	4		1		1	3		2
S. nuttalli																
S. auduboni																
Rodentia sp.																
Sciuridae sp.																
Marmota flaviventris																
Cynomys gunnisoni																
Citellus sp.						1	1									
C. variegatus					1								1			
cf. *grammurus*																
Eutamias sp.																
Geomyidae sp.																
Thomomys sp.								1								
T. umbrinus																
Dipodomys sp.																
Cricetidae sp.																
Peromyscus																
P. crinitus																
Neotoma sp.	1															2
N. cinerea	1					1	1									
Microtus sp.																
M. montanus																
cf. *fusus*																
M. mexicanus																
cf. *mogollonensis*																
Carnivora sp.			1													
Canidae sp.																
Canis sp.												1				
Canis lupus																
Canis familiaris														1		
Canis latrans			1													
Vulpes sp.																
Vulpes fulva																
Urocyon cinereoargenteus				1												
cf. *scotti*																
Mustelidae sp.																
Mustela (*Putorius*) sp.																
Taxidea taxus																
cf. *berlandieri*																
Spilogale gracilis																
Felidae							1									
Lynx sp.							1									
Lynx rufus																
cf. *baileyi*		1														
Perissodactyla																
Equus caballus																
Artiodactyla sp.							1				1			1		
Odocoileus sp.			2							1			1			
O. hemionus																
Ovis canadensis			2													
TOTALS	6	1	9	1	2	9	28	2	4	1	2	1	3	5	1	4

**Mammalia—Aves,* Unknown *not* counted in totals. General, head of West Trash Slope—1 specimen. (No mammals present.)

Table 43. Distribution of unworked mammal bones by feature. (Continued)

	12: Disturbed fill above west wall top	12: Level B	12: Level B, undisturbed fill	12: Subfloor fill	12: Burial 25	13: Fill	14: Level B	14: Crack, base of west (bedrock) wall	15: Disturbed fill	17: Disturbed fill	19: Fill	23: Undisturbed fill	24: Undisturbed fill	25: Undisturbed fill	26: Undisturbed fill	27: Undisturbed fill
**Mammalia—Aves*, Unknown			1													
Mammalia sp.					1											
Sorex sp.																
Lepus sp.																
L. californicus																
Sylvilagus sp.	13	34	97	1	4	6	2	1	4	3		2	1	3	7	5
S. nuttalli																
S. auduboni																
Rodentia sp.																1
Sciuridae sp.		1														
Marmota flaviventris																
Cynomys gunnisoni																
Citellus sp.	1	3	19												1	
C. variegatus	1	1														
cf. *grammurus*																
Eutamias sp.											1					
Geomyidae sp.																
Thomomys sp.									1							
T. umbrinus																
Dipodomys sp.																
Cricetidae sp.		2														
Peromyscus			1						1						1	
P. crinitus																
Neotoma sp.	1	2	13			1			4					3		6
N. cinerea		1			1	2			2	2						2
Microtus sp.																
M. montanus																
cf. *fusus*																
M. mexicanus																
cf. *mogollonensis*																
Carnivora sp.																
Canidae sp.			1													
Canis sp.	1		1													
Canis lupus																
Canis familiaris			1													
Canis latrans			4													
Vulpes sp.																
Vulpes fulva																
Urocyon cinereoargenteus																
cf. *scotti*																
Mustelidae sp.																
Mustela (*Putorius*) sp.																
Taxidea taxus																
cf. *berlandieri*																
Spilogale gracilis																
Felidae																
Lynx sp.					1										1	
Lynx rufus																
cf. *baileyi*																
Perissodactyla																
Equus caballus																
Artiodactyla sp.	1	3	1													
Odocoileus sp.			2						1							
O. hemionus																
Ovis canadensis										2						
TOTALS	18	48	145	1	7	9	2	1	13	7	1	2	1	6	10	14

**Mammalia—Aves*, Unknown *not* counted in totals.

Table 43. Distribution of unworked mammal bones by feature. (Continued)

	28: Fill	28: Burial 30	29: Trash fill	30: Floor	35: Fill above gray sandy clay	35: Fill	36: Disturbed fill	36: Undisturbed fill	36: Level C	37: Upper fill	37: Fill	37: Burial 33	39: Fill	40: Fill	42: Fill	43: Fill
**Mammalia—Aves,* Unknown																
Mammalia sp.																
Sorex sp.																
Lepus sp.																
L. californicus																
Sylvilagus sp.	5	6	5	24	5	9	3	2	1			1	1	4	75	52
S. nuttalli														1		
S. auduboni																
Rodentia sp.															36	
Sciuridae sp.															2	1
Marmota flaviventris																
Cynomys gunnisoni																
Citellus sp.	1															
C. variegatus						1					1				10	1
cf. *grammurus*																
Eutamias sp.																
Geomyidae sp.																1
Thomomys sp.				1											7	
T. umbrinus																
Dipodomys sp.																
Cricetidae sp.																1
Peromyscus				1											15	
P. crinitus																
Neotoma sp.	7	1		9	2	2		2						2	217	30
N. cinerea	1			1			3									9
Microtus sp.				1											13	
M. montanus																
cf. *fusus*																
M. mexicanus																
cf. *mogollonensis*																
Carnivora sp.																
Canidae sp.																
Canis sp.																
Canis lupus																
Canis familiaris																
Canis latrans																
Vulpes sp.																
Vulpes fulva																
Urocyon cinereoargenteus																
cf. *scotti*																
Mustelidae sp.																
Mustela (*Putorius*) sp.																
Taxidea taxus										1						
cf. *berlandieri*																
Spilogale gracilis																
Felidae																
Lynx sp.			1													
Lynx rufus																
cf. *baileyi*																
Perissodactyla																
Equus caballus																
Artiodactyla sp.																
Odocoileus sp.																
O. hemionus																
Ovis canadensis							1									
TOTALS	14	7	6	37	7	12	7	4	1	1	1	1	1	7	375	95

**Mammalia—Aves,* Unknown *not* counted in totals.

Table 43. Distribution of unworked mammal bones by feature. (Continued)

	44: Fill	45: Fill	46: Fill	47: Level I	47: Level II	47: Level III	48: Level A	48: Level B	48: Level C	48-P.H. 1: Level C	48: Dip in yellow soil back of cave, Level C	48: Level D	48: General Feature #3	48: N.E. corner, undisturbed fill	49: On floor	50: Fill
**Mammalia—Aves*, Unknown	3	2														
Mammalia sp.																
Sorex sp.									1							
Lepus sp.													1			
L. californicus									1							
Sylvilagus sp.	109	58	2				2	11	7	2			4	2	1	2
S. nuttalli																
S. auduboni		1														
Rodentia sp.	4	2														
Sciuridae sp.		1														
Marmota flaviventris						12		1	1	1	2	5		1	1	
Cynomys gunnisoni					1							1				
Citellus sp.																
C. variegatus								2						1		
cf. *grammurus*																
Eutamias sp.																
Geomyidae sp.																
Thomomys sp.	11															
T. umbrinus	1	3														
Dipodomys sp.	3															
Cricetidae sp.	1															
Peromyscus		1	3													
P. crinitus		2														
Neotoma sp.	211	35		1				3								1
N. cinerea	32	5	1			1		5			1					
Microtus sp.	1	2														
M. montanus																
cf. *fusus*																
M. mexicanus																
cf. *mogollonensis*																
Carnivora sp.																
Canidae sp.								1	1							
Canis sp.				1								1				
Canis lupus																
Canis familiaris																
Canis latrans																
Vulpes sp.																
Vulpes fulva																
Urocyon cinereoargenteus																
cf. *scotti*																
Mustelidae sp.																
Mustela (Putorius) sp.						1										
Taxidea taxus																
cf. *berlandieri*																
Spilogale gracilis																
Felidae																
Lynx sp.																
Lynx rufus																
cf. *baileyi*																
Perissodactyla																
Equus caballus																
Artiodactyla sp.																
Odocoileus sp.								1								
O. hemionus																
Ovis canadensis				1												
TOTALS	373	110	6	3	1	14	2	24	11	3	3	7	5	4	2	3

**Mammalia—Aves*, Unknown *not* counted in totals.

Table 43. Distribution of unworked mammal bones by feature. (Continued)

	52: Fill	54: Level II	54: Level III, subfloor	54: Level IV, subfloor	54: Level V, subfloor	54: Level VI, subfloor	54: Level VII, subfloor	55: Level VI, subfloor	55: Level VII, subfloor	55: Level VIII, subfloor	56: Fill	56: Level I	56: Level II	56: Level IV	56: Level V	57: Surface & fill
**Mammalia—Aves*, Unknown																
Mammalia sp.									2			1				
Sorex sp.																
Lepus sp.																
L. californicus																
Sylvilagus sp.	2	1					1		2	1	3	1	2		1	1
S. nuttalli																
S. auduboni																
Rodentia sp.													1			
Sciuridae sp.																
Marmota flaviventris				2		1	3		1	4						
Cynomys gunnisoni																
Citellus sp.			1													
C. variegatus							1									
cf. *grammurus*																
Eutamias sp.																
Geomyidae sp.																
Thomomys sp.																
T. umbrinus																
Dipodomys sp.																
Cricetidae sp.																
Peromyscus																
P. crinitus																
Neotoma sp.																
N. cinerea																
Microtus sp.																
M. montanus																
cf. *fusus*																
M. mexicanus																
cf. *mogollonensis*																
Carnivora sp.																
Canidae sp.													1			
Canis sp.																
Canis lupus																
Canis familiaris																
Canis latrans		2														
Vulpes sp.																
Vulpes fulva																
Urocyon cinereoargenteus					1			1								
cf. *scotti*																
Mustelidae sp.																
Mustela (Putorius) sp.																
Taxidea taxus																
cf. *berlandieri*																
Spilogale gracilis																
Felidae																
Lynx sp.																
Lynx rufus																
cf. *baileyi*																
Perissodactyla																
Equus caballus																
Artiodactyla sp.				1			1									
Odocoileus sp.																
O. hemionus																
Ovis canadensis														2		
TOTALS	3	3	1	3	1	1	6	1	5	5	3	2	4	2	1	1

**Mammalia—Aves*, Unknown *not* counted in totals.

Table 43. Distribution of unworked mammal bones by feature. (Continued)

	57: Fill	57-Kiva J: vent area, subfloor fill	58: Fill	60: Level III	60: Ash fill, NE. firepit	60: Subfloor fill	63: Surface and fill	64: Fill	65: Subfloor fill	66: Surface	66: E-W trench, subfloor fill	66: Subfloor beneath east wall, etc.	70: Fill	71: Fill	72: Fill	75: Level I, floor
**Mammalia—Aves*, Unknown				1												1
Mammalia sp.																
Sorex sp.																
Lepus sp.																
L. californicus																
Sylvilagus sp.		1	1	1		1	6	2	1		1	1	2	1	7	1
S. nuttalli																
S. auduboni																
Rodentia sp.																
Sciuridae sp.																
Marmota flaviventris																
Cynomys gunnisoni																
Citellus sp.			1													
C. variegatus			1		1	1	1		1							
cf. *grammurus*																
Eutamias sp.																
Geomyidae sp.																
Thomomys sp.																
T. umbrinus																
Dipodomys sp.																
Cricetidae sp.												1				
Peromyscus																
P. crinitus																
Neotoma sp.	1						2	4	4						2	
N. cinerea														4		
Microtus sp.																
M. montanus																
cf. *fusus*																
M. mexicanus																
cf. *mogollonensis*																
Carnivora sp.																
Canidae sp.																
Canis sp.																
Canis lupus																
Canis familiaris																
Canis latrans																1
Vulpes sp.																
Vulpes fulva																
Urocyon cinereoargenteus																
cf. *scotti*																
Mustelidae sp.																
Mustela (*Putorius*) sp.																
Taxidea taxus																
cf. *berlandieri*																
Spilogale gracilis																
Felidae																
Lynx sp.																1
Lynx rufus																
cf. *baileyi*																
Perissodactyla																
Equus caballus																
Artiodactyla sp.								2								
Odocoileus sp.										1						
O. hemionus								1								
Ovis canadensis																
TOTALS	1	1	3	1	1	2	9	9	6	1	1	2	2	1	13	3

**Mammalia—Aves*, Unknown *not* counted in totals.

Table 43. Distribution of unworked mammal bones by feature. (Continued)

	76: Level I	76: Level II, floor	76: Level IV	79: Levels IV, V, VI (subfloor)	80: Level II, floor	81: Level I	81: Level II	82: Level II	84: Level I	84: Level IV	85: Level II	85: Level III	85: Subfloor	87: Level III	87: Subfloor fill	Kiva A: fill
**Mammalia—Aves*, Unknown																
Mammalia sp.								1								
Sorex sp.																
Lepus sp.																
L. californicus													1			
Sylvilagus sp.	1	1	2	2				1	1	1	1	1				1
S. nuttalli																
S. auduboni																
Rodentia sp.					1											
Sciuridae sp.																
Marmota flaviventris							1						1		1	
Cynomys gunnisoni																
Citellus sp.																
C. variegatus						1										
cf. *grammurus*																
Eutamias sp.																
Geomyidae sp.																
Thomomys sp.																
T. umbrinus																
Dipodomys sp.					2											
Cricetidae sp.																
Peromyscus					1								2			
P. crinitus																
Neotoma sp.					8							1	1		1	
N. cinerea					2						1					
Microtus sp.																
M. montanus																
cf. *fusus*																
M. mexicanus																
cf. *mogollonensis*																
Carnivora sp.																1
Canidae sp.																1
Canis sp.																
Canis lupus																
Canis familiaris																
Canis latrans																
Vulpes sp.																
Vulpes fulva																
Urocyon cinereoargenteus																
cf. *scotti*																
Mustelidae sp.																
Mustela (*Putorius*) sp.																
Taxidea taxus																
cf. *berlandieri*																
Spilogale gracilis																
Felidae																
Lynx sp.																
Lynx rufus																
cf. *baileyi*																
Perissodactyla																7
Equus caballus																
Artiodactyla sp.																
Odocoileus sp.																
O. hemionus																
Ovis canadensis														1		
TOTALS	1	1	2	2	14	1	1	2	1	1	2	2	5	1	2	10

**Mammalia—Aves*, Unknown *not* counted in totals.

Table 43. Distribution of unworked mammal bones by feature. (Continued)

	Kiva A: vent shaft fill	Kiva B: approx. 2 ft. above floor	Kiva C: Fill between two walls	Kiva C: Upper fill	Kiva C: Southern recess, fill	Kiva D: Disturbed fill	Kiva D: immediately below floor	Kiva E: North side fill	Kiva E: Fill	Kiva E: Vent. shaft	Kiva F: Fill	Kiva G: Subfloor, fill between upper and 2nd floors	Kiva H: Level *A*	Kiva H: Level *B*	Kiva H: Level *C*	Kiva H: Vent shaft fill
**Mammalia—Aves*, Unknown											1					
Mammalia sp.						1			1							
Sorex sp.																
Lepus sp.																
L. californicus															1	
Sylvilagus sp.	1	2	2		1	2		6			4	3	6	1	4	1
S. nuttalli																
S. audubonі																
Rodentia sp.																
Sciuridae sp.																
Marmota flaviventris																
Cynomys gunnisoni																
Citellus sp.																
C. variegatus		1					3	1		1			1		1	
cf. *grammurus*																
Eutamias sp.																
Geomyidae sp.																
Thomomys sp.																
T. umbrinus																
Dipodomys sp.																
Cricetidae sp.																
Peromyscus																
P. crinitus																
Neotoma sp.						1		3			1		9		1	3
N. cinerea						3		1			1					
Microtus sp.																
M. montanus																
cf. *fusus*																
M. mexicanus																
cf. *mogollonensis*																
Carnivora sp.																
Canidae sp.																
Canis sp.								1			2					
Canis lupus				1												
Canis familiaris																
Canis latrans																
Vulpes sp.																
Vulpes fulva																
Urocyon cinereoargenteus																
cf. *scotti*																
Mustelidae sp.																
Mustela (*Putorius*) sp.																
Taxidea taxus																
cf. *berlandieri*																
Spilogale gracilis																
Felidae																
Lynx sp.																
Lynx rufus														1		
cf. *baileyi*																
Perissodactyla																
Equus caballus																
Artiodactyla sp.						1	1				1				1	
Odocoileus sp.																
O. hemionus															1	
Ovis canadensis																
TOTALS	1	3	2	1	1	8	4	12	1	1	9	3	16	2	9	4

**Mammalia—Aves*, Unknown *not* counted in totals.

Table 43. Distribution of unworked mammal bones by feature. (Continued)

	Kiva H: N.E. recess of vent. shaft, fill	Kiva H: Fill over floor	Kiva I: Surface	Kiva I: Level *A*	Kiva I: Level *B*	Kiva I: Vent. shaft, fill	Kiva I: general fill between walls	Kiva I: Probable fill over kiva	Kiva J: Upper level	Kiva J: Lower level	Kiva J: N. banquette around mug	Kiva J: Below N. bench	Kiva J: (Unknown)	Kiva K: Level I	Kiva K: Level III	Kiva K: Level IV
**Mammalia—Aves,* Unknown																
Mammalia sp.																
Sorex sp.																
Lepus sp.									1							
L. californicus														1		
Sylvilagus sp.	1	7	1	2	2	13	2			5				1		1
S. nuttalli																
S. auduboni																
Rodentia sp.																
Sciuridae sp.										1	1					
Marmota flaviventris								3	1	4		1				
Cynomys gunnisoni													1			
Citellus sp.																
C. variegatus cf. *grammurus*								1		3						
Eutamias sp.																
Geomyidae sp.																
Thomomys sp.																
T. umbrinus				1												
Dipodomys sp.																
Cricetidae sp.																
Peromyscus						1										
P. crinitus																
Neotoma sp.		1		1	1	7				2				1		
N. cinerea										1				1		1
Microtus sp.																
M. montanus cf. *fusus*																
M. mexicanus cf. *mogollonensis*																
Carnivora sp.																
Canidae sp.																
Canis sp.									1	2			1			
Canis lupus																
Canis familiaris																
Canis latrans																
Vulpes sp.																
Vulpes fulva																
Urocyon cinereoargenteus cf. *scotti*																
Mustelidae sp.																
Mustela (*Putorius*) sp.																
Taxidea taxus cf. *berlandieri*																
Spilogale gracilis																
Felidae					1											
Lynx sp.		1		1											1	
Lynx rufus cf. *baileyi*																
Perissodactyla																
Equus caballus																
Artiodactyla sp.																
Odocoileus sp.																
O. hemionus																
Ovis canadensis									1							
TOTALS	1	9	2	4	4	21	2	4	4	18	1	1	2	4	1	2

**Mammalia—Aves,* Unknown *not* counted in totals.

Table 43. Distribution of unworked mammal bones by feature. (Continued)

	Kiva K: Level V, floor	Kiva K: S. recess, fill	Kiva M: Level III	Kiva M: Level IV	Kiva M: Level VI	Kiva M: Level VII	Kiva M: vent. shaft fill	Kiva M: Subfloor fill	Kiva N: Level I	Kiva N: Level II	Kiva N: N. interpilaster space, fill	Kiva N: behind S.E. pilaster, fill	Kiva N: Subfloor, fill	Kiva N: S.E. interwall space, fill	Kiva O: Levels I, II	Kiva O: Level III
**Mammalia—Aves*. Unknown														1		
Mammalia sp.			1					2						2		
Sorex sp.																
Lepus sp.																
L. californicus																
Sylvilagus sp.	2	1			1	1	1	4		1	1			2	6	1
S. nuttalli																
S. auduboni																
Rodentia sp.								3								
Sciuridae sp.																
Marmota flaviventris														1		
Cynomys gunnisoni																
Citellus sp.																
C. variegatus								1						1		
cf. *grammurus*																
Eutamias sp.																
Geomyidae sp.																
Thomomys sp.																
T. umbrinus																
Dipodomys sp.																
Cricetidae sp.																
Peromyscus																
P. crinitus																
Neotoma sp.																
N. cinerea																
Microtus sp.												1				
M. montanus																
cf. *fusus*																
M. mexicanus																
cf. *mogollonensis*																
Carnivora sp.																
Canidae sp.																
Canis sp.														2		
Canis lupus																
Canis familiaris																
Canis latrans																
Vulpes sp.																
Vulpes fulva																
Urocyon cinereoargenteus																
cf. *scotti*																
Mustelidae sp.																
Mustela (Putorius) sp.																
Taxidea taxus																
cf. *berlandieri*																
Spilogale gracilis													1			
Felidae									1							
Lynx sp.	2			1	1				1							
Lynx rufus																
cf. *baileyi*																
Perissodactyla																
Equus caballus																
Artiodactyla sp.											1					
Odocoileus sp.																
O. hemionus																
Ovis canadensis																
TOTALS	4	1	1	1	2	1	1	10	1	1	2	1	1	8	6	1

**Mammalia—Aves*, Unknown *not* counted in totals.

Table 43. Distribution of unworked mammal bones by feature. (Continued)

	Kiva O: Level IV	Kiva O: Level V	Kiva O: Level VI	Kiva P: Level I	Kiva P: Level IV	Kiva Q: Level I	Kiva Q: Level II	Kiva Q: Level III	Kiva Q: Level IV	Kiva Q: Level V	Kiva Q: Level VI	Kiva Q: Level VII, (floor in shrine)	Kiva Q: In shrine, pit on E. side, niche behind, fill	Kiva Q: N. interpilaster space	Kiva Q: Foot drums, compact fill	Kiva R: Level I
**Mammalia—Aves*, Unknown															3	
Mammalia sp.			1			1	1					1				1
Sorex sp.																
Lepus sp.																
L. californicus																
Sylvilagus sp.			1	1	1	23	1	3					1		3	
S. nuttalli																
S. auduboni																
Rodentia sp.																
Sciuridae sp.																
Marmota flaviventris						2										
Cynomys gunnisoni																
Citellus sp.																
C. variegatus						6	1								3	
cf. *grammurus*																
Eutamias sp.																
Geomyidae sp.																
Thomomys sp.																
T. umbrinus																
Dipodomys sp.																
Cricetidae sp.																
Peromyscus																
P. crinitus																
Neotoma sp.						4										
N. cinerea													1			
Microtus sp.																
M. montanus																
cf. *fusus*																
M. mexicanus																
cf. *mogollonensis*																
Carnivora sp.																
Canidae sp.																
Canis sp.						1										
Canis lupus																
Canis familiaris																
Canis latrans																
Vulpes sp.																
Vulpes fulva		1							1	1						
Urocyon cinereoargenteus																
cf. *scotti*																
Mustelidae sp.																
Mustela (*Putorius*) sp.																
Taxidea taxus																
cf. *berlandieri*																
Spilogale gracilis																
Felidae																
Lynx sp.						2			1					4		
Lynx rufus																
cf. *baileyi*																
Perissodactyla																
Equus caballus																
Artiodactyla sp.						1					1					
Odocoileus sp.																
O. hemionus						1										
Ovis canadensis						3					1					
TOTALS	—	1	2	1	1	44	3	3	2	1	2	1	2	4	6	1

**Mammalia—Aves*, Unknown *not* counted in totals.

Table 43. Distribution of unworked mammal bones by feature. (Continued)

	Kiva R: Level III	Kiva R: Level V	Kiva R: Level VI	Kiva R: Level VII	Kiva R: Level IX	Kiva R: Level X, floor	Kiva R: Horizontal vent shaft, fill	Kiva R: Vent. shaft	Kiva S: Level V, floor	Kiva T: Level IV	Kiva T: Exterior, adjacent fill	Kiva U: Level I	Kiva U: Level II	Kiva U: Level III	Kiva U: Level IV	Kiva U: Level V
**Mammalia—Aves*, Unknown																
Mammalia sp.																
Sorex sp.																
Lepus sp.																
L. californicus																
Sylvilagus sp.		4		2		5		1	1		1	1	2	4	2	1
S. nuttalli																
S. auduboni																
Rodentia sp.																
Sciuridae sp.																
Marmota flaviventris				1		2										
Cynomys gunnisoni																
Citellus sp.																
C. variegatus														2		
cf. *grammurus*																
Eutamias sp.																
Geomyidae sp.																
Thomomys sp.																
T. umbrinus																
Dipodomys sp.																
Cricetidae sp.																
Peromyscus																
P. crinitus																
Neotoma sp.			1	1	2	3										
N. cinerea	1													1		
Microtus sp.																
M. montanus																
cf. *fusus*																
M. mexicanus																
cf. *mogollonensis*																
Carnivora sp.															1	
Canidae sp.																
Canis sp.																
Canis lupus																
Canis familiaris							1									
Canis latrans																
Vulpes sp.																
Vulpes fulva																
Urocyon cinereoargenteus																
cf. *scotti*																
Mustelidae sp.																
Mustela (*Putorius*) sp.																
Taxidea taxus																
cf. *berlandieri*																
Spilogale gracilis																
Felidae																
Lynx sp.										4						
Lynx rufus																
cf. *baileyi*																
Perissodactyla																
Equus caballus																
Artiodactyla sp.																
Odocoileus sp.																
O. hemionus																
Ovis canadensis									1							
TOTALS	1	4	1	4	2	10	1	1	2	4	1	1	2	7	3	1

**Mammalia—Aves*, Unknown *not* counted in totals.

Table 43. Distribution of unworked mammal bones by feature. (Continued)

	Great Kiva: Subfloor fill	Pithouse I: Fill	Pithouse I: Level I, floor I, 1' above	Area I: Fill	Area II: Subfloor	Area III	Area IV	Area IV: Level A	Area IV: Level B	Area IV: Level C	Area IV: Levels A, B, C	Area IV: Level I	Area IV: Level II	Area IV: Level III	Area V: Fill	Area V: Trash fill
**Mammalia—Aves*, Unknown																5
Mammalia sp.																
Sorex sp.																
Lepus sp.																
L. californicus			2													
Sylvilagus sp.	2		1	1	3	6	28	14	23	6	1	3	1	4	2	13
S. nuttalli																
S. auduboni																
Rodentia sp.							1									
Sciuridae sp.														1		
Marmota flaviventris			3													
Cynomys gunnisoni																
Citellus sp.																
C. variegatus						1	1	3	1							
cf. *grammurus*																
Eutamias sp.																
Geomyidae sp.		1														
Thomomys sp.																
T. umbrinus																
Dipodomys sp.																
Cricetidae sp.																
Peromyscus																
P. crinitus																
Neotoma sp.					1			1	1	1						4
N. cinerea																
Microtus sp.																
M. montanus																
cf. *fusus*																
M. mexicanus																
cf. *mogollonensis*																
Carnivora sp.																
Canidae sp.																
Canis sp.																
Canis lupus																
Canis familiaris	1															
Canis latrans																
Vulpes sp.																
Vulpes fulva																
Urocyon cinereoargenteus																
cf. *scotti*																
Mustelidae sp.																
Mustela (*Putorius*) sp.																
Taxidea taxus																
cf. *berlandieri*																
Spilogale gracilis																
Felidae																
Lynx sp.						1										2
Lynx rufus																
cf. *baileyi*							1									
Perissodactyla																
Equus caballus																
Artiodactyla sp.			1						1							1
Odocoileus sp.																
O. hemionus			1													
Ovis canadensis			1													
TOTALS	3	1	10	1	4	8	31	18	26	7	1	3	1	5	2	21

**Mammalia—Aves*, Unknown *not* counted in totals.

Table 43. Distribution of unworked mammal bones by feature. (Continued)

	Area VI: Surface	Area VI: Surface & fill	Area VI: Fill	Area VI: East side, fill	Area VII: Fill	Area VII: Behind w. wall	Area VII: Between 2 walls between Rm. 62 and Kiva G	Area VII: Below Rm. 33	Area VIII: A	Area VIII: B	Area VIII: C	Area VIII: (13122)	Area IX	Area IX: Level II	Area X: Surface	Area X: E. of Kiva P, surface
**Mammalia—Aves*, Unknown*	1									1	1				1	
Mammalia sp.	2													1		
Sorex sp.											1					
Lepus sp.																
L. californicus														2		
Sylvilagus sp.	3	1	26	1	9	1		1	17	107	64		3		9	1
S. nuttalli																
S. auduboni																
Rodentia sp.										15	16					
Sciuridae sp.					1				2							
Marmota flaviventris																
Cynomys gunnisoni																
Citellus sp.										3	2					
C. variegatus						1		1					1			1
cf. *grammurus*																
Eutamias sp.																
Geomyidae sp.																
Thomomys sp.			1						2	8	7					
T. umbrinus																
Dipodomys sp.																
Cricetidae sp.																
Peromyscus										9	1					
P. crinitus																
Neotoma sp.			3		1			1	17	106	40	2	1		1	
N. cinerea			3				1		4	13	6				1	
Microtus sp.										8	2					
M. montanus									6	1	1					
cf. *fusus*																
M. mexicanus										1						
cf. *mogollonensis*																
Carnivora sp.																
Canidae sp.																
Canis sp.																
Canis lupus																
Canis familiaris																
Canis latrans																
Vulpes sp.																
Vulpes fulva																
Urocyon cinereoargenteus															4	
cf. *scotti*																
Mustelidae sp.					1											
Mustela (Putorius) sp.																
Taxidea taxus																
cf. *berlandieri*																
Spilogale gracilis									1							
Felidae																
Lynx sp.	2				1		1									
Lynx rufus																
cf. *baileyi*																
Perissodactyla																
Equus caballus																
Artiodactyla sp.		1			3			2					1	2		
Odocoileus sp.					1								1			
O. hemionus	3			3										1	2	
Ovis canadensis				1											3	
TOTALS	10	2	33	5	17	2	2	5	49	271	140	2	6	5	22	2

**Mammalia—Aves*, Unknown *not* counted in totals.

Table 43. Distribution of unworked mammal bones by feature. (Continued)

	Area X: Surface & fill	Area X: E. of split boulder, surface and fill	Area X: Fill	Area X: Crevice W. of Rm. 83, fill	Area X: Crevice E. of Kiva D	Area X: E. of Kiva P and Rm. 82, Level II	Area X: Immed. S.E. of Kiva P, Level II	Area X: S. half, Levels I, II, mixed	Area X: S. half, Level I	Area X: S. half, Level II	Area X: S. half, Level III	Area X: S. half, Level III (IV b)	Area XI: Fill	Area XII: Surface & fill	Area XIII: Fill	Lower E. Trash Slope
**Mammalia—Aves,* Unknown									1							
Mammalia sp.																
Sorex sp.																
Lepus sp.																
L. californicus																1
Sylvilagus sp.	18	5	3	1		1		2	2	3	13	2		1	1	17
S. nuttalli																
S. auduboni																
Rodentia sp.																
Sciuridae sp.																
Marmota flaviventris																
Cynomys gunnisoni																
Citellus sp.																
C. variegatus										1	1					5
cf. *grammurus*																
Eutamias sp.																
Geomyidae sp.																
Thomomys sp.		1														
T. umbrinus																
Dipodomys sp.																
Cricetidae sp.																
Peromyscus																
P. crinitus																
Neotoma sp.	11	1														1
N. cinerea	1															4
Microtus sp.																
M. montanus																
cf. *fusus*																
M. mexicanus																
cf. *mogollonensis*																
Carnivora sp.																1
Canidae sp.																4
Canis sp.																
Canis lupus																
Canis familiaris																4
Canis latrans		1														1
Vulpes sp.																1
Vulpes fulva																
Urocyon cinereoargenteus																1
cf. *scotti*																
Mustelidae sp.																
Mustela (Putorius) sp.																
Taxidea taxus	4															
cf. *berlandieri*																
Spilogale gracilis																
Felidae																
Lynx sp.			1										1			9
Lynx rufus																
cf. *baileyi*																
Perissodactyla																
Equus caballus																
Artiodactyla sp.					1											
Odocoileus sp.		1														
O. hemionus																4
Ovis canadensis				1			1									3
TOTALS	34	9	4	2	1	1	1	2	2	4	14	2	1	1	1	56

**Mammalia—Aves,* Unknown *not* counted in totals.

Table 43. Distribution of unworked mammal bones by feature. (Continued)

	Lower E. Trash Slope: Test C	Lower E. Trash Slope: Burial 3	Lower E. Trash Slope: Burial 5	Lower E. Trash Slope: Burial 6	Lower E. Trash Slope: Burial 8	Lower E. Trash Slope: Burial 10	Lower E. Trash Slope: W. of Burial 12	Lower E. Trash Slope: Burial 13	Lower E. Trash Slope: Burial 20	Upper E. Trash Slope	Upper E. Trash Slope: Burial 23	Trash Slope: Below Area 5	W. Trash Slope	W. Trash Slope: Gray midden	W. Trash Slope: Brown midden	W. Trash Slope: Under BM "A"
**Mammalia—Aves*, Unknown										1						
Mammalia sp.															1	
Sorex sp.																
Lepus sp.																
L. californicus		1								4						
Sylvilagus sp.		4	1		1			2		37	1	13	5	12	7	1
S. nuttalli																
S. auduboni																
Rodentia sp.							1									
Sciuridae sp.																
Marmota flaviventris																
Cynomys gunnisoni										1						
Citellus sp.																
C. variegatus cf. *grammurus*									1	3		3	1			1
Eutamias sp.										1						
Geomyidae sp.																
Thomomys sp.		2								1						
T. umbrinus																
Dipodomys sp.																
Cricetidae sp.																
Peromyscus							1									
P. crinitus																
Neotoma sp.										2			1	2	1	
N. cinerea										1					1	
Microtus sp.																
M. montanus cf. *fusus*																
M. mexicanus cf. *mogollonensis*																
Carnivora sp.																
Canidae sp.		1								2						
Canis sp.										2						
Canis lupus										1						
Canis familiaris					2					6						
Canis latrans										1						
Vulpes sp.																
Vulpes fulva																
Urocyon cinereoargenteus cf. *scotti*										6						
Mustelidae sp.																
Mustela (*Putorius*) sp.																
Taxidea taxus cf. *berlandieri*													1			
Spilogale gracilis																
Felidae										1						
Lynx sp.		1		6						7		2		1	1	1
Lynx rufus cf. *baileyi*																
Perissodactyla																
Equus caballus													1			
Artiodactyla sp.												1	1			
Odocoileus sp.																
O. hemionus	1				1					1		1	3	1		
Ovis canadensis						1				10				1		
TOTALS	1	9	1	6	4	1	2	2	1	87	1	20	13	17	11	3

**Mammalia—Aves*, Unknown *not* counted in totals.

Table 43. Distribution of unworked mammal bones by feature. (Continued)

	W. Trash Slope: Below Rms. 5, 6, 7	Test F: vent. shaft fill	Burial 35 (South of Long House)	Back Dirt	Totals
**Mammalia—Aves*, Unknown					23
Mammalia sp.					23
Sorex sp.					1
Lepus sp.					5
L. californicus					13
Sylvilagus sp.	1	10		13	1,353
S. nuttalli					1
S. auduboni					1
Rodentia sp.					81
Sciuridae sp.					11
Marmota flaviventris					56
Cynomys gunnisoni					4
Citellus sp.					34
C. variegatus					79
cf. *grammurus*					
Eutamias sp.					2
Geomyidae sp.					2
Thomomys sp.					43
T. umbrinus				1	6
Dipodomys sp.					5
Cricetidae sp.					5
Peromyscus					38
P. crinitus					2
Neotoma sp.				4	825
N. cinerea				1	126
Microtus sp.				1	29
M. montanus					8
cf. *fusus*					
M. mexicanus					1
cf. *mogollonensis*					
Carnivora sp.					5
Canidae sp.					11
Canis sp.					17
Canis lupus					2
Canis familiaris					16
Canis latrans					11
Vulpes sp.					2
Vulpes fulva					2
Urocyon cinereoargenteus					15
cf. *scotti*					
Mustelidae sp.					1
Mustela (Putorius) sp.					1
Taxidea taxus					6
cf. *berlandieri*					
Spilogale gracilis					2
Felidae					6
Lynx sp.					73
Lynx rufus					
cf. *baileyi*					
Perissodactyla					
Equus caballus					3
Artiodactyla sp.					34
Odocoileus sp.					13
O. hemionus				2	26
Ovis canadensis			1		38
TOTALS	1	10	1	22	3,038

**Mammalia—Aves*, Unknown *not* counted in totals.

site on a reduced scale during the occupation is also obvious, particularly where individual rooms were either abandoned before the site was or were occupied intermittently. Included in the deposits are bones of reptiles and amphibians, Audubon's and Nuttall's cottontail, western chipmunk, southern pocket gopher, kangaroo rat, deer mouse, rock mouse, meadow mice, and voles. Some of these are also common to both occupation periods.

Mathews ascribed these post-occupational deposits " . . . to raptorine birds and the small to medium-sized carnivores"—with the evidence from the birds (disintegrated pellet material) making up the bulk of the specimens. The deposits contain most of the small rodents, the shrew, and certain other forms which, as Mathews stated, are " . . . not referable to any single environmental context but represent the hunting range of the raptores and carnivores."

Parts of the site, such as Area VIII (East Ledge Ruin) and Rooms 42, 44, and 45 (West Ledge Ruin), produced an especially large number of bones of small animals, such as rabbit, wood rat, pocket gopher, and mice. Room 12, immediately west of Kiva F, shows a similar pattern. We might assume that the ledge locations were easily reached by certain birds and carnivores and were not disturbed by man after abandonment, so that the material is not culturally related. However, the middle of the three levels excavated in Area VIII contains the largest amount of such bones. This suggests that the accumulation was made while Long House was occupied and the ledge was used at least intermittently. With abandonment, the concentration decreases.

It seems more likely, especially in the case of Room 12, that part of the collection represents rubbish from animals being prepared for food. Furthermore, Rooms 42, 44, and 45 might have been used for storage.

In considering possible environmental changes occurring between the late occupation and today, Mathews stated that " . . . study has thus far not completely convinced me of any real difference from that of the present-day environment on the mesa."

The large number of bone specimens from Long House provides raw data for correlations with the various classes of artifactual material and other data within the site, and for comparisons with similar material from Mug House, Step House, and other Mesa Verde sites.

Faunal Material—Avian

Desiccated remains (2 specimens). Two desiccated specimens of turkey, *Meleagris gallapavo*, were found in Long House, one (very juvenile) in the fill of Kiva B and the other (female) associated with Burial 30 in Room 28.

Feathers (180± specimens). Lyndon L. Hargrave, Collaborator in Ornithology and Archeology, identified the feathers and feather fragments from the ruin. Although the count is imprecise because it includes several lots and masses of feather material, it does show that only turkey and red-shafted flicker feathers were present in significant amounts in the fill.

The number of specimens of each kind is as follows:

17 turkey (*Meleagris gallopavo*)
25 red-shafted flicker (*Colaptes cafer*)
4 sparrow hawk (*Falco sparvarius*)
2 turkey vulture (*Cathartes aura*)

Hargrave's preliminary, macroscopic examination showed that most of the unidentified specimens are probably turkey, and that the following additional birds are probably represented by the number of specimens indicated:

4 eagle
2 grouse
2 jay
2 raven or crow
1 hawk or duck
1 turkey or hawk
1 hawk or eagle

The distribution closely follows that of other refuse materials, with most specimens coming from the western and central parts of the ruin. A few specimens were found on the east side (Rooms 47, 53, 89, and Kiva Q), and in both ledge ruins (Rooms 42, 44, and Area VIII).

Eggshell (40+ specimens). The numerous, tiny fragments of eggshell could not be identified. They were found in the foot drum of Kiva Q; in the fill directly above the floor of Room 30; with Burials 13 (Lower East Trash Slope), 25 (Room 12), and 32 (West Trash Slope); near the base of the fill in Area X; and on the surface of the West Trash Slope.

Feces (140± specimens). The specimens which Murie could identify were predominantly turkey, with only a few possibly assignable to sage grouse, prairie falcon, and quail. The west end and central room block produced the bulk of the material, with the few remaining specimens coming from Room 53, and the West Ledge Ruin (Rooms 40, 42, and 44), and the East Ledge Ruin (Area VIII).

In a separate section of this chapter, Charmion McKusick identifies and discusses both the worked and unworked bird bones from Long House.

Other Refuse Material

Reptiles and Amphibians (16 specimens). J. Alan Holman of Michigan State University, identified the following bones and desiccated remains:

rattlesnake (*Crotalis viridis*)—2 vertebrae (1 individual)
corn snake (*Elaphe guttata*)—1 vertebra, 1 precaudal vertebra
?(snake)—1 caudal vertebra
northern plateau lizard (*Sceloporus undulatus*)—2 vertebral columns, 4 "mummies" (desiccated)
? (lizard - probably *Sceloporus* sp.)—1 tibia
mountain short-horned lizard (*Phrynosoma douglasii*)—1 skull
Rocky Mountain toad (*Bufo woodhousei*)—1 right ilium

Several of these were obviously modern, and the rest—with one possible exception—could have been either recent intrusives in the fill or contemporaneous with the Pueblo occupation. Douglas (1966) does not include *Elaphe guttata* among the snakes found at Mesa Verde today.

Insects (12 specimens). Samuel A. Graham of the University of Michigan recovered five unbroken beetles of one species (*Polyphylla crenata* Lec) beneath the uppermost of several adobe floors of Kiva G in Long House. He has drawn several interesting conclusions about the possibility that the kiva was used, then abandoned for a considerable length of time, and then remodeled for additional use (Graham, 1965). He believes that the beetles developed from larva in fallen roof material and other debris, and then were unable to penetrate the floor laid above them when the kiva was repaired. Although the limited archeological data do not establish the length of time between construction periods, neither do they rule out the possibility of a considerable lapse in time between collapse and reconstruction.

Dr. Graham (op. cit., p. 172) also discusses, in general terms, his study of insect evidence in timbers from Long House and Mug House. He found tunneling and other evidence of insect attack in all of the Douglas-fir and ponderosa pine studied, and in 93 to 94 percent of the juniper and pinyon pine. Most of the species of insects involved belong to three families: flat-headed borers, round-headed or long-horned borers, and bark beetles.

Five insect cases, a ruptured cocoon, and a fragment of another were found in the ruin (Rooms 27, 36, 42, and Area VIII), but none were identified.

Mollusks (3 specimens). The two complete shells identified by Robert J. Drake, University of British Columbia, and a valve identified by Dr. Halsey W. Miller, Jr., University of Arizona, are as follows:

landsnail—*Microphysula ingersolli* (Bland), Kiva Q shrine, subfloor cist.
landsnail—*Retinella electrina* (Gould?), Kiva N, subfloor.
brachiopod—*Gryphaea newberryi* Stanton, Area X, surface, a fossil valve from the lower portion of the Mancos shale.

AVIAN REMAINS

Charmion R. McKusick

This paper deals with 273 bird bone artifacts and unworked bird bones, representing a minimum faunal count of 1,590, which were recovered during the excavation of Long House. The material was identified in 1962–64 by Lyndon L. Hargrave, then Collaborator in Archae-ornithology at the Southwest Archeological Center. Table 44 presents the avian list derived from identification studies of both worked and unworked bones. Levels of identification are summarized in table 45. Table 46 groups bird bone artifacts by elements and species.

A chart indicating distribution of species by provenience has not been prepared since, with one exception, only turkey bone (much of it worked) occurred on room and kiva floors and the stratigraphy is complicated by disturbed fill and inter-occupational and post-occupational deposits of remains of the birds inhabiting the cave. Instead, the Long House collections have been compared with artifact and unworked bone collections from two other cave sites and three mesa-top sites (tables 47 and 48) in order (1) to segregate culturally derived deposits from those which are inter-occupational and post-occupational, and (2) to determine if trends in bird usage can be suggested for Mesa Verde in general, if usage in cave sites differed from that at the mesa-top settlements, and if changes in usage can be observed at different times during the prehistoric occupation of the area.

Comments

Aves sp. Minimum faunal count—two; less than 1 percent of the collection. The two specimens are too immature to be identified.

Ducks

Anas sp. Minimal faunal count—one; less than 1 percent of the

Table 44. Avian list.

Scientific Name	Common Name	Worked	Unworked
Aves sp.	Bird, unknown		x
Anas sp.	Teel		x
Cathartes aura	Turkey Vulture	x	x
Falconiformes sp.	Hawk, unknown	x	
Accipiter gentilis	Goshawk	x	
Buteo sp.	Buteonine Hawk	x	
Buteo jamaicensis	Red-tailed Hawk	x	x
Buteo swainsoni	Swainson's Hawk		x
Buteo lagopus	Rough-legged Hawk		x
Aquila chrysaetos	Golden Eagle	x	x
Falco mexicanus	Prairie Falcon		x
Falco sparvarius	Sparrow Hawk		x
Centrocercus urophasianus	Sage Grouse		x
Odontophorinae sp.	Quail		x
Meleagris gallopavo	Large Indian Domestic Turkey	x	x
Zenaidura macroura	Mourning Dove		x
Otus asio	Screech Owl		x
Bubo virginianus	Great Horned Owl		x
Asio otus	Long-eared Owl		x
Asio flammeus	Short-eared Owl		x
Aegolius acadicus	Saw-whet Owl		x
Phalaenoptilus nuttallii	Poor-will		x
Aeronautes saxatalis	White-throated Swift		x
Colaptes auratus	Flicker		x
Passeriformes sp.	Passerine, unknown		x
Aphelocoma coerulescens	Scrub Jay		x
Corvus corax	Common Raven		x
Corvus brachyrhynchos	Common Crow		x
Lanius ludovicianus	Loggerhead Shrike		x
Vermivora sp.	Warbler		x
Agelaius phoeniceus	Red-winged Blackbird		x
Fringillidae sp.	Sparrow or Finch		x

Table 45. Avian list according to level of identification.

Group	Number of Taxa	Level of Identification
Aves	1	1 class
Anatidae	1	1 genus
Cathartidae	1	1 species
Falconiformes	1	1 order
Accipitridae	6	1 genus, 5 species
Falconidae	2	2 species
Tetraonidae	1	1 species
Phasianidae	1	1 sub family
Meleagrididae	1	1 species
Columbidae	1	1 species
Strigidae	5	5 species
Caprimulgidae	1	1 species
Apodidae	1	1 species
Picidae	1	1 species
Passeriformes	1	1 order
Corvidae	3	3 species
Laniidae	1	1 species
Parulidae	1	1 genus
Icteridae	1	1 species
Fringillidae	1	1 family
	32	
Classes	1	
Orders	2	
Families	1	
Sub families	1	
Genera	3	
Species	24	
	32	

collection. A teal of unknown species is represented by a fragmentary sternum and coracoid.

Vultures

Cathartes aura Minimum faunal count—12; less than 1 percent of the collection.

Artifacts: one specimen; less than 1 percent of the worked bone. The artifact is a long tube cut from the shaft of a right radius.

Of the 12 unworked bones, 10 are considered to be post-occupational. The other two are a left scapula and the distal end of a left humerus.

Hawks and Eagles

Accipitridae sp. No unworked bone.

Artifacts: one specimen; less than 1 percent of the worked bone. A tube was cut from the distal section of the left femoral shaft of a medium-sized hawk, Accipiter or Buteo.

Accipiter gentilis No unworked bone.

Artifacts: one specimen; less than 1 percent of the worked bird bone. A tube was cut from the right tibiotarsal shaft of a Goshawk.

Buteo (?) sp. No unworked bone.

Artifacts: one specimen; less than 1 percent of the worked bone. An awl was made from a sliver of bone which probably came from the ulna of a Buteonine Hawk.

Buteo jamaicensis Minimum faunal count—19; 1.2 percent of the collection.

Artifacts: one specimen; less than 1 percent of the collection.

The distal end of a right ulna was cut and ground.

The Red-tailed Hawk is the only breeding Buteo listed for Mesa Verde (Anon., 1959). Seven individuals are juveniles and five are immatures, indicating that this species may have nested in the cliffs above the ruin, and/or that the residents of Long House may have hand raised young hawks. In all but two cases, the individuals are represented by bones of the wings or legs. One Red-tailed Hawk was recovered from a Basketmaker III pithouse dating in the 600's; most of the others dated in the late 1200's.

Buteo swainsoni Minimum faunal count—one; less than 1 percent of the collection. Swainson's Hawk is represented by a right carpometacarpus and left humerus.

Buteo lagopus Minimum faunal count—two; less than 1 percent of the collection. The Rough-legged Hawk is identified from a right carpometacarpus and left humerus.

Aquila chrysaetos Minimum faunal count—three; less than 1 percent of the collection.

Artifacts: three specimens; less than 1 percent of the worked bird bone. A pendant was made by drilling an ungual; two other unguals were shaped on the articular heads and bore a green stain.

Unworked eagle bone consisted of two additional unguals and the shaft of a left radius.

Falcons

Falco mexicanus Minimum faunal count—two; less than 1 percent of the collection. Two Prairie Falcons, an adult and a juvenile, are represented by a left humerus and bones of the right legs.

Falco sparvarius Minimum faunal count—nine; less than 1 percent of the collection. These samples included three juveniles and

Table 46. Bird bone artifacts by element and species.

	Awls (193)					Tubes (48)					Pendants (2)	Cut-off ends (9)				Miscellaneous (20)							
	Ulna	Radius	Carpometacarpus	Tibiotarsus	Tarsometatarsus	Humerus	Ulna	Radius	Femur	Tibiotarsus	Ungual	Humerus	Ulna	Tibiotarsus	Tarsometatarsus	Humerus	Ulna	Radius	Scapula	Tibiotarsus	Tarsometatarsus	Element Unknown	Totals
Cathartes aura								1															1
Accipitridae									1														1
Accipiter gentilis										1													1
Buteo (?) sp.	1																						1
Buteo jamaicensus																		1					1
Aquila chrysaetos											2												2
Meleagris gallopavo	10	27	1	88	66	9	23	6	3	4		6	1	1	1	2	1	2	3	1	6	4	265
Totals	11	27	1	88	66	9	23	7	4	5	2	6	1	1	1	2	1	3	3	1	6	4	272

one immature. Only wing and leg bones of Sparrow Hawks were recovered.

Both falcons identified are resident forms which may have nested in crevices in the cliffs above Long House.

Grouse

Centrocercus urophasianus Minimum faunal count—10; less than 1 percent of the collection. Three juvenile and seven adult Sage Grouse are represented by random bones. Mesa Verde lies within the distribution of the eastern subspecies of Sage Grouse, *C. u. urophasianus* (Aldrich and Duvall, 1955, p. 12).

New World Quail

Odontophorinae sp. Minimum faunal count—one; less than 1 percent of the collection. The only quail bone recovered is the left tibiotarsus of a juvenile. Scaled Quail are native to Montezuma Valley around Towaoc, and they have been observed 2 miles from the mesa's edge (Alden C. Hayes, personal communication, 1970).

Pheasants

Phasianus colchicus Minimum faunal count—one; less than 1 percent of the collection. The Ring-necked Pheasant, a modern introduction, is identified from the left tibiotarsus of a juvenile.

Turkeys

Meleagris gallopavo Minimum faunal count—1,466; 92.2 percent of the collection.

Artifacts: 265 specimens; 97.4 percent of the worked bird bone.

Awls form the largest class of turkey bone artifacts: 88 from tibiotarsi, 66 from tarsometatarsi, 27 from radii, 10 from ulnae, and one from carpometacarpus. Tubes are second in frequency, with 23 cut from ulnae, nine from humeri, six from radii, four from tibiotarsi, and three from femora. The only cut-off ends found at Long House are turkey.

Turkey feather artifacts from Long House include strips of vane supported by the flexible, shiny covering of the rachis, which are commonly referred to as "fletching." However, an arrow from Long House was fletched with sections of turkey vane supported by the split rachis, which extended beyond the vane at each end so that they might be bound to the shaft with sinew. Eliminating this usage, a search was made of other feather artifacts. All utilized stripped vanes had been wound around vegetal fiber cords to make a coarse feather cord. Thus, in this area, both down and the vanes of flight feathers were made into feather cordage.

Long House turkey feathers include fragments from both light-colored and normally pigmented individuals. Specimens that can be identified at fairly low magnification on characters of rachis and barb are a light-colored semiplume from Room 47 (17425/700), dating between A.D. 1200 and 1300, and part of the vane of a flight feather from Kiva I (12200/700), dating between 1250 and 1300. Other specimens of light-colored turkeys from wetherill Mesa are a white-quilled flight feather from Room 29 (18271/700) and what appears to be a left primary covert with both rachis and white vane from Room 61 in Mug House (18635/703), both dating in the 1200's. The feather collection rocovered from excavations at Step House, also on Wetherill Mesa, provides further examples that are numerous and large enough for detailed study. One specimen of predominantly white vane stripped from a white rachis recovered from Pit Structure I is apparently contemporaneous with a pre-A.D. 700 specimen from San Dune Cave, Utah. This specimen has a predominantly white vane, with little black, and a white rachis (Hargrave, 1970, Fig. 27).

Specimens from the later occupation of Step House are more varied. Room 21 yielded a partially grown flight feather (36415/709) with one vane and rachis completely white, the other vane white splotched with black. The incomplete calamus of this specimen is drawn to a point similar to that of the Sand Dune Cave specimen noted above. Apparently in both instances, this malformation occurred because the feather was plucked or accidentally lost while it was still growing. This condition has not yet been noted in normally pigmented feathers and may be a weakness associated with the increased unpigmented areas in vane and rachis. Presumably, these turkeys were noticeably lighter than the predominantly black, normally pigmented fowl, and may indicate a Pied Mutation.

Table 47. Unworked bird bone by percentage of species.

Species	CLIFF SITES			MESA-TOP SITES		
	Long House	Mug House	Step House	Big Juniper House	Badger House	Site 1801
Aves sp.	[1]T	T	3.67	1.78	2.21	T
Anas sp. (Teal)	T					
Cathartes aura	T					
Accipiter cooperrii			T			
Buteo sp.					T	
Buteo jamaicensis	1.19	1.13			T	
Buteo swainsoni	T					
Buteo lagopus	T					
Buteo regalis		T				
Aquila chrysaetos	T					
Falco mexicanus	T					
Falco sparvarius	T		T			
Tetraonidae sp.		T				
Dendragapus obscurus		T				
Tympanuchus cupido			T			
Centrocercus urophasianus	T	1.70	T	T		
Odontophorinae sp.	T					
Phasianus colchicus	T					
Callipepla squamata				T		
Meleagris gallopavo	92.20	94.19	88.07	97.32	91.91	95.82
		Average 91.49			Average 95.02	
Zenaidura macroura	T	T	T			
Otus asio	T					
Bubo virginianus	T	T	T		2.21	2.05
Strix occidentalis			T			
Asio otus	T					
Asio flammeus	T					
Aegolius acadicus	T					
Phalaenoptilus nuttallii	T					
Aeronautes saxatalis	T					
Colaptes auratus	T					
Aphelocoma coerulescens	T					T
Passeriformes sp.	T	T				
Perisoreus canadensis		T				
Pica pica					1.47	
Corvus corax	T	T	T			
Corvus brachyrhynchos	T					
Oreoscoptes montanus					T	
Turdus migratorius			T			
Lanius ludovicianus	T					
Vermivora sp.	T					
Agelaius phoeniceus	T					
Fringillidae sp.	T					
Sample size	1,590	706	109	112	136	146

[1] T = Trace, or less than 1 percent.

Examples of an entirely different type of light-colored turkey were recovered from Rooms 21 and 30 in Long House. Turkeys are commonly described as black with white barring on the primaries and secondaries and brown barring on the rectrices. From these aberrant specimens, it is likely that the reverse is true. The basic color of turkey feathers is white, a schemochrome or structural color. Over this a wash of reddish-brown is deposited in appropriate areas, such as the rectrices. Black patterning is formed independently from the reddish-brown pigmentation. In these specimens, the genetic factor for deposition of black pigment may be absent or nonfunctional. There is a change from structural white to the areas where the black is normally deposited on the wing feathers, so a faint pattern can be discerned upon close inspection. However, the reddish-brown of the main body of the vane obscures this on the rectrices and only the subterminal band, which is usually black, may be easily outlined. This condition, resulting from the absence of one pigment, is called schizochromism. The more descriptive term, erythrism, pertaining to an excess of reddish-brown usually caused by partial albinism, is also applicable to these specimens. This anomaly is uncommon except in another gallinaceous bird, the Prairie Chicken (Van Tyne and Berger, 1959, p. 99).

Light-colored turkeys may have been widely known in the Southwest. The unpigmented dessicated left foot of a young female turkey (CC1097) has been recovered from Canyon de Chelly, Arizona. Excavations at Tularosa Cave in southwestern New Mexico yielded the unpigmented, dessicated foot of an adult female turkey as well as the dessicated remains of four juveniles. One medium and two small juveniles have white down with tan markings and unpig-

Table 48. Worked bird bone by percentage of species.

Species	CLIFF SITES			MESA-TOP SITES		
	Long House	Mug House	Step House	Big Juniper House	Badger House	Site 1801
Olor columbianus		[1]T				
Branta canadensis		[2]1.75				
Cathartes aura	T					
Falconiformes sp.	T					
Accipiter gentilis	T					
Buteo sp.	T					
Buteo jamaicensis	T					
Buteo regalis					12.50	
Aquila chrysaetos	T	[2]4.09		3.33	12.50	
Galliformes sp.				6.66		
Meleagris gallopavo	97.38	93.57	100.00	90.01	75.00	100.00
Sample size	273	171	20	30	8	1

[1] T = Trace, or less than 1 percent.
[2] All from the same necklace.

mented tarsi and feet. A larger juvenile has few feathers remaining, but down on the left side of the head, rachises of wing feathers, tarsi, and feet are all unpigmented. Downy young of wild turkeys are commonly darker in color; the natal plumage of eastern poults is described as shades of cinnamon marked with rich, dark brown (Bent, 1932, p. 333).

An additional specimen from Step House (31229/709), a right axillary of a female, has a greenish irridescence and a brown dorsal quill surface reminiscent of the brown-toned Turkey described by Hargrave (1970, pp. 24–25) from Sand Dune Cave.

Turkeys were utilized for six hundred years by the inhabitants of Wetherill and Chapin Mesas. Of the osteological specimens examined, none has been identified as Merriam's Wild Turkey. Variations in feather color present in early proveniences may indicate very early domestication in the Four Corners region. Schorger (1966, pp. 77, 115, and 146) has gathered information indicating that the turkey is a rather primitive, adaptable fowl that would be domesticated in as short a time as 20 to 30 years. Given a prolonged period of usage, the potential for quick domestication, and a group of people who ate turkeys and could easily remove less desirable phenotypes from the breeding population, it is not unexpected that a variety of plumages was present.

The basic breed raised at Wetherill Mesa sites was the large Indian Domestic Turkey. The antecedent of this breed can now be suggested. The Rio Grande Turkey (*M. g. intermedia*), Gould's Turkey (*M. g. mexicana*), and the South Mexican Turkey (*M. g. gallopavo*) have been eliminated on osteological characters. All archeological turkey tail feathers thus far examined have had light tips, eliminating the three eastern subspecies (*M. g. silvestris, M. g. osceola,* and *M. g. intermedia*), which have cinnamon tips. This leaves Merriam's Wild Turkey (*M. g. merriami*), slightly larger than the Large Indian Domestic Breed. The smaller size of the domestic form may be the result of smaller fowl possessing characteristics which better fitted them for life in close association with man, or an early admixture of a smaller, now extinct subspecies, the Tularosa Turkey (*M. g. tularosa*), which is known from Canyon del Muerto as early as A.D. 250. Statistical analysis of measurements of turkey tarsometatarsi from Wetherill Mesa sites suggests the possibility that some individuals from Long House and Mug House may be of the Small Indian Domestic Breed, which is believed to be directly descended from the Tularosa Turkey (cf. Schorger, 1970).

An assumption of long standing in Southwestern archeology is that the prehistoric inhabitants of the area did not eat turkey, or, in the opinion of some students, did not eat any birds at all. Although this generalization still appears true for the majority of groups, data from recent excavations indicate that, in a few areas, turkeys were a preconquest source of food. O'Bryan (1950, pp. 101 and 108–113) reported the finding of only turkey burials in pithouse clusters at Sites 1 and 102 in the Twin Trees area at Mesa Verde, which produced tree-ring dates in the early A.D. 800's, and only random turkey bones from the pueblos built on these sites, which yielded tree-ring dates from the middle to late 900's. He notes that bone tools from the pithouse villages were usually made from deer metapodials, and that turkey bone tools first appear in the pueblos at Sites 1 and 102. In O'Bryan's opinion, the few turkey bone artifacts from the Mancos Phase may be accounted for by the occasional eating of turkeys.

A scanning of the literature indicates that, prior to 900, artifacts which were later made from turkey bone were most often manufactured from the bones of jackrabbits. A re-examination of the Wetherill Mesa survey and excavation records revealed only two turkey bone artifacts which may be pre-900. One, the distal head of a left femur with a hole drilled through one side, was apparently in trash emanating from House 1 at Site 1676, with tree-ring dates around A.D. 840. The other is a splinter awl made from the fibular crest of a right tibiotarsus (31335/709), from Level I of Pit Structure I at Step House.

All relatively intact turkey humeri, tibiotarsi, and tarsometatarsi which pass through the Southwest Archeological Center are routinely measured. Early Wetherill Mesa sites yielded intact bones suitable for measurement, but they were too few in number to form a good series. Of the later sites that produced great numbers of turkey bones, only the tarsometatarsi from Mug House and Long House were sufficiently intact for measurement and numerous enough to provide adequate series. The use at Long House of 94 tibiotarsi, 73 tarsometatarsi, and 17 humeri for artifacts contributes to this shortage, but the removal of cancellous tissue from these bones, as discussed in detail by Hargrave (1965b), probably accounts for a greater number of specimens.

Mesa-top sites produced samples of bone in which cancellous material has been removed in a rather haphazard fashion. It is not until the later occupations of Long House and Step House that the proximal head of the tibiotarsus and both ends of the humerus were removed in a regular manner, apparently by a single blow with a straight-edge tool resembling a cleaver.

Hargrave (1965b, Fig. 6) illustrates a single tibiotarsus from Mug House which displays butchering marks on the distal end that were made while severing the tendons to disjoint the foot from the carcass. Since publication of this article, numerous tibiotarsi from Long House have been found to be similarly scarred.

Material from the Wetherill Mesa excavations which appears to predate food usage is from House 1 at Site 1676, which Alden Hayes dates between A.D. 840 and 850 (personal communication, 1970). Thus O'Bryan's placement of the beginning of food usage of turkeys in the Mancos Phase appears to be valid, and a date of post-950 to 1000 for the adoption of this trait seems probable.

There has been some uncertainty about the Indian's method of turkey culture. Analysis of samples of human and turkey fecal matter from Long House and Mug House by Dr. Bruno E. Sabels showed that in Long House manganese abundances decreased in human feces and increased in turkey feces, with time, and in Mug House both manganese and phosphorous abundances decreased in human feces from bottom to top of the excavation but manganese in turkey feces in the same levels showed an increase (Sabels, 1962, p. 40). Inferrably, people had less food, or less nourishing food, as the years passed, while turkeys continued to be well nourished on wild plants and insects (Osborne, D., 1964, p. 173). Insect parts occurred in Mesa Verde turkey droppings (Graham, 1965, p. 170), indicating that the birds were not kept confined at all times in the pens associated with the ruins. They may have been herded on the mesa top, as described in the Santa Clara story of Turkey Girl (Velarde, 1960, pp. 45–51), or, as suggested by Swannack (1969, pp. 141–142) and Wheeler (ch. 5, herein), they may have been tethered to stone weights so that they could forage much as hobbled horses do. Another possibility is that turkeys may have obtained sufficient minerals from the gradual wearing down and assimilation of the grit in their gizzards.

Doves

Zenaidura macroura Minimum faunal count—one; less than 1 percent of the collection. Mourning Dove is identified from the proximal end of the left tibiotarsus. This specimen is apparently from an owl pellet or a scat, and is probably post-occupational.

Owls

Of the five species of owls identified from Long House, four, the Screech Owl, Great Horned Owl, Long-eared Owl, and Saw-whet Owl, were probably resident in the area. The fifth, the Short-eared Owl, would have been present in the area during the winter. The Great Horned Owl, which is most numerous, probably nested in Long House cave.

Otus asio Minimum faunal count—one; less than 1 percent of the collection. The only Screech Owl bone recovered is a fragmentary left carpometacarpus.

Bubo virginianus Minimum faunal count—six; less than 1 percent of the collection. Great Horned Owls include an immature, a juvenile, and adults. Bones of adults present are a mandible and elements of wings and legs.

Asio otus Minimum faunal count—one; less than 1 percent of the collection. The Long-eared Owl specimen is the proximal end of a left ulna.

Asio flammeus Minimum faunal count—one; less than 1 percent of the collection. This specimen of Short-eared Owl, identified from elements of wings and the axial skeleton, is considered post-occupational.

Aegolius acadicus Minimum faunal count—one; less than 1 percent of the collection. The Saw-whet Owl, considered post-occupational, is represented by a left humerus, a coracoid, and a scapula.

Goatsuckers

Phalaenoptilus nuttallii Minimum faunal count—one; less than 1 percent of the collection. The Poor-will, which is common at Mesa Verde, is represented by a left humerus.

Swifts

Aeronautes saxatalis Minimum faunal count—one; less than 1 percent of the collection. The White-throated Swift is identified from a right tibiotarsus and a left ulna derived from an owl pellet, and is considered post-occupational. Since this species is a nesting obligate of cliffs, it is often recovered from rock shelters.

Woodpeckers

Colaptes auratus ssp. Minimum faunal count—one; less than 1 percent of the collection. Flicker is represented by a fragmentary right humerus. The Red-shafted Flicker is a common resident at Mesa Verde today.

Perching Birds

Passeriformes sp. Minimum faunal count—two; less than 1 percent of the collection. Two individuals, an adult and a juvenile, can be identified only as perching birds.

Corvids

Long House, and the Mesa Verde sites as a group, lack the conspicuous assemblages of corvids, particularly the Common Raven, which appear in some other areas.

Aphelocoma coerulescens Minimum faunal count—one; less than 1 percent of the collection. The crushed and dessicated carcass of an immature Scrub Jay was found in a high portion of the ruin accessible only by ladder. This ledge is much used by birds, and the specimen might have been carried there by a Goshawk or by a climbing mammal such as a Ringtail.

Corvus corax Minimum faunal count—13; less than 1 percent of the collection. Five juvenile and two immature individuals are included in the sample, indicating that Common Ravens may have nested in the rocky surfaces above Long House. Both young and adults are represented by random elements.

Corvus brachyrhynchos Minimum faunal count—one; less than 1 percent of the collection. Common Crow is identified from a left humerus.

Shrikes

Lanius ludovicianus Minimum faunal count—one; less than 1

percent of the collection. A fragmentary right tibiotarsus has been identified as Loggerhead Shrike, an uncommon summer resident of the area.

Warblers

Vermivora sp. Minimum faunal count—one; less than 1 percent of the collection. The ulna of a wood warbler was recovered in the shrine pit of Kiva Q. Orange-crowned, Nashville, and Virginia's Warblers are still found at Mesa Verde.

Blackbirds

Agelaius phoeniceus Minimum faunal count—one; less than 1 percent of the collection. Red-winged Blackbird is identified from a left tibiotarsus.

Finches and Sparrows

Fringillidae sp. Minimum faunal count—one; less than 1 percent of the collection. A fragmentary right humerus recovered from a scat is identifiable only to family. It is considered post-occupational.

Discussion

Of the 32 taxonomic categories to which avian remains from Long House have been assigned, 11 appear to have been affected by factors other than the human inhabitants of the site. The Ring-necked Pheasant is a recent introduction. Turkey Vulture, Red-tailed Hawk, Prairie Falcon, Sparrow Hawk, Great Horned Owl, and Common Raven may have nested in Long House cave. Therefore, the relatively high frequencies of some of these species probably do not reflect a true picture of cultural usage. Remains of the Mourning Dove, Scrub Jay, Short-eared Owl, White-throated Swift, and a sparrow or finch were recovered only from scats or owl pellets (tables 47 and 48). Some of these species have been recovered from proveniences in nearby sites which imply cultural usage, as outlined in table 49. Only two species, the Red-tailed Hawk and the Domestic Turkey, can be definitely associated with the pithouse occupation of Long House. All species listed, except those few from owl pellets or scats only, were found in proveniences relating to the 13th-century occupation.

As table 49 indicates, the Domestic Turkey is the only species for which there is evidence of continuous use during the entire period of occupation. Red-tailed Hawks and Common Ravens enter usage in the 600's, but bones of Great Horned Owls and Golden Eagles do not appear before the 900's, even though their feathers were used at least 200 years earlier (Hargrave, 1970, p. 41). The Greater Sandhill Crane bone on the floor of the pithouse on Chapin Mesa (Hargrave, 1965a, p. 158) is a unique occurrence of this species at Mesa Verde. All whistling Swan and Canada Goose and most Golden Eagle bones from Mesa Verde are artifacts and may be trade items.

From the 7th through the 11th centuries, bird species recovered from Mesa Verde fluctuated from a maximum of seven to a minimum of two species. Fifteen species were recovered from 12th-century proveniences, and 27 from those proveniences dating in the 13th century. Although relatively few species from Basketmaker sites have been identified from bones, at least 23 species have been identified from feathers (Hargrave, 1970), indicating that the low number of species identified from early Mesa Verde sites may not represent the full range of avifauna used. Most of the wild birds

Table 49. Cultural usage of bird species on Wetherill Mesa (x) and Chapin Mesa (*) from A.D. 600 to 1300.

	600's	700's	800's	900's	1000's	1100's	1200's
Olor columbianus			*				x
Branta canadensis							x
Anas platyrhynchos ssp.							*
Anas sp. (Teal)							x
Cathartes aura							x
Accipter gentilis							x
Accipiter cooperrii							x
Buteo jamaicensis	x		•	x		x	x
Buteo swainsoni							x
Buteo lagopus							x
Buteo regalis							x
Aquila chrysaetos				x	x	x	x
Falco mexicanus							x
Falco sparvarius						x	x
Dendragapus obscurus						x	x
Tympanuchus cupido						x	
Pedioecetes phasianellus					x		
Centrocercus urophasianus					x*	x	x
Callipepla squamata					x		
Meleagris gallopavo	x*	x*	x*	x*	x*	x*	x*
Grus canadensis	*						
Bubo virginianus				x	x	x	x*
Strix occidentalis						x	
Asio otus							x
Phalaenoptilus nuttallii							x
Colaptes auratus ssp.							x
Aphelocoma coerulescens			x		x	x	
Perisoreus canadensis							x
Pica pica				x	x	*	
Corvus corax	x	*				x	x
Corvus brachyrhynchos			*				x
Gymnorhinus cyanocephalus	x						
Oreoscoptes montanus				x			
Turdus migratorius						x	
Lanius ludovicianus							x
Agelaius phoeniceus							x
Zenaidura macroura						x	x

occurring in low frequencies were found at Long House; the large size of the collection from this site is no doubt a factor. While economic importance cannot be demonstrated for most of these species, wild birds are commonly used by modern Indians to provide feathers for socio-religious purposes. In view of the fact that Long House had 22 kivas, this type of usage appears most probable.

Mammal remains from Wetherill Mesa sites suggest that there might have been changes in usage from Basketmaker to Pueblo, or from mesa-top to cliff sites. No definite evidence of such shifts was observed in the avifauna. In all sites compared at all time-periods known, the Mesa Verdeans display a singleminded preoccupation with turkeys, first as a source of supply for feathers and artifacts, finally as an item of food. Mesa-top sites averaged 95 percent unworked turkey bone. In cliff sites, turkey bone averaged 91.5 percent, a slight drop which does not necessarily imply a decrease in turkey use but more likely increases in wild bird percentages for which raptors, predators, and birds nesting in the rock shelters are partly responsible.

There is no evidence in the avifauna for a drastic climatic shift since the prehistoric occupation of Mesa Verde. Although the only grouse listed for the park is the Blue Grouse (Anon., 1959, p. 3), Mesa Verde sites have yielded specimens of three other grouse. These sites are within the present range of the Sage Grouse and the former range of the Sharp-tailed Grouse (Aldrich and Duvall, 1955, pp. 11 and 12), but the Prairie Chicken has not been recorded in western Colorado or New Mexico in historic times. Tentative identifications of this species from archeological sites in New Mexico suggest that in prehistoric times it may have occurred in portions of the short grassland occupied today by Scaled Quail, extending from the San Juan Valley, up the Mancos River Valley, to a point very near Mesa Verde (cf. Bailey, 1928, Map 5).

STONE CHIPPING DEBRIS

Richard P. Wheeler

In 1963–64, Douglas Osborne analyzed samples of stone cores and flakes cataloged from Long House and six other large sites excavated by the Wetherill Mesa Project. Inasmuch as the edges of relatively few specimens showed evidence of utilization (pounding, scraping, or cutting), the samples were considered, overall, to be detritus that resulted from chipping done at the sites (D. Osborne, 1965).

The Long House samples total 518 cores and 4,757 flakes. Twelve cores and 117 flakes, from the floors of certain clan (?) kivas, the subfloor fill of the Great Kiva, and Pithouse 1, may be regarded with some confidence as representing the early occupancy of Long House. The other cores and flakes—the great bulk of the débitage—are attributable, with perhaps a slight admixture of earlier material, to the major occupation of the site during late Pueblo III times.

The cores of the larger, later group are, in the main, blocky flake cores of gray-green chert, of interior origin, with natural heels, weighing up to 300 gms. The flakes of the larger group are primarily of gray-green chert, blocky, of interior origin, with natural heels, and weigh up to 40+ gms.

As to the cores of the smaller, earlier group: the five specimens from kiva floors and the three from the subfloor fill of the Great Kiva are comparable to the larger group in shape, color and kind of material, and interior origin, but they have natural and artificial heels in about equal proportion and they weigh more (over 300 gms., from kiva floors) and less (up to 50 gms., subfloor fill of the Great Kiva). The four cores from Pithouse 1 are blocky and of interior origin. Three are brown to black claystone or siltstone, the fourth is gray-green chert. Two cores have natural heels and two have artificial heels. The four specimens weigh up to 200 gms.

The flakes of the smaller group are comparable to those of the larger group with respect to shape, weight, and the high proportions of natural heels and interior origin, but gray-green claystone or siltstone predominates over gray-green chert in the specimens from the kiva floors and the subfloor fill of the Great Kiva and is very nearly equal to gray-green chert in the flakes from Pithouse 1. The predominant color of this material is characteristic of the larger, mostly late Pueblo III group of flakes, but the material itself is that favored during Pueblo I and Pueblo II, as at Site 1676 (see Hayes and Lancaster, 1975).

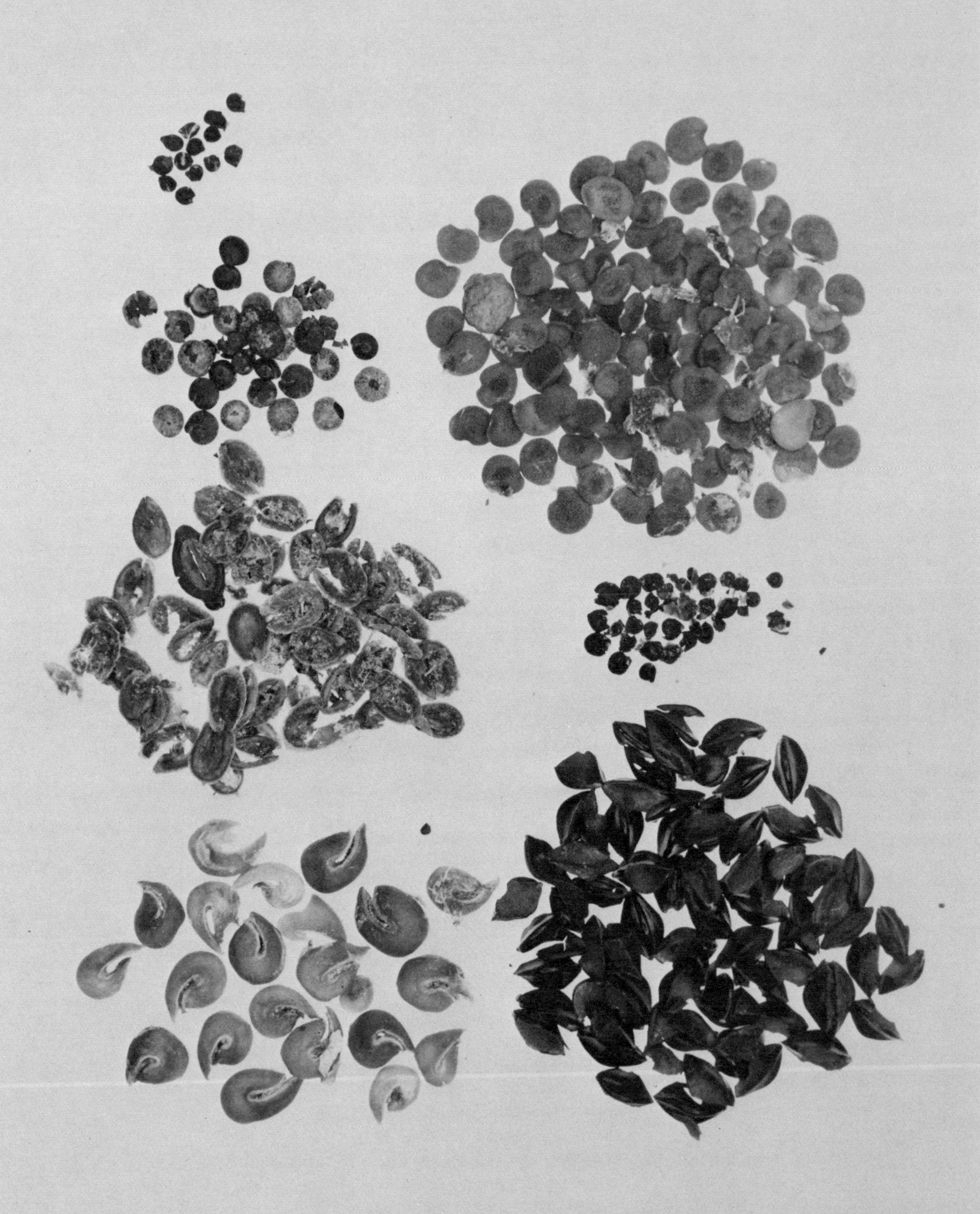

Chapter Nine

Pollen Analyses

POLLEN STRATIGRAPHY OF LONG HOUSE

Paul S. Martin
Geochronology Laboratories
University of Arizona

Four pollen profiles were constructed for samples that were collected by George Cattanach from four separate parts of Long House and that were extracted and counted by William Byers, using a sample size of 200 pollen grains at each level. Included are 14 levels in Kiva R, 13 levels in Kiva D–Room 78, 12 levels in Area II, and 4 levels in Room 54–Pithouse 1. The profiles are drawn from the relative numbers of each type and are subject to the contraint that all counts must total 100 percent. An increase or decrease in any pollen type may or may not reflect a true increase in the pollen of that plant from the sediment. Only when consistent trends are seen in different parts of the same pueblo and in different pueblos, as is the case of the post–occupation increase in tree pollen, is it clear that some change in regional vegetation is involved.

The post-occupation rise in tree pollen, mostly in juniper and pine, seldom in oak, is evident at Long House only above 0.40 m. in Kiva R (fig. 449). The rise marks pollen zone I from the Wetherill Mesa pollen chronology and, in addition to the maximum of pine and juniper, is characterized by a scarcity of economic pollen types, *Cleome, Zea,* and Cactaceae. Below 0.40 m. in Kiva R, *Cleome* increases. Tree pollen drops to the relatively low values found in pollen zones II in Mug House and elsewhere. The scarcity of *Zea* can be explained in terms of the pollen source—from a kiva rather than a work area or room within the pueblo.

Pollen samples from Kiva D and Room 78 were derived from subfloor fill, in each case (fig. 450). Unlike the samples from Kiva R, they do not extend into post-occupation time and do not reveal a rise in pine and juniper pollen. The high frequency of *Opuntia* (up to 10 percent) is unusual and must reflect some intensive prehistoric use of prickly pear in this particular subfloor.

In Area II, the pollen record shows a major decline in *Zea* from 60 to 20 percent but is otherwise undistinguished (fig. 451). The change in *Zea* proportions could mean one of many things, including a failing corn crop, a change in utilization of this area from storage to traffic (marked by development of the walking surfaces), or simply increased deposition of the other pollen types with accordant *apparent* reduction in abundance of *Zea*. Changes in *Zea* are not readily used in stratigraphic correlations, nor are such changes as the peak in *Artemisia* pollen found in the 9.2 cm. count.

The short pollen record from Room 54–Pithouse 1 (fig. 452) is of interest because it probably contains the oldest of the pollen samples in the four profiles. BM III, P I, and P III artifacts were associated with the pollen record The peak in pine pollen at 1.92 m. could be part of a pre–Pueblo pine maximum, suggested by some of the Mug House pollen counts, and recognized as Wetherill Mesa pollen zone IIb. The very low frequency of cheno–ams also indicates a minimum of disturbance and possibly limited occupation at the time. Cactus and squash (*Opuntia* and *Cucurbita*) pollen was found in a few levels, but the main economic types are corn (*Zea*) and beeplant (*Cleome*).

Preliminary pollen analysis by James Schoenwetter indicated a tendency for *Cleome* to replace *Zea* pollen toward the end of the occupation of Long House. Failure to find such a sequence at Mug House and in other parts of Wetherill Mesa dampened enthusiasm for a paleoecological interpretation of increased use of *Cleome* as a starvation plant during the last decade or decades of occupation of the Mesa Verde region. Nevertheless, *Cleome* appears to remain abundant while *Zea* declines in those profiles from Long House which contain sizeable amounts of both, and the possibility of true decreases in corn harvests should be kept in mind.

CORRELATION OF POLLEN PROFILES

The location from which the four pollen profiles discussed by Paul Martin were taken are among the most representative and significant of the 19 stratigraphic columns sampled in the field. An additional eight shorter profiles were analyzed by James Schoenwetter (MS.), with results that essentially complement the work by Martin and William Byers. Despite differences of opinion about events reflected by the pollen profiles, both Martin and Schoenwetter touched on points worth considering in our interpretation of the stratigraphy sampled.

Had time and funds permitted, pollen from the remaining seven profiles would have been extracted and counted. Although this might have strengthened my arguments for establishing a relative chronology and perhaps have provided additional information about the specific structures in which samples were taken, I feel that we have probably covered the occupation period of Long House as fully as is now possible.

Room 54–Pithouse 1

Presumably, the Room 54–Pithouse 1 profile spanned the period from A.D. 648 to almost 1300. Unfortunately, four factors complicate the picture. First, the burning of the pithouse may have destroyed pollen from the Basketmaker period in the area sampled, and it was not possible to correlate the pithouse sample with samples from other sections of the ruin which appear to date to this period.

Figure 449. *Pollen profile of Kiva R sample.*

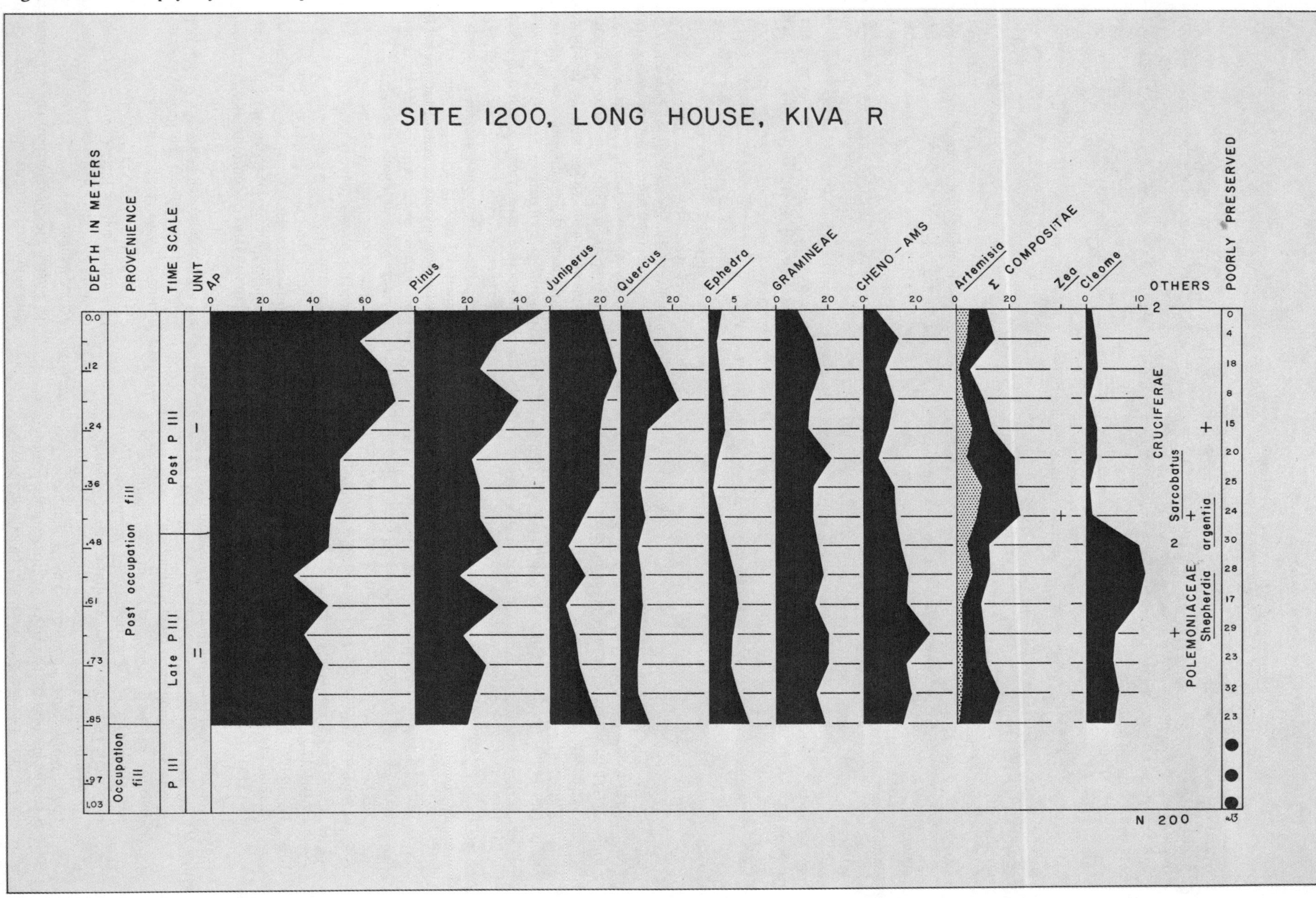

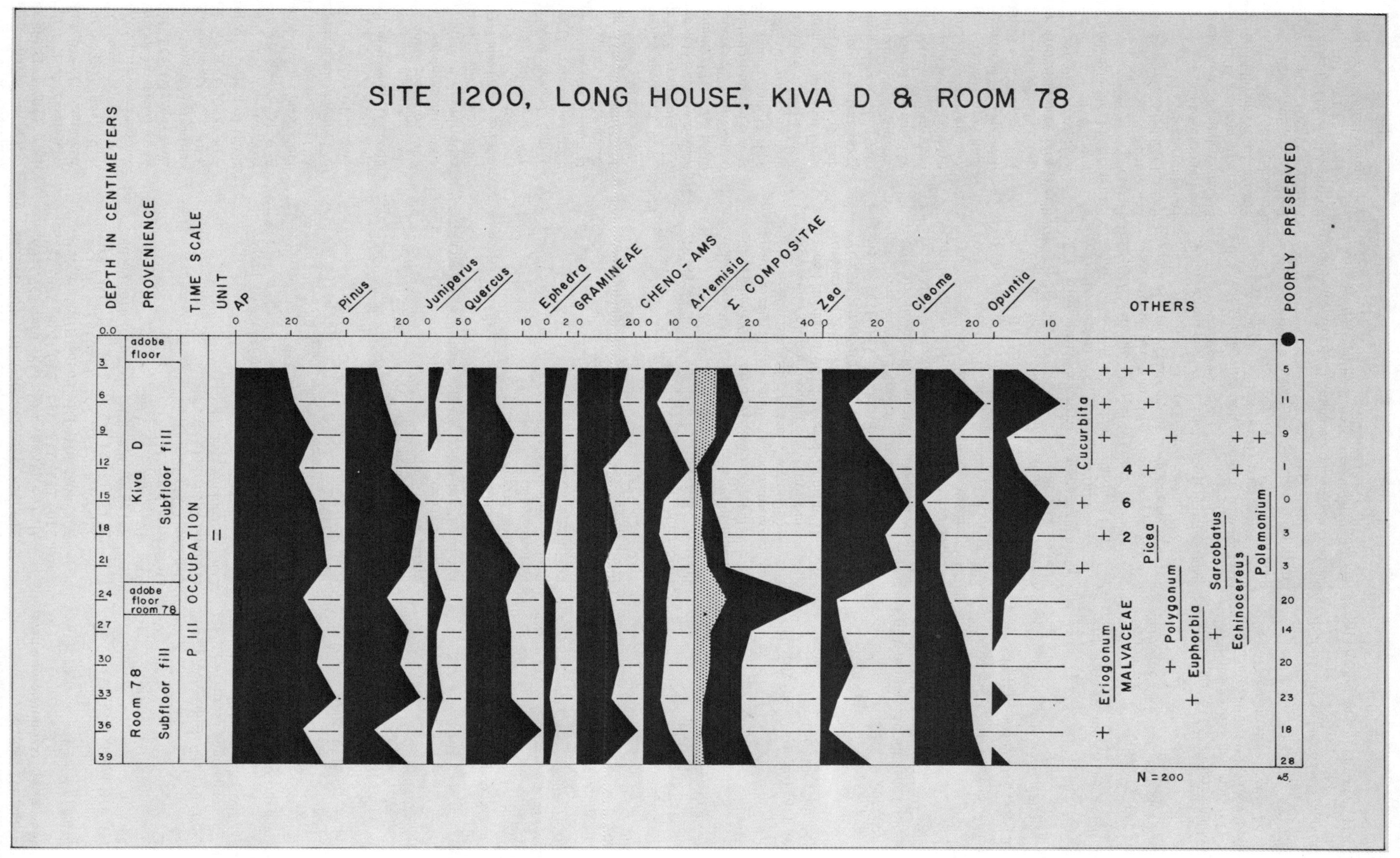

Figure 450. *Pollen profile of Kiva D-Room 78 samples.*

Figure 451. *Pollen profile of Area II sample.*

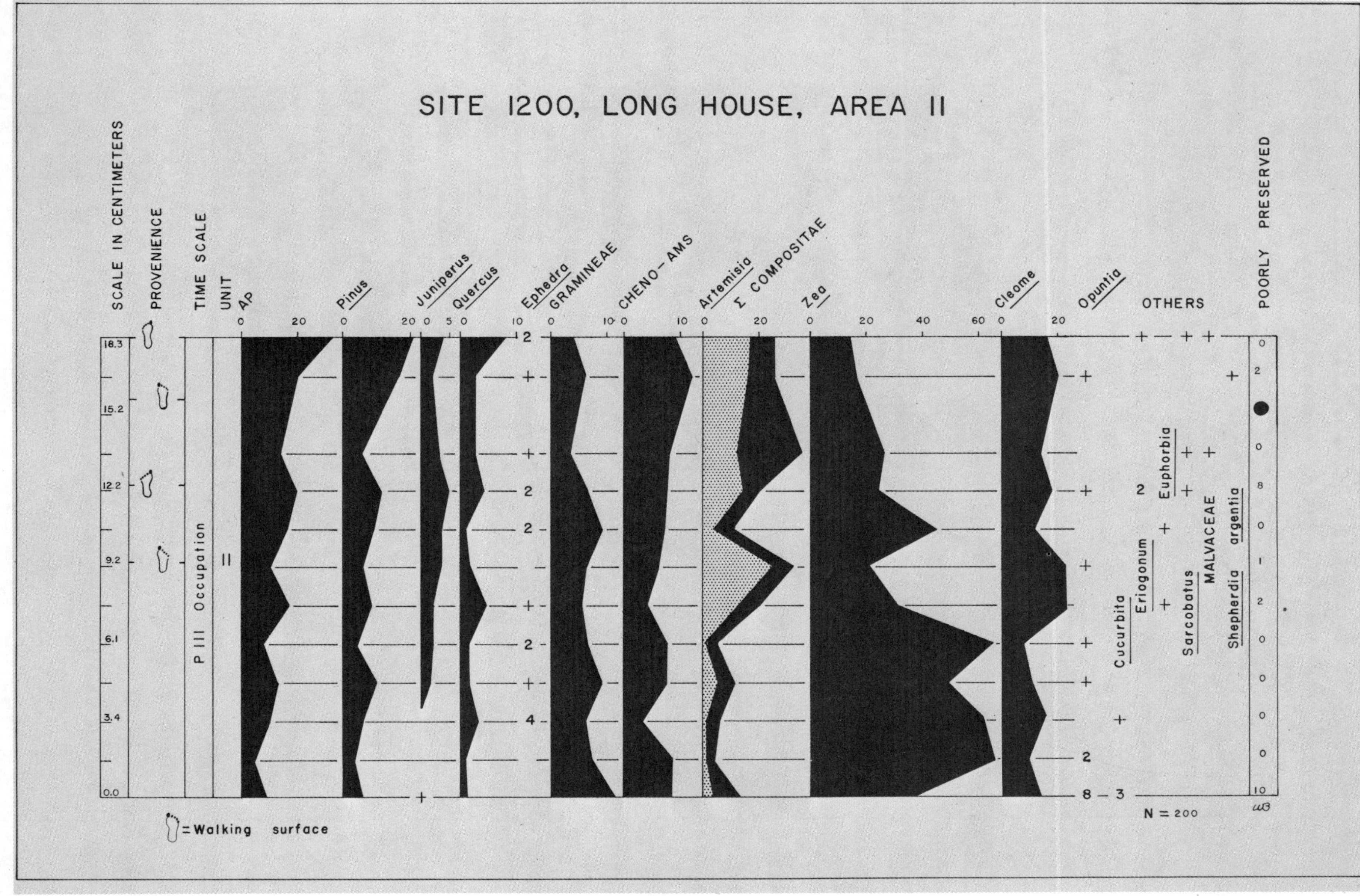

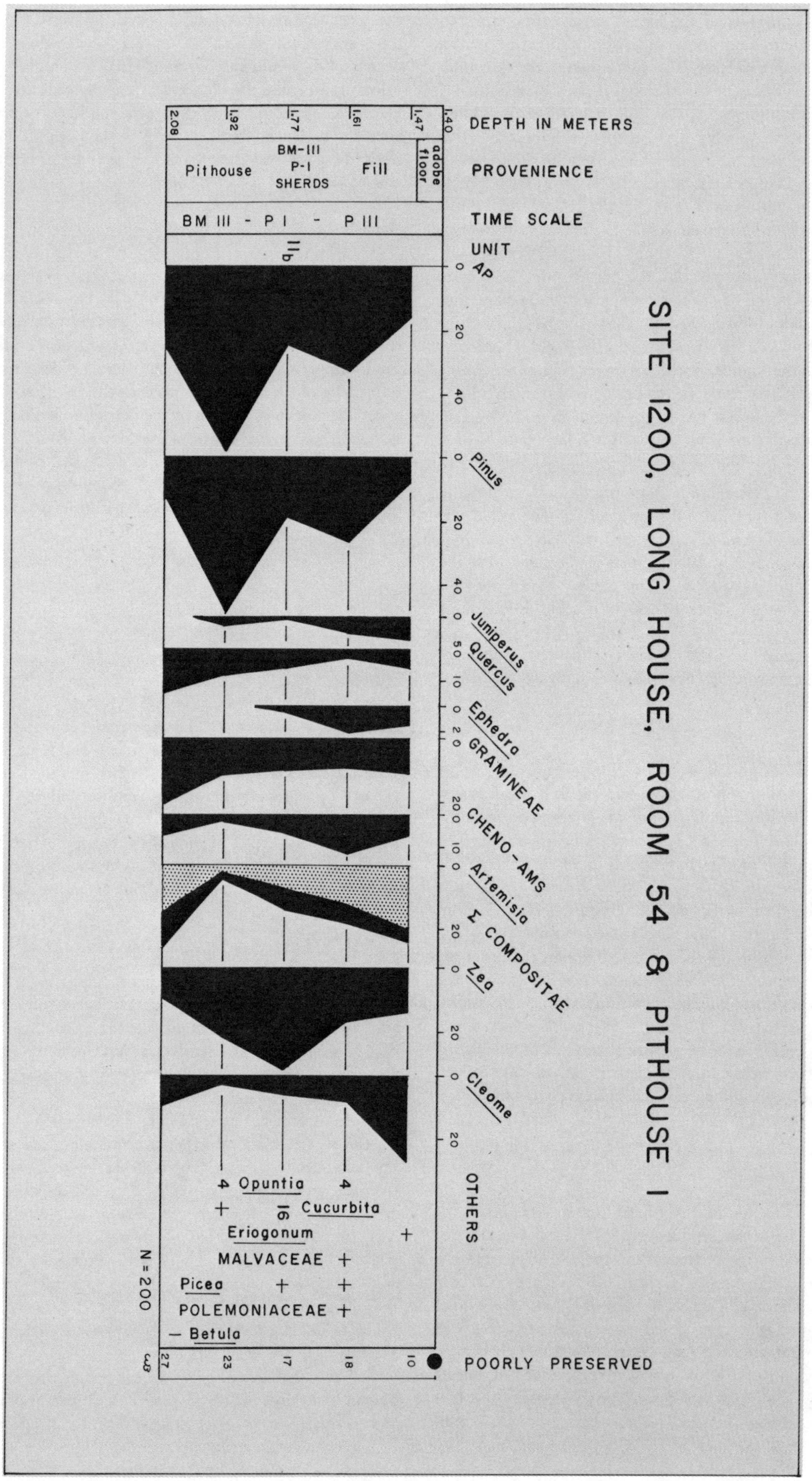

Figure 452. *Pollen profile of Room 54-Pithouse 1 sample.*

Secondly, several days after taking the specimens I discovered that reversed stratigraphy invalidated the lowest sample, from the pithouse floor, thus shortening the profile and losing one of our potentially most valuable samples. Thirdly, although the four middle deposits from two apparent occupational periods may accurately represent stratigraphic differences, they are probably from deliberately placed fill (source?) rather than natural soil deposition or accumulation of trash. And finally, the pollen from the floor adobe—the most accurately dated of the upper deposits—was too poorly preserved to identify and count.

The two lowest samples shown in Martin's profile were from fill derived from cave roof debris, rock-dressing spalls, and sterile, sandy soil which were probably dumped into the burned pithouse both to fill the large depression and to dispose of the material. The next two samples include, besides additional wood, charcoal, and ash from the pithouse superstructure, some Basketmaker III–Pueblo I pottery. This material, also, was probably thrown in as part of the filling process. The topmost layer in the pollen profile is apparently identical in composition to the lowest two levels. It was placed to level the site of the pithouse before building the walls and laying the floor of Room 54.

There are no good cultural indicators in any of this material to help us determine either the time of the filling or the source of all the material. Some of the early wood and pottery *could* have come from Basketmaker or later pre-Pueblo III structures at the east end of the cave in what are now rooms and kivas. This area is one of the few in Long House with a small concentration of Pueblo I–Pueblo II pottery.

Because of the above problems, it is very difficult to evaluate or correlate this profile with others from the site with any degree of confidence.

Kiva D–Room 78

Another stratigraphic column extending through two features, Kiva D and Room 78, was sampled to provide information from the west end of the pueblo through as long a time period as possible. The five lowest levels in the profile are probably from intentional fill, paralleling the situation in Pithouse 1. There is, next, one sample from the red adobe floor of Room 78. The seven samples from between the floors of Room 78 and Kiva D are from material which appears to be identical, with the addition of numerous chunks of red adobe, to that from beneath the floor of Room 78. Finally, there is a sample from Kiva D's floor, but the pollen proved to be too poorly preserved to be identified.

Most of the profile reflects, presumably, a later Pueblo III occupation. The lower deposits may or may not provide information of an earlier period, depending upon their source or sources and degree of intermixing.

Area II

Most intriguing to me, because of the location tested, was the profile for Area II. The section sampled was located 0.5 foot north of the northeast exterior corner of Room 25, and extended from the bedrock cave floor to the present surface, 0.6 foot above. It was thought that the main cave would have been used extensively quite early in the occupation because it offered both shelter and a source of water, and thus might present a long pollen record.

Careful dissection of the undisturbed occupation fill during collection of the 12 samples revealed six primary deposits and four clearly definable walking surfaces. At the base of the column, immediately above bedrock, is almost sterile soil. Trash content, and the concentration of organic material, increased steadily toward the top. There was almost no ceramic or building material in the deposit. We should keep in mind that this profile samples what was primarily an access corridor, at least during the latter part of the Long House occupation, rather than a room, kiva, or trash dump. The apparent presence of turkey dung in the upper levels of the deposit tested suggests that these birds may have been restricted to the back part of the cave.

Kiva R

Only here do we have a profile which may extend beyond the end of the prehistoric occupation. At the time of sampling, I thought the three lowest levels might represent cultural fill. Unfortunately, the pollen was too poorly preserved to identify. The remainder are from laminated post-occupational waterlaid deposits such as washed into many of the rooms and kivas in the ruin, especially on the east end. The thickness of each of the definable laminae was about 0.01 inch. Although the 3.5-foot-deep deposit could have been formed over a period of months or years, there was nothing of a cultural nature in the kiva fill to indicate the length of time represented or whether the pueblo was abandoned during or after the period of deposition.

Other Areas Sampled

Pollen profiles were constructed by Schoenwetter (but not reproduced here) for the following areas sampled early in the excavations: Area III, Area IV, Room 53, Room 35, Area I, Area II–III, Room 24, and Room 52. The first three seem to show, as would be expected, similarities to those for Area II and Kiva D–Room 78. The profile for Room 35 was considerably modified in some respects, perhaps by being exposed to rapid erosion and deposition through its position below the pour-off above Long House. In several respects, however, it also seems to parallel the pollen fluctuations seen in other profiles. I feel the remaining four profiles are built on too few samples to be of any real significance in a comparative analysis.

Correlation

The plants which seem to provide a basis for correlation of profiles are *Cleome, Zea, Artemisia* and other composites, the cheno-ams, and *Pinus.* These are among the weedy species which would occupy trampled and disturbed ground near the pueblo, as Martin and Byers (1965, p. 133) indicated in discussing the Mug House pollen record.

As Martin has pointed out, a paleoecological interpretation of the *Cleome-Zea* relationship is not possible because of lack of supporting data from other sites. The fact that one seems to vary inversely to the other in percentage of pollen present may still give us a significant time marker for correlating the various profiles. I believe that this, coupled with fluctuations in the pollen count from two other plants which are most likely to reflect cultural activity—cheno-ams and Compositae—make "cross-dating" possible within Long House.

The profiles for Area II and Kiva D-Room 78 are reproduced below to indicate a possible relative position of the four discussed by Martin.

The possible post-occupational rise in the arboreal pollen that Martin mentions, mainly in pine and juniper, is obvious in Kiva R, and perhaps in its early stages in Area II. Kiva D–Room 78 apparently overlaps the lower end of the profiles for Kiva R and Area II, and carries us farther back in time. Neither the Kiva D nor Room 54 profiles include, of course, pollen deposited during the occupation of these rooms or give any information about their time of abandonment.

Although both the main cave and the west end of the site may have been occupied almost simultaneously, the discrepancy in the profiles should not be surprising because of two factors: poorer preservation of Area II pollen in the lower levels of a very thin deposit where constant traffic would have crushed pollen against the cave floor; and the much larger amount of fill used to level the area where Room 78 was built undoubtedly contained pollen of an earlier period. A third factor must also be kept in mind: is there a significant difference in the pollen rain between the back of the cave and more exposed locations which would invalidate within-site cross-dating? I do not believe so in this case, judging by information derived from tree-ring dates.

Martin also pointed out a rise in pine pollen in the Room 54–Pithouse I profile at the 1.92-meter level which may indicate abandonment or a very small population in Long House after the Basketmaker III period. The upper three specimens in the profile appear to reflect the trends seen in the three other profiles checked by Martin, but by themselves would form a rather weak argument for such correlation. The lower two specimens *may* show the pollen rain at specific points during the Pueblo I–II, or early Pueblo III, period, but more likely are composite specimens from very mixed deposits. It is quite likely, however, that they show the general trend in a very rough fashion.

Taken in conjunction with tree-ring dates, the wall construction sequence, and temporal variations in ceramics and tools as indicated by stratigraphic data, the pollen profiles form one more link in relating chronologically the various phases of the occupation of Long House.

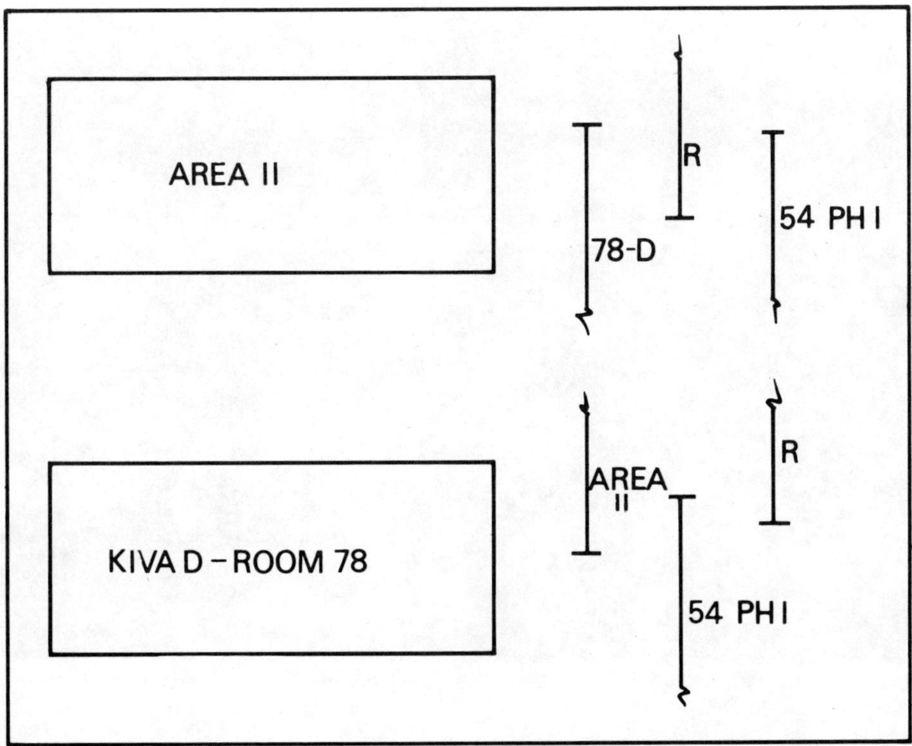

1200
KIVA I
VENT SHFT
ROOF
1201
7 16 59

Chapter Ten

Construction Sequence

TREE-RING DATES

An intensive program of collecting all wood and charcoal specimens which appeared to have any chance of being dated was carried on during the entire excavation program. Most of the collecting of samples, and all of the dating, was done by Robert Nichols.

About a sixth of the specimens collected—140 out of 796—were dated (Nichols and Harlan, 1967). The main types of wood represented, the numer of specimens of each collected, and the number dated (shown parenthetically) are as follows: juniper—468 (26); pinyon pine—146 (61); Douglas-fir—82 (36); ponderosa pine—19 (4); and other—81 (1).

The tree-ring dates for Long House—arranged numerically by specimen number—along with the form of the specimen, the species, and the inside dates have already been published (Nichols and Harlan, ibid., pp. 15–18). I have rearranged these dates by provenience, omitting all other information except the specimen number (table 50). The abbreviations and symbols used by Nichols and Harlan (ibid., pp. 13–14) immediately precede the list of dates.

Table 50. Tree-ring dates from Long House.

Abbreviations and Symbols Used (adapted from Nichols and Harlan, 1967, pp. 13-14).

Specimen No. "MV" specimens are cataloged in the collections of the Laboratory of Tree-Ring Research. Long House specimens MV-76 through MV-94 were collected in 1933 by H. T. Getty and have been reported previously (Getty 1935; Schulman 1946). All other "MV" specimens were collected by the Wetherill Mesa Project. "GP" specimens were collected by Deric O'Bryan of Gila Pueblo in 1941 and have been re-examined by Robert F. Nichols.

Outside Date:

v—outside shows erosion, outermost ring variable around circumference
vv—outside shows extreme erosion, outermost ring very variable
+—outer rings tight, possibly one or two rings absent from series
++—outer rings tight, possibly more than two rings absent from the series
r—outer ring constant over significant portion of circumference
c—outer ring constant around entire circumference
L—outside surface uniform in color and texture
G—bark beetle galleries present on outside
B—bark present on outside
(r, c, L, G, and B probably indicate cutting or "death" dates of the trees)

Provenience

*	—beam in place
D.N.	—Deric O'Bryan's field collection numbers
IPS	—interpilaster space (numbered clockwise from recess above the ventilator shaft)
Recess	—in kivas, the enlarged IPS above the ventilator shaft

Feature	Outside Date (A.D.) and Specimen No.	Provenience
Kiva B	1141L (GP-3220)	Surface (D.N. 77)
	1262cL (GP-3231)	Surface (D.N. 78)
Kiva D	1278v (MV-584)	Surface
	1278B (MV-586)	Surface
	1263L (MV-663)	Recess (IPS-1), fill
Kiva E	1264BG (MV-600)	Fallen roof material
Kiva H	1266r (MV-786)	Level I
	1256vv (MV-821)	Level II
	1194vv (MV-860)	Level III
	1263c (MV-658)	Level III
	1181vv (MV-885)	Level III
	1257r (MV-894)	Level III
	1253vv (MV-903)	Level III
	1223r (MV-906)	Level III
	1263vv (MV-907)	Level III

(continued)

Table 50. Tree-ring dates from Long House. (Continued)

	1270c (MV-912)	Fill
	1264r (MV-919)	On floor
	1280r (MV-925a,b)	Level III
	1257vv (MV-982)	Level III
	1264r (MV-985)	Level III
Kiva I	1253c (MV-1221)	*Roof
	1257c (MV-1234)	*S.W. IPS (IPS-1), roof
	1270+c (MV-1235)	*S.W. IPS (IPS-1), roof
	1253c (MV-1238)	*N.W. IPS (IPS-2), roof
	1272B (MV-2122)	*S.W. IPS (IPS-1), roof
Kiva J	648r (MV-930)	Upper fill (pithouse debris)
	1197vv (MV-1029)	*Roof
	1112c (MV-1030)	*Roof
	648r (MV-1454)	Subfloor fill (pithouse debris)
Kiva K	1242r (MV-1061)	Fill
	1147v (MV-1063)	Fill
	1178vv (MV-1213)	Below recess (IPS-1), fill
	1241L (MV-1291)	Level II
	1257r (MV-1243)	Level III
Kiva N	1255L (MV-1125)	Kiva N vicinity, surface
Kiva O	1229r (MV-1095)	Level III
	1229L (MV-1100)	Level IV
	1252L (MV-1102)	Level III
	1256v (MV-1103)	Level III
	1242vv (MV-1139)	N.E. IPS (IPS-5)
Pithouse 1	648r (MV-1078)	Level I (Room 56, Level IV)
	648v (MV-1079)	Level I (Room 56, Level IV)
	648r (MV-1086)	Level I (Room 56, Level V)
	648r (MV-1087)	Level I (Room 56, Level V)
	607r (MV-1093)	Level I (Room 56, Level VI)
	647vv (MV-1118)	Level I (Room 54, Level VI)
	648r (MV-1122)	Level I (Room 54, Level VII)
	644vv (MV-1124)	Level I (Room 54, Level VII)
	636r (MV-1130-2)	Level I (Room 54, Level VII)
	648v (MV-1146)	Level I (Room 55, Level IX)
	646+r (MV-1147)	Level I (Room 55, Level IX)
	610++r (MV-1149)	Level I (Room 55, Level IX)
	648r (MV-1287)	Fill
	648r (MV-1436)	Level I
	648r (MV-1437)	Level I
	648r (MV-1442)	Level I
	633r (MV-1451, 1452)	On floor
	604r (MV-1453)	On floor
	648vv (MV-1473)	Level I
	648B (MV-1474)	Level I
	648B (MV-1475)	Level I
Room 4	1266v (MV-2369)	*East wall
	1267 (GP-3235)	*Lintel in north wall recess (D.N. 7)
Room 5	1252cL (MV-1299)	Room 5 vicinity, fill
Room 6	1241+v (MV-587)	Surface
Room 12	1276r (MV-683)	Level II
Room 14	1278vv (MV-966)	On floor 1
Room 16	1248vv (GP-3227)	*Roof (D.N. 5)
Room 17	1267 (MV-1241)	*Roof
Room 19	1277B (MV-2125)	*Roof
Room 28	1231vv (MV-1013)	Fill
	1275B (MV-583)	Room 28 vicinity, fill
Room 29	1144vv (MV-2124)	*Lower roof
	1197v (MV-2127)	*Roof
	1200rL (MV-2128)	*Roof
Room 30	1249L (MV-1058)	Lower fill
Room 36	1257vv (MV-593)	Level I
Room 48	638+vv (MV-707)	Level II (pithouse debris)
	648r (MV-708)	Level II (pithouse debris)
	648v (MV-731)	Level III (pithouse debris)
	648r (MV-732)	Level III (pithouse debris)
	647v (MV-736)	Level III (pithouse debris)
	596vv (MV-743)	Level III (pithouse debris)
	596vv (MV-775)	Level IV (pithouse debris)
Room 60	1270L (MV1251)	Level IV
	1196vv (MV-1277)	Subfloor firepit, fill
Room 65	1261B (MV-2359)	*Door in west wall, lintel
	1261cL (MV-2360)	*Door in west wall, lintel
	1261cL (MV-2361)	*Door in west wall, lintel
Room 66	1262L (MV-2363)	*Door in south wall (plugged), lintel

Table 50. Tree-ring dates from Long House. (Continued)

	1259 (MV-2364)	*Door in south wall (plugged), lintel
Room 72	1277cL (MV-1033)	Roof beam
	1266cL (MV-1037)	Roof beam
Room 74	1274+L (MV-1233)	Level I
	1183vv (MV-2372)	Level II
Room 75	1246vv (MV-1138-2)	On floor
Room 76	1183L (MV-1040-9)	Lower roof material
	1253+B (MV-1044)	Upper roof material
	1204vv (MV-1049)	Upper roof material
	1053+R (MV-1050-2)	Upper roof material
	1267cL (MV-1054)	Upper roof material
	1077cL (MV-1055-2)	Upper roof material
	1274cL (MV-1121)	Roof material
	1024+L (MV-1128)	Upper roof material
Room 85	648r (MV-1465-2)	Subfloor fill (pithouse debris)
	647vv (MV-1465-5)	Subfloor fill (pithouse debris)
Room 87	1272cL (MV-1211)	Fill
Room 93	647r (MV-1350)	Fill (pithouse debris)
Area IV	1270B (MV-677)	Level I
Area VII	1225r (MV-672)	Fill
	1266rL (MV-1014)	Fill
	1258B (MV-1015)	Fill
Area IX	1131++v (MV-950)	Disturbed fill
	1273+B (MV-1182)	Level II
	1110+v (MV-1232)	Level II
	1264r (MV-1267)	Level II
Upper West Trash Slope	1250+vv (MV-613)	Surface
	1264vv (MV-1283)	Surface
Surface	1249v (MV-576)	(Previously sampled)
Burial 4	1236 (MV-579)	
Burial 26	1279+v (MV-1360)	(Room 12, Level II)
West end	1267cL (GP-3232)	(D.N. 79)
	1275+vv (GP-3234)	(D.N. 81)
North quarter	1268c (MV-76)	Near Kiva I (same as GP-3209)
	1204vv (MV-84)	
	1246vv (MV-85)	
	1274c (MV-86)	
	1211vv (MV-88)	
East quarter	1184v (MV-80)	
South quarter	1267v (MV-90)	
	1230+ (MV-92)	
West quarter	1273c (MV-93)	
	1267c (MV-94)	
Provenience unknown	1263c (MV-87)	
	1268vv (GP-3217)	(D.N. 66)
	1193 (GP-3218)	(D.N. 67)
	1240v (GP-3219)	(D.N. 68)
	1254B (GP-3210)	*(Kiva I, roof) (D.N. 4)

TIME PLACEMENT OF SITE COMPONENTS BY DATED WOOD SPECIMENS

Determining the significance of the dates is a much more difficult task, since few dated specimens were found in their original place in the ruin. Most of the roofs had collapsed, and the earlier excavations had disturbed some of the material found on the surface and in the upper fill.

In attempting to establish a construction sequence, I found that it was not possible to pinpoint either the precise year of construction of most rooms and kivas or the time of their subsequent repair or remodeling. We must recognize, of course, that even a precise cutting date may not give us the construction or repair date of a feature, especially when there is a chance that the timber may have been re-used. Wall abutment, one of the prime aids to accurate in-site dating, was of little help in Long House because of fallen or very badly eroded corners in key locations. Rooms 23–29, 70–72, and Kivas H and I are obvious exceptions to this, for here the relative—but not absolute—sequence can be determined readily.

It is easier to discuss the interpretation of the dates by first arbitrarily dividing the occupation span into five major periods. The first is manifested in Pithouse 1, a Basketmaker III structure dated at A.D. 648. The clustering of pithouse dates makes the structure one of the few in Long House dated fairly precisely. Some of the dated specimens recovered from subfloor levels of adjacent but later rooms were probably from the pithouse or at least associated with the Basketmaker III horizon. These included Rooms 48, 85, and 93, and, of course, Kiva J and Rooms 54–56, which overlay the pithouse.

There are no dates from the succeeding Pueblo I and Pueblo II periods, and probably not the early Pueblo III period. With a few exceptions, the next dates fall in the late part of the 12th century and the first half of the 13th century, and are probably from construction undertaken between 1200 and 1250 across the entire site. Because of the small number of dates involved, and the difficulty of accurately dating the structures concerned, this 50-year period forms the second arbitrary division of the occupation. Each of the remaining three periods embraces dates falling within ten-year intervals; the 1250's, 1260's, and 1270's.

The pueblo will be discussed by sections for convenience: (1) West—Kiva T through Rooms 18–20 and 32, as well as Rooms 39–45 (West Ledge Ruin); (2) Central—Rooms 23, 34, and 35 through Kiva I and Rooms 65–67, and Area VIII (East Ledge Ruin); and (3) East—Rooms 36, 91, 92 (Kiva L), 68, 69, and Kiva S through Kiva R and Rooms 21 and 52.

A.D. 1200–1250

West. Room 6 may have been built about 1241, while the room immediately west (in which Kiva A was later built) was constructed before 1262. Quite possibly the two are contemporaneous.

Central. The central block, from Room 23 to Room 29, was constructed at this time, as follows:

(1) Rooms 23 and 24, probably followed about the same time by Room 71 (between the two rooms) and 70 (built against Rooms 23 and 71).

(2) Room 29, although it may have been contemporaneous with Room 24 and, possibly, the retaining wall south of Kiva I. Construction date was about 1200.

(3) A possible room immediately west of Room 29 (perhaps one of two rooms between Rooms 28 and 29), later replaced by Kiva H. The room was probably built between 1200 and 1223.

(4) The retaining wall forming the south wall of Rooms 25 to 28, and a possible room immediately east of Room 28.

(5) Rooms 25 to 28, and the unnumbered possible room east of 28, in that order. Room 28 may have been built about 1231.

The Great Kiva may have been started as early as 1246. If so, it predates Rooms 64 to 67, which border it on the east side.

East. Kiva J, built about 1200, and Room 76/1, possibly dating to 1204, are the earliest dated rooms in the east side of the pueblo. The room in which Kiva O was built dates to 1229, and Kiva K shortly afterward, perhaps 1242.

Kiva M was probably built before 1246, and thus may be earlier than the Great Kiva. It definitely pre-dates Room 75, built in 1246, and Rooms 74, 73, 91, and 92, which were built west of Room 75, in that order. All may date to about 1246.

A.D. 1250's

West. Room 4/1 was built against the room later converted to Kiva A. The latter room was probably built at this time, although—as mentioned above—it may date to about 1241. Presumably, Room 3 was created when Room 4/1 was built, or shortly thereafter. Room 2, Kiva T, and Room 5 were constructed, the last about 1252 and the other two probably shortly before.

Central. The two possible rooms between Rooms 28 and 29 were torn out and Kiva H was built in 1257. Kiva I was built east of and against Room 29 at about the same time.

East. In 1257, Room 36 was probably built simultaneously with Kiva I and perhaps Kiva O, which was constructed within the earlier (1229) room. Kiva S, west of Kiva M, was built before 1262, probably in the 1250's. Kiva Q was constructed before Rooms 60 and 84–87, all of which it helps support, and probably also pre-dates Kiva N, adjacent on the west. The construction date falls before 1270 and—judging by internal features which appear early, such as the footdrum sealed during later remodelings—was probably in the 1250's. The adjoining rooms may have been built at this time or in the 1260's. (Room 85, at least, was built before 1270). Room 56 was built before Room 85 and after Rooms 54 and 55.

A.D. 1260's

West. Extensive construction was undertaken on the west end of the ruin during the 1260's. Kiva A was built before 1267, Kiva B after 1262, and Room 4/2 (and probably Rooms 4/3 and 4/4) after 1267. All may have been built about the same time. Quite likely Rooms 8, 9, and 10 and Kiva C were also built then, but there are no dated specimens to validate this conjecture. Kiva C's initial construction could have taken place at the time the room containing Kiva A was built.

Presumably, Rooms 39–45 were built after Kiva C was roofed, but the presence of the kiva would not have been a necessity for reaching the ledge. Room 78 probably came into existence in 1263, and Kiva F between 1264 and 1267, although the kiva may possibly date to the early 1270's. Kiva F was apparently built as a free-standing structure against the retaining wall east of Kiva E and Rooms 11, 46, 16, 17, and 19. Kiva E may have been built in 1264, but it is possible that it dates in the 1250's and was merely refloored in 1264. Room 11, also, was built sometime between 1250 and 1265. The Beer Cellar Complex may have been started in 1267 with the construction of Room 17.

Central. Room 72/1 was built against Room 28 and Kiva H in 1266. The rooms at the east side of the Great Kiva were built about 1262, as follows:

(1) Room 64 first? or with
(2) Room 66, which was built against Rooms 91 and 92.
(3) Room 65, which was built against Rooms 64 and 66.
(4) Room 67 was also built against Room 66.

About 1266, portions of the south walls of Kivas H and I and Room 29 collapsed, along with at least part of the initial tower (Room 64) structure.

East. No activity indicated by wood specimens.

A.D. 1270's

West. Kiva C was probably relined during the 1270's, but there are no substantiating tree-ring dates. Kiva D was possibly rebuilt or remodeled around 1278.

Room 12—a part of the Kiva F complex—was built in the late 1260's or early 1270's, and was apparently abandoned as a room and filled by 1276. Burial 26, dated to about 1279, was found in the room fill. Kiva F itself was remodeled and/or Rooms 13, 14, and 46 were added about 1278.

The major construction of the Beer Cellar Complex was undertaken in the 1270's. Room 17, possibly built in the 1260's, served as the nucleus, with the surrounding rooms being added as follows:

(1) Room 16 was built against Room 17, perhaps about 1273, leaving open the area between these rooms and the cave wall.

(2) Room 15 was closed in and Room 17/2 was added.

(3) Rooms 16/2, 19, and 20 were added between 1273 and 1277.

(4) Rooms 18/1 and 18/2 were built between Rooms 19 and 20 and the cave wall during this same period.

Central. Room 72/2 was constructed in 1277, creating a two-story structure adjacent to Kiva H on the northwest as well as on the east (Room 29). Kiva H was extensively remodeled after 1270 to repair damage resulting from the collapse of the room 64 tower. An additional support was added in 1280, the latest date from Long House. The southwest recess of Kiva I shows that this structure was repaired at about the same time as Kiva H. The Room 64 tower was probably reconstructed, ultimately reaching a height of five stories. Area VIII (East Ledge Ruin) was probably not built until the tower could be used as a platform for a ladder or pole.

East. Room 76/2 was added in 1274. Room 60 (round tower), partially above Kiva Q, was built in 1270, after Rooms 85 and 86. Its construction destroyed much of Room 88. Kiva N, between Kivas M and Q, probably postdates both. It may have been built about 1273. Room 87, which may date to the 1250's or 1260's, was possibly remodeled about 1273.

In the 1270's, or possibly the 1260's, but after collapse of the Room 64 tower, Rooms 91 and 92 were remodeled to create Kiva L and Room 69. After 1271, Room 92/2 was built against the south walls of Kiva I and Room 36.

There are a number of wood specimens dated in the early to late 1100's. Some may have been carried into Long House from other sites—probably early Pueblo III mesa–top villages. Others may indicate slightly earlier construction in Long House which has been almost entirely destroyed. For example, the early specimens from Kiva K (1147 and 1178) or Area IX–Kiva M (1110 and 1131) could be associated with features now represented only by wall stubs, such as one discovered below Room 76 and between Kivas O and K, or another present in the southeast pilaster of Kiva N.

The tree–ring dates give a broad, general idea of how the pueblo probably grew, despite the fact that few of the "dated" rooms can definitely be attributed to a specific year. Several areas produced no dates at all. Kiva R and the nearby rooms form one such location, and Kivas P, U, and G and the rooms between and immediately west another. A close study of these features—including the stratigraphy within each, the related ceramics and other artifacts, and the pollen profile in the case of Kiva R—helps establish a construction sequence within such areas and, to a limited extent, between the areas. However, since the major construction period in Long House is so short and several of these features (or the site on which the feature was built) reflect intermittent occupation, the exercise is not very productive. The construction sequence in the vicinity of each kiva and several of the rooms has been discussed in ch. 2 and will now be summarized insofar as the major undated areas are concerned.

Kiva R probably pre-dates Rooms 50, 52, 53, 58, 59, possibly 51. The Kiva D–Room 78 pollen profile overlaps the lower end of the Kiva R profile, suggesting that Kiva R was built after 1263.

Rooms 47–49 are three of the rooms which directly border on the pithouse. The area in which they were built—if not the rooms themselves—was undoubtedly used during the Basketmaker III occupation. Several features, such as the floor cists in Room 47 and the slabs used in the wall between Rooms 47 and 48, and again in the west wall of Room 49, suggest an earlier but undated occupation (see discussion of Rooms 47–56).

Kiva G was free standing, initially, and thus predates Room 31 on the south, the fill-retaining wall abutting it from the north, and Room 22, which extended out over part of the kiva roof from the ledge supporting the Beer Cellar Complex.

Kiva U predates and supports Kiva P and Rooms 82 and 83. Room 82, in turn, apparently was constructed before Rooms 61 and 62. Room 90 is an integral part of Kiva U and presumably was constructed at the same time. Kiva P was probably built before Room 82 but after Room 83.

Chapter Eleven

Summary Discussion

In an article entitled "The Cliff Dweller," published in the *Denver Republican* of January 22, 1893, an unknown author stated:

> Ever and again explorers have fortuned upon clearer evidences of that great tragedy of the past, in which a race went down in blood. Mr. Willmarth's party found one such testimony, which spoke of it in eloquent silence. In a dwelling in the wildest portion of the Mesa canons [sic] a skeleton was discovered. It lay in an oven, its legs stiffened and pushed up the big flue. Its skull projected from the oven's mouth and its long arms were stretched out upon the floor. In the back of the skull was a rugged hole, and close by lay a stone ax, from which the centuries had not entirely obliterated the pinkish tint of blood. What a story was there! What an echo of what high carnival of murder coming down from a voiceless past!

It is possible that violent death took place at some Mesa Verde pueblo in the distant past, but the story revealed by our excavations in Long House indicates that such sensational events must have been rare during the occupation of this pueblo. Rather, we have substantial evidence of peaceable, arduous work in developing a standard of living that allowed the people to devote considerable time to individual artistic endeavors as well as to clan and perhaps community ceremonial affairs and work projects. By community, we mean the estimated 150 men, women, and children who lived in Long House at any one time.

The mass of data collected in the ruin did not produce any startling finds, but the data made possible in–depth studies of the architectural features of Long House and of the ceramics, stone and bone tools, perishable objects, and detrital materials found therein. Because the short occupation periods of the site can be rather accurately dated, we now have a better knowledge of what we know to be late Basketmaker III and late Pueblo III materials in Mesa Verde. Through ancillary studies, we have learned much about the inhabitants physically, including their medical and dental problems and diet, and about the environmental conditions that obtained during the occupations.

From the architectural standpoint, Long House possesses several rather interesting though not unique features: a Basketmaker III pithouse, dating to A.D. 648, located beneath later rooms; the Great Kiva or ceremonial plaza complex (including Rooms 35 and 66), which resembles that of Fire Temple on Chapin Mesa; a low wall or defensive "breastwork," with 21 loopholes; a large number of small or clan(?) kivas; two kivas possessing probable foot drums; one kiva apparently remodeled from a Pueblo I pithouse; and three (possibly six) kivas with tunnels leading to another kiva (M–N) or room (N–87, R–50). The possible tunnels are those from Kiva T to Room 3, Kiva K to Room 81, and Kiva K to Kiva O. In addition, a tunnel would very likely have been installed between Kiva Q, and Room 60, the circular tower, if a large boulder had not prevented it. There is also a stairway leading from the Great Kiva to Room 66.

Several important questions call for answers: (1) why did the people move from the mesa top into Long House cave, (2) what was the relationship of these people to other Puebloan groups on the Mesa Verde, (3) why did these people and their neighbors abandon Mesa Verde, and (4) where did they go? Architecture and building techniques, art styles, tool manufacturing techniques, trade goods, items considered to be religious paraphernalia—these provide only partial, and highly speculative, answers to these questions.

It is possible to speculate that the later occupants of Long House moved into the rock shelter for defensive purposes, as suggested by the apertures not only in the breastwork but in the rooms of the West Ledge Ruin. The tunnels from kivas to rooms might possibly have been used as undercover avenues of retreat in case of a sudden attack. However, there is no evidence in the relatively few burials from Long House that an attack had ever been made directly upon the pueblo. And although some units had burned—Kivas M and S, for example—there is nothing to show that fires had been deliberately set.

The beginning of the late occupation of Long House, about A.D. 1200, overlaps the use of a number of the mesa-top pueblos such as Badger House, possibly by as much as 50 to 60 years. Obviously, there was no general exodus from the open sites.

It is interesting to note one temporal correlation between Badger House and Long House. There was an apparent footdrum still in use in Badger House at the time of abandonment; those in Kivas M and Q in Long House had been filled and floored over when abandoned. The time of construction of each was probably in the 1250's, judging by tree-ring dates from Badger House and the estimated date of construction for Kiva M (ca. 1246) and Kiva Q (1250's).

On the basis of dated wood specimens, estimated construction dates have been derived for parts of the pueblo. An attempt to correlate the construction sequence with the distribution of ceramics, especially the earlier ones, seems worthwhile.

Chapin Gray, a Basketmaker III pottery, was associated directly with the pithouse and occurred, logically, in several nearby structures such as Rooms 47–50, 57, 58, 60, 81, 84–88, and Kivas J, Q, and R. It was also found in other areas considered chronologically early (pre-1250), but not part of the Basketmaker III horizon: Rooms 6, 7, 28, 29, 69, 74, 75, and Kivas H, I, M, and the Great Kiva, for example. In addition, it was found in Rooms 12 and 14 and Kiva E.

This last group also produced sherds of most of the local pottery types, suggesting that either it saw considerable activity for a long period of time or was a dump for trash from areas showing a long occupation. We found Burial 26 in Room 12, along with an usually large number of rabbit, woodrat, and other small mammal bones, as commented upon in the discussion of unworked mammal bones.

Sherds of several other pottery types which precede McElmo-Mesa Verde Black-on-white and Mesa Verde Corrugated also turned up in the general pithouse-Kiva Q area. This suggests that the east end of the cave was the locus of a post-Basketmaker III but pre-1200 occupation. The ceramics involved are four black-on-white types—Chapin, Piedra, Cortez, and Mancos—and Moccasin Gray and Mancos Gray.

Pithouse 1 (and overlying Kiva J) and Kivas Q and R are low areas, and thus would tend to trap any trash from neighboring but higher rooms. However, on the basis of dated wood specimens, Kiva J (ca. A.D. 1200) and Kiva Q (1250's) were probably occupied early.

Other parts of the pueblo in which the earlier pottery types were well represented include several of the rooms and kivas at the extreme western end of the pueblo and at the eastern end of the central room block; the Great Kiva and the rooms adjoining it on the east; the kivas (including N) in the western part of the east section of the ruin; and a number of east end rooms, primarily those north and west of the pithouse. Although Kiva N may seem out of place here, the early construction in and around the kiva (and perhaps partially replaced by it) probably account for the presence of the early pottery.

In using the rather inclusive term "early pottery," I deliberately lump primarily the Pueblo I, II, and early Pueblo III local types. As mentioned before, there is little evidence to tie these to any structure. The latest types of this group, Mancos Black-on-white and Mancos Corrugated, would certainly be expected in the early stages of the late occupation along with McElmo-Mesa Verde Black-on-white and Mesa Verde Corrugated. A small amount of "heirloom" pottery is not surprising, although I doubt that all of the early material can be so classified. Some of this material was washed into Long House from sites in the drainage above. The source of the remainder will have to endure as an unresolved problem for the time being.

An attempt was made to correlate stylistic variations in two stone tool groups—manos and slabs—with probable construction dates and ceramic distribution. The results were inconclusive, probably because the samples were not really large enough for any patterns or trends to emerge.

The latest construction date for Long House is A.D. 1280, but the pueblo could easily have been occupied until 1300. The lack of coal-fired trade pottery from northeast Arizona in the Long House ceramic assemblage suggests that the occupation did not extend much beyond this date. The cultural and waterlaid sediments sampled for the Kiva R pollen profile may extend into the post-occupational period, but no correlations can be made at present which will help to date the time of abandonment.

Nothing emerged from our studies of the Long House material that shed much light upon the reasons for the abandonment of the pueblo. Several researchers have suggested that a slightly cooler climate reduced the marginal corn-growing seasons beyond the critical point, and thus may have contributed more to the exodus than the much-discussed dry years between A.D. 1276 and 1299. Lyndon L. Hargrave (personal communication to Douglas Osborne, 1962) states:

> Summarizing the results of my investigations from a study of biological material, it appears that the climate of the region was considerably warmer for some time prior to A.D. 1 to ca. A.D. 900. Thereafter temperatures seemed to average colder. These adverse conditions probably persisted until the early 1800's but appear to have been most severe from the mid-1200's to the 1300's, at least. The adverse cumulative effects of cold, short seasons was primarily responsible in my opinion for the explosive breakdown of our "pueblo cultures" in the 14th and 15th centuries.

Perhaps Dr. Harold C. Fritts, Laboratory of Tree-Ring Research, University of Arizona, will eventually provide some of the answers to this aspect of the problem through his computer-assisted paleoclimatic studies.

The work of Emma Lou Davis (MS) indicates late extensions of Mesa Verde culture (particularly as seen in ceramic designs) in several directions from the Four Corners area after 1300. Apparently the most likely route of departure for many of the Mesa Verde inhabitants was to the southeast toward the Rio Grande pueblos. It is likely that the Mesa Verde Indians drifted away over a period of many years—some being absorbed by Pueblo groups in New Mexico and Arizona, and others probably going in other directions and ultimately losing their identity.

References

ABEL, LELAND J.

1955. Pottery Types of the Southwest, Harold S. Colton, ed. Museum of Northern Arizona Ceramic Series, no. 3. Northern Arizona Society of Science and Art. Flagstaff.

ALDRICH, JOHN W., AND ALLEN J. DUVALL

1955. Distribution of American Gallinaceous Games Birds. Circular 34, Fish and Wildlife Service. Washington.

ADNRERSON, SYDNEY

1961. Mammals of Mesa Verde National Park, Colorado. University of Kansas Publications, Museum of Natural History, vol. 14, no. 3, pp. 26–67.Lawrence.

ANON.

1959. Check List of Birds of Mesa Verde National Park, Colorado. (Mimeographed) Southwest Archeological Center, National Park Service. Globe, Ariz.

BAILEY, FLORENCE M.

1928. Birds of New Mexico. New Mexico Department of Game and Fish. Santa Fe.

BEIDLEMAN, RICHARD G.

1949. Guide to the Birds of Prey of Colorado. University of Colorado Museum, Leaflet no. 6. Boulder.

BENT, ARTHUR CLEVELAND

1932. Life Histories of North American Gallinaceous Birds. United States National Museum, Bulletin 162. Washington.

BREW, JOHN OTIS

1946. Archaeology of Alkali Ridge, Southeastern Utah. Papers of the Peabody Museum of American Archaeology and Ethnology, Harvard University, volume 21. Cambridge.

BURKITT, MILES

1963. The Old Stone Age: A study of Palaeolithic Times. New York.

COLTON, HAROLD S.

1955. Check List of Southwestern Pottery Types. Museum of Northern Arizona, Ceramic Series, no. 2. Northern Arizona Society of Science and Art. Flagstaff.

COLTON, HAROLD S., ed.

1956. Pottery Types of the Southwest. Museum of Northern Arizona, Ceramic Series, no. 3C. Northern Arizona Society of Science and Art. Flagstaff.

COLTON, HAROLD S., AND LYNDON L. HARGRAVE

1937. Handbook of Northern Arizona Pottery Wares. Museum of Northern Arizona, Bulletin 11. Flagstaff.

COLYER, MARILYN, AND DOUGLAS OSBORNE

1965. Screening Soil and Fecal Samples for Recovery of Small Specimens. Memoirs of the Society for American Archaeology, no. 19; American Antiquity, vol. 31, no. 2, pt. 2, pp. 186–192. Salt Lake City.

COSGROVE, H. S., AND C.B.

1932. The Swarts Ruin, A Typical Mimbres Site in Southwestern New Mexico. Papers of the Peabody Museum of American Archaeology and Ethnology, Harvard University, vol. 15, no. 1. Cambridge.

COSNER, AARON J.

1956. The "Stone Scraper" and Arrow "Wrench." American Antiquity, vol. 21, no. 3, pp. 300–301. Salt Lake City.

CUTLER, HUGH C., AND WINTON MEYER

1965. Corn and Cucurbits from Wetherill Mesa. Memoirs of the Society for American Archaeology, no. 19; American Antiquity, vol. 31, no. 2, pt. 2, pp. 136–152. Salt Lake City.

DAVIS, EMMA LOU

MS. Anasazi Mobility (Wetherill Mesa Studies). Manuscript being edited for publication by the National Park Service. Washington.

DOUGLAS, CHARLES L.

1966. Amphibians and Reptiles of Mesa Verde National Park, Colorado. University of Kansas Publications, Museum of Natural History, vol. 15, no. 15, pp. 711–744. Lawrence.

ELLIS, FLORENCE H., AND MARY WALPOLE

1959. Possible Pueblo, Navajo, and Jicarilla Basketry Relationships. El Palacio, vol. 66, no. 6, pp. 181–198. Santa Fe

ERDMAN, JAMES A.

MS. Ecology of the Pinyon-Juniper Woodland of Wetherill Mesa, Mesa Verde National Park, Colorado. Unpublished M.A. thesis, 1962. University of Colorado. Boulder.

ERDMAN, JAMES A., CHARLES L. DOUGLAS, AND JOHN W. MARR

1969. Environment of Mesa Verde, Colorado (Wetherill Mesa Studies). Archeological Research Series 7–B, National Park Service. Washington.

FENENGA, FRANKLIN

1953. The Weights of Chipped Stone Points. A Clue to Their Functions. Southwestern Journal of Anthropology, vol. 9, no. 3, pp. 309–323. Albuquerque.

FEWKES, JESSE WALTER

1892. A Few Summer Ceremonials at the Tusayan Pueblos. Hemenway S. W. Archaeological Expendition. A Journal of American Ethnology and Archaeology vol. 2. Boston, Houghton, Mifflin & Co.

1901. Archeological Expedition to Arizona in 1895. Seventeenth Annual Report of the Bureau of American Ethnology, 1895–96, pt. 2, pp. 519–744. Washington.

FORDE, C. DARYLL

1950. Habitat, Economy and Society, 8th ed. Dutton, New York.

GETTY, HARRY T.

1935. New Dates from Mesa Verde. Tree-Ring Bulletin, vol. 1, no. 2, pp. 21–23. Tucson.

GLADWIN, HAROLD S.

1945. The Chaco Branch: Excavations at Whitemound and in the Red Mesa Valley. Medallion Papers, no. 33, Gila Pueblo, Globe, Arizona.

GRAHAM, SAMUEL A.

1965. Entomology: An aid in Archaeological Studies. Memoirs of the Society for American Archaeology, no. 19; American Antiquity, vol. 31, no. 2, pt. 2, pp. 167–174. Salt Lake City.

GRAUMONT, RAOUL, AND JOHN HENSEL

1946. Encyclopedia of Knots and Fancy Rope Work. Cornell Maritime Press. New York.

GUERNSEY, SAMUEL J.

1931. Explorations in Northeastern Arizona. Report on the Archaeological Fieldwork of 1920–23. Papers of the Peabody Museum of American Archaeology and Ethnology, Harvard University, vol. 12, no. 1. Cambridge.

HARGRAVE, LYNDON L.

1965a. Archaeological Bird Bones from Chapin Mesa, Mesa Verde National Park. Memoirs of the Society for American Archaeology, no. 19; American Antiquity, vol. 31, no. 2, pt. 2, pp. 156–160. Salt Lake City.

1965b. Turkey Bones From Wetherill Mesa. Memoirs of the Society for American Archaeology, no. 19; American Antiquity, vol. 31, no. 2, pt. 2, pp. 161–166. Salt Lake City.

1970. Feathers from Sand Dune Cave: A Basketmaker Cave Near Navajo Mountain, Utah. Museum of Northern Arizona, Technical Series, no. 9. Flagstaff.

HAYES, ALDEN C.

1964. The Archeological Survey of Wetherill Mesa, Mesa Verde National Park, Colorado. Archeological Research Series 7–A, National Park Service. Washington.

HAYES, ALDEN C., AND JAMES A. LANCASTER

1975. Badger House Community, Mesa Verde National Park, Colorado (Wetherill Mesa Excavations). Publication in Archeology 7–E, National Park Service. Washington.

HITCHCOCK, ROMYN

1891. The Ainus of Yezo, Japan. U.S. National Museum Report, *in* Annual Report of the Board of Regents of the Smithsonian Institution for the year ending June 30, 1890, pp. 436–502. Washington.

HODGE, FREDERICK WEBB

1920. Hawikuh Bonework. Museum of the American Indian, Heye Foundation; Indian Notes and Monographs, vol. 3, no. 3. New York.

1939. "A Square Kiva at Hawikuh," *in* So Live the Works of Men. University of New Mexico Press. Albuquerque.

HOUGH, WALTER

1897. The Hopi in Relation to Their Plant Environment. American Anthropologist, o.s., vol. 10, no. 2, pp. 33–44. Lancaster, Pa.

1914. Culture of the Ancient Pueblos of the Upper Gila River Region, New Mexico and Arizona. United States National Museum, Bulletin 87. Washington.

HURST, C.T., AND V.F. LOTRICH

1932. An Unusual Mug from Yellow Jacket Canyon. El Palacio, vol. 33 nos. 21–22. Santa Fe.

JUDD, NEIL M.

1954. The Material Culture of Pueblo Bonito. Smithsonian Miscellaneous Collections, vol. 124. Washington.

1964. The Architecture of Pueblo Bonito. Smithsonian Miscellaneous Collections, vol. 147, no. 1. Washington.

KAPLAN, LAWRENCE

1965. Beans of Wetherill Mesa. Memoirs of the Society for American Archaeology, no. 19; American Antiquity, vol. 31, no. 2, pt. 2, pp. 153–155. Salt Lake City.

KENT, KATE PECK

1957. The Cultivation and Weaving of Cotton in the Prehistoric Southwestern United States. Transactions of the American Philosophical Society, n.s. vol. 47, part 3. Philadelphia.

KIDDER, ALFRED VINCENT

1924. An Introduction to the Study of Southwestern Archaeology. Yale University Press. New Haven.

1932. The Artifacts of Pecos. Papers of the Southwestern Expedition, no. 6, Robert S. Peabody Foundation for Archaeology. Yale University Press. New Haven.

KIDDER, ALFRED VINCENT, AND SAMUEL J. GUERNSEY

1919. Archeological Explorations in Northeastern Arizona. Bureau of American Ethnology, Bulletin 65. Washington.

KRUMBEIN, W.C., AND F.J. PETTIJOHN

1938. Manual of Sedimentary Petrography. Appleton-Century Co., Inc. New York.

LEAVITT, ERNEST E., JR.

MS. Technical Differences in the Painted Decoration of Anasazi and Hohokam Pottery. Unpublished M.A. thesis, 1962. University of Arizona. Tucson.

LISTER, ROBERT H.

1968. Archeology for Layman and Scientist at Mesa Verde. Science, vol. 160, no. 3827, pp. 489–496. Washington.

LISTER, ROBERT H., J. RICHARD AMBLER, AND FLORENCE C. LISTER

1960. The Coombs Site. University of Utah Anthropological Papers, no. 41, pt. II. Salt Lake City.

MARTIN, PAUL S., AND WILLIAM BYERS

1965. Pollen and Archaeology at Wetherill Mesa. Memoirs of the Society for American Archaeology, no. 19; American Antiquity, vol. 31, no. 2, pt. 2, pp. 122–135. Salt Lake City.

MARTIN, PAUL S., AND JOHN RINALDO

1939. Modified Basket Maker Sites, Ackmen-Lowery Area, Southwestern Colorado, 1938. Field Museum of Natural History, Anthropological Series, vol. 23, no. 3, pp. 305–499. Chicago.

MARTIN, PAUL S., JOHN B. RINALDO, ELAINE BLUHM, HUGH C. CUTLER, AND ROGER GRANGE, JR.

1952. Mogollon Cultural Continuity and Change. The Stratigraphic Analysis of Tularosa and Cordoba Caves. Field Museum of Natural History. Fieldiana: Anthropology, vol. 40. Chicago.

MARTIN, PAUL S., L. ROYS, AND G. VON BONIN

1936. Lowry Ruin in Southwestern Colorado. Field Museum of Natural History, Anthropological Series, vol. 23, no. 1, pp. 1–216. Chicago.

MASON, C.C.

MS. The Story of the Discovery and Early Exploration of the Cliff Houses at the Mesa Verde. Manuscript presented to the State Historical Society of Colorado by author on May 5, 1918 (Acc. 11.278). Colorado State Museum. Denver.

MASON, OTIS TUFTON

1904. Aboriginal American Basketry: Studies in a Textile Art Without Machinery. Report of the U.S. National Museum for the year ending June 30, 1902. Washington.

MINDELEFF, VICTOR

1891. A Study of Pueblo Architecture: Tusayan and Cibola. Eighth Annual Report, Bureau of American Ethnology, pp. 3–228. Washington.

MORLEY, SYLVANUS G.

1908. The Excavation of Cannonball Ruins in Southwestern Colorado. American Anthropologist, vol. 10, no. 4, pp. 596–610. Lancaster, Pa.

MORRIS, EARL H.

1919a. The Aztec Ruin. Anthropological Papers of the American Museum of Natural History, vol. 26, pt. I. New York.

1919b. Preliminary Account of the Antiquities of the Region between the Mancos and La Plata Rivers in Southwestern Colorado. Thirty-third Annual Report of the Bureau of American Ethnology, pp. 155–206. Washington.

1939. Archaeological Studies in the La Plata District, Southwestern Colorado and Northwestern New Mexico. Carnegie Institution of Washington, Publication 519. Washington.

MORRIS, EARL H., AND ROBERT F. BURGH

1941. Anasazi Basketry. Carnegie Institution of Washington, Publiction 533. Washington.

1954. Basket Maker II Sites near Durango, Colorado. Carnegie Institution of Washington, Publication 604. Washington.

MORSS, NOEL

1931. The Ancient Culture of the Fremont River in Utah. Papers of the Peabody Museum of American Archaeology and Ethnology, Harvard University, vol. 12, no. 3. Cambridge.

NICHOLS, ROBERT F.

MS. Step House, Mesa Verde National Park, Colorado (Wetherill Mesa Excavations). Manuscript being edited for publication by the National Park Service. Washington.

NICHOLS, ROBERT F., AND THOMAS P. HARLAN

1967. Archaeological Tree-Ring Dates from Wetherill Mesa, *in* The Dendrochronology of the Wetheril Mesa Archeological Project, Tree-Ring Bulletin, vol. 28, nos. 1–4, pp. 12–40. Tucson, Ariz.

NORDENSKIÖLD, G.

1893. The Cliff Dwellers of the Mesa Verde, Southwestern Colorado. Their Pottery and Implements. Trans. by D. Lloyd Morgan. P.A. Norstedt and Söner. Stockholm and Chicago.

O'BRYAN, DERIC

1950. Excavations in Mesa Verde National Park, 1947–1948. Medallion Papers, no. 39. Gila Pueblo, Globe, Ariz.

O'NEALE, LILA M.

1945. Textiles of Highland Guatemala. Carnegie Institution of Washington, Publication 567. Washington.

OSBORNE, DOUGLAS

1964a. Solving the Riddles of Wetherill Mesa. National Geographic Magazine, vol. 125, no. 2. Washington.

1964b. Prologue to the Project, *in* The Archeological Survey of the Wetherill Mesa, Mesa Verde National Park, Colorado, by Alden C. Hayes. Archeological Research Series 7–A, National Park Service. Washington.

1965. Chipping Remains as an Indication of Cultural Change at Wetherill Mesa. Memoirs of the Society for American Archaeology, no. 19; American Antiquity, vol. 31, no. 2, pt. 2, pp. 30–44. Salt Lake City.

PARSONS, ORVILLE A.

MS. Soil Survey of Wetherill Mesa, Mesa Verde National Park, Colorado (Wetherill Mesa Studies). Manuscript being edited for publication by the National Park Service. Washington.

PEPPER, GEORGE H.

1920. Pueblo Bonito. American Museum of National History, Anthropological Papers, vol. 27. New York.

PESEL, LOUISA F.

n.d. Hitches from Eastern Embroideries. Percy Lund, Humphries and Co., Ltd. London, B.C. and the Country Press, Bradford.

-937. The Jemez Yucca Ring-Basket. El Palacio, vol. 42, nos. 7–9. School of American Research, Santa Fe.

PETTIJOHN, F. J.

1949. Sedimentary Rocks. Harper and Brothers. New York.

PHILLIPS PHILIP

1958. Application of the Wheat-Gifford-Wasley Taxonomy to Eastern Ceramics. American Antiquity, vol. 24, no. 2, pp. 117–125. Salt Lake City.

REED, ERID K.

1958. Excavations in Mancos Canyon, Colorado. University of Utah Anthropological Papers, no. 35. Salt Lake City.

ROBBINS, WILFRED WILLIAM, JOHN PEABODY HARRINGTON, AND BARBARA FREIRE-MARRECO

1916. Ethnobotany of the Tewa Indians. Bureau of American Ethnology, Bulletin 55. Washington.

ROBERTS, FRANK H. H., JR.

MS. The Ceramic Sequence in Chaco Canyon, New Mexico, and Its Relation to the Cultures of the San Juan Basin. Unpublished Ph.D. thesis, 1927. Harvard University. Cambridge.

1932. The Village of the Great Kivas on the Zuni Reservation, New Mexico. Bureau of American Ethnology, Bulletin 111. Washington.

ROEDIGER, VIRGINIA MORE

1961. Ceremonial Costumes of the Pueblo Indians; Their Evolution, Fabrication, and Significance in the Prayer Drama. University of California Press. Berkeley.

ROHN, ARTHUR H.

1959. A Tentative Classification of the Pottery from the Mesa Verde Region. (Mimeographed) Mesa Verde National Park, Colo.

SABELS, BRUNO E.

1962. Impurity Analysis on Wetherill Mesa Feces and Soils. 1961 Annual Report to the National Geographic Society on the Wetherill Mesa Project. U.S. Department of the Interior, National Park Service. Washington.

SCHOENWETTER, JAMES

MS. Pollen Stratigraphy of the Wetherill Mesa Region. Unpublished Manuscript (1961), Geochronology Laboratories, University of Arizona. Tucson.

SCHORGER, ARLIE WILLIAM

1966. The Wild Turkey: Its History and Domestication. Norman, Okla.

1970. A New Subspecies of *Meleagris gallopovo*. Auk, vol. 87. Gainesville, Fla.

SCHULMAN, EDMUND

1946. Dendrochronology at Mesa Verde National Park. Tree-Ring Bulletin, vol. 12, no. 3, pp. 18–24. Tucson.

SHEPARD, ANNA O.

1939. Technology of La Plata Potter, *in* Archaeological Studies in the La Plata District, Southwestern Colorado and Northwestern New Mexico, by Earl H. Morris. Carnegie Institution of Washington, Publication 519. Washington.

1948. The Symmetry of Abstract Design with Special Reference to Ceramic Decoration. Carnegie Institution of Washington, Publication 574, Contribution 47. Washington.

1957. Ceramics for the Archaeologist. Carnegie Institution of Washington, Publication 609. Washington.

STEVENSON, MATILDA COXE

1915. Ethnobotany of the Zuni Indians. Thirteenth Annual Report of the Bureau of American Ethnology, 1908–1909, pp. 31–102. Washington.

SWANNACK, JERVIS D., JR.

1969. Big Juniper House. Mesa Verde National Park, Colorado (Wetherill Mesa Excavations). Archeological Research Series 7–C, National Park Service. Washington.

MSS. Two Raven House and Four Tested Sites on Wetherill Mesa, Mesa Verde National Park Colorado (Wetherill Mesa Excavations). Manuscripts being edited for publication by the National Park Service. Washington.

TREWARTHA, GLENN T.

1954. An Introduction to Climate. McGraw-Hill. New York.

VAN TYNE, JOSSELYN, AND ANDRES J. BERGER

1959. Fundamentals of Ornithology. New York.

VELARDE, PABLITA

1960. Old Father the Story Teller. Dale Stuart King. Globe, Ariz.

VIVIAN, R. GORDON

1959. The Hubbard Site and Other Tri-Wall Structures in New Mexico and Colorado. Archeological Research Series 5, National Park Service. Washington.

VIVIAN, GORDON, AND PAUL REITER

1960. The Great Kivas of Chaco Canyon and Their Relationships. Monographs of the School of American Research and the Museum of New Mexico, no. 22. Santa Fe.

WANEK, ALEXANDER A.

1959. Geology and Fuel Resources of the Mesa Verde Area, Montezuma and La Plata Counties, Colorado. Geological Survey, Bulletin 1072–M, Washington.

WELSH, STANLEYL., AND JAMES A. ERDMAN

1964. Annotated Checklist of the Plants of Mesa Verde, Colorado. Brigham Young University Science Bulletin, Biological Series, vol. IV, no. 2. Provo.

WHEAT, JOE BEN, JAMES C. GIFFORD, AND WILLIAM W. WASLEY

1958. Ceramic Variety, Type Cluster, and Ceramic System in Southwestern Pottery Analysis. American Antiquity, vol. 24, no. 1, pp. 34–67. Salt Lake City.

WHEELER, RICHARD P.

1954. Selected Projectile Pointed Types of the United States: II. Bulletin of the Oklahoma Anthropological Society, vol. II, pp. 1–5. Norman, Okla.

1965. Edge-abraded Flakes, Blades, and Cores in the Puebloan Tool Assemblage. Memoirs of the Society for American Archaeology, no. 19; American Antiquity, vol. 31, no. 2, pt. 2, pp. 19–29. Salt Lake City.

WHITING, ALFRED F.

1950. Ethnobotany of the Hopi. Museum of Northern Arizona, Bulletin 15. Flagstaff.

WOODBURY, RICHARD B.

1954. Prehistoric Stone Implements of Northeastern Arizona. Papers of the Peabody Museum of American Archaeology and Ethnology, Harvard University, vol. 34. (Reports of the Awatovi Expedition, no. 6). Cambridge.

Index

Publications in Archeology

1. Archeology of the Bynum Mounds, Natchez Trace Parkway, Mississippi, by John L. Cotter and John M. Corbett. 1951. (PB 177 061)*
2. Archeological Excavations in Mesa Verde National Park, Colorado, 1950, by James A. Lancaster *et al.* 1954. (PB 177 062)*
3. Archeology of the Funeral Mound, Ocmulgee National Monument, Georgia, by Charles H. Fairbanks. 1956. (PB 177 063)*
4. Archeological Excavations at Jamestown, Virginia, by John L. Cotter. 1958 (PB 177 064)*
5. The Hubbard Site and Other Tri-wall Structures in New Mexico and Colorado, by R. Gordon Vivian. 1959. (PB 230 988/AS)*
6. Search for the Cittie of Ralegh, Archeological Excavations at Fort Raleigh National Historic Site, North Carolina, by Jean Carl Harrington. 1962.

7A. The Archeological Survey of Wetherill Mesa, Mesa Verde National Park, Colorado, by Alden C. Hayes. 1964. (PB 234 542/AS)*

7B. Environment of Mesa Verde, Colorado, by James A. Erdman *et al.* 1969. (PB 234 541/AS)*

7C. Big Juniper House, Mesa Verde National Park, Colorado, by Jervis D. Swannack, Jr. 1969. (PB 234 537/AS)*

7D. Mug House, Mesa Verde National Park, Colorado, by Arthur H. Rohn. 1971. (PB 234 539/AS)*

7E. Badger House Community, Mesa Verde National Park, Colorado, by Alden C. Hayes and James A. Lancaster. 1975.

7F. Skeletal Remains from Mesa Verde National Park, Colorado, by Kenneth A. Bennett. 1975.

7G. Orthopedic Problems of the Wetherill Mesa Populations, by James S. Miles, M.D. 1975.

7H. Long House, Mesa Verde National Park, Colorado, by George S. Cattanach, Jr. *et al.* 1980.

8. Excavations in a 17th-Century Jumano Pueblo, Gran Quivira, New Mexico, by Gordon Vivian. 1964.
9. Excavations at Tse-Ta'a, Canyon de Chelly National Monument, Arizona, by Charlie R. Steen. 1966. (PB 234 540/AS)*
10. Ruins Stabilization in the Southwestern United States, by Roland Von S. Richert and R. Gordon Vivian. 1974.
11. The Steamboat Bertrand: History, Excavation, and Architecture, by Jerome E. Petsche. 1974.
12. The Bertrand Bottles: A Study of 19th Century Glass and Ceramic Containers, by Ronald R. Switzer. 1974.
13. Investigations in Russell Cave, Russell Cave National Monument, Alabama, by John W. Griffin *et al.* 1974.
14. Casemates and Cannonballs: Archeological Investigations at Fort Stanwix National Monument, Rome, New York, by Lee H. Hanson and Dick Ping Hsu. 1975.
15. Woodland Complexes in Northeastern Iowa, by Wilfred D. Logan. 1976.

*These publications are no longer available from the Superintendent of Documents. They are available in microfiche or paper form from the National Technical Information Service. Cite the title and parenthetical code number, and apply for prices to NTIS, U.S. Department of Commerce, 5285 Port Royal Road, Springfield, Virginia 22161.

*U.S. Government Printing Office: 1979 0-214-930